D0604509

CALGARY PUBLIC LIBRARY

NOV - - 2011

WHAT WORKS ON WALL STREET

The Classic Guide to the Best-Performing Investment Strategies of All Time

JAMES P. O'SHAUGHNESSY

Fourth Edition

New York   Chicago   San Francisco   Lisbon   London
Madrid   Mexico City   Milan   New Delhi   San Juan
Seoul   Singapore   Sydney   Toronto

The McGraw·Hill Companies

Copyright © 2012 by James P. O'Shaughnessy. All rights reserved. Printed in the United States of America. Except as permitted under the United States Copyright Act of 1976, no part of this publication may be reproduced or distributed in any form or by any means, or stored in a database or retrieval system, without the prior written permission of the publisher.

1 2 3 4 5 6 7 8 9 10   QFR/QFR   1 6 5 4 3 2 1

ISBN	978-0-07-162576-0
MHID	0-07-162576-3
e-ISBN	978-0-07-175919-9
e-MHID	0-07-175919-0

This publication is designed to provide accurate and authoritative information in regard to the subject matter covered. It is sold with the understanding that neither the author nor the publisher is engaged in rendering legal, accounting, securities trading, or other professional services. If legal advice or other expert assistance is required, the services of a competent professional person should be sought.

—*From a Declaration of Principles Jointly Adopted by a Committee of the American Bar Association and a Committee of Publishers and Associations*

All information in this book is the property of O'Shaughnessy or the information providers and is protected by copyright and intellectual property laws. You may not reproduce, re-transmit, disseminate, sell, publish, broadcast, or circulate the information or material in this book without the express written consent of O'Shaughnessy or the other information providers herein. This book does not constitute investment advice from O'Shaughnessy, his publisher, affiliates, or O'Shaughnessy Asset Management LLC.

This book contains statements and statistics that have been obtained from sources believed to be reliable but are not guaranteed as to accuracy or completeness. Neither O'Shaughnessy nor the information providers can guarantee the accuracy, completeness, or timeliness of any of the information in the book, including, but not limited to, information originating with O'Shaughnessy, licensed by O'Shaughnessy from information providers, or gathered by O'Shaughnessy from publically available sources. There may be omissions or inaccuracies in the information contained in the book. Neither O'Shaughnessy, the publisher, nor any of the information providers shall have any liability, contingent or otherwise, for the accuracy, completeness, or timeliness of the information or for any decision made or action taken by you in reliance upon the information in this book. Neither O'Shaughnessy, the publisher, nor the information providers make any representations about the suitability of the information contained in the book and all such information is provided "as is" without warranty of any kind.

Library of Congress Cataloging-in-Publication Data

O'Sauhnessy, James P.
    What works on Wall Street : the classic guide to the best-performing investment strategies of all time / by James O'Shaughnessy. —4th ed.
        p. cm.
    Includes Index.
    ISBN-13: 978-0-07-162576-0 (alk. paper)
    ISBN-10: 0-07-162576-0 (alk. paper)
    1. Investments—United States.   2. Investment analysis—United States.   3. Stocks—United States.   I. Title.
    HG4910.O828 2012
    332.6—dc23   2011036391

McGraw-Hill books are available at special quantity discounts to use as premiums and sales promotions or for use in corporate training programs. To contact a representative, please e-mail us at bulksales@mcgraw-hill.com.

To Lael, Kathryn, Patrick, and Melissa

ABOUT THE AUTHOR

James P. O'Shaughnessy is the Chairman and CEO of O'Shaughnessy Asset Management LLC, a quantitative asset management company located in Stamford, Connecticut. He is the author of four books on investing. Long recognized as one of America's leading financial experts and a pioneer in quantitative equity analysis, he has been called a "world beater," a "statistical guru," and a "legendary investor" by *Barron's*. In February 2009, *Forbes* included Jim in a series on "Legendary Investors" along with Benjamin Graham, Warren Buffet, and Peter Lynch. O'Shaughnessy's investment strategies have been featured widely in the media, including *The Wall Street Journal, Barron's, The New York Times, The Washington Post, The Financial Times, CNN and CNBC.*

Wait for the wisest of all counselors, time.
—Pericles

C O N T E N T S

INTRODUCTION

The Chinese use two brush strokes to write the word "crisis." One brush stroke stands for danger; the other for opportunity. In a crisis, be aware of the danger—but recognize the opportunity.
—John F. Kennedy

This fourth edition of *What Works on Wall Street* has the dubious distinction of being published on the heels of the *worst* decade for U.S. stocks in 110 years! The first decade of 2000 began full of promise, with swarms of first-time equity buyers rushing into a market where the Nasdaq had increased nearly sevenfold (even after accounting for inflation) in the 1990s and the S&P 500 had risen nearly fourfold. As the first decade of the twenty-first century progressed, it became painfully clear that the early optimism investors had for equity returns was completely unjustified.

The decade ended with a real loss of –3.39 percent per year for the S&P 500, where $10,000 invested on December 31, 1999, was worth just $7,083 after taking the effects of inflation into account by the end of 2009. It was even worse for large-cap growth stocks as measured by the Russell 1000 Growth Index, where $10,000 invested on December 31, 1999, was cut virtually in half by December 31, 2009, declining in value to just $5,190. The Nasdaq—the darling of investors in the 1990s—did even worse, losing 7.96 percent per year, turning $10,000 invested on December 31, 1999, into just $4,364 on December 31, 2009, a peak to trough decline between February 2000 and September 2002 of –76.59 percent, very close to that of the S&P 500 during the crash of 1929–1932. Only small stocks had a good run during the decade, with the Russell 2000 Index eking out a gain of 0.96 percent and the Russell 2000 Value Index returning 5.60 percent a year, the only broad U.S. stock index to beat U.S. long-term bonds, which returned 5.04 percent per year.

Please note that for this introduction, I am looking at *real* returns after adjusting for inflation, since it allows me to use the returns generated by professors Dimson, Marsh, and Staunton for the 1900 through 1930 period and published in their excellent book, *Triumph of the Optimists: 101 Years of Global Returns*. What's more, I find the real rate of return to be far more informative than the nominal rate, since it takes the loss of purchasing power of the dollar into account and gives a more accurate account of how your portfolio *really* performed over time. Therefore, while we retain the conventional use of nominal returns for our reviews of each factor and multifactor strategy throughout the book, we include the inflation-adjusted rate of return for several of the strategies as well as other asset classes in Chapter 28, which summarizes our findings.

To put all these data in perspective, there have only been two other decades since 1900 in which U.S. stock prices have had real declines in value—1910 through 1919 and 1970 through 1979, where the losses were –2.46 percent and –1.41 percent, respectively. Table I.1 shows the real average annual return for U.S. large stocks from 1900 forward, arranged by the best decade to the worst nine. When we look at all *rolling* 10-year periods between 1900 and 2009, we find the only 10-year period worse than the one ending February 2009 was the 10 years ending May 31, 1920. See Table I.2 for all of the other awful 10-year periods investors have had to endure since 1900. Two things are especially important about the information in Table I.2: First, note that following these atrocious ten-year declines, *all* returns for three years through ten years are *positive*, with an average ten-year real gain of 14.55 percent after one of these horrible ten-year periods. Second, the *minimum* ten-year real rate of return was a real gain of 6.39 percent for the ten years following the loss of 3.48 percent for the ten years ending November 1974. What's important for this minimum return of 6.39 percent is that it *dwarfed* the returns for U.S. long-term bonds over the same period. An investor who got spooked out of the equity market in November 1974 and put his or her money in long bonds would have had a real loss of 0.27 percent per year for the same period.

T A B L E   I.1

Real Returns for U.S. Large Stocks 1900–2009, Sorted by Best to Worst Return

Decade	Real average annual compound Return large stocks *
1950–1959	16.78%
1990–1999	14.84%
1920–1929	14.37%
1980–1989	11.85%
1900–1909	9.32%
1960–1969	5.15%
1940–1949	3.57%
1930–1939	2.04%
1970–1979	−1.41%
1910–1919	−2.46%
2000–2009	−3.39%

*For the period 1900–1930, we use the Dimson-Marsh-Staunton Global Returns Data.
For 1930–2009, we use the Ibbotson Large Stocks Data.

T A B L E   I.2

Worst 50 Real Average Annual Compound Returns for U.S. Stocks Since 1900

For the 10 years ending:	Real 10-year average annual compound return	Real compound average annual returns over the next:			
		1-year period	3-year period	5-year period	10-year period
May–1920	−6.09	16.04	17.63	17.40	20.64
Feb–2009	−5.86	50.40	N/A	N/A	N/A
Dec–1920	−5.72	24.33	18.06	21.33	16.05
Jun–1920	−5.72	13.26	16.81	17.46	18.77
Nov–1920	−5.55	21.17	16.94	20.18	16.68
Jan–1920	−5.49	21.75	16.79	19.92	16.11
Mar–2009	−5.43	46.38			
Dec–1919	−5.35	−18.84	9.67	11.13	16.23
Jun–1921	−5.33	40.34	17.00	18.81	15.43
Feb–1921	−5.31	26.87	15.84	18.52	17.33
Jul–1920	−5.28	14.69	14.67	17.37	19.23
Mar–1921	−5.27	33.34	16.38	17.18	16.55
Aug–1920	5.18	6.30	15.14	17.25	19.07
Apr–1920	−5.14	2.83	14.43	14.27	19.59
Jul–1921	−5.13	40.52	17.62	19.53	14.30
Jan–1920	−5.13	4.35	12.79	18.82	15.87
Feb–1920	−5.10	−4.92	14.33	14.25	18.25
Jan–2009	−5.06	29.74			
Apr–1921	−5.00	33.72	15.38	16.79	15.11
Sep–1920	−5.00	7.48	13.14	17.58	16.91
Aug–1921	−4.97	55.48	20.04	21.29	15.03
May–1921	−4.94	33.85	13.88	16.65	13.34
Apr–2009	−4.88	35.80			
Nov–1919	−4.79	−19.53	9.51	10.62	15.68
Jun–2009	−4.74	13.22			
Jan–1921	−4.74	48.84	19.39	20.30	11.81
Jan–1920	−4.70	−10.37	11.63	12.40	17.48
Nov–1921	−4.35	34.70	19.32	19.13	10.13
Sep–1921	−4.35	45.72	18.68	20.52	10.52
Dec–1921	−4.34	30.71	18.87	19.09	8.36
Sep–1974	−4.29	28.08	12.51	8.11	7.47
Mar–1920	−4.21	−12.04	10.30	10.97	18.28
May–2009	−4.16	18.58			
Jan–1922	−4.11	27.47	18.02	17.93	7.88
Aug–2010	−4.09				
Jun–2010	−3.87				
Nov–1978	−3.82	4.85	3.86	8.62	9.76
Dec–2008	−3.81	23.12			
Jul–1982	−3.80	55.63	22.98	25.79	14.94
Aug–1919	−3.80	−21.69	8.98	7.57	19.76
Dec–1974	−3.77	28.20	9.61	6.12	6.92
Sep–1919	−3.75	−19.87	7.86	7.56	19.00
Jan–1919	−3.71	−21.01	7.05	7.00	16.17

(continued on next page)

T A B L E   I.2

Worst 50 Real Average Annual Compound Returns for U.S. Stocks Since 1900 *(Continued)*

For the 10 years ending:	Real 10-year average annual compound return	Real compound average annual returns over the next:			
		1-year period	3-year period	5-year period	10-year period
Jul–2009	−3.69	12.43			
Jan–1978	−3.56	2.71	3.17	8.59	10.15
Jun–1982	−3.54	56.97	22.03	23.95	14.20
Feb–1922	−3.49	23.89	17.30	17.83	7.94
Nov–1974	−3.48	26.79	8.67	5.41	6.39
May–1982	−3.48	47.27	20.32	22.13	14.06
Nov–2008	−3.46	23.13			
Average	−4.60	20.47	14.53	15.78	14.55
Minimum	−6.09	−21.69	3.17	5.41	6.39
Maximum	−3.46	56.97	22.98	25.79	20.64

Source: For 1900–1929, William N. Goetzmann, The National Bureau of Economic Research; for 1929–2010, Morningstar EnCorr Analyzer, a dataset of a variety of investment returns provided in this instance by the Ibbotson *Stocks, Bonds, Bills, and Inflation* dataset.

The returns for our various universes covered here in *What Works on Wall Street* fared better than the S&P 500, possibly because we equal-weight our universes and include American Depository Receipts, whereas indexes such as the S&P 500 are capitalization-weighted and based exclusively on U.S.-based stocks. The last decade's returns for our various universes from *What Works on Wall Street* are as follows: the All Stocks universe had a real average annual gain of 1.82 percent; Large Stocks had a slight loss of –0.10 percent; Market Leaders had a gain of 3.30 percent; and Small Stocks a gain of 2.36 percent.

While the loss for 2000 to 2009 is the *worst* by decade, and the *second* worst when looking at all rolling 10-year periods since 1900, when looking at peak to trough losses in the U.S. market, we see that there have been bigger declines. Table I.3 shows all peak to trough losses exceeding 20 percent since 1900; here we see that our recent crash was actually second to the crash of 1929 through 1932, in which the S&P 500 lost 79 percent of its value from the 1929 peak through the 1932 trough. Yet you can see that as far as the *duration* of this decline is concerned, it was the longest in 110 years, lasting 102 months (Table I.3).

A LOSS OF FAITH IN EQUITIES

This poor performance has caused many investors to lose faith in equities. Indeed, According to the Leuthold Group's Supply/Demand Flash reports that cover the net inflow and outflow to U.S. equity and bond mutual funds, between 2007 and 2009, U.S. equity mutual funds have seen more than $234 billion in net outflows, whereas U.S. bond funds have seen their assets swell by $504.6 billion. As we argue in later chapters, we think that this is exactly the *wrong* time to be abandoning stocks for bonds and other asset classes.

T A B L E   I.3

All Peak to Trough Losses Exceeding 20 Percent, 1900–2009*

Peak date	Peak index value	Trough date	Trough index value	Recovery date	Decline (%)	Decline duration	Recovery duration
Dec-1906	2.04	Dec–07	1.43	Dec–08	−30.04	12	12
Dec-1915	2.79	Dec–20	1.53	Dec–24	−45.35	60	48
Aug-1929	3.04	May–32	0.64	Nov–36	−79.00	33	54
Feb-1937	3.18	Mar–38	1.59	Feb–45	−49.93	13	83
May-1946	4.33	Feb–48	2.72	Oct–50	−37.18	21	32
Dec-1961	21.57	Jun–62	16.65	Apr–63	−22.80	6	10
Nov-1968	34.62	Jun–70	22.34	Nov–72	−35.46	19	29
Dec-1972	35.84	Sep–74	17.25	Dec–84	−51.86	21	123
Aug-1987	72.06	Nov–87	50.32	Jul–89	−30.16	3	20
Aug-2000	307.32	Feb–09	141.37		−54.00	102	NA

*For the period 1900–1930, we use the Dimson-Marsh-Staunton Global Returns Data, which are annual. For 1930–2009, we use the Ibbotson Large Stocks Data, which are monthly.

Look again at Table I.2: in each instance where we have data for what happened *after* the worst 10-year periods for equities, equities went on to post *positive* returns in the one-, three-, five-, and ten-year periods that followed huge declines.

Yet, the drumbeat became increasingly louder as stocks lost value—late in 2008, CNBC ran a multipart series titled "The Death of Buy and Hold"; *Barron's* Electronic Investor published an article on February 19, 2009, titled "Modern Portfolio Theory Ages Badly—The Death of Buy and Hold" where they said the following: "Buy-and-hold is a loser's game. Markets are likely to be too erratic in the future to rely only on nicely structured portfolios and secular growth to generate returns that keep up with inflation and taxes, says Ken Stern, eponymous founder of a San Diego money-management firm." And much like *BusinessWeek*'s "Death of Equities" article penned on August 13, 1979, *Institutional Investor's* January 2010 issue featured a story titled "R.I.P. Equities 1982–2008: The Equity Culture Loses Its Bloom," which states: "After two brutal stock market crashes, investors are questioning the conventional wisdom that stocks outperform bonds. They're systematically pulling back from equities, and Wall Street will never be the same." What's more, a Google search on "the death of buy and hold investing" on January 13, 2010, yielded 750,000 hits. Clearly, the average investor, as well as a good number of professionals, had jumped on this bandwagon.

Some investors started calling the abysmal returns the "new normal" and argued that returns for stocks would be substantially lower well into the future. Never mind that commentators dubbed the late 1990s a "new era" for stocks in which they would perpetually rise and droned on with mantras of, "It's different this time," it seems that the one thing that *doesn't change* is people's reaction to short-term conditions and their axiomatic ability to perpetuate them far into the future.

HISTORY IS A BETTER GUIDE

It's not surprising to see such negativity for the long-term prospects for stocks. The last time we suffered from a market that was as bleak as the one in the last decade was in the 1970s, when *BusinessWeek* wrote its infamous "The Death of Equities" cover story on August 13, 1979. As we will see in Chapters Two and Three, investors seem to be programmed by nature to fail at investing, forever chasing the asset class that has turned in the best performance recently and heavily discounting *anything* that occurred more than three to five years ago.

The whole purpose of *What Works on Wall Street* is to dissuade investors from this course of action. Only the fullness of time shows which investment strategies are the best long-term performers, and this is doubly true after the last decade's sorry performance. You will see that after we review the results of the various strategies, investors who diligently stuck with the best long-term strategies did significantly better than those who followed a hit and miss approach to investing. Indeed, the wholesale shift to bonds and other asset classes that has occurred over the last several years looks to be yet another bubble. We will make the case that equities—particularly those selected using the best long-term strategies—will go on to be the best performing assets over the next 10 and 20 years. We are at a historic crossroad for equities—the conditions prevailing currently offer investors an unusual opportunity. As of March 2009, stocks had been outperformed by bonds over the last 10-, 20-, and 40-year periods. To put this in perspective, this was the second worst 40-year period for stocks since 1900, and the first time since December 31, 1941, that this had occurred. Stocks returning less than 4 percent per year over a 40-year period is so rare that it has happened only four times since 1900—the 40 years ending December 1941, December 1942, February 2009, and March 2009. The last time this happened in the early 1940s, stocks went on to provide excellent returns over the next 5, 10, and 20 years. And as Figure I.1 shows, we also saw the largest negative 10-year equity premium since 1926.

Historically, we have always seen reversion to the mean—after stocks have had an unusually great 10 or 20 years, they typically turn in subpar results over the next 10 or 20, and after bad 10- to 20-year stretches, the next 10 to 20 tend to be above average. This makes sense economically. After a great 10- or 20-year run, stocks are characterized by high PE ratios and low dividend yields, whereas after horrible 10- or 20-year returns, the reverse is true, with low PEs and higher dividend yields typically the norm. Indeed, I wrote an entire book titled *Predicting the Markets of Tomorrow* based upon the mean-reverting tendencies in equity markets and how we can use them to our advantage.

In the past, the United States has endured far more perilous times than those we currently face, and I believe that you will never make money betting against the United States over the long term. We have come through far greater challenges to emerge stronger, more vibrant, and ready to face the future. I believe this time is no different and that investors who avail themselves of the superior stock selection strategies featured in this book will be delighted with the outcome over the long term.

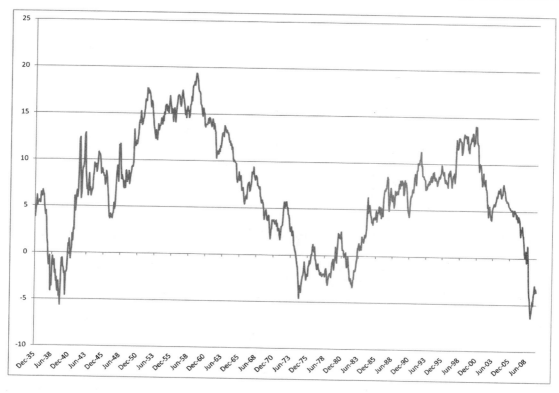

FIGURE I.1

US equity risk premium rolling 10-year percent return

EXTENDING OUR EARLIER STUDIES

This fourth edition of *What Works on Wall Street* continues to offer readers access to long-term studies of Wall Street's most effective investment strategies. Prior to its initial publication in 1996, no widely available, comprehensive guides were available to which stock selection strategies were long-term winners and which were not. Here, I show how careful readers of earlier editions of the book could have avoided much of the carnage visited upon investors in the two bear markets of the 2000s—simply by *avoiding* the types of stocks that, while popular during the stock market bubble of the 1990s, had historically proven themselves to be horrible long-term performers. We also show how readers of the first edition of the book would have fared simply by using the information presented as a guideline for which stocks to buy and which to avoid. Most of the advice derived from this long-term analysis is the same as when the book was originally published in 1996, yet we have also expanded the number of single-factor and multifactor strategies for this edition.

WHAT'S NEW

We've made significant changes to the way we analyze the data, and we've added several individual factors and multifactor models. Among the new changes:

- For all factor and multifactor models, we now present the composited returns for all months of the test. The first three versions of *What Works on Wall Street* presented the results of what an investor would have achieved if he or she had invested on December 31 of each year. While useful, it ignored any seasonality that might occur in a factor or strategy. We wanted to eliminate that concern by presenting the results for investments in each month and then compositing all returns to give a more accurate overall picture for how a factor or strategy performed, regardless of the month in which the investment was made. This makes the data more useful, since most of us do not confine our investments to December 31 of each year. This method also gives you a truer sense of what most investors will experience with the strategy, regardless of their starting date. To construct the composite returns for a given strategy, we begin with a portfolio in each month which will be held for one year, such that there are always 12 distinct portfolios for each strategy, all rebalanced annually. The composite monthly returns that we use for our analysis for any given month, then, are an average of the returns of those 12 portfolios. To make this switch, we were limited to the monthly data from Compustat, which began in 1963.

- Since the last publication of this book, O'Shaughnessy Asset Management has acquired the Center for Research in Security Prices (CRSP) dataset, which has monthly data going back to 1926. We now present returns for each factor for which we have data back to 1926. The factors include market capitalization, price-to-book ratio, dividend yield, buyback yield (a high buyback yield indicates that the company is aggressively repurchasing its shares in the market, signaling that management thinks the stock is undervalued), shareholder yield (which combines buyback and dividend yield), and price momentum. Using these long-term data, we have created several new multifactor models worth consideration. For all other factors and multifactor models, we begin with the Compustat monthly data beginning in 1963. This additional 37 years of data serves as an excellent holdout period. We also test if what was true for the 1963–2009 data is also true for the 1926–1963 data.

- For this edition of the book, we present the results for each individual factor looking at the top and bottom decile (10 percent) of stocks for each factor. A common criticism of the first several editions of the book was that we were focusing only on the extremes of each factor by presenting the result for the best and worst 50 stocks by factor. In order to give a more accurate representation of the returns of each factor and how they might contribute to your portfolio, for many of the multifactor tests we will continue to look at 25- and 50-stock portfolios.

- New single-factor reviews include: buyback yield, shareholder yield, EBITDA-to-enterprise value, cashflow-to-enterprise value, sales-to-enterprise value, accruals-to-price, cashflow-to-debt, annual sales growth, and a review of the efficacy of many accounting variables.

- We also present a new composited value factor that combines traditional value factors into a single ranking system to determine the overall condition of a stock, ranking stocks from the least expensive to the most. These composited value factors outperform all the single-value factors and do so with greater consistency. What's more, the spreads between best and worst decile are consistent and large; for example, the worst deciles for the various value composites in the Small Stocks universe all *lost money* over the last 46 years.

- New multifactor models include composited factors that are presented as a single factor that judges stocks on their combined scores on several factors; strategies that use price appreciation and shareholder yield; strategies that focus on investable microcap stocks that are cheap and have excellent price momentum; strategies that buy market-leading stocks with high dividend yields that serve as competition for bonds by offering yields consistent with or greater than the 10-year Treasury while also offering capital appreciation; among others.

- We also now include factor results for sectors, so you will know which group of factors works best at the individual sector level.

ORIGINS

It took the combination of fast computers and huge databases like Compustat and CRSP to prove that a portfolio's returns are essentially determined by the factors that define the portfolio. Before computers, it was almost impossible to determine what strategy guided any given portfolio. The number of underlying factors (characteristics that define a portfolio like PE ratio, dividend yield, etc.) an investor could consider seemed endless. The best you could do was look at portfolios in the most general ways. Sometimes even a *professional manager* didn't know what particular factors best characterized the stocks in his or her portfolio, relying more often on general descriptions and other qualitative measures.

Computers changed this. We can now analyze a portfolio and see which factors, if any, separate the best-performing strategies from the mediocre. With computers, we can also test combinations of factors over long periods of time, showing us what to expect in the future from any given investment strategy.

MOST STRATEGIES ARE MEDIOCRE

What Works on Wall Street shows that most investment strategies are mediocre and the majority, *particularly those most appealing to investors over the short term,* fail to beat the simple strategy of indexing to the S&P 500. The book also provides evidence that contradicts the academic theory that stock prices follow a "random walk."

Rather than moving about without rhyme or reason, the stock market methodically rewards certain investment strategies while punishing others. *What Works on Wall Street's* long-term returns show there's nothing random about long-term stock market returns. Investors can do *much better* than the market if they consistently use time-tested strategies that are based on sensible, rational methods for selecting stocks.

DISCIPLINE IS KEY

What Works on Wall Street shows that the only way to beat the market over the long term is to consistently use sensible investment strategies. Seventy percent of the mutual funds covered by Morningstar fail to beat the S&P 500 over almost any 10-year period because their managers lack the discipline to stick with one strategy through thick and thin. This lack of discipline devastates long-term performance.

HIGHLIGHTS

After reading *What Works on Wall Street,* investors will know that:

- Most small-capitalization strategies owe their superior returns to microcap stocks that have market capitalizations below $25 million. These stocks are too small for almost all investors to *actually buy*, making their returns on paper an illusion. That is why we cover stocks only with enough liquidity and capitalization for an investor to actually buy without huge market impact.
- Stocks with the worst price momentum are horrible long-term performers; the only time these stocks do well is in the first year after a severe (–40 percent or more) bear market when "junk" rallies have always occurred.
- Single value factors have vastly better returns and batting averages than pure growth factors. The one exception to this is price momentum, and even here it should always be used in connection with a value constraint.
- Using several value factors together in a composited value factor offers much better and more consistent returns than using individual value factors on their own.
- Accounting variables such as accruals to price, asset turnover, external financing, and percentage change in debt offer key insights into which stocks have higher-quality earnings. This translates directly into better performance for those stocks with higher-quality earnings and much lower returns for stocks with lower-quality earnings. Indeed, we have found that using several accounting variables together—total accruals to total assets, percentage change in net operating assets, total accruals to average assets, and depreciation expense to capital expense—dramatically improves the quality of stocks you are focusing on and also the return.
- The two least risky sectors—consumer staples and utilities—can nevertheless offer investors excellent returns at low levels of risk by focusing on composited value factors and shareholder yield. You'll find the results in Chapter Twenty-Four for a 50-stock portfolio from these two conservative sectors that nevertheless provides market-beating results with a much lower risk than the overall market.
- The poorest performing sector, returning an average annual compound return of 7.29 percent over the full period of our study, is also one of the most popular—information technologies.
- There are several large capitalization strategies that consistently beat the market while taking lower risks.

- Buying Wall Street's current darlings with the richest valuations is one of the worst things you can do.
- A simple strategy that buys the 25 best-performing stocks based on six-month price momentum from the stocks scoring in the upper 10 percent of one of our value composites earns more than 20 percent per year since 1963, with lower levels of risk than the All Stocks universe.
- Finding a workable investment plan and then working that plan, regardless of current conditions in the market, is the one sure way to success for long-term investors.

ACKNOWLEDGMENTS

This book would not have been possible without the help of many people. When I started this project almost 20 years ago, Jim Branscome, then head of S&P Compustat, was a champion of the project at every turn. His successor, Paul Cleckner, was also extraordinarily supportive and is an outstanding example of a businessman who understands that the best way to help the bottom-line of your business is to help the bottom-line of thousands of ordinary investors. Mitch Abeyta, the current head of Compustat, has also been wonderful to work with on the on-going effort to improve the strategies and data covered in the book.

I owe a special thanks to my colleagues Chris Meredith, Patrick O'Shaughnessy, Travis Fairchild, Scott Bartone, Ashvin Viswanathan, Amar Patel, and Nathan Przbylo. Virtual wizards at setting up backtests within the SAS and FactSet environment, this version would not have been possible without their considerable talent.

And for the first time I have a contributing author to *What Works on Wall Street*: my son, Patrick O'Shaughnessy, who wrote Chapter Three and assisted editorially on several others.

But this book would not have been finished without the continual help, support, and encouragement of my wife, Melissa. She earned her Summa Cum Laude degree in Journalism many years ago, yet I still reap the benefits decades later. Without her expert hand, this book might never have been finished. As Mark Twain said, "The difference between the right word and the almost right word is the difference between lightning and the lightning bug." In addition to loving her dearly, I owe any success I have as an author to her.

Thanks also to my entire team at O'Shaughnessy Asset Management for their support on this project.

STOCK INVESTMENT STRATEGIES: DIFFERENT METHODS, SIMILAR GOALS

Good intelligence is nine-tenths of any battle.

—Napoleon

There are two main approaches to equity investing: active and passive. The active approach is most common. With this approach managers attempt to maximize their returns at various levels of risk by buying stocks they believe are superior to others. Usually, the managers assess stocks in a traditional manner. They analyze the company, interview management, talk to customers and competitors, review historical trends and current forecasts, and then decide if the stock is worth buying.

Active investors are guided by styles, broadly called *growth and value*. The type of stocks they buy depends largely on their underlying philosophy. Growth investors buy stocks that have higher than average growth in sales and earnings with expectations for more of the same. Growth investors believe in the company's potential and think a stock's price will follow its earnings higher.

Value investors seek stocks with current market values substantially below liquidating value. They use factors like price-to-earnings (PE) ratio or price-to-sales ratios (PSR) to identify when a stock is selling below its intrinsic value. They bargain hunt, looking for stocks in which they can buy a dollar's worth of assets for less than a dollar. Value investors believe in the company's balance sheet, thinking that a stock's price will eventually rise to meet its intrinsic value.

Actively managed funds often use a hodgepodge of techniques from both schools of investing, but the most successful have strongly articulated strategies. The majority of mutual funds, professionally managed pension funds, and separately managed individual accounts are managed with an active approach.

TRADITIONAL ACTIVE MANAGEMENT DOESN'T WORK

Active management seems to make perfect sense until you review the record of traditional, actively managed funds. The majority does not beat the S&P 500. This is true over both short and long periods. Figure 1.1 shows the percentage of those actively managed diversified mutual funds in Morningstar's database that beat the S&P 500 over a 10-year period. While the record looks quite strong since 2007, the average—over all of the periods covered back to 1991—is just 30 percent. Thus, for all 10-year periods since 1991, 70 percent of actively managed funds failed to beat the S&P 500 over previous 10-year periods. What's more, this record overstates traditionally managed active fund performance, because it doesn't include all the funds that *failed to survive* for a 10-year period.

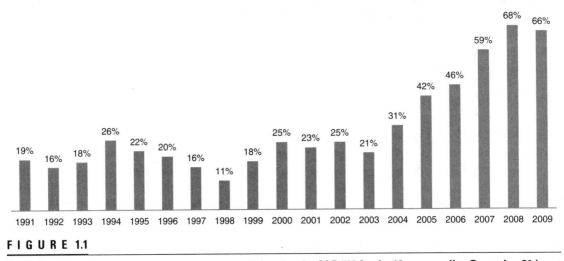

F I G U R E 1.1

Percent of all equity funds with 10-year track records beating the S&P 500 for the 10 years ending December 31 in each year

Source: For 1991–1996 *Morningstar OnDisc* for 1997–2009 Morningstar Inc. All Rights Reserved.

Passive indexing has exploded in the past two decades as a result. Investors buy an index that they think broadly represents the market, such as the S&P 500, and let it go at that. Their objective is to match the market, not outperform it. They're willing to give up their shot at outperforming the market for the security of not underperforming it. Since the publication of the first edition of this book in 1996, index managers have continued to see their assets under management soar. According to the September 21, 2009, issue of *Pensions & Investments*, an industry publication, "Worldwide index assets under management were $4.6 trillion as of June 30, 2009." What's more, since 1996 the popularity of exchange traded funds (ETFs)—index funds that are listed and traded on exchanges like stocks—has exploded, furthering what amounts to a revolution in investment management characterized by investors continuing to flock to more structured, disciplined investment strategies. *The Economist* magazine reported in its January 23, 2010, issue that, "At the end of 2009 ETF assets under management topped the $1 trillion mark for the first time, according to Blackrock, a fund-management firm. The industry's assets were just $40 billion at the end of 1999."

What's more, since the disappointing results of the last decade for equity returns, many institutions have planned to reduce their investments in equities, and those investments they do make will likely be made in low-cost index funds. According to a July 7, 2009, article in the industry publication *Fundfire*, "Institutional investors are expected to reduce their equity allocations to as low as 35 percent to 45 percent by 2015, down from the 55 percent they placed in equities in 2007, according to a survey released yesterday by The Boston Consulting Group."

WHAT'S THE PROBLEM?

Conventional academics aren't surprised that traditionally-managed funds fail to beat the market. Most have long held that markets are efficient and that current security prices reflect all available information; they argue that prices follow a *random walk* and move without rhyme or reason. According to their theories, you might as well have a monkey throw darts at a stock page as attempt security analysis because stock prices are random and cannot be predicted.

Yet the long-term evidence in this book contradicts the random walk theory. Far from following a random walk, the evidence continues to reveal a purposeful stride. The 46 years of data found in this edition proves strong return predictability. Indeed, the CRSP data included in this edition extends this to 83 years of historical data. What's more, this return predictability continues to persist even since the first edition of this book was published in 1996. The market clearly and consistently rewards certain attributes (e.g., stocks with low price-to-earnings, price-to-cash flow, and price-to-sales ratios) and clearly and consistently punishes others (e.g., stocks with high price-to-earnings, price-to-cash flow, and price-to-sales ratios) over long periods of time and over many market cycles. Indeed, the crash of October 2007 through March 2009, where the S&P 500 fell a dizzying 51 percent from peak to trough, has led many academics and portfolio managers to challenge the notion that markets are in any way efficient. According to the *New York Times*, "Market strategist Jeremy Grantham has stated flatly that the Efficient Market Theory is responsible for the current financial crisis (in 2008 and 2009), claiming that belief in the hypothesis caused financial leaders to have a 'chronic underestimation of the dangers of asset bubbles breaking.'" A careful review of the data suggests that the stock market is a complex, adaptive system with feedback loops that allows for bubbles and crashes and always follows similar patterns during both trends. We'll learn more about this in the coming chapters on behavioral finance and neurofinance.

Yet the paradox remains: if past historical tests—as well as the real-time results that were generated with the strategies featured in this book since its initial publication—show such high return predictability, why do 70 percent of traditionally managed mutual funds continually fail to beat the S&P 500 over long periods of time? Finding exploitable investment opportunities does not mean that it is easy to make money, however. To do so requires the ability to consistently, patiently, and slavishly stick with the strategy, even when it is performing poorly relative to other methods. One of the central themes of this book is that all strategies have performance cycles in which they over- and underperform their relevant benchmarks. The key to outstanding long-term performance is to find strategies that have the highest base rate, or batting average (more on that later), and then stick with that strategy, even when it's underperforming other strategies and benchmarks. Few people are capable of such action. Successful investors do not comply with nature; they defy it. Most investors react very emotionally to the short-term gyrations of the market, and I've seen many who follow my strategies and portfolios in real time say, "Well, the strategies used to work, but they don't anymore," after just a few months of underperformance. Indeed, history documents several periods in which factors have inverted, with the long-term factor that normally produces outstanding results being walloped by the factor that has historically led to disastrous results. What appears dull and boring in a long-term compilation of factor returns becomes emotional and frightening when investors live through it in real time, leading to doubt as to whether the long-term results will somehow change. Our very human nature leads us to believe that we live in unique times in which the lessons from the past no longer apply. Generation after generation has shared this outlook, and by ignoring the lessons of the past, each generation has repeated the same mistakes of its predecessors. In the next chapter, I argue that the reason traditional management doesn't work well is that decision making is *systematically flawed and unreliable*. This provides an opportunity to those of us who use rational, disciplined methods to buy and sell stocks using time-tested methods to do much better than a simple index like the S&P 500, essentially allowing the disciplined investor to arbitrage human nature.

Since this book was first published in 1996, a school of academic thought called Behavioral Economics has grown in popularity to explain why these performance anomalies continue to exist even after being documented and written about extensively. This work has received a great deal of public attention and centers around a new paradigm for evaluating how people *actually* make investment choices. In his book *Behavioral Finance: Insights into Your Irrational Mind and the Market*, James Montier writes:

> This is the world of behavioral finance, a world in which human emotions rule, logic has its place, but markets are moved as much by psychological factors as by information from corporate balance sheets… [T]he models of classical finance are fatally flawed. They fail to produce predictions that are even vaguely close to the outcomes we observe in real financial markets … of course, now we need some understanding of what causes markets to deviate from their fundamental value. The answer quite simply is human behavior.

While I examine some of the tenets of behavioral finance in Chapters 2 and 3, I think one of the principal reasons classically trained economists were getting the wrong answers was that they were asking the wrong questions.

STUDYING THE WRONG THINGS

It is no surprise that academics find traditionally managed stock portfolios following a random walk. The past records of most traditional managers cannot be predictive of future returns because their behavior is *inconsistent*. You cannot make forecasts based on inconsistent behavior, because when you behave inconsistently, *you are unpredictable*. Even if the manager is a perfectly consistent investor—a hallmark of the best money managers—if that manager leaves the fund, all predictive ability from past performance of the fund is lost. Moreover, if a manager changes his or her style, all predictive ability from past performance is also lost. Traditional academics, therefore, have been measuring the wrong things. They assumed perfect, rational behavior in a capricious environment ruled by greed, hope, and fear. They have been contrasting the returns of a passively held portfolio—the S&P 500—with the returns of portfolios managed in an inconsistent, shoot from the hip style. Track records are worthless unless you know what strategy the manager uses and if it is still being used. When you study traditionally managed funds, you're really looking at two things: first, the strategy used, and second, the ability of the manager to implement it successfully. It makes much more sense to contrast the one factor (in this case, market capitalization) S&P 500 portfolio with other one or multifactor portfolios.

WHY INDEXING WORKS

Indexing to the S&P 500 works because it sidesteps flawed decision making and automates the simple strategy of buying the big stocks that make up the S&P 500. The mighty S&P 500 consistently beat 70 percent of traditionally managed funds over the long term by doing nothing more than making a disciplined bet on large capitalization stocks. Figure 1.2 compares the returns of the S&P 500 with those of our Large Stocks universe, which consists of all the stocks in the Compustat database that have market capitalizations greater than the database mean in any given year. This effectively limits us to the top 16 percent of the companies in the database by market capitalization. Stocks are then bought in equal dollar amounts. The returns are virtually identical. $10,000 invested in the S&P 500 of December 31, 1926, was worth $23,171,851 on December 31, 2009, a compound return of 9.78 percent. The same $10,000 invested in our Large Stocks universe was worth $21,617,372, a compound return of 9.69 percent. (Both include the reinvestment of all dividends.) And it's not just the absolute returns that are so similar. Risk, as measured by the standard deviation of return, is also virtually identical for the two strategies. The S&P 500 had an annual standard deviation of return of 19.27 percent, whereas the Large Stocks universe had 19.35 percent. And remember that our Large Stock universe is equally weighted whereas the S&P 500 is cap weighted—the results would be even closer if we ran our Large Stocks universe on a cap-weighted basis.

Thus, far from being "the market," the S&P 500's returns are the result of a simple strategy that says, "Buy big stocks." The reason this works so well is that the S&P 500 *never varies* from this strategy. It doesn't wake up in the morning and say, "You know, small-cap stocks have been doing well recently. I think I will change and become a small-cap index,"

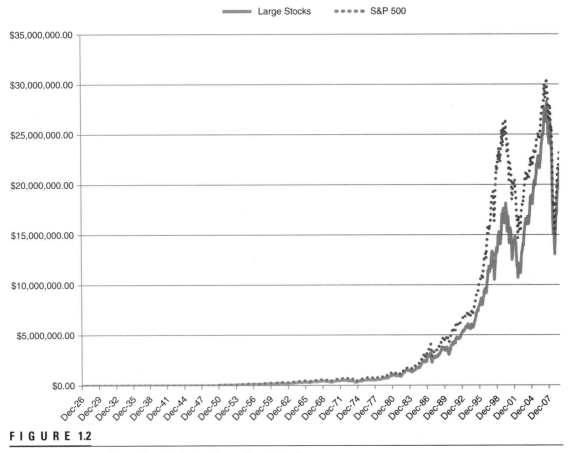

FIGURE 1.2

Comparative returns, December 31, 1926, to December 31, 2009

nor does it watch as Ben Bernanke gives testimony to Congress and say, "Yikes! Today I'm going to become the S&P cash and bond index!" It just continues to passively implement the strategy of buying big stocks, and that's why it's so effective. The S&P 500 beats 70 percent of conventionally managed funds because it never varies from its underlying strategy of buying large-capitalization stocks. It never panics, has second thoughts, or is envious when other indexes outperform it. The key to its long-term success is its unwavering disciplined implementation of an investment strategy.

Yet, indexing to the S&P 500 is just *one* form of a passive implementation of a strategy, in this case consistently buying big stocks. As you will see in later chapters, the S&P 500's long-term results are fairly mediocre, coming in the bottom third of all strategies we tested. There are numerous strategies that do vastly better than the S&P 500 over long periods of time. One example is called "Dogs of the Dow," which simply buys the 10 highest-yielding stocks in the Dow Jones Industrial Average each year. This is a great example of another strategy that works consistently over the long term. From 1928—when the Dow Jones Industrial was expanded to 30 stocks—through 2009, the strategy consistently beat the S&P 500.

Indeed, it beat the S&P 500 in almost all rolling 10-year periods, with only five 10-year rolling periods out of 72 underperforming the S&P 500. So $10,000 invested in the Dogs of the Dow on December 31, 1928 (when the Dow Jones Industrial Average was expanded to 30 stocks), was worth $55 million on December 31, 2009, an average annual compound return of 11.22 percent, compared to a $10,000 investment in the S&P 500 which would have grown to just $11.7 million or an average annual return of 9.12 percent. You'll find a number of other such winning strategies in this book.

PINPOINTING PERFORMANCE

It took the combination of fast computers and huge databases like Compustat and CRSP to prove that a portfolio's returns are essentially determined by the factors that define the portfolio. Before computers, it was virtually impossible to determine what strategy guided the development of a portfolio. The number of underlying factors an investor could consider (characteristics that define a portfolio like PE ratio, dividend yield, etc.) seemed endless. The best you could do was look at portfolios in the most general ways. Sometimes even a professional manager didn't know what particular factors characterized the stocks in his or her portfolio, relying more often on general descriptions and other qualitative measures. Traditional approaches to investing relied heavily on the portfolio manager's insights about prospects for the business and/or industry and often specifically what the manager thought about the management team of the corporation. As we will learn in coming chapters, intuitive-based management is almost always outperformed by the consistent application of time-tested strategies.

Indeed, it was the computer that changed our ability to prove this. We now can quickly analyze the factors that define any portfolio and see which, if any, separate the best-performing funds and strategies from the mediocre. With computers, we also can test combinations of factors over long periods, thus showing us what to expect in the future from any given investment strategy. This is because the *one* element that has not changed is human nature. We continue to price securities in the same way we did during the panic of 1907, the crash of 1929, the bull market of the 1950s and 1960s, the market malaise of the 1970s, the bull market of the 1980s and 1990s, the Internet bubble of 1999, and the bear markets of 2000–2002 and 2007–2009.

We now have the ability to empirically compare different investment strategies and their ongoing performance over time. What you will see in coming chapters is that almost all of them are deeply consistent with what common sense would tell you was true. Strategies that buy stocks that are selling at deep discounts to cash flow, sales, earnings, EBITDA to enterprise value, and so on do extraordinarily better than those that are willing to buy stocks with the richest valuations. If he had had access to today's powerful computers and huge databases, Ben Graham, the founder of modern securities analysis, would have been able to prove as much back in the 1930s.

This area of research has blossomed in the years since the original edition of this book was published, with many managers running a long-term test of their investment strategies in a manner similar to the tests in this book. One potential problem with the proliferation of this kind of research—which I expand on later—is the potential for *data mining*. When you test an infinite number of strategies, statistically you are bound to find several that have vastly outperformed the market, however odd they might be. That's why we insist on using great restraint when testing a strategy. Generally, the strategy must make intuitive sense, generate similar findings when using similar variables (i.e., low price-to-sales and low price-to-cash flow should demonstrate similar findings), and perform well in all hold-out periods. I cover this in greater depth in later chapters.

DISCIPLINE IS THE KEY

If you use a one-factor model based on market capitalization—as in the examples above—you get the same results as the seemingly mighty S&P 500. If, however, you change a portfolio's underlying factors so that they deviate significantly from the S&P 500, say by keeping price-to-sales ratios below one or dividend yields above a certain number, you can expect the portfolio to perform *very differently* from the market. S&P 500 index funds are nothing more than *structured portfolios* that make disciplined bets on a large capitalization factor. *Many other factors perform much better.* Systematic, structured investing is a hybrid of active and passive management that automates the buy and sell decisions. If a stock meets the criteria, it's bought. If not, not. No personal, emotional judgments enter into the process. Essentially, you're indexing a portfolio to a specific investment strategy and, by doing so, uniting the best of active and passive investing. The disciplined implementation of active strategies is the key to performance. Traditional managers usually follow a hit and miss approach to investing. Their lack of discipline accounts for their inability to beat simple approaches that never vary from the underlying strategy.

Imagine what the Dow would look like today if, in the 1920s, the editors of Dow Jones & Co. decided to revamp the Dow Jones Industrial Average, basing it on reasonably priced value stocks rather than just on big industrial companies. If they expanded the list to 50 names and in each year simply bought the 50 large stocks with the lowest price-to-book ratios, the "market" today would be three times higher than it is!

CONSISTENCY WINS

In a study for my book *Invest Like the Best*, I found that the one thing that unites the best managers is consistency. I am not alone. In the 1970s, AT&T did a study of its pension fund managers and found that successful investing requires, at a minimum, a structured decision-making process that can be easily defined and a stated investment philosophy that is consistently applied. John Neff, the long-time manager of the Windsor Fund, and Peter Lynch, of the Magellan Fund, became legends because their success was the result of slavish devotion to their investment strategies. The turmoil of the market crash between October 2007 and February 2009, when stocks plunged at a faster and steeper rate than at any time other than the early 1930s, led many investors to abandon their underlying approach to investing—which I believe will ultimately cause grave damage to their long-term performance. It's virtually impossible to remain stoic in the face of such market activity, but the consistent application of a time-tested investment strategy is the only way to ensure superior long-term results.

A STRUCTURED PORTFOLIO IN ACTION

Very few funds or managers stick with their strategies over long periods. Inevitably, events like the tech bubble of the late 1990s cause even the most value-oriented managers to sneak some growth stocks into their portfolios, and severely declining markets like those in 2007 through early 2009 cause even the most stalwart defenders of long-term equities to throw in the towel, raise loads of cash, and wonder when the assault will stop.

There is, however, *one* fund that I could find that truly stuck to its underlying investment strategy—the ING Corporate Leaders Trust (Ticker LEXCX). It's unusual in that it was set up as a unit investment trust and is a good example of a *structured portfolio* in action. Formed in 1935—during the depths of the Great Depression—the trust was designed to hold 30 stocks that its creators felt were the leading companies in their industry. The fund's portfolio is *share-weighted,* holding the same number of shares in each company regardless of price. Since 1935, 9 companies have been eliminated and or combined with others, so the portfolio currently holds just 21 stocks. You'll know every name in the portfolio—including ExxonMobil; Procter & Gamble; AT&T; General Electric, and Dow Chemical. Yet this single-factor portfolio is a market-slayer—since its inception in 1935, the fund has done significantly better than the S&P 500 and the average large stock value mutual fund, as well as besting the vast majority of traditionally managed funds. A review of the data at Morningstar.com shows that the fund is doing significantly better than both the S&P 500 and the average Morningstar Large Value category. Over the five years ending March 31, 2010, the fund is 1.17 percent ahead of the S&P 500 and 2.02 percent ahead of the average Large Value fund in the Morningstar universe. This performance put it ahead of 85 percent of its peers in the large value universe over the previous five years! The 10-year numbers are equally compelling. For the 10 years ending March 31, 2010, the fund is 5.66 percent ahead of the S&P 500 and 2.66 percent ahead of the average large value mutual fund covered by Morningstar. Finally, over the previous 15 years, the fund is 1.05 percent ahead of the S&P 500 and 1.68 percent ahead of the average Large Value fund in Morningstar, putting it ahead of 82 percent of its peers in the Morningstar Large Value universe. What's more, its charter prevents rebalancing the portfolio, which would allow it to reflect changes in corporate leadership since 1935. Imagine how it would have done with some of today's corporate leaders like Microsoft and Intel!

OVERWHELMED BY OUR NATURE

Knowing and doing are two very different things. As Goethe said, "In the realm of ideas, everything depends on enthusiasm; in the real world, all rests on perseverance." While we may *intellectually* understand what we should do, we usually are overwhelmed by our nature, allowing the intensely emotional present to overpower our better judgment. When someone questioned the general secretary of the former Soviet Union, Mikhail Gorbachev, about actions he had taken against his better judgment, he replied, "Your question is academic because it is abstract. People don't have the luxury of living in the abstract. They live in the real, emotional, full-blooded world of reality." Readers who personally experienced the recent "full-blooded" fear as equities tumbled from 2008 through the beginning of 2009 have only to look at their own behavior to understand this concept extremely well. It is in the full-blooded world of reality that our problems begin. Let's see why this is so.

C H A P T E R

THE UNRELIABLE EXPERTS: GETTING IN THE WAY OF OUTSTANDING PERFORMANCE

What ails the truth is that it is mainly uncomfortable, and often dull. The human mind seeks something more amusing, and more caressing.

—H. L. Mencken

Everyone is guilty of faulty decision making, not just the scions of Wall Street. An accountant must offer an opinion on the creditworthiness of a firm. A college administrator must decide which students to accept into a graduate program. A psychologist must decide whether the patient's problems are neurosis or psychosis. A doctor must decide if it's liver cancer or not. More prosaically, a bookie must try to handicap the next horse race.

All these are activities in which an expert predicts an outcome. They occur every day and make up the fabric of our lives. Generally, predictions are made in two ways. Most common is for a person to run through a variety of possible outcomes in his or her head, essentially relying on personal knowledge, experience, and common sense to reach a decision. This is known as a clinical or *intuitive* approach, and it is how most traditional active money managers make choices. Stock analysts may pore over a company's financial statements, interview management, talk to customers and competitors, and finally try to make an overall forecast for that company's health and long-term potential. The graduate school administrator might use a host of data, from college grade-point average and interviews with applicants, to determine whether a student should be accepted. This type of judgment relies on the perceptiveness of the forecaster. Psychologists have shown in numerous studies that when people are confronted with vast amounts of data, their brains create mental shortcuts to help them make decisions. The shortcuts, called *heuristics*, are the rules of thumb on which most intuitive forecasters rely when making any number of complex decisions or forecasts in their field.

The other way to reach a decision is the actuarial or *quantitative* approach. Here the forecaster makes no subjective judgments, nor does she rely on a rule of thumb heuristic. Rather, only empirical relationships between the data and the desired outcome are used to reach conclusions. This method relies solely on proven relationships using larger samples of data, in which the data are systematically weighed and integrated. It's similar to the structured portfolio selection process I discuss in Chapter 1. The graduate school administrator might use a model that finds college grade-point average highly correlated to graduate school success and admit only those who made a certain grade. A money manager might rely on a stock selection technique that employs long-term, empirical tests (like those in this book) that prove the strategies' efficacy over the span of 50 or more years. In almost every instance, we naturally prefer qualitative, intuitive methods. In almost every instance, *we're wrong.*

HUMAN JUDGMENT IS LIMITED

David Faust writes in his revolutionary book, *The Limits of Scientific Reasoning*, "Human judgment is far more limited than we think. We have a surprisingly restricted capacity to manage or interpret complex information." Studying a wide range of professionals, from medical doctors making diagnoses to experts making predictions of job success in academic or military training, Faust found that *human judges were consistently outperformed by simple actuarial models.* Like traditional money managers, most professionals cannot beat the passive implementation of time-tested formulas.

Another researcher, Paul Meehl, offered the first comprehensive review of statistical prediction (similar to an empirical, systematic approach) and clinical prediction (similar to an intuitive, traditional heuristic approach) in his 1954 study, *Clinical versus Statistical Prediction: A Theoretical Analysis and Review of the Literature.* He reviewed 20 studies that compared clinical and statistical predictions for three things: academic success, response to electric shock therapy, and criminal recidivism. In almost every instance, Meehl found that simple actuarial models outperformed the human judges. In predicting academic success in college, for example, a model using just high school grade-point average and the level attained on an aptitude test (such as the SAT) outperformed the judgment of admissions officers at several colleges. Robyn Dawes, in his book, *House of Cards: Psychology and Psychotherapy Built on Myth*, tells us more. He refers to Jack Sawyer, a researcher who published a review of 45 studies comparing the two forecasting techniques: in none was the clinical, intuitive method—the one favored by most people—found to be superior. What's more, Sawyer included instances in which the human judges had more information than the model and were given a result of the quantitative models before being asked for a prediction. The actuarial models still beat the human judges!

Psychology researcher L. R. Goldberg went further: he devised a simple model based on the results of the Minnesota Multiphasic Personality Inventory (MMPI), a personality test commonly used to distinguish between neurosis and psychosis, to determine into which category a patient falls. His test achieved a success rate of 70 percent. He found that no human expert could match his model's result. The best judge achieved an overall success ratio of 67 percent. Reasoning that his human judges might do better with practice, he gave training packets consisting of 300 additional MMPI profiles to his judges, along with immediate feedback on their accuracy. Even after the practice sessions, none of the human judges matched the model's success rate of 70 percent.

WHAT'S THE PROBLEM?

The problem doesn't seem to be lack of insight on the part of human judges. One study of pathologists predicting survival time following the initial diagnosis of Hodgkin's disease, a form of cancer, found that the human judges were vastly outperformed by a simple actuarial formula. Oddly, the model used exactly the same criteria that the judges themselves said they used. The judges were largely unable to use their own ideas properly. They used perceptive, intelligent criteria, but they were unable to take advantage of the predictive ability of the criteria. *The judges themselves, not the value of their insights, were responsible for their own dismal predictive performance.*

WHY MODELS BEAT HUMANS

In a famous cartoon, Walt Kelly's character Pogo says, "We've met the enemy, and he is us." This illustrates our dilemma. Models beat the human forecasters because they reliably and consistently apply the same criteria time after time. In almost every instance, it is the total reliability of application of the model that accounts for its superior performance. Models never vary. They are always consistent. They are never moody, never fight with their spouse, are never hung over from a night on the town, and never get bored. They don't favor vivid, interesting stories over reams of statistical data. They never take anything personally. They don't have egos. They're not out to prove anything. If they were people, they'd be the death of any party.

People, on the other hand, are far more interesting. It's far more natural to react emotionally or to personalize the problem than it is to dispassionately review broad statistical occurrences—and so much more fun! It's much more natural for us to look at the limited set of our personal experiences and then generalize from this small sample to create a rule-of-thumb heuristic. We are a bundle of inconsistencies, and although this tends to make us interesting, it plays havoc with our ability to successfully invest our money. In most instances, money managers, like the college administrators, doctors, and accountants mentioned above, favor the intuitive method of forecasting. They all follow the same path: analyze the company, interview the management, talk to customers and competitors, and so on. Most, if not all, money managers think that they have the superior insights and intelligence they need to help them to pick winning stocks, yet 70 percent of them are routinely outperformed by the S&P 500. They are victims of their own overconfidence in their ability to outsmart and outguess everyone else on Wall Street. Even though virtually every study conducted over the last 60 years has found that simple, actuarially based models created with a large data sample will outperform traditional active managers, the managers refuse to admit this simple fact, clinging to the belief that, while this may be true for other investors, it's not true for *them*.

Each of us, it seems, believes that we are above average. Sadly, this cannot be true statistically. Yet, in tests of people's belief in their own ability—typically people are asked to rank their ability as drivers—virtually everyone puts his or her own ability in the upper 10 to 20 percent. It may be tempting to dismiss this as a foible that highly trained professionals would not stumble into. Yet, as Professor Nick Bostrom of Oxford University points out in his paper *Existential Risks: Analyzing Human Extinction Scenarios and Related Hazards*, "Bias seems to be present even among highly educated people. According to one survey, almost half of all sociologists believed that they would become one of the top ten in their field, and 94% of sociologists thought they were better at their jobs than their average colleagues." In his 1998 paper *The Psychology of the Nonprofessional Investor*, Nobel laureate Daniel Kahneman says, "The biases of judgment and decision making have sometimes been called cognitive illusions. Like visual illusions, the mistakes of intuitive reasoning are not easily eliminated ... merely learning about illusions does not eliminate them." Kahneman goes on to say that, like our investors above, the majority of investors are dramatically over confident and optimistic, prone to the illusion of control where none exists. Kahneman also points out that the reason it is so difficult for investors to correct their false beliefs is that they also suffer from *hindsight* bias, a condition that he described thus: "Psychological evidence indicates people can rarely reconstruct, after the fact, what they thought about the probability of an event before it occurred. Most are honestly deceived when they exaggerate their earlier estimate of the probability that the event would occur ... because of another hindsight bias, events that the best informed experts did not anticipate often appear almost inevitable after they occur."

If Kahneman's insight seems hard to believe, go back and see how many of the "experts" were calling for a Nasdaq crash in the early part of the year 2000 and contrast that with the number of people who now say it was inevitable. Or go to the library and browse business magazines from the summer of 2007. Were any of them filled with dire warnings about the coming crash in real estate and credit markets and the worst stock market downturn since the Great Depression? On January 1, 2008, would a panel of Wall Street's top analysts, economists, market forecasters, stock pickers, and money managers ever have predicted that in less than two years, Bear Stearns would be forced to sell itself to JPMorgan Chase for a fraction of book value because of a run on the bank? That Lehman Brothers, a firm with more than 156 years of operating history, would collapse into bankruptcy? That Merrill Lynch—the thundering herd—would be forced to sell itself to the Bank of America to avoid its own collapse? That Goldman Sachs and Morgan Stanley, kings of the investment bankers, would be forced to declare themselves ordinary banks? My guess is that no matter how diligently you search, you will find no such warnings. *After the fact*, we see a plethora of books, articles, and documentaries that chronicle the crash, with many authors claiming it was inevitable. That's hindsight bias.

What's more, even investors who were guided by a quantitative stock selection system let their human inconsistencies hogtie them. A September 16, 2004, issue of the *Wall Street*

Journal includes an article titled "A Winning Stock Pickers Losing Fund" by Jeff D. Opdyke and Jane J. Kim. The story centers on the Value Line Investment Survey, which is one of the top independent stock research services and has a remarkable long-term record of identifying winners. According to the *Wall Street Journal*, "The company also runs a mutual fund, and in one of Wall Street's odd paradoxes, it has performed terribly. Investors following the Value Line approach to buying and selling stocks would've racked up cumulative gains of nearly 76% over the five years ended in December, according to the investment research firm. That period includes the worst bear market in a generation [Author's note: the article was referring to the downturn in 2000–2003, not what turned out to be the worse downturn of 2008–2009]. By contrast, the mutual fund—one of the nation's oldest, having started in 1950—lost a cumulative 19% over the same period. The discrepancy has a lot to do with the fact that the Value Line fund, despite its name, does not rigorously follow the weekly investment advice printed by its parent Value Line publishing." In other words, the managers of the fund ignore their own data, thinking that they can improve on the quantitative selection process. The article goes on to point out that another closed-end fund, the First Trust Value Line Fund, adheres closely to the Value Line survey advice and has earned gains more in line with the underlying research.

BASE RATES ARE BORING

Many investors, as well as anyone else using traditional, intuitive forecasting methods, are overwhelmed by their human nature. They use information unreliably, at one point including a stock in a portfolio and at another time excluding it, even though in each instance the information about the stock is the same. Our decision making is *systematically flawed* because we prefer gut reactions and individual, colorful stories to boring base rates. Base rates are among the most illuminating statistics that exist. They're just like batting averages. For example, if a town of 100,000 people had 70,000 lawyers and 30,000 engineers, the base rate for lawyers would be 70 percent. When used in the stock market, these rates tell you what to expect from a certain class of stocks (e.g., all stocks with high dividend yields) and what that variable shows for how that category of stocks has performed over many decades of data. We have found that since the original publication of this book in 1996, the performance of the various factors we studied has persisted. Remember that the base rates tell you nothing about how each individual member of that class will behave. Rather they indicate how *all* stocks with high dividend yields—or whatever factor is being reviewed—will behave.

Most statistical prediction techniques use base rates. For example, 75 percent of university students with grade-point averages above 3.50 go on to do well in graduate school; smokers are twice as likely to get cancer; the average 70-year-old in the United States can expect, based on actuarial tables, to live another 13$\frac{1}{2}$ years; stocks with low PE ratios outperformed the market in 99 percent of all rolling 10-year periods between 1964 and 2009. The best way to predict the future is to bet with the base rate that is derived from a large sample. Yet numerous studies have found that people make full use of base rate information only when there is a lack of descriptive data. In one example, people are told that out of a sample of 100 people, 70 are lawyers and 30 are engineers. When provided with no additional information and asked to guess the occupation of a randomly selected 10, people use the base rate information, saying that all 10 are lawyers, by doing so they ensure themselves of getting the most right.

However, when worthless yet descriptive data were added, such as, "Dick is a highly motivated 30-year-old married man who is well liked by his colleagues," people largely ignored the base rate information in favor of their "feel" for the person. They're certain that their unique insights will help them make a better forecast, even when the additional information is meaningless. We prefer descriptive data to impersonal statistics because they better represent our individual experience. Then when *stereotypical* information is added, such as, "Dick is 30 years old, married, shows no interest in politics or social issues, and likes to spend free time on his many hobbies, which include carpentry and mathematical puzzles," people *totally* ignore the base rate and say that Dick is an engineer, despite a 70 percent chance that he is a lawyer. This bias has been proven time and again with numerous tests over a range of subjects. People *always* default to making predictions based upon their individual experience and intuition.

It's difficult to blame people. Base rates are boring; experience is vivid and fun. The only way anyone will pay 100 times a company's earnings for a stock is if it has a tremendous story. Never mind that stocks with high PE ratios beat the market less than 1 percent of the time over all rolling 10-year periods between 1964 and 2009—the story is so compelling that you're happy to throw the base rates out the window.

THE INDIVIDUAL VERSUS THE GROUP

Human nature makes it virtually impossible to forgo the specific information of an individual case in favor of the results of a great number of cases. We're interested in *this* stock and *this* company, not with this *class* of stocks or with this *class* of companies. Large numbers mean nothing to us. As Stalin chillingly said, "One death is a tragedy; a million, a statistic." When making an investment, we almost always do so on a stock-by-stock basis, rarely thinking about the overall strategy. If a story about one stock is compelling enough, we're willing to ignore what the base rates tell us about an entire class of stocks.

Imagine if the life insurance industry made decisions on a case-by-case basis. An agent visits you at your home, checks out your spouse and children, and finally makes a judgment based on his gut feeling. How many people who should get coverage would be denied, and how many millions of dollars in premiums would be lost? The reverse is also true. Someone who should be denied life insurance might be extended coverage because the agent's gut feeling was that *this* individual is different, despite what actuarial tables say. The company would lose millions in additional payouts. The reason life insurance companies are so profitable, however, is that they base coverage and premiums solely on what the actuarial tables tell them. Actuarial tables are developed using huge databases of human mortality statistics based on underlying characteristics such as weight, family history of disease, blood work, blood pressure, smoking and drinking habits, and prior history.

They tell you what to expect the central tendencies of a large group will be. If you are 33 years old, have no family history of heart disease or cancer, are a nonsmoker and moderate drinker, have normal blood pressure and excellent blood work, your chances of being extended life insurance at a low rate are excellent. Why? Because the mortality tables say that it is highly unlikely for you to die anytime soon. Does this mean that the life insurance companies will make money on all 33-year-olds? No. There will be rare instances where a freak accident kills some of these healthy young people, but the vast majority of them will go on living and paying their premiums to the life insurance company.

The same thing happens when we think in terms of *individual* stocks, rather than stock selection strategies. A case-by-case approach wreaks havoc with returns, because it virtually guarantees that many of our choices will, at least partially, include our emotions. This is a highly unreliable, unsystematic way to buy stocks, yet it's the most natural and the most common. In the 13 years since the initial publication of this book, I have given hundreds of presentations about its findings. I always see people nodding their heads when I tell them that low price-to-sales stocks do vastly better than stocks with high price-to-sales. They agree because this is a simple fact, and it makes intuitive sense to them that paying less for every dollar of sales should lead to higher returns than paying more for every dollar of sales. But when I give them some of the actual names of stocks that meet these criteria, their demeanor visibly changes. Hands will go up with statements like, "What a dog," or, "I hate that industry," simply because we have now provided them with specific individual stocks about which they may have ingrained prejudices. Combating these personal feelings, even when we are aware of the bias, is a very difficult task indeed.

PERSONAL EXPERIENCE PREFERRED

We also place more reliance on personal experience than on impersonal base rates. An excellent example is the 1972 presidential campaign. The reporters on the campaign trail with George McGovern unanimously agreed that he could not lose by more than 10 percent, even though they knew he lagged in the polls by 20 percent and that no major poll had been wrong by more than 3 percent in 24 years. These tough, intelligent people bet against the base rate because the concrete evidence of their personal experience overwhelmed them. They *saw* huge crowds of supporters, *felt* their enthusiasm, and *trusted* their feelings. In much the same way, a market analyst who has visited the company and knows the president will largely ignore the statistical information that tells him that the company is a poor investment if the company's executives do a good job in persuading him that while that might be true in general, it does not hold for *their* company because of any number of colorful stories they might tell him. In social science terms, he's overweighting the vivid story and underweighting the pallid statistics.

Investors do this all the time, and a story told to me by a colleague clearly illustrates that this can lead to disastrous results. At an investment conference in 2001, a portfolio manager who owned a large stake in Enron was asked repeatedly what was going on with the company. Enron shares had fallen from an August 2000 high of $90 per share to the mid-$40s, and investors wanted to know what the portfolio manager's thoughts were about the future of the company. The manager responded that he felt everything was fine at Enron; in fact, he had recently attended a barbecue at the CFO's home where many upper-management executives were present and had assured him that all was well.

The manager went on to say that he was so relieved with their explanation that he was buying more Enron shares. Late in 2001, Enron filed for bankruptcy, and its shares traded at one dollar. Clearly, this manager's judgment was clouded by a reliance on stories and personal relationships, which blinded him to the facts. His relationship with the executives, many of whom went on to plead guilty to securities fraud and other fraudulent management practices, helped him turn a blind eye to what the market seemed to think—there was something rotten at Enron's core.

There are many similar examples to prove the point. According to Barton Biggs's book *Wealth, War and Wisdom*, there is ample evidence that so-called experts making intuitive forecasts *are right less than half the time* and that "they were worse than dart-throwing monkeys in forecasting outcomes when multiple probabilities were involved." And the study he was referring to did not use a small sample—it covered 284 experts who made 82,361 forecasts over a period of many years. The book concluded that most of these errors were made because analysts made decisions using intuitive, emotional heuristics. Biggs is not alone—in his book *Value Investing: Tools and Techniques for Intelligent Investment*, James Montier writes: "One of the recurring themes of my research is that we just can't forecast. There isn't a shred of evidence to suggest that we can. This, of course, doesn't stop everyone from trying. Last year, Rui Antunes of our quant team looked at the short-term forecasting ability of analysts. The results aren't kind to my brethren. The average 24-month forecast error is around 94%, the average 12-month forecast error is around 45%."

In his book *Expert Political Judgment*, Philip Tetlock said, "Human performance suffers because we are, deep down, deterministic thinkers with an aversion to probabilistic strategies that accept the inevitability of error." In other words, even though the rational thing to do is to bet with the base rate and accept that we will not always be right, we are forever rejecting the long-term evidence in the face of the short-term hunch, even though the probability of being correct plummets.

In regard to the stock market, many have hypothesized that analysts get much more confident about their predictions after they have met the members of management of the company and formed personal opinions about their talent—or lack thereof. The analysts often can be seen clinging to these opinions even after factual events have proved them wrong. Think of all of the investors who, at the end of the 1990s, based their investment decisions just on their most recent personal experience in the market. For this intuitive investor, the only game in town was technology stocks and other large-cap growth fare. Every bit of their personal experience suggested that it was different this time, that a "new era" had dawned, and that only those who implicitly rejected history would do well going forward. And the majority of them held on to that belief through the crash of 2000–2003, so certain were they that a rebound was right around the corner. Only after 2$^{1}/_{2}$ years of "new personal experience" did these hapless intuitive investors learn that it wasn't different this time. Indeed, investors began falling for new catchphrases after the heart-pounding losses of 2008 and early 2009, when many investors started buying into the concept that the bear market low in March 2009 was the "new normal." Proponents of this new normal believe that returns in the future are destined to be disappointing and that investors should once again ignore history and change their behavior based upon short-term market conditions. I believe that several years from now, that catchphrase will be found in the same historical dustbin where the "new era" currently languishes. Yet through it all, most investors held onto their inherent overconfidence in their own predictive abilities.

SIMPLE VERSUS COMPLEX

We also prefer the complex and artificial to the simple and unadorned. We are certain that investment success requires an incredibly complex ability to judge a host of variables correctly and then act upon that knowledge. Professor Alex Bavelas designed a fascinating experiment in which two subjects, Smith and Jones, face individual projection screens. They cannot see or communicate with each other. They're told that the purpose of the experiment is to learn to recognize the difference between healthy and sick cells. They must learn to distinguish between the two using trial and error. In front of each are two buttons marked Healthy and Sick, along with two signal lights marked Right and Wrong. Every time the slide is projected, they register their guess as to whether the cell is healthy or sick by pressing the button so marked. After they guess, their signal light will flash Right or Wrong, informing them whether they have guessed correctly.

Here's the hitch—only Smith gets true feedback. If he's correct, his light flashes Right; if he's wrong, it flashes Wrong. Because he's getting true feedback, Smith soon starts getting around 80 percent correct, because it's a matter of simple discrimination.

Jones's situation is entirely different. He doesn't get true feedback based on guesses. Rather, the feedback he gets is based on Smith's guesses! It doesn't matter if he's right or wrong about a particular slide; he's told he's right if Smith guessed right, or wrong if Smith guessed wrong. Of course, Jones doesn't know this. He's been told that a true order exists that he can discover from the feedback. He's left searching for order when there is no true order to be found.

The moderator then asks Smith and Jones to discuss the rules they use for judging healthy and sick cells. Smith, who got true feedback, offers rules that are simple, concrete, and to the point. Jones, on the other hand, uses rules that are, out of necessity, subtle, complex, and highly adorned. After all, he had to base his opinions on contradictory guesses and hunches.

The amazing thing is that Smith doesn't think Jones's explanations are absurd, crazy, or unnecessarily complicated. He's impressed by the "brilliance" of Jones's method and feels inferior and vulnerable because of the pedestrian simplicity of his own rules. The more complicated and ornate Jones's explanations, *the more likely they are to convince Smith*.

Before the next test with new slides, the two are asked to guess who will do better this time around. All Joneses and most Smiths say that Jones will. In fact, Jones shows no improvement at all. Smith, on the other hand, does significantly worse than he did the first time because he's now making guesses based on some of the complicated rules he learned from Jones.

A SIMPLE SOLUTION

William of Ockham, a fourteenth-century Franciscan monk from the village of Ockham, in Surrey, England, developed the *principle of parsimony*, now called Occam's razor. For centuries it has been a guiding principle of modern science. It's axioms—such as, "What can be done with fewer assumptions is done in vain with more," and, "Entities are not to be multiplied without necessity"—boil down to this: Keep it simple, sweetheart. Occam's razor shows that, most often, the simplest theory is the best.

This is also the key to successful investing. Yet being a successful investor runs contrary to human nature. We love to make the simple complex and follow the crowd. We allow our love of a story about some stock to inflame our emotions and dictate our decisions—buying and selling based on tips and hunches. We approach each investment decision on a case-by-case basis, with no underlying consistency or strategy. We are optimistically overconfident in our own abilities, prone to hindsight bias, and quite willing to ignore over 80 years of facts that show these things to be so. When making investment decisions, we do everything in the present tense. And, because we time-weight information, we give the most recent events the greatest import. Indeed, behavioral economists call this tendency *recency bias,* which is the tendency to remember more recent events or observations more clearly, and to overweight recent information and underweight events from the more distant past. We then extrapolate anything that has been working well *recently* very far out in time, assuming that it will always be so. How else could the majority of investors have concentrated their portfolios in large-cap growth stocks and technology shares right before the technology bubble burst in 2000 and the biggest bear market for the Nasdaq since the 1970s ensued?

More recently, on the heels of the market crash of 2008–2009, investors have learned a far different lesson. Because the decade from 2000 through 2009 was the worst for U.S. stock performance in 110 years, investors have pulled trillions of dollars from stocks and moved their investments into bonds—the asset class that has done the best recently—ignoring the fact that 110 years of market history show us that bonds almost never outperform equities over long periods of time.

It's extremely difficult not to make decisions this way. Think about the last time you really goofed. Time passes, and you say, "*What was I thinking*! It's so obvious that I was wrong, why didn't I see it?" The mistake becomes obvious when you see the situation historically, drained of emotion and feeling. When the mistake was made, you had to contend with emotion. Emotion often wins, since, as John Junor said, "An ounce of emotion is equal to a ton of facts."

This isn't a phenomenon reserved for the unsophisticated. Pension sponsors have access to the best research and talent that money can buy, yet they are notorious for investing heavily in stocks just as the bear market begins and for firing managers at the absolute bottom of their cycle. Institutional investors say that they make decisions objectively and unemotionally, but they don't. The authors of the book *Fortune and Folly: The Wealth and Power of Institutional Investing* found that, although institutional investors' desks are cluttered with in-depth, analytical reports, the majority of pension executives selects outside managers using gut feelings. They also retain managers with consistently poor performance simply because they have good personal relationships with them.

The path to achieving investment success is to study long-term results and find a strategy or group of strategies that makes sense. Remember to consider risk (the standard deviation of return, which I cover in detail later in this book) and choose a level that is acceptable.

Then stay on that path. To succeed, let history guide you. Successful investors look at history. They understand and react to the present in terms of the past. Yesterday and tomorrow, as well as today, make up their now. Something as simple as looking at a strategy's best and worst years is a good example. Knowing the potential parameters of a strategy gives investors a tremendous advantage over the uninformed. If the maximum expected losses from a strategy are 35 percent and the strategy is down 15 percent, instead of panicking, an informed investor can feel happy that things aren't as bad as they could be. This knowledge tempers expectations and emotions, giving informed investors a perspective that acts as an emotional pressure valve. Thinking historically, they let what they know transcend how they feel. This is the only way to perform well.

The information in this book gives perspective. It helps you understand that hills and valleys are part of every investment scheme and are to be expected, not feared. It tells you what to expect from various classes of stocks. Don't second-guess. Don't change your mind. Don't reject an individual stock—if it meets the criteria of your strategy—because you think that the particular individual security will do poorly. Don't try to outsmart. By looking at decades of data, you can see that many strategies have periods during which they underperform the S&P 500, but they also had many that did much better. Understand, see the long term, and let your strategy work. If you do, your chance of your succeeding is very high. If you don't, no amount of knowledge or data will help you see, and you'll find yourself with the 70 percent of underperformers thinking, "Don't try to outsmart the market."

USING HISTORICAL DATA TO FORECAST FUTURE MARKET RETURNS

Let's now look at case studies that focus on how I actually used data to make predictions about the market's direction, in which virtually all of the predictions were based on the idea that everything ultimately reverts to its long-term mean. The most ironclad rule I have been able to find studying masses of data on the stock market, both in the United States and developed foreign markets, is the idea of reversion to the mean. If the general market has enjoyed outstanding results over a 20-year period, we generally spend the next 20 years reverting downward to its long-term average annual return. If, on the other hand, markets have generated disappointing results over the previous 20 years, they go on to do quite well in the ensuing 20-year period.

The same holds true at the strategy level. When strategies that have historically generated abysmal results are on fire, it's fairly easy to forecast that they will go on to do quite poorly. During the bubble years of the late 1990s, I published a commentary called *The Internet Contrarian*. It was published on April 22, 1999, and I looked at the valuation of Internet stocks through the long-term data valuation metrics by which we judge all stocks. I wrote:

> We are currently witnessing the biggest bubble the stock market has ever created. When the Internet insanity ends, truckloads of books will be turned out; endless comparisons to Dutch tulip bulbs and Ponzi schemes will be made; and a whole generation of ex-daytraders will rue the day that they were seduced by the siren

song of the Internet. This mania is a creation of fantasy and ludicrous expectation and of the childlike notion that hope can prevail over experience. Legions of inexperienced people—many of whom can't even begin to understand the balance sheet—believe that all they need to do to secure their fortune is to plunk down their money on anything .com and watch the profits roll in. For the patient, educated, long-term investor who knows that over time the market is bound by the rules of economics, the last year and a half has been pretty sickening. Near the top of any mania, you'll often see outright stupidity rewarded. The current myopia cannot and will not last. After every other market mania—from tulip bulbs in 17th-century Holland, radio stocks in the 1920s, aluminum stocks in the 1950s, to computer stocks in the mid–1980s, and the biotech craze of the early 1990s—those boring laws of economics always rear their very sane heads. Ultimately, a stock's price must be tied to the future cash payments the company will make to you as an owner. History shows us that the more you pay for each dollar of a company's revenue, the lower your total return. It does this because it has to—that's why economics is called the dismal science.

After publishing this piece, I received numerous irate e-mails telling me, in effect, that I was way too young (I was 39 at the time) to be so committed to ideas that were so outmoded and dusty. All I did was look at history. Every single bubble ends the same way—that is, very, very badly. When you look at the annual returns for richly valued securities, those with the highest price-to-sales, price-to-earnings, price-to-cash flow, and price-to-book near the end of the Internet bubble, you will see why investors were so enthusiastic—the stocks with the highest price-to-book value, for example, soared 127 percent for the 12 months ending February 2000, while those with the highest price-to-sales ratios advanced an incredible 207 percent, the highest 12-month rolling return since 1964. All I did was review the historical returns of such richly valued strategies, found them to be among the worst performers over long periods of time, and forecast that they would revert to their long-term mean. I used a similar methodology for all forecasts: I simply reviewed the long-term data and assumed that the strategy would ultimately revert to its long-term average.

Using that methodology, I also:

- Forecast in 1999 that small-cap stocks were due for a long period of outperformance because they had performed well below their long-term average. They went on to be the only broad market cap group that actually went up in the next decade.
- Forecast in 1998 a return to prominence for the Dogs of the Dow strategy because of its recent underperformance. Between 1999 and 2009, the Dogs did indeed proceed to beat the S&P 500.
- Published a study in 2002 (later expanded into my book *Predicting the Markets of Tomorrow*) forecasting that returns for the U.S. market would be comparatively low from 2000–2020, since for the 20 years ending March 2000, the market had earned its highest real rate of return in history. Little did I know that almost all of the downward movement and mean reversion would happen between 2000 and 2009.

- Published a series of commentaries between September 2008 and March 2009 fore-casting that the market should excel over the next three, five, and ten years.

The point of reviewing these forecasts is not an attempt at self aggrandizement. *Any* investor with access to long-term data who understands that markets are ultimately rational and have demonstrated long-term reversion to the mean will be able to make similar forecasts. The key is to strip emotion from the analysis and understand that it's not different this time. Markets and strategies will always, ultimately, revert to their long-term average.

Now let's take an in-depth look at two new schools of thought that seek to examine and explain why we make decisions the way we do.

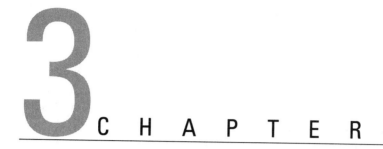

CHAPTER

THE PERSISTENCE OF IRRATIONALITY: HOW COMMON MISTAKES CREATE TREMENDOUS OPPORTUNITY

Nowhere does history indulge in repetitions so often or so uniformly as in Wall Street. When you read contemporary accounts of booms or panics, the one thing that strikes you most forcibly is how little either stock speculation or stock speculators today differ from yesterday. The game does not change and neither does human nature.

—Edwin Lefevre, *Reminiscences of a Stock Operator*, 1923

Investors looking to beat the market face a very daunting task. One study by John Bogle of Vanguard found that for the 20 years ending 2003, the S&P 500 returned 13 percent per year, while the average mutual fund returned just 10.3 percent and the average investor enjoyed just a 7.9 percent annualized return. The track record is so poor, in fact, that it seems feasible that those who do beat the market are simply lucky. The predominant explanation behind this poor rate of success is that markets are rational and efficient—meaning that prices always accurately reflect all publicly known information and therefore outsmarting the market is not possible. It is convenient for economic theorists to assume rational investor behavior because it makes the modeling of markets easier. A market that is efficient is one that lacks opportunity for outperformance, which seems to sync with Bogle's findings. Yet, the data in this book consistently demonstrate exploitable investment opportunities that have persisted even after becoming widely known.

The nature of our behavior and the biology of our brains have not significantly changed since the first market bubbles and collapses. The latest research in neuroeconomics and behavioral finance explains why we continually make foolish investment decisions and why it would be naïve to expect anything different in the future—evolution has hardwired our brains to be less than perfectly rational. Luckily for us, an irrational market is one rife with opportunities as investors misprice securities in both calm and turbulent market environments. As long as fallible people are responsible for security prices, there will be opportunities for the shrewd investor to profit from their mistakes. The key to successful investing is to recognize that *we* are just as susceptible to crippling behavioral biases as the next person. Simply being aware of our behavioral biases does not make them go away. If we can remove emotion and subjectivity from our investment strategies, we *can* beat the market in the long run.

This chapter highlights historical examples of market madness and inefficiency and explains several of the realities of our neurological makeup and behavioral biases which make the task of outperformance such a difficult one.

LESSONS FROM HISTORY

Douglas Adams said, "Human beings, who are almost unique in having the ability to learn from the experience of others, are also remarkable for their apparent disinclination to do so." Throughout history, examples of irrational behavior in the market abound. And while the circumstances of each mania or panic are generally unique, the psychology of the market participants has always been remarkably consistent. As researchers continue to improve their understanding of human decision making—both behaviorally and neurologically—we should no longer be surprised that irrational bubbles and panics persist despite the lessons of history. Our brains were engineered through natural selection to help us survive in an environment of small numbers and simple odds, not to evaluate complex financial decisions—let alone to be successful at doing so.

It is astonishing how frequently investors make the same mistakes that plagued those before them. Hindsight bias, overconfidence, and the prospect of great fortune have continually thwarted investors' rationality as the latest investing fad takes hold. From the Dutch tulip mania in 1637, to radio stocks in the 1920s, to aluminum stocks in the 1950s, to computer stocks in the mid–1980s, to the dot-com craze of the late 1990s, and to the recent unprecedented rise and collapse of real estate prices, there have been countless lessons that should have taught investors to avoid outlandishly priced assets—yet bubbles persist. By comparing one of the earliest major stock market bubbles to one of the most recent, it is easy to see just how little human nature has changed.

SOUTH SEA AND NASDAQ—A LITTLE BIT OF HISTORY REPEATING

One of the first and best-documented examples of irrational investor behavior is the South Sea Trading Company bubble which famously led Isaac Newton to say, "I can calculate the motion of heavenly bodies, but not the madness of men." It is an excellent example of the same irrational exuberance that led to the tech bubble in the late 1990s. The two manias, nearly three centuries apart, were eerily similar.

As Richard Dale describes in his book *The First Crash: Lessons from the South Sea Bubble,* the seeds for the trading bubble began with irresponsible spending by the British government, similar to that of many sovereign governments today. Between 1688 and 1713

England fought in both the Nine Years War and the War of Spanish Succession—enjoying just 4 years of peace in 25 years. As a result, military spending increased dramatically, absorbing up to 9 percent of England's national income. As the overall debt levels rose, the government had trouble making interest payments and saw its cost to borrow rise significantly. If they had been around, Moody's or S&P would likely have downgraded the credit rating of the British government.

In 1711, to reduce the debt level, Parliament created the South Sea Trading Company. The company was granted exclusive rights to trade with England's South American colonies and would take over 9.5 million pounds of debt from the government in exchange for annual interest payments on the debt. Holders of the government debt could convert their bonds into South Sea stock in a debt-equity swap. This was very attractive to the government debt holders because their interest payments were often in arrears, and they were not sure when to expect repayment of their principle. Owning shares of South Sea instead would give them a more reliable dividend payment, greater liquidity (as the shares would trade openly in Exchange Alley), and the potential for gains as the stock price rose. Richard Dale says:

> Given the entrepreneurial spirit of the times, the idea of a new company with a specific remit to trade in the Spanish West Indies held a particular attraction for investors. Ever since the buccaneering days of Elizabethan England, the New World had held out the prospect of untold riches ...

Perhaps because of the prospect of "untold riches," the conversion operation shifting investors from depreciated government debt to South Sea stock went well. However, even though South America was thought to have vast amounts of gold and silver, the actual trading operations of the company were not at all successful. In one telling episode, a 200,000 pound cargo shipment decayed in port because of delays—unsurprising considering that none of the directors of the company had any experience trading in the New World. As an operating company, South Sea was a failure by almost any measure. However, just as a sexy PowerPoint presentation could make investors open their wallets for a hot technology stock in the 1990s, the very idea of the South Sea company ignited the passions of early investors. Because of the success of the first debt conversion, in 1720 the South Sea Company proposed to privatize a large portion of the British national debt. Again, holders of debt would exchange relatively illiquid debt for lower-yielding but far more liquid stock which also had more upside price potential.

For the equity side of the deal, Parliament allowed South Sea to issue 315,000 shares at £100 per share for a total value of £31.5 million. Any shares not given to government debt holders in the conversion could be sold on the open market for profit. As a result, the company would profit from an inflated share price because it would have to convert fewer shares per debt holder, who were owed a set amount, measured in pounds not shares. The appetite for South Sea stock was strong, and investors began to bid up the price, which quickly took off. Soon after the debt privatization plan was announced on January 21, 1720, the stock quickly rose from £128 to £187. The rise attracted even more speculators, and in a month the price had reached £300. As shown in Figure 3.1, Isaac Newton sold his shares at this point for a healthy profit of £7,000, but the share price continued to rise.

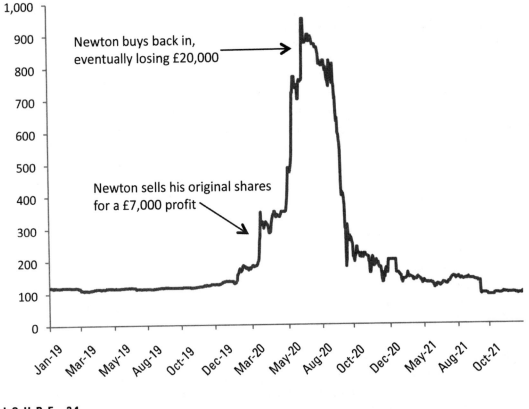

FIGURE 3.1

Rise and fall of South Sea Trading Co. share price

As Edward Chancellor notes in his excellent book, *Devil Take the Hindmost: A History of Financial Speculation*, the rise of the South Sea share price was not even the most glaring example of investor irrationality at the time. Concurrent with the South Sea bubble was the birth of a number of new companies, dubbed "bubble companies," whose fundamentals and rising stock prices were even more questionable than those of South Sea's. These companies advertised their equivalent of an initial public offering in the local newspapers, and in many cases they had no real prospects for profits. One company planned to convert salt water to fresh, and another planned to import jackasses from Spain. Other, more legitimate sounding companies were also offered, including a number dealing in property and insurance. Legitimate or not, these companies benefitted from the market's euphoric mindset, and investors continued to pile in. At its peak, the market value of the London stock exchange reached 500 million pounds—100 times its value just 25 years earlier, and 5 times the cash in all of Europe. Years later, only 4 of the 200 bubble companies survived.

The market euphoria extended beyond the South Sea Company stock and the related bubble companies. Well-established companies of the day saw similarly huge jumps in their share prices. John Castaing, a broker in London at the time, recorded daily prices for several large companies, including the Old East India Trading Company, Bank of England, the Royal African Company, Million Bank, and the South Sea Company. The rampant speculation surrounding South Sea's skyrocketing share price precipitated huge price jumps for these other companies as well. Based on Castaing's daily prices, Table 3.1 shows the percentage rise and fall of each stock's price during the bubble and subsequent bust. The meteoric rise of these share prices can be attributed only to greed and performance chasing. Later in this chapter we explore why our brains—and fundamental human nature—allow us to make such foolish decisions.

T A B L E 3.1

Major Stock Returns during the South Sea Bubble

	Bank of England	Royal African Co.	Million Bank	Old East India Co.	South Sea Co.	Average
Percentage rise • Jan 1, 1720, to July 1, 1720	58%	504%	231%	110%	640%	309%
Percentage decline • July 1, 1720, to Dec 23, 1720	−41%	−72%	−58%	−64%	−83%	−64%

Like the wrenching experience Nasdaq investors would suffer centuries later, the bursting of the South Sea bubble was swift and painful. One financially savvy British MP, Archebald Hutcheson, the Robert Schiller of his day, understood the company well and published a series of anti-South Sea pamphlets. He reminded investors that given parliament's obligation to make an unexciting and relatively low 5 percent interest payment annually and the poor record and prospects of the South Sea Company as an actual *trading* company, those who bought shares at inflated prices were "deprived of all common sense and understanding" because the value of the company was not supported by fundamentals. Many did not heed his warning. Isaac Newton, the author of the *Principia* which laid the foundation for modern physics, bought back into the stock at its peak. When the share price inevitably collapsed, Newton lost £20,000. He is said to have quivered at any mention of the South Sea Company for the rest of his life.

As with most manias, there was no one single reason the bubble burst. Experts such as Dale and Chancellor cite tightening credit, overstretched valuations, and meltdowns of similar bubble companies as triggers for the inevitable market crash. Ultimately, Richard Dale says, "The only conclusion to be drawn from these valuation anomalies is that, during the Bubble year, the behavior of South Sea investors became manic and irrational in a way that is difficult if not impossible to reconcile with modern finance theory."

Nearly three centuries later, in a far more sophisticated market with easier access to information and fundamental data, investors ignored history again—in a remarkably similar fashion. The dangerous mantra that, "It's different this time" was touted yet again, as investors became convinced that old rules did not apply to these new-age companies. The source of the excitement was very different, but surely the brain activity and resulting behavior of bubble speculators were the same. The rise and fall of the Nasdaq seen in Figure 3.2 mirrors that of the South Sea Company.

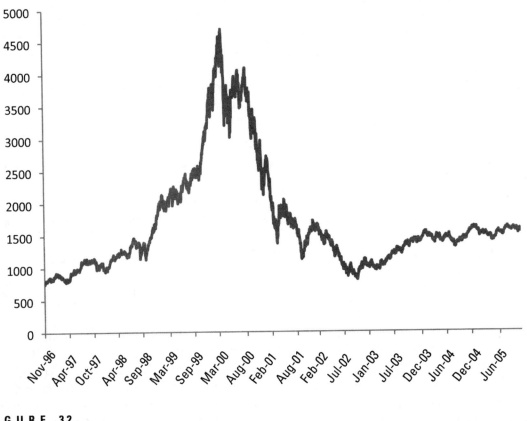

FIGURE   3.2

Rise and Fall of the NASDAQ 100

As of March 2000, companies like Constellation 3D, eNotes.com, simplayer.com, and Braintech saw their stock price appreciate by more than 1,000 percent despite having *zero* sales! The prospects of success for these companies were akin to those of the South Sea bubble companies. Indeed, over the next two years these stocks declined by an average of 98 percent. Some were driven by irrational greed; others subscribed to the "greater fool theory" which suggests that even though they felt the investments were overpriced, they would still be able to make a large profit provided that a greater fool buys their shares at a higher price sometime in the near future. Despite huge early profits, bubble investors ultimately shared the same fate as Sir Isaac Newton.

MATHEMATICAL PROOF OF MARKET INEFFICIENCY

South Sea, dot-com, and similar bubbles are extreme examples of irrationality—but inefficiencies persist during more normal market environments as well. The late Benoit Mandelbrot, a mathematician famous for his work in fractal geometry, turned his attention to the behavior of market prices to see if their historical movements did in fact follow a random walk. In his brilliant book *The (mis)Behavior of Markets*, Mandelbrot compares the volatility of the Dow Jones Industrial Average (DJIA) since 1916 to hypothetical market volatility predicted by a fully efficient, random walk market.

With daily index levels for the DJIA going back to 1896, we are able to extend his study even further back. Figure 3.3 represents the daily volatility (measured in standard deviations) of an efficient—or random walk—market. Notice that the days follow a normal distribution pattern, with very few days exceeding four standard deviations of the average change. This would be the sort of market which proponents of the efficient market hypothesis argue makes it so difficult for investors to outperform. Figure 3.4 is the *actual* daily market volatility of the DJIA back to 1896.

There are many observations between 5 and 10 standard deviations, and one in 1987 that exceeds 20 standard deviations. As Mandelbrot points out, the odds of Black Monday happening in an efficient market framework are one in 10^{50}. If markets were indeed fully efficient, the Dow could have traded every day since the big bang and we *still* would not expect to see a day like Black Monday. It should alarm investors that tools which are meant to help us quantify risk, such as Value at Risk (VaR) and options pricing models like Black-Scholes

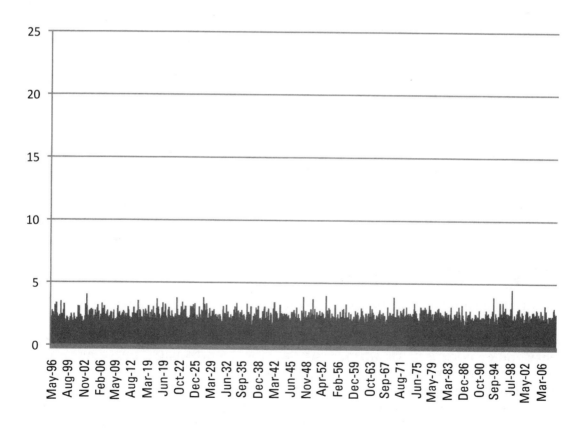

F I G U R E 3.3

Daily changes of random walk Dow Jones measured in standard deviations,1896–2009

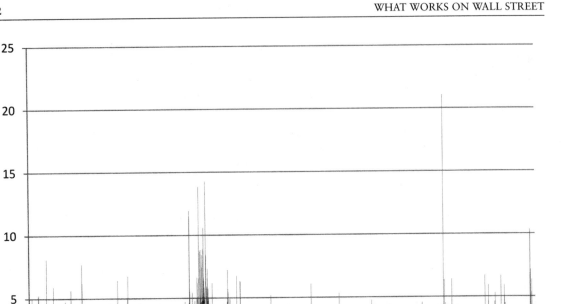

FIGURE 3.4

Daily changes in Dow Jones Industrial Average measured in standard deviations,1896–2009

assume that markets move randomly, as in Figure 3.3. Real market history is so at odds with the random walk assumption that this evidence represents a fatal blow to the idea of perfectly efficient markets.

INEFFICIENT MARKETS ROOTED IN NEUROLOGY

What is it about our basic biological makeup that makes us such bad investors and that keeps markets from being efficient? Researchers are now able to monitor the neurological activity of people while they are making financial decisions. Neuroscientists and behavioral economists agree: when we are faced with uncertainty of outcomes—a ubiquitous condition in financial markets—we are not calm, rational, or calculating. Instead, and usually to the detriment of our portfolios, we are emotional and often irrational. This is especially true in times of extreme greed, such as the South Sea or Nasdaq bubbles, and in times of extreme fear, such the credit crisis of 2008. Our brains are not only prone to making irrational reasoning mistakes, they are reliably and remarkably consistent in doing so.

Richard Peterson, author of *Inside the Investor's Brain*, says, "The human brain is the product of millions of years of evolution, and it is designed to efficiently and effectively interpret information, compete in a social hierarchy, and direct activity towards achieved goals while avoiding danger. However, our brains evolved in a stone-age world where dangers and opportunities were largely immediate, and social interactions were limited to other members of the clan. Now, as the modern world becomes more interconnected and fast paced, it is apparent that the stone-age brain is not optimized for managing the complexities of the modern life." Our environment is now full of cultural constructs—like financial markets—that have evolved very quickly. Because cultural constructs can, and have, evolve far faster than our brains, we must make decisions in a world that is far more complicated and nuanced than the world we evolved to survive and thrive in.

To understand how the brain affects our investment decisions, it is helpful to adopt P. D. MacLean's "triune" model of the brain, which divides our gray matter into three sections: The reptilian brain, the old mammalian brain, and the human brain. The reptilian brain controls our life-sustaining mechanisms like breathing and heartbeat. The old mammalian brain, which contains our emotional center known as the limbic system, controls our desires, drives, emotions, and motivations. Finally the human brain controls higher-order thinking such as reason and analytical decision making. Thanks to fMRI scanners, which reveal films of the brain—as opposed to the snapshots provided by more traditional MRI machines—we now understand just how intricately linked the emotional and rational centers of our brains are. We know that emotion is involved in most decision-making processes, yet we also know that this emotional involvement can significantly impair our investment choices. This is interesting in an experimental setting but can be devastating when it is applied to real world decisions such as investing for our children's education or our retirement.

WE ARE NOT RATIONAL

Socrates was not very accurate when he classified humans as a "rational animal." Our brains commit a plethora of reasoning mistakes over and over again. We make logically inconsistent decisions based on how our options are framed, we base decisions on meaningless numbers, and we make choices that are not in our own best interests.

Try answering the following two questions. What are the last four digits of your social security number? In what year did Genghis Khan die? When a large group of people are asked these two questions in this order, there will be a strong average relationship between the two answers, meaning those with higher social security numbers give higher guesses for the second answer and vice versa. If subjects are asked these questions in reverse order, there is no relationship between the answers. This phenomenon, known as *anchoring*, is amusing until you consider the influence that analyst earnings estimates have on the price of a stock. As we have already explored in Chapter Two and as David Dreman and others have shown, individual analyst estimates tend to be about as useful as our social security number in predicting a company's earnings, and yet people base their decisions on these estimates all the time.

Another classic example, originally conceived by Daniel Kahneman and Amos Tversky, is known as the "Asian disease problem." Imagine a disease indigenous to Asia which is going to migrate to the United States and is expected to kill 9,000 people. We have two options to fight this epidemic. The first option would result in 3,000 people being saved, while the second option offers a one-third probability that everyone will be saved and a two-thirds probability that no one will be saved. Most respondents, favoring the certainty of the first option, elect to save the 3,000 people. But what if the question is phrased differently? Again we have two options. The first option is that 6,000 people will die. The second option offers a one-third probability that nobody will die and a two-thirds probability that everyone will die. Now, faced with the certain death of 6,000 people, respondents prefer the second option. The expected outcome of these two scenarios is exactly the same, but most people would prefer to avoid a loss rather than ensure a gain of equal size.

BRAIN DAMAGE CAN CREATE SUPERIOR INVESTMENT RESULTS

Our brain activity determines who and what we are, and physical changes or damage to the brain can materially alter our decision making. In one study led by researcher Baba Shiv of Stanford University originally reported in a *Wall Street Journal* article titled "Lessons from the Brain-Damaged Investor," a group of 41 participants played an investment game in which each was given $20 and asked to make 20 rounds of $1 investing decisions based on a coin toss. They would choose either "invest" or "don't invest." The "don't invest" option was considered the conservative or risk-averse choice and simply meant that the subject kept his or her dollar for that round. When the subjects chose "invest," the researcher took the $1 and flipped a coin. If it came up heads, the dollar was lost; if it came up tails, the subject was rewarded with $2.50. Clearly the most profitable strategy would be to play every round, as the expected value of each $1 "invested" is $1.25. The twist in the study was that one group of participants had suffered brain damage, which affected key emotional centers in the brain such as the amygdala or the insula—mammalian brain regions that play a large role in our perception of fear and panic. The other participants had either no brain damage at all or brain damage that affected nonemotional centers of the brain.

The results were illuminating. Those participants without any emotional brain damage invested just 58 percent of the time, ending up with an average of $22.80, but participants *with* brain damage did much better, investing 84 percent of the time and ending up with an average of $25.70. The main reason participants with normal brains did so poorly was the result of how they reacted to a losing coin toss. Instead of recognizing the very simple positive expected value of choosing "invest," the normal group was scared of losing twice in a row and, as a result, immediately following a loss, invested just 41 percent of the time. The brain damaged group maintained their overall percentage after a loss, investing 85 percent of the time. This study illustrates that fear, recent loss, and irrational risk avoidance act as a tax on our portfolios if we do not take action to circumvent their influence. If the goal is to buy low in the stock market, then very often the very best time to invest is when stocks have done poorly, driving down their PE ratios and often increasing their dividend yields.

We have lived through a near-perfect example of this sort of irrational loss avoidance during the market crash of 2007–2009. In many ways, investing in stocks is very similar to choosing "invest" in the coin-toss game, except that the stock market goes up roughly 72 percent of the time, which are even better odds than those facing professor Shiv's participants. Still, since the market bottom in March 2009, investors have sold and shunned equity mutual funds and flocked to bond funds in record numbers. The price they have paid is extreme. In 2009, the S&P 500 (a real life proxy for choosing "invest") was up 26.4 percent, while the Barclay's Aggregate, a bond fund and a proxy for the risk avoidant "don't invest" option, returned just 5.9 percent. During this same time, total flows for equity funds were a *negative* $8.6 billion, while total flows into bond funds were a staggering $375 billion. Not only were equity flows negative, as Figure 3.5 shows, but most of the selling came at the worst possible time—near the market bottom in February and March. Investors acted just as professor Shiv's participants did after a loss—avoiding what has been demonstrated to be the better investment asset—largely because of fear.

The trouble is that our brains are wired the way they are for very good reasons. In most cases, avoiding behavior that previously led to a negative outcome is a good policy. Indeed brain damaged patients like those in Shiv's study often went bankrupt because a lack of emotional judgment made them *too* risk-seeking and susceptible to scams. If we

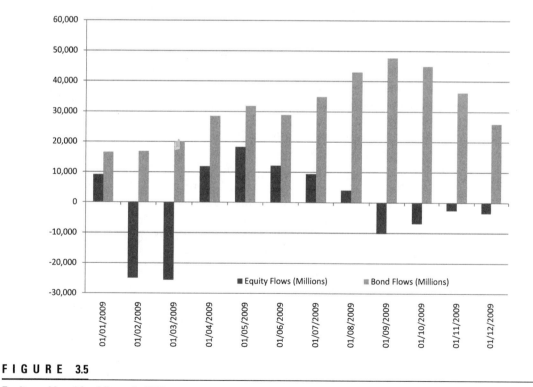

FIGURE   3.5

Equity and bond fund flows in 2009

didn't have this risk avoidance system, we would not learn our lesson after touching a burning hot stove. What's more, our fear of continued negative outcomes affects our behavior in all areas of life. Following the 9/11 attacks, a huge number of travelers opted to drive to their destinations rather than fly. Sadly, one study found that even after controlling for time trends, weather, road conditions, and other factors, as many as 2,300 people died during that time because they elected to drive instead of fly—nearly 75 percent of the number of deaths caused by the attacks themselves. These travelers misinterpreted the dangers of flying because of the recent terrorist attacks. Surely, the financial meltdown was not as tragic, but given how severely it hurt the financial lives of so many people, the misguided decisions of millions of investors in its aftermath are understandable.

The primary driver of the irrational behavior of Professor Shiv's participants was a phenomenon called *loss aversion*. This behavioral concept was first explored by Amos Tversky and Daniel Kahneman, who are regarded as the founding fathers of behavioral finance. Tversky and Kahneman pioneered psychological and economic studies that revolutionized the scientific approach to decision making. They published their original findings in the 1979 paper "Prospect Theory: An Analysis of Decision under Risk." They ultimately won many prestigious awards and honors, including the Nobel Memorial prize in Economic Sciences, awarded to Kahneman in 2002.

The pair discovered that people react very differently to financial gains and losses. Specifically, losses are much more painful than gains are pleasurable. Consider the following two scenarios:

Scenario 1: You can accept a guaranteed gain of $500 dollars *or* flip a coin. If it's heads, you win $1,000; if it's tails, you win nothing.

Scenario 2: You can accept a guaranteed loss of $500 dollars *or* flip a coin. If it's heads, you lose $1,000; if it's tails, you lose nothing.

In each scenario the expected value of each option is the same; the simple probabilities dictate that it does not matter which option is chosen. However, Tversky and Kahneman found that 84 percent of people take the guaranteed money in scenario 1, but 70 percent elect to gamble in scenario 2. People tend to be risk-*averse* when faced with gains, but risk-*seeking* when faced with losses. This bizarre contradiction is driven by an intense fear of loss. People are so afraid to realize or lock in a loss that they will go to irrational lengths to avoid it. By adjusting this test using different values, Tversky and Kahneman found subjects to be more than twice as sensitive to losses as to gains. Our brain is programmed to believe that a bird in the hand is worth two in the bush.

Benedetto de Martino, a London-based neuroscientist, conducted a study using fMRI scans to monitor the brain activity of subjects facing these sorts of financial decisions. He wanted to learn if the way a question was framed had an effect on his subjects' decisions. Subjects were given an initial amount of money, say $100, and offered a "sure" option or a "gamble" option, similar to Tversky and Kahneman's original study. Like the other examples already reviewed, the expected value of the two options was always the same.

When the subjects were given the choice between "keeping" $40 of the $100 (the "gain" frame) or gambling (where the expected value was also $40), the majority chose to keep the $40. But when given the option of "losing" $60 of the $100 (the "loss" frame), the majority chose to gamble. The offer was the same in both cases, but the wording of the question triggered loss-aversion behavior. More importantly, de Martino and his team were able to monitor the portions of the brain that showed the most activity while each decision was being made. When subjects were influenced by loss aversion, playing it safe in the gain frame or gambling in the loss frame, their brain activity was centered in the amygdala, the emotional fight-or-flight center of the brain. When subjects went against the grain, gambling in the gain frame or opting for the sure thing in the loss frame, it was the orbital prefrontal cortex and the anterior cingulate cortex—both responsible for rational cognitive functions—that were activated. Investors' overreaction to loss or the prospect of a loss triggers the emotional fear center of the brain instead of the rational portions.

Decisions that might help avoid losses or pain are often prioritized regardless of their rationality. Practically speaking, this brain bias has proven to be very bad for investors' portfolios. I was inspired by a table in Nassim Taleb's book *Fooled by Randomness* that looks at the chances that an investment goes up over different intervals of time. If you had invested $10,000 in the S&P 500 in January 1980, your investment would have grown to $243,754 by the end of 2009—a healthy return of 11.23 percent with a reasonable 15.52 percent volatility. Even with such a strong annualized return, Table 3.2 shows that if you checked your account daily or weekly, the chances that the account was up would be barely better than a coin toss. A fully rational investor might not be bothered by these probabilities, but an emotional one would have a very hard time sticking with his or her investment. Assuming that losses are indeed twice as painful as gains, then the emotional impact of the performance of that same portfolio over short periods of time might be too much to bear. A simple test demonstrates that investors should check their portfolios as infrequently as possible. Instead of just taking the various observation returns at face value, I assign a score of 1 for each positive return observation and a score of –2 for each negative return observation to represent what we know about losses being twice as painful as gains are pleasurable. Table 3.2 shows the emotion-adjusted average score for each observation period. It is not until we reach the annual portfolio observation that the pain/reward score turns positive. Just as a watched pot never boils, when accounting for the pain of losses relative to the pleasure of gains, it is fair to say that a watched portfolio never feels like it is rising.

T A B L E 3.2

Chances of Positive Returns on an S&P 500 Portfolio, 1980–2009

Observation frequency	Chance of positive return	Emotion-adjusted average pain/ reward score
Daily	53%	−0.41
Weekly	56%	−0.32
Monthly	61%	−0.16
Quarterly	66%	−0.01
Yearly	74%	0.21

Because of loss aversion, people hold onto losers too long and sell their winners too soon. They favor assets which have had low recent volatility and seem low in risk—especially following major losses. Investment plans that automatically rebalance portfolio asset weights, thereby taking loss aversion out of the equation, are superior and can help people overcome their fear of loss and the corrosive effect it has on their portfolio's value.

GREEDILY CHASING PERFORMANCE AND PATTERNS

At a purely chemical level, every experience humans find enjoyable—whether listening to music, embracing a lover, or savoring chocolate—amounts to little more than an explosion of dopamine in the nucleus accumbens as exhilarating and ephemeral as a firecracker.

—J. Madelaine Nash

Just as our brain is wired to make us behave in a manner that avoids losses, so too is it wired to encourage behavior that leads to gains. The downside of our gain-seeking tendencies is that we can ignore important risks to satisfy our desires. The feeling of pleasure from anticipating a future reward is a powerful driver of behavior, which makes a tremendous amount of evolutionary sense but can lead us to make very foolish investment choices. Many stock bubbles have fed on this tendency in the brain to seek out activity that may lead to huge payoffs. Buyers of Internet stocks in the late 1990s and South Sea stock in the 1720s were not rational investors. They were often caught up in the pleasure they felt from recent gains and the prospect of more to come. When we anticipate financial gains or rewards, the same areas of the brain light up that light up during sexual arousal or hardcore drug use—surely not the kind of mental state conducive to making sound investment decisions.

When an asset—be it a single stock, the overall stock market, or real estate—appreciates rapidly, it presents the perceived opportunity to realize huge returns in a short period of time. Once investors have committed money to asset bubbles, they often become blinded to underlying fundamentals because of how their brains interpret the pattern of consistently strong returns. Brian Knutson of Stanford University monitored the brain activity of people making money; he found that two key areas of the brain were activated: the nucleus accumbens (NAcc), a key anticipatory center, and the medial prefrontal cortex (MPFC) which helps us permanently learn what sorts of activities will lead to rewards. The trouble with this structure is that, as the rewards become somewhat consistent—for example, the returns on an investment in the Nasdaq in 1998–1999—the brain gets complacent and assumes that these rewards will continue into the future. Research by Hannah Bayer and Paul Glimcher shows that this brain bias is compounded by the fact that the dopamine neurons responsible for using past information to forecast future outcomes overweight more recent experiences. The strength of the signal sent by each individual dopamine neuron fades over time, so neurons associated with the most recent experiences fire most forcefully. We biologically lack the ability to learn well or equally from a long history. Instead, we rely too much on recent experience, which appears to be one biological reason for the recency bias discussed in Chapter Two. This complacency and mental emphasis on the recent past makes us less aware of risks. In the investing world, a complacent brain is a dangerous thing.

The NAcc clearly plays a large role in our financial choices. In his book *The Chemical Carousel: What Science Tells Us about Beating Addiction,* Dirk Hanson discusses the role of the NAcc in addiction to drugs. When parts of the NAcc were sliced out of rats with a heroin addiction, the craving for the drug stopped. When we crave or take a drug, it is the surge of dopamine into our NAcc that is responsible, and this is the same area of the brain that fires when we are anticipating making money. Of course investors in South Sea bubble companies and Internet stocks were willing to buy garbage stocks—it felt too good not to.

To make matters worse, most people are far too confident of their own abilities—be they as a driver, lover, or investor. Most people believe themselves to be better than average, which is of course impossible. This misplaced self-confidence further damages our abilities to deal rationally with potential market risks. We think that we know which stock will outperform, and we commit money accordingly. As a species we abhor randomness and seek patterns in any data set. Once we find a pattern, many of which have no real meaning, we become very confident that it does have meaning. In his book *Your Money and Your Brain,* Jason Zweig discusses one type of experiment in which even pigeons and rats are more successful at predicting outcomes than humans. In the experiment, there was a pair of flashing lights—one red and one green—which were flashed 20 times for the human and rodent subjects. The exact sequence of the flashes was randomized, but the green light flashed 80 percent of the time. Similar to the game played by the brain damaged investors where it was wisest to choose "invest" every time, the easiest way to predict the most flashes correctly would be to guess green every time. While pigeons and rats tend to follow this logical strategy and guess right close to 80 percent of the time, human subjects get caught up in trying to predict when the next red light will flash and correctly predict only 68 percent of the flashes. Even after being informed that the lights flash at random, human subjects continued to try to outsmart the odds, and their performance tended to get worse over time.

Read Montague, a neuroscience professor at the Baylor College of Medicine, has performed studies analyzing the brain during hypothetical financial bubbles. An article by Jonah Lehrer in the *New York Times* summarizes his experiment. Subjects are given $100 and a synopsis of the "market" they will be investing in. Based on this information, the subjects can invest as much or as little of their $100 as they like and then watch the value of their portfolios rise and fall over the course of 20 rounds. The fantastic twist to this study is that instead of having the subjects invest their $100 in random markets, Montague uses the patterns of real bubbles like the Dow of 1929 and the Nasdaq of 1999. In the early phases of each bubble, the dopamine reward anticipation system is firing on all cylinders— driving the subjects to increase their investment as they watch their $100 grow with the bubble. However, near the peak of the bubbles, Montague found that the dopamine neurons quieted down significantly. Montague says, "It's as if the cells were getting anxious . . . they knew something wasn't right." At this stage, the subjects were no longer driven by the dopamine surges that got them into the mess in the first place. Instead, it became the prefrontal cortex's turn to sabotage the subjects' portfolio. Now the investors' higher-order brains began rationalizing their investment, fabricating reasons for holding on instead of taking gains. This study is an eye-opening example of both our primal and our higher-order brains contributing to poor investment choices.

The key lesson from these studies is that the combination of emotional pleasure produced by realized and prospective gains and our overconfidence in our own ability to predict the future can prove deadly in certain market conditions.

WE CANNOT ESCAPE OUR MINDS

Like many activities in life, investing is all about seeking gains and avoiding losses. Research by Cameilia Kuhnen and Brian Knutson of Stanford University has conclusively identified the centers of the brain that are responsible for risk-seeking and risk-aversion mistakes. For investors, what is most interesting is what else these regions of the brain are responsible for. The NAcc is responsible for feelings of intense positive emotional pleasure, the euphoria associated with heavy drug use, and the anticipatory thrill of, say, being with your significant other. As Kuhnen and Knutson state, "This may explain why casinos surround their guests with reward cues (e.g., inexpensive food, free liquor, surprise gifts, potential jackpot prizes)—anticipation of rewards activates the NAcc, which may lead to an increase in the likelihood of individuals switching from risk-averse to risk-seeking behavior." Considering that this pleasure center in our brain is firing as we are making money, it makes sense that people chase asset bubbles. Investors in early 2000 had to pay $175 for every dollar of Nasdaq earnings, and there were no economically sound arguments for this truly inflated price. Still, many people continued to buy, and they were likely driven by surges of dopamine to their NAcc. At the opposite end of the spectrum, investors faced with market panic, economic contraction and uncertainty, and declining portfolio values—a description all too familiar to investors in 2008—must battle brain activation in their anterior insula and amygdala—emotional brain centers responsible for feelings of pain, disgust, and fear which often lead us to be overly cautious.

The most important lesson from this cutting edge research is that, because of the interrelated nature of the emotional and rational centers of our brain, we will never be able to fully overcome our tendency to make irrational choices. Simply being aware of this problem does not make it go away. To break from our all too human tendencies to avoid losses even when it is disadvantageous to do so, chase performance, and perceive patterns where there are none, we must find an investment strategy that removes subjective, human decision making from the process and relies instead on smart, empirically proven systematic strategies. With this deeper understanding of the human mind, we can become wise by realizing just how unwise we truly are. This realization is the first and most difficult step toward investment success.

CHAPTER 4

RULES OF THE GAME

It is amazing to reflect how little systematic knowledge Wall Street has to draw upon as regards the historical behavior of securities with defined characteristics. We do, of course, have charts showing the long-term price movements of stock groups and individual stocks. But there is no real classification here, except by type of business. Where is the continuous, ever growing body of knowledge and technique handed down by the analysts of the past to those of the present and future? When we contrast the annals of medicine with those of finance, the paucity of our recorded and digested experience becomes a reproach. We lack the codified experience which will tell us whether codified experience is valuable or valueless. In the years to come we analysts must go to school to the older established disciplines. We must study their ways of amassing and scrutinizing facts and from this study develop methods of research suited to the peculiarities of our own field of work.

—Ben Graham, the father of securities analysis, in 1946

In the early 1990s when I began the research for what became *What Works on Wall Street*, little had been done to address Graham's challenge. Now, nearly 20 years later, real strides have been made. The first edition of *What Works on Wall Street*, published in 1996, covered many of the variables that Graham was looking for 50 years earlier. Another money manager, Tweedy, Browne Company LLC, also published a booklet titled *What Has Worked in Investing: Studies of Investment Approaches and Characteristics Associated with Exceptional Returns* in 1992 and has continually updated the research. The booklet was a review and description of over 50 studies that were found to be most relevant in determining which investment strategies worked the best over long periods of time. Academics, of course, were also churning out research concerning the efficacy of various investment strategies. Over the past several years, many academics have also reviewed decades of stock market data and offered their findings to the general public. Of particular note is the brilliant *Triumph of the Optimists: 101 Years of Global Investment Returns*, by Elroy Dimson, Paul Marsh, and Mike Staunton, which catalogs returns over the last 101 years in 16 different countries. The book also looks at country-by-country results for various investment strategies, such as growth and value. Some noteworthy academic papers published since the first edition of *What Works on Wall Street* include: Charles M. C. Lee and Bhaskaran Swaminathan's 1998 *Price Momentum and Trading Volume*; Cliff Asness's 1997 *The Interaction of Value and Momentum Strategies*; and Joseph D. Piotroski's 2000 paper, *Value Investing: The Use of Historical Financial Statement Information to Separate Winners and Losers*. Other academics, such as Eugene Fama and Ken French have built growth and value indices for small and large cap stocks going back to 1927. Fama and French use the price-to-book ratio of a company to assign the stock to the value or growth camp, with stocks with low price-to-book ratios falling into the value index and stocks with high price-to-book ratios going into growth. Their data gave us the longest return history on the two main styles of investing available. For this edition of this book, we also use the CRSP dataset for several of our single and multifactor models. The CRSP dataset was compiled starting in 1959 by the University of Chicago Graduate School of Business. The University compiled the first machine-readable files of month-end price and total return, as well as several additional data items, for stocks listed on the New York Stock Exchange between 1926 and 1960. The Center for Research in Security Prices has expanded the dataset to include additional exchanges and information. Now that we have the CRSP dataset, we will be able to show that, much as we found in earlier editions of this book, uniting value and growth characteristics often leads to vastly better results than relying on simply pure growth or pure value.

Over the past several decades, many academics have taken their own research and started money management firms to take advantage of the results their findings demonstrated. After publishing their seminal paper, *Contrarian Investment, Extrapolation and Risk*, Professors Josef Lakonishok, Andrei Shleifer, and Robert W. Vishny formed LSV Asset Management, which currently manages over $53 billion using strategies perfected through long-term research. And as their Web site claims, they stick very close to the strategies tested: "The quantitative investment strategies offered by LSV Asset Management are the result of over 20 years of academic research, rigorous testing of techniques and strict application of risk controls."

Yet all this research is valuable precisely because it covers returns over decades—not days or years. Many investors believe that a five-year track record is sufficient to judge a manager's abilities. But like Alexander Pope's maxim that a little learning is a dangerous thing, too little time gives investors extremely misleading information. Richard Brealey, a respected data analysis researcher and British economist, estimated that to make reasonable assumptions about a strategy's validity (i.e., to assume it was 95 percent likely to be statistically relevant), you would need more than 25 years of data.

SHORT PERIODS ARE VALUELESS

Consider the "soaring sixties." The go-go growth managers of the era switched stocks so fast that they were called gunslingers. Performance was the name of the game, and buying stocks with outstanding growth was the way to achieve it. The hot investors of the era focused on the most rapidly growing companies without even considering how much they were paying for every dollar of growth.

In hindsight, look at how misleading a five-year period can be. Between January 1, 1964, and December 31, 1968, $10,000 invested in a portfolio that annually bought the 50 stocks in the Compustat database with the best annual growth in sales soared to $33,500 in value, a compound return of 27.34 percent a year. That more than doubled the S&P 500's 10.16 percent annual return, which saw $10,000 grow to just $16,220. Unfortunately, the strategy didn't fare so well over the next five years. It went on to *lose* more than half its value between January 1, 1969, and December 31, 1973, *losing* 15.7 percent per year, compared to a gain of two percent for the S&P 500. Think of the hapless investor who watched these types of stocks *soar* in value for the five years ending December 31, 1968; doing what they considered "homework" by reading all the glowing reports in the press about the impressive returns generated by the "gunslingers" on Wall Street and finally taking the plunge in 1969. In that scenario, their $10,000 would have shrunk to just $4,260; so much for paying attention to just a five-year record.

Had this same hapless investor had access to long-term returns, he or she would have seen that buying stocks based just on their annual growth of sales was a horrible way to invest—the strategy returned just 3.88 percent per year between 1964 and 2009. In addition, $10,000 invested in the 50 stocks from All Stocks with the best annual sales growth grew to just $57,631 at the end of 2009, whereas the same $10,000 invested in U.S. T-bills compounded at 5.57 percent per year, turning $10,000 into $120,778. In contrast, if the investor had simply put the money in an index like the S&P 500, the $10,000 would have earned 9.46 percent per year, with the $10,000 growing to $639,144! An investment in All Stocks would have done significantly better, earning 11.22 percent per year and turning the $10,000 into $1.33 million!

This is not simply an academic exercise—people base much of their retirement savings on how a fund or a strategy has performed only recently. Imagine the difference to someone starting to save for retirement in 1964 using this strategy. This person would not ever have enough money to retire.

If the 1960s seem too long ago, let's look at the same factors' performance more recently—the five years between January 1, 1995, and December 31, 1999. The mania of the late 1990s provided yet another example of people extrapolating shorter-term results well into the future. People once again were drunk with the prospects of rapidly growing companies, only the names changed from Polaroid, Mohawk Data, and Zimmer Homes to Pets.com, Webvan, and eToys.com. So $10,000 invested on January 1, 1995, in the 50 stocks from the All Stocks universe with the best annual growth in sales soared by 35.42 percent per year through December 31, 1999, growing to $45,539. That was nearly double the All Stocks universe return of 20.72 percent per year, where the same $10,000 grew to $25,644. And much like the 1960s, all the popular media outlets, "experts," and ordinary enthusiasts fell for the short-term outsized returns and poured their money into those stocks, with the same disastrous results that investors had suffered 30 years earlier. Over the next five years, the 50 stocks with the best annual sales gains plummeted by 20.72 percent per year through December 31, 2004, turning $10,000 into just $3,132, a total loss of 69 percent, a catastrophic event for anyone saving for retirement. In contrast, an investment in All Stocks over the same period grew by 6.68 percent per year—turning $10,000 into $13,818. Needless to say, those who forget history are doomed to repeat it.

IT'S DIFFERENT THIS TIME

People want to believe that the present is different from the past. Markets are now computerized, and high-frequency and block traders dominate. Individual investors are gone, and in their place sit a plethora of huge mutual and hedge funds to which individual investors have given their money. Some people think these masters of money make decisions differently from the rest of us, and they believe that looking at how a strategy performed in the 1950s or 1960s offers little insight into how it will perform in the future.

But while we humans passionately believe that our own current circumstances are somehow unique, not much has really changed since the inarguably brilliant Isaac Newton lost a fortune in the South Sea Trading Company bubble of 1720. Newton lamented that he could "calculate the motions of heavenly bodies but not the madness of men." Herein lies the key to why basing investment decisions on long-term results is vital: the price of a stock is still determined by *people*. Figures 3.1 and 3.2 in Chapter 3 compares the South Sea Company's stratospheric rise with the Nasdaq in the 1990s. As long as people let fear, greed, hope, and ignorance cloud their judgment, they will continue to misprice stocks and provide opportunities to those who rigorously use simple, time-tested strategies to pick stocks. Newton lost his money because he let himself get caught up in the hoopla of the moment and invested in a colorful story rather than the dull facts. Names change. Industries change. Styles come in and out of fashion. But the underlying characteristics that identify a good or bad investment remain the same.

Each era has its own group of stocks that people flock to, usually those with the most intoxicating story. Investors of the 1920s sent the Dow Jones Industrial Average up 497 percent between 1921 and 1929, buying into the "new era" industries such as radio and movie companies. In 1928 alone, gullible investors sent Radio Corporation from $85 to $420 per share, all based on the hope that this new marvel would revolutionize the world. In that same year, speculators sent Warner Brothers Corporation up 962 percent—from $13 to $138—based on their excitement about talking pictures and a new Al Jolson contract. The 1950s saw a similar fascination in new technologies, with Texas Instruments soaring from $16 to $194 between 1957 and 1959, with other companies like Haloid-Xerox, Fairchild Camera, Polaroid, and IBM being beneficiaries of the speculative fever. Closer to home, remember all the dot-coms of the late 1990s that soared on little more than a PowerPoint presentation and a lot of sizzle?

The point is simple. Far from being an anomaly, the euphoria of the late 1960s and 1990s was a predictable end to a long bull market, where the silliest investment strategies often do extraordinarily well, only to go on to crash and burn. A long view of returns is essential because only the fullness of time uncovers basic relationships that short-term gyrations conceal. It also lets us analyze how the market responds to a large number of events, such as inflation, stock market crashes, stagflation, recessions, wars, and new discoveries. From the past the future flows. History never repeats *exactly*, but the same *types* of events continue to occur. Investors who had taken this essential message to heart in the last speculative bubble were the ones least hurt in the aftermath.

The same is true after devastating bear markets. Investors behave as irrationally after protracted bear markets as they do after market manias, leaving the equity markets in droves, usually at or near the market's bottom. By the time they gather enough courage to venture back into equities, a good portion of the recovery has often already taken place. Investors who stayed out of the fray in 2009 left between 50 and 75 percent of gains on the table, making it very difficult for them to catch up with the market.

We are always trying to second-guess the market, but the facts are clear: there are no market timers on the Forbes 500 list of the richest people, whereas there are many, many investors.

ANECDOTAL EVIDENCE IS NOT ENOUGH

Investment advice bombards us from many directions with little to support it but anecdotes. Many times, a manager will suggest a handful of stocks as examples, demonstrating how well they went on to perform. Unfortunately, these managers conveniently ignore the many *other stocks* that also possessed the preferred characteristics but *failed*. A common error identified in behavioral research on the stock market is this tendency to generalize from the particular, with evidence showing that people often "delete" from their memory those instances in which they did poorly. This leaves them with the strongest memories centered on the few stocks that performed very well for them and only the faintest memory of those that performed badly. We therefore must look at how well overall *strategies,* not individual stocks, perform. There's often a chasm of difference between what we *think* might work and what really *does* work.

My goal in this book is to bring a more methodical, scientific method to stock market decisions and portfolio construction. To do this, I have tried to stay true to those scientific rules that distinguish a method from a less rigorous model. Among these rules are:

1. *An explicit method:* All models must use explicitly stated rules. There must be no ambiguity in the statement of the rule to be tested. There is no allowance for a private or unique interpretation of the rule.
2. *A public rule:* The rule must be stated explicitly and publicly so anyone with the time, money, data, equipment, and inclination can reproduce the results. The rule must make sense and must not be derived from the data.
3. *A reliable method:* Someone using the same rules and the same database must get the same results. Also, the results must be consistent over time. Long-term results cannot owe all their benefit to a few years.

4. *An objective rule:* I have attempted to use only rules that are intuitive and logical and that appeal to sensibility, but in all cases are objective. They are independent of the social position, financial status, and cultural background of the investor and do not require superior insight, information, or interpretation.

5. *A reliable database:* There are many problems with back-testing, and the quality of data is the primary concern. *All* large collections of historical data contain many errors. While Standard & Poor's Compustat Active and Research Database and CRSP datasets are the gold standard datasets for back-testing, we must remain mindful of the limits of each. Undoubtedly, the databases contain stocks in which a split was unaccounted for, in which a bad book value persisted for several years, in which earnings were misstated and went uncorrected, in which a price was inverted from 31 to 13, and so on. These problems will be present for *any* test of stock market methods and must not be discounted, especially when a method shows just a slight advantage over the market in general. For this edition we use the CRSP dataset for the first time, which covers securities back to 1926.

Remember that the limits of the datasets are not trivial, and should be kept in mind as you review the results presented in this book. Edward F. McQuarrie published an article titled, "The Myth of 1926: How Much Do We Know about Long-Term Returns on U.S. Stocks?" in the Winter 2009 edition of *The Journal of Investing* in which he outlines some of the things to keep in mind when reviewing back-test results for various strategies. He points out that even comprehensive datasets like CRSP are faced with problems that include:

- *Timeframe limitations:* While the CRSP starts in 1926, McQuarrie notes that this still does not cover more than "50 percent of the historical record of widespread, large-scale stock trading in the United States, which goes back almost 200 years." Obviously, the monthly data from Compustat, starting in 1963, is even more limited in scope.
- *Lack of coverage for all traded stocks:* McQuarrie notes that, "For more than 50 percent of its timeframe, the CRSP dataset excludes the majority of stocks trading in the United States, especially the smaller and more vulnerable enterprises."

Compustat also added many small stocks to its dataset in the late 1970s that could have caused an upward bias to result, since many of the stocks added were added *because* they had been successful.

Thus, even though these datasets are among the best for analyzing the results of various styles of investing, it is important to keep their limitations in mind and contrast the results to those derived from other data series such as the Dimson, Marsh, Staunton Global Returns Series featured in the book *Triumph of the Optimists: 101 Years of Global Investment Returns*, markets outside the United States such as those covered by MSCI, and finally additional U.S. datasets such as the Value Line and Worldscope databases.

POTENTIAL PITFALLS

Many studies of Wall Street's favorite investment methods have been seriously flawed. Among their problems are the following.

DATA MINING

It takes approximately 40 minutes for an express train to go from Greenwich, Connecticut, to Grand Central Station in Manhattan. In that time, you could look around your car and find all sorts of statistically relevant characteristics about your fellow passengers. Perhaps there are a huge number of blondes, or 75 percent of the people have blue eyes, or the majority were born in May. These relationships, however, are most likely the result of chance occurrences and probably wouldn't be true for the car in front of or behind you. When you went looking for these relationships, you went data mining. You've found a statistical relationship that fits *one set of data very well, but will not translate to another.* As statisticians have been known to quip, if you torture the data long enough, it will confess to anything. Thus, if there is no sound theoretical, economic, or intuitive, common sense reason for the relationship, it's most likely a chance occurrence. If you see strategies that require that you buy stocks only on a Wednesday and hold them for $16^{1}/_{2}$ months, you're looking at the results of data mining. The best way to confirm that the excess returns are genuine is to test them on different periods or subperiods or in different markets, such as those of European countries. Indeed, we can look at the new results from the CRSP data between 1926 and 1963 as a validation of our previous findings. Research we have conducted using the MSCI EAFE dataset (Europe, Australia and Far East) shows the strategies performing with a level of excess returns similar to those in the United States.

Another technique that we employ is bootstrapping the data. Bootstrapping randomly resamples the overall results for the various strategies we test. We run 100 randomly selected subperiods to make certain that none of the randomly selected periods vary to any significant degree from the overall results shown for the various strategies. Typically, we view a factor as useful or predictive when there is a large spread between the annualized returns of the best and worst decile of that factor. The fact that the best decile of stocks with the best (highest) six-month price momentum beats the worst decile (stocks with the worst price momentum) by 9.96 percent per year for the last 83 years is powerful information that greatly influences how we advocate managing money. To eliminate any potential sample bias in this analysis, we run a test on randomly selected subsamples of the data to make sure that similar decile return spreads exist regardless of the group of stocks that we are considering. For each of the 100 iterations of each bootstrap test, we first randomly select 50 percent of the possible monthly dates in our back-test and discard the other 50 percent. We then randomly select 50 percent of the stocks available on each of those dates and discard the rest. This gives us just 25 percent of our original universe on which to run our decile analysis. We do this 100 times for each factor and analyze the decile return spreads. It so happens that for our best factors, the return spread between the best and the worst decile remains consistent in these 100 iterations. Said another way, for the six-month price appreciation factor, no matter which group of stocks are possible investments, it is always better to buy the decile with the best price momentum. If we discovered that there were large inconsistencies in the bootstrapped data, we would have less confidence in the results and investigate whether there was any evidence of unintentional data mining inherent in the test.

A LIMITED TIME PERIOD

Anything can look good for five or even ten years. There are innumerable strategies that look great during some time periods but that perform horribly over the long term. Even zany strategies can work in any given year. For example, a portfolio of stocks with ticker symbols that are vowels—A, E, I, O, U, and sometimes Y—beat the S&P 500 by more than 11 percent in 1996, but that doesn't make it a good strategy! It simply means that in 1996, chance led it to outperform the S&P 500. This is referred to in the literature as *small sample bias*, whereby people look at a recent five-year return and expect it to hold true for *all* five-year periods. The *more* time studied it is, the greater the chance a strategy will continue to work in the future. Statistically, you will always have greater confidence in results derived from large samples than in those derived from small ones.

SURVIVORSHIP BIAS: THEN IT WAS THERE; NOW IT'S THIN AIR

Many studies don't include stocks that fail, thus producing an upward bias to their results. Numerous companies disappear from the database because of bankruptcy, or more brightly, a takeover. While most new studies include a research file made up of delisted stocks, many early ones did not.

LOOK-AHEAD BIAS: HINDSIGHT IS BETTER THAN 20/20

Many studies assumed that fundamental information was available when it was not. For example, researchers often assumed that you received annual earnings data in January; in reality, they might not be available until March. This biases results upward.

RULES OF THE GAME

I have attempted to correct these problems by using the methodology discussed below.

1. UNIVERSE

For this edition of this book, we use two datasets—the Standard & Poor's Compustat Active and Research Database from 1963 through 2009 and the Center for Research in Security Price (CRSP) dataset from 1926 through 2009. The S&P Compustat Database currently covers nearly 13,000 securities in North America and keeps historical records of financial and statistical information for the vast majority of traded securities—since 1950 for annual data and since 1963 for quarterly data. The CRSP dataset provides U.S. daily corporate actions, price, volume, return, and shares outstanding data for securities with primary listings on the NYSE, Nasdaq, and Amex exchanges. Both Compustat's and CRSP's research files include stocks that were originally listed in the dataset but were removed because of merger, bankruptcy, or some other reason. This avoids *survivorship* bias, which occurs when failed companies are excluded from studies because they no longer exist.

I cannot overstate the importance of testing strategies over long periods of time. Any study from the early 1970s to the early 1980s will find strong results for value investing, just as any study from the 1960s and 1990s will favor growth stocks. Styles come in and out of fashion on Wall Street, so the longer the time period studied, the more illuminating the results. From a statistical viewpoint, the strangest results come from the smallest samples. Large samples always provide better conclusions than small ones. Some pension consultants use a branch of statistics called *reliability mathematics* that use past returns to predict future performance. They've found that you need a *minimum* of 14 periods to even *begin* to make accurate predictions about the future.

2. MARKET CAPITALIZATION

Except for specific small capitalization tests, I review stocks from two distinct groups. The first includes only stocks with market capitalizations in excess of $200 million (adjusted for inflation), called "All Stocks" throughout this book. Table 4.1 shows how I created the deflated minimums. The second group includes larger, better-known stocks with market capitalizations greater than the database average (usually the top 17 percent of the database by market capitalization). These larger stocks are called "Large Stocks" throughout this book. Table 4.2 shows the number of stocks with market capitalizations above the database mean.

T A B L E   4.1

Inflation-Adjusted Value of $200 Million

Date	Inflation	Inflation adjustment factor	Value of $200 million
Dec–09	2.72	1.03	$205,442,662.25
Dec–08	0.09	1.00	$200,000,000.00
Dec–07	4.08	1.00	$199,817,341.17
Dec–06	2.54	0.96	$191,982,038.55
Dec–05	3.42	0.94	$187,225,298.25
Dec–04	3.26	0.91	$181,041,535.86
Dec–03	1.88	0.88	$175,333,447.50
Dec–02	2.38	0.86	$172,098,864.09
Dec–01	1.55	0.84	$168,103,202.24
Dec–00	3.39	0.83	$165,534,562.48
Dec–99	2.68	0.80	$160,111,878.53
Dec–98	1.61	0.78	$155,925,947.07
Dec–97	1.70	0.77	$153,452,442.11
Dec–96	3.32	0.75	$150,883,802.35
Dec–95	2.54	0.73	$146,031,927.24
Dec–94	2.67	0.71	$142,416,804.61
Dec–93	2.75	0.69	$138,706,547.18
Dec–92	2.90	0.67	$134,996,289.74
Dec–91	3.06	0.66	$131,190,897.50

(continued on next page)

T A B L E   4.1

Inflation-Adjusted Value of $200 Million *(Continued)*

Date	Inflation	Inflation adjustment factor	Value of $200 million
Dec–90	6.11	0.64	$127,290,370.45
Dec–89	4.65	0.60	$119,964,990.39
Dec–88	4.42	0.57	$114,637,441.25
Dec–87	4.41	0.55	$109,785,566.15
Dec–86	1.13	0.53	$105,123,960.65
Dec–85	3.77	0.52	$103,982,342.98
Dec–84	3.95	0.50	$100,176,950.74
Dec–83	3.80	0.48	$96,371,558.50
Dec–82	3.87	0.46	$92,851,570.68
Dec–81	8.94	0.45	$89,426,717.66
Dec–80	12.40	0.41	$82,101,337.60
Dec–79	13.31	0.36	$72,968,396.22
Dec–78	9.03	0.32	$64,406,263.68
Dec–77	6.77	0.30	$59,078,714.54
Dec–76	4.81	0.28	$55,368,457.10
Dec–75	7.01	0.26	$52,799,817.34
Dec–74	12.20	0.25	$49,374,964.32
Dec–73	8.80	0.22	$43,952,280.38
Dec–72	3.41	0.20	$40,432,292.56
Dec–71	3.36	0.20	$39,100,405.27
Dec–70	5.49	0.19	$37,863,652.80
Dec–69	6.11	0.18	$35,865,821.87
Dec–68	4.72	0.17	$33,772,856.14
Dec–67	3.04	0.16	$32,250,699.24
Dec–66	3.35	0.16	$31,299,351.18
Dec–65	1.92	0.15	$30,252,868.31
Dec–64	1.19	0.15	$29,682,059.48
Dec–63	1.65	0.15	$29,396,655.06
Dec–62	1.22	0.14	$28,920,981.03
Dec–61	0.67	0.14	$28,540,441.81
Dec–60	1.48	0.14	$28,350,172.19
Dec–59	1.50	0.14	$27,969,632.97
Dec–58	1.76	0.14	$27,493,958.94
Dec–57	3.02	0.14	$27,018,284.91
Dec–56	2.86	0.13	$26,257,206.46
Dec–55	0.37	0.13	$25,496,128.01
Dec–54	(0.50)	0.13	$25,400,993.21
Dec–53	0.62	0.13	$25,591,262.82
Dec–52	0.88	0.13	$25,400,993.21
Dec–51	5.87	0.13	$25,210,723.60
Dec–50	5.79	0.12	$23,783,701.51
Dec–49	(1.80)	0.11	$22,451,814.22
Dec–48	2.71	0.11	$22,927,488.25
Dec–47	9.01	0.11	$22,261,544.61
Dec–46	18.16	0.10	$20,453,983.29

(continued on next page)

T A B L E   4.1

Inflation-Adjusted Value of $200 Million *(Continued)*

Date	Inflation	Inflation adjustment factor	Value of $200 million
Dec–45	2.25	0.09	$17,314,534.70
Dec–44	2.11	0.08	$16,933,995.47
Dec–43	3.16	0.08	$16,553,456.25
Dec–42	9.29	0.08	$16,077,782.22
Dec–41	9.72	0.07	$14,745,894.93
Dec–40	0.96	0.07	$13,414,007.65
Dec–39	(0.48)	0.07	$13,318,872.84
Dec–38	(2.78)	0.07	$13,318,872.84
Dec–37	3.10	0.07	$13,699,412.07
Dec–36	1.21	0.07	$13,318,872.84
Dec–35	2.99	0.07	$13,128,603.23
Dec–34	2.03	0.06	$12,748,064.01
Dec–33	0.51	0.06	$12,557,794.39
Dec–32	(10.30)	0.06	$12,462,659.59
Dec–31	(9.52)	0.07	$13,889,681.68
Dec–30	(6.03)	0.08	$15,316,703.77
Dec–29	0.20	0.08	$16,363,186.64
Dec–28	(0.97)	0.08	$16,268,051.83
Dec–27	(2.08)	0.08	$16,458,321.44
Dec–26	(1.49)	0.08	$16,838,860.67

T A B L E   4.2

Number of Stocks with a Market Capitalization above the Database Mean

Year ending	Number of stocks with a market capitalization above the database mean	Number of stocks in the database	Percent
Dec 31, 1962	162	751	21.57%
Dec 31, 1963	164	785	20.89%
Dec 31, 1964	175	836	20.93%
Dec 31, 1965	231	1,073	21.53%
Dec 30, 1966	333	1,676	19.87%
Dec 29, 1967	385	1,961	19.63%
Dec 31, 1968	483	2,556	18.90%
Dec 31, 1969	493	2,668	18.48%
Dec 31, 1970	462	2,528	18.28%
Dec 31, 1971	528	2,766	19.09%
Dec 29, 1972	550	3,037	18.11%
Dec 31, 1973	454	2,551	17.80%
Dec 31, 1974	405	2,211	18.32%
Dec 31, 1975	446	2,387	18.68%
Dec 31, 1976	481	2,482	19.38%
Dec 30, 1977	516	2,620	19.69%

(continued on next page)

TABLE 4.2

Number of Stocks with a Market Capitalization above the Database Mean *(Continued)*

Year ending	Number of stocks with a market capitalization above the database mean	Number of stocks in the database	Percent
Dec 29, 1978	530	2,607	20.33%
Dec 31, 1979	550	2,682	20.51%
Dec 31, 1980	557	2,942	18.93%
Dec 31, 1981	581	2,829	20.54%
Dec 31, 1982	595	2,913	20.43%
Dec 30, 1983	678	3,416	19.85%
Dec 31, 1984	458	3,235	14.16%
Dec 31, 1985	469	3,339	14.05%
Dec 31, 1986	521	3,575	14.57%
Dec 31, 1987	518	3,408	15.20%
Dec 30, 1988	628	3,513	17.88%
Dec 29, 1989	615	3,470	17.72%
Dec 31, 1990	527	2,965	17.77%
Dec 31, 1991	614	3,395	18.09%
Dec 31, 1992	675	3,908	17.27%
Dec 31, 1993	790	4,684	16.87%
Dec 30, 1994	818	4,941	16.56%
Dec 29, 1995	882	5,442	16.21%
Dec 31, 1996	920	6,013	15.30%
Dec 31, 1997	923	6,457	14.29%
Dec 31, 1998	767	5,923	12.95%
Dec 31, 1999	768	6,053	12.69%
Dec 29, 2000	720	5,498	13.10%
Dec 31, 2001	709	5,043	14.06%
Dec 31, 2002	657	4,655	14.11%
Dec 31, 2003	771	5,122	15.05%
Dec 31, 2004	815	5,314	15.34%
Dec 30, 2005	815	5,307	15.36%
Dec 29, 2006	805	5,405	14.89%
Dec 31, 2007	777	5,279	14.72%
Dec 31, 2008	622	3,981	15.62%
Dec 31, 2009	651	4,150	15.69%
Average	583	3,549	17.32%

In all cases, I remove the smallest stocks in the database from consideration. For example, at the end of 2009, of the 6,705 stocks in our dataset, more than 2,555 stocks were jettisoned because their market capitalization fell below an inflation-adjusted minimum of $200 million. In the same year, only 651 stocks had market capitalizations exceeding the database average. We also remove stocks that appear in the Compustat but have no market capitalization, duplicate issues, shares of mutual funds, and the like.

I originally chose a $150 million value in 1995 (now an inflation-adjusted $200 million) after consulting traders at several large Wall Street brokerages. They felt that it was the minimum necessary if they were investing $100 million in a large portfolio of stocks in 1995. Because of inflation, the number now stands at $200 million. I use this figure to avoid microcap stocks and focus only on those stocks that a professional investor could buy without running into liquidity problems. Inflation has taken its toll: A stock with a market capitalization of $29.40 million in 1963 was the equivalent of $200 million at the end of 2009. The same $200 million deflated back to 1926 was the equivalent of a $16.8 million.

Eliminating microcap stocks considerably reduces the returns for several of the factors we study. It also puts the results featured in this book at a disadvantage when compared with many academic studies that include microcap stocks. We have found that by eliminating microcaps, our results appear to be significantly lower than those of studies that include them. But I think it is both appropriate and honest to do, in order to capture results that are far more likely to be replicated in the real world. Microcap stocks possess virtually no trading liquidity, and a large order would send their prices skyrocketing. Thus, while it is easy to *assume* that you could purchase and sell these securities at their listed price in the historical dataset, I believe that this is an illusion and unnecessarily gives an upward bias to the results of studies that allow their inclusion.

3. AVOIDING LOOK-AHEAD BIAS

We use only publicly available monthly information. To ensure that we are not selecting stocks based on information that is *not* publicly known, we lag quarterly data by three months and annual data by six months. While this can have the effect of making information slightly stale, it is necessary in order to avoid look-ahead bias.

One potential problem with the earlier data is the changing nature of the Compustat dataset. As Table 4.2 shows, Standard & Poor's Compustat has continually expanded the database. Many smaller stocks have been added, including up to five years of retroactive data. And since these firms were usually added *because* they were successful, the likelihood of a look-ahead bias becomes a real concern. Though this book may suffer from this bias, I think because I eliminate the smallest stocks from consideration, the problem is greatly diminished.

4. REBALANCE METHODOLOGY

In the first three editions of this book, all portfolios were formed on December 31 of each calendar year and held for one year. While this was a useful approach, especially for the period between 1950 and 1963 when only annual data were available, it is lacking in two key respects. First, in an era of quarterly financial reporting, forming portfolios only once a year ignores a significant amount of new information that emerges over the course of any given year. The same model will select a variety of different securities throughout the year based on changing quarterly financial statement information. Second, by forming portfolios only in December, the results may have seasonal biases. The reality is that investors invest continually throughout the year, not just on December 31. To address these two issues, and thereby gain an even stronger understanding of our factors and strategies, we are now compositing all of our results. To do this, we form 12 separate portfolios each year for each strategy, one every month, and then we average the results of each of the 12 to produce our portfolio return. The rebalance period for each monthly portion of the portfolio remains one year. Dynamic rebalancing (composited back-testing) is superior to single-month analysis because it captures the entire profile of a factor rather than a single data point. If the December series of a factor just happens to be better than those for a different month, you may draw an incomplete or incorrect inference as to the efficacy of the overall effectiveness of a factor. Conversely, if the December series of a factor is weak, even if all of the other months have a superior return, you will miss the ability to make use of a superior factor.

Look at Table 4.3, which we created in early 2009 as we began to explore the benefits of composited back-testing. It shows the various results to buying 10 percent of stocks from All Stocks with the lowest PE ratios—quite a difference! An investor in the January series would have enjoyed an average annual compound return of 19.03 percent, turning $10,000 into $30.7 million, whereas an investor in the March series—again, buying the stocks with the lowest PE ratios from All Stocks—would have earned 13.81 percent, turning the same $10,000 into just $3.9 million, a tenfold difference. Indeed, the excess return over All Stocks generated by purchasing the 10 percent of stocks from the group with the lowest PE ratios went from a minimum of 4.73 percent for the March series up to 9.91 percent for the January series. What's more, the monthly base rates of beating the All Stocks universe are also different. Tests that use one data point—such as the December series—and exclude all others don't tell you how low PE stocks might perform in all other months. Using a composited back-test, you can get a much better sense of the true base rate of the

TABLE 4.3

Summary Statistics: PE Decile One December 1962 through December 2008, Various Months Ranked by Return

	N periods	Geometric mean (%)	Arithmetic mean (%)	Standard deviation (%)	T statistic	Ending index value	Sharpe ratio	Maximum decline (%)
Jan	553	19.03	19.36	18.92	6.9461	$30,695,522.02	0.76	−56.74
Dec	553	16.38	16.87	17.86	6.4133	$10,877,646.98	0.66	−58.6
Nov	553	15.73	16.31	17.87	6.195	$8,389,183.87	0.63	−59.68
Oct	553	15.44	16.09	18.04	6.0519	$7,466,607.98	0.61	−58.93
August	553	15.4	16.08	18.19	5.9984	$7,358,622.01	0.61	−59.1
Sept	553	15.05	15.77	18.17	5.8903	$6,392,296.59	0.59	−57.7
May	553	15.03	15.84	18.77	5.7288	$6,344,822.28	0.58	−58.79
July	553	15.03	15.82	18.58	5.779	$6,337,902.47	0.58	−60.01
Feb	553	14.84	15.63	18.38	5.7707	$5,887,275.31	0.58	−62.06
June	553	14.83	15.63	18.54	5.7225	$5,863,131.31	0.57	−58.1
April	553	14.74	15.53	18.45	5.716	$5,651,325.05	0.57	−58.67
March	553	13.81	14.7	18.3	5.4514	$3,878,612.77	0.53	−60.58
Average		15.44	16.14	18.34	5.97195	$8,761,912.39	0.61	−59.08

underlying factor. Also, I caution you to avoid the impulse to say, "I will make my investments only in January, since that was the best month to rebalance low PE stocks in between 1963 and 2008" because the best month often *changes* over time. If we look at the 10 years between January 1, 1999, and December 31, 2008, featured in Table 4.4, we see that for those 10 years, the best monthly data series was in September, with January sinking to the middle of the pack.

T A B L E   4.4

Summary Statistics: PE Decile One Returns December 1999 through December 2008, Various Months Ranked by Return

	N periods	Geometric mean (%)	Arithmetic mean (%)	Standard deviation (%)	T statistic	Ending index value	Sharpe ratio	Maximum decline (%)
Sept	120	13.78	15.3	21.28	2.27	$36,369.10	0.48	−57.7
August	120	13.74	15.27	21.36	2.26	$36,241.10	0.48	−59.1
Dec	120	13.71	15.12	20.73	2.31	$36,139.77	0.49	−58.6
Oct	120	13.48	15.07	21.46	2.22	$35,412.70	0.47	−58.93
Nov	120	13.06	14.58	20.84	2.21	$34,141.20	0.46	−59.68
July	120	12.22	14	21.85	2.03	$31,687.76	0.41	−60.01
Jan	120	11.9	13.76	21.85	1.99	$30,778.75	0.40	−56.74
May	120	11.71	13.65	22.65	1.91	$30,270.96	0.38	−58.79
June	120	10.88	12.8	22.11	1.83	$28,085.63	0.35	−58.1
April	120	10.01	11.93	21.82	1.73	$25,950.10	0.32	−58.67
March	120	8.21	10.17	20.99	1.53	$22,017.78	0.25	−60.58
Feb	120	8.13	10.19	21.35	1.51	$21,858.69	0.24	−62.06
Average		11.74	13.49	21.52	1.98	$30,746.13	0.394703	−59.08

We also find that, in general, base rates improve when you look at the monthly composited results. This is so because the December series now accounts for only $1/12$ of the composited portfolio. Back-tested strategies or factors that are rebalanced just once a year in December may over- or understate the efficacy of that factor or strategy and lead us to make mistakes in choosing the best factors for investment.

If, for example, the low price/earnings portfolios formed and rebalanced once per year in December underperform other value metrics, we would avoid using that value factor in favor of superior alternatives. However, as we have learned is indeed the case, price/earnings do very well when people invest in months other than December.

Instead, by forming portfolios 12 times per year, one in each month, we gain a much more complete understanding of how a factor or strategy works. After all, these factors and strategies are all about information, and information changes over the course of a year. December-only portfolios ignore 11 months of information. By incorporating information throughout the year, we can understand which factors work the best regardless of what time of year the initial investment and subsequent rebalances are made.

All strategies are rebalanced annually, and stocks are equally weighted with no adjustments for beta, industry, or other variable. Foreign stocks (in the form of American Depository Receipts, or ADRs) included in the Compustat Universe are allowed.

For this edition of this book, I am also including risk statistics obtained through the monthly data. These allow me to focus on things like how often the strategy performed well, what the worst-case scenario was, how long it took for the strategy to recover, and so on.

I assume that no trades are made throughout the year, with one exception—if a stock goes bankrupt or is acquired before the formal rebalance, we invest the proceeds of that stock on a pro rata basis across the remaining stocks in the portfolio. This may bias my results slightly as it rewards trade-averse strategies, but I believe that many excellent strategies that require numerous trades turn mediocre once trading costs are included. I also examine annual returns and remove stocks with extreme returns or data that were inconsistent with outside information.

In real time, we have a list of six "red flags" that alert us to remove a stock from a portfolio and replace it with a new one that meets the criteria of the strategy. These are:

1. If a company fails to verify its numbers as required by Sarbanes-Oxley, we replace the stock in the portfolio.
2. If a company is charged with fraud by the Federal government, we replace the stock in the portfolio.
3. If a company restates numbers such that they would not have qualified at the time of purchase, we replace the stock in the portfolio.
4. If a company receives a takeover offer from a third party, we replace the stock if the price of the stock moves to within 95 percent of the takeover offer price.
5. If a company drops by 50 percent from point of purchase *and* is in the bottom 10 percent of all stocks for the previous 12 months of price performance, we replace the stock in the portfolio.
6. If a stock from one of our dividend strategies cuts its dividend by 50 percent or more, it is replaced in the portfolio.

I also compare absolute and risk-adjusted returns and look at the beta generated by each strategy. Beta theoretically measures how closely a security or portfolio of securities performs relative to the market as a whole. A stock or portfolio with a beta of 1 would suggest that it would have similar risk and returns to the market as a whole, whereas a security or a portfolio with a beta of 1.4 would be considered much more risky and have higher return potential than the market as a whole. Risk-adjusted returns take the volatility of a portfolio—as measured by the standard deviation of return—into account, and not just absolute returns. Generally, investors prefer a portfolio earning 15 percent a year with a standard deviation of 20 percent to one earning 16 percent a year with a standard deviation of 30 percent. A 1 percent absolute advantage doesn't compensate for the terror of the wild ride. I use the well-known Sharpe ratio of reward-to-risk for my calculations, with higher numbers indicating better risk-adjusted returns. To arrive at the Sharpe ratio, simply take the average return from a strategy, subtract the risk-free rate of interest (we use a constant 5 percent risk-free rate of interest which allows us to compare strategies over all subperiods with a consistent risk-free interest rate), and then divide that number by the standard deviation of return. The ratio is important because it reflects risk. Table 4.5 provides an example of a strategy that outperforms the S&P 500 on an *absolute* basis but fails to beat it on a risk-adjusted basis. Generally speaking, you will want to use only strategies that outperform their benchmark on both an absolute and a risk-adjusted basis. I also show *downside risk*—which is measured by the semistandard deviation below zero—allowing me to measure how risky a strategy is when stock prices are declining. I believe that this is a more exact way to measure risk. Along that line, along with the Sharpe ratio, we will also look at the Sortino ratio which is a modification of the Sharpe ratio that penalizes only downside risk. You calculate it by taking the return of the portfolio and subtracting a constant required rate of return of 10 percent divided by downside risk.

TABLE 4.5

Determining a Strategy's Risk-Adjusted Return

Year ending	S&P 500	Strategy	Constant risk-free rate	S&P 500-constant risk-free rate	Strategy-constant risk-free rate
Dec 31, 1993	9.99%	7.00%	5.00%	4.99%	2.00%
Dec 31, 1994	1.31%	5.00%	5.00%	−3.69%	0.00%
Dec 31, 1995	37.43%	42.00%	5.00%	32.43%	37.00%
Dec 31, 1996	23.07%	18.00%	5.00%	18.07%	13.00%
Dec 31, 1997	33.36%	24.00%	5.00%	28.36%	19.00%
Dec 31, 1998	28.58%	16.80%	5.00%	23.58%	11.80%
Dec 31, 1999	21.04%	23.57%	5.00%	16.04%	18.57%
Dec 31, 2000	−9.11%	−5.00%	5.00%	−14.11%	−10.00%
Dec 31, 2001	−11.88%	−5.18%	5.00%	−16.88%	−10.18%
Dec 31, 2002	−22.10%	−28.00%	5.00%	−27.10%	−33.00%
Dec 31, 2003	28.70%	48.00%	5.00%	23.70%	43.00%
Average	12.76%	13.29%	5.00%	7.76%	8.29%
Standard deviation	19.43%	20.83%	0.00%		

Risk-adjusted ratio for the S&P 500 equals 7.76% divided by 19.43%, or 0.40.
Risk-adjusted ratio for the strategy equals 8.29% divided by 20.83%, or 0.39.

5. MINIMUM AND MAXIMUM EXPECTED RETURNS

In all summary information about a strategy, I provide the maximum and minimum projected returns, as well as the actual maximum and minimum over the past 52 years. This is *extremely* useful information, since investors can glance at the worst loss and decide if they can stomach the volatility of any particular strategy.

6. SUMMARY STATISTICS

For each strategy I now include a number of measurements not available in earlier editions of this book. I generate all the summary statistical information using the Morningstar

EnCorr Analyzer program. In addition to the concepts already covered, each summary result report includes the following:

- *Arithmetic average:* The average return over the period.
- *Geometric average:* The average annual compound return over the period.
- *Median return:* The return that has 50 percent of all returns above it and below it.
- *Standard deviation of return:* The extent to which observations in a data series differ from the average return for the entire series. The larger the standard deviation, the "riskier" the strategy. But since approximately 70 percent of all observations are positive, I think that using this to measure overall risk in a portfolio can be misleading. After all, when stocks are going your way, you want as much "risk" as possible. Therefore, I prefer to look at:
  - *Semistandard deviation of return below zero (downside risk):* I believe that this is a much better measurement of the risk of a strategy because it focuses on the portion of risk that is to the left of all observations below zero return. It essentially focuses on downside risk and the *lower* this number is, the lower the risk of the strategy when stock prices are falling.
  - *T-statistic:* Measures how likely it is that results are due to the result of chance. Typically, a T-statistic of +/−1.96 (where there are at least 20 observations) indicates a statistically significant selection return at the 95 percent level of confidence. The higher the T-statistic, the less likely that the results were due to chance. You can test this by generating a series of random numbers over the period being analyzed. For example, a randomly generated list of numbers over the period 1963–2009 generates a T-statistic of −1.02.
  - *Tracking error with the universe from which the strategy is drawn:* Tracking error measures how close a portfolio's return is to an index or a universe to which it benchmarked. The higher the tracking error, the less the portfolio is like the benchmark.

7. DECILES AND 25–TO–50 STOCK PORTFOLIOS

All multifactor portfolios contain 25–to–50 stocks. For all single factor results, we compare the results for the best decile with results for the worst decile.

8. DISCIPLINE

I test investment disciplines, not trading strategies. My results show that universe equity markets are not perfectly efficient. Investors *can* outperform the market by sticking with superior strategies over long periods of time. Simple, disciplined strategies—such as buying the top 10 *yielding* stocks in the Dow Jones Industrial Average—have worked over the *last* 75 years because they are immune to the emotions of the market and *force* investors to buy industrial stocks when they are under distress. No one wanted to buy Union Carbide after Bhopal or Exxon after the Valdez oil spill, yet it is precisely these kinds of times that often offer the best buys.

9. COSTS

Transaction costs and bid/ask spreads are not included. Each reader faces different transaction costs. Institutional investors making million-dollar trades face substantially lower costs than an individual, odd-lot trader. Thus, each investor will be able to review raw data and factor in the appropriate transaction costs. Since the first edition of this book was published in 1996, however, online brokers have seriously reduced the transaction costs that individual investors pay for trading stocks. In many instances, an individual can now trade any number of shares for a flat $7 commission. There are also services available from companies like Sharebuilder.com and FolioInvesting.com that allow you to make unlimited trades during the year for a flat, annual fee. This makes buying a large number of stocks far less expensive for the individual than in years past, since they now pay trading costs that are in line with those of large institutional investors.

In terms of gains lost to the bid/ask spread, an excellent paper by Charles M. Jones of the Columbia Graduate School of Business titled *A Century of Stock Market Liquidity and Trading Costs* published in May 2002, finds that when looking at the 30 stocks in the Dow Jones Industrial Average (certainly among the most liquid stocks trading on U.S. exchanges), "It is perhaps surprising that spreads on Dow Jones stocks were around 0.60% for sustained periods around 1910 and in the 1920's and were at similar levels in the 1950's and in the 1980's. Spreads have fallen dramatically over the last twenty years." A chart from his paper shows that spreads in these stocks in the year 2000 had dropped to under 0.20 percent. This demonstrates that if even the most liquid stocks on U.S. exchanges had spreads of 0.60 percent as recently as the 1980s, those on smaller issues were certainly higher. Thus, wisdom would dictate that you should subtract as much as 1 percent of gains (or add 1 percent of losses) for the data for the 1960s through the 1980s that you might now hope to achieve when implementing these strategies in the real world. Currently, our traders at O'Shaughnessy Asset Management have found that bid/ask spreads on small-cap trades average 0.50 percent and 0.15 percent on large-cap trades.

Now let's look at the tests. We'll start with a review of return by market capitalization and then look at returns by single and multifactor combinations.

CHAPTER 5

RANKING STOCKS BY MARKET CAPITALIZATION: SIZE MATTERS

Order and simplification are the first steps toward the mastery of a subject.

—Thomas Mann

In this new edition of this book, we use the CRSP dataset to look at stocks by market capitalization between 1926 and 2009. First, I review the returns for the two universes I use as benchmarks against which I measure all other strategies. These benchmarks, based on market capitalization, are called All Stocks and Large Stocks. All Stocks are those with market capitalizations in excess of a deflated $200 million. Large Stocks are those with a market capitalization greater than the dataset average (usually the top 17 percent of the entire dataset by market capitalization). I also look at a universe of small capitalization stocks that have adequate liquidity to allow large-scale trading. Finally, we use the Compustat dataset to look at a universe of large capitalization stocks composed of market-leading companies. We need the Compustat dataset for our market-leading companies—which I call Market Leaders—because several of the factors we use to create Market Leaders are not available in the CRSP dataset. In addition to these investable groups, I also focus on shares of investable companies (market capitalizations greater than a deflated $200 million) by various levels of market capitalization, ranking them by decile from the smallest to the largest investable stocks.

With the exception of the Market Leaders universe, in all cases I start with a $10,000 investment on December 31, 1926, and rebalance the portfolio annually using the compositing methodology discussed in Chapter Four. As with all my tests, the stocks are equally weighted, all dividends are reinvested, and all variables such as common shares outstanding are time-lagged to avoid look-ahead bias. I also use the monthly data to show worst-case scenarios over the last 83 years.

Table 5.1 shows the results for All Stocks, Large Stocks, and the S&P 500. As mentioned in Chapter 1, there is virtually no difference in performance between stocks with market capitalizations above the CRSP and Compustat mean (Large Stocks) and the S&P 500. The $10,000 invested in the S&P 500 on December 31, 1926, was worth $23,171,851 on December 31, 2009, and $21,617,372 if invested in the Large Stocks universe. This is not surprising since investing in the S&P 500 is nothing more than a bet on big, well-known companies. Table 5.1 summarizes the results for each universe. The average annual compound return for the S&P 500 over the period was 9.78 percent versus 9.69 percent for the Large Stocks universe.

The All Stocks group did considerably better then the S&P 500 and, Large Stocks universe: $10,000 grew to $38,542,780, an average annual compound return of 10.46 percent. The performance was not without bumps, however. The All Stocks portfolio had a higher standard deviation of return at 21.67 percent, as well as a higher downside risk than the Large Stocks portfolio. Also, if you look at rolling returns over the entire period, you will see that there were several periods where All Stocks significantly outperformed Large Stocks, and several times where the reverse was true. Large Stocks did better on a five-year basis than All Stocks during the early 1930s, but All Stocks did significantly better after the market bottomed in May 1932. For example, the five years ending May 1937 saw All Stocks with a cumulative gain of 461 percent over the previous five years, or a compound average annual return of 41.17 percent, whereas Large Stocks earned 370 percent, or a compound average annual return of 36.26 percent and a cumulative advantage of 91 percent for All Stocks over Large Stocks.

T A B L E   5.1

Summary Annual Return and Risk Results Data: S&P 500, Large Stocks, and All Stocks, January 1, 1927, to December 31, 2009

	S&P 500	Large Stocks	All Stocks
Arithmetic average	11.81%	11.75%	13.06%
Geometric average	9.78%	9.69%	10.46%
Median return	16.58%	16.75%	18.54%
Standard deviation	19.27%	19.35%	21.67%
Upside deviation	13.65%	13.10%	14.78%
Downside deviation	14.43%	14.40%	16.03%
Tracking error	4.22	0.00	4.76
Number of positive periods	615	609	606
Number of negative periods	380	387	390
Maximum peak-to-trough decline	−83.41%	−84.33%	−85.45%
Beta	0.97	1.00	1.10
T-statistic (m = 0)	5.30	5.25	5.19
Sharpe ratio (Rf = 5%)	0.25	0.24	0.25
Sortino ratio (MAR = 10%)	−0.01	−0.02	0.03

(continued on next page)

T A B L E   5.1

Summary Annual Return and Risk Results Data: S&P 500, Large Stocks, and All Stocks, January 1, 1927, to December 31, 2009 *(Continued)*

	S&P 500	Large Stocks	All Stocks
$10,000 becomes	$23,171,851	$21,617,372	$38,542,780
Minimum 1-year return	−67.56%	−66.63%	−66.72%
Maximum 1-year return	162.89%	159.52%	201.69%
Minimum 3-year return	−42.35%	−43.53%	−45.99%
Maximum 3-year return	43.35%	45.64%	51.03%
Minimum 5-year return	−17.36%	−20.15%	−23.07%
Maximum 5-year return	36.12%	36.26%	41.17%
Minimum 7-year return	−6.12%	−6.95%	−7.43%
Maximum 7-year return	25.82%	22.83%	23.77%
Minimum 10-year return	−4.95%	−5.70%	−5.31%
Maximum 10-year return	21.43%	19.57%	22.05%
Minimum expected return*	−26.73%	−26.96%	−30.28%
Maximum expected return†	50.35%	50.46%	56.39%

* Minimum expected return is arithmetic return minus 2 times the standard deviation.

† Maximum expected return is arithmetic return plus 2 times the standard deviation.

Large Stocks did quite a bit worse than All Stocks between December 31, 1975, and December 31, 1983, only to turn around and do better between December 31, 1984, and December 31, 1990. The All Stocks universe had a worst-case scenario similar to that of Large Stocks: Between August 1929 and June 1932, All Stocks lost 85.45 percent, whereas Large Stocks lost 84.33 percent. Between 1926 and 2009, each of the two universes lost 20 percent or more nine times. All Stocks had nine peak-to-trough declines exceeding 20 percent, with the largest occurring between August 1929 and June 1932 when the group lost 85.45 percent. The most recent decline occurred between May 2007 and February 2009, with All Stocks losing 55.54 percent. Table 5.1 summarizes the results for each group for the period 1926–2009 and Table 5.2 shows the returns by decade. Figure 5.1 shows the rolling average annual compound excess return for the All Stocks universe minus the Large Stocks universe between 1926 and 2009.

T A B L E   5.2

Average Annual Compound Rates of Return by Decade

	1920s*	1930s	1940s	1950s	1960s	1970s	1980s	1990s	2000s†
All Stocks	12.33%	−0.03%	11.57%	18.07%	10.72%	7.56%	16.78%	15.35%	4.39%
Large Stocks	17.73%	−1.05%	9.65%	17.06%	8.31%	6.65%	17.34%	16.38%	2.42%
S&P 500	21.83%	−0.05%	9.17%	19.35%	7.81%	5.86%	17.55%	18.20%	−0.95%

* Returns for January 1, 1927, to December 31, 1929.

† Returns for January 1, 2000, to December 31, 2009.

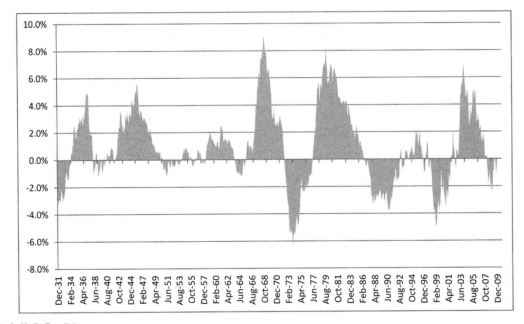

F I G U R E   5.1

Five-year average annual compound excess (deficient) return All Stocks minus Large Stocks, January 1, 1927, to December 31, 2009

WORST-CASE SCENARIOS AND BEST AND WORST RETURNS

I list the best and worst returns for the strategies for each one-, three-, five- and ten-year period. We also look at the worst-case scenario for each group and list any time they declined by more than 20 percent (the usual definition of a bear market), how long the decline lasted, and how long it took to recover.

Tables 5.3 through 5.5 show the worst-case scenarios for each of our universes and Tables 5.6 and 5.7 show best and worst returns for various holding periods. For example, an investor with a five-year time horizon who wanted to invest in the All Stocks universe might look and see that in all monthly periods over the last 83 years, the *worst* five-year period had a loss of 23.07 percent per year, whereas the *best* five years saw a gain of 41.17 percent. Both of these occurred in the 1930s, after the crash of 1929 led to the Great Depression, but as we've seen with recent market collapses, they are offered as examples of just how bad and how good a five-year experience can be for an investor. Translating this into dollars, as Table 5.7 demonstrates, if the investor put $10,000 in the All Stocks universe and got a return over the next five years that matched the *worst* ever recorded over the last 83 years, his portfolio would be worth $2,695, an overall loss 73.05 percent or a decline of 23.07 percent per year. Alternatively, if he received a return matching the *best* ever recorded over the last 83 years, his $10,000 would have grown to $56,062, an overall gain of 461 percent, or an increase of 41.17 percent per year. Investors should search for strategies that have the best upside potential with the lowest downside risk, so we feature these data for all our key strategies.

TABLE 5.3

Worst-Case Scenarios: All 20 Percent or Greater Declines for All Stocks, January 1, 1927, to December 31, 2009

Peak date	Peak index value	Trough date	Trough index value	Recovery date	Decline (%)	Decline duration	Recovery duration
Aug–29	2.09	Jun–32	0.30	May–44	−85.45%	34	143
May–46	4.31	May–47	3.02	Jan–50	−29.80%	12	32
Nov–61	28.62	Jun–62	21.68	Aug–63	−24.25%	7	14
Nov–68	78.28	Sep–74	36.94	Jun–77	−52.81%	70	33
Aug–87	541.36	Nov–87	365.98	Apr–89	−32.40%	3	17
Sep–89	617.58	Oct–90	459.03	Mar–91	−25.67%	13	5
Apr–98	2,159.90	Aug–98	1,526.20	Jun–99	−29.34%	4	10
Mar–00	2,767.91	Sep–02	1,748.78	Nov–03	−36.82%	30	14
May–07	4,859.84	Feb–09	2,160.86	N/A	−55.54%	21	N/A
Average					−41.34%	21.56	33.5

TABLE 5.4

Worst-Case Scenarios: All 20 Percent or Greater Declines for Large Stocks, January 1, 1927, to December 31, 2009

Peak date	Peak index value	Trough date	Trough index value	Recovery date	Decline (%)	Decline duration	Recovery duration
Aug–29	2.31	May–32	0.36	Feb–45	−84.33%	33	153
May–46	3.52	May–47	2.66	Dec–49	−24.57%	12	31
Nov–61	23.28	Jun–62	17.75	May–63	−23.76%	7	11
Nov–68	46.40	Jun–70	30.93	Dec–71	−33.33%	19	18
Nov–72	53.38	Sep–74	29.15	Sep–76	−45.39%	22	24
Aug–87	321.58	Nov–87	226.82	Apr–89	−29.47%	3	17
Apr–98	1,335.07	Aug–98	1,051.59	Dec–98	−21.23%	4	4
Aug–00	1,811.01	Sep–02	1,071.37	Nov–04	−40.84%	25	26
Oct–07	2,824.49	Feb–09	1,305.79	N/A	−53.77%	16	N/A
Average					−39.63%	15.67	35.5

TABLE 5.5

Worst-Case Scenarios: All 20 Percent or Greater Declines for S&P 500, January 1, 1927, to December 31, 2009

Peak date	Peak index value	Trough date	Trough index value	Recovery date	Decline (%)	Decline duration	Recovery duration
Aug–29	2.63	Jun–32	0.44	Jan–45	−83.41%	34	151
May–46	3.99	Nov–46	3.12	Oct–49	−21.76%	6	35
Dec–61	32.35	Jun–62	25.14	Apr–63	−22.28%	6	10
Nov–68	61.27	Jun–70	43.35	Mar–71	−29.25%	19	9
Dec–72	76.11	Sep–74	43.66	Jun–76	−42.63%	21	21
Aug–87	411.97	Nov–87	290.31	May–89	−29.53%	3	18
Aug–00	2,654.00	Sep–02	1466.79	Oct–06	−44.73%	25	49
Oct–07	3,056.44	Feb–09	1499.18	N/A	−50.95%	16	N/A
Average					−40.57%	16.25	41.86

TABLE 5.6

Best and Worst Average Annual Compound Returns over Period for Monthly Data, January 1, 1927, to December 31, 2009

For any	1-year period	3-year period	5-year period	7-year period	10-year period
S&P 500 minimum compound return	−67.56%	−42.35%	−17.36%	−6.12%	−4.95%
S&P 500 maximum compound return	162.89%	43.35%	36.12%	25.82%	21.43%
Large Stocks minimum compound return	−66.63%	−43.53%	−20.15%	−6.95%	−5.70%
Large Stocks maximum compound return	159.52%	45.64%	36.26%	22.83%	19.57%
All Stocks minimum compound return	−66.72%	−45.99%	−23.07%	−7.43%	−5.31%
All Stocks maximum compound return	201.69%	51.03%	41.17%	23.77%	22.05%

TABLE 5.7

Terminal Value of $10,000 Invested for Best and Worst Average Annual Compound Returns for Monthly Data, January 1, 1927, to December 31, 2009

For any	1-year period	3-year period	5-year period	7-year period	10-year period
S&P 500 minimum $10,000 value	$3,244	$1,916	$3,855	$6,427	$6,021
S&P 500 maximum $10,000 value	$26,289	$29,458	$46,736	$49,906	$69,692
Large Stocks minimum $10,000 value	$3,337	$1,800	$3,247	$6,041	$5,561
Large Stocks maximum $10,000 value	$25,952	$30,890	$46,970	$42,189	$59,747
All Stocks minimum $10,000 value	$3,328	$1,576	$2,695	$5,825	$5,793
All Stocks maximum $10,000 value	$30,169	$34,452	$56,062	$44,504	$73,345

If we ignore the Great Depression, where all four of these universes had their worst three-year declines ending June 1932, we see that the three major indexes featured here occasionally fall out of sync with each other. For example, the worst three-year decline the S&P 500 ever suffered since 1950 were the three years ending March 2003, where the index lost 41 percent, whereas the largest three-year decline for the All Stocks and Large Stocks universes were the three years ending February 2009, where they lost 46 and 41 percent, respectively. This tells us that the bear market of 2000 through March 2003 affected the S&P 500 more than it did the average stock traded in the United States. The data allow you to see just how far out of whack the S&P 500 got during the bubble years of 1997–2000. In those years, the S&P 500—or, more specifically, a handful of large growth names in the index—drove all performance and created a huge difference between it and almost every other stock in the market. Keep that in mind when you equate investing in the market with buying an S&P 500 Index fund.

Tables 5.3, 5.4, and 5.5 show various worst-case scenarios. Reviewing the data for the S&P 500 shows that in the last 83 years there were four instances when the S&P 500 lost more than 40 percent from high to low, which is how I define a *severe* bear market. Note that two of the four occurred in the last decade. The other two, August 1929 to June 1932 and December 1972 through September 1974, were separated by 42 years—quite enough time for investors to forget how terribly a severe bear market can fray investors' nerves. Investors in our current era were not so lucky, and back-to-back severe bear markets between 2000 and 2009 have actually incited investors to change their behavior. Even after the market's dramatic recovery beginning in March 2009, cash continued to pour into bond funds and flow out of equity funds. Equity investors have indeed had their nerves frayed, and this has led them to make very conservative investments, despite the fact that the U.S. stock market has recovered from *every* downturn since the founding of the New York Stock Exchange in the 1790s and then gone on to reach new highs.

Returning to Table 5.5, we see that for the S&P 500, the average decline for all losing periods was a loss of 40.57 percent and that it took an average of 16 months to post the decline. It also shows that the average recovery duration is 42 months, nearly three times as long as the decline. This information is extremely useful to review when we next find ourselves in a bear market, for it also shows that stocks always go on to recover from even the most frightening declines.

Finally, I always look at base rates for how well each of the strategies performed against our two main benchmarks, All Stocks and Large Stocks. Table 5.8 shows the base rates for All Stocks versus Large Stocks. Looking at returns for rolling five- and ten-year periods to establish a base rate, we see that All Stocks outperformed Large Stocks in 586 of the 937 rolling five-year periods, or 63 percent of the time. All Stocks also outperformed Large Stocks in 655 of the 877 rolling ten-year periods, or 75 percent of the time. Conversely, the Large Stocks universe beat All Stocks in 37 percent of all rolling five year periods and 25 percent of all rolling ten year periods. The returns show that, for most strategies, you're better off fishing in the larger pond of All Stocks—which includes many smaller-cap stocks—than exclusively buying large, well-known stocks.

T A B L E   5.8

Base Rates for All Stocks and Large Stocks, January 1, 1927, to December 31, 2009

Item	All Stocks beat Large Stocks	Percent	Average annual excess return
Single-year return	538 out of 985	55%	1.31%
Rolling three-year compound teturn	533 out of 961	55%	0.88%
Rolling five-year compound return	586 out of 937	63%	0.95%
Rolling seven-year compound return	627 out of 913	69%	0.97%
Rolling ten-year compound return	655 out of 877	75%	0.91%

HOW MUCH BETTER ARE SMALL-CAP STOCKS?

Most academic studies of market capitalization sort stocks by deciles (10 percent) and review how an investment in each decile fares over time. The studies are nearly unanimous in their findings that small stocks (those in the lowest two deciles) do significantly better than large ones. We too have found tremendous returns from tiny stocks.

The glaring problem with this method when used with the CRSP and Compustat datasets is that it's virtually impossible to *buy* the stocks that account for a large share of the performance advantage of small capitalization strategies. We did a deep analysis of the noninvestable microcap stocks (stocks with market capitalizations of less than a deflated $25 million) and found that the returns generated were highly contingent on which stocks were allowed into the test and which ones that were excluded. For example, looking at the Compustat universe, Table 5.9 shows a great disparity of returns, depending upon your assumptions. Between 1964 and 2009, if, as Compustat Scenario One illustrates, you required stock prices greater than $1 but put no return limit and allowed for stocks with missing data to be included, then the portfolio earned an average annual compound return of 28 percent. Yet, when you require that all stocks have share prices of greater than $1, have no missing return data, and have limited the monthly return on any security to 2,000 percent per month, as we see with Scenario Two, returns decline by approximately 10 percent, and the portfolio earns an average annual compound return of 18.2 percent. Finally, as Scenario Three illustrates, if you add no additional criteria and are willing to allow in any of the microcap names at any price with no return limit, you earn 63.2 percent per year.

T A B L E 5.9

Returns for Microcap Stocks (Market Cap Less Than Deflated $25 Million under Various Scenarios for CRSP and Compustat Datasets, 1964–2009

CRSP data	Return	Std dev	Trading status	Exchange	Share type	Price
Scenario One	17.8%	25.4%	Active	Major exchange	Equity or ADR	Any price
Scenario Two	17.7%	25.4%	Any status	Any exchange	Any type	Any price
Scenario Three	17.6%	24.1%	Any status	Any exchange	Any type	Price > $1

Compustat data	Return	Std dev	Null missing returns	Return limit	Price
Scenario One	28.0%	111.5%	Yes	None	>$1
Scenario Two	18.2%	24.8%	Yes	2,000%	>$1
Scenario Three	63.2%	139.3%	Yes	None	Any
Scenario Four	23.9%	27.4%	Yes	20	Any

Obviously, the data for these noninvestable microcap names will lead to very different returns based upon how realistic your assumptions are. Included with the Compustat data are the data from the CRSP dataset, leading me to conclude that *if* you could buy these tiny names, the most realistic average annual returns would be between 17.6 to 18.2 percent over the long term. When you extend the analysis to include the period from July 1926 through December 2009 using the CRSP dataset, the average annual compound return for noninvestable microcaps falls to 15 percent per year. Thus the returns for this group are highly unstable, and the results you see are highly contingent upon which stocks will be allowed and which ones will be excluded. On December 31, 2009, there were approximately 2,401 stocks in the combined CRSP and Compustat datasets that I define as noninvestable microcap stocks—where an investment of any size would send their bid/ask spread soaring, making the prices for those stocks a bit of a fiction. If investors of almost any size—be they an institution or an individual trying to buy a significant position—tried to buy them, their prices would skyrocket.

When you look at the results for *investable* microcap names, those with market capitalizations between a deflated $50 million and a deflated $250 million, you see that most of the return for tiny stocks disappears. Using the Compustat dataset, between 1964 and 2009 investable microcap stocks earned an average annual compound return of 12.70 percent, whereas when using the CRSP dataset over the same period microcap stocks earned 11.82 percent per year. When you use the CRSP dataset to review the full period between 1926 and 2009, the investable microcap stocks compound at 10.92 percent per year, slightly better than our Small Stocks universe. A far better way to analyze the effects of market capitalization on a company's returns is to evaluate all fully investable stocks by decile. When you look at the returns in the All Stocks universe by market capitalization decile, a fairly different picture emerges. Looking at Figure 5.2, we see that within the universe of investable stocks, there *is* an advantage to smaller-cap stocks, but it is not of the magnitude of other studies that allow noninvestable microcaps. Here, the smallest decile by market capitalization had the highest compound return between December 31, 1926, and December 31, 2009, and the largest two deciles had the lowest compound returns, but the amounts are not huge: The tenth decile had the highest return at 10.95 percent per year, whereas the first decile (largest stocks) had the lowest return at 8.82 percent, a difference of 2.13 percent. Table 5.Decile Addendum 1 shows what $10,000 grows to for each decile, from decile one—those 10 percent of stocks from All Stocks with the highest market capitalization—to decile ten, which is the 10 percent of the All Stocks universe with the smallest market capitalization. The table also shows the Sharpe ratio for each decile.

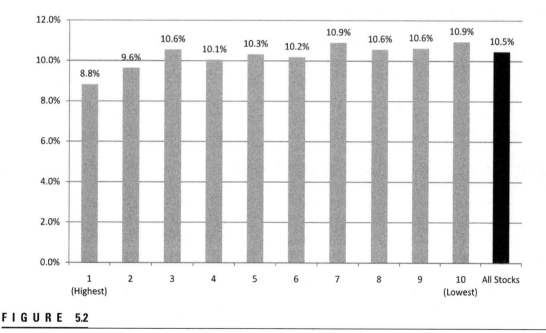

FIGURE 5.2

Average annual compound return by decile, All Stocks universe, January 1, 1927, to December 31, 2009

T A B L E   5. DECILE ADDENDUM 1

Summary Results for Market-Cap Decile Analysis of All Stocks Universe, January 1, 1927, to December 31, 2009

Decile	$10,000 Grows to	Average return	Compound return	Standard deviation	Sharpe ratio
1 (Highest)	$11,162,862	10.66%	8.82%	18.38%	0.21
2	$20,681,325	11.62%	9.63%	18.97%	0.24
3	$41,423,439	12.86%	10.56%	20.47%	0.27
4	$28,334,148	12.65%	10.05%	21.70%	0.23
5	$34,882,681	12.93%	10.33%	21.74%	0.25
6	$31,350,515	12.97%	10.19%	22.48%	0.23
7	$53,556,520	13.63%	10.90%	22.16%	0.27
8	$41,671,384	13.46%	10.56%	22.97%	0.24
9	$43,506,827	13.74%	10.62%	23.74%	0.24
10 (Lowest)	$55,516,858	14.22%	10.95%	24.36%	0.24
All Stocks	$38,542,780	13.06%	10.46%	21.67%	0.25

SMALL STOCKS AND MARKET LEADERS

I also look at two additional distinct groups of stocks—Small Stocks, or stocks that have market capitalizations greater than a deflated $200 million but less than the database average, and Market Leaders. Market Leaders are like Large Stocks on steroids. They come from the Large Stocks universe but also possess characteristics beyond mere size. To be a market leading company, you must be a nonutility stock with a market capitalization greater than the average—now with a minimum market capitalization of $50 million (Older versions of the book simply required greater than the database average, which included tiny stocks)—shares outstanding greater than the average, cash flow greater than average, and finally, sales 50 percent greater than the average stock. Applying these factors to the overall Compustat database leaves just 6 percent of the database qualifying as Market Leaders. Since we have data for the Small Stocks universe back to 1926, let's first look at that universe and then turn to the 1964 forward period and look at the Market Leaders universe.

SMALL STOCKS ARE THE WINNERS BY A HAIR

If we ignore the microcap stocks in Table 5.9 as unobtainable, the results—shown in Table 5.10—show that investors who pay no heed to risk or other factors are best off concentrating on smaller stocks. As we'll see later, this is appropriate only for investors who want to make market capitalization their sole criterion for stock selection. These results confirm the academic studies that demonstrate that smaller stocks beat large stocks, but once microcaps are removed, by not nearly the large margins that many studies have touted. The Small Stocks universe earned 10.82 percent a year between 1927 and 2009, whereas the All Stocks universe earned 10.46 percent, and Large Stocks earned 9.69 percent. So $10,000 invested in the Small Stocks universe on December 31, 1926, would have been worth $50,631,666 at the end of 2009, well ahead of Large Stocks and All Stocks. But the higher risk of Small Stocks of 23.09 percent brought in their Sharpe ratio at exactly the same figure as for All Stocks—.25. Table 5.11 shows the return by decade for our three major universes, and Tables 5.12 and 5.13 show the base rates for Small Stocks versus All Stocks and Large Stocks.

T A B L E 5.10

Summary Annual Return and Risk Results Data: All Stocks, Large Stocks, and Small Stocks, January 1, 1927, to December 31, 2009

	All Stocks	Large Stocks	Small Stocks
Arithmetic average	13.06%	11.75%	13.77%
Geometric average	10.46%	9.69%	10.82%
Median return	18.54%	16.75%	19.28%
Standard deviation	21.67%	19.35%	23.09%
Upside deviation	14.78%	13.10%	16.05%
Downside deviation	16.03%	14.40%	16.89%
Tracking error	0.00	4.76	2.22
Number of positive periods	606	609	605
Number of negative periods	390	387	391
Maximum peak-to-trough decline	−85.45%	−84.33%	−86.12%
Beta	1.00	0.87	1.06
T-statistic (m = 0)	5.19	5.25	5.12
Sharpe ratio (Rf = 5%)	0.25	0.24	0.25
Sortino ratio (MAR = 10%)	0.03	−0.02	0.05
$10,000 becomes	$38,542,780	$21,617,372	$50,631,666
Minimum 1-year return	−66.72%	−66.63%	−66.91%
Maximum 1-year return	201.69%	159.52%	233.48%
Minimum 3-year return	−45.99%	−43.53%	−47.28%
Maximum 3-year return	51.03%	45.64%	54.35%
Minimum 5-year return	−23.07%	−20.15%	−24.56%
Maximum 5-year return	41.17%	36.26%	44.18%
Minimum 7-year return	−7.43%	−6.95%	−7.64%
Maximum 7-year return	23.77%	22.83%	27.35%
Minimum 10-year return	−5.31%	−5.70%	−5.19%
Maximum 10-year return	22.05%	19.57%	24.47%
Minimum expected return*	−30.28%	−26.96%	−32.41%
Maximum expected return†	56.39%	50.46%	59.96%

* Minimum expected return is arithmetic return minus 2 times the standard deviation.
† Maximum expected return is arithmetic return plus 2 times the standard deviation.

T A B L E   5.11

Average Annual Compound Rates of Return by Decade

	1920s*	1930s	1940s	1950s	1960s	1970s	1980s	1990s	2000s†
All Stocks	12.33%	−0.03%	11.57%	18.07%	10.72%	7.56%	16.78%	15.35%	4.39%
Large Stocks	17.73%	−1.05%	9.65%	17.06%	8.31%	6.65%	17.34%	16.38%	2.42%
Small Stocks	9.81%	0.67%	12.79%	18.45%	11.61%	8.19%	16.46%	14.96%	4.95%

* Returns for January 1, 1927, to December 31, 1929.
† Returns for January 1, 2000, to December 31, 2009.

T A B L E   5.12

Base Rates for Small Stocks and All Stocks, January 1, 1927, to December 31, 2009

Item	Small Stocks beat All Stocks	Percent	Average annual excess return
Single-year return	534 out of 985	54%	0.75%
Rolling 3-year compound return	527 out of 961	55%	0.47%
Rolling 5-year compound return	571 out of 937	61%	0.48%
Rolling 7-year compound return	613 out of 913	67%	0.47%
Rolling 10-year compound return	625 out of 877	71%	0.44%

T A B L E   5.13

Base Rates for Small Stocks and Large Stocks, January 1, 1927, to December 31, 2009

Item	Small Stocks beat Large Stocks	Percent	Average annual excess return
Single-year return	538 out of 985	55%	2.06%
Rolling 3-year compound return	531 out of 961	55%	1.35%
Rolling 5-year compound return	579 out of 937	62%	1.43%
Rolling 7-year compound return	623 out of 913	68%	1.44%
Rolling 10-year compound return	652 out of 877	74%	1.35%

Ironically, we *have* found that when you use strategies like those featured in this book that are looking for maximum return, they *inevitably* lead you to stocks that are in the small and midcap category. I believe that this is not because of market capitalization alone, but rather because the stocks in this category are the least efficiently priced. Currently, around 400 stocks account for approximately 75 percent of the U.S. stock market capitalization, whereas there are literally thousands of stocks that make up the remaining 25 percent. The sheer number of companies in the small and midcap category makes them far more difficult for analysts to cover adequately, thus providing great opportunities to investors willing to use a systematic, disciplined approach to finding those companies that possess the factors that have a long association with higher returns.

WORST-CASE SCENARIOS AND BEST AND WORST RETURNS

Table 5.14 shows all declines greater than 20 percent for the Small Stocks universe between 1926 and 2009. The Small Stocks universe, like that for the All Stocks and Large Stocks universe, had nine separate declines of 20 percent or more since 1926, with the worst being the 86 percent decline between August 1929 and June 1932. Unlike the other indexes, the second worst drop for the Small Stocks universe was when it lost 58 percent between November 1968 and September 1974. The most recent beat between May 2007 and February 2009 saw the group decline 56 percent. In terms of the best and worst returns for the group, Table 5.15 shows the best and worst percentage gains and declines for a number of holding periods. You can see that if you had a five-year time horizon, the worst you could expect from an investment in the Small Stocks universe would be a loss of 24.56 percent per year. Looking at Table 5.16 to see how that translates into dollar terms, we see that if you got a five-year return equal to the worst Small Stocks have seen over the last 83 years, your $10,000 would have been reduced to just $2,444. Conversely, if you received a five-year return that was similar to the best we've seen since 1926, your $10,000 would soar to $62,313. Table 5.16 shows the results for all other holding periods. Figure 5.3 shows the five-year annual compound excess return for the Small Stocks universe minus the All Stocks universe.

TABLE 5.14

Worst-Case Scenarios: All 20 Percent or Greater Declines for Small Stocks, January 1, 1927. to December 31, 2009

Peak date	Peak index value	Trough date	Trough index value	Recovery date	Decline (%)	Decline duration	Recovery duration
Aug–29	1.99	Jun–32	0.28	May–43	−86.12%	34	131
May–46	4.99	May–47	3.37	Apr–50	−32.47%	12	35
Nov–61	32.82	Oct–62	24.73	Jan–64	−24.65%	11	15
Nov–68	100.99	Sep–74	41.93	Nov–77	−58.48%	70	38
Aug–87	713.67	Nov–87	472.29	Apr–89	−33.82%	3	17
Sep–89	803.90	Oct–90	572.17	Mar–91	−28.83%	13	5
Apr–98	2,776.53	Aug–98	1,894.96	Nov–99	−31.75%	4	15
Feb–00	3,511.27	Sep–02	2,235.24	Oct–03	−36.34%	31	13
May–07	6,352.93	Feb–09	2,765.42	N/A	−56.47%	21	N/A
Average					−43.21%	22.11	33.63

TABLE 5.15

Best and Worst Average Annual Compound Returns over Period for Monthly Data, January 1, 1927, to December 31, 2009

For any	1-year period	3-year period	5-year period	7-year period	10-year period
All Stocks minimum compound return	−66.72%	−45.99%	−23.07%	−7.43%	−5.31%
All Stocks maximum compound return	201.69%	51.03%	41.17%	23.77%	22.05%
Large Stocks minimum compound return	−66.63%	−43.53%	−20.15%	−6.95%	−5.70%
Large Stocks maximum compound return	159.52%	45.64%	36.26%	22.83%	19.57%
Small Stocks minimum compound return	−66.91%	−47.28%	−24.56%	−7.64%	−5.19%
Small Stocks maximum compound return	233.48%	54.35%	44.18%	27.35%	24.47%

T A B L E   5.16

Terminal Value of $10,000 Invested for Best and Worst Average Annual Compound Returns for Monthly Data, January 1, 1927, to December 31, 2009

For any	1-year period	3-year period	5-year period	7-year period	10-year period
All Stocks minimum $10,000 value	$3,328	$1,576	$2,695	$5,825	$5,793
All Stocks maximum $10,000 value	$30,169	$34,452	$56,062	$44,504	$73,345
Large Stocks minimum $10,000 value	$3,337	$1,800	$3,247	$6,041	$5,561
Large Stocks maximum $10,000 value	$25,952	$30,890	$46,970	$42,189	$59,747
Small Stocks minimum $10,000 value	$3,309	$1,465	$2,444	$5,733	$5,872
Small Stocks maximum $10,000 value	$33,348	$36,775	$62,313	$54,327	$89,249

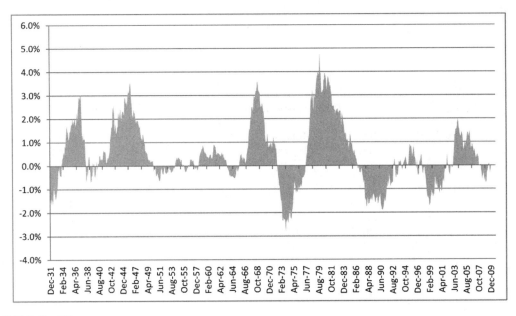

F I G U R E   5.3

Five-year average annual compound excess (deficient) return Small Stocks minus All Stocks, January 1, 1927, to December 31, 2009

MARKET LEADERS AND SMALL STOCKS: A BETTER WAY TO CREATE AN INDEX

Now we look at the Market Leaders universe as well as provide an example of how using quantitative rules to build indexes might be superior to current methodologies. As mentioned, Market Leaders are large, market-leading companies with annual sales 50 percent greater than average; shares outstanding greater than average and cash flow greater than average, and Small Stocks are all stocks in the CRSP and Compustat datasets with market capitalizations greater than a deflated $200 million but less than the database average. $200 million of today's dollars translate into a company with a market cap greater than $13.6 million in 1926. These universes offer a good approximation for the *category* of blue chip and small stocks. Table 5.17

shows the returns of all four of our universes as well as the S&P 500. Note that the Market Leaders universe offers better performance than all but the Small Stocks universe on an absolute basis and *the* best on a risk-adjusted basis, as it has the highest Sharpe ratio of all five universes at .39. Market Leaders also has the highest Sortino ratio—which looks only at downside risk—of the five at .12. Table 5.18 shows the return by decade for the Market Leaders universe as well as Large Stocks and the S&P 500. Tables 5.19 and 5.20 show the base rates for the Market Leaders versus the Large Stocks universe and the S&P 500. When comparing Market Leaders to Large Stocks, we see that they beat Large Stocks 75 percent of all rolling five-year periods and 89 percent of all rolling ten-year periods. Figure 5.4 shows the five-year average annual compound excess (deficient) return for Market Leaders versus Large Stocks since 1964. Market Leaders enjoy similar batting averages when compared to the S&P 500.

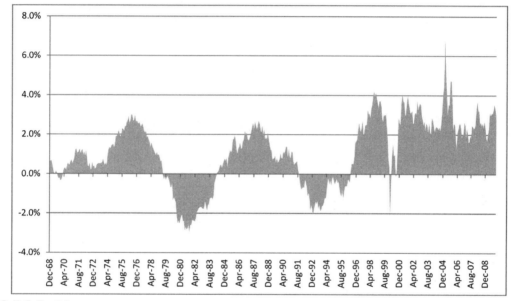

FIGURE 5.4

Five-year average annual compound excess (deficient) return Market Leaders minus Large Stocks, January 1, 1964, to December 31, 2009

TABLE 5.17

Summary Annual Return and Risk Results Data: All Stocks, Small Stocks, Large Stocks, Market Leaders, and S&P 500; January 1, 1964, to December 31, 2009

	All Stocks	Small Stocks	Large Stocks	Market Leaders	S&P 500
Arithmetic average	13.26%	13.94%	11.72%	12.82%	10.71%
Geometric average	11.22%	11.60%	10.20%	11.36%	9.46%
Median return	17.16%	19.28%	17.20%	14.62%	13.76%
Standard deviation	18.99%	20.31%	16.50%	16.13%	15.09%
Upside deviation	10.98%	11.87%	9.70%	10.00%	9.37%
Downside deviation	13.90%	14.83%	11.85%	11.66%	10.76%

(continued on next page)

T A B L E   5.17

Summary Annual Return and Risk Results Data: All Stocks, Small Stocks, Large Stocks, Market Leaders, and S&P 500; January 1, 1964, to December 31, 2009 *(Continued)*

	All Stocks	Small Stocks	Large Stocks	Market Leaders	S&P 500
Tracking error	5.41	7.56	0.00	4.09	4.63
Number of positive periods	329	329	332	335	342
Number of negative periods	223	223	220	217	210
Maximum peak-to-trough decline	−55.54%	−58.48%	−53.77%	−54.03%	−50.95%
Beta	1.11	1.15	1.00	0.95	0.88
T-statistic (m = 0)	4.47	4.38	4.58	5.10	4.59
Sharpe ratio (Rf = 5%)	0.33	0.32	0.32	0.39	0.30
Sortino ratio (MAR = 10%)	0.09	0.11	0.02	0.12	−0.05
$10,000 becomes	$1,329,513	$1,555,109	$872,861	$1,411,897	$639,147
Minimum 1-year return	−46.49%	−46.38%	−46.91%	−48.15%	−43.32%
Maximum 1-year return	84.19%	93.08%	68.96%	66.79%	61.01%
Minimum 3-year return	−18.68%	−19.53%	−15.89%	−13.61%	−16.10%
Maximum 3-year return	31.49%	34.00%	33.12%	34.82%	33.40%
Minimum 5-year return	−9.91%	−11.75%	−5.82%	−4.36%	−−6.64%
Maximum 5-year return	27.66%	31.37%	28.95%	31.52%	29.72%
Minimum 7-year return	−6.32%	−7.64%	−4.15%	−2.93%	−3.85%
Maximum 7-year return	23.77%	27.35%	22.83%	24.56%	23.08%
Minimum 10-year return	1.01%	1.08%	−0.15%	1.01%	−3.43%
Maximum 10-year return	22.05%	24.47%	19.57%	19.69%	19.48%
Minimum expected return*	−24.73%	−26.69%	−21.28%	−19.44%	−19.46%
Maximum expected return†	51.24%	54.57%	44.72%	45.07%	40.88%

* Minimum expected return is arithmetic return minus 2 times the standard deviation.
† Maximum expected return is arithmetic return plus 2 times the standard deviation.

T A B L E   5.18

Average Annual Compound Rates of Return by Decade

	1960s*	1970s	1980s	1990s	2000s†
Large Stocks	8.16%	6.65%	17.34%	16.38%	2.42%
Market Leaders	8.23%	7.32%	18.10%	16.54%	5.92%
S&P 500	6.80%	5.86%	17.55%	18.20%	−0.95%

* Returns for January 1, 1964, to December 31, 1969.
† Returns for January 1, 2000, to December 31, 2009.

T A B L E   5.19

Base Rates for Market Leaders and Large Stocks, January 1, 1964, to December 31, 2009

Item	Market Leaders beat Large Stocks	Percent	Average annual excess return
Single-year return	326 out of 541	60%	1.03%
Rolling 3-year compound return	364 out of 517	70%	1.12%
Rolling 5-year compound return	368 out of 493	75%	1.10%
Rolling 7-year compound return	351 out of 469	75%	1.09%
Rolling 10-year compound return	387 out of 433	89%	1.04%

T A B L E   5.20

Base Rates for Market Leaders and S&P 500; January 1, 1964, to December 31, 2009

Item	Market Leaders beat S&P 500	Percent	Average annual excess return
Single-year return	335 out of 541	62%	1.85%
Rolling 3-year compound return	368 out of 517	71%	1.73%
Rolling 5-year compound return	375 out of 493	76%	1.65%
Rolling 7-year compound return	340 out of 469	72%	1.54%
Rolling 10-year compound return	338 out of 433	78%	1.38%

WORST-CASE SCENARIOS AND BEST AND WORST RETURNS

Table 5.21 shows all of the times Market Leaders lost 20 percent or more. Remember that the data for Market Leaders begin in 1964 instead of 1926, because they use factors that are not in the CRSP dataset, so drawdowns will miss the Great Depression. Like many of our universes, the worst decline for the Market Leaders universe came between October 2007 and February 2009, when the group lost 54 percent. Table 5.22 shows the best and worst returns for the Market Leaders universe between 1963 and 2009 for a variety of holding periods, and Table 5.23 shows what $10,000 invested grows to under the best and worst returns for a variety of holding periods.

T A B L E   5.21

Worst-Case Scenarios: All 20 Percent or Greater Declines for Market Leaders, January 1, 1927, to December 31, 2009

Peak date	Peak index value	Trough date	Trough index value	Recovery date	Decline (%)	Decline duration	Recovery duration
Nov–68	1.91	Jun–70	1.27	Apr–71	−33.42%	19	10
Nov–72	2.20	Sep–74	1.29	Jan–76	−41.29%	22	16
Aug–87	14.87	Nov–87	10.50	Apr–89	−29.39%	3	17
Jan–01	85.39	Sep–02	60.48	Nov–03	−29.17%	20	14
Oct–07	177.00	Feb–09	81.37	N/A	−54.03%	16	N/A
Average					−37.46%	16	14.25

TABLE 5.22

Best and Worst Average Annual Compound Returns for Monthly Data, January 1, 1964, to December 31, 2009

For any	1-year period	3-year period	5-year period	7-year period	10-year period
Market Leaders minimum compound return	−48.15%	−13.61%	−4.36%	−2.93%	1.01%
Market Leaders maximum compound return	66.79%	34.82%	31.52%	24.56%	19.69%

TABLE 5.23

Terminal Value of $10,000 Invested for Best and Worst Average Annual Compound Returns for Monthly Data, January 1, 1964, to December 31, 2009

For any	1-year period	3-year period	5-year period	7-year period	10-year period
Market Leaders minimum $10,000 value	$5,185	$6,448	$8,001	$8,122	$11,061
Market Leaders maximum $10,000 value	$16,679	$24,506	$39,355	$46,514	$60,354

Returning to the example of what $10,000 would be worth over any five-year period, the best and worst case for Market Leaders would find your $10,000 declining to $8,001 over five years if you received a return equal to the *worst* seen since 1963, and appreciating to $39,355 if you got a return equal to the *best* seen in any five-year period. That compares favorably with the minimum and maximum generated by the All Stocks universe over the same time frame.

Returning to Table 5.17, we see that Market Leaders handily beat all the other large-cap indexes and even managed to beat the All Stocks universe, but it's really when you compare them to other style-specific indexes that you see that using quantitative selection rules like those followed here might be a much better way to construct an index. The Russell indexes are widely used capitalization and style-specific indexes created in 1979. Many institutional clients compare their managers to these indexes. Table 5.24 compares the large-cap Russell 1000 and the S&P 500 with the Market Leaders universe.

TABLE 5.24

Summary Annual Return and Risk Results Data: Market Leaders, S&P 500, and Russell 1000; January 1, 1979, to December 31, 2009

	Market Leaders	S&P 500	Russell 1000
Arithmetic average	15.24%	12.80%	12.86%
Geometric average	13.71%	11.46%	11.49%
Median return	20.48%	16.91%	17.72%
Standard deviation	16.30%	15.44%	15.62%
Upside deviation	9.67%	9.19%	9.12%
Downside deviation	12.85%	11.63%	11.84%
Tracking error	0.00	4.37	4.30
Number of positive periods	237	239	239

(continued on next page)

T A B L E 5.24

Summary Annual Return and Risk Results Data: Market Leaders, S&P 500, and Russell 1000; January 1, 1979, to December 31, 2009 *(Continued)*

	Market Leaders	S&P 500	Russell 1000
Number of negative periods	135	133	133
Maximum peak-to-trough decline	−54.03%	−50.95%	−51.13%
Beta	0.93	0.87	0.92
T-statistic (m = 0)	4.87	4.36	4.33
Sharpe ratio (Rf = 5%)	0.53	0.42	0.42
Sortino ratio (MAR = 10%)	0.29	0.13	0.13
$10,000 becomes	$536,002	$288,701	$290,853
Minimum 1-year return	−48.15%	−43.32%	−43.62%
Maximum 1-year return	66.79%	61.01%	63.47%
Minimum 3-year return	−13.61%	−16.10%	−16.20%
Maximum 3-year return	34.82%	33.40%	32.37%
Minimum 5-year return	−3.00%	−6.64%	−6.39%
Maximum 5-year return	31.52%	29.72%	28.60%
Minimum 7-year return	0.70%	−3.85%	−3.47%
Maximum 7-year return	24.56%	23.08%	22.44%
Minimum 10-year return	1.85%	−3.43%	−3.02%
Maximum 10-year return	19.15%	19.48%	19.89%
Minimum expected return*	−17.37%	−18.09%	−18.38%
Maximum expected return†	47.84%	43.69%	44.10%

* Minimum expected return is arithmetic return minus 2 times the standard deviation.
† Maximum expected return is arithmetic return plus 2 times the standard deviation.

In virtually every category, Market Leaders provide superior results to both the S&P 500 and Russell 1000 indexes. Between 1979 and 2009, Market Leaders provided nearly double the return of the other two large-cap indexes, and they had only slightly higher risk, as measured by standard deviation of return. So $10,000 invested on December 31, 1978 (when the Russell 1000 was created), in Market Leaders grows to $536,002, a compound average annual return of 13.71 percent, versus a $10,000 investment in the Russell 1000, which grew to $290,853, a return of 11.49 percent per year. The base rates for the Market Leaders universe versus the Russell 1000 are all positive, with Market Leaders beating the Russell 1000 in 74 percent of all rolling five-year periods and 79 percent of all rolling ten-year periods. What's more, once your holding period reaches seven years, the Market Leaders universe has *no* negative seven-year returns, whereas the Russell does, for both seven and ten years. (To be fair, if we had the data for both Market Leaders and the Russell 1000 back to 1926, no doubt both groups would show negative seven- and ten-year returns.) The only time the Russell 1000 bests Market Leaders is in maximum decline—between October 2007 and February 2009, Market Leaders fell 54 percent and the Russell 1000 declined 51 percent. I should also note that another possible reason that the Market Leaders universe beats the

Russell 1000 so handily is that it includes foreign-domiciled companies in the form of American Depository Receipts (ADRs) whereas the Russell 1000 is composed entirely of U.S.-based companies. Yet investors should not limit themselves to a stock simply because of where it is headquartered, and I therefore believe that the Market Leaders universe is a better place for investors interested in large, market leading companies. One final reason that the Market Leaders universe beats both the Russell 1000 index and the S&P 500 is that we equal-weight the universe, while both the Russell and S&P 500 are cap-weighted.

SMALL STOCKS

Our Small Stocks universe also outperforms the Russell 2000 index. Table 5.25 summarizes the return and risk results for Small Stocks versus the Russell 2000. So $10,000 invested on December 31, 1978, in our Small Stocks universe grew to $419,088 at the end of December 2009, a compound average annual return of 12.81 percent, whereas $10,000 invested in the Russell 2000 grew to $275,906, a return of 11.30 percent per year. The base rates for the Small Stocks universe versus the Russell 2000 were all positive, with the Small Stocks universe beating the Russell 2000 95 percent of all rolling five-year periods and 100 percent of all rolling ten- year periods.

T A B L E   5.25

Summary Annual Return and Risk Results Data: Small Stocks and Russell 2000; January 1, 1979, to December 31, 2009

	Small Stocks	Russell 2000
Arithmetic average	15.20%	13.57%
Geometric average	12.81%	11.30%
Median return	24.78%	22.94%
Standard deviation	20.35%	19.91%
Upside deviation	11.21%	10.78%
Downside deviation	15.57%	15.18%
Tracking error	0.00	3.89
Number of positive periods	230	229
Number of negative periods	142	143
Maximum peak-to-trough decline	−56.47%	−52.89%
Beta	1.00	0.96
T-statistic (m = 0)	3.90	2.58
Sharpe ratio (Rf = 5%)	0.38	0.32
Sortino ratio (MAR = 10%)	0.18	0.09
$10,000 becomes	$419,088	$275,906
Minimum 1-year return	−46.38%	−42.38%
Maximum 1-year return	93.08%	97.52%
Minimum 3-year return	−19.53%	−17.89%
Maximum 3-year return	33.27%	33.93%

(continued on next page)

T A B L E   5.25

Summary Annual Return and Risk Results Data: Small Stocks and Russell 2000; January 1, 1979, to December 31, 2009 *(Continued)*

	Small Stocks	**Russell 2000**
Minimum 5-year return	−7.72%	−6.68%
Maximum 5-year return	26.92%	26.69%
Minimum 7-year return	−0.63%	−1.39%
Maximum 7-year return	24.08%	22.64%
Minimum 10-year return	2.11%	1.22%
Maximum 10-year return	18.42%	17.14%
Minimum expected return*	−25.49%	−26.25%
Maximum expected return†	55.90%	53.38%

* Minimum expected return is arithmetic return minus 2 times the standard deviation.
† Maximum expected return is arithmetic return plus 2 times the standard deviation.

I think these results demonstrate that creators of equity indexes can do a better job than the current committee selection structure which drives much of index creation. If firms that create broad indexes were to use more explicitly stated rules, they could both test them historically and build a better model for investors who prefer a broad index to a style-specific or conventionally managed portfolio.

IMPLICATIONS FOR INVESTORS

Investors should be wary of small-stock strategies that promise high returns *simply* because they invest in smaller issues. The numbers show the smallest stocks—those with market capitalizations below $25 million—account for the lion's share of the difference between small and large stock returns, and those returns vary widely depending upon the criteria you use when selecting them. You get vastly higher results when you open the field to any stocks in the universe under a deflated $25 million than you do when requiring that their price be above $1 and limiting the amount they can go up or down in any given month. They're also impossible to buy and are therefore shunned by mutual funds and individual investors alike.

Small-cap stocks *do* outperform larger stocks on an absolute basis, but are virtually indistinguishable when risk is taken into account—their Sharpe ratio is .25 and identical to All Stocks and one point higher than Large Stocks.

The big surprise is the performance of Market Leaders. These large, well-known stocks outperformed All Stocks, Large Stocks, and the S&P 500, while taking less risk than All Stocks and Large Stocks and only slightly higher risk than the S&P 500. And while our Small Stocks universe outperformed Market Leaders on an absolute basis, once risk is taken into account, between 1964 and 2009 they have a lower Sharpe ratio than Market Leaders. Market Leaders had the highest Sharpe ratio of all stocks that you can actually invest in and proved to be excellent performers over a variety of market cycles. Between

1964 and 2009, Market Leaders had positive base rates for all three-, five-, seven-, and ten-year periods against All Stocks, Large Stocks, Small Stocks, and the S&P 500. They are superior to other large-cap indexes like the Russell 1000 and S&P 500 and offer a lesson to the creators of index funds, demonstrating that they may wish to bring a more objective, quantitative screening process to bear when devising new indexes.

We'll see later in this book that investors who want to beat the S&P 500 and are willing to take more risk should concentrate on all reasonably sized stocks—those in the All Stocks group with market capitalizations above $200 million—instead of focusing exclusively on just tiny or huge stocks. As of December 31, 2009, the All Stocks Universe included 2,879 stocks. The median market capitalization for All Stocks was $1.3 billion, and their average market capitalization was $8 billion—considerably smaller than Large Stocks' average market capitalization of $36.8 billion.

OUR TWO BENCHMARKS

In each coming chapter, I use the All Stocks and Large Stocks groups as benchmarks for all the strategies I cover. Each provides an excellent indication of what you can achieve in each capitalization class. For tests that expressly begin with either the Market Leaders universe or the Small Stocks universe, we include those as benchmarks as well.

6

C H A P T E R

PRICE-TO-EARNINGS RATIOS: SEPARATING THE WINNERS FROM THE LOSERS

When it comes to making money, everyone is of the same religion.

—Voltaire

For many on Wall Street, buying stocks with low price-to-earnings ratios (PE ratios) is the one true faith. You find a stock's current PE ratio by dividing the price by the current earnings per share. The higher the PE, the more investors are paying for earnings, and the larger the implied expectations for future earnings growth. A stock's PE ratio is the most common measurement of how cheap or expensive it is relative to others.

Investors who buy stocks with low PE ratios think they're getting a bargain. Generally, they believe that when a stock's PE ratio is high, investors have unrealistic expectations for the earnings growth of that stock. High hopes, the low PE investor reasons, are usually dashed, along with the price of the stock. Conversely, they believe that the prices of low PE stocks are unduly discounted and that when earnings recover, the price of the stock will follow.

THE RESULTS

Remember that we look at two distinct groups—those with high and low PE ratios drawn from the All Stocks universe (all stocks with market capitalizations greater than a deflated $200 million) and those with high and low PE ratios drawn from the Large Stocks universe (those stocks with market capitalizations greater than the Compustat mean).

As already discussed, we look at a composite return for all months, with each portfolio rebalanced annually. Let's look at low PE stocks first. We start with $10,000 on December 31, 1963, and buy the 10 percent (first decile) of stocks with the highest earnings-to-price ratios (i.e., the lowest PE ratios) from the All Stocks and Large Stocks universes. (Because of Compustat's internal math, we must rank stocks by the *highest* earnings/price ratios, which is the reciprocal of the PE ratio.) Remember that stocks with high earnings-to-price ratios are low PE stocks. With the new compositing methodology, we also look at an annually rebalanced portfolio in each of the subsequent 11 months. We rebalance the portfolios annually to hold the 10 percent of stocks with the lowest PE ratios in any given year. As with all the tests, the stocks are equally weighted, and the earnings variable is time-lagged to avoid look-ahead bias.

Tables 6.1 through 6.5 summarize the results for low PE investing.

T A B L E   6.1

Summary Annual Return and Risk Results Data: AS All Stocks (AS) Earnings/Price Decile 1 and All Stocks, January 1, 1964, to December 31, 2009

	All Stocks earnings/price decile 1	All Stocks
Arithmetic average	18.23%	13.26%
Geometric average	16.25%	11.22%
Median return	22.93%	17.16%
Standard deviation	18.45%	18.99%
Upside deviation	11.95%	10.98%
Downside deviation	13.62%	13.90%
Tracking error	7.40	0.00
Number of positive periods	351	329
Number of negative periods	201	223
Maximum peak-to-trough decline	−59.13%	−55.54%
Beta	0.90	1.00
T-statistic (m = 0)	6.20	4.47
Sharpe ratio (Rf = 5%)	0.61	0.33
Sortino ratio (MAR = 10%)	0.46	0.09
$10,000 becomes	$10,202,345	$1,329,513
Minimum 1-year return	−52.60%	−46.49%
Maximum 1year return	81.42%	84.19%
Minimum 3-year return	−18.31%	−18.68%
Maximum 3-year return	42.43%	31.49%
Minimum 5-year return	−4.15%	−9.91%
Maximum 5-year return	33.31%	27.66%
Minimum 7-year return	−0.64%	−6.32%
Maximum 7-year return	29.92%	23.77%
Minimum 10-year return	6.07%	1.01%
Maximum 10-year return	28.20%	22.05%
Minimum expected return*	−18.68%	−24.73%
Maximum expected return†	55.14%	51.24%

* Minimum expected return is arithmetic return minus 2 times the standard deviation.

† Maximum expected return is arithmetic return plus 2 times the standard deviation.

   The decile of the lowest PE stocks (decile one) from the All Stock universe turned $10,000 into $10,202,345, a compound rate of return of 16.25 percent per year. That's nearly $9 million more than you would have earned with an investment in the All Stocks universe, where $10,000 invested in 1963 grew to $1,329,513 at the end of 2009, an average annual compound return of 11.22 percent. What's more, the risk of the low PE stocks from the All Stocks universe was lower than the broad universe itself—the standard deviation of return for the low PE stocks from All Stocks was 18.45 percent compared with 18.99 percent for All Stocks. The higher return with lower risk led to a much higher Sharpe ratio for the low PE stocks of .61, compared to .33 for the All Stocks universe.

   The base rates for the low PE stocks from All Stocks are uniformly high—low PE stocks from All Stocks beat the All Stocks universe 92 percent of the time in all rolling five-year periods and 99 percent of the time in all rolling ten-year periods.

T A B L E 6.2

Base Rates for AS All Stocks (AS) Earnings/Price Decile 1 and All Stocks, January 1, 1964, to December 31, 2009

Item	All Stocks earnings/price decile 1 beat All Stocks	Percent	Average annual excess return
Single-year return	413 out of 541	76%	4.85%
Rolling 3-year compound return	443 out of 517	86%	4.97%
Rolling 5-year compound return	455 out of 493	92%	4.99%
Rolling 7-year compound return	450 out of 469	96%	4.88%
Rolling 10-year compound return	430 out of 433	99%	4.63%

   Using the base rates as odds for beating an investment in the All Stocks universe, we see that between 1963 and 2009, your chances of beating All Stocks with low PE stocks in any five-year period are 92 percent. If you look at the remaining 8 percent of rolling five-year periods where low PE stocks *don't* beat All Stocks, you see that the worst five-year return relative to the All Stocks universe was the five years ending February 2000, where the low PE stocks from All Stocks earned a cumulative return of 113 percent over the previous five years, whereas All Stocks gained 172 percent—a difference of 60 percent, or an average annual compound return of 16.32 percent gain for the low PE stocks versus a 22.18 percent gain for the All Stocks universe. If you average *all* the five-year periods where the low PE stocks from All Stocks underperformed the All Stocks universe, you see that the average underperformance was just a cumulative 16.87 percent.

   Conversely, if you look at the *best* five years for low PE stocks versus All Stocks, you find that in the five years ending February 2005, low PE stocks cumulatively gained 202 percent, compared to a gain of just 23 percent for the All Stocks universe. On an average annual compound basis, that is a gain of 24.76 percent for the low PE stocks and a gain of just 4.28 percent for the All Stocks universe. Readers should note that cumulative relative performance sometimes looks different from average annual compound excess returns that you will see in this and future chapters. While I used cumulative performance to calculate the relative performance between the factor and the universe, the charts feature the five-year average annual excess—or deficient—return for the factor minus the performance of the universe it comes

from, and sometimes the two are at odds. On average, when low PE stocks are outperforming
All Stocks over a five-year period, they have an average cumulative advantage of 49 percent
over All Stocks. Yet this analysis reminds us of one of the central points of this book—it is very
hard to embrace a strategy *after* it has suffered a run of underperformance. How likely would
average investors have been to embrace the low PE approach to investing at the end of
February 2000? Not very. The investors most likely would have been frightened off by the
recent underperformance of the low PE group compared to All Stocks and would have found
it virtually impossible to embrace them, thereby missing their great rebound over the next five
years. Indeed, if the investors were similar to typical investors, they would have been far more
seduced by the stellar performance of the dot-com stocks that dominated the period. For the
same five years ending February 2000, the stocks with the *highest* PE ratios had a cumulative
five-year return of 259 percent, more than doubling the return for the low PE group. Such daz-
zling short-term performance clouded many investors' minds and blinded them to the long-
term truth—stocks with very high PE ratios are almost never a good investment and tend to
perform well only at the end of unsustainable bubbles. Indeed, as we saw in the study featured
in Chapter Three, when investors witness strong short-term performance, their dopamine goes
crazy, but just as that effect wears off, the logical part of our brain takes over and we start
making excuses for why we should continue to invest in the stocks that had recently soared.
When you look at this PE data dispassionately, for example, you see what a dangerous combination of impulses this can be for the uninformed investor.

When we extend our odds to all rolling 10-year periods, we see that historically, low
PE stocks almost always beat All Stocks. There are only three 10-year periods out of 433
in which low PE stocks failed to beat the All Stocks universe. Yet very few investors are
capable of maintaining their investment discipline for 10-year periods. As Lord Keynes
said, "It is better to fail conventionally than succeed unconventionally"—and a consistent
10-year outlook is unconventional indeed!

WORST-CASE SCENARIOS AND BEST AND WORST RETURNS

Table 6.3 shows all the times that the low PE stocks from All Stocks declined by 20 percent or
more. There were seven in all, with the worst being the most recent drop of 59 percent between
May 2007 and February 2009. The low PE stocks did particularly well in the first bear market of the twenty-first century, dropping just 24 percent during the bear market of 2000–2003.
Examine Table 6.3 for all other declines greater than 20 percent. Table 6.4 shows the best and
worst gains and losses for the group over a variety of holding periods. If you have a five-year
time horizon, Table 6.4 shows that the worst you could do if you matched the worst five-year
return for low PE stocks (decile one) would be a loss of 4.15 percent a year. Conversely,
the best you could do if you matched returns for the group since 1963 would be a gain of
33.31 percent per year. Turning to Table 6.5 to translate that into dollars, the worst five-year
return would see your $10,000 shrink to $8,089, while the best five years would see it soar to
$42,109. Consult both tables for additional holding periods. We return to these tables when
we examine stocks with the highest PE ratios. Figure 6.1 shows the five-year average annual
compound excess (deficient) return for the low PE stocks from All Stocks minus the return of
the All Stocks universe; this is commonly called the *alpha* of the strategy.

TABLE 6.3

Worst-Case Scenarios: All 20 Percent or Greater Declines for AS All Stocks (AS) Earnings/Price Decile 1, January 1, 1964, to December 31, 2009

Peak date	Peak index value	Trough date	Trough index value	Recovery date	Decline (%)	Decline duration	Recovery duration
Jan–69	3.25	Jun–70	2.11	Mar–71	−35.16%	17	9
Nov–72	3.63	Dec–74	2.20	Jan–76	−39.50%	25	13
Aug–87	52.28	Nov–87	37.93	Mar–89	−27.45%	3	16
Aug–89	62.94	Oct–90	39.13	Jul–91	−37.84%	14	9
Apr–98	267.36	Aug–98	194.43	Aug–00	−27.28%	4	24
Apr–02	385.89	Sep–02	294.48	May–03	−23.69%	5	8
May–07	1,153.21	Feb–09	471.36	N/A	−59.13%	21	N/A
Average					−35.72%	12.71	13.17

TABLE 6.4

Best and Worst Average Annual Compound Returns for Monthly Data, January 1, 1964, to December 31, 2009

For any	1-year period	3-year period	5-year period	7-year period	10-year period
All Stocks earnings/price decile 1 minimum compound return	−52.60%	−18.31%	−4.15%	−0.64%	6.07%
All Stocks earnings/price decile 1 maximum compound return	81.42%	42.43%	33.31%	29.92%	28.20%
All Stocks minimum compound return	−46.49%	−18.68%	−9.91%	−6.32%	1.01%
All Stocks maximum compound return	84.19%	31.49%	27.66%	23.77%	22.05%
All Stocks earnings/price decile 10 minimum compound return	−59.04%	−40.45%	−17.89%	−13.19%	−8.13%
All Stocks earnings/price decile 10 maximum compound return	139.77%	43.72%	29.10%	22.36%	17.75%

TABLE 6.5

Terminal Value of $10,000 Invested for Best and Worst Average Annual Compound Returns for Monthly Data, January 1, 1964, to December 31, 2009

For any	1-year period	3-year period	5-year period	7-year period	10-year period
All Stocks earnings/price decile 1 minimum $10,000 value	$4,740	$5,452	$8,089	$9,558	$18,029
All Stocks earnings/price decile 1 maximum $10,000 value	$18,142	$28,894	$42,109	$62,488	$119,902
All Stocks minimum $10,000 value	$5,351	$5,379	$5,936	$6,330	$11,054
All Stocks maximum $10,000 value	$18,419	$22,734	$33,903	$44,504	$73,345
All Stocks earnings/price decile 10 minimum $10,000 value	$4,096	$2,112	$3,732	$3,714	$4,283
All Stocks earnings/price decile 10 maximum $10,000 value	$23,977	$29,684	$35,868	$41,059	$51,246

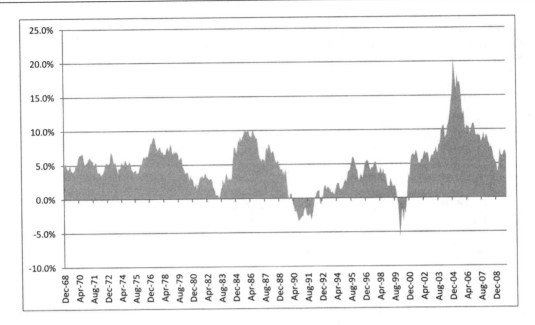

FIGURE   6.1

Five-year average annual compound excess (deficient) return All Stocks (AS) earnings/ price decile 1 minus All Stocks, January 1, 1964, to December 31, 2009

LARGE STOCKS

A $10,000 investment in the decile of low PE stocks from Large Stocks made in 1963 grew to $3,463,712, $2.59 million more than the Large Stock universe's $872,861 total return. The compound return of the low PE stocks was 13.56 percent, 3.36 percent better than the Large Stock's return of 10.20 percent a year. Moreover, the low PE stocks from Large Stocks had a better risk-adjusted return, sporting a Sharpe ratio of .50, compared to the Large Stocks universe's Sharpe ratio of .32. Table 6.6 shows all the summary information for the low PE stocks from Large Stocks. The base rates for low PE stocks from Large Stocks are also uniformly high. As Table 6.7 shows, low PE stocks from Large Stocks beat the broad universe 83 percent of the time in all rolling five-year periods and 95 percent of the time in all rolling ten-year periods.

TABLE   6.6

Summary Annual Return and Risk Results Data: Large Stocks Earnings/Price Decile 1 and Large Stocks, January 1, 1964, to December 31, 2009

	Large Stocks earnings/price decile 1	Large Stocks
Arithmetic average	15.22%	11.72%
Geometric average	13.56%	10.20%
Median return	19.71%	17.20%

(continued on next page)

TABLE 6.6

Summary Annual Return and Risk Results Data: Large Stocks Earnings/Price Decile 1 and Large Stocks, January 1, 1964, to December 31, 2009 *(Continued)*

	Large Stocks earnings/price decile 1	Large Stocks
Standard deviation	17.12%	16.50%
Upside deviation	11.15%	9.70%
Downside deviation	12.05%	11.85%
Tracking error	8.25	0.00
Number of positive periods	337	332
Number of negative periods	215	220
Maximum peak-to-trough decline	−65.62%	−53.77%
Beta	0.91	1.00
T-statistic (m = 0)	5.65	4.58
Sharpe ratio (Rf = 5%)	0.50	0.32
Sortino ratio (MAR = 10%)	0.30	0.02
$10,000 becomes	$3,463,712	$872,861
Minimum 1-year return	−59.71%	−46.91%
Maximum 1-year return	66.75%	68.96%
Minimum 3-year return	−19.39%	−15.89%
Maximum 3-year return	40.94%	33.12%
Minimum 5-year return	−2.95%	−5.82%
Maximum 5-year return	32.51%	28.95%
Minimum 7-year return	−0.35%	−4.15%
Maximum 7-year return	25.17%	22.83%
Minimum 10-year return	2.39%	−0.15%
Maximum 10-year return	21.76%	19.57%
Minimum expected return*	−19.02%	−21.28%
Maximum expected return†	49.46%	44.72%

* Minimum expected return is arithmetic return minus 2 times the standard deviation.
† Maximum expected return is arithmetic return plus 2 times the standard deviation.

TABLE 6.7

Base Rates for Large Stocks Earnings/Price Decile 1 and Large Stocks, January 1, 1964, to December 31, 2009

Item	Large Stocks earnings/price decile 1 beat Large Stocks	Percent	Average annual excess return
Single-year return	365 out of 541	67%	3.48%
Rolling 3-year compound return	371 out of 517	72%	3.54%
Rolling 5-year compound return	408 out of 493	83%	3.59%
Rolling 7-year compound return	411 out of 469	88%	3.49%
Rolling 10-year compound return	412 out of 433	95%	3.33%

Using the base rates as odds for beating an investment in the Large Stocks universe, we see that between 1963 and 2009, your chances of beating Large Stocks were 83 percent. If you look at the 17 percent of rolling five-year periods where low PE stocks *didn't* beat Large Stocks, you see that, like low PE stocks from All Stocks, the worst five-year return relative to the Large Stocks universe was the five years ending February 2000, where the low PE stocks earned a cumulative return over the previous five years of 124 percent while Large Stocks gained 180 percent—a difference of 56 percent. On an average annual compound basis, the low PE stocks earned 17.48 percent compared to 22.86 percent for the Large Stocks universe. If you average all of the five-year periods where low PE stocks from Large Stocks underperformed, the average underperformance was just a cumulative 13.42 percent.

Conversely, if you look at the *best* five years for low PE stocks versus Large Stocks you see that in the five years ending October 2007, low PE stocks from Large Stocks cumulatively gained 309 percent versus a gain of 149 percent for Large Stocks, a difference of 160 percent. On an average annual compound return basis, this means a gain of 32.51 percent for the low PE stocks and 19.99 percent for the Large Stocks universe. On average, when low PE stocks from Large Stocks are outperforming, they have an average cumulative advantage of 38.60 percent over Large Stocks.

WORST-CASE SCENARIOS AND BEST AND WORST RETURNS

Looking at Tables 6.8, 6.9, and 6.10, we see that the worst-case scenario for low PE stocks from both All Stocks and Large Stocks occurred during the market meltdown between 2007 and early 2009, with the low PE stocks from All Stocks dropping 59.13 percent and the low PE stocks from Large Stocks declining 65.62 percent. Like many value factors, low PE stocks suffered more in this recent bear market than they did in the earlier bear markets of 1973–1974 and 2000 through early 2003. The low PE stocks from All Stocks had four declines exceeding 30 percent, while the low PE stocks from Large Stocks suffered declines greater than 30 percent three times since 1963.

T A B L E   6.8

Worst-Case Scenarios: All 20 Percent or Greater Declines for Large Stocks Earnings/Price Decile 1, January 1, 1964, to December 31, 2009

Peak date	Peak index value	Trough date	Trough index value	Recovery date	Decline (%)	Decline duration	Recovery duration
Jan–66	1.44	Sep–66	1.14	Apr–67	−20.68%	8	7
Jan–69	2.01	Jun–70	1.39	Apr–71	−30.72%	17	10
Nov–72	2.35	Sep–74	1.56	Jun–75	−33.58%	22	9
Aug–87	23.54	Nov–87	17.57	Apr–89	−25.38%	3	17
Aug–89	28.13	Oct–90	19.84	May–91	−29.48%	14	7
Mar–98	111.40	Aug–98	89.02	Apr–99	−20.08%	5	8
May–01	152.00	Sep–02	118.02	Jul–03	−22.35%	16	10
Oct–07	496.48	Feb–09	170.69	N/A	−65.62%	16	N/A
Average					−30.99%	12.63	9.71

Table 6.9 shows the best and worst percentage decline over a variety of holding periods, and Table 6.10 shows the terminal value of a $10,000 investment matching the best- and worst-case scenarios for low PE stocks from the Large Stocks universe over the previous 46 years.

TABLE 6.9

Best and Worst Average Annual Compound Returns for Monthly Data, January 1, 1964, to December 31, 2009

For any	1-year period	3-year period	5-year period	7-year period	10-year period
Large Stocks earnings/price decile 1 minimum compound return	−59.71%	−19.39%	−2.95%	−0.35%	2.39%
Large Stocks earnings/price decile 1 maximum compound return	66.75%	40.94%	32.51%	25.17%	21.76%
Large Stocks minimum compound return	−46.91%	−15.89%	−5.82%	−4.15%	−0.15%
Large Stocks maximum compound return	68.96%	33.12%	28.95%	22.83%	19.57%
Large Stocks earnings/price decile 10 minimum compound return	−64.59%	−39.39%	−17.27%	−8.65%	−7.82%
Large Stocks earnings/price decile 10 maximum compound return	82.09%	43.99%	30.66%	26.34%	21.94%

TABLE 6.10

Terminal Value of $10,000 Invested for Best and Worst Average Annual Compound Returns for Monthly Data, January 1, 1964, to December 31, 2009

For any	1-year period	3-year period	5-year period	7-year period	10-year period
Large Stocks earnings/price decile 1 minimum $10,000 value	$4,029	$5,237	$8,609	$9,757	$12,663
Large Stocks earnings/price decile 1 maximum $10,000 value	$16,675	$27,996	$40,862	$48,136	$71,596
Large Stocks minimum $10,000 value	$5,309	$5,951	$7,409	$7,434	$9,848
Large Stocks maximum $10,000 value	$16,896	$23,591	$35,656	$42,189	$59,747
Large Stocks earnings/price decile 10 minimum $10,000 value	$3,541	$2,226	$3,876	$5,310	$4,427
Large Stocks earnings/price decile 10 maximum $10,000 value	$18,209	$29,854	$38,075	$51,387	$72,674

The best five-year return for low PE stocks from Large Stocks was in October 2007, where $10,000 invested five years earlier grew to $40,862, an average annual compound return of 32.51 percent. The worst five years for low PE stocks from Large Stocks were those ending February 2009, where $10,000 invested five years earlier shrank to $8,609, an average loss of 2.95 percent per year. We will return to these tables when we look at buying high PE stocks from Large Stocks.

The performance of low PE stocks for the ten years ending December 31, 2009, illustrates the importance of a long-term perspective. Even though low PE stocks suffered their largest drawdown in 46 years during this time, a long-term investor who simply stuck with low PE stocks for the entire decade would have done well—between January 1, 2000, and December 31, 2009, the low PE stocks from All Stocks sported a gain of 14.86 percent per year, turning $10,000 invested at the start of the decade into $39,977, and leaving an investor who pursued this strategy comfortably ahead of one who chose to index to the S&P 500, where the same $10,000 invested at the start of the decade was worth just $9,089, a loss of 0.95 percent a year.

Yet how difficult would it have been for investors to sit passively by while their portfolio plunged by 59 percent between 2007 and February 2009? To illustrate the difference between the typical investor and the disciplined, impassive one, imagine that both had started investing in low PE stocks in 2000. By May 2007, their portfolios would have swelled in value to $45,196, an average annual return of 22.55 percent. Fast forward to February 2009, near the end of the ferocious bear market: each portfolio would have fallen to $18,473. The height of outflows from equity funds came right around this time. Investors who panicked and bailed out of their low PE portfolio and invested in T-bills would have given up more than $21,000 in terminal value, while investors who simply stuck with their investment would have a portfolio worth more than double that of the jittery investor—the final value for each portfolio at the end of December 2009 was $39,983 for the investors who stuck with their low PE stocks and $18,488 for the investors who sold out in February and put their money in T-bills.

Clearly, this kind of behavior can be catastrophic when it comes to saving and investing for retirement: those investors who stuck with a low PE investing strategy wound up with portfolios worth twice as much as those who abandoned the strategy and fled the equity market in a fit of short-term emotion. While it is nearly impossible to ignore our underlying emotions during extreme market volatility, the lesson of today remains the same as the lessons learned from the first edition of *What Works on Wall Street*: the single best thing you can do to succeed is to find the right underlying investment strategy and then *stick with it through everything*. Figure 6.2 shows the five-year average annual compound excess (deficient) return for the low PE stocks from Large Stocks minus the return of the Large Stocks universe.

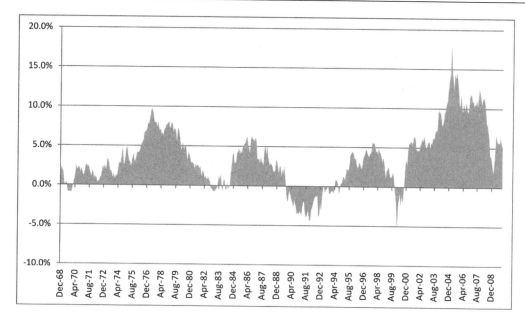

FIGURE 6.2

Five-year average annual compound excess (deficient) return. Large Stocks earning/price decile 1 minus Large Stocks, January 1, 1964, to December 31, 2009

HIGH PE RATIOS ARE DANGEROUS

Buying high PE stocks, regardless of their market capitalization, is a dangerous endeavor. You shouldn't let the flash of the latest glamour stock draw you in to paying ridiculous prices for earnings, yet investors do this frequently and seemingly with greater determination as the years have gone by. Witness investors pushing Polaroid's PE to 164 in 1961; Best Buy to 712 in 1997; and Yahoo to 4,900 in 1999.

As Table 6.11 shows, starting with the All Stocks universe, $10,000 invested in 1963 in the decile of stocks with the highest PE ratios (decile 10) and rebalanced annually grew to just $118,820 by the end of 2009, $1.2 million less than if you had bought the All Stocks universe itself. The compound return of 5.53 percent was well behind All Stocks' 11.22 percent annual return. It also did worse than an investment in U.S. T-bills, where $10,000 invested on December 31, 1963, grew to $120,778, an average annual compound return of 5.57 percent. When you adjust for risk, the news gets even grimmer. The top decile of high PE stocks' Sharpe ratio of .02 was a fraction of that of the All Stocks universe. The high PE stocks beat the All Stock group just *one* time out of 433 rolling 10-year periods—and even then it did only 69 basis points better than All Stocks annually in that single winning 10-year period. Table 6.12 shows the base rates for all holding periods.

T A B L E   6.11

Summary Annual Return and Risk Results Data: All Stocks Earnings/Price Decile 10 and All Stocks, January 1, 1964, to December 31, 2009

	All Stocks earnings/price decile 10	All Stocks
Arithmetic average	9.37%	13.26%
Geometric average	5.53%	11.22%
Median return	14.66%	17.16%
Standard deviation	26.52%	18.99%
Upside deviation	16.24%	10.98%
Downside deviation	19.08%	13.90%
Tracking error	10.71	0.00
Number of positive periods	310	329
Number of negative periods	242	223
Maximum peak-to-trough decline	−82.14%	−55.54%
Beta	1.32	1.00
T-statistic (m = 0)	2.30	4.47
Sharpe ratio (Rf = 5%)	0.02	0.33
Sortino ratio (MAR = 10%)	−0.23	0.09
$10,000 becomes	$118,820	$1,329,513
Minimum 1-year return	−59.04%	−46.49%
Maximum 1-year return	139.77%	84.19%
Minimum 3-year return	−40.45%	−18.68%
Maximum 3-year return	43.72%	31.49%
Minimum 5-year return	−17.89%	−9.91%
Maximum 5-year return	29.10%	27.66%
Minimum 7-year return	−13.19%	−6.32%
Maximum 7-year return	22.36%	23.77%
Minimum 10-year return	−8.13%	1.01%
Maximum 10-year return	17.75%	22.05%
Minimum expected return*	−43.67%	−24.73%
Maximum expected return†	62.40%	51.24%

* Minimum expected return is arithmetic return minus 2 times the standard deviation.
† Maximum expected return is arithmetic return plus 2 times the standard deviation.

T A B L E   6.12

Base Rates for All Stocks Earnings/Price Decile 10 and All Stocks, January 1, 1964, to December 31, 2009

Item	All Stocks earnings/price decile 1 beat All Stocks	Percent	Average annual excess return
Single-year return	176 out of 541	33%	−3.29%
Rolling 3-year compound return	101 out of 517	20%	−5.31%
Rolling 5-year compound return	50 out of 493	10%	−5.90%
Rolling 7-year compound return	11 out of 469	2%	−6.18%
Rolling 10-year compound return	1 out of 433	0%	−6.26%

What's more, high PE stocks show *extreme* volatility and concentration of returns and typically only perform well in speculative markets heading toward their peaks. For example, investors who got caught up in the frenzy of the Internet and technology boom of the late 1990s and put $10,000 in the high-PE "story" stocks from the All Stocks universe at the end of 1997 would have seen their investment of $10,000 soar to $24,943 at the end of February 2000, an average annual gain of 50.11 percent in just over two years. Such outstanding short-term performance made these stocks irresistible to investors, despite what they might have known about the long-term prospects for such pricey fare. The price moves in these names were extraordinary. For example, look at the shares of Xcelera Inc., a technology–E-commerce company that made the list. On December 31, 1999, it was trading at $17.44 per share. By March 22, 2000, its price had soared to $110. That's a move of over 530 percent in less than three months. Investors who lacked access to long-term data on high PE stocks based all their hopes on what they had witnessed over the previous few years and kept buying the stock. But the story had an unsurprising ending—the shares plunged in value to $0.31 in September 2002 and by 2006 the company went kaput. There were innumerable stocks that faced similar fates, of course, and the dot-com collapse wiped out more than $5 trillion in market value between 2000 and 2002. As George Santayana said, "Those who cannot remember the past are condemned to repeat it." [*The Life of Reason: Phases of Human Progress*, University of Toronto Libraries reprint, 2011. Originally published 1905.]

After the bubble popped, high PE stocks went into a death spiral from which they have not yet recovered—between February 2000 and February 2009, high PE stocks from All Stocks plunged by 82 percent, with no recovery in sight. Table 6.13 catalogs the woe. Figure 6.3 shows the five-year average annual compound excess (or in this case, deficient) return for the high PE stocks from All Stocks minus the return of the All Stocks universe.

TABLE 6.13

Worst-Case Scenarios: All 20 Percent or Greater Declines for All Stocks Earnings/Price Decile 10, January 1, 1964, to December 31, 2009

Peak date	Peak Index value	Trough date	Trough index value	Recovery date	Decline (%)	Decline duration	Recovery duration
Apr–66	1.59	Oct–66	1.24	Jan–67	−22.53%	6	3
Dec–68	3.07	Sep–74	0.87	Feb–80	−71.54%	69	65
Feb–80	3.10	Mar–80	2.36	Jul–80	−24.14%	1	4
Nov–80	4.36	Jul–82	2.59	Feb–83	−40.56%	20	7
Jun–83	5.63	Jul–84	3.69	Apr–87	−34.36%	13	33
Aug–87	6.28	Nov–87	4.07	May–89	−35.29%	3	18
Aug–89	6.76	Oct–90	4.38	Jan–92	−35.26%	14	15
May–96	13.01	Apr–97	9.96	Sep–97	−23.48%	11	5
Apr–98	14.42	Aug–98	9.22	Apr–99	−36.06%	4	8
Feb–00	30.81	Feb–09	5.50	N/A	−82.14%	108	N/A
Average					−40.54%	24.9	17.56

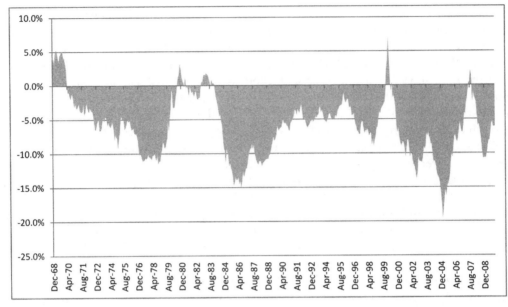

F I G U R E   6.3

Five-year average annual compound excess (deficient) return. All Stocks earnings/price decile 10 minus All Stocks, January 1, 1964, to December 31, 2009

LARGE STOCKS FAIR NO BETTER

As Table 6.14 demonstrates, the high PE damage is similar in the Large Stocks group. The $10,000 invested in the decile of Large Stocks with the highest PE ratios grew to $185,848 at the end of 2009, a fraction of the $872,861 terminal value of an investment in Large Stocks. The Sharpe ratio of .07 is abysmal next to that of .32 for Large Stocks.

T A B L E   6.14

Summary Annual Return and Risk Results Data: Large Stocks Earnings/Price Decile 10 and Large Stocks, January 1, 1964, to December 31, 2009

	Large Stocks earnings/price decile 10	Large Stocks
Arithmetic average	9.06%	11.72%
Geometric average	6.56%	10.20%
Median return	16.87%	17.20%
Standard deviation	21.38%	16.50%
Upside deviation	12.60%	9.70%
Downside deviation	16.04%	11.85%
Tracking error	9.75	0.00
Number of positive periods	328	332
Number of negative periods	224	220
Maximum peak-to-trough decline	−79.88%	−53.77%
Beta	1.16	1.00

(continued on next page)

T A B L E   6.14

Summary Annual Return and Risk Results Data: Large Stocks Earnings/Price Decile 10 and Large Stocks, January 1, 1964, to December 31, 2009 *(Continued)*

	Large Stocks earnings/price decile 10	Large Stocks
T-statistic (m = 0)	2.76	4.58
Sharpe ratio (Rf = 5%)	0.07	0.32
Sortino ratio (MAR = 10%)	−0.21	0.02
$10,000 becomes	$185,848	$872,861
Minimum 1-year return	−64.59%	−46.91%
Maximum 1-year return	82.09%	68.96%
Minimum 3-year return	−39.39%	−15.89%
Maximum 3-year return	43.99%	33.12%
Minimum 5-year return	−17.27%	−5.82%
Maximum 5-year return	30.66%	28.95%
Minimum 7-year return	−8.65%	−4.15%
Maximum 7-year return	26.34%	22.83%
Minimum 10-year return	−7.82%	−0.15%
Maximum 10-year return	21.94%	19.57%
Minimum expected return*	−33.69%	−21.28%
Maximum expected return†	51.81%	44.72%

* Minimum expected return is arithmetic return minus 2 times the standard deviation.
† Maximum expected return is arithmetic return plus 2 times the standard deviation.

Table 6.15 shows that adding insult to injury, the Large Stocks with the highest PE ratios beat the Large Stocks universe just 11 percent of the time over all rolling ten-year periods. Over rolling five-year periods, high PE stocks from Large Stocks beat the universe 24 percent of the time, but this was generally a good indicator that the market was near a top. The best five years for the high PE Large Stocks versus the Large Stocks universe was the five years ending February 2000, right at the top of the Internet and technology bubble. They returned a cumulative gain of 281 percent versus 180 percent for Large Stocks. The *second* best performance for high PE stocks over a five-year period was December 1969, near the end of *that* bubble which saw investors willing to pay stratospheric prices for growth stocks. On average, when high PE Large Stocks are beating the universe over a five-year period, they do only about 22 percent better (cumulatively over those five year) than the Large Stocks universe, hardly worth the risk you are taking in investing in such a volatile group. For all five-year periods where high PE stocks are *underperforming* Large Stocks, we see that, on average, they do 35 percent worse on a cumulative basis. Figure 6.4 shows the five-year average annual compound excess (deficient) return for the high PE stocks from Large Stocks minus the return of the Large Stocks universe.

T A B L E   6.15

Base Rates for Large Stocks Earnings/Price Decile 10 and Large Stocks, January 1, 1964, to December 31, 2009

Item	Large Stocks earnings/price decile 10 beat Large Stocks	Percent	Average annual excess return
Single-year return	233 out of 541	43%	−1.83%
Rolling 3-year compound return	170 out of 517	33%	−3.14%
Rolling 5-year compound return	120 out of 493	24%	−3.81%
Rolling 7-year compound return	91 out of 469	19%	−4.19%
Rolling 10-year compound return	46 out of 433	11%	−4.34%

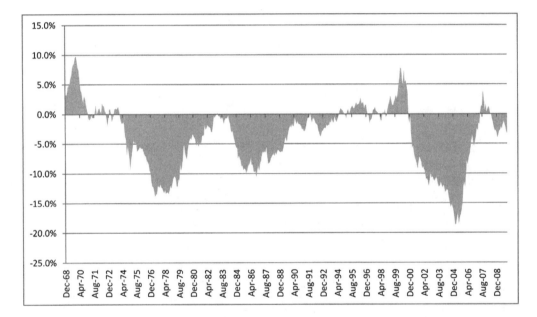

F I G U R E   6.4

Five-year average annual compound excess (deficient) return Large Stocks earnings/price decile 10 minus Large Stocks, January 1, 1964, to December 31, 2009

WORST-CASE SCENARIOS AND BEST AND WORST YEARS

As Table 6.13 shows, High PE stocks from All Stocks peaked in February 2000 and have not recovered their old highs—they were down an astounding 82 percent between February 2000 and February 2009! Since 1963, they have lost more than 20 percent from peak to trough ten times, and lost more than 70 percent twice. *Not* a group of stocks you want to bet on, even when the siren song of short-term performance makes them look irresistible. As Table 6.16 shows, high PE stocks from Large Stocks suffered five separate declines greater than 30 percent between 1963 and 2009, with the largest being the nearly 80 percent drop between

T A B L E 6.16

Worst-Case Scenarios: All 20 Percent or Greater Declines for Large Stocks Earnings/Price Decile 10, January 1, 1964, to December 31, 2009

Peak date	Peak index value	Trough date	Trough index value	Recovery date	Decline (%)	Decline duration	Recovery duration
Dec–69	2.32	Jun–70	1.47	Jan–72	−36.47%	6	19
May–72	2.79	Sep–74	1.10	Oct–80	−60.58%	28	73
Nov–80	3.16	Jul–82	2.14	Dec–82	−32.36%	20	5
Jun–83	3.98	Jul–84	2.95	Jan–86	−25.86%	13	18
Sep–87	6.14	Nov–87	4.13	Mar–89	−32.75%	2	16
Dec–89	7.51	Oct–90	5.49	Oct–91	−26.92%	10	12
Mar–00	46.27	Sep–02	9.31	N/A	−79.88%	30	N/A
Average					−42.12%	15.57	23.83

March 2000 and September 2002. They still have not recovered from this drop. Tables 6.4, 6.5, 6.9, and 6.10 show each scenario for All Stocks and Large Stocks.

Tables 6.5 and 6.10 show the terminal value of a $10,000 investment matching the best- and worst-case returns for the time periods enumerated. The best five years for high PE stocks from both All Stocks and Large Stocks were the five years ending February 2000, where the high PE stocks from All Stocks turned $10,000 into $35,868, an average annual compound return of 29.10 percent. The best five years for the high PE stocks from Large Stocks—also ending February 2000—saw $10,000 grow to $38,075, an average annual compound return of 30.66 percent.

The worst five-year return for high PE stocks from All Stocks were the five-years ending September 1974, where $10,000 invested five years earlier shrank to $3,732, an average annual loss of 17.89 percent. (The second worst five-year period, ending in February 2009, saw an almost identical decline.) The worst five-year declines for high PE stocks from Large Stocks were those ending March 2005, where $10,000 shrank to $3,876, an average annual loss of 17.27 percent. Tables 6.17 and 6.18 show the return for each decile by decade.

T A B L E 6.17

Average Annual Compound Rates of Return by Decade

	1960s*	1970s	1980s	1990s	2000s†
All Stocks earnings/price decile 1	17.68%	13.03%	20.38%	16.02%	14.86%
All Stocks earnings/price decile 10	14.74%	1.61%	9.21%	13.73%	−6.55%
All Stocks	13.36%	7.56%	16.78%	15.35%	4.39%

* Returns for January 1, 1964, to December 31, 1969.
† Returns for January 1, 2000, to December 31, 2009.

T A B L E   6.18

Average Annual Compound Rates of Return by Decade

	1960s*	1970s	1980s	1990s	2000s†
Large Stocks earnings/price decile 1	8.48%	11.38%	18.48%	16.04%	11.60%
Large Stocks earnings/price decile 10	15.07%	−0.93%	13.52%	18.53%	−7.64%
Large Stocks	8.16%	6.65%	17.34%	16.38%	2.42%

* Returns for January 1, 1964, to December 31, 1969.
† Returns for January 1, 2000, to December 31, 2009.

ALL DECILES

As Figure 6.5 and Table 6.19 show, for the All Stocks universe, all four of the cheapest deciles outperform the All Stocks universe, while having lower standard deviation of returns than the All Stocks universe itself. Deciles 5 through 10 all underperform with deciles 7 through 10 having significantly higher standard deviations than the All Stocks universe. Decile 10—the most expensive stocks with the highest PE ratios—underperforms an investment in U.S. T-bills.

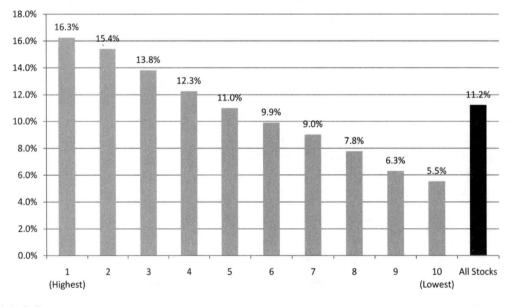

F I G U R E   6.5

All Stocks average annual compound return by decile, Earnings/Price universe, January 1, 1964, to December 31, 2009

TABLE 6.19

Summary Results for Earnings/Price Decile Analysis of All Stocks Universe, January 1, 1964, to December 31, 2009

Decile	$10,000 grows to	Average return	Compound return	Standard deviation	Sharpe ratio
1 (highest)	$10,202,345	18.23%	16.25%	18.45%	0.61
2	$7,256,873	16.89%	15.40%	16.10%	0.65
3	$3,835,747	15.19%	13.81%	15.56%	0.57
4	$2,037,160	13.68%	12.25%	15.85%	0.46
5	$1,209,030	12.50%	10.99%	16.40%	0.37
6	$771,740	11.58%	9.91%	17.27%	0.28
7	$530,331	11.08%	9.02%	19.28%	0.21
8	$313,515	10.43%	7.78%	21.95%	0.13
9	$166,562	9.35%	6.31%	23.59%	0.06
10 (lowest)	$118,820	9.37%	5.53%	26.52%	0.02
All Stocks	$1,329,513	13.26%	11.22%	18.99%	0.33

For Large Stocks, as Figure 6.6 and Table 6.20 show, we see that the four cheapest deciles by PE all do better than the Large Stocks universe, whereas the bottom six all underperform Large Stocks, with decile 10 doing just slightly better than T-bills.

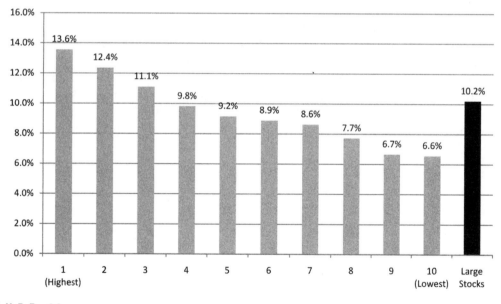

FIGURE 6.6

Large Stocks average annual compound return by decile, Earnings/Price universe, January 1, 1964. to December 31, 2009

T A B L E   6.20

Summary Results for Earnings/Price Decile Analysis of Large Stocks Universe, January 1, 1964, to December 31, 2009

Decile	$10,000 grows to	Average return	Compound return	Standard deviation	Sharpe ratio
1 (highest)	$3,463,712	15.22%	13.56%	17.12%	0.50
2	$2,129,844	13.67%	12.36%	15.25%	0.48
3	$1,272,353	12.31%	11.11%	14.68%	0.42
4	$743,184	11.08%	9.82%	15.09%	0.32
5	$561,623	10.38%	9.15%	14.91%	0.28
6	$500,099	10.13%	8.88%	15.11%	0.26
7	$448,787	10.02%	8.62%	16.01%	0.23
8	$305,717	9.38%	7.72%	17.50%	0.16
9	$194,076	8.69%	6.66%	19.31%	0.09
10 (lowest)	$185,848	9.06%	6.56%	21.38%	0.07
Large Stocks	$872,861	11.72%	10.20%	16.50%	0.32

IMPLICATIONS

Figures 6.5 and 6.6, as well as Tables 6.19 and 6.20 summarize what you can expect when buying stocks with low and high PE ratios. The results are striking. Both All Stocks and Large Stocks with high PE ratios perform substantially worse than the market. Companies with low PE ratios from both the All Stocks and Large Stocks universes do much better than the universe. In both groups, *stocks with low PE ratios do much better than stocks with high PE ratios.* Moreover, there's not much difference in risk. All the low PE groups provided higher returns over the periods, with lower risk than that of the universe.

But you could have learned about this 70 years ago if you had carefully read Graham and Dodd; Ben Graham and David Dodd were absolutely right in their 1940 book *Security Analysis: Principles and Techniques.* They said: "People who habitually purchase common stocks at more than about 20 times their average earnings are likely to lose considerable money in the long run."

7

C H A P T E R

EBITDA TO ENTERPRISE VALUE

Follow the course that is opposite to custom and you will almost always do well.

—Jean-Jacques Rousseau

Many investors believe that analyzing a stock's EBITDA (see below for definition) to enterprise value ("EBITDA/EV") is a better way to assess value—that is, how cheap or expensive it is—than looking at the PE ratio alone. The reason they find EBITDA/EV more compelling than other ratios is that it is neutral to a company's capital structure and capital expenditures. Stocks that have very high debt levels often have low PE ratios, but this does not necessarily mean that they are cheap in relation to other securities. Stocks that are highly leveraged tend to have far more volatile PE ratios than those that are not. A stock's PE ratio is greatly affected by debt levels and tax rates, whereas its EBITDA/EV is not. To compare valuations on a level playing field, you need to account for how a company is financing itself and then compare how relatively cheap or expensive it is after accounting for all balance sheet items.

You calculate EBITDA by looking at a company's earnings *before* interest, taxes, depreciation, and amortization. This offers you an approximation of the firm's operating cash flow. You calculate enterprise value by taking the common equity at market value and then adding debt, minority interest, and preferred equity at market value. From this you *subtract* any associate company at market value and all cash and cash equivalents.

As with all of our tests, we look at the composited returns for an investment in deciles 1 and 10 from both the All Stocks and Large Stocks universe. We start with $10,000 on December 31, 1963, and end on December 31, 2009.

THE RESULTS

Tables 7.1 through 7.5 summarize the results for high EBITDA/EV investing. As you can see from Table 7.1, the decile of stocks with the highest EBITDA/EV turned $10,000 invested on December 31, 1963, into $11,614,717 at the end of 2009, an average annual compound return of 16.58 percent, the best on an absolute basis for all the individual value factors we examined. That's $10 million *more* than the $1,329,513 you would have earned with a similar investment in the All Stocks universe over the same period. Risk, as measured by the standard deviation of return, was 17.71 percent, more than 1 percent below that of All Stocks 18.99 percent. The much higher returns coupled with lower risk led to a Sharpe ratio of .65, nearly double the .33 Sharpe ratio of the All Stocks universe over the same period.

T A B L E   7.1

Summary Annual Return and Risk Results Data: All Stocks EBITDA/ Enterprise Value Decile 1 and All Stocks, January 1, 1964, to December 31, 2009

	All Stocks EBITDA/ enterprise value decile 1	All Stocks
Arithmetic average	18.41%	13.26%
Geometric average	16.58%	11.22%
Median return	22.80%	17.16%
Standard deviation	17.71%	18.99%
Upside deviation	11.12%	10.98%
Downside deviation	13.10%	13.90%
Tracking error	6.26	0.00
Number of positive periods	354	329
Number of negative periods	198	223
Maximum peak-to-trough decline	−54.29%	−55.54%
Beta	0.88	1.00
T-statistic (m = 0)	6.52	4.47
Sharpe ratio (Rf = 5%)	0.65	0.33
Sortino ratio (MAR = 10%)	0.50	0.09
$10,000 becomes	$11,614,717	$1,329,513
Minimum 1-year return	−47.13%	−46.49%
Maximum 1-year return	80.66%	84.19%
Minimum 3-year return	−14.62%	−18.68%
Maximum 3-year return	42.92%	31.49%
Minimum 5-year return	−2.73%	−9.91%
Maximum 5-year teturn	32.61%	27.66%

(continued on next page)

T A B L E 7.1

Summary Annual Return and Risk Results Data: All Stocks EBITDA/ Enterprise Value Decile 1 and All Stocks, January 1, 1964, to December 31, 2009 *(Continued)*

	All Stocks EBITDA/ enterprise value decile 1	All Stocks
Minimum 7-year return	−0.58%	−6.32%
Maximum 7-year return	29.58%	23.77%
Minimum 10-year return	5.05%	1.01%
Maximum 10-year return	25.95%	22.05%
Minimum expected return*	−17.01%	−24.73%
Maximum expected return†	53.84%	51.24%

* Minimum expected return is arithmetic return minus 2 times the standard deviation.
† Maximum expected return is arithmetic return plus 2 times the standard deviation.

As you can see from Table 7.2, the decile 1 base rates of EBITDA/EV are uniformly high, with the stocks with the highest EBITDA/EV beating All Stocks 96 percent of all rolling five-year periods and 100 percent of all rolling 10-year periods.

T A B L E 7.2

Base Rates for All Stocks EBITDA/Enterprise Value Decile 1 and All Stocks, January 1, 1964, to December 31, 2009

Item	All Stocks EBITDA/enterprise value decile 1 beat All Stocks	Percent	Average annual excess return
Single-year return	411 out of 541	76%	4.96%
Rolling 3-year compound return	439 out of 517	85%	5.22%
Rolling 5-year compound return	475 out of 493	96%	5.36%
Rolling 7-year compound return	468 out of 469	100%	5.37%
Rolling 10-year compound return	433 out of 433	100%	5.23%

Using the base rates as odds for beating an investment in the All Stocks universe, we see that between 1963 and 2009, your chance of beating All Stocks with high EBITDA/EV stocks in any five-year period are 96 percent. If you look at the 4 percent of the time where high EBITDA/EV stocks *don't* beat All Stocks, you see that the worst five-year return relative to All Stocks was the five-years ending February 2000, where the high EBITDA/EV earned a cumulative return of 140 percent over the previous five years, whereas All Stocks gained 172 percent over the same period, a difference of 33 percent. On an average annual compound basis, that translates into a gain of 19.09 percent for the stocks with the best EBITDA/EV and 22.18 percent for the All Stocks universe. If you average *all* the five-year periods in which high EBITDA/EV stocks lost to All Stocks, you see that when underperforming, they only do so by 9.79 percent cumulatively.

Conversely, the *best* five-year period for high EBITDA/EV stocks versus All Stocks was for the five-years ending February 2005. Here, they returned a cumulative gain of 190 percent versus just 23 percent for All Stocks, a difference of 167 percent. That translates to an average annual compound return of 23.70 percent for decile 1 of EBITDA/EV versus 4.28 percent for the All Stocks universe. On average, when stocks with high EBITDA/EV are outperforming All Stocks over a five-year period, they have an average cumulative advantage of 48 percent over All Stocks. But much like we saw with low PE stocks, it is very difficult to embrace an investment strategy after it has performed poorly relative to its benchmark for five years. You'll note that low PE stocks and high EBITDA/EV stocks have very similar performance patterns—both had their worst five years versus All Stocks in the five years ending February 2000, and both had their *best* relative five years for the five years ending February 2005. This means that for an investor to enjoy the great five years ending February 2005, he or she would have had to stay committed to the approach just as it was coming off its worst relative performance since 1963.

As I mention in the last chapter, that would have been *extremely unlikely* for all but the most disciplined investor. February 2000 was the month that the tech-rich Nasdaq reached its peak valuation; hordes of investors had chucked out any concerns about a stock's valuation and had fallen prey to the most dubious of bubble logic. It is worth constantly reminding yourself that these types of ups and downs for a strategy are all part of the bargain you must strike with yourself as a strategic investor. Even if you read all three of the previous versions of *What Works on Wall Street*, my guess is that you would have been sorely tempted to ignore all the evidence and buy into the "new era" nonsense— because it probably didn't sound so nonsensical at the time. If nothing else, remember that buying into a strategy after it has underperformed is often both extremely difficult and extremely wise. As you can see from Table 7.3, which we revisit shortly when looking at best- and worst-case scenarios, there were several opportunities to buy into the strategy after some steep declines.

T A B L E   7.3

Worst-Case Scenarios: All 20 Percent or Greater Declines for All Stocks EBITDA/Enterprise Value Decile, January 1, 1964, to December 31, 2009

Peak date	Peak Index value	Trough date	Trough index value	Recovery date	Decline (%)	Decline duration	Recovery duration
Jan–69	2.91	Jun–70	1.81	Apr–71	−37.76%	17	10
Nov–72	3.20	Dec–74	2.04	Jun–75	−36.30%	25	6
Aug–87	42.07	Nov–87	30.53	Jan–89	−27.45%	3	14
Aug–89	52.31	Oct–90	37.71	Mar–91	−27.91%	14	5
Apr–98	269.06	Aug–98	199.29	Jun–99	−25.93%	4	10
Apr–02	431.95	Sep–02	321.15	Jun–03	−25.65%	5	9
May–07	1277.49	Feb–09	584.00	N/A	−54.29%	21	N/A
Average					−33.61%	12.71	9

When we look at rolling 10-year periods since 1963, stocks with the highest EBITDA/EV always outperform the All Stocks universe. When we look at the relative outperformance of All Stocks for all rolling 10-year periods, we find that, on average, the decile of stocks with the best EBITDA/EV outperforms All Stocks by a cumulative 181 percent. The best 10-year performance relative to All Stocks was the 10 years ending July 2006, where the first decile of EBITDA/EV returned a cumulative 575 percent, versus 193 percent for All Stocks. The worst 10-year relative performance for the first decile of EBITDA/EV was the 10 years ending December 1974, where it gained a cumulative 64 percent versus All Stocks 17 percent. Thus, if you are that extraordinary investor who can make 10-year commitments, stocks with great EBITDA/EV will serve you well. Tables 7.4 and 7.5 show the best and worst returns on both a percentage basis and what happens to a $10,000 investment under the best- and worst-case scenarios. We revisit these tables when we are looking at decile 10, those stocks with the *worst* EBITDA/EV. Figure 7.1 shows the five-year average annual compound excess (deficient) return for decile 1 minus the return for the All Stocks universe, generally referred to as alpha.

TABLE 7.4

Best and Worst Average Annual Compound Returns for Monthly Data, January 1, 1964, to December 31, 2009

For any	1-year period	3-year period	5-year period	7-year period	10-year period
All Stocks EBITDA/enterprise value decile 1 minimum compound return	−47.13%	−14.62%	−2.73%	−0.58%	5.05%
All Stocks EBITDA/enterprise value decile 1 maximum compound return	80.66%	42.92%	32.61%	29.58%	25.95%
All Stocks minimum compound return	−46.49%	−18.68%	−9.91%	−6.32%	1.01%
All Stocks maximum compound return	84.19%	31.49%	27.66%	23.77%	22.05%
All Stocks EBITDA/enterprise value decile 10 minimum compound return	−65.28%	48.12%	−23.93%	−16.69%	−11.98%
All Stocks EBITDA/enterprise value decile 10 minimum compound return	194.94%	50.63%	35.57%	23.68%	18.64%

TABLE 7.5

Terminal Value of $10,000 Invested for Best and Worst Average Annual Compound Returns for Monthly Data, January 1, 1964, to December 31, 2009

For any	1-year period	3-year period	5-year period	7-year period	10-year period
All Stocks EBITDA/enterprise value decile 1 minimum $10,000 value	$5,287	$6,224	$8,706	$9,603	$16,359
All Stocks EBITDA/enterprise value decile 1 maximum $10,000 value	$18,066	$29,194	$41,008	$61,327	$100,428
All Stocks minimum $10,000 value	$5,351	$5,379	$5,936	$6,330	$11,054
All Stocks maximum $10,000 value	$18,419	$22,734	$33,903	$44,504	$73,345
All Stocks EBITDA/enterprise value decile 10 minimum $10,000 value	$3,472	$1,396	$2,547	$2,784	$2,790
All Stocks EBITDA/enterprise value decile 10 maximum $10,000 value	$29,494	$34,176	$45,796	$44,261	$55,232

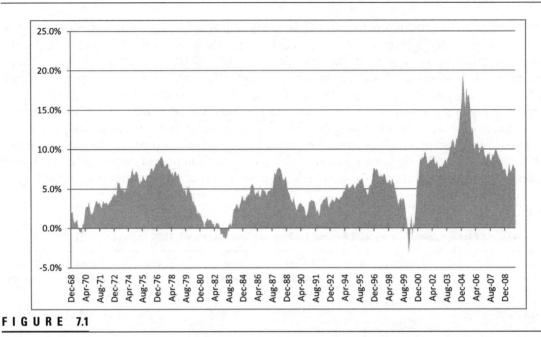

FIGURE   7.1

Five-year average annual compound excess (deficient) return All Stocks EBITDA/enterprise value Decile 1 minus All Stocks, January 1, 1964, to December 31, 2009

LARGE STOCKS

As you can see in Table 7.6, there is a similar performance advantage to Large Stocks with the best EBITDA/EV: $10,000 invested on December 31, 1963, grows to $4,003,309 at the end of December 2009, an average annual compound return of 13.91 percent. That compares exceptionally well with the $872,861 you would have earned with an investment in the Large Stocks universe, which compounded at 10.20 percent over the same period. The risk of the Large Stocks with the best EBITDA/EV was slightly higher than Large Stocks, with a standard deviation of return of 16.82 percent, compared to 16.50 percent for the Large Stock universe. Nevertheless, the excess returns generated by the strategy brought its Sharpe ratio to .53, much higher than the Sharpe ratio of .32 earned by Large Stocks over the same period.

T A B L E   7.6

Summary Annual Return and Risk Results Data: Large Stocks EBITDA/Enterprise Value Decile 1 and Large Stocks, January 1, 1964, to December 31, 2009

	Large Stocks EBITDA/enterprise value decile 1	Large Stocks
Arithmetic average	15.52%	11.72%
Geometric average	13.91%	10.20%
Median return	19.14%	17.20%
Standard deviation	16.82%	16.50%
Upside deviation	10.74%	9.70%
Downside deviation	11.37%	11.85%

(continued on next page)

T A B L E   7.6

Summary Annual Return and Risk Results Data: Large Stocks EBITDA/Enterprise Value Decile 1 and Large Stocks, January 1, 1964, to December 31, 2009 *(Continued)*

	Large Stocks EBITDA/enterprise value decile 1	Large Stocks
Tracking error	8.30	0.00
Number of positive periods	350	332
Number of negative periods	202	220
Maximum peak-to-trough decline	−52.85%	−53.77%
Beta	0.89	1.00
T-statistic (m = 0)	5.85	4.58
Sharpe ratio (Rf = 5%)	0.53	0.32
Sortino ratio (MAR = 10%)	0.34	0.02
$10,000 becomes	$4,003,309	$872,861
Minimum 1-year return	−46.65%	−46.91%
Maximum 1-year return	67.17%	68.96%
Minimum 3-year return	−10.69%	−15.89%
Maximum 3-year return	39.50%	33.12%
Minimum 5-year return	−0.82%	−5.82%
Maximum 5-year teturn	34.82%	28.95%
Minimum 7-year return	−0.82%	−4.15%
Maximum 7-year return	27.48%	22.83%
Minimum 10-year return	0.79%	−0.15%
Maximum 10-year return	22.54%	19.57%
Minimum expected return*	−18.11%	−21.28%
Maximum expected return†	49.15%	44.72%

* Minimum expected return is arithmetic return minus 2 times the standard deviation.

† Maximum expected return is arithmetic return plus 2 times the standard deviation.

As you can see by looking at Table 7.7, base rates for the Large Stocks with the best EBITDA/EV were strong—the group beat Large Stocks 87 percent of all rolling five-year periods and 99 percent of all rolling ten-year periods. Using the base rates as odds for beating the Large Stocks universe in any given five-year period, we see that the EBITDA/EV stocks failed to beat Large Stocks in 13 percent of all rolling five-year periods. Much like the All Stocks example, the *worst* five years for the Large Stocks with the best EBITDA/EV relative to the Large Stocks universe were the five years ending February 2000, where Large Stocks had a cumulative gain of 180 percent, compared to a gain of 130 percent for the Large Stocks with the best EBITDA/EV, a deficit of 50 percent. Translating the cumulative gains to average annual compound returns, decile 1 earned 18.15 percent compared to 22.86 percent for the Large Stocks universe. The average underperformance for the best Large Stocks by EBITDA/EV versus Large Stocks when underperforming on a five-year basis was an 11 percent cumulative lag.

TABLE 7.7

Base Rates for Large Stocks EBITDA/Enterprise Value Decile 1 and Large Stocks, January 1, 1964, to December 31, 2009

Item	Large Stocks EBITDA/enterprise value decile 1 beat Large Stocks	Percent	Average annual excess return
Single-year return	379 out of 541	70%	3.77%
Rolling 3-year compound return	412 out of 517	80%	3.94%
Rolling 5-year compound return	427 out of 493	87%	4.02%
Rolling 7-year compound return	433 out of 469	92%	3.97%
Rolling 10-year compound return	429 out of 433	99%	3.91%

The *best* five-year results for the Large Stocks with the best EBITDA/EV were the five years ending October 2007, where Large Stocks returned a cumulative gain of 149 percent and the best Large Stocks on EBITDA/EV gained 289 percent, a 140 percent advantage over the Large Stocks universe. Translating the cumulative gains to average annual compound returns saw decile 1 of Large Stocks by EBITDA/EV earn 30.81 percent, compared to 20.63 percent for the All Stocks universe. In the 87 percent of rolling five-year returns when the best EBITDA/EV stocks beat Large Stocks, they beat them, on average, by a cumulative 43 percent. Figure 7.2 shows the five-year average annual compound excess (deficient) return for decile 1 from Large Stocks minus the return for the Large Stocks universe.

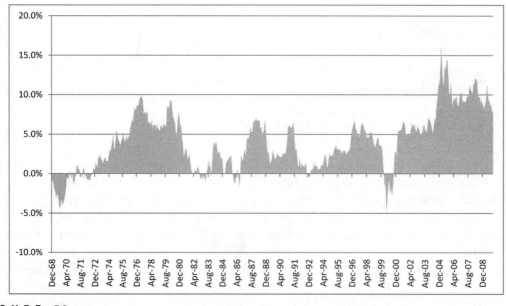

FIGURE 7.2

Five-year average annual compound excess (deficient) return Large Stocks EBITDA/enterprise value decile 1 minus Large Stocks, January 1, 1964, to December 31, 2009

BEST- AND WORST-CASE SCENARIOS AND BEST AND WORST RETURNS

Looking at Tables 7.3, 7.4, and 7.5, we see that the worst-case scenario for decile 1 of EBITDA/EV from All Stocks is a loss of 54 percent for the period of May 2007 through February 2009. That actually is *less* than the decline suffered by the All Stocks universe, which swooned 55 percent between October 2007 and February 2009. It also highlights something that I have noticed when bear markets are beginning—value-oriented strategies tend to start declining a few months ahead of the general market. Decile 1 for EBITDA/EV had seven separate occasions where the drop was more than 20 percent from peak to trough, whereas the All Stocks universe had six declines of similar or greater magnitude. Thus, unlike some of the other value factors we examine, stocks with the best EBITDA/EV look like they manage to soften the blow of serious bear markets.

Table 7.5 shows the terminal value of a $10,000 investment in decile 1 of EBITDA/EV from All Stocks: The worst five-year return was for the five years ending December 31, 1973, where $10,000 invested five years earlier shrank to $8,706, a cumulative loss of 13 percent over the period. The best five years came at the end of July 1987, where $10,000 invested five years earlier soared to $48,008, a cumulative return of 310 percent. Table 7.5 shows best- and worst-case absolute returns for all other holding periods.

For decile 1 of EBITDA/EV from Large Stocks, the worst-case scenario was a loss of 53 percent between October 2007 and February 2009. As we saw with All Stocks, this was actually a bit less than the 54 percent drawdown experienced by the Large Stocks universe over the same period. Decile 1 of EBITDA/EV from Large Stocks had seven losses that exceeded 20 percent between December 31, 1963, and December 31, 2009. You can see them all in Table 7.8.

T A B L E 7.8

Worst-Case Scenarios: All 20 Percent or Greater Declines for Large Stocks (LS) EBITDA/Enterprise Value Decile 1, January 1, 1964, to December 31, 2009

Peak date	Peak index value	Trough date	Trough index value	Recovery date	Decline (%)	Decline duration	Recovery duration
Jan–66	1.35	Sep–66	1.06	Jul–67	−21.40%	8	10
Jan–69	1.77	Jun–70	1.16	Apr–71	−34.31%	17	10
Oct–73	2.03	Sep–74	1.36	Jun–75	−32.88%	11	9
Nov–80	6.44	Jul–82	4.72	Jan–83	−26.79%	20	6
Aug–87	21.43	Nov–87	15.57	Jan–89	−27.34%	3	14
May–01	161.39	Sep–02	124.22	Aug–03	−23.03%	16	11
Oct–07	504.03	Feb–09	237.66	N/A	−52.85%	16	N/A
Average					−31.23%	13	10

Table 7.9 shows the best and worst average annual compound returns for deciles 1 and 10 of Large Stocks whereas Table 7.10 shows the terminal value of $10,000 invested in deciles 1 and 10 of EBITDA/EV from Large Stocks: The worst five years were those ending September 1974, where $10,000 invested five years earlier dipped to $9,594. This demonstrates the strategy's excellent downside protection, as the bear market of 1973–1974 was equal in severity to that of 2008–2009. The best five years for decile 1 of EBITDA/EV from Large Stocks were the five years ending July 1987, where $10,000 invested soared to $44,544, an average annual compound gain of 34.82 percent. The table also shows best- and worst-case results for other holding periods.

T A B L E   7.9

Best and Worst Average Annual Compound Returns for Monthly Data, January 1, 1964, to December 31, 2009

For any	1-year period	3-year period	5-year period	7-year period	10-year period
Large Stocks EBITDA/enterprise value decile 1 minimum compound return	−46.65%	−10.69%	−0.82%	−0.82%	0.79%
Large Stocks EBITDA/enterprise value decile 1 maximum compound return	67.17%	39.50%	34.82%	27.48%	22.54%
Large Stocks minimum compound return	−46.91%	−15.89%	−5.82%	−4.15%	−0.15%
Large Stocks maximum compound return	68.96%	33.12%	28.95%	22.83%	19.57%
Large Stocks EBITDA/enterprise value decile 10 minimum compound return	−80.16%	−49.78%	−27.19%	−17.69%	−14.40%
Large Stocks EBITDA/enterprise value decile 10 maximum compound return	100.74%	56.32%	39.89%	28.78%	25.30%

T A B L E   7.10

Terminal Value of $10,000 Invested for Best and Worst Average Annual Compound Returns for Monthly Data, January 1, 1964, to December 31, 2009

For any	1-year period	3-year period	5-year period	7-year period	10-year period
Large Stocks EBITDA/enterprise value decile 1 minimum $10,000 value	$5,335	$7,124	$9,594	$9,437	$10,816
Large Stocks EBITDA/enterprise value decile 1 maximum $10,000 value	$16,717	$27,148	$44,544	$54,707	$76,366
Large Stocks minimum $10,000 value	$5,309	$5,951	$7,409	$7,434	$9,848
Large Stocks maximum $10,000 value	$16,896	$23,591	$35,656	$42,189	$59,747
Large Stocks EBITDA/enterprise value decile 10 minimum $10,000 value	$1,984	$1,266	$2,047	$2,559	$2,112
Large Stocks EBITDA/enterprise value decile 10 maximum $10,000 value	$20,074	$38,196	$53,574	$58,731	$95,380

STOCKS WITH THE WORST EBITDA/EV ARE HORRIBLE INVESTMENTS

My mother used to say that when you paid less and got more, you'd end up doing well in the long run. Conversely, when you pay more and get less, anticipate being continually disappointed. Buying decile 10 by EBITDA/EV from All Stocks focuses on paying the most for the smallest amount of value—and the results are predictable. As you can see from Table 7.11, $10,000 invested on December 31, 1963, in decile 10 of EBITDA/EV from All Stocks grew to just $109,001, an anemic average annual compound return of just 5.33 percent. To put that in perspective, had you simply held your $10,000 in 30-day U.S. T-bills, you would have had $120,778 at the end of 2009, an average annual compound return of 5.57 percent. If you had simply bought the All Stocks universe, your $10,000 would have been worth $1,329,513, a compound average annual return of 11.22 percent. (Remember these returns are nominal and do not take the effects of inflation into account.) Just to break even with inflation, the $10,000 you invested in 1963 would have to be worth nearly $70,000, so after adjusting for inflation, you got very little real return from the worst stocks by EBITDA/EV from All Stocks. To add insult to injury, while giving you very little overall return, they managed to take you on a wild ride to nowhere. The standard deviation of return for decile 10 of EBITDA/EV from All Stocks was 26.71 percent, more than 7 percent higher than that of the All Stocks universe. That volatility, combined with dismal returns, gave the strategy a Sharpe ratio of just .01, compared with .33 for the All Stocks universe.

T A B L E   7.11

Summary Annual Return and Risk Results Data: All Stocks (AS) EBITDA/Enterprise Value Decile 10 and All Stocks, January 1, 1964, to December 31, 2009

	All Stocks EBITDA/ enterprise value decile 1	All Stocks
Arithmetic average	9.20%	13.26%
Geometric average	5.33%	11.22%
Median return	15.22%	17.16%
Standard deviation	26.71%	18.99%
Upside deviation	17.12%	10.98%
Downside deviation	19.74%	13.90%
Tracking error	12.48	0.00
Number of positive periods	318	329
Number of negative periods	234	223
Maximum peak-to-trough decline	−89.54%	−55.54%
Beta	1.27	1.00
T-statistic (m = 0)	2.24	4.47
Sharpe ratio (Rf = 5%)	0.01	0.33
Sortino ratio (MAR = 10%)	−0.24	0.09
$10,000 becomes	$109,001	$1,329,513
Minimum 1-year return	−65.28%	−46.49%
Maximum 1-year return	194.94%	84.19%

(continued on next page)

T A B L E   7.11

Summary Annual Return and Risk Results Data: AS EBITDA/Enterprise Value Decile 10 and All Stocks, January 1, 1964, to December 31, 2009 *(Continued)*

	All Stocks EBITDA/ enterprise value decile 1	All Stocks
Minimum 3-year return	−48.12%	−18.68%
Maximum 3-year return	50.63%	31.49%
Minimum 5-year return	−23.93%	−9.91%
Maximum 5-year teturn	35.57%	27.66%
Minimum 7-year return	−16.69%	−6.32%
Maximum 7-year return	23.68%	23.77%
Minimum 10-year return	−11.98%	1.01%
Maximum 10-year return	18.64%	22.05%
Minimum expected return*	−44.21%	−24.73%
Maximum expected return†	62.62%	51.24%

* Minimum expected return is arithmetic return minus 2 times the standard deviation.
† Maximum expected return is arithmetic return plus 2 times the standard deviation.

As you might have expected, base rates for the strategy, featured in Table 7.12, are also abysmal—it manages to beat All Stocks just 11 percent of the time over all rolling five-year periods and 6 percent of the time over all rolling ten-year periods. Using the base rates as odds for the worst EBITDA/EV stocks from All Stocks, you would anticipate winning only a handful of times over any five-year period—and when you did, you could be fairly certain that you were in the middle of a stock market bubble that was just about to burst. The *best* five-year relative performance versus All Stocks was the five years ending February 2000, at the absolute peak of the dot-com bubble. For those five years, All Stocks with the worst EBITDA/EV gained 358 percent cumulatively, compared to a gain of 172 percent for the All Stocks universe, a cumulative advantage of 186 percent. On an average annual compound return basis, that translates to a gain of 35.57 percent for the stocks with the worst EBITDA/EV and 22.18 percent for the All Stocks universe. The next best series of excess returns for decile 10 of EBITDA/EV came in the five-year periods ending in 1968 and 1969, the last major bubble in stock prices prior to the dot-com period. In other words, whenever these stocks do appreciably better than All Stocks, it is time to watch out below! On average, for the 11 percent of five-year periods where the stocks with the worst EBITDA/EV beat All Stocks, they do so by a cumulative 41 percent. This average is a bit higher than you might expect because of the bubble blast-off that fuels these stocks during extremely speculative markets. Don't be deceived into thinking that you can identify when those times will be, however. It's very difficult to *know* you are in a bubble until after it has popped; although one clue would be that stocks with the highest valuations have performed uncharacteristically well.

T A B L E   7.12

Base Rates for AS EBITDA/ Enterprise Value Decile 10 and All Stocks, January 1, 1964, to December 31, 2009

Item	All Stocks EBITDA/enterprise value decile 10 beat All Stocks	Percent	Average annual excess return
Single-year return	172 out of 541	32%	−3.18%
Rolling 3-year compound return	79 out of 517	15%	−5.25%
Rolling 5-year compound return	53 out of 493	11%	−5.95%
Rolling 7-year compound return	43 out of 469	9%	−6.18%
Rolling 10-year compound return	28 out of 433	6%	−6.14%

For the 89 percent of rolling five-year periods when decile 10 of EBITDA/EV *under-performs* All Stocks, you can expect to earn 47 percent *less* than All Stocks over those five years. The worst relative performance for decile 10 of EBITDA/EV from All Stocks were the five years ending November 2005, where decile 10 of EBITDA/EV *lost* 35 percent cumulatively over the previous five years compared to a gain of 71 percent for All Stocks. Table 7.13 shows the worst-case scenarios for decile 10 of EBITDA/EV for All Stocks. Figure 7.3 shows the five-year average annual compound excess (or, in this case, mostly deficient) return for decile 10 minus the return for the All Stocks universe.

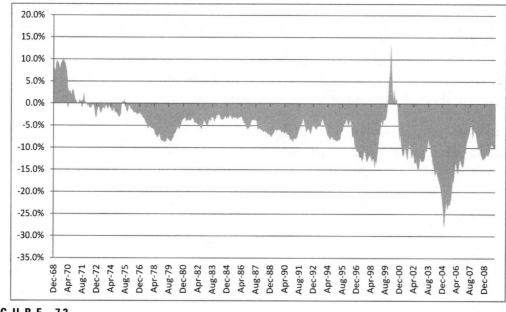

F I G U R E   7.3

Five-year average annual compound excess (deficient) return All Stocks EBITDA/enterprise value decile 10 minus All Stocks, January 1, 1964, to December 31, 2009

T A B L E   7.13

Worst-Case Scenarios: All 20 Percent or Greater Declines for All Stocks EBITDA/Enterprise Value Decile 10, January 1, 1964, to December 31, 2009

Peak date	Peak index value	Trough date	Trough index value	Recovery date	Decline (%)	Decline duration	Recovery duration
Apr–66	1.62	Oct–66	1.24	Jan–67	−23.36%	6	3
Jan–69	3.57	Sep–74	1.47	Dec–79	−58.75%	68	63
May–81	5.38	Jul–82	3.90	Nov–82	−27.51%	14	4
Jun–83	7.51	Jul–84	5.99	Feb–85	−20.27%	13	7
Aug–87	11.62	Nov–87	7.46	Aug–89	−35.78%	3	21
Sep–89	11.85	Oct–90	7.49	Aug–91	−36.84%	13	10
Oct–93	16.15	Jun–94	12.31	Jul–95	−23.80%	8	13
May–96	21.79	Aug–98	11.81	Mar–99	−45.81%	27	7
Feb–00	58.29	Feb–09	6.10	N/A	−89.54%	108	N/A
Average					−40.19%	28.89	16

LARGE STOCKS UNIVERSE STOCKS DO EVEN WORSE

As you can see from Table 7.14, $10,000 invested in decile 10 of EBITDA/EV from the Large Stocks universe does even worse than those from All Stocks, eking out an average annual compound return of 5.13 percent and growing the $10,000 into just $99,989 at the end of 2009. Remember, as with All Stocks, this is worse than the return you would earn by keeping your money in U.S. T-bills. As we saw with All Stocks, the standard deviation of return for decile 10 by EBITDA/EV is vastly higher than that of Large Stocks, coming in at 23.56 percent compared to 16.50 for the Large Stocks universe. That type of volatility—married to abysmal returns—provides a Sharpe ratio of just .01, compared to .32 for Large Stocks.

T A B L E   7.14

Summary Annual Return and Risk Results Data: Large Stocks EBITDA/Enterprise Value Decile 10 and Large Stocks, January 1, 1964, to December 31, 2009

	Large Stocks EBITDA/enterprise value decile 10	Large Stocks
Arithmetic average	8.19%	11.72%
Geometric average	5.13%	10.20%
Median return	13.29%	17.20%
Standard deviation	23.56%	16.50%
Upside deviation	14.31%	9.70%
Downside deviation	18.45%	11.85%
Tracking error	12.15	0.00
Number of positive periods	309	332
Number of negative periods	243	220
Maximum peak-to-trough decline	−89.48%	−53.77%
Beta	1.25	1.00

(continued on next page)

T A B L E   7.14

Summary Annual Return and Risk Results Data: Large Stocks EBITDA/Enterprise Value Decile 10 and Large Stocks, January 1, 1964, to December 31, 2009 *(Continued)*

	Large Stocks EBITDA/enterprise value decile 10	Large Stocks
T-statistic (m = 0)	2.27	4.58
Sharpe ratio (Rf = 5%)	0.01	0.32
Sortino ratio (MAR = 10%)	−0.26	0.02
$10,000 becomes	$99,989	$872,861
Minimum 1-year return	−80.16%	−46.91%
Maximum 1-year return	100.74%	68.96%
Minimum 3-year return	−49.78%	−15.89%
Maximum 3-year return	56.32%	33.12%
Minimum 5-year return	−27.19%	−5.82%
Maximum 5-year teturn	39.89%	28.95%
Minimum 7-year return	−17.69%	−4.15%
Maximum 7-year return	28.78%	22.83%
Minimum 10-year return	−14.40%	−0.15%
Maximum 10-year return	25.30%	19.57%
Minimum expected return*	−38.92%	−21.28%
Maximum expected return†	55.30%	44.72%

* Minimum expected return is arithmetic return minus 2 times the standard deviation.
† Maximum expected return is arithmetic return plus 2 times the standard deviation.

As you can see in Table 7.15, the base rates for decile 10 by EBITDA/EV are surprisingly better for Large Stocks than for All Stocks—decile 10 by EBITDA/EV beats Large Stocks in 19 percent of all rolling five-year periods and 11 percent of all rolling ten-year periods. The best five years—relative to the performance of the Large Stocks universe—were the five years ending February 2000, where decile 10 by EBITDA/EV from Large Stocks had a gain of 436 percent versus 180 for Large Stocks, a cumulative advantage of 256 percent. Translating that into average annual compound returns, the decile 10 stocks earned 39.89 percent per year versus 22.86 percent for the Large Stocks universe. Such eye-popping returns turned many an investor's head, enticing many to abandon any dispassionate assessment of valuation and begin to truly believe that we had entered a "new era" for investing. Interestingly, the last chasm that opened up between decile 10 by EBITDA/EV from Large Stocks and the Large Stocks universe was in the bubble period of the late 1960s. On average, when decile 10 by EBITDA/EV from Large Stocks was outperforming Large Stocks over all five-year periods, the gain was a cumulative 41 percent advantage over the Large Stocks universe. But as we saw with All Stocks, the triple digit excess performance periods were highly concentrated in the year 2000. Without the biggest bubble in nearly 60 years, most of the advantage to the worst stocks by EBITDA/EV from Large Stocks would evaporate.

TABLE 7.15

Base Rates for Large Stocks EBITDA/Enterprise Value Decile 10 and Large Stocks, January 1, 1964, to December 31, 2009

Item	Large Stocks EBITDA/enterprise value decile 1 beat Large Stocks	Percent	Average annual excess return
Single-year return	196 out of 541	36%	−2.53%
Rolling 3-year compound return	120 out of 517	23%	−4.35%
Rolling 5-year compound return	95 out of 493	19%	−5.21%
Rolling 7-year compound return	78 out of 469	17%	−5.64%
Rolling 10-year compound return	46 out of 433	11%	−5.74%

The worst five-year relative performance versus Large Stocks were the five years ending July 1987, where the stocks in decile 10 by EBITDA/EV from Large Stocks had a cumulative return of 139 percent, 116 percent behind the Large Stocks universe gain of 257 percent. Translating that into average annual compound returns, decile 10 earned 19.05 percent, compared to a gain of 28.95 percent for the Large Stocks universe. On average, when decile 10 by EBITDA/EV from Large Stocks is underperforming the Large Stocks universe, it does so by a cumulative 44 percent over all rolling five-year periods. Figure 7.4 shows the five-year average annual compound excess (or, in this case, mostly deficient) return for decile 10 minus the return for the Large Stocks universe.

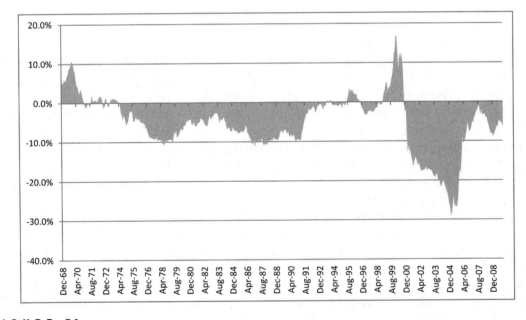

FIGURE 7.4

Five-year average annual compound excess (deficient) return Large Stocks EBITDA/enterprise value decile 10 minus Large Stocks, January 1, 1964, to December 31, 2009

WORST-CASE SCENARIOS AND BEST AND WORST YEARS

Tables 7.13 and 7.16 show drawdowns for decile 10 by EBITDA/EV from All Stocks and Large Stocks. Ouch! The stocks with the worst EBITDA/EV from All Stocks peaked in February 2000, and then went into a headlong crash through February 2009, losing 90 percent of their value from peak to trough. Since 1963, they lost more than 20 percent in value nine times. If Table 7.16 does not scare you away from such richly valued stocks, I don't know what will.

T A B L E   7.16

Worst-Case Scenarios: All 20 Percent or Greater Declines for Large Stocks EBITDA/Enterprise Value Decile 10, January 1, 1964, to December 31, 2009

Peak date	Peak index value	Trough date	Trough index value	Recovery date	Decline (%)	Decline duration	Recovery duration
Apr–66	1.73	Oct–66	1.37	Feb–67	−20.73%	6	4
Dec–69	2.40	Jun–70	1.52	Jan–72	−36.69%	6	19
Dec–72	3.01	Sep–74	1.29	Sep–80	−57.09%	21	72
May–81	3.33	Jul–82	2.38	Nov–82	−28.42%	14	4
Jun–83	4.50	Jul–84	3.20	Dec–85	−28.86%	13	17
Sep–87	6.00	Nov–87	4.12	May–89	−31.34%	2	18
Sep–89	6.88	Oct–90	4.41	Aug–91	−35.86%	13	10
Jul–98	23.28	Aug–98	18.48	Dec–98	−20.64%	1	4
Feb–00	54.48	Feb–09	5.73	N/A	−89.48%	108	N/A
Average					−38.79%	20.44	18.5

The tale for decile 10 by EBITDA/EV from Large Stocks is much the same as we see with All Stocks—they peak in February 2000 and plunge throughout the ensuing nine years, hitting bottom in February 2009 with a loss of 89 percent. Like those from All Stocks, decile 10 by EBITDA/EV from Large Stocks suffered nine separate declines of more than 20 percent between 1963 and 2009.

Tables 7.5 and 7.10 show the terminal value of a $10,000 investment matching the best and worst years for the stocks in decile 10 by EBITDA/EV for All Stocks and Large Stocks. The best five years for decile 10 by EBITDA/EV from All Stocks were the five years ending February 2000, where $10,000 invested five years earlier grew to $45,796, an average annual compound gain of 35.57 percent. The worst five years for decile 10 by EBITDA/EV from All Stocks were the five years ending February 2005, where $10,000 invested five years earlier shrank to $2,547, an average annual compound loss of 23.93 percent.

The best five years for decile 10 by EBITDA/EV from Large Stocks was February 2000, where $10,000 invested five years earlier grew to $53,574, an average annual compound return of 39.89 percent. The worst five years for decile 10 by EBITDA/EV from Large Stocks were the five years ending February 2005, where $10,000 invested five years earlier shrank to $2,047, a compound average annual loss of 27.18 percent. Tables 7.17 and 7.18 show the average annual compound return by decade for each decile within All Stocks and Large Stocks.

T A B L E   7.17

Average Annual Compound Rates of Return by Decade—All Stocks

	1960s*	1970s	1980s	1990s	2000s†
All Stocks EBITDA/enterprise value decile 1	14.14%	13.82%	19.95%	18.59%	15.55%
All Stocks EBITDA/enterprise value decile 10	18.72%	2.61%	11.97%	13.28%	−11.98%
All Stocks	13.36%	7.56%	16.78%	15.35%	4.39%

* Returns for January 1, 1964, to December 31, 1969.
† Returns for January 1, 2000, to December 31, 2009.

T A B L E   7.18

Average Annual Compound Rates of Return by Decade—Large Stocks

	1960s*	1970s	1980s	1990s	2000s†
Large Stocks EBITDA/enterprise value decile 1	5.35%	12.75%	19.31%	16.96%	12.15%
Large Stocks EBITDA/enterprise value decile 10	15.70%	0.41%	10.03%	21.78%	−14.27%
Large Stocks	8.16%	6.65%	17.34%	16.38%	2.42%

* Returns for January 1, 1964, to December 31, 1969.
† Returns for January 1, 2000, to December 31, 2009.

DECILES

As Figures 7.5 and 7.6 and Tables 7.19 and 7.20 show, deciles 1 through 5 of EBITDA/EV from All Stocks all outperform the All Stocks universe, whereas deciles 6 through 10 all underperform the All Stocks universe. Deciles 9 and 10 have the dubious distinction of also underperforming 30-day U.S. T-bills.

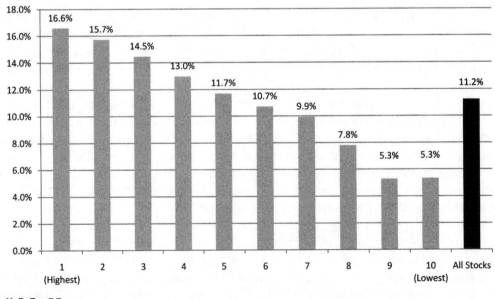

F I G U R E   7.5

Average annual compound return by EBITDA/enterprise value decile, All Stocks universe, January 1, 1964, to December 31, 2009

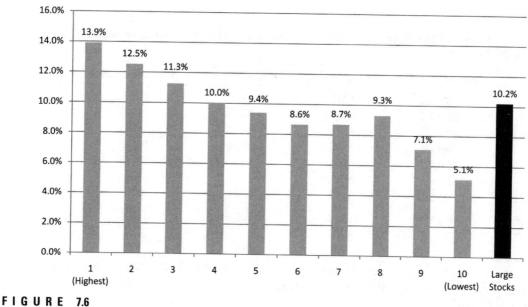

FIGURE 7.6

Average annual compound return by EBITDA/enterprise value decile, Large Stocks universe, January 1, 1964, to December 31, 2009

TABLE 7.19

Summary Results for EBITDA/Enterprise Value Decile Analysis of All Stocks Universe, January 1, 1964, to December 31, 2009

Decile	$10,000 grows to	Average return	Compound return	Standard deviation	Sharpe ratio
1 (highest)	$11,614,717	18.41%	16.58%	17.71%	0.65
2	$8,275,696	17.57%	15.73%	17.82%	0.60
3	$4,972,919	16.17%	14.45%	17.26%	0.55
4	$2,734,277	14.66%	12.97%	17.19%	0.46
5	$1,620,973	13.40%	11.70%	17.34%	0.39
6	$1,072,150	12.46%	10.70%	17.70%	0.32
7	$775,885	11.82%	9.92%	18.41%	0.27
8	$316,267	10.11%	7.80%	20.46%	0.14
9	$106,512	8.54%	5.28%	24.44%	0.01
10 (lowest)	$109,001	9.20%	5.33%	26.71%	0.01
All Stocks	$1,329,513	13.26%	11.22%	18.99%	0.33

TABLE 7.20

Summary Results for EBITDA/Enterprise Value Decile Analysis of Large Stocks Universe, January 1, 1964, to December 31, 2009

Decile	$10,000 grows to	Average return	Compound return	Standard deviation	Sharpe ratio
1 (highest)	$4,003,309	15.52%	13.91%	16.82%	0.53
2	$2,273,260	13.88%	12.52%	15.58%	0.48
3	$1,357,246	12.53%	11.27%	15.09%	0.42

(continued on next page)

T A B L E   7.20

Summary Results for EBITDA/Enterprise Value Decile Analysis of Large Stocks Universe, January 1, 1964, to December 31, 2009 *Continued)*

Decile	$10,000 grows to	Average return	Compound return	Standard deviation	Sharpe ratio
4	$808,224	11.30%	10.02%	15.17%	0.33
5	$623,765	10.72%	9.40%	15.47%	0.28
6	$452,578	9.99%	8.64%	15.68%	0.23
7	$461,233	10.11%	8.69%	16.11%	0.23
8	$594,472	10.82%	9.29%	16.71%	0.26
9	$233,431	9.04%	7.09%	18.88%	0.11
10 (lowest)	$99,989	8.19%	5.13%	23.56%	0.01
Large Stocks	$872,861	11.72%	10.20%	16.50%	0.32

For Large Stocks, deciles 1 through 3 all outperform the Large Stocks universe, whereas deciles 4 through 10 all underperform. Here, decile 10 also loses to cash invested in 30-day U.S. T-bills.

IMPLICATIONS

For All Stocks, stocks with the best EBITDA/EV have earned the best absolute return over the 1963–2009 time period, unseating all the other value ratios—and doing so with relatively low volatility and excellent base rates. I will resist the impulse to crown it the new "king" of value factors (as I did with my original findings on price-to-sales ratios), since my ongoing research suggests that the horse race between value factors will likely continue to ebb and flow, and the next version of *What Works on Wall Street* might find a new "king" edging out EBITDA/EV. As we'll see on the longer-term data we use with the price-to-book ratio, there may be a long stretch of time when a traditional value factor fails to add value on its own. That's why we will later look at *combining* value factors so that we always can take advantage of those that are working well.

For Large Stocks, we see that EBITDA/EV also earns first place in terms of absolute performance since 1963. As we'll see in Chapter Sixteen, "The Value of Value Factors," there is much more clustering with the value factors when applied to the Large Stocks universe. For example, Large Stocks with the best EBITDA/EV earned an annual compound average return of 13.91 percent between December 31, 1963, and December 31, 2009, whereas low PE stocks from Large Stocks earned 13.56 percent per year over the same time period, very close to those with the best EBITDA/EV.

For now, EBITDA/EV has proven itself very useful in ferreting out both stocks that go on to do very well and those that go on to do very poorly.

CHAPTER SEVEN CASE STUDY

USING ENTERPRISE VALUE TO CREATE OTHER RATIOS

While EBITDA/EV turns in the best performance over our study period, using it in other ratios works well also. For example, measuring free cash flow to enterprise value for the All Stocks universe finds the first decile returning a 16.10 percent compound average annual return between December 31, 1963, and December 31, 2009. So $10,000 invested grows to $9,607,437, and the base rates compared to All Stocks are all positive, with the group beating All Stocks in 88 percent of all rolling five-year periods and in 96 percent of all rolling ten-year periods. The worst-case scenario occurred during the most recent bear market, where the group declined by 57 percent between May 2007 and February 2009.

Looking at the *worst* decile by free cash flow to enterprise value, we see performance similar to that dismal performance generated by the worst decile by EBITDA/EV—with the group returning an average annual compound return of 7.27 percent and $10,000 growing to $252,497. Base rates for the strategy are also poor, with the group beating All Stocks in just 3 percent of all rolling ten-year periods. And the few times they *did* beat All Stocks over a ten-year period it was only by a fraction, with the best relative performance coming in February 1974, where their average annual return over the previous ten years was 7.48 percent compared to 7.03 percent for the All Stocks universe. Thus the group—like the worst stocks from All Stocks by EBITDA/EV—should always be avoided.

The performance spread between decile 1 and decile 10 is not as dramatic when measuring free cash flow to enterprise value using the Large Stocks universe. The best decile returned 13.11 percent between 1963 and 2009—compared to Large Stocks' 9.6—whereas the worst decile returned 8.20 percent. The base rates for the best free cash flow to enterprise value were all positive, with the group beating Large Stocks 85 percent of all rolling five-year periods and 99 percent of all rolling ten-year periods. The Large Stocks with the worst free cash flow to enterprise value had uniformly negative base rates, but not as pronounced as those from the All Stocks group—they beat Large Stocks 33 percent of all rolling five-year periods and 37 percent of all rolling ten-year periods.

SALES TO ENTERPRISE VALUE

As we saw with free cash flow to enterprise value, the concept works well with virtually all ratios. When we rank stocks on sales to enterprise value, we see similar outperformance for decile 1 and significant underperformance for decile 10. Hence $10,000 invested in the stocks from All Stocks with the best sales to enterprise value on December 31, 1963, grows to $8,472,839 at the end of 2009, an average annual compound return of 15.79 percent. The group was similar to other factors in terms of drawdown, the worst case occurring during the recent bear market, where the stocks with the best sales to enterprise value declined by 62 percent between May 2007 and February 2009. The base rates for decile 1 were all positive, with the group beating All Stocks in 96 percent of all rolling five-year periods and 99 percent of all rolling ten-year periods.

Looking at the worst decile by sales to enterprise value, we see those now all too familiar dismal returns. The $10,000 invested in the stocks with the worst sales to enterprise value in 1963 grew to just $96,684 at the end of 2009, an average annual compound return of 5.06 percent. That's worse than the $120,778 you'd have earned by keeping all your money in cash invested in 30-day T-bills. To show you how truly awful the group did, if you adjusted returns for inflation, the $10,000 invested in 1963 in decile 10 by sales to enterprise value would have been worth $13,825 after inflation at the end of 2009, an average annual return of 0.77 percent. The same $10,000 invested in T-bills adjusted for inflation would have been worth $17,270, an annual after-inflation return of 1.19 percent, whereas $10,000 invested in the stocks with the best sales to enterprise value would have been worth $1,211,518, a 10.99 percent annual return since 1963. The lessons are clear—avoid the priciest stocks—and T-bills!

The worst-case scenario for the stocks with the worst sales to enterprise value from All Stocks was an almost fatal decline of 92 percent that took place between February 2000 and February 2009. Base rates were uniformly negative, with the group beating All Stocks in just 19 percent of all rolling five-year periods and 6 percent of all rolling ten-year periods.

Ranking Large Stocks by sales to enterprise value has similar results. The $10,000 invested in 1963 in the group with the best sales to enterprise value grew to $2,429,387 at the end of 2009, an average annual compound return of 12.68 percent, which is considerably better than the $682,195 an investment in the Large Stocks universe would have earned. The worst-case scenario for decile 1 of Large Stocks by sales to enterprise value was a loss of 53 percent between October 2007 and February 2009. That's actually a *smaller* drop then the Large Stocks universe suffered over the same period, when it lost 54 percent. The base rates were all positive, with the group beating Large Stocks 81 percent of all rolling five-year periods and 97 percent of all rolling ten-year periods.

When we look at the Large Stocks with the worst sales to enterprise value, we see something that is rare—they actually do *worse* than the group from All Stocks, with $10,000 invested in 1963 growing to just $75,146, an average annual compound return of just 4.48 percent. Again, like the worst group from All Stocks, you would have been better off in cash. The worst-case scenario for the group was a drop of 88 percent between February 2000 and February 2009. Base rates were all negative, with the group beating Large Stocks in just 22 percent of all rolling five-year periods and 10 percent of all rolling ten-year periods.

IMPLICATIONS

Enterprise value works well as a guide to under- and overvaluation when contrasted to EBITDA, free cash flow, and sales. If nothing else, it shows that investors should avoid the priciest stocks ranked on EBITDA/EV, free cash flow/EV, and sales/EV, and those that are the most reasonably priced can do significantly better than the market.

C H A P T E R

PRICE-TO-CASH FLOW RATIOS: USING CASH TO DETERMINE VALUE

Losing an illusion makes you wiser than finding a truth.
—Ludwig Borne

The price-to-cash flow ratio is yet another measure of whether a stock is cheap or not. *Cash flow* is defined as Net Income plus Depreciation and other non-cash expenses. The price-to-cash flow ratio is the market value of the stock divided by total cash flow. Let's look at it on a per share basis.

Some value investors prefer using price-to-cash flow ratios to find bargain-priced stocks because cash flow is traditionally more difficult to manipulate than earnings. We exclude utility stocks here, since utilities show up frequently, and we want to avoid bias to one industry.

As usual, we look at both the low and high price-to-cash flow ratio stocks from our All Stocks and Large Stocks universes. We start with $10,000 on December 31, 1963, and buy the top decile of stocks with the highest cash flow-to-price ratios from the All Stocks universe. We also rank both All Stocks and Large Stocks by price-to-cash flow decile. (Again, because of Compustat's ranking function, we must rank stocks by the decile with the highest cash flow-to-price ratios, the inverse of the price-to-cash flow ratio.) We'll rebalance the portfolio annually, and, as with all our tests, the results will be from our composited results. The stocks are equally weighted, and all variables except price are time-lagged to avoid look-ahead bias.

THE RESULTS

Like other value criteria, investors reward stocks with low price-to-cash flow ratios and punish those with high ones. Let's look at the returns of low price-to-cash flow ratio stocks first. Tables 8.1 through 8.5 summarize the results for the All Stocks universe. Thus $10,000 invested on December 31, 1963, in the decile of stocks with the lowest price-to-cash flow ratios from the All Stocks universe was worth $10,187,545 on December 31, 2009, a compound return of 16.25 percent a year, significantly better than the $1,329,513 you'd earn from the same investment in the All Stocks universe. Risk was actually a few basis points lower than that for All Stocks. The standard deviation of return for the decile of stocks with the lowest price-to-cash flow was 18.47 percent, slightly lower than the All Stocks universe's 18.99 percent. Because of this, the low price-to-cash flow portfolio came in with a significantly higher Sharpe ratio than All Stocks—with the low price-to-cash flow decile sporting a Sharpe ratio of .61 versus .33 for the All Stocks universe.

T A B L E   8.1

Summary Annual Return and Risk Results Data: All Stocks Net Operating Cash Flow to Price Decile 1 and All Stocks, January 1, 1964, to December 31, 2009

	All Stocks net operating cash flow to price decile 1	All Stocks
Arithmetic average	18.23%	13.26%
Geometric average	16.25%	11.22%
Median return	22.64%	17.16%
Standard deviation	18.47%	18.99%
Upside deviation	12.15%	10.98%
Downside deviation	14.04%	13.90%
Tracking error	7.63	0.00
Number of positive periods	357	329
Number of negative periods	195	223
Maximum peak-to-trough decline	−60.87%	−55.54%
Beta	0.89	1.00
T-statistic (m = 0)	6.19	4.47
Sharpe ratio (Rf = 5%)	0.61	0.33
Sortino ratio (MAR = 10%)	0.45	0.09
$10,000 becomes	$10,187,545	$1,329,513
Minimum 1-year return	−54.24%	−46.49%
Maximum 1-year return	89.55%	84.19%
Minimum 3-year return	−18.63%	−18.68%
Maximum 3-year return	45.20%	31.49%
Minimum 5-year return	−3.86%	−9.91%
Maximum 5-year return	32.98%	27.66%
Minimum 7-year return	−0.39%	−6.32%
Maximum 7-year return	27.49%	23.77%
Minimum 10-year return	5.90%	1.01%
Maximum 10-year return	25.86%	22.05%
Minimum expected return*	−18.70%	−24.73%
Maximum expected return†	55.16%	51.24%

* Minimum expected return is arithmetic return minus 2 times the standard deviation.

† Maximum expected return is arithmetic return plus 2 times the standard deviation.

The base rates for the lowest price-to-cash flow stocks from All Stocks are featured in Table 8.2. The base rates are uniformly high—low price-to-cash flow stocks from All Stocks beat the All Stocks universe in 100 percent of all rolling ten-year periods and in 91 percent of all rolling five-year periods.

T A B L E 8.2

Base Rates for All Stocks Net Operating Cash Flow to Price Decile 1 and All Stocks, January 1, 1964, to December 31, 2009

Item	All Stocks net opearating cash flow to price decile 1 beat All Stocks	Percent	Average annual excess return
Single-year return	396 out of 541	73%	4.56%
Rolling 3-year compound return	449 out of 517	87%	4.80%
Rolling 5-year compound return	449 out of 493	91%	4.86%
Rolling 7-year compound return	461 out of 469	98%	4.78%
Rolling 10-year compound return	432 out of 433	100%	4.59%

Using the base rates as odds for beating an investment in the All Stocks universe, we see that between 1963 and 2009, if you managed to rigorously hold onto the stocks with the lowest price-to-cash flow ratios from All Stocks, you won in every ten-year period, with an average excess gain of 4.59 percent on an average annual compound basis better than the All Stocks universe. When we look at all rolling five-year periods, we see that the worst that low price-to-cash flow stocks did on a relative basis were the five years ending February 2000, when they earned a cumulative return of 122 percent compared to a cumulative gain of 172 percent for the All Stocks universe, a cumulative deficit of 50 percent. Translating that into average annual compound returns, the low price-to-cash flow stocks earned 17.29 percent compared to an annual gain of 22.18 percent for the All Stocks universe. The best that the low price-to-cash flow stocks did versus the All Stocks universe were the five years ending February 2005, when they gained a cumulative 202 percent, compared to a gain of just 23 percent for the All Stocks universe. That's a cumulative advantage of 179 percent over those five years. Translating those returns into average annual compound returns, the low price-to-cash flow stocks earned 24.74 percent a year compared to 4.28 percent for the All Stocks universe. We revisit Tables 8.3 through 8.5 later in the chapter when we analyze worst-case scenarios and best and worst returns.

T A B L E 8.3

Worst-Case Scenarios: All 20 Percent or Greater Declines for All Stocks Net Operating Cash Flow to Price Decile 1, January 1, 1964, to December 31, 2009

Peak date	Peak index value	Trough date	Trough index value	Recovery date	Decline (%)	Decline duration	Recovery duration
Jan–69	3.20	Jun–70	1.96	Nov–72	−38.83%	17	29
Nov–72	3.35	Sep–74	2.23	May–75	−33.46%	22	8

(continued on next page)

TABLE 8.3

Worst-Case Scenarios: All 20 Percent or Greater Declines for All Stocks Net Operating Cash Flow to Price Decile 1, January 1, 1964, to December 31, 2009 *(Continued)*

Peak date	Peak index value	Trough date	Trough index value	Recovery date	Decline (%)	Decline duration	Recovery duration
Aug–87	43.97	Nov–87	30.24	Mar–89	−31.22%	3	16
Aug–89	53.60	Oct–90	36.93	Mar–91	−31.10%	14	5
Apr–98	235.65	Aug–98	174.76	Jun–99	−25.84%	4	10
Apr–02	371.69	Sep–02	268.66	Jul–03	−27.72%	5	10
May–07	1141.14	Feb–09	446.53	N/A	−60.87%	21	N/A
Average					−35.58%	12.29	13

TABLE 8.4

Best and Worst Average Annual Compound Returns for Monthly Data, January 1, 1964, to December 31, 2009

For any	1-year period	3-year period	5-year period	7-year period	10-year period
All Stocks net operating cash flow to price decile 1 mnimum compound return	−54.24%	−18.63%	−3.86%	−0.39%	5.90%
All Stocks net operating cash flow to price decile 1 maximum compound return	89.55%	45.20%	32.98%	27.49%	25.86%
All Stocks minimum compound return	−46.49%	−18.68%	−9.91%	−6.32%	1.01%
All Stocks maximum compound return	84.19%	31.49%	27.66%	23.77%	22.05%
All Stocks net operating cash flow to price decile 10 minimum compound return	−58.46%	−43.45%	−19.26%	−12.72%	−11.15%
All Stocks net operating cash flow to price decile 10 maximum compound return	126.83%	36.00%	25.37%	18.35%	14.23%

TABLE 8.5

Terminal Value of $10,000 Invested for Best and Worst Average Annual Compound Returns for Monthly Data, January 1, 1964, to December 31, 2009

For any	1-year period	3-year period	5-year period	7-year period	10-year period
All Stocks net operating cash flow to price decile 1 minimum $10,000 value	$4,576	$5,387	$8,215	$9,728	$17,736
All Stocks net operating cash flow to price decile 1 maximum $10,000 value	$18,955	$30,610	$41,583	$54,740	$99,764
All Stocks minimum $10,000 value	$5,351	$5,379	$5,936	$6,330	$11,054
All Stocks maximum $10,000 value	$18,419	$22,734	$33,903	$44,504	$73,345
All Stocks net operating cash flow to price decile 10 minimum $10,000 value	$4,154	$1,808	$3,432	$3,860	$3,065
All Stocks net operating cash flow to price decile 10 maximum $10,000 value	$22,683	$25,155	$30,975	$32,517	$37,831

Let me reiterate a caution I've made in regard to the other value ratios we've examined thus far. While we always want to bet on the factors that have the best results over the long term, remember that factors come in and out of favor. The better lesson to learn from the results of all of our factor tests is that certain groups of factors—such as stocks with the best value characteristics—do substantially better over long periods of times than others, and it is on these factors that we wish to concentrate our portfolio's profile. Yet it is precisely when they are underperforming that we question whether they will continue to do well in the future, and it is at these times that you must remind yourself of the long-term data featured in this book. Figure 8.1 shows the five-year average annual compound excess (deficient) return for decile 1 minus the return for the All Stocks universe.

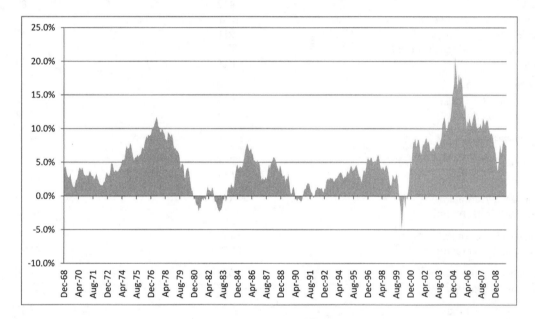

FIGURE 8.1

Five-year average annual compound excess (deficient) return All Stocks net operating cash flow to price decile 1 minus All Stocks, January 1, 1964, to December 31, 2009

LARGE STOCKS ARE LESS PROFITABLE, LESS VOLATILE

Tables 8.6 through 8.10 summarize the results for the Large Stock universe. The original $10,000 invested in the decile of stocks with the lowest price-to-cash flow from Large Stocks in 1963 grew to $3,470,690 at the end of 2009, a compound return of 13.56 percent a year. That's five times the $872,861 you'd earn from $10,000 invested in the Large Stocks universe, where the compound return was 10.20 percent per year. The standard deviation of return of 16.22 percent is slightly lower than the Large Stocks' 16.50 percent, and lower than the low price-to-cash flow stocks from the All Stocks category. The Sharpe ratio for the low price-to-cash flow stocks from Large Stocks was .53, compared to .32 for the Large Stocks universe.

T A B L E   8.6

Summary Annual Return and Risk Results Data: Large Stocks Net Operating Cash Flow to Price Decile 1 and Large Stocks, January 1, 1964, to December 31, 2009

	Large Stocks net operating cash flow to price decile 1	Large Stocks
Arithmetic average	15.05%	11.72%
Geometric average	13.56%	10.20%
Median return	18.93%	17.20%
Standard deviation	16.22%	16.50%
Upside deviation	10.69%	9.70%
Downside deviation	11.63%	11.85%
Tracking error	8.02	0.00
Number of positive periods	341	332
Number of negative periods	211	220
Maximum peak-to-trough decline	−62.15%	−53.77%
Beta	0.86	1.00
T-statistic (m = 0)	5.90	4.58
Sharpe ratio (Rf = 5%)	0.53	0.32
Sortino ratio (MAR = 10%)	0.31	0.02
$10,000 becomes	$3,470,690	$872,861
Minimum 1-year return	−56.00%	−46.91%
Maximum 1-year return	62.39%	68.96%
Minimum 3-year return	−16.60%	−15.89%
Maximum 3-year return	37.30%	33.12%
Minimum 5-year return	−1.90%	−5.82%
Maximum 5-year return	31.70%	28.95%
Minimum 7-year return	−0.36%	−4.15%
Maximum 7-year return	25.59%	22.83%
Minimum 10-year return	2.54%	−0.15%
Maximum 10-year return	21.44%	19.57%
Minimum expected return*	−17.39%	−21.28%
Maximum expected return†	47.49%	44.72%

* Minimum expected return is arithmetic return minus 2 times the standard deviation.
† Maximum expected return is arithmetic return plus 2 times the standard deviation

Table 8.7 summarizes the Large Stocks base rates. The base rates for the low price-to-cash flow stocks from the Large Stocks universe are uniformly high. Over all rolling five-year periods, the decile with the lowest price-to-cash flow stocks from the Large Stocks group beat the universe 75 percent of the time. Returning to the concept of using the long-term base rates as an indicator of what your odds are for any five-year period, this would tell us that we have a 75 percent chance of beating the Large Stocks universe if we consistently stick with Large Stocks with low price-to-cash flow ratios. Again using the average over- and underperformance from all rolling five-year periods, we see that if

TABLE   8.7

Base Rates for Large Stocks Net Operating Cash Flow to Price Decile 1 and Large Stocks, January 1, 1964, to December 31, 2009

Item	Large Stocks net operating cash flow to price decile 1 beat Large Stocks	Percent	Average annual excess return
Single-year return	354 out of 541	65%	3.31%
Rolling 3-year compound return	371 out of 517	72%	3.54%
Rolling 5-year compound return	371 out of 493	75%	3.59%
Rolling 7-year compound return	396 out of 469	84%	3.55%
Rolling 10-year compound return	415 out of 433	96%	3.48%

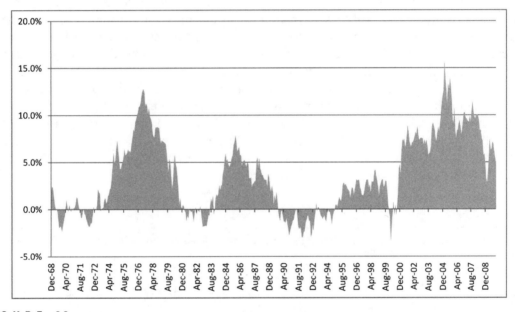

FIGURE   8.2

Five-year average compound excess (deficient) return Large Stocks net operating cash flow to price decile 1 minus Large Stocks, January 1, 1964, to December 31, 2009

we were unlucky and found ourselves in the 25 percent of the time that low price-to-cash flow Large Stocks underperform the Large Stocks universe, we would, on average, have a portfolio whose cumulative value was 8 percent less than one invested in the Large Stocks universe. On the other hand, if the five-year period was among the 75 percent of observations where low price-to-cash flow Large Stocks outperformed the Large Stocks universe, we would, on average, have a portfolio worth 41 percent *more* than one invested in the Large Stocks universe. The *worst* five-year period for the decile of stocks from Large Stocks with the lowest price-to-cash flows versus Large Stocks was the five years ending February 2000, where the low price-to-cash flow group gained a cumulative 144 percent versus a cumulative gain of 180 percent for the Large Stocks universe. On an average annual compound return basis, the low price-to-cash flow group earned 19.56 percent per year, and the Large Stocks universe earned 22.86 percent per year. The *best* five years were the five years ending October 2007, where the low price-to-cash flow group gained a cumulative 292 percent versus a gain of 149 percent for Large Stocks. The annual average compound returns were 31.4 percent a year for the low price-to-cash flow stocks versus 19.99 percent for the Large Stocks universe. Sticking with this strategy has very compelling odds indeed.

WORST-CASE SCENARIOS AND BEST AND WORST RETURNS

Looking at Tables 8.3 and 8.8, we see that the worst-case scenario for low price-to-cash flow stocks from both the All Stocks and Large Stocks universes came in the bear market of 2007 through early 2009, with the low price-to-cash flow stocks from All Stocks losing 61 percent and the low price-to-cash flow stocks from Large Stocks falling 62 percent. Like several of our other value factors, low price-to-cash flow ratios suffered more during the bear market of 2007–2009 than in previous bear markets. For both All Stocks and Large Stocks, the decline was much less pronounced in the bear market of 1973–1974, where each dropped less than 40 percent from peak to trough. The low price-to-cash flow stocks from All Stocks had seven declines exceeding 20 percent, whereas the low price-to-cash flow stocks from Large Stocks had six declines of more than 20 percent, making them the better choice for the more risk-averse investor.

T A B L E   8.8

Worst-Case Scenarios: All 20 Percent or Greater Declines for Large Stocks Net Operating Cash Flow Price Decile 1, January 1, 1964, to December 31, 2009

Peak date	Peak index value	Trough date	Trough index value	Recovery date	Decline (%)	Decline duration	Recovery duration
Jan–69	2.04	Jun–70	1.27	Nov–72	−37.87%	17	29
Nov–72	2.14	Sep–74	1.58	May–75	−26.24%	22	8
Aug–87	23.54	Nov–87	17.12	Jan–89	−27.30%	3	14
Sep–89	29.12	Oct–90	20.47	Oct–91	−29.71%	13	12
May–01	156.58	Sep–02	117.33	Aug–03	−25.06%	16	11
Oct–07	478.28	Feb–09	181.00	N/A	−62.15%	16	N/A
Average					−34.72%	14.5	14.8

Tables 8.4, 8.5, 8.9, and 8.10 summarize the best- and worst-case scenarios for both All Stocks and Large Stocks for various holding periods. Investors with five-year time horizons should be indifferent to selecting stocks from All Stocks or Large Stocks—the worst five years for the stocks with the lowest price-to-cash flow from All

Stocks were those ending November 1973, shrinking $10,000 to $8,215, whereas the worst five years for stocks with the lowest price-to-cash flows from Large Stocks were those ending February 2009, shrinking $10,000 invested five years earlier to $9,085. Stretching the horizon to 10 years, we see that the lowest price-to-cash flow stocks from All Stocks do better than those from Large Stocks, with the worst 10-year return—earned during the 10 years ending September 1974—turned $10,000 into $17,736. For Large Stocks, the worst 10 years for the lowest price-to-cash flow stocks was also for the 10 years ending September 1974, when the $10,000 invested earlier grew to $12,852.

T A B L E   8.9

Best and Worst Average Annual Compound Returns for Monthly Data, January 1, 1964, to December 31, 2009

For any	1-year period	3-year period	5-year period	7-year period	10-year period
Large Stocks net operating cash flow to price decile 1 minimum compound return	−56.00%	−16.60%	−1.90%	−0.36%	2.54%
Large Stocks net operating cash flow to price decile 1 maximum compound return	62.39%	37.30%	31.70%	25.59%	21.44%
Large Stocks minimum compound return	−46.91%	−15.89%	−5.82%	−4.15%	−0.15%
Large Stocks maximum compound return	68.96%	33.12%	28.95%	22.83%	19.57%
Large Stocks net operating cash flow to price decile 10 minimum compound return	−60.95%	−37.26%	−15.89%	−7.31%	−8.54%
Large Stocks net operating cash flow to price decile 10 maximum compound return	79.14%	39.67%	28.37%	22.59%	19.16%

T A B L E   8.10

Terminal Value of $10,000 Invested for Best and Worst Average Annual Compound Returns for Monthly Data, January 1, 1964, to December 31, 2009

For any	1-year period	3-year period	5-year period	7-year period	10-year period
Large Stocks net operating cash flow to price decile 1 minimum $10,000 value	$4,400	$5,800	$9,085	$9,749	$12,852
Large Stocks net operating cash flow to price decile 1 maximum $10,000 value	$16,239	$25,885	$39,628	$49,276	$69,780
Large Stocks minimum $10,000 value	$5,309	$5,951	$7,409	$7,434	$9,848
Large Stocks maximum $10,000 value	$16,896	$23,591	$35,656	$42,189	$59,747
Large Stocks net operating cash flow to price decile 10 minimum $10,000 value	$3,905	$2,470	$4,209	$5,878	$4,094
Large Stocks net operating cash flow to price decile 10 maximum $10,000 value	$17,914	$27,248	$34,858	$41,597	$57,716

HIGH PRICE-TO-CASH FLOW RATIOS ARE DANGEROUS

As with the other value factors, we see that stocks with high price-to-cash flow ratios are usually bad investments. Tables 8.11 through 8.13 summarize the data, and Tables 8.4 and 8.5 show the best- and worst-case scenarios for high price-to-cash flow stocks.

T A B L E 8.11

Summary Annual Return and Risk Results Data: All Stocks Net Operating Cash Flow to Price Decile 10 and All Stocks, January 1, 1964, to December 31, 2009

	All Stocks net operating cash flow to price decile 10	All Stocks
Arithmetic average	7.15%	13.26%
Geometric average	3.49%	11.22%
Median return	12.66%	17.16%
Standard deviation	26.09%	18.99%
Upside deviation	15.82%	10.98%
Downside deviation	18.70%	13.90%
Tracking error	10.71	0.00
Number of positive periods	312	329
Number of negative periods	240	223
Maximum peak-to-trough decline	−86.49%	−55.54%
Beta	1.28	1.00
T-statistic (m = 0)	1.80	4.47
Sharpe ratio (Rf = 5%)	−0.06	0.33
Sortino ratio (MAR = 10%)	−0.35	0.09
$10,000 becomes	$48,471	$1,329,513
Minimum 1-year return	−58.46%	−46.49%
Maximum 1-year return	126.83%	84.19%
Minimum 3-year return	−43.45%	−18.68%
Maximum 3-year return	36.00%	31.49%
Minimum 5-year return	−19.26%	−9.91%
Maximum 5-year return	25.37%	27.66%
Minimum 7-year return	−12.72%	−6.32%
Maximum 7-year return	18.35%	23.77%
Minimum 10-year return	−11.15%	1.01%
Maximum 10-year return	14.23%	22.05%
Minimum expected return*	−45.04%	−24.73%
Maximum expected return†	59.33%	51.24%

* Minimum expected return is arithmetic return minus 2 times the standard deviation.
† Maximum expected return is arithmetic return plus 2 times the standard deviation.

The decile of stocks from All Stocks with the highest price-to-cash flow ratios had eight calendar years in which they underperformed All Stocks by more than 15 percent, but only three years in which they beat All Stocks by 15 percent or more. They also exhibit a concentration of good returns in brief periods of time, characterized by very speculative market environments. Generally, great relative performance in any one year is followed by a plunge in the next. In the very speculative year of 1967, the high price-to-cash flow stocks soared by 73.21 percent, doing 28.26 percent better than All Stocks, but then they went on to dramatically underperform over the next three years. And the several years that followed 1999's stellar return of 69.95 percent should serve as fair warning to any investor tempted to forget the odds and buy the hottest story stocks. In 2000, the decile with the highest price-to-cash flow stocks from All Stocks lost 41 percent; in 2001 it lost 14 percent; and in 2002 it lost 47 percent.

The same is true over the long term. The $10,000 invested on December 31, 1963, in the decile of stocks with the highest price-to-cash flow ratios from All Stocks grew to just $48,471 by the end of 2009, an average annual compound gain of just 3.49 percent. That return is dwarfed by a simple investment in the All Stocks universe. The Sharpe ratio is a dismal –.06. What's more, an investment in U.S. T-bills did vastly better than investing in the decile of stocks from All Stocks with the highest price-to-cash flow ratios: $10,000 invested in T-bills on December 31, 1963, was worth $120,778 at the end of 2009, an average annual compound return of 5.57 percent.

As Table 8.12 shows, all base rates were uniformly negative, with the high price-to-cash flow stocks from All Stocks beating the All Stocks universe in just 6 percent of all rolling five-year periods and 2 percent of all rolling ten-year periods. What's worse is that high price-to-cash flow stocks from All Stocks posted an average annual compound loss of 11.15 percent for the 10 years ending February 2009. Had you invested $10,000 10 years earlier, it would have been worth just $3,065 at the end of February 2009. Figure 8.3 shows the five-year average annual compound excess (or, in this case, mostly deficient) return for decile 10 minus the return for the All Stocks universe. Table 8.13 shows all declines greater than 20 percent for the stocks from All Stocks with the highest price-to-cash flows.

T A B L E 8.12

Base Rates for All Stocks Net Operating Cash Flow to Price Decile 10 and All Stocks, January 1, 1964, to December 31, 2009

Item	All Stocks net opearating cash flow to decile 10 beat All Stocks	Percent	Average annual excess return
Single-year return	163 out of 541	30%	−5.53%
Rolling 3-year compound return	77 out of 517	15%	−7.43%
Rolling 5-year compound return	29 out of 493	6%	−7.99%
Rolling 7-year compound return	30 out of 469	6%	−8.29%
Rolling 10-year compound return	10 out of 433	2%	−8.48%

T A B L E   8.13

Worst-Case Scenarios: All 20 Percent or Greater Declines for All Stocks Net Operating Cash Flow to Price Decile 10, January 1, 1964, to December 31, 2009

Peak date	Peak index value	Trough date	Trough index value	Recovery date	Decline (%)	Decline duration	Recovery duration
Apr–66	1.65	Oct–66	1.30	Jan–67	−21.14%	6	3
Dec–68	3.10	Sep–74	1.06	Jul–80	−65.79%	69	70
Nov–80	4.32	Jul–82	2.66	Jan–83	−38.38%	20	6
Jun–83	5.85	Jul–84	3.61	Jul–87	−38.21%	13	36
Aug–87	6.03	Nov–87	3.74	May–89	−38.06%	3	18
Sep–89	6.38	Oct–90	3.92	Oct–91	−38.44%	13	12
Feb–92	7.34	Aug–92	5.75	Oct–93	−21.64%	6	14
Jan–94	7.81	Jan–95	6.22	Aug–95	−20.41%	12	7
May–96	9.49	Apr–97	7.00	Sep–97	−26.28%	11	5
Apr–98	10.10	Aug–98	6.25	Apr–99	−38.08%	4	8
Feb–00	19.72	Feb–09	2.66	N/A	−86.49%	108	N/A
Average					−39.36%	24.09	17.9

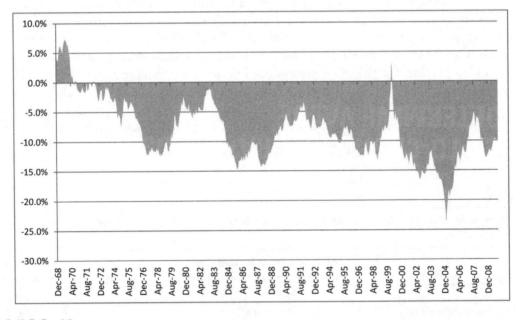

F I G U R E   8.3

Five-year average annual compound excess (deficient) return All Stocks net operating cash flow to price decile 10 minus All Stocks, January 1, 1964, to December 31, 2009

LARGE STOCKS HIT, TOO

Large Stocks with high price-to-cash flow ratios fared little better. Tables 8.14 through 8.16 summarize the results. Here, $10,000 invested on December 31, 1963, grew to $165,494 by the end of 2009, four times less than what you'd have earned from an investment in the Large Stocks universe. The Sharpe ratio was a paltry .06. As Table 8.15 shows, all base rates were negative, with the group beating the Large Stocks universe 18 percent of all rolling five-year periods and 7 percent of all rolling ten-year periods.

T A B L E 8.14

Summary Annual Return and Risk Results Data: Large Stocks Net Operating Cash Flow to Price Decile 10 and Large Stocks, January 1, 1964, to December 31, 2009

	Large Stocks net operating cash flow to price decile 10	Large Stocks
Arithmetic average	8.72%	11.72%
Geometric average	6.29%	10.20%
Median return	15.33%	17.20%
Standard deviation	21.08%	16.50%
Upside deviation	12.44%	9.70%
Downside deviation	15.82%	11.85%
Tracking error	9.58	0.00
Number of positive periods	312	332
Number of negative periods	240	220
Maximum peak-to-trough decline	−77.33%	−53.77%
Beta	1.15	1.00
T-statistic (m = 0)	2.70	4.58
Sharpe ratio (Rf = 5%)	0.06	0.32
Sortino ratio (MAR = 10%)	−0.23	0.02
$10,000 becomes	$165,494	$872,861
Minimum 1-year return	−60.95%	−46.91%
Maximum 1-year return	79.14%	68.96%
Minimum 3-year return	−37.26%	−15.89%
Maximum 3-year return	39.67%	33.12%
Minimum 5-year return	−15.89%	−5.82%
Maximum 5-year return	28.37%	28.95%
Minimum 7-year return	−7.31%	−4.15%
Maximum 7-year return	22.59%	22.83%
Minimum 10-year return	−8.54%	−0.15%
Maximum 10-year return	19.16%	19.57%
Minimum expected return*	−33.45%	−21.28%
Maximum expected return†	50.89%	44.72%

* Minimum expected return is arithmetic return minus 2 times the standard deviation.
† Maximum expected return is arithmetic return plus 2 times the standard deviation.

T A B L E   8.15

Base Rates for Large Stocks Net Operating Cash Flow to Price Decile 10 and Large Stocks, January 1, 1964, to
December 31, 2009

Item	Large Stocks net operating cash flow to price decile 10 beat Large Stocks	Percent	Average annual excess return
Single-year return	228 out of 541	42%	−2.36%
Rolling 3-year compound return	134 out of 517	26%	−3.44%
Rolling 5-year compound return	90 out of 493	18%	−3.98%
Rolling 7-year compound return	53 out of 469	11%	−4.33%
Rolling 10-year compound return	31 out of 433	7%	−4.62%

Like many of our findings concerning pricey stocks with rich valuations, focusing on the returns of Large Stocks with high price-to-cash flow ratios helps you understand why scrutinizing long-term results is the only way to understand the value of a strategy.

This book first came out in 1996 and offered the same advice concerning high price-to-cash flow stocks—avoid them. Yet, if you had read the book then and actually *watched* your favorite stocks with high price-to-cash flow ratios in real time, you might have been inclined to think that while those types of stocks performed poorly historically, they were doing very well in the boom markets of the late 1990s. From the end of 1996 through September 2000 (when high price-to-cash flow stocks from Large Stocks had their best 5-year performance), you would have seen the highest price-to-cash flow stocks from Large Stocks gain nearly 23 percent a year, compared to a gain of 18.65 percent for Large Stocks. The evidence from this book might have appeared to ring hollow. Yet if you understood the much more important long-term data, you would have resolutely avoided them and in so doing, missed getting nearly wiped out over the next few years.

As Table 8.16 shows, between 2000 and 2002, Large Stocks with the highest price-to-cash flows plunged 77 percent, nearly as badly as the market decline during the great crash of 1929–1932! Yet even if the long-term performance data didn't dissuade you, the

T A B L E   8.16

Worst-Case Scenarios: All 20 Percent or Greater Declines for Large Stocks Net Operating Cash Flow to
Price Decile 10, January 1, 1964, to December 31, 2009

Peak date	Peak index value	Trough date	Trough index value	Recovery date	Decline (%)	Decline duration	Recovery duration
Dec–69	2.36	Jun–70	1.58	Apr–71	−32.98%	6	10
Dec–72	3.26	Sep–74	1.29	Nov–80	−60.29%	21	74
May–81	3.49	Jul–82	2.63	Nov–82	−24.66%	14	4
Jun–83	4.83	Jul–84	3.55	Jan–86	−26.50%	13	18
Sep–87	7.16	Nov–87	4.92	May–89	−31.24%	2	18
May–90	8.11	Oct–90	6.08	Apr–91	−25.03%	5	6
Jun–98	23.78	Aug–98	18.80	Dec–98	−20.96%	2	4
Feb–00	42.86	Sep–02	9.72	N/A	−77.33%	31	N/A
Average					−37.37%	11.75	19.14

base rates might have. When we review the base rates for high price-to-cash flow stocks found in Tables 8.12 and 8.15, we see that you have only a 7 percent chance to outperform Large Stocks in any 10-year period. Figure 8.4 shows the five-year average annual compound excess (or, in this case, mostly deficient) return for decile 10 minus the return for the Large Stocks universe.

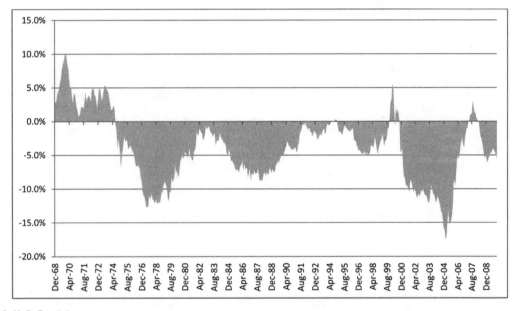

FIGURE 8.4

Five-year average annual compound excess (deficient) return Large Stocks net operating cash flow to price decile 10 minus Large Stocks, January 1, 1964, to December 31, 2009

WORST-CASE SCENARIO AND BEST AND WORST RETURNS

Unlike the low price-to-cash flow stocks, returns here are abysmal. As Table 8.13 illustrates, high price-to-cash flow stocks from All Stocks lost more than 20 percent from peak to trough more than 11 times, with bear market years doing particular damage. In the bear market of the early 1970s, the high price-to-cash flow stocks from All Stocks lost 66 percent of their value, and in the most recent bear market of 2000–2002, they lost a whopping 86 percent from top to bottom, worse than the decline for the S&P 500 between 1929 and 1932. As of March 10, 2010, they still have not recovered from this drawdown. Their best- and worst-case returns from the last 40 years showed them well behind All Stocks and dramatically behind the stocks from All Stocks with the lowest price-to-cash flows. Someone investing for a 10-year period and getting a return similar to the *worst* 10-year return over the prior 40 years would see $10,000 dwindle to a little more than $3,000. Tables 8.4 and 8.5 have the returns for all holding periods.

Large Stocks fared little better. As Table 8.16 illustrates, the high price-to-cash flow stocks from Large Stocks declined by more than 20 percent eight times over the last

46 years and performed abysmally in the bear markets of 1973–1974 and 2000–2002, where they lost 60 and 77 percent, respectively. The best- and worst-case scenarios for the group lag behind the broad Large Stocks universe and have very little to recommend them—with the dangerous exception of performing well during speculative market frenzies. Tables 8.9 and 8.10 feature best and worst returns for all rolling holding periods. Tables 8.17 and 8.18 feature the average annual compound return by decade for each group from All Stocks and Large Stocks.

T A B L E   8.17

Average Annual Compound Rates of Return by Decade

	1960s*	1970s	1980s	1990s	2000s†
All Stocks net operating cash flow to price decile 1	15.86%	13.64%	19.27%	16.62%	15.78%
All Stocks net operating cash flow to price decile 10	16.70%	0.96%	7.79%	9.36%	−10.32%
All Stocks	13.36%	7.56%	16.78%	15.35%	4.39%

* Returns for January 1, 1964, to December 31, 1969.
† Returns for January 1, 2000, to December 31, 2009

T A B L E   8.18

Average Annual Compound Rates of Return by Decade

	1960s*	1970s	1980s	1990s	2000s†
Large Stocks net operating cash flow to price decile 1	6.89%	11.89%	19.71%	16.22%	10.79%
Large Stocks net operating cash flow to price decile 10	15.40%	0.33%	12.51%	17.69%	−8.54%
Large Stocks	8.16%	6.65%	17.34%	16.38%	2.42%

* Returns for January 1, 1964, to December 31, 1969.
† Returns for January 1, 2000, to December 31, 2009.

DECILES

The full decile analysis of All Stocks by price-to-cash flow ratios tells the same story as it does with our other value ratios. Stocks in the lowest deciles have *much* higher returns than stocks in the highest deciles. As we move from the lowest decile to the highest, risk skyrockets and returns plummet. As shown in Figure 8.5 and Table 8.19, the decile with the stocks with the lowest price-to-cash flows turned $10,000 invested in 1963 into $10,187,545 at the end of 2009, whereas the those in the top decile grew to just $48,471— less than T-bills. What's more, the highest decile stocks had *a significantly greater risk* than the lowest, with the highest price-to-cash flow stocks having a standard deviation of return of 26.09 percent, and the lowest price-to-cash flow stocks having a 18.47 percent return. Downside risk was also significantly lower for the low price-to-cash flow stocks. Looking at the graph in Figure 8.5, you can see that as you pay more for every dollar of cash flow, your returns decline until you get to the most expensive stocks by price-to-cash flow, where your returns underperform T-bills.

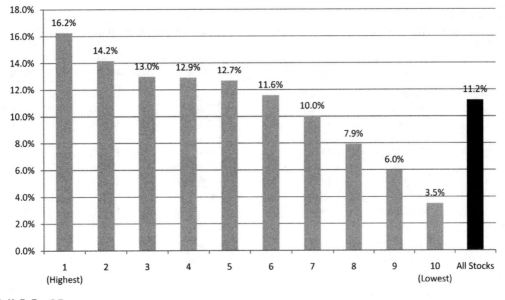

FIGURE 8.5

Average annual compound return by net operating cash flow to price decile, All Stocks universe, January 1, 1964, to December 31, 2009

TABLE 8.19

Summary Results for Net Operating Cash Flow to Price Decile Analysis of All Stocks Universe, January 1, 1964, to December 31, 2009

Decile	$10,000 grows to	Average return	Compound return	Standard deviation	Sharpe ratio
1 (highest)	$10,187,545	18.23%	16.25%	18.47%	0.61
2	$4,424,631	15.60%	14.16%	15.85%	0.58
3	$2,730,088	14.45%	12.97%	16.12%	0.49
4	$2,651,411	14.47%	12.90%	16.61%	0.48
5	$2,416,830	14.27%	12.67%	16.75%	0.46
6	$1,538,825	13.26%	11.57%	17.31%	0.38
7	$805,018	11.97%	10.01%	18.74%	0.27
8	$332,293	10.49%	7.91%	21.59%	0.13
9	$144,235	9.10%	5.97%	23.96%	0.04
10 (lowest)	$48,471	7.15%	3.49%	26.09%	−0.06
All Stocks	$1,329,513	13.26%	11.22%	18.99%	0.33

We see a similar progression with Large Stocks, although it doesn't have the perfect symmetry exhibited by All Stocks. Here, the decile made up of the stocks from Large Stocks with the lowest price-to-cash flows turned the $10,000 into $3,470,690 by the end of 2009, nearly $2.6 million more than an investment in the Large Stocks universe. Tables 8.19 and 8.20, as well as Figures 8.5 and 8.6 summarize the results.

T A B L E   8.20

Summary Results for Net Operating Cash Flow to Price Decile Analysis of Large Stocks Universe, January 1, 1964, to December 31, 2009

Decile	$10,000 grows to	Average return	Compound return	Standard deviation	Sharpe ratio
1 (highest)	$3,470,690	15.05%	13.56%	16.22%	0.53
2	$1,361,303	12.45%	11.27%	14.56%	0.43
3	$796,263	11.19%	9.98%	14.77%	0.34
4	$663,741	10.85%	9.55%	15.35%	0.30
5	$984,904	11.86%	10.49%	15.64%	0.35
6	$787,794	11.35%	9.96%	15.87%	0.31
7	$559,672	10.59%	9.14%	16.25%	0.25
8	$316,980	9.40%	7.80%	17.15%	0.16
9	$228,099	9.09%	7.03%	19.30%	0.11
10 (lowest)	$165,494	8.72%	6.29%	21.08%	0.06
Large Stocks	$872,861	11.72%	10.20%	16.50%	0.32

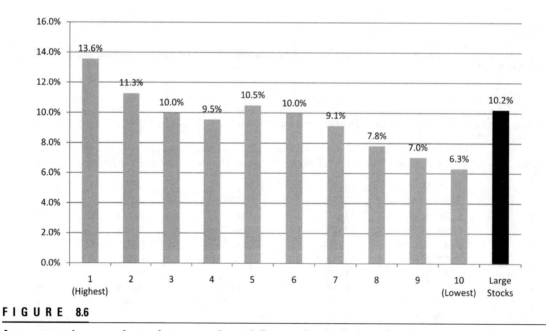

F I G U R E   8.6

Average annual compound return by net operating cash flow to price decile, Large Stocks universe, January 1, 1964, to December 31, 2009

IMPLICATIONS

The odds strongly favor stocks with low price-to-cash flow ratios. Unless there are additional compelling factors (e.g., the stock is selected by a successful growth model's criteria which can absorb some high price-to-cash flow risk), you should avoid stocks with the highest price-to-cash flow ratios and concentrate on the lower end of the price-to-cash flow spectrum.

CHAPTER EIGHT CASE STUDY

WHAT ABOUT PRICE-TO-FREE CASH FLOW?

Many analysts have taken to measuring a stock's price-to-free cash flow as a better measurement than net cash flow, reasoning that the most important number for a company is the cash flow that the firm is free to distribute to its shareholders either in the form of an increase in cash dividends or for buying back shares in the open market. We define free cash flow as net cash flow minus capital expenditures, dividends, and preferred dividends. It is essentially the money left over from operations after accounting for all of the firm's other obligations. Let's see how much different they are by testing net cash flow against free cash flow. Table 8CS.1 shows the results for an investment in the best deciles for both net and free cash flow between December 31, 1963, and December 31, 2009.

T A B L E   8.CS1

Summary Annual Return and Risk Results Data: All Stocks Net Operating Cash Flow to Price Decile 1 and All Stocks Free Cash Flow to Price Decile 1, January 1, 1964, to December 31, 2009

	All Stocks net operating cash flow to price decile 1	All Stocks free cash flow to price decile 1
Arithmetic average	18.23%	17.53%
Geometric average	16.25%	15.49%
Median return	22.64%	22.10%
Standard deviation	18.47%	18.75%
Upside deviation	12.15%	11.98%
Downside deviation	14.04%	14.14%
Tracking error	7.63	7.21
Number of positive periods	357	359
Number of negative periods	195	193
Maximum peak-to-trough decline	−60.87%	−61.66%
Beta	0.89	0.91
T-statistic (m = 0)	6.19	5.88
Sharpe ratio (Rf = 5%)	0.61	0.56
Sortino ratio (MAR = 10%)	0.45	0.39
$10,000 becomes	$10,187,545	$7,532,596

(continued on next page)

TABLE 8.CS1

**Summary Annual Return and Risk Results Data: All Stocks Net Operating Cash Flow to Price Decile 1 and
All Stocks Free Cash Flow to Price Decile 1, January 1, 1964, to December 31, 2009** *(Continued)*

	All Stocks net operating cash flow to price decile 1	All Stocks free cash flow to price decile 1
Minimum 1-year return	−54.24%	−51.68%
Maximum 1-year return	89.55%	83.93%
Minimum 3-year return	−18.63%	−20.76%
Maximum 3-year return	45.20%	41.35%
Minimum 5-year return	−3.86%	−7.12%
Maximum 5-year return	32.98%	36.33%
Minimum 7-year return	−0.39%	−3.81%
Maximum 7-year return	27.49%	29.68%
Minimum 10-year return	5.90%	3.58%
Maximum 10-year return	25.86%	27.18%
Minimum expected return*	−18.70%	−19.96%
Maximum expected return†	55.16%	55.02%

* Minimum expected return is arithmetic return minus 2 times the standard deviation.

† Maximum expected return is arithmetic return plus 2 times the standard deviation.

For these 46 years, net cash flow beats free cash flow by 76 basis points per year, turning $10,000 invested on December 31, 1963, into $10,187,545, an average annual compound return of 16.25 percent, compared with the $7,532,596 you'd have had you invested in the best decile by free cash flow over the same period. As Tables 8CS.2 and 8CS.3 show, the base rates for net cash flow are also better, if only marginally. Thus, when used as a single factor, you are best off sticking with the traditional net cash flow number. We learn later in this book, however, that sometimes free cash flow works better in multifactor models where the interaction effect with other factors comes into play.

TABLE 8.CS2

Base Rates for All Stocks Free Cash Flow to Price Decile 1 and All Stocks, January 1, 1968, to December 31, 2009

Item	All Stocks free cash flow to price decile 1 beat All Stocks	Percent	Average annual excess return
Single-year return	355 out of 493	72%	4.37%
Rolling 3-year compound return	375 out of 469	80%	4.62%
Rolling 5-year compound return	407 out of 445	91%	4.79%
Rolling 7-year compound return	414 out of 421	98%	4.87%
Rolling 10-year compound return	385 out of 385	100%	4.66%

T A B L E   8.CS3

Base Rates for All Stocks Net Operating Cash Flow to Price Decile 1 and All Stocks, January 1, 1968, to December 31, 2009

Item	All Stocks net operating cash flow to price decile 1 beat All Stocks	Percent	Average annual excess return
Single-year return	356 out of 493	72%	4.76%
Rolling 3-year compound return	401 out of 469	86%	5.03%
Rolling 5-year compound return	401 out of 445	90%	5.07%
Rolling 7-year compound return	413 out of 421	98%	4.94%
Rolling 10-year compound return	384 out of 385	100%	4.51%

9
C H A P T E R

PRICE-TO-SALES RATIOS

If you do not change direction, you may end up where you are heading.

—Lao Tzu

In the original edition of *What Works on Wall Street*, I found that the single-best value factor was a stock's price-to-sales ratio (PSR). With our new compositing methodology, we see that this is no longer the case. While PSR continues to perform well as both an individual factor and in combination with other factors in multifactor models, EBITDA-to-enterprise value has displaced it as the best-performing single factor when you include all monthly data in the analysis. The unseating of PSR as the top value factor can be attributed to two things: (1) By analyzing the price-to-sales ratio's composited decile data, as opposed to simply reviewing the 50 lowest price-to-sales ratios stocks on a single December rebalance cycle, we broaden the scope of analysis. That broader scope improves the results of certain factors like PE ratio, where focusing on all available months yields better results than simply looking at the 50 stocks with the lowest PE ratios. (2) Two very bad years for the price-to-sales ratio in 2007 and 2008.

One thing has troubled me about all single-factor returns is the speed with which a few years can change the results of our findings. While directionally the results remain the same—stocks with low PEs, low EBITDA/EV low price-to-cash flows and low PSRs do vastly better than those with high valuations—it is still troubling to see a few bad years change the relative return of a factor over a 46-year period. When we were still using 50-stock portfolios in the last edition of this book as the basis for our research, we saw that between 1963 and December 31, 2003 (using monthly data), the 50 stocks with the lowest PSRs compounded at 15.19 percent per year and had a maximum drawdown of 46.93. The 50 stocks with the lowest PE ratios compounded at 14.64 percent and had a maximum drawdown of 44.81 percent. Convention holds that after you have 25 years or more of data, you can safely infer how the factor with those data will perform in the future. From 1963 to 2003 makes up 40 years of data. Yet over the next six years, this convention has been upended—since 2003 the 50 stocks with the lowest PSRs compounded at 7.29 percent and their maximum drawdown grew to –75.04 percent, whereas the 50 stocks with the lowest PE ratios earned 14.26 percent a year while their maximum decline climbed to –64.42 percent. Granted, we faced market conditions more similar to the crash of 1929–1932 than we had ever seen previously, but the ability of a single factor like PSR—especially concentrated into the 50 names with the lowest ratios—to be so affected by six years led me to conclude that we must work toward a more broadly inclusive composited value factor that is less subject to violent changes over a few short years. We consider several of these later in the book. For now, let's look at the results for PSR alone.

A stock's PSR is similar to its price-to-earnings ratio, but it measures the price of the company against annual sales instead of earnings. Like investors who favor low PE stocks, investors buy low PSR stocks because they believe they're getting a bargain. Ken Fisher popularized the use of the PSR in his 1984 book *Super Stocks*. In the book, he says that a stock's PSR is, "An almost perfect measure of popularity," warning that only hope and hype will increase the price of a stock with a high PSR.

I'll again look at both the decile of lowest PSR stocks and the decile of the highest PSR stocks from both the All Stocks and Large Stocks universes. As with the other ratios, I'll also look at how the two universes stack up when ranked by all price-to-sales deciles. All accounting data are time-lagged to avoid look-ahead bias and the portfolios are rebalanced annually. Finally, because of Compustat's ranking function, I rank stocks by the decile of the *highest* sales/price ratios, the inverse of the price-to-sale ratio. I'll refer to them, however, as high and low PSR stocks throughout the chapter.

THE RESULTS

As Table 9.1 shows, $10,000 invested on December 31, 1963, in the decile of the lowest PSR stocks from the All Stocks universe grew to $5,044,457 by December 31, 2009, a compound return of 14.49 percent. This is four times the $1,329,513 earned from the $10,000 invested in the All Stocks universe. As Table 9.2 shows, the strategy also performs well over time, with the low PSR stocks from All Stocks beating the universe in 89 percent of all rolling 10-year periods. The low PSR stocks also do well on a risk-adjusted basis, with a Sharpe ratio of .46. Table 9.1 summarizes the returns of low PSR stocks from the All Stocks universe, and Table 9.2 compares the base rates for the strategy with All Stocks.

Using the base rates as odds for winning over all the various holding periods, we see that for all rolling five-year periods, we could expect to beat the All Stocks universe 75 percent of the time. If you look at all of the times historically where the low PSR group beat

TABLE 9.1

Summary Annual Return and Risk Results Data: All Stocks Sales to Price Decile 1 and All Stocks, January 1, 1964, to December 31, 2009

	All Stocks Sales/price decile 1	All Stocks
Arithmetic average	16.95%	13.26%
Geometric average	14.49%	11.22%
Median return	20.06%	17.16%
Standard deviation	20.68%	18.99%
Upside deviation	13.41%	10.98%
Downside deviation	15.38%	13.90%
Tracking error	7.68	0.00
Number of positive periods	343	329
Number of negative periods	209	223
Maximum peak-to-trough decline	−65.98%	−55.54%
Beta	1.01	1.00
T-statistic (m = 0)	5.17	4.47
Sharpe ratio (Rf = 5%)	0.46	0.33
Sortino ratio (MAR = 10%)	0.29	0.09
$10,000 becomes	$5,044,457	$1,329,513
Minimum 1-year return	−54.83%	−46.49%
Maximum 1-year return	98.93%	84.19%
Minimum 3-year return	−22.44%	−18.68%
Maximum 3-year return	46.36%	31.49%
Minimum 5-year return	−9.51%	−9.91%
Maximum 5-year return	33.53%	27.66%
Minimum 7-year return	−4.58%	−6.32%
Maximum 7-year return	28.58%	23.77%
Minimum 10-year return	4.05%	1.01%
Maximum 10-year return	26.95%	22.05%
Minimum expected return*	−24.41%	−24.73%
Maximum expected return†	58.32%	51.24%

* Minimum expected return is arithmetic return minus 2 times the standard deviation.

† Maximum expected return is arithmetic return plus 2 times the standard deviation.

TABLE 9.2

Base Rates for All Stocks Sales to Price Decile 1 and All Stocks, January 1, 1964, to December 31, 2009

Item	All Stocks sales to price decile 1 beat "All Stocks"	Percent	Average annual excess return
Single-year return	368 out of 541	68%	3.58%
Rolling 3-year compound return	371 out of 517	72%	3.03%
Rolling 5-year compound return	372 out of 493	75%	2.94%
Rolling 7-year compound return	374 out of 469	80%	2.83%
Rolling 10-year compound return	386 out of 433	89%	2.70%

All Stocks, you can see that, on average, it did 40 percent better on a cumulative basis than the All Stocks universe. For the 25 percent of the time that the low PSR group was underperforming All Stocks, the differential is much smaller, with the low PSR group, on average, losing to All Stocks by a cumulative 14 percent.

For all rolling five-year periods, the best that the low PSR stocks performed relative to the All Stocks universe were the five years ending February 2005, when the low PSR stocks earned a cumulative gain of 157 percent compared to 23 percent for the All Stocks universe. Translating that into average annual compound returns shows a gain of 20.76 percent for the low PSR stocks and a 2.28 percent gain for the All Stocks universe. The worst they ever performed relative to the All Stocks universe were the five years ending February 2000, when the low PSR stocks had a cumulative gain of 84 percent compared to a cumulative gain of 172 percent for the All Stocks universe. That amounts to an 88 percent deficit for the low-price group. On an average annual compound basis, the low PSR stocks earned 13.02 percent a year, compared with 22.18 percent for the All Stocks universe.

When we look at all rolling 10-year holding periods, we see that low PSR stocks beat All Stocks by an average cumulative 108 percent, whereas in the 11 percent of all rolling 10-year periods when they lost to All Stocks they did so, on average, by a cumulative 38 percent. Keep in mind that that figure has been seriously inflated by several months in the year 2000, when they lagged All Stocks in the triple digits. Figure 9.1 shows the five-year average annual compound excess (deficient) return for decile 1 minus the return for the All Stocks universe. Table 9.3 shows the worst-case scenarios for the All Stocks group, and Tables 9.4 and 9.5 show the best- and worst-case returns over a variety of holding periods.

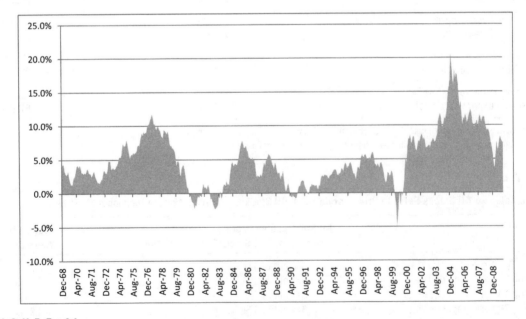

F I G U R E   9.1

Five-year average annual compound excess (deficient) return All Stocks sales to price decile 1 minus All Stocks, January 1, 1964, to December 31, 2009

TABLE 9.3

Worst-Case Scenarios: All 20 Percent or Greater Declines for All Stocks Sales to Price Decile 1, January 1, 1964, to December 31, 2009

Peak date	Peak index value	Trough date	Trough index value	Recovery date	Decline (%)	Decline duration	Recovery duration
Feb–66	1.97	Sep–66	1.57	Mar–67	−20.28%	7	6
Nov–68	3.60	Jun–70	1.83	Jan–76	−49.15%	19	67
Aug–87	42.55	Nov–87	27.94	Jan–89	−34.34%	3	14
Aug–89	52.32	Oct–90	30.89	Jan–92	−40.97%	14	15
Apr–98	178.70	Aug–98	129.94	Apr–01	−27.29%	4	32
Apr–02	234.56	Feb–03	152.64	Aug–03	−34.92%	10	6
May–07	628.57	Feb–09	213.83	N/A	−65.98%	21	N/A
Average					−38.99%	11.14	23.33

TABLE 9.4

Best and Worst Average Annual Compound Returns for Monthly Data, January 1, 1964, to December 31, 2009

For any	1-year period	3-year period	5-year period	7-year period	10-year period
All Stocks sales to price decile 1 minimum compound return	−54.83%	−22.44%	−9.51%	−4.58%	4.05%
All Stocks sales to price decile 1 maximum compound return	98.93%	46.36%	33.53%	28.58%	26.95%
All Stocks minimum compound return	−46.49%	−18.68%	−9.91%	−6.32%	1.01%
All Stocks maximum compound return	84.19%	31.49%	27.66%	23.77%	22.05%
All Stocks sales to price decile 10 minimum compound return	−73.19%	−51.96%	−29.96%	−21.38%	−14.79%
All Stocks sales to price decile 10 maximum compound return	207.00%	52.33%	37.51%	25.11%	18.47%

TABLE 9.5

Terminal Value of $10,000 Invested for Best and Worst Average Annual Compound Returns for Monthly Data, January 1, 1964, to December 31, 2009

For any	1-year period	3-year period	5-year period	7-year period	10-year period
All Stocks sales to price decile 1 minimum $10,000 value	$4,517	$4,667	$6,068	$7,202	$14,878
All Stocks sales to price decile 1 maximum $10,000 value	$19,893	$31,353	$42,448	$58,094	$108,710
All Stocks minimum $10,000 value	$5,351	$5,379	$5,936	$6,330	$11,054
All Stocks maximum $10,000 value	$18,419	$22,734	$33,903	$44,504	$73,345
All Stocks sales to price decile 10 minimum $10,000 value	$2,681	$1,108	$1,686	$1,857	$2,018
All Stocks sales to price decile 10 maximum $10,000 value	$30,700	$35,347	$49,172	$47,987	$54,462

LARGE STOCKS WITH LOW PRICE-TO-SALES RATIOS DO WELL

As Table 9.6 shows, Large Stocks with low PSRs also beat the Large Stocks universe, but not by as much as those from the smaller-cap All Stocks universe. Ten thousand dollars invested on December 31, 1963, was worth $1,470,652 at the end of 2009, a compound return of 11.46 percent. The return was considerably better than the $872,861 you'd have earned if you invested $10,000 in the Large Stocks universe itself. The low PSR stocks had a Sharpe ratio of .37 versus .32 for the Large Stocks universe.

T A B L E   9.6

Summary Annual Return and Risk Results Data: Large Stocks Sales to Price Decile 1 and Large Stocks, January 1, 1964, to December 31, 2009

	Large Stocks sales to price decile 1	Large Stocks
Arithmetic average	13.16%	11.72%
Geometric average	11.46%	10.20%
Median return	14.05%	17.20%
Standard deviation	17.38%	16.50%
Upside deviation	11.22%	9.70%
Downside deviation	12.89%	11.85%
Tracking error	8.01	0.00
Number of positive periods	336	332
Number of negative periods	216	220
Maximum peak-to-trough decline	−59.89%	−53.77%
Beta	0.94	1.00
T-statistic (m = 0)	4.85	4.58
Sharpe ratio (Rf = 5%)	0.37	0.32
Sortino ratio (MAR = 10%)	0.11	0.02
$10,000 becomes	$1,470,652	$872,861
Minimum 1-year return	−53.11%	−46.91%
Maximum 1-year return	71.13%	68.96%
Minimum 3-year return	−15.98%	−15.89%
Maximum 3-year return	37.52%	33.12%
Minimum 5-year return	−6.15%	−5.82%
Maximum 5-year return	32.78%	28.95%
Minimum 7-year return	−5.08%	−4.15%
Maximum 7-year return	25.34%	22.83%
Minimum 10-year return	−0.88%	−0.15%
Maximum 10-year return	20.80%	19.57%
Minimum expected return*	−21.61%	−21.28%
Maximum expected return†	47.92%	44.72%

* Minimum expected return is arithmetic return minus 2 times the standard deviation.
† Maximum expected return is arithmetic return plus 2 times the standard deviation.

The rolling five- and ten-year base rates for both groups of low PSR stocks are strong, with the low PSR stocks from Large Stocks beating the universe 74 percent of all rolling ten-year periods. Table 9.7 summarizes the results. Figure 9.2 shows the five-year average annual compound excess (deficient) return for decile 1 minus the return for the Large Stocks universe.

TABLE 9.7

Base Rates for Large Stocks Sales to Price Decile 1 and Large Stocks, January 1, 1964, to December 31, 2009

Item	Large Stocks sales to price decile 1 beat Large Stocks	Percent	Average annual excess return
Single-year return	310 out of 541	57%	1.60%
Rolling 3-year compound return	307 out of 517	59%	1.41%
Rolling 5-year compound return	312 out of 493	63%	1.34%
Rolling 7-year compound return	326 out of 469	70%	1.31%
Rolling 10-year compound return	320 out of 433	74%	1.34%

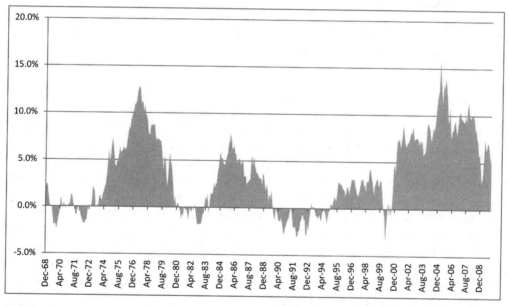

FIGURE 9.2

Five-year average annual compound excess (deficient) return Large Stocks sales to price decile 1 minus Large Stocks, January 1, 1964, to December 31, 2009

WORST-CASE SCENARIOS AND BEST AND WORST RETURNS

Tables 9.3 and 9.8 show that low PSR stocks from both the All Stocks and Large Stocks universes experienced their worst declines ever during the bear market of 2007 through early 2009. The low PSR stocks from All Stocks lost 65.98 percent between May 2007 and

February 2009, approximately 10 percent more than the 55.30 percent decline for All Stocks over the same period. The low PSR stocks from Large Stocks declined 59.89 percent between October 2007 and February 2009, whereas the Large Stocks universe fell 54.21 percent over the same period. Over the last 46 years, the lowest PSR stocks from All Stocks lost more than 20 percent from high to low on seven occasions, and several of these declines came rapidly. Looking at Table 9.3, you can see that the group lost more than 20 percent in seven or fewer months in three instances. Anyone pursuing a low PSR strategy should keep this in mind. As Table 9.8 shows, low PSR stocks from Large Stocks exhibit similar declines.

T A B L E   9.8

Worst-Case Scenarios: All 20 Percent or Greater Declines for Large Stock Sales to Price Decile 1, January 1, 1964, to December 31, 2009

Peak date	Peak index value	Trough date	Trough index value	Recovery date	Decline (%)	Decline duration	Recovery duration
Nov–68	1.94	Sep–74	1.14	Jan–76	−41.21%	70	16
Aug–87	16.51	Nov–87	10.78	Mar–89	−34.70%	3	16
Aug–89	18.97	Oct–90	12.22	Feb–92	−35.55%	14	16
May–01	87.58	Mar–03	56.21	Nov–03	−35.82%	22	8
Oct–07	208.48	Feb–09	83.62	N/A	−59.89%	16	N/A
Average					−41.43%	25	14

During the worst five-year period, which ended in December 1973, $10,000 invested in the stocks with the lowest PSR from All Stocks declined to $6,068, an average annual compound loss of –9.51 percent. The worst five-year return for the low PSR stocks from Large Stocks was for the five years ending November 1973, when $10,000 invested five years earlier shrank to $7,279, an average annual compound loss of –6.15 percent. The *best* five-year returns for low PSR stocks from All Stocks were the five years ending July 1987, when $10,000 invested soared to $42,448, an average annual compound gain of 33.53 percent. Low PSR stocks from Large Stocks also had their best five-year performance for the five years ending July 1987, when $10,000 invested five years earlier grew to $41,276, a gain of 32.78 percent per year. Tables 9.4 and 9.5 as well as Tables 9.9 and 9.10 show returns for all other holding periods.

On a relative basis, the best five years for the low PSR stocks from All Stocks versus the All Stocks universe were the five years ending February 2005, when the low PSR group earned a cumulative return of 157 percent, while All Stocks earned just 24 percent, a 133 percent cumulative advantage for the low PSR group. The worst five years for the low PSR group came at the period ending in February 2000—at the height of the bubble—when the low PSR stocks had a cumulative gain of 84 percent compared to 176 percent for the All Stocks universe, a deficit of 92 percent. Figure 9.1 shows the excess (or deficient) five-year return ("alpha") for the low PSR stocks from All Stocks compared to the return from the All Stocks universe.

TABLE 9.9

Best and Worst Average Annual Compound Returns for Monthly Data, January 1, 1964, to December 31, 2009

For any	1-year period	3-year period	5-year period	7-year period	10-year period
Large Stocks sales to price decile 1 minimum compound return	−53.11%	−15.98%	−6.15%	−5.08%	−0.88%
Large Stocks sales to price decile 1 maximum compound return	71.13%	37.52%	32.78%	25.34%	20.80%
Large Stocks minimum compound return	−46.91%	−15.89%	−5.82%	−4.15%	−0.15%
Large Stocks maximum compound return	68.96%	33.12%	28.95%	22.83%	19.57%
Large Stocks sales to price decile 10 minimum compound return	−79.08%	−46.46%	−25.76%	−16.84%	−11.37%
Large Stocks sales to price decile 10 minimum compound return	105.17%	48.15%	35.67%	25.67%	20.02%

TABLE 9.10

Terminal Value of $10,000 Invested for Best and Worst Average Annual Compound Returns for Monthly Data, January 1, 1964, to December 31, 2009

For any	1-year period	3-year period	5-year period	7-year period	10-year period
Large Stocks sales to price decile 1 minimum $10,000 value	$4,689	$5,932	$7,279	$6,944	$9,152
Large Stocks sales to price decile 1 maximum $10,000 value	$17,113	$26,006	$41,276	$48,605	$66,155
Large Stocks minimum $10,000 value	$5,309	$5,951	$7,409	$7,434	$9,848
Large Stocks maximum $10,000 value	$16,896	$23,591	$35,656	$42,189	$59,747
Large Stocks sales to price decile 10 minimum $10,000 value	$2,092	$1,535	$2,255	$2,750	$2,991
Large Stocks sales to price decile 10 maximum $10,000 value	$20,517	$32,514	$45,962	$49,490	$62,025

For the low PSR stocks from Large Stocks, the best five years were those ending in October 1995, when the low PSR stocks rose by 190 percent compared to a gain of 111 percent for the Large Stocks universe, a cumulative advantage of 79 percent. The worst five years were those ending in February 2000, when the low PSR stocks from Large Stocks gained a cumulative 109 percent, but the Large Stocks universe was up by 185 percent, a cumulative deficit of 73 percent.

HIGH PSR STOCKS ARE TOXIC

As Table 9.11 shows, the dubious honor of worst performance to date goes to the decile of stocks with the highest price-to-sales ratios from the All Stocks universe: $10,000 invested

TABLE 9.11

Summary Annual Return and Risk Results Data: All Stocks Sales to Price Decile 10 and All Stocks, January 1, 1964, to December 31, 2009

	All Stocks sales to price decile 10	All Stocks
Arithmetic average	7.05%	13.26%
Geometric average	3.36%	11.22%
Median return	12.29%	17.16%
Standard deviation	26.24%	18.99%
Upside deviation	16.57%	10.98%
Downside deviation	19.73%	13.90%
Tracking error	13.16	0.00
Number of positive periods	312	329
Number of negative periods	240	223
Maximum peak-to-trough decline	−91.41%	−55.54%
Beta	1.21	1.00
T-statistic (m = 0)	1.77	4.47
Sharpe ratio (Rf = 5%)	−0.06	0.33
Sortino ratio (MAR = 10%)	−0.34	0.09
$10,000 becomes	$45,711	$1,329,513
Minimum 1-year return	−73.19%	−46.49%
Maximum 1-year return	207.00%	84.19%
Minimum 3-year return	−51.96%	−18.68%
Maximum 3-year return	52.33%	31.49%
Minimum 5-year return	−29.96%	−9.91%
Maximum 5-year return	37.51%	27.66%
Minimum 7 Year return	−21.38%	−6.32%
Maximum 7-year return	25.11%	23.77%
Minimum 10-year return	−14.79%	1.01%
Maximum 10-year return	18.47%	22.05%
Minimum expected return*	−45.44%	−24.73%
Maximum expected return†	59.53%	51.24%

* Minimum expected return is arithmetic return minus 2 times the standard deviation.
† Maximum expected return is arithmetic return plus 2 times the standard deviation.

on December 31, 1963, was worth just $45,711 at the end of 2009. That's an average annual compound return of 3.36 percent. You'd be vastly better off with T-bills, where the same $10,000 grew to $120,778. The Sharpe ratio is –.06, the bottom of the barrel.

Table 9.12 helps catalog the carnage. The All Stocks universe beat the highest PSR stocks 69 percent of the time in any given rolling 12-month period. December 31, 1980, through December 31, 1984, was particularly gruesome. Ten thousand dollars invested in the

All Stocks universe grew by more than 50 percent to $15,915, but an investment in the decile of stocks with the highest PSRs *fell* by nearly 7 percent per year, turning $10,000 into $6,759. Unfortunately, such horrendous performance is not unique—the decile of stocks with the highest price-to-sales ratios routinely underperforms the All Stocks universe, regardless of what is going on in the market. Once again, the only real exceptions are during extremely speculative markets. If you look at the calendar year returns for the high PSR stocks from All Stocks, you'll see that their best year was at the peak of the stock market bubble in 1999. And on a rolling 12-month basis, their best year was that ending February 2000, where they gained an astonishing 207 percent. No wonder people became intoxicated by these ultimately deadly stocks. Yet those who *did* get excited and bought them would have had to deal with the 12-months ending September 2001, when the high PSR stocks plunged more than 73 percent. In virtually all other market environments, these stocks are at the very bottom of the return barrel, rarely posting positive returns, regardless of the stock market environment.

T A B L E 9.12

Base Rates for All Stocks Sales to Price Decile 10 and All Stocks, January 1, 1964, to December 31, 2009

Item	All Stocks sales to price decile 10 "beat All Stocks"	Percent	Average annual excess return
Single-year return	170 out of 541	31%	−5.21%
Rolling 3-year compound return	110 out of 517	21%	−7.15%
Rolling 5-year compound return	70 out of 493	14%	−7.63%
Rolling 7-year compound return	38 out of 469	8%	−7.90%
Rolling 10-year compound return	10 out of 433	2%	−7.87%

Looking at five-year rolling returns, the All Stocks universe beat the high PSR stocks 86 percent of the time. On a rolling 10-year basis the All Stocks universe beat high PSR stocks 98 percent of the time.

Yet, look again at the year ending February 2000—at the height of the stock market bubble—when they gained 207 percent, and December 1999, when they gained 111 percent. The overhyped stocks that typically dominate the highest PSR group from All Stocks soared in value: February 2000's gain swamped All Stocks gain of 53 percent, whereas the 1999 gain was 79 percent better than All Stocks return of 32 percent. Imagine how you would feel looking at the one-year performance of these sexy story stocks. The urge to join the bandwagon would be overwhelming, but the fullness of time shows how disastrous that decision would have been. Following the stellar gains of 207 percent in February 2000, the group went on to *lose* 71 percent over the next 12 months. And finally, the high PSR stocks' swan song: Between February 2000 and February 2009, they lost 91 percent—and they have not yet recovered. Tables 9.11 through 9.13 catalog the woe. Also, refer back to Tables 9.4 and 9.5 to see the best- and worst-case outcomes for all holding periods. Figure 9.3 shows the five-year average annual compound excess (in this case, mostly deficient) return for decile 10 on minus the return for the All Stocks universe.

T A B L E   9.13

Worst-Case Scenarios: All 20 Percent or Greater Declines for All Stocks Sales to Price Decile 10, January 1, 1964, to December 31, 2009

Peak date	Peak index value	Trough date	Trough index value	Recovery date	Decline (%)	Decline duration	Recovery duration
May–69	2.24	Jun–70	1.20	Feb–72	−46.22%	13	20
Dec–72	2.45	Sep–74	1.04	Jun–79	−57.70%	21	57
Feb–80	3.77	Mar–80	2.92	Jul–80	−22.61%	1	4
Nov–80	5.58	Jul–82	2.96	Jun–83	−47.02%	20	11
Jun–83	5.80	Jul–84	3.49	Feb–87	−39.80%	13	31
Aug–87	6.55	Nov–87	4.26	Nov–89	−34.91%	3	24
Jun–90	6.79	Oct–90	5.23	Feb–91	−22.93%	4	4
Jan–92	9.17	Jun–94	6.46	Sep–95	−29.57%	29	15
May–96	12.15	Aug–98	7.23	Mar–99	−40.45%	27	7
Feb–00	34.36	Feb–09	2.95	N/A	−91.41%	108	N/A
Average					−43.26%	23.9	19.22

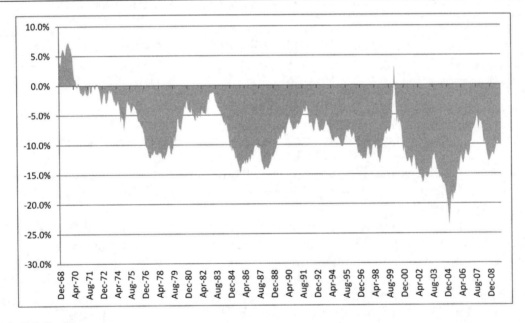

F I G U R E   9.3

Five-year average annual compound excess (deficient) return All Stocks sales to price decile 10 minus All Stocks, January 1, 1964, to December 31, 2009

LARGE STOCKS DO LITTLE BETTER

As Table 9.14 makes clear, high PSR stocks from the Large Stocks universe suffer a similar fate. Here, $10,000 invested in the decile of stocks with the highest PSRs on December 31, 1963, grows to $82,579, a compound return of 4.70 percent. That's a fraction of what you'd earn from the Large Stocks universe, and only nominally better than the decile of high PSR stocks from the All Stocks universe. Like the high PSR stocks from All Stocks, those in the tenth decile by PSR in Large Stocks also are bested by an investment in U.S. T-bills. The Sharpe ratio is –.01, considerably below the Large Stocks universe's .32. As you can see in Table 9.15, all base rates are negative, with the decile of the highest price-to-sales ratio stocks from Large Stocks underperforming the Large Stocks universe 96 percent of the time over all 10-year periods. As you can see in Table 9.16, Large Stocks with the highest PSRs lost more than 20 percent on seven occasions, with the worst coming after the tech-wreck of the early 2000s when they lost 86 percent between February 2000 and September 2002—a loss from which they still have not recovered. Figure 9.4 shows the five-year average annual compound excess (in this case, mostly deficient) return for decile 10 on minus the return for the Large Stocks universe.

T A B L E   9.14

Summary Annual Return and Risk Results Data: Large Stocks Sales to Price Decile 10 and Large Stocks, January 1, 1964, to December 31, 2009

	Large Stocks sales to price decile 10	Large Stocks
Arithmetic average	7.39%	11.72%
Geometric average	4.70%	10.20%
Median return	11.43%	17.20%
Standard deviation	22.14%	16.50%
Upside deviation	13.35%	9.70%
Downside deviation	17.78%	11.85%
Tracking error	11.83	0.00
Number of positive periods	318	332
Number of negative periods	234	220
Maximum peak-to-trough decline	−86.24%	−53.77%
Beta	1.14	1.00
T-statistic (m = 0)	2.19	4.58
Sharpe ratio (Rf = 5%)	−0.01	0.32
Sortino ratio (MAR = 10%)	−0.30	0.02
$10,000 becomes	$82,579	$872,861
Minimum 1-year return	−79.08%	−46.91%
Maximum 1-year return	105.17%	68.96%
Minimum 3-year return	−46.46%	−15.89%
Maximum 3-year return	48.15%	33.12%
Minimum 5-year return	−25.76%	−5.82%
Maximum 5-year return	35.67%	28.95%
Minimum 7-year return	−16.84%	−4.15%
Maximum 7-year return	25.67%	22.83%
Minimum 10-year return	−11.37%	−0.15%
Maximum 10-year return	20.02%	19.57%
Minimum expected return*	−36.88%	−21.28%
Maximum expected return†	51.67%	44.72%

* Minimum expected return is arithmetic return minus 2 times the standard deviation.
† Maximum expected return is arithmetic return plus 2 times the standard deviation.

T A B L E   9.15

Base Rates for Large Stocks Sales to Price Decile 10 and Large Stocks, January 1, 1964, to December 31, 2009

Item	Large Stocks sales to price decile 10 beat Large Stocks	Percent	Average annual excess return
Single-year return	213 out of 541	39%	−3.55%
Rolling 3-year compound return	141 out of 517	27%	−5.18%
Rolling 5-year compound return	74 out of 493	15%	−5.88%
Rolling 7-year compound return	50 out of 469	11%	−6.27%
Rolling 10-year compound return	16 out of 433	4%	−6.44%

T A B L E   9.16

Worst-Case Scenarios: All 20 Percent or Greater Declines for Large Stocks Sales to Price Decile 10, January 1, 1964, to December 31, 2009

Peak date	Peak index value	Trough date	Trough index value	Recovery date	Decline (%)	Decline duration	Recovery duration
Dec–69	1.91	Jun–70	1.32	Apr–71	−30.95%	6	10
Dec–72	2.65	Sep–74	1.05	Nov–80	−60.39%	21	74
Nov–80	2.91	Jul–82	1.73	May–83	−40.46%	20	10
Jun–83	3.13	Jul–84	2.36	Dec–85	−24.51%	13	17
Aug–87	5.18	Nov–87	3.50	Jul–89	−32.50%	3	20
Apr–98	14.51	Aug–98	11.34	Dec–98	−21.84%	4	4
Feb–00	33.58	Sep–02	4.62	N/A	−86.24%	31	N/A
Average					−42.41%	14	22.5

F I G U R E   9.4

Five-year average annual compound excess (deficient) return Large Stocks sales to price decile 10 minus Large Stocks, January 1, 1964, to December 31, 2009

WORST-CASE SCENARIOS AND BEST AND WORST RETURNS

While we've already cataloged most of the damage, Table 9.13 shows the worst-case scenarios for decile 10—the 10 percent of stocks with the highest PSRs—from the All Stocks universe. The group lost 20 percent or more 10 times since 1963, with the worst drop being the 91 percent decline that began in February 2000. Table 9.13 shows all other declines for the Large Stocks group greater than 20 percent.

The best five-year performance for the group on an absolute basis came after the five years ending February 2000, when it earned an average annual compound return of 37.51 percent and turned $10,000 into $49,172. The worst five-year performance for the group on an absolute basis came after the five years ending February 2005, when it lost 29.96 percent per year, turning $10,000 into $1,686. Consult Tables 9.4 and 9.5 for other best- and worst-case returns for all holding periods.

The best relative five-year performance for the group was the same as its best absolute return—the five years ending February 2000, when it earned a cumulative return of 392 percent versus All Stocks' 176 percent, a cumulative advantage of 216 percent for the high PSR group. Translating that into average annual compound return shows the high PSR stocks from All Stocks earning 37.51 percent compared to 22.18 percent for the All Stocks universe. The worst relative five-year performance versus All Stocks was the five years ending August 1986, when the group gained a cumulative 11.18 percent compared to 148 percent for the All Stocks universe, a cumulative deficit of 137 percent. On an average annual compound return basis, the high PSR stocks earned 2.14 percent compared to 19.95 percent for the All Stocks universe. Table 9.5 shows the terminal value of a $10,000 investment made for differing best- and worst-case holding periods. Figure 9.3 shows the five-year excess (or deficient) return for the high PSR group from All Stocks versus the All Stocks universe.

Table 9.16 shows the seven times since 1963 that the high PSR stocks from Large Stocks declined by 20 percent or more. The worst, a drop of 86 percent, was between February 2000 and September 2002, and still persists as of this writing; they have yet to recover from that drop.

For the Large Stocks group with the highest PSRs, the best absolute five-year return occurred with the five years ending February 2000, when it earned an average annual compound return of 35.67 percent, turning $10,000 into $45,962. The worst absolute five-year return for the group was those five years ending February 2005, when it lost 25.76 percent per year and turned $10,000 into $2,255. Consult Tables 9.9 and 9.10 to see the best and worst for other holding periods.

The best five-year relative performance for the group versus Large Stocks was the same as the best absolute return, the five years ending February 2000. Over that period, the high PSR stocks from Large Stocks earned a cumulative 360 percent compared to a cumulative gain of 182 percent for Large Stocks, a cumulative 178 percent advantage over Large Stocks. The worst relative five-year performance for the group versus Large Stocks was the five years ending July 2001, when the group lost a cumulative 9 percent compared to a gain of 88 percent for Large Stocks, a cumulative deficit of 97 percent. Translating that into average annual compound returns, the high PSR stocks from Large Stocks lost

1.90 percent versus a gain of 13.44 percent for the Large Stocks universe. Figure 9.4 shows the five-year excess (or deficient) returns over the Large Stocks universe for the entire period. Tables 9.17 and 9.18 show the average annual compound return by decade for each group from All Stocks and Large Stocks.

T A B L E   9.17

Average Annual Compound Rates of Return by Decade

	1960s*	1970s	1980s	1990s	2000s†
All Stocks sales to price decile 1	16.90%	11.44%	20.03%	12.82%	12.43%
All Stocks sales to price decile 10	11.58%	5.60%	7.23%	12.98%	−14.79%
All Stocks	13.36%	7.56%	16.78%	15.35%	4.39%

* Returns for January 1, 1964, to December 31, 1969.
† Returns for January 1, 2000, to December 31, 2009.

T A B L E   9.18

Average Annual Compound Rates of Return by Decade

	1960s*	1970s	1980s	1990s	2000s†
Large Stocks sales to price decile 1	5.99%	8.80%	18.54%	14.95%	7.30%
Large Stocks sales to price decile 10	11.40%	0.16%	11.40%	17.05%	−11.37%
Large Stocks	8.16%	6.65%	17.34%	16.38%	2.42%

* Returns for January 1, 1964, to December 31, 1969.
† Returns for January 1, 2000, to December 31, 2009.

DECILES

The decile returns for price-to-sales ratios demonstrate that you would be better off concentrating on the 20 percent of All Stocks with the lowest price-to-sales ratios. Look at Table 9.19 and Figure 9.5. Decile 2 actually does better than decile 1, with an average annual compound return of 14.53 percent between 1963 and 2009, compared to decile 1's return of 14.49. While it is only four basis points, the All Stocks base rates are actually better for decile 2 then for decile 1—decile 2 beats All Stocks in 90 percent of all rolling five-year periods and 97 percent of all rolling ten-year periods. The two together provide better returns with higher base rates. Despite the slight inversion of decile 2 performing better than decile 1, total returns march downhill from there, with a compound return of 14.54 percent for a combined decile 1 and 2 to an abysmal 3.36 percent return for decile 10, which is made up of the stocks with the highest PSRs.

Large Stocks show similar—although more muted—findings. As with the All Stocks group, decile 2 from Large Stocks does better than decile 1, returning 11.77 percent per year versus 11.46 percent for decile 1. Here too, investors would be better off concentrating on

T A B L E 9.19

Summary Results for Sales to Price Decile Analysis of All Stocks Universe, January 1, 1964, to December 31, 2009

Decile	$10,000 grows to	Average return	Compound return	Standard deviation	Sharpe ratio
1 (highest)	$5,044,457	16.95%	14.49%	20.68%	0.46
2	$5,128,129	16.61%	14.53%	18.98%	0.50
3	$3,587,828	15.57%	13.64%	18.32%	0.47
4	$2,744,842	14.78%	12.98%	17.74%	0.45
5	$2,075,249	13.97%	12.30%	17.12%	0.43
6	$1,465,785	12.95%	11.45%	16.32%	0.40
7	$806,593	11.51%	10.01%	16.37%	0.31
8	$365,406	9.89%	8.14%	17.89%	0.18
9	$173,591	8.84%	6.40%	21.16%	0.07
10 (lowest)	$45,711	7.05%	3.36%	26.24%	−0.06
All Stocks	$1,329,513	13.26%	11.22%	18.99%	0.33

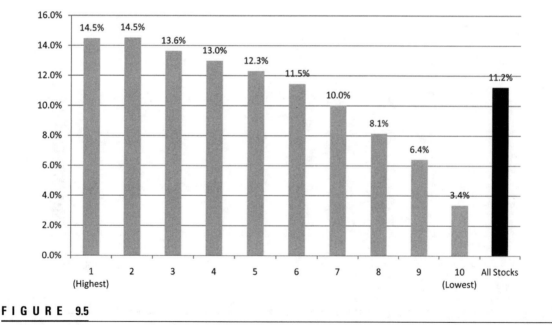

F I G U R E 9.5

Average annual compound return by Sales to Price decile, All Stocks universe, January 1, 1964 to December 31, 2009

the 20 percent of Large Stocks with the lowest PSRs. Base rates are also better for decile 2, with that group beating Large Stocks in 81 percent of all rolling five-year periods and in 94 percent of all rolling ten-year periods. Yet, as we saw with All Stocks, after the decile 1 and 2 inversion, each decile declines in returns as you climb the PSR mountain, with decile 10's returns behind those from U.S. T-bills. Table 9.20 and Figure 9.6 summarize the findings for Large Stocks.

T A B L E   9.20

Summary Results for Sales to Price Decile Analysis of Large Stocks Universe, January 1, 1964, to December 31, 2009

Decile	$10,000 grows to	Average return	Compound return	Standard deviation	Sharpe ratio
1 (highest)	$1,470,652	13.16%	11.46%	17.38%	0.37
2	$1,672,056	13.36%	11.77%	16.77%	0.40
3	$1,324,507	12.76%	11.21%	16.59%	0.37
4	$1,158,334	12.19%	10.88%	15.33%	0.38
5	$1,037,505	11.86%	10.62%	14.99%	0.37
6	$553,407	10.27%	9.12%	14.53%	0.28
7	$486,962	10.04%	8.81%	14.95%	0.26
8	$369,957	9.55%	8.17%	15.97%	0.20
9	$304,900	9.43%	7.71%	17.77%	0.15
10 (lowest)	$82,579	7.39%	4.70%	22.14%	−0.01
Large Stocks	$872,861	11.72%	10.20%	16.50%	0.32

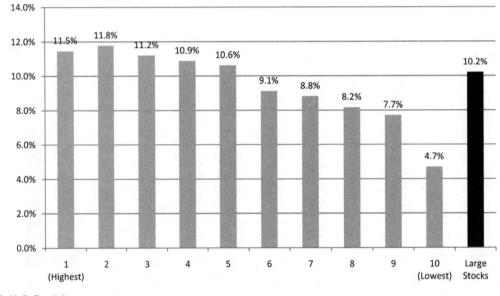

F I G U R E   9.6

Average annual compound return by Sales to Price decile, Large Stocks universe, January 1, 1964, to December 31, 2009

IMPLICATIONS

While no longer the king of the hill, stocks with low price-to-sales ratios beat the market consistently over time. The only time high PSR stocks manage to beat their benchmarks is when investors are in an irrational and exuberant frenzy, throwing caution (and smart investment decisions) to the wind and dashing headlong into stocks with the sexiest stories. Yet as we've seen, those times are brief and there was hell to pay after the party, with both the All Stocks and Large Stocks high PSR deciles doing worse than keeping your money in cash. Both suffered extreme declines from which they have not yet recovered. We'll see later how incorporating PSR into a group of other value ratios provides even better protection for investors.

PRICE-TO-BOOK VALUE RATIOS: A LONG-TERM WINNER WITH LONG PERIODS OF UNDERPERFORMANCE

We can easily represent things as we wish them to be.

—Aesop

Many investors believe that price-to-book value ratios are more important than price-to-earnings (PE) ratios when they're looking for a bargain. They argue that earnings can be easily manipulated by a clever chief financial officer. Here's an old joke as an example: A company wants to hire a new chief financial officer. Each candidate is asked just one question: "What does two plus two equal?" Each candidate answers four, with the exception of the one they hire. Her answer was, "What number did you have in mind?"

You find the price-to-book ratio by dividing the current price of the stock by the book value per share. Here we use the common equity liquidating value per share as a proxy for book value per share. Essentially, investors who buy stocks with low price-to-book value ratios believe they are getting stocks at a price close to their liquidating value and that they will be rewarded for not paying high prices for assets.

Price-to-book has long been a favorite value ratio. Ben Graham, the founder of modern securities analysis, made it a central factor in his rules for investing featured in *The Intelligent Investor: A Book of Practial Counsel*, saying that to maintain a "margin of safety," one should pay no more than 1.2 times book value for a stock. (Graham realized that companies with a lot of intangible assets, such as brand recognition, could be profitable investments, and he argued that for such companies one could pay as much as 2.5 times book and still do well.)

Eugene Fama and Ken French immortalized price-to-book in their three-factor model published as "The Cross-Section of Expected Stock Returns," in which they claimed that a simple three-factor model could explain almost all of a portfolio's return. The three factors were:

1. The portfolio's exposure to the market itself.
2. The portfolio's exposure to small-cap stocks.
3. The portfolio's price-to-book ratio.

Fama and French went on to create both large-cap and small-cap value and growth portfolios using price-to-book value ratios as their guide. Large- and small-cap value portfolios were composed of the large and small stocks that were in the bottom 30 percent by price-to-book (i.e., the 30 percent of stocks with the *lowest* price-to-book value ratios), whereas large- and small-cap growth portfolios were those with stocks in the *highest* 30 percent based upon price-to-book ratios. These portfolios originated in 1927 and show the long-term efficacy of value, as opposed to growth, investing.

Several other studies confirmed these findings, but over shorter periods of time. One featured in the January 11, 1989, edition of *The Wall Street Journal* was a study conducted by Professor Marc Reinganum, then a professor at the University of Iowa and currently a senior managing director at State Street Global Advisors. Reinganum's study looked at the common characteristics of 222 stocks that tripled in price in a calendar year in the 1970–1983 period. One of his findings was that many of the winners had a per-share price that was less than the per-share book value. Finally, in his "Decile Portfolios of the New York Stock Exchange, 1967–1984," Roger Ibbotson showed that the decile of stocks with the lowest price-to-book value ratio earned compound annual returns of 14.36 percent, whereas the stocks in the decile of stocks with the highest price-to-book ratios earned compound annual returns of just 6.06 percent.

WHAT WORKS ON WALL STREET HAS SIMILAR FINDINGS, BUT ...

When we look at the composited results for our All Stocks and Large Stocks universes over the entire 1927–2009 period, we also find that buying stocks with low price-to-book value ratios works, but we find that there are long subperiods where low price-to-book value ratios, *especially the lowest 10 percent,* do not work well at all. For example, using our data to look at the same period that Roger Ibbotson studied, 1967–1984, we find very similar results to Ibbotson's. Table 10.1 shows the results for each of the 10 deciles from the All Stocks universe by price-to-book value, with decile 1 containing the 10 percent of stocks with the lowest price-to-book value ratios and decile 10 containing the 10 percent with the highest price-to-book value ratios. They descend in near perfect order for the 18 years studied, with the stocks with the lowest price-to-book ratios earning 16.60 percent and then declining with each dollar more an investor is willing to pay for book value to deciles 9 and 10, which earn 6.54 percent and 6.90 percent, respectively. As you can see by looking at the table, in each instance, an investor in decile 8, 9, or 10 would have been better off investing in U.S. T-bills, which earned 7.43 percent over the same period.

TABLE 10.1

Summary Results for Book-to-Price Decile Analysis of All Stocks Universe, January 1, 1967, to December 31, 1984

Decile	$10,000 grows to	Average return	Compound return	Standard deviation	Sharpe ratio
1 (highest)	$158,792	19.03%	16.60%	20.69%	0.56
2	$152,607	18.25%	16.35%	18.33%	0.62
3	$109,027	15.83%	14.19%	17.15%	0.54
4	$77,946	13.78%	12.08%	17.53%	0.40
5	$64,544	12.77%	10.92%	18.40%	0.32
6	$62,868	12.77%	10.75%	19.17%	0.30
7	$47,530	11.15%	9.05%	19.68%	0.21
8	$35,503	9.61%	7.29%	20.76%	0.11
9	$31,285	9.10%	6.54%	21.87%	0.07
10 (lowest)	$33,246	10.13%	6.90%	24.47%	0.08
All Stocks	$67,282	13.22%	11.17%	19.29%	0.32

Yet over longer periods of time, the results do *not hold to the pattern found for these 18 years*. Indeed, we see in a moment that analyzing the results for stocks based on their price-to-book value ratios underlines and highlights why we should always seek access to the longest datasets we can find because they offer much better indications of what investors should expect from various types of investing.

Now that we have the CRSP data and the Fama and French price-to-book value data, we can see that for the 36-year period from 1927 through 1963 (when our Compustat dataset begins), featured in Table 10.2, the decile of stocks with the lowest price-to-book value ratios *was actually the worst performing of all the deciles*. (Please keep in mind that the stocks with the highest book-to-price are actually those with the lowest price-to-book.) Deciles 2, 3, and 4 all outperformed the All Stocks universe, showing that stocks with lower price-to-book value ratios did well, but *not* those with the lowest.

TABLE 10.2

Summary Results for Book-to-Price Decile Analysis of All Stocks Universe, January 1, 1927, to December 31, 1963

Decile	$10,000 grows to	Average return	Compound return	Standard deviation	Sharpe ratio
1 (highest)	$144,371	14.62%	7.48%	37.21%	0.07
2	$317,579	14.41%	9.80%	29.70%	0.16
3	$399,400	14.28%	10.48%	26.70%	0.21
4	$374,866	13.72%	10.29%	25.42%	0.21
5	$317,254	12.87%	9.79%	23.95%	0.20
6	$287,508	12.40%	9.50%	23.04%	0.20
7	$231,167	11.76%	8.86%	22.96%	0.17
8	$248,432	11.65%	9.07%	21.62%	0.19
9	$228,206	11.29%	8.82%	21.07%	0.18
10 (lowest)	$169,542	10.55%	7.95%	21.57%	0.14
All Stocks	$289,901	12.81%	9.53%	24.62%	0.18

Over the same period, an examination of the Fama-French Large Value and Small Value indexes returns, available through Morningstar's EnCorr Analyzer, earned an average annual compound return of 10.81 percent and 11.77 percent, respectively. There are two reasons why this might be so: First, Fama and French allowed microcap stocks that *What Works on Wall Street* excludes, and second, as mentioned earlier, the Fama and French data look at the lowest 30 percent by price-to-book value (essentially deciles 1, 2, and 3 combined.) Finally, to get a sense of what buying stocks with low price-to-book ratios looks like post-World War II, look at Table 10.3, where we see once again the familiar pattern of stocks with the lowest price-to-book ratios handily beating both the All Stocks universe and stocks with the highest price-to-book ratios. Deciles 1 and 2 each beat the All Stocks universe by an average annual compound return of 2.35 percent or more, whereas deciles 9 and 10 both underperform the All Stocks universe by an average annual compound return of 2.33 percent or more.

TABLE   10.3

Summary Results for Book-to-Price Decile Analysis of All Stocks Universe, January 1, 1946, to December 31, 2009

Decile	$10,000 grows to	Average return	Compound return	Standard deviation	Sharpe ratio
1 (highest)	$40,122,085	16.14%	13.84%	20.12%	0.44
2	$50,429,660	15.87%	14.25%	16.84%	0.55
3	$33,859,330	14.94%	13.54%	15.70%	0.54
4	$16,188,434	13.64%	12.24%	15.72%	0.46
5	$10,839,492	13.02%	11.54%	16.21%	0.40
6	$8,868,366	12.80%	11.19%	16.92%	0.37
7	$4,672,115	11.80%	10.08%	17.52%	0.29
8	$2,909,845	11.16%	9.27%	18.45%	0.23
9	$2,739,699	11.36%	9.17%	19.90%	0.21
10 (lowest)	$2,326,032	11.64%	8.89%	22.27%	0.17
All Stocks	$10,561,110	13.25%	11.49%	17.63%	0.37

WHAT SUBPERIOD ANALYSIS TEACHES US

By looking at the various subperiods, we learn three important lessons:

1. The results for shorter periods of time should be taken with a large grain of salt. If we looked only at the 1967–1984 results, we would think that buying stocks with the lowest price-to-book value ratios was a fantastic way to buy stocks, whereas if we looked at the 1927–1963 data, featured in Table 10.2, we would see that, while stocks with lower price-to-book value ratios did well, you should actually avoid the stocks with the *lowest* price-to-book value ratios at all costs because they were the worst-performing decile for that period. Later, when we examine the full 1926–2009 period, we see what I believe is the truest lesson about this value factor because we will be studying the longest period of time.

2. Factors that exhibit such variance over various time periods should be used carefully. We see later that other factors, such as buyback yield, shareholder yield,

and price momentum do *not* exhibit such erratic performance patterns and are therefore more stable than those factors—like price-to-book—which do.

3. It may be best to combine factors in a composited format so that if one is underperforming—as we saw with stocks from All Stocks with the lowest price-to-book value ratios between 1926 and 1963—the other factors, such as PE, price-to-sales, price-to-cash flow, and so on may be working better and therefore strengthen the efficacy of an overall value approach. We revisit this approach in Chapter Fifteen.

Finally, we might also note that one horrific period for any factor can ripple forward for quite some time, perhaps masking the overall value of the factor. Looking at Table 10.4, we see that almost all of the damage done to the stocks from All Stocks with the lowest price-to-book value ratios was done during the Great Depression. Between 1927 and 1939, the stocks in decile 1—the 10 percent of stocks from All Stocks with the lowest price-to-book value ratios—actually lost 6.55 percent per year, whereas stocks in decile 9—those stocks from All Stocks with the second-highest price-to-book value ratios actually gained 4.78 percent per year. This could be the result of value stocks being a proxy for companies in distress. As Robert Haugen points out in his paper "The Effects of Intrigue, Liquidity, Imprecision, and Bias on the Cross-Section of Expected Stock Returns," "They [Fama and French] argue that firms with low price-to-book ratios (value stocks) tend to be companies in distress. This being the case, the high returns to these stocks may come as no surprise to the market. The high expected returns to value stocks may be risk premiums that investors require as compensation for investing in companies that are in relatively weak financial condition."

T A B L E   10.4

Summary Results for Book-to-Price Decile Analysis of All Stocks Universe, January 1, 1927, to December 31, 1939

Decile	$10,000 grows to	Average return	Compound return	Standard deviation	Sharpe ratio
1 (highest)	$4,142	8.16%	−6.55%	56.69%	−0.20
2	$12,124	11.34%	1.49%	45.07%	−0.08
3	$14,167	10.71%	2.72%	40.14%	−0.06
4	$14,623	10.12%	2.97%	38.07%	−0.05
5	$15,060	9.56%	3.20%	35.51%	−0.05
6	$15,275	9.25%	3.31%	33.95%	−0.05
7	$16,392	9.87%	3.87%	33.74%	−0.03
8	$17,720	9.78%	4.50%	31.55%	−0.02
9	$18,349	9.75%	4.78%	30.29%	−0.01
10 (lowest)	$14,671	7.74%	2.99%	29.64%	−0.07
All Stocks	$14,126	9.46%	2.69%	36.50%	−0.06

Obviously, if stocks with low price-to-book ratios are a proxy for weak, risky companies, it would be no surprise that a great economic depression might send many of them into bankruptcy, thus sending them to the bottom of the performance list. Indeed, the performance of stocks with low price-to-book ratios during the recent market crash of 2007–2009 exhibit similar performance—investors, perhaps for the first time since the Great Depression, were expecting extremely weak economic conditions, and the performance of low price-to-book stocks ended up at the bottom, as Table 10.5 illustrates.

TABLE 10.5

Summary Results for Book-to-Price Decile Analysis of All Stocks Universe, May 1, 2007, to February 28, 2009

Decile	$10,000 grows to	Average return	Compound return	Standard deviation	Sharpe ratio
1 (highest)	$3,203	−43.59%	−46.26%	29.65%	−1.73
2	$4,433	−33.73%	−35.83%	24.58%	−1.66
3	$4,763	−31.34%	−33.27%	23.15%	−1.65
4	$4,874	−30.46%	−32.43%	23.27%	−1.61
5	$4,994	−29.56%	−31.53%	23.17%	−1.58
6	$5,001	−29.39%	−31.47%	23.79%	−1.53
7	$5,227	−27.72%	−29.81%	23.53%	−1.48
8	$5,151	−28.15%	−30.36%	24.28%	−1.46
9	$5,184	−27.80%	−30.12%	24.75%	−1.42
10 (lowest)	$4,729	−31.21%	−33.53%	25.30%	−1.52
All Stocks	$4,618	−32.23%	−34.39%	24.56%	−1.60

THE FULL TIME PERIOD

Now let's look at the results for buying stocks based on the full 1926–2009 time period. The composited portfolios for All Stocks by price-to-book value ratios start on December 31, 1926, and run through December 31, 2009, a full 83 years of data. As Table 10.6 shows, over the entire time period, the best-performing decile is actually decile 2, which earned an average annual compound return of 12.68 and turned $10,000 into $200 million, significantly ahead of the return for All Stocks, which gained 10.46 percent per year and turned $10,000 into $38.5 million. The worst-performing decile was decile 10, containing those stocks with the highest price-to-book value. Table 10.7 contrasts deciles 1, 2, and 10 with All Stocks. For consistency's sake, we elaborate on deciles 1 and 10, even though decile 2 did better than decile 1.

TABLE 10.6

Summary Results for Book-to-Price Decile Analysis of All Stocks Universe, January 1, 1927, to December 31, 2009

Decile	$10,000 grows to	Average return	Compound return	Standard deviation	Sharpe ratio
1 (highest)	$74,047,642	15.94%	11.33%	29.26%	0.22
2	$200,324,516	15.74%	12.68%	23.73%	0.32
3	$149,843,701	14.83%	12.28%	21.58%	0.34
4	$66,442,393	13.59%	11.19%	20.99%	0.29
5	$41,728,068	12.88%	10.57%	20.55%	0.27
6	$31,212,269	12.52%	10.18%	20.55%	0.25
7	$15,157,464	11.65%	9.22%	20.90%	0.20
8	$10,270,496	11.13%	8.71%	20.91%	0.18
9	$8,789,844	11.09%	8.51%	21.57%	0.16
10 (lowest)	$6,440,263	11.09%	8.10%	23.14%	0.13
All Stocks	$38,542,780	13.06%	10.46%	21.67%	0.25

THE RESULTS

Table 10.7 shows the results of buying decile 1 of All Stocks by the 10 percent of stocks with the lowest price-to-book ratios. I also include decile 2 to show that even over the long term, you are better off in the 10 to 20 percent of stocks with the lowest price-to-book ratios. The $10,000 invested in decile 1—those stocks from All Stocks with the lowest price-to-book value ratios—on December 31, 1926, grew to $74 million by the end of 2009, an average annual compound return of 11.33 percent, some 87 basis points better

T A B L E   10.7

Summary Annual Return and Risk Results Data: All Stocks Book-to-Price Decile 1, All Stocks Book-to-Price Decile 2 and All Stocks, January 1, 1927, to December 31, 2009

	All Stocks book-to-price decile 1	All Stocks book-to-price decile 2	All Stocks
Arithmetic average	15.94%	15.74%	13.06%
Geometric average	11.33%	12.68%	10.46%
Median return	17.51%	18.76%	18.54%
Standard deviation	29.26%	23.73%	21.67%
Upside deviation	23.60%	18.47%	14.78%
Downside deviation	20.75%	16.88%	16.03%
Tracking error	12.16	7.23	0.00
Number of positive periods	603	622	606
Number of negative periods	393	374	390
Maximum peak-to-trough decline	−92.09%	−89.45%	−85.45%
Beta	1.25	1.04	1.00
T-statistic (m = 0)	4.63	5.64	5.19
Sharpe ratio (Rf = 5%)	0.22	0.32	0.25
Sortino ratio (MAR = 10%)	0.06	0.16	0.03
$10,000 becomes	$74,047,642	$200,324,516	$38,542,780
Minimum 1-year return	−78.25%	−75.10%	−66.72%
Maximum 1-year return	314.58%	292.62%	201.69%
Minimum 3-year return	−55.17%	−50.53%	−45.99%
Maximum 3-year return	57.73%	54.57%	51.03%
Minimum 5-year return	−34.61%	−28.56%	−23.07%
Maximum 5-year return	42.38%	50.78%	41.17%
Minimum 7-year return	−21.07%	−10.98%	−7.43%
Maximum 7-year return	30.70%	28.05%	23.77%
Minimum 10-year return	−15.55%	−6.43%	−5.31%
Maximum 10-year return	28.03%	26.71%	22.05%
Minimum expected return*	−42.58%	−31.73%	−30.28%
Maximum expected return†	74.45%	63.21%	56.39%

* Minimum expected return is arithmetic return minus 2 times the standard deviation.

† Maximum expected return is arithmetic return plus 2 times the standard deviation.

per year than the All Stocks annual return of 10.46 percent, which turned $10,000 into $38.5 million. Risk, as measured by the standard deviation of return, at 29.26 percent, was much higher for decile 1, compared to 21.67 for the All Stocks universe. The higher risk married to the marginally higher return brought the Sharpe ratio to .22, compared to a Sharpe ratio of .25 for the All Stocks universe. This shows that when selecting stocks with low price-to-book ratios, you are better off looking at the lowest 10 to 20 percent than concentrating on the absolute lowest 10 percent. All the base rates for decile 1 are positive, with the group beating the All Stocks universe 66 percent of all rolling five-year periods and 77 percent of all rolling ten-year periods. Table 10.8 shows the base rates for all periods. Figure 10.1 shows the five-year average annual compound excess (deficient) return for decile 1 minus the return for the All Stocks universe. This is commonly referred to as *alpha*.

T A B L E   10.8

Base Rates for All Stocks Book-to-Price Decile 1 and All Stocks, January 1, 1927, to December 31, 2009

Item	All Stocks book-to-price decile 1 beat "All Stocks"	Percent	Average annual excess return
Single-year return	573 out of 985	58%	2.73%
Rolling 3-year compound return	570 out of 961	59%	1.48%
Rolling 5-year compound return	617 out of 937	66%	1.52%
Rolling 7-year compound return	664 out of 913	73%	1.55%
Rolling 10-year compound return	673 out of 877	77%	1.69%

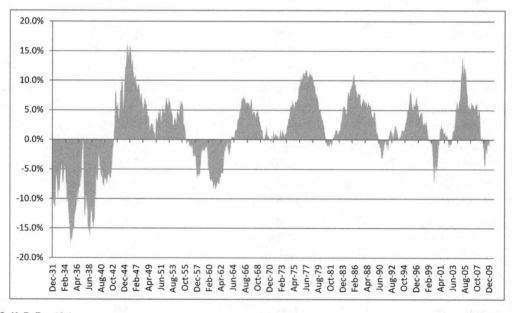

F I G U R E   10.1

Five-year average annual compound excess (deficient) return All Stocks book-to-price decile 1 minus All Stocks, January 1, 1927, to December 31, 2009

LARGE STOCKS WITH LOW PRICE-TO-BOOK RATIOS SIMILAR TO ALL STOCKS

Table 10.9 shows the returns of price-to-book ratios by deciles for the Large Stocks universe. As we saw with the All Stocks group, the second decile is actually the best performing of all 10 deciles. Nevertheless, for continuity's sake we focus on decile 1, the group of Large Stocks with the lowest price-to-book ratios. The $10,000 invested on December 31, 1926, in decile 1 grew to $44 million by the end of 2009, an average annual compound return of 10.63 percent. That's an annual 94 basis points better than the return for the Large Stocks universe, where $10,000 invested over the same period grew to $22 million, an average annual compound return of 9.69 percent. Risk, as measured by the standard deviation of return, was higher for the low price-to-book stocks from Large Stocks. The standard deviation of return for the group was 25.96 percent, compared to 19.35 percent for the Large Stocks universe. The higher risk, married to only slightly higher returns, brought the Sharpe ratio to .22 for the low price-to-book stocks from Large Stocks, compared to .24 for the Large Stocks universe. As Table 10.10 shows, all base rates were positive for the low price-to-book stocks from Large Stocks, with the group beating the Large Stocks universe in 71 percent of all rolling five-year periods and 83 percent of all rolling ten-year periods. Figure 10.2 shows the five-year average annual compound excess (deficient) return for decile 1 minus the return for the Large Stocks universe.

T A B L E   10.9

Summary Results for Book-to-Price Decile Analysis of Large Stocks Universe, January 1, 1927, to December 31, 2009

Decile	$10,000 grows to	Average return	Compound return	Standard deviation	Sharpe ratio
1 (highest)	$43,856,220	14.24%	10.63%	25.96%	0.22
2	$56,571,661	13.53%	10.97%	21.79%	0.27
3	$36,137,654	12.56%	10.37%	20.10%	0.27
4	$32,295,187	12.26%	10.22%	19.34%	0.27
5	$17,180,598	11.46%	9.39%	19.43%	0.23
6	$15,713,733	11.34%	9.27%	19.40%	0.22
7	$18,382,056	11.54%	9.48%	19.35%	0.23
8	$14,882,149	11.36%	9.20%	19.76%	0.21
9	$7,500,437	10.56%	8.30%	20.29%	0.16
10 (lowest)	$4,728,676	10.22%	7.70%	21.38%	0.13
Large Stocks	$21,617,372	11.75%	9.69%	19.35%	0.24

T A B L E   10.10

Base Rates for Large Stocks Book-to-Price Decile 1 and Large Stocks, January 1, 1927, to December 31, 2009

Item	Large Stocks book-to-price decile 1 beat Large Stocks	Percent	Average annual excess return
Single-year return	569 out of 985	58%	2.84%
Rolling 3-year compound return	589 out of 961	61%	1.67%
Rolling 5-year compound return	667 out of 937	71%	1.66%
Rolling 7-year compound return	707 out of 913	77%	1.78%
Rolling 10-year compound return	727 out of 877	83%	2.02%

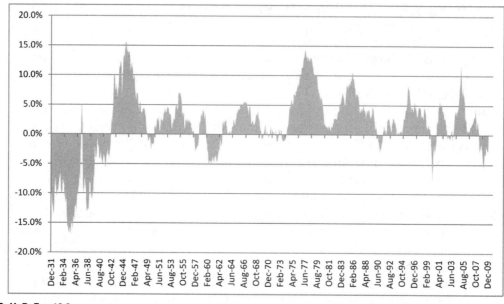

F I G U R E   10.2

Five-year average annual compound excess (deficient) return Large Stocks book-to-price decile 1 minus Large
Stocks, January 1, 1927, to December 31, 2009

WORST-CASE SCENARIOS AND BEST AND WORST RETURNS

As we saw in the beginning of this chapter, stocks with low price-to-book ratios had some
very trying times over the 84 years of our study. For both All Stocks and Large Stocks, the
worst-case scenario was from August 1929 through May 1932, when the lowest price-to-
book stocks from All Stocks lost 92 percent of their value, and the lowest price-to-book
stocks from Large Stocks lost 93 percent. Indeed, over the entire 84-year time period, the
lowest price-to-book stocks from All Stocks had 13 separate occasions when they lost 20
percent or more. The second worst period for the group was the recent bear market
between May 2007 and February 2009, when the group lost 69 percent from peak to
trough. Table 10.11 shows all drops greater than 20 percent for the low price-to-book
stocks from All Stocks. The low price-to-book stocks from Large Stocks suffered 10 losses
greater than 20 percent, and like the group from All Stocks, their second-worst decline
was also during the May 2007 through February 2009 period, where they lost 67 percent.
Table 10.12 summarizes the results for large stocks.

When we look at Tables 10.13 and 10.14, we can see that the best absolute five-year
return for the low price-to-book stocks from All Stocks occurred in the five years ending
May 1946, where the group earned an average annual compound return of 42.38 percent,
turning $10,000 into $58,512. The worst absolute five-year return for the low price-to-
book stocks from All Stocks came in the five years ending May 1932, when they suffered
an average annual compound loss of 34.61 percent, turning $10,000 into a mere $1,196.

T A B L E   10.11

Worst-Case Scenarios: All 20 Percent or Greater Declines for All Stocks Book-to-Price Decile 1, January 1, 1927, to December 31, 2009

Peak date	Peak index value	Trough date	Trough index value	Recovery date	Decline (%)	Decline duration	Recovery duration
Aug–29	1.81	May–32	0.14	Nov–45	−92.09%	33	162
May–46	2.19	May–47	1.42	Apr–50	−35.28%	12	35
Mar–56	8.70	Dec–57	5.98	Sep–58	−31.28%	21	9
Jul–59	11.89	Oct–60	9.12	Feb–62	−23.31%	15	16
Feb–62	11.96	Jun–62	9.26	Mar–63	−22.56%	4	9
Feb–66	26.77	Sep–66	20.33	Mar–67	−24.03%	7	6
Nov–68	45.99	Jun–70	25.01	Jun–75	−45.61%	19	60
Aug–87	687.27	Nov–87	479.51	Jan–89	−30.23%	3	14
Aug–89	867.71	Oct–90	501.08	Jan–92	−42.25%	14	15
Apr–98	3,445.35	Aug–98	2,490.25	Jan–01	−27.72%	4	29
Jun–01	3,971.13	Sep–01	3,111.64	Mar–02	−21.64%	3	6
Apr–02	4,104.00	Sep–02	2,652.83	Jul–03	−35.36%	5	10
May–07	10,227.81	Feb–09	3,150.42	N/A	−69.20%	21	N/A
Average					−38.50%	12	30.92

T A B L E   10.12

Worst-Case Scenarios: All 20 Percent or Greater Declines for Large Stocks Book-to-Price Decile 1, January 1, 1927, to December 31, 2009

Peak date	Peak index value	Trough date	Trough index value	Recovery date	Decline (%)	Decline duration	Recovery duration
Aug–29	1.93	May–32	0.14	May–46	−92.85%	33	168
May–46	1.95	May–47	1.30	Apr–50	−33.39%	12	35
Mar–56	8.29	Dec–57	5.92	Aug–58	−28.55%	21	8
Jul–59	11.68	Sep–60	9.04	Aug–61	−22.63%	14	11
Jan–69	34.40	Jun–70	19.76	Nov–72	−42.57%	17	29
Nov–72	35.13	Sep–74	25.24	Apr–75	−28.15%	22	7
Aug–87	491.83	Nov–87	367.32	Oct–88	−25.32%	3	11
Aug–89	667.71	Oct–90	414.92	Aug–91	−37.86%	14	10
May–01	3,623.29	Sep–02	2,047.84	Feb–04	−43.48%	16	17
May–07	6,664.50	Feb–09	2,167.83	N/A	−67.47%	21	N/A
Average					−42.23%	17.3	32.89

T A B L E   10.13

Best and Worst Average Annual Compound Returns for Monthly Data, January 1, 1927, to December 31, 2009

For any	1-year period	3-year period	5-year period	7-year period	10-year period
All Stocks book-to-price decile 1 minimum compound return	−78.25%	−55.17%	−34.61%	−21.07%	−15.55%
All Stocks book-to-price decile 1 maximum compound return	314.58%	57.73%	42.38%	30.70%	28.03%
All Stocks minimum compound return	−66.72%	−45.99%	−23.07%	−7.43%	−5.31%
All Stocks maximum compound return	201.69%	51.03%	41.17%	23.77%	22.05%

T A B L E   10.14

Terminal Value of $10,000 Invested for Best and Worst Average Annual Compound Returns for Monthly Data, January 1, 1927, to December 31, 2009

For any	1-year period	3-year period	5-year period	7-year period	10-year period
All Stocks book-to-price decile 1 minimum $10,000 value	$2,175	$901	$1,196	$1,908	$1,845
All Stocks book-to-price decile 1 maximum $10,000 value	$41,458	$39,243	$58,512	$65,138	$118,330
All Stocks minimum $10,000 value	$3,328	$1,576	$2,695	$5,825	$5,793
All Stocks maximum $10,000 value	$30,169	$34,452	$56,062	$44,504	$73,345

The best five-year *relative* performance versus the All Stocks universe occurred in the five years ending January 1946, when the low price-to-book stocks gained 463.62 percent, compared to a gain of 211.18 percent for the All Stocks universe, a cumulative advantage of 252 percent over All Stocks. That translates to an average annual compound return of 41.32 percent for the low price-to-book group versus an average annual compound return of 25.49 percent for the All Stocks universe.

The worst five-year relative performance for the low price-to-book group from All Stocks versus the All Stocks universe occurred in the five years ending August 1937, when the group gained 65.66 percent versus a gain of 180.60 percent for the All Stocks universe, a cumulative five-year deficit of −114.94 percent. That translates to an average annual compound return of 10.62 percent for the low price-to-book stocks versus an average annual gain of 22.92 percent for the All Stocks universe. Figure 10.1 shows the rolling five-year average annual compound excess (or deficient) return for the stocks from All Stocks with the lowest price-to-book ratios, minus the average annual compound return for the All Stocks universe, or the five-year rolling alpha earned by the strategy.

Looking at Tables 10.15 and 10.16, you can see that the best five-year absolute return for the low price-to-book stocks from Large Stocks occurred in the five years ending May 1937, when the low price-to-book stocks from Large Stocks earned an average annual

TABLE 10.15

Best and Worst Average Annual Compound Returns for Monthly Data, January 1, 1927, to December 31, 2009

For any	1-year period	3-year period	5-year period	7-year period	10-year period
Large Stocks book-to-price decile 1 minimum compound return	−83.47%	−56.45%	−33.65%	−20.02%	−15.27%
Large Stocks book-to-price decile 1 maximum compound return	285.97%	49.80%	41.36%	28.27%	24.64%
Large Stocks minimum compound return	−66.63%	−43.53%	−20.15%	−6.95%	−5.70%
Large Stocks maximum compound return	159.52%	45.64%	36.26%	22.83%	19.57%

TABLE 10.16

Terminal Value of $10,000 Invested for Best and Worst Average Annual Compound Returns for Monthly Data, January 1, 1927, to December 31, 2009

For any	1-year period	3-year period	5-year period	7-year period	10-year period
Large Stocks book-to-price decile 1 minimum $10,000 value	$1,653	$826	$1,286	$2,094	$1,907
Large Stocks book-to-price decile 1 maximum $10,000 value	$38,597	$33,612	$56,442	$57,119	$90,463
Large Stocks minimum $10,000 value	$3,337	$1,800	$3,247	$6,041	$5,561
Large Stocks maximum $10,000 value	$25,952	$30,890	$46,970	$42,189	$59,747

compound return of 41.36 percent over the previous five years, turning $10,000 into $56,442. The worst five-year absolute return for the low price-to-book stocks from Large Stocks came in the five years ending May 1932, when they had an average annual compound loss of 33.65 percent, turning $10,000 invested five years earlier into $1,286.

The best five-year relative return for the low price-to-book stocks from Large Stocks occurred in the five years ending May 1945, when they gained 304 percent versus a gain of 117 percent for the Large Stocks universe, a cumulative advantage of 187 percent. This translates into an average annual compound return of 32.23 percent compared with 16.81 percent for the Large Stocks universe. The worst five-year relative return for the low price-to-book stocks from Large Stocks was for the five years ending September 1936, when they gained 42 percent versus 126 percent for Large Stocks, a cumulative deficit of 84 percent. This translates into an average annual compound return of 7.31 percent for the low price-to-book group versus an average annual compound return of 17.70 percent for the Large Stocks universe. Figure 10.2 shows the rolling five-year average annual compound excess (or deficient) return of the low price-to-book stocks from Large Stocks minus the average annual compound return for the Large Stocks universe, or the rolling five-year alpha earned by the strategy.

STOCKS WITH HIGH PRICE-TO-BOOK RATIOS ARE POOR PERFORMERS

As we've already seen by looking at the deciles for both All Stocks and Large Stocks, the decile of stocks with the highest price-to-book ratios—decile 10—is a poor performer both in All Stocks and Large Stocks. Let's look at the All Stocks group first.

THE RESULTS

As Table 10.17 shows, $10,000 invested on December 31, 1926, in decile 10—those stocks in the All Stocks universe with the highest price-to-book ratios—grew to $6,440,263 by the end of 2009, an average annual compound return of 8.10 percent. That's about $32 million less than you'd have earned with a $10,000 investment in the All Stocks universe, where it grew to $38.5 million, an average annual compound return of 10.46 percent. Risk, as measured by the standard deviation of return, was 23.14 percent, higher than All Stocks risk of 21.67 percent. The lower return combined with the higher risk brought the Sharpe ratio for decile 10 to .13, compared to .25 for the All Stocks universe. Table 10.17 shows the relevant statistics. All base rates for the group were negative, with the high price-to-book stocks from All Stocks beating the All Stocks universe just 26 percent of all rolling five-year periods and 12 percent of all rolling ten-year periods. Table 10.18 shows the base rates for all holding periods. Figure 10.3 shows the five-year average annual compound excess (or, in this case, mostly deficient) return for decile 10 minus the return for the All Stocks universe.

TABLE   10.17

Summary Annual Return and Risk Results Data: All Stocks Book-to-Price Decile 10 and All Stocks, January 1, 1927, to December 31, 2009

	All Stocks book-to-price decile 10	All Stocks
Arithmetic average	11.09%	13.06%
Geometric average	8.10%	10.46%
Median return	15.63%	18.54%
Standard deviation	23.14%	21.67%
Upside deviation	14.26%	14.78%
Downside deviation	17.44%	16.03%
Tracking error	9.63	0.00
Number of positive periods	596	606
Number of negative periods	400	390
Maximum peak-to-trough decline	−83.37%	−85.45%
Beta	0.97	1.00
T-statistic (m = 0)	4.16	5.19
Sharpe ratio (Rf = 5%)	0.13	0.25
Sortino ratio (MAR = 10%)	−0.11	0.03
$10,000 becomes	$6,440,263	$38,542,780
Minimum 1-year return	−59.59%	−66.72%
Maximum 1-year return	124.23%	201.69%
Minimum 3-year return	−44.02%	−45.99%
Maximum 3-year return	50.10%	51.03%

(continued on next page)

T A B L E   10.17

Summary Annual Return and Risk Results Data: All Stocks Book-to-Price Decile 10 and All Stocks, January 1, 1927, to December 31, 2009 *(Continued)*

	All Stocks book-to-price decile 10	All Stocks
Minimum 5-year return	−18.83%	−23.07%
Maximum 5-year return	37.16%	41.17%
Minimum 7-year return	−8.95%	−7.43%
Maximum 7-year return	28.34%	23.77%
Minimum 10-year return	−6.28%	−5.31%
Maximum 10-year return	24.07%	22.05%
Minimum expected return*	−35.20%	−30.28%
Maximum expected return†	57.38%	56.39%

* Minimum expected return is arithmetic return minus 2 times the standard deviation.
† Maximum expected return is arithmetic return plus 2 times the standard deviation.

T A B L E   10.18

Base Rates for All Stocks Book-to-Price Decile 10 and All Stocks, January 1, 1927, to December 31, 2009

Item	All Stocks book-to-price decile 10 beat all Stocks	Percent	Average annual excess return
Single-year return	423 out of 985	43%	−1.85%
Rolling 3-year compound return	290 out of 961	30%	−2.46%
Rolling 5-year compound return	243 out of 937	26%	−2.60%
Rolling 7-year compound return	159 out of 913	17%	−2.64%
Rolling 10-year compound return	103 out of 877	12%	−2.55%

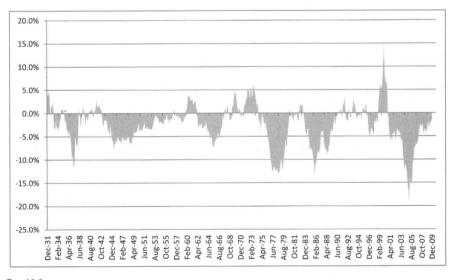

F I G U R E   10.3

Five-year average annual compound excess (deficient) return All Stocks book-to-price decile 10 minus All Stocks, January 1, 1927, to December 31, 2009

LARGE STOCKS ALSO SUFFER

The news is no better for the high price-to-book stocks from the Large Stocks universe; $10,000 invested on December 31, 1926, grew to just $4,728,676, an average annual compound return of 7.70 percent. That's about $17 million less than you would have earned with a $10,000 investment in the Large Stocks universe itself, where it grew to $21.6 million, an average annual compound return of 9.69 percent. Risk, once again measured by the standard deviation of return, was 21.38, higher than that of Large Stocks, where the standard deviation of return over the same period was 19.35 percent. The vastly lower return combined with the higher risk brought the Sharpe ratio for the high price-to-book stocks from Large Stocks to .13, compared to .24 for the Large Stocks universe itself. Table 10.19 shows all the

T A B L E   10.19

Summary Annual Return and Risk Results Data: Large Stocks Book-to-Price Decile 10 and Large Stocks, January 1, 1927, to December 31, 2009

	Large Stocks book-to-price decile 10	Large Stocks
Arithmetic average	10.22%	11.75%
Geometric average	7.70%	9.69%
Median return	14.35%	16.75%
Standard deviation	21.38%	19.35%
Upside deviation	13.68%	13.10%
Downside deviation	15.86%	14.40%
Tracking error	10.23	0.00
Number of positive periods	581	609
Number of negative periods	415	387
Maximum peak-to-trough decline	−83.70%	−84.33%
Beta	0.97	1.00
T-statistic (m = 0)	4.16	5.25
Sharpe ratio (Rf = 5%)	0.13	0.24
Sortino ratio (MAR = 10%)	−0.14	−0.02
$10,000 becomes	$4,728,676	$21,617,372
Minimum 1-year return	−62.21%	−66.63%
Maximum 1-year return	100.70%	159.52%
Minimum 3-year return	−44.40%	−43.53%
Maximum 3-year return	53.03%	45.64%
Minimum 5-year return	−21.48%	−20.15%
Maximum 5-year return	38.92%	36.26%
Minimum 7-year return	−11.37%	−6.95%
Maximum 7-year return	29.33%	22.83%
Minimum 10-year return	−7.65%	−5.70%
Maximum 10-year return	25.98%	19.57%
Minimum expected return*	−32.55%	−26.96%
Maximum expected return†	52.99%	50.46%

* Minimum expected return is arithmetic return minus 2 times the standard deviation.
† Maximum expected return is arithmetic return plus 2 times the standard deviation.

T A B L E   10.20

Base Rates for LS Book-to-Price Decile 10 and Large Stocks, January 1, 1927, to December 31, 2009

Item	Large Stocks book-to-price decile 10 beat all stocks	Percent	Average annual excess return
Single-year return	427 out of 985	43%	−1.40%
Rolling 3-year compound return	355 out of 961	37%	−1.85%
Rolling 5-year compound return	301 out of 937	32%	−1.92%
Rolling 7-year compound return	195 out of 913	21%	−1.96%
Rolling 10-year compound return	160 out of 877	18%	−1.88%

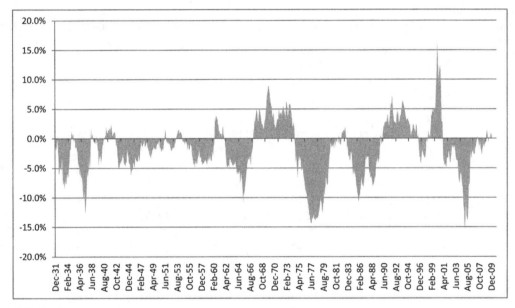

F I G U R E   10.4

Five-year average annual compound excess (deficient) return Large Stocks book-to-price Decile 10 minus Large Stocks, January 1, 1927, to December 31, 2009

relevant statistics. All base rates were negative, with the high price-to-book stocks from Large Stocks beating the Large Stocks universe in 32 percent of all rolling five-year periods and in 18 percent of all rolling ten-year periods. Table 10.20 shows the base rates for all holding periods. Figure 10.4 shows the five-year average annual compound excess (deficient) return for decile 1 minus the return for the Large Stocks universe.

WORST-CASE SCENARIOS AND BEST AND WORST RETURNS

The stocks with the highest price-to-book ratios from All Stocks had 14 separate declines of 20 percent or more. The worst drawdown came between August 1929 and May 1932, when the group lost 83.37 percent. The second worst decline came during the bear market between February 2000 and September 2002, when the group plunged 73.67 percent, a loss it has not recovered from as I write. Table 10.21 shows all drawdowns exceeding 20 percent for the group.

On an absolute basis, the best five-year return for the high price-to-book stocks from All Stocks came with the five years ending February 2000, when the group earned an average annual compound return of 37.16 percent, turning $10,000 into $48,545. The worst absolute five-year performance for the group occurred in the five years ending July 1934, when the group posted an average annual compound loss of 18.83 percent, turning $10,000 into $3,524 (see Tables 10.22 and 10.23).

T A B L E   10.21

Worst-Case Scenarios: All 20 Percent or Greater Declines for All Stocks Book-to-Price Decile 10, January 1, 1927, to December 31, 2009

Peak date	Peak index value	Trough date	Trough index value	Recovery date	Decline (%)	Decline duration	Recovery duration
Aug–29	2.44	May–32	0.41	Oct–45	−83.37%	33	161
May–46	3.27	Nov–48	2.27	May–50	−30.52%	30	18
Jul–57	10.09	Dec–57	7.88	Aug–58	−21.90%	5	8
Nov–61	20.41	Oct–62	12.06	Sep–65	−40.92%	11	35
Apr–66	25.77	Oct–66	20.55	Jan–67	−20.26%	6	3
Dec–68	42.59	Jun–70	24.00	Jan–72	−43.64%	18	19
May–72	52.13	Sep–74	19.55	Jan–80	−62.50%	28	64
Nov–80	89.55	Jul–82	54.33	Jan–83	−39.33%	20	6
Jun–83	121.55	Jul–84	76.03	Apr–86	−37.45%	13	21
Aug–87	163.87	Nov–87	102.29	Aug–89	−37.58%	3	21
Jun–90	172.47	Oct–90	127.83	Feb–91	−25.88%	4	4
May–96	473.89	Apr–97	354.03	Sep–97	−25.29%	11	5
Apr–98	548.69	Aug–98	394.82	Dec–98	−28.04%	4	4
Feb–00	1324.42	Sep–02	348.69	N/A	−73.67%	31	N/A
Average					−40.74%	15.5	28.38

T A B L E   10.22

Best and Worst Average Annual Compound Returns for Monthly Data, January 1, 1927, to December 31, 2009

For any	1-year period	3-year period	5-year period	7-year period	10-year period
All Stocks book-to-price decile 10 minimum compound return	−59.59%	−44.02%	−18.83%	−8.95%	−6.28%
All Stocks book-to-price decile 10 maximum compound return	124.23%	50.10%	37.16%	28.34%	24.07%
All Stocks minimum compound return	−66.72%	−45.99%	−23.07%	−7.43%	−5.31%
All Stocks maximum compound return	201.69%	51.03%	41.17%	23.77%	22.05%

TABLE 10.23

Terminal Value of $10,000 Invested for Best and Worst Average Annual Compound Returns for Monthly Data, January 1, 1927, to December 31, 2009

For any	1-year period	3-year period	5-year period	7-year period	10-year period
All Stocks book-to-price decile 10 minimum $10,000 value	$4,041	$1,754	$3,524	$5,188	$5,229
All Stocks book-to-price decile 10 maximum $10,000 value	$22,423	$33,820	$48,545	$57,345	$86,454
All Stocks minimum $10,000 value	$3,328	$1,576	$2,695	$5,825	$5,793
All Stocks maximum $10,000 value	$30,169	$34,452	$56,062	$44,504	$73,345

The best relative five-year performance for the high price-to-book stocks from All Stocks was the five years ending February 2000, when the group gained 385.45 percent versus a gain of 172.30 percent for All Stocks, providing a 213.15 percent cumulative advantage over the All Stocks universe. On an average annual compound basis, that translates into a return of 37.16 percent for the high price-to-book All Stocks group versus 22.18 percent for the All Stocks universe.

The worst relative five-year performance on a cumulative basis for price-to-book stocks versus the All Stocks group occurred in the five years ending May 1937, when the high price-to-book stocks from All Stocks earned 266.98 percent compared to 460.62 percent for the All Stocks universe, a cumulative deficit of 193.64 percent. On an average annual compound return basis, the high price-to-book stocks earned 29.70 percent over the period versus 41.17 percent a year for the All Stocks universe. Figure 10.3 shows the rolling five-year excess (or deficient) average annual returns (alpha) for the high price-to-book stocks from All Stocks minus the return for All Stocks.

LARGE STOCKS

Between 1926 and 2009, the 10 percent of Large Stocks with the highest price-to-book ratios had 10 separate occasions when they fell by 20 percent or more. The worst decline was during the bear market between August 1929 and June 1932, when the high price-to-book stocks from Large Stocks fell by 83.70 percent from peak to trough. Like the pricey All Stocks group, their second worst decline occurred between February 2000 and September 2002, when they lost 70.70 percent in value. Like the All Stocks group, they have yet to recover from this decline. Table 10.24 shows all losses of 20 percent or more for the high price-to-book stocks from Large Stocks.

The best absolute five-year performance for the high price-to-book stocks from Large Stocks occurred in the five years ending February 2000, when the group earned an average annual compound return of 38.92 percent, turning $10,000 into $51,747. The worst absolute return for the group occurred in the five years ending March 1933, when the group had an average annual compound loss of 21.48 percent, turning $10,000 into $2,985 (see Tables 10.25 and 10.26).

T A B L E 10.24

Worst-Case Scenarios: All 20 Percent or Greater Declines for Large Stocks Book-to-Price Decile 10, January 1, 1927, to December 31, 2009

Peak date	Peak index value	Trough date	Trough index value	Recovery date	Decline (%)	Decline duration	Recovery duration
Aug–29	2.07	Jun–32	0.34	Dec–49	−83.70%	34	210
Jul–57	6.75	Dec–57	5.21	Sep–58	−22.86%	5	9
Nov–61	11.76	Oct–62	7.11	Aug–65	−39.58%	11	34
Dec–69	21.51	Jun–70	15.13	Mar–71	−29.66%	6	9
Dec–72	30.88	Sep–74	11.92	Sep–80	−61.41%	21	72
Nov–80	37.32	Jul–82	23.71	Feb–83	−36.47%	20	7
Jun–83	48.36	May–84	32.42	Mar–86	−32.96%	11	22
Aug–87	78.13	Nov–87	51.52	Jul–89	−34.05%	3	20
Jun–98	349.36	Aug–98	278.94	Nov–98	−20.16%	2	3
Feb–00	809.32	Sep–02	237.15	N/A	−70.70%	31	N/A
Average					−43.15%	14.4	42.89

T A B L E 10.25

Best and Worst Average Annual Compound Returns for Monthly Data, January 1, 1927, to December 31, 2009

For any	1-year period	3-year period	5-year period	7-year period	10-year period
Large Stocks book-to-price decile 10 minimum compound return	−62.21%	−44.40%	−21.48%	−11.37%	−7.65%
Large Stocks book-to-price decile 10 maximum compound return	100.70%	53.03%	38.92%	29.33%	25.98%
Large Stocks minimum compound return	−66.72%	−45.99%	−23.07%	−7.43%	−5.31%
Large Stocks maximum compound return	201.69%	51.03%	41.17%	23.77%	22.05%

T A B L E 10.26

Terminal Value of $10,000 Invested for Best and Worst Average Annual Compound Returns for Monthly Data, January 1, 1927, to December 31, 2009

For any	1-year period	3-year period	5-year period	7-year period	10-year period
Large Stocks book-to-price decile 10 minimum $10,000 value	$3,779	$1,719	$2,985	$4,297	$4,511
Large Stocks book-to-price decile 10 maximum $10,000 value	$20,070	$35,839	$51,747	$60,509	$100,730
Large Stocks minimum $10,000 value	$3,337	$1,800	$3,247	$6,041	$5,561
Large Stocks maximum $10,000 value	$25,952	$30,890	$46,970	$42,189	$59,747

The best relative five-year return for the group was for the five years ending February 2000, when the group earned 417.47 percent compared to 179.90 percent for the Large Stocks universe, a cumulative advantage of 237.57 percent. In terms of average annual return, that was an average annual compound return of 38.92 percent for the high price-to-book Large Stocks and an average annual gain of 22.18 percent for the Large Stocks universe itself.

The worst relative five-year return on a cumulative basis versus Large Stocks was during the five years ending May 1937, when the group earned 196.49 percent versus 369.71 percent for the Large Stocks universe, a cumulative deficit of 173.22 percent. In terms of average annual return, that translates to an average annual compound gain of 24.28 percent for the high price-to-book stocks from Large Stocks versus an average annual compound return of 41.17 percent for the Large Stocks universe. Figure 10.4 shows the rolling five-year excess (or deficient) average annual returns (alpha) for the high price-to-book stocks from Large Stocks minus the return for Large Stocks itself.

IMPLICATIONS

As we saw when we previously examined the deciles for both All Stocks and Large Stocks, deciles 2 and 3—those groups of stocks that are the second and third cheapest when ranked on price-to-book ratios—do substantially better than stocks in decile 1—those stocks that are in the 10 percent of stocks that are cheapest based upon price-to-book ratio (Figures 10.5 and 10.6). The second decile earned an average annual compound return of 12.71 percent between 1926 and 2009, well ahead of decile 1, which earned 11.26 percent per year. Deciles 2 and 3 also had better base rates, with decile 2 beating All Stocks in 79 percent of all rolling five-year periods and in 87 percent of all rolling ten-year periods and decile 3 beating All Stocks in 78 percent of all rolling five-year periods and 93 percent of all rolling ten-year periods. That is substantially better than the base rates earned by decile 1. As Table 10.4 shows, much of that advantage was earned between 1926 and 1939 when decile 1—those stocks with the lowest price-to-book ratios—suffered mightily compared with deciles 2 and 3. The dislocations of the crash and Great Depression hit the riskiest stocks the hardest, and no doubt many were sent into bankruptcy during that time. Yet, the addition of these data now is very timely. The recent crash of 2007–2009 saw investors exhibiting much the same terror that investors experienced 80 years ago, and this was manifested in the severity with which they punished risky stocks. Tables 10.27 and 10.28 summarize returns by decade for high and low price-to-book companies in All Stocks and Large Stocks. It's also instructive to see that the more data we have access to, the more we are able to learn. In the case of picking stocks on price-to-book value ratios, here's what the last 84 years demonstrate:

- Be wary of studies that cover only a limited period of time. For instance, Roger Ibbotson's "Decile Portfolios of the New York Stock Exchange, 1967–1984," showed that the decile of stocks with the lowest price-to-book value ratios earned compound annual returns of 14.36 percent, whereas the stocks in the decile of stocks with the highest price-to-book ratios earned compound annual returns of just 6.06 percent. But that was only 18 years of data, and as we have seen, such

T A B L E   10.27

Average Annual Compound Rates of Return by Decade

	1920s*	1930s	1940s	1950s	1960s	1970s	1980s	1990s	2000s†
All Stocks book-to-price decile 1	9.79%	−10.97%	17.34%	18.53%	11.34%	13.29%	21.25%	14.68%	9.12%
All Stocks book-to-price decile 10	13.26%	0.10%	7.31%	17.38%	10.27%	2.84%	12.31%	20.31%	−4.79%
All Stocks	12.33%	−0.03%	11.57%	18.07%	10.72%	7.56%	16.78%	15.35%	4.39%

* Returns for January 1, 1927, to December 31, 1929.
† Returns for January 1, 2000, to December 31, 2009.

T A B L E   10.28

Average Annual Compound Rates of Return by Decade

	1920s*	1930s	1940s	1950s	1960s	1970s	1980s	1990s	2000s†
Large Stocks book-to-price decile 1	17.17%	−11.63%	14.45%	19.77%	8.84%	12.71%	22.07%	15.67%	5.12%
Large Stocks book-to-price decile 10	8.38%	−2.13%	7.45%	15.42%	9.31%	0.26%	14.39%	22.78%	−3.27%
Large Stocks	17.73%	−1.05%	9.65%	17.06%	8.31%	6.65%	17.34%	16.38%	2.42%

* Returns for January 1, 1927, to December 31, 1929.
† Returns for January 1, 2000, to December 31, 2009.

a small dataset limits your ability to draw true conclusions as to how robust the results actually are.

- It is not always the lowest absolute rankings of a value factor that do the best. One of the reasons we moved to decile analysis for this version of the book was because looking at the highest and lowest 50 stocks might be too restrictive. Here we see that most of the value of price-to-book is unlocked in the second and third deciles. It is worth studying all the deciles for all the factors we cover to see how uniform the return patterns are for each decile.

- Because of the skewed nature of the returns to decile 1 in the 1920s and 1930s, an analysis of the group between 1926 and 1963 shows that buying low price-to-book stocks failed to beat the All Stocks universe. As we dug deeper, we saw that this was largely a result of the beating they took in the 1930s and serves as a reminder that we should always go as deep into the data as possible.

- Finally, this highlights the dangers of relying on a single factor. Had you conducted a study in 1963 for the period 1926 through 1963, you would have concluded that price-to-book was truly erratic, with both the cheapest stocks—decile 1—and the most expensive stocks—decile 10—underperforming the All Stocks universe. Between 1926 and 1963, an investment in the All Stocks universe earned an average annual compound return of 9.43 percent, whereas an investment in decile 1 by price-to-book earned just 7.41 percent, but decile 10 earned 7.71 percent. Only the fullness of time revealed the erratic nature of the price-to-book ratio. This also argues the importance of looking at a variety of factors, as we do in Chapter Fifteen. Finally, Figures 10.5 and 10.6 revisit the return by decile for the All Stocks universe and the Large Stocks universe.

Now let's move on to dividend yield to see what it tells us about a stock's prospects.

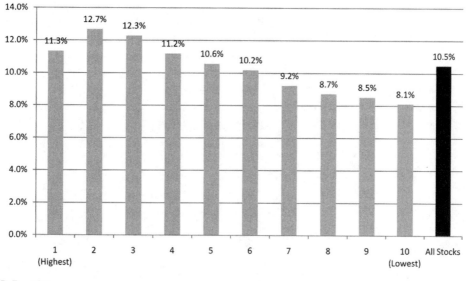

FIGURE 10.5

Average annual compound return by book-to-price decile, All Stocks universe, January 1, 1927, to December 31, 2009

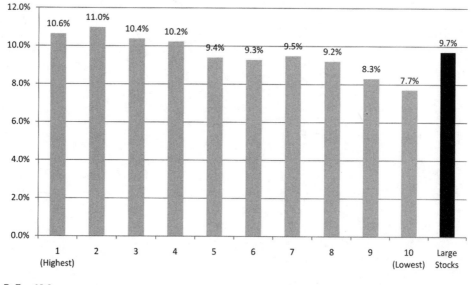

FIGURE 10.6

Average annual compound return by book-to-price decile, Large Stocks universe, January 1, 1927, to December 31, 2009

DIVIDEND YIELDS: BUYING AN INCOME

October. This is one of the peculiarly dangerous months to speculate in stocks. The others are July, January, September, April, November, May, March, June, December, August and February.

—Mark Twain

Investors who find all months peculiarly dangerous often seek redemption in stocks with high dividend yields. Since dividends have historically accounted for more than half a stock's total return, investors think it wise to concentrate on stocks paying high dividends. What's more, it's impossible to monkey with a dividend yield, since a company must pay, defer, or cancel it.

You find a stock's dividend yield by dividing the indicated annual dividend rate by the current price of the stock. The result is then multiplied by 100 to make it a percentage. Thus, if a company pays an annual dividend of $1.00 and the current price of the stock is $10.00, the dividend yield is 10 percent.

We look at buying the decile of highest-yielding stocks from the All Stocks and Large Stocks universes, and since we use data from CRSP, we can begin our study in 1926.

THE RESULTS

As Table 11.1 shows, a $10,000 investment in the decile of highest-yielding stocks from the All Stocks universe on December 31, 1926, was worth $102,331,244 at the end of 2009, an average annual compound return of 11.77 percent. That's $63 million more than

T A B L E   11.1

Summary Annual Return and Risk Results Data: All Stocks Dividend Yield Decile 1 and All Stocks, January 1, 1927, to December 31, 2009

	All Stocks dividend yield decile 1	All Stocks
Arithmetic average	14.00%	13.06%
Geometric average	11.77%	10.46%
Median return	17.23%	18.54%
Standard deviation	20.15%	21.67%
Upside deviation	15.15%	14.78%
Downside deviation	15.91%	16.03%
Tracking error	9.29	0.00
Number of positive periods	638	606
Number of negative periods	358	390
Maximum peak-to-trough decline	−90.03%	−85.45%
Beta	0.84	1.00
T-statistic (m = 0)	5.96	5.19
Sharpe ratio (Rf = 5%)	0.34	0.25
Sortino ratio (MAR = 10%)	0.11	0.03
$10,000 becomes	$102,331,244	$38,542,780
Minimum 1-year return	−74.39%	−66.72%
Maximum 1-year return	214.52%	201.69%
Minimum 3-year return	−51.80%	−45.99%
Maximum 3-year return	58.05%	51.03%
Minimum 5-year return	−29.24%	−23.07%
Maximum 5-year return	44.41%	41.17%
Minimum 7-year return	−10.39%	−7.43%
Maximum 7-year return	27.58%	23.77%
Minimum 10-year return	−7.84%	−5.31%
Maximum 10-year return	22.60%	22.05%
Minimum expected return*	−26.29%	−30.28%
Maximum expected return†	54.30%	56.39%

* Minimum expected return is arithmetic return minus 2 times the standard deviation.
† Maximum expected return is arithmetic return plus 2 times the standard deviation.

an investment in the All Stocks universe, where $10,000 grew to $38.5 million, an average annual compound return of 10.46 percent. Risk, as measured by the standard deviation of return, was 20.15 percent, compared with 21.67 percent for the All Stocks universe. The strategy has a higher Sharpe ratio than All Stocks because it took less risk to generate the better absolute performance. The Sharpe ratio for the decile of highest-yielding stocks from All Stocks was .34, compared to .25 for the All Stocks universe. As Table 11.2 shows, all the base rates for the highest-yielding stocks are positive, with the group beating All Stocks in 67 percent of all rolling five-year periods and 75 percent of all rolling ten-year periods.

TABLE 11.2

Base Rates for All Stocks Dividend Yield Decile 1 and All Stocks, January 1, 1927, to December 31, 2009

Item	All Stocks dividend yield decile 1 beat All Stocks	Percent	Average annual excess return
Single-year return	535 out of 985	54%	1.21%
Rolling 3-year compound return	611 out of 961	64%	1.50%
Rolling 5-year compound return	628 out of 937	67%	1.49%
Rolling 7-year compound return	610 out of 913	67%	1.57%
Rolling 10-year compound return	659 out of 877	75%	1.59%

On the downside, the group suffers deeper declines than those from the All Stocks universe over all one-, three-, five-, seven-, and ten-year periods. For example, the minimum three-year return for the highest-yielding stocks was an annual loss of 51.80 percent, compared to a loss of 45.99 percent per year for All Stocks. Even when you extend the time frame to 10 years, the worst 10 years for the high-yielding stocks was an annual decline of 7.84 percent versus a decline of 5.31 percent for the All Stocks universe. As we'll see when we examine the deciles, the highest-yielding stocks from All Stocks are actually outperformed by deciles 2, 3, and 4, suggesting that stocks with the highest yields might exhibit risks that other stocks—which also pay above-average dividends—might not possess.

For example, the best-performing decile was decile 3, where $10,000 invested on December 31, 1926, grew to $145 million by the end of 2009, an average annual compound return of 12.23 percent. The risk was also considerably lower for the third decile of highest-yielding stocks from All Stocks, which sported a standard deviation of return of just 18.71 percent. The decile also had better minimum returns for all rolling periods between one and ten years. See Tables 11.1 and 11.2 for a complete review of these summary statistics. Figure 11.1 shows the five-year average annual compound excess (deficient) return for decile 1 minus the return for the All Stocks universe.

LARGE STOCKS

A $10,000 investment in the decile of highest-yielding stocks from the Large Stocks universe on December 31, 1926, grew to $51,678,232 by the end of 2009. That's a compound return of 10.85 percent, some 1.16 percent better on an average annual compound basis than the Large Stocks universe's return of 9.69 percent, which grew from $10,000 to $21,617,372 over the same period. The decile of highest-yielding stocks from Large Stocks had a standard deviation of return of 19.36 percent, a virtual dead heat with Large Stocks' 19.35 percent. This, coupled with the higher absolute return, accounts for the high Sharpe ratio of .30. Over shorter holding periods, the high-yielding stocks from Large Stocks had greater absolute losses than the Large Stocks universe itself, but also had significantly higher absolute gains. After your holding period reaches 10 years or longer, the high-yielding Large Stocks provide better protection on the downside than the Large Stocks universe while also providing better maximum returns on the upside. Table 11.3 shows the relevant numbers for both groups between 1926 and 2009.

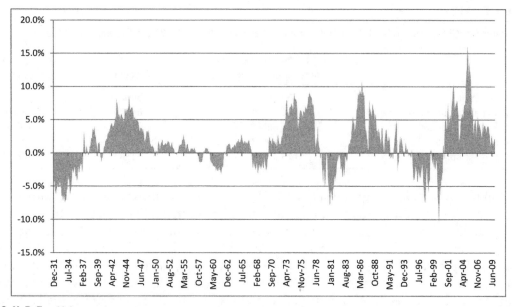

F I G U R E   11.1

Five-year average annual compound excess (deficient) return All Stocks dividend yield decile 1 minus All Stocks, January 1, 1927, to December 31, 2009

T A B L E   11.3

Summary Annual Return and Risk Results Data: Large Stocks Dividend Yield Decile 1 and Large Stocks, January 1, 1927, to December 31, 2009

	Large Stocks dividend yield-decile 1	Large Stocks
Arithmetic average	12.90%	11.75%
Geometric average	10.85%	9.69%
Median return	13.89%	16.75%
Standard deviation	19.36%	19.35%
Upside deviation	14.57%	13.10%
Downside deviation	14.45%	14.40%
Tracking error	9.29	0.00
Number of positive periods	605	609
Number of negative periods	391	387
Maximum peak-to-trough decline	−88.81%	−84.33%
Beta	0.89	1.00
T-statistic (m = 0)	5.74	5.25
Sharpe ratio (Rf = 5%)	0.30	0.24
Sortino ratio (MAR = 10%)	0.06	−0.02
$10,000 becomes	$51,678,232	$21,617,372
Minimum 1-year return	−73.79%	−66.63%
Maximum 1-year return	241.44%	159.52%

(continued on next page)

T A B L E   11.3

Summary Annual Return and Risk Results Data: Large Stocks Dividend Yield Decile 1 and Large Stocks, January 1, 1927, to December 31, 2009 *(Continued)*

	Large Stocks dividend yield-decile 1	Large Stocks
Minimum 3-year return	−50.25%	−43.53%
Maximum 3-year return	57.13%	45.64%
Minimum 5-year return	−27.58%	−20.15%
Maximum 5-year return	44.16%	36.26%
Minimum 7-year return	−9.53%	−6.95%
Maximum 7-year return	27.31%	22.83%
Minimum 10-year return	−5.64%	−5.70%
Maximum 10-year return	22.25%	19.57%
Minimum expected return*	−25.83%	−26.96%
Maximum expected return†	51.62%	50.46%

* Minimum expected return is arithmetic return minus 2 times the standard deviation.
† Maximum expected return is arithmetic return plus 2 times the standard deviation.

T A B L E   11.4

Base Rates for Large Stocks Dividend Yield Decile 1 and Large Stocks, January 1, 1927, to December 31, 2009

Item	Large Stocks dividend yield decile 1 beat Large Stocks	Percent	Average annual excess return
Single-year return	513 out of 985	52%	1.50%
Rolling 3-year compound return	611 out of 961	64%	1.35%
Rolling 5-year compound return	652 out of 937	70%	1.42%
Rolling 7-year compound return	670 out of 913	73%	1.49%
Rolling 10-year compound return	713 out of 877	81%	1.45%

The high-yield strategy is also slightly more consistent when used with Large Stocks. Here, the decile of highest-yielding stocks beat the universe 81 percent of the time over all rolling ten-year periods. Table 11.4 shows the base rates versus Large Stocks. As we saw with the All Stocks high-yielding decile, the top decile in Large Stocks by dividend yield is actually outperformed by the third decile, implying that sometimes high dividend yield is not an ideal metric to use on its own. The third decile of Large Stocks by dividend yield earned 11.06 percent per year and had a standard deviation of return of 18.05 percent, giving it a higher Sharpe ratio of .34. We'll see in Chapter Twenty-Six that dividend yield can be an even stronger strategy when combined with market-leading companies. Figure 11.2 shows the five-year average annual compound excess (deficient) return for decile 1 minus the return for the Large Stocks universe.

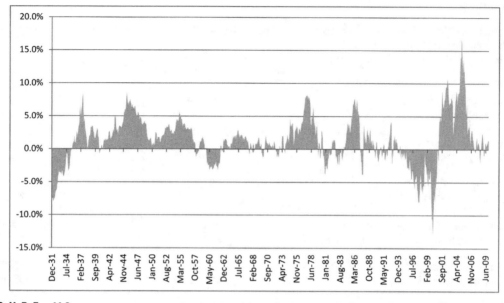

FIGURE   11.2

Five-year average annual compound excess (deficient) return Large Stocks dividend yield decile 1 minus Large Stocks, January 1, 1927, to December 31, 2009

WORST-CASE SCENARIOS AND BEST AND WORST RETURNS

The high-yielding stocks from the All Stocks universe suffered six declines exceeding 20 percent, the worst being a loss of 90 percent during the bear market between August 1929 and May 1932. It was a drop so severe that they did not regain their old highs until March 1944. In our most recent bear market, the group lost 61 percent between October 2007 and February 2009. Looking at best- and worst-case scenarios on an annualized basis, the worst five-year period for the high-yielding stocks from All Stocks were those ending May 1932, where they had an average annual compound loss of 29.24 percent and turned $10,000 into $1,774. This is hardly the type of return that a risk-averse investor would be able to stomach, and it serves as a reminder that capitalization really matters when searching for returns through higher dividend yields. Table 11.5 shows the worst-case scenarios for decile 1 from All Stocks.

The best five-year return for the high-yielding stocks from All Stocks occurred in the five years ending May 1937, when they earned an average annual compound return of 44.41 percent, turning $10,000 into $62,799. Tables 11.6 and 11.7 feature the best and worst returns for all other holding periods.

The best the group ever performed on a relative basis to All Stocks was the five years ending February 2005, where they earned 154 percent, compared to an All Stocks gain of just 23 percent, giving the high-yielders a 131 percent cumulative advantage over All Stocks for those five years. That translates to an average annual compound return of

T A B L E   11.5

Worst-Case Scenarios: All 20 Percent or Greater Declines for All Stocks Dividend Yield Decile 1, January 1, 1927, to December 31, 2009

Peak date	Peak index value	Trough date	Trough index value	Recovery date	Decline (%)	Decline duration	Recovery duration
Aug–29	1.97	May–32	0.20	Mar–44	−90.03%	33	142
May–46	4.48	May–47	3.11	Jan–50	−30.45%	12	32
May–57	16.81	Dec–57	13.11	Jul–58	−22.03%	7	7
Jan–69	80.98	Jun–70	56.47	Apr–71	−30.27%	17	10
Nov–72	89.62	Sep–74	64.03	Jun–75	−28.55%	22	9
Oct–07	13,652.95	Feb–09	5,301.97	N/A	−61.17%	16	N/A
Average					−43.75%	17.83	40

T A B L E   11.6

Best and Worst Average Annual Compound Returns for Monthly Data, January 1, 1927, to December 31, 2009

For any	1-year period	3-year period	5-year period	7-year period	10-year period
All Stocks dividend yield decile 1 minimum compound return	−74.39%	−51.80%	−29.24%	−10.39%	−7.84%
All Stocks dividend yield decile 1 maximum compound return	214.52%	58.05%	44.41%	27.58%	22.60%
All Stocks minimum compound return	−66.72%	−45.99%	−23.07%	−7.43%	−5.31%
All Stocks maximum compound return	201.69%	51.03%	41.17%	23.77%	22.05%

T A B L E   11.7

Terminal Value of $10,000 Invested for Best and Worst Average Annual Compound Returns for Monthly Data, January 1, 1927, to December 31, 2009

For any	1-year period	3-year period	5-year period	7-year period	10-year period
All Stocks dividend yield decile 1 minimum $10,000 value	$2,561	$1,119	$1,774	$4,638	$4,420
All Stocks dividend yield decile 1 maximum $10,000 value	$31,452	$39,482	$62,799	$55,000	$76,707
All Stocks minimum $10,000 value	$3,328	$1,576	$2,695	$5,825	$5,793
All Stocks maximum $10,000 value	$30,169	$34,452	$56,062	$44,504	$73,345

20.52 percent for the highest-yielding stocks from All Stocks versus an average annual gain of 4.28 percent for the All Stocks universe. It seems that the period between the top of the bubble in February 2000 and February 2005 was a mini-golden age for value investing, when many of the value factors covered in previous chapters also enjoyed their best performance relative to the overall market. Perhaps it was a reaction to the ridiculous valuations reached during the bubble, but during that time investors seemed to go back to the basics.

The worst relative performance versus All Stocks occurred in the five years ending—you guessed it—February 2000, where the high-yielders earned 75 percent, whereas All Stocks earned 172 percent, a cumulative deficit for the high-yielders of 97 percent. Translating this into average annual compound returns, the highest yielders from All Stocks earned 11.80 percent, whereas the All Stocks universe earned 22.18 percent. Tables 11.5 through 11.7 and Figure 11.1 show the results for all worst-case scenarios and best and worst returns for a number of holding periods.

LARGE STOCKS

While the high-yielding stocks from Large Stocks lost more than 20 percent from peak to trough eight times, they also demonstrate the ability to snap back quickly from their losses. With the exception of their 89 percent loss between August 1929 and June 1932 and their 59 percent loss between October 2007 and February 2009, the high-yielding stocks from Large Stocks experienced less severe declines in other bear markets. Look at Table 11.8 and you can see that they lost only 29 percent in the bear market of 1972 to 1974 and 26 percent in the bear market of 2000–2003. Looking at the best- and worst-case scenarios on an annualized basis, featured in Tables 11.9 and 11.10, we see that on an absolute return basis their best five years came with the five years ending May 1937, when they earned an annualized return of 44.16 percent, turning $10,000 into $62,267. Their worst five years were those ending in May 1932, when they lost 27.58 percent per year, turning $10,000 invested into $1,992. The tables show additional best and worst case returns for other holding periods.

T A B L E   11.8

Worst-Case Scenarios: All 20 Percent or Greater Declines for Large Stocks Dividend Yield Decile 1, January 1, 1927, to December 31, 2009

Peak date	Peak index value	Trough date	Trough index value	Recovery date	Decline (%)	Decline duration	Recovery duration
Aug–29	1.96	Jun–32	0.22	May–44	−88.81%	34	143
May–46	4.06	May–47	2.91	Dec–49	−28.28%	12	31
Jul–56	17.85	Dec–57	13.82	Jul–58	−22.58%	17	7
Jan–69	65.54	Jun–70	45.94	Jan–72	−29.89%	17	19
Nov–72	71.94	Sep–74	51.12	Jun–75	−28.95%	22	9
May–99	2,311.57	Feb–00	1,847.93	Aug–00	−20.06%	9	6
Mar–02	3,338.43	Feb–03	2,480.85	Dec–03	−25.69%	11	10
Oct–07	6,674.33	Feb–09	2,766.36	N/A	−58.55%	16	N/A
Average					−37.85%	17.25	32.14

TABLE 11.9

Best and Worst Average Annual Compound Returns for Monthly Data, January 1, 1927, to December 31, 2009

For any	1-year period	3-year period	5-year period	7-year period	10-year period
Large Stocks dividend yield decile 1 minimum compound return	−73.79%	−50.25%	−27.58%	−9.53%	−5.64%
Large Stocks dividend yield decile 1 maximum compound return	241.44%	57.13%	44.16%	27.31%	22.25%
Large Stocks minimum compound return	−66.63%	−43.53%	−20.15%	−6.95%	−5.70%
Large Stocks maximum compound return	159.52%	45.64%	36.26%	22.83%	19.57%

TABLE 11.10

Terminal Value of $10,000 Invested for Best and Worst Average Annual Compound Returns for Monthly Data, January 1, 1927, to December 31, 2009

For any	1-year period	3-year period	5-year period	7-year period	10-year period
Large Stocks dividend yield decile 1 minimum $10,000 value	$2,621	$1,231	$1,992	$4,959	$5,596
Large Stocks dividend yield decile 1 maximum $10,000 value	$34,144	$38,793	$62,267	$54,196	$74,569
Large Stocks minimum $10,000 value	$3,337	$1,800	$3,247	$6,041	$5,561
Large Stocks maximum $10,000 value	$25,952	$30,890	$46,970	$42,189	$59,747

The best five-year performance on a relative basis for the high-yielding stocks from Large Stocks was those for years ending in June 1937, when the high-yielding stocks from Large Stocks gained 501 percent versus the Large Stocks universe's 346 percent, a cumulative advantage of 155 percent. Translated to average annual compound returns, that's a gain of 43.14 percent for the first decile group and a return of 34.85 percent for the Large Stocks universe. The worst relative five-year performance for the group occurred during the five years ending in February 2000, when the group gained 62 percent versus the Large Stocks universe's 180 percent, a 118 percent cumulative deficit. Translated into average annual compound returns, that's a gain of 10.11 percent for the high-yielding stocks versus 22.86 percent for the Large Stocks universe.

The high-yielders from Large Stocks do best in market environments in which value is outperforming growth, winning 74 percent of the time. They also do well in markets in which bonds are outperforming stocks, winning 65 percent of the time in those environments.

DECILES

The high-dividend yield full decile analysis paints a somewhat different picture, however. Here we see the top eight deciles performing better than the All Stocks universe itself, while deciles 9 and 10—with lower dividend yields—underperform the benchmark. Yet deciles 2, 3, and 4 all do better than decile 1, indicating that you would be better off simply selecting *broadly* from higher-yielding stocks from All Stocks rather than focusing solely on the stocks with the *absolute* highest yields. We see in later chapters that buying stocks with high-dividend yields *after* they have met a number of other requirements is a much better way to approach high-dividend stocks. In the case study at the end of this chapter, I show why you're probably better off focusing on larger, market-leading companies when selecting high dividend stocks.

The Large Stocks full decile analysis shows that decile 2 actually outperforms decile 1, but only marginally. With the Large Stocks universe ranked by dividend yield, we see that deciles 1 through 5 all outperform Large Stocks, with deciles 1 through 4 doing so in a meaningful way. The bottom five all underperformed Large Stocks, but only decile 10 does significantly worse. Tables 11.11 through 11.14 along with Figures 11.3 and 11.4 summarize the results.

T A B L E   11.11

Average Annual Compound Rates of Return by Decade

	1920s*	1930s	1940s	1950s	1960s	1970s	1980s	1990s	2000s†
All Stocks dividend yield decile 1	13.02%	−2.61%	14.82%	18.33%	10.75%	10.63%	20.41%	11.76%	11.23%
All Stocks dividend yield-decile 10	15.30%	0.80%	8.11%	18.63%	10.76%	5.04%	15.31%	13.34%	5.16%
All Stocks	12.33%	−0.03%	11.57%	18.07%	10.72%	7.56%	16.78%	15.35%	4.39%

* Returns for January 1, 1927, to December 31, 1929.
† Returns for January 1, 2000, to December 31, 2009.

T A B L E   11.12

Average Annual Compound Rates of Return by Decade

	1920s*	1930s	1940s	1950s	1960s	1970s	1980s	1990s	2000s†
Large Stocks-dividend yield decile 1	14.13%	−1.60%	12.68%	18.60%	8.79%	8.85%	19.08%	10.83%	9.98%
Large Stocks dividend yield decile 10	12.65%	−1.95%	7.63%	19.60%	10.11%	2.30%	13.27%	14.85%	2.40%
Large Stocks	17.73%	−1.05%	9.65%	17.06%	8.31%	6.65%	17.34%	16.38%	2.42%

* Returns for January 1, 1927, to December 31, 1929.
† Returns for January 1, 2000, to December 31, 2009.

T A B L E   11.13

Summary Results for Dividend Yield Decile Analysis of All Stocks Universe, January 1, 1927, to December 31, 2009

Decile	$10,000 grows to	Average return	Compound return	Standard deviation	Sharpe ratio
1 (highest)	$102,331,244	14.00%	11.77%	20.15%	0.34
2	$121,953,398	13.96%	12.00%	18.78%	0.37
3	$144,731,790	14.19%	12.23%	18.71%	0.39
4	$129,380,536	13.99%	12.08%	18.49%	0.38

(continued on next page)

TABLE 11.13

Summary Results for Dividend Yield Decile Analysis of All Stocks Universe, January 1, 1927, to December 31, 2009
(Continued)

Decile	$10,000 grows to	Average return	Compound return	Standard deviation	Sharpe ratio
5	$86,874,622	13.45%	11.55%	18.51%	0.35
6	$65,007,160	13.14%	11.16%	18.91%	0.33
7	$50,304,616	12.85%	10.81%	19.10%	0.30
8	$41,851,221	12.73%	10.57%	19.67%	0.28
9	$32,351,872	12.59%	10.23%	20.61%	0.25
10 (lowest)	$21,823,869	12.46%	9.71%	22.18%	0.21
All Stocks	$38,542,780	13.06%	10.46%	21.67%	0.25

TABLE 11.14

Summary Results for Dividend Yield Decile Analysis of Large Stocks Universe, January 1, 1927, to December 31, 2009

Decile	$10,000 grows to	Average return	Compound return	Standard deviation	Sharpe ratio
1 (highest)	$51,678,232	12.90%	10.85%	19.36%	0.30
2	$59,523,837	12.91%	11.04%	18.45%	0.33
3	$60,461,472	12.87%	11.06%	18.05%	0.34
4	$50,153,882	12.59%	10.81%	17.96%	0.32
5	$29,632,548	11.96%	10.11%	18.35%	0.28
6	$23,573,631	11.62%	9.81%	18.10%	0.27
7	$19,314,301	11.44%	9.54%	18.56%	0.24
8	$19,021,660	11.60%	9.52%	19.39%	0.23
9	$18,186,725	11.80%	9.46%	20.57%	0.22
10 (lowest)	$8,485,983	11.18%	8.46%	22.13%	0.16
Large Stocks	$21,617,372	11.75%	9.69%	19.35%	0.24

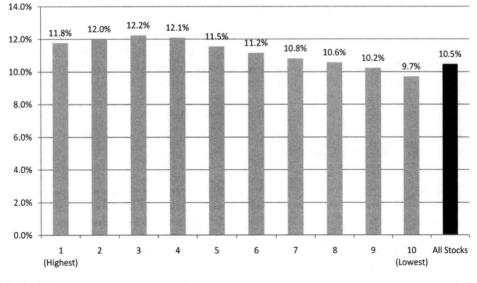

FIGURE 11.3

Average annual compound return by dividend yield decile, All Stocks universe, January 1, 1927, to December 31, 2009

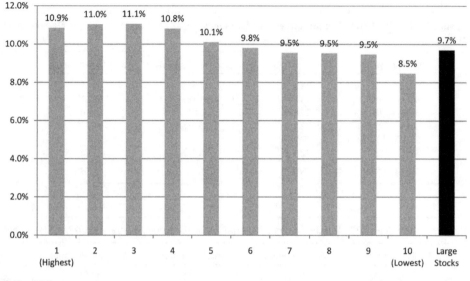

Average annual compound return by dividend yield decile, Large Stocks universe, January 1, 1927, to December 31, 2009

IMPLICATIONS

High-dividend yields alone do not provide a constant panacea for investments in broader indexes or a more specific strategy that includes other factors. In other words, you're not going to want to rely *just* on dividend yield to make your investment choice. We see in Chapter Thirteen that shareholder yield does a better job and offers a smoother ride than dividend yield alone. Most investors' maximum time horizon is five years, and after reviewing Figure 11.1 we see that there have been a significant number of five-year periods in which high-yielding stocks did substantially worse than the market. Indeed, between 1980 and 2000, the highest-yielding stocks from All Stocks actually *underperformed* the All Stocks universe, if only by a small margin of five basis points. Investors who want to use dividend yields as a sole determinant of value should stick to large, better-known companies, since those companies typically have stronger balance sheets and longer operating histories. Indeed, in the second case study at the end of this chapter, we see that when you include other criteria such as strong cash flows, large sales, and large numbers of shares outstanding, large stocks with high-dividend yields offer excellent risk-adjusted returns.

CHAPTER ELEVEN CASE STUDY 1

DO HIGH PAYOUT YIELD AND DIVIDEND CUTS EFFECT DIVIDEND STRATEGIES?

People who favor stocks with high dividend yields often pay close attention to how much of a company's earnings are being paid out in dividends. The reasonable assumption is that stocks that payout a great deal of their earnings in the form of dividends might not perform as well as those that choose instead to reinvest in the company's business. While I do not have payout data in the CRSP dataset, when studying stocks with high-dividend yields, I do have the data in the Compustat dataset, starting in 1963.

A review of the returns for stocks based upon the payout ratio finds that the middle deciles do the best—specifically deciles 5, 6, and 7. This partially confirms the theory that stocks with high payout ratios might be poor investments. I say partially because the only three deciles that do not outperform the All Stocks universe are deciles 1—those with the highest payout ratio—and 9 and 10—those with the *lowest* payout ratios. It appears that investors favor stocks that pay *some* earnings out in the form of dividends but don't want to invest in the 10 percent of the universe that has the highest payout ratios. The fifth decile by payout ratio performed the best. Between 1964 and 2009, it had an average annual compound return of 12.81 percent compared with All Stocks' 11.24 percent return. Decile 1—those stocks with the highest payout ratios—returned 10.40 percent per year, but the worst performer was decile 10—those stocks with the *lowest* payout ratios—which returned 10.33 percent per year. Thus, when looking at stocks purely by dividend yield, the data suggest that you should probably avoid those stocks with the highest dividend yields that are also in the highest decile based on their payout ratio.

A study of dividend yields that my research team at O'Shaughnessy Asset Management (OSAM) conducted found that in the 4,722 instances when a company cut its dividend by between >0 and 50 percent, the stock's average performance in the year following the cut was a modest –0.7 percent drop. However, in the 801 instances when a company cut the dividend by 50 to <100 percent, the stocks lost to their benchmarks by an average of 3.6 percent in the following year. The worst returns came from companies that suspended their dividends altogether; there were 3,329 instances when this occurred, and the stocks, lost an average 5.1 percent to their benchmark.

On the other hand, stocks that increased their dividends (over the course of our study there were 46,358 instances when this occurred) beat their benchmark, on average, by 4.5 percent in the following year. The biggest winners were stocks that had paid no dividend but then started to pay one. In the 6,035 observations in which a firm initiated a dividend, the stocks, on average, went on to beat their benchmark by 9.2 percent in the following year.

These data suggest that dividend investors should sell any of their holdings where the dividend is cut by more than 50 percent and/or if it is suspended and replace the stock with another high-dividend yield company.

CHAPTER ELEVEN CASE STUDY 2

MARKET LEADING COMPANIES WITH HIGH-DIVIDEND YIELDS

We've found that investors interested in stocks with high-dividend yields are best served by limiting their search to market-leading stocks, and then concentrating on those with the highest dividend yields. You'll recall that a stock must meet the following criteria to be included in our Market Leaders universe:

- All nonutility stocks in the Large Stocks universe.
- Shares outstanding greater than the dataset average.

- Cash flow greater than the dataset average.
- Sales greater than 1.5 times the dataset average (50 percent higher than average).

When you apply these criteria to the Compustat dataset, you usually end up with 350 to 400 stocks from the Compustat universe that are all large, well-known companies, and we use that group as the starting point for this enhanced dividend strategy. From the Market Leaders universe we then exclude the bottom half of stocks ranked by their EBITDA/EV score, allowing us to focus on the 50 percent of Market Leaders with the very best financial conditions. We do this to ensure the highest probability that the remaining stocks will be able to continue to maintain—and perhaps increase—their dividend payout. From this group of stocks, we focus on the 50 with the highest-dividend yields. Since we are attempting to maximize our income, we will *overweight* the stocks with the highest-dividend yields in the following manner:

- The 25 percent of stocks with the highest-dividend yields will receive a 1.5 times weight in the portfolio.
- The next 25 percent by dividend yield will receive a 1.25 times weight in the portfolio.
- The next 25 percent by dividend yield will receive a .75 times weight in the portfolio.
- The final 25 percent by dividend yield will receive a .50 times weight in the portfolio.

A portfolio generated using these criteria in October 2010 has a dividend yield of 4.51 percent, substantially higher than the current 10-year Treasury note yield of 2.63 percent. Historically, this enhanced dividend portfolio has offered a dividend yield that is competitive with bonds yet also offers the potential for capital appreciation. Table 11CS2.1 shows the summary results for the enhanced dividend portfolio versus the Market Leaders universe. An investment of $10,000 on December 31, 1963, grows to $4,655,000 at the end of 2009 (assuming the reinvestment of all dividends), generating an average annual compound return of 14.29 percent, significantly ahead of the $1,411,897 you'd have earned from an investment in the Market Leaders universe itself. The strategy's risk of 15.38 percent is lower than the Market Leaders' 16.13 percent, bringing the Sharpe ratio to .60, versus .39 for the Market Leaders universe. What's more, the strategy never had a five-year period in which it lost money—an extremely enticing characteristic for risk-averse investors. The base rates for the strategy, featured in Table 11CS2.2, are all positive, with the strategy beating Market Leaders in 84 percent of all rolling five-year periods and 96 percent of all rolling ten-year periods. Figure 11CS2.1 shows the rolling five-year average annual compound excess (deficient return for the enhanced dividend strategy minus the returns for the Market Leaders universe.

We also tested this strategy purely for its income producing potential—starting with a lump sum investment in 1963 and *consuming all dividend income* produced through 2009. The strategy managed to increase income, on average, by 10 percent per year. Between 1963 and 2009, there were only five occasions in which your income declined from the previous year. What's more, this consistent increase in income occurred despite the fact that the principal value of the portfolio declined in 10 of the 46 years of the study. Indeed, when you focus on just the income portion of the portfolio, you see that the rolling 10-year increase in income increased nearly 148 percent over all rolling 10-year periods and that the

T A B L E 11CS2.1

Summary Annual Return and Risk Results Data: Enhanced Dividend and Market Leaders, January 1, 1964, to December 31, 2009

	Enhanced dividend	Market Leaders
Arithmetic average	15.63%	12.82%
Geometric average	14.29%	11.36%
Median return	20.14%	14.62%
Standard deviation	15.38%	16.13%
Upside deviation	10.03%	10.00%
Downside deviation	10.44%	11.66%
Tracking error	5.86	0.00
Number of positive periods	343	335
Number of negative periods	209	217
Maximum peak-to-trough decline	−52.44%	−54.03%
Beta	0.89	1.00
T-statistic (m = 0)	6.44	5.10
Sharpe ratio (Rf = 5%)	0.60	0.39
Sortino ratio (MAR = 10%)	0.41	0.12
$10,000 becomes	$4,655,000	$1,411,897
Minimum 1-year return	−45.86%	−48.15%
Maximum 1-year return	65.28%	66.79%
Minimum 3-year return	−9.23%	−13.61%
Maximum 3-year return	39.15%	34.82%
Minimum 5-year return	0.01%	−4.36%
Maximum 5-year return	36.38%	31.52%
Minimum 7-year return	0.83%	−2.93%
Maximum 7-year return	28.89%	24.56%
Minimum 10-year return	3.11%	1.01%
Maximum 10-year return	23.92%	19.69%
Minimum expected return*	−15.13%	−19.44%
Maximum expected return†	46.39%	45.07%

* Minimum expected return is arithmetic return minus 2 times the standard deviation.
† Maximum expected return is arithmetic return plus 2 times the standard deviation.

T A B L E 11CS2.2

Base Rates for Enhanced Dividend and Market Leaders, January 1, 1964, to December 31, 2009

Item	Enhanced dividend beat Market Leaders	Percent	Average annual excess return
Single-year return	353 out of 541	65%	2.69%
Rolling 3-year compound return	401 out of 517	78%	2.88%
Rolling 5-year compound return	413 out of 493	84%	2.98%
Rolling 7-year compound return	408 out of 469	87%	3.04%
Rolling 10-year compound return	416 out of 433	96%	3.09%

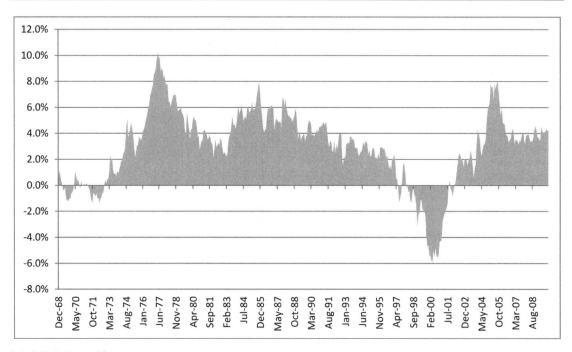

FIGURE   11CS2.1

Five-year average annual compound excess (deficient) return enhanced dividend minus Market Leaders, January 1, 1964, to December 31, 2009

minimum 10-year increase in income was 69 percent. The reason this works so well is that in years in which stock prices declined, dividend yields increased. Thus this strategy gives investors who want both bondlike income and the chance for capital appreciation a real alternative to use stocks instead of bonds. What's more, over the 46 years of the study, the principal value of the portfolio increased by a cumulative 5,538 percent. You can find the full study at http://www.osam.com/commentary.aspx.

C H A P T E R

BUYBACK YIELD

Vision is the art of seeing what is invisible to others.

—Jonathan Swift

While many investors focus on a stock's dividend yield, fewer look at a stock's buyback yield. A stock's buyback yield is determined by contrasting shares outstanding today with those outstanding one year earlier. If a stock has 90 shares outstanding today and had 100 outstanding a year earlier, it would have a buyback yield of 10 percent, which you derive by dividing the 10 fewer shares by the 100 from a year earlier. Conversely, if a stock has 100 shares outstanding today while it had 90 shares outstanding one year earlier, it has a buyback yield of –11 percent, indicating that the company has issued additional shares.

The theory is that if a company is buying back its shares, the company's management must believe that those shares are undervalued, and so managers are therefore availing themselves of the opportunity to purchase their shares at a discount. It is also another way for the company to support the share price for shareholders. It therefore can be seen as the company making a "payment" to shareholders in place of a cash dividend. Share buybacks have become increasingly popular since the 1990s. In their paper "Share Repurchases and Stock Valuation Models," authors John D. Stowe, Dennis W. McLeavey, and Jerald E. Pinto point out that, "The amounts of repurchases relative to dividends has grown substantially over this time period [1987–2006], with the ratio of repurchases to cash dividends roughly doubling in the second half of the period." They mention that "for the first 70 years of the twentieth century, repurchases represented an almost insignificant portion of the firm payout. During the 1990s, repurchases grew rapidly compared to dividend distributions, and repurchases were increasingly substituted for dividends as the method to distribute earnings." Thus the theory is that stocks with high buyback yields should provide better performance than those with low buyback yields. Let's see who is right.

THE RESULTS

Since we are able to use the CRSP dataset to calculate buyback yields, we begin on December 31, 1926, and invest $10,000 in the deciles of stocks with both the highest and lowest buyback yields from both the All Stock and Large Stocks universes. The reason we are also looking at stocks with the *lowest* buyback yield is that in most instances they are net *issuers* of shares, which might indicate that management thinks the market has priced its stock too high and is taking advantage of these valuations by issuing additional shares. Let's look at the high buyback yield stocks from All Stocks and Large Stocks first. As always, we use our composited portfolio methodology to avoid any seasonality and time-lag all data to avoid look-ahead bias.

The $10,000 invested on December 31, 1926, in the All Stocks group with the highest buyback yield grew to $421,203,905 by the end of 2009, an average annual compound return of 13.69 percent. The same $10,000 invested in All Stocks grew to $38,542,780, an average annual compound return of 10.46 percent. The stocks with the highest buyback yield from All Stocks had a higher risk—as measured by standard deviation of return—than All Stocks, coming in at 24.32 percent compared to 21.67 percent for the All Stocks universe. The high buyback yield stocks also had a slightly higher downside risk—17.56 percent versus 16.03 percent for the All Stocks universe. Despite this slightly higher risk, the high buyback yield group had a Sharpe ratio of .36, considerably higher than the .25 earned by the All Stocks universe. Table 12.1 shows the relevant statistics.

All base rates are positive, with the high buyback decile beating All Stocks in 89 percent of all rolling five-year periods and 89 percent of all rolling ten-year periods. Table 12.2 lists the base rates over several holding periods. The group performs particularly well when large-cap value is performing well, as well as when bonds are outperforming stocks. It also does well in markets with neutrality between the performance of U.S. markets and international ones. Figure 12.1 shows the five-year average annual compound excess (deficient) return for the high buyback yielding stocks from All Stocks minus the returns of the All Stocks universe.

T A B L E   12.1

Summary Annual Return and Risk Results Data: All Stocks Buyback Yield Decile 1 and All Stocks, January 1, 1927, to December 31, 2009

	All Stocks buyback yield decile 1	All Stocks
Arithmetic average	16.86%	13.06%
Geometric average	13.69%	10.46%
Median return	20.94%	18.54%
Standard deviation	24.32%	21.67%
Upside deviation	19.94%	14.78%

(continued on next page)

T A B L E   12.1

Summary Annual Return and Risk Results Data: All Stocks Buyback Yield Decile 1 and All Stocks, January 1, 1927, to December 31, 2009 *(Continued)*

	All Stocks buyback yield decile 1	All Stocks
Downside deviation	17.56%	16.03%
Tracking error	8.97	0.00
Number of positive periods	630	606
Number of negative periods	366	390
Maximum peak-to-trough decline	−85.43%	−85.45%
Beta	1.04	1.00
T-statistic (m = 0)	5.87	5.19
Sharpe ratio (Rf = 5%)	0.36	0.25
Sortino ratio (MAR = 10%)	0.21	0.03
$10,000 becomes	$421,203,905	$38,542,780
Minimum 1-year return	−65.20%	−66.72%
Maximum 1-year return	248.23%	201.69%
Minimum 3-year return	−44.28%	−45.99%
Maximum 3-year return	59.81%	51.03%
Minimum 5-year return	−20.80%	−23.07%
Maximum 5-year return	41.35%	41.17%
Minimum 7-year return	−3.79%	−7.43%
Maximum 7-year return	30.22%	23.77%
Minimum 10-year return	−7.45%	−5.31%
Maximum 10-year return	27.95%	22.05%
Minimum expected return*	−31.79%	−30.28%
Maximum expected return†	65.50%	56.39%

* Minimum expected return is arithmetic return minus 2 times the standard deviation.
† Maximum expected return is arithmetic return plus 2 times the standard deviation.

T A B L E   12.2

Base Rates for All Stocks Buyback Yield Decile 1 and All Stocks, January 1, 1927, to December 31, 2009

Item	All Stocks buyback yield decile 1 beat All Stocks	Percent	Average annual excess return
Single-year return	700 out of 985	71%	3.41%
Rolling 3-year compound return	830 out of 961	86%	3.18%
Rolling 5-year compound return	835 out of 937	89%	3.18%
Rolling 7-year compound return	827 out of 913	91%	3.17%
Rolling 10-year compound return	784 out of 877	89%	3.13%

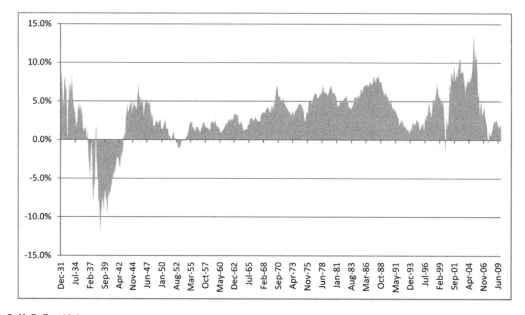

FIGURE 12.1

Five-year average annual compound excess (deficient) return All Stocks buyback yield decile 1 minus All Stocks, January 1, 1927, to December 31, 2009

LARGE STOCKS ARE STRONG PERFORMERS AS WELL

The $10,000 invested in the highest decile by buyback yield from the Large Stocks universe on December 31, 1926, grew to $250,019,446 by the end of 2009, an average annual compound return of 12.98 percent. That's significantly better than the $21,617,372 you'd have earned from an investment in the Large Stocks universe itself, which generated a return of 9.69 percent over the same time period. Risk was higher for the high buyback yield group from Large Stocks however, with a standard deviation of return of 23.11 percent compared with 19.35 percent for the Large Stocks universe. Downside risk was also greater for the high buyback group, coming in at 17.13 percent versus 14.40 for the Large Stocks universe. Yet the higher absolute return for the group brought the Sharpe ratio to .35, compared to .24 for the Large Stocks universe. Table 12.3 shows the relevant statistics.

All base rates were positive, with the high buyback yield group from Large Stocks beating the Large Stocks universe in 85 percent of all rolling five-year periods and 88 percent of all rolling ten-year periods. Table 12.4 shows the base rates for all holding periods. And while the authors I cited at the beginning of the chapter said that repurchases were not common during the first 70 years of the twentieth century, the returns to companies using them were strong. Between 1927 and 1963, the highest-yielding buyback stocks from the All Stocks universe compounded at 11.11 percent, compared to 9.53 for All Stocks. The highest-yielding buyback stocks from Large Stocks compounded at 10.58 percent, versus 9.06 percent for the Large Stocks universe. Figure 12.2 shows the five-year average annual compound excess (deficient) return for the high buyback yielding stocks from Large Stocks minus the returns of the Large Stocks universe.

T A B L E 12.3

Summary Annual Return and Risk Results Data: Large Stocks Buyback Yield Decile 1 and Large Stocks, January 1, 1927, to December 31, 2009

	Large Stocks buyback yield decile 1	Large Stocks
Arithmetic average	15.88%	11.75%
Geometric average	12.98%	9.69%
Median return	20.93%	16.75%
Standard deviation	23.11%	19.35%
Upside deviation	18.26%	13.10%
Downside deviation	17.13%	14.40%
Tracking error	8.96	0.00
Number of positive periods	621	609
Number of negative periods	375	387
Maximum peak-to-trough decline	−85.95%	−84.33%
Beta	1.11	1.00
T-statistic (m = 0)	5.85	5.25
Sharpe ratio (Rf = 5%)	0.35	0.24
Sortino ratio (MAR = 10%)	0.17	−0.02
$10,000 becomes	$250,019,446	$21,617,372
Minimum 1-year return	−66.57%	−66.63%
Maximum 1-year return	204.71%	159.52%
Minimum 3-year return	−45.01%	−43.53%
Maximum 3-year return	47.23%	45.64%
Minimum 5-year return	−19.46%	−20.15%
Maximum 5-year return	38.25%	36.26%
Minimum 7-year return	−8.78%	−6.95%
Maximum 7-year return	29.94%	22.83%
Minimum 10-year return	−10.19%	−5.70%
Maximum 10-year return	26.96%	19.57%
Minimum expected return*	−30.34%	−26.96%
Maximum expected return†	62.11%	50.46%

* Minimum expected return is arithmetic return minus 2 times the standard deviation.
† Maximum expected return is arithmetic return plus 2 times the standard deviation.

T A B L E 12.4

Base Rates for Large Stocks Buyback Yield—Decile 1 and Large Stocks, January 1, 1927, to December 31, 2009

Item	Large Stocks buyback yield decile 1 beat Large Stocks	Percent	Average annual excess return
Single-year return	715 out of 985	73%	3.61%
Rolling 3-year compound return	783 out of 961	81%	3.04%
Rolling 5-year compound return	793 out of 937	85%	3.04%
Rolling 7-year compound return	800 out of 913	88%	3.06%
Rolling 10-year compound return	776 out of 877	88%	3.06%

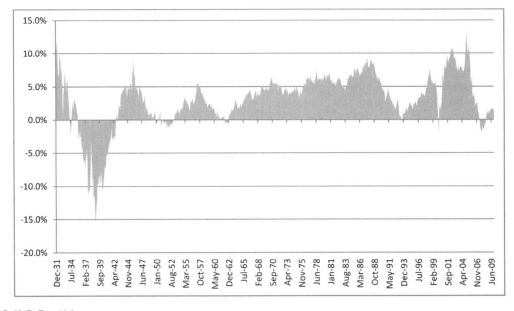

F I G U R E   12.2

Five-year average annual compound excess (deficient) return Large Stocks buyback yield decile 1 minus Large Stocks, January 1, 1927, to December 31, 2009

WORST-CASE SCENARIOS AND BEST AND WORST RETURNS

The highest buyback yield stocks from All Stocks had nine separate times when they dropped by 20 percent or more. The worst decline occurred between September 1929 and May 1932, when these stocks plummeted by 85.43 percent. In the most recent bear market between May 2007 and February 2009, the group lost 53.28 percent, slightly less than the All Stocks universe's decline of 55.54 percent. Table 12.5 shows all declines for the group greater than 20 percent between 1927 and 2009.

On an absolute basis, the best five-year period was the one ending in May 1937, when $10,000 grew to $56,424, an average annual compound return of 41.35 percent. The worst five years were those ending in March 1933, where $10,000 invested shrank to $3,115, an average annual compound loss of 20.80 percent.

Relative to the All Stocks universe, the best five-year period for the group was that ending July 1987, when the high buyback yield group gained 363 percent versus a 239 percent gain for the All Stocks universe, a 124 percent cumulative advantage over All Stocks. Translating that into average annual compound returns, the stocks from All Stocks with the highest buyback yields earned 35.88 percent, whereas the All Stocks universe earned 27.66 percent. The worst relative five-year period for the group was that ending in December 1938, when the group lost 2.39 percent while the All Stocks universe enjoyed a gain of 72 percent, a cumulative deficit of 74 percent and an average annual compound loss of –0.48 for the high buyback stocks versus a gain of 11.44 percent for the All Stocks universe. Tables 12.6 and 12.7 show the terminal value of $10,000 invested over a variety

T A B L E   12.5

Worst-Case Scenarios: All 20 Percent or Greater Declines for All Stocks Buyback Yield Decile 1, January 1, 1927, to December 31, 2009

Peak date	Peak index value	Trough date	Trough index value	Recovery date	Decline (%)	Decline duration	Recovery duration
Sep–29	2.74	May–32	0.40	Jun–44	−85.43%	32	145
May–46	5.77	May–47	4.12	Dec–49	−28.61%	12	31
Feb–62	46.93	Jun–62	36.67	May–63	−21.84%	4	11
Nov–68	156.90	Jun–70	100.81	Jan–72	−35.75%	19	19
Nov–72	170.81	Sep–74	96.36	Jan–76	−43.58%	22	16
Aug–87	2,730.86	Nov–87	1,859.87	Mar–89	−31.89%	3	16
Aug–89	3,287.60	Oct–90	2,512.94	Feb–91	−23.56%	14	4
Apr–98	14,643.54	Aug–98	11,579.48	May–99	−20.92%	4	9
May–07	52,090.76	Feb–09	24,336.60	N/A	−53.28%	21	N/A
Average					−38.32%	14.56	31.38

T A B L E   12.6

Best and Worst Average Annual Compound Returns over Period for Monthly Data, January 1, 1927, to December 31, 2009

For any	1-year period	3-year period	5-year period	7-year period	10-year period
All Stocks buyback yield decile 1 minimum compound return	−65.20%	−44.28%	−20.80%	−3.79%	−7.45%
All Stocks buyback yield decile 1 maximum compound return	248.23%	59.81%	41.35%	30.22%	27.95%
All Stocks minimum compound return	−66.72%	−45.99%	−23.07%	−7.43%	−5.31%
All Stocks maximum compound return	201.69%	51.03%	41.17%	23.77%	22.05%

T A B L E   12.7

Terminal Value of $10,000 Invested for Best and Worst Average Annual Compound Returns for Monthly Data, January 1, 1927, to December 31, 2009

For any	1-year period	3-year period	5-year period	7-year period	10-year period
All Stocks buyback yield decile 1 minimum $10,000 value	$3,480	$1,730	$3,115	$7,629	$4,612
All Stocks buyback yield decile 1 maximum $10,000 value	$34,823	$40,815	$56,424	$63,495	$117,555
All Stocks minimum $10,000 value	$3,328	$1,576	$2,695	$5,825	$5,793
All Stocks maximum $10,000 value	$30,169	$34,452	$56,062	$44,504	$73,345

of other periods with best- and worst-case outcomes, and Figure 12.1 shows the rolling excess (or deficient) returns for the group from All Stocks with the highest buyback yield compared to the All Stocks universe for the entire period studied.

LARGE STOCKS

Table 12.8 shows the worst-case scenarios for the best buyback yield group from Large Stocks. It suffered its largest decline between August 1929 and May 1932, dropping 85.95 percent over the period. The group had seven separate times when it lost 20 percent or more, with the most recent significant decline of 51.56 percent occurring between May 2007 and February 2009.

T A B L E   12.8

Worst-Case Scenarios: All 20 Percent or Greater Declines for Large Stocks Buyback Yield Decile 1, January 1, 1927, to December 31, 2009

Peak date	Peak index value	Trough date	Trough index value	Recovery date	Decline (%)	Decline duration	Recovery duration
Aug–29	3.91	May–32	0.55	Nov–45	−85.95%	33	162
May–46	4.70	May–47	3.58	Dec–49	−23.95%	12	31
Nov–68	96.03	Jun–70	70.12	Jan–71	−26.98%	19	7
Nov–72	123.95	Sep–74	78.26	Jun–75	−36.86%	22	9
Aug–87	1,768.36	Nov–87	1,211.45	Jan–89	−31.49%	3	14
Aug–89	2,202.89	Oct–90	1,723.00	Feb–91	−21.78%	14	4
May–07	30,304.22	Feb–09	14,679.98	N/A	−51.56%	21	N/A
Average					−39.80%	17.71	37.83

The best five-year period for the group was the five years ending July 1987, when $10,000 invested grew to $50,511, an average annual compound gain of 38.25 percent. The worst five years for the group were the five years ending August 1934, where $10,000 invested shrank to $3,390, an average annual compound loss of 19.46 percent.

On a relative basis, the best five years were the same as those on an absolute basis, the five-year period ending July 1987, when the group gained 405 percent versus a gain of 257 for the Large Stocks universe, a cumulative advantage of 148 percent. The worst five years for the group relative to the Large Stocks universe were those ending August 1937, when the group earned 58 percent versus 152 percent for the Large Stocks universe, a deficit of 94 percent. Tables 12.9 and 12.10 show the terminal value of $10,000 invested over various other holding periods, and Figure 12.2 shows the rolling excess (or deficient) returns for the group from Large Stocks with the highest buyback yield over the Large Stocks universe for the entire period studied

T A B L E 12.9

Best and Worst Average Annual Compound Returns for Monthly Data, January 1, 1927, to December 31, 2009

For any	1-year period	3-year period	5-year period	7-year period	10-year period
Large Stocks buyback yield decile 1 minimum compound return	−66.57%	−45.01%	−19.46%	−8.78%	−10.19%
Large Stocks buyback yield decile 1 maximum compound return	204.71%	47.23%	38.25%	29.94%	26.96%
Large Stocks minimum compound return	−66.63%	−43.53%	−20.15%	−6.95%	−5.70%
Large Stocks maximum compound return	159.52%	45.64%	36.26%	22.83%	19.57%

T A B L E 12.10

Terminal Value of $10,000 Invested for Best and Worst Average Annual Compound Returns for Monthly Data, January 1, 1927, to December 31, 2009

For any	1-year period	3-year period	5-year period	7-year period	10-year period
Large Stocks buyback yield decile 1 minimum $10,000 value	$3,343	$1,663	$3,390	$5,256	$3,412
Large Stocks buyback yield decile 1 maximum $10,000 value	$30,471	$31,917	$50,511	$62,547	$108,818
Large Stocks minimum $10,000 value	$3,337	$1,800	$3,247	$6,041	$5,561
Large Stocks maximum $10,000 value	$25,952	$30,890	$46,970	$42,189	$59,747

BUYING THE STOCKS WITH THE LOWEST BUYBACK YIELD OFFERS HORRIBLE RESULTS

Stocks with the lowest buyback yield represent the firms that are issuing stock as opposed to buying it back. These stocks do not make good investments. We look first at All Stocks and then at Large Stocks. For All Stocks, $10,000 invested on December 31, 1926, in the lowest buyback yield group grew to just $1,204,517, an average annual compound return of 5.94 percent and some $37 million *less* than an investment in the All Stocks universe, which compounded at 10.46 percent over that period. The group also had a higher standard deviation of return—24.05 percent versus All Stocks' 21.67 percent. That, coupled with the much lower absolute return, brought the Sharpe ratio to a very low .04, compared to .25 for the All Stocks universe. All base rates were negative, with the group beating All Stocks in just 2 percent of all rolling five-year periods and in none of the rolling ten-year periods. Table 12.11 shows the relevant statistics and Table 12.12 shows the base rates for all periods.

Figure 12.3 shows the rolling five-year average annual compound excess (deficient) return for the group minus the return of the All Stocks universe.

T A B L E   12.11

Summary Annual Return and Risk Results Data: All Stocks Buyback Yield Decile 10 and All Stocks, January 1, 1927, to December 31, 2009

	All Stocks buyback yield decile 10	All Stocks
Arithmetic average	9.02%	13.06%
Geometric average	5.94%	10.46%
Median return	15.77%	18.54%
Standard deviation	24.05%	21.67%
Upside deviation	16.83%	14.78%
Downside deviation	17.65%	16.03%
Tracking error	4.77	0.00
Number of positive periods	580	606
Number of negative periods	416	390
Maximum peak-to-trough decline	−88.38%	−85.45%
Beta	1.09	1.00
T-statistic (m = 0)	3.28	5.19
Sharpe ratio (Rf = 5%)	0.04	0.25
Sortino ratio (MAR = 10%)	−0.23	0.03
$10,000 becomes	$1,204,517	$38,542,780
Minimum 1-year return	−68.72%	−66.72%
Maximum 1-year return	211.93%	201.69%
Minimum 3-year return	−49.95%	−45.99%
Maximum 3-year return	47.88%	51.03%
Minimum 5-year return	−26.38%	−23.07%
Maximum 5-year return	39.21%	41.17%
Minimum 7-year return	−13.15%	−7.43%
Maximum 7-year return	21.28%	23.77%
Minimum 10-year return	−8.01%	−5.31%
Maximum 10-year return	17.67%	22.05%
Minimum expected return*	−39.08%	−30.28%
Maximum expected return†	57.13%	56.39%

* Minimum expected return is arithmetic return minus 2 times the standard deviation.
† Maximum expected return is arithmetic return plus 2 times the standard deviation.

T A B L E   12.12

Base Rates for All Stocks Buyback Yield Decile 10 and All Stocks, January 1, 1927, to December 31, 2009

Item	All Stocks buyback yield decile 10 beat All Stocks	Percent	Average annual excess return
Single-year return	219 out of 985	22%	−4.07%
Rolling 3-year compound return	89 out of 961	9%	−4.33%
Rolling 5-year compound return	20 out of 937	2%	−4.42%
Rolling 7-year compound return	0 out of 913	0%	−4.50%
Rolling 10-year compound return	0 out of 877	0%	−4.51%

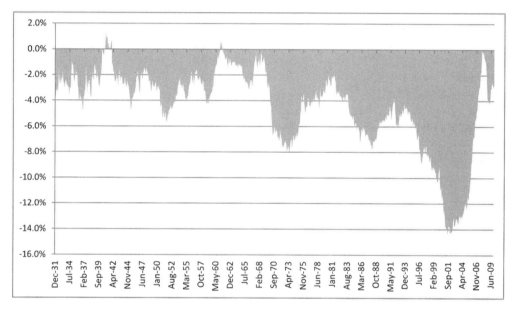

F I G U R E   12.3

Five-year average annual compound excess (deficient) return All Stocks buyback yield decile 10 minus All Stocks, January 1, 1927, to December 31, 2009

LARGE STOCKS ARE LITTLE BETTER

The $10,000 invested on December 31, 1926, in Large Stocks with the lowest buyback yields grew to just $1,397,168 by the end of 2009, an average annual compound return of 6.13 percent. That's more than $20 million less than the $21,617,372 you'd have earned by investing in the Large Stocks universe itself. The standard deviation for the Large Stocks with the lowest buyback yields was 21.93 percent, compared to the Large Stocks universe's 19.35. The higher standard deviation coupled with the lower return brought the Sharpe ratio to .05 for the low buyback yield group compared to .24 for the Large Stock universe. Table 12.13

shows the relevant statistics. All base rates were negative, with the group beating the Large Stocks universe in 11 percent of all rolling five-year periods and just 4 percent of all rolling ten-year periods. Table 12.14 shows the base rates for all holding periods. Figure 12.4 shows the rolling five-year average annual compound excess (deficient) return for the group minus the return of the Large Stocks universe.

T A B L E   12.13

Summary Annual Return and Risk Results Data: Large Stocks Buyback Yield Decile 10 and Large Stocks, January 1, 1927, to December 31, 2009

	Large Stocks buyback yield decile 10	Large Stocks
Arithmetic average	8.67%	11.75%
Geometric average	6.13%	9.69%
Median return	13.50%	16.75%
Standard deviation	21.93%	19.35%
Upside deviation	16.00%	13.10%
Downside deviation	16.07%	14.40%
Tracking error	5.90	0.00
Number of positive periods	585	609
Number of negative periods	411	387
Maximum peak-to-trough decline	−88.05%	−84.33%
Beta	1.10	1.00
T-statistic (m = 0)	3.47	5.25
Sharpe ratio (Rf = 5%)	0.05	0.24
Sortino ratio (MAR = 10%)	−0.24	−0.02
$10,000 becomes	$1,397,168	$21,617,372
Minimum 1-year return	−68.72%	−66.63%
Maximum 1-year return	209.17%	159.52%
Minimum 3-year return	−48.96%	−43.53%
Maximum 3-year return	51.99%	45.64%
Minimum 5-year return	−25.95%	−20.15%
Maximum 5-year return	38.38%	36.26%
Minimum 7-year return	−12.05%	−6.95%
Maximum 7-year return	21.37%	22.83%
Minimum 10-year return	−7.69%	−5.70%
Maximum 10-year return	15.59%	19.57%
Minimum expected return*	−35.19%	−26.96%
Maximum expected return†	52.53%	50.46%

* Minimum expected return is arithmetic return minus 2 times the standard deviation.
† Maximum expected return is arithmetic return plus 2 times the standard deviation.

T A B L E   12.14

Base Rates for Large Stocks Buyback Yield Decile 10 and Large Stocks, January 1, 1927, to December 31, 2009

Item	Large Stocks buyback yield decile 10 beat Large Stocks	Percent	Average annual excess return
Single-year return	300 out of 985	30%	−3.04%
Rolling 3-year compound return	216 out of 961	22%	−3.26%
Rolling 5-year compound return	105 out of 937	11%	−3.29%
Rolling 7-year compound return	47 out of 913	5%	−3.39%
Rolling 10-year compound return	37 out of 877	4%	−3.46%

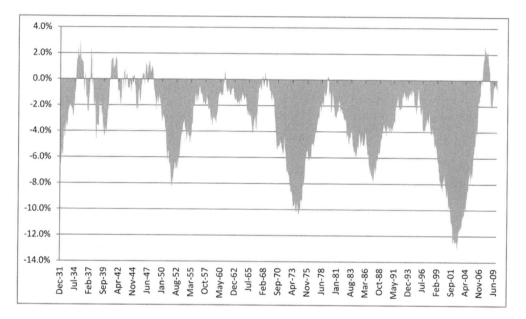

F I G U R E   12.4

Five-year average annual compound excess (deficient) return Large Stocks buyback yield decile 10 minus Large Stocks, January 1, 1927, to December 31, 2009

WORST-CASE SCENARIOS AND BEST AND WORST RETURNS

The stocks with the lowest buyback yields from All Stocks had 10 separate declines of 20 percent or more between 1927 and 2009. Their worst decline came between August 1929 and June 1932, when the group lost 88 percent from peak to trough. It suffered a huge drop of 71 percent between November 1968 and September 1974, and never recovered from the 65 percent drop that began in February 2000. Table 12.15 features all of the worst-case scenarios for the group.

TABLE 12.15

Worst-Case Scenarios: All 20 Percent or Greater Declines for All Stocks Buyback Yield Decile 10, January 1, 1927, to December 31, 2009

Peak date	Peak index value	Trough date	Trough index value	Recovery date	Decline (%)	Decline duration	Recovery duration
Aug–29	1.94	Jun–32	0.22	Oct–45	−88.38%	34	160
May–46	2.66	May–47	1.75	Jan–51	−34.18%	12	44
Nov–61	12.49	Jun–62	8.86	Jun–64	−29.09%	7	24
Nov–68	30.05	Sep–74	8.74	Jul–80	−70.91%	70	70
May–81	39.88	Jul–82	29.95	Nov–82	−24.91%	14	4
Jun–83	54.64	Jul–84	39.82	Nov–85	−27.12%	13	16
Aug–87	78.79	Nov–87	50.44	Aug–89	−35.98%	3	21
Sep–89	80.01	Oct–90	57.08	Mar–91	−28.65%	13	5
Apr–98	162.27	Aug–98	108.29	Dec–99	−33.27%	4	16
Feb–00	184.13	Feb–09	64.42	N/A	−65.01%	108	N/A
Average					−43.75%	27.8	40

The group's best absolute five-year performance came during the five years ending May 1937, when it compounded at 39.21 percent and turned $10,000 into $52,273. Its worst absolute five-year performance came during the five years ending May 1932, when it dropped 26.38 percent per year, turning $10,000 into $2,162.

On a relative basis versus All Stocks, its best five-year performance occurred in the five years ending December 1940, when it gained 6 percent versus All Stocks −0.3 percent decline, a 6 percent cumulative advantage over All Stocks. Its worst relative five-year performance versus All Stocks occurred during the five years ending March 2000, when it gained 71 percent versus All Stocks gain of 156 percent, a cumulative deficit of 85 percent. Tables 12.16 and 12.17 show the terminal value for $10,000 invested over various best- and worst-case holding periods. Figure 12.3 shows the rolling five-year excess (or deficient) returns for the group versus the All Stocks universe.

TABLE 12.16

Best and Worst Average Annual Compound Returns for Monthly Data, January 1, 1927, to December 31, 2009

For any	1-year period	3-year period	5-year period	7-year period	10-year period
All Stocks buyback yield decile 10 maximum compound return	−68.72%	−49.95%	−26.38%	−13.15%	−8.01%
All Stocks buyback yield decile 10 minimum compound return	211.93%	47.88%	39.21%	21.28%	17.67%
All Stocks minimum compound return	−66.72%	−45.99%	−23.07%	−7.43%	−5.31%
All Stocks maximum compound return	201.69%	51.03%	41.17%	23.77%	22.05%

T A B L E   12.17

Terminal Value of $10,000 Invested for Best and Worst Average Annual Compound Returns for Monthly Data, January 1, 1927, to December 31, 2009

For any	1-year period	3-year period	5-year period	7-year period	10-year period
All Stocks buyback yield decile 10 minimum $10,000 value	$3,128	$1,254	$2,162	$3,727	$4,339
All Stocks buyback yield decile 10 maximum $10,000 value	$31,193	$32,341	$52,273	$38,587	$50,909
All Stocks minimum $10,000 value	$3,328	$1,576	$2,695	$5,825	$5,793
All Stocks maximum $10,000 value	$30,169	$34,452	$56,062	$44,504	$73,345

LARGE STOCKS

The stocks with the lowest buyback yields from Large Stocks had 10 separate declines of 20 percent or more. Their worst decline occurred between August 1929 and May 1932, when they lost 88.05 percent. They actually lost a point more in the August 2000 through September 2002 bear market—61 percent—than they did in the most recent bear market of October 2007 through February 2009, when they lost 60 percent. Table 12.18 features all of the worst-case scenarios for the group.

The group's best absolute five-year performance occurred during the five years ending May 1937, when it compounded at 38.38 percent per year, turning $10,000 into $50,747. The group's worst absolute performance occurred during the five years ending May 1932, when it lost 25.95 percent per year and turned $10,000 into $2,227. Tables 12.19 and 12.20 show the terminal value of a $10,000 investment for other holding periods.

T A B L E   12.18

Worst-Case Scenarios: All 20 Percent or Greater Declines for Large Stocks Buyback Yield Decile 10, January 1, 1927, to December 31, 2009

Peak date	Peak index value	Trough date	Trough index value	Recovery date	Decline (%)	Decline duration	Recovery duration
Aug–29	1.87	May–32	0.22	Nov–45	−88.05%	33	162
May–46	2.36	May–47	1.71	Jan–51	−27.38%	12	44
Dec–61	10.33	Jun–62	7.68	Jan–64	−25.63%	6	19
Nov–68	19.42	Sep–74	6.72	Sep–80	−65.37%	70	72
Jun–83	29.84	Jul–84	22.96	May–85	−23.04%	13	10
Aug–87	50.26	Nov–87	34.62	May–89	−31.12%	3	18
Aug–89	56.63	Oct–90	42.21	Feb–91	−25.45%	14	4
Apr–98	161.95	Aug–98	120.20	Apr–99	−25.78%	4	8
Aug–00	175.56	Sep–02	68.59	Apr–07	−60.93%	25	55
Oct–07	199.66	Feb–09	80.17	N/A	−59.85%	16	N/A
Average					−43.26%	19.6	43.56

T A B L E   12.19

Best and Worst Average Annual Compound Returns for Monthly Data, January 1, 1927, to December 31, 2009

For any	1-year period	3-year period	5-year period	7-year period	10-year period
Large Stocks buyback yield decile 10 minimum compound return	−68.72%	−48.96%	−25.95%	−12.05%	−7.69%
Large Stocks buyback yield decile 10 maximum compound return	209.17%	51.99%	38.38%	21.37%	15.59%
Large Stocks minimum compound return	−66.63%	−43.53%	−20.15%	−6.95%	−5.70%
Large Stocks maximum compound return	159.52%	45.64%	36.26%	22.83%	19.57%

T A B L E   12.20

Terminal Value of $10,000 Invested for Best and Worst Average Annual Compound Returns for Monthly Data, January 1, 1927, to December 31, 2009

For any	1-year period	3-year period	5-year period	7-year period	10-year period
Large Stocks buyback yield decile 10 minimum $10,000 value	$3,128	$1,329	$2,227	$4,072	$4,491
Large Stocks buyback yield decile 10 maximum $10,000 value	$30,917	$35,113	$50,747	$38,804	$42,574
Large Stocks minimum $10,000 value	$3,337	$1,800	$3,247	$6,041	$5,561
Large Stocks maximum $10,000 value	$25,952	$30,890	$46,970	$42,189	$59,747

On a relative basis versus the Large Stocks universe, the best the group ever performed was during the five years ending June 1937, when it gained 386 percent versus a gain of 346 percent for the Large Stocks universe, a cumulative advantage of 40 percent. The worst five years were those ending July 1987, when the group gained 164 percent compared to a gain of 257 percent for the Large Stocks universe, a cumulative deficit of 93 percent. Figure 12.4 shows the rolling excess (or deficient) performance for the group versus Large Stocks over the entire period.

FULL DECILE ANALYSIS

Buyback yield is unlike the other factors in that there are several companies with exactly the same value creating several ties. Any company that neither issues nor repurchases stock will have a zero value for buyback yield. This makes it difficult to provide statistics for stocks in the middle deciles for buyback yield because there are several months with over 10 percent of the companies in the All Stocks and Large Stocks universe that have a zero buyback yield. This causes some deciles to be clumped together. For example, there might not be a decile 6 because decile 7 includes 20 percent of the population that has a zero buyback. In this case we set decile 6 and decile 7 equal to each other so that there are no gaps in the monthly decile returns. Deciles 1 and 10 are unaffected because they contain the stocks with the highest buyback activity and the lowest (i.e., those stocks that are issuing shares).

The full decile analysis is unusual in that the top eight deciles beat the All Stocks universe, and we see that only deciles 9 and 10 dramatically underperform All Stocks—with decile 10 earning a compound average annual rate of return of 5.94 percent and decile 9 earning 8.60 percent. Yet the significantly higher returns for decile 1 lead us to the conclusion that you should be interested in only the top 10 percent of stocks doing massive repurchasing of their shares and that you should be wary of the 20 percent of companies issuing a lot of new shares to the public. Tables 12.21 and 12.22 show the results by decade for decile 1 and 10 for both All Stocks and Large Stocks while Table 12.23 and Figure 12.5 show the results for all the deciles in All Stocks.

T A B L E   12.21

Average Annual Compound Rates of Return by Decade

	1920s*	1930s	1940s	1950s	1960s	1970s	1980s	1990s	2000s†
All Stocks buyback yield decile 1	21.36%	−1.89%	14.69%	19.82%	13.51%	12.97%	22.42%	17.52%	10.02%
All stocks buyback yield decile 10	5.31%	−1.59%	8.48%	15.11%	8.24%	2.80%	11.15%	7.94%	−3.09%
All Stocks	12.33%	−0.03%	11.57%	18.07%	10.72%	7.56%	16.78%	15.35%	4.39%

* Returns for January 1, 1927, to December 31, 1929.
† Returns for January 1, 2000, to December 31, 2009.

T A B L E   12.22

Average Annual Compound Rates of Return by Decade

	1920s*	1930s	1940s	1950s	1960s	1970s	1980s	1990s	2000s†
Large Stocks buyback yield decile 1	31.00%	−3.72%	11.91%	19.56%	11.40%	12.10%	23.43%	18.40%	8.00%
Large Stocks buyback yield decile 10	4.65%	−1.80%	8.34%	13.75%	6.86%	0.83%	12.93%	11.77%	−1.77%
Large Stocks	17.73%	−1.05%	9.65%	17.06%	8.31%	6.65%	17.34%	16.38%	2.42%

* Returns for January 1, 1927, to December 31, 1929.
† Returns for January 1, 2000, to December 31, 2009.

T A B L E   12.23

Summary Results for Buyback Yield Decile Analysis of All Stocks Universe, January 1, 1927, to December 31, 2009

Decile	$10,000 grows to	Average return	Compound return	Standard deviation	Sharpe ratio
1 (highest)	$421,203,905	16.86%	13.69%	24.32%	0.36
2	$119,843,583	15.14%	11.98%	24.46%	0.29
3	$85,516,305	14.59%	11.53%	24.17%	0.27
4	$75,029,995	14.38%	11.35%	24.07%	0.26
5	$68,380,894	13.65%	11.23%	20.92%	0.30
6	$59,335,635	13.56%	11.04%	21.32%	0.28
7	$81,823,740	14.19%	11.47%	22.09%	0.29
8	$45,119,547	13.49%	10.67%	22.52%	0.25
9	$9,388,666	11.30%	8.60%	22.17%	0.16
10 (lowest)	$1,204,517	9.02%	5.94%	24.05%	0.04
All Stocks	$38,542,780	13.06%	10.46%	21.67%	0.25

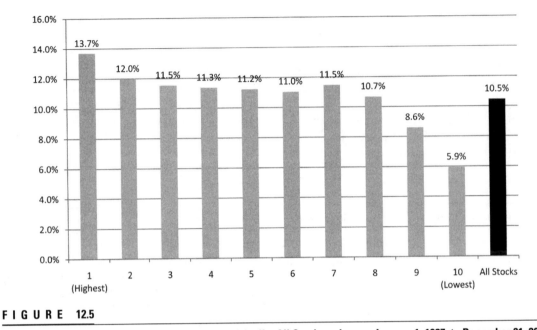

F I G U R E   12.5

Average annual compound return by buyback yield decile, All Stocks universe, January 1, 1927, to December 31, 2009

For Large Stocks, deciles 1 through 7 all beat Large Stocks, but deciles 4 and 6 do so only marginally most likely because of the problem mentioned above on placing stocks with zero values in the right decile. As with All Stocks, only deciles 9 and 10 should be completely avoided (see Table 12.24 and Figure 12.6).

T A B L E   12.24

Summary Results for Buyback Yield Decile Analysis of Large Stocks Universe, January 1, 1927, to December 31, 2009

Decile	$10,000 grows to	Average return	Compound return	Standard deviation	Sharpe ratio
1 (highest)	$250,019,446	15.88%	12.98%	23.11%	0.35
2	$145,516,544	15.15%	12.24%	23.22%	0.31
3	$113,823,003	14.68%	11.91%	22.76%	0.30
4	$25,737,268	12.51%	9.92%	22.24%	0.22
5	$38,376,139	12.46%	10.45%	19.09%	0.29
6	$22,742,972	11.90%	9.76%	19.72%	0.24
7	$53,593,671	13.19%	10.90%	20.32%	0.29
8	$19,536,117	11.84%	9.56%	20.28%	0.22
9	$8,615,546	10.90%	8.48%	21.18%	0.16
10 (lowest)	$1,397,168	8.67%	6.13%	21.93%	0.05
Large Stocks	$21,617,372	11.75%	9.69%	19.35%	0.24

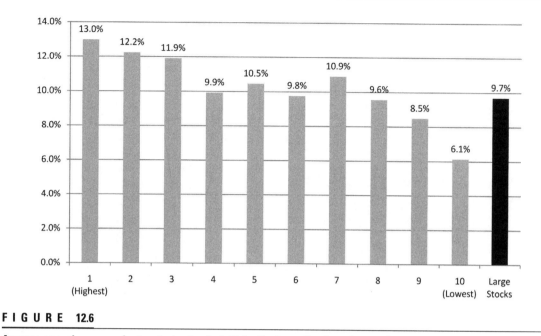

FIGURE 12.6

Average annual compound return by buyback yield decile, Large Stocks universe, January 1, 1927, to December 31, 2009

IMPLICATIONS

When studying the most effective way to return cash to shareholders, repurchasing shares in the open market provides higher returns than paying cash in the form of dividends. Stocks with the highest buyback yields do significantly better than the market—over the past 83 years besting the All Stocks universe by 3.23 percent on an average annual compound basis. Stocks with the lowest buyback yields perform horribly, losing 4.52 percent per year to the All Stocks universe. The spread between the best buyback group and the worst is 7.75 percent per year and seems to be very consistent when we analyze the rolling alpha generated over all five-year holding periods. In that analysis, we see that the group with the worst buyback yields consistently lose to the All Stock universe over 98 percent of all rolling five-year periods. All in all, buyback yield is an excellent factor to look at when determining a stock's relative attractiveness.

C H A P T E R

SHAREHOLDER YIELD

Better to be wise by the misfortunes of others than by your own.

—Aesop

Now we turn our attention to a ratio called *shareholder yield*. Shareholder yield unites a stock's dividend yield with its buyback yield to show what percentage of total cash the company is paying out to shareholders, either in the form of a cash dividend or as expended cash to repurchase its shares in the open market. Thus, if a company is paying a 5 percent dividend yield and has a buyback yield of 10 percent, its shareholder yield would be 15 percent. The theory is that stocks with higher shareholder yields might be more attractive than those with lower ones. Let's see if this holds true.

THE RESULTS

As always, we use our composited portfolios to review the deciles of stocks from All Stocks and Large Stocks with the highest and lowest shareholder yields. Since we have the data we need to conduct this analysis in the CRSP dataset, we start with a $10,000 investment on December 31, 1926, and hold it through to December 31, 2009. The $10,000 invested in the stocks from All Stocks with the highest shareholder yield would be worth $298,363,138 at the end of 2009, a compound average annual return of 13.22 percent. The $10,000 invested in the All Stocks universe grew to $38,542,780 over the same period, a compound average annual return of 10.46 percent. Risk, as measured by the standard deviation of return, was actually lower for the high shareholder yield stocks than for the All Stocks universe, coming in at 20.19 percent versus 21.67 percent for All Stocks. The downside risk for the group was also lower, coming in at 15.90 percent compared with 16.03 percent for All Stocks. Tables 13.1 through 13.5 outline all the statistics on the high shareholder yield group.

TABLE   13.1

Summary Annual Return and Risk Results Data: All Stocks Shareholder Yield Decile 1 and All Stocks, January 1, 1927, to December 31, 2009

	All Stocks shareholder yield decile 1	All Stocks
Arithmetic average	15.50%	13.06%
Geometric average	13.22%	10.46%
Median return	19.52%	18.54%
Standard deviation	20.19%	21.67%
Upside deviation	14.68%	14.78%
Downside deviation	15.90%	16.03%
Tracking error	6.79	0.00
Number of positive periods	648	606
Number of negative periods	348	390
Maximum peak-to-trough decline	−88.98%	−85.45%
Beta	0.89	1.00
T-statistic (m = 0)	6.54	5.19
Sharpe ratio (Rf = 5%)	0.41	0.25
Sortino ratio (MAR = 10%)	0.20	0.03
$10,000 becomes	$298,363,138	$38,542,780
Minimum 1-year return	−72.39%	−66.72%
Maximum 1-year return	210.02%	201.69%
Minimum 3-year return	−50.26%	−45.99%
Maximum 3-year return	57.28%	51.03%
Minimum 5-year return	−27.92%	−23.07%
Maximum 5-year return	43.17%	41.17%
Minimum 7-year Return	−9.38%	−7.43%
Maximum 7-year return	31.00%	23.77%
Minimum 10-year return	−7.42%	−5.31%
Maximum 10-year return	27.18%	22.05%
Minimum expected return*	−24.89%	−30.28%
Maximum expected return†	55.89%	56.39%

* Minimum expected return is arithmetic return minus 2 times the standard deviation.
† Maximum expected return is arithmetic return plus 2 times the standard deviation.

Base rates were all positive, with the group beating All Stocks in 86 percent of all rolling five-year periods and in 93 percent of all rolling ten-year periods. Table 13.2 shows the base rates for all holding periods. The strategy works particularly well when small-cap value is outperforming small-cap growth, and when large-cap value is outperforming large-cap growth. It also works well in market environments in which bonds are outperforming stocks. Figure 13.1 shows the five-year average annual compound excess return for decile 1 minus the return of the All Stocks universe.

TABLE 13.2

Base Rates for All Stocks Shareholder Yield Decile 1 and All Stocks, January 1, 1927, to December 31, 2009

Item	All Stocks shareholder yield decile 1 beat All Stocks	Percent	Average annual excess return
Single-year return	654 out of 985	66%	2.63%
Rolling 3-year compound return	783 out of 961	81%	2.90%
Rolling 5-year compound return	810 out of 937	86%	2.96%
Rolling 7-year compound return	833 out of 913	91%	3.08%
Rolling 10-year compound return	815 out of 877	93%	3.13%

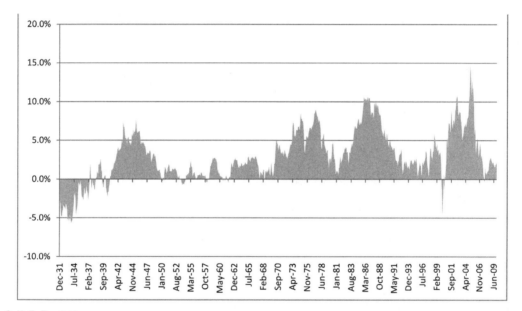

FIGURE 13.1

Five-year average annual compound excess (deficient) return All Stocks shareholder yield decile 1 minus All Stocks, January 1, 1927, to December 31, 2009

LARGE STOCKS ALSO PERFORM WELL

The $10,000 invested on December 31, 1926, in the stocks from Large Stocks with the highest shareholder yields grew to $217,331,288 by the end of 2009, an average annual compound return of 12.79 percent. The group had a slightly lower standard deviation of return than Large Stocks, coming in at 19.31 percent versus 19.35 percent for the Large Stocks universe. The higher return married to the lower risk provided a good Sharpe ratio of .40 compared to .24 for the Large Stocks universe. Tables 13.6 through 13.10 summarize the results.

All base rates were positive, with the group beating Large Stocks in 90 percent of all rolling five-year periods and in 97 percent of all rolling ten-year periods. Table 13.7 shows the base rates for all holding periods. The group performs particularly well when large-cap value is outperforming large-cap growth and when bonds are outperforming stocks. Figure 13.2 shows the five-year average annual compound excess return for decile 1 minus the return of the Large Stocks universe.

WORST-CASE SCENARIOS AND BEST AND WORST RETURNS

Between 1926 and 2009, the highest shareholder yield stocks from All Stocks declined by 20 percent or more seven times. The worst decline occurred between August 1929 and May 1932, when the group lost 89 percent. With the exception of the most recent bear market—when the group declined 55 percent between May 2007 and February 2009—most other declines were more muted than for many of the strategies we have examined. For example, in the 2000–2003 bear market, the group declined by less than 20 percent, making it one of the few single factors that didn't show up on a worst-case scenario list during that time period. Table 13.3 provides information on each of the decline periods.

T A B L E   13.3

Worst-Case Scenarios: All 20 Percent or Greater Declines for All Stocks Shareholder Yield Decile 1, January 1, 1927, to December 31, 2009

Peak date	Peak index value	Trough date	Trough index value	Recovery date	Decline (%)	Decline duration	Recovery duration
Aug–29	2.05	May–32	0.23	May–43	−88.98%	33	132
May–46	4.73	May–47	3.34	Dec–49	−29.51%	12	31
Jan–69	108.40	Jun–70	75.43	Apr–71	−30.42%	17	10
Nov–72	120.51	Sep–74	82.91	Jun–75	−31.20%	22	9
Aug–87	2,004.81	Nov–87	1,476.23	Jan–89	−26.37%	3	14
Aug–89	2,451.44	Oct–90	1,924.29	Feb–91	−21.50%	14	4
May–07	36,406.26	Feb–09	16,490.49	N/A	−54.70%	21	N/A
Average					−40.38%	17.43	33.33

The best absolute five-year period for the strategy occurred in the five years ending May 1937 when the group earned an average annual compound return of 43.17 percent and turned $10,000 into $60,161. The worst absolute five-year period occurred in the five years ending May 1932, when it lost 27.92 percent per year and turned $10,000 into $1,945. Table 13.4 shows the minimum and maximum average annual compound return for various periods and Table 13.5 shows the terminal value of $10,000 invested for the best and worst of all these holding periods.

TABLE 13.4

Best and Worst Average Annual Compound Returns for Monthly Data, January 1, 1927, to December 31, 2009

For any	1-year period	3-year period	5-year period	7-year period	10-year period
All Stocks shareholder yield decile 1 minimum compound return	−72.39%	−50.26%	−27.92%	−9.38%	−7.42%
All Stocks shareholder yield decile 1 maximum compound return	210.02%	57.28%	43.17%	31.00%	27.18%
All Stocks minimum compound return	−66.72%	−45.99%	−23.07%	−7.43%	−5.31%
All Stocks maximum compound return	201.69%	51.03%	41.17%	23.77%	22.05%
All Stocks shareholder yield decile 10 minimum compound return	−68.26%	−49.89%	−27.07%	−13.76%	−6.90%
All Stocks shareholder yield decile 10 minimum compound return	234.90%	48.95%	43.55%	23.60%	17.80%

TABLE 13.5

Terminal Value of $10,000 Invested for Best and Worst Average Annual Compound Returns for Monthly Data, January 1, 1927, to December 31, 2009

For any	1-year period	3-year period	5-year period	7-year period	10-year period
All Stocks shareholder yield decile 1 minimum $10,000 value	$2,761	$1,231	$1,945	$5,017	$4,626
All Stocks shareholder yield decile 1 maximum $10,000 value	$31,002	$38,910	$60,161	$66,193	$110,679
All Stocks minimum $10,000 value	$3,328	$1,576	$2,695	$5,825	$5,793
All Stocks maximum $10,000 value	$30,169	$34,452	$56,062	$44,504	$73,345
All Stocks shareholder yield decile 10 minimum $10,000 value	$3,174	$1,258	$2,063	$3,548	$4,894
All Stocks shareholder yield decile 10 maximum $10,000 value	$33,490	$33,045	$60,946	$44,069	$51,450

On a relative basis versus the All Stocks universe, the best five years for the group occurred in the five years ending July 1987, when it earned a cumulative return of 371 percent, whereas the All Stocks universe earned a cumulative 239 percent, giving the high shareholder yield group a 132 percent cumulative advantage over All Stocks. The worst five-year period for the group versus All Stocks occurred in the five years ending February 2000, when it earned a cumulative 127 percent versus All Stocks cumulative gain of 172 percent, a cumulative deficit of 45 percent for the high shareholder yield group. Figure 13.1 shows the excess (or deficient) returns compared to All Stocks for the entire period.

Between 1929 and 2009, the high shareholder yield stocks from Large Stocks lost 20 percent or more seven times. The largest drawdown was between August 1929 and June 1932, when they lost 87 percent. With the exception of the most recent bear market between October 2007 and February 2009 when they lost 53 percent, the high shareholder yield stocks from Large Stocks experienced more declines just like their All Stocks brethren did. Like the group from All Stocks, the high shareholder yield stocks from Large Stocks did not suffer a

20 percent decline during the bear market of 2000–2003 and lost only 28 percent in the 1973–1974 bear market. Table 13.8 lists all declines greater than 20 percent for the group.

T A B L E   13.6

Summary Annual Return and Risk Results Data: Large Stocks Shareholder Yield Decile 1 and Large Stocks, January 1, 1927, to December 31, 2009

	Large Stocks shareholder yield decile 1	Large Stocks
Arithmetic average	14.86%	11.75%
Geometric average	12.79%	9.69%
Median return	18.03%	16.75%
Standard deviation	19.31%	19.35%
Upside deviation	14.07%	13.10%
Downside deviation	14.59%	14.40%
Tracking error	6.54	0.00
Number of positive periods	628	609
Number of negative periods	368	387
Maximum peak-to-trough decline	−87.43%	−84.33%
Beta	0.94	1.00
T-statistic (m = 0)	6.57	5.25
Sharpe ratio (Rf = 5%)	0.40	0.24
Sortino ratio (MAR = 10%)	0.19	−0.02
$10,000 becomes	$217,331,288	$21,617,372
Minimum 1-year return	−73.02%	−66.63%
Maximum 1-year return	234.00%	159.52%
Minimum 3-year return	−48.31%	−43.53%
Maximum 3-year return	58.49%	45.64%
Minimum 5-year return	−25.54%	−20.15%
Maximum 5-year return	44.08%	36.26%
Minimum 7-year return	−7.66%	−6.95%
Maximum 7-year return	29.52%	22.83%
Minimum 10-year return	−4.17%	−5.70%
Maximum 10-year return	25.50%	19.57%
Minimum expected return*	−23.75%	−26.96%
Maximum expected return†	53.47%	50.46%

* Minimum expected return is arithmetic return minus 2 times the standard deviation.
† Maximum expected return is arithmetic return plus 2 times the standard deviation.

T A B L E   13.7

Base Rates for Large Stocks Shareholder Yield Decile 1 and Large Stocks, January 1, 1927, to December 31, 2009

Item	Large Stocks shareholder yield-decile 1 beat Large Stocks	Percent	Average annual excess return
Single-year return	658 out of 985	67%	3.29%
Rolling 3-year compound return	777 out of 961	81%	3.24%
Rolling 5-year compound return	843 out of 937	90%	3.33%
Rolling 7-year compound return	869 out of 913	95%	3.42%
Rolling 10-year compound return	855 out of 877	97%	3.41%

T A B L E   13.8

Worst-Case Scenarios: All 20 Percent or Greater Declines for Large Stocks Shareholder Yield Decile 1, January 1, 1927, to December 31, 2009

Peak date	Peak index value	Trough date	Trough index value	Recovery date	Decline (%)	Decline duration	Recovery duration
Aug–29	2.11	Jun–32	0.26	Mar–43	−87.43%	34	129
May–46	5.07	May–47	3.75	Dec–49	−26.10%	12	31
Nov–68	85.84	Jun–70	60.64	Jan–72	−29.36%	19	19
Nov–72	97.80	Sep–74	70.09	Jun–75	−28.34%	22	9
Aug–87	1,378.44	Nov–87	1,020.06	Oct–88	−26.00%	3	11
Aug–89	1,796.96	Oct–90	1,422.98	Feb–91	−20.81%	14	4
Oct–07	25,856.5	Feb–09	12,239.88	N/A	−52.66%	16	N/A
Average					−38.67%	17.14	33.83

On an absolute basis, the best five-year return for the group occurred in the five years ending May 1937, when it earned an average annual compound return of 44.08 percent and turned $10,000 into $62,095. Their worst absolute return occurred in the five years ending May 1932, when it declined by 25.54 percent a year and turned $10,000 into $2,288. Tables 13.9 and 13.10 show the results for best and worst returns for all holding periods.

T A B L E   13.9

Best and Worst Average Annual Compound Returns for Monthly Data, January 1, 1927, to December 31, 2009

For any	1-year period	3-year period	5-year period	7-year period	10-year period
Large Stocks shareholder yield decile 1 minimum compound return	−73.02%	−48.31%	−25.54%	−7.66%	−4.17%
Large Stocks shareholder yield decile 1 maximum compound return	234.00%	58.49%	44.08%	29.52%	25.50%
Large Stocks minimum compound return	−66.63%	−43.53%	−20.15%	−6.95%	−5.70%
Large Stocks maximum compound return	159.52%	45.64%	36.26%	22.83%	19.57%
Large Stocks shareholder yield decile 10 minimum compound return	−68.79%	−48.88%	−26.55%	−13.44%	−7.94%
Large Stocks shareholder yield decile 10 maximum compound return	253.61%	55.40%	41.34%	22.39%	15.85%

T A B L E   13.10

Terminal Value of $10,000 Invested for Best and Worst Average Annual Compound Returns for Monthly Data, January 1, 1927, to December 31, 2009

For any	1-year period	3-year period	5-year period	7-year period	10-year period
Large Stocks shareholder yield decile 1 minimum $10,000 value	$2,698	$1,381	$2,288	$5,723	$6,533
Large Stocks shareholder yield decile 1 maximum $10,000 value	$33,400	$39,810	$62,095	$61,149	$96,932

(continued on next page)

TABLE 13.10

Terminal Value of $10,000 Invested for Best and Worst Average Annual Compound Returns for Monthly Data, January 1, 1927, to December 31, 2009 *(Continued)*

For any	1-year period	3-year period	5-year period	7-year period	10-year period
Large Stocks minimum $10,000 value	$3,337	$1,800	$3,247	$6,041	$5,561
Large Stocks maximum $10,000 value	$25,952	$30,890	$46,970	$42,189	$59,747
Large Stocks shareholder yield decile 10 minimum $10,000 value	$3,121	$1,336	$2,138	$3,642	$4,370
Large Stocks shareholder yield decile 10 maximum $10,000 value	$35,361	$37,529	$56,416	$41,130	$43,533

On a relative basis, the best five years were those ending June 1937, when the group earned a cumulative 498 percent versus Large Stocks' 346 percent, providing a 152 percent cumulative advantage for the group.

Their worst relative five-year return versus Large Stocks occurred in the five years ending February 2000, when it gained a cumulative return of 137 percent versus 180 percent for Large Stocks, a cumulative deficit of 43 percent. Figure 13.2 shows the excess (or deficient) five-year returns for the group compared to Large Stocks for the entire period.

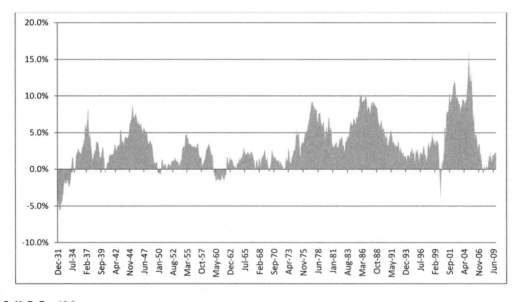

FIGURE 13.2

Five-year average annual compound excess (deficient) return Large Stocks shareholder yield decile 1 minus Large Stocks, January 1, 1927, to December 31, 2009

BUYING THE STOCKS FROM ALL STOCKS WITH THE LOWEST SHAREHOLDER YIELD OFFERS POOR RETURNS

Let's now look at an investment in the decile of stocks with the lowest shareholder yield. The $10,000 invested on December 31, 1926, was worth $1,334,762 at the end of 2009, an average annual compound return of 6.07 percent. Needless to say, that pales in comparison to the $38,542,780 you'd have earned with an investment in the All Stocks universe itself. Risk was substantially higher, with the group sporting a standard deviation of return of 25.78 compared to All Stocks' 21.67 percent. Downside risk was also higher, at 18.38 percent compared to 16.03 for All Stocks. The much lower return married to the higher risk brought the Sharpe ratio down to .04, paltry compared to All Stocks' Sharpe ratio of .25. Tables 13.11 through 13.13 list all the statistics for the lowest shareholder yield group versus All Stocks.

T A B L E   13.11

Summary Annual Return and Risk Results Data: All Stocks Shareholder Yield Decile 10 and All Stocks, January 1, 1927, to December 31, 2009

	All Stocks shareholder yield decile 10	All Stocks
Arithmetic average	9.58%	13.06%
Geometric average	6.07%	10.46%
Median return	16.52%	18.54%
Standard deviation	25.78%	21.67%
Upside deviation	18.72%	14.78%
Downside deviation	18.38%	16.03%
Tracking error	6.15	0.00
Number of positive periods	580	606
Number of negative periods	416	390
Maximum peak-to-trough decline	−88.56%	−85.45%
Beta	1.17	1.00
T-statistic (m = 0)	3.25	5.19
Sharpe ratio (Rf = 5%)	0.04	0.25
Sortino ratio (MAR = 10%)	−0.21	0.03
$10,000 becomes	$1,334,762	$38,542,780
Minimum 1-year return	−68.26%	−66.72%
Maximum 1-year return	234.90%	201.69%
Minimum 3-year return	−49.89%	−45.99%
Maximum 3-year return	48.95%	51.03%
Minimum 5-year return	−27.07%	−23.07%
Maximum 5-year return	43.55%	41.17%
Minimum 7-year return	−13.76%	−7.43%
Maximum 7-year return	23.60%	23.77%

(continued on next page)

TABLE 13.11

Summary Annual Return and Risk Results Data: All Stocks Shareholder Yield Decile 10 and All Stocks, January 1, 1927, to December 31, 2009 *(Continued)*

	All Stocks shareholder yield decile 10	All Stocks
Minimum 10-year return	−6.90%	−5.31%
Maximum 10-year return	17.80%	22.05%
Minimum expected return*	−41.97%	−30.28%
Maximum expected return†	61.13%	56.39%

* Minimum expected return is arithmetic return minus 2 times the standard deviation.
† Maximum expected return is arithmetic return plus 2 times the standard deviation.

All base rates for the strategy were negative, with the group beating All Stocks in just 9 percent of all rolling five-year periods and 4 percent of all rolling ten-year periods. Table 13.12 gives the base rates for all holding periods. Figure 13.3 shows the five-year average annual compound excess (or, in this case, deficient) return minus the return for the All Stocks universe. Table 13.13 shows all declines for the group greater than 20 percent.

TABLE 13.12

Base Rates for All Stocks Shareholder Yield Decile 10 and All Stocks, January 1, 1927, to December 31, 2009

Item	All Stocks shareholder yield decile 10 beat All Stocks	Percent	Average annual excess return
Single-year return	263 out of 985	27%	−3.57%
Rolling 3-year compound return	171 out of 961	18%	−4.12%
Rolling 5-year compound return	83 out of 937	9%	−4.23%
Rolling 7-year compound return	56 out of 913	6%	−4.33%
Rolling 10-year compound return	36 out of 877	4%	−4.37%

TABLE 13.13

Worst-Case Scenarios: All 20 Percent or Greater Declines for All Stock Shareholder Yield Decile 10, January 1, 1927, to December 31, 2009

Peak date	Peak index value	Trough date	Trough index value	Recovery date	Decline (%)	Decline duration	Recovery duration
Aug–29	1.88	May–32	0.22	Feb–45	−88.56%	33	153
May–46	3.45	May–47	2.18	Jan–51	−36.83%	12	44
Nov–61	15.60	Jun–62	10.88	Jan–65	−30.25%	7	31
Apr–66	21.90	Oct–66	17.15	Jan–67	−21.66%	6	3
Nov–68	37.00	Sep–74	10.22	Jul–80	−72.38%	70	70
May–81	52.20	Jul–82	35.45	Jan–83	−32.09%	14	6
Jun–83	67.61	Jul–84	47.17	Feb–86	−30.23%	13	19
Aug–87	90.43	Nov–87	57.30	Aug–89	−36.63%	3	21
Sep–89	91.29	Oct–90	64.65	Mar–91	−29.18%	13	5
Apr–98	181.75	Aug–98	120.75	Dec–99	−33.56%	4	16
Feb–00	208.17	Feb–09	70.79	N/A	−65.99%	108	N/A
Average					−43.40%	26	37

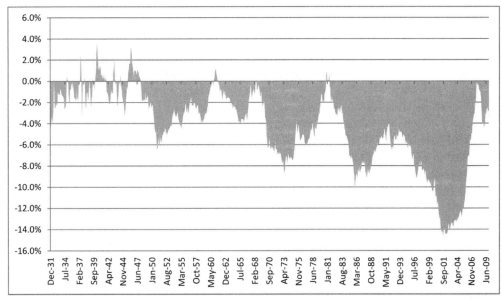

FIGURE 13.3

Five-year average annual compound excess (deficient) return All Stocks shareholder yield decile 10 minus All Stocks, January 1, 1927, to December 31, 2009

LARGE STOCKS WORSE THAN ALL STOCKS

Between December 31, 1926, and December 31, 2009, $10,000 invested in the decile of stocks from Large Stocks with the lowest shareholder yield grew to $1,182,249, an average annual compound return of 5.92 percent. That's a long way from the $21,617,372 you'd have earned with an investment in the Large Stocks universe itself, which compounded at 9.69 percent over the same period. Risk for the low shareholder yield group from Large Stocks was high, with a standard deviation of 23.90 percent versus Large Stocks' 19.35 percent. The higher risk married to the lower return brought the Sharpe ratio to .04, considerably lower than the .24 Sharpe ratio for the Large Stocks universe. Tables 13.14 through 13.16 list all the statistics for the low shareholder yield group versus Large Stocks.

TABLE 13.14

Summary Annual Return and Risk Results Data: Large Stocks Shareholder Yield Decile 10 and Large Stocks, January 1, 1927, to December 31, 2009

	Large Stocks shareholder yield decile 10	Large Stocks
Arithmetic average	8.89%	11.75%
Geometric average	5.92%	9.69%
Median return	12.56%	16.75%

(continued on next page)

T A B L E   13.14

Summary Annual Return and Risk Results Data: Large Stocks Shareholder Yield Decile 10 and Large Stocks, January 1, 1927, to December 31, 2009 *(Continued)*

	Large Stocks shareholder yield decile 10	Large Stocks
Standard deviation	23.90%	19.35%
Upside deviation	18.21%	13.10%
Downside deviation	16.89%	14.40%
Tracking error	7.30	0.00
Number of positive periods	579	609
Number of negative periods	417	387
Maximum peak-to-trough decline	−88.63%	−84.33%
Beta	1.19	1.00
T-statistic (m = 0)	3.26	5.25
Sharpe ratio (Rf = 5%)	0.04	0.24
Sortino ratio (MAR = 10%)	−0.24	−0.02
$10,000 becomes	$1,182,249	$21,617,372
Minimum 1-year return	−68.79%	−66.63%
Maximum 1-year return	253.61%	159.52%
Minimum 3-year return	−48.88%	−43.53%
Maximum 3-year return	55.40%	45.64%
Minimum 5-year return	−26.55%	−20.15%
Maximum 5-year return	41.34%	36.26%
Minimum 7-year return	−13.44%	−6.95%
Maximum 7-year return	22.39%	22.83%
Minimum 10-year return	−7.94%	−5.70%
Maximum 10-year return	15.85%	19.57%
Minimum expected return*	−38.91%	−26.96%
Maximum expected return†	56.68%	50.46%

* Minimum expected return is arithmetic return minus 2 times the standard deviation.
† Maximum expected return is arithmetic return plus 2 times the standard deviation.

All base rates for the strategy are negative, with the group beating Large Stocks in just 14 percent of all rolling five-year periods and a mere 4 percent of all rolling ten-year periods. Table 13.15 shows all base rates for of the rolling five- and ten-year holding periods. Figure 13.4 shows the five-year average annual compound excess (or, in this case, deficient) return minus the return for the Large Stocks universe.

T A B L E   13.15

Base Rates for Large Stocks Shareholder Yield Decile 10 and Large Stocks, January 1, 1927, to December 31, 2009

Item	Large Stocks shareholder yield-decile 10 beat Large Stocks	Percent	Average annual excess return
Single-year return	280 out of 985	28%	−2.98%
Rolling 3-year compound return	200 out of 961	21%	−3.49%
Rolling 5-year compound return	131 out of 937	14%	−3.54%
Rolling 7-year compound return	65 out of 913	7%	−3.68%
Rolling 10-year compound return	34 out of 877	4%	−3.79%

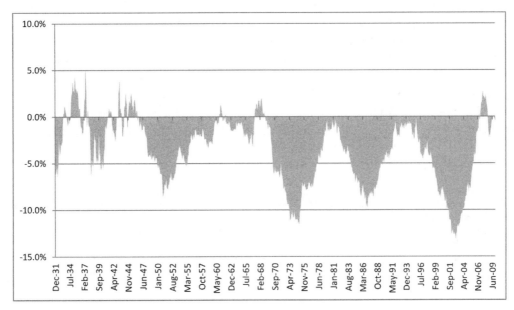

F I G U R E   13.4

Five-year average annual compound excess (deficient) return Large Stocks shareholder yield decile 10 minus Large Stocks, January 1, 1927, to December 31, 2009

WORST-CASE SCENARIOS AND BEST AND WORST RETURNS

The decile of stocks with the lowest shareholder yield from All Stocks had 11 separate declines of 20 percent or more. The worst decline occurred between August 1929 and May 1932, when the group lost 89 percent. The group was also badly hit in the bear market of November 1968 through September 1974, when it lost 72 percent. The group's most current decline occurred between February 2000 and February 2009, losing 66 percent over the period. Table 13.13 shows all declines greater than 20 percent over the entire period.

The best five years on an absolute basis were those ending May 1937, when the group earned an average annual compound return of 43.55 percent and turned $10,000 into $60,946. The worst five-year absolute return occurred in the five years ending May 1932, when it dropped by 27.07 percent per year, turning $10,000 into $2,063. Tables 13.4 and 13.5 show the best- and worst-case returns for all holding periods.

On a relative basis, the best five-years for the group versus All Stocks were also those ending in May 1937, when it earned a cumulative return of 509 percent versus All Stocks' 461 percent, a cumulative 48 percent advantage over All Stocks. The worst five years for the group versus All Stocks were those ending in March 2000, when it earned a cumulative return of 71 percent versus All Stocks' 165 percent, a cumulative deficit of 94 percent. Figure 13.3 shows the excess (or deficient) return compared to the All Stocks universe for all rolling five-year periods. It does not paint a pretty picture.

The decile of stocks from Large Stocks with the lowest shareholder yield had 11 separate declines exceeding 20 percent between 1926 and 2009, with the worst occurring between August 1929 and May 1932, when it lost 89 percent. The group was also hard hit during the bear market between November 1968 and September 1974, when it lost 68 percent. It was again hit hard between August 2000 and September 2002, when it lost 62 percent, and in the bear market between October 2007 and February 2009, when it lost 59 percent. Table 13.16 lists all declines greater than 20 percent since 1926.

T A B L E   13.16

Worst-Case Scenarios: All 20 Percent or Greater Declines for Large Stocks Shareholder Yield Decile 10, January 1, 1927, to December 31, 2009

Peak date	Peak index value	Trough date	Trough index value	Recovery date	Decline (%)	Decline duration	Recovery duration
Aug–29	1.90	May–32	0.22	Oct–45	−88.63%	33	161
May–46	2.43	May–47	1.64	Feb–51	−32.70%	12	45
Nov–61	10.22	Jun–62	7.37	Dec–63	−27.91%	7	18
Nov–68	19.71	Sep–74	6.21	Nov–80	−68.49%	70	74
May–81	22.04	Jul–82	15.74	Jan–83	−28.59%	14	6
Jun–83	27.15	Jul–84	20.13	Nov–85	−25.86%	13	16
Aug–87	41.56	Nov–87	28.60	May–89	−31.18%	3	18
May–90	47.07	Oct–90	34.76	Feb–91	−26.16%	5	4
Apr–98	134.61	Aug–98	99.42	Apr–99	−26.14%	4	8
Aug–00	146.87	Sep–02	56.55	Apr–07	−61.50%	25	55
Oct–07	165.07	Feb–09	67.61	N/A	−59.04%	16	N/A
Average					−43.29%	18	41

The best five-year absolute performance for the group occurred during the five years ending May 1937, when it earned an average annual compound return of 41.34 percent and turned $10,000 into $56,416. The worst absolute five-year return for the group occurred in the five years ending May 1932, when it lost 26.55 percent per year and turned

$10,000 into $2,138. Tables 13.9 and 13.10 show the best- and worst-case returns for all holding periods.

On a relative basis versus Large Stocks, the best five years were those ending in June 1937, when the group gained a cumulative 414 percent compared to a gain of 346 percent for the Large Stocks universe, a cumulative advantage of 68 percent. The worst relative performance versus the Large Stocks universe occurred in the five years ending July 1987, when the group gained a cumulative 158 percent compared to 257 percent for Large Stocks, a 99 percent cumulative deficit over the period. Figure 13.4 shows the five-year excess (or deficient) return for the low shareholder yield group versus Large Stocks for the entire period. As we saw with All Stocks, the picture is not a pretty one. Tables 13.17 and 13.18 show the average annual compound return for each group from All Stocks and Large Stocks by decade.

T A B L E   13.17

Average Annual Compound Rates of Return by Decade

	1920s*	1930s	1940s	1950s	1960s	1970s	1980s	1990s	2000s†
All Stocks shareholder yield decile 1	14.39%	−2.11%	14.62%	19.32%	12.25%	13.09%	23.15%	16.33%	10.53%
All Stocks	12.33%	−0.03%	11.57%	18.07%	10.72%	7.56%	16.78%	15.35%	4.39%
All Stocks shareholder yield decile 10	4.31%	0.05%	9.37%	15.30%	8.02%	2.73%	10.32%	7.77%	−3.23%

* Returns for January 1, 1927, to December 31, 1929.
† Returns for January 1, 2000, to December 31, 2009.

T A B L E   13.18

Average Annual Compound Rates of Return by Decade

	1920s*	1930s	1940s	1950s	1960s	1970s	1980s	1990s	2000s†
Large Stocks shareholder yield decile 1	16.34%	−0.07%	12.55%	19.20%	8.96%	11.84%	23.42%	17.37%	9.63%
Large Stocks	17.73%	−1.05%	9.65%	17.06%	8.31%	6.65%	17.34%	16.38%	2.42%
Large Stocks shareholder yield decile 10	4.86%	−1.41%	7.39%	14.03%	7.28%	−0.10%	11.60%	11.83%	−1.61%

* Returns for January 1, 1927, to December 31, 1929.
† Returns for January 1, 2000, to December 31, 2009.

FULL DECILE ANALYSIS

The full decile analysis for shareholder yield shows more uniformity than we saw with buyback yield. Figure 13.5 and Table 13.19 show that here the deciles descend in order, with those stocks from All Stocks with the highest shareholder yield providing the best returns, and those with the lowest shareholder yields earning the worst returns. The spread between decile 1 and decile 10 is 7.14 percent a year over the 83 years studied, creating a gulf in terminal value between the two portfolios.

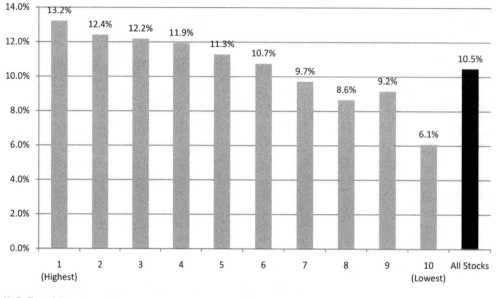

FIGURE   13.5

Average annual compound return by shareholder yield decile, All Stocks universe, January 1, 1927, to December 31, 2009

TABLE   13.19

Summary Results for Shareholder Yield Decile Analysis of All Stocks Universe, January 1, 1927, to December 31, 2009

Decile	$10,000 grows to	Average return	Compound return	Standard deviation	Sharpe ratio
1 (highest)	$298,363,138	15.50%	13.22%	20.19%	0.41
2	$164,632,206	14.35%	12.41%	18.66%	0.40
3	$138,927,917	14.08%	12.18%	18.43%	0.39
4	$116,208,174	13.93%	11.94%	18.91%	0.37
5	$71,061,645	13.42%	11.28%	19.61%	0.32
6	$47,745,959	13.15%	10.75%	20.71%	0.28
7	$21,930,224	12.55%	9.71%	22.60%	0.21
8	$9,775,556	11.97%	8.65%	24.65%	0.15
9	$14,358,062	13.01%	9.15%	26.68%	0.16
10 (lowest)	$1,334,762	9.58%	6.07%	25.78%	0.04
All Stocks	$38,542,780	13.06%	10.46%	21.67%	0.25

The full decile analysis for the Large Stocks universe is similar to that for All Stocks. Figure 13.6 and Table 13.20 show that the returns by decile again decline in order, with the 10 percent of stocks in decile 1 with the highest shareholder yield strongly outperforming those in decile 10 with the lowest shareholder yield. The spread between decile 1 and decile 10 is 6.87 percent a year over the 83 years studied, also creating a huge gulf in terminal portfolio value.

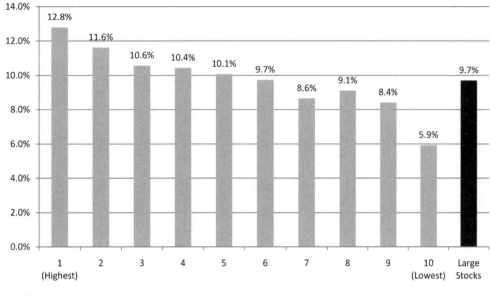

F I G U R E   13.6

Average annual compound return by shareholder yield decile, Large Stocks universe, January 1, 1927, to December 31, 2009

T A B L E   13.20

Summary Results for Shareholder Yield Decile Analysis of Large Stocks Universe, January 1, 1927, to December 31, 2009

Decile	$10,000 grows to	Average return	Compound return	Standard deviation	Sharpe ratio
1 (highest)	$217,331,288	14.86%	12.79%	19.31%	0.40
2	$91,230,690	13.40%	11.61%	17.93%	0.37
3	$41,546,263	12.32%	10.56%	17.91%	0.31
4	$37,632,925	12.22%	10.43%	18.07%	0.30
5	$28,687,731	11.94%	10.07%	18.37%	0.28
6	$22,224,338	11.76%	9.73%	19.11%	0.25
7	$9,720,068	11.00%	8.64%	20.73%	0.18
8	$13,821,435	11.71%	9.10%	21.71%	0.19
9	$8,115,199	11.42%	8.41%	23.57%	0.14
10 (lowest)	$1,182,249	8.89%	5.92%	23.90%	0.04
Large Stocks	$21,617,372	11.75%	9.69%	19.35%	0.24

IMPLICATIONS

Both shareholder yield and buyback yield are superior to dividend yield alone in selecting stocks. While buyback yield alone beats dividend yield and shareholder yield, shareholder yield has more muted declines than buyback yield and superior base rates to buyback yield.

Investors who couldn't withstand a five-year period when their portfolio lagged its benchmark by 74 percent might prefer the shareholder yield approach, since its worst cumulative loss to its benchmark was 45 percent. Both buyback yield and shareholder yield are good performers and should be considered by both value investors who want the best buyback yield and shareholder yield and by growth investors who want to make certain to avoid the risks associated with the bottom deciles of each group.

14 CHAPTER

ACCOUNTING RATIOS

Remind people that profit is the difference between revenue and expense. This makes you look smart.
—Scott Adams

Now let's look at the efficacy of using various accounting variables to help us pick which stocks look attractive and which should be avoided. Several academic papers have suggested that paying closer attention to accounting variables such as accruals-to-price and asset turnover can help investors make better stock selections. For the purposes of this chapter, we summarize a variety of accounting variables and look at which variables have empirical evidence supporting them and which do not. We feature only those items that may be of real use in determining whether a stock should be considered for purchase or should be avoided. Many of the variables we tested offered no clear empirical evidence of their efficacy. For example, ratios like assets to equity and debt to assets reveal no systematic evidence that they are worth consideration. Yet several variables do offer meaningful and predictive evidence of a stock's future performance, with the first being accruals-to-price.

ACCRUALS-TO-PRICE

Many analysts believe that a company's accruals-to-price ratio is a good proxy for the quality of a company's earnings, with those stocks having a low accruals-to-price ratio offering higher-quality earnings because a high accruals-to-price ratio indicates that the firm may be under pressure to "pad" sales by doing such things as sending excess inventory to stores even though the company knows that it will be unable to sell its products but it then accrues those "sales" to create a number that might be ultimately bogus. For this reason, many believe that stocks with the highest accruals-to-price ratios will ultimately be the most likely to have negative earnings surprises that will adversely affect a stock's price. Let's see if this is true.

Table 14.1 shows the results for $10,000 invested between 1963 and 2009 in each decile from All Stocks ranked by accruals-to-price, with the tenth decile being the 10 percent of stocks from All Stocks with the lowest accruals-to-price. Stocks with the lowest accruals-to-price clearly do better than the market, with the three deciles with the lowest accruals-to-price all beating the All Stocks universe, and the two deciles with the lowest accruals-to-price doing so by a significant margin. At the same time, the two deciles with the highest accruals-to-price do significantly worse than the All Stocks universe. Table 14.2 shows the detailed results for deciles 1 and 10.

T A B L E   14.1

Summary Results for Accruals-to-Price Decile Analysis of All Stocks Universe, January 1, 1964, to December 31, 2009

Decile	$10,000 grows to	Average return	Compound return	Standard deviation	Sharpe ratio
1 (highest)	$482,948	11.37%	8.79%	21.47%	0.18
2	$463,666	11.12%	8.70%	20.84%	0.18
3	$585,626	11.85%	9.25%	21.65%	0.20
4	$708,911	12.13%	9.71%	20.86%	0.23
5	$947,994	12.57%	10.40%	19.66%	0.27
6	$1,244,211	12.97%	11.06%	18.45%	0.33
7	$1,105,662	12.44%	10.77%	17.24%	0.33
8	$1,467,435	12.94%	11.45%	16.23%	0.40
9	$2,874,786	14.66%	13.10%	16.51%	0.49
10 (lowest)	$4,800,813	16.70%	14.36%	20.13%	0.47
All Stocks	$1,329,513	13.26%	11.22%	18.99%	0.33

T A B L E   14.2

Summary Annual Return and Risk Results Data: All Stocks Accruals-to-Price Decile 1, All Stocks Accruals-to-Price Decile 10, and All Stocks, January 1, 1964, to December 31, 2009

	All Stocks accruals-to-price decile 1	All Stocks accruals-to-price decile 10	All Stocks
Arithmetic average	11.37%	16.70%	13.26%
Geometric average	8.79%	14.36%	11.22%
Median return	13.62%	19.06%	17.16%
Standard deviation	21.47%	20.13%	18.99%
Upside deviation	12.57%	13.10%	10.98%
Downside deviation	15.47%	14.94%	13.90%

(continued on next page)

T A B L E 14.2

Summary Annual Return and Risk Results Data: All Stocks Accruals-to-Price Decile 1, All Stocks Accruals-to-Price Decile 10, and All Stocks, January 1, 1964, to December 31, 2009 *(Continued)*

	All Stocks accruals-to-price decile 1	All Stocks accruals-to-price decile 10	All Stocks
Tracking error	4.96	6.75	0.00
Number of positive periods	316	345	329
Number of negative periods	236	207	223
Maximum peak-to-trough decline	−60.25%	−63.33%	−55.54%
Beta	1.10	1.00	1.00
T-statistic (m = 0)	3.42	5.24	4.47
Sharpe ratio (Rf = 5%)	0.18	0.47	0.33
Sortino ratio (MAR = 10%)	−0.08	0.29	0.09
$10,000 becomes	$482,948	$4,800,813	$1,329,513
Minimum 1-year return	−51.98%	−54.53%	−46.49%
Maximum 1-year return	86.79%	112.37%	84.19%
Minimum 3-year return	−22.33%	−20.77%	−18.68%
Maximum 3-year return	35.84%	47.50%	31.49%
Minimum 5-year return	−11.31%	−6.68%	−9.91%
Maximum 5-year return	28.55%	34.00%	27.66%
Minimum 7-year return	−7.05%	−0.86%	−6.32%
Maximum 7-year return	24.78%	25.06%	23.77%
Minimum 10-year return	−0.65%	4.74%	1.01%
Maximum 10-year return	21.36%	24.43%	22.05%
Minimum expected return*	−31.57%	−23.56%	−24.73%
Maximum expected return†	54.31%	56.96%	51.24%

* Minimum expected return is arithmetic return minus 2 times the standard deviation.
† Maximum expected return is arithmetic return plus 2 times the standard deviation

The base rates for decile 10—the stocks with the lowest accruals-to-price—are all positive, with the group beating the All Stocks universe in 86 percent of all rolling five-year periods and 91 percent of all rolling ten-year periods. The base rates for decile 1—the stocks with the highest accruals-to-price—are all negative, with the group beating the All Stocks universe in just 25 percent of all rolling five-year periods and 12 percent of all rolling ten-year periods. Tables 14.3 and 14.4 show the base rates for each group for all rolling periods.

T A B L E   14.3

Base Rates for All Stocks Accruals-to-Price Decile 10 and All Stocks, January 1, 1964, to December 31, 2009

Item	All Stocks accruals-to-price decile 10 beat All Stocks	Percent	Average annual excess return
Single-year return	346 out of 541	64%	3.04%
Rolling 3-year compound return	400 out of 517	77%	2.92%
Rolling 5-year compound return	422 out of 493	86%	2.90%
Rolling 7-year compound return	404 out of 469	86%	2.81%
Rolling 10-year compound return	396 out of 433	91%	2.72%

T A B L E   14.4

Base Rates for All Stocks Accruals-to-Price Decile 1 and All Stocks, January 1, 1964, to December 31, 2009

Item	All Stocks accruals-to-price decile 10 beat All Stocks	Percent	Average annual excess return
Single-year return	218 out of 541	40%	−1.90%
Rolling 3-year compound return	168 out of 517	32%	−2.51%
Rolling 5-year compound return	123 out of 493	25%	−2.78%
Rolling 7-year compound return	90 out of 469	19%	−3.02%
Rolling 10-year compound return	51 out of 433	12%	−3.40%

LARGE STOCKS

Table 14.5 shows the results for all deciles by accruals-to-price for the Large Stocks universe. As we saw with All Stocks, Large Stocks with low accruals-to-price perform much better than those with the highest accruals to price, yet the return differentials are not as significant as we saw with All Stocks. Here, decile 10, those Large Stocks with the lowest accruals-to-price returned 12.67 percent per year between 1963 and 2009, whereas those with the highest accruals-to-price returned 8.48 percent. The Large Stocks universe itself earned 10.20 percent per year over the same period. Table 14.6 shows the detailed results for deciles 1 and 10.

T A B L E   14.5

Summary Results for Accruals-to-Price Decile Analysis of Large Stocks Universe, January 1, 1964, to December 31, 2009

Decile	$10,000 grows to	Average return	Compound return	Standard deviation	Sharpe ratio
1 (highest)	$423,609	10.18%	8.48%	17.53%	0.20
2	$378,951	9.95%	8.22%	17.74%	0.18
3	$639,736	11.09%	9.46%	17.19%	0.26
4	$571,142	10.74%	9.19%	16.79%	0.25
5	$617,850	10.88%	9.38%	16.50%	0.27
6	$413,896	9.83%	8.43%	15.96%	0.21
7	$730,698	11.09%	9.78%	15.46%	0.31
8	$470,284	9.91%	8.73%	14.72%	0.25
9	$1,286,892	12.29%	11.14%	14.44%	0.43
10 (lowest)	$2,415,916	14.08%	12.67%	15.85%	0.48
Large Stocks	$872,861	11.72%	10.20%	16.50%	0.32

T A B L E 14.6

Summary Annual Return and Risk Results Data: Large Stocks Accruals-to-Price Decile 1, Large Stocks Accruals-to-Price Decile 10, and Large Stocks, January 1, 1964 to December 31, 2009

	Large Stocks accruals-to-price decile 1	Large Stocks accruals-to-price decile 10	Large Stocks
Arithmetic average	10.18%	14.08%	11.72%
Geometric average	8.48%	12.67%	10.20%
Median return	14.01%	18.70%	17.20%
Standard deviation	17.53%	15.85%	16.50%
Upside deviation	10.33%	9.99%	9.70%
Downside deviation	12.98%	11.10%	11.85%
Tracking error	5.90	7.38	0.00
Number of positive periods	322	339	332
Number of negative periods	230	213	220
Maximum peak-to-trough decline	−54.83%	−53.48%	−53.77%
Beta	1.00	0.86	1.00
T-statistic (m = 0)	3.77	5.67	4.58
Sharpe ratio (Rf = 5%)	0.20	0.48	0.32
Sortino ratio (MAR = 10%)	−0.12	0.24	0.02
$10,000 becomes	$423,609	$2,415,916	$872,861
Minimum 1-year return	−49.21%	−45.26%	−46.91%
Maximum 1-year return	70.19%	72.99%	68.96%
Minimum 3-year return	−19.18%	−10.83%	−15.89%
Maximum 3-year return	35.68%	39.51%	33.12%
Minimum 5-year return	−9.61%	−0.66%	−5.82%
Maximum 5-year return	29.41%	32.88%	28.95%
Minimum 7-year return	−4.29%	−0.25%	−4.15%
Maximum 7-year return	23.53%	25.99%	22.83%
Minimum 10-year return	−1.71%	2.75%	−0.15%
Maximum 10-year return	20.79%	20.36%	19.57%
Minimum expected return*	−24.87%	−17.61%	−21.28%
Maximum expected return†	45.24%	45.78%	44.72%

* Minimum expected return is arithmetic return minus 2 times the standard deviation.
† Maximum expected return is arithmetic return plus 2 times the standard deviation.

Tables 14.7 and 14.8 show the base rates for each group. The Large Stocks with the lowest accruals-to-price from decile 10 have positive base rates across all periods, beating the Large Stocks universe in 74 percent of all rolling five-year periods and in 89 percent of all rolling ten-year periods. For Large Stocks with the *highest* accruals-to-price, all base rates are negative, with the group beating Large Stocks in just 37 percent of all rolling five-year periods and 19 percent of all rolling ten-year periods.

TABLE 14.7

Base Rates for Large Stocks Accruals-to-Price Decile 10 and Large Stocks, January 1, 1964, to December 31, 2009

Item	Large Stocks accruals-to-price decile 10 beat Large Stocks	Percent	Average annual excess return
Single-year return	330 out of 541	61%	2.51%
Rolling 3-year compound return	369 out of 517	71%	2.59%
Rolling 5-year compound return	365 out of 493	74%	2.55%
Rolling 7-year compound return	350 out of 469	75%	2.47%
Rolling 10-year compound return	384 out of 433	89%	2.41%

TABLE 14.8

Base Rates for Large Stocks Accruals-to-Price Decile 1 and Large Stocks, January 1, 1964, to December 31, 2009

Item	Large Stocks accruals-to-price decile 1 beat Large Stocks	Percent	Average annual excess return
Single-year return	207 out of 541	38%	−1.36%
Rolling 3-year compound return	202 out of 517	39%	−1.66%
Rolling 5-year compound return	181 out of 493	37%	−1.90%
Rolling 7-year compound return	132 out of 469	28%	−2.11%
Rolling 10-year compound return	83 out of 433	19%	−2.34%

IMPLICATIONS

Investors would be rewarded by sticking with stocks that have low accruals-to-price and avoiding those with high accruals-to-price. The lower accruals-to-price group appears to offer higher-quality earnings than those with high accruals-to-price, which is more likely to have negative earnings surprises and should therefore be avoided.

ASSETS-TO-EQUITY

The assets-to-equity ratio measures the relationship of the total assets of a company to the portion owned by its shareholders, which is often called shareholder or owner's equity. It essentially measures the company's use of leverage—the amount of debt used by a company to finance the firm's operations. Firms with high asset-to-equity ratios have taken on substantial amounts of debt to finance the firm's operations, whereas firms with low asset-to-equity ratios are financing most of the firm's operations through cash flow rather than debt. Let's see what a decile analysis of this ratio reveals.

Table 14.9 shows the results from an investment made in each composited portfolio by decile, with decile 1 made up of the 10 percent of stocks from All Stocks with the *highest* assets-to-equity ratios and decile 10 composed of the 10 percent of stocks from All Stocks with the *lowest* asset-to-equity ratios. Essentially, stocks in decile 10 have the lowest leverage and least amount of debt, whereas stocks in decile 1 have the highest leverage and most debt. At first glance, the only thing we learn from this analysis is that we should avoid decile 10, those stocks with the lowest asset-to-equity ratios. Essentially this tells us that using *some* leverage is beneficial, and using little or none can actually be damaging to the prospects of a stock's price. Table 14.10 shows the detailed results for deciles 1 and 10. Note that using very

T A B L E 14.9

Summary Results for Assets-to-Equity Decile Analysis of All Stocks Universe, January 1, 1964, to December 31, 2009

Decile	$10,000 grows to	Average return	Compound return	Standard deviation	Sharpe ratio
1 (highest)	$1,299,802	12.90%	11.16%	17.59%	0.35
2	$1,146,410	12.88%	10.86%	18.94%	0.31
3	$1,374,211	12.91%	11.30%	16.87%	0.37
4	$1,027,534	12.08%	10.59%	16.27%	0.34
5	$1,360,122	12.90%	11.27%	16.97%	0.37
6	$1,333,908	13.12%	11.22%	18.32%	0.34
7	$1,535,471	13.67%	11.56%	19.28%	0.34
8	$1,071,593	12.96%	10.70%	20.09%	0.28
9	$967,971	13.03%	10.45%	21.49%	0.25
10 (lowest)	$254,268	10.14%	7.29%	22.81%	0.10
All Stocks	$1,329,513	13.26%	11.22%	18.99%	0.33

T A B L E 14.10

Summary Annual Return and Risk Results Data: All Stocks Assets-to-Equity Decile 1, All Stocks Assets-to-Equity Decile 10, and All Stocks, January 1, 1964, to December 31, 2009

	All Stocks assets-to-equity decile 1	All Stocks assets-to-equity decile 10	All Stocks
Arithmetic average	12.90%	10.14%	13.26%
Geometric average	11.16%	7.29%	11.22%
Median return	15.78%	16.92%	17.16%
Standard deviation	17.59%	22.81%	18.99%
Upside deviation	10.83%	14.23%	10.98%
Downside deviation	13.54%	16.54%	13.90%
Tracking error	9.84	8.62	0.00
Number of positive periods	337	326	329
Number of negative periods	215	226	223
Maximum peak-to-trough decline	−64.20%	−79.51%	−55.54%
Beta	0.79	1.12	1.00
T-statistic (m = 0)	4.70	2.88	4.47
Sharpe ratio (Rf = 5%)	0.35	0.10	0.33
Sortino ratio (MAR = 10%)	0.09	−0.16	0.09
$10,000 becomes	$1,299,802	$254,268	$1,329,513
Minimum 1-year return	−54.34%	−58.70%	−46.49%
Maximum 1-year return	83.27%	151.77%	84.19%
Minimum 3-year return	−26.05%	−39.82%	−18.68%
Maximum 3-year return	46.01%	41.62%	31.49%
Minimum 5-year return	−11.85%	−17.83%	−9.91%
Maximum 5-year return	32.59%	30.85%	27.66%
Minimum 7-year return	−4.60%	−10.87%	−6.32%
Maximum 7-year return	34.80%	22.39%	23.77%
Minimum 10-year return	−0.83%	−6.69%	1.01%
Maximum 10-year return	25.58%	18.29%	22.05%
Minimum expected return*	−22.28%	−35.47%	−24.73%
Maximum expected return†	48.08%	55.75%	51.24%

* Minimum expected return is arithmetic return minus 2 times the standard deviation.
† Maximum expected return is arithmetic return plus 2 times the standard deviation.

high leverage is not necessarily a good thing either. It could signify an unusually aggressive company to willing to pile on debt to pursue opportunities that might not be realized, as it compounded at 11.16 percent, a hair below the return for the All Stocks universe.

Tables 14.11 and 14.12 show the base rates for deciles 1 and 10.

T A B L E   14.11

Base Rates for All Stocks Assets-to-Equity Decile 1 and All Stocks, January 1, 1964, to December 31, 2009

Item	All Stocks assets-to-equity decile 1 beat All Stocks	Percent	Average annual excess return
Single-year return	279 out of 541	52%	0.39%
Rolling 3-year compound return	280 out of 517	54%	1.09%
Rolling 5-year compound return	295 out of 493	60%	1.50%
Rolling 7-year compound return	279 out of 469	59%	1.64%
Rolling 10-year compound return	271 out of 433	63%	1.55%

T A B L E   14.12

Base Rates for All Stocks Assets-to-Equity Decile 10 and All Stocks, January 1, 1964, to December 31, 2009

Item	All Stocks assets-to-equity decile 10 beat All Stocks	Percent	Average annual excess return
Single-year return	191 out of 541	35%	−2.99%
Rolling 3-year compound return	116 out of 517	22%	−3.93%
Rolling 5-year compound return	103 out of 493	21%	−4.11%
Rolling 7-year compound return	91 out of 469	19%	−4.24%
Rolling 10-year compound return	84 out of 433	19%	−4.29%

LARGE STOCKS

Table 14.13 shows the ranked assets-to-equity ratio deciles for Large Stocks. Decile one features the Large Stocks with the highest asset-to-equity ratios and decile 10 features the Large Stocks with the lowest asset-to-equity ratios. As we saw with All Stocks, the only really significant conclusion that we can draw from this analysis is that Large Stocks with the lowest asset-to-equity ratios (and therefore the least leverage) should be avoided. As we saw with the All Stocks group, decile 7 actually showed the best performance, indicating that reasonable levels of leverage are helpful to a company's prospects. Table 14.14 shows the detailed results for deciles 1 and 10, and Tables 14.15 and 14.16 show the base rates for deciles 1 and 10 compared to Large Stocks.

T A B L E   14.13

Summary Results for Assets-to-Equity Decile Analysis of Large Stocks Universe, January 1, 1964, to December 31, 2009

Decile	$10,000 grows to	Average return	Compound return	Standard deviation	Sharpe ratio
1 (highest)	$571,201	11.48%	9.19%	20.30%	0.21
2	$574,361	10.82%	9.21%	17.07%	0.25
3	$397,276	9.57%	8.33%	15.06%	0.22
4	$546,167	10.21%	9.09%	14.37%	0.28

(continued on next page)

T A B L E   14.13

Summary Results for Assets-to-Equity Decile Analysis of Large Stocks Universe, January 1, 1964, to December 31, 2009
(Continued)

Decile	$10,000 grows to	Average return	Compound return	Standard deviation	Sharpe ratio
5	$900,896	11.47%	10.28%	14.65%	0.36
6	$808,299	11.30%	10.02%	15.23%	0.33
7	$936,552	11.77%	10.37%	15.92%	0.34
8	$813,004	11.57%	10.03%	16.67%	0.30
9	$514,567	10.68%	8.94%	17.71%	0.22
10 (lowest)	$317,916	9.91%	7.81%	19.57%	0.14
Large Stocks	$872,861	11.72%	10.20%	16.50%	0.32

T A B L E   14.14

Summary Annual Return and Risk Results Data: Large Stocks Assets-to-Equity Decile 1, Large Stocks Assets-to-Equity Decile 10, and Large Stocks, January 1, 1964, to December 31, 2009

	Large Stocks assets-to-equity decile 1	Large Stocks assets-to-equity decile 10	Large Stocks
Arithmetic average	11.48%	9.91%	11.72%
Geometric average	9.19%	7.81%	10.20%
Median return	12.35%	9.92%	17.20%
Standard deviation	20.30%	19.57%	16.50%
Upside deviation	13.45%	12.79%	9.70%
Downside deviation	14.61%	14.41%	11.85%
Tracking error	10.00	8.83	0.00
Number of positive periods	324	325	332
Number of negative periods	228	227	220
Maximum peak-to-trough decline	−74.87%	−72.53%	−53.77%
Beta	1.07	1.06	1.00
T-statistic (m = 0)	3.65	3.29	4.58
Sharpe ratio (Rf = 5%)	0.21	0.14	0.32
Sortino ratio (MAR = 10%)	−0.06	−0.15	0.02
$10,000 becomes	$571,201	$317,916	$872,861
Minimum 1-year return	−67.28%	−63.16%	−46.91%
Maximum 1-year return	77.49%	110.51%	68.96%
Minimum 3-year return	−31.13%	−31.52%	−15.89%
Maximum 3-year return	47.08%	43.54%	33.12%
Minimum 5-year return	−14.00%	−12.49%	−5.82%
Maximum 5-year return	31.87%	33.66%	28.95%
Minimum 7-year return	−6.55%	−6.34%	−4.15%
Maximum 7-year return	30.28%	27.95%	22.83%
Minimum 10-year return	−3.15%	−3.04%	−0.15%
Maximum 10-year return	26.47%	23.05%	19.57%
Minimum expected return*	−29.13%	−29.24%	−21.28%
Maximum expected return†	52.08%	49.05%	44.72%

* Minimum expected return is arithmetic return minus 2 times the standard deviation.
† Maximum expected return is arithmetic return plus 2 times the standard deviation.

T A B L E   14.15

Base Rates for Large Stocks Assets-to-Equity Decile 1 and Large Stocks, January 1, 1964, to December 31, 2009

Item	Large Stocks assets-to-equity decile 1 beat Large Stocks	Percent	Average annual excess return
Single-year return	292 out of 541	54%	−0.06%
Rolling 3-year compound return	266 out of 517	51%	0.09%
Rolling 5-year compound return	218 out of 493	44%	0.33%
Rolling 7-year compound return	181 out of 469	39%	0.35%
Rolling 10-year compound return	159 out of 433	37%	0.24%

T A B L E   14.16

Base Rates for Large Stocks Assets-to-Equity Decile 10 and Large Stocks, January 1, 1964, to December 31, 2009

Item	Large Stocks assets-to-equity decile 10 beat Large Stocks	Percent	Average annual excess return
Single-year return	204 out of 541	38%	−1.60%
Rolling 3-year compound return	154 out of 517	30%	−2.41%
Rolling 5-year compound return	112 out of 493	23%	−2.54%
Rolling 7-year compound return	101 out of 469	22%	−2.64%
Rolling 10-year compound return	42 out of 433	10%	−2.75%

IMPLICATIONS

Leverage is not necessarily a bad thing—decile 7 was actually the best performer—showing that the use of *some* leverage can be helpful to a company's prospects. Companies that used very little leverage—those in decile 10—actually were the worst performers, indicating that a company that is too conservative might be missing out on opportunities in the marketplace. For both the All Stocks and Large Stocks universes, decile 10—those stocks with the lowest asset-to-equity ratios—underperformed their respective universes. The use of a little leverage, then, seems to be a good thing.

ASSET TURNOVER

The asset turnover ratio measures a company's sales divided by its average total assets. It measures the efficiency of a company's use of its assets. Companies with high asset turnover ratios are presumed to be using their assets more efficiently than those with lower asset turnover ratios. Table 14.17 shows the ten deciles from the All Stocks universe based on the asset turnover ratio. Deciles 1 and 2—those with the highest asset turnover ratios—clearly beat the All Stocks universe, whereas deciles 9 and 10—those with the lowest asset turnover ratios—clearly underperform it. Table 14.18 shows deciles 1 and 10 versus the All Stocks universe. The base rates for the stocks with the highest asset turnover ratios, featured in Tables 14.19 and 14.20, are all positive, but not as high as those for the accruals-to-price ratio. Stocks with the highest asset turnover ratios beat the All Stocks universe in 76 percent of all rolling five-year periods and in 87 percent of all rolling ten-year periods. The base rates for the stocks with the lowest asset turnover ratios are all negative, but not severely so. They beat All Stocks in 42 percent of all rolling five-year periods and in 42 percent of all rolling ten-year periods.

T A B L E   14.17

Summary Results for Asset Turnover Decile Analysis of All Stocks Universe, January 1, 1964, to December 31, 2009

Decile	$10,000 grows to	Average return	Compound return	Standard deviation	Sharpe ratio
1 (highest)	$2,761,259	15.26%	13.00%	19.87%	0.40
2	$2,005,972	14.45%	12.21%	19.78%	0.36
3	$1,642,909	13.90%	11.73%	19.60%	0.34
4	$1,566,766	13.76%	11.61%	19.43%	0.34
5	$1,566,380	13.83%	11.61%	19.79%	0.33
6	$1,291,645	13.28%	11.15%	19.47%	0.32
7	$1,488,492	13.43%	11.49%	18.56%	0.35
8	$1,017,147	12.15%	10.57%	16.80%	0.33
9	$295,650	9.27%	7.64%	17.27%	0.15
10 (lowest)	$521,728	10.60%	8.98%	17.16%	0.23
All Stocks	$1,329,513	13.26%	11.22%	18.99%	0.33

T A B L E   14.18

Summary Annual Return and Risk Results Data: All Stocks Asset Turnover Decile 1, All Stocks Asset Turnover Decile 10, and All Stocks, January 1, 1964, to December 31, 2009

	All Stocks asset turnover decile 1	All Stocks asset turnover decile 10	All Stocks
Arithmetic average	15.26%	10.60%	13.26%
Geometric average	13.00%	8.98%	11.22%
Median return	18.01%	14.26%	17.16%
Standard deviation	19.87%	17.16%	18.99%
Upside deviation	11.92%	10.45%	10.98%
Downside deviation	14.37%	13.14%	13.90%
Tracking error	5.97	8.81	0.00
Number of positive periods	342	342	329
Number of negative periods	210	210	223
Maximum peak-to-trough decline	−62.08%	−63.29%	−55.54%
Beta	1.00	0.80	1.00
T-statistic (m = 0)	4.88	4.00	4.47
Sharpe ratio (Rf = 5%)	0.40	0.23	0.33
Sortino ratio (MAR = 10%)	0.21	−0.08	0.09
$10,000 becomes	$2,761,259	$521,728	$1,329,513
Minimum 1-year return	−46.39%	−52.75%	−46.49%
Maximum 1-year return	107.27%	82.38%	84.19%
Minimum 3-year return	−24.00%	−27.49%	−18.68%
Maximum 3-year return	42.07%	41.60%	31.49%
Minimum 5-year return	−11.35%	−14.79%	−9.91%
Maximum 5-year return	32.05%	29.53%	27.66%
Minimum 7-year return	−5.92%	−6.33%	−6.32%
Maximum 7-year return	29.32%	29.67%	23.77%
Minimum 10-year return	1.61%	−4.63%	1.01%
Maximum 10-year return	25.14%	22.15%	22.05%
Minimum expected return*	−24.48%	−23.71%	−24.73%
Maximum expected return†	55.00%	44.92%	51.24%

* Minimum expected return is arithmetic return minus 2 times the standard deviation.
† Maximum expected return is arithmetic return plus 2 times the standard deviation.

TABLE 14.19

Base Rates for All Stocks Asset Turnover Decile 1 and All Stocks, January 1, 1964, to December 31, 2009

Item	All Stocks asset turnover decile 1 beat All Stocks	Percent	Average annual excess return
Single-year return	321 out of 541	59%	2.37%
Rolling 3-year compound return	343 out of 517	66%	2.04%
Rolling 5-year compound return	373 out of 493	76%	2.05%
Rolling 7-year compound return	384 out of 469	82%	1.98%
Rolling 10-year compound return	376 out of 433	87%	1.79%

TABLE 14.20

Base Rates for All Stocks Asset Turnover Decile 10 and All Stocks, January 1, 1964, to December 31, 2009

Item	All Stocks asset turnover decile 10 beat All Stocks	Percent	Average annual excess return
Single-year return	224 out of 541	41%	−1.91%
Rolling 3-year compound return	214 out of 517	41%	−1.28%
Rolling 5-year compound return	206 out of 493	42%	−0.88%
Rolling 7-year compound return	196 out of 469	42%	−0.73%
Rolling 10-year compound return	180 out of 433	42%	−0.72%

LARGE STOCKS

Table 14.21 shows the results for the 10 deciles from Large Stocks by asset turnover. Much as we saw with All Stocks, the Large Stocks with the highest asset turnover (in decile 1) beat the Large Stocks universe, whereas the stocks with the lowest asset turnover (in deciles 9 and 10) significantly underperformed the universe. Yet here, we see that decile 8 shows the worst overall performance. Thus, much as we saw with All Stocks, this measure is not as clearly defined as it is when looking at the accruals-to-price of a stock. Table 14.22 shows the detailed results for deciles 1 and 10.

TABLE 14.21

Summary Results for Asset Turnover Decile Analysis of Large Stocks Universe, January 1, 1964, to December 31, 2009

Decile	$10,000 grows to	Average return	Compound return	Standard deviation	Sharpe ratio
1 (highest)	$1,194,287	12.49%	10.96%	16.56%	0.36
2	$865,900	11.79%	10.18%	17.02%	0.30
3	$830,433	11.62%	10.08%	16.63%	0.31
4	$849,555	11.70%	10.14%	16.75%	0.31
5	$793,584	11.57%	9.98%	16.97%	0.29
6	$561,131	10.67%	9.15%	16.63%	0.25
7	$695,511	11.10%	9.66%	16.16%	0.29
8	$345,274	9.26%	8.00%	15.21%	0.20
9	$432,955	9.97%	8.54%	16.18%	0.22
10 (lowest)	$380,644	10.29%	8.23%	19.39%	0.17
Large Stocks	$872,861	11.72%	10.20%	16.50%	0.32

T A B L E   14.22

Summary Annual Return and Risk Results Data: Large Stocks Asset Turnover Decile 1, Large Stocks Asset Turnover Decile 10, and Large Stocks, January 1, 1964, to December 31, 2009

	Large Stocks asset turnover decile 1	Large Stocks asset turnover decile 10	Large Stocks
Arithmetic average	12.49%	10.29%	11.72%
Geometric average	10.96%	8.23%	10.20%
Median return	11.31%	12.23%	17.20%
Standard deviation	16.56%	19.39%	16.50%
Upside deviation	10.45%	13.13%	9.70%
Downside deviation	11.48%	13.87%	11.85%
Tracking error	6.81	10.49	0.00
Number of positive periods	323	323	332
Number of negative periods	229	229	220
Maximum peak-to-trough decline	−54.64%	−75.82%	−53.77%
Beta	0.92	0.99	1.00
T-statistic (m = 0)	4.84	3.44	4.58
Sharpe ratio (Rf = 5%)	0.36	0.17	0.32
Sortino ratio (MAR = 10%)	0.08	−0.13	0.02
$10,000 becomes	$1,194,287	$380,644	$872,861
Minimum 1-year return	−45.03%	−67.52%	−46.91%
Maximum 1-year return	65.03%	74.96%	68.96%
Minimum 3-year return	−19.20%	−33.06%	−15.89%
Maximum 3-year return	36.30%	49.44%	33.12%
Minimum 5-year return	−7.97%	−16.99%	−5.82%
Maximum 5-year return	30.79%	31.53%	28.95%
Minimum 7-year return	−5.50%	−8.57%	−4.15%
Maximum 7-year return	25.20%	31.39%	22.83%
Minimum 10-year return	−0.17%	−5.66%	−0.15%
Maximum 10-year return	22.53%	26.06%	19.57%
Minimum expected return*	−20.64%	−28.49%	−21.28%
Maximum expected return†	45.61%	49.07%	44.72%

* Minimum expected return is arithmetic return minus 2 times the standard deviation.
† Maximum expected return is arithmetic return plus 2 times the standard deviation.

Table 14.23 shows the base rates for decile 1—those Large Stocks with the highest asset turnover. Table 14.24 shows the base rates for decile 10—those with the lowest asset turnover. For the Large Stocks with the highest asset turnover, all base rates are positive, but not nearly as high as we saw with accruals-to-price, beating the Large Stocks universe in 60 percent of all rolling ten-year periods. For the Large Stocks with the lowest asset turnover, all base rates are negative, but not as low as we saw with accruals-to-price.

T A B L E   14.23

Base Rates for Large Stocks Asset Turnover Decile 1 and Large Stocks, January 1, 1964, to December 31, 2009

Item	Large Stocks asset turnover decile 1 beat Large Stocks	Percent	Average annual excess return
Single-year return	304 out of 541	56%	1.03%
Rolling 3-year compound return	322 out of 517	62%	0.89%
Rolling 5-year compound return	306 out of 493	62%	0.76%
Rolling 7-year compound return	300 out of 469	64%	0.72%
Rolling 10-year compound return	261 out of 433	60%	0.65%

T A B L E   14.24

Base Rates for Large Stocks Asset Turnover Decile 10 and Large Stocks, January 1, 1964, to December 31, 2009

Item	Large Stocks asset turnover decile 10 beat Large Stocks	Percent	Average annual excess return
Single-year return	255 out of 541	47%	−1.17%
Rolling 3-year compound return	220 out of 517	43%	−0.94%
Rolling 5-year compound return	205 out of 493	42%	−0.68%
Rolling 7-year compound return	172 out of 469	37%	−0.61%
Rolling 10-year compound return	148 out of 433	34%	−0.71%

IMPLICATIONS

Stocks with higher asset turnover ratios beat both stocks with lower asset turnover ratios and the All Stocks universe, but they don't exhibit the same consistency of performance as those with lower accruals-to-price. We see the same results using the Large Stocks universe. Therefore, investors should prefer stocks with higher asset turnover ratios, yet not necessarily shun stocks with lower asset turnover ratios if other factors contribute to making the stock attractive.

CASH FLOW TO DEBT RATIO

A company's cash flow to debt ratio, also known as the coverage ratio, measures a company's annual cash flow in relation to its total debt. It gives an indication of a company's ability to cover its debt obligations with its annual cash flow. The higher the ratio, the more the company is able to cover its debt. Table 14.25 shows the deciles of All Stocks based on their cash flow to debt ratios. The real significance of the table is demonstrated by the returns for deciles 9 and 10, those with the lowest coverage ratios. Their returns are significantly below the All Stocks universe. Over the 46 years studied, the compound average annual return for decile 10—stocks with the lowest coverage ratio—is 2.41 percent, much lower than that for the All Stocks universe and also lower than an investment in U.S. T-bills. Its Sharpe ratio is a −.10, among the worst we've seen. It's interesting that decile 6 does the best and that decile 1—those companies with the highest coverage ratios—do only slightly better than the All Stocks universe. This implies that the market rewards companies that are fairly aggressive with debt, but severely punish those that take on too much debt with insufficient cash flow to cover it. Table 14.26 shows the detailed results for deciles 1 and 10.

T A B L E   14.25

Summary Results for Cash Flow to Debt (%) Decile Analysis of All Stocks Universe, January 1, 1964, to December 31, 2009

Decile	$10,000 grows to	Average return	Compound return	Standard deviation	Sharpe ratio
1 (highest)	$1,709,196	14.22%	11.83%	20.65%	0.33
2	$2,142,515	14.44%	12.38%	19.09%	0.39
3	$2,286,232	14.38%	12.53%	17.99%	0.42
4	$2,715,232	14.77%	12.96%	17.80%	0.45
5	$2,498,614	14.58%	12.75%	17.88%	0.43
6	$3,123,742	15.14%	13.30%	17.89%	0.46
7	$2,359,119	14.36%	12.61%	17.52%	0.43
8	$1,122,794	12.47%	10.81%	17.20%	0.34
9	$172,921	8.53%	6.39%	19.70%	0.07
10 (lowest)	$29,894	6.24%	2.41%	26.84%	−0.10
All Stocks	$1,329,513	13.26%	11.22%	18.99%	0.33

T A B L E   14.26

Summary Annual Return and Risk Results Data: All Stocks Cash Flow to Debt (%) Decile 1, All Stocks Cash Flow to Debt (%) Decile 10, and All Stocks, January 1, 1964, to December 31, 2009

	All Stocks cash flow to debt (%) decile 1	All Stocks cash flow to debt (%) decile 10	All Stocks
Arithmetic average	14.22%	6.24%	13.26%
Geometric average	11.83%	2.41%	11.22%
Median return	17.07%	10.49%	17.16%
Standard deviation	20.65%	26.84%	18.99%
Upside deviation	13.17%	17.38%	10.98%
Downside deviation	14.29%	20.16%	13.90%
Tracking error	6.26	12.28	0.00
Number of positive periods	336	309	329
Number of negative periods	216	243	223
Maximum peak-to-trough decline	−54.66%	−92.73%	−55.54%
Beta	1.04	1.29	1.00
T-statistic (m = 0)	4.39	1.53	4.47
Sharpe ratio (Rf = 5%)	0.33	−0.10	0.33
Sortino ratio (MAR = 10%)	0.13	−0.38	0.09
$10,000 becomes	$1,709,196	$29,894	$1,329,513
Minimum 1-year return	−46.86%	−71.56%	−46.49%
Maximum 1-year return	121.96%	173.31%	84.19%
Minimum 3-year return	−17.81%	−52.46%	−18.68%
Maximum 3-year return	42.20%	40.27%	31.49%
Minimum 5-year return	−7.18%	−28.23%	−9.91%
Maximum 5-year return	33.26%	27.86%	27.66%
Minimum 7-year return	−3.13%	−20.10%	−6.32%
Maximum 7-year return	26.88%	23.45%	23.77%
Minimum 10-year return	3.09%	−14.93%	1.01%
Maximum 10-year return	24.91%	20.52%	22.05%
Minimum expected return*	−27.08%	−47.44%	−24.73%
Maximum expected return†	55.52%	59.93%	51.24%

* Minimum expected return is arithmetic return minus 2 times the standard deviation.
† Maximum expected return is arithmetic return plus 2 times the standard deviation.

The base rates for deciles 1 and 10 are featured in Tables 14.27 and 14.28. As noted, decile 10 offers atrocious returns, beating the All Stocks universe in just 5 percent of all rolling five-year periods and in not even one rolling ten-year period. As you might guess, one of the best five-year periods for the stocks with the lowest coverage ratio—the very definition of a highly speculative stock—were the five years ending February 2000, when the group earned an average annual compound return of 27.08 percent. It has not yet recovered—losing 93 percent of its value through February 2009.

T A B L E 14.27

Base Rates for All Stocks Cash Flow to Debt (%) Decile 1 and All Stocks, January 1, 1964, to December 31, 2009

Item	All Stocks cash flow to debt (%) decile 1 beat All Stocks	Percent	Average annual excess return
Single-year return	253 out of 541	47%	0.87%
Rolling 3-year compound return	229 out of 517	44%	0.47%
Rolling 5-year compound return	262 out of 493	53%	0.43%
Rolling 7-year compound return	261 out of 469	56%	0.41%
Rolling 10-year compound return	253 out of 433	58%	0.30%

T A B L E 14.28

Base Rates for All Stocks Cash Flow to Debt (%) Decile 10 and All Stocks, January 1, 1964, to December 31, 2009

Item	All Stocks cash flow to debt (%) decile 10 beat All Stocks	Percent	Average annual excess return
Single-year return	132 out of 541	24%	−6.64%
Rolling 3-year compound return	53 out of 517	10%	−8.35%
Rolling 5-year compound return	27 out of 493	5%	−8.62%
Rolling 7-year compound return	9 out of 469	2%	−8.78%
Rolling 10-year compound return	0 out of 433	0%	−8.62%

LARGE STOCKS

Table 14.29 shows the results for the deciles from Large Stocks based on cash flow to debt. As we saw with All Stocks, the only group to be seriously punished is decile 9 and 10, those Large Stocks with the lowest coverage ratios. As with the other factors tested, the results are more muted with the Large Stocks universe. Table 14.30 shows the detailed results for deciles 1 and 10. As we saw with All Stocks, the Large Stocks with the worst coverage ratios only excel in frothy, speculative markets—their three best rolling five-year returns were for the five years ending in December 1999, February 2000, and March 2000.

Tables 14.31 and 14.32 show the base rates for deciles 1 and 10. As we saw with the All Stocks group, it appears that the *best* coverage ratios are not rewarded, perhaps because the market views these stocks as too conservatively managed: They beat the Large Stocks group just 15 percent of the time over all rolling ten-year periods. The group with the worst coverage ratio also shows negative base rates, beating the Large Stocks universe in just 28 percent of all rolling five-year periods and 16 percent of all rolling ten-year periods.

T A B L E   14.29

Summary Results for Cash Flow to Debt (%) Decile Analysis of Large Stocks Universe, January 1, 1964, to December 31, 2009

Decile	$10,000 grows to	Average return	Compound return	Standard deviation	Sharpe ratio
1 (highest)	$483,462	10.94%	8.80%	19.70%	0.19
2	$1,357,088	12.80%	11.27%	16.61%	0.38
3	$1,190,025	12.39%	10.95%	16.05%	0.37
4	$1,204,561	12.40%	10.98%	15.99%	0.37
5	$1,105,736	12.19%	10.77%	15.97%	0.36
6	$694,449	11.02%	9.66%	15.70%	0.30
7	$783,434	11.28%	9.94%	15.55%	0.32
8	$463,146	9.93%	8.70%	15.01%	0.25
9	$376,237	9.53%	8.21%	15.58%	0.21
10 (lowest)	$180,177	8.61%	6.49%	19.72%	0.08
Large Stocks	$872,861	11.72%	10.20%	16.50%	0.32

T A B L E   14.30

Summary Annual Return and Risk Results Data: Large Stocks Cash Flow to Debt (%) Decile 1, Large Stocks Cash Flow to Debt (%) Decile 10, and Large Stocks, January 1, 1964, to December 31, 2009

	Large Stocks cash flow to debt (%) decile 1	Large Stocks cash flow to debt (%) decile 10	Large Stocks
Arithmetic average	10.94%	8.61%	11.72%
Geometric average	8.80%	6.49%	10.20%
Median return	12.36%	10.31%	17.20%
Standard deviation	19.70%	19.72%	16.50%
Upside deviation	12.57%	12.41%	9.70%
Downside deviation	14.22%	15.21%	11.85%
Tracking error	8.66	9.05	0.00
Number of positive periods	311	323	332
Number of negative periods	241	229	220
Maximum peak-to-trough decline	−71.34%	−77.96%	−53.77%
Beta	1.07	1.06	1.00
T-statistic (m = 0)	3.59	2.85	4.58
Sharpe ratio (Rf = 5%)	0.19	0.08	0.32
Sortino ratio (MAR = 10%)	−0.08	−0.23	0.02
$10,000 becomes	$483,462	$180,177	$872,861
Minimum 1-year return	−62.64%	−66.18%	−46.91%
Maximum 1-year return	86.88%	70.98%	68.96%
Minimum 3-year return	−29.12%	−31.88%	−15.89%
Maximum 3-year return	47.76%	35.62%	33.12%
Minimum 5-year return	−11.47%	−16.60%	−5.82%
Maximum 5-year return	34.75%	30.94%	28.95%
Minimum 7-year return	−4.98%	−8.72%	−4.15%
Maximum 7-year return	27.72%	25.78%	22.83%
Minimum 10-year return	−1.95%	−10.64%	−0.15%
Maximum 10-year return	25.19%	21.42%	19.57%
Minimum expected return*	−28.45%	−30.83%	−21.28%
Maximum expected return†	50.33%	48.06%	44.72%

* Minimum expected return is arithmetic return minus 2 times the standard deviation.
† Maximum expected return is arithmetic return plus 2 times the standard deviation.

T A B L E   14.31

Base Rates for Large Stocks Cash Flow to Debt (%) Decile 1 and Large Stocks, January 1, 1964, to December 31, 2009

Item	Large Stocks cash flow to debt (%) decile 1 beat Large Stocks	Percent	Average annual excess return
Single-year return	238 out of 541	44%	−0.59%
Rolling 3-year compound return	177 out of 517	34%	−1.22%
Rolling 5-year compound return	172 out of 493	35%	−1.45%
Rolling 7-year compound return	148 out of 469	32%	−1.58%
Rolling 10-year compound return	67 out of 433	15%	−1.63%

T A B L E   14.32

Base Rates for Large Stocks Cash Flow to Debt (%) Decile 10 and Large Stocks, January 1, 1964, to December 31, 2009

Item	Large Stocks cash flow to debt (%) decile 10 beat Large Stocks	Percent	Average annual excess return
Single-year return	206 out of 541	38%	−2.45%
Rolling 3-year compound return	180 out of 517	35%	−2.71%
Rolling 5-year compound return	138 out of 493	28%	−2.65%
Rolling 7-year compound return	105 out of 469	22%	−2.64%
Rolling 10-year compound return	70 out of 433	16%	−2.44%

IMPLICATIONS

Investors should avoid the 10 percent of stocks with the lowest coverage ratio since they do well only in speculative, frothy markets and might serve as the canary in the coal mine for investors. Any time they mark a significantly better return than the All Stocks universe for any length of time, this is likely to be followed by a devastating bear market. We see similar return patterns with the Large Stocks universe, yet not as severe as with the results from All Stocks.

DEBT TO EQUITY

Debt to equity measures the amount of financial leverage a company is using by dividing the total liabilities of a company by shareholder's equity. Essentially, it measures how aggressive a company is being with its use of debt. As you will see as we review the results, this is a good example of a factor that everyone knows about, but it provides little empirical help in directing investors to the best stocks *based on just this single factor.* We see later that combining this factor with *others* in a composited portfolio can be helpful, but it's not much use on its own. Table 14.33 shows the detailed results for deciles 1 and 10. and Tables 14.34 and 14.35 show the base rates for each. Table 14.36 shows the results for all 10 deciles from the All Stocks universe. As you can see from the tables, both deciles 1 and 10 *underperform* the All Stocks universe. The decile analysis offers little in the way of specific guidance, other than that the market appears to reward companies that use debt efficiently and are neither ultra-conservative nor ultra-aggressive.

T A B L E   14.33

Summary Annual Return and Risk Results Data: All Stocks Debt to Equity Decile 1, All Stocks Debt to Equity Decile 10, and All Stocks, January 1, 1964 to December 31, 2009

	All Stocks debt to equity decile 1	All Stocks debt to equity decile 10	All Stocks
Arithmetic average	12.90%	13.15%	13.26%
Geometric average	10.90%	10.54%	11.22%
Median return	18.24%	15.78%	17.16%
Standard deviation	18.83%	21.70%	18.99%
Upside deviation	11.60%	14.09%	10.98%
Downside deviation	14.52%	15.18%	13.90%
Tracking error	7.29	7.57	0.00
Number of positive periods	339	330	329
Number of negative periods	213	222	223
Maximum peak-to-trough decline	−66.85%	−63.65%	−55.54%
Beta	0.92	1.07	1.00
T-statistic (m = 0)	4.39	3.88	4.47
Sharpe ratio (Rf = 5%)	0.31	0.26	0.33
Sortino ratio (MAR = 10%)	0.06	0.04	0.09
$10,000 becomes	$1,166,094	$1,003,009	$1,329,513
Minimum 1-year return	−57.49%	−46.65%	−46.49%
Maximum 1-year return	86.83%	149.23%	84.19%
Minimum 3-year return	−25.57%	−26.80%	−18.68%
Maximum 3-year return	36.95%	45.60%	31.49%
Minimum 5-year return	−10.74%	−7.70%	−9.91%
Maximum 5-year return	27.88%	35.17%	27.66%
Minimum 7-year return	−3.78%	−2.50%	−6.32%
Maximum 7-year return	27.82%	26.79%	23.77%
Minimum 10-year return	−0.94%	0.45%	1.01%
Maximum 10-year return	22.06%	22.96%	22.05%
Minimum expected return*	−24.77%	−30.24%	−24.73%
Maximum expected return†	50.56%	56.55%	51.24%

* Minimum expected return is arithmetic return minus 2 times the standard deviation.
† Maximum expected return is arithmetic return plus 2 times the standard deviation.

T A B L E   14.34

Base Rates for All Stocks Debt to Equity Decile 1 and All Stocks, January 1, 1964, to December 31, 2009

Item	All Stocks debt to equity decile 1 beat All Stocks	Percent	Average annual excess return
Single-year return	303 out of 541	56%	−0.05%
Rolling 3-year compound return	317 out of 517	61%	0.41%
Rolling 5-year compound return	293 out of 493	59%	0.79%
Rolling 7-year compound return	264 out of 469	56%	0.81%
Rolling 10-year compound return	240 out of 433	55%	0.68%

T A B L E 14.35

Base Rates for All Stocks Debt to Equity Decile 10 and All Stocks, January 1, 1964, to December 31, 2009

Item	All Stocks debt to equity decile 10 beat All Stocks	Percent	Average annual excess return
Single-year return	232 out of 541	43%	−0.08%
Rolling 3-year compound return	176 out of 517	34%	−0.73%
Rolling 5-year compound return	167 out of 493	34%	−0.80%
Rolling 7-year compound return	137 out of 469	29%	−0.85%
Rolling 10-year compound return	106 out of 433	24%	−0.94%

T A B L E 14.36

Summary Results for Debt to Equity Decile Analysis of All Stocks Universe, January 1, 1964, to December 31, 2009

Decile	$10,000 grows to	Average return	Compound return	Standard deviation	Sharpe ratio
1 (highest)	$219,325	12.90%	10.90%	18.83%	0.31
2	$745,636	11.54%	9.83%	17.47%	0.28
3	$886,549	11.58%	10.24%	15.50%	0.34
4	$1,018,729	12.17%	10.57%	16.90%	0.33
5	$1,297,926	13.06%	11.16%	18.35%	0.34
6	$1,820,955	13.92%	11.98%	18.48%	0.38
7	$1,962,633	14.11%	12.16%	18.51%	0.39
8	$1,152,898	13.05%	10.87%	19.70%	0.30
9	$577,042	11.81%	9.22%	21.58%	0.20
10 (lowest)	$1,003,009	13.15%	10.54%	21.70%	0.26
All Stocks	$1,329,513	13.26%	11.22%	18.99%	0.33

LARGE STOCKS

Tables 14.37 and Table 14.38 demonstrate that the same is true for the efficacy of debt to equity in the Large Stocks universe. Tables 14.39 and 14.40 show the base rates for deciles 1 and 10.

T A B L E 14.37

Summary Annual Return and Risk Results Data: Large Stocks Debt to Equity Decile 1, Large Stocks Debt to Equity Decile 10, and Large Stocks, January 1, 1964, to December 31, 2009

	Large Stocks debt to equity decile 1	Large Stocks debt to equity decile 10	Large Stocks
Arithmetic average	10.78%	11.00%	11.72%
Geometric average	8.75%	8.87%	10.20%
Median return	11.19%	11.69%	17.20%
Standard deviation	19.26%	19.63%	16.50%
Upside deviation	12.94%	12.40%	9.70%
Downside deviation	13.52%	14.63%	11.85%

(continued on next page)

T A B L E   14.37

Summary Annual Return and Risk Results Data: Large Stocks Debt to Equity Decile 1, Large Stocks Debt to Equity Decile 10, and Large Stocks, January 1, 1964, to December 31, 2009 *(Continued)*

	Large Stocks debt to equity decile 1	Large Stocks debt to equity decile 10	Large Stocks
Tracking error	8.87	8.49	0.00
Number of positive periods	321	323	332
Number of negative periods	231	229	220
Maximum peak-to-trough decline	−73.17%	−72.61%	−53.77%
Beta	1.04	1.08	1.00
T-statistic (m = 0)	3.62	3.62	4.58
Sharpe ratio (Rf = 5%)	0.19	0.20	0.32
Sortino ratio (MAR = 10%)	−0.09	−0.08	0.02
$10,000 becomes	$473,838	$498,044	$872,861
Minimum 1-year return	−64.73%	−64.69%	−46.91%
Maximum 1-year return	73.85%	84.86%	68.96%
Minimum 3-year return	−29.26%	−32.21%	−15.89%
Maximum 3-year return	44.13%	40.82%	33.12%
Minimum 5-year return	−13.20%	−12.38%	−5.82%
Maximum 5-year return	29.92%	31.06%	28.95%
Minimum 7-year return	−5.98%	−4.97%	−4.15%
Maximum 7-year return	28.13%	24.97%	22.83%
Minimum 10-year return	−3.78%	−2.74%	−0.15%
Maximum 10-year return	24.91%	22.23%	19.57%
Minimum expected return*	−27.74%	−28.26%	−21.28%
Maximum expected return†	49.30%	50.27%	44.72%

* Minimum expected return is arithmetic return minus 2 times the standard deviation.
† Maximum expected return is arithmetic return plus 2 times the standard deviation.

T A B L E   14.38

Summary Results for Debt to Equity Decile Analysis of Large Stocks Universe, January 1, 1964, to December 31, 2009

Decile	$10,000 grows to	Average return	Compound return	Standard deviation	Sharpe ratio
1 (highest)	$473,838	10.78%	8.75%	19.26%	0.19
2	$498,126	10.17%	8.87%	15.37%	0.25
3	$397,269	9.43%	8.33%	14.18%	0.24
4	$432,889	9.84%	8.54%	15.42%	0.23
5	$677,925	11.00%	9.60%	15.94%	0.29
6	$771,443	11.34%	9.91%	16.06%	0.31
7	$865,571	11.63%	10.18%	16.13%	0.32
8	$1,227,251	12.49%	11.02%	16.21%	0.37
9	$719,520	11.35%	9.74%	17.07%	0.28
10 (lowest)	$498,044	11.00%	8.87%	19.63%	0.20
Large Stocks	$872,861	11.72%	10.20%	16.50%	0.32

T A B L E   14.39

Base Rates for Large Stocks Debt to Equity Decile 1 and Large Stocks, January 1, 1964, to December 31, 2009

Item	Large Stocks debt to equity decile 1 beat Large Stocks	Percent	Average annual excess return
Single-year return	257 out of 541	48%	−0.69%
Rolling 3-year compound return	225 out of 517	44%	−0.56%
Rolling 5-year compound return	191 out of 493	39%	−0.35%
Rolling 7-year compound return	159 out of 469	34%	−0.37%
Rolling 10-year compound return	147 out of 433	34%	−0.41%

T A B L E   14.40

Base Rates for Large Stocks Debt to Equity Decile 10 and Large Stocks, January 1, 1964, to December 31, 2009

Item	Large Stocks debt to equity decile 10 beat Large Stocks	Percent	Average annual excess return
Single-year return	240 out of 541	44%	−0.66%
Rolling 3-year compound return	189 out of 517	37%	−1.23%
Rolling 5-year compound return	184 out of 493	37%	−1.51%
Rolling 7-year compound return	159 out of 469	34%	−1.70%
Rolling 10-year compound return	103 out of 433	24%	−1.79%

IMPLICATIONS

On its own, debt to equity offers investors little help in determining whether a stock is worth buying or not. We see at the end of this chapter that using debt to equity in conjunction with several other factors can be very helpful in judging the financial strength of a company, but it is of little use on its own.

EXTERNAL FINANCING

Academic research has clearly established that companies using a great deal of external financing face weak future stock returns. In their paper "The Relation between Corporate Financing Activities, Analysts' Forecasts and Stock Returns," authors Bradshaw, Richardson, and Sloan say, "A large body of evidence documents a negative relation between external financing activities and future stock returns. Future stock returns are unusually low in the years following initial public offerings (Ritter, 1991), seasoned equity offerings (Loughran and Ritter, 1997), debt offerings (Spiess and Affleck-Graves, 1999) and bank borrowings (Billett et al., 2001)." You determine how much a company is using external financing (through debt or the issuance of shares) compared to internally generated cash flow from business operations by dividing cash flow from financing by average assets. Companies that use a lot of external financing might presumably be at greater risk than companies that are able to finance their activities through internally generated cash flow. Let's see if this is correct.

For this decile analysis, we have data only from September 30, 1971, so this study covers just over 38 years. Table 14.41 shows the 10 deciles from All Stocks based upon external financing. Decile 1 is made up of the 10 percent of companies from All Stocks that have the *highest* external financing, whereas decile 10 is made up of the 10 percent of companies with the *lowest* use of external financing. Clearly, as Table 14.41 shows, high levels of external financing are toxic to a company's stock returns. Decile 1—the 10 percent of stocks from All Stocks with the highest external financing—actually *loses money* over the entire period studied, whereas decile 10—the stocks with the lowest external financing—performs significantly better than the All Stocks universe. Over the full period of the study, $10,000 invested in decile 1 shrank to $9,759, an average annual compound loss of –.06 percent. And that's *before* taking inflation into account. If you did consider inflation, the actual value of the $10,000 would have been a mere $1,843. So much for buying stocks that don't generate their own financing from cash flow.

T A B L E   14.41

Summary Results for External Financing Decile Analysis of All Stocks Universe, October 1, 1971, to December 31, 2009

Decile	$10,000 grows to	Average return	Compound return	Standard deviation	Sharpe ratio
1 (highest)	$9,759	4.16%	−0.06%	28.28%	−0.18
2	$95,130	8.97%	6.07%	22.98%	0.05
3	$348,976	12.02%	9.73%	20.17%	0.23
4	$588,344	13.46%	11.24%	19.82%	0.31
5	$853,099	14.67%	12.33%	20.31%	0.36
6	$1,348,145	15.79%	13.68%	19.20%	0.45
7	$1,078,799	14.75%	13.02%	17.43%	0.46
8	$1,645,795	15.90%	14.27%	16.83%	0.55
9	$1,443,403	15.47%	13.88%	16.62%	0.53
10 (lowest)	$1,535,774	15.80%	14.07%	17.34%	0.52
All Stocks	$587,200	13.35%	11.24%	19.34%	0.32

Decile one also has the dubious distinction of having a maximum decline of 92 percent from peak to trough; you can find all the other summary information in Table 14.42. All base rates for decile 1—featured in Table 14.43—are negative, with the group beating All Stocks in just 7 percent of all rolling five-year periods and not even one rolling ten-year period. The only time that stocks with high external financing do well is during times of very high inflation. Their best five years were the five years ending November 1980, when they earned an average annual compound return of 30.22 percent.

Decile 10—featuring the stocks with the lowest external financing—tells a completely different story. Here, $10,000 invested grows to $1,535,774, an average annual compound return of 14.07 percent and nearly three times the $587,200 you'd have earned from an investment in the All Stocks universe. The base rates—featured in Table 14.44—are overwhelmingly positive, with the group beating All Stocks in 91 percent of all rolling five-year periods and in 100 percent of all rolling ten-year periods.

T A B L E   14.42

Summary Annual Return and Risk Results Data: All Stocks External Financing Decile 1, All Stocks External Financing Decile 10, and All Stocks, October 1, 1971, to December 31, 2009

	All Stocks external financing decile 1	All Stocks external financing decile 10	All Stocks
Arithmetic average	4.16%	15.80%	13.35%
Geometric average	−0.06%	14.07%	11.24%
Median return	11.38%	18.71%	17.02%
Standard deviation	28.28%	17.34%	19.34%
Upside deviation	16.86%	10.42%	11.21%
Downside deviation	20.90%	13.28%	14.21%
Tracking error	12.46	4.85	0.00
Number of positive periods	258	288	272
Number of negative periods	201	171	187
Maximum peak-to-trough decline	−91.78%	−50.35%	−55.54%
Beta	1.36	0.87	1.00
T-statistic (m = 0)	0.89	5.26	4.03
Sharpe ratio (Rf = 5%)	−0.18	0.52	0.32
Sortino ratio (MAR = 10%)	−0.48	0.31	0.09
$10,000 becomes	$9,759	$1,535,774	$587,200
Minimum 1-year return	−72.97%	−39.90%	−46.49%
Maximum 1-year return	142.44%	76.60%	84.19%
Minimum 3-year return	−52.51%	−14.51%	−18.68%
Maximum 3-year return	36.94%	30.47%	31.49%
Minimum 5-year return	−28.55%	−4.38%	−7.00%
Maximum 5-year return	30.22%	28.74%	27.66%
Minimum 7-year return	−20.53%	1.07%	−0.67%
Maximum 7-year return	23.92%	25.12%	23.77%
Minimum 10-year return	−15.05%	5.62%	1.65%
Maximum 10-year return	16.80%	23.14%	22.05%
Minimum expected return*	−52.40%	−18.88%	−25.32%
Maximum expected return†	60.71%	50.49%	52.03%

* Minimum expected return is arithmetic return minus 2 times the standard deviation.
† Maximum expected return is arithmetic return plus 2 times the standard deviation.

T A B L E   14.43

Base Rates for All Stocks External Financing Decile 1 and All Stocks, October 1, 1971, to December 31, 2009

Item	All Stocks external financing decile 1 beat All Stocks	Percent	Average annual excess return
Single-year return	93 out of 448	21%	−9.00%
Rolling 3-year compound return	41 out of 424	10%	−10.96%
Rolling 5-year compound return	26 out of 400	7%	−11.50%
Rolling 7-year compound return	12 out of 376	3%	−11.98%
Rolling 10-year compound return	0 out of 340	0%	−12.31%

TABLE 14.44

Base Rates for All Stocks External Financing Decile 10 and All Stocks, October 1, 1971, to December 31, 2009

Item	All Stocks external financing decile 10 beat All Stocks	Percent	Average annual excess return
Single-year return	307 out of 448	69%	2.14%
Rolling 3-year compound return	365 out of 424	86%	2.38%
Rolling 5-year compound return	365 out of 400	91%	2.45%
Rolling 7-year compound return	368 out of 376	98%	2.56%
Rolling 10-year compound return	340 out of 340	100%	2.62%

LARGE STOCKS

Table 14.45 shows the decile results for Large Stocks grouped by external financing with decile 1 featuring the 10 percent of Large Stocks with the highest external financing and decile 10 featuring the 10 percent of Large Stocks with the lowest external financing. As we saw with the All Stocks universe, the worst performance comes from the Large Stocks with the highest external financing. The $10,000 invested on September 30, 1971, in decile 1 grew to just $33,769 by the end of 2009, an average annual compound return of 3.23 percent and a return that was significantly bested if you had kept all your money in T-bills. Unlike Large Stocks that used less external financing, decile 1 had a maximum decline of 87 percent from peak to trough. Table 14.46 shows the detailed summary information for deciles 1 and 10. All the base rates for decile 1—featured in Table 14.47—are negative, with the group beating Large Stocks in just 2 percent of all rolling five-year periods and in no rolling ten-year periods.

TABLE 14.45

Summary Results for External Financing Decile Analysis of Large Stocks Universe, October 1, 1971, to December 31, 2009

Decile	$10,000 grows to	Average return	Compound return	Standard deviation	Sharpe ratio
1 (highest)	$33,769	6.14%	3.23%	23.10%	−0.08
2	$198,753	9.95%	8.13%	18.14%	0.17
3	$295,478	10.94%	9.26%	17.45%	0.24
4	$479,333	12.36%	10.65%	17.60%	0.32
5	$403,146	11.65%	10.15%	16.47%	0.31
6	$849,698	13.85%	12.32%	16.48%	0.44
7	$853,317	13.66%	12.33%	15.40%	0.48
8	$635,094	12.78%	11.46%	15.39%	0.42
9	$783,726	13.41%	12.08%	15.42%	0.46
10 (lowest)	$621,863	12.74%	11.40%	15.52%	0.41
Large Stocks	$481,960	12.29%	10.66%	17.03%	0.33

TABLE 14.46

Summary Annual Return and Risk Results Data: Large Stocks External Financing Decile 1, Large Stocks External Financing Decile 10, and Large Stocks, October 1, 1971, to December 31, 2009

	Large Stocks external financing decile 1	Large Stocks external financing decile 10	Large Stocks
Arithmetic average	6.14%	12.74%	12.29%
Geometric average	3.23%	11.40%	10.66%
Median return	11.34%	14.12%	16.49%
Standard deviation	23.10%	15.52%	17.03%
Upside deviation	13.46%	9.98%	10.04%
Downside deviation	18.25%	10.85%	12.30%
Tracking error	10.24	6.21	0.00
Number of positive periods	255	281	274
Number of negative periods	204	178	185
Maximum peak-to-trough decline	−86.85%	−47.48%	−53.77%
Beta	1.24	0.85	1.00
T-statistic (m = 0)	1.60	4.80	4.23
Sharpe ratio (Rf = 5%)	−0.08	0.41	0.33
Sortino ratio (MAR = 10%)	−0.37	0.13	0.05
$10,000 becomes	$33,769	$621,863	$481,960
Minimum 1-year return	−78.50%	−44.24%	−46.91%
Maximum 1-year return	71.06%	51.89%	68.96%
Minimum 3-year return	−48.14%	−11.77%	−15.89%
Maximum 3-year return	32.01%	39.25%	33.12%
Minimum 5-year return	−25.81%	−3.80%	−4.67%
Maximum 5-year return	26.15%	31.21%	28.95%
Minimum 7-year return	−16.30%	−0.29%	−0.96%
Maximum 7-year return	19.09%	22.62%	22.83%
Minimum 10-year return	−14.70%	1.37%	−0.15%
Maximum 10-year return	17.16%	19.98%	19.57%
Minimum expected return*	−40.05%	−18.29%	−21.78%
Maximum expected return†	52.33%	43.78%	46.35%

* Minimum expected return is arithmetic return minus 2 times the standard deviation.
† Maximum expected return is arithmetic return plus 2 times the standard deviation.

TABLE 14.47

Base Rates for Large Stocks External Financing Decile 1 and Large Stocks, October 1, 1971, to December 31, 2009

Item	Large Stocks external financing decile 1 beat Large Stocks	Percent	Average annual excess return
Single-year return	109 out of 448	24%	−5.53%
Rolling 3-year compound return	21 out of 424	5%	−6.82%
Rolling 5-year compound return	8 out of 400	2%	−7.45%
Rolling 7-year compound return	2 out of 376	1%	−7.96%
Rolling 10-year compound return	0 out of 340	0%	−8.03%

Unlike what we saw with All Stocks, decile 10, the 10 percent of Large Stocks with the lowest external financing, outperformed the Large Stocks universe by only 0.74 percent annually. The $10,000 invested in the group was worth $621,863 at the end of 2009, an average annual compound return of 11.40 percent. In contrast, decile 7 compounded at 12.33 percent per year. But the base rates for decile 10—featured in Table 14.48—were all positive, with decile 10 beating Large Stocks in 56 percent of all rolling five-year periods and in 74 percent of all rolling ten-year periods. Unlike decile 1, the largest maximum decline suffered by decile 10 was a drop of 47 percent from peak to trough.

T A B L E   14.48

Base Rates for Large Stocks External Financing Decile 10 and Large Stocks, October 1, 1971, to December 31, 2009

Item	Large Stocks external financing decile 10 beat Large Stocks	Percent	Average annual excess return
Single-year return	240 out of 448	54%	0.27%
Rolling 3-year compound return	211 out of 424	50%	0.29%
Rolling 5-year compound return	223 out of 400	56%	0.35%
Rolling 7-year compound return	234 out of 376	62%	0.58%
Rolling 10-year compound return	250 out of 340	74%	0.73%

IMPLICATIONS

For both All Stocks and Large Stocks, investors would do well to avoid companies that finance themselves from external sources rather than through internally generated cash flow. The All Stocks group with the highest external financing actually *lost* money, whereas the Large Stocks group earned less than T-bills. In both cases, the companies with the lowest use of external financing did better than the universe, with the All Stocks group doing significantly better than the All Stocks universe. Both groups had positive base rates, whereas the companies that used the most external financing never beat either universe in any of the rolling ten-year periods of the study. The implication is crystal clear—avoid stocks with big debt and the habit of issuing shares to cover the financing needs of the company.

PERCENTAGE CHANGE IN DEBT

As the name implies, this is a straightforward look at what happens when a company piles on debt. As you can see from Table 14.49, companies with the highest percentage change in debt do significantly worse than the market. Decile 1—the 10 percent of companies in All Stocks with the highest growth in debt—returns 6.64 percent per year over the 46 years of the study, significantly less than the All Stocks universe. Its base rates, featured in Table 14.50, are horrible, beating All Stocks in only 4 percent of all rolling five-year periods and not once in any rolling ten-year period. Table 14.51 shows the detailed results for deciles 1 and 10, and Table 14.52 shows the base rates for decile 10.

T A B L E   14.49

Summary Results for Debt Change (%) Decile Analysis of All Stocks Universe, January 1, 1964, to December 31, 2009

Decile	$10,000 grows to	Average return	Compound return	Standard deviation	Sharpe ratio
1 (highest)	$192,676	9.33%	6.64%	22.09%	0.07
2	$731,127	11.88%	9.78%	19.36%	0.25
3	$982,781	12.24%	10.49%	17.66%	0.31
4	$1,258,342	12.64%	11.08%	16.61%	0.37
5	$1,400,209	12.77%	11.34%	15.96%	0.40
6	$1,923,115	13.52%	12.11%	15.79%	0.45
7	$2,708,537	14.45%	12.95%	16.21%	0.49
8	$2,904,657	14.84%	13.12%	17.34%	0.47
9	$3,403,915	15.61%	13.51%	19.10%	0.45
10 (lowest)	$1,141,501	13.61%	10.85%	22.14%	0.26
All Stocks	$1,329,513	13.26%	11.22%	18.99%	0.33

T A B L E   14.50

Base Rates for All Stocks Debt Change (%) Decile 1 and All Stocks, January 1, 1964, to December 31, 2009

Item	All Stocks debt change (%) decile 1 beat All Stocks	Percent	Average annual excess return
Single-year return	135 out of 541	25%	−3.74%
Rolling 3-year compound return	60 out of 517	12%	−4.65%
Rolling 5-year compound return	22 out of 493	4%	−5.13%
Rolling 7-year compound return	0 out of 469	0%	−5.35%
Rolling 10-year compound return	0 out of 433	0%	−5.52%

T A B L E   14.51

Summary Annual Return and Risk Results Data: All Stocks Debt Change (%) Decile 1, All Stocks Debt Change (%) Decile 10, and All Stocks, January 1, 1964, to December 31, 2009

	All Stocks debt change (%) decile 1	All Stocks debt change (%) decile 10	All Stocks
Arithmetic average	9.33%	13.61%	13.26%
Geometric average	6.64%	10.85%	11.22%
Median return	14.58%	18.11%	17.16%
Standard deviation	22.09%	22.14%	18.99%
Upside deviation	12.93%	13.56%	10.98%
Downside deviation	16.20%	15.79%	13.90%
Tracking error	5.05	6.36	0.00
Number of positive periods	321	333	329
Number of negative periods	231	219	223
Maximum peak-to-trough decline	−69.24%	−66.25%	−55.54%
Beta	1.14	1.12	1.00

(continued on next page)

T A B L E   14.51

Summary Annual Return and Risk Results Data: All Stocks Debt Change (%) Decile 1, All Stocks Debt Change (%) Decile 10, and All Stocks, January 1, 1964, to December 31, 2009 *(Continued)*

	All Stocks debt change (%) decile 1	All Stocks debt change (%) decile 10	All Stocks
T-statistic (m = 0)	2.75	3.93	4.47
Sharpe ratio (Rf = 5%)	0.07	0.26	0.33
Sortino ratio (MAR = 10%)	−0.21	0.05	0.09
$10,000 becomes	$192,676	$1,141,501	$1,329,513
Minimum 1-year return	−52.74%	−48.68%	−46.49%
Maximum 1-year return	83.43%	110.21%	84.19%
Minimum 3-year return	−27.08%	−29.70%	−18.68%
Maximum 3-year return	31.54%	39.31%	31.49%
Minimum 5-year return	−15.96%	−9.56%	−9.91%
Maximum 5-year return	26.78%	31.74%	27.66%
Minimum 7-year return	−12.34%	−3.83%	−6.32%
Maximum 7-year return	22.09%	24.99%	23.77%
Minimum 10-year return	−3.68%	−1.85%	1.01%
Maximum 10-year return	17.75%	21.96%	22.05%
Minimum expected return*	−34.85%	−30.67%	−24.73%
Maximum expected return†	53.51%	57.88%	51.24%

* Minimum expected return is arithmetic return minus 2 times the standard deviation.
† Maximum expected return is arithmetic return plus 2 times the standard deviation.

T A B L E   14.52

Base Rates for All Stocks Debt Change (%) Decile 10 and All Stocks, January 1, 1964, to December 31, 2009

Item	All Stocks debt change (%) decile 10 beat All Stocks	Percent	Average annual excess return
Single-year return	277 out of 541	51%	0.34%
Rolling 3-year compound return	270 out of 517	52%	−0.22%
Rolling 5-year compound return	236 out of 493	48%	−0.41%
Rolling 7-year compound return	206 out of 469	44%	−0.50%
Rolling 10-year compound return	194 out of 433	45%	−0.47%

LARGE STOCKS

Table 14.53 shows the results for all 10 deciles from Large Stocks based upon their percentage change in debt. As we saw with All Stocks, Large Stocks that pile on debt do worse than the Large Stocks universe as well those companies that are more prudent with debt. But here we see that the most conservative companies, those in decile 10, are outperformed by deciles 7, 8, and 9, indicating the market's preference for stocks that are not the most conservative in terms of their approach to debt. Table 14.54 shows the detailed returns for deciles 1 and 10.

T A B L E   14.53

Summary Results for Debt Change (%) Decile Analysis of Large Stocks Universe, January 1, 1964, to December 31, 2009

Decile	$10,000 grows to	Average return	Compound return	Standard deviation	Sharpe ratio
1 (highest)	$250,512	9.09%	7.25%	18.37%	0.12
2	$494,002	10.39%	8.85%	16.77%	0.23
3	$425,858	9.91%	8.50%	16.04%	0.22
4	$519,169	10.22%	8.97%	15.12%	0.26
5	$611,814	10.54%	9.36%	14.67%	0.30
6	$682,149	10.79%	9.61%	14.61%	0.32
7	$1,216,176	12.21%	11.00%	14.75%	0.41
8	$1,371,176	12.54%	11.29%	14.97%	0.42
9	$1,598,403	13.12%	11.66%	16.11%	0.41
10 (lowest)	$1,006,941	12.30%	10.55%	17.69%	0.31
Large Stocks	$872,861	11.72%	10.20%	16.50%	0.32

T A B L E   14.54

Summary Annual Return and Risk Results Data: Large Stocks Debt Change (%) Decile 1, Large Stocks Debt Change (%) Decile 10, and Large Stocks, January 1, 1964, to December 31, 2009

	Large Stocks debt change (%) decile 1	Large Stocks debt change (%) decile 10	Large Stocks
Arithmetic average	9.09%	12.30%	11.72%
Geometric average	7.25%	10.55%	10.20%
Median return	13.70%	15.92%	17.20%
Standard deviation	18.37%	17.69%	16.50%
Upside deviation	10.98%	10.60%	9.70%
Downside deviation	13.26%	12.94%	11.85%
Tracking error	5.62	4.90	0.00
Number of positive periods	317	326	332
Number of negative periods	235	226	220
Maximum peak-to-trough decline	−63.62%	−55.95%	−53.77%
Beta	1.06	1.03	1.00
T-statistic (m = 0)	3.22	4.47	4.58
Sharpe ratio (Rf = 5%)	0.12	0.31	0.32
Sortino ratio (MAR = 10%)	−0.21	0.04	0.02
$10,000 becomes	$250,512	$1,006,941	$872,861
Minimum 1-year return	−51.38%	−44.94%	−46.91%
Maximum 1-year return	69.05%	63.25%	68.96%
Minimum 3-year return	−27.99%	−21.98%	−15.89%
Maximum 3-year return	34.45%	34.83%	33.12%
Minimum 5-year return	−11.54%	−5.92%	−5.82%
Maximum 5-year return	28.86%	29.44%	28.95%
Minimum 7-year return	−4.45%	−3.04%	−4.15%
Maximum 7-year return	21.29%	22.35%	22.83%
Minimum 10-year return	−4.29%	−0.46%	−0.15%
Maximum 10-year return	16.41%	20.63%	19.57%
Minimum expected return*	−27.65%	−23.07%	−21.28%
Maximum expected return†	45.84%	47.67%	44.72%

* Minimum expected return is arithmetic return minus 2 times the standard deviation.

† Maximum expected return is arithmetic return plus 2 times the standard deviation

Tables 14.55 and 14.56 show the base rates for deciles 1 and 10. As expected, all base rates for decile 1—those Large Stocks with the greatest percentage change in debt—are negative, with the group beating Large Stocks in 18 percent of all rolling five-year periods and in only 3 percent of all rolling ten-year periods. The base rates for decile 10—those Large Stocks with the smallest percentage increase in debt—are not great, with the group beating the Large Stocks universe in only 38 percent of all rolling ten-year periods. Yet as previously mentioned, it's really the companies piling on debt that you should avoid.

T A B L E   14.55

Base Rates for Large Stocks Debt Change (%) Decile 1 and Large Stocks, January 1, 1964, to December 31, 2009

Item	Large Stocks debt change (%) decile 1 beat Large Stocks	Percent	Average annual excess return
Single-year return	191 out of 541	35%	−2.48%
Rolling 3-year compound return	119 out of 517	23%	−3.04%
Rolling 5-year compound return	90 out of 493	18%	−3.38%
Rolling 7-year compound return	55 out of 469	12%	−3.66%
Rolling 10-year compound return	12 out of 433	3%	−3.86%

T A B L E   14.56

Base Rates for Large Stocks Debt Change (%) Decile 10 and Large Stocks, January 1, 1964, to December 31, 2009

Item	Large Stocks debt change (%) decile 10 beat Large Stocks	Percent	Average annual excess return
Single-year return	328 out of 541	61%	0.56%
Rolling 3-year compound return	314 out of 517	61%	0.29%
Rolling 5-year compound return	281 out of 493	57%	0.11%
Rolling 7-year compound return	228 out of 469	49%	−0.04%
Rolling 10-year compound return	166 out of 433	38%	−0.12%

IMPLICATIONS

Keep an eye on how rapidly companies in your portfolio accumulate debt, and avoid the 10 percent in All Stocks that are adding it the fastest.

DEPRECIATION EXPENSE TO CAPITAL EXPENSE

The depreciation to capital expenditures ratio measures the pace at which a company is writing down its physical assets versus the amount of cash it needs to replenish them. If a company's management is conservative, it will likely write down the asset values more quickly than the pace of replenishing them. This will suppress earnings in the short term but will allow for bigger earnings in the future. If management is aggressive, it might overestimate the usefulness of equipment and therefore write down asset values more slowly, thus negatively affecting future earnings.

As Table 14.57 shows, stocks with the lowest depreciation expense to capital expense ratios do very poorly, earning a compound average annual return of 5.3 percent per year, much worse than the All Stocks universe and even worse than keeping cash in 30-day U.S. T-bills. This shows us that very aggressive companies that delay writing down the equipment eventually pay the price for this by producing large negative earnings in the future. Table 14.58 shows the detailed results for deciles 1 and 10. Tables 14.59 and 14.60 show the base rates for deciles 1 and 10 versus the All Stocks universe. Stocks in decile 10 have horrible base rates, beating the All Stocks universe in just 12 percent of all rolling five-year periods and in none of the rolling ten-year periods.

T A B L E   14.57

Summary Results for Depreciation Expense to Capital Expense Decile Analysis of All Stocks Universe, January 1, 1964, to December 31, 2009

Decile	$10,000 grows to	Average return	Compound return	Standard deviation	Sharpe ratio
1 (highest)	$1,931,495	14.86%	12.12%	21.90%	0.33
2	$2,820,689	15.21%	13.05%	19.44%	0.41
3	$2,550,921	14.74%	12.80%	18.38%	0.42
4	$2,580,867	14.74%	12.83%	18.30%	0.43
5	$1,830,339	13.81%	11.99%	17.91%	0.39
6	$1,622,204	13.58%	11.70%	18.26%	0.37
7	$1,140,232	12.73%	10.85%	18.34%	0.32
8	$965,810	12.41%	10.45%	18.72%	0.29
9	$504,411	11.07%	8.90%	19.75%	0.20
10 (lowest)	$107,705	8.15%	5.30%	22.88%	0.01
All Stocks	$1,329,513	13.26%	11.22%	18.99%	0.33

T A B L E   14.58

Summary Annual Return and Risk Results Data: All Stocks Depreciation Expense to Capital Expense Decile 1, All Stocks Depreciation Expense to Capital Expense Decile 10, and All Stocks, January 1, 1964, to December 31, 2009

	All Stocks depreciation expense to capital expense decile 1	All Stocks depreciation expense to capital expense decile 10	All Stocks
Arithmetic average	14.86%	8.15%	13.26%
Geometric average	12.12%	5.30%	11.22%
Median return	21.99%	12.08%	17.16%
Standard deviation	21.90%	22.88%	18.99%
Upside deviation	13.04%	13.53%	10.98%
Downside deviation	15.71%	16.81%	13.90%
Tracking error	6.06	7.25	0.00
Number of positive periods	326	319	329
Number of negative periods	226	233	223

(continued on next page)

T A B L E   14.58

Summary Annual Return and Risk Results Data: All Stocks Depreciation Expense to Capital Expense Decile 1, All Stocks Depreciation Expense to Capital Expense Decile 10, and All Stocks, January 1, 1964, to December 31, 2009 *(Continued)*

	All Stocks depreciation expense to capital expense decile 1	All Stocks depreciation expense to capital expense decile 10	All Stocks
Maximum peak-to-trough decline	−65.18%	−71.68%	−55.54%
Beta	1.11	1.15	1.00
T-statistic (m = 0)	4.32	2.33	4.47
Sharpe ratio (Rf = 5%)	0.33	0.01	0.33
Sortino ratio (MAR = 10%)	0.14	−0.28	0.09
$10,000 becomes	$1,931,495	$107,705	$1,329,513
Minimum 1-year return	−44.19%	−56.41%	−46.49%
Maximum 1-year return	99.09%	86.53%	84.19%
Minimum 3-year return	−27.98%	−34.19%	−18.68%
Maximum 3-year return	37.41%	34.28%	31.49%
Minimum 5-year return	−11.75%	−16.09%	−9.91%
Maximum 5-year return	33.82%	26.76%	27.66%
Minimum 7-year return	−4.82%	−10.53%	−6.32%
Maximum 7-year return	27.38%	19.90%	23.77%
Minimum 10-year return	−3.58%	−5.29%	1.01%
Maximum 10-year return	25.69%	15.37%	22.05%
Minimum expected return*	−28.94%	−37.60%	−24.73%
Maximum expected return†	58.65%	53.91%	51.24%

* Minimum expected return is arithmetic return minus 2 times the standard deviation.
† Maximum expected return is arithmetic return plus 2 times the standard deviation.

T A B L E   14.59

Base Rates for All Stocks Depreciation Expense to Capital Expense Decile 1 and All Stocks, January 1, 1964, to December 31, 2009

Item	All Stocks depreciation expense to capital expense decile 1 beat All Stocks	Percent	Average annual excess return
Single-year return	314 out of 541	58%	1.54%
Rolling 3-year compound return	326 out of 517	63%	1.07%
Rolling 5-year compound return	308 out of 493	62%	0.97%
Rolling 7-year compound return	295 out of 469	63%	1.00%
Rolling 10-year compound return	314 out of 433	73%	1.21%

TABLE 14.60

Base Rates for All Stocks Depreciation Expense to Capital Expense Decile 10 and All Stocks, January 1, 1964, to December 31, 2009

Item	All Stocks depreciation expense to capital expense decile 10 beat All Stocks	Percent	Average annual excess return
Single-year return	156 out of 541	29%	−4.77%
Rolling 3-year compound return	94 out of 517	18%	−5.87%
Rolling 5-year compound return	58 out of 493	12%	−6.49%
Rolling 7-year compound return	26 out of 469	6%	−6.97%
Rolling 10-year compound return	0 out of 433	0%	−7.33%

LARGE STOCKS

As Table 14.61 shows, the only Large Stocks deciles that really suffer are 9 and 10, those with the lowest depreciation expense to capital expense ratios. Here, deciles 2 and 3 do better than decile 1, perhaps proving that the market wants companies to be at least *a little* aggressive with their accounting. Table 14.62 shows the detailed results for deciles 1 and 10 versus Large Stocks.

TABLE 14.61

Summary Results for Depreciation Expense to Capital Expense Decile Analysis of Large Stocks Universe, January 1, 1964, to December 31, 2009

Decile	$10,000 grows to	Average return	Compound return	Standard deviation	Sharpe ratio
1 (highest)	$718,161	11.55%	9.74%	18.05%	0.26
2	$1,052,498	12.07%	10.65%	15.96%	0.35
3	$1,243,777	12.43%	11.05%	15.69%	0.39
4	$848,074	11.51%	10.13%	15.76%	0.33
5	$666,059	10.94%	9.56%	15.87%	0.29
6	$846,052	11.52%	10.13%	15.86%	0.32
7	$639,233	10.85%	9.46%	15.88%	0.28
8	$497,939	10.23%	8.87%	15.79%	0.24
9	$422,308	10.05%	8.48%	16.93%	0.21
10 (lowest)	$296,664	9.56%	7.65%	18.70%	0.14
Large Stocks	$872,861	11.72%	10.20%	16.50%	0.32

TABLE 14.62

Summary Annual Return and Risk Results Data: Large Stocks Depreciation Expense to Capital Expense Decile 1, Large Stocks Depreciation Expense to Capital Expense Decile 10, and Large Stocks, January 1, 1964, to December 31, 2009

	Large Stocks depreciation expense to capital expense decile 1	Large Stocks depreciation expense to capital expense decile 10	Large Stocks
Arithmetic average	11.55%	9.56%	11.72%
Geometric average	9.74%	7.65%	10.20%

(continued on next page)

T A B L E   14.62

Summary Annual Return and Risk Results Data: Large Stocks Depreciation Expense to Capital Expense Decile 1, Large Stocks Depreciation Expense to Capital Expense Decile 10, and Large Stocks, January 1, 1964, to December 31, 2009
(Continued)

	Large Stocks depreciation expense to capital expense decile 1	Large Stocks depreciation expense to capital expense decile 10	Large Stocks
Median return	15.69%	11.42%	17.20%
Standard deviation	18.05%	18.70%	16.50%
Upside deviation	10.89%	11.17%	9.70%
Downside deviation	12.94%	13.61%	11.85%
Tracking error	5.82	8.20	0.00
Number of positive periods	325	313	332
Number of negative periods	227	239	220
Maximum peak-to-trough decline	−57.70%	−66.24%	−53.77%
Beta	1.04	1.02	1.00
T-statistic (m = 0)	4.13	3.32	4.58
Sharpe ratio (Rf = 5%)	0.26	0.14	0.32
Sortino ratio (MAR = 10%)	−0.02	−0.17	0.02
$10,000 becomes	$718,161	$296,664	$872,861
Minimum 1-year return	−50.86%	−53.66%	−46.91%
Maximum 1-year return	73.50%	50.79%	68.96%
Minimum 3-year return	−20.79%	−28.81%	−15.89%
Maximum 3-year return	34.49%	34.29%	33.12%
Minimum 5-year return	−9.83%	−10.55%	−5.82%
Maximum 5-year return	29.82%	26.21%	28.95%
Minimum 7-year return	−4.02%	−6.24%	−4.15%
Maximum 7-year return	22.89%	19.41%	22.83%
Minimum 10-year return	−4.22%	−2.84%	−0.15%
Maximum 10-year return	20.13%	18.28%	19.57%
Minimum expected return*	−24.55%	−27.84%	−21.28%
Maximum expected return†	47.65%	46.97%	44.72%

* Minimum expected return is arithmetic return minus 2 times the standard deviation.

† Maximum expected return is arithmetic return plus 2 times the standard deviation

Tables 14.63 and 14.64 show the base rates for each decile. As expected, the base rates for decile 10—those stocks from Large Stocks with the lowest depreciation expense to capital expense ratios—are all negative, with the group beating Large Stocks in just 18 percent of all rolling five-year periods and in no rolling ten-year periods.

T A B L E   14.63

Base Rates for Large Stocks Depreciation Expense to Capital Expense Decile 1 and Large Stocks, January 1, 1964, to December 31, 2009

Item	Large Stocks depreciation expense to capital expense decile 1 beat Large Stocks	Percent	Average annual excess return
Single-year return	272 out of 541	50%	−0.01%
Rolling 3-year compound return	285 out of 517	55%	−0.09%
Rolling 5-year compound return	243 out of 493	49%	−0.01%
Rolling 7-year compound return	265 out of 469	57%	0.05%
Rolling 10-year compound return	260 out of 433	60%	0.14%

T A B L E   14.64

Base Rates for Large Stocks Depreciation Expense to Capital Expense Decile 10 and Large Stocks, January 1, 1964, to December 31, 2009

Item	Large Stocks depreciation expense to capital expense decile 10 beat Large Stocks	Percent	Average annual excess return
Single-year return	213 out of 541	39%	−1.94%
Rolling 3-year compound return	166 out of 517	32%	−2.50%
Rolling 5-year compound return	88 out of 493	18%	−2.90%
Rolling 7-year compound return	45 out of 469	10%	−3.17%
Rolling 10-year compound return	2 out of 433	0%	−3.28%

IMPLICATIONS

Investors should be wary of companies that delay writing down their equipment. The delay usually leads to future negative earnings and historically this group has earned less than U.S. T-bills.

PERCENTAGE CHANGE IN NET OPERATING ASSETS

Net operating assets (NOA) are a company's operating assets minus operating liabilities. You derive them by separating operating activity from financing activity to isolate the operating performance of a company and not its gains from financing activities. In their paper "Do Investors Overvalue Firms with Bloated Balance Sheets?" David Hirshleifer, Kewei Hou, Siew Hong Teoh, and Yinglei Zhang state, "When cumulative net operating income (accounting value-added) outstrips cumulative free cash flow (cash value-added), subsequent earnings growth is weak. If investors with limited attention focus on accounting profitability, and neglect information about cash profitability, then net operating assets, the cumulation of the discrepancies between the two, measures the extent to which reporting outcomes provoke over-optimism. During the 1964–2002 sample period, net operating assets scaled by total assets is a strong negative predictor of long-run stock returns." They go on to state that, "The level of net operation assets ... measures the extent to which operating/reporting outcomes provoke excessive investor optimism … In other words, a high level of net operating assets, scaled to control for firm size, indicates a lack of sustainability of recent earnings performance."

Looking at Table 14.65, we see that the data confirm their hypothesis. Decile 1, those firms with the highest change in net operating assets, earned an average annual compound return of just 3.5 percent, significantly worse than the All Stocks universe and worse than an investment in U.S. T-bills. Deciles with the lowest change in net operating assets—especially deciles 9 and 8—significantly outperformed an investment in All Stocks, earning 14.42 and 14.09 percent, respectively. The detailed information on deciles 1 and 10 is featured in Table 14.66. The base rates for decile 1—those stocks with the highest change in net operating margins—are atrocious. They managed to beat the All Stocks universe in just 3 percent of all rolling five-year periods and in none of the rolling ten-year periods and are featured in Table 14.67. The base rates for the best performing decile—decile 9—is featured in Table 14.68 and reveals the opposite, beating All Stocks in 98 percent of all rolling five-year periods and in 100 percent of all rolling ten-year periods. Table 14.69 shows the base rates for decile 10.

T A B L E   14.65

Summary Results for NOA Change (%) Decile Analysis of All Stocks Universe, January 1, 1964, to December 31, 2009

Decile	$10,000 grows to	Average return	Compound return	Standard deviation	Sharpe ratio
1 (highest)	$48,617	6.86%	3.50%	24.94%	−0.06
2	$317,719	10.53%	7.81%	22.16%	0.13
3	$619,971	11.60%	9.39%	19.90%	0.22
4	$1,101,751	12.59%	10.76%	17.98%	0.32
5	$1,561,767	13.17%	11.61%	16.61%	0.40
6	$1,804,138	13.38%	11.96%	15.91%	0.44
7	$2,741,662	14.38%	12.98%	15.72%	0.51
8	$4,303,364	15.74%	14.09%	16.93%	0.54
9	$4,915,954	16.43%	14.42%	18.60%	0.51
10 (lowest)	$1,859,794	14.76%	12.03%	21.93%	0.32
All Stocks	$1,329,513	13.26%	11.22%	18.99%	0.33

T A B L E   14.66

Summary Annual Return and Risk Results Data: All Stocks NOA Change (%) Decile 1, All Stocks NOA Change (%) Decile 10, and All Stocks, January 1, 1964, to December 31, 2009

	All Stocks NOA change (%) decile 1	All Stocks NOA change (%) decile 10	All Stocks
Arithmetic average	6.86%	14.76%	13.26%
Geometric average	3.50%	12.03%	11.22%
Median return	12.47%	20.88%	17.16%
Standard deviation	24.94%	21.93%	18.99%
Upside deviation	14.47%	13.58%	10.98%
Downside deviation	18.64%	15.91%	13.90%

(continued on next page)

TABLE 14.66

Summary Annual Return and Risk Results Data: All Stocks NOA Change (%) Decile 1, All Stocks NOA Change (%) Decile 10, and All Stocks, January 1, 1964, to December 31, 2009 *(Continued)*

	All Stocks NOA change (%) decile 1	All Stocks NOA change (%) decile 10	All Stocks
Tracking error	8.89	6.49	0.00
Number of positive periods	319	336	329
Number of negative periods	233	216	223
Maximum peak-to-trough decline	−83.42%	−68.42%	−55.54%
Beta	1.25	1.11	1.00
T-statistic (m = 0)	1.81	4.28	4.47
Sharpe ratio (Rf = 5%)	−0.06	0.32	0.33
Sortino ratio (MAR = 10%)	−0.35	0.13	0.09
$10,000 becomes	$48,617	$1,859,794	$1,329,513
Minimum 1-year return	−66.27%	−50.68%	−46.49%
Maximum 1-year return	104.57%	118.44%	84.19%
Minimum 3-year return	−44.30%	−29.94%	−18.68%
Maximum 3-year return	34.49%	41.45%	31.49%
Minimum 5-year return	−21.14%	−13.35%	−9.91%
Maximum 5-year return	26.76%	34.59%	27.66%
Minimum 7-year return	−13.62%	−5.26%	−6.32%
Maximum 7-year return	22.22%	28.44%	23.77%
Minimum 10-year return	−9.75%	−3.39%	1.01%
Maximum 10-year return	15.86%	24.38%	22.05%
Minimum expected return*	−43.01%	−29.09%	−24.73%
Maximum expected return†	56.74%	58.62%	51.24%

* Minimum expected return is arithmetic return minus 2 times the standard deviation.

† Maximum expected return is arithmetic return plus 2 times the standard deviation.

TABLE 14.67

Base Rates for All Stocks NOA Change (%) Decile 1 and All Stocks, January 1, 1964, to December 31, 2009

Item	All Stocks NOA change (%) decile 1 beat All Stocks	Percent	Average annual excess return
Single-year return	142 out of 541	26%	−6.09%
Rolling 3-year compound return	64 out of 517	12%	−7.68%
Rolling 5-year compound return	14 out of 493	3%	−8.37%
Rolling 7-year compound return	0 out of 469	0%	−8.78%
Rolling 10-year compound return	0 out of 433	0%	−9.00%

T A B L E 14.68

Base Rates for All Stocks NOA Change (%) Decile 9 and All Stocks, January 1, 1964, to December 31, 2009

Item	All Stocks NOA change (%) decile 9 beat All Stocks	Percent	Average annual excess return
Single-year return	412 out of 541	76%	3.01%
Rolling 3-year compound return	447 out of 517	86%	3.06%
Rolling 5-year compound return	484 out of 493	98%	3.14%
Rolling 7-year compound return	466 out of 469	99%	3.23%
Rolling 10-year compound return	433 out of 433	100%	3.32%

T A B L E 14.69

Base Rates for All Stocks NOA Change (%) Decile 10 and All Stocks, January 1, 1964, to December 31, 2009

Item	All Stocks NOA change (%) decile 10 beat All Stocks	Percent	Average annual excess return
Single-year return	318 out of 541	59%	1.56%
Rolling 3-year compound return	336 out of 517	65%	0.99%
Rolling 5-year compound return	340 out of 493	69%	1.03%
Rolling 7-year compound return	331 out of 469	71%	1.17%
Rolling 10-year compound return	331 out of 433	76%	1.38%

LARGE STOCKS

Table 14.70 shows the results for the deciles of Large Stocks separated by percentage change in NOA. The story is the same as with All Stocks. Decile 1, those firms from Large Stocks with the highest change in net operating assets, returned just 5.79 percent, whereas decile 9, the stocks with the second-lowest percentage change in net operating assets, earned 12.22 percent, well ahead of Large Stocks. Decile 10, those stocks with the *lowest* percentage change in net operating assets, also beat Large Stocks, but not by the same magnitude as decile 9 did. Table 14.71 shows the detailed results for deciles 1 and 10.

T A B L E 14.70

Summary Results for NOA Change (%) Decile Analysis of Large Stocks Universe, January 1, 1964, to December 31, 2009

Decile	$10,000 grows to	Average return	Compound return	Standard deviation	Sharpe ratio
1 (highest)	$132,953	7.87%	5.79%	19.54%	0.04
2	$246,147	9.09%	7.21%	18.54%	0.12
3	$398,181	9.92%	8.34%	16.94%	0.20
4	$500,413	10.19%	8.88%	15.43%	0.25
5	$595,644	10.46%	9.29%	14.58%	0.29
6	$877,239	11.32%	10.22%	14.17%	0.37
7	$1,066,589	11.79%	10.68%	14.17%	0.40
8	$1,648,166	12.84%	11.74%	14.07%	0.48
9	$2,007,746	13.55%	12.22%	15.40%	0.47
10 (lowest)	$1,406,317	12.98%	11.35%	16.99%	0.37
Large Stocks	$872,861	11.72%	10.20%	16.50%	0.32

TABLE 14.71

Summary Annual Return and Risk Results Data: Large Stocks NOA Change (%) Decile 1, Large Stocks NOA Change (%) Decile 10, and Large Stocks, January 1, 1964, to December 31, 2009

	Large Stocks NOA change (%) decile 1	Large Stocks NOA change (%) decile 10	Large Stocks
Arithmetic average	7.87%	12.98%	11.72%
Geometric average	5.79%	11.35%	10.20%
Median return	11.25%	15.09%	17.20%
Standard deviation	19.54%	16.99%	16.50%
Upside deviation	11.57%	10.15%	9.70%
Downside deviation	15.04%	12.71%	11.85%
Tracking error	7.57	5.57	0.00
Number of positive periods	317	345	332
Number of negative periods	235	207	220
Maximum peak-to-trough decline	−78.05%	−58.76%	−53.77%
Beta	1.10	0.97	1.00
T-statistic (m = 0)	2.64	4.90	4.58
Sharpe ratio (Rf = 5%)	0.04	0.37	0.32
Sortino ratio (MAR = 10%)	−0.28	0.11	0.02
$10,000 becomes	$132,953	$1,406,317	$872,861
Minimum 1-year return	−67.89%	−46.51%	−46.91%
Maximum 1-year return	74.43%	63.59%	68.96%
Minimum 3-year return	−39.29%	−22.64%	−15.89%
Maximum 3-year return	30.06%	43.60%	33.12%
Minimum 5-year return	−18.44%	−4.39%	−5.82%
Maximum 5-year return	25.53%	34.03%	28.95%
Minimum 7-year return	−9.21%	−0.73%	−4.15%
Maximum 7-year return	19.91%	26.33%	22.83%
Minimum 10-year return	−7.38%	−1.02%	−0.15%
Maximum 10-year return	16.53%	22.57%	19.57%
Minimum expected return*	−31.22%	−21.01%	−21.28%
Maximum expected return†	46.95%	46.97%	44.72%

* Minimum expected return is arithmetic return minus 2 times the standard deviation.
† Maximum expected return is arithmetic return plus 2 times the standard deviation.

Tables 14.72, 14.73, and 14.74 show the base rates for deciles 1, 10, and 9. I include 9 to demonstrate that its base rates improve significantly from decile 10, so perhaps investors would be better served following NOA by looking at the upper, middle, and bottom thirds rather than by decile. Nevertheless, the base rates for decile 1 are atrocious, with the group beating Large Stocks in just 10 percent of all rolling five-year periods and in no rolling ten-year periods.

T A B L E   14.72

Base Rates for Large Stocks NOA Change (%) Decile 1 and Large Stocks, January 1, 1964, to December 31, 2009

Item	Large Stocks NOA change (%) decile 1 beat Large Stocks	Percent	Average annual excess return
Single-year return	193 out of 541	36%	−3.42%
Rolling 3-year compound return	129 out of 517	25%	−4.30%
Rolling 5-year compound return	48 out of 493	10%	−4.88%
Rolling 7-year compound return	33 out of 469	7%	−5.32%
Rolling 10-year compound return	0 out of 433	0%	−5.52%

T A B L E   14.73

Base Rates for Large Stocks NOA Change (%) Decile 10 and Large Stocks, January 1, 1964, to December 31, 2009

Item	Large Stocks NOA change (%) decile 10 beat Large Stocks	Percent	Average annual excess return
Single-year return	324 out of 541	60%	1.49%
Rolling 3-year compound return	341 out of 517	66%	1.38%
Rolling 5-year compound return	330 out of 493	67%	1.32%
Rolling 7-year compound return	316 out of 469	67%	1.26%
Rolling 10-year compound return	328 out of 433	76%	1.31%

T A B L E   14.74

Base Rates for Large Stocks NOA Change (%) Decile 9 and Large Stocks, January 1, 1964, to December 31, 2009

Item	Large Stocks NOA change (%) decile 9 beat Large Stocks	Percent	Average annual excess return
Single-year return	318 out of 541	59%	1.85%
Rolling 3-year compound return	397 out of 517	77%	2.04%
Rolling 5-year compound return	426 out of 493	86%	2.12%
Rolling 7-year compound return	433 out of 469	92%	2.19%
Rolling 10-year compound return	392 out of 433	91%	2.22%

IMPLICATIONS

As we proceed with our review of balance sheet items, we see that we can learn a great deal about the prospects for stocks based solely on their books and records. Percentage change in net operating assets, like accruals-to-price, offers investors an excellent measurement for determining whether stocks that might otherwise look attractive might be poised to disappoint investors.

TOTAL ACCRUALS TO TOTAL ASSETS (TATA)

In an article titled "Measuring Company Quality" Richard Lawson said, "The first quality signal, accruals, measures income quality. It has attracted much attention in the U.S. and increasingly world-wide over the last decade. In particular, academic and industry research in the U.S. found that accruals are an effective contrarian signal because they measure the extent to which earnings do not reflect operating fundamentals, which markets seem to misprice." Much as we saw with accrual-to-price, our hypothesis is that the *lower* the total change in total accruals to total assets, the more sound the company's earnings. On the other hand, companies with the *highest* relative change in total accruals to total assets are far more likely to experience negative earnings surprises in the future. Thus we would expect decile 1—with the highest changes—to do poorly and decile 10—with the lowest changes—to do well. Let's see if that is true.

Table 14.75 shows the returns of each decile over the period from December 31, 1963, to December 31, 2009. The $10,000 invested in decile 10—those with the lowest changes in total accruals to total assets—grew to $3,178,230 by the end of 2009, an average annual compound return of 13.34 percent. That's three times the $1.3 million you'd have earned with an investment in the All Stocks universe, which compounded at 11.22 percent. Table 14.76 shows the base rates for decile 10, all of which are positive, with the group beating All Stocks in 70 percent of all rolling five-year periods and in 78 percent of all rolling ten-year periods.

The results for buying the group from decile 1, those with the highest change in total accruals to total assets, tells a significantly different story. Here, the $10,000 grows to just $71,913, an average annual compound return of 4.38 percent. An investment in U.S. T-bills would have done significantly better. As for the base rates, as you can see by examining Table 14.77, they are abysmal, with the group beating All Stocks in just 4 percent of all rolling five-year periods and in no rolling ten-year period. Table 14.78 provides a detailed summary for deciles 1 and 10 as well as for All Stocks.

T A B L E   14.75

Summary Results for TATA Decile Analysis of All Stocks Universe, January 1, 1964, to December 31, 2009

Decile	$10,000 grows to	Average return	Compound return	Standard deviation	Sharpe ratio
1 (highest)	$71,913	7.69%	4.38%	24.75%	−0.02
2	$627,508	11.83%	9.42%	20.79%	0.21
3	$1,050,321	12.72%	10.65%	19.15%	0.29
4	$1,509,326	13.33%	11.52%	17.87%	0.36
5	$2,233,050	14.10%	12.48%	16.89%	0.44
6	$2,468,826	14.34%	12.72%	16.88%	0.46
7	$2,030,988	13.89%	12.25%	17.02%	0.43
8	$2,271,665	14.37%	12.52%	18.05%	0.42
9	$2,884,961	15.24%	13.10%	19.27%	0.42
10 (lowest)	$3,178,230	16.12%	13.34%	21.92%	0.38
All Stocks	$1,329,513	13.26%	11.22%	18.99%	0.33

T A B L E   14.76

Base Rates for All Stocks TATA Decile 10 and All Stocks, January 1, 1964, to December 31, 2009

Item	All Stocks TATA decile 10 beat All Stocks	Percent	Average annual excess return
Single-year return	379 out of 541	70%	2.99%
Rolling 3-year compound return	372 out of 517	72%	2.14%
Rolling 5-year compound return	347 out of 493	70%	1.92%
Rolling 7-year compound return	321 out of 469	68%	1.84%
Rolling 10-year compound return	338 out of 433	78%	1.94%

T A B L E   14.77

Base Rates for All Stocks TATA Decile 1 and All Stocks, January 1, 1964, to December 31, 2009

Item	All Stocks TATA decile 1 beat All Stocks	Percent	Average annual excess return
Single-year return	148 out of 541	27%	−5.57%
Rolling 3-year compound return	56 out of 517	11%	−6.94%
Rolling 5-year compound return	19 out of 493	4%	−7.64%
Rolling 7-year compound return	6 out of 469	1%	−8.02%
Rolling 10-year compound return	0 out of 433	0%	−8.43%

T A B L E   14.78

Summary Annual Return and Risk Results Data: All Stocks TATA Decile 1, All Stocks TATA Decile 10, and All Stocks, January 1, 1964, to December 31, 2009

	All Stocks TATA decile 1	All Stocks TATA decile 10	All Stocks
Arithmetic average	7.69%	16.12%	13.26%
Geometric average	4.38%	13.34%	11.22%
Median return	12.61%	22.50%	17.16%
Standard deviation	24.75%	21.92%	18.99%
Upside deviation	14.77%	12.98%	10.98%
Downside deviation	17.41%	16.24%	13.90%
Tracking error	8.18	6.20	0.00
Number of positive periods	314	335	329
Number of negative periods	238	217	223
Maximum peak-to-trough decline	−77.80%	−69.09%	−55.54%
Beta	1.26	1.11	1.00
T-statistic (m = 0)	2.04	4.65	4.47
Sharpe ratio (Rf = 5%)	−0.02	0.38	0.33
Sortino ratio (MAR = 10%)	−0.32	0.21	0.09
$10,000 becomes	$71,913	$3,178,230	$1,329,513
Minimum 1-year return	−59.71%	−53.01%	−46.49%
Maximum 1-year return	97.43%	115.44%	84.19%

(continued on next page)

T A B L E   14.78

Summary Annual Return and Risk Results Data: All Stocks TATA Decile 1, All Stocks TATA Decile 10, and All Stocks, January 1, 1964, to December 31, 2009 *(Continued)*

	All Stocks TATA decile 1	All Stocks TATA decile 10	All Stocks
Minimum 3-year return	−32.09%	−30.42%	−18.68%
Maximum 3-year return	35.79%	44.52%	31.49%
Minimum 5-year return	−21.15%	−8.69%	−9.91%
Maximum 5-year return	25.29%	35.90%	27.66%
Minimum 7-year return	−17.50%	−3.33%	−6.32%
Maximum 7-year return	20.89%	29.82%	23.77%
Minimum 10-year return	−7.01%	−1.03%	1.01%
Maximum 10-year return	15.56%	26.06%	22.05%
Minimum expected return*	−41.81%	−27.72%	−24.73%
Maximum expected return†	57.19%	59.97%	51.24%

* Minimum expected return is arithmetic return minus 2 times the standard deviation.
† Maximum expected return is arithmetic return plus 2 times the standard deviation.

LARGE STOCKS

Table 14.79 shows the results for the deciles by total accruals to total assets for Large Stocks. As we saw with All Stocks, Large Stocks with the lowest change in total accruals to total assets did significantly better than those with the highest change in total accruals to total assets. Decile 10—stocks from Large Stocks with the lowest change in total accruals to total assets— earned 11.99 percent per year, whereas those in decile 1—stocks from Large Stocks with the highest change in total accruals to total assets—earned just 6.18 percent. Table 14.80 shows the detailed summary results for investments made in deciles 1 and 10.

T A B L E   14.79

Summary Results for TATA Decile Analysis of Large Stocks Universe, January 1, 1964, to December 31, 2009

Decile	$10,000 grows to	Average return	Compound return	Standard deviation	Sharpe ratio
1 (highest)	$157,901	8.18%	6.18%	19.22%	0.06
2	$426,474	9.98%	8.50%	16.45%	0.21
3	$375,261	9.53%	8.20%	15.65%	0.20
4	$657,927	10.71%	9.53%	14.65%	0.31
5	$1,122,873	12.00%	10.81%	14.63%	0.40
6	$1,073,892	11.90%	10.70%	14.68%	0.39
7	$1,217,792	12.25%	11.00%	14.96%	0.40
8	$1,034,194	12.03%	10.61%	15.98%	0.35
9	$1,261,567	12.59%	11.09%	16.35%	0.37
10 (lowest)	$1,830,510	13.87%	11.99%	18.17%	0.38
Large Stocks	$872,861	11.72%	10.20%	16.50%	0.32

T A B L E   14.80

Summary Annual Return and Risk Results Data: Large Stocks TATA Decile 1, Large Stocks TATA Decile 10, and Large Stocks, January 1, 1964, to December 31, 2009

	Large Stocks TATA decile 1	Large Stocks TATA decile 10	Large Stocks
Arithmetic average	8.18%	13.87%	11.72%
Geometric average	6.18%	11.99%	10.20%
Median return	9.86%	18.02%	17.20%
Standard deviation	19.22%	18.17%	16.50%
Upside deviation	11.60%	10.72%	9.70%
Downside deviation	13.79%	13.55%	11.85%
Tracking error	6.85	7.03	0.00
Number of positive periods	305	344	332
Number of negative periods	247	208	220
Maximum peak-to-trough decline	−58.61%	−69.58%	−53.77%
Beta	1.09	1.02	1.00
T-statistic (m = 0)	2.78	4.87	4.58
Sharpe ratio (Rf = 5%)	0.06	0.38	0.32
Sortino ratio (MAR = 10%)	−0.28	0.15	0.02
$10,000 becomes	$157,901	$1,830,510	$872,861
Minimum 1-year return	−49.87%	−51.37%	−46.91%
Maximum 1-year return	67.88%	78.34%	68.96%
Minimum 3-year return	−21.48%	−31.01%	−15.89%
Maximum 3-year return	27.99%	46.11%	33.12%
Minimum 5-year return	−10.02%	−8.45%	−5.82%
Maximum 5-year return	25.49%	35.06%	28.95%
Minimum 7-year return	−7.99%	−2.84%	−4.15%
Maximum 7-year return	18.68%	30.00%	22.83%
Minimum 10-year return	−2.93%	−0.83%	−0.15%
Maximum 10-year return	15.19%	23.24%	19.57%
Minimum expected return*	−30.26%	−22.48%	−21.28%
Maximum expected return†	46.62%	50.21%	44.72%

* Minimum expected return is arithmetic return minus 2 times the standard deviation.
† Maximum expected return is arithmetic return plus 2 times the standard deviation.

As Table 14.81 makes clear, the base rates for decile 1 are atrocious and very consistent. The stocks with the highest change in total accruals to total assets beat Large Stocks in just 6 percent of all rolling five-year periods and in no rolling ten-year periods. Table 14.82 shows the base rates for decile 10—all are positive, and the group beat Large Stocks in 82 percent of all rolling ten-year periods.

T A B L E   14.81

Base Rates for Large Stocks TATA Decile 1 and Large Stocks, January 1, 1964, to December 31, 2009

Item	Large Stocks TATA decile 1 beat Large Stocks	Percent	Average annual excess return
Single-year return	159 out of 541	29%	−3.70%
Rolling 3-year compound return	74 out of 517	14%	−4.33%
Rolling 5-year compound return	32 out of 493	6%	−4.74%
Rolling 7-year compound return	22 out of 469	5%	−4.98%
Rolling 10-year compound return	1 out of 433	0%	−5.24%

T A B L E   14.82

Base Rates for Large Stocks TATA Decile 10 and Large Stocks, January 1, 1964, to December 31, 2009

Item	Large Stocks TATA decile 10 beat Large Stocks	Percent	Average annual excess return
Single-year return	345 out of 541	64%	2.64%
Rolling 3-year compound return	380 out of 517	74%	2.03%
Rolling 5-year compound return	384 out of 493	78%	1.63%
Rolling 7-year compound return	363 out of 469	77%	1.42%
Rolling 10-year compound return	353 out of 433	82%	1.45%

IMPLICATIONS

Much as we saw with accruals to price, companies that are playing games with the books end up disappointing investors with negative earnings surprises. Indeed, while we are more focused on what attributes identify attractive stocks, several of these accounting variables might be very helpful for investors interested in shorting stocks, as several of them do an excellent job of identifying stocks that go on to crash and burn.

TOTAL ACCRUALS TO AVERAGE ASSETS (TAAA)

Another take on the total accruals phenomenon is to compare them with a company's average assets, using the same assumption that companies with lower total accruals to average assets will provide higher-quality earnings and that companies with higher total accruals to average assets will have lower-quality earnings and might therefore be bad investments. In order to get the figure for average assets through the Compustat dataset, we must use quarterly data that start in 1971. So, for this test, we start on September 30, 1971, and invest $10,000 in the various deciles by total accruals to average assets.

As Table 14.83 makes clear, much as we saw with total accruals to total assets, the lower, the better. The $10,000 invested in decile 10—those stocks from All Stocks with the lowest total accruals to average assets—grows to $1,188,797, an average annual compound return of 13.31 percent. That's over two times the $587,200 you'd have earned investing in the All Stocks universe over the same period, where the universe compounded at 11.24 percent. All base rates, featured in Table 14.84, are positive, with the stocks with the lowest total accruals to average assets beating the All Stocks universe in 71 percent of all rolling five-year periods and in 73 percent of all rolling ten-year periods.

TABLE   14.83

Summary Results for TAAA Decile Analysis of All Stocks Universe, October 1, 1971, to December 31, 2009

Decile	$10,000 grows to	Average return	Compound return	Standard deviation	Sharpe ratio
1 (highest)	$17,835	5.91%	1.52%	28.78%	−0.12
2	$163,775	10.65%	7.58%	23.49%	0.11
3	$458,772	12.91%	10.52%	20.58%	0.27
4	$710,848	13.75%	11.79%	18.54%	0.37
5	$773,494	13.81%	12.04%	17.63%	0.40
6	$808,397	13.81%	12.17%	17.01%	0.42
7	$1,082,229	14.67%	13.03%	17.01%	0.47
8	$1,270,308	15.23%	13.50%	17.40%	0.49
9	$1,252,980	15.29%	13.46%	17.85%	0.47
10 (lowest)	$1,188,797	15.66%	13.31%	20.29%	0.41
All Stocks	$587,200	13.35%	11.24%	19.34%	0.32

TABLE   14.84

Base Rates for All Stocks TAAA Decile 10 and All Stocks, October 1, 1971, to December 31, 2009

Item	All Stocks TAAA decile 10 beat All Stocks	Percent	Average annual excess return
Single-year return	258 out of 448	58%	2.19%
Rolling 3-year compound return	269 out of 424	63%	1.76%
Rolling 5-year compound return	284 out of 400	71%	1.80%
Rolling 7-year compound return	276 out of 376	73%	1.86%
Rolling 10-year compound return	247 out of 340	73%	1.94%

The $10,000 invested in decile 1—those stocks with the highest total accruals to average assets—tells quite a different story. Here $10,000 grows to a mere $17,835, an average annual compound return of just 1.52 percent. That's significantly worse than keeping your money in T-bills. And if you adjusted the return for inflation, you would find yourself in the poor house. All base rates, featured in Table 14.85, are negative, with the stocks with the highest total accruals to average assets beating All Stocks in just 8 percent of all rolling five-year periods and in no rolling ten-year periods. You definitely want to stay away from companies playing with the numbers. Table 14.86 shows the detailed results for deciles 1 and 10.

T A B L E   14.85

Base Rates for All Stocks TAAA Decile 1 and All Stocks, October 1, 1971, to December 31, 2009

Item	All Stocks TAAA decile 1 beat All Stocks	Percent	Average annual excess return
Single-year return	131 out of 448	29%	−7.43%
Rolling 3-year compound return	45 out of 424	11%	−9.43%
Rolling 5-year compound return	31 out of 400	8%	−9.79%
Rolling 7-year compound return	16 out of 376	4%	−10.02%
Rolling 10-year compound return	1 out of 340	0%	−10.23%

T A B L E   14.86

Summary Annual Return and Risk Results Data: All Stocks TAAA Decile 1, All Stocks TAAA Decile 10, and All Stocks, October 1, 1971, to December 31, 2009

	All Stocks TAAA decile 1	All Stocks TAAA decile 10	All Stocks
Arithmetic average	5.91%	15.66%	13.35%
Geometric average	1.52%	13.31%	11.24%
Median return	10.83%	19.61%	17.02%
Standard deviation	28.78%	20.29%	19.34%
Upside deviation	17.67%	12.59%	11.21%
Downside deviation	20.16%	14.36%	14.21%
Tracking error	32.33	26.06	0.00
Number of positive periods	256	280	272
Number of negative periods	203	179	187
Maximum peak-to-trough decline	−89.41%	−51.34%	−55.54%
Beta	0.21	0.14	1.00
T-statistic (m = 0)	1.24	4.46	4.03
Sharpe ratio (Rf = 5%)	−0.12	0.41	0.32
Sortino ratio (MAR = 10%)	−0.42	0.23	0.09
$10,000 becomes	$17,835	$1,188,797	$587,200
Minimum 1-year return	−68.33%	−45.86%	−46.49%
Maximum 1-year return	146.70%	93.05%	84.19%
Minimum 3-year return	−49.09%	−15.36%	−18.68%
Maximum 3-year return	36.70%	36.90%	31.49%
Minimum 5-year return	−25.47%	−4.92%	−7.00%
Maximum 5-year return	28.83%	30.74%	27.66%
Minimum 7-year return	−17.77%	−0.06%	−0.67%
Maximum 7-year return	24.78%	26.11%	23.77%
Minimum 10-year return	−13.02%	4.89%	1.65%
Maximum 10-year return	19.96%	24.61%	22.05%
Minimum expected return*	−51.64%	−24.92%	−25.32%
Maximum expected return†	63.47%	56.25%	52.03%

* Minimum expected return is arithmetic return minus 2 times the standard deviation.
† Maximum expected return is arithmetic return plus 2 times the standard deviation.

LARGE STOCKS

Table 14.87 shows the returns for the 10 deciles by total accruals to average assets for stocks in the Large Stocks universe. Here we see that the results are not as smooth as they were with the All Stocks group. Like the All Stocks group, deciles 9 and 8 both do better than decile 10, but in the case of All Stocks the three top deciles with the lowest total accruals to average assets all performed roughly the same. Here, deciles 9 and 8 do significantly better than decile 10. Decile 10 still beats the Large Stocks universe, but not by the same magnitude we saw with All Stocks. Decile 10—those Large Stocks with the lowest total accruals to average assets—turned $10,000 invested in 1971 into $563,915, an average annual compound return of 11.12 percent. That's better than the $481,960 you would have earned had you invested in the Large Stocks universe over the same period, which earned an annual compound gain of 10.66 percent. The base rates, featured in Table 14.88, were mostly positive, but not by a significant margin. The group beat the Large Stocks universe in 48 percent of all rolling five-year periods and in 70 percent of all rolling ten-year periods.

T A B L E 14.87

Summary Results for TAAA Decile Analysis of Large Stocks Universe, October 1, 1971, to December 31, 2009

Decile	$10,000 grows to	Average return	Compound return	Standard deviation	Sharpe ratio
1 (highest)	$49,304	7.33%	4.26%	23.68%	−0.03
2	$204,802	10.15%	8.21%	18.72%	0.17
3	$298,729	10.88%	9.29%	17.11%	0.25
4	$477,735	12.04%	10.64%	15.92%	0.35
5	$434,451	11.74%	10.36%	15.78%	0.34
6	$655,943	12.96%	11.56%	15.84%	0.41
7	$950,182	13.98%	12.64%	15.39%	0.50
8	$1,015,254	14.22%	12.84%	15.64%	0.50
9	$1,508,368	15.38%	14.01%	15.52%	0.58
10 (lowest)	$563,915	12.87%	11.12%	17.77%	0.34
Large Stocks	$481,960	12.29%	10.66%	17.03%	0.33

T A B L E 14.88

Base Rates for Large Stocks TAAA Decile 10 and Large Stocks, October 1, 1971, to December 31, 2009

Item	Large Stocks TAAA decile 10 beat Large Stocks	Percent	Average annual excess return
Single-year return	226 out of 448	50%	0.81%
Rolling 3-year compound return	220 out of 424	52%	0.47%
Rolling 5-year compound return	190 out of 400	48%	0.44%
Rolling 7-year compound return	186 out of 376	49%	0.48%
Rolling 10-year compound return	239 out of 340	70%	0.66%

Where the total accruals to average assets ratio really shines is in showing you the stocks to *avoid*. The $10,000 invested in 1971 in decile 1—those stocks from Large Stocks with the highest total accruals to average assets—grew to only $49,304, an average annual compound return of just 4.26 percent. That's worse than T-bills and well behind the 10.66 percent return per year you would have earned with an investment in the Large Stocks universe. Decile 1 was also significantly riskier than an investment in Large Stocks, with a standard deviation of return of 23.68 percent versus 17.03 percent for the Large Stocks universe. The higher risk married to the lower return brought the Sharpe ratio to an anemic –0.03. The maximum decline for the group was also huge, with the group losing 84 percent from peak to trough. You can view all the detailed data for deciles 1 and 10 in Table 14.89. As Table 14.90 shows, the base rates for the group were all negative, with decile 1 beating Large Stocks in only 19 percent of all rolling five-year periods and in 10 percent of all rolling ten-year periods.

T A B L E   14.89

Summary Annual Return and Risk Results Data: Large Stocks TAAA Decile 1, Large Stocks TAAA Decile 10, and Large Stocks, October 1, 1971, to December 31, 2009

	Large Stocks TAAA decile 1	Large Stocks TAAA decile 10	Large Stocks
Arithmetic average	7.33%	12.87%	12.29%
Geometric average	4.26%	11.12%	10.66%
Median return	10.69%	14.36%	16.49%
Standard deviation	23.68%	17.77%	17.03%
Upside deviation	14.19%	11.22%	10.04%
Downside deviation	18.38%	11.99%	12.30%
Tracking error	27.74	23.63	0.00
Number of positive periods	257	269	274
Number of negative periods	202	190	185
Maximum peak-to-trough decline	−83.64%	−55.41%	−53.77%
Beta	0.14	0.08	1.00
T-statistic (m = 0)	1.85	4.23	4.23
Sharpe ratio (Rf = 5%)	−0.03	0.34	0.33
Sortino ratio (MAR = 10%)	−0.31	0.09	0.05
$10,000 becomes	$49,304	$563,915	$481,960
Minimum 1-year return	−74.68%	−50.49%	−46.91%
Maximum 1-year return	72.65%	65.19%	68.96%
Minimum 3-year return	−43.26%	−16.33%	−15.89%
Maximum 3-year return	31.64%	39.63%	33.12%
Minimum 5-year return	−22.45%	−2.84%	−4.67%
Maximum 5-year return	24.59%	32.03%	28.95%
Minimum 7-year return	−12.51%	−0.18%	−0.96%
Maximum 7-year return	21.59%	26.14%	22.83%
Minimum 10-year return	−12.55%	0.93%	−0.15%
Maximum 10-year return	19.02%	21.41%	19.57%
Minimum expected return*	−40.03%	−22.67%	−21.78%
Maximum expected return†	54.69%	48.41%	46.35%

* Minimum expected return is arithmetic return minus 2 times the standard deviation.

† Maximum expected return is arithmetic return plus 2 times the standard deviation.

T A B L E   14.90

Base Rates for Large Stocks TAAA Decile 1 and Large Stocks, October 1, 1971, to December 31, 2009

Item	Large Stocks TAAA decile 1 beat Large Stocks	Percent	Average annual excess return
Single-year return	179 out of 448	40%	−4.40%
Rolling 3-year compound return	114 out of 424	27%	−5.36%
Rolling 5-year compound return	76 out of 400	19%	−5.80%
Rolling 7-year compound return	53 out of 376	14%	−6.10%
Rolling 10-year compound return	33 out of 340	10%	−6.13%

IMPLICATIONS

As we saw with total accruals to total assets, you want to avoid stocks that have high total accruals to average assets. Companies that are playing games with the books end up with far more opportunities to disappoint investors with negative earnings surprises than companies that take a more conservative approach to bookkeeping.

A COMPOSITED ACCOUNTING RATIO

We spend the entire next chapter investigating whether we might get better, more consistent results by looking at how stocks score on *all* value factors rather than just looking at the factors individually. It is reasonable to assume that a stock that scores very well on PE ratio *and* EBITDA-to-enterprise value *and* price-to-sales might do better than a stock that scores well on one but not another. Let's start the investigation with our accounting variables and see if the results of combining several accounting variables do better than they do individually.

Specifically, we look at a combination of the following:

- Total accruals to total assets
- Percentage change in net operating assets (NOA)
- Total accruals to average assets
- Depreciation expense to capital expense

Here we're looking for stocks with high earnings quality. For each combined group of factors, we assign a percentile ranking for each stock in the All Stocks and Large Stocks universes on a scale of 1 to 100. If a stock has a total accruals to total assets ratio that is in the lowest 1 percent for the universe, it receives a rank of 100; if a stock has a total accruals to total assets ratio in the highest 1 percent for the universe it receives a rank of 1. We follow a similar convention for each of the factors. Thus, if a stock is in the lowest 1 percent of the universe based on its NOA change, it gets 100; if in the highest 1 percent, it gets a 1. For instances in which *higher is better*, we reverse the rankings, so if a stock ranks in the upper 1 percent of depreciation expense to capital expense, it gets a 100, whereas if it is in the lowest 1 percent, it gets a rank of 1. If a value is missing for a factor, we assign a neutral rank of 50. Once all factors are ranked, we add up all the factors' ranks and assign the stocks to deciles based upon their overall cumulative ranking. Those with the highest scores are assigned to decile 1, and those with the lowest scores are assigned to decile 10.

Let's call this composited group of accounting variables the Earnings Quality Composite. As Table 14.91 demonstrates, by combining several accounting variables into a single master composite, you increase the robustness of the analysis and get better, more consistent overall results. Starting on December 31, 1963, $10,000 invested in the stocks in decile 1 with the best scores for each of the accounting variables grew to $8,992,076 by the end of 2009, a robust average annual compound return of 15.93 percent. It's also $8 million more than the $1,329,513 you'd have earned with an investment in the All Stocks universe, which compounded at 11.24 percent over the same period. Risk was slightly higher for the stocks with the best accounting scores, with the standard deviation of return of 19.11 percent, slightly higher than that of All Stocks' 18.99 percent. Yet the much higher absolute return from the stocks with the best accounting variables generated a much higher Sharpe ratio of .57 versus .33 for the All Stocks universe.

T A B L E   14.91

Summary Results for COMP Earnings Quality Composite Decile Analysis of All Stocks Universe, January 1, 1964, to December 31, 2009

Decile	$10,000 grows to	Average return	Compound return	Standard deviation	Sharpe ratio
1 (highest)	$8,992,076	18.07%	15.93%	19.11%	0.57
2	$4,902,190	16.23%	14.42%	17.74%	0.53
3	$2,837,680	14.79%	13.06%	17.36%	0.46
4	$1,532,421	13.15%	11.56%	16.79%	0.39
5	$1,313,455	12.77%	11.19%	16.81%	0.37
6	$1,616,169	13.14%	11.69%	16.05%	0.42
7	$1,020,448	12.30%	10.58%	17.51%	0.32
8	$592,812	11.32%	9.28%	19.12%	0.22
9	$407,634	10.81%	8.39%	20.84%	0.16
10 (lowest)	$60,037	7.29%	3.97%	24.79%	−0.04
All Stocks	$1,329,513	13.26%	11.22%	18.99%	0.33

The base rates for the Earnings Quality Composite are all positive, with decile 1 beating All Stocks in 94 percent of all rolling five-year periods and in 100 percent of all rolling ten-year periods. Table 14.92 shows the base rates for all other rolling periods. As you can see from Table 14.91, the stocks with the *worst* scores from the Earnings Quality Composite do horribly. The same $10,000 invested on December 31, 1963, grows to just $60,037, an average annual compound return of a mere 3.97 percent. That's worse than an investment in T-bills. What's more, it also has a high standard deviation of return of 24.79 percent, bringing its Sharpe ratio to an anemic –.04. Its maximum decline is also dreadful, with a maximum peak-to-trough decline of 73.54 percent, compared to 54.83 percent for decile 1 and 55.30 percent for the All Stocks universe. The base rates for decile 10—those stocks with the worst collective scores on the four accounting variables and featured in Table 14.93—were atrocious, beating the All Stocks universe in just 6 percent of all rolling five-year periods and in no rolling ten-year periods.

T A B L E   14.92

Base Rates for All Stocks Combined Earnings Quality Decile 1 and All Stocks, January 1, 1964, to December 31, 2009

Item	All Stocks combined earnings quality decile 1 beat All Stocks	Percent	Average annual excess return
Single-year return	455 out of 541	84%	4.69%
Rolling 3-year compound return	460 out of 517	89%	4.78%
Rolling 5-year compound return	466 out of 493	95%	4.94%
Rolling 7-year compound return	459 out of 469	98%	5.13%
Rolling 10-year compound return	433 out of 433	100%	5.34%

T A B L E   14.93

Base Rates for All Stocks Combined Earnings Quality Composite Decile 10 and All Stocks, January 1, 1964, to December 31, 2009

Item	All Stocks combined earnings quality Composite decile 10 beat All Stocks	Percent	Average annual excess return
Single-year return	154 out of 541	28%	−5.89%
Rolling 3-year compound return	84 out of 517	16%	−7.29%
Rolling 5-year compound return	28 out of 493	6%	−7.97%
Rolling 7-year compound return	15 out of 469	3%	−8.46%
Rolling 10-year compound return	0 out of 433	0%	−8.82%

ALSO HELPFUL FOR THE INDIVIDUAL STOCK INVESTOR

If you pare down the number of stocks to 25 or 50 names, you see that results get even better. An individual investor who simply bought the 25 stocks that scored the best on the Earnings Quality Composite could do significantly better than simply investing in the All Stocks universe. As Table 14.94 shows, investing in the 25 stocks from All Stocks with the best score would turn $10,000 invested in 1963 into $19,611,978, an average annual compound return of 17.92 percent. That's $18 million more than you would have earned from investing in the All Stocks universe, where $10,000 grew to $1,342,499. Risk—with a standard deviation of return of 22.17 percent—was higher than in the All Stocks universe, but the much higher absolute return brought the Sharpe ratio to .58, compared to .33 for the All Stocks universe. This 25-stock portfolio had a maximum decline of 57.26 percent, which is not much worse than All Stocks' maximum 55.30 percent decline.

All base rates for the 25-stock portfolio from the Earnings Quality Composite are positive, with the group beating All Stocks in 90 percent of all rolling five-year periods and in 100 percent of all rolling ten-year periods. Table 14.95 shows the base rates for all holding periods.

TABLE 14.94

Summary Annual Return and Risk Results Data: All Stocks Combined Earnings Quality Composite High 25, All Stocks Combined Earnings Quality Low 25, and All Stocks, January 1, 1964, to December 31, 2009

	All Stocks combined earnings quality composite low 25	All Stocks combined earnings quality composite high 25	All Stocks
Arithmetic average	4.86%	20.83%	13.26%
Geometric average	0.08%	17.92%	11.22%
Median return	8.99%	26.12%	17.16%
Standard deviation	30.18%	22.17%	18.99%
Upside deviation	18.38%	13.87%	10.98%
Downside deviation	20.83%	15.75%	13.90%
Tracking error	15.35	8.60	0.00
Number of positive periods	298	344	329
Number of negative periods	254	208	223
Maximum peak-to-trough decline	−90.10%	−57.26%	−55.54%
Beta	1.44	1.08	1.00
T-statistic (m = 0)	1.07	5.84	4.47
Sharpe ratio (Rf = 5%)	−0.16	0.58	0.33
Sortino ratio (MAR = 10%)	−0.48	0.50	0.09
$10,000 becomes	$10,389	$19,611,978	$1,329,513
Minimum 1-year return	−68.25%	−43.19%	−46.49%
Maximum 1-year return	94.42%	120.34%	84.19%
Minimum 3-year return	−49.24%	−21.52%	−18.68%
Maximum 3-year return	45.31%	49.64%	31.49%
Minimum 5-year return	−25.80%	−9.05%	−9.91%
Maximum 5-year return	27.52%	40.75%	27.66%
Minimum 7-year return	−20.99%	−1.46%	−6.32%
Maximum 7-year return	21.44%	37.29%	23.77%
Minimum 10-year return	−15.19%	2.88%	1.01%
Maximum 10-year return	14.65%	35.04%	22.05%
Minimum expected return*	−55.49%	−23.50%	−24.73%
Maximum expected return†	65.21%	65.17%	51.24%

* Minimum expected return is arithmetic return minus 2 times the standard deviation.
† Maximum expected return is arithmetic return plus 2 times the standard deviation.

TABLE 14.95

Base Rates for All Stocks Combined Earnings Quality Composite High 25 and All Stocks, January 1, 1964, to December 31, 2009

Item	All Stocks combined earnings quality composite high 25 beat All Stocks	Percent	Average annual excess return
Single-year return	395 out of 541	73%	7.73%
Rolling 3-year compound return	416 out of 517	80%	7.26%
Rolling 5-year compound return	446 out of 493	90%	7.38%
Rolling 7-year compound return	438 out of 469	93%	7.71%
Rolling 10-year compound return	431 out of 433	100%	8.28%

Looking at the 25-stock Earnings Quality Composite portfolio from All Stocks that scored the *worst*, we see that it helps investors to know which stocks to *avoid*. The $10,000 invested in the 25 stocks with the worst scores grew to just $10,389 between 1962 and 2009, an average annual compound return of 0.08 percent! If you took inflation into account, the investment would have been nearly wiped out. Indeed, accounting for inflation over the period would have seen the real value of that initial $10,000 investment worth just $1,485 at the end of 2009. What's worse, the risk of the strategy was huge—the 25 stocks with the worst scores had a standard deviation of return of 30.18 percent. That brings its Sharpe ratio to an abysmal –0.16. The maximum decline for the group was a portfolio-crushing 90.10 percent. As Table 14.96 shows, all base rates for the group were negative, with the group beating All Stocks in just 7 percent of all rolling five-year periods and in no rolling ten-year periods. The results for investors who want a more widely diversified 50-stock portfolio are similar, with the 50-stock portfolio with the best scores from the Earnings Quality Composite earning 16.78 percent a year between 1963 and 2009 and the 50-stock portfolio with the worst scores earning just 0.83 percent per year.

T A B L E   14.96

Base Rates for All Stocks Combined Earnings Quality Low 25 and All Stocks, January 1, 1964, to December 31, 2009

Item	All Stocks combined earnings quality composite low 25 beat All Stocks	Percent	Average annual excess return
Single-year return	159 out of 541	29%	−7.99%
Rolling 3-year compound return	76 out of 517	15%	−10.75%
Rolling 5-year compound return	35 out of 493	7%	−11.79%
Rolling 7-year compound return	17 out of 469	4%	−12.30%
Rolling 10-year compound return	0 out of 433	0%	−12.63%

LARGE STOCKS

The results from the Earnings Quality Composite work well with Large Stocks as well, but the returns are more muted. As you can see by looking at Table 14.97, decile 1—those Large Stocks with the best combined scores—performs the best of all of the deciles, with $10,000 invested on December 31, 1963, growing to $2,575,924, an average annual compound return of 12.83 percent. That's much better than the $872,861 you would have earned with a similar investment in the Large Stocks universe, which compounded at 10.20 percent over the same period. The standard deviation of return for the Earnings Quality Composite group was 15.91 percent, slightly lower than Large Stocks' 16.50 percent. The higher return married to a relatively low standard deviation of return generated a Sharpe ratio of .49 for the group, compared to .32 for the Large Stocks universe. The maximum decline of 49 percent was actually slightly better than Large Stocks' 53.77 percent. Table 14.98 shows all summary information for deciles 1 and 10. All base rates, featured in Table 14.100, were positive, with the group beating the Large Stocks universe in 88 percent of all rolling five-year periods and 100 percent of all rolling ten-year periods.

T A B L E   14.97

Summary Results for COMP Earnings Quality Composite Decile Analysis of Large Stocks Universe, January 1, 1964, to December 31, 2009

Decile	$10,000 grows to	Average return	Compound return	Standard deviation	Sharpe ratio
1 (highest)	$2,575,924	14.25%	12.83%	15.91%	0.49
2	$1,716,641	13.01%	11.84%	14.45%	0.47
3	$1,116,015	12.02%	10.79%	14.84%	0.39
4	$1,173,365	12.18%	10.91%	15.06%	0.39
5	$837,890	11.39%	10.11%	15.25%	0.33
6	$784,911	11.37%	9.95%	16.05%	0.31
7	$488,031	10.35%	8.82%	16.71%	0.23
8	$393,881	9.74%	8.31%	16.14%	0.21
9	$313,195	9.37%	7.77%	17.11%	0.16
10 (lowest)	$136,740	7.76%	5.85%	18.75%	0.05
Large Stocks	$872,861	11.72%	10.20%	16.50%	0.32

T A B L E   14.98

Summary Annual Return and Risk Results Data: Large Stock COMP Earnings Quality Decile 10, Large Stocks COMP Earnings Quality Composite Decile 1, and Large Stocks, January 1, 1964, to December 31, 2009

	Large Stocks COMP earnings quality decile 10	Large Stocks COMP earnings quality decile 1	Large Stocks
Arithmetic average	7.76%	14.25%	11.72%
Geometric average	5.85%	12.83%	10.20%
Median return	11.37%	17.31%	17.20%
Standard deviation	18.75%	15.91%	16.50%
Upside deviation	10.99%	9.81%	9.70%
Downside deviation	13.76%	10.91%	11.85%
Tracking error	6.24	6.35	0.00
Number of positive periods	304	342	332
Number of negative periods	248	210	220
Maximum peak-to-trough decline	−61.33%	−49.00%	−53.77%
Beta	1.07	0.89	1.00
T-statistic (m = 0)	2.71	5.71	4.58
Sharpe ratio (Rf = 5%)	0.05	0.49	0.32
Sortino ratio (MAR = 10%)	−0.30	0.26	0.02
$10,000 becomes	$136,740	$2,575,924	$872,861
Minimum 1-year return	−52.05%	−43.38%	−46.91%
Maximum 1-year return	66.70%	56.88%	68.96%
Minimum 3-year return	−25.76%	−12.96%	−15.89%
Maximum 3-year return	29.46%	42.92%	33.12%
Minimum 5-year return	−12.30%	−2.90%	−5.82%
Maximum 5-year return	25.85%	34.95%	28.95%

(continued on next page)

T A B L E   14.98

Summary Annual Return and Risk Results Data: Large Stock COMP Earnings Quality Decile 10, Large Stocks COMP Earnings Quality Composite Decile 1, and Large Stocks, January 1, 1964, to December 31, 2009 *(Continued)*

	Large Stocks COMP earnings quality decile 10	Large Stocks COMP earnings quality decile 1	Large Stocks
Minimum 7-year return	−8.13%	−1.24%	−4.15%
Maximum 7-year return	19.99%	27.57%	22.83%
Minimum 10-year return	−5.70%	2.21%	−0.15%
Maximum 10-year return	14.63%	23.45%	19.57%
Minimum expected return*	−29.75%	−17.56%	−21.28%
Maximum expected return†	45.26%	46.07%	44.72%

* Minimum expected return is arithmetic return minus 2 times the standard deviation.
† Maximum expected return is arithmetic return plus 2 times the standard deviation.

T A B L E   14.99

Base Rates for Large Stocks COMP Earnings Quality Composite Decile 10 and Large Stocks, January 1, 1964, to December 31, 2009

Item	Large Stocks COMP earnings quality decile 10 beat Large Stocks	Percent	Average annual excess return
Single-year return	139 out of 541	26%	−3.86%
Rolling 3-year compound return	78 out of 517	15%	−4.20%
Rolling 5-year compound return	30 out of 493	6%	−4.46%
Rolling 7-year compound return	7 out of 469	1%	−4.69%
Rolling 10-year compound return	0 out of 433	0%	−4.89%

T A B L E   14.100

Base Rates for Large Stocks COMP Earnings Quality Decile 1 and Large Stocks, January 1, 1964, to December 31, 2009

Item	Large Stocks COMP earnings quality decile 1 beat Large Stocks	Percent	Average annual excess return
Single-year return	377 out of 541	70%	2.75%
Rolling 3-year compound return	428 out of 517	83%	2.85%
Rolling 5-year compound return	433 out of 493	88%	2.88%
Rolling 7-year compound return	434 out of 469	93%	2.88%
Rolling 10-year compound return	432 out of 433	100%	2.95%

Decile 10—those Large Stocks with the worst scores from the Earnings Quality Composite—turned $10,000 into $136,740, an average annual compound return of 5.85 percent, just slightly better than the 5.57 percent annual return you would have earned from an investment in U.S. T-bills. The group with the worst scores from the Earnings

Quality Composite were also riskier—with a standard deviation of return of 18.75 percent versus 16.50 for the Large Stocks universe. The higher risk married to the lower returns brought the Sharpe ratio to .05, compared to .32 for the Large Stocks universe. All base rates for the group, featured in Table 14.99, were negative, with decile 10 beating the Large Stocks universe in only 6 percent of all rolling five-year periods and in no rolling ten-year periods.

IMPLICATIONS

Accounting variables matter. How companies account for accruals, how quickly they depreciate capital expenses and their additions to debt all have a serious impact on the health of their stock price. We have seen that, in many instances, it is just as important to know what to avoid: for example, be very wary of any stock that suddenly lands in the top decile by percentage increase in debt. Equally as troublesome are companies with poor coverage ratios; they do well only in speculative, frothy markets, and their success is an excellent warning that the market may be headed for a fall. Above all, we've seen that by combining several individual accounting variables into a master Earnings Quality Composite leads to even better results than using any accounting factor individually. We see later in the book how these composited factors can be extremely useful in developing multifactor strategies that do significantly better than the market. Now let's see if that is also true for the traditional valuation ratios such as PE and price-to-sales ratios.

15
C H A P T E R

COMBINING VALUE FACTORS INTO A SINGLE COMPOSITE FACTOR

The rational man—like the Loch Ness monster—is sighted often, but photographed rarely.
—David Dreman

As I point out in earlier chapters, there appears to be an ongoing horse race among the individual factors—such as PE ratios, price-to-cashflow, and EBITDA/EV—as to which is the single best performing ratio. In the original version of this book my research was conducted using annual returns with a single December data series because that was all that was available in 1996. Then I found that price-to-sales was the single best-performing factor. Yet now, using the much larger databases that include monthly data and our more sophisticated compositing methodology, I have found that EBITDA/EV has unseated the price-to-sales ratio (PSR) as the single best-performing factor. There are three reasons for this: (1) our new methodology and data have changed the way we look at single factors; (2) because the stocks with the lowest price-to-sales ratios from All Stocks suffered a larger hit between May 2007 and February 2009 than several of the other value factors; and (3) because when we study the various time periods, which factor provides the "best" return continues to change, with one period being won by PSR, while another is EBITDA/EV, and yet another cash flow to enterprise value.

The idea of building a master value composite factor came to me after reading "Returns to Trading Strategies Based on Price-to-Earnings and Price-to-Sales Ratios."

In the article, authors Siva Nathan, Kumar Sivakumar, and Jayaraman Vijayakumar argue that combining PE and price-to-sales ratios provided better returns than either factor alone. Indeed, they claimed that, "We show that an investment strategy using both P/E and P/S ratios simultaneously, and going long or short stocks based on the magnitudes of these ratios, yields an average annual *excess return* of 28.89%. This far exceeds the annual *raw returns* of 16.01% reported by O'Shaughnessy using a strategy of going long the 50 stocks with the lowest P/S ratios each year."

I was intrigued by this notion of merging value variables, even though I felt that the time period of their study—1990 through 1996—wasn't long enough to truly test the efficacy or robustness of the strategy. The period they studied did not include the technology bubble between 1997 and February 2000, and it was also a period when value factors generally enjoyed excellent returns. For example, between January 1, 1990, and December 31, 1996, the decile of All Stocks with the lowest PE ratios returned 17 percent per year, and the decile of stocks with the best EBITDA/EV returned 19.37 percent; whereas the decile with the lowest PSRs returned 13.74 percent, and the All Stocks universe gained 13.80 percent. Of the three value factors, PSR actually *underperformed* the All Stocks universe while the other two did significantly better. Nevertheless, I felt it was a compelling idea and decided to run a test over the full period for which we have monthly data for all the factors, from 1963 to 2009.

First, we analyze just balance sheet and cash flow factors for a "pure play" combined value factor that we will call Value Factor One. It is made up of the following factors:

1. Price-to-book
2. Price-to-earnings
3. Price-to-sales
4. EBITDA/EV
5. Price-to-cash flow

Next, we see if the addition of shareholder yield can improve the results of the pure play Value Factor One. Thus our second factor combination tests the five listed above but also includes shareholder yield (buyback yield plus dividend yield).

For each combined group of factors, we assign a percentile ranking (from 1 to 100) for each stock in the All Stocks and Large Stocks universes. If a stock has a PE ratio that is in the lowest 1 percent for the universe, it receives a rank of 100; if a stock has a PE ratio in the highest 1 percent for the universe, it receives a rank of 1. We follow a similar convention for each of the factors. Thus, if a stock is in the lowest 1 percent of the universe based on its price-to-sales ratio, it gets 100; if it's in the highest 1 percent, it gets a 1. If a value is missing for a factor, we assign it a neutral rank of 50. For shareholder yield and EBITDA/EV, those stocks in the 1 percent of the universe with the *highest* values are ranked 100, whereas those within the lowest 1 percent are be ranked 1. Once all factors are ranked, we add up all their rankings and assign the stocks to deciles based upon their overall cumulative ranking. Those with the highest scores are assigned to decile 1, while those with the lowest scores are assigned to decile 10.

Thus the stocks in decile 1 would feature the best combined score and would have the lowest PEs, PSRs, and so on, whereas the stocks in decile 10 would have the *highest* PEs, PSRs, and so on. Let's first look at the performance of the pure-play Value Factor One compared to All Stocks and Large Stocks.

THE RESULTS

$10,000 invested in decile 1 of Value Factor One (price-to-book; PE; price-to-cash flow; PSR, and EBITDA/EV) on December 31, 1963, grew to $14,688,089 by the end of 2009, an average annual compound return of 17.18 percent. That's better than any of the single value factors we have studied and dwarfs the return of a similar investment in the All Stocks universe, where the same $10,000 grew to $1,329,513, a compound average annual return of 11.22 percent. Value Factor One's risk, as measured by the standard deviation of return, was lower than that of the All Stocks universe, coming in at 18.09 percent versus 18.99 percent for the All Stocks universe. Value Factor One's downside risk of 13.50 percent was also lower than All Stocks' 13.90 percent. What's more, with the exception of some one-year returns, all three-, five-, seven-, and ten-year minimum returns and maximum returns are superior to the All Stocks universe. Thus the stocks in decile 1 of Value Factor One delivered better downside protection while offering superior maximum returns. The higher returns married to lower risk yielded a Sharpe ratio of .67, among the highest we've seen for any factor. That Sharpe ratio is nearly double the .33 earned by the All Stocks universe itself. Table 15.1 details all the relevant statistical information for Value Factor One and the All Stocks universe. Note that in the table, we refer to Value Factor One as VC1.

T A B L E   15.1

Summary Return and Risk Results for Annual Data: All Stocks VC1 Decile 1 and All Stocks, January 1, 1964 to December 31, 2009

	All Stocks VC 1 decile 1	All Stocks
Arithmetic average	19.09%	13.26%
Geometric average	17.18%	11.22%
Median return	23.52%	17.16%
Standard deviation	18.09%	18.99%
Upside deviation	11.77%	10.98%
Downside deviation	13.50%	13.90%
Tracking error	7.50	0.00
Number of positive periods	363	329
Number of negative periods	189	223
Maximum peak-to-trough decline	−57.78%	−55.54%
Beta	0.88	1.00

(continued on next page)

T A B L E   15.1

Summary Return and Risk Results for Annual Data: All Stocks VC1 Decile 1 and All Stocks, January 1, 1964 to December 31, 2009 *(Continued)*

	AS VC 1 decile 1	All Stocks
T-statistic (m = 0)	6.60	4.47
Sharpe ratio (Rf = 5%)	0.67	0.33
Sortino ratio (MAR = 10%)	0.53	0.09
$10,000 becomes	$14,688,089	$1,329,513
Minimum 1-year return	−48.24%	−46.49%
Maximum 1-year return	81.40%	84.19%
Minimum 3-year return	−17.00%	−18.68%
Maximum 3-year return	41.09%	31.49%
Minimum 5-year return	−5.33%	−9.91%
Maximum 5-year return	35.49%	27.66%
Minimum 7-year return	−1.25%	−6.32%
Maximum 7-year return	30.19%	23.77%
Minimum 10-year return	6.08%	1.01%
Maximum 10-year return	29.41%	22.05%
Minimum expected return*	−17.10%	−24.73%
Maximum expected return†	55.28%	51.24%

* Minimum expected return is arithmetic return minus 2 times the standard deviation.
† Maximum expected return is arithmetic return plus 2 times the standard deviation.

All base rates are positive, with Value Factor One beating the All Stocks universe in 98 percent of all rolling five-year periods and in 100 percent of all rolling ten-year periods. Table 15.2 shows the base rates for all holding periods. Table 15.3 shows all drops exceeding 20 percent since 1963, whereas Tables 15.4 and 15.5 show the best and worst returns for a variety of holding periods. We revisit these tables when we look at worst-case scenarios for Value Factor One later in the chapter. Figure 15.1 shows the five-year average annual excess (deficient) return for Value Factor One minus the returns for All Stocks.

T A B L E   15.2

Base Rates for All Stocks VC1 Decile 1 and All Stocks, January 1, 1964, to December 31, 2009

Item	All Stocks VC1 decile 1 beat All Stocks	Percent	Average annual excess return
Single-year return	420 out of 541	78%	5.70%
Rolling 3-year compound return	481 out of 517	93%	5.82%
Rolling 5-year compound return	484 out of 493	98%	5.88%
Rolling 7-year compound return	462 out of 469	99%	5.89%
Rolling 10-year compound return	431 out of 433	100%	5.80%

T A B L E   15.3

Worst-Case Scenarios: All 20 Percent or Greater Declines for All Stocks VC1 Decile 1, January 1, 1964, to December 31, 2009

Peak date	Peak index value	Trough date	Trough index value	Recovery date	Decline (%)	Decline duration	Recovery duration
Jan–69	3.39	Jun–70	2.02	Feb–72	−40.38%	17	20
Nov–72	3.51	Sep–74	2.23	May–75	−36.56%	22	8
Aug–87	61.55	Nov–87	45.41	Jan–89	−26.23%	3	14
Aug–89	77.09	Oct–90	54.46	Mar–91	−29.35%	14	5
Apr–98	356.62	Aug–98	280.06	Jun–99	−21.47%	4	10
Apr–02	591.59	Sep–02	444.05	Jul–03	−24.94%	5	10
May–07	1,638.90	Feb–09	691.91	N/A	−57.78%	21	N/A
Average					−33.82%	12.29	11.17

T A B L E   15.4

Best and Worst Average Annual Compound Returns for Monthly Data, January 1, 1964, to December 31, 2009

For any	1-year period	3-year period	5-year period	7-year period	10-year period
All Stocks VC1 decile 1 minimum compound return	−48.24%	−17.00%	−5.33%	−1.25%	6.08%
All Stocks VC1 decile 1 maximum compound return	81.40%	41.09%	35.49%	30.19%	29.41%
All Stocks minimum compound return	−46.49%	−18.68%	−9.91%	−6.32%	1.01%
All Stocks maximum compound return	84.19%	31.49%	27.66%	23.77%	22.05%
All Stocks VC1 decile 10 minimum compound return	−71.59%	−53.72%	−31.25%	−22.49%	−16.22%
All Stocks VC1 decile 10 maximum compound return	215.77%	56.66%	38.69%	26.29%	19.09%

T A B L E   15.5

Terminal Value of $10,000 Invested for Best and Worst Average Annual Compound Returns for Monthly Data, January 1, 1964, to December 31, 2009

For any	1-year period	3-year period	5-year period	7-year period	10-year period
All Stocks VC1 decile 1 minimum $10,000 value	$5,176	$5,717	$7,604	$9,155	$18,041
All Stocks VC1 decile 1 maximum $10,000 value	$18,140	$28,085	$45,658	$63,377	$131,777
All Stocks minimum $10,000 value	$5,351	$5,379	$5,936	$6,330	$11,054
All Stocks maximum $10,000 value	$18,419	$22,734	$33,903	$44,504	$73,345
All Stocks VC1 decile 10 minimum $10,000 value	$2,841	$991	$1,536	$1,681	$1,704
All Stocks VC1 decile 10 maximum $10,000 value	$31,577	$38,450	$51,319	$51,223	$57,396

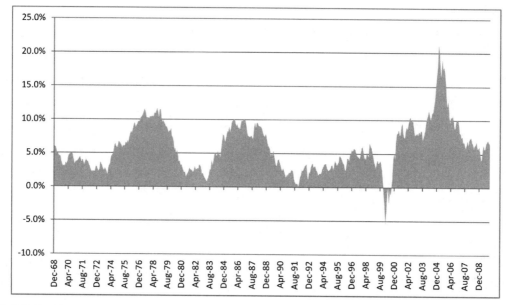

FIGURE 15.1

Five-year average annual compound excess (deficient) return All Stocks VC1 Decile 1 minus All Stocks, January 1, 1964, to December 31, 2009

LARGE STOCKS ALSO STRONG

The $10,000 invested in decile 1 of Value Factor One from Large Stocks grew to $3,335,373, an average annual compound return of 13.46 percent, vastly better than the $872,861 you'd have earned with an investment in the Large Stocks universe, which earned an average annual compound return of 10.20 percent. Unlike the All Stocks group, the standard deviation of return for Value Factor One from Large Stocks was higher than the universe's standard deviation, coming in at 16.68 percent compared to 16.50 percent for the Large Stocks universe. Downside risk was largely similar—11.87 percent compared to 11.85 percent for the Large Stocks universe. The Sharpe ratio for the value factor group was a strong .51, well ahead of the .32 earned by the Large Stocks universe. Table 15.6 shows the relevant statistics for Value Factor One and Large Stocks.

TABLE 15.6

Summary Return and Risk Results for Annual Data: Large Stocks VC1 Decile 1 (High) and Large Stocks, January 1, 1964, to December 31, 2009

	Large Stocks VC1 Decile 1 (High)	Large Stocks
Arithmetic average	15.04%	11.72%
Geometric average	13.46%	10.20%

(continued on next page)

TABLE 15.6

Summary Return and Risk Results for Annual Data: Large Stocks VC1 Decile 1 (High) and Large Stocks, January 1, 1964, to December 31, 2009 *(Continued)*

	Large Stocks VC1 Decile 1 (High)	Large Stocks
Median return	18.42%	17.20%
Standard deviation	16.68%	16.50%
Upside deviation	10.63%	9.70%
Downside deviation	11.87%	11.85%
Tracking error	8.20	0.00
Number of positive periods	344	332
Number of negative periods	208	220
Maximum peak-to-trough decline	−61.86%	−53.77%
Beta	0.89	1.00
T-statistic (m = 0)	5.73	4.58
Sharpe ratio (Rf = 5%)	0.51	0.32
Sortino ratio (MAR = 10%)	0.29	0.02
$10,000 becomes	$3,335,373	$872,861
Minimum 1-year return	−55.57%	−46.91%
Maximum 1-year return	72.36%	68.96%
Minimum 3-year return	−16.99%	−15.89%
Maximum 3-year return	37.73%	33.12%
Minimum 5-year return	−2.03%	−5.82%
Maximum 5-year return	35.12%	28.95%
Minimum 7-year return	0.26%	−4.15%
Maximum 7-year return	27.27%	22.83%
Minimum 10-year return	2.36%	−0.15%
Maximum 10-year return	22.19%	19.57%
Minimum expected return*	−18.31%	−21.28%
Maximum expected return†	48.40%	44.72%

* Minimum expected return is arithmetic return minus 2 times the standard deviation.
† Maximum expected return is arithmetic return plus 2 times the standard deviation.

All base rates were positive, with the group beating the Large Stocks universe in 78 percent of all rolling five-year periods and in 97 percent of all rolling ten-year periods. Table 15.7 shows the base rates for all holding periods. Figure 15.2 shows the five-year average annual excess (deficient) return for Value Factor One minus the returns for Large Stocks.

T A B L E   15.7

Base Rates for Large Stocks VC1 Decile 1 (High) and Large Stocks, January 1, 1964, to December 31, 2009

Item	Large Stocks VC1 decile 1 (high) beat Large Stocks	Percent	Average annual excess return
Single-year return	339 out of 541	63%	3.35%
Rolling 3-year compound return	377 out of 517	73%	3.50%
Rolling 5-year compound return	385 out of 493	78%	3.61%
Rolling 7-year compound return	404 out of 469	86%	3.61%
Rolling 10-year compound return	420 out of 433	97%	3.56%

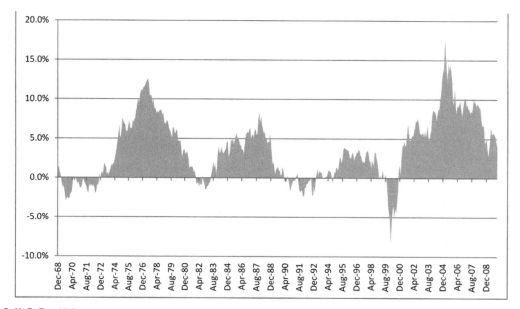

F I G U R E   15.2

Five-year average annual compound excess (deficient) return Large Stocks VC1 decile 1 (high) minus Large Stocks, January 1, 1964, to December 31, 2009

WORST-CASE SCENARIOS AND BEST AND WORST RETURNS

Decile 1 for the Value Factor One group from All Stocks had seven declines of 20 percent or more between 1964 and 2009. The largest decline occurred between May 2007 and February 2009, when the group lost 58 percent. Table 15.3 shows all declines greater than 20 percent for the period.

The best absolute five-year return for the group occurred in the five years ending September 1979, when it earned 35.49 percent and turned $10,000 into $45,658. Table 15.5 shows the terminal value of $10,000 invested in other best- and worst-case periods.

The worst five-year absolute return for the Value Factor One group occurred in the five years ending December 1973, when the group lost an average 5.33 percent per year and turned $10,000 into $7,604.

The best relative five-year performance for the Value Factor One group versus All Stocks occurred in the five years ending February 2005, when the group earned an average annual compound return of 25.45 percent, while the All Stocks universe compounded at just 4.38 percent a year, an average annual advantage for the group of 21.07 percent per year and a five-year cumulative advantage of 186 percent over the All Stocks universe.

The worst relative five-year performance for the group versus All Stocks occurred in the five-years ending February 2000, when the group earned an average annual compound return of 16.74 percent compared to 22.54 percent for the All Stocks universe compounded, an average annual deficit for the group of 5.8 percent per year and a cumulative deficit of 59 percent. Figure 15.1 shows the average annual compound excess return (alpha) of the group minus the average annual return for the All Stocks universe.

Looking at decile 1 of Value Factor One from the Large Stocks universe, we see that there were seven instances between 1964 and 2009 when it declined by 20 percent or more. The worst decline occurred between October 2007 and February 2009, when the group lost 62 percent. As with the group from All Stocks, all other declines were more muted than those we have seen with other individual factors. Table 15.8 shows all declines greater than 20 percent since 1964.

T A B L E 15.8

Worst-Case Scenarios: All 20 Percent or Greater Declines for Large Stocks VC1 Decile 1 (High), January 1, 1964, to December 31, 2009

Peak date	Peak index value	Trough date	Trough index value	Recovery date	Decline (%)	Decline duration	Recovery duration
Jan–69	1.92	Jun–70	1.22	Aug–72	−36.07%	17	26
Oct–73	2.11	Sep–74	1.58	Mar–75	−24.88%	11	6
Jun–81	6.73	Jul–82	5.33	Oct–82	−20.74%	13	3
Aug–87	24.77	Nov–87	18.70	Jan–89	−24.51%	3	14
Aug–89	30.27	Oct–90	22.38	May–91	−26.07%	14	7
Mar–02	159.66	Sep–02	125.42	Jul–03	−21.44%	6	10
Oct–07	474.69	Feb–09	181.04	N/A	−61.86%	16	N/A
Average					−30.80%	11.43	11

The best absolute five-year performance for the group occurred in the five years ending July 1987, when it earned an average annual compound return of 35.12 percent per year, turning $10,000 invested into $45,044.

The worst absolute five-year return occurred during the five years ending February 2009, when it lost an average annual compound return of 2.03 percent, turning $10,000 into $9,027. Tables 15.9 and 15.10 show the best and worst returns for a variety of holding periods.

T A B L E   15.9

Best and Worst Average Annual Compound Returns for Monthly Data, January 1, 1964, to December 31, 2009

For any	1-year period	3-year period	5-year period	7-year period	10-year period
Large Stocks VC1 decile 1 (high) minimum compound return	−55.57%	−16.99%	−2.03%	0.26%	2.36%
Large Stocks VC1 decile 1 (high) maximum compound return	72.36%	37.73%	35.12%	27.27%	22.19%
Large Stocks minimum compound return	−46.91%	−15.89%	−5.82%	−4.15%	−0.15%
Large Stocks maximum compound return	68.96%	33.12%	28.95%	22.83%	19.57%
Large Stocks VC1 decile 10 (low) minimum compound return	−78.05%	−45.26%	−25.22%	−16.48%	−11.49%
Large Stocks VC1 decile 10 (low) maximum compound return	91.71%	51.26%	35.39%	24.91%	20.36%

T A B L E   15.10

Terminal Value of $10,000 Invested for Best and Worst Average Annual Compound Returns for Monthly Data, January 1, 1964, to December 31, 2009

For any	1-year period	3-year period	5-year period	7-year period	10-year period
Large Stocks VC1 decile 1 (high) minimum $10,000 value	$4,443	$5,720	$9,027	$10,180	$12,626
Large Stocks VC1 decile 1 (high) maximum $10,000 value	$17,236	$26,125	$45,044	$54,099	$74,174
Large Stocks minimum $10,000 value	$5,309	$5,951	$7,409	$7,434	$9,848
Large Stocks maximum $10,000 value	$16,896	$23,591	$35,656	$42,189	$59,747
Large Stocks VC1 decile 10 (low) minimum $10,000 value	$2,195	$1,640	$2,339	$2,835	$2,951
Large Stocks VC1 decile 10 (low) maximum $10,000 value	$19,171	$34,609	$45,495	$47,447	$63,795

The best relative five-year performance for the group occurred during the five years ending February 2005, when it earned an average annual compound return of 19.30 percent versus Large Stocks' 1.80 percent. That's a 17.50 percent average annual compound return advantage and a cumulative advantage of 134 percent.

The worst relative five-year performance for the Value Factor One group occurred in the five years ending February 2000, when it earned an average annual compound return of 14.67 percent compared to the Large Stocks universe's 22.87 percent, an average annual compound deficit of 8.2 percent for the group versus Large Stocks, and a cumulative deficit to Large Stocks of 84 percent. Figure 15.2 shows the excess return (alpha) over Large Stocks for all five-year holding periods.

THE WORST DECILE FOR VALUE FACTOR ONE LIVES UP TO ITS NAME

The $10,000 invested in decile 10 from Value Factor One from the All Stocks universe—the 10 percent of stocks from All Stocks with the *highest* PEs, PSRs, and so on—grew to just $38,481 by the end of 2009, a measly average annual compound return of 2.97 percent. That awful return was dwarfed by an investment in the All Stocks universe, where $10,000 grew to $1,329,513 over the same period, an average annual compound return of 11.22 percent. It's also less than half the $120,778 you'd have earned if you simply invested in 30-day U.S. T-bills, which compounded at 5.57 percent over the period. Risk—as determined by the standard deviation of return—was a very high 27.80 percent compared to 18.99 percent for the All Stocks universe. The combination of dreadful returns with high risk brought the Sharpe ratio in at −.07 for the group, compared to a Sharpe ratio of .33 for the All Stocks universe. The minimum returns for tenth decile are also deplorable, with their minimum 10-year return at an astounding *loss* of 16.22 percent a year compared with a *gain* of 1.01 percent per year for the All Stocks universe. Table 15.11 shows all the relevant statistics for the group and for the All Stocks universe.

T A B L E 15.11

Summary Return and Risk Results for Annual Data: All Stocks VC1 Decile 10 and All Stocks, January 1, 1964, to December 31, 2009

	All Stocks VC1 Decile 10	All Stocks
Arithmetic average	7.11%	13.26%
Geometric average	2.97%	11.22%
Median return	10.97%	17.16%
Standard deviation	27.80%	18.99%
Upside deviation	17.39%	10.98%
Downside deviation	20.32%	13.90%
Tracking error	14.03	0.00
Number of positive periods	312	329
Number of negative periods	240	223
Maximum peak-to-trough decline	−92.81%	−55.54%
Beta	1.30	1.00
T-statistic (m = 0)	1.68	4.47
Sharpe ratio (Rf = 5%)	−0.07	0.33
Sortino ratio (MAR = 10%)	−0.35	0.09
$10,000 becomes	$38,481	$1,329,513
Minimum 1-year return	−71.59%	−46.49%
Maximum 1-year return	215.77%	84.19%
Minimum 3-year return	−53.72%	−18.68%
Maximum 3-year return	56.66%	31.49%
Minimum 5-year return	−31.25%	−9.91%
Maximum 5-year return	38.69%	27.66%

(continued on next page)

TABLE 15.11

Summary Return and Risk Results for Annual Data: All Stocks VC1 Decile 10 and All Stocks, January 1, 1964, to December 31, 2009 *(Continued)*

	All Stocks VC1 Decile 10	All Stocks
Minimum 7-year return	−22.49%	−6.32%
Maximum 7-year return	26.29%	23.77%
Minimum 10-year return	−16.22%	1.01%
Maximum 10-year return	19.09%	22.05%
Minimum expected return*	−48.49%	−24.73%
Maximum expected return†	62.71%	51.24%

* Minimum expected return is arithmetic return minus 2 times the standard deviation.
† Maximum expected return is arithmetic return plus 2 times the standard deviation.

Base rates were all negative, with the group beating the All Stocks universe in only 15 percent of rolling five-year periods and in just 4 percent of all rolling ten-year periods. Table 15.12 shows the base rates for all holding periods. Table 15.13 shows all declines of 20 percent or more since 1963, which we revisit when we discuss worst-case scenarios. Figure 15.3 shows the five-year average annual compound excess (or, in this case, mostly deficient) return for decile 10 of All Stocks for Value Composite One minus the return for the All Stocks universe.

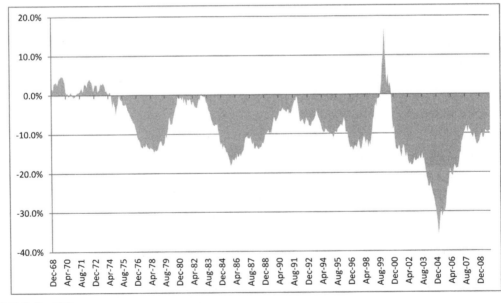

FIGURE 15.3

Five-year average annual compound excess (deficient) return All Stocks VC1 decile 10 minus All Stocks, January 1, 1964, to December 31, 2009

TABLE 15.12

Base Rates for All Stocks VC1 Decile 10 and All Stocks, January 1, 1964, to December 31, 2009

Item	All Stocks VC1 decile 10 beat All Stocks	Percent	Average annual excess return
Single-year return	186 out of 541	34%	−5.02%
Rolling 3-year compound return	121 out of 517	23%	−7.57%
Rolling 5-year compound return	76 out of 493	15%	−8.30%
Rolling 7-year compound return	47 out of 469	10%	−8.62%
Rolling 10-year compound return	18 out of 433	4%	−8.69%

TABLE 15.13

Worst-Case Scenarios: All 20 Percent or Greater Declines for All Stocks VC1 Decile 10, January 1, 1964, to December 31, 2009

Peak date	Peak index value	Trough date	Trough index value	Recovery date	Decline (%)	Decline duration	Recovery duration
Dec–68	2.82	Jun–70	1.42	Feb–72	−49.82%	18	20
May–72	3.11	Sep–74	1.18	Jan–80	−61.97%	28	64
Feb–80	3.38	Mar–80	2.64	Jul–80	−21.99%	1	4
Nov–80	5.02	Jul–82	2.85	Apr–83	−43.26%	20	9
Jun–83	6.02	Nov–84	3.52	Mar–87	−41.57%	17	28
Aug–87	6.33	Nov–87	4.03	May–90	−36.24%	3	30
May–90	6.40	Oct–90	4.61	Mar–91	−28.07%	5	5
Jan–92	8.54	Jun–94	5.89	Sep–95	−31.11%	29	15
May–96	11.43	Aug–98	6.24	Mar–99	−45.41%	27	7
Feb–00	33.15	Feb–09	2.38	N/A	−92.81%	108	N/A
Average					−45.23%	25.6	20.22

LARGE STOCKS ALSO HIT

The $10,000 invested in decile 10 of Value Factor One from Large Stocks grew to $93,708 by the end of 2009, an average annual compound return of 4.98 percent. That return was dwarfed by a similar investment in the Large Stocks universe, where $10,000 grew to $872,861, an average annual compound return of 10.20 percent. Like its All Stocks brothers, the Large Stocks group with the highest valuations was again outperformed by U.S. T-bills, which earned 5.57 percent a year over the period. Risk, as measured by the standard deviation of return, was 22.43 percent compared to 16.50 percent for the Large Stocks universe. The combination of low returns with high risk brought the Sharpe ratio to 0.0, compared to .32 for that of the Large Stocks universe. As we saw with the All Stocks group, the minimum returns over all holding periods were much worse for the strategy than for the Large Stocks universe. Table 15.14 shows the relevant statistics for the group versus the Large Stocks universe.

T A B L E   15.14

Summary Return and Risk Results for Annual Data: Large Stocks VC1 Decile 10 (Low) and Large Stocks, January 1, 1964, to December 31, 2009

	Large Stocks VC1 decile 10 (low)	Large Stocks
Arithmetic average	7.75%	11.72%
Geometric average	4.98%	10.20%
Median return	12.79%	17.20%
Standard deviation	22.43%	16.50%
Upside deviation	13.82%	9.70%
Downside deviation	17.47%	11.85%
Tracking error	12.01	0.00
Number of positive periods	314	332
Number of negative periods	238	220
Maximum peak-to-trough decline	−85.28%	−53.77%
Beta	1.16	1.00
T-statistic (m = 0)	2.26	4.58
Sharpe ratio (Rf = 5%)	0.00	0.32
Sortino ratio (MAR = 10%)	−0.29	0.02
$10,000 becomes	$93,708	$872,861
Minimum 1-year return	−78.05%	−46.91%
Maximum 1-year return	91.71%	68.96%
Minimum 3-year return	−45.26%	−15.89%
Maximum 3-year return	51.26%	33.12%
Minimum 5-year return	−25.22%	−5.82%
Maximum 5-year return	35.39%	28.95%
Minimum 7-year return	−16.48%	−4.15%
Maximum 7-year return	24.91%	22.83%
Minimum 10-year return	−11.49%	−0.15%
Maximum 10-year return	20.36%	19.57%
Minimum expected return*	−37.12%	−21.28%
Maximum expected return†	52.61%	44.72%

* Minimum expected return is arithmetic return minus 2 times the standard deviation.
† Maximum expected return is arithmetic return plus 2 times the standard deviation.

All base rates for the group are negative, with the high valuation Value Factor One from Large Stocks beating the universe in 18 percent of all rolling five-year periods and in 7 percent of all rolling ten-year periods. Table 15.15 shows the base rates for all holding periods. Figure 15.4 shows the five-year average annual compound excess (or, in this case, mostly deficient) return for decile 10 of Large Stocks for Value Composite One minus the return for the Large Stocks universe.

T A B L E 15.15

Base Rates for Large Stocks VC1 Decile 10 (Low) and Large Stocks, January 1, 1964, to December 31, 2009

Item	Large Stocks VC1 decile 10 (low) beat Large Stocks	Percent	Average annual excess return
Single-year return	211 out of 541	39%	−3.26%
Rolling 3-year compound return	132 out of 517	26%	−4.96%
Rolling 5-year compound return	90 out of 493	18%	−5.79%
Rolling 7-year compound return	55 out of 469	12%	−6.24%
Rolling 10-year compound return	29 out of 433	7%	−6.52%

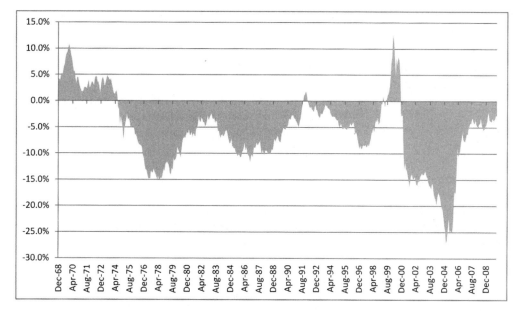

F I G U R E 15.4

Five-year average annual compound excess (deficient) return Large Stocks VC1 decile10 (low) minus Large Stocks, January 1, 1964, to December 31, 2009

WORST-CASE SCENARIOS AND BEST AND WORST RETURNS

Decile 10 of Value Factor One from All Stocks had 10 declines of 20 percent or more between 1964 and 2009. The worst decline began in February 2000, and the group has yet to recover—suffering a loss of 92.81 percent. The group has six separate losses of 40 percent or more since 1964—quite a horror show. Table 15.13 shows all declines greater than 20 percent for the group.

The best absolute five-year return for the group occurred in the five years ending February 2000, when the group earned an average annual compound return of 38.69 percent, turning $10,000 into $51,319.

The worst absolute five-year return for the group occurred in the five years ending February 2005, when the group lost an average annual 31.25 percent, turning $10,000 into $1,536. Table 15.5 shows the terminal value of $10,000 invested over other best- and worst-case periods.

The best relative five-year performance for the group was the same as the best absolute period, the five years ending February 2000, when the group earned an average annual compound return of 38.69 percent versus All Stocks 22.54 percent, an average annual compound advantage of 16.15 percent and a 237 percent cumulative outperformance.

The worst relative five-year return versus All Stocks occurred in the five years ending November 2005, when the group lost an average annual compound 14.44 percent compared to the All Stocks universe's *gain* of 11.07 percent per year, an average annual compound deficit of 25.51 percent, and a 123 percent cumulative loss to the All Stocks universe. Figure 15.3 shows the five-year average annual excess return (alpha) for the group for the entire period. In this case, it is almost all negative alpha. By plotting the five-year excess returns for decile 1 and decile 10 of Value Factor One from All Stocks, Figure 15.4 makes the case more dramatically.

By looking at decile 10 of Value Factor One from Large Stocks, we see that the group had five occasions when it declined by 20 percent or more between 1964 and 2009. The worst decline occurred between February 2000 and September 2002, when it plummeted 85 percent. It has still not recovered from this decline. Table 15.16 shows all declines of 20 percent or more for the group between 1964 and 2009.

T A B L E 15.16

Worst-Case Scenarios: All 20 Percent or Greater Declines for Large Stocks VC1 Decile 10 (Low), January 1, 1964, to December 31, 2009

Peak date	Peak index value	Trough date	Trough index value	Recovery date	Decline (%)	Decline duration	Recovery duration
Dec–69	2.48	Jun–70	1.66	Jun–71	−33.11%	6	12
Dec–72	3.36	Sep–74	1.35	Feb–83	−59.85%	21	101
Jun–83	4.06	May–84	2.86	Feb–86	−29.64%	11	21
Aug–87	5.84	Nov–87	3.85	Jul–89	−34.02%	3	20
Feb–00	37.43	Sep–02	5.51	N/A	−85.28%	31	N/A
Average					−48.38%	14.4	38.5

The best five-year absolute return for the group occurred in the five years ending February 2000, when the group earned an average annual compound return of 35.39 percent and turned $10,000 into $45,495.

The worst absolute five-year return for the group occurred in the five years ending February 2005, when the group lost an average annual compound return of 25.22 percent and turned $10,000 into $2,339. We can refer back to Table 15.10 to show the terminal value of $10,000 invested for other best- and worst-case holding periods.

The best relative five-year return for the group versus Large Stocks also occurred in the period ending February 2000, when it earned an average annual compound return of 35.39 percent versus the Large Stocks universe's 23.06 percent, an average annual compound advantage of 12.33 percent and a cumulative advantage of 173 percent over Large Stocks.

The worst five-year relative return for the group versus Large Stocks occurred in the five years ending January 1987, when the group earned an average annual compound return of 11.83 percent versus a gain of 22.54 percent per year for the Large Stocks universe, an average annual deficit of 10.71 percent and a cumulative deficit of 101 percent. Figure 15.4 show the five-year average annual compound excess return (alpha) for decile 10 of Value Factor One compared to the Large Stocks universe for the entire period.

FULL DECILE ANALYSIS

Tables 15.17 and 15.18 show the average annual compound return for deciles 1 and 10 from All Stocks and Large Stocks by decade. Looking at the results for all 10 deciles—featured in Figures 15.5 and 15.6, as well as Tables 15-Decile Addendum 1 and 15-Decile Addendum 2, we see a near perfect staircase of declining returns, with the highest returns coming from decile 1 and the lowest from decile 10. Deciles 1 through 5 all outperform the All Stocks universe, whereas deciles 6 through 10 all underperform, with decile 9 and 10 also losing to an investment in U.S. T-bills. We see much the same picture with the Large Stocks deciles, with deciles 1 through 4 all outperforming the Large Stocks universe, while deciles 5 through 10 all underperform, with decile 10 also underperforming U.S. T-bills.

T A B L E 15.17

Average Annual Compound Rates of Return by Decade

	1960s*	1970s	1980s	1990s	2000s†
All Stocks VC1 decile 1	16.84%	14.78%	22.21%	16.34%	15.73%
All Stocks VC1 decile 10	15.88%	2.22%	7.42%	13.85%	−16.22%
All Stocks	13.36%	7.56%	16.78%	15.35%	4.39%

* Returns for January 1, 1964, to December 31, 1969.
† Returns for January 1, 2000, to December 31, 2009.

T A B L E 15.18

Average Annual Compound Rates of Return by Decade

	1960s*	1970s	1980s	1990s	2000s†
Large Stocks VC1 decile 1 (high)	6.54%	12.75%	19.84%	14.64%	11.10%
Large Stocks VC1 decile 10 (low)	16.37%	−0.97%	10.73%	17.66%	−11.49%
Large Stocks	8.16%	6.65%	17.34%	16.38%	2.42%

* Returns for January 1, 1964, to December 31, 1969.
† Returns for January 1, 2000, to December 31, 2009.

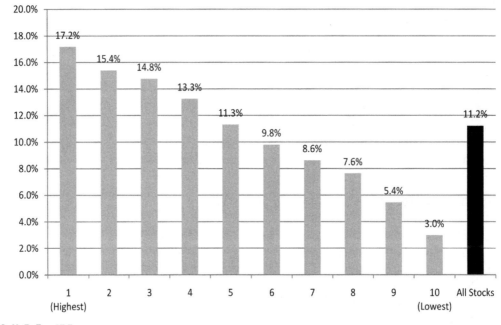

F I G U R E 15.5

Average annual compound return by VC1 decile, All Stocks universe, January 1, 1964, to December 31, 2009

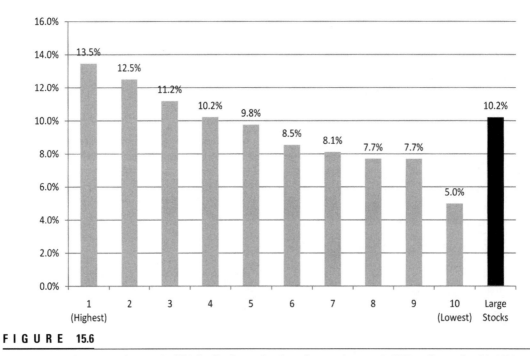

F I G U R E 15.6

Average annual compound return by VC1 decile, Large Stocks universe, January 1, 1964, to December 31, 2009

T A B L E   15-DECILE ADDENDUM 1

Summary Results for VC Decile Analysis of All Stocks Universe, January 1, 1964, to December 31, 2009

Decile	$10,000 grows to	Average return	Compound return	Standard deviation	Sharpe ratio
1 (highest)	$14,688,089	19.09%	17.18%	18.09%	0.67
2	$7,262,781	17.13%	15.40%	17.30%	0.60
3	$5,634,919	16.40%	14.76%	16.83%	0.58
4	$3,066,959	14.81%	13.26%	16.46%	0.50
5	$1,380,234	12.81%	11.31%	16.30%	0.39
6	$735,230	11.36%	9.79%	16.75%	0.29
7	$449,449	10.42%	8.62%	17.98%	0.20
8	$295,378	9.84%	7.64%	19.99%	0.13
9	$114,369	8.43%	5.44%	23.46%	0.02
10 (lowest)	$38,481	7.11%	2.97%	27.80%	−0.07
All Stocks	$1,329,513	13.26%	11.22%	18.99%	0.33

T A B L E   15-DECILE ADDENDUM 2

Summary Results for VC Decile Analysis of Large Stocks Universe, January 1, 1964, to December 31, 2009

Decile	$10,000 grows to	Average return	Compound return	Standard deviation	Sharpe ratio
1 (highest)	$3,335,373	15.04%	13.46%	16.68%	0.51
2	$2,256,400	13.86%	12.50%	15.52%	0.48
3	$1,311,085	12.48%	11.18%	15.26%	0.41
4	$877,032	11.47%	10.21%	15.04%	0.35
5	$724,818	11.01%	9.76%	15.02%	0.32
6	$433,301	9.81%	8.54%	15.24%	0.23
7	$360,891	9.45%	8.11%	15.72%	0.20
8	$302,571	9.23%	7.69%	16.80%	0.16
9	$301,635	9.50%	7.69%	18.23%	0.15
10 (lowest)	$93,708	7.75%	4.98%	22.43%	0.00
Large Stocks	$872,861	11.72%	10.20%	16.50%	0.32

DOES ADDING SHAREHOLDER YIELD IMPROVE RESULTS?

We now add shareholder yield to the five factors tested in Value Factor One and compare the results. We scale the composited Value Factor Two exactly as we did Value Factor One, but now we also include shareholder yield.

As Table 15.19 shows, if you add shareholder yield to Value Factor One, you gain an improvement in overall average annual compound return of 12 basis points over the entire period studied. What's more, the standard deviation of return declines by .99 percent, and the downside risk improves by .69 percent. If you look at the minimum returns, you'll see that after you reach a five-year holding period, the minimum return generated by including shareholder yield with the other five value factors also improves.

T A B L E   15.19

Summary Return and Risk Results for Annual Data: All Stocks VC2 Decile 1 and All Stocks VC1 Decile 1, January 1, 1964, to December 31, 2009

	All Stocks VC2 decile 1	All Stocks VC1 decile 1
Arithmetic average	19.00%	19.09%
Geometric average	17.30%	17.18%
Median return	22.74%	23.52%
Standard deviation	17.10%	18.09%
Upside deviation	11.32%	11.77%
Downside deviation	12.81%	13.50%
Tracking error	8.10	7.50
Number of positive periods	368	363
Number of negative periods	184	189
Maximum peak-to-trough decline	−58.07%	−57.78%
Beta	0.81	0.88
T-statistic (m = 0)	6.95	6.60
Sharpe ratio (Rf = 5%)	0.72	0.67
Sortino ratio (MAR = 10%)	0.57	0.53
$10,000 becomes	$15,416,651	$14,688,089
Minimum 1-year return	−48.60%	−48.24%
Maximum 1-year return	77.27%	81.40%
Minimum 3-year return	−17.13%	−17.00%
Maximum 3-year return	41.33%	41.09%
Minimum 5-year return	−3.65%	−5.33%
Maximum 5-year return	35.99%	35.49%
Minimum 7-year return	−0.10%	−1.25%
Maximum 7-year return	31.35%	30.19%
Minimum 10-year return	6.17%	6.08%
Maximum 10-year return	29.77%	29.41%
Minimum expected return*	−15.20%	−17.10%
Maximum expected return†	53.20%	55.28%

* Minimum expected return is arithmetic return minus 2 times the standard deviation.
† Maximum expected return is arithmetic return plus 2 times the standard deviation.

Base rates against All Stocks remain similar; however, when you compare the base rates for how often Value Factor Two—which includes shareholder yield—beats Value Factor One, we see that it does so in 59 percent of all rolling five-year periods and in 71 percent of all rolling ten-year periods. Table 15.20 shows the base rates for Value Factor Two versus Value Factor One for all rolling periods. Additionally, Table 15.21 shows the returns within each decade for each value factor.

T A B L E   15.20

Base Rates for All Stocks VC2 Decile 1 and All Stocks VC1 Decile 1, January 1, 1964, to December 31, 2009

Item	All Stocks VC2 Decile 1 beat All Stocks VC1 Decile 1	Percent	Average annual excess return
Single-year return	276 out of 541	51%	−0.02%
Rolling 3-year compound return	301 out of 517	58%	0.15%
Rolling 5-year compound return	289 out of 493	59%	0.25%
Rolling 7-year compound return	324 out of 469	69%	0.31%
Rolling 10-year compound return	306 out of 433	71%	0.33%

T A B L E   15.21

Average Annual Compound Rates of Return by Decade

	1960s*	1970s	1980s	1990s	2000s†
All Stocks VC1 Decile 1	16.84%	14.78%	22.21%	16.34%	15.73%
All Stocks VC2 Decile 1	15.49%	15.35%	23.21%	16.10%	15.82%
All Stocks VC3 Decile 1	16.50%	15.62%	22.56%	16.69%	15.36%
All Stocks	13.36%	7.56%	16.78%	15.35%	4.39%

* Returns for January 1, 1964, to December 31, 1969.
† Returns for January 1, 2000, to December 31, 2009.

The difference is even more pronounced with Large Stocks. Table 15.22 compares Value Factor One to Value Factor Two from Large Stocks. The average annual compound return increases from 13.46 to 14.21 percent, or .75 percent per year on a compounded basis. Standard deviation of return and downside risk also improve, as do minimum seven- and ten-year returns. As Table 15.23 shows, base rates improve by adding shareholder yield to Value Factor One, with Value Factor Two beating Value Factor One in 79 percent of all rolling five-year periods and in 95 percent of all rolling ten-year periods. Thus, you would add value to total return, risk, and overall base rates for All Stocks and Large Stocks by adding shareholder yield to the factor mix.

T A B L E   15.22

Summary Return and Risk Results for Annual Data: Large Stocks VC2 Decile 1 and Large Stocks VC1 Decile 1, January 1, 1964, to December 31, 2009

	Large Stocks VC2 decile 1	Large Stocks VC1 decile 1
Arithmetic average	15.72%	15.04%
Geometric average	14.21%	13.46%
Median return	18.82%	18.42%
Standard deviation	16.26%	16.68%
Upside deviation	10.61%	10.63%

(continued on next page)

T A B L E   15.22

Summary Return and Risk Results for Annual Data: Large Stocks VC2 Decile 1 and Large Stocks VC1 Decile 1, January 1, 1964, to December 31, 2009 *(Continued)*

	Large Stocks VC2 decile 1	Large Stocks VC1 decile 1
Downside deviation	11.53%	11.87%
Tracking error	8.60	8.20
Number of positive periods	343	344
Number of negative periods	209	208
Maximum peak-to-trough decline	−62.69%	−61.86%
Beta	0.85	0.89
T-statistic (m = 0)	6.13	5.73
Sharpe ratio (Rf = 5%)	0.57	0.51
Sortino ratio (MAR = 10%)	0.36	0.29
$10,000 becomes	$4,509,506	$3,335,373
Minimum 1-year return	−56.23%	−55.57%
Maximum 1-year return	72.26%	72.36%
Minimum 3-year return	−18.46%	−16.99%
Maximum 3-year return	38.87%	37.73%
Minimum 5-year return	−3.29%	−2.03%
Maximum 5-year return	37.09%	35.12%
Minimum 7-year return	1.22%	0.26%
Maximum 7-year return	29.30%	27.27%
Minimum 10-year return	2.74%	2.36%
Maximum 10-year return	24.02%	22.19%
Minimum expected return*	−16.80%	−18.31%
Maximum expected return†	48.23%	48.40%

* Minimum expected return is arithmetic return minus 2 times the standard deviation.
† Maximum expected return is arithmetic return plus 2 times the standard deviation.

T A B L E   15.23

Base Rates for Large Stocks VC2 Decile 1 and Large Stocks VC1 Decile 1, January 1, 1964, to December 31, 2009

Item	Large Stocks VC2 decile 1 beat Large Stocks VC1 Decile 1	Percent	Average annual excess return
Single-year return	337 out of 541	62%	0.65%
Rolling 3-year compound return	392 out of 517	76%	0.79%
Rolling 5-year compound return	390 out of 493	79%	0.89%
Rolling 7-year compound return	389 out of 469	83%	0.95%
Rolling 10-year compound return	413 out of 433	95%	1.02%

SUBSTITUTING BUYBACK YIELD FOR SHAREHOLDER YIELD IN VALUE FACTOR TWO

What if you are interested only in stocks that have the best value characteristics, but you are indifferent as to whether they pay a dividend yield? In this case, you could add *just* buyback yield to the equation and create a new composited value factor that we will call Value Factor Three. In this instance, we combine the following factors:

1. Price-to-book
2. Price-to-earnings
3. Price-to-sales
4. EBITDA/EV
5. Price-to-cash flow
6. Buyback yield

Just as we did with the first two composited value factors, we assign a percentile rank to each of the six factors. Thus a stock with a PE ratio in the lowest 1 percent of the universe will receive a score of 100, and a stock with a PE in the highest 1 percent of the universe will receive a rank of 1. We follow a similar convention for each of the six factors. If a value is missing for a factor, we assign a neutral score of 50. Once all factors are ranked, we add the scores and assign them to deciles, with the 10 percent of stocks with the highest scores going into decile 1 and the ten percent of stocks with the lowest scores going into decile 10. Remember that decile 1 features the stocks with the lowest PEs, PSRs, and highest buyback yields, whereas decile 10 is made up of the stocks with the highest PEs, PSRs, and lowest buyback yields.

Table 15.24 shows the results for decile 1 of Value Factor Three, and Table 15.25 shows the base rates comparing decile 1 of Value Factor Three to decile 1 of Value Factor One. Much as with Value Factor Two, including buyback yield enhances the performance of the original Value Factor One—now the average annual compound return goes up to 17.39 percent. The standard deviation decreases to 17.68 percent and the Sharpe ratio increases to .70. The base rates are virtually identical to Value Factor One, with the exception that the base rate for all three-year rolling periods increases to 96 percent against All Stocks, whereas the base rates against Value Composite One, featured in Table 15.25, improve a bit over Value Composite Two.

T A B L E   15.24

Summary Return and Risk Results for Annual Data: All Stocks VC3 Decile 1 (High) and All Stocks VC1 Decile 1, January 1, 1964, to December 31, 2009

	All Stocks VC3 decile 1 (high)	All Stocks VC1 decile 1
Arithmetic average	19.22%	19.09%
Geometric average	17.39%	17.18%
Median return	24.91%	23.52%
Standard deviation	17.68%	18.09%

(continued on next page)

T A B L E   15.24

Summary Return and Risk Results for Annual Data: All Stocks VC3 Decile 1 (High) and All Stocks VC1 Decile 1, January 1, 1964, to December 31, 2009 *(Continued)*

	All Stocks VC3 decile 1 (high)	All Stocks VC1 decile 1
Upside deviation	11.48%	11.77%
Downside deviation	13.30%	13.50%
Tracking error	7.52	7.50
Number of positive periods	368	363
Number of negative periods	184	189
Maximum peak-to-trough decline	−58.04%	−57.78%
Beta	0.85	0.88
T-statistic (m = 0)	6.79	6.60
Sharpe ratio (Rf = 5%)	0.70	0.67
Sortino ratio (MAR = 10%)	0.56	0.53
$10,000 becomes	$15,940,452	$14,688,089
Minimum 1-year return	−47.88%	−48.24%
Maximum 1-year return	83.26%	81.40%
Minimum 3-year return	−17.37%	−17.00%
Maximum 3-year return	42.57%	41.09%
Minimum 5-year return	−3.94%	−5.33%
Maximum 5-year return	36.16%	35.49%
Minimum 7-year return	−0.11%	−1.25%
Maximum 7-year return	30.43%	30.19%
Minimum 10-year return	6.47%	6.08%
Maximum 10-year return	29.54%	29.41%
Minimum expected return*	−16.14%	−17.10%
Maximum expected return†	54.57%	55.28%

* Minimum expected return is arithmetic return minus 2 times the standard deviation.
† Maximum expected return is arithmetic return plus 2 times the standard deviation.

T A B L E   15.25

Base Rates for All Stocks VC3 Decile 1 and All Stocks VC1 Decile1, January 1, 1964, to December 31, 2009

Item	All Stocks VC3 Decile 1 beat All Stocks VC1 Decile 1	Percent	Average annual excess return
Single-year return	276 out of 541	51%	0.17%
Rolling 3-year compound return	303 out of 517	59%	0.28%
Rolling 5-year compound return	346 out of 493	70%	0.36%
Rolling 7-year compound return	358 out of 469	76%	0.40%
Rolling 10-year compound return	368 out of 433	85%	0.41%

Adding just buyback yield also helps to isolate stocks that you should avoid. As Table 15.26 shows, decile 10 of Value Factor Three compounds at just 2.47 percent per year, and Table 15.27 shows that the base rates of decile 10 of Value Factor Three beats All Stocks just 11 percent of all rolling five-year periods and 3 percent of all rolling ten-year periods. Tables 15.28, 15.29, and 15.30 show the results for decile 10 of Value Factor Three in Large Stocks and the base rates for deciles 1 and 10.

T A B L E   15.26

Summary Return and Risk Results for Annual Data: All Stocks VC3 Decile 10 and All Stocks, January 1, 1964, to December 31, 2009

	All Stocks VC3 decile 10	All Stocks
Arithmetic average	6.69%	13.26%
Geometric average	2.47%	11.22%
Median return	10.69%	17.16%
Standard deviation	28.14%	18.99%
Upside deviation	17.62%	10.98%
Downside deviation	20.32%	13.90%
Tracking error	14.03	0.00
Number of positive periods	308	329
Number of negative periods	244	223
Maximum peak-to-trough decline	−92.77%	−55.54%
Beta	1.32	1.00
T-statistic (m = 0)	1.56	4.47
Sharpe ratio (Rf = 5%)	−0.09	0.33
Sortino ratio (MAR = 10%)	−0.37	0.09
$10,000 becomes	$30,733	$1,329,513
Minimum 1-year return	−70.35%	−46.49%
Maximum 1-year return	216.74%	84.19%
Minimum 3-year return	−52.67%	−18.68%
Maximum 3-year return	53.69%	31.49%
Minimum 5-year return	−30.57%	−9.91%
Maximum 5-year return	36.42%	27.66%
Minimum 7-year return	−22.02%	−6.32%
Maximum 7-year return	24.75%	23.77%
Minimum 10-year return	−15.95%	1.01%
Maximum 10-year return	17.97%	22.05%
Minimum expected return*	−49.59%	−24.73%
Maximum expected return†	62.97%	51.24%

* Minimum expected return is arithmetic return minus 2 times the standard deviation.
† Maximum expected return is arithmetic return plus 2 times the standard deviation.

T A B L E   15.27

Base Rates for All Stocks VC3 Decile 10 and All Stocks, January 1, 1964, to December 31, 2009

Item	All Stocks VC3 Decile 10 beat All Stocks	Percent	Average annual excess return
Single-year return	176 out of 541	33%	−5.46%
Rolling 3-year compound return	115 out of 517	22%	−8.12%
Rolling 5-year compound return	52 out of 493	11%	−8.86%
Rolling 7-year compound return	37 out of 469	8%	−9.16%
Rolling 10-year compound return	11 out of 433	3%	−9.21%

T A B L E   15.28

Summary Return and Risk Results for Annual Data: Large Stocks VC3 Decile 10 (Low) and Large Stocks, January 1, 1964, to December 31, 2009

	Large Stocks VC1 decile 10 (low)	Large Stocks
Arithmetic average	7.57%	11.72%
Geometric average	4.74%	10.20%
Median return	11.85%	17.20%
Standard deviation	22.77%	16.50%
Upside deviation	14.17%	9.70%
Downside deviation	17.61%	11.85%
Tracking error	12.04	0.00
Number of positive periods	319	332
Number of negative periods	233	220
Maximum peak-to-trough decline	−85.90%	−53.77%
Beta	1.19	1.00
T-statistic (m = 0)	2.18	4.58
Sharpe ratio (Rf = 5%)	−0.01	0.32
Sortino ratio (MAR = 10%)	−0.30	0.02
$10,000 becomes	$84,019	$872,861
Minimum 1-year return	−78.70%	−46.91%
Maximum 1-year return	91.71%	68.96%
Minimum 3-year return	−46.12%	−15.89%
Maximum 3-year return	50.10%	33.12%
Minimum 5-year return	−25.57%	−5.82%
Maximum 5-year return	33.58%	28.95%
Minimum 7-year return	−16.41%	−4.15%
Maximum 7-year return	24.00%	22.83%
Minimum 10-year return	−11.32%	−0.15%
Maximum 10-year return	19.33%	19.57%
Minimum expected return*	−37.96%	−21.28%
Maximum expected return†	53.10%	44.72%

* Minimum expected return is arithmetic return minus 2 times the standard deviation.
† Maximum expected return is arithmetic return plus 2 times the standard deviation.

T A B L E 15.29

Base Rates for Large Stocks VC3 Decile 1 and Large Stocks, January 1, 1964, to December 31, 2009

Item	Large Stocks VC3 decile 1 beat Large Stocks	Percent	Average annual excess return
Single-year return	363 out of 541	67%	4.00%
Rolling 3-year compound return	402 out of 517	78%	4.26%
Rolling 5-year compound return	447 out of 493	91%	4.46%
Rolling 7-year compound return	439 out of 469	94%	4.52%
Rolling 10-year compound return	424 out of 433	98%	4.53%

T A B L E 15.30

Base Rates for Large Stocks VC3 Decile 10 and Large Stocks, January 1, 1964, to December 31, 2009

Item	Large Stocks VC3 decile 10 beat Large Stocks	Percent	Average annual excess return
Single-year return	206 out of 541	38%	−3.46%
Rolling 3-year compound return	135 out of 517	26%	−5.20%
Rolling 5-year compound return	80 out of 493	16%	−6.04%
Rolling 7-year compound return	54 out of 469	12%	−6.54%
Rolling 10-year compound return	28 out of 433	6%	−6.83%

IMPLICATIONS

Investors would be well served to consider how stocks score on *all* value factors and not just on one or two. By using a methodology that includes all the value factors, you avoid the inevitable performance variations of individual factors and smooth out the attendant risk of betting on a single factor. Yes, there will be times when you would have been better off focusing on a single factor, but the problem is that you don't know when that time will be. For example, EBITDA/EV—the best single factor for the composited 1963–2009 period—beats Value Factor One in only 45 percent of all rolling one-year periods and in 46 percent of all rolling five-year periods.

The only time it makes sense to favor a single factor over the composited value factors is when it is a key element of a multifactor strategy. For example, we use a strategy called Enhanced Divided that buys market leading companies with high-dividend yields. Since the ability to continually pay that high dividend is of the utmost importance to the strategy, we narrow the field of market-leading companies by eliminating the 50 percent with the worst EBITDA/EV. Since this factor looks at what the company is earning versus what it owes, this factor helps us determine how likely it is that the company will be able to continue to pay or increase its dividend. Yet, even here, we have discovered that the combined value factors also work exceedingly well.

CHAPTER FIFTEEN CASE STUDY

USING THE COMPOSITED VALUE FACTOR FOR INDIVIDUAL INVESTORS' PORTFOLIOS

We've been focusing on how the best and worst decile for each factor performs in order to give the reader a good idea of how stocks with low and high valuations perform in general. Yet experience has taught me that rarely do investors buy or sell securities based on a single factor. Since Value Factors One and Two are more robust multifactor models, I thought it would be worth reviewing how more concentrated portfolios derived from them would perform. Let's take a quick look at how both Value Factor One and Value Factor Two perform when the names in decile 1 are narrowed down to just 25 or 50 stocks. And for those investors interested in shorting securities, I review the performance of the 25 and 50 stocks in decile 10.

Table 15CS.1 shows the results of investing $10,000 in the 25 and 50 names with the highest scores from decile 1 of Value Factor One. Both perform slightly better than decile 1 in its entirety, but at a cost—both the 25- and 50-stock portfolios have higher volatility. The 25-stock portfolio has a standard deviation of return of 20.54 percent, compared to 18.09 percent for decile 1 of Value Factor One, and the 50-stock portfolio has a slightly lower standard deviation of return of 19.47. Because of the higher volatility, both have Sharpe ratios less than that earned by decile 1—the Sharpe ratio for the 25-stock version is .59 and .63 for the 50-stock portfolio compared to .67 for decile 1. Both the 25- and 50-stock portfolios have higher maximum drawdowns, with the top 25 having a maximum decline of −64.09 percent, and the top 50 having a maximum decline of −60.33 percent.

T A B L E   15CS.1

Summary Return and Risk Results for Annual Data: All Stocks VC1 High 25, All Stocks VC1 High 50, and All Stocks VC1 Decile 1, January 1, 1964, to December 31, 2009

	All Stocks VC1 high 25	All Stocks VC1 high 50	All Stocks VC1 decile 1
Arithmetic average	19.64%	19.53%	19.09%
Geometric average	17.20%	17.32%	17.18%
Median return	20.91%	22.12%	23.52%
Standard deviation	20.54%	19.47%	18.09%
Upside deviation	14.29%	13.16%	11.77%
Downside deviation	14.35%	14.06%	13.50%
Tracking error	10.06	8.81	7.50
Number of positive periods	355	356	363
Number of negative periods	197	196	189
Maximum peak-to-trough decline	−64.09%	−60.33%	−57.78%
Beta	0.94	0.92	0.88
T-statistic (m = 0)	5.97	6.26	6.60
Sharpe ratio (Rf = 5%)	0.59	0.63	0.67
Sortino ratio (MAR = 10%)	0.50	0.52	0.53
$10,000 becomes	$14,842,204	$15,547,632	$14,688,089
Minimum 1-year return	−52.46%	−50.76%	−48.24%
Maximum 1-year return	102.70%	92.25%	81.40%
Minimum 3-year return	−19.06%	−16.86%	−17.00%
Maximum 3-year return	48.12%	45.60%	41.09%

(continued on next page)

T A B L E   15CS.1

Summary Return and Risk Results for Annual Data: All Stocks VC1 High 25, All Stocks VC1 High 50, and All Stocks VC1 Decile 1, January 1, 1964, to December 31, 2009 *(Continued)*

	All Stocks VC1 high 25	All Stocks VC1 high 50	All Stocks VC1 decile 1
Minimum 5-year return	−6.67%	−6.83%	−5.33%
Maximum 5-year return	38.16%	36.32%	35.49%
Minimum 7-year return	−1.97%	−2.37%	−1.25%
Maximum 7-year return	31.45%	30.33%	30.19%
Minimum 10-year return	5.22%	5.15%	6.08%
Maximum 10-year return	25.48%	27.71%	29.41%
Minimum expected return*	−21.43%	−19.42%	−17.10%
Maximum expected return†	60.71%	58.48%	55.28%

* Minimum expected return is arithmetic return minus 2 times the standard deviation.
† Maximum expected return is arithmetic return plus 2 times the standard deviation.

In Tables 15CS.2 and 15CS.3, you can see the base rates for the top 25 and 50 stocks from decile 1 of Value Factor One. Over short periods of time, the top 25 stocks from Value Composite One have a *slight* advantage over the full decile, with the top 25 beating the decile 54 percent of all rolling five-year periods, but when you get to the longer ten-year holding period, we see a slight disadvantage to the top 25 stocks as they beat the full decile just 48 percent of the time. As with decile 1 of Value Factor One, both portfolios beat the All Stocks universe in 100 percent of all rolling ten-year periods, but do not perform quite as well as decile 1 when you look at the five-year base rates. Tables 15CS.4 and 15CS.5 show all base rates for each of the portfolios.

TABLE 15CS.2

Base Rates for All Stocks VC1 High 25 and All Stocks VC1 Decile 1, January 1, 1964, to December 31, 2009

Item	All Stocks VC1 high 25 beat All Stocks VC1 decile 1	Percent	Average annual excess return
Single-year return	270 out of 541	50%	0.19%
Rolling 3-year compound return	264 out of 517	51%	−0.26%
Rolling 5-year compound return	264 out of 493	54%	−0.29%
Rolling 7-year compound return	248 out of 469	53%	−0.37%
Rolling 10-year compound return	206 out of 433	48%	−0.41%

T A B L E   15CS.3

Base Rates for All Stocks VC1 High 50 and All Stocks VC1 Decile 1, January 1, 1964, to December 31, 2009

Item	All Stocks VC1 high 50 beat All Stocks VC1 decile 1	Percent	Average annual excess return
Single-year return	274 out of 541	51%	0.20%
Rolling 3-year compound return	264 out of 517	51%	−0.04%
Rolling 5-year compound return	241 out of 493	49%	−0.10%
Rolling 7-year compound return	224 out of 469	48%	−0.15%
Rolling 10-year compound return	182 out of 433	42%	−0.18%

T A B L E   CS15.4

Base Rates for All Stocks VC1 High 25 and All Stocks, January 1, 1964, to December 31, 2009

Item	All Stocks VC1 high 25 beat All Stocks	Percent	Average annual excess return
Single-year return	381 out of 541	70%	5.89%
Rolling 3-year compound return	418 out of 517	81%	5.57%
Rolling 5-year compound return	412 out of 493	84%	5.59%
Rolling 7-year compound return	431 out of 469	92%	5.52%
Rolling 10-year compound return	433 out of 433	100%	5.39%

T A B L E   CS15.5

Base Rates for All Stocks VC1 High 50 and All Stocks, January 1, 1964, to December 31, 2009

Item	All Stocks VC1 high 50 beat All Stocks	Percent	Average annual excess return
Single-year return	403 out of 541	74%	5.90%
Rolling 3-year compound return	422 out of 517	82%	5.78%
Rolling 5-year compound return	434 out of 493	88%	5.79%
Rolling 7-year compound return	460 out of 469	98%	5.74%
Rolling 10-year compound return	432 out of 433	100%	5.62%

BOTTOM 25 AND 50 OF DECILE 10 OFFER HORRIBLE RETURNS

Table 15CS.6 shows the results of investing $10,000 in the 25- and 50-stock portfolios with the worst scores from decile 10—in short, the priciest securities from the All Stocks universe. As you can see from the table, it is not a pretty picture. Over the 46 years of the study, each portfolio *lost money*, with the bottom 25 losing 2.94 percent a year and turning $10,000 invested on December 31, 1963, into $2,535 by the end of 2009. Remember, these are nominal returns that do not take the effects of inflation into account. If inflation was considered, an investor in the bottom 25 stocks would have *nothing* left after 46 years. The 50-stock portfolio from decile 10 of Value Factor One also lost money, turning $10,000 invested into $5,296, a loss of 1.37 percent a year. Like the bottom 25, if inflation was factored in to the returns, an investor in the bottom 50 would also have been wiped out. As Tables 15CS.7 and 15CS.8 show, all base rates are negative with the bottom 25 losing to All Stocks in every single rolling ten-year period and the bottom 50 beating All Stocks only three times over the 46 years.

T A B L E   15CS.6

Summary Return and Risk Results for Annual Data: All Stocks VC1 Low 25, All Stocks VC1 Low 50, and All Stocks VC1 Decile 10, January 1, 1964, to December 31, 2009

	All Stocks VC1 low 25	All Stocks VC1 low 50	All Stocks VC1 decile 10
Arithmetic average	2.29%	3.39%	7.11%
Geometric average	−2.94%	−1.37%	2.97%
Median return	6.45%	6.91%	10.97%

(continued on next page)

T A B L E   15CS.6

Summary Return and Risk Results for Annual Data: All Stocks VC1 Low 25, All Stocks VC1 Low 50, and All Stocks VC1 Decile 10, January 1, 1964, to December 31, 2009 *(Continued)*

	All Stocks VC1 low 25	All Stocks VC1 low 50	All Stocks VC1 decile 10
Standard deviation	31.98%	30.34%	27.80%
Upside deviation	20.08%	18.99%	17.39%
Downside deviation	21.54%	21.12%	20.32%
Tracking error	18.94	17.10	14.03
Number of positive periods	285	285	312
Number of negative periods	267	267	240
Maximum peak-to-trough decline	−96.51%	−95.38%	−92.81%
Beta	1.42	1.37	1.30
T-statistic (m = 0)	0.48	0.75	1.68
Sharpe ratio (Rf = 5%)	−0.25	−0.21	−0.07
Sortino ratio (MAR = 10%)	−0.60	−0.54	−0.35
$10,000 becomes	$2,535	$5,296	$38,481
Minimum 1-year return	−67.75%	−70.05%	−71.59%
Maximum 1-year return	230.25%	231.01%	215.77%
Minimum 3-year return	−50.79%	−52.51%	−53.72%
Maximum 3-year return	49.91%	50.85%	56.66%
Minimum 5-year return	−29.13%	−30.56%	−31.25%
Maximum 5-year return	29.90%	31.14%	38.69%
Minimum 7-year return	−22.50%	−23.86%	−22.49%
Maximum 7-year return	14.62%	15.98%	26.29%
Minimum 10-year return	−17.41%	−19.18%	−16.22%
Maximum 10-year return	5.55%	10.87%	19.09%
Minimum expected return*	−61.67%	−57.29%	−48.49%
Maximum expected return†	66.25%	64.07%	62.71%

* Minimum expected return is arithmetic return minus 2 times the standard deviation.
† Maximum expected return is arithmetic return plus 2 times the standard deviation.

T A B L E   15CS.7

Base Rates for All Stocks VC1 Low 25 and All Stocks, January 1, 1964, to December 31, 2009

Item	All Stocks VC1 low 25 beat All Stocks	Percent	Average annual excess return
Single-year return	154 out of 541	28%	−9.58%
Rolling 3-year compound return	73 out of 517	14%	−14.00%
Rolling 5-year compound return	25 out of 493	5%	−15.06%
Rolling 7-year compound return	24 out of 469	5%	−15.56%
Rolling 10-year compound return	0 out of 433	0%	−15.99%

TABLE   15CS.8

Base Rates for All Stocks VC1 Low 50 and All Stocks, January 1, 1964, to December 31, 2009

Item	All Stocks VC1 low 50 beat All Stocks	Percent	Average annual excess return
Single-year return	162 out of 541	30%	−8.51%
Rolling 3-year compound return	96 out of 517	19%	−12.09%
Rolling 5-year compound return	26 out of 493	5%	−12.94%
Rolling 7-year compound return	27 out of 469	6%	−13.28%
Rolling 10-year compound return	3 out of 433	1%	−13.47%

For those interested in shorting these stocks, it is wise to remember that they are the very type of securities that soar during market bubbles. Looking at Table 15CS.9, we see that in 1999, as the dot-com bubble neared its end, the stocks in the 50- and 25-stock portfolios soared by 175 percent and 189 percent, respectively. As we will see in Chapter Twenty when we study price momentum, these stocks also perform well coming out of bear markets, since during those periods the speculative, frothy names often attract the short-term attention of investors. But in bear market years, the stocks are crushed—look at the back-to-back-to-back declines in 2000, 2001, and 2002. Thus, if you are interested in using these names as the basis of a shorting strategy, I advise that you couple it with additional mechanical strategies such as moving averages and stop-loss orders so as to avoid the havoc they might wreak on a shorting strategy during market bubbles and the immediate aftermath of bear markets. Look again at Table 15CS.6 and note that the *best* one-year return for these stocks was a gain of 230.25 percent for the worst 25 stocks and 231.01 percent for the worst 50 stocks. Even if you extend the holding period to three years' yields gains of 49.91 percent and 50.85 percent, respectively, for the worst 25- and 50-stock portfolios. Remember that markets can remain irrational longer than most investors can remain solvent, so if you want to use these value composite strategies for shorting, you *must* marry them to some additional form of analysis.

TABLE   15CS.9

Annual Return January 1, 1998 to December 31, 2002

Year	All Stocks VC1 low 25	All Stocks VC1 low 50
1998	2%	1%
1999	189%	175%
2000	−51%	−53%
2001	−46%	−28%
2002	−67%	−52%

VALUE FACTOR TWO 25- AND 50-STOCK PORTFOLIOS

Table 15CS.10 shows the results of buying the top 25 and 50 stocks from decile 1 of Value Factor Two—which, as you will recall, includes shareholder yield. Here we see that including shareholder yield improves the returns of the 25- and 50-stock portfolios. Both do significantly better than decile 1 of Value Factor Two and have lower maximum declines than decile 1.

The Sharpe ratio of .76 for the 50-stock portfolio is actually higher than the Sharpe ratio for decile 1 of Value Factor Two of .72.

T A B L E   15CS.10

Summary Return and Risk Results for Annual Data: All Stocks VC2 High 25, All Stocks VC2 High 50, and All Stocks VC2 Decile 1, January 1, 1964, to December 31, 2009

	All Stocks VC2 high 25	All Stocks VC2 high 50	All Stocks VC2 decile 1
Arithmetic average	20.00%	20.46%	19.00%
Geometric average	18.02%	18.61%	17.30%
Median return	22.16%	21.72%	22.74%
Standard deviation	18.48%	17.80%	17.10%
Upside deviation	12.79%	12.08%	11.32%
Downside deviation	13.16%	12.84%	12.81%
Tracking error	9.94	9.08	8.10
Number of positive periods	358	369	368
Number of negative periods	194	183	184
Maximum peak-to-trough decline	−55.64%	−54.25%	−58.07%
Beta	0.84	0.82	0.81
T-statistic (m = 0)	6.74	7.15	6.95
Sharpe ratio (Rf = 5%)	0.70	0.76	0.72
Sortino ratio (MAR = 10%)	0.61	0.67	0.57
$10,000 becomes	$20,385,881	$25,656,756	$15,416,651
Minimum 1-year return	−48.62%	−45.40%	−48.60%
Maximum 1-year return	89.56%	84.67%	77.27%
Minimum 3-year return	−13.17%	−12.91%	−17.13%
Maximum 3-year return	46.84%	44.32%	41.33%
Minimum 5-year return	−4.47%	−3.52%	−3.65%
Maximum 5-year return	38.79%	37.09%	35.99%
Minimum 7-year return	−0.82%	0.19%	−0.10%
Maximum 7-year return	31.68%	30.44%	31.35%
Minimum 10-year return	5.15%	6.30%	6.17%
Maximum 10-year return	26.62%	28.78%	29.77%
Minimum expected return*	−16.96%	−15.13%	−15.20%
Maximum expected return†	56.97%	56.06%	53.20%

* Minimum expected return is arithmetic return minus 2 times the standard deviation.
† Maximum expected return is arithmetic return plus 2 times the standard deviation.

Tables 15CS.11 and 15CS.12 show the base rates for each of the portfolios versus the All Stocks universe. Like decile 1, both beat the All Stocks universe in 100 percent of all rolling ten-year periods, but unlike the top 50 from Value Factor One, the top 50 here also beat the All Stocks universe in 99 percent of all rolling seven-year periods, nine points better than decile 1. Table 15CS.13 shows the results for the top 25- and 50-stock portfolio from Value Composites One and Two by decade.

T A B L E   15CS.11

Base Rates for All Stocks VC2 High 25 and All Stocks, January 1, 1964, to December 31, 2009

Item	All Stocks VC2 High 25 beat All Stocks	Percent	Average annual excess return
Single-year return	400 out of 541	74%	6.45%
Rolling 3-year compound return	421 out of 517	81%	6.41%
Rolling 5-year compound return	432 out of 493	88%	6.46%
Rolling 7-year compound return	440 out of 469	94%	6.42%
Rolling 10-year compound return	433 out of 433	100%	6.34%

T A B L E   15CS.12

Base Rates for All Stocks VC2 High 50 and All Stocks, January 1, 1964, to December 31, 2009

Item	All Stocks VC2 high 50 beat All Stocks	Percent	Average annual excess return
Single-year return	420 out of 541	78%	6.93%
Rolling 3-year compound return	454 out of 517	88%	7.00%
Rolling 5-year compound return	474 out of 493	96%	7.12%
Rolling 7-year compound return	465 out of 469	99%	7.13%
Rolling 10-year compound return	433 out of 433	100%	7.07%

T A B L E   15CS.13

Average Annual Compound Rates of Return by Decade

	1960s*	1970s	1980s	1990s	2000s†
All Stocks VC1 high 25	14.60%	13.78%	20.38%	17.71%	18.64%
All Stocks VC1 high 50	15.49%	14.39%	20.72%	17.08%	18.30%
All Stocks VC2 high 25	13.88%	13.97%	22.53%	18.37%	19.89%
All Stocks VC2 high 50	14.97%	15.62%	23.26%	18.28%	19.63%
All Stocks	13.36%	7.56%	16.78%	15.35%	4.39%

* Returns for January 1, 1964, to December 31, 1969.
† Returns for January 1, 2000, to December 31, 2009.

VALUE FACTOR TWO BOTTOM 25 AND 50 STOCKS FROM DECILE 10

Table 15CS.14 shows the returns of the bottom 25 and 50 stocks from decile 10 of Value Factor Two. As with the decile 10 stocks from Value Factor One, the returns are atrocious. The bottom 25 stocks lost 3.16 percent per year and turned $10,000 invested on December 31, 1963, into $2,288—and again, this return does *not* take inflation into account. Worse yet, the maximum decline for the bottom 25 stocks of decile 10 is 97 percent. Consult the table for all other relevant statistics.

T A B L E   15CS.14

Summary Return and Risk Results for Annual Data: All Stocks VC2 Low 25, All Stocks VC2 Low 50, and All Stocks VC2 Decile 10, January 1, 1964, to December 31, 2009

	All Stocks VC2 low 25	All Stocks VC2 low 50	All Stocks VC1 decile 10
Arithmetic average	1.98%	3.65%	6.89%
Geometric average	−3.16%	−1.23%	2.63%
Median return	4.15%	8.19%	10.16%
Standard deviation	31.69%	30.71%	28.26%
Upside deviation	19.92%	19.48%	17.66%
Downside deviation	21.66%	20.99%	20.35%
Tracking error	18.57	17.41	14.16
Number of positive periods	284	290	305
Number of negative periods	268	262	247
Maximum peak-to-trough decline	−97.01%	−94.16%	−92.67%
Beta	1.41	1.39	1.33
T-statistic (m = 0)	0.42	0.79	1.60
Sharpe ratio (Rf = 5%)	−0.26	−0.20	−0.08
Sortino ratio (MAR = 10%)	−0.61	−0.53	−0.36
$10,000 becomes	$2,288	$5,671	$33,018
Minimum 1-year return	−68.56%	−64.60%	−69.93%
Maximum 1-year return	188.42%	201.60%	218.30%
Minimum 3-year return	−49.28%	−47.99%	−52.39%
Maximum 3-year return	45.98%	44.85%	53.82%
Minimum 5-year return	−30.58%	−26.68%	−30.36%
Maximum 5-year return	30.82%	28.28%	36.62%
Minimum 7-year return	−26.28%	−22.73%	−21.89%
Maximum 7-year return	17.34%	17.56%	24.78%
Minimum 10-year return	−19.09%	−16.99%	−15.80%
Maximum 10-year return	8.59%	11.34%	18.11%
Minimum expected return*	−61.39%	−57.76%	−49.64%
Maximum expected return†	65.35%	65.07%	63.42%

* Minimum expected return is arithmetic return minus 2 times the standard deviation.
† Maximum expected return is arithmetic return plus 2 times the standard deviation.

As Tables 15CS.15 and 15CS.16 show, all base rates are negative, yet the same caution is required here as we offer with the stocks from Value Factor One—many of these stocks *soar* during market bubbles and in the immediate aftermaths of bear markets, so the same advice given on shorting the worst stocks from Value Factor One applies to investors interested in shorting these stocks. Table 15CS.17 shows the results by decade.

T A B L E   15CS.15

Base Rates for All Stocks VC2 Low 25 and All Stocks, January 1, 1964, to December 31, 2009

Item	All Stocks VC2 low 25 beat All Stocks	Percent	Average annual excess return
Single-year return	150 out of 541	28%	−10.64%
Rolling 3-year compound return	83 out of 517	16%	−14.25%
Rolling 5-year compound return	42 out of 493	9%	−15.23%
Rolling 7-year compound return	38 out of 469	8%	−15.64%
Rolling 10-year compound return	12 out of 433	3%	−16.01%

T A B L E   15CS.16

Base Rates for All Stocks VC2 Low 50 and All Stocks, January 1, 1964, to December 31, 2009

Item	All Stocks VC2 low 50 beat All Stocks	Percent	Average annual excess return
Single-year return	157 out of 541	29%	−8.65%
Rolling 3-year compound return	102 out of 517	20%	−11.99%
Rolling 5-year compound return	33 out of 493	7%	−12.84%
Rolling 7-year compound return	33 out of 469	7%	−13.16%
Rolling 10-year compound return	10 out of 433	2%	−13.41%

T A B L E   15CS.17

Average Annual Compound Rates of Return by Decade

	1960s*	1970s	1980s	1990s	2000s†
All Stocks VC1 low 25	16.81%	−5.26%	−0.61%	2.13%	−17.41%
All Stocks VC1 low 50	16.18%	−1.28%	4.69%	2.69%	−19.18%
All Stocks VC2 low 25	19.40%	−2.17%	0.78%	−3.34%	−18.61%
All Stocks VC2 low 50	17.61%	−0.60%	2.84%	1.02%	−16.99%
All Stocks	13.36%	7.56%	16.78%	15.35%	4.39%

* Returns for January 1, 1964, to December 31, 1969.
† Returns for January 1, 2000, to December 31, 2009.

VALUE FACTOR THREE 25- AND 50-STOCK PORTFOLIOS

Table 15CS.18 shows the results of buying the top 25 and 50 stocks from decile 1 of Value Factor Three. As we saw with the first two value factors, the returns improve compared to the decile in its entirety. Buying the 50 stocks with the best scores from Value Factor Three earns an average annual compound return of 18.64 percent and never loses money over any rolling seven- or ten-year period. As we saw with the 50 best stocks from Value Factor Two, base rates ten-year periods are 100 percent. Tables 15CS.19 and 15CS.20 show the base rates for the best 25 and 50 stocks from Value Factor Three versus All Stocks.

T A B L E   15CS.18

Summary Return and Risk Results for Annual Data: All Stocks VC3 High 25, All Stocks VC3 High 50, and All Stocks VC3 Decile 1 (High), January 1, 1964, to December 31, 2009

	All Stocks VC3 high 25	All Stocks VC3 high 50	All Stocks VC3 decile 1 (high)
Arithmetic average	20.60%	20.63%	19.22%
Geometric average	18.46%	18.64%	17.39%
Median return	21.49%	24.01%	24.91%
Standard deviation	19.06%	18.37%	17.68%
Upside deviation	12.72%	12.10%	11.48%
Downside deviation	13.64%	13.56%	13.30%
Tracking error	9.38	8.61	7.52
Number of positive periods	361	365	368
Number of negative periods	191	187	184
Maximum peak-to-trough decline	−56.92%	−55.86%	−58.04%
Beta	0.88	0.86	0.85
T-statistic (m = 0)	6.72	6.98	6.79
Sharpe ratio (Rf = 5%)	0.71	0.74	0.70
Sortino ratio (MAR = 10%)	0.62	0.64	0.56
$10,000 becomes	$24,248,981	$26,017,798	$15,940,452
Minimum 1-year return	−46.24%	−44.88%	−47.88%
Maximum 1-year return	88.53%	85.38%	83.26%
Minimum 3-year return	−15.12%	−14.22%	−17.37%
Maximum 3-year return	45.74%	44.50%	42.57%
Minimum 5-year return	−3.92%	−3.76%	−3.94%
Maximum 5-year return	39.98%	38.71%	36.16%
Minimum 7-year return	−0.43%	0.21%	−0.11%
Maximum 7-year return	32.20%	30.91%	30.43%
Minimum 10-year return	5.81%	6.92%	6.47%
Maximum 10-year return	29.09%	29.15%	29.54%
Minimum expected return*	−17.53%	−16.10%	−16.14%
Maximum expected return†	58.72%	57.36%	54.57%

* Minimum expected return is arithmetic return minus 2 times the standard deviation.
† Maximum expected return is arithmetic return plus 2 times the standard deviation.

T A B L E   15CS.19

Base Rates for All Stocks VC3 High 25 and All Stocks, January 1, 1964, to December 31, 2009

Item	All Stocks VC3 high 25 beat All Stocks	Percent	Average annual excess return
Single-year return	420 out of 541	78%	6.98%
Rolling 3-year compound return	456 out of 517	88%	6.94%
Rolling 5-year compound return	471 out of 493	96%	7.07%
Rolling 7-year compound return	467 out of 469	100%	7.08%
Rolling 10-year compound return	433 out of 433	100%	7.02%

T A B L E   15CS.20

Base Rates for All Stocks VC3 High 50 and All Stocks, January 1, 1964, to December 31, 2009

Item	All Stocks VC3 high 50 beat All Stocks	Percent	Average annual excess return
Single-year return	439 out of 541	81%	7.11%
Rolling 3-year compound return	461 out of 517	89%	7.18%
Rolling 5-year compound return	478 out of 493	97%	7.27%
Rolling 7-year compound return	468 out of 469	100%	7.26%
Rolling 10-year compound return	433 out of 433	100%	7.17%

VALUE FACTOR THREE BOTTOM 25 AND 50 STOCKS FROM DECILE 10

Once again, the bottom 25 and 50 stocks from decile 10 of Value Factor Three perform horribly. As Table 15CS.21 shows, the bottom 25 and 50 stocks from Value Factor Three lose money over the entire period. The bottom 25 lost 3 percent per year, turning $10,000 invested on December 31, 1963, into $2,468 by the end of 2009. The bottom 50 lost 1.29 percent per year and turned $10,000 into $5,498. As we saw with the other Value Factor Composites, all base rates are negative, with both the bottom 25 and 50 almost never beating the All Stocks universe in rolling ten-year periods. Tables 15CS.22 and 15CS.23 show the base rates for both. Once again I caution investors interested in shorting these stocks to remember that they can perform very well in bubbles and as bear markets end. For example, the bottom 50 stocks from Value Factor Three soared 28.78 percent per year for the five years ending February 2000, and anyone shorting them during that time would have been in real trouble. Yet this very performance could be used as a contrarian signal, since they went on to *decline* 66 percent in the following 12 months and lost an astounding 48 percent *per year* over the next three years. Table 15CS.24 shows the returns for the best and worst from Value Composite Three by decade.

T A B L E   15CS.21

Summary Return and Risk Results for Annual Data: All Stocks VC3 Low 25, All Stocks VC3 Low 50, and All Stocks VC3 Decile 10, January 1, 1964, to December 31, 2009

	All Stocks VC3 low 25	All Stocks VC3 low 50	All Stocks VC3 decile 10
Arithmetic average	2.11%	3.53%	6.69%
Geometric average	−3.00%	−1.29%	2.47%
Median return	6.64%	9.98%	10.69%
Standard deviation	31.55%	30.53%	28.14%
Upside deviation	19.95%	19.42%	17.62%
Downside deviation	21.70%	20.99%	20.32%
Tracking error	18.44	17.22	14.03
Number of positive periods	289	295	308
Number of negative periods	263	257	244
Maximum peak-to-trough decline	−96.87%	−94.14%	−92.77%
Beta	1.41	1.38	1.32

(continued on next page)

T A B L E   15CS.21

Summary Return and Risk Results for Annual Data: All Stocks VC3 Low 25, All Stocks VC3 Low 50, and All Stocks VC3 Decile 10, January 1, 1964, to December 31, 2009 *(Continued)*

	All Stocks VC3 low 25	All Stocks VC3 low 50	All Stocks VC3 decile 10
T-statistic (m = 0)	0.45	0.77	1.56
Sharpe ratio (Rf = 5%)	−0.25	−0.21	−0.09
Sortino ratio (MAR = 10%)	−0.60	−0.54	−0.37
$10,000 becomes	$2,468	$5,498	$30,733
Minimum 1-year return	−69.69%	−65.58%	−70.35%
Maximum 1-year return	189.70%	202.19%	216.74%
Minimum 3-year return	−49.79%	−48.49%	−52.67%
Maximum 3-year return	43.83%	43.88%	53.69%
Minimum 5-year return	−31.10%	−27.22%	−30.57%
Maximum 5-year return	28.11%	28.78%	36.42%
Minimum 7-year return	−26.74%	−23.07%	−22.02%
Maximum 7-year return	17.52%	18.88%	24.75%
Minimum 10-year return	−19.16%	−17.27%	−15.95%
Maximum 10-year return	11.25%	11.52%	17.97%
Minimum expected return*	−61.00%	−57.52%	−49.59%
Maximum expected return†	65.22%	64.58%	62.97%

* Minimum expected return is arithmetic return minus 2 times the standard deviation.
† Maximum expected return is arithmetic return plus 2 times the standard deviation.

T A B L E   15CS.22

Base Rates for All Stocks VC3 Low 25 and All Stocks, January 1, 1964, to December 31, 2009

Item	All Stocks VC3 low 25 beat All Stocks	Percent	Average annual excess return
Single-year return	152 out of 541	28%	−10.38%
Rolling 3-year compound return	87 out of 517	17%	−13.90%
Rolling 5-year compound return	30 out of 493	6%	−14.87%
Rolling 7-year compound return	29 out of 469	6%	−15.21%
Rolling 10-year compound return	4 out of 433	1%	−15.49%

T A B L E   15CS.23

Base Rates for All Stocks VC3 Low 50 and All Stocks, January 1, 1964, to December 31, 2009

Item	All Stocks VC3 low 50 beat All Stocks	Percent	Average annual excess return
Single-year return	156 out of 541	29%	−8.85%
Rolling 3-year compound return	101 out of 517	20%	−12.05%
Rolling 5-year compound return	39 out of 493	8%	−12.86%
Rolling 7-year compound return	31 out of 469	7%	−13.19%
Rolling 10-year compound return	5 out of 433	1%	−13.45%

T A B L E   15CS.24

Average Annual Compound Rates of Return by Decade

	1960s*	1970s	1980s	1990s	2000st
All Stocks VC3 high 25	15.00%	17.42%	21.78%	18.07%	18.74%
All Stocks VC3 high 50	16.54%	17.00%	21.82%	18.19%	18.91%
All Stocks VC3 low 25	18.03%	−2.92%	3.00%	−2.84%	−18.98%
All Stocks VC3 low 50	18.00%	−1.38%	3.14%	1.36%	−17.27%
All Stocks	13.36%	7.56%	16.78%	15.35%	4.39%

* Returns for January 1, 1964, to December 31, 1969.
† Returns for January 1, 2000, to December 31, 2009.

IMPLICATIONS

Because Value Factors One, Two, and Three are multifactor models, individuals might find buying the top 25 or 50 stocks an attractive way to put together a portfolio with excellent long-term returns, reasonable levels of risk, and outstanding base rates. Conversely, investors interested in a basic framework for shorting securities could start with the 25 or 50 worst stocks from decile 10, remembering to use sell-stop orders in frothy markets. At the very least, individual investors should be aware of the historically disappointing returns from these securities and avoid them at almost any cost.

16

C H A P T E R

THE VALUE OF VALUE FACTORS

Discovery consists in seeing what everybody has seen and thinking what nobody has thought.
  —Albert Szent-Gyorgyi

An analysis of the past behavior of stocks grouped by defining factors such as PE ratio, price-to-sales ratio, and EBITDA/EV shows that rather than careening about like a drunken monkey, the stock market methodically rewards certain types of stocks while punishing others. What's more, had you simply read and followed the advice in the second edition of this book you could have avoided the carnage that investors in the highest valued stocks suffered between 2000 and 2003. The severe bear market of 2007 through 2009 was more difficult to avoid, since the panic selling that caused much of the decline affected all stocks, regardless of their valuations. Nevertheless, paying attention to valuations would have left you better positioned to take advantage of the resurgence of stock prices in the last three quarters of 2009. And even though this book has been been available to the public since 1996, nothing has really changed regarding the longer-term performance of overpriced companies: They do *horribly* over the long term.

There's nothing random about Figure 16.1. Stocks with the best scores from our composited value ratios (as well as all the other value ratios tested) dramatically outperform the All Stocks universe. Just as important, those with the worst scores from our composited value ratios (as well as stocks with high price-to-book, high price-to-cash flow and high price-to-sales ratios) dramatically underperform. The symmetry is striking. Indeed, 12 of the 15 groups with very high valuations—such as earnings-to-price, EBITDA-to-enterprise value, sales-to-price, and all of our value composites—underperformed U.S. T-bills. What's more, the underperforming and overvalued strategies had higher standard deviations of return than the value strategies that significantly outperformed the All Stocks universe.

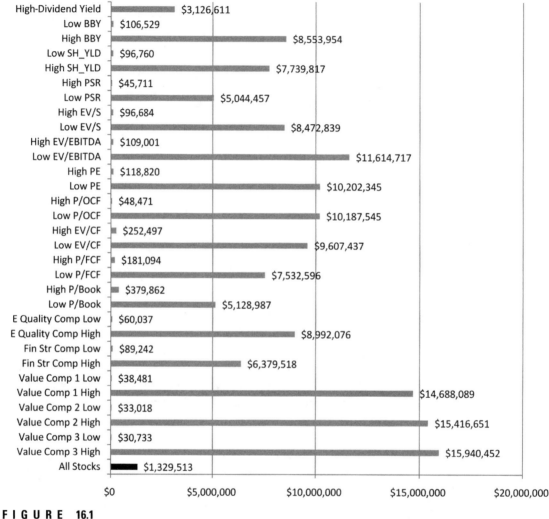

FIGURE   16.1

December 31, 2009, value of $10,000 invested in various strategies on January 1, 1964, using the All Stocks universe

RISK DOESN'T ALWAYS EQUAL REWARD

An important principle of the Capital Asset Pricing Model is that risk is compensated. It steers investors seeking higher returns to stocks with higher standard deviations. Yet the results of this evidence conflict with that principle. Twelve of the 16 strategies that outperform the All Stocks universe did so with *lower* standard deviations of return than the

All Stocks universe. However, higher risk does not always lead to higher returns. As Figure 16.2 shows, the higher risk of the *high* price-to-earnings, price-to-book, price-to-cash flow, and price-to-sales ratios went uncompensated. Indeed, each of the strategies significantly underperformed the All Stocks universe. Buying the stocks in decile 1 of our Value Composite Three turns $10,000 into $15,940,452 with a standard deviation of return of 17.68 percent, but buying the stocks in Value Composite Three in decile 10—those securities with the richest valuations—turns $10,000 into just $30,733, *yet with a higher standard deviation of return of 28.14 percent.*

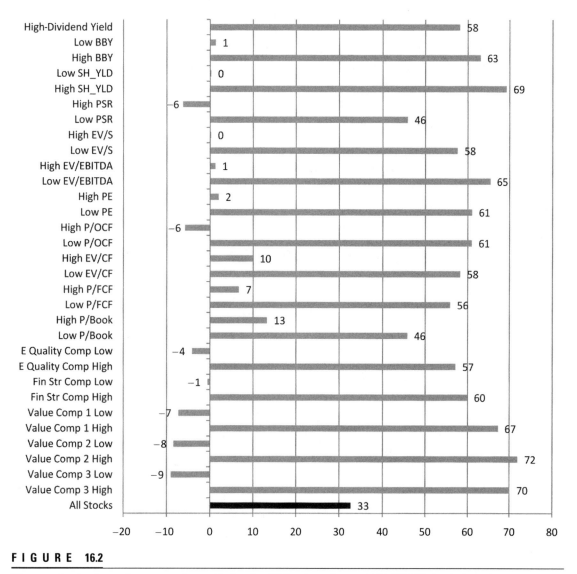

FIGURE   16.2

Sharpe ratios for the various strategies applied to the All Stocks universe, 1964–2009 (higher is better)

This remains largely true even when you use the CRSP dataset to analyze an additional 37 years of data. Between 1926 and 2009, buying the decile of stocks from All Stocks with the highest shareholder yield earned an average annual compound return of 13.22 percent and had a standard deviation of return of 20.19 percent. That's a higher return and lower standard deviation of return than an investment in the All Stocks universe itself, with its average annual compound return of 10.46 percent and standard deviation of 21.67 percent. In keeping with the 1963–2009 returns, an investment in the decile of stocks from All Stocks with the lowest shareholder yield—that is, those companies that were issuing the most stock and had a low dividend yield—had an average annual compound return of 5.06 percent and a standard deviation of return of 22.53 percent. Thus, for both the shorter period between 1963 and 2009 and the longer one between 1926 through 2009, the high shareholder yield strategy had much higher returns and a lower standard deviation of return than both the All Stocks universe and the low shareholder yield strategy.

IS IT WORTH THE RISK?

Figure 16.2 shows the risk-adjusted returns for all the factors, and Figure 16.3 shows the Sortino ratio for each factor. Many of the sexiest stocks with the most compelling stories also come with high PEs, price-to-book, price-to-cash flow, or price-to-sales ratios and have abysmal absolute *and* risk-adjusted returns. Nothing demonstrated this more forcefully then the performance of the strategies between January 1997 and March of 2000 and then after that particular speculative bubble burst. During the stock market bubble of the late 1990s, investors pushed the prices of richly valued stocks to unprecedented levels. An investor who believed the market-bubble mantra that it was "different this time" and focused on buying the "story" stocks with no earnings, little sales, but *great* stories about a bright future (think Anything.com) would have done extraordinarily well in the three years after the revised edition of *What Works on Wall Street* came out in 1997. An investor who stuck with the time-tested strategies featured in that book would have felt like an old fogey comparing his or her portfolio's performance to the high-ratio "story" stocks in March of 2000, the top of the stock market bubble.

Between January 1, 1997, and March 31, 2000, the decile of stocks from the All Stocks universe with the *worst scores* from Value Composite One compounded at *39.47 percent per year*, more than doubling $10,000 into $29,482 in three years and three months. Other speculative names did equally as well, with the decile of stocks from All Stocks with the highest price-to-book ratios growing a $10,000 investment into $28,286, a compound return of 37.70 percent. *All* the highest valuation stocks trounced All Stocks over that brief period, leaving those focusing on the shorter term to think that maybe it *was* different this time. But anyone familiar with past market bubbles knows that ultimately the laws of economics reassert their grip on market activity. Investors back in 2000 would have done well to remember Horace's *Ars Poetica*, in which he states: "Many shall be restored that are now fallen, and many shall fall that now are in honor."

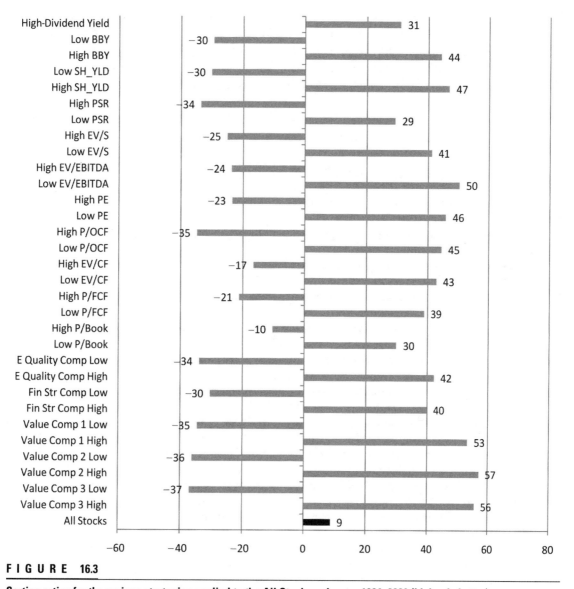

Sortino ratios for the various strategies applied to the All Stocks universe, 1964–2009 (higher is better)

For fall they did, and they fell hard. A near-sighted investor entering the market at its peak in March of 2000 would have faced true devastation. A $10,000 investment in decile 10 of Value Composite One on March 31, 2000, would have been worth just $1,441 at the end of 2009, an average annual compound loss of 18.02 percent. A similar $10,000 investment in the 10 percent of stocks from All Stocks with the worst sales-to-enterprise value would have been worth just $1,647, a loss of 16.89 percent a year. A similar fate befell all the other stocks with sky-high valuations.

You must *always* consider risk before investing in strategies that buy stocks that are significantly different from the market. Remember that high risk does not always mean high reward. Figures 16.4 and 16.5 show the compound average annual return and standard deviations for the All Stocks strategies. All the higher-risk strategies are eventually dashed on the rocks, as Figures 16.2, 16.3, and 16.6 make clear.

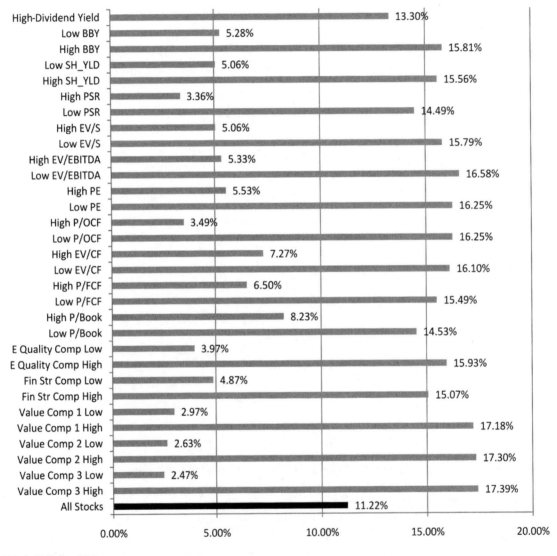

FIGURE 16.4

Compound average annual rates of return for the 46 years ending December 31, 2009, results of applying strategies on the All Stocks universe

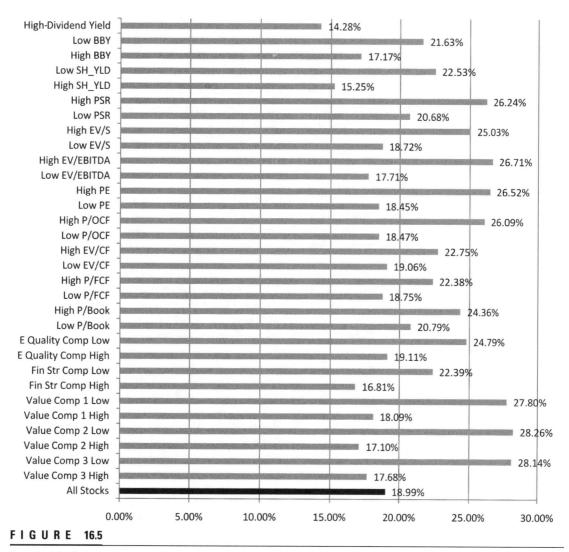

High-Dividend Yield	14.28%
Low BBY	21.63%
High BBY	17.17%
Low SH_YLD	22.53%
High SH_YLD	15.25%
High PSR	26.24%
Low PSR	20.68%
High EV/S	25.03%
Low EV/S	18.72%
High EV/EBITDA	26.71%
Low EV/EBITDA	17.71%
High PE	26.52%
Low PE	18.45%
High P/OCF	26.09%
Low P/OCF	18.47%
High EV/CF	22.75%
Low EV/CF	19.06%
High P/FCF	22.38%
Low P/FCF	18.75%
High P/Book	24.36%
Low P/Book	20.79%
E Quality Comp Low	24.79%
E Quality Comp High	19.11%
Fin Str Comp Low	22.39%
Fin Str Comp High	16.81%
Value Comp 1 Low	27.80%
Value Comp 1 High	18.09%
Value Comp 2 Low	28.26%
Value Comp 2 High	17.10%
Value Comp 3 Low	28.14%
Value Comp 3 High	17.68%
All Stocks	18.99%

FIGURE 16.5

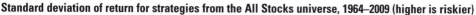

Standard deviation of return for strategies from the All Stocks universe, 1964–2009 (higher is riskier)

EMBRACE CONSISTENCY

You should also look for strategies that do well over time and have the highest base rates compared to their universes. Stocks that score well on the various composited value factors as well as those with the best EBITDA/EV, the highest buyback and shareholder yield, the lowest PE ratios and price-to-sales and price-to-cash flow ratios all have excellent long-term base rates. On the other hand, stocks with the worst scores on the composited value factors, as well as those with high PE ratios and price-to-sales ratios and low shareholder and buyback yield all have *horrible* base rates and usually only do well in unsustainable market bubbles. You must remember this the next time some hot sector is soaring and you are hearing all of the predictably short-term reasons why the old rules of valuation no longer apply. They *always* apply—and have for the entire time for which we have records of the stock market. Another thing to focus on is how badly various strategies suffered in the past. Figure 16.6 shows the maximum decline for each of the strategies tested between 1963 and 2009. The bear market of 2007–2009 was the second-worst decline for stocks since the great stock market crash of 1929–1932. The results shown in Figure 16.6 make this painfully evident. Even strategies that have performed brilliantly over the long-term have suffered *severe* drops in price—for example, all of the value composites dropped by

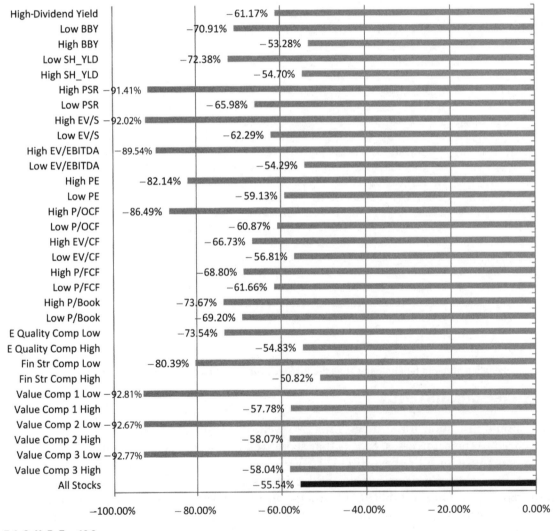

FIGURE 16.6

Maximum peak-to-trough decline—maximum percentage decline for strategies from the All Stocks universe, 1964–2009

more than 57 percent from peak to trough during the bear market of 2007–2009. Investors need to focus their attention on these worst-case scenarios and plan on how they will take action if another should occur in the future. We've seen that the U.S. stock market has recovered from *every* severe decline in history, but that will be of little use to us if we panic when the markets are moving against us. Study Table 16.6 closely the next time stocks are in a bear market and remember what comes afterward.

LARGE STOCKS RESULTS CONSISTENT WITH ALL STOCKS

As Figure 16.7 makes clear, when looking at the Large Stocks universe, we see similar results to those for All Stocks, only more muted. All the value strategies with low ratios beat the market, and all the strategies with high ratios do considerably worse. All the pricy, high-ratio strategies had higher standard deviations than their low ratio counterparts—and performed

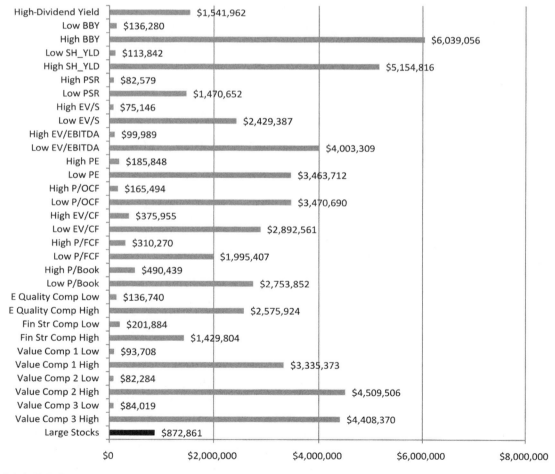

FIGURE 16.7

December 31, 2009 value of $10,000 invested in various strategies on January 1, 1964 using the Large Stocks universe.

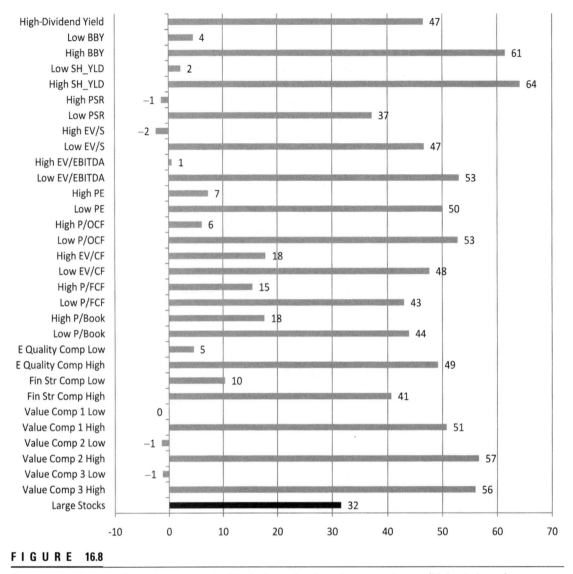

Sharpe ratios for the various strategies applied to the Large Stocks universe, 1964–2009 (higher is better)

significantly worse. But the absolute amounts are more modest. With Large Stocks, the best-performing strategy is to buy the decile of stocks with highest buyback yield. There, a $10,000 investment on January 1, 1964, grows to $6,039,056 by the end of 2009. We also see Large Stocks with good EBITDA/EV and high scores in Value Composite Two beating the Large Stocks universe by wide margins. Figure 16.7 shows the terminal value of $10,000 invested on January 1, 1964, in the various value strategies. Figures 16.8 and 16.9 show the risk-adjusted returns for all of the Large Stocks strategies, and Figure 16.10 shows the average annual compound returns for all of the Large Stocks strategies.

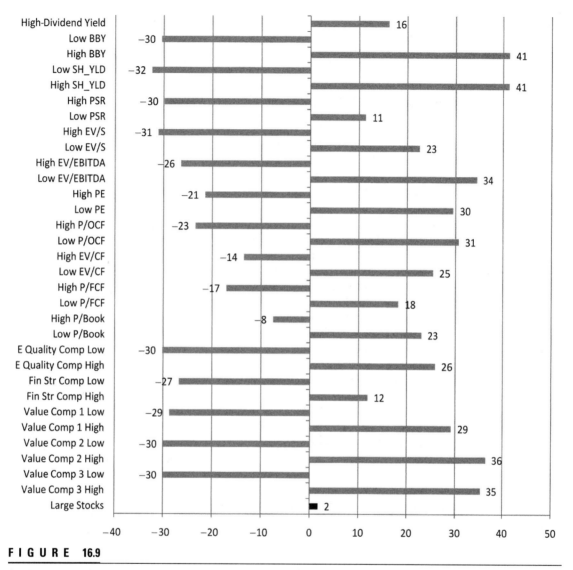

FIGURE 16.9

Sortino ratios for the various strategies applied to the Large Stocks universe, 1964–2009 (higher is better)

As you look at Figure 16.7, note that within the Large Stocks universe, *all* of the pricy, high ratios strategies did worse than the Large Stocks universe itself, and seven did worse than an investment in U.S. T-bills. In other words, over the last 46 years, you would have been better off making no investment in the stock market at all than to invest in these high-priced Large Stocks. Worse yet, if you took inflation into account, these high-priced stocks from the Large Stocks universe would have earned *no real return* over the last 46 years. So $10,000 invested in decile 10 of sales-to-enterprise value from Large Stocks—the priciest stocks by this measure—would have been worth $10,788 at the end of 2009, a miniscule

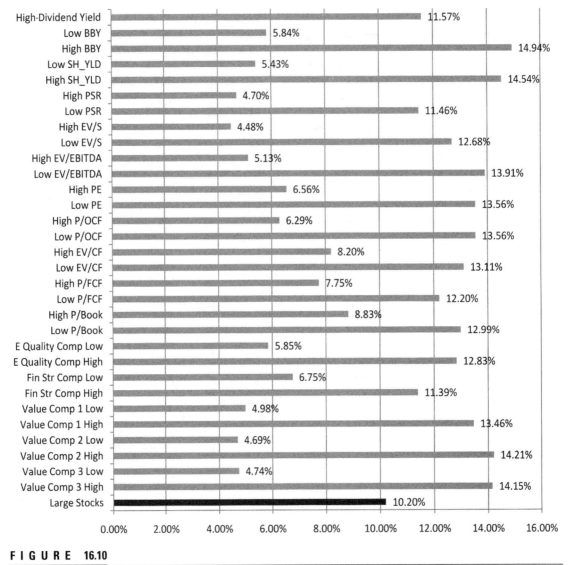

F I G U R E   16.10

Compound average annual rates of return for the 46 years ending December 31, 2009, results of applying strategies on the Large Stocks universe

average annual compound return of 0.17 percent after inflation. Even an investment in riskless U.S. T-bills turned $10,000 invested over the same period into $17,238, an after-inflation average annual compound return of 1.19 percent.

As far as risk is concerned, several of the Large Stocks strategies that did very well *also* had lower standard deviations of return. As Figure 16.11 shows, nine of the strategies that outperformed the Large Stocks universe did so at lower levels of risk, which is very

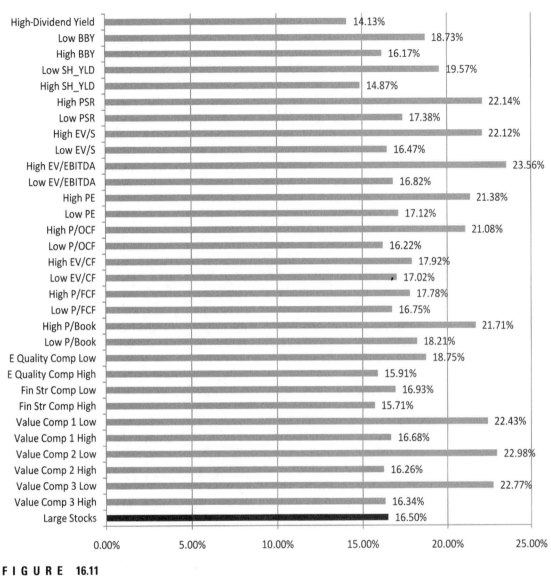

FIGURE 16.11

Standard deviation of return for strategies from the Large Stocks universe, 1964–2009 (higher is riskier)

helpful for their standings as we review the risk-adjusted Sharpe ratios and Sortino ratios found in Figures 16.8 and 16.9.

The highest Sharpe ratios in the Large Stocks universe were earned by the strategies with the highest shareholder yields, the highest buyback yield, and the best scores on Value Composite Two. Yet all the strategies that bought stocks with reasonable valuations managed to earn higher Sharpe ratios than the Large Stocks universe itself, and all the strategies

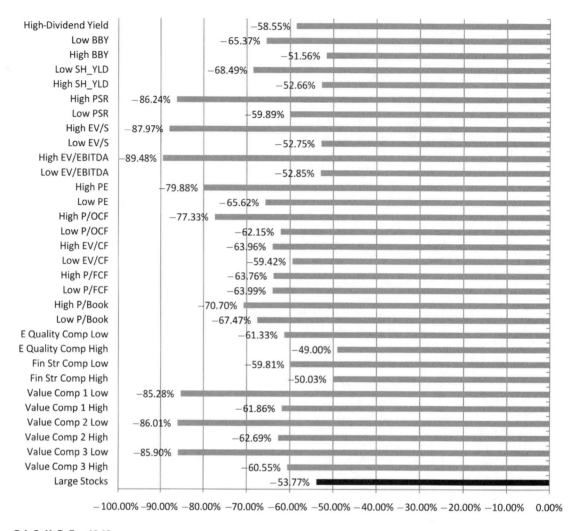

FIGURE   16.12

Maximum peak-to-trough decline—maximum percentage decline for strategies from the Large Stocks universe 1964–2009

that bought stocks with the richest valuations had Sharpe ratios much lower than that of the Large Stocks universe.

When reviewing the worst-case scenarios of our Large Stocks strategies, found in Figure 16.12, we see that six of the strategies that performed significantly better than the Large Stocks universe did so with smaller maximum declines. In the cases of larger higher returns and larger drawdowns, they declined only a few percentage points more than the Large Stocks universe. Yet the strategies from Large Stocks that failed to beat the universe had uniformly larger maximum declines, with six of the richly valued strategies losing more than 85 percent from peak to trough.

IMPLICATIONS

Value strategies work, rewarding patient investors who stick with them through bull and bear markets and through bubble and burst. But it's sticking with them that is extraordinarily hard. Since we all filter *today's* market performance through our decision-making process, it's almost always the glamorous, high-expectations, high-ratio stocks that grab our attention. They are the stocks we see zooming up in price, they are the ones that our friends and fellow investors talk about, and they are the ones on which investors focus their attention and buying power. Yet they are the very stocks that consistently disappoint investors over the long term.

All of the Large Stock value strategies beat the Large Stocks universe on an absolute and risk-adjusted basis, and in several cases did four times as well as Large Stocks. That's an extraordinary track record. The full decile analysis confirms our top and bottom decile findings, showing that you are almost always better off confining your search for market-beating stocks to the lower deciles from each of the ratios.

Conversely, high-ratio strategies (e.g., high PE, high price-to-book, etc.) consistently underperform their universes over the long term. They are both riskier and offer less reward. They have some spectacular runs that encourage investors to pay unwarranted prices for the stocks, but they consistently disappoint and should be avoided unless there are *extremely compelling* strategic reasons for buying them.

LEARNING TO FOCUS ON THE LONG TERM

Let's say that you bought the second edition of this book in 1998 and truly understood the dangers of investing in overvalued stocks. Yet in real time you would have watched those very stocks soar—month in and month out—for the next two years. Two years feels like an eternity to the average investor, and I believe that even armed with all the information in the book, you would have had a tough time staying away from those high-flying story stocks. Yes, the long-term data say to avoid these issues, but they are the only ones moving up in price, so maybe there really is something to this "new economy" paradigm shift that everyone is talking and writing about.

If you were like the typical investor, little by little you would relax the rules, becoming more and more willing to take a chance on some of the sexy stocks being touted on CNBC or in research reports. And then, much like the drug user who thinks he's just experimenting, you'd have been hooked. Unfortunately, in all likelihood you'd have gotten hooked nearer the end of the speculative market environment—and it would have cost you a fortune. To truly take advantage of the evidence presented in this book, you have to internalize this message and stay focused on the much longer term. In *no period* over the last 46 years did the high-flying, richly valued stocks *stay* ahead over the long term. They *always* ended up crashing and burning. The hot stocks of 1997–2000 were technology and Internet issues, but the hot stocks of tomorrow will quite likely come from a different industry with a new hot story. Remember that the market always reverts to basic economics and that it will be no different for those future hot stocks than it was for those in the past. Only then will you be able to take full advantage of all the long-term evidence presented in this book.

You'll also need to think about the long-term results of our strategies after bear markets like those of 2000–2003 and 2007–2009. The back-to-back severe bear markets of the last decade soured many people on *ever* investing in the stock market, and such an asset allocation mistake will most certainly radically reduce the returns you earn on your investments. According to the Investment Company Institute, between December 31, 2006, and August 11, 2010, investors yanked nearly $159 billion from equity funds and poured more than $709 billion into bond funds. Given that bond yields are close to historic lows, that is almost certainly going to be a losing investment as time goes on because, when yields increase, bond prices decline. It's hard to remember the long-term prospects for equities after suffering such a serious rout, yet it is when equities are priced well with low valuations and high-dividend yields that they go on to offer great returns for investors who had the courage to stay true to their long-term asset allocation. Tables 16.1 and 16.2 show the returns for the various strategies from All Stocks and Large Stocks by decades.

T A B L E   16.1

Average Annual Compound Rates of Return by Decade, All Stocks Universe

	1960s*	1970s	1980s	1990s	2000s†
All Stocks	13.36%	7.56%	16.78%	15.35%	4.39%
VC3 high	16.50%	15.62%	22.56%	16.69%	15.36%
VC3 low	15.54%	1.46%	6.76%	12.68%	−15.95%
VC2 high	15.49%	15.35%	23.21%	16.10%	15.82%
VC2 low	16.29%	1.48%	6.79%	12.80%	−15.80%
VC1 high	16.84%	14.78%	22.21%	16.34%	15.73%
VC1 low	15.88%	2.22%	7.42%	13.85%	−16.22%
Financial Strength Comp high	15.13%	10.41%	19.67%	21.09%	9.56%
Financial Strength Comp low	14.71%	4.78%	10.34%	7.12%	−7.44%
Earnings Quality Comp high	17.30%	14.36%	20.46%	22.47%	6.33%
Earnings Quality Comp low	14.95%	0.63%	5.89%	6.87%	−3.37%
Low P/Book	14.69%	13.29%	21.25%	14.68%	9.12%
High P/Book	14.99%	2.84%	12.31%	20.31%	−4.79%
Low P/Free Cash Flow	14.40%	13.59%	17.27%	18.88%	12.99%
High P/Free Cash Flow	11.51%	7.11%	11.32%	7.69%	−2.54%
Low Enterprise Value/Cash Flow	21.61%	11.89%	15.92%	21.31%	12.31%
High EnterpriseValue/Cash Flow	15.00%	7.12%	11.90%	7.05%	−1.03%
Low Price/Operating Cash Flow	15.86%	13.64%	19.27%	16.62%	15.78%
High Price/Operating Cash Flow	16.70%	0.96%	7.79%	9.36%	−10.32%
Low PE	17.68%	13.03%	20.38%	16.02%	14.86%
High PE	14.74%	1.61%	9.21%	13.73%	−6.55%
Low Enterprise Value/EBITDA	14.14%	13.82%	19.95%	18.59%	15.55%
High Enterprise Value/EBITDA	18.72%	2.61%	11.97%	13.28%	−11.98%
Low Enterprise Value/Sales	16.39%	12.44%	22.86%	15.60%	12.20%
High Enterprise Value/Sales	16.41%	5.74%	12.95%	13.49%	−15.50%
Low PSR	16.90%	11.44%	20.03%	12.82%	12.43%
High PSR	11.58%	5.60%	7.23%	12.98%	−14.79%
High SH_YLD	14.74%	13.09%	23.15%	16.33%	10.53%

(continued on next page)

T A B L E   16.1

Average Annual Compound Rates of Return by Decade, All Stocks Universe *(Continued)*

	1960s*	1970s	1980s	1990s	2000s†
Low SH_YLD	10.48%	2.73%	10.32%	7.77%	−3.23%
High Buyback Yield	16.94%	12.97%	22.42%	17.52%	10.02%
Low Buyback Yield	10.20%	2.80%	11.15%	7.94%	−3.09%
High-dividend yield	12.38%	10.63%	20.41%	11.76%	11.23%

*Returns for January 1, 1964, to December 31, 1969.
†Returns for January 1, 2000, to December 31, 2009.

T A B L E   16.2

Average Annual Compound Rates of Return by Decade, Large Stocks Universe

	1960s*	1970s	1980s	1990s	2000s†
All Stocks	8.16%	6.65%	17.34%	16.38%	2.42%
VC3 high	6.67%	13.80%	21.57%	15.56%	10.62%
VC3 low	15.89%	−0.58%	10.00%	16.77%	−11.32%
VC2 high	6.40%	13.65%	22.22%	15.04%	11.10%
VC2 low	16.00%	−1.13%	9.84%	17.32%	−11.36%
VC1 high	6.54%	12.75%	19.84%	14.64%	11.10%
VC1 low	16.37%	−0.97%	10.73%	17.66%	−11.49%
Financial Strength Comp high	8.21%	7.35%	16.66%	17.69%	6.30%
Financial Strength Comp low	6.92%	3.01%	14.85%	12.85%	−2.82%
Earnings Quality Comp high	9.26%	8.40%	22.75%	18.45%	4.82%
Earnings Quality Comp low	7.72%	1.08%	12.94%	12.89%	−3.60%
Low P/Book	8.20%	12.71%	22.07%	15.67%	5.12%
High P/Book	14.31%	0.26%	14.39%	22.78%	−3.27%
Low P/Free Cash Flow	2.98%	11.91%	17.47%	17.48%	8.03%
High P/Free Cash Flow	4.14%	5.38%	18.48%	12.92%	−2.40%
Low Enterprise Value/Cash Flow	7.75%	11.06%	18.58%	18.16%	8.30%
High EnterpriseValue/Cash Flow	3.90%	7.97%	17.27%	12.73%	−1.60%
Low P/Operating Cash Flow	6.89%	11.89%	19.71%	16.22%	10.79%
High P/Operating Cash Flow	15.40%	0.33%	12.51%	17.69%	−8.54%
Low PE	8.48%	11.38%	18.48%	16.04%	11.60%
High PE	15.07%	−0.93%	13.52%	18.53%	−7.64%
Low Enterprise Value/EBITDA	5.35%	12.75%	19.31%	16.96%	12.15%
High Enterprise Value/EBITDA	15.70%	0.41%	10.03%	21.78%	−14.27%
Low Enterprise Value/Sales	6.38%	10.01%	20.96%	15.62%	8.47%
High Enterprise Value/Sales	13.49%	1.34%	8.67%	19.04%	−13.50%
Low PSR	5.99%	8.80%	18.54%	14.95%	7.30%
High PSR	11.40%	0.16%	11.40%	17.05%	−11.37%
High SH_YLD	8.71%	11.84%	23.42%	17.37%	9.63%
Low SH_YLD	6.70%	−0.10%	11.60%	11.83%	−1.61%
High Buyback Yield	12.35%	12.10%	23.43%	18.40%	8.00%
Low Buyback Yield	6.52%	0.83%	12.93%	11.77%	−1.77%
High-dividend yield	8.04%	8.85%	19.08%	10.83%	9.98%

*Returns for January 1, 1964, to December 31, 1969.
†Returns for January 1, 2000, to December 31, 2009.

Now let's turn to growth variables and look for any compelling strategies that might overcome the dangers of investing in high-ratio stocks.

17 CHAPTER

ONE-YEAR EARNINGS PER SHARE PERCENTAGE CHANGES: DO HIGH EARNINGS GAINS MEAN HIGH PERFORMANCE?

It ain't so much what people know that hurts as what they know that ain't so.
—Artemus Ward

Now let's look at factors commonly associated with growth investing. Generally, growth investors like high growth, while value investors like low-value ratios like low PEs and low PSRs. Growth investors want high earnings and sales growth with prospects for more of the same. They usually don't care if a stock has a high PE ratio, reasoning that a company can grow its way out of short-term overvaluations. Growth investors often award high prices to stocks with rapidly increasing earnings.

Unfortunately, Compustat lacks long-term data on earnings forecasts. Many growth investors make substantial use of earnings forecasts when constructing their portfolios, so our inability to do a long-term test is somewhat limiting. However, some studies have found that forecasts are remarkably undependable. In the October 11, 1993, issue of *Forbes Magazine*, David Dreman recounts a study that used a sample of 67,375 analysts' quarterly estimates for the New York and American Stock Exchange listed companies between 1973 and 1990. It found that analysts' average forecast error was 40 percent and that estimates were misleading (i.e., missed their mark by more than 10 percent) two-thirds of the time. Therefore, I look at actual earnings changes, not earnings forecasts.

EXAMINING ANNUAL EARNINGS CHANGES

First, we look at buying the top decile of stocks with the best and the worst one-year earnings per share percentage changes from the All Stocks and Large Stocks universes. For this edition of the book, we have updated the formula within FactSet and are now able to look at stocks whose earnings went from positive to negative and vice versa. We accomplish this using the following formula to generate earnings changes: earnings per share (EPS) for current year minus earnings per share from one year ago, divided by the absolute value of earnings per share from one year ago. (The formula looks like this: EPS – EPS(–1 year)/absolute value [EPS (–1 year)].

Let's look at the returns from buying the top decile (decile 1) of stocks from the All Stocks universe with the best one-year earnings-per-share percentage gains. As usual, we start with $10,000 and rebalance the composited portfolio annually. As Tables 17.1 and 17.2 show, there's very little difference in buying stocks with the biggest annual gain in earnings and buying a broad universe like All Stocks. The $10,000 invested on December 31, 1963, in the top decile of one-year earnings gainers from All Stocks grew to $1,750,567 by the end of 2009. That's an average annual compound return of 11.88 percent. This is just slightly better return than a similar investment in All Stocks, where $10,000 grew to $1,329,513, an average annual compound return of 11.22 percent. The highest one-year earnings gainers from decile 1 were also riskier—their standard deviation was 22.10 percent compared to All Stocks' 18.99 percent. The higher risk brings the Sharpe ratio to .31, two points shy of All Stocks' Sharpe ratio of .33.

The strategy has had some magnificent runs, however. In the four-year period between December 31, 1963, and December 31, 1967, the strategy did significantly better than the

TABLE 17.1

Summary Annual Return and Risk Results Data: All Stocks and All Stocks EPS Change (%), Decile 1, January 1, 1964, to December 31, 2009

	All Stocks EPS change (%), decile 1	All Stocks
Arithmetic average	14.68%	13.26%
Geometric average	11.88%	11.22%
Median return	20.02%	17.16%
Standard deviation	22.10%	18.99%
Upside deviation	12.81%	10.98%
Downside deviation	15.77%	13.90%
Tracking error	6.59	0.00
Number of positive periods	331	329
Number of negative periods	221	223
Maximum peak-to-trough decline	−58.60%	−55.54%
Beta	1.12	1.00
T-statistic (m = 0)	4.23	4.47
Sharpe ratio (Rf = 5%)	0.31	0.33
Sortino ratio (MAR = 10%)	0.12	0.09

(continued on next page)

TABLE 17.1

Summary Annual Return and Risk Results Data: All Stocks and All Stocks EPS Change (%), Decile 1, January 1, 1964, to December 31, 2009 *(Continued)*

	All Stocks EPS change (%), decile 1	All Stocks
$10,000 becomes	$1,750,567	$1,329,513
Minimum 1-year return	−50.36%	−46.49%
Maximum 1-year return	89.75%	84.19%
Minimum 3-year return	−17.47%	−18.68%
Maximum 3-year return	44.57%	31.49%
Minimum 5-year return	−12.12%	−9.91%
Maximum 5-year return	34.81%	27.66%
Minimum 7-year return	−8.46%	−6.32%
Maximum 7-year return	25.99%	23.77%
Minimum 10-year return	0.58%	1.01%
Maximum 10-year return	20.64%	22.05%
Minimum expected return*	−29.52%	−24.73%
Maximum expected return†	58.88%	51.24%

* Minimum expected return is arithmetic return minus 2 times the standard deviation.
† Maximum expected return is arithmetic return plus 2 times the standard deviation.

TABLE 17.2

Base Rates for All Stocks EPS Change (%), Decile 1, and All Stocks, January 1, 1964, to December 31, 2009

Item	All Stocks EPS change (%) decile 1 beat All Stocks	Percent	Average annual excess return
Single-year return	303 out of 541	56%	1.43%
Rolling 3-year compound return	297 out of 517	57%	0.74%
Rolling 5-year compound return	288 out of 493	58%	0.30%
Rolling 7-year compound return	264 out of 469	56%	0.05%
Rolling 10-year compound return	262 out of 433	61%	−0.01%

All Stocks universe, turning $10,000 into $31,189, an annual compound return of 32.89 percent. It had another terrific streak between 1976 and 1980, when it gained 33.03 percent a year compared to All Stocks' 24.33 percent a year gain, but it lacks long-term consistency. Right after these great runs, the strategy performed significantly worse than All Stocks. Table 17.3 summarizes all the declines of 20 percent or more, and Tables 17.4 and 17.5 summarize the best and worst periods for the top decile of earnings gainers.

Think how maddening it would be to watch the biggest earnings gainers from All Stocks light up the board between 1976 and 1980, only to watch them return just 5.32 percent over the next five years, just as a bull market was roaring and the All Stocks universe itself gained a whopping 16.13 percent per year during the same period. Look at Figure 17.1, which features the rolling five-year excess (deficient) return for the top decile of stocks from All Stocks with the highest earnings gains. You'll see that the five years of double-digit excess returns in the periods ending in 1968 and 1980 were followed by years of bitter disappointment. It's also interesting to look at the recent dot-com market bubble, when earnings really ceased to matter. In Figure 17.1 you see that during the bubble years, the top decile by earnings gains received virtually no advantage over the All Stock universe. The base rates in Table 17.2 show that you might as well have been flipping a coin, with the biggest earnings gainers from All Stocks beating All Stocks in 58 percent of all rolling five-year periods and in 61 percent of all rolling ten-year periods.

T A B L E   17.3

Worst-Case Scenarios: All 20 Percent or Greater Declines for All Stocks EPS Change (%), Decile 1, January 1, 1964, to December 31, 2009

Peak date	Peak index value	Trough date	Trough index value	Recovery date	Decline (%)	Decline duration	Recovery duration
Apr–66	1.98	Oct–66	1.48	Jan–67	−24.91%	6	3
Nov–68	3.91	Sep–74	1.62	Apr–78	−58.60%	70	43
Aug–78	4.98	Oct–78	3.87	Mar–79	−22.28%	2	5
Feb–80	7.39	Mar–80	5.79	Jul–80	−21.59%	1	4
Nov–80	10.41	Jul–82	6.66	Feb–83	−36.04%	20	7
Jun–83	13.11	Jul–84	9.45	Feb–86	−27.92%	13	19
Aug–87	19.31	Nov–87	12.78	Apr–89	−33.81%	3	17
Sep–89	21.86	Oct–90	16.30	Mar–91	−25.44%	13	5
Apr–98	83.20	Aug–98	56.71	Nov–99	−31.83%	4	15
Feb–00	109.50	Sep–02	71.46	Dec–03	−34.74%	31	15
Oct–07	230.01	Feb–09	98.10	N/A	−57.35%	16	N/A
Average					−34.05%	16.27	13.3

T A B L E   17.4

Best and Worst Average Annual Compound Returns for Monthly Data, January 1, 1964, to December 31, 2009

For any	1-year period	3-year period	5-year period	7-year period	10-year period
All Stocks EPS change (%), decile 1, minimum compound return	−50.36%	−17.47%	−12.12%	−8.46%	0.58%
All Stocks EPS change (%), decile 1, maximum compound return	89.75%	44.57%	34.81%	25.99%	20.64%
All Stocks minimum compound return	−46.49%	−18.68%	−9.91%	−6.32%	1.01%
All Stocks maximum compound return	84.19%	31.49%	27.66%	23.77%	22.05%
All Stocks EPS change (%), decile 10, minimum compound return	−59.14%	−31.94%	−12.47%	−8.31%	−4.25%
All Stocks EPS change (%), decile 10, maximum compound return	106.63%	36.89%	27.29%	21.85%	19.03%

T A B L E   17.5

Terminal Value of $10,000 Invested for Best and Worst Average Annual Compound Returns for Monthly Data, January 1, 1964, to December 31, 2009

For any	1-year period	3-year period	5-year period	7-year period	10-year period
All Stocks EPS change (%), decile 1, minimum $10,000 value	$4,964	$5,621	$5,240	$5,388	$10,600
All Stocks EPS change (%), decile 1, maximum $10,000 value	$18,975	$30,216	$44,530	$50,400	$65,301
All Stocks minimum $10,000 value	$5,351	$5,379	$5,936	$6,330	$11,054
All Stocks maximum $10,000 value	$18,419	$22,734	$33,903	$44,504	$73,345
All Stocks EPS change (%), decile 10, minimum $10,000 value	$4,086	$3,152	$5,138	$5,450	$6,477
All Stocks EPS change (%), decile 10, maximum $10,000 value	$20,663	$25,649	$33,423	$39,887	$57,099

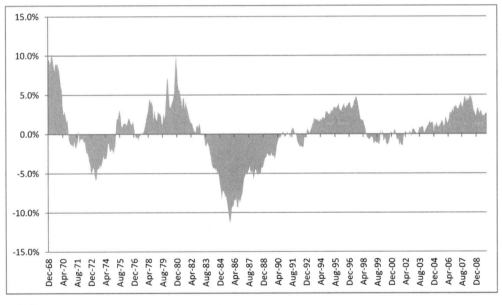

F I G U R E   17.1

Five-year average annual compound excess (deficient) return All Stocks EPS change (%) decile 1 minus All Stocks, January 1, 1964, to December 31, 2009

LARGE STOCKS DO WORSE

The top decile of stocks with the highest one-year earnings gains from the Large Stocks universe did not perform as well. Here, $10,000 invested on December 31, 1963, grew to $555,651 by the end of 2009, a compound return of 9.13 percent. That's slightly less than the $872,861 you'd have earned investing $10,000 in the Large Stocks universe, which had a return of 10.20 percent a year. The Sharpe ratio is .22, compared to Large Stocks' .32. All base rates are negative, with the top decile of highest one-year earnings gainers beating Large Stocks in just 14 percent of all rolling ten-year periods. Tables 17.6 and 17.7 show the summary information as well as the base rates for the stocks from Large Stocks with the best one-year earnings gains.

T A B L E   17.6

Summary Annual Return and Risk Results Data: Large Stocks and Large Stocks EPS Change (%), Decile 1, January 1, 1964, to December 31, 2009

	Large Stocks EPS change (%), decile 1	Large Stocks
Arithmetic average	11.09%	11.72%
Geometric average	9.13%	10.20%
Median return	13.71%	17.20%
Standard deviation	18.83%	16.50%
Upside deviation	11.03%	9.70%
Downside deviation	13.00%	11.85%
Tracking error	6.78	0.00
Number of positive periods	324	332
Number of negative periods	228	220
Maximum peak-to-trough decline	−53.41%	−53.77%
Beta	1.07	1.00
T-statistic (m = 0)	3.80	4.58
Sharpe ratio (Rf = 5%)	0.22	0.32
Sortino ratio (MAR = 10%)	−0.07	0.02
$10,000 becomes	$555,651	$872,861
Minimum 1-year return	−47.02%	−46.91%
Maximum 1-year return	69.02%	68.96%
Minimum 3-year return	−19.06%	−15.89%
Maximum 3-year return	34.20%	33.12%
Minimum 5-year return	−8.00%	−5.82%
Maximum 5-year return	26.67%	28.95%
Minimum 7-year return	−7.09%	−4.15%
Maximum 7-year return	20.58%	22.83%
Minimum 10-year return	−1.24%	−0.15%
Maximum 10-year return	18.74%	19.57%
Minimum expected return*	−26.57%	−21.28%
Maximum expected return†	48.74%	44.72%

* Minimum expected return is arithmetic return minus 2 times the standard deviation.
† Maximum expected return is arithmetic return plus 2 times the standard deviation.

T A B L E   17.7

Base Rates for Large Stocks EPS Change (%), Decile 1, and Large Stocks, January 1, 1964, to December 31, 2009

Item	Large Stocks EPS change (%), decile 1 beat Large Stocks	Percent	Average annual excess return
Single-year return	239 out of 541	44%	−0.56%
Rolling 3-year compound return	186 out of 517	36%	−0.97%
Rolling 5-year compound return	142 out of 493	29%	−1.28%
Rolling 7-year compound return	116 out of 469	25%	−1.48%
Rolling 10-year compound return	62 out of 433	14%	−1.57%

The record shows that buying stocks with the highest one-year earnings gains has very little long-term consistency. This probably occurs because high expectations are hard to meet. Seduced by stellar earnings gains, investors bid the stocks to unsustainable levels. When earnings growth fails to continue, they become disenchanted and sell their shares in disgust. Figure 17.2 shows the five-year average annual excess (or in this case, mostly deficient) return for decile 1 minus the return for the Large Stocks universe. It's pretty disappointing.

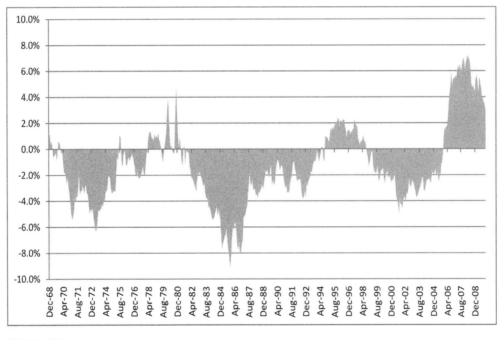

F I G U R E   17.2

Five-year average annual compound excess (deficient) return Large Stocks EPS change (%) decile 1 minus Large Stocks, January 1, 1964, to December 31, 2009

BEST- AND WORST-CASE SCENARIOS AND BEST AND WORST RETURNS

Between December 31, 1963, and December 31, 2009, the decile of stocks from the All Stocks universe with the highest earnings per share percentage gains lost more than 20 percent of its value 11 times. The largest peak-to-trough decline was a loss of 58.60 percent between November 1968 and September 1974. That loss was nearly matched between October 2007 and February 2009, when it lost 57.35 percent. It also proved more volatile when stock prices were declining, with a downside risk of 15.77 percent compared to 13.90 percent for All Stocks.

Table 17.5 shows the terminal value of $10,000 invested in decile 1 of the best one-year earnings gainers from All Stocks: Its best five-year return came at the end of November 1980, when it turned $10,000 into $44,530, an average annual compound return of 34.81 percent. Its worst five years were those ending September 1974, when it reduced the same $10,000 to $5,240, an average annual compound loss of –12.12 percent.

Large Stocks with the highest one-year earnings gains lost more than 20 percent nine times between December 31, 1963, and December 31, 2009 (Table 17.8). Their largest peak-to-trough decline was between October 2007 and February 2009, when they lost 53.41 percent. Like the group from All Stocks, they were also more volatile when prices were declining, with a downside risk of 13 percent compared to 11.85 for Large Stocks. Their best five-year return occurred in the period ending October 2007, when a $10,000 investment grew to $32,611, a compound return of 26.67 percent per year. Their worst five years occurred in the period ending September 1974, when the same $10,000 declined to $6,592, an average annual compound loss of –8.0 percent. Table 17.8 shows the worst-case scenarios, and Tables 17.9 and 17.10 the best and worst returns for all periods. Figures 17.1 and 17.2 graph all rolling five-year excess returns from 1964 through 2009 for the top earnings growth decile of All Stocks and Large Stocks.

T A B L E   17.8

Worst-Case Scenarios: All 20 Percent or Greater Declines for Large Stocks EPS Change (%), Decile 1, January 1, 1964, to December 31, 2009

Peak date	Peak index value	Trough date	Trough index value	Recovery date	Decline (%)	Decline duration	Recovery duration
Apr–66	1.58	Oct–66	1.19	Apr–67	−25.02%	6	6
Nov–68	1.96	Sep–74	1.04	Dec–76	−46.59%	70	27
Nov–80	4.15	Jul–82	2.61	Apr–83	−36.96%	20	9
Jun–83	4.65	May–84	3.66	Jan–85	−21.32%	11	8
Sep–87	8.61	Nov–87	6.07	May–89	−29.42%	2	18
Aug–89	10.13	Oct–90	7.51	Sep–91	−25.82%	14	11
Apr–98	32.61	Aug–98	25.59	Jan–99	−21.53%	4	5
Aug–00	45.74	Feb–03	23.19	Aug–05	−49.29%	30	30
Oct–07	79.16	Feb–09	36.88	N/A	−53.41%	16	N/A
Average					−34.37%	19.22	14.25

TABLE 17.9

Best and Worst Average Annual Compound Returns for Monthly Data, January 1, 1964, to December 31, 2009

For any	1-year period	3-year period	5-year period	7-year period	10-year period
Large Stocks EPS change (%), decile 1, minimum compound return	−47.02%	−19.06%	−8.00%	−7.09%	−1.24%
Large Stocks EPS change (%), decile 1, maximum compound return	69.02%	34.20%	26.67%	20.58%	18.74%
Large Stocks minimum compound return	−46.91%	−15.89%	−5.82%	−4.15%	−0.15%
Large Stocks maximum compound return	68.96%	33.12%	28.95%	22.83%	19.57%
Large Stocks EPS change (%), decile 10, minimum compound return	−55.59%	−27.26%	−9.55%	−6.21%	−4.26%
Large Stocks EPS change (%), decile 10, maximum compound return	62.25%	33.14%	27.10%	22.58%	20.99%

TABLE 17.10

Terminal Value of $10,000 Invested for Best and Worst Average Annual Compound Returns for Monthly Data, January 1, 1964, to December 31, 2009

For any	1-year period	3-year period	5-year period	7-year period	10-year period
Large Stocks EPS change (%), decile 1, minimum $10,000 value	$5,298	$5,303	$6,592	$5,978	$8,828
Large Stocks EPS change (%), decile 1, maximum $10,000 value	$16,902	$24,169	$32,611	$37,068	$55,698
Large Stocks minimum $10,000 value	$5,309	$5,951	$7,409	$7,434	$9,848
Large Stocks maximum $10,000 value	$16,896	$23,591	$35,656	$42,189	$59,747
Large Stocks EPS change (%), decile 10, minimum $10,000 value	$4,441	$3,849	$6,053	$6,383	$6,473
Large Stocks EPS change (%), decile 10, maximum $10,000 value	$16,225	$23,600	$33,169	$41,574	$67,211

On a *relative basis* to their benchmarks, the best five-year relative performance for the best earnings gainers from All Stocks versus the All Stocks Universe occurred in the period ending November 1980, when they had a cumulative return of 345 percent compared to 203 percent for the All Stocks universe, an excess cumulative return of 142 percent. The worst five years versus All Stocks occurred in the period ending in December 1985, when they had a cumulative gain of 30 percent versus All Stocks' cumulative gain of 113 percent, producing a deficit of 83 percent for the best earnings gainers from All Stocks.

For the Large Stocks group, the best five-year relative performance against the Large Stocks universe occurred in the period ending November 1980, when the best earnings gainers from Large Stocks had a cumulative return of 177 percent versus a gain of 128 percent for Large Stocks, a cumulative excess over Large Stocks of 49 percent. The worst five-year relative performance against Large Stocks occurred in the period ending in August 1986, when they earned a cumulative return of 79 percent compared to a gain of 150 percent for the Large Stocks universe, a deficit of 71 percent.

BUYING STOCKS WITH THE WORST EARNINGS CHANGES

Perhaps you'd be better off buying the decile of stocks with the *worst* annual earnings changes. At least expectations for these stocks are modest. Remember that we are also now looking at stocks for which earnings go from positive to negative, thus really huge declines into negative territory will dominate decile 10.

The $10,000 invested on December 31, 1963, in the decile of stocks from the All Stocks universe with the worst one-year earnings changes grew to $350,708 by the end of 2009, an average annual compound return of 8.04 percent. That return falls significantly short of the $1,329,513 you'd have earned from the same investment in All Stocks alone. Risk was 23.34 percent, a good bit higher than the All Stocks universe's 18.99 percent. The Sharpe ratio for the worst decile by earnings changes was .13, compared to .33 for the All Stocks universe. Base rates were uniformly negative with the worst annual earnings changes group from All Stocks, beating the All Stocks universe in only 16 percent of all rolling five-year periods and in just 2 percent of all rolling ten-year periods. Tables 17.11, 17.12, and 17.13 summarize the results. Figure 17.3 shows the rolling five-year average annual compound excess (deficient) return for decile 10 minus the All Stocks universe return.

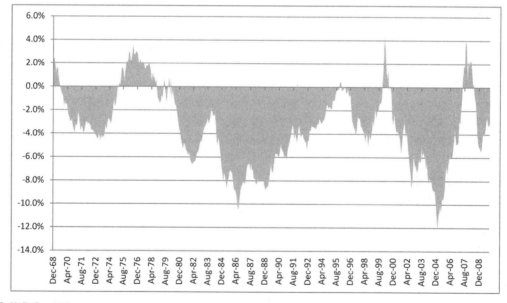

FIGURE   17.3

Five-year average annual compound excess (deficient) return All Stocks EPS change (%) decile 10 minus All Stocks, January 1, 1964, to December 31, 2009

TABLE 17.11

Summary Annual Return and Risk Results Data: All Stocks and All Stocks EPS Change (%), Decile 10, January 1, 1964, to December 31, 2009

	All Stocks EPS change (%) decile 10	All Stocks
Arithmetic average	11.05%	13.26%
Geometric average	8.04%	11.22%
Median return	16.09%	17.16%
Standard deviation	23.34%	18.99%
Upside deviation	14.64%	10.98%
Downside deviation	16.90%	13.90%
Tracking error	7.28	0.00
Number of positive periods	325	329
Number of negative periods	227	223
Maximum peak-to-trough decline	−71.22%	−55.54%
Beta	1.18	1.00
T-statistic (m = 0)	3.06	4.47
Sharpe ratio (Rf = 5%)	0.13	0.33
Sortino ratio (MAR = 10%)	−0.12	0.09
$10,000 becomes	$350,708	$1,329,513
Minimum 1-year return	−59.14%	−46.49%
Maximum 1-year return	106.63%	84.19%
Minimum 3-year return	−31.94%	−18.68%
Maximum 3-year return	36.89%	31.49%
Minimum 5-year return	−12.47%	−9.91%
Maximum 5-year return	27.29%	27.66%
Minimum 7-year return	−8.31%	−6.32%
Maximum 7-year return	21.85%	23.77%
Minimum 10-year return	−4.25%	1.01%
Maximum 10-year return	19.03%	22.05%
Minimum expected return*	−35.64%	−24.73%
Maximum expected return†	57.74%	51.24%

* Minimum expected return is arithmetic return minus 2 times the standard deviation.
† Maximum expected return is arithmetic return plus 2 times the standard deviation.

TABLE 17.12

Base Rates for All Stocks EPS Change (%), Decile 10, and All Stocks, January 1, 1964, to December 31, 2009

Item	All Stocks EPS change (%), decile, 10 beat All Stocks	Percent	Average annual excess return
Single-year return	209 out of 541	39%	−2.14%
Rolling 3-year compound return	145 out of 517	28%	−3.17%
Rolling 5-year compound return	80 out of 493	16%	−3.44%
Rolling 7-year compound return	52 out of 469	11%	−3.58%
Rolling 10-year compound return	10 out of 433	2%	−3.52%

TABLE 17.13

Worst-Case Scenarios: All 20 Percent or Greater Declines for All Stocks EPS Change (%) Decile 10, January 1, 1964, to December 31, 2009

Peak date	Peak index value	Trough date	Trough index value	Recovery date	Decline (%)	Decline duration	Recovery duration
Jan–69	2.94	Sep–74	1.19	May–78	−59.46%	68	44
May–81	5.67	Jul–82	4.01	Nov–82	−29.36%	14	4
Jun–83	7.95	Jul–84	6.02	Feb–86	−24.23%	13	19
Aug–87	10.65	Nov–87	7.00	May–89	−34.27%	3	18
Aug–89	11.49	Oct–90	7.42	Jan–92	−35.39%	14	15
Apr–98	29.52	Aug–98	19.66	Apr–99	−33.42%	4	8
Feb–00	54.32	Sep–02	15.63	N/A	−71.22%	31	N/A
Average					−41.05%	21	18

LARGE STOCKS DO WORSE

The $10,000 invested in the decile of the Large Stocks universe with the worst one-year earnings grew to just $285,002 on December 31, 2009, a compound return of 7.55 percent. And the $10,000 invested on December 31, 1963, in Large Stocks grew to $872,861, a compound return of 10.20 percent a year. The Sharpe ratio of the worst one-year earnings group was just .14, compared to the Large Stocks' ratio of .32. Tables 17.14, 17.15, and 17.16 summarize the results. The base rates are slightly better than they were for the worst earnings gainers from All Stocks, with the worst earnings gainers beating the Large Stocks universe in 25 percent of all rolling five-year periods and in 9 percent of all rolling ten-year periods. Figure 17.4 shows the rolling five-year average annual compound excess (deficient) return for decile 10 minus the Large Stocks universe return, Tables 17.17 and 17.18 summarize the average compound rates of return by decade for best and worst deciles of earnings change for the All Stocks and the Large Stocks universes.

TABLE 17.14

Summary Annual Return and Risk Results Data: Large Stocks and Large Stocks EPS Change (%), Decile 10, January 1, 1964, to December 31, 2009

	Large Stocks EPS change (%), decile 10	Large Stocks
Arithmetic average	9.43%	11.72%
Geometric average	7.55%	10.20%
Median return	13.63%	17.20%
Standard deviation	18.56%	16.50%
Upside deviation	11.21%	9.70%
Downside deviation	13.29%	11.85%
Tracking error	6.79	0.00
Number of positive periods	319	332
Number of negative periods	233	220
Maximum peak-to-trough decline	−67.30%	−53.77%
Beta	1.05	1.00

(continued on next page)

T A B L E 17.14

Summary Annual Return and Risk Results Data: Large Stocks and Large Stocks EPS Change (%), Decile 10, January 1, 1964, to December 31, 2009 *(Continued)*

	Large Stocks EPS change (%), decile 10	Large Stocks
T-statistic (m = 0)	3.31	4.58
Sharpe ratio (Rf = 5%)	0.14	0.32
Sortino ratio (MAR = 10%)	−0.18	0.02
$10,000 becomes	$285,002	$872,861
Minimum 1-year return	−55.59%	−46.91%
Maximum 1-year return	62.25%	68.96%
Minimum 3-year return	−27.26%	−15.89%
Maximum 3-year return	33.14%	33.12%
Minimum 5-year return	−9.55%	−5.82%
Maximum 5-year return	27.10%	28.95%
Minimum 7-year return	−6.21%	−4.15%
Maximum 7-year return	22.58%	22.83%
Minimum 10-year return	−4.26%	−0.15%
Maximum 10-year return	20.99%	19.57%
Minimum expected return*	−27.68%	−21.28%
Maximum expected return†	46.55%	44.72%

* Minimum expected return is arithmetic return minus 2 times the standard deviation.

† Maximum expected return is arithmetic return plus 2 times the standard deviation.

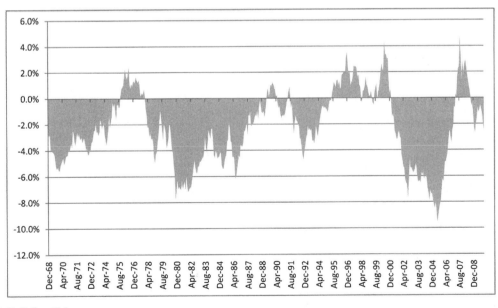

F I G U R E 17.4

Five-year average annual compound excess (deficient) return Large Stocks EPS change (%) decile 10 minus Large Stocks, January 1, 1964, to December 31, 2009

TABLE 17.15

Base Rates for Large Stocks EPS Change (%), Decile 10, and Large Stocks, January 1, 1964, to December 31, 2009

Item	Large Stocks EPS change (%), decile 10 beat Large Stocks	Percent	Average annual excess return
Single-year return	200 out of 541	37%	−1.85%
Rolling 3-year compound return	160 out of 517	31%	−2.17%
Rolling 5-year compound return	122 out of 493	25%	−2.26%
Rolling 7-year compound return	57 out of 469	12%	−2.34%
Rolling 10-year compound return	37 out of 433	9%	−2.22%

TABLE 17.16

Worst-Case Scenarios: All 20 Percent or Greater Declines for Large Stocks EPS Change (%) Decile 10, January 1, 1964, to December 31, 2009

Peak date	Peak index value	Trough date	Trough index value	Recovery date	Decline (%)	Decline duration	Recovery duration
Jan–66	1.24	Sep–66	0.99	Apr–67	−20.15%	8	7
Jan–69	1.61	Sep–74	0.86	Feb–76	−46.73%	68	17
Mar–81	2.57	Jul–82	1.99	Nov–82	−22.57%	16	4
Sep–87	6.71	Nov–87	4.75	Jan–89	−29.11%	2	14
Aug–89	8.21	Oct–90	5.85	May–91	−28.67%	14	7
Aug–00	42.69	Sep–02	13.96	Sep–07	−67.30%	25	60
Oct–07	44.70	Feb–09	17.16	N/A	−61.62%	16	N/A
Average					−39.45%	21.29	18.17

TABLE 17.17

Average Annual Compound Rates of Return by Decade

	1960s*	1970s	1980s	1990s	2000s†
All Stocks EPS change (%), decile 1	19.66%	8.30%	12.25%	17.02%	5.80%
All Stocks EPS change (%), decile 10	11.85%	7.38%	10.55%	14.67%	−1.97%
All Stocks	13.36%	7.56%	16.78%	15.35%	4.39%

* Returns for January 1, 1964, to December 31, 1969.
† Returns for January 1, 2000, to December 31, 2009.

TABLE 17.18

Average Annual Compound Rates of Return by Decade

	1960s*	1970s	1980s	1990s	2000s†
Large Stocks EPS change (%), decile 1	8.30%	5.40%	13.32%	15.94%	2.88%
Large Stocks EPS change (%), decile 10	3.13%	4.76%	15.60%	16.29%	−2.55%
Large Stocks	8.16%	6.65%	17.34%	16.38%	2.42%

* Returns for January 1, 1964, to December 31, 1969.
† Returns for January 1, 2000, to December 31, 2009.

BEST- AND WORST-CASE SCENARIOS

Between December 31, 1963, and December 31, 2009, the decile of stocks from the All Stocks universe with the biggest annual drop in earnings per share declined by more than 20 percent from peak to trough seven times. The largest decline of 71.22 percent occurred between February 2000 and September 2002, and it has yet to recover from the February 2000 highs. Table 17.13 shows all declines since 1963. As with the decile of stocks from All Stocks with the biggest earnings per share gains, the decile with the worst earnings per share gains was also more volatile when stock prices were declining, with a downside risk of 16.90 percent versus 13.90 percent for All Stocks. The best five-year period for the decile of stocks with the worst earnings per share changes occurred in the period ending December 1979, when a $10,000 investment grew to $33,423, a compound return of 27.29 percent per year. The worst five-year period occurred in the period ending February 2009, when the $10,000 dropped to $5,138, an average annual compound loss of −12.47 percent.

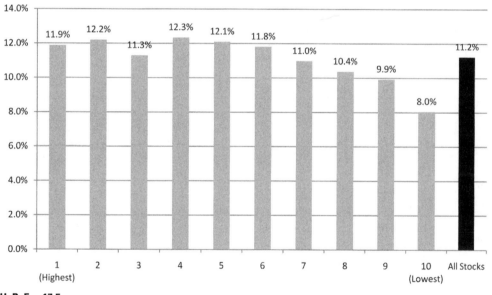

FIGURE 17.5

Average annual compound return by EPS Change (%) decile, All Stocks universe, January 1, 1964 to December 31, 2009

TABLE 17.19

Summary Results for EPS Change (%) Decile Analysis of All Stocks Universe, January 1, 1964, to December 31, 2009

Decile	$10,000 grows to	Average return	Compound return	Standard deviation	Sharpe ratio
1 (highest)	$1,750,567	14.68%	11.88%	22.10%	0.31
2	$1,995,466	14.76%	12.20%	21.14%	0.34
3	$1,371,466	13.38%	11.29%	19.17%	0.33
4	$2,107,751	14.04%	12.34%	17.28%	0.42

(continued on next page)

T A B L E   17.19

Summary Results for EPS Change (%) Decile Analysis of All Stocks Universe, January 1, 1964, to December 31, 2009
(Continued)

Decile	$10,000 grows to	Average return	Compound return	Standard deviation	Sharpe ratio
5	$1,907,735	13.53%	12.09%	15.97%	0.44
6	$1,696,234	13.14%	11.81%	15.41%	0.44
7	$1,200,373	12.32%	10.97%	15.57%	0.38
8	$932,374	11.91%	10.36%	16.67%	0.32
9	$773,000	11.85%	9.91%	18.68%	0.26
10 (lowest)	$350,708	11.05%	8.04%	23.34%	0.13
All Stocks	$1,329,513	13.26%	11.22%	18.99%	0.33

The decile of stocks from the Large Stocks universe with the worst earnings per share declines dropped by more than 20 percent seven times, with the largest decline—67.3 percent—occurring between August 2000 and September 2002. That maximum drawdown was almost matched by the 61.62 percent decline it suffered between October 2007 and February 2009. Like the decile of Large Stocks with the best earnings gains, those with the worst were riskier when stock prices were declining, with a downside risk of 13.29 percent versus 11.85 percent for Large Stocks. The best five-year return occurred in the period ending July 1987, when a $10,000 investment grew to $33,169, a compound return of 27.10 percent. The worst five-year period occurred in the period ending September 2002, when the $10,000 declined to $6,053. Tables 17.9 and 17.10 catalog the worst-case scenarios and best and worst case returns over all time periods, and Table 17.20 shows the return for all deciles of Large Stocks by earnings per share percentage change.

T A B L E   17.20

Summary Results for EPS Change (%) Decile Analysis of Large Stocks Universe, January 1, 1964, to December 31, 2009

Decile	$10,000 grows to:	Average return	Compound return	Standard deviation	Sharpe ratio
1 (highest)	$555,651	11.09%	9.13%	18.83%	0.22
2	$887,075	12.01%	10.24%	17.77%	0.29
3	$795,618	11.46%	9.98%	16.31%	0.31
4	$939,305	11.73%	10.38%	15.61%	0.34
5	$746,951	11.10%	9.83%	15.16%	0.32
6	$803,736	11.19%	10.01%	14.66%	0.34
7	$687,816	10.78%	9.63%	14.47%	0.32
8	$624,773	10.66%	9.41%	15.11%	0.29
9	$826,689	11.48%	10.07%	15.94%	0.32
10 (lowest)	$285,002	9.43%	7.55%	18.56%	0.14
Large Stocks	$872,861	11.72%	10.20%	16.50%	0.32

On a relative basis, the best five years for the decile of stocks with the worst earnings changes from All Stocks versus the All Stocks universe occurred in the period ending in February 2000, when the decile returned a cumulative 223 percent versus 172 percent for All Stocks, a cumulative advantage of 51 percent. The worst five-year relative performance occurred in the period ending in June 1986, when the group earned a cumulative 51 percent compared to a cumulative gain of 136 percent for All Stocks, a cumulative deficit of 85 percent.

When we look at the worst decile by earnings change from Large Stocks, we see that the best five-year relative performance versus Large Stocks occurred in October 1995, when it earned a cumulative 154 percent versus 143 percent for the Large Stocks universe, an 11 percent cumulative advantage. The worst relative performance versus Large Stocks occurred in the period ending June 1986, when the group earned a cumulative 80 percent versus a gain of 134 percent for the Large Stocks universe, a deficit of 54 percent. Figures 17.3 and 17.4 graph all rolling five-year excess returns from 1964 through 2009 for the worst decile earnings growth of All Stocks and Large Stocks.

DECILES

This full decile analysis shows that earnings gains aren't a very good variable to use when selecting stocks. Looking at the All Stocks decile analysis for the full period, decile 4 is actually the best performer, with an average annual compound return of 12.34 percent. The returns are very concentrated between deciles 1 and 6, all beating All Stocks, but by very slight margins and with much greater volatility. Deciles 7 through 10—the ones with increasingly bad earnings changes—all lost to All Stocks. This should come as no big surprise, since consistently poor earnings changes are not much of an enticement to investors.

The full decile analysis for Large Stocks is even more confusing. As we saw with All Stocks, decile 4 was the best performing on an absolute basis, earning 10.38 percent per year. But unlike All Stocks, we find that only deciles 2 and 4 manage to beat the Large Stocks universe. This relative bizarre pattern tells us that earnings changes in the Large Stocks universe alone should not be used to select or rule out stocks. The irony, of course, is that earnings are among the most closely followed numbers on Wall Street. Tables 17.19 and 17.20 and Figures 17.5 and 17.6 all show the full decile analysis.

IMPLICATIONS

Buying stocks simply because they had great earnings gains is a losing proposition. While stocks from All Stocks with great earnings gains have subperiods where they are on fire, we've seen that their ensuing performance plummets and that they wind up doing *worse* than the universe itself. Their lack of consistency makes them a poor choice for making intelligent investment decisions. As much of what we have found with this research, earnings *can* be useful, but only in concert with other variables like how much you are paying for earnings gains and how much the market has validated them with relative price appreciation.

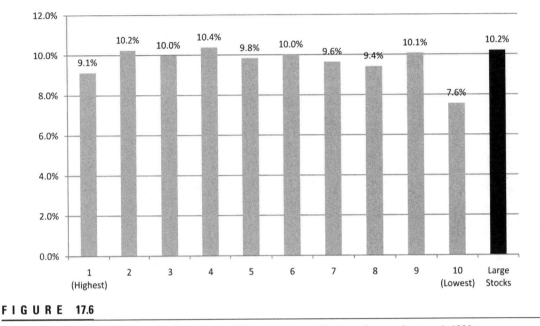

F I G U R E   17.6

Average annual compound return by EPS Change (%) decile, Large Stocks universe, January 1, 1964 to
December 31, 2009

One reason you should not look at earnings gains in isolation is that investors often
get overly excited about companies with dramatic earnings gains and project these earnings assumptions too far into the future. It's interesting to note that the stocks with the
highest one-year earnings gains almost always have the highest price-to-earnings ratios,
another indicator that poor performance lies ahead. We see later that strong earnings gains
coupled with strong price momentum will lead you to high-performing stocks, but for
now, remember that you shouldn't buy a stock simply because it has outstanding one-year
earnings gains.

You're even worse off buying stocks with the worst earnings changes. On their own,
there is no compelling reason to buy them. History suggests that you should not make
investment decisions on using either one of these variables alone.

C H A P T E R

PROFIT MARGINS: DO INVESTORS PROFIT FROM CORPORATE PROFITS?

The same thing happened today that happened yesterday, only to different people.

—Walter Winchell

Net profit margins are an excellent gauge of a company's operating efficiency and ability to compete successfully with other firms in its field. Many believe that firms with high net profit margins are better investments, since they are the leaders in their industries. You find net profit margins by dividing net income before extraordinary items (a company's income after all expenses but before provisions for dividends) by net sales. This is then multiplied by 100 to make it a percentage.

THE RESULTS

I test this strategy by buying the decile of stocks from the All Stocks and Large Stocks universes with the highest net profit margins. We begin on December 31, 1963, with $10,000 and, as usual, time-lag all accounting data to avoid look-ahead bias. The composited portfolio is rebalanced annually.

A $10,000 investment on December 31, 1963, in the decile of stocks from the All Stocks universe with the highest net profit margins grew to $911,179 by the end of 2009, a compound return of 10.31 percent. That's $418,334 less than you'd have earned investing in the All Stocks universe alone. There, $10,000 grew to $1,329,513, a return of 11.22 percent per year.

The decile of high profit margin stocks' risk was virtually the same as the All Stocks universe, with a standard deviation of return of 17.05 percent, slightly lower than All

Stocks' 18.99 percent. Downside risk for the group was also close to that of All Stocks, coming in at 12.82 percent versus the universe's 13.90 percent. The slightly lower return married to the slightly lower risk brought the Sharpe ratio for the high net profit margin stocks close to All Stocks—its Sharpe ratio was .31 versus .33 for All Stocks. Base rates look like a coin toss—the decile of stocks with the highest net profit margins beat All Stocks in 47 percent of all rolling five-year periods and in 48 percent of all rolling ten-year periods. Tables 18.1 through 18.5 summarize the returns.

T A B L E   18.1

Summary Annual Return and Risk Results Data: All Stocks Net Margin, Decile 1, and All Stocks, January 1, 1964, to December 31, 2009

	All Stocks net margin, decile 1	All Stocks
Arithmetic average	11.93%	13.26%
Geometric average	10.31%	11.22%
Median return	13.44%	17.16%
Standard deviation	17.05%	18.99%
Upside deviation	10.19%	10.98%
Downside deviation	12.82%	13.90%
Tracking error	6.50	0.00
Number of positive periods	334	329
Number of negative periods	218	223
Maximum peak-to-trough decline	−53.32%	−55.54%
Beta	0.84	1.00
T-statistic (m = 0)	4.51	4.47
Sharpe ratio (Rf = 5%)	0.31	0.33
Sortino ratio (MAR = 10%)	0.02	0.09
$10,000 becomes	$911,179	$1,329,513
Minimum 1-year return	−46.92%	−46.49%
Maximum 1-year return	59.62%	84.19%
Minimum 3-year return	−15.05%	−18.68%
Maximum 3-year return	32.22%	31.49%
Minimum 5-year return	−6.26%	−9.91%
Maximum 5-year return	27.91%	27.66%
Minimum 7-year return	−2.81%	−6.32%
Maximum 7-year return	21.40%	23.77%
Minimum 10-year return	0.05%	1.01%
Maximum 10-year return	19.42%	22.05%
Minimum expected return*	−22.17%	−24.73%
Maximum expected return†	46.04%	51.24%

* Minimum expected return is arithmetic return minus 2 times the standard deviation.
† Maximum expected return is arithmetic return plus 2 times the standard deviation.

TABLE 18.2

Base Rates for All Stocks Net Margin, Decile 1, and All Stocks, January 1, 1964, to December 31, 2009

Item	All Stocks net margin, decile 1 beat All Stocks	Percent	Average annual excess return
Single-year return	233 out of 541	43%	−1.29%
Rolling 3-year compound return	270 out of 517	52%	−0.85%
Rolling 5-year compound return	232 out of 493	47%	−0.66%
Rolling 7-year compound return	225 out of 469	48%	−0.64%
Rolling 10-year compound return	209 out of 433	48%	−0.71%

TABLE 18.3

Worst-Case Scenarios: All 20 Percent or Greater Declines for All Stocks Net Margin Decile 1, January 1, 1964, to December 31, 2009

Peak date	Peak index value	Trough date	Trough index value	Recovery date	Decline (%)	Decline duration	Recovery duration
Jan–69	1.85	Jun–70	1.27	Feb–72	−31.36%	17	20
Dec–72	2.14	Sep–74	1.16	Jan–77	−45.60%	21	28
Nov–80	5.36	Jul–82	3.84	Feb–83	−28.39%	20	7
Jun–83	6.27	Jul–84	4.84	Jun–85	−22.77%	13	11
Aug–87	9.75	Nov–87	7.08	May–89	−27.44%	3	18
Apr–98	39.43	Aug–98	28.66	Jun–99	−27.30%	4	10
Aug–00	56.99	Sep–02	42.27	Oct–03	−25.83%	25	13
Oct–07	115.91	Feb–09	54.11	N/A	−53.32%	16	N/A
Average					−32.75%	14.88	15.29

TABLE 18.4

Best and Worst Average Annual Compound Returns for Monthly Data, January 1, 1964, to December 31, 2009

For any	1-year period	3-year period	5-year period	7-year period	10-year period
All Stocks net margin, decile 1, minimum compound return	−46.92%	−15.05%	−6.26%	−2.81%	0.05%
All Stocks net margin, decile 1, maximum compound return	59.62%	32.22%	27.91%	21.40%	19.42%
All Stocks minimum compound return	−46.49%	−18.68%	−9.91%	−6.32%	1.01%
All Stocks maximum compound return	84.19%	31.49%	27.66%	23.77%	22.05%

T A B L E   18.5

Terminal Value of $10,000 Invested for Best and Worst Average Annual Compound Returns for Monthly Data, January 1, 1964, to December 31, 2009

For any	1-year period	3-year period	5-year period	7-year period	10-year period
All Stocks net margin, decile 1, minimum $10,000 value	$5,308	$6,131	$7,238	$8,193	$10,046
All Stocks net margin, decile 1, maximum $10,000 value	$15,962	$23,116	$34,238	$38,866	$58,969
All Stocks minimum $10,000 value	$5,351	$5,379	$5,936	$6,330	$11,054
All Stocks maximum $10,000 value	$18,419	$22,734	$33,903	$44,504	$73,345

As you can see from Figure 18.1, stocks with high net profit margins never really experienced any five-year streaks relative to All Stocks that might entice investors. Their strongest performance came in the five years ending in 1980, a time when stocks with the best earnings gains were also soaring. Remember as I note in Chapter Six that there is a difference in the way cumulative returns look versus average annual compound returns, so while the period in the earlier 1970s looks better on an excess return basis, on a cumulative basis the five years ending 1980 saw really good returns for stocks with high profit margins. While it makes intuitive sense that stocks with great earnings gains and high profit margins should be good investments,

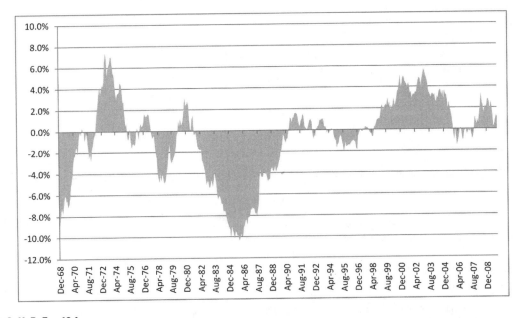

F I G U R E   18.1

Five-year average annual compound excess (deficient) return All Stocks net margin decile 1 minus All Stocks, January 1, 1964, to December 31, 2009

the long-term data suggest otherwise. That's because successful investing relies heavily on buying stocks that have good *prospects*, but for which investors currently have *low* expectations. Stocks with great earnings gains and high net profit margins are basically high-expectations stocks. These high expectations often lead investors to overpay, and when these "super" stocks inevitably stumble, their prices swoon and they become victims of their own success.

LARGE STOCKS RESULTS SIMILAR TO ALL STOCKS

The performance of high net profit margin stocks from the Large Stocks universe fare no better than those from All Stocks. Between December 31, 1963, and December 31, 2009, a $10,000 investment in decile 1 grew to $434,494, a compound average annual return of 8.54 percent. That's significantly less than the $872,861 you'd have earned from the same investment in the Large Stocks universe, which earned 10.20 percent per year with a standard deviation of 16.50 percent versus 16.60 percent for decile 1. The Sharpe ratio for decile 1 was .21, compared to .32 for the Large Stocks. All base rates are negative, with the decile of stocks with the highest net profit margins beating the Large Stocks universe in just 30 percent of all rolling ten-year periods. Tables 18.6 through 18.10 summarize the returns for the high net profit margin stocks from Large Stocks. Figure 18.2 shows the rolling five-year average annual compound excess (deficient) return for the highest profit margin stocks from Large Stocks minus the return for the Large Stocks universe.

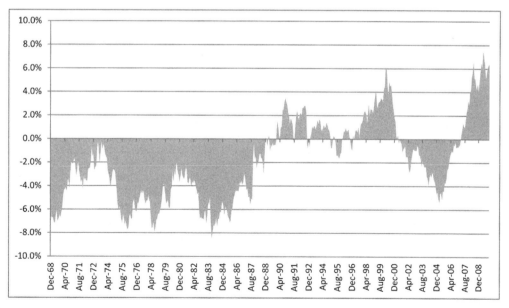

F I G U R E   18.2

Five-year average annual compound excess (deficient) return Large Stocks net margin decile 1 minus Large Stocks, January 1, 1964, to December 31, 2009

TABLE 18.6

Summary Annual Return and Risk Results Data: Large Stocks Net Margin, Decile 1, and Large Stocks, January 1, 1964, to December 31, 2009

	Large Stocks net margin, decile 1	Large Stocks
Arithmetic average	10.05%	11.72%
Geometric average	8.54%	10.20%
Median return	12.26%	17.20%
Standard deviation	16.60%	16.50%
Upside deviation	10.11%	9.70%
Downside deviation	11.83%	11.85%
Tracking error	7.30	0.00
Number of positive periods	325	332
Number of negative periods	227	220
Maximum peak-to-trough decline	−52.15%	−53.77%
Beta	0.91	1.00
T-statistic (m = 0)	3.93	4.58
Sharpe ratio (Rf = 5%)	0.21	0.32
Sortino ratio (MAR = 10%)	−0.12	0.02
$10,000 becomes	$434,494	$872,861
Minimum 1-year return	−47.91%	−46.91%
Maximum 1-year return	49.86%	68.96%
Minimum 3-year return	−19.63%	−15.89%
Maximum 3-year return	31.68%	33.12%
Minimum 5-year return	−8.66%	−5.82%
Maximum 5-year return	28.97%	28.95%
Minimum 7-year return	−6.87%	−4.15%
Maximum 7-year return	23.06%	22.83%
Minimum 10-year return	−4.41%	−0.15%
Maximum 10-year return	20.02%	19.57%
Minimum expected return*	−23.15%	−21.28%
Maximum expected return†	43.25%	44.72%

* Minimum expected return is arithmetic return minus 2 times the standard deviation.
† Maximum expected return is arithmetic return plus 2 times the standard deviation.

TABLE 18.7

Base Rates for Large Stocks Net Margin, Decile 1, and Large Stocks, January 1, 1964, to December 31, 2009

Item	Large Stocks net margin, decile 1, beat Large Stocks	Percent	Average annual excess return
Single-year return	250 out of 541	46%	−1.61%
Rolling 3-year compound return	169 out of 517	33%	−1.66%
Rolling 5-year compound return	153 out of 493	31%	−1.78%
Rolling 7-year compound return	144 out of 469	31%	−1.90%
Rolling 10-year compound return	132 out of 433	30%	−1.92%

T A B L E   18.8

Worst-Case Scenarios: All 20 Percent or Greater Declines for Large Stocks Net Margin Decile 1, January 1, 1964, to December 31, 2009

Peak date	Peak index value	Trough date	Trough index value	Recovery date	Decline (%)	Decline duration	Recovery duration
Sep–65	1.22	Aug–66	0.95	Sep–67	−22.48%	11	13
Nov–68	1.37	Jun–70	0.97	Mar–71	−29.24%	19	9
Nov–72	1.55	Sep–74	0.74	Jan–80	−52.15%	22	64
Nov–80	2.02	Jul–82	1.58	Jan–83	−21.47%	20	6
Aug–87	4.72	Nov–87	3.70	Apr–89	−21.71%	3	17
Apr–98	22.25	Aug–98	17.28	Dec–98	−22.31%	4	4
Aug–00	34.79	Sep–02	17.22	Jan–06	−50.51%	25	40
May–08	51.24	Feb–09	26.32	N/A	−48.64%	9	N/A
Average					−33.56%	14.13	21.86

T A B L E   18.9

Best and Worst Average Annual Compound Returns for Monthly Data, January 1, 1964, to December 31, 2009

For any	1-year period	3-year period	5-year period	7-year period	10-year period
Large Stocks net margin, decile 1, minimum compound return	−47.91%	−19.63%	−8.66%	−6.87%	−4.41%
Large Stocks net margin, decile 1, maximum compound return	49.86%	31.68%	28.97%	23.06%	20.02%
Large Stocks minimum compound return	−46.91%	−15.89%	−5.82%	−4.15%	−0.15%
Large Stocks maximum compound return	68.96%	33.12%	28.95%	22.83%	19.57%

T A B L E   18.10

Terminal Value of $10,000 Invested for Best and Worst Average Annual Compound Returns for Monthly Data, January 1, 1964, to December 31, 2009

For any	1-year period	3-year period	5-year period	7-year period	10-year period
Large Stocks net margin, decile 1, minimum $10,000 value	$5,209	$5,192	$6,358	$6,076	$6,368
Large Stocks net margin, decile 1, maximum $10,000 value	$14,986	$22,833	$35,681	$42,747	$62,031
Large Stocks minimum $10,000 value	$5,309	$5,951	$7,409	$7,434	$9,848
Large Stocks maximum $10,000 value	$16,896	$23,591	$35,656	$42,189	$59,747

BEST- AND WORST-CASE SCENARIOS AND BEST AND WORST RETURNS

The worst-case scenario tables show us that stocks with the highest profit margins, especially those from Large Stocks, don't suffer such dramatic declines as many of the other strategies we've looked at. As Table 18.3 shows, since 1963 the decile of stocks with the highest profit margins from the All Stocks universe lost more than 20 percent from peak to trough eight times, with the biggest loss of 53.32 percent occurring between October 2007 and February 2009. Looking at Tables 18.4 and 18.5, we see that during their best five-year period the high margin stocks turned $10,000 into $34,238 for the period ending in November 1980, and their worst five years reduced the same $10,000 to $7,238.

The high-margin stocks from Large Stocks also had eight declines exceeding 20 percent, with the largest, 52.15 percent, coming during the bear market of 1972 through 1974. During the best five-year period—ending in November 1980—$10,000 grew to $35,681, and during the worst five-year period—ending in September 1974—the same investment shrank to $6,358. Tables 18.8 through 18.10 show the worst-case scenarios as well as the best and worst returns over several time periods.

On a relative basis, the best five years for the high margin stocks from All Stocks also occurred during the period ending November 1980, when they returned a cumulative 242 percent compared to All Stocks' 191 percent, a cumulative advantage of 51 percent. The worst relative performance of All Stocks occurred in the five years ending March 1985, when the high margin stocks returned a cumulative 82 percent, compared to All Stocks' 165 percent, an 83 percent deficit.

Looking at Figure 18.2, the relative performance of high profit margin stocks from Large Stocks is not unlike that from All Stocks. The best relative five-year performance of the high margin group versus Large Stocks occurred in the period ending in February 2000, when it earned a cumulative 257 percent versus Large Stocks' 182 percent, a 75 percent cumulative advantage. The worst relative five-year performance versus Large Stocks occurred in the period ending in July 1987, when the high margin stocks had a cumulative return of 187 percent versus Large Stocks' gain of 255 percent, a 68 percent deficit. Tables 18.11 and 18.12 show the return for deciles 1 and 10 for both All Stocks and Large Stocks by decade.

T A B L E   18.11

Average Annual Compound Rates of Return by Decade

	1960s*	1970s	1980s	1990s	2000s†
All Stocks net margin, decile 1	8.09%	8.91%	11.51%	16.04%	6.34%
All Stocks net margin, decile 10	17.10%	8.87%	11.04%	14.54%	−15.04%
All Stocks	13.36%	7.56%	16.78%	15.35%	4.39%

* Returns for January 1, 1964, to December 31, 1969.
† Returns for January 1, 2000, to December 31, 2009.

T A B L E   18.12

Average Annual Compound Rates of Return by Decade

	1960s*	1970s	1980s	1990s	2000st
Large Stocks net margin, decile 1	2.86%	2.46%	14.54%	18.47%	3.13%
Large Stocks net margin, decile 10	8.92%	6.18%	18.19%	20.34%	−8.62%
Large Stocks	8.16%	6.65%	17.34%	16.38%	2.42%

* Returns for January 1, 1964, to December 31, 1969.
† Returns for January 1, 2000, to December 31, 2009.

DECILES

The decile analysis confirms that it's not a good idea to buy a stock simply because it has a high profit margin. The decile analysis in fact shows the opposite, with stocks in some of the lowest profit margin deciles outperforming those toward the top (the exceptions being the ninth and tenth deciles). For example, $10,000 invested in the 10 percent of stocks with the highest profit margins from All Stocks grew to $911,179, well behind the All Stocks universe and *considerably* behind those in the seventh decile, where $10,000 grew to $2,056,372. What's more, every decile *except* the tenth performed better than the first decile. Only the tenth suffers greatly, earning a compound average annual rate of return of 5.75 percent, barely ahead of the 5.57 percent you would have earned from an investment in 30-day T-bills. Much the same is true with Large Stocks, where lower profit margin deciles outperform higher deciles. Tables 18.11 through 18.14 along with Figures 18.3 and 18.4 summarize the results.

T A B L E   18.13

Summary Results for Net Margin Decile Analysis of All Stocks Universe, January 1, 1964, to December 31, 2009

Decile	$10,000 grows to	Average return	Compound return	Standard deviation	Sharpe ratio
1 (highest)	$911,179	11.93%	10.31%	17.05%	0.31
2	$1,110,574	12.07%	10.78%	15.22%	0.38
3	$1,552,337	12.97%	11.59%	15.66%	0.42
4	$1,958,226	13.74%	12.16%	16.71%	0.43
5	$1,405,711	13.11%	11.35%	17.65%	0.36
6	$1,440,360	13.29%	11.41%	18.20%	0.35
7	$2,056,372	14.29%	12.28%	18.81%	0.39
8	$1,951,536	14.35%	12.15%	19.64%	0.36
9	$927,218	13.22%	10.35%	22.52%	0.24
10 (lowest)	$130,773	9.83%	5.75%	27.29%	0.03
All Stocks	$1,329,513	13.26%	11.22%	18.99%	0.33

T A B L E   18.14

Summary Results for Net Margin Decile Analysis of Large Stocks Universe, January 1, 1964, to December 31, 2009

Decile	$10,000 grows to	Average return	Compound return	Standard deviation	Sharpe ratio
1 (highest)	$434,494	10.05%	8.54%	16.60%	0.21
2	$494,767	10.05%	8.85%	14.83%	0.26
3	$627,112	10.66%	9.41%	15.07%	0.29
4	$914,208	11.60%	10.31%	15.24%	0.35
5	$924,229	11.76%	10.34%	16.00%	0.33
6	$836,921	11.53%	10.10%	16.09%	0.32
7	$673,795	11.07%	9.58%	16.40%	0.28
8	$784,618	11.54%	9.95%	16.89%	0.29
9	$781,507	11.50%	9.94%	16.79%	0.29
10 (lowest)	$418,270	10.67%	8.45%	19.92%	0.17
Large Stocks	$872,861	11.72%	10.20%	16.50%	0.32

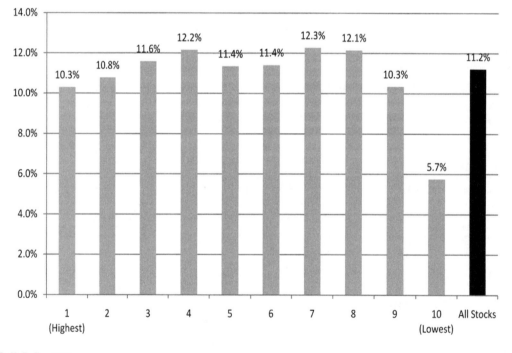

F I G U R E   18.3

Average annual compound return by net margin decile, All Stocks universe, January 1, 1964, to December 31, 2009

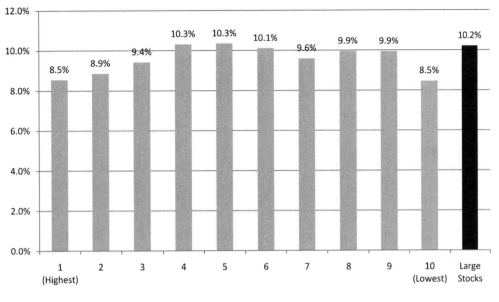

FIGURE 18.4

Average annual compound return by net margin decile, Large Stocks universe, January 1, 1964, to December 31, 2009

IMPLICATIONS

History shows that using high profit margins as the sole determinant for buying a stock leads to disappointing results. The only real lesson here is that it is best to avoid stocks in decile 10 with the lowest net profit margins.

19

C H A P T E R

RETURN ON EQUITY

I'd rather see folks doubt what's true than accept what isn't.

—Frank A. Clark

High return on equity is a hallmark of a growth stock. You calculate return on equity by dividing common stock equity into income before extraordinary items (a company's income after all expenses but before provisions for dividends). You then multiply that by 100 to express the term as a percentage.

Like high profit margins, many believe that a high return on equity (ROE) is an excellent gauge of how effectively a company invests shareholders' money. The higher the ROE, the better the company's ability to reinvest your money in itself, and presumably, the better an investment the stock will be.

THE RESULTS

We look at the results for both high and low ROE stocks from the All Stocks and Large Stocks universes. We start on December 31, 1963, with a $10,000 investment in the decile of stocks from All Stocks with the highest ROE. We also review all 10 deciles by ROE from both All Stocks and Large Stocks. As usual, we rebalance the composited portfolio annually and time lag all accounting data to avoid look-ahead bias.

As Table 19.1 shows, as of December 31, 2009, $10,000 invested in the group of stocks with the highest ROE is worth $2,066,648, a compound average annual return of 12.29 percent, slightly better than an investment in All Stocks, where $10,000 grows to $1,329,513. And even though the decile of stocks with the highest ROE had a standard deviation of return of 20.74 percent, slightly higher than All Stocks' 18.99 percent, the Sharpe ratio is just two basis points higher at .35, versus .33 for All Stocks. The highest ROE stocks were slightly riskier, with a downside of 15 percent compared to 13.9 percent for All Stocks.

T A B L E 19.1

Summary Annual Return and Risk Results Data: All Stocks ROE, Decile 1, and All Stocks, January 1, 1964, to December 31, 2009

	All Stocks ROE, Decile 1	All Stocks
Arithmetic average	14.75%	13.26%
Geometric average	12.29%	11.22%
Median return	18.08%	17.16%
Standard deviation	20.74%	18.99%
Upside deviation	12.36%	10.98%
Downside deviation	15.00%	13.90%
Tracking error	6.28	0.00
Number of positive periods	334	329
Number of negative periods	218	223
Maximum peak-to-trough decline	−63.88%	−55.54%
Beta	1.04	1.00
T-statistic (m = 0)	4.53	4.47
Sharpe ratio (Rf = 5%)	0.35	0.33
Sortino ratio (MAR = 10%)	0.15	0.09
$10,000 becomes	$2,066,648	$1,329,513
Minimum 1-year return	−53.89%	−46.49%
Maximum 1-year return	97.64%	84.19%
Minimum 3-year return	−22.01%	−18.68%
Maximum 3-year return	37.49%	31.49%
Minimum 5-year return	−11.82%	−9.91%
Maximum 5-year return	29.63%	27.66%
Minimum 7-year return	−6.42%	−6.32%
Maximum 7-year return	24.22%	23.77%
Minimum 10-year return	0.88%	1.01%
Maximum 10-year return	20.58%	22.05%
Minimum expected return*	−26.73%	−24.73%
Maximum expected return†	56.23%	51.24%

* Minimum expected return is arithmetic return minus 2 times the standard deviation.
† Maximum expected return is arithmetic return plus 2 times the standard deviation.

The base rates for decile 1 (the highest ROE stocks) are very interesting. As you can see from Table 19.2, they outperform All Stocks more often over shorter periods than over longer periods. For decile 1 versus All Stocks, the three- and five-year base rates are 63 percent and 66 percent, respectively, whereas the seven- and ten-year base rates are 57 percent and 51 percent, respectively. Table 19.3 shows the worst case scenarios for the group from All Stocks and Tables 19.4 and 19.5 show the best and worst returns for a variety of holding periods. Figure 19.1 shows the five-year average annual compound excess (deficient) return of decile one minus the return for the All Stocks universe.

T A B L E   19.2

Base Rates for All Stocks ROE, Decile 1, and All Stocks, January 1, 1964, to December 31, 2009

Item	All Stocks ROE, decile 1, beat All Stocks	Percent	Average annual excess return
Single-year return	325 out of 541	60%	1.61%
Rolling 3-year compound return	324 out of 517	63%	1.04%
Rolling 5-year compound return	327 out of 493	66%	0.76%
Rolling 7-year compound return	267 out of 469	57%	0.57%
Rolling 10-year compound return	220 out of 433	51%	0.25%

T A B L E   19.3

Worst-Case Scenarios: All 20 Percent or Greater Declines for for All Stocks ROE Decile 1, January 1, 1964, to December 31, 2009

Peak date	Peak index value	Trough date	Trough index value	Recovery date	Decline (%)	Decline duration	Recovery duration
Nov–68	3.24	Jun–70	1.78	Dec–71	−45.21%	19	18
May–72	4.12	Sep–74	1.49	Aug–78	−63.88%	28	47
Aug–78	4.32	Oct–78	3.34	Jun–79	−22.71%	2	8
May–81	8.30	Jul–82	5.62	Dec–82	−32.28%	14	5
Jun–83	11.47	May–84	8.26	Dec–85	−27.93%	11	19
Aug–87	18.67	Nov–87	11.72	Jul–89	−37.22%	3	20
Jun–90	20.37	Oct–90	15.60	Feb–91	−23.43%	4	4
Apr–98	79.73	Aug–98	57.86	Jun–99	−27.43%	4	10
Aug–00	105.19	Sep–01	80.56	Aug–03	−23.42%	13	23
Oct–07	252.05	Feb–09	116.29	N/A	−53.86%	16	N/A
Average					−35.74%	11.4	17.11

T A B L E   19.4

Best and Worst Average Annual Compound Returns for Monthly Data, January 1, 1964, to December 31, 2009

For any	1-year period	3-year period	5-year period	7-year period	10-year period
All Stocks ROE, decile 1, minimum compound return	−53.89%	−22.01%	−11.82%	−6.42%	0.88%
All Stocks ROE, decile 1, maximum compound return	97.64%	37.49%	29.63%	24.22%	20.58%
All Stocks minimum compound return	−46.49%	−18.68%	−9.91%	−6.32%	1.01%
All Stocks maximum compound return	84.19%	31.49%	27.66%	23.77%	22.05%
All Stocks ROE, decile 10, minimum compound return	−68.28%	−49.47%	−24.34%	−16.02%	−11.65%
All Stocks ROE, decile 10, maximum compound return	175.93%	47.89%	33.66%	24.75%	20.65%

TABLE   19.5

Terminal Value of $10,000 Invested for Best and Worst Average Annual Compound Returns for Monthly Data, January 1, 1964, to December 31, 2009

For any	1-year period	3-year period	5-year period	7-year period	10-year period
All Stocks ROE, decile 1, minimum $10,000 value	$4,611	$4,744	$5,332	$6,284	$10,916
All Stocks ROE, decile 1, maximum $10,000 value	$19,764	$25,992	$36,610	$45,631	$64,998
All Stocks minimum $10,000 value	$5,351	$5,379	$5,936	$6,330	$11,054
All Stocks maximum $10,000 value	$18,419	$22,734	$33,903	$44,504	$73,345
All Stocks ROE, decile 10, minimum $10,000 value	$3,172	$1,290	$2,480	$2,945	$2,898
All Stocks ROE, decile 10, maximum $10,000 value	$27,593	$32,346	$42,662	$47,015	$65,379

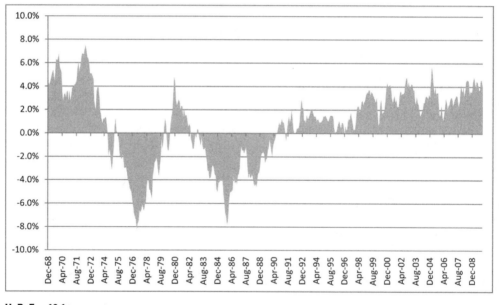

FIGURE   19.1

Five-year average annual compound excess (deficient) return All Stocks ROE decile 1 minus All Stocks, January 1, 1964, to December 31, 2009

LARGE STOCKS DO SLIGHTLY WORSE

On the other hand, the decile with the highest ROE stocks from Large Stocks do slightly worse than an investment in the Large Stocks universe (Table 19.6). Here, a $10,000 investment made on December 31, 1963, grows to $656,810 by the end of 2009, a compound return of 9.52 percent a year. That's worse than the $872,861 you'd have earned investing in the Large Stocks universe itself. The decile with the highest ROE stocks from Large Stocks was also riskier; its standard deviation of return was 17.50 percent, compared to 16.50 percent for the Large Stocks universe. Because of its lower return and higher risk, the top decile by ROE had a Sharpe ratio of .26, six points behind that of the Large Stocks universe's .32.

T A B L E 19.6

Summary Annual Return and Risk Results Data: Large Stocks ROE, Decile 1, and Large Stocks, January 1, 1964, to December 31, 2009

	Large Stocks ROE, decile 1	Large Stocks
Arithmetic average	11.21%	11.72%
Geometric average	9.52%	10.20%
Median return	11.89%	17.20%
Standard deviation	17.50%	16.50%
Upside deviation	10.88%	9.70%
Downside deviation	11.94%	11.85%
Tracking error	9.44	5.41
Number of positive periods	332	332
Number of negative periods	220	220
Maximum peak-to-trough decline	−58.46%	−53.77%
Beta	0.80	0.84
T-statistic (m = 0)	4.14	4.58
Sharpe ratio (Rf = 5%)	0.26	0.32
Sortino ratio (MAR = 10%)	−0.04	0.02
$10,000 becomes	$656,810	$872,861
Minimum 1-year return	−53.07%	−46.91%
Maximum 1-year return	63.93%	68.96%
Minimum 3-year return	−19.26%	−15.89%
Maximum 3-year return	36.49%	33.12%
Minimum 5-year return	−10.07%	−5.82%
Maximum 5-year return	29.20%	28.95%
Minimum 7-year return	−8.05%	−4.15%
Maximum 7-year return	23.54%	22.83%
Minimum 10-year return	−2.67%	−0.15%
Maximum 10-year return	21.19%	19.57%
Minimum expected return*	−23.79%	−21.28%
Maximum expected return†	46.22%	44.72%

* Minimum expected return is arithmetic return minus 2 times the standard deviation.
† Maximum expected return is arithmetic return plus 2 times the standard deviation.

Base rates for decile 1 from Large Stocks looks like a coin toss, with the group beating the Large Stocks universe in 48 percent of all rolling seven-year periods and in 50 percent of all rolling ten-year periods. Tables 19.6 through 19.10 summarize the returns for the Large Stocks group. As we will see when we examine the results for all 10 deciles, there is little rhyme or reason for investing in Large Stocks by ROE. Figure 19.2 shows the five year average annual compound excess (deficient) return of decile 1 minus the return for the Large Stocks universe.

T A B L E   19.7

Base Rates for Large Stocks ROE, Decile 1, and Large Stocks, January 1, 1964, to December 31, 2009

Item	Large Stocks ROE, decile 1, beat Large Stocks	Percent	Average annual excess return
Single-year return	282 out of 541	52%	−0.14%
Rolling 3-year compound return	235 out of 517	45%	−0.55%
Rolling 5-year compound return	222 out of 493	45%	−0.79%
Rolling 7-year compound return	225 out of 469	48%	−0.86%
Rolling 10-year compound return	215 out of 433	50%	−0.97%

T A B L E   19.8

Worst-Case Scenarios: All 20 Percent or Greater Declines for for Large Stocks ROE Decile 1, January 1, 1964, to December 31, 2009

Peak date	Peak index value	Trough date	Trough index value	Recovery date	Decline (%)	Decline duration	Recovery duration
Nov–68	1.55	Jun–70	1.06	Mar–71	−31.64%	19	9
Dec–72	2.04	Sep–74	0.85	Jun–80	−58.46%	21	69
Nov–80	2.92	Jul–82	1.72	Jun–83	−41.09%	20	11
Jun–83	2.97	May–84	2.35	Jan–85	−20.98%	11	8
Aug–87	6.51	Nov–87	4.33	Jul–89	−33.51%	3	20
Oct–00	45.74	Sep–02	29.32	Dec–04	−35.89%	23	27
Oct–07	80.81	Feb–09	41.40	N/A	−48.78%	16	N/A
Average					−38.62%	16.14	24

T A B L E   19.9

Best and Worst Average Annual Compound Returns for Monthly Data, January 1, 1964, to December 31, 2009

For any	1-year period	3-year period	5-year period	7-year period	10-year period
Large Stocks ROE, decile 1, minimum compound return	−53.07%	−19.26%	−10.07%	−8.05%	−2.67%
Large Stocks ROE, decile 1, maximum compound return	63.93%	36.49%	29.20%	23.54%	21.19%
Large Stocks minimum compound return	−46.91%	−15.89%	−5.82%	−4.15%	−0.15%
Large Stocks maximum compound return	68.96%	33.12%	28.95%	22.83%	19.57%

(continued on next page)

T A B L E   19.9

Best and Worst Average Annual Compound Returns for Monthly Data, January 1, 1964, to December 31, 2009 *(Continued)*

For any	1-year period	3-year period	5-year period	7-year period	10-year period
Large Stocks ROE, decile 10, minimum compound return	−62.47%	−38.53%	−16.41%	−7.84%	−7.73%
Large Stocks ROE, decile 10, maximum compound return	74.65%	37.66%	27.27%	23.81%	19.83%

T A B L E   19.10

Terminal Value of $10,000 Invested for Best and Worst Average Annual Compound Returns for Monthly Data, January 1, 1964, to December 31, 2009

For any	1-year period	3-year period	5-year period	7-year period	10-year period
Large Stocks ROE, decile 1, minimum $10,000 value	$4,693	$5,263	$5,880	$5,559	$7,629
Large Stocks ROE, decile 1, maximum $10,000 value	$16,393	$25,429	$36,003	$43,913	$68,341
Large Stocks minimum $10,000 value	$5,309	$5,951	$7,409	$7,434	$9,848
Large Stocks maximum $10,000 value	$16,896	$23,591	$35,656	$42,189	$59,747
Large Stocks ROE, decile 10, minimum $10,000 value	$3,753	$2,323	$4,082	$5,645	$4,473
Large Stocks ROE, decile 10, maximum $10,000 value	$17,465	$26,088	$33,386	$44,589	$61,047

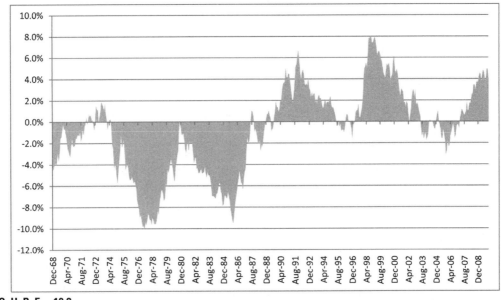

F I G U R E   19.2

Five-year average annual compound excess (deficient) return Large Stocks ROE decile 1 minus Large Stocks, January 1, 1964, to December 31, 2009

WORST-CASE SCENARIOS AND BEST AND WORST RETURNS

As Tables 19.3, 19.4, and 19.5 reveal, high ROE stocks do not exhibit much volatility. Their worst drop occurred during the bear market between May 1972 and September 1974, when they fell 64 percent from peak to trough. They had a similar drop in the most recent bear market, with a 54 percent decline occurring between October 2007 and February 2009. There were five separate occasions when the top decile of stocks by ROE from All Stocks dropped by more than 30 percent and two occasions when they fell by more than 50 percent. Looking at Table 19.5, you see the best five years for the high ROE stocks turned $10,000 into $36,610 for the period ending November 1980, whereas the worst five years reduced the $10,000 to $5,332 for the period ending September 1974.

Relative to the All Stocks universe, the best five years for the high ROE stocks were those ending in November 1980, when they gained a cumulative 266 percent compared to All Stocks' 191 percent, a 75 percent cumulative advantage. The worst five years versus All Stocks occurred in the period ending November 1985, when the high ROE stocks returned a cumulative 39 percent versus All Stocks' 97 percent, a cumulative deficit of 58 percent.

As Table 19.8 shows, the decile of stocks with the highest ROE from Large Stocks was slightly less volatile. Its worst decline of 58 percent occurred during the 1970's bear market. Highest ROE within Large stocks had six 30 percent peak to trough declines, although only one drop exceeded 50 percent. An investment during the best five-year period ending in July 1987 turned $10,000 into $36,003, whereas the worst five years, ending in September 1974, reduced $10,000 to $5,880.

On a relative basis, the best five years for the high ROE stocks from Large Stocks versus the Large Stocks universe occurred in the period ending June 1999, when the high ROE stocks gained a cumulative 253 percent versus a 168 percent gain for Large Stocks, a cumulative advantage of 85 percent. The worst five years occurred in the period ending November 1985, when the high ROE stocks from Large Stocks gained a cumulative 21 percent versus a gain of 87 percent for the Large Stocks universe, a 66 percent deficit.

BUYING STOCKS WITH THE WORST ROE

As Table 19.11 shows, $10,000 invested in 1963 in the decile of stocks from All Stocks with the lowest ROE grew to just $156,535 by the end of 2009, an average annual compound return of 6.16 percent. That's a fraction of the $1,329,513 you'd have earned from investing in the All Stocks universe, which compounded at 11.22 percent. Risk, as measured by standard deviation of return, was 26.37 percent versus 18.99 percent for All Stocks. The higher risk married to the lower return brought the Sharpe ratio to .04, well below the .33 earned by All Stocks. As Table 19.12 shows, all base rates were negative, with the low ROE group beating the All Stocks universe in just 22 percent of all rolling five-year periods and in 29 percent of all rolling ten-year periods. Figure 19.3 shows the five-year average annual compound excess (deficient) return of decile 10 minus the return for the All Stocks universe.

T A B L E   19.11

Summary Annual Return and Risk Results Data: All Stocks ROE, Decile 10, and All Stocks, January 1, 1964, to December 31, 2009

	All Stocks ROE, Decile 10	All Stocks
Arithmetic average	9.97%	13.26%
Geometric average	6.16%	11.22%
Median return	15.82%	17.16%
Standard deviation	26.37%	18.99%
Upside deviation	16.72%	10.98%
Downside deviation	19.55%	13.90%
Tracking error	11.44	0.00
Number of positive periods	318	329
Number of negative periods	234	223
Maximum peak-to-trough decline	−89.50%	−55.54%
Beta	1.28	1.00
T-statistic (m = 0)	2.46	4.47
Sharpe ratio (Rf = 5%)	0.04	0.33
Sortino ratio (MAR = 10%)	−0.20	0.09
$10,000 becomes	$156,535	$1,329,513
Minimum 1-year return	−68.28%	−46.49%
Maximum 1-year return	175.93%	84.19%
Minimum 3-year return	−49.47%	−18.68%
Maximum 3-year return	47.89%	31.49%
Minimum 5-year return	−24.34%	−9.91%
Maximum 5-year return	33.66%	27.66%
Minimum 7-year return	−16.02%	−6.32%
Maximum 7-year return	24.75%	23.77%
Minimum 10-year return	−11.65%	1.01%
Maximum 10-year return	20.65%	22.05%
Minimum expected return*	−42.76%	−24.73%
Maximum expected return†	62.71%	51.24%

* Minimum expected return is arithmetic return minus 2 times the standard deviation.

† Maximum expected return is arithmetic return plus 2 times the standard deviation.

T A B L E   19.12

Base Rates for All Stocks ROE, Decile 10, and All Stocks, January 1, 1964, to December 31, 2009

Item	All Stocks ROE, decile 10, beat All Stocks	Percent	Average annual excess return
Single-year return	201 out of 541	37%	−2.82%
Rolling 3-year compound return	133 out of 517	26%	−4.76%
Rolling 5-year compound return	106 out of 493	22%	−5.20%
Rolling 7-year compound return	112 out of 469	24%	−5.39%
Rolling 10-year compound return	126 out of 433	29%	−5.24%

TABLE   19.13

Worst-Case Scenarios: All 20 Percent or Greater Declines for for All Stocks ROE Decile 10, January 1, 1964, to December 31, 2009

Peak date	Peak index value	Trough date	Trough index value	Recovery date	Decline (%)	Decline duration	Recovery duration
Jan–69	3.06	Jun–70	1.44	Mar–76	−52.97%	17	69
May–81	7.56	Jul–82	5.66	Nov–82	−25.06%	14	4
Jun–83	11.50	Jul–84	7.97	Mar–87	−30.70%	13	32
Aug–87	13.31	Nov–87	8.58	May–89	−35.52%	3	18
Aug–89	14.32	Oct–90	9.53	Oct–91	−33.42%	14	12
May–96	26.69	Apr–97	19.14	Apr–98	−28.28%	11	12
Apr–98	26.98	Aug–98	17.08	Jan–99	−36.68%	4	5
Feb–00	73.06	Feb–09	7.67	N/A	−89.50%	108	N/A
Average					−41.51%	23	21.71

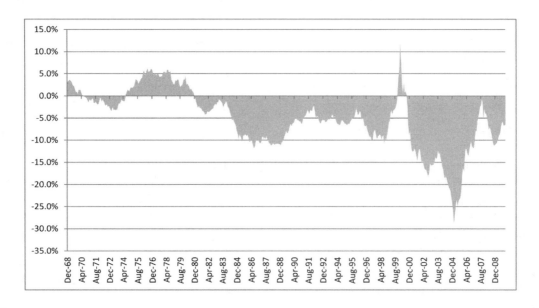

FIGURE   19.3

Five-year average annual compound excess (deficient) return All Stocks ROE decile 10 minus All Stocks, January 1, 1964, to December 31, 2009

LARGE STOCKS

Looking at the Large Stocks group with the lowest ROE, we see a similar pattern: the lowest ROE decile from Large Stocks turned $10,000 into $340,047 between 1963 and 2009, an average annual compound return of 7.97 percent and well below the $872,861 you'd have earned investing in the Large Stocks universe itself. Risk for the group was 19.51 percent, well above the Large Stocks universe's 16.50 percent (Table 19.14). The lower returns coupled with the higher risk brought the Sharpe ratio to .15 versus .32 for Large Stocks. Base rates, as detailed in Table 19.15, were slightly worse than a coin toss, with the group beating the universe in 34 percent of all rolling five-year periods and in 41 percent of all rolling 10-year periods. Table 19.16 shows the worst case scenarios for Large Stocks with the worst ROE. Figure 19.4 shows the five-year average annual compound excess (deficient) return of decile 10 minus the return for the Large Stocks universe.

T A B L E   19.14

Summary Annual Return and Risk Results Data: Large Stocks ROE, Decile 10, and Large Stocks, January 1, 1964, to December 31, 2009

	Large Stocks ROE, Decile 10	Large Stocks
Arithmetic average	10.07%	11.72%
Geometric average	7.97%	10.20%
Median return	15.14%	17.20%
Standard deviation	19.51%	16.50%
Upside deviation	11.87%	9.70%
Downside deviation	14.73%	11.85%
Tracking error	8.72	0.00
Number of positive periods	325	332
Number of negative periods	227	220
Maximum peak-to-trough decline	−79.66%	−53.77%
Beta	1.06	1.00
T-statistic (m = 0)	3.35	4.58
Sharpe ratio (Rf = 5%)	0.15	0.32
Sortino ratio (MAR = 10%)	−0.14	0.02
$10,000 becomes	$340,047	$872,861
Minimum 1-year return	−62.47%	−46.91%
Maximum 1-year return	74.65%	68.96%
Minimum 3-year return	−38.53%	−15.89%
Maximum 3-year return	37.66%	33.12%
Minimum 5-year return	−16.41%	−5.82%
Maximum 5-year return	27.27%	28.95%
Minimum 7-year return	−7.84%	−4.15%
Maximum 7-year return	23.81%	22.83%
Minimum 10-year return	−7.73%	−0.15%
Maximum 10-year return	19.83%	19.57%
Minimum expected return*	−28.94%	−21.28%
Maximum expected return†	49.08%	44.72%

* Minimum expected return is arithmetic return minus 2 times the standard deviation.
† Maximum expected return is arithmetic return plus 2 times the standard deviation.

TABLE 19.15

Base Rates for Large Stocks ROE, Decile 10, and Large Stocks, January 1, 1964, to December 31, 2009

Item	Large Stocks ROE, decile 10, beat Large Stocks	Percent	Average annual excess return
Single-year return	238 out of 541	44%	−1.11%
Rolling 3-year compound return	229 out of 517	44%	−1.57%
Rolling 5-year compound return	170 out of 493	34%	−1.76%
Rolling 7-year compound return	183 out of 469	39%	−1.89%
Rolling 10-year compound return	178 out of 433	41%	−1.69%

TABLE 19.16

Worst-Case Scenarios: All 20 Percent or Greater Declines for for Large Stocks ROE, Decile 10, January 1, 1964, to December 31, 2009

Peak date	Peak index value	Trough date	Trough index value	Recovery date	Decline (%)	Decline duration	Recovery duration
Jan–69	1.77	Jun–70	1.06	Nov–75	−40.18%	17	65
Dec–83	6.31	Jul–84	4.93	May–85	−21.95%	7	10
Sep–87	12.18	Nov–87	8.39	Jan–89	−31.11%	2	14
Dec–89	15.02	Oct–90	11.21	Jan–92	−25.35%	10	15
Feb–00	79.99	Sep–02	16.27	N/A	−79.66%	31	N/A
Average					−39.65%	13.4	26

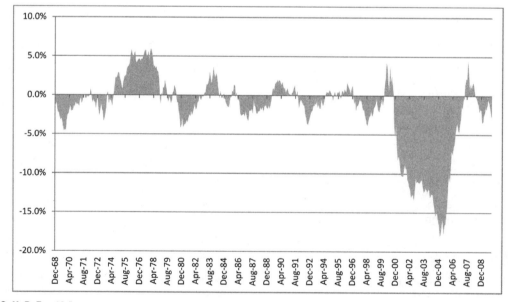

FIGURE 19.4

Five-year average annual compound excess (deficient) return Large Stocks ROE decile 10 minus Large Stocks, January 1, 1964, to December 31, 2009

WORST-CASE SCENARIOS AND BEST AND WORST RETURNS

The best absolute return for the group of stocks with the lowest ROE from All Stocks occurred during the five years ending February 2000, when $10,000 grew to $42,662. The worst absolute five years occurred during the period ending February 2005, when the $10,000 shrank to $2,480.

The best five years for the low ROE stocks from Large Stocks occurred during the period ending July 1987, when $10,000 grew to $33,386. The worst five years occurred during the period ending March 2005, when $10,000 shrank to $4,082. Table 19.10 shows the terminal value of $10,000 for other holding periods.

Relative to the All Stocks universe, the best five years for the lowest ROE group occurred in the period ending February 2000 when it gained a cumulative 327 percent compared to 176 percent for All Stocks, a 151 percent cumulative advantage. The worst relative performance for the group occurred in the five years ending November 2004, when it lost a cumulative 55 percent compared to a *gain* of 48 percent for the All Stocks universe, a deficit of 103 percent.

For the group with the lowest ROE from Large Stocks, the best relative five-year performance occurred in the period ending December 1983, when it gained a cumulative 193 percent versus a cumulative gain of 129 percent for Large Stocks, a 64 percent advantage. The group's worst relative five-year performance occurred in the period ending February 2005, when the low ROE stocks from Large Stocks lost 59 percent versus Large Stocks *gain* of 7.37 percent, a 66 percent cumulative deficit.

The worst peak-to-trough loss for the lowest ROE stocks from All Stocks occurred between February 2000 and February 2009, when they plunged 89.5 percent. The group lost more than 30 percent on six occasions. Table 19.13 shows all drawdowns for the low ROE group from All Stocks.

The worst peak-to-trough loss for the lowest ROE stocks from Large Stocks occurred between February 2000 and September 2002, when they lost 79.66 percent—a decline from which they have yet to recover. Between 1963 and 2009 the group lost more than 30 percent from peak to trough on three occasions. Table 19.16 shows all drawdowns for the low ROE group from Large Stocks. Tables 19.17 and 19.18 show the returns for both groups from All Stocks and Large Stocks by decade.

T A B L E   19.17

Average Annual Compound Rates of Return by Decade

	1960s*	1970s	1980s	1990s	2000s†
All Stocks ROE, decile 1	19.21%	6.24%	13.80%	17.58%	7.89%
All Stocks ROE, decile 10	12.94%	10.09%	9.73%	13.96%	−11.10%
All Stocks	13.36%	7.56%	16.78%	15.35%	4.39%

* Returns for January 1, 1964, to December 31, 1969.
† Returns for January 1, 2000, to December 31, 2009.

T A B L E   19.18

Average Annual Compound Rates of Return by Decade

	1960s*	1970s	1980s	1990s	2000s†
Large Stocks ROE, decile 1	7.43%	2.06%	14.00%	19.77%	4.47%
Large Stocks ROE, decile 10	4.55%	7.81%	18.42%	16.99%	−7.25%
Large Stocks	8.16%	6.65%	17.34%	16.38%	2.42%

*Returns for January 1, 1964, to December 31, 1969.
† Returns for January 1, 2000, to December 31, 2009.

DECILE

The decile analysis of the ROE stocks from All Stocks sees the top four deciles outperform the universe, but not by huge margins. Decile 5 matches the return for All Stocks, yet decile 6 does somewhat better. It is not until deciles 9 and 10 that we see significant underperformance. The oddness of this distribution pattern seems to imply that investors should simply avoid stocks with the lowest ROE. Tables 19.19 and 19.20, as well as Figures 19.5 and 19.6 summarize the results.

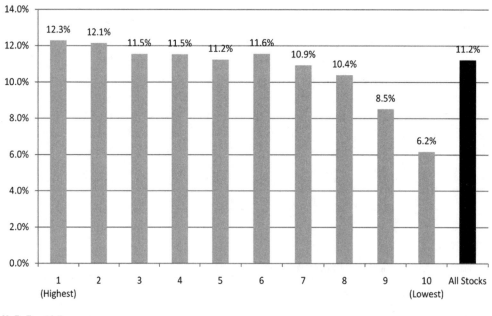

F I G U R E   19.5

Average annual compound return by ROE decile, All Stocks universe, January 1, 1964, to December 31, 2009

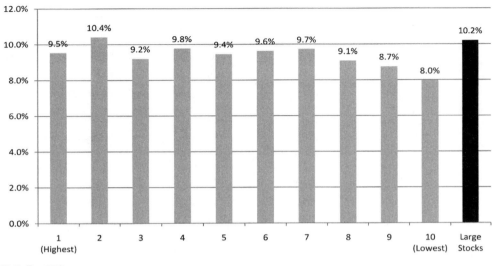

FIGURE 19.6

Average annual compound return by ROE decile, Large Stocks universe, January 1, 1964, to December 31, 2009

TABLE 19.19

Summary Results for ROE Decile Analysis of All Stocks Universe, January 1, 1964, to December 31, 2009

Decile	$10,000 grows to	Average return	Compound return	Standard deviation	Sharpe ratio
1 (highest)	$2,066,648	14.75%	12.29%	20.74%	0.35
2	$1,952,085	14.21%	12.15%	19.00%	0.38
3	$1,522,719	13.32%	11.54%	17.70%	0.37
4	$1,511,730	13.10%	11.53%	16.70%	0.39
5	$1,341,995	12.66%	11.24%	15.92%	0.39
6	$1,529,022	12.96%	11.55%	15.78%	0.42
7	$1,178,248	12.38%	10.92%	16.10%	0.37
8	$942,856	12.08%	10.39%	17.37%	0.31
9	$429,189	10.92%	8.52%	20.80%	0.17
10 (lowest)	$156,535	9.97%	6.16%	26.37%	0.04
All Stocks	$1,329,513	13.26%	11.22%	18.99%	0.33

TABLE 19.20

Summary Results for ROE Decile Analysis of Large Stocks Universe, January 1, 1964, to December 31, 2009

Decile	$10,000 grows to	Average return	Compound return	Standard deviation	Sharpe ratio
1 (highest)	$656,810	11.21%	9.52%	17.50%	0.26
2	$950,133	12.01%	10.41%	17.01%	0.32

(continued on next page)

TABLE 19.20

Summary Results for ROE Decile Analysis of Large Stocks Universe, January 1, 1964, to December 31, 2009 *(Continued)*

Decile	$10,000 grows to	Average return	Compound return	Standard deviation	Sharpe ratio
3	$570,816	10.69%	9.19%	16.51%	0.25
4	$727,485	11.20%	9.77%	16.12%	0.30
5	$634,558	10.79%	9.44%	15.64%	0.28
6	$684,187	10.89%	9.62%	15.18%	0.30
7	$713,593	10.96%	9.72%	14.96%	0.32
8	$541,295	10.37%	9.06%	15.39%	0.26
9	$472,148	10.13%	8.74%	15.92%	0.23
10 (lowest)	$340,047	10.07%	7.97%	19.51%	0.15
Large Stocks	$872,861	11.72%	10.20%	16.50%	0.32

IMPLICATIONS

Return on equity is not a great factor to use on its own when you're trying to decide whether a stock is a good investment or not. The data simply seem to tell us that it is wise to avoid stocks with the lowest return on equity.

CHAPTER NINETEEN CASE STUDY

IS RETURN ON ASSETS A BETTER GAUGE FOR STOCKS THAN ROE?

When you analyze stocks based on return on assets (ROA) instead of return on equity (ROE), you see that while the top decile from All Stocks does not perform as well as the top decile for ROE, the bottom decile actually does considerably worse. The $10,000 invested in the group of stocks from All Stocks with the lowest ROA grows to just $94,087, an average annual compound return of 4.99 percent. That's worse than keeping your money invested in 30-day U.S. T-bills. But note that it's *only* the 10 percent of stocks with the lowest ROA that get clobbered. When you look at all the ROA deciles, you see that their performance is tightly clustered between deciles 1 and 9, with decile 5 actually turning in the best performance (Table 19CS.1). Between 1963 and 2009, decile 5 earned 12.67 percent per year, whereas decile 1 earned 11.81 percent. But the spread in performance from decile 1 to decile 9 is only 2.52 percent. It's only when you get to the worst decile by ROA that you find stock that should be avoided. Thus you might simply exclude stocks in that decile from consideration.

For Large Stocks, the deciles show similar confusion, with decile 4 providing the best annual return at 10.72 percent and deciles 1–3 and 5 through 9 offering returns between 10.29 percent and 9.16 percent. As we saw with All Stocks, the only decile to truly avoid is decile 10, made up of the stocks from Large Stocks with the lowest ROA. Thus return on assets is of value only when you're screening out stocks to avoid (Table 19CS.2).

T A B L E   19CS.1

Summary Results for ROA Decile Analysis of All Stocks Universe, January 1, 1964, to December 31, 2009

Decile	$10,000 grows to	Average return	Compound return	Standard deviation	Sharpe ratio
1 (highest)	$1,701,127	14.21%	11.81%	20.54%	0.33
2	$1,705,054	13.83%	11.82%	18.82%	0.36
3	$1,678,191	13.67%	11.78%	18.25%	0.37
4	$1,845,855	13.84%	12.01%	17.94%	0.39
5	$2,414,564	14.29%	12.67%	16.89%	0.45
6	$1,704,225	13.31%	11.82%	16.22%	0.42
7	$1,481,986	12.84%	11.48%	15.52%	0.42
8	$927,033	11.94%	10.35%	16.86%	0.32
9	$852,108	12.82%	10.15%	21.74%	0.24
10 (lowest)	$94,087	8.69%	4.99%	26.09%	0.00
All Stocks	$1,329,513	13.26%	11.22%	18.99%	0.33

T A B L E   19CS.2

Summary Results for ROA Decile Analysis of Large Stocks Universe, January 1, 1964, to December 31, 2009

Decile	$10,000 grows to	Average return	Compound return	Standard deviation	Sharpe ratio
1 (highest)	$706,761	11.57%	9.70%	18.40%	0.26
2	$797,887	11.53%	9.99%	16.66%	0.30
3	$904,311	11.73%	10.29%	16.09%	0.33
4	$1,081,541	12.06%	10.72%	15.54%	0.37
5	$759,824	11.18%	9.87%	15.42%	0.32
6	$649,230	10.75%	9.50%	15.07%	0.30
7	$570,490	10.36%	9.19%	14.58%	0.29
8	$563,438	10.41%	9.16%	15.09%	0.28
9	$617,474	11.03%	9.38%	17.28%	0.25
10 (lowest)	$281,146	10.00%	7.52%	21.17%	0.12
Large Stocks	$872,861	11.72%	10.20%	16.50%	0.32

RELATIVE PRICE STRENGTH: WINNERS CONTINUE TO WIN

It may be that the race is not always to the swift, nor the battle to the strong—but that's the way to bet.

—Damon Runyon

"Don't fight the tape."

"Make the trend your friend."

"Cut your losses and let your winners run."

These Wall Street maxims all mean the same thing—bet on price momentum. Of all the beliefs on Wall Street, price momentum makes efficient market theorists howl the loudest. The defining principle of their theory is that you *cannot* use past prices to predict future prices. A stock may triple in a year, but according to efficient market theory, that will not affect next year. Efficient market theorists also hate price momentum because it is independent of all accounting variables. If buying winning stocks works, then stock prices have "memories" and carry useful information about the future direction of a stock.

In his book, "The Wisdom of Crowds," James Surowiecki argues that, "Under the right circumstances, groups are remarkably intelligent, and are often smarter than the smartest people in them." Surowiecki says that if four conditions are met, a crowd's "collective intelligence" will prove superior to the judgments of a smaller group of experts. The four conditions are: (1) diversity of opinion; (2) independence of members from one another; (3) decentralization; and (4) a good method for aggregating opinions. He then goes on to list several accounts where crowds were far more accurate than any individual trying to make a correct forecast.

Generally speaking, these four conditions are present in market-based price auctions, with the final price of a stock serving as an aggregator of all market opinion about the prospects for that stock. The only time this is not true is when markets are either in a bubble or a bust. At these market extremes a uniformity of opinion occurs, which impairs the ability of a group to offer good collective judgment.

Conversely, another school of thought says you should buy stocks that have been the *most* battered by the market. This is the argument of Wall Street's bottom feeders, who use absolute price change as their guide, buying issues after they've performed poorly. If Surowiecki is correct, this approach would only work after a bubble has turned into a bust, when the collective wisdom got the answer wrong. Let's see who is right.

THE RESULTS

For this test, we use the CRSP data that go back to 1926. After 1963, when the monthly Compustat data became available, we merge the two datasets in order to get the most comprehensive look at the factor's performance. We measure both six-month and twelve-month momentum. We look at buying the deciles of stocks with the *best* and the *worst* six-month and twelve-month price changes from both the All Stocks and Large Stocks universes, thereby contrasting the biggest winners with the biggest losers. We also review all 10 deciles for each universe. (In this and future chapters, I use the terms "relative strength" and "price appreciation" interchangeably. Stocks with the best relative strength are the biggest winners in terms of their previous six-month and twelve-month price appreciation.) Let's start with a look at buying the stocks with the best and worst six-month price momentum.

BUYING STOCKS WITH THE BEST SIX-MONTH PRICE APPRECIATION

In order to compare both six-month and twelve-month price appreciation from the same start date, we begin on January 1, 1927, and buy the decile of stocks with the largest price appreciation over the previous six months. As with all our tests, all the portfolios are composited so that every month is represented, and even though we are basing this on six-month price appreciation, we use an annual holding period for the portfolios.

As Table 20.1 shows, a $10,000 investment on December 31, 1926, in the decile of stocks from All Stocks with the best six-month price appreciation is worth $572,831,563 at the end of 2009, a compound return of 14.11 percent a year. This return dwarfed an investment in the All Stock universe, which turned $10,000 into $38,542,780 over the same period, an average annual compound return of 10.46 percent. The performance of the group of stocks from All Stocks with the best six-month price appreciation had higher risk, with a standard deviation of return of 24.54 percent versus All Stocks 21.67 percent. The Sharpe ratio for the best-performing stocks from All Stocks by six-month price appreciation was .37, a good bit higher than the .25 earned by the All Stocks universe over the same time period. As Table 20.2 shows, the base rates for the top performers were excellent, with the group beating All Stocks in 87 percent of all rolling five-year periods and in 98 percent of all rolling ten-year periods. Table 20.2 shows the base rates for all other holding periods.

T A B L E   20.1

Summary Annual Return and Risk Results Data: All Stocks and All Stocks 6-Month Momentum, Decile 1, January 1, 1927, to December 31, 2009

	All Stocks 6-month momentum, decile 1	All Stocks
Arithmetic average	17.60%	13.06%
Geometric average	14.11%	10.46%
Median return	24.79%	18.54%
Standard deviation	24.54%	21.67%
Upside deviation	15.24%	14.78%
Downside deviation	17.90%	16.03%
Tracking error	9.92	0.00
Number of positive periods	620	606
Number of negative periods	376	390
Maximum peak-to-trough decline	−78.26%	−85.45%
Beta	1.04	1.00
T-statistic (m = 0)	6.06	5.19
Sharpe ratio (Rf = 5%)	0.37	0.25
Sortino ratio (MAR = 10%)	0.23	0.03
$10,000 becomes	$572,831,563	$38,542,780
Minimum 1-year return	−59.29%	−66.72%
Maximum 1-year return	175.23%	201.69%
Minimum 3-year return	−38.12%	−45.99%
Maximum 3-year return	59.15%	51.03%
Minimum 5-year return	−15.54%	−23.07%
Maximum 5-year return	43.45%	41.17%
Minimum 7-year return	−3.32%	−7.43%
Maximum 7-year return	33.36%	23.77%
Minimum 10-year return	−3.90%	−5.31%
Maximum 10-year return	29.64%	22.05%
Minimum expected return*	−31.48%	−30.28%
Maximum expected return†	66.68%	56.39%

* Minimum expected return is arithmetic return minus 2 times the standard deviation.

† Maximum expected return is arithmetic return plus 2 times the standard deviation.

T A B L E   20.2

Base Rates for All Stocks 6-Month Momentum, Decile 1, and All Stocks, January 1, 1927, to December 31, 2009

Item	All Stocks 6-month momentum, decile 1, beat All Stocks	Percent	Average annual excess return
Single-year return	666 out of 985	68%	4.91%
Rolling 3-year compound return	761 out of 961	79%	4.21%
Rolling 5-year compound return	814 out of 937	87%	4.19%
Rolling 7-year compound return	863 out of 913	95%	4.16%
Rolling 10-year compound return	862 out of 877	98%	4.26%

If we look at the base rates for the stocks with the best six-month price appreciation, we see that in the 87 percent of all rolling five-year periods in which the group outperforms All Stocks, it does so by an average 49 percent. What's more, in the 13 percent of instances in which they underperform, the group's average cumulative loss to All Stocks is just 10 percent. Tables 20.3 and 20.4 catalog the the best and worst returns.

T A B L E   20.3

Best and Worst Average Annual Compound Returns for Monthly Data, January 1, 1927, to December 31, 2009

For any	1-year period	3-year period	5-year period	7-year period	10-year period
All Stocks 6-month momentum, decile 1, minimum compound return	−59.29%	−38.12%	−15.54%	−3.32%	−3.90%
All Stocks 6-month momentum, decile 1, maximum compound return	175.23%	59.15%	43.45%	33.36%	29.64%
All Stocks 6-month momentum decile 10 minimum compound return	−77.67%	−55.33%	−33.99%	−16.53%	−11.34%
All Stocks 6-month momentum, decile 10, maximum compound return	296.01%	50.90%	43.52%	24.87%	17.71%
All Stocks minimum compound return	−66.72%	−45.99%	−23.07%	−7.43%	−5.31%
All Stocks maximum compound return	201.69%	51.03%	41.17%	23.77%	22.05%

T A B L E   20.4

Terminal Value of $10,000 Invested for Best and Worst Average Annual Compound Returns for Monthly Data, January 1, 1927, to December 31, 2009

For any	1-year period	3-year period	5-year period	7-year period	10-year period
All Stocks 6-month momentum, decile 1, minimum $10,000 value	$4,071	$2,369	$4,298	$7,893	$6,719
All Stocks 6-month momentum, decile 1, maximum $10,000 value	$27,523	$40,308	$60,736	$75,006	$134,125
All Stocks 6-month momentum, decile 10, minimum $10,000 value	$2,233	$891	$1,253	$2,822	$3,000
All Stocks 6-month momentum, decile 10, maximum $10,000 value	$39,601	$34,363	$60,885	$47,347	$51,077
All Stocks minimum $10,000 value	$3,328	$1,576	$2,695	$5,825	$5,793
All Stocks maximum $10,000 value	$30,169	$34,452	$56,062	$44,504	$73,345

I cannot overstate how difficult it can be to stick with strategies that are as volatile as this one. Investors are drawn to these strategies by their outstanding performance, like when the top decile of stocks with the best six-month relative strength from All Stocks gained 66 percent in 1991 and an eye-popping 101 percent in 1999. Indeed, the 1990s proved to be the best decade for six-month relative strength stocks between 1926 and 2009. We see later in the book that uniting relative strength with other factors works *much better* than using relative strength alone. But for now, it appears that six-month relative strength significantly outperforms All Stocks, adding 3.65 percent annualized to the performance of the All Stocks universe over the last 83 years. We'll also revisit Tables 20.3 and 20.4 when looking at buying the *worst* decile by six-month relative strength. Finally, Figure 20.1 shows the five-year excess return of decile one minus the five-year returns for the All Stocks universe.

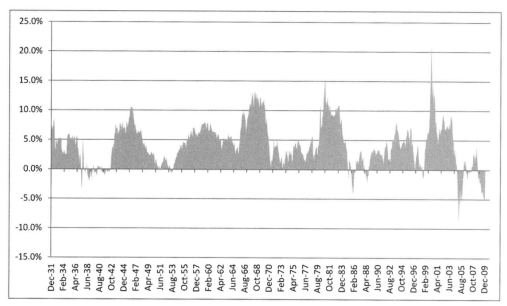

F I G U R E   20.1

Five-year average annual compound excess (deficient) return All Stocks 6-month momentum decile 1 minus All Stocks, January 1, 1927, to December 31, 2009

BUYING STOCKS WITH THE BEST 12-MONTH PRICE APPRECIATION

Now let's look at the results of buying the stocks from All Stocks with the best 12-month price appreciation. We again look at the period between December 31, 1926, and December 31, 2009. As Table 20.5 shows, $10,000 invested in the decile of stocks with the best 12-month price appreciation grew to $156,230,201, an average annual compound return of 12.34 percent and vastly better than the $38,542,780 you'd have earned from an investment in the All Stocks universe. Risk was higher for the decile of stocks with the best 12-month price appreciation, with a standard deviation of return of 24.78 percent versus 21.67 for the All Stocks universe. The Sharpe ratio for the group of best-performing stocks based on 12-month price appreciation was .30 versus .25 for All Stocks. As Table 20.6 shows, the base rates for the twelve-month relative strength group were not as strong as those of the six-month relative strength group, but were very positive still, with the group beating All Stocks in 72 percent of all rolling five-year periods and 84 percent of all rolling ten-year periods. Tables 20.7 and 20.8 detail the results for buying stocks with the highest twelve-month price appreciation over holding periods of one to ten years, the first showing the minimum and maximum percentage change and the second showing the performance of a $10,000 investment over the various holding periods. We revisit these tables when we review the results of buying the stocks with the *worst* relative strength from All Stocks, since those results are included here as well. Figure 20.2 shows the rolling five-year average annual compound return excess (deficient) return for decile 1 (the 10 percent of stocks with the best twelve-month price appreciation) minus the return for All Stocks.

T A B L E   20.5

Summary Annual Return and Risk Results Data: All Stocks and All Stocks 12-Month Momentum, Decile 1, January 1, 1927, to December 31, 2009

	All Stocks 12-month momentum, decile 1	All Stocks
Arithmetic average	15.88%	13.06%
Geometric average	12.34%	10.46%
Median return	25.50%	18.54%
Standard deviation	24.78%	21.67%
Upside deviation	14.75%	14.78%
Downside deviation	18.45%	16.03%
Tracking error	10.82	0.00
Number of positive periods	610	606
Number of negative periods	386	390
Maximum peak-to-trough decline	−79.58%	−85.45%
Beta	1.03	1.00
T-statistic (m = 0)	5.45	5.19
Sharpe ratio (Rf = 5%)	0.30	0.25
Sortino ratio (MAR = 10%)	0.13	0.03
$10,000 becomes	$156,230,201	$38,542,780
Minimum 1-year return	−64.71%	−66.72%
Maximum 1-year return	157.56%	201.69%
Minimum 3-year return	−39.36%	−45.99%
Maximum 3-year return	52.96%	51.03%
Minimum 5-year return	−16.35%	−23.07%
Maximum 5-year return	39.45%	41.17%
Minimum 7-year return	−4.94%	−7.43%
Maximum 7-year return	29.78%	23.77%
Minimum 10-year return	−5.76%	−5.31%
Maximum 10-year return	27.22%	22.05%
Minimum expected return*	−33.68%	−30.28%
Maximum expected return†	65.45%	56.39%

* Minimum expected return is arithmetic return minus 2 times the standard deviation.
† Maximum expected return is arithmetic return plus 2 times the standard deviation.

T A B L E 20.6

Base Rates for All Stocks 12-Month Momentum, Decile 1, and All Stocks, January 1, 1927, to December 31, 2009

Item	All Stocks 12-month momentum, decile 1, beat All Stocks	Percent	Average annual excess return
Single-year return	603 out of 985	61%	3.37%
Rolling 3-year compound return	598 out of 961	62%	2.45%
Rolling 5-year compound return	675 out of 937	72%	2.45%
Rolling 7-year compound return	679 out of 913	74%	2.41%
Rolling 10-year compound return	734 out of 877	84%	2.51%

T A B L E 20.7

Best and Worst Average Annual Compound Returns for Monthly Data, January 1, 1927, to December 31, 2009

For any	1-year period	3-year period	5-year period	7-year period	10-year period
All Stocks 12-month momentum, decile 1, minimum compound return	−64.71%	−39.36%	−16.35%	−4.94%	−5.76%
All Stocks 12-month momentum decile 1 maximum compound return	157.56%	52.96%	39.45%	29.78%	27.22%
All Stocks 12-month momentum, decile 10, minimum compound return	−77.93%	−53.98%	−32.90%	−16.37%	−10.14%
All Stocks 12-month momentum decile 10 maximum compound return	294.88%	54.61%	41.31%	23.70%	19.31%
All Stocks minimum compound return	−66.72%	−45.99%	−23.07%	−7.43%	−5.31%
All Stocks maximum compound return	201.69%	51.03%	41.17%	23.77%	22.05%

T A B L E 20.8

Terminal Value of $10,000 Invested for Best and Worst Average Annual Compound Returns for Monthly Data, January 1, 1927, to December 31, 2009

For any	1-year period	3-year period	5-year period	7-year period	10-year period
All Stocks 12-month momentum, decile 1, minimum $10,000 value	$3,529	$2,230	$4,096	$7,015	$5,528
All Stocks 12-month momentum, decile 1, maximum $10,000 value	$25,756	$35,784	$52,737	$62,011	$111,029
All Stocks 12-month momentum decile 10 minimum $10,000 value	$2,207	$975	$1,360	$2,861	$3,433
All Stocks 12-month momentum, decile 10, maximum $10,000 value	$39,488	$36,960	$56,352	$44,326	$58,449
All Stocks minimum $10,000 value	$3,328	$1,576	$2,695	$5,825	$5,793
All Stocks maximum $10,000 value	$30,169	$34,452	$56,062	$44,504	$73,345

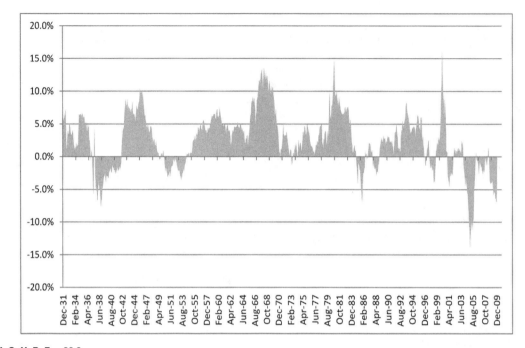

FIGURE   20.2

Five-year average annual compound excess (deficient) return All Stocks 12-month momentum decile 1 minus All Stocks, January 1, 1927, to December 31, 2009

LARGE STOCKS ALSO DO WELL

The decile of stocks from the Large Stocks universe with high six-month relative strength also performed well. As Table 20.9 shows, a $10,000 investment on December 31, 1926, in the decile of stocks from the Large Stocks universe with the best six-month price appreciation grew to $232,092,755, more than 10 times the $21,617,372 you'd have earned by investing in the Large Stocks universe, which compounded at 9.69 percent over the same period. Decile 1 of Large Stocks based on six-month price momentum compounded at 12.88 percent over the same period. Risk was higher for the best six-month performers from Large Stocks, with a standard deviation of return of 22.65 percent versus Large Stocks' 19.35 percent. The higher return offset the higher risk, however, bringing the Sharpe ratio to .35 compared to .24 for the Large Stocks universe.

As you can see from Table 20.10, all of the base rates are positive, with the best six-month relative strength stocks from Large Stocks beating the universe in 82 percent of all rolling five-year periods and in 93 percent of all rolling ten-year periods. Tables 20.11 and 20.12 detail the best and worst results for the best decile of six-month price performers from Large Stocks over various holding periods. Figure 20.3 shows the five-year average annual compound excess (deficient) return of decile 1 of the Large Stocks universe minus the Large Stock's return.

T A B L E   20.9

Summary Annual Return and Risk Results Data: Large Stocks 6-Month Momentum, Decile 1, and Large Stocks, January 1, 1927, to December 31, 2009

	Large Stocks 6-month momentum, decile 1	Large Stocks
Arithmetic average	15.81%	11.75%
Geometric average	12.88%	9.69%
Median return	22.40%	16.75%
Standard deviation	22.65%	19.35%
Upside deviation	14.44%	13.10%
Downside deviation	16.90%	14.40%
Tracking error	9.62	0.00
Number of positive periods	615	609
Number of negative periods	381	387
Maximum peak-to-trough decline	−81.81%	−84.33%
Beta	1.06	1.00
T-statistic (m = 0)	5.94	5.25
Sharpe ratio (Rf = 5%)	0.35	0.24
Sortino ratio (MAR = 10%)	0.17	−0.02
$10,000 becomes	$232,092,755	$21,617,372
Minimum 1-year return	−57.73%	−66.63%
Maximum 1-year return	150.84%	159.52%
Minimum 3-year return	−40.90%	−43.53%
Maximum 3-year return	67.35%	45.64%
Minimum 5-year return	−19.02%	−20.15%
Maximum 5-year return	48.55%	36.26%
Minimum 7-year return	−6.52%	−6.95%
Maximum 7-year return	37.36%	22.83%
Minimum 10-year return	−6.79%	−5.70%
Maximum 10-year return	32.45%	19.57%
Minimum expected return*	−29.49%	−26.96%
Maximum expected return†	61.12%	50.46%

* Minimum expected return is arithmetic return minus 2 times the standard deviation.
† Maximum expected return is arithmetic return plus 2 times the standard deviation.

T A B L E   20.10

Base Rates for Large Stocks 6-Month Momentum, Decile 1, and Large Stocks, January 1, 1927, to December 31, 2009

Item	Large Stocks 6-month momentum, decile 1, beat Large Stocks	Percent	Average annual excess return
Single-year return	663 out of 985	67%	4.51%
Rolling 3-year compound return	745 out of 961	78%	3.55%
Rolling 5-year compound return	771 out of 937	82%	3.42%
Rolling 7-year compound return	792 out of 913	87%	3.40%
Rolling 10-year compound return	816 out of 877	93%	3.50%

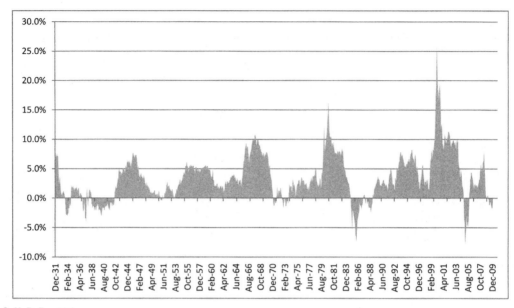

F I G U R E   20.3

Five-year average annual compound excess (deficient) return Large Stocks 6-month momentum decile 1 minus Large Stocks, January 1, 1927, to December 31, 2009

T A B L E   20.11

Best and Worst Average Annual Compound Returns for Monthly Data, January 1, 1927, to December 31, 2009

For any	1-year period	3-year period	5-year period	7-year period	10-year period
Large Stocks 6-month momentum, decile 1, minimum compound return	−57.73%	−40.90%	−19.02%	−6.52%	−6.79%
Large Stocks 6-month momentum, decile 1, maximum compound return	150.84%	67.35%	48.55%	37.36%	32.45%
Large Stocks 6-month momentum, decile 10, minimum compound return	−76.20%	−52.90%	−33.20%	−15.72%	−10.09%
Large Stocks 6-month momentum, decile 10, maximum compound return	248.01%	46.25%	41.27%	24.82%	16.40%
Large Stocks minimum compound return	−66.63%	−43.53%	−20.15%	−6.95%	−5.70%
Large Stocks maximum compound return	159.52%	45.64%	36.26%	22.83%	19.57%

T A B L E   20.12

Terminal Value of $10,000 Invested for Best and Worst Average Annual Compound Returns for Monthly Data, January 1, 1927, to December 31, 2009

For any	1-year period	3-year period	5-year period	7-year period	10-year period
Large Stocks 6-month momentum, decile 1, minimum $10,000 value	$4,227	$2,065	$3,482	$6,238	$4,953

(continued on next page)

T A B L E   20.12

Terminal Value of $10,000 Invested for Best and Worst Average Annual Compound Returns for Monthly Data, January 1, 1927, to December 31, 2009 *(Continued)*

For any	1-year period	3-year period	5-year period	7-year period	10-year period
Large Stocks 6-month momentum, decile 1, maximum $10,000 value	$25,084	$46,865	$72,338	$92,281	$166,173
Large Stocks 6-month momentum, decile 10, minimum $10,000 value	$2,380	$1,045	$1,330	$3,020	$3,453
Large Stocks 6-month momentum, decile 10, maximum $10,000 value	$34,801	$31,280	$56,273	$47,215	$45,667
Large Stocks minimum $10,000 value	$3,337	$1,800	$3,247	$6,041	$5,561
Large Stocks maximum $10,000 value	$25,952	$30,890	$46,970	$42,189	$59,747

BUYING LARGE STOCKS WITH THE BEST 12-MONTH PRICE APPRECIATION

As Table 20.13 shows, $10,000 invested in the stocks with the best 12-month price appreciation from Large Stocks grew to $90,010,397 between 1926 and 2009, an average annual compound return of 11.59 percent, vastly higher than the $21,617,372 you would have earned from an investment in the Large Stocks universe. Risk, with a standard deviation of return of 23.11 percent, was higher for the group than for the Large Stocks universe, where the standard deviation of return was 19.35 percent. Nevertheless, the Sharpe ratio for the group with the best 12-month price appreciation was .29, versus .24 for the Large Stocks universe. As Table 20.14 shows, all the base rates were positive, yet as we saw with the All Stocks group, not quite as strong as those of the six-month price performers. The group beat the Large Stocks universe in 72 percent of all rolling five-year periods and in 84 percent of all rolling ten-year periods. Figure 20.4 shows the five-year average annual compound excess (deficient) returns of decile one based on 12-month price appreciation minus the Large Stocks universe.

T A B L E   20.13

Summary Annual Return and Risk Results Data: Large Stocks 12-Month Momentum, Decile 1, and Large Stocks, January 1, 1927, to December 31, 2009

	Large Stocks 12-month momentum, decile 1	Large Stocks
Arithmetic average	14.65%	11.75%
Geometric average	11.59%	9.69%
Median return	21.31%	16.75%
Standard deviation	23.11%	19.35%
Upside deviation	14.38%	13.10%
Downside deviation	17.46%	14.40%

(continued on next page)

T A B L E 20.13

Summary Annual Return and Risk Results Data: Large Stocks 12-Month Momentum, Decile 1, and Large Stocks, January 1, 1927, to December 31, 2009 *(Continued)*

	Large Stocks 12-month momentum, decile 1	Large Stocks
Tracking error	11.14	0.00
Number of positive periods	606	609
Number of negative periods	390	387
Maximum peak-to-trough decline	−81.56%	−84.33%
Beta	1.05	1.00
T-statistic (m = 0)	5.42	5.25
Sharpe ratio (Rf = 5%)	0.29	0.24
Sortino ratio (MAR = 10%)	0.09	−0.02
$10,000 becomes	$90,010,397	$21,617,372
Minimum 1-year return	−59.67%	−66.63%
Maximum 1-year return	148.43%	159.52%
Minimum 3-year return	−40.38%	−43.53%
Maximum 3-year return	66.27%	45.64%
Minimum 5-year return	−18.40%	−20.15%
Maximum 5-year return	47.14%	36.26%
Minimum 7-year return	−7.62%	−6.95%
Maximum 7-year return	35.36%	22.83%
Minimum 10-year return	−7.97%	−5.70%
Maximum 10-year return	31.44%	19.57%
Minimum expected return*	−31.58%	−26.96%
Maximum expected return†	60.87%	50.46%

* Minimum expected return is arithmetic return minus 2 times the standard deviation.
† Maximum expected return is arithmetic return plus 2 times the standard deviation.

T A B L E 20.14

Base Rates for Large Stocks 12-Month Momentum, Decile 1, and Large Stocks, January 1, 1927, to December 31, 2009

Item	Large Stocks 12-month momentum, decile 1, beat Large Stocks	Percent	Average annual excess return
Single-year return	603 out of 985	61%	3.51%
Rolling 3-year compound return	630 out of 961	66%	2.30%
Rolling 5-year compound return	675 out of 937	72%	2.18%
Rolling 7-year compound return	690 out of 913	76%	2.11%
Rolling 10-year compound return	741 out of 877	84%	2.18%

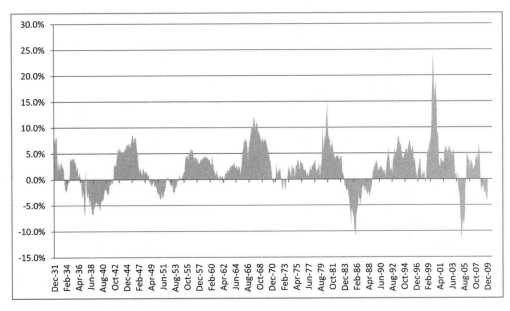

F I G U R E   20.4

Five-year average annual compound excess (deficient) return Large Stocks 12-month momentum decile 1 minus Large Stocks, January 1, 1927, to December 31, 2009

WHY PRICE PERFORMANCE WORKS WHILE OTHER MEASURES DO NOT

Price momentum conveys different information about the prospects of a stock and is a much better indicator than factors such as earnings growth rates. Many look at the disappointing results of buying stocks with the highest earnings gains and wonder why they differ from the best price performers. First, price momentum is the market putting its money where its mouth is. Second, the common belief that stocks with strong relative strength also have the highest PE ratios or earnings growth is incorrect. When you look at the top performers over time, you find that they are *rarely* the highest valued in terms of PE or PSR. The same is true for five-year earnings per share growth rates and one-year earnings per share growth rates. As a group, they are usually higher than lower momentum stocks than the market, but not by extraordinary amounts. Also, Surowiecki's concept of "wise crowds" is proven out in the longer-term data for price momentum, with price movement being an excellent measure of what the overall market opinion is of the current price.

   The only time that strong price momentum leads you astray is at the peak of a bubble or when the market is emerging from a severe bear market (greater than a 40 percent drop). Take the bubble that occurred between December 31, 1995 and February 2000—the group of stocks from All Stocks with the best six-month relative strength soared by 42.24 percent a year, turning $10,000 into $43,407 in a little over four years. That performance doubled the 20.13 percent annual gains for an investment in the All Stocks universe. But the conditions for group intelligence that Surowiecki outlined in his book had broken down.

Everyone was of the same opinion that stocks would continue to soar, and as we all know, that opinion was wrong. Over the next three years, the stocks with the best six-month price momentum from All Stocks went on to lose nearly half their value, losing 15.52 percent per year compared to a loss of 9.01 percent per year for the All Stocks universe.

As we see when we look at stocks with the *worst* price momentum, the best performers also do poorly coming out of a severe bear market. What tends to happen then is that price momentum inverts, with the *worst* performers doing vastly better than the best. For example, after stocks bottomed in May of 1932, over the next year decile 1 of All Stocks by six-month price momentum went up 69.3 percent whereas decile 10—those with the worst six-month price momentum—went up 127.1 percent. The All Stocks universe itself went up 91.4 percent. This happens because investors collectively realize that all the companies that they had priced for extinction may in fact not go out of business, so they rush in and quickly bid up their prices. We saw a similar phenomenon after the 1973–1974 bear market and after the most recent bear market that ended in February 2009. Indeed, the inversion that occurred most recently was almost as severe as that of the early 1930s—between February 2009 and December 2009, the worst six-month price performers from All Stocks soared 132.21 percent, turning $10,000 invested in February into $21,647 just 11 months later. The best decile of six-month performers from the All Stocks universe grew just 32 percent over the same period, turning $10,000 invested in February into $12,868. The All Stocks universe itself gained 66 percent over the same period, turning $10,000 into $15,883.

Typically, this inversion is a short-term event and usually lasts about only a year. We then see things return to normal, with the best price performers vastly outdistancing all other stocks.

WORST-CASE SCENARIOS AND BEST AND WORST RETURNS

Looking at Tables 20.15 through 20.18, we see that for both All Stocks and Large Stocks the biggest drawdown for the top decile by six-month price appreciation occurred during the mother of all bear markets: between August 1929 and May 1932, the group lost 78 percent. Yet, as harrowing as that looks, it was actually 7 percent better than the drawdown suffered by the All Stocks universe itself, which plunged 85 percent over the same period. During the most recent bear market, the best six-month price appreciation group from All Stocks dropped 62 percent, 6 percent more than All Stocks' decline of 56 percent. All told, between 1926 and 2009, the group of best six-month price performers had 18 periods in which they lost more than 20 percent from peak to trough. Table 20.15 shows the worst-case scenarios for the best six-month price performers.

We see similar declines when looking at the top 12-month price appreciation performers from All Stocks. The worst decline occurred between August 1929 and May 1932, when the group lost 80 percent, 5 percent less than All Stocks' decline. More recently, between February 2000 and February 2009, the 12-month price performers dropped by 66 percent and have not yet retaken the highs attained in February 2000. Table 20.16 shows all the worst-case scenarios for the 12-month price appreciation group from All Stocks. All told, the group had 16 separate drops exceeding 20 percent between 1926 and 2009.

T A B L E 20.15

Worst-Case Scenarios: All 20 Percent or Greater Declines for All Stocks 6-Month Momentum Decile 1, January 1, 1927, to December 31, 2009

Peak date	Peak index value	Trough date	Trough index value	Recovery date	Decline (%)	Decline duration	Recovery duration
Aug–29	2.50	May–32	0.54	Oct–36	−78.26%	33	53
Mar–37	3.14	Mar–38	1.28	Mar–43	−59.29%	12	60
May–46	9.51	May–47	6.22	Feb–50	−34.60%	12	33
Jun–57	44.77	Oct–57	35.77	Jul–58	−20.10%	4	9
Nov–61	105.65	Jun–62	75.85	Aug–63	−28.21%	7	14
Apr–66	251.21	Oct–66	178.48	Mar–67	−28.95%	6	5
Nov–68	481.45	Jun–70	253.33	May–72	−47.38%	19	23
May–72	487.44	Sep–74	260.92	Jun–76	−46.47%	28	21
Aug–78	856.81	Oct–78	646.13	Apr–79	−24.59%	2	6
Feb–80	1,391.01	Mar–80	1,050.19	Jul–80	−24.50%	1	4
Nov–80	2,132.17	Mar–82	1593.53	Nov–82	−25.26%	16	8
Jun–83	3,363.92	Jul–84	2,369.97	Nov–85	−29.55%	13	16
Aug–87	6,048.80	Nov–87	3,964.43	Apr–89	−34.46%	3	17
May–90	7,100.84	Oct–90	5,223.89	Feb–91	−26.43%	5	4
May–96	24,155.26	Jul–96	19,103.51	Jul–97	−20.91%	2	12
Apr–98	29,247.49	Aug–98	20,394.35	Dec–98	−30.27%	4	4
Feb–00	82,912.64	Feb–03	34,645.93	Jan–06	−58.21%	36	35
Oct–07	103,850.95	Feb–09	39,011.26	N/A	−62.44%	16	N/A
Average					−37.77%	12.17	19.06

T A B L E 20.16

Worst-Case Scenarios: All 20 Percent or Greater Declines for All Stocks 12-Month Momentum Decile 1, January 1, 1927, to December 31, 2009

Peak date	Peak index value	Trough date	Trough index value	Recovery date	Decline (%)	Decline duration	Recovery duration
Aug–29	2.52	May–32	0.52	Jan–37	−79.58%	33	56
Mar–37	2.77	Mar–38	0.98	Apr–43	−64.71%	12	61
May–46	7.58	May–47	4.72	May–50	−37.76%	12	36
Jun–57	29.27	Dec–57	22.77	Aug–58	−22.19%	6	8
Nov–61	66.77	Jun–62	45.95	Dec–63	−31.18%	7	18
Apr–66	152.40	Oct–66	106.83	Mar–67	−29.90%	6	5
Nov–68	294.31	Sep–74	147.29	Dec–76	−49.95%	70	27
Aug–78	491.36	Oct–78	369.18	Apr–79	−24.87%	2	6
Feb–80	763.58	Mar–80	578.02	Jul–80	−24.30%	1	4
Nov–80	1,206.64	Mar–82	821.35	Jan–83	−31.93%	16	10
Jun–83	1,707.68	May–84	1,160.41	Nov–85	−32.05%	11	18
Aug–87	2,993.02	Nov–87	1,898.79	May–89	−36.56%	3	18
May–90	3,482.48	Oct–90	2,550.81	Feb–91	−26.75%	5	4
May–96	11,467.48	Apr–97	8,625.93	Aug–97	−24.78%	11	4
Apr–98	12,927.70	Aug–98	8,760.95	Jan–99	−32.23%	4	5
Feb–00	33,099.41	Feb–09	11,156.51	N/A	−66.29%	108	N/A
Average					−38.44%	19.19	18.67

T A B L E   20.17

Worst-Case Scenarios: All 20 Percent or Greater Declines for Large Stocks 6-Month Momentum, Decile 1, January 1, 1927, to December 31, 2009

Peak date	Peak index value	Trough date	Trough index value	Recovery date	Decline (%)	Decline duration	Recovery duration
Aug–29	3.21	Feb–33	0.58	Dec–44	−81.81%	42	142
May–46	6.01	May–47	4.21	Dec–49	−30.00%	12	31
Nov–61	55.69	Jun–62	40.40	May–63	−27.45%	7	11
Apr–66	119.63	Oct–66	91.95	Mar–67	−23.14%	6	5
Nov–68	166.09	Jun–70	104.03	Feb–72	−37.36%	19	20
May–72	185.87	Sep–74	113.62	Jan–76	−38.87%	28	16
Feb–80	474.82	Mar–80	365.28	Jun–80	−23.07%	1	3
Nov–80	715.67	Mar–82	488.30	Mar–83	−31.77%	16	12
Jun–83	880.50	Jul–84	634.28	Jun–85	−27.96%	13	11
Aug–87	1,774.29	Nov–87	1,230.70	Apr–89	−30.64%	3	17
Jun–98	10,047.71	Aug–98	7,851.02	Nov–98	−21.86%	2	3
Feb–00	31,098.19	Sep–02	12,511.88	Mar–07	−59.77%	31	54
May–08	39,866.89	Feb–09	16,024.94	N/A	−59.80%	9	N/A
Average					−37.96%	15	27.08

T A B L E   20.18

Worst-Case Scenarios: All 20 Percent or Greater Declines for Large Stocks 12-Month Momentum, Decile 1, January 1, 1927, to December 31, 2009

Peak date	Peak index value	Trough date	Trough index value	Recovery date	Decline (%)	Decline duration	Recovery duration
Aug–29	3.36	May–32	0.62	Jan–45	−81.56%	33	152
May–46	5.65	May–47	3.72	May–50	−34.19%	12	36
Jul–56	22.94	Oct–57	17.72	Sep–58	−22.73%	15	11
Nov–61	42.52	Jun–62	29.19	Aug–63	−31.35%	7	14
Apr–66	85.78	Oct–66	63.94	Mar–67	−25.46%	6	5
Nov–68	121.18	Jun–70	76.53	Jan–72	−36.85%	19	19
May–72	139.34	Sep–74	82.13	Feb–76	−41.06%	28	17
Feb–80	322.28	Mar–80	247.94	Jun–80	−23.07%	1	3
Nov–80	492.63	Jul–82	300.65	May–83	−38.97%	20	10
Jun–83	535.11	Jul–84	366.45	Nov–85	−31.52%	13	16
Aug–87	1,038.15	Nov–87	698.11	May–89	−32.75%	3	18
Sep–89	1,221.49	Oct–90	958.45	Feb–91	−21.53%	13	4
Jun–98	5,324.91	Aug–98	4,131.38	Dec–98	−22.41%	2	4
Feb–00	16,305.59	Sep–02	5,731.03	Oct–07	−64.85%	31	61
Oct–07	17,380.34	Feb–09	6,454.09	N/A	−62.87%	16	N/A
Average					−38.08%	14.6	26.43

For the best six-month price performers from Large Stocks, the worst decline occurred between August 1929 and February 1933 when they lost 82 percent, yet the loss was actually 2 percent better than that suffered by the Large Stocks universe, which declined 84 percent over the same period. More recently, the group lost 60 percent between May 2008 and February 2009. The group lost more than 20 percent 13 times between 1926 and 2009. Table 20.17 shows all the worst-case scenarios for the group.

For the best 12-month performers from Large Stocks, the worst decline occurred between August 1929 and May 1932, when the group lost 82 percent. More recently, the group lost 63 percent between October 2007 and February 2009. Between 1926 and 2009, the group lost more than 20 percent on 15 separate occasions. Table 20.18 details all the worst-case scenarios for the group.

In terms of the best and worst absolute performance for the various groups, the best five-year return for the best six-month price performers from All Stocks occurred in the period ending February 2000, when $10,000 invested five years earlier grew to $60,736, a compound return of 43.45 percent a year. The worst absolute five-year return for the group occurred in the period ending March 1933, when $10,000 invested five years earlier declined to $4,298, a compound loss of 15.54 percent per year. Tables 20.19 and 20.20 show the results for other holding periods.

T A B L E   20.19

Best and Worst Average Annual Compound Returns for Monthly Data, January 1, 1927, to December 31, 2009

For any	1-year period	3-year period	5-year period	7-year period	10-year period
All Stocks 6-month momentum, decile 1, minimum compound return	−59.29%	−38.12%	−15.54%	−3.32%	−3.90%
All Stocks 6-month momentum, decile 1, maximum compound return	175.23%	59.15%	43.45%	33.36%	29.64%
All Stocks 12-month momentum, decile 1, minimum compound return	−64.71%	−39.36%	−16.35%	−4.94%	−5.76%
All Stocks 12-month momentum, decile 1, maximum compound return	157.56%	52.96%	39.45%	29.78%	27.22%
All Stocks minimum compound return	−66.72%	−45.99%	−23.07%	−7.43%	−5.31%
All Stocks maximum compound return	201.69%	51.03%	41.17%	23.77%	22.05%

T A B L E   20.20

Terminal Value of $10,000 Invested for Best and Worst Average Annual Compound Returns for Monthly Data, January 1, 1927, to December 31, 2009

For any	1-year period	3-year period	5-year period	7-year period	10-year period
All Stocks 6-month momentum, decile 1, minimum $10,000 value	$4,071	$2,369	$4,298	$7,893	$6,719
All Stocks 6-month momentum, decile 1, maximum $10,000 value	$27,523	$40,308	$60,736	$75,006	$134,125

(continued on next page)

TABLE 20.20

Terminal Value of $10,000 Invested for Best and Worst Average Annual Compound Returns for Monthly Data, January 1, 1927, to December 31, 2009 *(Continued)*

For any	1-year period	3-year period	5-year period	7-year period	10-year period
All Stocks 12-month momentum, decile 1, minimum $10,000 value	$3,529	$2,230	$4,096	$7,015	$5,528
All Stocks 12-month momentum, decile 1, maximum $10,000 value	$25,756	$35,784	$52,737	$62,011	$111,029
All Stocks minimum $10,000 value	$3,328	$1,576	$2,695	$5,825	$5,793
All Stocks maximum $10,000 value	$30,169	$34,452	$56,062	$44,504	$73,345

Looking at the best six-month performers from All Stocks, we see that the best relative cumulative performance over all rolling five-year periods occurred in the period ending February 2000. The worst five-year relative performance versus All Stocks occurred in the period ending February 2005, when the group suffered a cumulative loss of 20 percent compared to a gain of 20 percent for the All Stock universe.

The best absolute five-year gains for the best 12-month price performers from All Stocks occurred in the period ending November 1980, when $10,000 grew to $52,737, a compound gain of 39.45 percent per year. The worst absolute five-year return for the group occurred in the period ending May 1932, when an average annual loss of 16.35 percent shrank a $10,000 investment to $4,096. Tables 20.19 and 20.20 show the results for other holding periods.

The best relative five-year performance for the 12-month price appreciation group versus All Stocks occurred in the period ending February 2000, when the best 12-month performers gained a cumulative 406 percent compared to a gain of 172 percent for All Stocks, a cumulative advantage of 234 percent. The worst relative five-year performance for the group occurred in the period ending June 1937, when the group gained a cumulative 333 percent compared to a gain of 431 percent for All Stocks, a cumulative deficit of 98 percent.

LARGE STOCKS

For the best six-month price performers from Large Stocks, the best absolute five-year gains occurred in the period ending February 2000, when $10,000 grew to $72,338, an average annual compound return of 48.55 percent. The worst five years for the group occurred in the period ending August 1934, when $10,000 invested five years earlier shrank to $3,482, an average annual compound loss of −19.02 percent. Table 20.21 and 20.22 shows the results for other holding periods.

The best relative five-year performance for the twelve-month price appreciation group versus Large Stocks also occurred during the period ending February 2000. The worst relative five-year performance versus Large Stocks occurred in the period ending June 1937, when the best six-month performers from Large Stocks had a cumulative gain of 284 percent versus a gain of 346 percent for Large Stocks, a cumulative deficit of 62 percent.

The best absolute five-year returns for the best twelve-month performers from Large Stocks occurred in the period ending February 2000, when $10,000 grew to $68,962, a compound average annual gain of 47.14 percent. The worst absolute five-year returns for the group occurred in the period ending August 1934, when $10,000 shrank to $3,618, an average annual compound loss of 18.40 percent. Tables 20.21 and 20.22 show the results for other holding periods.

The best relative five-year returns for the best twelve-month performers versus Large Stocks also occurred in the period ending February 2000. The worst relative five-year returns for the group versus the Large Stocks occurred in the period ending June 1937, when the group earned a cumulative 241 percent versus a gain of 346 percent for the Large Stocks universe, a cumulative deficit of 105 percent.

TABLE 20.21

Best and Worst Average Annual Compound Returns for Monthly Data, January 1, 1927, to December 31, 2009

For any	1-year period	3-year period	5-year period	7-year period	10-year period
Large Stocks 6-month momentum, decile 1, minimum compound return	−57.73%	−40.90%	−19.02%	−6.52%	−6.79%
Large Stocks 6-month momentum, decile 1, maximum compound return	150.84%	67.35%	48.55%	37.36%	32.45%
Large Stocks 12-month momentum, decile 1, minimum compound return	−59.67%	−40.38%	−18.40%	−7.62%	−7.97%
Large Stocks 12-month momentum, decile 1, maximum compound return	148.43%	66.27%	47.14%	35.36%	31.44%
Large Stocks minimum compound return	−66.63%	−43.53%	−20.15%	−6.95%	−5.70%
Large Stocks maximum compound return	159.52%	45.64%	36.26%	22.83%	19.57%

TABLE 20.22

Terminal Value of $10,000 Invested for Best and Worst Average Annual Compound Returns for Monthly Data, January 1, 1927, to December 31, 2009

For any	1-year period	3-year period	5-year period	7-year period	10-year period
Large Stocks 6-month momentum, decile 1, minimum $10,000 value	$4,227	$2,065	$3,482	$6,238	$4,953
Large Stocks 6-month momentum, decile 1, maximum $10,000 value	$25,084	$46,865	$72,338	$92,281	$166,173
Large Stocks 12-month momentum, decile 1, minimum $10,000 value	$4,033	$2,119	$3,618	$5,743	$4,356
Large Stocks 12-month momentum, decile 1, maximum $10,000 value	$24,843	$45,964	$68,962	$83,273	$153,965
Large Stocks minimum $10,000 value	$3,337	$1,800	$3,247	$6,041	$5,561
Large Stocks maximum $10,000 value	$25,952	$30,890	$46,970	$42,189	$59,747

BUYING THE WORST-PERFORMING STOCKS

If you're looking for a great way to underperform the market, look no further. A $10,000 investment on December 31, 1926, in the decile of stocks from the All Stocks universe with the worst six-month price performance was worth just $292,547 at the end of 2009, a measly compound return of 4.15 percent a year (Table 20.23). That's a long way from the $38,542,780 you would have earned investing in the All Stocks universe. The standard deviation of return for the six-month losers was 29.26 percent, considerably higher than All Stocks' 21.67 percent. With such abysmal returns, *any* risk will wreak havoc on the Sharpe ratio, and here it's a pathetic −.03. To further illustrate how horrible this return is,

T A B L E   20.23

Summary Annual Return and Risk Results Data: All Stocks 6-Month Momentum, Decile 10, and All Stocks, January 1, 1927, to December 31, 2009

	All Stocks 6-month momentum, decile 10	All Stocks
Arithmetic average	8.50%	13.06%
Geometric average	4.15%	10.46%
Median return	8.10%	18.54%
Standard deviation	29.26%	21.67%
Upside deviation	23.67%	14.78%
Downside deviation	19.83%	16.03%
Tracking error	10.74	0.00
Number of positive periods	559	606
Number of negative periods	437	390
Maximum peak-to-trough decline	−91.78%	−85.45%
Beta	1.29	1.00
T-statistic (m = 0)	2.55	5.19
Sharpe ratio (Rf = 5%)	−0.03	0.25
Sortino ratio (MAR = 10%)	−0.30	0.03
$10,000 becomes	$292,547	$38,542,780
Minimum 1-year return	−77.67%	−66.72%
Maximum 1-year return	296.01%	201.69%
Minimum 3-year return	−55.33%	−45.99%
Maximum 3-year return	50.90%	51.03%
Minimum 5-year return	−33.99%	−23.07%
Maximum 5-year return	43.52%	41.17%
Minimum 7-year return	−16.53%	−7.43%
Maximum 7-year return	24.87%	23.77%
Minimum 10-year return	−11.34%	−5.31%
Maximum 10-year return	17.71%	22.05%
Minimum expected return*	−50.01%	−30.28%
Maximum expected return†	67.02%	56.39%

* Minimum expected return is arithmetic return minus 2 times the standard deviation.
† Maximum expected return is arithmetic return plus 2 times the standard deviation.

remember that $10,000 in 1926 is the equivalent of $123,966 on December 31, 2009. Table 20.23 catalogs the woe.

Base rates, featured in Table 20.24, are atrocious as well, with the six-month losers beating All Stocks in only 2 percent of all rolling five-year periods and in 1 percent of all rolling ten-year periods. What's more, the *magnitude* of all rolling five-year losses was huge, with the decile of the worst six-month price performers, on average, lagging All Stocks by over 42 percent in any five-year period. But the booby prize goes to the ten-year returns: over all ten-year periods, the six-month biggest losers had cumulative ten-year returns that were 142 percent *less* than All Stocks. Figure 20.5 shows the average annual compound excess—or in this case, deficient—return for decile 10 of six-month price appreciation group minus the All Stocks universe's return.

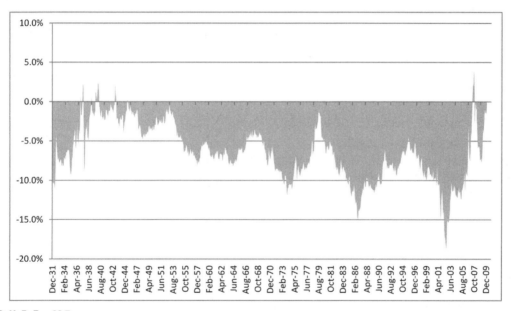

F I G U R E   20.5

Five-year average annual compound excess (deficient) return All Stocks 6-month momentum decile 10 minus All Stocks, January 1, 1927, to December 31, 2009

T A B L E   20.24

Base Rates for All Stocks 6-Month Momentum, Decile 10, and All Stocks, January 1, 1927, to December 31, 2009

Item	All Stocks 6-month momentum, decile 10, beat All Stocks	Percent	Average annual excess return
Single-year return	178 out of 985	18%	−5.20%
Rolling 3-year compound return	64 out of 961	7%	−6.24%
Rolling 5-year compound return	22 out of 937	2%	−6.36%
Rolling 7-year compound return	16 out of 913	2%	−6.45%
Rolling 10-year compound return	5 out of 877	1%	−6.48%

BUYING THE BIGGEST 12-MONTH LOSERS

As Table 20.25 makes clear, the news isn't much better when investing in the decile of biggest 12-month losers. The $10,000 invested on December 31, 1926, grew to $1,038,156, an average annual compound return of 5.75 percent. Risk was a very high 29.91 versus 21.67 for All Stocks. The poor return married to the high risk brought the Sharpe ratio to .03, compared to .25 for All Stocks. Table 20.26 shows base rates. All are negative, with the group beating All Stocks in just 7 percent of all rolling five-year periods and in 1 percent of all rolling ten-year periods.

T A B L E   20.25

Summary Annual Return and Risk Results Data: All Stocks 12-Month Momentum, Decile 10 and All Stocks, January 1, 1927, to December 31, 2009

	All Stocks 12-month momentum, decile 10	All Stocks
Arithmetic average	10.34%	13.06%
Geometric average	5.75%	10.46%
Median return	10.94%	18.54%
Standard deviation	29.91%	21.67%
Upside deviation	24.66%	14.78%
Downside deviation	20.30%	16.03%
Tracking error	11.94	0.00
Number of positive periods	557	606
Number of negative periods	439	390
Maximum peak-to-trough decline	−90.94%	−85.45%
Beta	1.30	1.00
T-statistic (m = 0)	3.01	5.19
Sharpe ratio (Rf = 5%)	0.03	0.25
Sortino ratio (MAR = 10%)	−0.21	0.03
$10,000 becomes	$1,038,156	$38,542,780
Minimum 1-year return	−77.93%	−66.72%
Maximum 1-year return	294.88%	201.69%
Minimum 3-year return	−53.98%	−45.99%
Maximum 3-year return	54.61%	51.03%
Minimum 5-year return	−32.90%	−23.07%
Maximum 5-year return	41.31%	41.17%
Minimum 7-year return	−16.37%	−7.43%
Maximum 7-year return	23.70%	23.77%
Minimum 10-year return	−10.14%	−5.31%
Maximum 10-year return	19.31%	22.05%
Minimum expected return*	−49.48%	−30.28%
Maximum expected return†	70.17%	56.39%

* Minimum expected return is arithmetic return minus 2 times the standard deviation.
† Maximum expected return is arithmetic return plus 2 times the standard deviation.

T A B L E 20.26

Base Rates for All Stocks 12-Month Momentum, Decile 10, and All Stocks, January 1, 1927, to December 31, 2009

Item	All Stocks 12-month momentum, decile 10, beat All Stocks	Percent	Average annual excess return
Single-year return	265 out of 985	27%	−3.58%
Rolling 3-year compound return	125 out of 961	13%	−4.64%
Rolling 5-year compound return	61 out of 937	7%	−4.73%
Rolling 7-year compound return	25 out of 913	3%	−4.79%
Rolling 10-year compound return	11 out of 877	1%	−4.80%

As I mentioned when reviewing the best price performing stocks, the only time either of these groups of losers do well is right after a crushing bear market (with a loss of more than 40 percent). To wit: the best months for the 12-month price losers occurred in August 1932, when they soared 82 percent in just one month, and in April 2009, when they gained 38 percent. And when you look at the groups' performance one year after a severe bear market, the returns take your breath away: in the one year ending June 1933, the 12-month price losers posted a return of 295 percent, and in the year ending September 2003, they gained 112 percent. But as we've seen before, those unsustainable returns are indeed unsustainable, with returns quickly fading and the losers soon reverting to their atrocious performance. Thus, the *only* time to consider purchasing these stocks is right as the market emerges from a serious decline. Figure 20.6 shows the five-year average annual compound— mostly deficient—returns for the group minus the returns from the All Stocks universe.

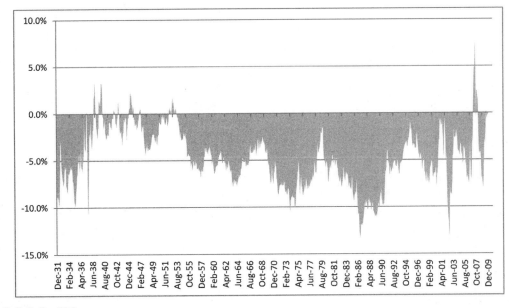

F I G U R E 20.6

Five-year average annual compound excess (deficient) return All Stocks 12-month momentum decile 10 minus All Stocks, January 1, 1927, to December 31, 2009

LARGE STOCKS ALSO HIT

The price losers from the Large Stocks universe also suffered, and the results were nearly as fatal. A $10,000 investment on December 21, 1926, in the decile of stocks with the worst six-month price performance from the Large Stocks universe grew to only $629,553 by the end of 2009, a compound return of 5.12 percent a year. That's much worse than the return for the Large Stocks universe, which compounded at 9.69 percent over the same period. Risk was also higher for the group, with the six-month losers' standard deviation being 25.31 percent. The Sharpe ratio was a low .00. Table 20.27 shows all the summary data.

T A B L E   20.27

Summary Annual Return and Risk Results Data: Large Stocks 6-Month Momentum, Decile 10, and Large Stocks, January 1, 1927, to December 31, 2009

	Large Stocks 6-month momentum, decile 10	Large Stocks
Arithmetic average	8.44%	11.75%
Geometric average	5.12%	9.69%
Median return	9.07%	16.75%
Standard deviation	25.31%	19.35%
Upside deviation	19.86%	13.10%
Downside deviation	17.92%	14.40%
Tracking error	9.92	0.00
Number of positive periods	557	609
Number of negative periods	439	387
Maximum peak-to-trough decline	−91.07%	−84.33%
Beta	1.22	1.00
T-statistic (m = 0)	2.93	5.25
Sharpe ratio (Rf = 5%)	0.00	0.24
Sortino ratio (MAR = 10%)	−0.27	−0.02
$10,000 becomes	$629,553	$21,617,372
Minimum 1-year return	−76.20%	−66.63%
Maximum 1-year return	248.01%	159.52%
Minimum 3-year return	−52.90%	−43.53%
Maximum 3-year return	46.25%	45.64%
Minimum 5-year return	−33.20%	−20.15%
Maximum 5-year return	41.27%	36.26%
Minimum 7-year return	−15.72%	−6.95%
Maximum 7-year return	24.82%	22.83%
Minimum 10-year return	−10.09%	−5.70%
Maximum 10-year return	16.40%	19.57%
Minimum expected return*	−42.18%	−26.96%
Maximum expected return†	59.05%	50.46%

* Minimum expected return is arithmetic return minus 2 times the standard deviation.
† Maximum expected return is arithmetic return plus 2 times the standard deviation.

The base rates of the group from Large Stocks were slightly better than those from All Stocks, as Table 20.28 shows. The six-month losers from Large Stocks beat the universe in just 6 percent of all rolling five-year periods and in 2 percent of all rolling ten-year periods. Figure 20.7 shows the five-year average annual compound (mostly deficient) returns for the group minus the returns from the Large Stocks universe.

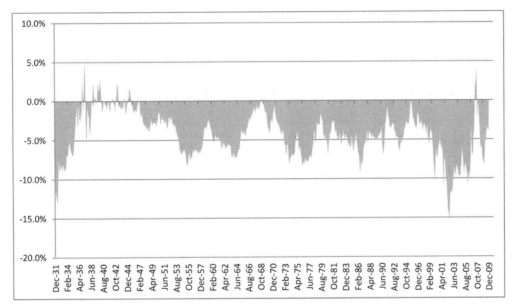

F I G U R E   20.7

Five-year average annual compound excess (deficient) return Large Stocks 6-month momentum decile 10 minus Large Stocks, January 1, 1927, to December 31, 2009

T A B L E   20.28

Base Rates for Large Stocks 6-Month Momentum, Decile 10, and Large Stocks, January 1, 1927, to December 31, 2009

Item	Large Stocks 6-month momentum, decile 10, beat Large Stocks	Percent	Average annual excess return
Single-year return	269 out of 985	27%	−3.72%
Rolling 3-year compound return	106 out of 961	11%	−4.30%
Rolling 5-year compound return	53 out of 937	6%	−4.26%
Rolling 7-year compound return	40 out of 913	4%	−4.28%
Rolling 10-year compound return	19 out of 877	2%	−4.24%

BUYING THE BIGGEST 12-MONTH LOSERS FROM LARGE STOCKS

As Table 20.29 shows, you would do slightly better with the biggest 12-month losers from Large Stocks—$10,000 invested on December 31, 1926, grew to $1,581,383 by the end of 2009, an average annual compound return of 6.29 percent. Obviously, it's over $20 million less than you would have earned with an investment in the Large Stocks universe, but it's better than the six-month losers' performance. The standard deviation of return for the group was 25.66, much higher than Large Stocks' 19.35 percent. The Sharpe ratio was .05, and all base rates were negative, with the group beating Large Stocks in 13 percent of all rolling five-year periods and in 8 percent of all rolling ten-year periods. Table 20.30 shows the base rates for all other holding periods. Figure 20.8 shows the five-year average annual compound (mostly deficient) returns for the group minus the returns from the Large Stocks universe.

T A B L E   20.29

Summary Annual Return and Risk Results Data: Large Stocks 12-Month Momentum, Decile 10, and Large Stocks, January 1, 1927, to December 31, 2009

	Large Stocks 12-month momentum, decile 10	Large Stocks
Arithmetic average	9.73%	11.75%
Geometric average	6.29%	9.69%
Median return	8.32%	16.75%
Standard deviation	25.66%	19.35%
Upside deviation	20.44%	13.10%
Downside deviation	18.10%	14.40%
Tracking error	10.85	0.00
Number of positive periods	554	609
Number of negative periods	442	387
Maximum peak-to-trough decline	−88.68%	−84.33%
Beta	1.22	1.00
T-statistic (m = 0)	3.31	5.25
Sharpe ratio (Rf = 5%)	0.05	0.24
Sortino ratio (MAR = 10%)	−0.20	−0.02
$10,000 becomes	$1,581,383	$21,617,372
Minimum 1-year return	−75.47%	−66.63%
Maximum 1-year return	245.23%	159.52%
Minimum 3-year return	−49.52%	−43.53%
Maximum 3-year return	49.31%	45.64%
Minimum 5-year return	−30.18%	−20.15%
Maximum 5-year return	39.71%	36.26%
Minimum 7-year return	−14.62%	−6.95%
Maximum 7-year return	24.64%	22.83%
Minimum 10-year return	−7.44%	−5.70%
Maximum 10-year return	19.27%	19.57%
Minimum expected return*	−41.59%	−26.96%
Maximum expected return†	61.06%	50.46%

* Minimum expected return is arithmetic return minus 2 times the standard deviation.
† Maximum expected return is arithmetic return plus 2 times the standard deviation.

T A B L E   20.30

Base Rates for Large Stocks 12-Month Momentum, Decile 10, and Large Stocks, January 1, 1927, to December 31, 2009

Item	Large Stocks 12-month momentum, decile 10, beat Large Stocks	Percent	Average annual excess return
Single-year return	326 out of 985	33%	−2.48%
Rolling 3-year compound return	196 out of 961	20%	−3.14%
Rolling 5-year compound return	125 out of 937	13%	−3.08%
Rolling 7-year compound return	73 out of 913	8%	−3.07%
Rolling 10-year compound return	67 out of 877	8%	−3.03%

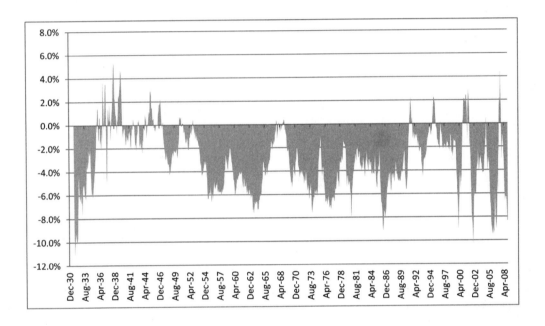

F I G U R E   20.8

Five-year average annual compound excess (deficient) return Large Stocks 12-month momentum decile 10 minus Large Stocks, January 1, 1927, to December 31, 2009

BEST- AND WORST-CASE RETURNS

Looking at Tables 20.31 through 20.38, we see a very unattractive picture. The decile of stocks with the worst six-month performance from All Stocks is simply dreadful—it lost 92 percent between August 1929 and May 1932, 77 percent between November 1968 and September 1974, and 73 percent between February 2000 and September 2002, a drop from which they have yet to recover. Table 20.31 catalogs the woe. What about the biggest 12-month relative strength losers from All Stocks? They're not much better. When you look at the best- and worst-case returns for any five-year period, what you *don't* see on the surface is that over all rolling five-year periods between 1926 and 2009, the *absolute return* for this group of stocks was *negative* 19 percent of the time. The group also lost to U.S. T-bills in 35 percent of all rolling five-year periods. Its declines were almost as bad as the six-month losers: the 12-month losers from All Stocks dropped 91 percent between August 1929 and May 1932, 75 percent between November 1968 and September 1974, and 70 percent between May 2007 and February 2009. Clearly, this paints a terrifying picture. Table 20.32 shows the worst-case scenarios for the biggest 12-month losers from All Stocks.

T A B L E 20.31

Worst-Case Scenarios: All 20 Percent or Greater Declines for All Stocks 6-Month Momentum Decile 10, January 1, 1927, to December 31, 2009

Peak date	Peak index value	Trough date	Trough index value	Recovery date	Decline (%)	Decline duration	Recovery duration
Aug–29	1.65	May–32	0.14	Nov–45	−91.78%	33	162
May–46	1.98	Feb–48	1.25	Aug–50	−36.76%	21	30
Mar–56	4.48	Dec–57	3.33	Jul–58	−25.63%	21	7
May–61	6.47	Oct–62	4.38	Jan–65	−32.32%	17	27
Nov–68	12.71	Sep–74	2.87	Apr–83	−77.42%	70	103
Jun–83	14.80	Jul–84	11.54	Mar–86	−22.03%	13	20
Aug–87	18.37	Oct–90	10.50	Feb–92	−42.85%	38	16
Apr–98	34.19	Aug–98	20.23	Dec–99	−40.84%	4	16
Feb–00	37.91	Sep–02	10.38	N/A	−72.61%	31	N/A
Average					−49.14%	27.56	47.63

T A B L E 20.32

Worst-Case Scenarios: All 20 Percent or Greater Declines for All Stocks 12-Month Momentum, Decile 10, January 1, 1927, to December 31, 2009

Peak date	Peak index value	Trough date	Trough index value	Recovery date	Decline (%)	Decline duration	Recovery duration
Aug–29	1.63	May–32	0.15	Oct–45	−90.94%	33	161
May–46	2.09	Feb–48	1.38	Apr–50	−34.01%	21	26
May–57	5.55	Dec–57	4.27	Jul–58	−22.96%	7	7
May–61	8.76	Oct–62	5.87	Jan–65	−33.06%	17	27
Nov–68	17.93	Sep–74	4.44	May–81	−75.22%	70	80
May–81	18.14	Jul–82	13.17	Jan–83	−27.39%	14	6
Aug–87	31.21	Oct–90	18.50	Jan–92	−40.72%	38	15
Sep–97	72.86	Aug–98	43.61	Dec–99	−40.15%	11	16
Jun–01	92.46	Sep–02	31.49	Dec–04	−65.94%	15	27
May–07	127.56	Feb–09	38.21	N/A	−70.04%	21	N/A
Average					−50.04%	24.7	40.56

T A B L E   20.33

Worst-Case Scenarios: All 20 Percent or Greater Declines for Large Stocks 6-Month Momentum, Decile 10, January 1, 1927, to December 31, 2009

Peak date	Peak Index value	Trough date	Trough Index value	Recovery date	Decline (%)	Decline duration	Recovery duration
Aug–29	1.63	May–32	0.15	Apr–46	−91.07%	33	167
May–46	1.73	Feb–48	1.20	Apr–50	−30.76%	21	26
Dec–61	5.75	Oct–62	4.14	Jun–64	−27.97%	10	20
Nov–68	10.34	Sep–74	4.08	Jul–80	−60.57%	70	70
May–81	12.30	Jul–82	8.93	Dec–82	−27.39%	14	5
Aug–87	27.16	Nov–87	19.61	Jan–89	−27.78%	3	14
Aug–89	31.32	Oct–90	20.01	May–91	−36.11%	14	7
Apr–98	81.83	Aug–98	56.84	Apr–99	−30.53%	4	8
Jan–01	95.01	Sep–02	29.60	N/A	−68.85%	20	N/A
Average					−44.56%	21	39.63

T A B L E   20.34

Worst-Case Scenarios: All 20 Percent or Greater Declines for Large Stocks 12-Month Momentum, Decile 10, January 1, 1927, to December 31, 2009

Peak date	Peak Index value	Trough date	Trough Index value	Recovery date	Decline (%)	Decline duration	Recovery duration
Aug–29	1.59	May–32	0.18	Sep–45	−88.68%	33	160
May–46	2.10	Feb–48	1.47	Jan–50	−30.16%	21	23
Aug–61	8.18	Oct–62	5.79	Jun–64	−29.30%	14	20
Nov–68	14.85	Sep–74	5.95	Jul–80	−59.95%	70	70
May–81	18.41	Jul–82	13.63	Nov–82	−25.96%	14	4
Aug–87	42.36	Nov–87	29.71	Jan–89	−29.86%	3	14
Aug–89	49.56	Oct–90	32.59	Apr–91	−34.26%	14	6
Apr–98	147.04	Aug–98	107.11	Jan–99	−27.16%	4	5
Jan–01	217.31	Sep–02	71.41	Apr–07	−67.14%	20	55
May–07	229.40	Feb–09	70.25	N/A	−69.38%	21	N/A
Average					−46.18%	21.4	39.67

T A B L E   20.35

Best and Worst Average Annual Compound Returns for Monthly Data, January 1, 1927, to December 31, 2009

For any	1-year period	3-year period	5-year period	7-year period	10-year period
All Stocks 6-month momentum, decile 10, minimum compound return	−77.67%	−55.33%	−33.99%	−16.53%	−11.34%
All Stocks 6-month momentum, decile 10, maximum compound return	296.01%	50.90%	43.52%	24.87%	17.71%

(continued on next page)

T A B L E   20.35

Best and Worst Average Annual Compound Returns for Monthly Data, January 1, 1927, to December 31, 2009
(Continued)

For any	1-year period	3-year period	5-year period	7-year period	10-year period
All Stocks 12-month momentum, decile 10, minimum compound return	−77.93%	−53.98%	−32.90%	−16.37%	−10.14%
All Stocks 12-month momentum, decile 10, maximum compound return	294.88%	54.61%	41.31%	23.70%	19.31%
All Stocks minimum compound return	−66.72%	−45.99%	−23.07%	−7.43%	−5.31%
All Stocks maximum compound return	201.69%	51.03%	41.17%	23.77%	22.05%

T A B L E   20.36

Terminal Value of $10,000 Invested for Best and Worst Average Annual Compound Returns for Monthly Data, January 1, 1927, to December 31, 2009

For any	1-year period	3-year period	5-year period	7-year period	10-year period
All Stocks 6-month momentum, decile 10, minimum $10,000 value	$2,233	$891	$1,253	$2,822	$3,000
All Stocks 6-month momentum, decile 10, maximum $10,000 value	$39,601	$34,363	$60,885	$47,347	$51,077
All Stocks 12-month momentum, decile 10, minimum $10,000 value	$2,207	$975	$1,360	$2,861	$3,433
All Stocks 12-month momentum, decile 10, maximum $10,000 value	$39,488	$36,960	$56,352	$44,326	$58,449
All Stocks minimum $10,000 value	$3,328	$1,576	$2,695	$5,825	$5,793
All Stocks maximum $10,000 value	$30,169	$34,452	$56,062	$44,504	$73,345

T A B L E   20.37

Best and Worst Average Annual Compound Returns for Monthly Data, January 1, 1927 to December 31, 2009

For any	1-year period	3-year period	5-year period	7-year period	10-year period
Large Stocks 6-month momentum, decile 10, minimum compound return	−76.20%	−52.90%	−33.20%	−15.72%	−10.09%
Large Stocks 6-month momentum, decile 10, maximum compound return	248.01%	46.25%	41.27%	24.82%	16.40%
Large Stocks 12-month momentum, decile 10, minimum compound return	−75.47%	−49.52%	−30.18%	−14.62%	−7.44%
Large Stocks 12-month momentum, decile 10, maximum compound return	245.23%	49.31%	39.71%	24.64%	19.27%
Large Stocks minimum compound return	−66.63%	−43.53%	−20.15%	−6.95%	−5.70%
Large Stocks maximum compound return	159.52%	45.64%	36.26%	22.83%	19.57%

TABLE 20.38

Terminal Value of $10,000 Invested for Best and Worst Average Annual Compound Returns for Monthly Data, January 1, 1927, to December 31, 2009

For any	1-year period	3-year period	5-year period	7-year period	10-year period
Large Stocks 6-month momentum, decile 10, minimum $10,000 value	$2,380	$1,045	$1,330	$3,020	$3,453
Large Stocks 6-month momentum, decile 10, maximum $10,000 value	$34,801	$31,280	$56,273	$47,215	$45,667
Large Stocks 12-month momentum, decile 10, minimum $10,000 value	$2,453	$1,286	$1,659	$3,309	$4,618
Large Stocks 12-month momentum, decile 10, maximum $10,000 value	$34,523	$33,288	$53,231	$46,733	$58,265
Large Stocks minimum $10,000 value	$3,337	$1,800	$3,247	$6,041	$5,561
Large Stocks maximum $10,000 value	$25,952	$30,890	$46,970	$42,189	$59,747

The *only* time you would want to buy stocks in this group is right after a severe bear market. These stocks really shine for about one year after a bear market ends. For example, when the market bottomed in mid–1932, the decile of six-month biggest losers from All Stocks shot up 295 percent for the year ending June 1933, but I cannot point out strongly enough that this is a short-term phenomenon. The stocks will inevitably revert to their losing ways. You can review all the tables for best- and worst-case returns for a number of holding periods and for the worst-case scenarios for both groups from the All Stocks and Large Stocks universes. Tables 20.33 and 20.34 show all declines in excess of 20 percent for the six-month and 12-month losers from Large Stocks, and Tables 20.35 and 20.36 show the best and worst returns for the All Stocks losers. Tables 20.37 and 20.38 show the best and worst returns for the Large Stocks losers.

DECILES

The decile returns for All Stocks by six-month price appreciation reveal a perfect staircase, with the performance of decile 1—containing the best six-month price performing stocks—at the top and returns of the other deciles descending in step to the tenth decile, which contains the worst six-month price performers. The top six deciles all beat All Stocks, with the bottom four all underperforming the universe. You can also see how much earning an additional 9.96 percent per year over 83 years affects your total portfolio value, with the best-performing group turning $10,000 into $573 million and the worst performing group turning it into $293,000. As Albert Einstein said, "Compound interest is the eighth wonder of the world. He who understands it, earns it. He who doesn't, pays it."

We see a similar symmetry for the deciles of six-month price appreciation from Large Stocks. with the top five deciles beating Large Stocks and the bottom five underperforming them. Tables 20.39 through 20.42 and Figures 20.9 through 20.12 detail the decile returns for both All Stocks and Large Stocks by 6- and 12-month price appreciation Finally, Tables 20.43 and 20.44 show the returns for both groups from All Stocks and Large Stocks by decade.

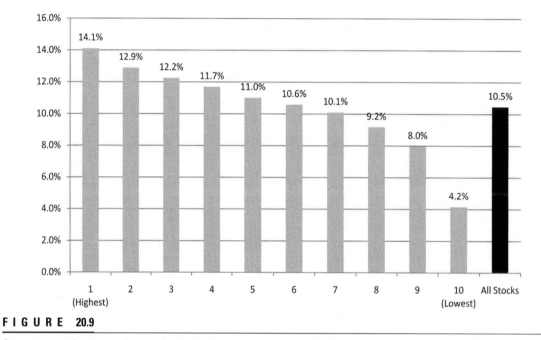

FIGURE 20.9

Average annual compound return by decile, 6-month momentum, All Stocks universe, January 1, 1927, to December 31, 2009

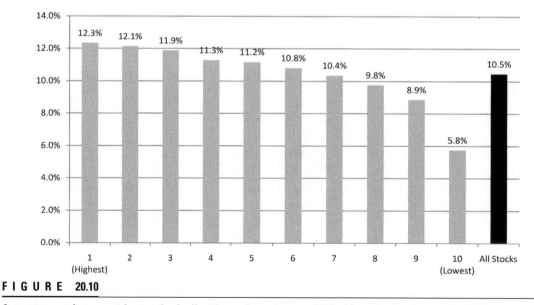

FIGURE 20.10

Average annual compound return by decile, 12-month momentum, All Stocks universe, January 1, 1927, to December 31, 2009

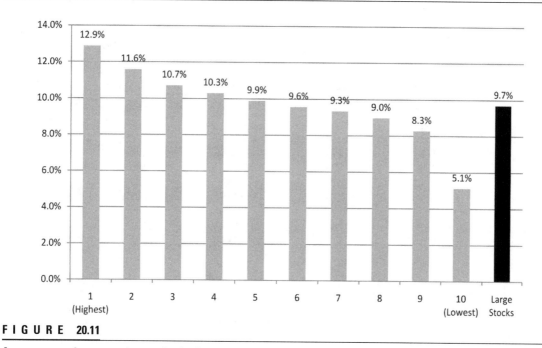

FIGURE 20.11

Average annual compound return by decile, 6-month momentum, Large Stocks universe, January 1, 1927, to December 31, 2009

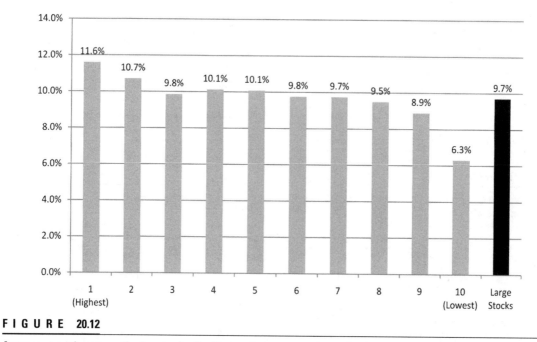

FIGURE 20.12

Average annual compound return by decile, 12-month momentum, Large Stocks universe, January 1, 1927, to December 31, 2009

T A B L E   20.39

Summary Results for 6-Month Momentum Decile Analysis of All Stocks Universe, January 1, 1927, to December 31, 2009

Decile	$10,000 grows to	Average return	Compound return	Standard deviation	Sharpe ratio
1 (highest)	$572,831,563	17.60%	14.11%	24.54%	0.37
2	$233,586,271	15.42%	12.88%	21.08%	0.37
3	$145,736,021	14.45%	12.24%	19.72%	0.37
4	$96,512,411	13.79%	11.69%	19.37%	0.35
5	$58,103,875	13.09%	11.01%	19.34%	0.31
6	$42,142,030	12.76%	10.58%	19.96%	0.28
7	$29,379,380	12.43%	10.10%	20.69%	0.25
8	$14,494,301	11.73%	9.17%	21.79%	0.19
9	$5,786,567	11.06%	7.96%	24.28%	0.12
10 (lowest)	$292,547	8.50%	4.15%	29.26%	−0.03
All Stocks	$38,542,780	13.06%	10.46%	21.67%	0.25

T A B L E   20.40

Summary Results for 12-Month Momentum Decile Analysis of All Stocks Universe, January 1, 1927, to December 31, 2009

Decile	$10,000 grows to	Average return	Compound return	Standard deviation	Sharpe ratio
1 (highest)	$156,230,201	15.88%	12.34%	24.78%	0.30
2	$134,035,688	14.61%	12.13%	20.85%	0.34
3	$110,707,814	14.08%	11.87%	19.76%	0.35
4	$71,040,889	13.35%	11.28%	19.20%	0.33
5	$65,466,534	13.22%	11.17%	19.21%	0.32
6	$49,893,393	12.97%	10.80%	19.86%	0.29
7	$35,520,440	12.70%	10.35%	20.79%	0.26
8	$22,713,816	12.44%	9.76%	22.37%	0.21
9	$11,442,307	12.04%	8.86%	24.53%	0.16
10 (lowest)	$1,038,156	10.34%	5.75%	29.91%	0.03
All Stocks	$38,542,780	13.06%	10.46%	21.67%	0.25

T A B L E   20.41

Summary Results for 6-Month Momentum Decile Analysis of Large Stocks Universe, January 1, 1927, to December 31, 2009

Decile	$10,000 grows to	Average return	Compound return	Standard deviation	Sharpe ratio
1 (highest)	$232,092,755	15.81%	12.88%	22.65%	0.35
2	$89,230,630	13.77%	11.58%	19.73%	0.33
3	$46,577,967	12.66%	10.71%	18.66%	0.31
4	$33,882,890	12.14%	10.29%	18.26%	0.29
5	$24,961,686	11.69%	9.88%	18.09%	0.27
6	$19,542,852	11.39%	9.56%	18.27%	0.25

(continued on next page)

T A B L E 20.41

Summary Results for 6-Month Momentum Decile Analysis of Large Stocks Universe, January 1, 1927, to December 31, 2009 *(Continued)*

Decile	$10,000 grows to	Average return	Compound return	Standard deviation	Sharpe ratio
7	$16,522,196	11.29%	9.34%	18.95%	0.23
8	$12,587,294	11.10%	8.98%	19.90%	0.20
9	$7,351,529	10.73%	8.28%	21.58%	0.15
10 (lowest)	$629,553	8.44%	5.12%	25.31%	0.00
Large Stocks	$21,617,372	11.75%	9.69%	19.35%	0.24

T A B L E 20.42

Summary Results for 12-Month Momentum Decile Analysis of Large Stocks Universe, January 1, 1927, to December 31, 2009

Decile	$10,000 grows to	Average return	Compound return	Standard deviation	Sharpe ratio
1 (highest)	$90,010,397	14.65%	11.59%	23.11%	0.29
2	$46,324,623	12.94%	10.70%	19.93%	0.29
3	$24,317,249	11.85%	9.85%	19.00%	0.26
4	$29,752,173	11.96%	10.12%	18.24%	0.28
5	$28,856,078	11.89%	10.08%	18.08%	0.28
6	$22,675,942	11.53%	9.76%	17.96%	0.26
7	$22,364,844	11.74%	9.74%	19.33%	0.25
8	$18,561,262	11.68%	9.49%	20.22%	0.22
9	$11,729,923	11.47%	8.89%	22.09%	0.18
10 (lowest)	$1,581,383	9.73%	6.29%	25.66%	0.05
Large Stocks	$21,617,372	11.75%	9.69%	19.35%	0.24

T A B L E 20.43

Average Annual Compound Rates of Return by Decade

	1920s*	1930s	1940s	1950s	1960s	1970s	1980s	1990s	2000s†
All Stocks 6-month momentum, decile 1	15.45%	2.74%	16.31%	23.61%	17.77%	11.73%	18.94%	24.28%	−0.29%
All Stocks 6-month momentum, decile 10	0.55%	−3.22%	8.82%	12.86%	3.99%	0.67%	6.29%	7.63%	−1.70%
All Stocks 12-month momentum, decile 1	12.05%	2.00%	14.87%	21.72%	16.87%	10.90%	17.37%	22.33%	−4.36%
All Stocks 12-month momentum, decile 10	1.92%	−3.62%	10.13%	14.34%	4.95%	1.31%	7.95%	10.60%	2.66%
All Stocks	12.33%	−0.03%	11.57%	18.07%	10.72%	7.56%	16.78%	15.35%	4.39%

* Returns for January 1, 1927, to December 31, 1929.
† Returns for January 1, 2000, to December 31, 2009.

TABLE 20.44

Average Annual Compound Rates of Return by Decade

	1920s*	1930s	1940s	1950s	1960s	1970s	1980s	1990s	2000s†
Large Stocks 6-month momentum, decile 1	25.14%	−1.00%	13.00%	20.90%	13.47%	10.70%	17.83%	27.63%	−0.01%
Large Stocks 6-month momentum, decile 10	5.21%	−4.13%	7.98%	12.14%	4.15%	1.97%	12.17%	11.04%	−2.94%
Large Stocks 12-month momentum, decile 1	23.61%	−1.26%	12.23%	19.11%	12.98%	10.03%	15.82%	26.79%	−3.20%
Large Stocks 12-month momentum, decile 10	7.07%	−3.14%	8.65%	13.55%	3.83%	2.70%	13.20%	13.24%	−0.48%
Large Stocks	17.73%	−1.05%	9.65%	17.06%	8.31%	6.65%	17.34%	16.38%	2.42%

* Returns for January 1, 1927, to December 31, 1929.
† Returns for January 1, 2000, to December 31, 2009.

ADDITIONAL METRICS TO CONSIDER WITH PRICE MOMENTUM

I want to point out a few additional factors that might be beneficial to consider in conjunction with price momentum. The first is the average daily volume of a stock over a six-month period. While we don't have volume statistics available in the CRSP dataset, we do have them in the Compustat dataset beginning in 1964. Analyzing stocks by average six-month dollar volume, we find that the stocks with the greatest average six-month dollar trading volume have the lowest returns, while stocks with the lowest six-month trading volume have the highest returns. $10,000 invested on December 31, 1963, in the decile of stocks with the highest average dollar volume over the last six months becomes $357,900 by the end of 2009, an average annual compound return of 8.09 percent. That's well below the 11.24 percent earned by the All Stocks universe over the same period, while the same $10,000 grows to $1.32 million. Conversely, an investment in the decile of stocks with the *lowest* six-month trading volume turned $10,000 into $2.9 million, an average annual compound return of 13.16 percent. The theory is that stocks with huge trading volumes are the subjects of greater speculation than those with lower trading volumes, and according to our results, the speculative names go on to do poorly in the future.

Thus, linking pure price momentum to trading volume is a strategy worth considering. By adding points if the stock is in the seventh to tenth decile by average trading volume and subtracting points from the deciles with the highest trading volume, particularly deciles 1 and 2, you penalize stocks with the highest trading volume and reward those with lower trading volume. This might allow you to smooth out your ride if you are using price momentum exclusively to make stock selections.

Another possible addition to the price momentum tool kit is price volatility, but here you would want to avoid the decile of stocks with the *greatest* price volatility—the group had an average annual compound return of 6.94 percent between 1964 and 2009, well behind All Stocks' gain of 11.24 percent a year. By avoiding the most volatile stocks, you might also smooth the returns to a pure price momentum strategy.

Finally, we continue to conduct tests using multiple versions of price momentum, giving the highest points to six-month price momentum but also awarding points to stocks with *poor* five-year momentum.

IMPLICATIONS

Damon Runyon's quote at the beginning of this chapter is apt. Over six-month and twelve-month periods, winners generally continue to win and losers generally continue to lose. Remember that when we say losers, we're *not* talking about stocks that lost some ground, but about the 10 percent of the *worst* casualties from the entire universe. Yet the full decile analysis shows that investors are best off avoiding stocks in the lowest price appreciation deciles.

The advice is simple—unless financial ruin is your goal, avoid the biggest losers. The *only* time you should buy stocks from this group is in the first year following a severe bear market, because that is the only time that they soar in value and actually outperform not only the market but the best performers as well. Buy stocks with the *best* relative strength, but understand that their volatility will continually test your emotional endurance. In coming chapters, we see how relative strength is an excellent factor to use in conjunction with other factors, helping us steer clear of the most richly valued stocks. For now, we see that relative strength is among the only pure growth factors that actually beats the market consistently, and by a wide margin.

21 CHAPTER

USING MULTIFACTOR MODELS TO IMPROVE PERFORMANCE

It is not who is right, but what is right, that is important.

—Thomas Huxley

Thus far, with the exception of the value, earnings quality, and financial strength composites, we have been reviewing the performance of single factors, such as EBITDA to enterprise value, price-to-sales ratios, and PE ratios. In this chapter, we look at using two or more criteria to create portfolios. Depending on your goal, using several factors allows you to enhance performance or reduce risk, or, hopefully, both. Here we use the CRSP dataset to analyze multifactor strategies. While CRSP is somewhat limited in the number of factors it covers, the fact that it goes all the way back to 1926 allows us to look at how multifactor strategies performed during the worst period for U.S. stocks—the Great Depression. Seeing how multifactor strategies performed over the last eight decades should offer investors broad insights into how these strategies perform in all kinds of market conditions. In coming chapters, we return to the Compustat dataset in order to review several of the factors not included in the CRSP dataset. For now, let's look at how select multifactor strategies performed over the last 80 years.

COMBINING PRICE MOMENTUM AND SHAREHOLDER YIELD

Price momentum married to high shareholder yield (SY) gave us one of the best performing long-term strategies that we've seen. Table 21.1 shows the results for the following model:

1. Starting universe is the Small Stocks universe.
2. Three-month price momentum must exceed the median for the Small Stocks universe.
3. Six-month price momentum must exceed the median for the Small Stocks universe.
4. Buy the 25 stocks with the highest shareholder yield.

The portfolio is rebalanced annually to again hold the top 25 stocks by shareholder yield that also meet the price momentum criteria. As we review Table 21.1, we see that by combining price momentum with shareholder yield, we considerably improve the results generated by price momentum or shareholder yield alone. Starting on December 31, 1927 (the date from which we can generate fully composited portfolios for the multifactor model), we see that $10,000 invested on December 31, 1927, grows to $1.9 *billion* by the end of 2009, an average annual compound return of 15.98 percent. As Table 21.2 shows, investing $10,000 in the 25 stocks from the Small Stocks universe with the best six-month price momentum grew to $240 million, an average annual compound return of 13.09 percent, and a $10,000 investment in the 25 stocks from the Small Stocks universe with the highest shareholder yield grew to $183 million, an average annual compound return of 12.71 percent. A $10,000 investment in the Small Stocks universe over the same period grew to $37.4 million, an average annual compound return of 10.55 percent.

T A B L E   21.1

Summary Annual Return and Risk Results Data: Small Stocks, 3 and 6 mo.>med, top 25 SY; Small Stocks, 3 and 6 mo.>med, top 50 SY; and Small Stocks, January 1, 1928 to December 31, 2009

	Small Stocks, 3 and 6 mo.>med, top 25 SY	Small Stocks, 3 and 6 mo.>med, top 50 SY	Small Stocks
Arithmetic average	18.10%	17.27%	13.52%
Geometric average	15.98%	15.22%	10.55%
Median return	25.29%	25.28%	19.28%
Standard deviation	19.10%	18.89%	23.19%
Upside deviation	12.40%	12.40%	16.14%
Downside deviation	14.80%	14.72%	16.93%
Tracking error	7.95	7.47	1.00
Number of positive periods	640	640	596
Number of negative periods	344	344	388
Maximum peak-to-trough decline	−76.86%	−76.36%	−86.12%
Beta	0.78	0.78	1.0
T-statistic (m = 0)	7.94	7.69	4.98
Sharpe ratio (Rf = 5%)	0.58	0.54	0.24
Sortino ratio (MAR = 10%)	0.40	0.35	0.03

(continued on next page)

TABLE 21.1

Summary Annual Return and Risk Results Data: Small Stocks, 3 and 6 mo.>med, top 25 SY; Small Stocks, 3 and 6 mo.>med, top 50 SY; and Small Stocks, January 1, 1928 to December 31, 2009 *(Continued)*

	Small Stocks, 3 and 6 mo.>med, top 25 SY	Small Stocks, 3 and 6 mo.>med, top 50 SY	Small Stocks
$10,000 becomes	$1,909,317,736	$1,108,399,700	$37,383,049
Minimum 1-year return	−55.29%	−54.88%	−66.91%
Maximum 1-year return	160.02%	163.19%	233.48%
Minimum 3-year return	−37.01%	−36.54%	−47.28%
Maximum 3-year return	52.05%	49.41%	54.35%
Minimum 5-year return	−13.52%	−13.37%	−21.72%
Maximum 5-year return	39.98%	38.02%	44.18%
Minimum 7-year return	0.20%	−0.49%	−7.64%
Maximum 7-year return	34.29%	32.96%	27.35%
Minimum 10-year return	−1.43%	−1.90%	−5.19%
Maximum 10-year return	32.00%	29.09%	24.47%
Minimum expected return*	−20.10%	−20.50%	−32.86%
Maximum expected return†	56.30%	55.05%	59.90%

* Minimum expected return is arithmetic return minus 2 times the standard deviation.

† Maximum expected return is arithmetic return plus 2 times the standard deviation.

TABLEE 21.2

Summary Annual Return and Risk Results Data: Small Stocks SY, Best 25; Small Stocks, 6 mo. Momentum, Best 25; and Small Stocks, January 1, 1928, to December 31, 2009

	Small Stocks SY best 25	Small Stocks 6 Mo. momentum best 25	Small Stocks
Arithmetic average	15.38%	18.07%	13.52%
Geometric average	12.71%	13.09%	10.55%
Median return	20.05%	28.40%	19.28%
Standard deviation	21.74%	29.39%	23.19%
Upside deviation	15.10%	19.08%	16.14%
Downside deviation	16.86%	21.00%	16.93%
Tracking error	7.65	15.32	0.00
Number of positive periods	634	603	596
Number of negative periods	350	381	388
Maximum peak-to-trough decline	−89.32%	−84.50%	−86.12%
Beta	0.88	1.08	1.00
T-statistic (m = 0)	6.00	5.15	4.98
Sharpe ratio (Rf = 5%)	0.35	0.28	0.24
Sortino ratio (MAR = 10%)	0.16	0.15	0.03
$10,000 becomes	$182,749,970	$240,040,089	$37,383,049

(continued on next page)

T A B L E E   21.2

Summary Annual Return and Risk Results Data: Small Stocks SY, Best 25; Small Stocks, 6 Mo, Momentum, Best 25; and Small Stocks, January 1, 1928, to December 31, 2009 *(Continued)*

	Small Stocks SY best 25	Small Stocks 6 mo. momentum best 25	Small Stocks
Minimum 1-year return	−71.26%	−70.32%	−66.91%
Maximum 1-year return	187.52%	256.16%	233.48%
Minimum 3-year return	−50.54%	−39.47%	−47.28%
Maximum 3-year return	55.01%	81.25%	54.35%
Minimum 5-year return	−25.41%	−19.46%	−21.72%
Maximum 5-year return	40.41%	52.06%	44.18%
Minimum 7-year return	−9.16%	−9.43%	−7.64%
Maximum 7-year return	32.84%	38.83%	27.35%
Minimum 10-year return	−8.29%	−10.50%	−5.19%
Maximum 10-year return	29.90%	32.97%	24.47%
Minimum expected return*	−28.09%	−40.70%	−32.86%
Maximum expected return†	58.85%	76.85%	59.90%

* Minimum expected return is arithmetic return minus 2 times the standard deviation.
† Maximum expected return is arithmetic return plus 2 times the standard deviation.

LOWER RISK, HIGHER BASE RATES

Combining price momentum with shareholder yield not only improves total returns dramatically, but it also lowers overall risk and thereby results in significantly better base rates. The standard deviation of return for buying the 25 stocks from Small Stocks with the best six-month price momentum was 29.39 percent, and 21.74 percent for those with the highest shareholder yield. Better yet, by combining price momentum and shareholder yield, the standard deviation drops to 19.10 percent. Thus we are able to reduce the standard deviation of return of the multifactor strategy to less than that for each individual factor, but also to below that of the Small Stocks universe, which had a standard deviation of return of 23.19 percent over the same period. The lower risk married to higher returns gave the combined momentum and shareholder yield portfolio a Sharpe ratio of .58, more than double the .24 earned by the Small Stocks universe. As Tables 21.1 and 21.2 show, the minimum return earned by each of the four portfolios was also significantly better with the combined price momentum and shareholder yield portfolio—all minimum returns from one to ten years were superior to the Small Stocks universe.

The base rates for the combined portfolio, featured in Table 21.3, are also superior to those for either factor alone. The combined price momentum and shareholder yield portfolio beat the Small Stocks universe in 95 percent of all rolling five-year periods and 99 percent of all rolling ten-year periods. Table 21.3 shows all other rolling periods. For comparison's sake, Tables 21.4 and 21.5 show the base rates for the single factors.

T A B L E 21.3

Base Rates for Small Stocks, 3 and 6 mo>med, top 25 SY and Small Stocks, January 1, 1928, to December 31, 2009

Item	Small Stocks, 3 and 6 mo.>med, top 25 SY beat Small Stocks	Percent	Average annual excess return
Single-year return	729 out of 973	75%	4.88%
Rolling 3-year compound return	886 out of 949	93%	5.51%
Rolling 5-year compound return	875 out of 925	95%	5.47%
Rolling 7-year compound return	866 out of 901	96%	5.44%
Rolling 10-year compound return	859 out of 865	99%	5.39%

T A B L E 21.4

Base Rates for Small Stocks SY, Best 25, and Small Stocks, January 1, 1928, to December 31, 2009

Item	Small Stocks SY best, 25 beat Small Stocks	Percent	Average annual excess return
Single-year return	559 out of 973	57%	2.21%
Rolling 3-year compound return	725 out of 949	76%	2.47%
Rolling 5-year compound return	723 out of 925	78%	2.41%
Rolling 7-year compound return	735 out of 901	82%	2.43%
Rolling 10-year compound return	763 out of 865	88%	2.53%

T A B L E 21.5

Base Rates for Small Stocks 6-Month Momentum, Best 25, and Small Stocks, January 1, 1928, to December 31, 2009

Item	Small Stocks, 6-month momentum, best 25 beat Small Stocks	Percent	Average annual excess return
Single-year return	599 out of 973	62%	5.23%
Rolling 3-year compound return	645 out of 949	68%	3.78%
Rolling 5-year compound return	714 out of 925	77%	3.71%
Rolling 7-year compound return	782 out of 901	87%	3.77%
Rolling 10-year compound return	805 out of 865	93%	3.99%

WORST-CASE SCENARIOS AND BEST AND WORST RETURNS

As Table 21.6 shows, the worst decline for the combined strategy occurred between August 1929 and May 1932, when it lost 77 percent. While that is a breathtaking drop, it's not as bad as the Small Stocks universe's 86 percent decline over the same period. Most price drops for the combined strategy were fairly muted, and there were only two other instances in which the strategy lost more than 50 percent: the February 1937 through March 1938 period, when it lost just over 55 percent, and the more recent October 2007 through February 2009 period, when it dropped 53 percent.

T A B L E   21.6

Worst-Case Scenarios: All 20 Percent or Greater Declines for Small Stocks, 3 and 6 mo.>med, top 25 SY, January 1, 1928, to December 31, 2009

Peak date	Peak index value	Trough date	Trough index value	Recovery date	Decline (%)	Decline duration	Recovery duration
Aug–29	1.63	May–32	0.38	Jan–36	−76.86%	33	44
Feb–37	2.26	Mar–38	1.01	Feb–43	−55.38%	13	59
May–46	6.81	May–47	4.81	May–48	−29.40%	12	12
May–48	6.83	Jun–49	5.44	Jan–50	−20.30%	13	7
Apr–66	150.09	Sep–66	118.60	Mar–67	−20.98%	5	6
Jan–69	281.70	Jun–70	205.99	Mar–71	−26.88%	17	9
Nov–72	324.49	Sep–74	233.21	May–75	−28.13%	22	8
Aug–78	786.59	Oct–78	628.88	Mar–79	−20.05%	2	5
Aug–87	8,372.99	Nov–87	6,021.27	Mar–89	−28.09%	3	16
Oct–07	259,667.21	Feb–09	123,154.99	N/A	−52.57%	16	N/A
Average					−35.86%	14	18

The best absolute five-year returns for the strategy all occurred in the 1930s or the 1980s, with the best returns occurring in the five years ending May 1937, when the strategy earned 39.98 percent and turned $10,000 invested into $53,745. The worst absolute five-year returns for the strategy occurred in the period ending February 1933, when the strategy lost 13.52 percent per year, turning $10,000 invested five years earlier into $4,837. Tables 21.7 and 21.8 show best and worst percentage and dollar returns for all periods.

On a relative basis versus the Small Stocks universe, the best five years were those ending December 1982, when the strategy earned an absolute return 171 percent greater than that of the Small Stocks universe, earning an average annual compound return of 35.63 percent versus an average annual compound return of 23.57 percent for the Small Stocks

T A B L E   21.7

Best and Worst Average Annual Compound Returns for Monthly Data, January 1, 1928, to December 31, 2009

For any	1-year period	3-year period	5-year period	7-year period	10-year period
Small Stocks, 3 and 6 mo.>med, top 25 SY minimum compound return	−55.29%	−37.01%	−13.52%	0.20%	−1.43%
Small Stocks, 3 and 6 mo.>med, top 25 SY maximum compound return	160.02%	52.05%	39.98%	34.29%	32.00%
Small Stocks, 3 and 6 mo.>med, top 50 SY minimum compound return	−54.88%	−36.54%	−13.37%	−0.49%	−1.90%
Small Stocks, 3 and 6 mo.>med, top 50 SY maximum compound return	163.19%	49.41%	38.02%	32.96%	29.09%
Small Stocks minimum compound return	−66.91%	−47.28%	−21.72%	−7.64%	−5.19%
Small Stocks maximum compound return	233.48%	54.35%	44.18%	27.35%	24.47%

TABLE 21.8

Terminal Value of $10,000 Invested for Best and Worst Average Annual Compound Returns for Monthly Data, January 1, 1928, to December 31, 2009

For any	1-year period	3-year period	5-year period	7-year period	10-year period
Small Stocks, 3 and 6 mo.>med, top 25 SY minimum $10,000 value	$4,471	$2,499	$4,837	$10,144	$8,660
Small Stocks, 3 and 6 mo.>med, top 25 SY maximum $10,000 value	$26,002	$35,153	$53,745	$78,745	$160,589
Small Stocks, 3 and 6 mo.>med, top 50 SY minimum $10,000 value	$4,512	$2,556	$4,880	$9,661	$8,255
Small Stocks, 3 and 6 mo.>med, top 50 SY maximum $10,000 value	$26,319	$33,355	$50,088	$73,441	$128,530
Small Stocks minimum $10,000 value	$3,309	$1,465	$2,940	$5,733	$5,872
Small Stocks maximum $10,000 value	$33,348	$36,775	$62,313	$54,327	$89,249

universe. The worst five years on a relative basis versus the Small Stocks universe were those ending June 1937, when the strategy suffered a 99.1 percent absolute loss against Small Stocks, earning an average annual compound return of 37.57 percent versus 42.70 percent for the Small Stocks universe. Figure 21.1 shows the rolling excess (deficient) return for the strategy versus the Small Stocks universe.

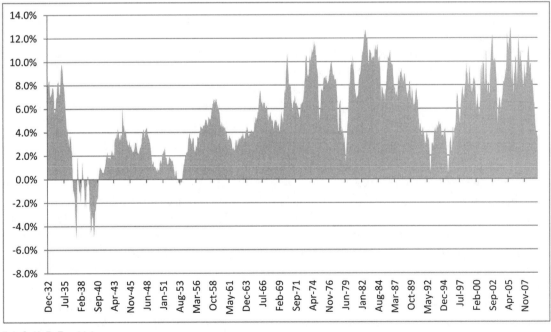

FIGURE 21.1

Five-year average annual compound excess (deficient) return Small Stocks, 3 and 6 mo. >med, top 25 SY minus Small Stocks; January 1, 1928, to December 31, 2009

50-STOCK VERSION ALSO DOES WELL

The 50-stock version of this strategy did almost as well as the more concentrated 25-stock strategy. Here, $10,000 invested in 1927 grows to $1.1 billion, an average annual compound return of 15.22 percent. The standard deviation of return for the 50-stock strategy drops to 18.89 percent and the total number of drawdowns drops from ten for the 25-stock strategy to seven for the 50-stock version. The maximum decline for the 50-stock strategy was a slightly lower 76.36 percent. Thus, by increasing the number of stocks in the strategy to 50 from 25, you slightly reduce overall volatility at the expense of an annual 76 basis points in total return. See Table 21.1 for all the specifics on the 50-stock version of the strategy.

MICROCAP STOCKS WITH GOOD VALUE CHARACTERISTICS AND PRICE MOMENTUM

When looking at the best growth strategies in Chapter Twenty-Five, we'll see that uniting value factors with growth factors can offer outstanding performance. Essentially, you are looking for cheap stocks on the mend; they are still cheaply valued but are gaining price momentum. You can improve the performance further by focusing on investable microcap stocks. (Currently, we believe that individual investors with portfolios of between $10 and $25 million can successfully invest in stocks with market capitalizations in the $50 to $250 million range.) For our next multifactor portfolio we create a concentrated portfolio of 25 stocks with the following characteristics:

- Market capitalization between a deflated $50 million and $250 million at time of purchase.
- Price-to-book (or, book to price, BP) ratio in the three cheapest deciles (i.e., lowest 30 percent of the universe by price-to-book ratio).
- Three- and six-month price appreciation greater than zero.
- The 25 stocks with the best 12-month price appreciation are the ones to buy.

Let's take a look at the strategy's performance. As Table 21.9 shows, $10,000 invested on December 31, 1927, would have grown to $8.78 billion by the end of 2009. That's an average annual compound return of 18.16 percent, swamping the 10.55 percent return you would have earned with an investment in the Small Stocks universe. Granted, you could never *actually* grow a portfolio to that level since the tiny stocks could not withstand such huge investments, yet the strategy is well worth considering as a wealth-generating component of a more diversified portfolio. You also need to keep the strategy's volatility in mind before investing—this strategy had a relatively high standard deviation of return of 26.88 percent, compared to 23.19 percent for the Small Stocks universe. And unlike the more value-oriented strategy focusing on shareholder yield, this strategy had a ten-year period when it *lost* 7.23 percent per year, a downside few investors could stomach. Imagine losing 7.23 percent per year for ten years, and watching your $10,000 dwindle to $4,724. The maximum peak-to-trough decline for this strategy is a whopping 88 percent, and between 1927 and 2009, the strategy had 11 separate drawdowns exceeding 20 percent, several of them extremely severe. For example, that 88 percent decline occurred between February 1929 and May 1932, yet, as Table 21.10 shows, just when you thought the worst was over, the strategy went on to lose another 70 percent of its value between March 1937 and March 1938. Few investors could withstand that nightmare. The volatile strategy's most recent decline of nearly 54 percent occurred between October 2007 and February 2009. Thus, this is a high-octane strategy that only the most aggressive investors should pursue.

TABLE 21.9

Summary Annual Return and Risk Results Data: 25 Stocks Microcap BP Top 3 Deciles, 3 and 6 mo.>0, Top 25 by 12m mom; 50 Stocks Microcap BP top 3 deciles, 3 and 6 mo.>0, Top 50 by 12m mom; and Small Stocks, January 1, 1928, to December 31, 2009

	25 stocks microcap BP top 3 deciles, 3 and 6 mo>0, top 25 by 12m mom	50 stocks microcap BP top 3 deciles, 3 and 6 mo.>0, top 50 by 12m mom	Small Stocks
Arithmetic average	22.31%	21.34%	13.52%
Geometric average	18.16%	17.39%	10.55%
Median return	24.54%	26.12%	19.28%
Standard deviation	26.88%	26.33%	23.19%
Upside deviation	20.21%	19.98%	16.14%
Downside deviation	19.37%	19.24%	16.93%
Tracking error	10.27	9.74	0.00
Number of positive periods	636	638	596
Number of negative periods	348	346	388
Maximum peak-to-trough decline	−87.69%	−88.08%	−86.12%
Beta	1.07	1.06	1.00
T-statistic (m = 0)	6.84	6.71	4.98
Sharpe ratio (Rf = 5%)	0.49	0.47	0.24
Sortino ratio (MAR = 10%)	0.42	0.38	0.03
$10,000 becomes	$8,784,360,432	$5,130,796,619	$37,383,049
Minimum 1-year return	−70.17%	−69.55%	−66.91%
Maximum 1-year return	308.05%	286.06%	233.48%
Minimum 3-year return	−47.75%	−48.20%	−47.28%
Maximum 3-year return	67.92%	66.00%	54.35%
Minimum 5-year return	−24.77%	−25.64%	−21.72%
Maximum 5-year return	52.74%	49.59%	44.18%
Minimum 7-year return	−10.97%	−12.07%	−7.64%
Maximum 7-year return	40.79%	36.74%	27.35%
Minimum 10-year return	−7.23%	−7.80%	−5.19%
Maximum 10-year return	35.52%	32.86%	24.47%
Minimum expected return*	−31.44%	−31.32%	−32.86%
Maximum expected return†	76.07%	74.00%	59.90%

* Minimum expected return is arithmetic return minus 2 times the standard deviation.
† Maximum expected return is arithmetic return plus 2 times the standard deviation.

T A B L E   21.10

Worst-Case Scenarios: All 20 Percent or Greater Declines for 25 Stocks Microcap BP top 3 deciles, 3 and 6 mo.>0, Top 25 by 12m mom, January 1, 1928, to December 31, 2009

Peak date	Peak index value	Trough date	Trough index value	Recovery date	Decline (%)	Decline duration	Recovery duration
Feb–29	1.55	May–32	0.19	Dec–36	−87.69%	39	55
Mar–37	1.87	Mar–38	0.56	May–43	−70.17%	12	62
May–46	6.37	May–47	4.18	Apr–50	−34.34%	12	35
Feb–62	60.70	Jun–62	48.08	Mar–63	−20.79%	4	9
Apr–66	166.56	Oct–66	124.74	Mar–67	−25.10%	6	5
Nov–68	373.97	Jun–70	188.00	Jan–76	−49.73%	19	67
Aug–78	1,032.23	Oct–78	795.42	Mar–79	−22.94%	2	5
Sep–87	11,166.19	Nov–87	7,716.16	Apr–89	−30.90%	2	17
Aug–89	12,453.84	Oct–90	9,451.78	Mar–91	−24.11%	14	5
Apr–98	112,735.55	Aug–98	84,250.35	Jun–99	−25.27%	4	10
Oct–07	1,330,836.88	Feb–09	613,609.69	N/A	−53.89%	16	N/A
Average					−40.45%	12	27

Base rates, as featured in Table 21.11, are all positive, with the strategy beating the Small Stocks universe in 91 percent of all rolling five-year periods and in 95 percent of all rolling ten-year periods. When analyzing the strategy's best absolute five-year returns, it is interesting to note that most occurred in the 1930s and 1940s, but the strategy also had a strong run in the five years ending March 2006, when it earned an average annual compound return of 45.30 percent. Tables 21.12 and 21.13 show the best and worst returns for the strategy. Figure 21.2 shows the average annual compound excess (or deficient) return for the strategy versus the Small Stocks universe. Remember that this is an extremely volatile strategy that should only be used for the most aggressive portion of your portfolio.

Finally, a few more caveats:

- Because the strategy requires three- and six-month price appreciation to be greater than zero, the strategy generates far fewer than 25 stocks during bear markets, with the very fewest generated near market lows. For example, in March 2009, only three stocks made it through the filter. Assuming you are equal-weighting your portfolio, you might argue that having fewer stocks reduces your exposure during bear markets. Yet it is precisely at market bottoms that you should think about overweighting stocks in your portfolio. For example, in March 2009, assuming you are making $10,000 available for investment in the 25 stocks in this strategy, your deployed capital would be just $1,200, since there were only three stocks that met the strategy's criteria.
- Microcap stocks are notoriously at odds with other equities, so much so that you might want to consider them as an alternate asset class. They are often going up when larger stocks are heading down or sideways, and they are declining when there is a big rally in larger stocks. It might be difficult for even the most aggressive

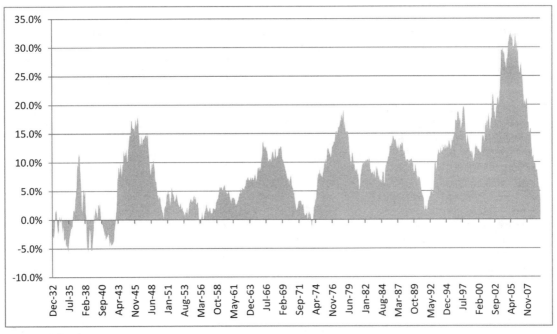

FIGURE 21.2

Five-year average annual compound excess (deficient) return 25 Stocks Microcap BP Top 3 Deciles, 3 and 6 mo. >0, Top 25 by 12m mom minus Small Stocks; January 1, 1928, to December 31, 2009

investor to stick by this microcap portfolio when it behaves so bizarrely compared to the general market.

- A large portion of the gains this strategy offers come from the microcap stocks. A similar strategy used on the Small Stocks universe generates a return of just 13.32 percent over the same period, significantly less than the microcap version. You would, perhaps, be better served with the first strategy we cover in this chapter which combines price momentum and shareholder yield.

TABLE 21.11

Base Rates for 25 Stocks Microcap BP Top 3 Deciles, 3 and 6 mo.>0, Top 25 by 12m mom and Small Stocks, January 1, 1928 to December 31, 2009

Item	25 stocks, microcap BP top 3 deciles, 3 and 6 mo.>0, top 25 by 12m mom beat Small Stocks	Percent	Average annual excess return
Single-year return	716 out of 973	74%	9.55%
Rolling 3-year compound return	800 out of 949	84%	8.73%
Rolling 5-year compound return	839 out of 925	91%	8.72%
Rolling 7-year compound return	850 out of 901	94%	8.63%
Rolling 10-year compound return	819 out of 865	95%	8.43%

T A B L E   21.12

Best and Worst Average Annual Compound Returns for Monthly Data, January 1, 1928, to December 31, 2009

For any	1-year period	3-year period	5-year period	7-year period	10-year period
25 stocks microcap BP top 3 deciles, 3 and 6 mo.>0, top 25 by 12m mom minimum compound return	−70.17%	−47.75%	−24.77%	−10.97%	−7.23%
25 stocks microcap BP top 3 deciles, 3 and 6 mo.>0, top 25 by 12m mom maximum compound return	308.05%	67.92%	52.74%	40.79%	35.52%
50 stocks microcap BP top 3 deciles, 3 and 6 mo.>0, top 50 by 12m mom minimum compound return	−69.55%	−48.20%	−25.64%	−12.07%	−7.80%
50 stocks microcap BP top 3 deciles, 3 and 6 mo.>0, top 50 by 12m mom maximum compound return	286.06%	66.00%	49.59%	36.74%	32.86%
Small Stocks minimum compound return	−66.91%	−47.28%	−21.72%	−7.64%	−5.19%
Small Stocks maximum compound return	233.48%	54.35%	44.18%	27.35%	24.47%

T A B L E   21.13

Terminal Value of $10,000 Invested for Best and Worst Average Annual Compound Returns for Monthly Data, January 1, 1928, to December 31, 2009

For any	1-year period	3-year period	5-year period	7-year period	10-year period
25 stocks microcap BP top 3 deciles, 3 and 6 mo.>0, top 25 by 12m mom minimum $10,000 value	$2,983	$1,426	$2,409	$4,432	$4,724
25 stocks microcap BP top 3 deciles, 3 and 6 mo.>0, top 25 by 12m mom maximum $10,000 value	$40,805	$47,350	$83,125	$109,637	$208,872
50 stocks microcap BP top 3 deciles, 3 and 6 mo.>0, top 50 by 12m mom minimum $10,000 value	$3,045	$1,390	$2,273	$4,064	$4,439
50 stocks microcap BP top 3 deciles, 3 and 6 mo.>0, top 50 by 12m mom maximum $10,000 value	$38,606	$45,746	$74,913	$89,371	$171,339
Small Stocks minimum $10,000 value	$3,309	$1,465	$2,940	$5,733	$5,872
Small Stocks maximum $10,000 value	$33,348	$36,775	$62,313	$54,327	$89,249

AN ALL STOCKS VERSION OF STRONG THREE- AND SIX-MONTH PRICE APPRECIATION AND HIGH SHAREHOLDER YIELD

Lest you think that the only good gains come from Small Stocks and microcap names, let's revisit the first strategy we looked at, but let's use the All Stocks universe instead of the Small Stocks universe. The All Stocks version of the first strategy we looked at—focusing on stocks whose three- and six-month price appreciation was greater than the median and then buying the top 25 stocks with the highest shareholder yield—earned an average annual compound return of 15.93 percent. Risk was a similar 19.07 percent, and the Sharpe ratio was .57, all very similar to the returns earned from the Small Stocks' version. Table 21.14 shows the summary statistics for the All Stocks version of the strategy. Note that with the All Stocks version the minimum seven- and ten-year returns for the strategy are lower (meaning you lost more) than they are for the Small Stocks version.

T A B L E   21.14

Summary Annual Return and Risk Results Data: All Stocks 3 and 6 Mo Mom.>med, Top 25 SY and All Stocks, January 1, 1928, to December 31, 2009

	All Stocks 3 and 6 mo. mom.>med, top 25 SY	All Stocks
Arithmetic average	18.05%	12.81%
Geometric average	15.93%	10.20%
Median return	25.20%	18.54%
Standard deviation	19.07%	21.75%
Upside deviation	12.25%	14.85%
Downside deviation	14.85%	16.07%
Tracking error	7.54	0.00
Number of positive periods	637	597
Number of negative periods	347	387
Maximum peak-to-trough decline	−78.14%	−85.45%
Beta	0.82	1.00
T-statistic (m = 0)	7.93	5.04
Sharpe ratio (Rf = 5%)	0.57	0.24
Sortino ratio (MAR = 10%)	0.40	0.01
$10,000 becomes	$1,838,450,713	$28,805,557
Minimum 1-year return	−57.85%	−66.72%
Maximum 1-year return	152.96%	201.69%
Minimum 3-year return	−37.88%	−45.99%
Maximum 3-year return	56.92%	51.03%
Minimum 5-year return	−13.50%	−20.67%
Maximum 5-year return	43.57%	41.17%
Minimum 7-year return	−2.18%	−7.43%
Maximum 7-year return	35.05%	23.77%
Minimum 10-year return	−3.08%	−5.31%
Maximum 10-year return	34.04%	22.05%
Minimum expected return*	−20.09%	−30.70%
Maximum expected return†	56.19%	56.32%

* Minimum expected return is arithmetic return minus 2 times the standard deviation.
† Maximum expected return is arithmetic return plus 2 times the standard deviation.

The All Stocks version of the strategy also has similar maximum declines and base rates. The maximum decline was 78 percent, and the strategy beat the All Stocks universe in 93 percent of all rolling five-year periods and in 99 percent of all rolling ten-year periods (Table 21.15). Table 21.16 shows all declines greater than 20 percent since 1928 and Tables 21.17 and 21.18 show the best- and worst-case results. Thus you can safely use this strategy on the larger All Stocks universe and expect similar results to those from the Small Stocks universe. Table 21.19 shows the average annual compound returns for the strategy by decade, and Figure 21.3 shows the rolling five-year average annual compound excess (deficient) return for the strategy minus the return for the All Stocks universe.

T A B L E   21.15

Base Rates for All Stocks 3 and 6 Mo. Mom.>med, Top 25 SY and All Stocks, January 1, 1928, to December 31, 2009

Item	All Stocks 3 and 6 mo. mom.>med, top 25 SY beat All Stocks	Percent	Average annual excess return
Single-year return	754 out of 973	77%	5.61%
Rolling 3-year compound return	877 out of 949	92%	5.94%
Rolling 5-year compound return	856 out of 925	93%	5.88%
Rolling 7-year compound return	846 out of 901	94%	5.85%
Rolling 10-year compound return	858 out of 865	99%	5.82%

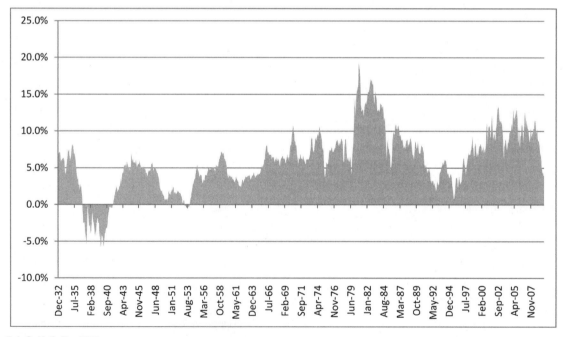

F I G U R E   21.3

Five-year average annual compound excess (deficient) return All Stocks 3 and 6M Mom >Med, Top 25 SY minus Small Stocks; January 1, 1928, to December 31, 2009

T A B L E 21.16

Worst-Case Scenarios: All 20 Percent or Greater Declines for All Stocks 3 and 6 Mo. Mom.>med, Top 25 SY, January 1, 1928, to December 31, 2009

Peak date	Peak index value	Trough date	Trough index value	Recovery date	Decline (%)	Decline duration	Recovery duration
Aug–29	1.68	May–32	0.37	Aug–36	−78.14%	33	51
Feb–37	1.93	Mar–38	0.87	Feb–43	−54.80%	13	59
May–46	5.66	May–47	4.07	May–48	−27.99%	12	12
Nov–61	56.24	Jun–62	44.97	Mar–63	−20.04%	7	9
Apr–66	125.82	Sep–66	100.33	Mar–67	−20.26%	5	6
Jan–69	224.68	Jun–70	167.71	Feb–71	−25.36%	17	8
Nov–72	265.15	Sep–74	193.66	May–75	−26.96%	22	8
Feb–80	1,133.15	Mar–80	898.11	Jun–80	−20.74%	1	3
Aug–87	7,539.72	Nov–87	5,166.63	Apr–89	−31.47%	3	17
Oct–07	247,468.17	Feb–09	118,125.09	N/A	−52.27%	16	N/A
Average					−35.80%	12.9	19.22

T A B L E 21.17

Best and Worst Average Annual Compound Returns for Monthly Data, January 1, 1928, to December 31, 2009

For any	1-year period	3-year period	5-year period	7-year period	10-year period
All Stocks 3 and 6 mo. mom.>med, top 25 SY minimum compound return	−57.85%	−37.88%	−13.50%	−2.18%	−3.08%
All Stocks 3 and 6 mo. mom.>med, top 25 SY maximum compound return	152.96%	56.92%	43.57%	35.05%	34.04%
All Stocks minimum compound return	−66.72%	−45.99%	−20.67%	−7.43%	−5.31%
All Stocks maximum compound return	201.69%	51.03%	41.17%	23.77%	22.05%

T A B L E 21.18

Terminal Value of $10,000 Invested for Best and Worst Average Annual Compound Returns for Monthly Data, January 1, 1928, to December 31, 2009

For any	1-year period	3-year period	5-year period	7-year period	10-year period
All Stocks 3 and 6 mo. mom.>med, top 25 SY minimum $10,000 value	$4,215	$2,397	$4,844b	$8,570	$7,314
All Stocks 3 and 6 mo. mom.>med, top 25 SY maximum $10,000 value	$25,296	$38,642	$60,995	$81,948	$187,183
All Stocks minimum $10,000 value	$3,328	$1,576	$3,142	$5,825	$5,793
All Stocks maximum $10,000 value	$30,169	$34,452	$56,062	$44,504	$73,345

T A B L E   21.19

Average Annual Compound Rates of Return by Decade

	1920s*	1930s	1940s	1950s	1960s	1970s	1980s	1990s	2000st
All Stocks 3 and 6 mo. mom.>med, top 25 SY	11.89%	1.27%	14.95%	22.51%	16.36%	17.24%	25.20%	21.24%	11.27%
All Stocks	2.93%	−0.03%	11.57%	18.07%	10.72%	7.56%	16.78%	15.35%	4.39%

* Returns for January 1, 1928, to December 31, 1929.
† Returns for January 1, 2000, to December 31, 2009.

MORE LONG-TERM MULTIFACTOR STRATEGIES USING THE VARIOUS UNIVERSES

Tables 21.20 through 21.25 summarize the returns and base rates for a variety of multifactor strategies using the CRSP dataset. As you can see by reviewing the tables, the strategy of focusing on stocks with three- and six-month price appreciation better than the median and then buying the 25 stocks with the highest shareholder yield also worked well when applied to the Large Stocks universe. Consulting Table 21.24, we see that it was also the best-performing of all the strategies tested on the Large Stocks universe, earning an average annual compound return of 13.17 percent compared to 9.45 percent for the Large Stocks universe itself. The Large Stocks strategy's standard deviation of return of 17.98 percent was also lower than that of the Large Stocks universe, bringing its Sharpe ratio in at .45, much higher than the .23 earned by the Large Stocks universe. The base rates for the strategy, featured in Table 21.25, were all positive, with the strategy beating the Large Stocks universe in 88 percent of all rolling five-year periods and in 96 percent of all rolling ten-year periods.

T A B L E   21.20

Summary Results for Strategies Benchmarked against the Returns of Small Stocks (Jan–28 to Dec–09); Strategies Sorted by Compound Return

Strategy	Geometric mean	Standard deviation (%)	Excess returns	Sharpe ratio	Tracking error	Largest drawdown	Beta
Microcap BP top 3 deciles, 3 and 6 mo.>0, top 25 by 12m mom	18.16%	26.88%	7.61%	0.49	10.27	−87.69%	1.07
Microcap BP top 3 deciles, 3 and 6 mo.>median top 25 by 12m mom	17.84%	24.98%	7.28%	0.51	9.71	−88.20%	0.99
Microcap BP top 3 deciles, 3 and 6 mo.>median top 25 by 12m mom	17.39%	24.60%	6.84%	0.50	9.44	−88.20%	0.98
Microcap BP top 3 deciles, 3 and 6 mo.>0, top 50 by 12m mom	17.39%	26.33%	6.84%	0.47	9.74	−88.08%	1.06

(continued on next page)

T A B L E   21.20

Summary Results for Strategies Benchmarked against the Returns of Small Stocks (Jan–28 to Dec–09); Strategies Sorted by Compound Return *(Continued)*

Strategy	Geometric mean	Standard deviation (%)	Excess returns	Sharpe ratio	Tracking error	Largest drawdown	Beta
Small Stocks>med by SY, 6 mo. top 25 BP	15.99%	20.22%	5.44%	0.54	8.54	−78.80%	0.81
Small Stocks, 3 and 6 mo.>med, top 25 SY	15.98%	19.10%	5.43%	0.58	7.95	−76.86%	0.78
Small Stocks>med by BP, 6 mo. top 25 BBY	15.67%	22.16%	5.12%	0.48	7.88	−82.73%	0.90
Small Stocks >med by 3m, 6m: top 50 BP	15.61%	20.93%	5.06%	0.51	7.07	−79.00%	0.86
Small Stocks, PB in top 3 deciles, 3 and 6 mo. mom>median, top 25 by SY	15.51%	22.76%	4.96%	0.46	9.05	−86.37%	0.91
Small Stocks>med by SY, 6 mo. top 50 BP	15.49%	19.39%	4.94%	0.54	8.21	−78.77%	0.79
Small Stocks >med by 3 and 6 mo., top 25 BP	15.35%	22.39%	4.80%	0.46	7.73	−81.60%	0.91
Small Stocks, PB in top 3 deciles, 3 and 6 mo. mom>median, top 25 by 12m mom	15.30%	24.29%	4.75%	0.42	8.66	−86.27%	0.98
Small Stocks, 3 and 6 mo.>med, top 50 SY	15.22%	18.89%	4.67%	0.54	7.47	−76.36%	0.78
Small Stocks >med by BP, SY, top 25 6 mo.	15.21%	22.18%	4.66%	0.46	6.89	−84.67%	0.91
Small Stocks, PB in top 3 deciles, 3 and 6 mo. mom>median, top 50 by SY	15.15%	23.10%	4.60%	0.44	8.69	−86.37%	0.93
Small Stocks>med by BP, 6 mo., top 25 SY	15.14%	20.59%	4.59%	0.49	8.18	−81.96%	0.83
Small Stocks, PB in top 3 deciles, 3 and 6 mo. mom>median, top 50 by 12m mom	15.06%	23.66%	4.50%	0.42	8.22	−86.27%	0.96
Small Stocks>med by BP, 6 mo., top 50 BBY	14.79%	22.01%	4.24%	0.44	7.17	−83.52%	0.90
Small Stocks>med by BP, 6 mo., top 50 SY	14.59%	21.21%	4.04%	0.45	7.95	−83.52%	0.86
Small Stocks>med by BP, SY top 50 6 mo.	14.40%	21.74%	3.85%	0.43	6.54	−87.36%	0.90
Small Stock >med by BP, 3 and 6 mo., top 25 12 mo.	14.29%	23.79%	3.74%	0.39	7.67	−82.92%	0.97
Small Stocks>med by SY, 3 and 6 mo., top 50 12 mo.	14.24%	21.21%	3.69%	0.44	7.74	−77.24%	0.86
Small Stocks>med by BP, 3 and 6 mo., top 50 12 mo.	14.15%	22.87%	3.60%	0.40	6.94	−82.80%	0.94
Small Stocks>med by BP, BBY, top 25 6 mo.	13.94%	29.96%	3.39%	0.30	14.63	−91.60%	1.14

(continued on next page)

T A B L E   21.20

Summary Results for Strategies Benchmarked against the Returns of Small Stocks (Jan–28 to Dec–09). Strategies Sorted by Compound Return *(Continued)*

Strategy	Geometric mean	Standard deviation (%)	Excess returns	Sharpe ratio	Tracking error	Largest drawdown	Beta
Small Stocks>med by SY, 3 and 6 mo., top 25 12 mo.	13.90%	22.60%	3.34%	0.39	9.23	−76.45%	0.90
Small Stocks>med by BP, BBY, top 50 6 mo.	13.59%	29.36%	3.03%	0.29	14.44	−91.60%	1.11
Small Stocks>med by BP, BBY, 3 mo., top 25 6 mo.	13.52%	26.67%	2.97%	0.32	13.76	−90.97%	1.00
Small Stocks, PB in top 3 deciles, 3 and 6 mo. mom>0, top 25 by 12m mom	13.26%	26.45%	2.71%	0.31	12.86	−94.82%	1.00
Small Stocks, PB in top 3 deciles, 3 and 6 mo. mom>0, top 25 by SY	13.24%	24.86%	2.69%	0.33	13.14	−94.82%	0.91
Small Stocks, PB in top 3 deciles, 3 and 6 mo. mom>0, top 50 by 12m mom	13.14%	25.80%	2.59%	0.32	12.58	−94.82%	0.97
Small Stocks>med by BP, BBY, 3 mo., top 50 6 mo.	13.09%	26.04%	2.54%	0.31	14.33	−90.97%	0.98
Small Stocks, PB in top 3 deciles, 3 and 6 mo. mom>0, top 50 by SY	12.96%	25.02%	2.41%	0.32	12.90	−94.82%	0.93
Small Stocks>med by BBY, 3 mo., top 50 12 mo.	12.21%	25.07%	1.66%	0.29	11.78	−82.88%	0.99
Small Stocks>med by BBY, 3 mo., top 25 12 mo.	12.06%	26.45%	1.50%	0.27	12.27	−82.88%	1.03
Small Stocks	10.56%	23.19%	N/A	0.24	N/A	−86.12%	N/A

T A B L E   21.21

Summary Base Rate Information for all Rolling One-, Three-, Five-, Seven-, and Ten-Year Periods for Strategies Benchmarked against the Returns of Small Stocks (Jan–28 to Dec–09); Strategies Sorted by Compound Return

Strategy	Percent of time				
	1 year	3 years	5 years	7 years	10 years
Microcap BP top 3 deciles, 3 and 6 mo.>0, top 25 by 12m mom	73.6%	84.3%	90.7%	94.3%	94.7%
Microcap BP top 3 deciles, 3 and 6 mo.>median top 25 by 12m mom	71.1%	82.8%	91.0%	93.2%	94.3%
Microcap BP top 3 deciles, 3 and 6 mo.>median top 25 by 12m mom	69.7%	82.0%	90.2%	92.6%	94.0%
Microcap BP top 3 deciles, 3 and 6 mo.>0, top 50 by 12m mom	73.7%	85.1%	90.2%	93.1%	94.1%
Small Stocks>med by SY, 6 mo. top 25 BP	74.0%	88.2%	94.4%	94.8%	99.0%
Small Stocks, 3 and 6 mo.>med, top 25 SY	74.9%	93.4%	94.6%	96.1%	99.3%

(continued on next page)

T A B L E 21.21

Summary Base Rate Information for all Rolling One-, Three-, Five-, Seven-, and Ten-Year Periods for Strategies Benchmarked against the Returns of Small Stocks (Jan–28 to Dec–09); Strategies Sorted by Compound Return
(Continued)

	Percent of time				
Strategy	**1 year**	**3 years**	**5 years**	**7 years**	**10 years**
Small Stocks>med by BP, 6 mo. top 25 BBY	74.1%	87.7%	91.6%	96.3%	98.0%
Small Stocks >med by 3M, 6M: top 50 BP	75.2%	89.6%	93.5%	95.0%	98.6%
Small Stocks, PB in top 3 deciles, 3 and 6 mo. mom>median, top 25 by SY	73.1%	83.1%	87.4%	90.1%	91.8%
Small Stocks>med by SY, 6 mo. top 50 BP	73.7%	90.0%	93.9%	94.8%	97.3%
Small Stocks >med by 3 and 6 mo., top 25 BP	71.9%	81.0%	88.3%	90.7%	94.0%
Small Stocks, PB in top 3 deciles, 3 and 6 mo. mom>median, top 25 by 12m mom	74.1%	84.3%	88.4%	90.6%	91.8%
Small Stocks, 3 and 6 mo.>med, top 50 SY	74.2%	92.1%	95.2%	96.8%	98.4%
Small Stocks >med by BP, SY, top 25 6 mo.	74.8%	89.3%	92.4%	92.1%	96.1%
Small Stocks, PB in top 3 deciles, 3 and 6 mo. mom>median, top 50 by SY	71.8%	83.9%	86.6%	89.7%	91.8%
Small Stocks>med by BP, 6 mo., top 25 SY	70.8%	85.1%	92.6%	95.9%	99.2%
Small Stocks, PB in top 3 deciles, 3 and 6 mo. mom>median, top 50 by 12m mom	73.2%	83.9%	87.1%	90.5%	91.8%
Small Stocks>med by BP, 6 mo., top 50 BBY	72.4%	85.8%	91.5%	91.1%	93.5%
Small Stocks>med by BP, 6 mo., top 50 SY	70.1%	84.8%	89.3%	90.7%	93.5%
Small Stocks>med by BP, SY, top 50 6 mo.	71.7%	87.9%	89.9%	92.1%	94.2%
Small Stock >med by BP, 3 and 6 mo., top 25 12 mo.	74.3%	85.0%	90.6%	92.2%	93.5%
Small Stocks>med by SY, 3 and 6 mo., top 50 12 mo.	77.7%	92.2%	93.3%	94.5%	97.2%
Small Stocks>med by BP, 3 and 6 mo., top 50 12 mo.	73.5%	88.5%	91.8%	92.5%	94.9%
Small Stocks>med by BP, BBY, top 25 6 mo.	66.5%	76.6%	81.9%	83.1%	89.1%
Small Stocks>med by SY, 3 and 6 mo., top 25 12 mo.	72.7%	85.5%	89.3%	91.8%	96.3%

(continued on next page)

T A B L E   21.21

Summary Base Rate Information for all Rolling One-, Three-, Five-, Seven-, and Ten-Year Periods for Strategies Benchmarked against the Returns of Small Stocks (Jan–28 to Dec–09); Strategies Sorted by Compound Return *(Continued)*

	Percent of time				
Strategy	**1 year**	**3 years**	**5 years**	**7 years**	**10 years**
Small Stocks>med by BP, BBY, top 50 6 mo.	64.4%	76.0%	80.5%	81.9%	88.2%
Small Stocks>med by BP, BBY, 3 mo., top 25 6 mo.	69.0%	83.8%	90.7%	93.0%	95.1%
Small Stocks, PB in top 3 deciles, 3 and 6 mo. mom>0, top 25 by 12m mom	69.1%	79.1%	82.4%	85.8%	88.6%
Small Stocks, PB in top 3 deciles, 3 and 6 mo. mom>0, top 25 by SY	66.7%	78.7%	81.3%	86.1%	88.6%
Small Stocks, PB in top 3 deciles, 3 and 6 mo. mom>0, top 50 by 12m mom	68.9%	78.9%	81.0%	84.0%	87.2%
Small Stocks>med by BP, BBY, 3 mo., top 50 6 mo.	67.5%	81.9%	89.3%	91.6%	94.7%
Small Stocks, PB in top 3 deciles, 3 and 6 mo. mom>0, top 50 by SY	66.7%	76.5%	78.7%	83.9%	87.2%
Small Stocks>med by BBY, 3 mo., top 50 12 mo.	65.8%	76.8%	83.7%	88.8%	96.4%
Small Stocks>med by BBY, 3 mo., top 25 12 mo.	61.3%	70.4%	79.1%	86.5%	95.3%
Small Stocks	0.0%	0.0%	0.0%	0.0%	0.0%

T A B L E   21.22

Summary Results for Strategies Benchmarked against the Returns of All Stocks (Jan–28 to Dec–09); Strategies Sorted by Compound Return

Strategy	**Geometric mean**	**Standard deviation (%)**	**Excess returns**	**Sharpe ratio**	**Tracking error**	**Largest drawdown**	**Beta**
All Stocks>med by 3 and 6 mo., top 25 SY	15.93%	19.07%	5.73%	0.57	7.54	−78.14%	0.82
All Stocks >med by SY, 6 mo., top 25 BP	15.54%	20.28%	5.34%	0.52	7.98	−82.43%	0.87
All Stocks, PB in top 3 deciles, 3 and 6 mo. mom>median, top 25 by SY	15.43%	21.28%	5.23%	0.49	8.34	−85.93%	0.90
All Stocks>med by SY, 6 mo., top 50 BP	15.35%	19.18%	5.15%	0.54	7.47	−80.20%	0.83
All Stocks>med by BP, 6 mo., top 25 SY	15.32%	19.37%	5.12%	0.53	7.39	−82.19%	0.84

(continued on next page)

T A B L E   21.22

Summary Results for Strategies Benchmarked against the Returns of All Stocks (Jan–28 to Dec–09); Strategies Sorted by Compound Return *(Continued)*

Strategy	Geometric mean	Standard deviation (%)	Excess returns	Sharpe ratio	Tracking error	Largest drawdown	Beta
All Stocks >med by BP, 6 mo., top 25 BBY	15.29%	21.22%	5.09%	0.49	7.79	−83.20%	0.91
All Stocks>med by 3 and 6 mo., top 50 SY	15.26%	18.37%	5.06%	0.56	6.87	−77.83%	0.81
All Stocks>med by BP, SY, top 25 6 mo.	15.26%	20.97%	5.06%	0.49	6.55	−82.44%	0.92
All Stocks, PB in top 3 deciles, 3 and 6 mo. mom>median, top 25 by 12m mom	15.21%	23.34%	5.01%	0.44	8.08	−86.28%	1.01
All Stocks>med by 3 and 6 mo., top 50 BP	15.04%	20.90%	4.84%	0.48	6.54	−81.32%	0.92
All Stocks>med by BP, BBY, top 25 6mo	14.82%	27.74%	4.61%	0.35	12.38	−85.31%	1.15
All Stocks, PB in top 3 deciles, 3 and 6 mo. mom>median, top 50 by SY	14.79%	21.57%	4.59%	0.45	8.11	−86.04%	0.92
All Stocks, PB in top 3 deciles, 3 and 6 mo. mom>median, top 50 by 12m mom	14.75%	22.62%	4.55%	0.43	7.58	−86.00%	0.98
All Stocks>med by BP, 6 mo., top 50 BBY	14.75%	21.32%	4.54%	0.46	6.48	−83.88%	0.94
All Stocks>med by 3 and 6 mo., top 25 BP	14.65%	22.66%	4.45%	0.43	7.70	−84.63%	0.98
All Stocks>med by BP, BBY, 3 mo., top 25 6 mo.	14.63%	26.27%	4.43%	0.37	11.87	−83.38%	1.08
All Stocks>med by BP, 6 mo., top 50 SY	14.50%	20.09%	4.30%	0.47	7.27	−83.63%	0.87
All Stocks>med by BP, SY, top 50 6 mo.	14.40%	20.88%	4.20%	0.45	5.96	−85.90%	0.92
All Stocks>med by BP, BBY, top 50 6 mo.	14.38%	27.11%	4.18%	0.35	12.00	−85.31%	1.13
All Stocks>med by BP, BBY, 3 mo., top 50 6 mo.	14.29%	25.62%	4.09%	0.36	11.50	−83.38%	1.05
All Stocks>med by SY, 3 and 6 mo., top 25 12 mo.	14.04%	22.36%	3.84%	0.40	9.38	−74.29%	0.94
All Stocks>med by SY, 3 and 6 mo., top 50 12 mo.	13.93%	20.94%	3.73%	0.43	7.56	−78.27%	0.90
All Stocks>med by BP, 3 and 6 mo., top 25 12 mo.	13.88%	23.48%	3.68%	0.38	7.86	−83.26%	1.02
All Stocks>med by BP, 3 and 6 mo., top 50 12 mo.	13.39%	22.55%	3.19%	0.37	6.66	−83.35%	0.99
All Stocks, PB in top 3 deciles, 3 and 6 mo. mom>0, top 25 by SY	12.98%	24.15%	2.78%	0.33	12.73	−94.51%	0.94

(continued on next page)

T A B L E   21.22

Summary Results for Strategies Benchmarked against the Returns of All Stocks (Jan–28 to Dec–09); Strategies Sorted by Compound Return *(Continued)*

Strategy	Geometric mean	Standard deviation (%)	Excess returns	Sharpe ratio	Tracking error	Largest drawdown	Beta
All Stocks, PB in top 3 deciles, 3 and 6 mo. mom>0, top 25 by 12m mom	12.96%	25.93%	2.76%	0.31	12.66	−94.51%	1.04
All Stocks>med by BBY, 3 mo., top 50 12 mo.	12.94%	26.27%	2.74%	0.30	10.75	−81.42%	1.11
All Stocks,PB in top 3 deciles, 3 and 6 mo. mom>0, top 50 by 12m mom	12.86%	25.24%	2.66%	0.31	12.26	−94.53%	1.01
All Stocks, PB in top 3 deciles, 3 and 6 mo. m mom>0, top 50 by SY	12.76%	24.25%	2.55%	0.32	12.59	−94.53%	0.95
All Stocks>med by BBY, 3 mo., top 25 12 mo.	12.67%	27.66%	2.47%	0.28	12.39	−81.42%	1.15
All Stocks	10.20%	21.75%	N/A	0.24	N/A	−85.45%	N/A

T A B L E   21.23

Summary Base Rate Information for all Rolling One-, Three-, Five-, Seven-, and Ten-Year Periods for Strategies Benchmarked against the Returns of All Stocks (Jan–28 to Dec–09); Strategies Sorted by Compound Return

	Percent of time				
Strategy	1 year	3 years	5 years	7 years	10 years
All Stocks>med by 3 and 6 mo., top 25 SY	77.5%	92.4%	92.5%	93.9%	99.2%
All Stocks >med by SY, 6 mo., top 25 BP	71.4%	85.6%	92.1%	93.2%	99.3%
All Stocks,PB in top 3 deciles, 3 and 6 mo. mom>median, top 25 by SY	73.6%	86.6%	91.1%	91.0%	94.5%
All Stocks>med by SY, 6 mo., top 50 BP	76.8%	90.8%	93.7%	94.2%	99.4%
All Stocks>med by BP, 6 mo., top 25 SY	72.6%	87.5%	94.5%	98.8%	100.0%
All Stocks >med by BP, 6 mo.: Top 25 BBY	72.0%	84.6%	87.6%	89.8%	91.7%
All Stocks>med by 3 and 6 mo., top 50 SY	78.4%	94.4%	95.0%	96.1%	99.3%
All Stocks>med by BP, SY, top 25 6 mo.	80.6%	92.0%	95.7%	97.6%	100.0%
All Stocks, PB in top 3 deciles, 3 and 6 mo. mom>median, top 25 by 12m mom	75.5%	85.0%	91.9%	92.2%	94.6%
All Stocks>med by 3 and 6 mo., top 50 BP	75.4%	87.5%	92.9%	94.2%	96.4%
All Stocks>med by BP, BBY, top 25 6M	70.9%	84.1%	89.3%	94.3%	96.9%
All Stocks, PB in top 3 deciles, 3 and 6 mo. mom>median, top 50 by SY	72.7%	84.5%	89.9%	90.7%	94.3%
All Stocks, PB in top 3 deciles, 3 and 6 mo. mom>median, top 50 by 12m mom	74.5%	85.1%	90.7%	91.6%	94.3%
All Stocks>med by BP, 6 mo, top 50 BBY	74.5%	89.6%	92.0%	93.8%	95.3%
All Stocks>med by 3 and 6 mo., top 25 BP	70.1%	78.0%	83.9%	87.0%	91.0%

(continued on next page)

T A B L E   21.23

Summary Base Rate Information for all Rolling One-, Three-, Five-, Seven-, and Ten-Year Periods for Strategies Benchmarked against the Returns of All Stocks (Jan–28 to Dec–09); Strategies Sorted by Compound Return *(Continued)*

Strategy	Percent of time				
	1 year	3 years	5 years	7 years	10 years
All Stocks>med by BP, BBY, 3 mo., top 25 6 mo.	72.4%	82.6%	90.4%	95.2%	97.6%
All Stocks>med by BP, 6 mo., top 50 SY	71.7%	87.9%	94.6%	96.0%	99.0%
All Stocks>med by BP, SY, top 50 6 mo.	76.1%	91.8%	95.1%	96.8%	98.5%
All Stocks>med by BP, BBY, top 50 6 mo.	69.7%	83.5%	87.5%	92.0%	94.1%
All Stocks>med by BP, BBY, 3 mo., top 50 6 mo.	71.8%	84.3%	91.7%	95.8%	97.2%
All Stocks>med by SY, 3 and 6 mo., top 25 12 mo.	69.7%	81.7%	85.8%	91.2%	98.2%
All Stocks>med by SY, 3 and 6 mo., top 50 12 mo.	76.9%	90.3%	91.0%	93.7%	97.2%
All Stocks>med by BP, 3 and 6 mo., top 25 12 mo.	74.2%	86.0%	88.6%	92.6%	94.0%
All Stocks>med by BP, 3 and 6 mo., top 50 12 mo.	74.6%	86.4%	91.2%	91.8%	94.3%
All Stocks, PB in top 3 deciles, 3 and 6 mo. mom>0, top 25 by SY	66.8%	78.6%	83.2%	87.6%	90.9%
All Stocks, PB in top 3 deciles, 3 and 6 mo. mom>0, top 25 by 12m mom	70.2%	78.0%	83.2%	86.2%	89.7%
All Stocks>med by BBY, 3 mo., top 50 12 mo.	63.9%	74.6%	79.7%	85.8%	89.4%
All Stocks, PB in top 3 deciles, 3 and 6 mo. mom>0, top 50 by 12m mom	70.1%	79.5%	81.9%	86.1%	88.2%
All Stocks, PB in top 3 deciles, 3 and 6 mo. m mom>0, top 50 by SY	66.6%	76.9%	80.6%	85.0%	88.1%
All Stocks>med by BBY, 3 mo., top 25 12 mo.	60.0%	68.7%	75.2%	83.6%	83.7%
All Stocks	0.0%	0.0%	0.0%	0.0%	0.0%

T A B L E   21.24

Summary Results for Strategies Benchmarked against the Returns of Large Stocks (Jan–28 to Dec–09); Strategies Sorted by Compound Return

Strategy	Geometric mean	Standard deviation (%)	Excess returns	Sharpe ratio	Tracking error	Largest drawdown	Beta
Large Stocks>med by 3 and 6 mo., top 25 SY	13.17%	17.98%	3.72%	0.45	5.90	−79.32%	0.88
Large Stocks>med by BBY, 3 mo., top 25 12 mo.	12.87%	25.44%	3.42%	0.31	11.74	−83.19%	1.18
Large Stocks>med by BP, BBY, 3 mo., top 25 6 mo.	12.78%	26.45%	3.32%	0.29	13.71	−83.87%	1.18

(continued on next page)

T A B L E   21.24

Summary Results for Strategies Benchmarked against the Returns of Large Stocks (Jan–28 to Dec–09); Strategies Sorted by Compound Return *(Continued)*

Strategy	Geometric mean	Standard deviation (%)	Excess returns	Sharpe ratio	Tracking error	Largest drawdown	Beta
Large Stocks>med by SY, 3 and 6 mo., top 25 12 mo.	12.78%	18.97%	3.32%	0.41	6.14	−80.08%	0.93
Large Stocks>med by 3 and 6 mo., top 25 BP	12.66%	19.00%	3.20%	0.40	5.79	−82.18%	0.93
Large Stocks>med by BP, BBY, top 25 6 mo.	12.57%	24.69%	3.11%	0.31	11.17	−80.31%	1.14
Large Stocks>med by BP, BBY, 3 mo., top 50 6 mo.	12.56%	26.26%	3.10%	0.29	13.68	−83.87%	1.16
Large Stocks>med by BP, 6 mo., top 25 BBY	12.54%	20.28%	3.08%	0.37	5.87	−86.70%	1.00
Large Stocks>med by BBY, 3 mo., top 50 12 mo.	12.47%	24.64%	3.01%	0.30	10.95	−83.19%	1.15
Large Stocks>med by SY, 6 mo., top 25 BP	12.37%	18.15%	2.92%	0.41	6.54	−82.43%	0.88
Large Stocks>med by SY, 3 and 6 mo., top 50 12 mo.	12.28%	18.09%	2.83%	0.40	5.27	−80.22%	0.90
Large Stocks>med by BBY, top 25 DIVY	12.23%	23.83%	2.77%	0.30	13.25	−85.17%	1.02
Large Stocks>med by 3 and 6 mo., top 50 SY	12.20%	18.13%	2.75%	0.40	5.15	−80.48%	0.90
Large Stocks>med by BBY, top 50 DIVY	12.17%	23.67%	2.72%	0.30	12.52	−85.17%	1.03
Large Stocks>med by BP, 6 mo., top 25 SY	12.11%	19.53%	2.65%	0.36	6.54	−86.69%	0.95
Large Stocks>med by BP, SY, top 25 6 mo.	12.06%	19.77%	2.61%	0.36	6.19	−88.57%	0.97
Large Stocks>med by BP, BBY, top 50 6 mo.	11.96%	24.41%	2.50%	0.28	11.25	−80.31%	1.13
Large Stocks>med by BP, 6 mo., top 50 BBY	11.93%	19.99%	2.47%	0.35	5.47	−86.68%	0.99
Large Stocks>med by 3 and 6 mo., top 50 BP	11.85%	18.63%	2.39%	0.37	5.12	−81.63%	0.93
Large Stock >med by BP, 6 mo., top 50 SY	11.83%	19.60%	2.37%	0.35	6.02	−86.68%	0.96
Large Stocks>med by SY, 6 mo., top 50 BP	11.80%	17.82%	2.35%	0.38	5.88	−82.54%	0.88
Large Stocks>med by BP, SY, top 50 6 mo.	11.50%	19.51%	2.04%	0.33	6.13	−88.75%	0.95
Large Stocks>med by BP, 3 and 6 mo., top 50 12 mo.	11.32%	20.12%	1.86%	0.31	5.64	−86.25%	0.99
Large Stocks>med by BP, 3 and 6 mo., top 25 12 mo.	11.28%	20.72%	1.83%	0.30	6.28	−86.16%	1.02
Large Stocks>med by BP, top 50 DIVY	10.34%	19.36%	0.89%	0.28	9.56	−88.30%	0.88
Large Stocks>med by BP, top 25 DIVY	10.28%	19.96%	0.83%	0.26	10.45	−90.20%	0.88
Large Stocks	9.45%	19.42%	N/A	0.23	N/A	−84.33%	N/A

T A B L E 21.25

Summary Base Rate Information for all Rolling One-, Three-, Five-, Seven-, and Ten-Year Periods for Strategies Benchmarked against the Returns of Large Stocks (Jan–28 to Dec–09); Strategies Sorted by Compound Return

	Percent of time				
Strategy	1 year	3 years	5 years	7 years	10 years
Large Stocks>med by 3 and 6 mo., top 25 SY	71.7%	86.8%	88.2%	91.6%	96.0%
Large Stocks>med by BBY, 3 mo., top 25 12 mo.	66.4%	79.3%	85.9%	90.9%	93.9%
Large Stocks>med by BP, BBY, 3 mo., top 25 6 mo.	69.9%	84.0%	93.7%	98.6%	100.0%
Large Stocks>med by SY, 3 and 6 mo., top 25 12 mo.	72.1%	85.9%	92.5%	96.1%	99.8%
Large Stocks>med by 3 and 6 mo., top 25 BP	69.6%	82.8%	91.8%	93.1%	97.5%
Large Stocks>med by BP, BBY, top 25 6 mo.	69.9%	81.5%	91.1%	95.0%	97.6%
Large Stocks>med by BP, BBY, 3 mo., top 50 6 mo.	68.3%	82.8%	92.5%	97.7%	99.5%
Large Stocks>med by BP, 6 mo., top 25 BBY	68.2%	77.3%	86.9%	87.8%	94.0%
Large Stock >med by BBY, 3 mo., top 50 12 mo.	69.5%	81.5%	88.9%	92.0%	95.5%
Large Stocks>med by SY, 6 mo., top 25 BP	67.4%	82.1%	86.2%	91.7%	99.0%
Large Stocks>med by SY, 3 and 6 mo., top 50 12 mo.	70.8%	85.6%	88.4%	93.0%	99.8%
Large Stocks>med by BBY, top 25 DIVY	57.6%	68.7%	75.1%	84.2%	88.6%
Large Stocks>med by 3 and 6 mo., top 50 SY	68.3%	83.0%	85.5%	88.3%	94.1%
Large Stocks>med by BBY, top 50 DIVY	59.0%	69.1%	76.6%	83.6%	89.4%
Large Stocks>med by BP, 6 mo., top 25 SY	63.9%	72.0%	82.9%	84.6%	92.1%
Large Stocks>med by BP, SY, top 25 6 mo.	69.6%	82.3%	88.2%	91.3%	94.7%
Large Stocks>med by BP, BBY, top 50 6 mo.	67.3%	79.1%	86.6%	92.8%	95.4%
Large Stocks>med by BP, 6 mo., top 50 BBY	69.5%	78.5%	87.8%	88.3%	94.3%
Large Stocks>med by 3 and 6 mo., top 50 BP	65.0%	79.6%	85.4%	88.9%	93.8%
Large Stocks>med by BP, 6 mo., top 50 SY	65.1%	73.0%	85.0%	87.2%	92.9%
Large Stocks>med by SY, 6 mo., top 50 BP	65.4%	78.0%	83.9%	86.9%	93.9%
Large Stocks>med by BP, SY, top 50 6 mo.	66.0%	76.0%	85.5%	86.3%	91.6%
Large Stocks>med by BP, 3 and 6 mo., top 50 12 mo.	64.4%	73.3%	82.1%	87.6%	94.7%
Large Stocks>med by BP, 3 and 6 mo., top 25 12 mo.	66.1%	74.7%	80.1%	87.3%	94.0%
Large Stocks>med by BP, top 50 DIVY	56.8%	63.6%	61.9%	66.3%	77.7%
Large Stocks>med by BP, top 25 DIVY	55.2%	67.3%	68.9%	70.9%	78.7%
Large Stocks	0.0%	0.0%	0.0%	0.0%	0.0%

DOUBLE VALUE WITH MOMENTUM

As Table 21.23 shows, between 1928 and 2009, there are two strategies from the All Stocks universe that have perfect ten-year base rates. The first strategy requires that stocks have a book-to-price greater than the median (i.e., eliminate the half of the stocks where investors are paying the most for every dollar of book value); have six-month price appreciation greater than the median; and finally, buy the 25 stocks with the highest shareholder yield.

Not only does this strategy beat the All Stocks universe in 100 percent of all rolling ten-year periods, but it also beats the universe in seven out of every ten one-year holding periods. There is a price for the consistency however, as the strategy earned an average annual compound return of 15.32 percent, some 61 basis points behind the best-performing strategy. It also has a larger maximum decline of 82 percent and a lower Sharpe ratio. Nevertheless, a 100 percent base rate over all rolling ten-year periods between 1928 and 2009 is a rarity.

The second strategy requires that stocks have both a book-to-price and shareholder yield greater than the median stock in All Stocks, and then buys the 25 stocks with the best 12-month price appreciation. This strategy beat the All Stocks universe in eight out of ten rolling one-year periods and in 100 percent of all rolling ten-year periods. As with the strategy above, you would pay a price for the strategy's greater consistency—this strategy earned an average annual compound return of 15.26 percent, some 67 basis points behind the best-performing All Stocks strategy requiring three- and six-month price appreciation greater than the universe median and buying the 25 stocks with the best shareholder yield. See Tables 21.20 through 21.25 for the summary results for other strategies.

LONG-TERM SUCCESS OF MULTIFACTOR STRATEGIES

For all three of our universes, history demonstrates that you can do *vastly* better than a passive investment in any given universe itself by using more than one factor to select a portfolio of stocks. Buying stocks with great price momentum or high shareholder yield alone works quite well, but we've seen that by combining these factors—first requiring good price appreciation and then focusing on the stocks with the best shareholder yield—generates significantly higher returns at *lower levels of risk*. This combination of value and growth characteristics is one we revisit when we look at even more multifactor models using research from the Compustat dataset. For now, the long-term data show that uniting several factors provides higher returns and lower risk than using single factor criteria.

IMPLICATIONS

Investors are best served by buying stocks that have jumped a series of hurdles rather than just one. It is often best to marry both value and growth characteristics when looking for stocks that will go on to offer investors the best absolute and risk-adjusted returns. We've seen that by combining single factors like price momentum and shareholder yield we can generate far better returns than using either individually, and we can lower our risk at the same time. We'll see in the coming chapters that we can also substantially improve returns in both growth and value strategies by adding accounting factors to the mix, looking not only for stocks with good price momentum or shareholder yield, but also those that are not fiddling with the books, taking on too much debt, or turning to external financing to run the company. Next, let's look at what factors have been successful when applied to our two additional universes: Market Leaders and Small Stocks.

22 CHAPTER

DISSECTING THE MARKET LEADERS UNIVERSE: THE RATIOS THAT ADD THE MOST VALUE

Numbers serve to discipline rhetoric. Without them it is too easy to follow flights of fancy, to ignore the world as it is and to remold it nearer the heart's desire.
—Ralph Waldo Emerson

In the previous chapter we saw that we can enhance returns and lower risk by using several factors to build a model portfolio. In this chapter I take a look at the Market Leaders universe—a multifactor model itself—and then apply single factors or groups of factors to enhance its performance. You will recall from Chapter Five that the Market Leaders universe is a bit like the S&P 500 on steroids and that these large, well-known stocks outperformed All Stocks, Large Stocks, and the S&P 500. The Market Leaders universe had the highest Sharpe ratio of all the broader-based, index-like portfolios and proved to be an excellent performer over a variety of market cycles. Market Leaders also outperformed other large-cap indexes like the Russell 1000.

Market leading companies are nonutility stocks with greater-than-average market capitalization. (We now use a minimum market capitalization of $50 million.) Older versions of this book required only a market capitalization greater than the database average, which included tiny stocks. By eliminating noninvestable microcap stocks, we bring the average market-cap up and include only investable stocks), shares outstanding, cash flows, and finally, sales 50 percent greater than the average stock. Applying these factors to the Compustat dataset qualifies just 6 percent of the stocks as Market Leaders. It is important to note that Market Leaders allow the inclusion of American Depository Receipts (ADRs), which are dollar denominated overseas shares, which trade in the United States. Thus, giant companies like Germany's Deutsche Telekom, Japan's NTT, and the United Kingdom's British Petroleum are included for consideration. This is an important distinction, especially when comparing performance with the S&P 500, which is made up of only U.S. companies. In the new global economy, the ability to purchase shares of companies domiciled outside the United States might be an advantage. Indeed, the number of ADRs in the Market Leaders universe has grown considerably over the years—in 1995, they made up approximately 20 percent of the universe; at the end of 2003, they accounted for 35 percent, and by May 2010, they accounted for 48 percent of the Market Leaders universe. Also important to note is that the Market Leaders universe is equally weighted, whereas the S&P 500 is cap-weighted, giving far greater weight to the largest companies in the index. Currently, the Market Leaders universe contains 331 stocks with a weighted market capitalization of $46.4 billion and a median market-cap of $27.3 billion. In contrast, the S&P 500 has a weighted market capitalization of $21.12 billion and a median market-cap of $9.35 billion, so Market Leaders focus on even larger stocks than those in the S&P 500. Over longer periods of time, equal-weighted indexes have outperformed cap-weighted indexes, another important fact when comparing the S&P 500 to Market Leaders. Table 22.1 offers a refresher on how the Market Leaders universe compared to All Stocks, Large Stocks, Small Stocks, and the S&P 500 between 1963 and 2009.

Typically, large, broad-based indexes like the S&P 500—and the other universes featured here—earn positive monthly returns about 60 percent of the time, with negative returns accounting for the remaining 40 percent. Interestingly, this 60–40 balance tends to persist no matter what time frame you look at—for example, for all monthly returns for the S&P 500 between January 1, 1926, and December 31, 2009, about 62 percent are positive and 38 percent are negative. The figure is similar for our Large Stocks universe, with 61 percent of the returns being positive and 39 percent negative. All Stocks also shows a 61 percent positive and 39 percent negative balance over those 84 years. If you choose to look at the market only after World War II, the figure barely budges, moving up to 63 percent positive and 37 percent negative. And if you look at the dismal 1926 through 1944 time period—dominated by the Great Depression of the 1930s—you would still see that 58 percent of all monthly returns for the S&P 500 were positive.

T A B L E   22.1

Summary Annual Return and Risk Results Data: Market Leaders, S&P 500, Large Stocks, All Stocks, and Small Stocks, January 1, 1964, to December 31, 2009

	Market Leaders	S&P 500	Large Stocks	All Stocks	Small Stocks
Arithmetic average	12.82%	10.71%	11.72%	13.26%	13.94%
Geometric average	11.36%	9.46%	10.20%	11.22%	11.60%
Median return	14.62%	13.76%	17.20%	17.16%	19.28%
Standard deviation	16.13%	15.09%	16.50%	18.99%	20.31%
Upside deviation	10.00%	9.37%	9.70%	10.98%	11.87%
Downside deviation	11.66%	10.76%	11.85%	13.90%	14.83%

(continued on next page)

TABLE 22.1

Summary Annual Return and Risk Results Data: Market Leaders, S&P 500, Large Stocks, All Stocks, and Small Stocks, January 1, 1964, to December 31, 2009 *(Continued)*

	Market Leaders	S&P 500	Large Stocks	All Stocks	Small Stocks
Tracking error	7.63	8.69	5.41	0.00	2.21
Number of positive periods	335	342	332	329	329
Number of negative periods	217	210	220	223	223
Maximum peak-to-trough decline	−54.03%	−50.95%	−53.77%	−55.54%	−58.48%
Beta	0.78	0.71	0.84	1.00	1.07
T-statistic (m = 0)	5.10	4.59	4.58	4.47	4.38
Sharpe ratio (Rf = 5%)	0.39	0.30	0.32	0.33	0.32
Sortino ratio (MAR = 10%)	0.12	−0.05	0.02	0.09	0.11
$10,000 becomes	$1,411,897	$639,147	$872,861	$1,329,513	$1,555,109
Minimum 1-year return	−48.15%	−43.32%	−46.91%	−46.49%	−46.38%
Maximum 1-year return	66.79%	61.01%	68.96%	84.19%	93.08%
Minimum 3-year return	−13.61%	−16.10%	−15.89%	−18.68%	−19.53%
Maximum 3-year return	34.82%	33.40%	33.12%	31.49%	34.00%
Minimum 5-year return	−4.36%	−6.64%	−5.82%	−9.91%	−11.75%
Maximum 5-year return	31.52%	29.72%	28.95%	27.66%	31.37%
Minimum 7-year return	−2.93%	−3.85%	−4.15%	−6.32%	−7.64%
Maximum 7-year return	24.56%	23.08%	22.83%	23.77%	27.35%
Minimum 10-year return	1.01%	−3.43%	−0.15%	1.01%	1.08%
Maximum 10-year return	19.69%	19.48%	19.57%	22.05%	24.47%
Minimum expected return*	−19.44%	−19.46%	−21.28%	−24.73%	−26.69%
Maximum expected return†	45.07%	40.88%	44.72%	51.24%	54.57%

* Minimum expected return is arithmetic return minus 2 times the standard deviation.

† Maximum expected return is arithmetic return plus 2 times the standard deviation.

When examining Table 22.1, you'll see that, with the exception of the Small Stocks universe, the Market Leaders universe earned the best absolute return. On a risk-adjusted basis, the Market Leaders universe provides the best return, sporting a Sharpe ratio of .39, higher than any of the others. Market Leaders also has better minimum returns over almost all of the various holding periods, indicating that they hold up better in market downturns. You'll also recall that over most rolling five-year periods, the Market Leaders universe outperforms both the S&P 500 and the Large Stocks universe. Indeed, as we found in Chapter Five, the Market Leaders universe beat the S&P 500 in 76 percent of all rolling five-year periods and in 78 percent of all rolling ten-year periods, and it beat the Large Stocks universe in 75 percent of all rolling five-year periods and in 89 percent of all rolling ten-year periods. Figures 22.1 and 22.2 show the rolling five-year average annual compound excess (deficient) return for Market Leaders minus the S&P 500 and Large Stocks' returns, respectively.

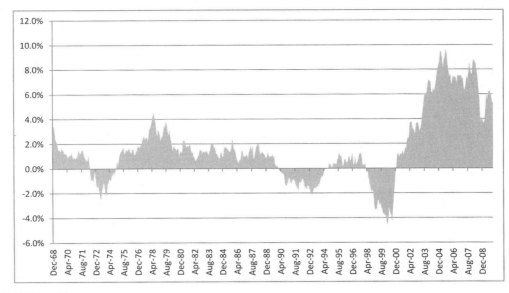

FIGURE 22.1

Five-year average annual compound excess (deficient) return Market Leaders minus S&P 500, January 1, 1964, to December 31, 2009

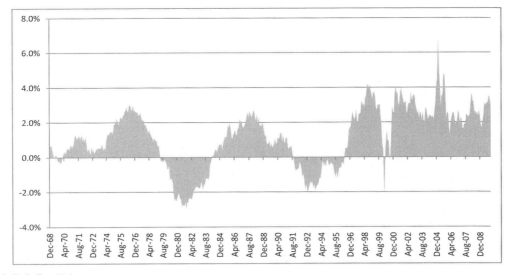

FIGURE 22.2

Five-year average annual compound excess (deficient) return Market Leaders minus Large Stocks, January 1, 1964, to December 31, 2009

SUMMARY RESULTS FOR MARKET LEADERS STRATEGIES

Here I confine myself to reviewing the summary data for each strategy, as my goal is to show you that what holds true for the broad All Stocks and Large Stocks universes is equally as compelling within the Market Leaders universe. In order to accommodate all the factors tested, the data here start on September 1965. Table 22.2 lists the various strategies and is sorted by average annual compound return. Notice that the high valuations for the factors are not as devastating to Market Leaders as they are for All Stocks and Large Stocks, primarily because of the sheer size of the market leading companies. For example, the three worst-performing Market Leaders strategies are buying the stocks from Market Leaders with the *worst* scores on Value Composite Three, which returned 7.71 percent per year; buying the decile of Market Leaders with the lowest shareholder yield, which returned 7.25 percent per year and, in last place, buying the 10 percent of stocks from Market Leaders with the lowest buyback yield (essentially those Market Leaders that were net issuers of shares), which returned 6.76 percent.

T A B L E   22.2

Summary Results for Strategies Benchmarked against the Returns of Market Leaders Universe USA (Sep–65 to Dec–09); Strategies Sorted by Compound Return

Strategy	Geometric mean	Standard deviation (%)	Excess returns	Sharpe ratio	Tracking error	Largest drawdown	Beta
Market Leaders, top two deciles Value Comp 2, top 25 by 6 mo. PA	15.34%	17.17%	4.70%	0.60	6.03	−52.74%	0.98
Market Leaders, top two deciles Value Comp 2, top 50 by 6 mo. PA	15.00%	17.16%	3.73%	0.58	5.27	−53.43%	1.00
Market Leaders top 25 by shareholder yld	14.94%	17.00%	3.66%	0.58	6.52	−57.57%	0.96
Market Leaders Composite Value 2 decile 1 (high)	14.84%	18.52%	3.57%	0.53	7.10	−62.16%	1.05
Market Leaders shareholder yield (%) decile 1	14.72%	16.77%	3.44%	0.58	6.38	−56.44%	0.95
Market Leaders, 3/6 mo. PA>median, top 25 by shareholder yld	14.65%	16.32%	3.38%	0.59	5.09	−56.33%	0.95
Cornerstone Value improved 50	14.55%	16.19%	3.28%	0.59	5.11	−56.01%	0.94
Market Leaders Composite Value 3 decile 1 (high)	14.49%	18.29%	3.21%	0.52	6.90	−60.13%	1.03
Market Leaders EBITDA/EV decile 1	14.39%	18.15%	3.12%	0.52	7.53	−52.21%	1.01
Market Leaders buyback Yield (%) decile 1	14.28%	16.52%	3.01%	0.56	5.24	−53.60%	0.96
Market Leaders Composite Value decile 1 (high)	14.27%	18.69%	3.00%	0.50	6.75	−60.56%	1.07
Market Leaders free CF to enterprise value decile 1	13.75%	18.60%	2.48%	0.47	7.15	−62.79%	1.05

(continued on next page)

T A B L E   22.2

Summary Results for Strategies Benchmarked against the Returns of Market Leaders Universe USA (Sep–65 to Dec–09); Strategies Sorted by Compound Return *(Continued)*

Strategy	Geometric mean	Standard deviation (%)	Excess returns	Sharpe ratio	Tracking error	Largest drawdown	Beta
Market Leaders net operating cash flow to price decile 1	13.72%	18.76%	2.44%	0.46	7.09	−64.38%	1.06
Market Leaders earnings/price decile 1	13.67%	19.07%	2.39%	0.45	7.25	−62.69%	1.08
Market Leaders TATA decile 10	13.54%	17.66%	2.26%	0.48	6.89	−56.44%	0.99
Cornerstone Value 25 div yld	13.49%	17.22%	2.21%	0.49	7.91	−65.01%	0.94
Market Leaders return 6 mo. decile 1	13.41%	18.27%	2.14%	0.46	8.67	−58.00%	0.98
MF Market Leaders, PSR<avg top 25 12 mo. ret	13.35%	17.01%	2.08%	0.49	6.12	−48.31%	0.97
Market Leaders accruals-to-price decile 10	13.17%	18.38%	1.90%	0.44	7.28	−54.81%	1.03
Market Leaders NOA change (%) decile 10	13.17%	16.62%	1.90%	0.49	5.24	−52.95%	0.96
Market Leaders dividend yield (%) decile 1	13.13%	16.96%	1.85%	0.48	7.59	−64.59%	0.93
Market Leaders sales to enterprise value decile 1	13.04%	17.27%	1.76%	0.47	6.08	−51.07%	0.99
MF Market Leaders, top 10 PCF	12.89%	21.74%	1.62%	0.36	11.17	−75.55%	1.15
MF Market Leaders, PSR<avg top 50 12 mo. ret	12.79%	16.68%	1.52%	0.47	4.27	−52.04%	0.99
Market Leaders return 12 mo. decile 1	12.71%	19.38%	1.44%	0.40	10.42	−60.88%	1.00
Market Leaders free cash flow to price decile 1	12.68%	19.44%	1.41%	0.40	7.79	−65.82%	1.09
Market Leaders sales to price decile 1	12.28%	18.76%	1.00%	0.39	6.96	−58.12%	1.07
Market Leaders book/price decile 1	12.21%	19.95%	0.93%	0.36	8.20	−67.38%	1.12
Market Leaders debt change (%) decile 10	12.17%	17.29%	0.90%	0.41	4.69	−48.85%	1.02
Market Leaders ROA decile 1	11.77%	16.81%	0.50%	0.40	7.83	−48.00%	0.91
Market Leaders net margin decile 1	11.63%	15.77%	0.35%	0.42	6.33	−46.73%	0.89
Market Leaders asset turnover decile 1	11.60%	16.84%	0.32%	0.39	7.00	−49.88%	0.94
Market Leaders operating margin decile 1	11.52%	16.92%	0.24%	0.39	6.91	−57.34%	0.95
Market Leaders yoy sales growth decile 1	11.48%	19.11%	0.20%	0.34	7.67	−61.47%	1.07
Market Leaders universe USA	11.27%	16.37%	N/A	0.38	N/A	−54.03%	N/A

(continued on next page)

T A B L E   22.2

Summary Results for Strategies Benchmarked against the Returns of Market Leaders Universe USA (Sep–65 to Dec–09); Strategies Sorted by Compound Return *(Continued)*

Strategy	Geometric mean	Standard deviation (%)	Excess returns	Sharpe ratio	Tracking error	Largest drawdown	Beta
Market Leaders working capital decile 10	11.27%	15.83%	−0.01%	0.40	5.89	−52.21%	0.90
Market Leaders depr exp to cap exp decile 1	11.21%	17.99%	−0.06%	0.35	6.07	−57.97%	1.03
Market Leaders ROE decile 1	10.95%	16.86%	−0.33%	0.35	6.79	−51.13%	0.94
Market Leaders depr exp to cap exp decile 10	10.68%	18.29%	−0.60%	0.31	6.43	−55.30%	1.05
Market Leaders yoy net operating CF PS growth decile 1	10.60%	19.34%	−0.67%	0.29	6.46	−65.37%	1.12
Market Leaders asset turnover decile 10	10.35%	20.82%	−0.93%	0.26	10.60	−78.30%	1.10
Market Leaders ROE decile 10	10.34%	18.95%	−0.93%	0.28	7.48	−61.32%	1.07
Market Leaders accruals-to-price decile 1	10.09%	16.55%	−1.18%	0.31	5.80	−51.92%	0.95
Market Leaders free CF to enterprise value decile 10	10.07%	18.10%	−1.21%	0.28	6.41	−60.38%	1.03
Market Leaders ROA decile 10	10.06%	21.02%	−1.21%	0.24	8.75	−73.38%	1.18
Market Leaders yoy sales growth decile 10	10.06%	18.49%	−1.22%	0.27	6.21	−63.69%	1.07
Market Leaders working capital decile 1	9.84%	16.98%	−1.44%	0.28	6.49	−63.97%	0.96
Market Leaders net margin decile 10	9.79%	18.53%	−1.48%	0.26	6.57	−59.32%	1.06
Market Leaders free cash flow to price decile 10	9.75%	17.90%	−1.52%	0.27	6.31	−59.72%	1.02
Market Leaders EPS change (%) decile 1	9.74%	18.26%	−1.53%	0.26	6.36	−53.81%	1.05
Market Leaders book/price decile 10	9.66%	17.15%	−1.62%	0.27	8.78	−51.30%	0.90
Market Leaders yoy net operating CF PS growth decile 10	9.55%	18.43%	−1.72%	0.25	5.10	−63.85%	1.08
Market Leaders debt change (%) decile 1	9.40%	17.27%	−1.88%	0.25	4.17	−54.87%	1.02
Market Leaders operating margin decile 10	9.31%	18.06%	−1.96%	0.24	6.81	−54.95%	1.02
Market Leaders dividend yield (%) decile 10	9.25%	20.39%	−2.03%	0.21	9.73	−56.42%	1.10
Market Leaders EBITDA/EV decile 10	8.90%	19.44%	−2.37%	0.20	8.62	−65.29%	1.07
Market Leaders EPS change (%) decile 10	8.83%	19.25%	−2.44%	0.20	6.78	−64.96%	1.11

(continued on next page)

T A B L E   22.2

Summary Results for Strategies Benchmarked against the Returns of Market Leaders Universe USA (Sep–65 to Dec–09); Strategies Sorted by Compound Return *(Continued)*

Strategy	Geometric mean	Standard deviation (%)	Excess returns	Sharpe ratio	Tracking error	Largest drawdown	Beta
Market Leaders earnings/price decile 10	8.74%	19.18%	−2.53%	0.20	8.21	−58.63%	1.06
Market Leaders Composite Value 1 decile 10 (low)	8.64%	17.55%	−2.63%	0.21	9.28	−57.66%	0.91
Market Leaders NOA change (%) decile 1	8.58%	17.67%	−2.69%	0.20	5.85	−53.01%	1.02
Market Leaders sales to price decile 10	8.57%	17.39%	−2.71%	0.21	9.02	−58.92%	0.91
Market Leaders sales to enterprise value decile 10	8.53%	17.97%	−2.75%	0.20	7.84	−64.70%	0.99
Market Leaders return 12 mo. decile 10	8.52%	21.39%	−2.75%	0.16	9.05	−65.66%	1.20
Market Leaders return 6 mo. decile 10	8.30%	20.52%	−2.98%	0.16	7.54	−65.20%	1.18
Market Leaders Composite Value 2 decile 10 (low)	7.85%	18.03%	−3.43%	0.16	9.13	−60.68%	0.95
Market Leaders TATA decile 1	7.82%	18.06%	−3.46%	0.16	5.78	−56.09%	1.05
Market Leaders net operating cash flow to price decile 10	7.80%	17.54%	−3.47%	0.16	8.41	−59.89%	0.94
Market Leaders Composite Value 3 decile 10 (low)	7.71%	17.86%	−3.56%	0.15	8.87	−59.42%	0.95
Market Leaders shareholder yield (%) decile 10	7.25%	19.26%	−4.02%	0.12	6.48	−61.88%	1.11
Market Leaders buyback yield (%) decile 10	6.76%	18.93%	−4.52%	0.09	5.49	−63.96%	1.11
US 30 day T-bill USD	5.64%	0.82%	−5.64%	0.78	16.41	0.00%	0.00

Yet, even here, the difference between high and low is extraordinary. The best of the decile strategies, buying the top decile of Market Leaders with the highest scores on Value Factor Two (see Chapter Fifteen to review Value Factor Two) turned a $10,000 investment into over $4.6 million, an average annual compound return of 14.84 percent whereas the worst, buying the decile of Market Leaders with the lowest buyback yield (i.e., those market leading companies that were issuing large amounts of new shares rather than buying them back), saw the same $10,000 grow to just $181,791, an average annual compound return of just 6.76 percent. The Value Factor Two strategy performs 15 times better! A $10,000 investment in the Market Leaders universe itself grew to $1.1 million over the same period, an average annual compound return of 11.27 percent.

I've sorted the strategies by average annual compound returns, and much like the returns seen in the All Stocks and Large Stocks universes, the *highest* returns are awarded to the Market Leaders with the *lowest* price-to-book, price-to-earnings, price-to-sales, and price-to-cash flow ratios, or composite factors like Value Factor Two, whereas the *lowest* returns are awarded to the market leading companies with the *highest* price-to-book, price-to-earnings, price-to-sales, and price-to-cash flow ratios. Here we see the same symmetry that we found in our review of all the value factors covered in Chapter Sixteen.

MULTIFACTOR STRATEGIES ALSO DO WELL

Some of the same multifactor strategies we looked at in the last chapter also perform well with Market Leaders. The best-performing strategy is one we cover in greater detail in Chapter Twenty-Five: buying the 25 stocks with the best six-month price appreciations from Market Leaders that are also in the top two deciles of Value Composite Two. This strategy turned $10,000 invested August 31, 1965, into $5,585,470 by the end of 2009, an average annual compound return of 15.34 percent. That's considerably better than the $1.1 million you'd have earned with an investment in the Market Leaders universe itself, which compounded at 11.27 percent over the same period. All the base rates for the strategy—featured in Table 22.3—were positive, with the group beating the Market Leaders universe in 92 percent of all rolling five-year periods and in 100 percent of all rolling ten-year periods. What's more, it has the highest risk-adjusted return of all the Market Leaders' strategies, with a Sharpe ratio of .60. In Chapter Twenty-Three, we'll see that you can earn even better absolute returns using this strategy on a smaller capitalization universe, but here we see that it provided excellent overall returns with one of the lowest maximum declines and a perfect ten-year base rate. This type of strategy essentially buys cheap stocks on the mend. You never pay more than the average for every dollar of sales, and you buy them when their prices are heading up. Keep in mind that this type of momentum strategy almost always works best when you include a value factor in the model.

T A B L E   22.3

Summary Base Rate Information for all Rolling One-, Three-, Five-, Seven-, and Ten-Year Periods for Strategies Benchmarked against the Returns of Market Leaders Universe USA (Sep–65 to Dec–09); Strategies Sorted by Compound Return

Strategy	Percent of time				
	1-year	3-year	5-year	7-year	10-year
Market Leaders, top two deciles Value Comp 2, top 25 by 6 mo. PA	73%	85%	92%	98%	100.0%
Market Leaders, top two deciles Value Comp 2, top 50 by 6 mo. PA	75%	86%	93%	97%	100.0%
Market Leaders top 25 by shareholder yld	65.3%	82.1%	90.3%	98.4%	100.0%
Market Leaders Composite Value 2 decile1 (high)	64.1%	71.2%	79.7%	92.9%	98.8%
Market Leaders shareholder yield (%) decile 1	64.9%	80.3%	91.3%	97.3%	100.0%

(continued on next page)

T A B L E   22.3

Summary Base Rate Information for all Rolling One-, Three-, Five-, Seven-, and Ten-Year Periods for Strategies Benchmarked against the Returns of Market Leaders Universe USA (Sep–65 to Dec–09); Strategies Sorted by Compound Return *(Continued)*

Strategy	Percent of time				
	1-year	3-year	5-year	7-year	10-year
Market Leaders, 3/6 mo. PA>MI median, top 25 by shareholder yld	67.0%	86.0%	98.0%	100.0%	100.0%
ML CSV improved 50	69.1%	84.9%	96.6%	99.1%	100.0%
Market Leaders Composite Value 3 decile 1 (high)	63.3%	67.8%	78.9%	91.3%	96.9%
Market Leaders EBITDA/EV decile 1	68.1%	77.7%	83.5%	93.5%	99.5%
Market Leaders buyback Yield (%) decile 1	71.8%	86.9%	91.5%	95.1%	100.0%
Market Leaders Composite Value 1 decile 1 (high)	62.0%	70.6%	70.8%	88.0%	96.4%
Market Leaders free CF to enterprise value decile 1	63.0%	73.6%	87.5%	87.1%	90.6%
Market Leaders net operating cash flow to price decile 1	60.7%	66.0%	73.8%	87.8%	97.1%
Market Leaders earnings/price decile 1	61.4%	67.6%	65.1%	71.5%	64.6%
Market Leaders TATA decile 10	66.2%	74.8%	81.2%	83.1%	92.5%
ML CSV 25 div yld	57.4%	65.2%	67.4%	72.4%	84.3%
Market Leaders return 6 mo. decile 1	62.6%	71.0%	83.7%	93.8%	96.9%
Market Leaders, PSR<avg top 25 12 mo. ret	67.2%	77.9%	84.8%	88.2%	98.3%
Market Leaders accruals-to-price decile 10	59.7%	65.2%	72.9%	80.8%	91.5%
Market Leaders NOA change (%) decile 10	61.8%	73.8%	79.1%	84.6%	85.5%
Market Leaders dividend yield (%) decile 1	55.7%	61.2%	67.2%	74.2%	86.0%
Market Leaders sales to enterprise value decile 1	63.5%	68.6%	75.1%	74.2%	81.4%
Market Leaders, top 10 PCF	57.2%	62.8%	68.5%	81.5%	91.0%
Market Leaders, PSR<avg top 50 12 mo. ret	64.1%	70.2%	73.2%	75.1%	80.1%
Market Leaders return 12 mo. decile 1	60.1%	66.0%	78.6%	83.1%	86.2%
Market Leaders free cash flow to price decile 1	58.3%	61.8%	69.1%	71.3%	72.9%
Market Leaders sales to price decile 1	57.6%	53.3%	60.0%	57.0%	64.4%
Market Leaders book/price decile 1	56.2%	55.5%	57.3%	64.1%	66.8%
Market Leaders debt change (%) decile 10	60.3%	64.6%	73.6%	79.7%	86.9%
Market Leaders ROA decile 1	51.2%	45.7%	47.8%	52.8%	52.8%
Market Leaders net margin decile 1	48.6%	52.1%	48.6%	54.8%	55.4%
Market Leaders asset turnover decile 1	49.3%	52.9%	54.8%	56.1%	67.1%
Market Leaders operating margin decile 1	45.7%	46.5%	45.0%	50.8%	53.3%
Market Leaders yoy sales growth decile 1	49.5%	43.5%	42.5%	45.7%	42.4%
Market Leaders universe USA	0.0%	0.0%	0.0%	0.0%	0.0%
Market Leaders working capital decile 10	55.1%	51.9%	56.9%	55.7%	59.8%
Market Leaders depr exp to cap exp decile 1	54.3%	61.4%	65.1%	70.2%	76.8%
Market Leaders ROE decile 1	50.9%	43.9%	46.3%	44.3%	50.6%

(continued on next page)

T A B L E   22.3

Summary Base Rate Information for all Rolling One-, Three-, Five-, Seven-, and Ten-Year Periods for Strategies Benchmarked against the Returns of Market Leaders Universe USA (Sep–65 to Dec–09); Strategies Sorted by Compound Return *(Continued)*

Strategy	1-year	3-year	Percent of time 5-year	7-year	10-year
Market Leaders depr exp to cap exp decile 10	45.3%	40.2%	38.3%	39.6%	39.5%
Market Leaders yoy net operating CF PS growth decile 1	46.8%	39.4%	45.0%	48.3%	40.2%
Market Leaders asset turnover decile 10	51.2%	50.9%	56.4%	53.2%	49.2%
Market Leaders ROE decile 10	50.1%	45.7%	38.7%	36.1%	38.7%
Market Leaders accruals-to-price decile 1	42.6%	37.4%	40.0%	37.6%	25.4%
Market Leaders free CF to enterprise value decile 10	44.9%	40.0%	39.7%	38.3%	33.4%
Market Leaders ROA decile 10	48.9%	34.0%	36.4%	37.4%	31.2%
Market Leaders yoy sales growth decile 10	45.7%	33.4%	32.1%	26.7%	22.8%
Market Leaders working capital decile 1	41.8%	41.2%	41.0%	38.8%	37.5%
Market Leaders net margin decile 10	47.4%	42.5%	40.4%	37.4%	44.1%
Market Leaders free cash flow to price decile 10	42.6%	34.0%	33.0%	27.2%	28.3%
Market Leaders EPS change (%) decile 1	40.3%	32.4%	27.9%	22.5%	21.1%
Market Leaders book/price decile 10	43.4%	38.4%	34.9%	35.2%	20.8%
Market Leaders yoy net operating CF PS growth decile 10	39.5%	29.8%	22.6%	24.9%	19.4%
Market Leaders debt change (%) decile 1	38.4%	30.0%	22.2%	11.8%	1.7%
Market Leaders operating margin decile 10	42.2%	37.6%	25.2%	26.5%	15.3%
Market Leaders dividend yield (%) decile 10	39.3%	25.8%	22.4%	18.5%	22.5%
Market Leaders EBITDA/EV decile 10	41.8%	32.0%	27.7%	26.9%	20.3%
Market Leaders EPS change (%) decile 10	34.0%	24.7%	16.5%	10.2%	3.4%
Market Leaders earnings/price decile 10	40.7%	31.8%	28.1%	14.7%	8.7%
Market Leaders Composite Value 1 decile 10 (low)	39.0%	33.4%	32.1%	25.2%	9.7%
Market Leaders NOA change (%) decile 1	35.5%	25.6%	16.1%	8.2%	1.7%
Market Leaders sales to price decile 10	40.9%	37.8%	30.9%	28.3%	9.9%
Market Leaders sales to enterprise value decile 10	36.5%	33.8%	34.7%	33.6%	24.0%
Market Leaders return 12 mo. decile 10	33.2%	20.9%	13.1%	5.3%	1.5%
Market Leaders return 6 mo. decile 10	33.6%	13.3%	6.8%	1.3%	0.0%
Market Leaders Composite Value 2 decile 10 (low)	34.9%	32.2%	20.3%	11.6%	5.8%
Market Leaders TATA decile 1	26.5%	8.9%	1.1%	0.0%	0.0%
Market Leaders net operating cash flow to price decile 10	34.9%	28.2%	17.8%	14.3%	1.9%
Market Leaders Composite Value 3 decile 10 (low)	34.4%	29.0%	20.3%	10.0%	4.8%
Market Leaders shareholder yield (%) decile 10	21.9%	13.1%	3.2%	0.2%	0.0%
Market Leaders buyback yield (%) decile 10	23.2%	14.5%	4.4%	0.9%	0.0%
US 30-day T-bill USD	32.4%	23.5%	16.7%	12.5%	10.7%

You also see several value strategies, such as buying the 25 Market Leaders with the highest shareholder yield near the top of the list. That strategy earned 14.94 percent per year with a Sharpe ratio of .58.

BASE RATES

When we examine the strategies' underlying base rates, we see that they rank similarly to the strategies' compound returns. The strategies with the best average annual compound returns have the highest long-term base rates, and those with the lowest average annual compound returns have the worst. The top-ten performing strategies all had ten-year base rates of 96 percent or better, with seven strategies beating the Market Leaders universe over all ten-year periods. Of the ten worst-performing strategies, only two managed double-digit ten-year base rates, and four *never* beat the Market Leaders universe in any rolling ten-year period. As we saw with the Large and All Stocks universes, over time the underlying base rate gets stronger with the winning strategies and weaker with the losing ones.

Some of the strategies that beat the Market Leaders universe over the 44-year course of this study were marked by erratic returns. For example, buying the decile of stocks from the Market Leaders universe with the best year-over-year growth in sales compounded at 11.48 percent per year, yet earned much of that in the three years ending March 2000, when it compounded at 41.76 percent per year. This strategy's erratic behavior and tendency toward huge, concentrated run-ups can be seen when looking at its ten-year base rate—despite its good overall returns, it beat the Market Leaders universe in just 42 percent of all rolling ten-year periods. This illustrates why you must look at not just *overall* returns, but the long-term consistency of those returns as well.

WORST-CASE SCENARIOS

Consistent with what we see with base rates, we find that the strategies with the worst overall performance and consistency also delivered the *worst* declines to investors. The stocks with the worst asset turnover, cash flow to debt, and return on assets all had peak-to-trough declines exceeding 70 percent. Some of the better performing strategies, such as buying the Market Leaders with the best EBITDA/EV; highest sales / enterprise value, and highest buyback yields all had better worst-case scenarios than the Market Leaders universe. Table 22.2 shows all maximum declines for all of the Market Leaders strategies.

IMPLICATIONS

With the Market Leaders universe we see exactly the same thing we see with the broader All and Large Stocks universes—focusing on the most expensive popular stocks delivers the worst overall returns, while concentrating on the cheapest stocks delivers the best returns. In addition, the strategies that provided the best overall compound returns also did so with the highest degree of consistency.

23 CHAPTER

DISSECTING THE SMALL STOCKS UNIVERSE: THE RATIOS THAT ADD THE MOST VALUE

The degree of one's emotions varies inversely with one's knowledge of the facts—the less you know, the hotter you get.

—Bertrand Russell

Let's now turn our attention to the Small Stocks universe and examine it in detail, much as we did the Market Leaders universe. You'll recall from Chapter Five that the smallest capitalization stocks are often almost impossible to buy because of their lack of liquidity. The smallest stocks in the CRSP and Compustat datasets provided the best overall returns mainly because their prices were essentially a mirage.

For this reason, we define our Small Stocks universe as any company within the CRSP or Compustat universes with a market capitalization greater than an inflation-adjusted $200 million but *less* than the database average. Unlike Market Leaders, whose constraints lead us to just a handful of stocks, the Small Stocks universe is much larger. As of December 31, 2009, there were 2,355 stocks in the Small Stocks universe, with a weighted market capitalization of $1.66 billion and a median market capitalization of $871 million. To put that in perspective, as of June 2010, the median market capitalization of the Russell 2000 index was $1.2 billion, making the weighted market capitalization of our Small Stocks universe roughly $460 million more than that of the Russell 2000.

Table 23.1 will refresh your memory on how the Small Stocks universe compares with the All Stocks and Large Stocks universes between 1926 and 2009. Table 23.2 shows the results from 1963–2009, similar to the strategies we review here. Remember that the All Stocks universe includes *every* company in the CRSP and Compustat datasets with market capitalizations exceeding an inflation-adjusted $200 million. Thus All Stocks include many large companies that Small Stocks explicitly excludes. Because both are equal-weighted indexes, their returns are closer than you might expect, with the far more numerous small-cap stocks in the All Stocks universe driving much of its performance. Between December 31, 1926, and December 31, 2009, the Small Stocks universe beat the All Stocks universe by just 36 basis points. Because they each had a relatively high standard deviation of return, the Sharpe ratio for both was .25. Yet the base rates for the Small Stocks universe versus All Stocks were all positive, with Small Stocks beating the All Stocks universe in 61 percent of all rolling five-year periods and in 71 percent of all rolling ten-year periods. When we compare Small Stocks to Large Stocks over the same period, we see Small Stocks' outperformance increasing to 1.13 percent. Figure 23.1 shows the rolling five-year average annual compound excess (deficient) return for Small Stocks minus the return for the All Stocks universe, whereas Figure 23.2 show the excess return over Large Stocks.

T A B L E   23.1

Summary Annual Return and Risk Results Data: Small Stocks, All Stocks, and Large Stocks, January 1, 1927, to December 31, 2009

	Small Stocks	All Stocks	Large Stocks
Arithmetic average	13.77%	13.06%	11.75%
Geometric average	10.82%	10.46%	9.69%
Median return	19.28%	18.54%	16.75%
Standard deviation	23.09%	21.67%	19.35%
Upside deviation	16.05%	14.78%	13.10%
Downside deviation	16.89%	16.03%	14.40%
Tracking error	0.00	2.22	6.91
Number of positive periods	605	606	609
Number of negative periods	391	390	387
Maximum peak-to-trough decline	−86.12%	−85.45%	−84.33%
Beta	1.00	0.94	0.81
T-statistic (m = 0)	5.12	5.19	5.25
Sharpe ratio (Rf = 5%)	0.25	0.25	0.24
Sortino ratio (MAR = 10%)	0.05	0.03	−0.02
$10,000 becomes	$50,631,666	$38,542,780	$21,617,372
Minimum 1-year return	−66.91%	−66.72%	−66.63%
Maximum 1-year return	233.48%	201.69%	159.52%
Minimum 3-year return	−47.28%	−45.99%	−43.53%
Maximum 3-year return	54.35%	51.03%	45.64%
Minimum 5-year return	−24.56%	−23.07%	−20.15%
Maximum 5-year return	44.18%	41.17%	36.26%
Minimum 7-year return	−7.64%	−7.43%	−6.95%
Maximum 7-year return	27.35%	23.77%	22.83%

(continued on next page)

T A B L E   23.1

Summary Annual Return and Risk Results Data: Small Stocks, All Stocks, and Large Stocks, January 1, 1927, to December 31, 2009 *(Continued)*

	Small Stocks	All Stocks	Large Stocks
Minimum 10-year return	−5.19%	−5.31%	−5.70%
Maximum 10-year return	24.47%	22.05%	19.57%
Minimum expected return*	−32.41%	−30.28%	−26.96%
Maximum expected return†	59.96%	56.39%	50.46%

* Minimum expected return is arithmetic return minus 2 times the standard deviation.
† Maximum expected return is arithmetic return plus 2 times the standard deviation.

T A B L E   23.2

Summary Annual Return and Risk Results Data: Small Stocks, All Stocks, and Large Stocks, January 1, 1964, to December 31, 2009

	Small Stocks	All Stocks	Large Stocks
Arithmetic average	13.94%	13.26%	11.72%
Geometric average	11.60%	11.22%	10.20%
Median return	19.28%	17.16%	17.20%
Standard deviation	20.31%	18.99%	16.50%
Upside deviation	11.87%	10.98%	9.70%
Downside deviation	14.83%	13.90%	11.85%
Tracking error	0.00	2.21	7.56
Number of positive periods	329	329	332
Number of negative periods	223	223	220
Maximum peak-to-trough decline	−58.48%	−55.54%	−53.77%
Beta	1.00	0.93	0.76
T-statistic (m = 0)	4.38	4.47	4.58
Sharpe ratio (Rf = 5%)	0.32	0.33	0.32
Sortino ratio (MAR = 10%)	0.11	0.09	0.02
$10,000 becomes	$1,555,109	$1,329,513	$872,861
Minimum 1-year return	−46.38%	−46.49%	−46.91%
Maximum 1-year return	93.08%	84.19%	68.96%
Minimum 3-year return	−19.53%	−18.68%	−15.89%
Maximum 3-year return	34.00%	31.49%	33.12%
Minimum 5-year return	−11.75%	−9.91%	−5.82%
Maximum 5-year return	31.37%	27.66%	28.95%
Minimum 7-year return	−7.64%	−6.32%	−4.15%
Maximum 7-year return	27.35%	23.77%	22.83%
Minimum 10-year return	1.08%	1.01%	−0.15%
Maximum 10-year return	24.47%	22.05%	19.57%
Minimum expected return*	−26.69%	−24.73%	−21.28%
Maximum expected return†	54.57%	51.24%	44.72%

* Minimum expected return is arithmetic return minus 2 times the standard deviation.
† Maximum expected return is arithmetic return plus 2 times the standard deviation.

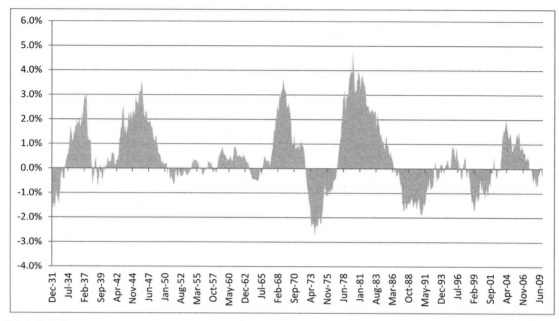

FIGURE 23.1

Five-year average annual compound excess (deficient) return Small Stocks minus All Stocks, January 1, 1927, to December 31, 2009

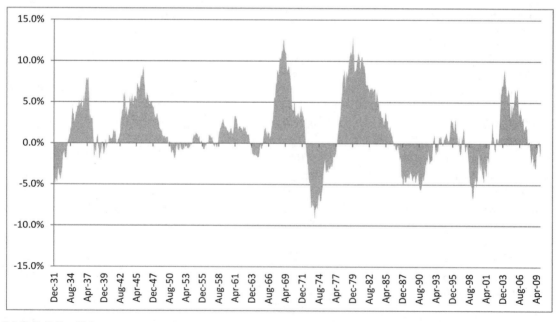

FIGURE 23.2

Five-year average annual compound excess (deficient) return Small Stocks minus Large Stocks, January 1, 1927, to December 31, 2009

Table 23.2 compares the universes' performance for the Compustat dataset, which covers the 1963 to 2009 time period. Here we see that Small Stocks beats All Stocks by just 38 basis points, but actually had a lower Sharpe ratio, since Small Stocks were more volatile than All Stocks. Over the same 46-year period, Small Stocks beat the Large Stocks universe by 1.40 percent. And while the Small Stocks universe beat the All Stocks universe on an absolute basis, its base rates were worse than for those from the longer-term CRSP data, beating All Stocks in 53 percent of all rolling five- and in 55 percent of all rolling ten-year periods. Nevertheless, as we are about to see, if you are searching for strategies that deliver the highest absolute total returns, the Small Stocks universe is a good place to start.

MONTHLY DATA REVIEWED; SUMMARY DATA ACCESSED

The start date that allows a full test of all Small Stocks strategies is August 31, 1965—the nearly 44 years between August 31, 1965, and December 31, 2009.

Table 23.3 shows the returns for all Small Stocks strategies. I must offer a disclaimer here—the five best-performing strategies do not actually come from our Small Stocks universe, but from a universe of microcap stocks that I created to see what types of returns individual investors might achieve investing in the tiniest stocks. We've already discussed several of these strategies in Chapter Twenty-One, so you can refer back to the broader analysis in that chapter.

TABLE 23.3

Summary Results for Strategies Benchmarked against the Returns of Small Stocks (Sep–65 to Dec–09); Strategies Sorted by Compound Return

Strategy	Geometric mean	Standard deviation (%)	Excess returns	Sharpe ratio	Tracking error	Largest drawdown	Beta
Microcap BP top 3 deciles, 3 and 6 mo.>0, top 25 by 12m mom	22.33%	20.38%	10.97%	0.85	9.73	−53.89%	0.88
Microcap PSR<1, pos 3 and 6 mo. ret top 10 12 mo. ret	22.29%	27.57%	10.93%	0.63	15.14	−57.64%	1.13
Microcap BP top 3 deciles, 3 and 6 mo.>median top 25 by 12m mom	21.78%	20.01%	10.42%	0.84	10.05	−55.64%	0.85
Microcap BP top 3 deciles, 3 and 6 mo.>0, top 50 by 12m mom	21.43%	19.17%	10.07%	0.86	8.86	−55.26%	0.84
Microcap PSR<1 top 25 12 mo. ret	20.33%	27.14%	8.97%	0.56	15.45	−59.22%	1.09
Small Stocks Value Comp 3, decile 1	19.37%	18.92%	8.01%	0.76	7.95	−59.68%	0.85
Small Stocks Value Comp 2, decile 1	19.03%	18.14%	7.66%	0.77	8.29	−60.05%	0.81
Small Stocks EBITDA/EV decile 1	18.96%	18.70%	7.60%	0.75	6.67	−55.94%	0.86
Small Stocks Value Comp 1, decile 1	18.85%	19.37%	7.49%	0.72	7.86	−60.23%	0.87
Small Stocks, PB in top 3 deciles, 3 and 6 mo. mom>median, top 25 by SY	18.84%	16.35%	7.48%	0.85	9.66	−49.20%	0.70
Small Stocks psr<1 3 and 6 mo.>0, top 50, 12 mo. ret	18.80%	23.29%	7.44%	0.59	9.96	−56.62%	1.02

(continued on next page)

T A B L E   23.3

Summary Results for Strategies Benchmarked against the Returns of Small Stocks (Sep–65 to Dec–09); Strategies Sorted by Compound Return *(Continued)*

Strategy	Geometric mean	Standard deviation (%)	Excess returns	Sharpe ratio	Tracking error	Largest drawdown	Beta
Small Stocks>med by SY, 6 mo., top 25 BP	18.49%	18.70%	7.13%	0.72	9.29	−59.17%	0.81
Small Stocks>med by BP, 6 mo., top 25 BBY	18.44%	17.92%	7.07%	0.75	8.66	−50.98%	0.79
Small Stocks, 3 and 6 mo.>med, top 25 SY	18.37%	16.72%	7.00%	0.80	8.39	−52.57%	0.75
Small Stocks, PB in top 3 deciles, 3 and 6 mo. mom>median, top 25 by 12m mom	18.34%	19.87%	6.97%	0.67	8.86	−59.85%	0.87
Small Stocks, PB in top 3 deciles, 3 and 6 mo. mom>0, top 25 by 12m mom	18.33%	19.79%	6.97%	0.67	8.84	−59.65%	0.87
Small Stocks, PB in top 3 deciles, 3 and 6 mo. mom>0, top 25 by SY	18.28%	16.09%	6.92%	0.83	9.82	−52.42%	0.69
Small Stocks, PB in top 3 deciles, 3 and 6 mo. mom>0, top 50 by 12m mom	18.16%	18.42%	6.80%	0.71	8.31	−56.04%	0.82
Small Stocks, PB in top 3 deciles, 3 and 6 mo. mom>median, top 50 by SY	18.15%	17.08%	6.79%	0.77	9.00	−49.60%	0.75
Small Stocks >med by 3 and 6 mo, top 25 BP	18.00%	19.84%	6.64%	0.66	8.48	−59.60%	0.88
Small Stocks, PB in top 3 deciles, 3 and 6 mo. mom>median, top 50 by 12m mom	17.97%	18.48%	6.61%	0.70	8.16	−54.41%	0.82
Small Stocks>med by 3 and 6 mo., top 50 BP	17.92%	18.75%	6.55%	0.69	7.63	−56.80%	0.85
Small Stocks, PB in top 3 deciles, 3 and 6 mo. mom>0, top 50 by SY	17.85%	16.36%	6.49%	0.79	9.20	−55.34%	0.72
Small Stocks>Med by SY, 6 mo., top 50 BP	17.84%	17.59%	6.48%	0.73	8.89	−56.52%	0.77
Small Stocks>med by BP, 6 mo., top 25 SY	17.64%	15.77%	6.28%	0.80	9.69	−50.87%	0.68
Small Stocks free CF to enterprise value decile 1	17.54%	20.60%	6.17%	0.61	6.67	−59.25%	0.95
Small Stocks earnings/price decile 1	17.53%	19.58%	6.17%	0.64	7.56	−56.31%	0.88
Small Stocks>med by BP, BBY, 3 mo., top 25 6 mo.	17.47%	20.09%	6.10%	0.62	7.75	−59.70%	0.91
Small Stocks>med by BP, BBY, top 25 6 mo.	17.42%	20.49%	6.05%	0.61	7.83	−61.12%	0.92
Small Stocks net operating cash flow to price decile 1	17.39%	20.53%	6.03%	0.60	7.99	−65.23%	0.92
Small Stocks>med by BP, 6 mo., top 50 BBY	17.30%	17.24%	5.94%	0.71	8.24	−49.81%	0.77
Small Stocks>med by BP, SY, top 25 6 mo.	17.26%	19.40%	5.90%	0.63	7.72	−59.63%	0.87

(continued on next page)

TABLE 23.3

Summary Results for Strategies Benchmarked against the Returns of Small Stocks (Sep–65 to Dec–09); Strategies Sorted by Compound Return *(Continued)*

Strategy	Geometric mean	Standard deviation (%)	Excess returns	Sharpe ratio	Tracking error	Largest drawdown	Beta
Small Stocks, 3 and 6 mo.>med, top 50 SY	17.26%	15.94%	5.90%	0.77	7.97	−50.21%	0.72
Small Stocks>med by BP, BBY, 3 mo., top 50 6 mo.	17.24%	18.54%	5.87%	0.66	7.19	−56.03%	0.84
Small Stocks sales to enterprise value decile 1	17.13%	20.02%	5.77%	0.61	7.00	−64.82%	0.91
Small Stocks > med by BP, BBY, top 50 6 mo.	17.05%	18.91%	5.68%	0.64	7.19	−56.68%	0.86
Small Stocks >med by BP, 6 mo., top 50 SY	16.85%	15.48%	5.49%	0.77	9.51	−48.74%	0.68
Small Stocks free cash flow to price decile 1	16.77%	20.92%	5.41%	0.56	7.61	−63.76%	0.95
Small Stocks>med by BP, SY, top 50 6 mo.	16.68%	17.96%	5.31%	0.65	7.49	−55.06%	0.81
Small Stocks>med by BP, 3 and 6 mo., top 25 12 mo.	15.76%	21.47%	4.39%	0.50	8.68	−65.51%	0.95
Small Stocks>med by BP, 3 and 6 mo., top 50 12 mo.	15.62%	19.60%	4.26%	0.54	7.70	−61.91%	0.88
Small Stocks buyback yield-decile 1	15.55%	18.17%	4.19%	0.58	6.33	−54.20%	0.84
Small Stocks shareholder yield-decile 1	15.45%	15.96%	4.09%	0.65	8.20	−55.73%	0.72
Small Stocks>med by SY, 3 and 6 mo., top 50 12 mo.	14.95%	21.24%	3.58%	0.47	7.83	−58.10%	0.96
Small Stocks sales to price decile 1	14.84%	22.46%	3.48%	0.44	8.79	−70.68%	1.00
Small Stocks 3 and 6 month return positive, ROE>avg 50 best 12 mo. ret	14.66%	29.34%	3.30%	0.33	15.31	−74.82%	1.24
Small Stocks accruals to price decile 10	14.47%	22.86%	3.10%	0.41	7.93	−66.72%	1.04
Small Stocks 6-month momentum-decile 1	14.38%	26.32%	3.01%	0.36	11.03	−63.10%	1.17
Small Stocks>med by SY, 3 and 6 mo., top 25 12 mo.	14.30%	23.54%	2.94%	0.40	9.92	−63.04%	1.04
Small Stocks>med by BBY, 3 mo., top 50 12 mo.	14.28%	24.14%	2.92%	0.38	9.42	−58.74%	1.08
Small Stocks book to price decile 1	14.26%	22.11%	2.90%	0.42	8.49	−69.88%	0.99
Small Stocks 60-mo. mom. decile 10	14.12%	24.83%	2.76%	0.37	9.51	−69.84%	1.12
Small Stocks dividend yield decile 1	13.83%	14.83%	2.47%	0.60	11.50	−62.48%	0.60
Small Stocks asset turnover decile 1	13.70%	21.31%	2.34%	0.41	5.93	−64.74%	0.99
Small Stocks>med by BBY, 3 mo. top 25 12 mo.	13.67%	26.48%	2.31%	0.33	12.09	−63.25%	1.15
Small Stocks cash flow to debt (%) decile 1	13.36%	20.72%	2.00%	0.40	5.50	−54.47%	0.97
Small Stocks ROA decile 1	13.10%	22.08%	1.74%	0.37	5.79	−61.96%	1.03
Small Stocks ROE decile 1	13.08%	22.87%	1.72%	0.35	6.51	−65.72%	1.07
Small Stocks EPS change (%) decile 1	12.86%	23.35%	1.50%	0.34	6.88	−64.25%	1.09
Small Stocks TATA decile 10	12.65%	24.78%	1.29%	0.31	8.55	−70.06%	1.14

(continued on next page)

T A B L E   23.3

Summary Results for Strategies Benchmarked against the Returns of Small Stocks (Sep–65 to Dec–09); Strategies Sorted by Compound Return *(Continued)*

Strategy	Geometric mean	Standard deviation (%)	Excess returns	Sharpe ratio	Tracking error	Largest drawdown	Beta
Small Stocks 12-mo. mom decile 1	12.14%	26.95%	0.78%	0.27	11.67	−67.06%	1.20
Small Stocks operating margin decile 1	11.81%	16.07%	0.45%	0.42	8.78	−53.55%	0.71
Small Stocks net margin decile 1	11.70%	17.63%	0.34%	0.38	7.06	−52.87%	0.81
Small Stocks depr exp to cap exp decile 1	11.69%	24.23%	0.33%	0.28	8.72	−69.57%	1.10
Small Stocks	11.36%	20.60%	N/A	0.31	N/A	−58.48%	N/A
Small Stocks debt change (%) decile 10	11.03%	23.89%	−0.33%	0.25	7.52	−67.10%	1.11
Small Stocks NOA change (%) decile 10	10.83%	25.57%	−0.54%	0.23	10.03	−75.46%	1.15
Small Stocks 60-mo. mom decile 1	8.78%	24.09%	−2.59%	0.16	8.19	−68.08%	1.11
Small Stocks accruals to price decile 1	8.64%	23.17%	−2.72%	0.16	6.08	−64.22%	1.09
Small Stocks book to price-decile 10	8.12%	26.81%	−3.24%	0.12	10.66	−74.79%	1.21
Small Stocks asset turnover decile 10	7.83%	17.68%	−3.54%	0.16	8.57	−62.16%	0.78
Small Stocks EPS change (%) decile 10	6.93%	26.17%	−4.44%	0.07	9.57	−72.16%	1.20
Small Stocks free CF to enterprise value decile 10	6.39%	26.05%	−4.98%	0.05	10.27	−73.23%	1.18
Small Stocks free cash flow to price decile 10	5.36%	25.22%	−6.00%	0.01	9.24	−72.60%	1.15
Small Stocks debt change (%) decile 1	5.25%	23.86%	−6.11%	0.01	6.38	−75.29%	1.12
Small Stocks 12-mo. mom decile 10	5.20%	27.41%	−6.16%	0.01	11.34	−79.12%	1.23
Small Stocks buyback yield decile 10	5.10%	23.37%	−6.27%	0.00	4.97	−71.57%	1.11
Small Stocks shareholder yield-decile 10	4.88%	24.17%	−6.48%	0.00	5.60	−74.59%	1.15
Small Stocks earnings/price decile 10	4.78%	29.59%	−6.58%	−0.01	13.76	−82.67%	1.31
Small Stocks TATA decile 1	3.47%	26.62%	−7.89%	−0.06	9.13	−81.88%	1.24
Small Stocks EBITDA/EV decile 10	3.28%	28.75%	−8.09%	−0.06	14.21	−87.57%	1.24
Small Stocks depr exp to cap exp decile 10	3.27%	24.38%	−8.10%	−0.07	7.93	−72.64%	1.13
Small Stocks ROE decile 10	2.66%	30.11%	−8.70%	−0.08	14.66	−91.45%	1.32
Small Stocks 6-mo, mom decile 10	2.60%	27.07%	−8.77%	−0.09	10.20	−80.22%	1.24
Small Stocks sales to enterprise value decile 10	2.52%	25.98%	−8.84%	−0.10	12.13	−91.71%	1.12
Small Stocks net operating cash flow to price decile 10	2.39%	28.72%	−8.97%	−0.09	13.22	−85.02%	1.27
Small Stocks cash flow to debt (%) decile 10	2.16%	29.59%	−9.20%	−0.10	14.44	−87.81%	1.29
Small Stocks NOA change (%) decile 1	1.84%	26.83%	−9.52%	−0.12	9.65	−85.63%	1.24
Small Stocks ROA decile 10	1.11%	29.56%	−10.26%	−0.13	15.07	−93.32%	1.26
Small Stocks operating margin decile 10	0.90%	29.92%	−10.46%	−0.14	15.36	−93.74%	1.28
Small Stocks net margin decile 10	0.81%	30.39%	−10.55%	−0.14	15.58	−94.14%	1.30
Small Stocks sales to price decile 10	0.16%	27.71%	−11.20%	−0.17	13.99	−93.67%	1.17
Small Stocks Value Comp 1 decile 10	−0.80%	29.92%	−12.16%	−0.19	15.39	−94.37%	1.28
Small Stocks Value Comp 2 decile 10	−0.92%	30.35%	−12.29%	−0.20	15.42	−94.46%	1.31
Small Stocks Value Comp 3 decile 10	−1.35%	30.18%	−12.71%	−0.21	15.25	−94.72%	1.30

T A B L E   23.4

Summary Base Rate Information for all Rolling One-, Three-, Five-, Seven-, and Ten-Year Periods for Strategies Benchmarked against the Returns of Small Stocks (Sep–65 to Dec–09); Strategies Sorted by Compound Return

Strategy	Percent of Time				
	1-Year	3-Year	5-Year	7-Year	10-Year
Microcap BP top 3 deciles, 3 and 6 mo.>0, top 25 by 12m mom	78.9%	90.3%	98.9%	100.0%	100.0%
Microcap PSR<1, pos 3 and 6 mo. ret top 10 12 mo. ret	69.3%	88.9%	98.1%	99.1%	100.0%
Microcap BP top 3 deciles, 3 and 6 mo.> median top 25 by 12m mom	77.2%	90.1%	99.2%	100.0%	100.0%
Microcap BP top 3 deciles, 3 and 6 mo.>0, top 50 by 12m mom	82.3%	93.4%	100.0%	100.0%	100.0%
Microcap PSR<1 top 25 12 mo. ret	72.6%	85.1%	95.8%	99.6%	99.8%
Small Stocks Value Comp 3, decile 1	83.3%	94.2%	99.4%	100.0%	100.0%
Small Stocks Value Comp 2, decile 1	80.6%	93.4%	99.4%	99.8%	100.0%
Small Stocks EBITDA/EV decile 1	82.0%	95.2%	100.0%	100.0%	100.0%
Small Stocks Value Comp 1,decile 1	80.8%	92.6%	99.4%	100.0%	100.0%
Small Stocks, PB in top 3 deciles, 3 and 6 mo. mom>median, top 25 by SY	75.0%	91.3%	97.5%	98.7%	100.0%
Small Stocks psr<1 pos 3 and 6 mo. ret top 50, 12 mo. ret	74.1%	89.1%	97.5%	98.9%	100.0%
Small Stocks>med by SY, 6 mo., top 25 BP	74.5%	89.9%	98.9%	98.4%	100.0%
Small Stocks>med by BP, 6 mo., top 25 BBY	77.9%	95.2%	99.6%	100.0%	100.0%
Small Stocks, 3 and 6 mo.>med, top 25 SY	74.9%	98.4%	100.0%	100.0%	100.0%
Small Stocks, PB in top 3 deciles, 3 and 6 mo. mom>median, top 25 by 12m mom	77.0%	93.8%	100.0%	99.6%	100.0%
Small Stocks, PB in top 3 deciles, 3 and 6 mo. mom>0, top 25 by 12m mom	77.2%	91.5%	99.6%	99.6%	100.0%
Small Stocks, PB in top 3 deciles, 3 and 6 mo. mom>0, top 25 by SY	73.7%	91.3%	96.0%	98.4%	100.0%
Small Stocks, PB in top 3 deciles, 3 and 6 mo. mom>0, top 50 by 12m mom	78.5%	94.4%	99.6%	99.6%	100.0%
Small Stocks, PB in top 3 deciles, 3 and 6 mo. mom>median, top 50 by SY	75.0%	93.8%	98.7%	98.4%	100.0%
Small Stocks >med by 3 and 6 mo, top 25 BP	75.8%	88.3%	99.6%	99.6%	100.0%
Small Stocks, PB in top 3 deciles, 3 and 6 mo. mom>median, top 50 by 12m mom	77.4%	93.8%	99.8%	99.6%	100.0%
Small Stocks>med by 3 and 6 mo., top 50 BP	75.0%	93.0%	99.4%	99.3%	100.0%
Small Stocks, PB in top 3 deciles, 3 and 6 mo. mom>0, top 50 by SY	74.1%	89.5%	95.8%	99.3%	100.0%
Small Stocks>med by SY, 6 mo., top 50 BP	72.4%	90.7%	97.3%	97.8%	100.0%
Small Stocks>med by BP, 6 mo., top 25 SY	70.2%	89.3%	95.6%	99.1%	100.0%
Small Stocks free CF to enterprise value decile 1	73.5%	81.9%	83.9%	87.1%	92.0%
Small Stocks earnings/price decile 1	76.0%	86.7%	91.1%	95.3%	99.5%

(continued on next page)

T A B L E   23.4

Summary Base Rate Information for all Rolling One-, Three-, Five-, Seven-, and Ten-Year Periods for Strategies Benchmarked against the Returns of Small Stocks (Sep–65 to Dec–09); Strategies Sorted by Compound Return
(Continued)

	Percent of Time				
Strategy	**1-Year**	**3-Year**	**5-Year**	**7-Year**	**10-Year**
Small Stocks>med by BP, BBY, 3 mo., top 25 6 mo.	74.9%	93.8%	99.2%	99.8%	100.0%
Small Stocks>med by BP, BBY, top 25 6 mo.	75.2%	93.4%	98.7%	99.3%	100.0%
Small Stocks net operating cash flow to price decile 1	72.4%	82.3%	90.3%	94.0%	100.0%
Small Stocks>med by BP, 6 mo., top 50 BBY	74.1%	92.0%	99.4%	99.6%	100.0%
Small Stocks>med by BP, SY, top 25 6 mo.	76.8%	95.4%	98.7%	99.6%	100.0%
Small Stocks, 3 and 6 mo.>med, top 50 SY	74.1%	97.2%	99.4%	100.0%	100.0%
Small Stocks>med by BP, BBY, 3 mo., top 50 6 mo.	74.7%	94.0%	100.0%	100.0%	100.0%
Small Stocks sales to enterprise value decile 1	73.1%	86.9%	97.0%	99.8%	100.0%
Small Stocks > med by BP, BBY, top 50 6 mo.	74.7%	95.2%	99.6%	100.0%	100.0%
Small Stocks >med by BP, 6 mo., top 50 SY	67.9%	86.9%	94.1%	98.7%	100.0%
Small Stocks free cash flow to price decile 1	68.3%	77.7%	86.0%	87.8%	90.6%
Small Stocks>med by BP, SY, top 50 6 mo.	71.2%	94.2%	100.0%	100.0%	100.0%
Small Stocks>med by BP, 3 and 6 mo., top 25 12 mo.	75.8%	87.1%	96.6%	98.0%	98.8%
Small Stocks>med by BP, 3 and 6 mo., top 50 12 mo.	73.9%	93.6%	98.3%	98.0%	100.0%
Small Stocks buyback yield decile 1	77.7%	96.0%	98.9%	99.8%	100.0%
Small Stocks shareholder yield decile 1	70.2%	88.1%	94.9%	98.4%	99.3%
Small Stocks>med by SY, 3 and 6 mo., top 50 12 mo.	77.9%	94.2%	96.0%	96.9%	97.8%
Small Stocks sales to price decile 1	68.1%	68.4%	75.9%	75.5%	79.4%
Small Stocks 3 and 6 mo. return positive, ROE>avg 50 best 12 mo. ret	64.5%	74.4%	82.9%	88.0%	94.2%
Small Stocks accruals to price decile 10	61.2%	69.0%	67.7%	70.2%	68.0%
Small Stocks 6-mo. mom. decile 1	61.4%	72.6%	85.6%	91.1%	97.6%
Small Stocks>med by SY, 3 and 6 mo., top 25 12 mo.	72.2%	84.9%	91.8%	92.4%	97.1%
Small Stocks>med by BBY, 3 mo., top 50 12 mo.	69.1%	81.7%	87.3%	93.5%	98.3%
Small Stocks book to price decile 1	61.0%	68.6%	75.9%	90.0%	97.6%
Small Stocks 60-mo. mom decile 10	61.6%	71.6%	75.7%	78.2%	72.9%
Small Stocks dividend yield decile 1	55.3%	69.2%	71.9%	73.1%	87.2%
Small Stocks asset turnover decile 1	60.1%	63.0%	68.7%	71.7%	77.7%
Small Stocks>med by BBY, 3 mo. top 25 12 mo.	63.3%	71.6%	77.6%	87.5%	95.6%
Small Stocks cash flow to debt (%) decile 1	53.7%	62.0%	70.0%	68.2%	62.7%
Small Stocks ROA decile 1	57.0%	64.8%	69.1%	65.5%	60.0%

(continued on next page)

T A B L E 23.4

Summary Base Rate Information for all Rolling One-, Three-, Five-, Seven-, and Ten-Year Periods for Strategies Benchmarked against the Returns of Small Stocks (Sep–65 to Dec–09); Strategies Sorted by Compound Return
(Continued)

	Percent of Time				
Strategy	**1-Year**	**3-Year**	**5-Year**	**7-Year**	**10-Year**
Small Stocks ROE decile 1	58.2%	62.2%	64.1%	59.7%	58.4%
Small Stocks EPS change (%) decile 1	58.5%	56.7%	63.0%	65.9%	66.6%
Small Stocks TATA decile 10	49.9%	56.1%	52.2%	53.9%	47.2%
Small Stocks 12-mo. mom. decile 1	58.0%	57.1%	66.6%	69.3%	74.1%
Small Stocks operating margin decile 1	46.6%	51.7%	58.1%	58.1%	58.1%
Small Stocks net margin decile 1	49.5%	59.6%	61.1%	58.8%	57.4%
Small Stocks depr exp to cap exp decile 1	49.1%	50.1%	45.9%	39.6%	37.3%
Small Stocks	0.0%	0.0%	0.0%	0.0%	0.0%
Small Stocks debt change (%) decile 10	47.6%	43.1%	37.4%	37.4%	38.3%
Small Stocks NOA change (%) decile 10	49.3%	50.1%	46.1%	44.1%	39.7%
Small Stocks 60-mo. mom decile 1	36.1%	32.8%	30.0%	24.3%	27.1%
Small Stocks accruals to price decile 1	39.5%	35.8%	33.4%	34.5%	23.0%
Small Stocks book to price-decile 10	41.7%	27.4%	21.4%	12.0%	5.6%
Small Stocks asset turnover decile 10	35.1%	33.0%	19.7%	17.8%	9.4%
Small Stocks EPS change (%) decile 10	32.1%	24.1%	17.8%	8.9%	4.8%
Small Stocks free CF to enterprise value decile 10	29.4%	23.3%	18.2%	12.5%	9.0%
Small Stocks free cash flow to price decile 10	27.3%	22.1%	16.1%	6.0%	1.7%
Small Stocks debt change (%) decile 1	22.5%	9.7%	2.1%	0.9%	0.0%
Small Stocks 12-mo. mom decile 10	20.9%	7.0%	3.4%	1.8%	0.0%
Small Stocks buyback yield decile 10	16.5%	3.4%	0.8%	0.0%	0.0%
Small Stocks shareholder yield decile 10	18.4%	7.0%	2.5%	0.0%	0.0%
Small Stocks earnings/price decile 10	29.4%	18.7%	10.1%	1.6%	0.2%
Small Stocks TATA decile 1	23.0%	8.5%	3.2%	1.3%	0.0%
Small Stocks EBITDA/EV decile 10	23.6%	12.3%	4.9%	4.9%	1.2%
Small Stocks depr exp to cap exp decile 10	29.6%	19.9%	13.1%	4.5%	0.0%
Small Stocks ROE decile 10	29.9%	26.0%	20.3%	17.6%	13.8%
Small Stocks 6-mo, mom decile 10	11.3%	3.0%	1.1%	1.3%	0.0%
Small Stocks sales to enterprise value decile 10	31.1%	18.3%	16.5%	10.7%	10.9%
Small Stocks net operating cash flow to price decile 10	23.8%	10.3%	2.1%	0.7%	0.0%
Small Stocks cash flow to debt (%) decile 10	26.7%	17.1%	10.4%	2.4%	0.0%
Small Stocks NOA change (%) decile 1	25.5%	12.7%	6.1%	2.7%	0.0%
Small Stocks ROA decile 10	23.8%	11.1%	6.3%	6.2%	3.6%
Small Stocks operating margin decile 10	26.3%	17.9%	17.1%	11.8%	7.3%
Small Stocks net margin decile 10	28.6%	20.3%	18.6%	12.0%	8.0%
Small Stocks sales to price decile 10	30.7%	20.9%	16.7%	11.8%	8.5%
Small Stocks Value Comp 1 decile 10	28.2%	14.9%	9.7%	4.9%	1.0%
Small Stocks Value Comp 2 decile 10	28.8%	13.5%	8.9%	4.2%	0.5%
Small Stocks Value Comp 3 decile 10	27.6%	13.5%	7.4%	3.8%	0.5%

From the Small Stocks universe, the best five strategies are buying the highest deciles of Value Composites One, Two, and Three, buying the decile of stocks with the highest EBITDA/EV, and finally the multifactor model that selects Small Stocks with price-to-book ratios in the lowest 30 percent that also have three- and six-month price appreciation higher than the median, and then buys the 25 stocks with the highest shareholder yield. Of those five strategies, the one with the best base rates—featured in Table 23.4—is buying the Small Stocks with the highest EBITDA/EV, which beat the Small Stocks universe in eight out of ten rolling one-year periods and in 100 percent of all rolling five- and ten-year periods. However, as we learned in Chapter Fifteen, even though the base rates are highest for this single value factor, you're probably better off with the multifactor value composites. They too have very high base rates and higher absolute average annual compound returns, as well as the benefit of betting on *all* the value factors and not just one. As you can see from Table 23.3, virtually all the multifactor strategies as well as all of the other single value factors do significantly better than the Small Stocks universe.

THE WORST STRATEGIES

We also find the usual suspects at the bottom of the list, but here again, we find a larger magnitude of difference—the three worst strategies actually *lost* money over the last 44 years. In addition, the 22 worst-performing strategies all returned *less* than T-bills over the same period. For the 44 years ending December 31, 2009, an investor in T-bills would have seen her investment compound at 5.64 percent per year, turning $10,000 into $113,721. All of the 22 worst-performing strategies did drastically worse than the no-risk T-bill investment. As you can see in the base rate table, they also were *very* consistent in their underperformance, with the bottom 26 strategies never beating the Small Stocks universe in more than 15 percent of all rolling ten-year period. Seven of the 26 *never* had a rolling ten-year period when they beat the Small Stocks universe.

The worst three strategies, buying stocks from Small Stocks with the worst scores on Value Composites One, Two, and Three all lost money over the 44 years, draining a $10,000 investment to $7,012, $6,623 and $5,468, respectively. Remember that all our returns are *nominal* and do not adjust for the effects of inflation—if we adjusted for inflation, the $10,000 invested in these three strategies would have an actual real value of $1,025, $969, and $800, respectively. The Small Stocks in decile 10 of Value Composites One, Two, and Three also have terrifying worst-case scenarios. All three have drawdowns exceeding 90 percent between February 2000 and 2009, and were essentially in complete freefall for most of the bull market years between the early 1980s and the 2000s, *losing* 80 percent during the biggest bull market since the 1950s. When investing in small-cap stocks, it appears that having the worst value composite scores can essentially wipe you out. This makes sense. Smaller companies tend to be single- or dual-line business models, and if the company is vastly overpriced, the graveyard is the most probable destination. Yet for those readers who might want to use these strategies to short stocks, keep in mind that they do have one-year periods when they soar in value—gains in excess of 200 percent are often seen in the data—generally during stock market bubbles.

In general, we see the same things happening in the Small Stocks universe that we did in the Market Leaders universe—cheap stocks do vastly better than expensive stocks, and multifactor relative strength models that marry value with growth end up at or near the top of the performance tables.

BASE RATES

All three of the value composites also had excellent base rates compared to the Small Stocks universe. Each beat the Small Stocks universe in 99 percent of all rolling five-year periods and in 100 percent of all rolling ten-year periods. The odds are clearly in favor of these strategies. Remember that our mantra is to focus not only on absolute performance, but also on the consistency of that performance. Great performance alone is not enough; if you want to invest in a strategy that you can actually stick with through all the market's gyrations, you must marry it to consistency. We should also expect that these strategies might not always generate 100 percent base rates. For example, when examining some of the strategies with the longer-term CRSP dataset, we find several factors that do not earn those 100 percent scores, that is, the five-year base rate for Small Stocks with the best buyback yield drops to 89 percent, and the ten-year base rate to 87 percent. While these are still very good numbers, they are not as stellar as the 1963–2009 data indicate. The same can be said for many of the other strategies. Look at the Small Stocks strategy with three- and six-month price appreciation greater than the median of the universe and then buying the 25 stocks with the highest shareholder yield. As Table 23.4 shows, between 1965 and 2009, the strategy's base rates were outstanding, beating the Small Stocks universe in 98 percent of all rolling three-year periods and in 100 percent of all rolling five- and ten-year periods. When we look at the longer-term base rates between 1927 and 2009, however, the three-year base rate falls from 98 percent to 93 percent; the five-year base rate falls from 100 percent to 95 percent, and the ten-year base rate falls from 100 percent to 99 percent. Keep this in mind for *all* the strategies that have 100 percent long-term base rates over the shorter 1965–2009 period. The base rates for the strategy over the longer-term data remain incredibly impressive, but we should exercise some restraint in our hopes when looking at shorter periods of time.

THE WORST BASE RATES

Ten of the Small Stocks strategies *never* beat the Small Stocks universe on a rolling ten-year basis. From a base rate perspective, the two worst strategies were buying the decile of stocks from Small Stocks with the lowest buyback yield and buying the decile of Small Stocks with the worst six-month price appreciation. Buying the decile of stocks with the worst buyback yield—essentially those small companies that issued a ton of new shares—beat the Small Stocks universe in just 3 percent of all rolling three-year periods; in under 1 percent of all rolling five-year periods; and in no rolling seven- or ten-year period. Buying the decile of stocks from Small Stocks with the worst six-month price appreciation was next. It managed to beat the Small Stocks universe in just 3 percent of all rolling three-year periods; 1 percent of all rolling five-year periods, and in no rolling ten-year periods. Remember that the worst decile by price appreciation *only* does well following severe bear markets, so it will come as no surprise that triple-digit returns were earned by this group in the one-year period following the bear markets of 2000–2003 and 2007–2008. As with all of the other universes, don't let these phenomenal one-year returns fool you—these stocks are toxic.

Want more proof? These are two Small Stocks strategies for which we have data going back to 1926, and when we include these additional data, we find very similar base rates. Here, the Small Stocks with the worst buyback yield beat the universe in just 26 of 937 rolling five-year periods—or 3 percent of all rolling five-year periods—and in *no* rolling ten-year periods. For the Small Stocks with the worst six-month price appreciation there were only 15 rolling five-year periods out of 937 when they beat Small Stocks, or just 2 percent of the time. And, like the data from 1963 forward, there are *no* rolling ten-year periods when they beat the Small Stocks universe since 1927.

Almost every strategy that underperformed the Small Stocks universe did so consistently, so you'll want to carefully review where any small-cap stock you are considering for purchase falls in the continuum. The worst-case offenders are the usual suspects—stocks with balance sheet shenanigans—such as decile 1 of Small Stocks by total accruals to total assets, decile 1 of NOA and debt change, and those with the worst price performance over the last 6 and 12 months. All these strategies fall to the bottom of the barrel—avoid them like the plague.

WORST-CASE SCENARIOS

Table 23.3 lists maximum declines for the various Small Stocks strategies. The first thing you notice is that almost all of the strategies had maximum declines exceeding 50 percent. If you want the upside that small-cap investing offers, you're almost certain to face some wild declines. As a group, small-cap stocks are inherently more volatile than stocks from Large Stocks and Market Leaders.

Virtually all these biggest drops occurred during the bear market of 2007–2008, and while it is unlikely that we will suffer through another of such magnitude any time soon, it is something that a small-cap investor must be prepared for. History shows that the best thing you could do is *buy more* as the decline is happening. Yet history also suggests that this is something precious few investors are actually able to do. The great investor Sir John Templeton used to set limit buy orders for stocks that he liked at levels well below prevailing prices. He knew that if and when the stocks hit those low prices, even *he* might be tempted to come up with new reasons why he should not buy them. Thus it is wise to remember that even one of the greatest investors of all time knew that his emotions could get in the way of smart investing during a severe bear market. My advice is to use only those strategies that have done significantly better than the Small Stocks universe consistently (those with the highest base rates) and limit your strategy selections to those that had maximum declines within 10 percent of those of the Small Stocks universe itself. That leaves you with the majority of the best-performing strategies and helps you avoid those that you would never be able to stick with should another severe bear market come our way. Forewarned is forearmed.

IMPLICATIONS

Over the past 44 years, the best-performing small-cap strategy performed nine times as well as the Small Stocks universe, and many of the commonly successful strategies like buying stocks with the lowest price-to-earnings, price-to-cashflow or price-to-sales ratios significantly enhanced the returns of a small capitalization strategy. The value composites proved to be excellent measures of the health of small-cap stocks, with those in decile 1 doing very well over the long term and those in decile 10 getting crushed. The best-performing strategies also perform consistently, with excellent base rates over all rolling five- and ten-year periods. For two of the best performing strategies—buying Small Stocks with the best buyback yield and buying Small Stocks with the best six-month price appreciation—we are able to further verify their outperformance by looking at the CRSP dataset between 1926 and 1963, where the Compustat dataset begins, thus adding 37 years of confirming data.

There is a red flag here, however. Even the best strategies suffered declines of 50 percent or more, a reality all small-cap investors must face. If you don't think you can stomach those drops, consider using the more tranquil Market Leaders or Large Stocks strategies. If you can take the roller coaster ride, however, small-cap strategies can play an important role in diversifying your portfolio while greatly enhancing overall performance.

Finally, think *very carefully* about volatility before using a more concentrated version of these small-cap strategies—concentration enhances both return *and* volatility, but it is the volatility that you should think about the most. Many an investor has been lured by performance, only to crack and throw in the towel when the strategy takes a dive. Always look at the worst-case scenario for *any* strategy before you take the leap.

24 CHAPTER

SECTOR ANALYSIS

All truths are easy to understand once they are discovered; the point is to discover them.
    —Galileo Galilei

Let's now look at how the factors we have examined thus far perform on the sector level. Because the scope of this chapter is admittedly ambitious—and could easily be a book in its own right—out of necessity we will have to simplify the discussion in order to cover all 10 economic sectors concisely and within this single chapter. Here, rather than review factor performance by decile, as we have done so far with All Stocks and Large Stocks, we review and summarize the results from the All Stocks universe by quintile (20 percent increments). (We use quintiles here because several of the factors have too few constituents to make decile analysis feasible; by looking at 20 percent chunks of data, we are more able to draw reasonable conclusions about the efficacy of each factor by sector.) We also must begin our analysis on December 31, 1967, since prior to that there is no adequate data for all 10 sectors. For each of the 10 sectors, we provide:

- The compound average annual return (geometric mean) for the best and worst quintile
- The standard deviation of return for the best quintile
- The Sharpe ratio for the best quintile
- The spread on the return of the best quintile minus the worst quintile
- The spread of the return of the best quintile minus the sector benchmark

- The worst drawdown for the best quintile
- The beta of the best quintile

We also feature the base rates—in table format—for the best and worst quintiles versus their relevant sector benchmark. We begin with the All Stocks universe and generate the returns for each sector by using the same composited methodology used elsewhere in this book, and all stocks within the sector are equal-weighted.

THE 10 ECONOMIC SECTORS IN 2009

As most investors know, the economy is broadly split into 10 individual economic sectors. They are:

1. **Consumer discretionary**. Currently composed of 430 stocks, this sector is made up of industries that offer products or services that are not necessities. Examples include luxury goods, high-end retailers, and travel industries such as hotels and resorts. Some companies in this category include Abercrombie & Fitch, Amazon.com, Bed Bath and Beyond, Ford Motor Company, Home Depot, InterContinental Hotels Group, Marriott International, McDonald's, and Starbucks.

2. **Consumer staples.** Currently composed of 141 stocks, this sector is made up of industries that offer the most common consumer products such as food, housewares, tobacco, and drugs. Some companies in this category include Anheuser-Busch, Campbell Soup Company, Coca-Cola, Dole Foods Company, General Mills, Kraft Foods, Philip Morris, Procter & Gamble, Walmart, and USANA Health Sciences.

3. **Energy.** Currently composed of 220 stocks, this sector is made up of energy industries. Some companies in this category include American Oil & Gas, Chevron, Exxon Mobil, Halliburton, Nordic American Tanker Shipping, Precision Drilling, Sunoco, TransAtlantic Petroleum, Valero Energy, and Williams Companies.

4. **Financials.** Currently composed of 408 stocks, this sector is made up of industries offering financial services to individuals and institutions. Some companies in this category include AFLAC, American Express, Bank of New York Mellon, Chubb, Citigroup, E*Trade, Goldman Sachs, Huntington Bancshares, JPMorgan Chase, MetLife, State Street, U.S. Bancorp, Wells Fargo, and Zions Bancorporation.

5. **Health care.** Currently composed of 323 stocks, this sector is made up of industries providing health-care products and services to individuals and institutions. Some companies in this category include Abbott Laboratories, Baxter International, Biogen, Bristol-Myers Squibb, Eli Lilly, GlaxoSmithKline, Humana, Lifepoint Hospitals, Medtronic, Merck, Owens & Minor, Pfizer, St. Jude Medical, UnitedHealth Group, WellPoint and Zoll Medical Group.

6. **Industrials.** Currently composed of 424 stocks, this sector is made up of industries engaged in manufacturing products. Some companies in this category include 3M,

American Woodmark Corp, Boeing, Caterpillar, Deere & Company, Delta Air Lines, Emerson Electric, Fastenal, GE, Goodrich, Honeywell International, Ingersoll-Rand, Lockheed Martin, Navistar, Precision CastParts, Rollins, Teledyne Technologies, UAL, Waste Management, and World Color Press.

7. **Information technology.** Currently composed of 501 stocks, this sector is made up of industries that create or sell information technology to individuals and corporations. Some companies in this category include Adobe Systems, Apple, BMC Software, Checkpoint Systems, Cisco Systems, CoreLogic, Dell, eBay, Google, Hewlett-Packard, Intel, IBM, Jabil Circuit, Lattice Semiconductor, McAfee, Microsoft, NETGEAR, Palm, QUALCOMM, Red Hat, Silicon Graphics, Symantec, VeriSign, Western Digital, and Yahoo!

8. **Materials.** Currently composed of 240 stocks, this sector is made up of industries involved in discovering, developing, or processing raw materials. Some companies in this category include AK Steel, Alcoa, Calgon Carbon, CGA Mining Ltd., Dow Chemical, Freeport-McMoRan Copper & Gold, Goldcorp, H.B. Fuller, International Paper, Monsanto, Newmont Mining, Potash, Rio Tinto PLC, Sherwin-Williams, Weyerhaeuser, and Yamana Gold.

9. **Telecommunication services.** Currently composed of 96 stocks, this sector is made up of industries that provide telecommunication services to individuals and corporations. Some companies in this category include AT&T, BCE, Cincinnati Bell, Global Crossing, Leap Wireless International, Level 3 Communications, Nippon Telegraph & Telephone, Qwest Communications International, Rogers Communications, Sprint Nextel, TELUS, U.S. Cellular, Verizon Communications, and Vonage Holdings.

10. **Utilities.** Currently composed of 114 stocks, this sector is made up of industries that provide electricity, natural gas, and water to individuals and corporations. Some companies in this category include Allegheny Energy, American Electric Power Company, American Water Works, Calpine, CMS Energy, Consolidated Edison, Dynergy, El Paso Electric, Exelon, Nicor, NSTAR, PG&E, Southern Companies, UGI Corp., Westar Energy, and Xcel Energy.

THE CONSUMER DISCRETIONARY SECTOR

Table 24.1 features the factor return summary for the consumer discretionary sector. The best performing factor in the sector is enterprise value/free cash flow, returning 13.89 percent per year, compared to the 9.60 percent per year earned by investing in the entire sector. As Table 24.2 shows, the base rates for the best quintile by EV/free cash flow are all positive, with the best quintile beating the sector in 96.6 percent of all rolling five-year periods and in 100 percent of all rolling ten-year periods. The spread between the best quintile and the worst is nearly 9 percent per year, and the base rates for the worst quintile of consumer discretionary stocks by EV/free cash flow, featured in Table 24.3, are horrible. The stocks in the quintile with the worst EV/free cash flow fail to beat the sector in *any* rolling five- or ten-year period.

T A B L E   24.1

Summary Results for Various Strategies Applied to the Consumer Discretionary Sector (Strategies Benchmarked against the Returns of All Stocks in the Sector) December 31, 1967–December 31, 2009 (Strategies Sorted by Compound Return of the Best Quintile)

Strategy	Geometric mean		Best quintile					
	Best quintile	Worst quintile	Standard deviation (%)	Sharpe ratio	Spread (Best-worst)	Spread (Best-benchmark)	Worst drawdown	Beta
EV/free Cash Flow	13.89%	4.92%	21.36%	0.42	8.97%	4.29%	−65.39%	0.95
Price/cash flow (free)	13.79%	4.33%	22.15%	0.40	9.46%	4.18%	−68.13%	0.98
Value Composite 3	13.73%	4.47%	21.17%	0.41	9.26%	4.12%	−69.11%	0.92
Value Composite 2	13.65%	4.62%	21.06%	0.41	9.03%	4.05%	−69.53%	0.92
6-mo. momentum	13.65%	2.95%	23.03%	0.38	10.70%	4.04%	−65.23%	1.00
Value Composite 1	13.50%	5.23%	21.76%	0.39	8.27%	3.90%	−70.10%	0.95
Buyback yield	13.41%	3.88%	20.14%	0.42	9.52%	3.80%	−64.78%	0.90
NOA change	13.32%	3.56%	21.72%	0.38	9.76%	3.72%	−70.81%	0.97
Shareholder yield	13.10%	4.79%	19.53%	0.41	8.31%	3.49%	−66.48%	0.86
EV/EBITDA	13.10%	3.83%	20.78%	0.39	9.27%	3.49%	−69.05%	0.91
EV/sales	13.03%	6.75%	22.89%	0.35	6.28%	3.43%	−76.07%	1.00
9-mo. momentum	12.98%	3.37%	23.32%	0.34	9.61%	3.37%	−64.22%	1.01
3-mo. momentum	12.84%	3.61%	22.85%	0.34	9.23%	3.23%	−67.55%	1.01
Price/cash flow	12.47%	2.80%	22.14%	0.34	9.67%	2.86%	−74.75%	0.97
12-mo. momentum	12.34%	4.37%	23.52%	0.31	7.98%	2.74%	−64.80%	1.01
Debt change	12.16%	5.70%	22.22%	0.32	6.45%	2.55%	−66.89%	1.00
Price/earnings	12.03%	4.63%	21.58%	0.33	7.40%	2.43%	−70.48%	0.95
Total assets to total accruals (TATA)	11.98%	4.38%	22.07%	0.32	7.60%	2.38%	−65.57%	0.99
Cash flow/debt	11.71%	3.59%	21.02%	0.32	8.11%	2.10%	−69.97%	0.93
Debt/capital	11.52%	6.43%	21.76%	0.30	5.09%	1.91%	−70.42%	0.97
Asset turnover	11.30%	8.85%	24.59%	0.26	2.45%	1.70%	−73.86%	1.08
ROA	11.30%	6.07%	22.09%	0.29	5.22%	1.69%	−72.38%	0.97
ROE	11.18%	6.70%	23.09%	0.27	4.48%	1.58%	−74.29%	1.02
Price/accruals	10.79%	7.25%	22.86%	0.25	3.54%	1.18%	−75.93%	1.01
1-mo. momentum	10.76%	5.76%	22.75%	0.25	4.99%	1.15%	−69.26%	1.02
Dividend yield	10.67%	7.04%	19.24%	0.29	3.64%	1.07%	−67.86%	0.84
EPS change	10.49%	6.12%	23.98%	0.23	4.37%	0.88%	−70.34%	1.06
Price/book	10.15%	9.02%	22.84%	0.23	1.13%	0.55%	−76.72%	0.99
Price/sales	10.13%	7.05%	24.26%	0.21	3.08%	0.53%	−79.93%	1.05
Sector benchmark	9.60%	N/A	21.97%	0.21	N/A	N/A	−68.53%	N/A
Market cap	8.82%	8.16%	23.81%	0.16	0.65%	−0.79%	−71.61%	1.06

T A B L E   24.2

Best Quintile: Summary Base Rate Information for All Rolling One-, Three-, Five-, Seven-, and Ten-Year Periods for the Consumer Discretionary Sector's Best Quintile (Strategies Benchmarked against the Returns of All Stocks in the Sector) December 31, 1967–December 31, 2009 (Strategies Sorted by Compound Return of the Best Quintile)

Strategy	Percent of time				
	1 year	3 years	5 years	7 years	10 years
EV/free Cash Flow	73.7%	89.6%	96.6%	100.0%	100.0%
Price/cash flow (free)	70.9%	88.9%	91.9%	94.5%	96.6%

(continued on next page)

T A B L E   24.2

Best Quintile: Summary Base Rate Information for All Rolling One-, Three-, Five-, Seven-, and Ten-Year Periods for the Consumer Discretionary Sector's Best Quintile (Strategies Benchmarked against the Returns of All Stocks in the Sector) December 31, 1967–December 31, 2009 (Strategies Sorted by Compound Return of the Best Quintile) *(Continued)*

Strategy	Percent of time				
	1 year	3 years	5 years	7 years	10 years
Value Composite 3	65.0%	85.1%	91.7%	98.1%	99.0%
Value Composite 2	64.6%	83.6%	91.0%	97.6%	98.3%
6-mo. momentum	76.7%	91.3%	95.7%	97.2%	99.5%
Value Composite 1	65.2%	84.7%	94.4%	98.1%	98.3%
Buyback yield	70.2%	84.7%	91.3%	98.1%	100.0%
NOA change	77.1%	89.8%	93.3%	95.0%	94.6%
Shareholder yield	64.4%	81.7%	90.8%	98.6%	99.3%
EV/EBITDA	61.7%	79.4%	86.8%	96.0%	99.5%
EV/sales	63.2%	77.2%	87.4%	90.5%	97.5%
9-mo. momentum	71.9%	87.4%	89.9%	93.8%	96.6%
3-mo. momentum	76.9%	93.0%	96.2%	98.6%	99.5%
Price/cash flow	63.0%	82.1%	91.0%	95.5%	99.3%
12-mo. momentum	70.0%	77.0%	87.7%	91.5%	94.1%
Debt change	71.1%	80.4%	88.3%	94.1%	93.8%
Price/earnings	58.5%	68.9%	74.2%	80.6%	82.3%
Total assets to total accruals (TATA)	73.1%	84.0%	88.1%	84.6%	83.5%
Cash flow/debt	61.7%	70.9%	77.6%	80.6%	82.0%
Debt/capital	59.7%	74.5%	85.9%	87.0%	86.9%
Asset turnover	55.3%	59.8%	62.1%	76.3%	78.3%
ROA	59.7%	53.4%	63.5%	66.8%	67.7%
ROE	59.7%	60.4%	54.5%	58.8%	55.7%
Price/accruals	57.9%	72.6%	79.8%	83.9%	89.9%
1-mo. momentum	61.1%	70.2%	81.2%	86.0%	87.4%
Dividend yield	53.2%	65.5%	54.0%	56.2%	64.5%
EPS change	56.7%	63.2%	67.0%	70.9%	71.9%
Price/book	47.8%	52.3%	59.2%	62.8%	60.3%
Price/sales	52.2%	55.3%	65.5%	76.1%	78.8%
Sector benchmark	0.0%	0.0%	0.0%	0.0%	0.0%
Market cap	37.4%	33.0%	39.0%	38.6%	32.5%

T A B L E   24.3

Worst Quintile: Summary Base Rate Information for All Rolling One-, Three-, Five-, Seven-, and Ten-Year Periods for the Consumer Discretionary Sector's Worst Quintile (Strategies Benchmarked against the Returns of All Stocks in the Sector) December 31, 1967–December 31, 2009 (Strategies Sorted by Compound Return of the Best Quintile)

Strategy	Percent of time				
	1 year	3 years	5 years	7 years	10 years
EV/free Cash Flow	18.6%	7.4%	0.0%	0.0%	0.0%
Price/cash flow (free)	17.6%	9.1%	0.0%	0.0%	0.0%
Value Composite 3	33.6%	23.2%	11.2%	2.4%	1.5%
Value Composite 2	34.4%	26.4%	11.2%	2.4%	1.5%

(continued on next page)

TABLE 24.3

Worst Quintile: Summary Base Rate Information for All Rolling One-, Three-, Five-, Seven-, and Ten-Year Periods for the Consumer Discretionary Sector's Worst Quintile (Strategies Benchmarked against the Returns of All Stocks in the Sector) December 31, 1967–December 31, 2009 (Strategies Sorted by Compound Return of the Best Quintile) *(Continued)*

Strategy	Percent of time				
	1 year	3 years	5 years	7 years	10 years
6-mo. momentum	10.1%	0.4%	0.0%	0.0%	0.0%
Value Composite 1	36.6%	27.7%	13.2%	3.8%	3.0%
Buyback yield	22.3%	16.8%	9.6%	0.0%	0.0%
NOA change	17.6%	7.2%	4.0%	0.5%	0.0%
Shareholder yield	28.1%	15.1%	8.1%	0.0%	0.0%
EV/EBITDA	29.1%	17.2%	6.5%	1.2%	1.2%
EV/sales	39.1%	33.8%	21.7%	13.7%	8.9%
9-mo. momentum	11.7%	0.2%	0.0%	0.0%	0.0%
3-mo. momentum	8.5%	0.0%	0.0%	0.0%	0.0%
Price/cash flow	22.1%	7.9%	2.5%	0.0%	0.0%
12-mo. momentum	14.4%	1.3%	0.0%	0.0%	0.0%
Debt change	26.9%	8.9%	2.7%	1.2%	0.0%
Price/earnings	31.2%	17.0%	7.0%	6.2%	4.9%
Total assets to total accruals (TATA)	17.8%	9.8%	3.1%	4.3%	4.2%
Cash flow/debt	26.5%	16.0%	14.1%	17.1%	14.0%
Debt/capital	35.6%	23.4%	13.2%	3.8%	3.0%
Asset turnover	49.2%	38.9%	43.7%	39.6%	40.9%
ROA	39.3%	38.9%	26.7%	28.4%	25.4%
ROE	36.6%	36.2%	25.1%	30.1%	26.8%
Price/accruals	38.5%	24.0%	23.3%	17.1%	14.5%
1-mo. momentum	9.9%	2.6%	0.4%	0.0%	0.0%
Dividend yield	42.7%	30.9%	24.7%	18.7%	14.0%
EPS change	32.8%	15.7%	6.3%	1.2%	0.5%
Price/book	43.7%	45.1%	42.2%	30.3%	29.1%
Price/sales	40.7%	33.0%	23.5%	9.2%	7.6%
Sector benchmark	0.0%	0.0%	0.0%	0.0%	0.0%
Market cap	44.3%	48.5%	40.4%	35.1%	35.0%

Both Value Composites Two and Three also perform well, as does buying the stocks from the sector with the best six-month price appreciation. Indeed, of all the factors, six-month price appreciation works very well on consumer discretionary stocks. We see later in this chapter that six-month price momentum actually *doesn't work* in several of the sectors, but for now, notice that not only does it really work well on an absolute basis; but it also has the highest base rate for all rolling three-year periods and the third highest base rate for all rolling one-year periods. It also serves as one of the clearest signals for the consumer discretionary sector—the quintile with the worst six-month price appreciation earns just 2.95 percent a year over the 42 years covered in this study. That's significantly worse than T-bills and should serve as a dramatic warning for anyone thinking about buying a stock from the consumer discretionary sector in the bottom quintile. I believe that six-month price appreciation works so well here because of the diversity of the industries included in the sector—companies as varied as automobiles, diversified consumer services, Internet and catalog retailing, media, and retailing. Being the least concentrated of the sectors probably makes it a very good candidate for price momentum.

The only factor that does *not* improve on the full sector return is market capitalization, where the best-performing quintile was made up of the smallest market-cap stocks, and the worst-performing quintile was made up of companies with the largest market caps. In both instances, neither managed to beat the performance of the broad sector.

THE DOWNSIDE

The downside to investing exclusively in the consumer discretionary sector is that all the strategies, as well as the sector itself, sport maximum declines exceeding 60 percent. Even the *best*-performing factors have drawdowns of between 65 and 70 percent. All these declines occurred during the bear markets of the last decade. Thus, even the ability to generate a return 4.29 percent higher than the sector would still have you suffering huge declines. Thus, keep the volatility of the sector in mind before committing money to this specific sector on its own.

Also, a note about Table 24.3, which features the base rates for the worst quintiles. Investors would do well to study this table very carefully because it illustrates how badly stocks with the worst EV/free cash flow, six-month price momentum, or buyback yields might perform within each of the 10 economic sectors. The stocks in the consumer discretionary sector with the worst EV/free cash flow *never* beat the sector in any rolling five- or ten-year period. Stocks with the worst six-month price appreciation (i.e., the 20 percent that have declined the most in price) almost *never* beat the sector in any rolling three-, five-, or ten-year period. Table 24.3 offers a cautionary tale of just how badly the odds are stacked against you if you are considering buying a stock that falls in the worst quintile.

IMPLICATIONS

If you are interested in investing in the consumer discretionary sector, your best bet is to concentrate on enterprise value to free cash flow, price to cash flow, the Value Composites Two or Three, or six-month price appreciation. Generally, you might adopt a model that incorporates all the above, perhaps by concentrating on stocks in the best deciles of the composite value factors and then selecting those stocks with the best six-month price appreciation. Finally, keep its volatility in mind before investing exclusively in the consumer discretionary sector.

THE CONSUMER STAPLES SECTOR

As Table 24.4 shows, the best returns in the consumer staples sector come from our value factors. Shareholder yield tops the list with an average annual compound return of 17.80 percent, some 4.22 percent better than what an investor would earn investing in the sector itself. What's more, it would have earned that return with remarkably low volatility—the best quintile by shareholder yield had a standard deviation of return of 14.73 percent, lower than the 15.76 percent generated by the overall sector. Finally, the worst-case scenario for the best quintile by shareholder yield of the consumer staples sector was just 33.71 percent, significantly less than the maximum loss of 52.15 percent suffered by the overall sector. The lower volatility married to high returns gives the strategy a high Sharpe ratio of .87, the highest of any of the factors tested on all 10 sectors. What's more, when looking at Table 24.5 we see that the base rates for buying the stocks with the highest shareholder yield from the consumer staples sector are uniformly high, beating the sector in 98.7 percent of all rolling five-year periods and in 100 percent of all rolling ten-year periods.

T A B L E   24.4

Summary Results for Various Strategies Applied to the Consumer Staples Sector (Strategies Benchmarked against the Returns of All Stocks in the Sector) December 31, 1967–December 31, 2009 (Strategies Sorted by Compound Return of the Best Quintile)

	Geometric mean		Best quintile					
Strategy	**Best quintile**	**Worst quintile**	**Standard deviation (%)**	**Sharpe ratio**	**Spread (Best-worst)**	**Spread (Best-benchmark)**	**Worst drawdown**	**Beta**
Shareholder yield	17.80%	10.19%	14.73%	0.87	7.61%	4.22%	−33.71%	0.87
Dividend yield	17.75%	10.11%	14.88%	0.86	7.64%	4.18%	−35.16%	0.86
EV/free cash flow	17.25%	9.48%	16.63%	0.74	7.77%	3.68%	−49.02%	1.00
Value Composite 3	17.25%	6.76%	15.94%	0.77	10.49%	3.67%	−41.49%	0.95
Value Composite 2	17.19%	6.63%	15.86%	0.77	10.56%	3.62%	−41.60%	0.94
EV/EBITDA	16.96%	7.36%	15.95%	0.75	9.60%	3.38%	−43.60%	0.93
Price/cash flow (free)	16.67%	9.29%	17.11%	0.68	7.38%	3.09%	−48.73%	1.03
Value Composite 1	16.55%	7.01%	16.12%	0.72	9.53%	2.97%	−43.33%	0.96
Price/earnings	16.20%	7.49%	15.84%	0.71	8.71%	2.62%	−46.07%	0.94
NOA change	16.15%	9.01%	15.53%	0.72	7.14%	2.58%	−49.10%	0.94
Buyback yield	16.14%	9.85%	15.18%	0.73	6.30%	2.57%	−39.65%	0.90
Price/cash flow	15.92%	6.79%	16.56%	0.66	9.13%	2.35%	−41.25%	0.98
EV/sales	15.66%	7.89%	17.08%	0.62	7.76%	2.08%	−46.24%	0.98
Total assets to total accruals (TATA)	15.65%	10.04%	15.39%	0.69	5.62%	2.08%	−49.58%	0.92
Debt change	15.00%	10.08%	16.22%	0.62	4.93%	1.43%	−49.37%	0.99
Price/book	14.99%	10.87%	17.01%	0.59	4.12%	1.42%	−46.45%	0.99
Price/sales	14.85%	8.27%	17.44%	0.57	6.58%	1.28%	−48.77%	1.01
Price/accruals	14.81%	10.28%	17.02%	0.58	4.52%	1.23%	−46.03%	1.01
Debt/capital	14.36%	9.52%	16.24%	0.58	4.84%	0.79%	−49.76%	0.97
Asset turnover	13.82%	10.41%	17.03%	0.52	3.41%	0.25%	−50.07%	0.98
Sector benchmark	13.57%	N/A	15.76%	0.54	N/A	N/A	−52.15%	N/A
EPS change	13.44%	11.57%	17.78%	0.47	1.87%	−0.13%	−52.92%	1.07
6-mo. momentum	13.23%	11.66%	16.88%	0.49	1.57%	−0.35%	−49.44%	1.01

(continued on next page)

T A B L E   24.4

Summary Results for Various Strategies Applied to the Consumer Staples Sector (Strategies Benchmarked against the Returns of All Stocks in the Sector) December 31, 1967–December 31, 2009 (Strategies Sorted by Compound Return of the Best Quintile) *(Continued)*

	Geometric mean		Best quintile					
Strategy	**Best quintile**	**Worst quintile**	**Standard deviation (%)**	**Sharpe ratio**	**Spread (Best-worst)**	**Spread (Best-benchmark)**	**Worst drawdown**	**Beta**
3-mo. momentum	12.97%	11.20%	16.58%	0.48	1.77%	−0.61%	−48.90%	1.01
ROE	12.89%	10.92%	16.83%	0.47	1.97%	−0.68%	−66.03%	0.99
9-mo. momentum	12.82%	11.93%	17.15%	0.46	0.89%	−0.75%	−48.86%	1.02
Market cap	12.67%	12.38%	18.63%	0.41	0.29%	−0.91%	−56.34%	1.09
1-mo. momentum	12.54%	11.69%	16.42%	0.46	0.85%	−1.04%	−52.78%	1.02
12-mo. momentum	12.51%	12.73%	17.35%	0.43	−0.22%	−1.06%	−51.01%	1.03
ROA	12.29%	10.64%	16.40%	0.44	1.65%	−1.29%	−64.71%	0.97
Cash flow/debt	11.58%	9.03%	15.63%	0.42	2.55%	−1.99%	−59.94%	0.92

T A B L E   24.5

Best Quintile: Summary Base Rate Information for All Rolling One-, Three-, Five-, Seven-, and Ten-Year Periods for the Consumer Staples Sector's Best Quintile (Strategies Benchmarked against the Returns of All Stocks in the Sector) December 31, 1967–December 31, 2009 (Strategies Sorted by Compound Return of the Best Quintile)

	Percent of time				
Strategy	**1 year**	**3 years**	**5 years**	**7 years**	**10 years**
Shareholder yield	77.3%	88.1%	98.7%	100.0%	100.0%
Dividend yield	73.7%	86.6%	95.7%	98.8%	100.0%
EV/free cash flow	72.9%	84.3%	94.6%	100.0%	100.0%
Value Composite 3	70.4%	77.7%	86.1%	92.2%	95.1%
Value Composite 2	69.2%	77.9%	87.9%	91.0%	92.9%
EV/EBITDA	69.0%	75.7%	84.1%	92.9%	92.9%
Price/cash flow (free)	68.4%	78.7%	90.8%	100.0%	99.3%
Value Composite 1	69.0%	75.3%	84.5%	89.6%	91.4%
Price/earnings	63.6%	74.7%	81.4%	88.2%	91.6%
NOA change	69.2%	77.7%	85.4%	95.7%	97.5%
Buyback yield	65.2%	80.6%	82.7%	92.9%	97.5%
Price/cash flow	65.2%	78.3%	84.5%	92.7%	95.1%
EV/sales	61.1%	70.6%	77.6%	86.5%	92.9%
Total assets to total accruals (TATA)	67.6%	80.4%	85.7%	97.9%	96.6%
Debt change	64.4%	65.1%	73.5%	82.5%	82.3%
Price/book	54.3%	63.6%	64.8%	64.7%	68.5%
Price/sales	57.5%	61.9%	61.4%	68.0%	68.2%
Price/accruals	57.5%	65.7%	65.9%	71.1%	79.6%
Debt/capital	60.7%	55.5%	67.5%	76.3%	83.7%

(continued on next page)

T A B L E   24.5

Best Quintile: Summary Base Rate Information for All Rolling One-, Three-, Five-, Seven-, and Ten-Year Periods for the Consumer Staples Sector's Best Quintile (Strategies Benchmarked against the Returns of All Stocks in the Sector) December 31, 1967–December 31, 2009 (Strategies Sorted by Compound Return of the Best Quintile) *(Continued)*

	Percent of time				
Strategy	1 year	3 years	5 years	7 years	10 years
Asset turnover	53.6%	61.1%	61.2%	57.6%	62.3%
Sector benchmark	0.0%	0.0%	0.0%	0.0%	0.0%
EPS change	52.0%	52.8%	57.4%	47.6%	55.4%
6-mo. momentum	50.6%	47.2%	46.2%	39.3%	30.8%
3-mo. momentum	45.3%	39.4%	37.0%	30.3%	21.2%
ROE	46.4%	45.5%	41.0%	32.2%	27.3%
9-mo. momentum	49.2%	44.5%	41.9%	35.3%	25.4%
Market cap	46.4%	44.3%	41.5%	36.7%	37.2%
1-mo. momentum	34.6%	30.2%	32.3%	22.0%	14.8%
12-mo. momentum	47.4%	39.8%	38.1%	30.6%	22.2%
ROA	41.7%	34.7%	25.8%	17.3%	11.8%
Cash flow/debt	39.3%	27.4%	20.6%	7.3%	1.2%

All five of the best-performing factors generated returns exceeding 17 percent over the full period covered. As we will see as we proceed with all 10 sectors, our composited value factors are generally at or near the top of the performance tables. All of the top five also had excellent base rates as well.

THE DOWNSIDE

Buying stocks with the best earnings gains, price momentum, or highest return on equity all failed to beat the sector average returns. It's unusual to see price momentum performing poorly, but price momentum works best on cyclical stocks, which consumer staples decidedly are not. Notice that the sector itself boasts an average annual compound return of 13.57 percent, the highest of all 10 sectors. Thus conservative investors using value factors such as shareholder yield might be very happy hunting in consumer staples. You also want to avoid the stocks in this sector that score poorly and fall in the worst quintile. Looking at Table 24.6, we see that stocks in the worst quintile in any of the composite value factors never beat the index in any rolling seven- or ten-year period, and that the stocks with the worst buyback yields never beat the sector average in any rolling five-, seven- or ten-year period. However, stocks in the consumer staples sector that fall in the worst quintile are not punished nearly as severely as those bottom quartile stocks from other sectors. While they do underperform, they still do reasonably well—the largest spread between best and worst quintile is 10.56 percent for Value Composite Two. Thus, the sector as a whole represents a solid choice for more risk-averse investors.

T A B L E   24.6

Worst Quintile: Summary Base Rate Information for All Rolling One-, Three-, Five-, Seven-, and Ten-Year Periods for the Consumer Staples Sector's Worst Quintile (Strategies Benchmarked against the Returns of All Stocks in the Sector) December 31, 1967–December 31, 2009 (Strategies Sorted by Compound Return of the Best Quintile)

Strategy	Percent of time				
	1 year	3 years	5 years	7 years	10 years
Shareholder yield	28.3%	16.0%	6.1%	2.8%	0.7%
Dividend yield	33.0%	20.9%	17.0%	6.2%	1.0%
EV/free cash flow	21.5%	11.5%	4.0%	0.0%	1.2%
Value Composite 3	16.0%	10.6%	4.7%	0.0%	0.0%
Value Composite 2	17.8%	11.7%	4.7%	0.0%	0.0%
EV/EBITDA	19.6%	13.0%	4.9%	0.0%	0.0%
Price/cash flow (free)	21.3%	11.5%	0.7%	0.0%	0.0%
Value Composite 1	16.8%	12.1%	4.9%	0.0%	0.0%
Price/earnings	22.9%	11.1%	4.7%	0.0%	0.0%
NOA change	25.7%	11.7%	2.7%	0.0%	0.0%
Buyback yield	22.5%	6.4%	0.0%	0.0%	0.0%
Price/cash flow	16.4%	8.9%	4.7%	0.0%	0.0%
EV/sales	26.9%	18.3%	7.6%	0.0%	0.0%
Total assets to total accruals (TATA)	20.9%	8.7%	2.9%	0.0%	0.0%
Debt change	20.9%	5.1%	0.0%	0.0%	0.0%
Price/book	39.3%	29.4%	25.3%	20.9%	19.0%
Price/sales	26.3%	16.6%	9.2%	0.2%	0.0%
Price/accruals	22.9%	9.1%	0.0%	0.0%	0.0%
Debt/capital	28.9%	15.1%	4.9%	0.0%	0.0%
Asset turnover	32.6%	19.6%	11.7%	6.6%	6.7%
Sector benchmark	0.0%	0.0%	0.0%	0.0%	0.0%
EPS change	35.6%	25.3%	23.3%	19.9%	20.0%
6-mo. momentum	30.6%	18.1%	14.8%	9.2%	6.4%
3-mo. momentum	25.5%	11.3%	7.2%	2.8%	3.2%
ROE	36.4%	28.7%	26.2%	24.4%	23.2%
9-mo. momentum	32.2%	19.4%	12.3%	7.8%	6.2%
Market cap	45.3%	51.5%	50.9%	40.5%	41.1%
1-mo. momentum	28.5%	7.7%	0.2%	0.9%	0.0%
12-mo. momentum	36.4%	31.1%	22.0%	15.4%	9.9%
ROA	35.2%	33.6%	28.5%	21.3%	22.4%
Cash flow/debt	26.5%	24.3%	14.6%	8.8%	9.1%

IMPLICATIONS

Conservative investors are well served by the consumer staples sector. It has the highest average annual compound return of all 10 economic sectors, which can be considerably improved upon by your concentrating on the stocks within the sector with the highest shareholder yield, dividend yield, or the best scores from any of our composited value factors. We see later in this chapter how a conservative investor might want to make the consumer staples sector a staple of his or her portfolio.

THE ENERGY SECTOR

As you will see when you consult Table 24.7, the energy sector is the home of the best-performing strategy on an absolute basis. Buying the quintile of energy sector stocks with the highest score on Value Factor Three earned an average annual compound return of 18.50 percent between 1967 and 2009. It also proved to have the largest spread—18.02 percent—between those energy stocks with the best and worst scores from Value Factor Three. The worst quintile of energy stocks by Value Factor Three earned just 0.48 percent per year between 1967 and 2009, a dashing disappointment to anyone who consistently purchased them. All the usual suspects are at the top of the performance tables, with the other two value factors and EV/EBITDA and PE ratio rounding out the top five performers. Note that all top five factors had drawdowns exceeding 60 percent, so investors must keep volatility in mind when they are investing in these high-performing energy stocks.

T A B L E   24.7

Summary Results for Various Strategies Applied to the Energy Sector (Strategies Benchmarked against the Returns of All Stocks in the Sector) December 31, 1967–December 31, 2009 (Strategies Sorted by Compound Return of the Best Quintile)

Strategy	Geometric mean		Best quintile					
	Best quintile	Worst quintile	Standard deviation (%)	Sharpe ratio	Spread (best-worst)	Spread (best-benchmark)	Worst drawdown	Beta
Value Composite 3	18.50%	0.48%	22.47%	0.60	18.02%	6.93%	−61.14%	0.84
Value Composite 2	18.36%	0.67%	21.84%	0.61	17.69%	6.79%	−60.31%	0.81
Value Composite 1	18.14%	0.94%	22.85%	0.58	17.20%	6.57%	−61.61%	0.85
EV/EBITDA	16.94%	2.20%	23.25%	0.51	14.75%	5.38%	−65.11%	0.87
Price/earnings	16.53%	3.01%	23.26%	0.50	13.52%	4.96%	−64.34%	0.87
EV/free cash flow	16.52%	8.00%	24.63%	0.47	8.52%	4.95%	−64.57%	0.94
EV/sales	16.35%	1.83%	22.46%	0.51	14.51%	4.78%	−60.32%	0.83
Price/cash flow (free)	16.11%	7.18%	24.51%	0.45	8.93%	4.55%	−65.32%	0.93
Price/cash flow	16.04%	3.58%	25.75%	0.43	12.46%	4.47%	−73.32%	0.97
Price/sales	15.78%	2.94%	22.95%	0.47	12.84%	4.21%	−61.43%	0.85
Buyback yield	15.33%	4.58%	22.31%	0.46	10.75%	3.76%	−60.16%	0.85
Shareholder yield	15.13%	5.75%	19.37%	0.52	9.38%	3.56%	−57.12%	0.71
Price/book	14.97%	4.10%	25.12%	0.40	10.87%	3.41%	−69.83%	0.95
Dividend yield	14.20%	6.78%	18.74%	0.49	7.42%	2.63%	−54.46%	0.67
Asset turnover	13.59%	5.24%	23.24%	0.37	8.35%	2.03%	−57.89%	0.86
Price/accruals	13.10%	8.42%	27.48%	0.29	4.68%	1.53%	−77.39%	1.04
NOA change	12.78%	6.41%	24.52%	0.32	6.36%	1.21%	−68.32%	0.93
ROE	12.05%	5.05%	25.28%	0.28	7.01%	0.49%	−64.05%	0.95
Total assets to total accruals (TATA)	11.92%	10.15%	25.86%	0.27	1.77%	0.35%	−72.12%	0.99
3-mo. momentum	11.79%	8.23%	26.56%	0.26	3.56%	0.23%	−72.67%	1.01

(continued on next page)

T A B L E   24.7

Summary Results for Various Strategies Applied to the Energy Sector (Strategies Benchmarked against the Returns of All Stocks in the Sector) December 31, 1967–December 31, 2009 (Strategies Sorted by Compound Return of the Best Quintile) *(Continued)*

	Geometric mean		Best quintile					
Strategy	Best quintile	Worst quintile	Standard deviation (%)	Sharpe ratio	Spread (best-worst)	Spread (best-benchmark)	Worst drawdown	Beta
Debt/capital	11.78%	6.33%	26.15%	0.26	5.45%	0.22%	−69.21%	0.99
ROA	11.62%	5.99%	24.65%	0.27	5.62%	0.05%	−63.55%	0.93
Sector benchmark	11.57%	N/A	25.48%	0.26	N/A	N/A	−68.87%	N/A
6-mo. momentum	11.46%	8.30%	26.98%	0.24	3.16%	−0.11%	−73.28%	1.01
Debt change	11.34%	8.60%	25.75%	0.25	2.74%	−0.23%	−67.61%	0.99
9-mo. momentum	10.99%	8.63%	27.34%	0.22	2.36%	−0.58%	−72.67%	1.02
Cash flow/debt	10.71%	6.07%	23.67%	0.24	4.65%	−0.85%	−60.71%	0.90
Market cap	10.49%	12.22%	28.83%	0.19	−1.73%	−1.08%	−75.84%	1.09
1-mo. momentum	10.18%	9.37%	26.26%	0.20	0.80%	−1.39%	−71.44%	1.02
12-mo. momentum	10.08%	9.83%	27.69%	0.18	0.25%	−1.49%	−72.33%	1.03
EPS change	9.29%	8.60%	27.83%	0.15	0.69%	−2.27%	−74.15%	1.07

As Table 24.8 makes clear, the base rates for the top-performing strategies are all positive, with the three composite value factors all beating the sector in 100 percent of all rolling ten-year periods.

T A B L E   24.8

Best Quintile: Summary Base Rate Information for All Rolling One-, Three-, Five-, Seven-, and Ten-Year Periods for the Energy Sector's Best Quintile (Strategies Benchmarked against the Returns of All Stocks in the Sector) December 31, 1967–December 31, 2009 (Strategies Sorted by Compound Return of the Best Quintile)

	Percent of time				
Strategy	1 year	3 years	5 years	7 years	10 years
Value Composite 3	74.1%	84.0%	90.1%	99.1%	100.0%
Value Composite 2	73.5%	81.9%	86.8%	98.3%	100.0%
Value Composite 1	74.3%	85.7%	93.5%	98.3%	100.0%
EV/EBITDA	71.7%	76.8%	80.5%	91.5%	92.6%
Price/earnings	69.6%	78.3%	85.9%	96.0%	100.0%
EV/free cash flow	73.9%	87.0%	91.7%	97.4%	100.0%
EV/sales	65.0%	78.1%	87.2%	93.4%	94.6%
Price/cash flow (free)	66.8%	87.9%	92.4%	99.3%	100.0%
Price/cash flow	68.6%	79.1%	85.0%	91.5%	96.8%
Price/sales	61.9%	78.3%	83.0%	94.8%	95.3%
Buyback yield	66.6%	83.6%	91.7%	99.1%	99.5%

(continued on next page)

T A B L E   24.8

Best Quintile: Summary Base Rate Information for All Rolling One-, Three-, Five-, Seven-, and Ten-Year Periods for the Energy Sector's Best Quintile (Strategies Benchmarked against the Returns of All Stocks in the Sector) December 31, 1967–December 31, 2009 (Strategies Sorted by Compound Return of the Best Quintile) *(Continued)*

Strategy	Percent of time				
	1 year	3 years	5 years	7 years	10 years
Shareholder yield	58.3%	67.0%	80.3%	86.7%	84.0%
Price/book	65.0%	71.1%	87.2%	92.2%	90.6%
Dividend yield	57.1%	62.1%	72.4%	73.9%	74.9%
Asset turnover	52.8%	62.3%	65.9%	64.2%	66.7%
Price/accruals	55.9%	66.2%	68.8%	69.2%	68.0%
NOA change	59.3%	68.3%	74.0%	78.7%	76.6%
ROE	51.4%	51.1%	47.1%	44.1%	38.2%
Total assets to total accruals (TATA)	50.8%	52.1%	54.0%	53.8%	50.5%
3-mo. momentum	58.1%	55.5%	67.3%	74.9%	82.0%
Debt/capital	48.6%	45.3%	48.4%	50.2%	50.0%
ROA	50.4%	46.8%	45.1%	40.5%	38.2%
Sector benchmark	0.0%	0.0%	0.0%	0.0%	0.0%
6-mo. momentum	54.0%	51.7%	60.3%	74.6%	83.0%
Debt change	50.8%	48.9%	43.7%	41.5%	42.4%
9-mo. momentum	50.2%	54.5%	54.3%	50.0%	52.5%
Cash flow/debt	38.7%	30.4%	28.7%	24.9%	22.2%
Market cap	50.4%	48.5%	49.3%	50.5%	52.5%
1-mo. momentum	36.4%	33.0%	24.9%	15.2%	11.8%
12-mo. momentum	47.2%	48.7%	43.0%	42.9%	37.2%
EPS change	44.5%	40.4%	35.4%	24.6%	18.5%

THE DOWNSIDE

As we saw with the consumer staples sector, with the exception of the 3 month momentum price momentum fails to beat the sector average return over our test period. Also lagging are debt change, cash flow to debt, and earnings per share gains. Price momentum lags only fractionally, yet actually has positive base rates for all periods analyzed. However, its maximum decline of 73 percent serves as a warning that these stocks can be extraordinarily volatile in down markets.

As for the bottom quintiles, none of the composite value factors ever beat the broad sector in any rolling five-, seven-, or ten-year period, and they beat the sector in only 1 percent of all rolling three-year periods. Worse is how badly these stocks suffer when markets are declining—the maximum decline for energy stocks in the bottom quintile of Value Factor Three was 91 percent! As Table 24.9 makes clear, investors would be well advised to avoid all the energy stocks that fall in the bottom quintile of the value composites. Clearly the energy sector is one where valuation truly matters.

T A B L E   24.9

Worst Quintile: Summary Base Rate Information for All Rolling One-, Three-, Five-, Seven-, and Ten-Year Periods for the Energy Sector's Worst Quintile (Strategies Benchmarked against the Returns of All Stocks in the Sector) December 31, 1967–December 31, 2009 (Strategies Sorted by Compound Return of the Best Quintile)

	Percent of time				
Strategy	1 year	3 years	5 years	7 years	10 years
Value Composite 3	11.9%	0.9%	0.0%	0.0%	0.0%
Value Composite 2	13.6%	0.9%	0.0%	0.0%	0.0%
Value Composite 1	13.0%	0.6%	0.0%	0.0%	0.0%
EV/EBITDA	20.2%	5.5%	2.5%	0.0%	0.0%
Price/earnings	25.1%	11.5%	4.5%	0.0%	0.0%
EV/free cash flow	28.7%	16.4%	14.6%	10.7%	5.2%
EV/sales	16.0%	8.9%	3.1%	0.0%	0.0%
Price/cash flow (free)	29.4%	14.9%	13.5%	10.0%	3.7%
Price/cash flow	25.3%	10.2%	0.4%	0.0%	0.0%
Price/sales	12.1%	6.2%	2.9%	0.0%	0.0%
Buyback yield	15.8%	8.1%	0.2%	0.0%	0.0%
Shareholder yield	18.8%	8.9%	1.1%	0.0%	0.0%
Price/book	18.4%	3.0%	0.0%	0.0%	0.0%
Dividend yield	30.6%	20.2%	13.7%	9.0%	6.9%
Asset turnover	24.7%	20.2%	13.9%	4.3%	0.0%
Price/accruals	38.5%	27.2%	22.6%	12.3%	7.9%
NOA change	20.6%	12.3%	5.8%	4.5%	3.7%
ROE	30.8%	17.2%	10.1%	9.0%	6.9%
Total assets to total accruals (TATA)	44.3%	36.8%	30.5%	16.1%	8.1%
3-mo. momentum	23.1%	10.0%	3.4%	1.4%	0.5%
Debt/capital	29.1%	18.7%	13.2%	5.7%	0.0%
ROA	33.4%	21.5%	15.9%	17.5%	18.2%
Sector benchmark	0.0%	0.0%	0.0%	0.0%	0.0%
6-mo. momentum	29.6%	13.4%	4.5%	4.0%	1.0%
Debt change	34.2%	28.1%	27.6%	17.3%	13.3%
9-mo. momentum	28.7%	16.4%	12.8%	7.8%	6.4%
Cash flow/debt	36.6%	28.1%	12.1%	10.2%	9.9%
Market cap	49.4%	47.2%	52.0%	46.2%	41.9%
1-mo. momentum	34.2%	21.5%	8.7%	6.4%	6.2%
12-mo. momentum	37.0%	34.5%	23.1%	19.4%	17.5%
EPS change	36.0%	22.1%	11.4%	8.8%	7.1%

IMPLICATIONS

Investing in the energy sector using Value Factor Three is a clear winner, offering the best absolute performance of any of the factors we've tested in any sector. Its higher volatility, however, lowers the risk-adjusted return, generating a Sharpe ratio of .60. The strategy also faced a maximum decline of 61 percent, so it might be best used in concert with a lower volatility strategy like buying consumer staples stocks with the highest shareholder yields.

Investors should shun any energy company that falls in the bottom quintile of any of the composited value factors—these stocks do very poorly and almost never beat the overall sector. Indeed, the bottom quintiles of virtually *all* of the factors we tested should probably be avoided; they offer little in the way of sector-beating performance and carry substantially increased risk.

THE FINANCIAL SECTOR

At one point in the last decade, the financial sector accounted for more than 40 percent of the S&P 500, although it now makes up just 16.05 percent. Oh, how the mighty have fallen! Yet investors can still earn good returns from the sector by focusing on the composited value factors, PE ratios, and buyback yield. By consulting Table 24.10, we see that the best-performing strategy in the financial sector is the same as it was in the energy sector—buying those stocks from the first quintile of Value Factor Three. Between December 31, 1967, and December 31, 2009, the group compounded at an average annual 15.96 percent, 3.59 percent ahead of the sector's 12.37 percent average annual return. As Table 24.11 makes clear, all base rates for the strategy were positive, with the group beating the sector in 94 percent of all rolling five-year periods and in 100 percent of all rolling ten-year periods. Other winning factors in the financial sector were buying financial stocks with the lowest PE ratios and the highest buyback yield. What's more, the financial stocks with the highest buyback yield had the highest Sharpe ratio of any of the other factors tested, coming in with a Sharpe ratio of .64, well ahead of the Sharpe of .42 for the overall sector.

T A B L E 24.10

Summary Results for Various Strategies Applied to the Financials Sector (Strategies Benchmarked against the Returns of All Stocks in the Sector) December 31, 1967–December 31, 2009 (Strategies Sorted by Compound Return of the Best Quintile)

Strategy	Geometric mean		Best quintile					
	Best quintile	Worst quintile	Standard deviation (%)	Sharpe ratio	Spread (best-worst)	Spread (best-benchmark)	Worst drawdown	Beta
Value Composite 3	15.96%	6.36%	18.65%	0.59	9.60%	3.59%	−61.73%	1.02
Value Composite 1	15.72%	6.96%	19.22%	0.56	8.77%	3.35%	−62.84%	1.05
Price/earnings	15.66%	7.39%	18.92%	0.56	8.27%	3.29%	−65.80%	1.03
Value Composite 2	15.66%	6.28%	18.55%	0.57	9.37%	3.28%	−62.67%	1.01
Buyback yield	15.65%	8.95%	16.69%	0.64	6.71%	3.28%	−55.99%	0.92
EV/EBITDA	14.92%	11.10%	18.25%	0.54	3.82%	2.55%	−54.17%	0.97
Debt/capital	14.87%	7.72%	22.96%	0.43	7.15%	2.50%	−59.81%	1.10
Price/cash flow	14.81%	7.16%	20.03%	0.49	7.65%	2.44%	−68.15%	1.09
Price/cash flow (free)	14.78%	6.67%	21.63%	0.45	8.11%	2.41%	−65.75%	1.13
EV/free cash flow	14.43%	8.59%	20.11%	0.47	5.84%	2.06%	−56.90%	1.04
Shareholder yield	14.36%	9.26%	16.50%	0.57	5.10%	1.98%	−58.58%	0.90
EV/sales	13.73%	12.06%	18.18%	0.48	1.67%	1.36%	−55.55%	0.97

(continued on next page)

T A B L E   24.10

Summary Results for Various Strategies Applied to the Financials Sector (Strategies Benchmarked against the Returns of All Stocks in the Sector) December 31, 1967–December 31, 2009 (Strategies Sorted by Compound Return of the Best Quintile) *(Continued)*

| Strategy | Geometric mean | | Best quintile | | | | | |
	Best quintile	Worst quintile	Standard deviation (%)	Sharpe ratio	Spread (best-worst)	Spread (best-benchmark)	Worst drawdown	Beta
Price/sales	13.36%	7.11%	21.82%	0.38	6.25%	0.99%	−73.75%	1.18
Price/book	13.17%	8.20%	20.26%	0.40	4.96%	0.79%	−74.68%	1.09
Debt change	13.05%	9.79%	17.38%	0.46	3.26%	0.68%	−57.69%	0.95
9-mo. momentum	12.92%	7.24%	18.32%	0.43	5.68%	0.55%	−53.43%	0.96
12-mo. momentum	12.87%	7.72%	18.56%	0.42	5.15%	0.49%	−54.05%	0.97
EPS change	12.67%	9.33%	19.61%	0.39	3.35%	0.30%	−59.74%	1.06
Dividend yield	12.63%	8.07%	17.58%	0.43	4.56%	0.26%	−66.33%	0.95
6-mo. momentum	12.51%	7.72%	18.20%	0.41	4.78%	0.13%	−53.34%	0.97
Sector benchmark	12.37%	N/A	17.74%	0.42	N/A	N/A	−62.46%	N/A
ROE	12.09%	10.07%	19.77%	0.36	2.02%	−0.28%	−61.15%	1.06
Cash flow/debt	12.07%	9.86%	18.46%	0.38	2.21%	−0.30%	−63.94%	0.93
Asset turnover	11.96%	13.19%	19.73%	0.35	−1.23%	−0.41%	−59.68%	1.03
Market cap	11.94%	10.80%	17.37%	0.40	1.14%	−0.43%	−60.74%	0.93
3-mo. momentum	11.89%	8.77%	18.12%	0.38	3.13%	−0.48%	−56.76%	0.98
ROA	11.87%	10.53%	19.14%	0.36	1.34%	−0.50%	−61.71%	1.00
1-mo. momentum	11.24%	10.02%	18.22%	0.34	1.22%	−1.13%	−60.43%	1.01

T A B L E   24.11

Best Quintile: Summary Base Rate Information for All Rolling One-, Three-, Five-, Seven-, and Ten-Year Periods for the Financials Sector's Best Quintile (Strategies Benchmarked against the Returns of All Stocks in the Sector) December 31, 1967–December 31, 2009 (Strategies Sorted by Compound Return of the Best Quintile)

| Strategy | Percent of time | | | | |
	1 year	3 years	5 years	7 years	10 years
Value Composite 3	78.7%	88.7%	94.4%	97.2%	100.0%
Value Composite 1	76.7%	82.8%	90.8%	93.4%	98.0%
Price/earnings	74.1%	79.4%	87.2%	87.2%	94.3%
Value Composite 2	79.8%	88.9%	89.9%	95.7%	99.3%
Buyback yield	77.7%	91.7%	97.3%	100.0%	100.0%
EV/EBITDA	69.4%	76.6%	85.2%	91.0%	91.1%
Debt/capital	56.5%	65.1%	67.7%	71.8%	75.4%
Price/cash flow	68.2%	67.7%	73.8%	79.9%	79.6%
Price/cash flow (free)	64.4%	71.1%	85.7%	91.7%	92.9%
EV/free cash flow	62.6%	66.4%	71.7%	81.8%	87.9%
Shareholder yield	67.6%	68.1%	75.6%	78.0%	83.5%
EV/sales	54.3%	58.7%	56.5%	64.7%	69.2%
Price/sales	56.5%	58.7%	64.1%	64.5%	65.3%

(continued on next page)

T A B L E   24.11

Best Quintile: Summary Base Rate Information for All Rolling One-, Three-, Five-, Seven-, and Ten-Year Periods for the Financials Sector's Best Quintile (Strategies Benchmarked against the Returns of All Stocks in the Sector) December 31, 1967–December 31, 2009 (Strategies Sorted by Compound Return of the Best Quintile) *(Continued)*

	Percent of time				
Strategy	1 year	3 years	5 years	7 years	10 years
Price/book	61.1%	60.9%	64.8%	60.9%	63.3%
Debt change	59.1%	67.2%	62.3%	66.8%	76.6%
9-mo. momentum	59.7%	61.5%	63.9%	66.8%	73.9%
12-mo. momentum	57.9%	62.3%	61.4%	65.4%	72.4%
EPS change	53.4%	44.9%	46.0%	52.4%	56.9%
Dividend yield	55.5%	57.2%	61.4%	58.5%	53.0%
6-mo. momentum	56.3%	54.0%	51.8%	57.3%	68.0%
Sector benchmark	0.0%	0.0%	0.0%	0.0%	0.0%
ROE	52.2%	38.7%	41.3%	41.0%	38.4%
Cash flow/debt	46.0%	38.7%	40.6%	35.8%	39.9%
Asset turnover	46.2%	43.2%	39.9%	37.9%	38.4%
Market cap	48.0%	43.4%	48.0%	54.0%	50.2%
3-mo. momentum	51.0%	45.7%	37.2%	39.3%	36.2%
ROA	42.3%	38.9%	35.7%	41.2%	38.2%
1-mo. momentum	41.7%	34.7%	25.8%	16.4%	10.8%

THE DOWNSIDE

ROE, cash flow to debt, asset turnover, and short-term momentum all failed to beat the sector average. Most of these had negative base rates and should not be used to identify stocks to buy in the financial sector. As for the worst quintiles, financial stocks in the value composite factors' bottom quintile *never* beat the sector in any rolling ten-year period and had very low win rates for any of the periods we examined. Table 24.12 lists the base rates for the worst quintiles for all factors applied to financial sector stocks. The only redeeming quality of financial stocks in the composited value factors' worst quintile was that their maximum declines were more subdued than what we see with other sectors—in this case, a maximum decline of a more modest 61 percent. Yet, as we are finding with the other sectors, investors are well advised to avoid stocks in the financial sector that score in the bottom quintile.

T A B L E   24.12

Worst Quintile: Summary Base Rate Information for All Rolling One-, Three-, Five-, Seven-, and Ten-Year Periods for the Financials Sector's Worst Quintile (Strategies Benchmarked against the Returns of All Stocks in the Sector) December 31, 1967–December 31, 2009 (Strategies Sorted by Compound Return of the Best Quintile)

	Percent of time				
Strategy	1 year	3 years	5 years	7 years	10 years
Value Composite 3	18.6%	9.6%	0.4%	0.0%	0.0%
Value Composite 1	21.1%	12.8%	4.5%	0.0%	0.0%

(continued on next page)

TABLE 24.12

Worst Quintile: Summary Base Rate Information for All Rolling One-, Three-, Five-, Seven-, and Ten-Year Periods for the Financials Sector's Worst Quintile (Strategies Benchmarked against the Returns of All Stocks in the Sector) December 31, 1967–December 31, 2009 (Strategies Sorted by Compound Return of the Best Quintile) *(Continued)*

Strategy	Percent of time				
	1 year	3 years	5 years	7 years	10 years
Price/earnings	28.3%	18.9%	9.9%	1.9%	0.0%
Value Composite 2	18.2%	10.4%	0.9%	0.0%	0.0%
Buyback yield	20.2%	16.6%	1.1%	0.0%	0.0%
EV/EBITDA	38.5%	38.7%	44.6%	47.2%	44.3%
Debt/capital	34.8%	20.4%	17.3%	11.6%	4.4%
Price/cash flow	24.1%	17.4%	11.2%	5.9%	1.5%
Price/cash flow (free)	26.5%	12.1%	7.6%	5.7%	3.0%
EV/free cash flow	35.2%	24.3%	16.6%	19.7%	20.4%
Shareholder yield	27.3%	20.0%	9.4%	2.1%	0.0%
EV/sales	49.2%	46.0%	50.9%	47.9%	53.7%
Price/sales	18.8%	11.3%	3.4%	0.2%	0.0%
Price/book	28.3%	24.3%	14.6%	0.7%	0.0%
Debt change	28.5%	14.5%	1.1%	0.0%	0.0%
9-mo. momentum	23.3%	5.5%	0.9%	0.0%	0.0%
12-mo. momentum	24.3%	12.6%	1.1%	0.0%	0.0%
EPS change	27.5%	21.3%	18.2%	13.3%	10.1%
Dividend yield	37.2%	33.6%	26.9%	10.9%	3.2%
6-mo. momentum	22.7%	7.2%	1.1%	0.0%	0.0%
Sector benchmark	0.0%	0.0%	0.0%	0.0%	0.0%
ROE	34.8%	31.9%	23.8%	14.2%	9.9%
Cash flow/debt	32.4%	26.0%	19.5%	21.3%	24.6%
Asset turnover	50.4%	63.6%	69.5%	78.0%	78.8%
Market cap	45.5%	42.8%	35.2%	26.1%	11.3%
3-mo. momentum	25.3%	15.5%	7.0%	0.2%	0.0%
ROA	38.3%	39.1%	25.1%	12.3%	9.6%
1-mo. momentum	30.4%	18.9%	14.8%	5.9%	3.0%

IMPLICATIONS

Investors in the financial sector who want good returns married to lower volatility should consider buying those financial stocks with the highest buyback yield. They offer sector-beating returns with a lower maximum declines than the sector itself. For investors with a higher risk tolerance, buying the financial stocks with the highest score on Value Factor Three should be pursued.

All investors will want to avoid financial stocks that fall into the bottom quintile by most of the factors analyzed. The three composited value factors are particularly good at identifying financial stocks to avoid, as is buyback yield and negative price appreciation.

THE HEALTH-CARE SECTOR

With this sector much in the news in 2009 and 2010, it's helpful to see that like the other sectors we analyzed, it is always good policy to focus on the stocks with the best valuations or highest shareholder yield. As Table 24.13 shows, the best strategy for health-care stocks is buying the quintile with the lowest price to cash flow. This group earned an average annual compound return of 17.59 percent, significantly better than the 10.55 percent earned by the sector as a whole. Its standard deviation of return of 20.85 percent was lower than the overall sector's 23.16 percent, offering a Sharpe ratio of .60. Rounding out the top five were all three composited value factors and price to free cash flow.

T A B L E 24.13

Summary Results for Various Strategies Applied to the Health-Care Sector (Strategies Benchmarked against the Returns of All Stocks in the Sector) December 31, 1967–December 31, 2009 (Strategies Sorted by Compound Return of the Best Quintile)

| | Geometric mean | | Best quintile | | | | | |
Strategy	Best quintile	Worst quintile	Standard deviation (%)	Sharpe ratio	Spread (best-worst)	Spread (best-benchmark)	Worst drawdown	Beta
Price/cash flow	17.59%	1.14%	20.85%	0.60	16.45%	7.03%	−62.86%	0.76
Value Composite 2	17.50%	0.33%	20.01%	0.62	17.17%	6.94%	−55.29%	0.72
Price/cash flow (free)	17.13%	3.57%	21.86%	0.55	13.56%	6.58%	−63.12%	0.83
Value Composite 3	17.01%	0.24%	20.14%	0.60	16.78%	6.46%	−56.06%	0.73
Value Composite 1	16.74%	0.42%	20.62%	0.57	16.31%	6.18%	−60.04%	0.74
EV/free cash flow	16.20%	4.32%	21.67%	0.52	11.87%	5.64%	−62.83%	0.83
Shareholder yield	16.02%	3.05%	17.27%	0.64	12.97%	5.47%	−46.79%	0.63
Price/earnings	16.00%	2.33%	19.46%	0.57	13.67%	5.45%	−61.23%	0.71
Price/sales	15.52%	−0.25%	22.15%	0.48	15.77%	4.97%	−63.64%	0.79
EV/EBITDA	15.44%	1.62%	20.35%	0.51	13.82%	4.89%	−58.68%	0.73
EV/sales	15.09%	−0.83%	21.62%	0.47	15.92%	4.54%	−61.44%	0.78
Buyback yield	14.91%	1.88%	18.56%	0.53	13.03%	4.36%	−57.07%	0.69
Dividend yield	14.91%	5.28%	16.60%	0.60	9.63%	4.36%	−43.37%	0.60
Price/accruals	14.38%	7.53%	24.15%	0.39	6.85%	3.83%	−65.91%	0.98
Total assets to total accruals (TATA)	14.01%	4.51%	25.17%	0.36	9.50%	3.46%	−55.46%	1.04
Price/book	13.65%	3.99%	21.92%	0.39	9.67%	3.10%	−62.57%	0.85
ROE	12.52%	3.28%	20.79%	0.36	9.24%	1.97%	−57.64%	0.80
Asset turnover	12.03%	2.85%	22.46%	0.31	9.18%	1.48%	−67.07%	0.86
6-mo. momentum	11.95%	6.14%	27.72%	0.25	5.81%	1.40%	−56.85%	1.13
Cash flow/debt	11.77%	4.60%	22.70%	0.30	7.18%	1.22%	−68.24%	0.91
9-mo. momentum	11.73%	6.57%	28.04%	0.24	5.16%	1.18%	−60.93%	1.14
Debt/capital	11.48%	3.21%	25.93%	0.25	8.27%	0.93%	−55.53%	1.06
NOA change	11.44%	2.09%	25.91%	0.25	9.35%	0.89%	−67.35%	1.07
EPS change	11.41%	7.26%	24.49%	0.26	4.16%	0.86%	−68.43%	0.97
12-mo. momentum	11.39%	7.33%	27.63%	0.23	4.06%	0.84%	−65.12%	1.12
Debt change	11.26%	4.53%	25.01%	0.25	6.72%	0.70%	−66.91%	1.04

(continued on next page)

T A B L E   24.13

Summary Results for Various Strategies Applied to the Health-Care Sector (Strategies Benchmarked against the Returns of All Stocks in the Sector) December 31, 1967–December 31, 2009 (Strategies Sorted by Compound Return of the Best Quintile) *(Continued)*

Strategy	Geometric mean		Best quintile					
	Best quintile	Worst quintile	Standard deviation (%)	Sharpe ratio	Spread (best-worst)	Spread (best-benchmark)	Worst drawdown	Beta
3-mo. momentum	10.88%	6.06%	27.08%	0.22	4.82%	0.33%	−60.15%	1.12
ROA	10.80%	3.62%	20.51%	0.28	7.19%	0.25%	−54.87%	0.80
Sector benchmark	10.55%	N/A	23.16%	0.24	N/A	N/A	−62.71%	N/A
1-mo. momentum	9.59%	7.15%	26.06%	0.18	2.44%	−0.96%	−63.21%	1.10
Market cap	6.88%	11.14%	29.24%	0.06	−4.26%	−3.68%	−79.99%	1.20

Investors who want lower downside risk and a higher Sharpe ratio should consider buying health-care stocks with the highest shareholder yield. While they compound annually at 16.02 percent, 1.57 percent less than health-care stocks with the lowest price to cash flow, the maximum decline falls to a loss of 47 percent versus 63 percent for the health-care stocks with the lowest price to cash flow. They are also much less volatile, with a standard deviation of return of 17.27 percent, resulting in a higher Sharpe ratio of .64. As Table 24.14 shows, they also have slightly higher base rates.

T A B L E   24.14

Best Quintile: Summary Base Rate Information for All Rolling One-, Three-, Five-, Seven-, and Ten-Year Periods for the Health-Care Sector's Best Quintile (Strategies Benchmarked against the Returns of All Stocks in the Sector) December 31, 1967–December 31, 2009 (Strategies Sorted by Compound Return of the Best Quintile)

Strategy	Percent of time				
	1 year	3 years	5 years	7 years	10 years
Price/cash flow	70.4%	81.7%	87.7%	95.7%	99.3%
Value Composite 2	71.1%	85.1%	93.5%	98.3%	100.0%
Price/cash flow (free)	68.0%	81.7%	90.6%	95.7%	98.5%
Value Composite 3	69.8%	83.0%	91.9%	97.9%	100.0%
Value Composite 1	66.8%	79.6%	90.8%	96.9%	100.0%
EV/free cash flow	61.3%	75.5%	84.8%	78.4%	79.3%
Shareholder yield	73.1%	81.9%	89.7%	96.7%	99.5%
Price/earnings	68.4%	76.2%	89.5%	96.4%	100.0%
Price/sales	61.1%	70.0%	81.4%	84.8%	93.3%
EV/EBITDA	61.9%	74.3%	85.2%	92.9%	99.5%
EV/sales	61.9%	71.7%	85.0%	90.5%	98.0%
Buyback yield	70.0%	80.0%	82.5%	94.1%	96.8%
Dividend yield	67.8%	74.5%	77.6%	91.9%	97.8%
Price/accruals	62.8%	70.9%	78.3%	84.1%	89.7%
Total assets to total accruals (TATA)	64.8%	82.6%	90.6%	92.2%	94.1%
Price/book	60.3%	62.3%	73.8%	81.8%	87.7%

(continued on next page)

TABLE 24.14

Best Quintile: Summary Base Rate Information for All Rolling One-, Three-, Five-, Seven-, and Ten-Year Periods for the Health-Care Sector's Best Quintile (Strategies Benchmarked against the Returns of All Stocks in the Sector) December 31, 1967–December 31, 2009 (Strategies Sorted by Compound Return of the Best Quintile) *(Continued)*

Strategy	Percent of time				
	1 year	**3 years**	**5 years**	**7 years**	**10 years**
ROE	58.9%	64.9%	64.1%	66.6%	59.6%
Asset turnover	54.5%	58.9%	57.4%	54.0%	61.6%
6-mo. momentum	56.3%	64.3%	74.2%	86.5%	90.4%
Cash flow/debt	56.5%	68.3%	63.9%	62.6%	60.1%
9-mo. momentum	56.7%	60.6%	71.3%	74.9%	74.6%
Debt/capital	47.8%	55.3%	53.8%	57.6%	58.6%
NOA change	56.3%	57.0%	64.8%	73.0%	75.1%
EPS change	65.0%	71.1%	76.9%	82.0%	86.7%
12-mo. momentum	54.9%	59.8%	67.3%	69.4%	72.4%
Debt change	57.5%	57.7%	56.5%	62.1%	60.1%
3-mo. momentum	49.0%	51.7%	61.4%	74.6%	78.1%
ROA	48.4%	55.1%	56.1%	51.2%	49.0%
Sector benchmark	0.0%	0.0%	0.0%	0.0%	0.0%
1-mo. momentum	36.4%	33.6%	40.8%	41.7%	38.9%
Market cap	36.0%	24.3%	18.8%	12.6%	13.8%

THE DOWNSIDE

As we saw with the consumer discretionary sector, almost all of the best quintiles of the health-care factors improve performance over the sector itself—only one month price performance and the smallest-cap stocks from the sector failed to beat the sector's return.

As for the worst quintiles, the spreads in the health-care sector are enormous. Looking at Table 24.13, we see that the health-care stocks with the highest price to sales ratios and enterprise value to sales actually have negative returns over the entire period. They also each have huge peak-to-trough declines of 91 percent. The worst quintiles of price to cash flow and the three composited value factors also help identify which health-care stocks to avoid. As Table 24.15 makes clear, stocks in these categories almost never beat the sector itself.

TABLE 24.15

Worst Quintile: Summary Base Rate Information for All Rolling One-, Three-, Five-, Seven-, and Ten-Year Periods for the Health-Care Sector's Worst Quintile (Strategies Benchmarked against the Returns of All Stocks in the Sector) December 31, 1967–December 31, 2009 (Strategies Sorted by Compound Return of the Best Quintile)

Strategy	Percent of time				
	1 year	**3 years**	**5 years**	**7 years**	**10 years**
Price/cash flow	18.6%	2.6%	0.2%	0.0%	0.0%
Value Composite 2	23.1%	5.3%	0.9%	0.0%	0.0%
Price/cash flow (free)	27.9%	3.2%	0.0%	0.0%	0.0%

(continued on next page)

T A B L E 24.15

Worst Quintile: Summary Base Rate Information for All Rolling One-, Three-, Five-, Seven-, and Ten-Year Periods for the Health-Care Sector's Worst Quintile (Strategies Benchmarked against the Returns of All Stocks in the Sector) December 31, 1967–December 31, 2009 (Strategies Sorted by Compound Return of the Best Quintile) *(Continued)*

Strategy	Percent of time				
	1 year	3 years	5 years	7 years	10 years
Value Composite 3	21.5%	4.9%	0.9%	0.0%	0.0%
Value Composite 1	21.9%	6.8%	1.1%	0.0%	0.0%
EV/free cash flow	30.4%	10.0%	0.4%	0.0%	0.0%
Shareholder yield	23.1%	15.1%	14.1%	15.4%	14.3%
Price/earnings	23.1%	5.3%	0.9%	0.0%	0.0%
Price/sales	23.5%	9.4%	0.9%	0.0%	0.0%
EV/EBITDA	20.2%	8.1%	2.2%	0.0%	0.0%
EV/sales	21.5%	5.1%	0.9%	0.0%	0.0%
Buyback yield	20.2%	12.1%	7.6%	3.6%	1.7%
Dividend yield	23.1%	8.1%	3.6%	0.0%	0.0%
Price/accruals	34.8%	17.9%	11.2%	2.8%	3.4%
Total assets to total accruals (TATA)	23.3%	9.4%	3.1%	0.0%	0.7%
Price/book	26.7%	13.6%	4.7%	0.0%	0.0%
ROE	33.8%	15.5%	16.6%	19.7%	20.9%
Asset turnover	34.8%	23.2%	17.3%	18.5%	19.2%
6-mo. momentum	24.9%	9.6%	6.5%	4.3%	3.2%
Cash flow/debt	37.2%	30.2%	26.9%	28.2%	28.1%
9-mo. momentum	30.2%	14.5%	7.8%	5.0%	4.2%
Debt/capital	22.3%	10.9%	4.0%	0.2%	0.0%
NOA change	14.2%	6.0%	0.4%	0.0%	0.0%
EPS change	34.2%	23.6%	10.8%	2.8%	0.0%
12-mo. momentum	33.2%	23.6%	13.7%	9.2%	8.4%
Debt change	18.8%	6.8%	0.0%	0.0%	0.0%
3-mo. momentum	22.3%	8.9%	6.1%	3.8%	2.2%
ROA	38.7%	23.0%	21.3%	26.8%	27.8%
Sector benchmark	0.0%	0.0%	0.0%	0.0%	0.0%
1-mo. momentum	22.1%	9.6%	4.7%	2.6%	0.0%
Market cap	54.7%	53.6%	56.3%	48.1%	49.0%

IMPLICATIONS

Investors in the health-care sector should concentrate on those stocks with the lowest price to cash flow or the highest scores on the composited value factors. Risk-averse investors should concentrate on health-care stocks with the highest shareholder yield, because they offer the highest Sharpe ratio of any of the factors tested.

As with the other sectors, health-care investors should shun stocks that fall into the bottom quintile of any of the composited value factors, as they rarely beat the sector's return. Indeed, with very few exceptions, investors should avoid any health-care stock that finds itself in worst quintile of any of the factors analyzed.

THE INDUSTRIAL SECTOR

While the world famous Dow Jones Industrial Average now includes many nonindustrial companies, let's look at the more purely "industrial" industrial sector. As you can see from Table 24.16, the composited value factors are the top three performers, followed by enterprise value to EBITDA and shareholder yield. The composited Value Factor Two served up the best returns, earning an average annual compound return of 15.34 percent versus 9.82 percent for the industrial sector itself. It offered this return with a lower standard deviation of return than for the sector itself, coming in at 19.89 percent versus 20.55 percent. That led to the highest Sharpe ratio for all the factors tested of .52. With the industrial sector, the best absolute performer is also the best risk-adjusted performer. The base rates for Value Factor Two—featured in Table 24.17—are also excellent, with the strategy beating the sector in 82 percent of all rolling one-year periods and in 100 percent of all rolling five-, seven-, and ten-year periods.

T A B L E   24.16

Summary Results for Various Strategies Applied to the Industrial Sector (Strategies Benchmarked against the Returns of All Stocks in the Sector) December 31, 1967–December 31, 2009 (Strategies Sorted by Compound Return of the Best Quintile)

| Strategy | Geometric mean | | Best quintile | | | | | |
	Best quintile	Worst quintile	Standard deviation (%)	Sharpe ratio	Spread (best-worst)	Spread (best-benchmark)	Worst drawdown	Beta
Value Composite 2	15.34%	1.35%	19.89%	0.52	13.99%	5.52%	−56.23%	0.93
Value Composite 3	15.01%	1.46%	20.30%	0.49	13.55%	5.20%	−56.51%	0.95
Value Composite 1	14.65%	2.00%	20.67%	0.47	12.65%	4.84%	−56.86%	0.97
EV/EBITDA	14.37%	1.41%	20.10%	0.47	12.96%	4.55%	−58.83%	0.94
Shareholder yield	13.85%	2.53%	17.86%	0.50	11.32%	4.04%	−54.00%	0.84
EV/sales	13.48%	4.17%	20.56%	0.41	9.31%	3.66%	−55.28%	0.97
Price/earnings	13.27%	3.18%	20.66%	0.40	10.09%	3.45%	−58.79%	0.97
Dividend yield	13.09%	3.53%	18.15%	0.45	9.56%	3.27%	−61.03%	0.84
Price/cash flow	13.05%	1.72%	21.78%	0.37	11.33%	3.24%	−61.07%	1.02
Price/Book	12.99%	4.94%	21.01%	0.38	8.05%	3.18%	−56.68%	0.98
Buyback yield	12.94%	2.72%	18.21%	0.44	10.22%	3.13%	−52.61%	0.86
EV/free cash flow	12.88%	5.56%	20.74%	0.38	7.31%	3.06%	−57.48%	0.99
Price/cash flow (free)	12.72%	4.65%	21.80%	0.35	8.07%	2.90%	−58.54%	1.03
NOA change	11.72%	3.50%	20.17%	0.33	8.22%	1.90%	−60.65%	0.96
Price/sales	11.68%	4.25%	22.23%	0.30	7.43%	1.86%	−58.85%	1.04
Price/accruals	11.60%	6.09%	21.95%	0.30	5.51%	1.78%	−60.05%	1.03
Debt/capital	11.01%	4.39%	20.61%	0.29	6.62%	1.20%	−56.81%	0.98
Total assets to total accruals (TATA)	10.83%	4.68%	20.70%	0.28	6.15%	1.01%	−60.83%	0.99
Debt change	10.69%	4.83%	20.52%	0.28	5.86%	0.87%	−58.28%	0.98
Asset turnover	10.08%	7.71%	20.63%	0.25	2.37%	0.27%	−56.00%	0.98

(continued on next page)

T A B L E 24.16

Summary Results for Various Strategies Applied to the Industrial Sector (Strategies Benchmarked against the Returns of All Stocks in the Sector) December 31, 1967–December 31, 2009 (Strategies Sorted by Compound Return of the Best Quintile) *(Continued)*

	Geometric mean		Best quintile					
Strategy	Best quintile	Worst quintile	Standard deviation (%)	Sharpe ratio	Spread (best-worst)	Spread (best-benchmark)	Worst drawdown	Beta
Sector benchmark	9.82%	N/A	20.55%	0.23	N/A	N/A	−57.79%	N/A
6-mo. momentum	9.76%	5.74%	21.91%	0.22	4.03%	−0.05%	−65.63%	1.02
Cash flow/debt	9.58%	3.73%	19.07%	0.24	5.85%	−0.24%	−54.34%	0.90
3-mo. momentum	9.46%	5.98%	21.54%	0.21	3.49%	−0.35%	−62.67%	1.02
ROE	9.35%	7.80%	21.37%	0.20	1.55%	−0.47%	−60.98%	1.01
9-mo. momentum	9.21%	5.93%	22.16%	0.19	3.28%	−0.61%	−67.11%	1.02
Market cap	9.16%	8.95%	21.95%	0.19	0.21%	−0.65%	−63.06%	1.04
ROA	8.97%	6.84%	19.84%	0.20	2.13%	−0.85%	−56.49%	0.93
12-mo. momentum	8.47%	6.73%	22.38%	0.16	1.75%	−1.34%	−67.70%	1.03
1-mo. momentum	8.38%	7.08%	21.28%	0.16	1.31%	−1.43%	−61.59%	1.02
EPS change	8.31%	7.37%	22.33%	0.15	0.95%	−1.50%	−63.23%	1.06

T A B L E 24.17

Best Quintile: Summary Base Rate Information for All Rolling One-, Three-, Five-, Seven-, and Ten-Year Periods for the Industrial Sector's Best Quintile (Strategies Benchmarked against the Returns of All Stocks in the Sector) December 31, 1967–December 31, 2009 (Strategies Sorted by Compound Return of the Best Quintile)

	Percent of time				
Strategy	1 year	3 years	5 years	7 years	10 years
Value Composite 2	82.0%	93.4%	100.0%	100.0%	100.0%
Value Composite 3	79.1%	93.2%	100.0%	100.0%	100.0%
Value Composite 1	78.9%	91.3%	100.0%	100.0%	100.0%
EV/EBITDA	80.4%	93.2%	99.1%	100.0%	100.0%
Shareholder yield	70.6%	90.0%	95.7%	99.1%	99.8%
EV/sales	71.3%	77.9%	86.8%	91.5%	98.8%
Price/earnings	71.9%	82.8%	94.8%	97.6%	98.5%
Dividend yield	65.0%	82.8%	84.3%	92.9%	93.8%
Price/cash flow	72.1%	83.8%	87.2%	98.1%	100.0%
Price/Book	66.0%	71.9%	78.3%	78.2%	85.2%
Buyback yield	71.9%	90.0%	94.2%	96.4%	99.8%
EV/free cash flow	69.8%	73.8%	87.2%	100.0%	100.0%
Price/cash flow (free)	71.5%	77.2%	80.5%	95.5%	97.8%
NOA change	69.2%	81.3%	86.3%	94.8%	93.6%
Price/sales	62.6%	60.6%	60.5%	70.4%	70.4%
Price/accruals	62.8%	74.7%	78.3%	79.4%	80.5%
Debt/capital	57.5%	58.5%	66.8%	78.7%	76.1%
Total assets to total accruals (TATA)	62.6%	64.5%	69.3%	73.2%	71.2%

(continued on next page)

T A B L E   24.17

Best Quintile: Summary Base Rate Information for All Rolling One-, Three-, Five-, Seven-, and Ten-Year Periods for the Industrial Sector's Best Quintile (Strategies Benchmarked against the Returns of All Stocks in the Sector) December 31, 1967–December 31, 2009 (Strategies Sorted by Compound Return of the Best Quintile) *(Continued)*

	Percent of time				
Strategy	1 year	3 years	5 years	7 years	10 years
Debt change	56.3%	68.7%	74.0%	78.0%	79.6%
Asset turnover	53.8%	61.3%	60.8%	69.4%	79.6%
Sector benchmark	0.0%	0.0%	0.0%	0.0%	0.0%
6-mo. momentum	54.9%	53.4%	55.2%	57.6%	61.1%
Cash flow/debt	45.3%	48.3%	41.0%	40.5%	45.8%
3-mo. momentum	46.6%	45.3%	46.6%	45.3%	46.6%
ROE	49.8%	47.0%	49.8%	43.8%	47.5%
9-mo. momentum	52.6%	54.5%	54.7%	56.2%	57.1%
Market cap	42.7%	37.4%	36.5%	43.6%	43.3%
ROA	46.2%	36.2%	38.6%	35.5%	35.5%
12-mo. momentum	49.4%	49.6%	52.7%	52.8%	52.2%
1-mo. momentum	34.6%	21.5%	9.2%	4.7%	1.7%
EPS change	46.4%	47.9%	47.5%	41.7%	36.2%

THE DOWNSIDE

Price momentum, ROE, cash flow to debt, and earnings per share percentage gains all failed to beat the sector itself. With the exceptions of six-month price momentum and cash flow to debt, all spreads between the best and worst deciles for these factors are less than 4 percent.

As Table 24.18 makes clear, investors should avoid any industrial company that finds itself in the worst quintile for any of the composited value factors. The base rates for all rolling three-year periods are in the single digits and are zero for all rolling five-, seven-, and ten-year rolling periods. You'll also want to avoid any industrial stock with the lowest shareholder and buyback yields, as they rarely beat the industrial sector itself. And even though the stocks with the best price momentum fail to beat the overall sector, the worst price momentum stocks almost never beat the sector and should be avoided.

T A B L E   24.18

Worst Quintile: Summary Base Rate Information for All Rolling One-, Three-, Five-, Seven-, and Ten-Year Periods for the Industrial Sector's Worst Quintile (Strategies Benchmarked against the Returns of All Stocks in the Sector) December 31, 1967–December 31, 2009 (Strategies Sorted by Compound Return of the Best Quintile)

	Percent of time				
Strategy	1 year	3 years	5 years	7 years	10 years
Value Composite 2	19.6%	4.7%	0.0%	0.0%	0.0%
Value Composite 3	19.6%	4.0%	0.0%	0.0%	0.0%
Value Composite 1	20.6%	6.2%	0.2%	0.0%	0.0%

(continued on next page)

TABLE 24.18

Worst Quintile: Summary Base Rate Information for All Rolling One-, Three-, Five-, Seven-, and Ten-Year Periods for the Industrial Sector's Worst Quintile (Strategies Benchmarked against the Returns of All Stocks in the Sector) December 31, 1967–December 31, 2009 (Strategies Sorted by Compound Return of the Best Quintile) *(Continued)*

	Percent of time				
Strategy	1 year	3 years	5 years	7 years	10 years
EV/EBITDA	20.0%	4.5%	0.2%	0.0%	0.0%
Shareholder yield	12.3%	3.4%	0.0%	0.0%	0.0%
EV/sales	27.7%	13.2%	2.2%	0.0%	0.0%
Price/earnings	21.5%	8.3%	0.9%	0.2%	0.0%
Dividend yield	21.3%	7.2%	0.7%	0.0%	0.0%
Price/cash flow	15.4%	3.0%	0.0%	0.0%	0.0%
Price/Book	29.8%	13.4%	5.8%	1.9%	0.0%
Buyback yield	7.1%	0.2%	0.0%	0.0%	0.0%
EV/free cash flow	23.5%	8.5%	6.3%	5.2%	5.4%
Price/cash flow (free)	15.0%	1.3%	0.0%	0.0%	0.0%
NOA change	14.4%	1.5%	0.0%	0.0%	0.0%
Price/sales	27.5%	16.2%	5.4%	0.0%	0.0%
Price/accruals	24.9%	21.1%	4.7%	0.0%	0.0%
Debt/capital	16.8%	3.0%	1.3%	0.0%	0.0%
Total assets to total accruals (TATA)	14.4%	1.3%	0.0%	0.0%	0.0%
Debt change	13.4%	8.7%	0.2%	0.0%	0.0%
Asset turnover	32.4%	22.8%	15.2%	4.7%	3.9%
Sector benchmark	0.0%	0.0%	0.0%	0.0%	0.0%
6-mo. momentum	19.6%	4.7%	2.5%	1.4%	0.0%
Cash flow/debt	19.0%	11.1%	8.7%	1.2%	0.0%
3-mo. momentum	17.4%	4.7%	0.7%	1.2%	0.0%
ROE	37.9%	28.7%	24.2%	22.5%	22.4%
9-mo. momentum	20.9%	6.4%	2.5%	1.4%	0.0%
Market cap	48.2%	49.6%	40.4%	41.2%	36.0%
ROA	34.2%	18.3%	18.8%	15.4%	15.3%
12-mo. momentum	23.3%	13.0%	5.2%	1.7%	0.0%
1-mo. momentum	15.2%	2.1%	0.0%	0.0%	0.0%
EPS change	31.6%	20.2%	15.0%	5.5%	0.0%

IMPLICATIONS

Investors focusing on the industrial sector should buy those industrial stocks with the highest scores on composited Value Factor Two, which includes shareholder yield. It offers the best absolute and risk-adjusted returns and has excellent base rates.

Conversely, investors should shun those industrial stocks that fall into the bottom quintile of composited Value Factor Two. Their return over the 42 years of the study was a scant 1.35 percent, and their maximum decline was 72 percent. They also never beat the sector itself for all rolling five-, seven-, and ten-year periods.

THE INFORMATION TECHNOLOGIES SECTOR

It is ironic that one of the sexiest sectors of all is the one that offers investors the lowest average annual compound return. Yes, the information technologies sector came in last of the ten sectors in terms of total return, with the sector earning an average annual compound return of just 7.29 percent between December 31, 1967, and December 31, 2009. While the information technologies sector led the market bubble between 1995 and March 2000, it suffered dramatic reversals when the bubble burst. The overall sector suffered a maximum decline of 85 percent.

It is perhaps not surprising that one of the most innovative sectors is an unstable investment environment. The relentless innovation and change in the sector make it a difficult place for investors. Remember Atari when it was king of the gamers? Remember Wang Computer, Netscape, Gateway, Pets.com, Webvan, and eToys.com? They all ultimately stumbled, several into the graveyard. Let's take a look at which factors help identify the best and worst stocks in the sector.

As Table 24.19 shows, technology stocks with the lowest enterprise value to sales and price-to-sales did the best, followed by enterprise value to free cash flow and Value Composites Two and Three. By focusing on enterprise value to sales, an investor would have earned an average annual compound return of 13.01 percent, some 5.72 percent ahead of an investor who bought the entire sector. The strategy's standard deviation of return of 27.68 percent was actually *below* that of the sector, which had a standard deviation of return of 31.14 percent. Such high variability gave the strategy a disappointing Sharpe ratio of just .29, and even that is the *highest* Sharpe ratio that any information technology strategy managed to achieve in the sector. Its maximum decline of 64 percent was well below that of the overall sector. Composited Value Factors Two and Three provided slightly lower absolute returns but lower maximum declines and identical Sharpe ratios. As Table 24.20 shows, all five have positive base rates for all rolling one-, three-, five-, seven-, and ten-year rolling periods.

T A B L E   24.19

Summary Results for Various Strategies Applied to the Information Technology Sector (Strategies Benchmarked against the Returns of All Stocks in the Sector) December 31, 1967–December 31, 2009 (Strategies Sorted by Compound Return of the Best Quintile)

Strategy	Geometric mean		Best quintile					
	Best quintile	Worst quintile	Standard deviation (%)	Sharpe ratio	Spread (best-worst)	Spread (best-benchmark)	Worst drawdown	Beta
EV/sales	13.01%	3.42%	27.68%	0.29	9.59%	5.72%	−64.22%	0.83
Price/sales	12.76%	4.03%	28.03%	0.28	8.74%	5.47%	−65.25%	0.84
EV/free cash flow	12.70%	3.08%	28.52%	0.27	9.62%	5.40%	−65.89%	0.88
Value Composite 2	12.55%	2.72%	25.83%	0.29	9.82%	5.25%	−60.66%	0.78
Value Composite 3	12.53%	2.55%	26.14%	0.29	9.98%	5.24%	−60.41%	0.78

(continued on next page)

T A B L E   24.19

Summary Results for Various Strategies Applied to the Information Technology Sector (Strategies Benchmarked against the Returns of All Stocks in the Sector) December 31, 1967–December 31, 2009 (Strategies Sorted by Compound Return of the Best Quintile) *(Continued)*

Strategy	Geometric mean		Best quintile					
	Best quintile	Worst quintile	Standard deviation (%)	Sharpe ratio	Spread (best-worst)	Spread (best-benchmark)	Worst drawdown	Beta
EV/EBITDA	12.36%	2.32%	27.66%	0.27	10.05%	5.07%	−68.39%	0.83
Buyback yield	12.26%	2.34%	25.19%	0.29	9.93%	4.97%	−61.64%	0.77
Price/cash flow (free)	12.11%	2.63%	28.59%	0.25	9.48%	4.82%	−71.25%	0.88
Value Composite 1	11.90%	2.67%	26.89%	0.26	9.23%	4.60%	−63.81%	0.81
Shareholder yield	11.30%	3.12%	25.39%	0.25	8.17%	4.00%	−77.16%	0.78
6-mo. momentum	11.24%	3.40%	33.83%	0.18	7.84%	3.94%	−85.47%	1.05
Price/earnings	11.13%	2.54%	27.39%	0.22	8.59%	3.84%	−68.93%	0.82
Asset turnover	11.06%	−0.04%	31.45%	0.19	11.10%	3.77%	−71.76%	0.97
3-mo. momentum	11.00%	2.74%	32.94%	0.18	8.26%	3.70%	−83.93%	1.03
Cash flow/debt	10.93%	0.92%	31.62%	0.19	10.01%	3.64%	−73.49%	0.98
Price/book	10.92%	7.79%	29.09%	0.20	3.13%	3.63%	−78.80%	0.88
Dividend yield	10.84%	7.22%	24.90%	0.23	3.62%	3.55%	−74.78%	0.76
Price/cash flow	10.81%	1.74%	28.05%	0.21	9.07%	3.51%	−75.10%	0.85
NOA change	10.64%	1.59%	31.01%	0.18	9.04%	3.34%	−85.44%	0.97
9-mo. momentum	10.61%	3.62%	34.11%	0.16	6.99%	3.32%	−87.02%	1.05
Total assets to total accruals (TATA)	10.50%	1.97%	30.80%	0.18	8.53%	3.21%	−88.10%	0.96
ROE	9.99%	3.10%	32.35%	0.15	6.89%	2.69%	−80.61%	0.99
12-mo. momentum	9.87%	4.28%	34.34%	0.14	5.59%	2.58%	−88.08%	1.06
ROA	9.84%	2.04%	31.20%	0.16	7.81%	2.55%	−71.31%	0.96
Debt/capital	9.55%	4.51%	31.33%	0.15	5.04%	2.25%	−88.42%	0.98
EPS change	9.38%	3.23%	35.47%	0.12	6.15%	2.09%	−85.64%	1.09
1-mo. momentum	8.93%	3.82%	32.30%	0.12	5.11%	1.63%	−85.05%	1.02
Market cap	7.48%	7.11%	32.34%	0.08	0.37%	0.18%	−84.32%	1.01
Debt change	7.47%	3.20%	31.87%	0.08	4.27%	0.17%	−86.91%	1.00
Sector benchmark	7.29%	N/A	31.14%	0.07	N/A	N/A	−85.42%	N/A
Price/accruals	6.87%	7.15%	31.39%	0.06	−0.28%	−0.43%	−84.67%	0.98

T A B L E   24.20

Best Quintile: Summary Base Rate Information for All Rolling One-, Three-, Five-, Seven-, and Ten-Year Periods for the Information Technology Sector's Best Quintile (Strategies Benchmarked against the Returns of All Stocks in the Sector) December 31, 1967–December 31, 2009 (Strategies Sorted by Compound Return of the Best Quintile)

Strategy	Percent of time				
	1 year	3 years	5 years	7 years	10 years
EV/sales	66.6%	77.7%	87.7%	93.6%	99.8%
Price/sales	64.8%	76.2%	85.9%	90.0%	99.3%
EV/free cash flow	68.0%	80.9%	80.9%	79.4%	79.1%

(continued on next page)

TABLE 24.20

Best Quintile: Summary Base Rate Information for All Rolling One-, Three-, Five-, Seven-, and Ten-Year Periods for the Information Technology Sector's Best Quintile (Strategies Benchmarked against the Returns of All Stocks in the Sector) December 31, 1967–December 31, 2009 (Strategies Sorted by Compound Return of the Best Quintile) *(Continued)*

Strategy	Percent of time				
	1 year	3 years	5 years	7 years	10 years
Value Composite 2	59.9%	72.8%	81.6%	85.5%	88.2%
Value Composite 3	59.1%	72.6%	79.6%	85.1%	89.4%
EV/EBITDA	59.1%	74.0%	83.9%	88.9%	91.4%
Buyback yield	69.0%	83.0%	91.0%	98.3%	99.8%
Price/cash flow (free)	65.2%	72.1%	81.6%	80.3%	81.5%
Value Composite 1	56.7%	70.6%	76.5%	83.2%	87.2%
Shareholder yield	67.8%	74.5%	82.5%	85.1%	95.8%
6-mo. momentum	64.2%	75.3%	80.3%	88.9%	90.9%
Price/earnings	55.3%	69.8%	72.6%	77.7%	80.8%
Asset turnover	62.8%	78.1%	90.8%	96.2%	99.3%
3-mo. momentum	65.6%	76.8%	85.7%	89.8%	93.6%
Cash flow/debt	61.7%	75.1%	79.8%	75.6%	76.4%
Price/book	58.5%	68.3%	77.4%	88.9%	97.3%
Dividend yield	61.7%	71.5%	75.8%	79.4%	87.9%
Price/cash flow	56.7%	63.4%	74.2%	79.4%	77.8%
NOA change	61.5%	77.9%	85.0%	86.5%	89.9%
9-mo. momentum	58.7%	69.4%	75.3%	86.5%	84.7%
Total assets to total accruals (TATA)	60.9%	68.7%	77.8%	84.8%	89.7%
ROE	61.9%	66.8%	78.3%	81.3%	84.5%
12-mo. momentum	57.1%	67.7%	69.7%	80.3%	79.8%
ROA	60.7%	67.2%	76.5%	79.6%	82.8%
Debt/capital	65.2%	60.4%	60.1%	63.3%	73.6%
EPS change	51.2%	63.6%	67.3%	76.1%	79.6%
1-mo. momentum	58.1%	68.3%	75.6%	84.4%	90.1%
Market cap	47.4%	41.9%	45.3%	45.0%	40.9%
Debt change	51.2%	54.5%	56.7%	58.8%	60.8%
Sector benchmark	0.0%	0.0%	0.0%	0.0%	0.0%
Price/accruals	42.7%	40.4%	52.2%	53.6%	57.1%

THE DOWNSIDE

The only factor that didn't improve the sector's returns was price-to-accruals. Also Investors who want to identify which technology stocks to avoid should pay attention to a technology company's asset turnover. This was the only factor in which the worst quintile actually lost money over the 42 years of our study, earning an average annual compound return of –.04 percent. The technology stocks with the worst asset turnover also had a whopping maximum decline of 96 percent. Indeed, the maximum declines for most of the factors in the worst quintile were large enough to consign these information technology stocks to the graveyard. The technology stocks in Value Factor Two's worst quintile had a maximum decline of 97 percent, those in the worst quintile by price-to-sales plummeted 95 percent, and those in the worst quintile by PE ratios plunged 94 percent. To navigate this treacherous sector, investors *must* avoid those stocks in the bottom quintile; they are toxic. Table 24.21 shows the base rates for the worst quintiles.

T A B L E   24.21

Worst Quintile: Summary Base Rate Information for All Rolling One-, Three-, Five-, Seven-, and Ten-Year Periods for the Information Technology Sector's Worst Quintile (Strategies Benchmarked against the Returns of All Stocks in the Sector) December 31, 1967–December 31, 2009 (Strategies Sorted by Compound Return of the Best Quintile)

	Percent of time				
Strategy	**1 year**	**3 years**	**5 years**	**7 years**	**10 years**
EV/sales	43.5%	39.6%	33.6%	30.1%	23.2%
Price/sales	44.3%	37.4%	33.4%	27.7%	11.1%
EV/free cash flow	35.8%	26.4%	22.4%	25.6%	28.3%
Value Composite 2	44.1%	31.1%	35.4%	29.1%	26.8%
Value Composite 3	43.3%	30.4%	35.4%	28.9%	26.4%
EV/EBITDA	39.1%	29.8%	27.8%	24.4%	24.4%
Buyback yield	24.5%	20.2%	16.8%	14.2%	13.5%
Price/cash flow (free)	39.5%	27.0%	28.9%	29.9%	30.0%
Value Composite 1	42.9%	29.1%	33.4%	27.7%	29.6%
Shareholder yield	27.5%	17.2%	15.9%	16.6%	14.3%
6-mo. momentum	33.2%	17.7%	11.9%	2.6%	0.2%
Price/earnings	35.6%	18.7%	15.5%	16.4%	19.5%
Asset turnover	27.1%	17.0%	4.9%	5.0%	0.2%
3-mo. momentum	21.5%	11.3%	5.6%	2.1%	0.0%
Cash flow/debt	30.0%	20.6%	17.3%	19.4%	18.5%
Price/book	52.4%	48.3%	48.4%	54.3%	55.4%
Dividend yield	39.7%	38.5%	41.0%	47.2%	45.1%
Price/cash flow	32.6%	17.9%	13.7%	12.6%	14.0%
NOA change	28.7%	15.1%	6.3%	2.8%	0.0%
9-mo. momentum	40.7%	26.6%	24.2%	13.7%	10.8%
Total assets to total accruals (TATA)	26.7%	14.3%	11.9%	2.8%	0.5%
ROE	38.7%	33.2%	26.9%	28.0%	26.4%
12-mo. momentum	43.1%	33.4%	37.4%	38.4%	41.6%
ROA	36.8%	31.7%	22.2%	28.9%	26.4%
Debt/capital	41.1%	36.2%	28.9%	20.9%	12.1%
EPS change	35.8%	24.9%	11.7%	2.6%	2.2%
1-mo. momentum	18.2%	11.5%	7.8%	2.4%	0.0%
Market cap	51.0%	54.0%	52.0%	54.0%	54.2%
Debt change	30.0%	9.4%	2.2%	2.4%	0.0%
Sector benchmark	0.0%	0.0%	0.0%	0.0%	0.0%
Price/accruals	49.8%	45.7%	46.9%	45.3%	41.4%

IMPLICATIONS

The information technologies sector is the most treacherous of the 10 sectors. It offered the lowest average annual returns along with huge maximum declines for both the overall sector and for those stocks in the various factors' worst quintile. The most successful strategies all revolve around technology stocks with the cheapest valuations. Investors in technology stocks are best served by looking at enterprise value to sales, price-to-sales, and the composited value factors. Even then, the overall volatility leads to the *best* strategy providing a compound return of only 13.01 percent and a Sharpe ratio of .29. You would have done better just buying the entire consumer staples sector. No wonder Warren Buffett avoids technology stocks.

Investors in the technology sector need to pay very close attention to stocks in the worst quintiles—and avoid them like the plague. The peak-to-trough declines are huge, and the total returns are horrible. Nevertheless, despite the volatility, there are times when technology stocks are outstanding investments. I have found that a better way to get to the best technology stocks is to start with the All Stocks universe and then use multifactor models to select across all economic sectors. When technology stocks make it through that filter, they tend to offer much better performance.

THE MATERIALS SECTOR

As Table 24.22 shows, the best returns from the materials sector come from the stocks that score highest on composited Value Factor Three. That strategy earned an average annual compound return of 16.48 percent, some 4.89 percent higher than the overall sector. Its standard deviation of return of 21.71 percent was slightly higher than that of the overall sector's 20.83 percent, and its Sharpe ratio is a decent .53. As Table 24.23 shows, the base rates for the strategy are all positive, with the strategy beating the sector in 93 percent of all rolling five-year periods and in 100 percent of all rolling ten-year periods. Rounding out the top five are the other two value factors—EV/EBITDA and shareholder yield. While shareholder yield had a lower absolute return, it had a higher Sharpe ratio because of its lower volatility. The worst-case maximum decline for the best strategy of buying the quintile of stocks that scored highest on Value Factor Three was 63 percent, just two points higher than the maximum decline for the overall sector, which was a loss of 61 percent.

T A B L E   24.22

Summary Results for Various Strategies Applied to the Materials Sector (Strategies Benchmarked against the Returns of All Stocks in the Sector) December 31, 1967–December 31, 2009 (Strategies Sorted by Compound Return of the Best Quintile)

| Strategy | Geometric mean | | Best quintile | | | | | |
	Best quintile	Worst quintile	Standard deviation (%)	Sharpe ratio	Spread (best-worst)	Spread (best-benchmark)	Worst drawdown	Beta
Value Composite 3	16.48%	5.56%	21.71%	0.53	10.92%	4.89%	−63.42%	0.99
Value Composite 2	16.48%	5.32%	21.58%	0.53	11.16%	4.89%	−63.53%	0.98
EV/EBITDA	16.02%	5.27%	21.87%	0.50	10.75%	4.43%	−67.13%	1.00
Value Composite 1	15.72%	5.88%	22.08%	0.49	9.85%	4.13%	−64.05%	1.01
Shareholder yield	15.36%	4.87%	19.29%	0.54	10.49%	3.77%	−57.89%	0.88

(continued on next page)

T A B L E   24.22

Summary Results for Various Strategies Applied to the Materials Sector (Strategies Benchmarked against the Returns of All Stocks in the Sector) December 31, 1967–December 31, 2009 (Strategies Sorted by Compound Return of the Best Quintile) *(Continued)*

	Geometric mean		Best quintile					
Strategy	**Best quintile**	**Worst quintile**	**Standard deviation (%)**	**Sharpe ratio**	**Spread (best-worst)**	**Spread (best-benchmark)**	**Worst drawdown**	**Beta**
Price/cash flow	15.19%	5.53%	22.61%	0.45	9.66%	3.60%	−64.69%	1.04
Dividend yield	14.54%	5.99%	19.45%	0.49	8.55%	2.95%	−58.83%	0.88
Price/earnings	14.54%	6.40%	22.04%	0.43	8.14%	2.95%	−66.67%	1.01
Price/cash flow (free)	14.08%	7.58%	22.27%	0.41	6.50%	2.49%	−62.71%	1.02
Buyback yield	14.02%	6.63%	19.52%	0.46	7.39%	2.43%	−55.97%	0.89
EV/free cash flow	13.66%	7.67%	21.31%	0.41	5.99%	2.07%	−63.31%	0.98
EV/sales	13.55%	6.05%	22.42%	0.38	7.50%	1.96%	−64.92%	1.00
Price/sales	13.52%	6.69%	23.52%	0.36	6.83%	1.93%	−65.14%	1.05
Price/book	13.48%	7.15%	23.95%	0.35	6.33%	1.89%	−65.24%	1.09
Price/accruals	13.44%	8.62%	23.18%	0.36	4.82%	1.85%	−62.93%	1.06
Total assets to total accruals (TATA)	13.12%	7.87%	21.17%	0.38	5.25%	1.53%	−64.03%	0.99
Debt change	12.98%	9.36%	21.59%	0.37	3.62%	1.39%	−62.77%	1.01
NOA change	12.76%	7.41%	21.21%	0.37	5.35%	1.17%	−62.67%	0.99
Cash flow/debt	12.50%	5.70%	20.04%	0.37	6.81%	0.91%	−60.36%	0.90
Debt/capital	12.50%	6.93%	21.71%	0.35	5.57%	0.91%	−61.04%	0.99
6-mo. momentum	12.21%	8.64%	22.51%	0.32	3.57%	0.62%	−64.23%	1.01
3-mo. momentum	12.09%	8.68%	21.99%	0.32	3.41%	0.50%	−62.54%	1.01
9-mo. momentum	11.75%	9.49%	22.81%	0.30	2.26%	0.16%	−65.22%	1.01
Sector benchmark	11.59%	N/A	20.83%	0.32	N/A	N/A	−61.36%	N/A
Asset turnover	11.40%	7.01%	20.66%	0.31	4.39%	−0.19%	−60.59%	0.91
1-mo. momentum	11.37%	9.91%	21.57%	0.30	1.47%	−0.22%	−60.09%	1.01
Market cap	11.35%	9.44%	22.29%	0.28	1.91%	−0.24%	−63.43%	1.02
ROA	11.14%	7.85%	20.86%	0.29	3.29%	−0.45%	−66.78%	0.95
12-mo. momentum	10.92%	10.13%	22.99%	0.26	0.80%	−0.67%	−65.33%	1.01
EPS change	10.37%	8.99%	22.77%	0.24	1.38%	−1.22%	−60.49%	1.05
ROE	9.63%	8.08%	21.37%	0.22	1.55%	−1.96%	−65.84%	0.97

T A B L E   24-23

Best Quintile: Summary Base Rate Information for All Rolling One-, Three-, Five-, Seven-, and Ten-Year Periods for the Materials Sector's Best Quintile (Strategies Benchmarked against the Returns of All Stocks in the Sector) December 31, 1967–December 31, 2009 (Strategies Sorted by Compound Return of the Best Quintile)

	Percent of time				
Strategy	**1 year**	**3 years**	**5 years**	**7 years**	**10 years**
Value Composite 3	73.3%	86.2%	92.6%	98.8%	100.0%
Value Composite 2	72.9%	86.8%	93.7%	100.0%	100.0%
EV/EBITDA	68.0%	84.9%	91.3%	99.8%	100.0%

(continued on next page)

TABLE 24–23

Best Quintile: Summary Base Rate Information for All Rolling One-, Three-, Five-, Seven-, and Ten-Year Periods for the Materials Sector's Best Quintile (Strategies Benchmarked against the Returns of All Stocks in the Sector) December 31, 1967–December 31, 2009 (Strategies Sorted by Compound Return of the Best Quintile) *(Continued)*

	Percent of time				
Strategy	1 year	3 years	5 years	7 years	10 years
Value Composite 1	67.2%	78.3%	86.8%	99.8%	100.0%
Shareholder yield	73.1%	90.0%	96.6%	100.0%	100.0%
Price/cash flow	66.0%	74.5%	83.4%	94.1%	99.3%
Dividend yield	68.0%	77.0%	80.7%	88.4%	97.3%
Price/earnings	63.4%	73.4%	76.2%	84.4%	87.7%
Price/cash flow (free)	64.6%	69.6%	79.1%	91.2%	94.3%
Buyback yield	64.4%	71.9%	80.0%	87.9%	93.3%
EV/free cash flow	63.8%	67.7%	78.3%	92.2%	96.8%
EV/sales	58.5%	68.3%	77.8%	78.4%	87.2%
Price/sales	54.3%	63.6%	70.9%	79.1%	89.4%
Price/book	49.8%	56.6%	65.9%	63.7%	53.9%
Price/accruals	54.7%	57.9%	65.2%	63.5%	65.0%
Total assets to total accruals (TATA)	61.9%	68.3%	77.4%	86.3%	87.9%
Debt change	67.2%	78.3%	83.2%	87.0%	91.1%
NOA change	56.3%	60.9%	71.7%	78.9%	80.5%
Cash flow/debt	54.3%	64.0%	58.1%	47.9%	46.3%
Debt/capital	54.9%	55.1%	51.6%	56.4%	56.2%
6-mo. momentum	57.9%	66.4%	77.1%	85.5%	82.8%
3-mo. momentum	53.4%	54.7%	59.9%	60.4%	62.8%
9-mo. momentum	60.7%	61.1%	68.8%	75.4%	73.6%
Sector benchmark	0.0%	0.0%	0.0%	0.0%	0.0%
Asset turnover	58.5%	59.1%	60.5%	62.3%	74.1%
1-mo. momentum	44.1%	47.2%	46.4%	41.0%	34.2%
Market cap	48.6%	44.5%	42.6%	42.9%	43.1%
ROA	48.6%	48.7%	50.7%	44.3%	43.6%
12-mo. momentum	57.5%	54.9%	57.4%	58.5%	64.0%
EPS change	43.3%	45.7%	41.3%	31.0%	26.1%
ROE	40.9%	39.8%	27.4%	21.8%	22.2%

THE DOWNSIDE

Short-term and long-term momentum failed to beat the overall sector's returns, as did asset turnover, ROA, ROE, and stocks with the best percentage earnings gains. The stocks in the *worst* quintile by Value Factor Two, Value Factor Three, and EV/EBITDA all failed to beat an investment in 30-day U.S. T-bills, and also had very low base rates. As Table 24.24 shows, the stocks from the materials sectors with the worst scores on composited Value Factors Two and Three had single-digit base rates for all rolling five-year periods and no wins in any rolling seven- or ten-year periods. The maximum declines for the worst quintiles in Value Factors Two and Three exceeded 72 percent.

T A B L E   24.24

Worst Qquintile: Summary Base Rate Information for All Rolling One-, Three-, Five-, Seven-, and Ten-Year Periods for the Materials Sector's Worst Quintile (Strategies Benchmarked against the Returns of All Stocks in the Sector) December 31, 1967–December 31, 2009 (Strategies Sorted by Compound Return of the Best Quintile)

	Percent of time				
Strategy	1 year	3 years	5 years	7 years	10 years
Value Composite 3	27.5%	14.9%	6.5%	0.0%	0.0%
Value Composite 2	25.9%	14.0%	6.3%	0.0%	0.0%
EV/EBITDA	27.7%	18.3%	10.5%	0.7%	0.0%
Value Composite 1	27.5%	15.3%	6.7%	1.2%	0.0%
Shareholder yield	20.2%	8.1%	5.4%	1.7%	0.0%
Price/cash flow	24.5%	13.6%	7.0%	0.2%	0.0%
Dividend yield	25.3%	25.5%	9.2%	3.6%	0.0%
Price/earnings	32.6%	27.4%	15.9%	2.4%	0.0%
Price/cash flow (free)	27.7%	18.9%	6.1%	0.0%	0.0%
Buyback yield	22.5%	6.4%	5.6%	1.2%	0.0%
EV/free cash flow	23.5%	17.0%	7.8%	0.5%	0.0%
EV/sales	30.4%	21.7%	11.9%	5.0%	0.5%
Price/sales	31.8%	22.3%	11.9%	4.7%	0.5%
Price/book	28.7%	17.4%	4.0%	0.0%	0.0%
Price/accruals	29.6%	20.4%	8.7%	5.0%	5.4%
Total assets to total accruals (TATA)	25.5%	14.9%	11.2%	10.9%	8.9%
Debt change	38.1%	36.8%	29.1%	18.7%	16.0%
NOA change	29.4%	17.4%	14.8%	5.9%	1.7%
Cash flow/debt	29.1%	21.9%	6.3%	2.6%	3.0%
Debt/capital	31.4%	15.5%	2.9%	0.7%	0.0%
6-mo. momentum	29.8%	13.0%	2.2%	1.9%	1.5%
3-mo. momentum	25.7%	12.3%	2.2%	1.4%	0.2%
9-mo. momentum	33.2%	20.0%	8.7%	5.0%	6.4%
Sector benchmark	0.0%	0.0%	0.0%	0.0%	0.0%
Asset turnover	32.0%	27.9%	24.2%	14.9%	11.8%
1-mo. momentum	27.5%	16.6%	6.1%	1.9%	1.5%
Market cap	38.3%	39.8%	36.5%	24.9%	14.5%
ROA	36.6%	28.9%	22.9%	15.6%	18.0%
12-mo. momentum	35.6%	22.1%	13.7%	8.3%	8.9%
EPS change	39.1%	26.0%	14.6%	2.4%	0.2%
ROE	37.7%	30.2%	24.7%	19.2%	19.2%

IMPLICATIONS

As the emerging pattern continues to show, focusing on the best quintile from composited Value Factors Two or Three offers the best returns for investors in the materials sector. For investors in the materials sector willing to give up some overall return for a slightly smoother ride, focusing on stocks with the highest shareholder yield offers the highest Sharpe ratio and a maximum decline of 58 percent.

As we have seen with the other sectors, investors should avoid those materials stocks that fall into the worst quintile for any of the composited value factors, EV/EBITDA, and shareholder yield. They offer little in the way of return and much in the way of increased risk.

THE TELECOMMUNICATIONS SECTOR

Welcome to the second toughest sector—telecommunications. While the sector itself offers some strategies that provide sector-beating performance and the overall sector provides a reasonable compound average annual return of 11.86 percent, stocks in the worst quintiles suffer *huge* maximum declines, which lead many of them to seek bankruptcy protection in the first decade of the 2000s. According to ZDNet, between 2000 and April 2004, 68 publicly traded telecom companies filed for Chapter 11 bankruptcy, with some of the largest and best known—Worldcom, MCI, Global Crossing, and XO Communications—all going bankrupt. Table 24.25 summarizes the results for all of the various factors.

T A B L E   24.25

Summary Results for Various Strategies Applied to the Telecommunication Services Sector (Strategies Benchmarked against the Returns of All Stocks in the Sector) December 31, 1967–December 31, 2009 (Strategies Sorted by Compound Return of the Best Quintile)

	Geometric mean		Best quintile					
Strategy	Best quintile	Worst quintile	Standard deviation (%)	Sharpe ratio	Spread (best-worst)	Spread (best-benchmark)	Worst drawdown	Beta
Value Composite 1	17.00%	5.08%	17.07%	0.70	11.92%	5.14%	−67.05%	0.68
Price/cash flow	16.74%	5.52%	19.00%	0.62	11.22%	4.88%	−76.98%	0.79
Value Composite 3	16.59%	4.01%	16.92%	0.68	12.58%	4.73%	−66.05%	0.68
Value Composite 2	16.53%	4.56%	16.76%	0.69	11.97%	4.67%	−65.14%	0.66
Price/earnings	16.06%	5.09%	17.14%	0.65	10.97%	4.20%	−62.54%	0.69
EV/EBITDA	15.80%	5.09%	18.06%	0.60	10.71%	3.94%	−65.90%	0.70
Price/cash flow (free)	14.79%	5.03%	19.36%	0.51	9.76%	2.93%	−76.11%	0.79
Price/book	14.48%	7.31%	20.96%	0.45	7.17%	2.62%	−86.35%	0.88
Shareholder yield	14.13%	6.62%	16.94%	0.54	7.51%	2.27%	−66.59%	0.67
Dividend yield	14.02%	9.12%	16.08%	0.56	4.90%	2.16%	−63.29%	0.62
Price/sales	13.91%	6.31%	23.27%	0.38	7.60%	2.05%	−86.53%	0.98
EV/free cash flow	13.69%	4.08%	20.16%	0.43	9.61%	1.83%	−70.54%	0.79
3-mo. momentum	13.63%	7.41%	22.59%	0.38	6.22%	1.77%	−82.64%	0.97
6-mo. momentum	13.53%	7.02%	23.12%	0.37	6.51%	1.67%	−79.42%	0.96
9-mo. momentum	13.27%	7.98%	23.43%	0.35	5.30%	1.41%	−80.13%	0.96
NOA change	13.11%	5.26%	20.39%	0.40	7.85%	1.25%	−78.09%	0.87
Price/accruals	13.03%	8.88%	24.61%	0.33	4.15%	1.17%	−94.77%	1.06
12-mo. momentum	12.86%	8.36%	23.90%	0.33	4.50%	1.00%	−82.21%	0.97
Buyback yield	12.52%	7.51%	19.02%	0.40	5.01%	0.66%	−70.87%	0.79
ROE	12.48%	5.57%	21.13%	0.35	6.91%	0.62%	−61.16%	0.79
Debt change	12.46%	6.76%	20.09%	0.37	5.69%	0.60%	−73.74%	0.84
1-mo. momentum	12.05%	9.24%	22.43%	0.31	2.81%	0.19%	−85.72%	1.00
Sector benchmark	11.86%	N/A	21.44%	0.32	N/A	N/A	−88.05%	N/A

(continued on next page)

TABLE 24.25

Summary Results for Various Strategies Applied to the Telecommunication Services Sector (Strategies Benchmarked against the Returns of All Stocks in the Sector) December 31, 1967–December 31, 2009 (Strategies Sorted by Compound Return of the Best Quintile) *(Continued)*

	Geometric mean		Best quintile					
Strategy	Best quintile	Worst quintile	Standard deviation (%)	Sharpe ratio	Spread (best-worst)	Spread (best-benchmark)	Worst drawdown	Beta
Market cap	11.80%	9.60%	27.64%	0.25	2.19%	−0.06%	−91.41%	1.16
EV/sales	11.24%	6.58%	22.86%	0.27	4.66%	−0.62%	−83.50%	0.91
ROA	10.87%	8.10%	20.73%	0.28	2.77%	−0.99%	−67.71%	0.78
Cash flow/debt	10.63%	7.86%	19.78%	0.28	2.77%	−1.23%	−66.03%	0.76
EPS change	10.63%	10.24%	22.48%	0.25	0.39%	−1.23%	−81.94%	0.92
Total assets to total accruals (TATA)	10.59%	8.13%	22.57%	0.25	2.46%	−1.27%	−85.97%	0.97
Debt/capital	9.98%	5.58%	22.75%	0.22	4.40%	−1.87%	−86.25%	0.93
Asset turnover	9.42%	7.33%	23.82%	0.19	2.09%	−2.44%	−78.93%	0.93

Even the *best* performing strategies had huge maximum declines; all with drops exceeding 60 percent and the overall sector suffering a peak-to-trough loss of 88 percent. It's best to keep this at the top of your mind as we look for strategies that offer sector- and market-beating returns. As usual, we find all three of the composited value factors in the top five best-performing strategies, with Value Factor One leading the way. Between 1967 and 2009, an investor who consistently bought the telecom stocks that were in the best quintile of Value Factor One would have earned an average annual compound return of 17 percent, some 5.14 percent better than an investment in the telecom sector itself. Its standard deviation of return of 17.07 percent was well below that of the overall sector's 21.44 percent. That led to a robust Sharpe ratio of .70. The base rates for the strategy—featured in Table 24.26—were all positive, but not as high as we've seen with the other sectors. Here, buying the best quintile from Value Factor One beat the telecom sector in 79 percent of all rolling five-year periods and in 83 percent of all rolling ten-year periods. Rounding out the top five performers were composited Value Factors Two and Three, as well as buying the telecom stocks with the lowest price-to-cash flows and PE ratios.

TABLE 24.26

Best Quintile: Summary Base Rate Information for All Rolling One-, Three-, Five-, Seven-, and Ten-Year Periods for the Telecommunication Services Sector's Best Quintile (Strategies Benchmarked against the Returns of All Stocks in the Sector) December 31, 1967–December 31, 2009 (Strategies Sorted by Compound Return of the Best Quintile)

	Percent of time				
Strategy	1 year	3 years	5 years	7 years	10 years
Value Composite 1	65.4%	66.6%	78.7%	79.9%	82.5%
Price/cash flow	68.2%	72.8%	75.3%	80.1%	80.8%
Value Composite 3	63.4%	65.5%	70.6%	76.1%	78.3%

(continued on next page)

T A B L E   24.26

Best Quintile: Summary Base Rate Information for All Rolling One-, Three-, Five-, Seven-, and Ten-Year Periods for the Telecommunication Services Sector's Best Quintile (Strategies Benchmarked against the Returns of All Stocks in the Sector) December 31, 1967–December 31, 2009 (Strategies Sorted by Compound Return of the Best Quintile) (Continued)

	Percent of time				
Strategy	**1 year**	**3 years**	**5 years**	**7 years**	**10 years**
Value Composite 2	64.0%	66.4%	73.3%	75.8%	75.4%
Price/earnings	58.7%	69.8%	72.4%	83.6%	85.0%
EV/EBITDA	60.5%	61.5%	65.2%	65.9%	70.9%
Price/cash flow (free)	58.3%	64.7%	66.8%	71.6%	74.6%
Price/book	67.4%	71.3%	70.0%	76.8%	78.6%
Shareholder yield	56.3%	53.4%	58.7%	67.3%	74.4%
Dividend yield	53.4%	51.9%	57.4%	65.2%	74.9%
Price/sales	57.1%	62.3%	69.3%	71.8%	72.2%
EV/free cash flow	60.3%	62.3%	65.2%	64.5%	65.5%
3-mo. momentum	52.8%	66.2%	71.1%	79.1%	80.3%
6-mo. momentum	51.8%	59.1%	67.7%	67.8%	73.6%
9-mo. momentum	50.6%	56.6%	64.3%	67.5%	74.4%
NOA change	53.0%	61.7%	70.9%	80.6%	82.5%
Price/accruals	59.5%	59.1%	54.9%	47.6%	47.3%
12-mo. momentum	52.0%	53.6%	63.0%	67.5%	73.4%
Buyback yield	44.5%	40.2%	42.2%	50.0%	53.7%
ROE	51.8%	49.8%	48.2%	51.9%	52.2%
Debt change	52.6%	58.7%	70.9%	74.6%	78.1%
1-mo. momentum	47.2%	51.1%	56.3%	52.1%	58.6%
Sector benchmark	0.0%	0.0%	0.0%	0.0%	0.0%
Market cap	50.0%	45.5%	45.7%	49.1%	61.6%
EV/sales	52.2%	46.8%	49.6%	50.7%	53.4%
ROA	41.9%	35.5%	43.9%	41.2%	41.6%
Cash flow/debt	45.3%	38.5%	38.1%	35.5%	32.3%
EPS change	47.0%	43.6%	42.2%	36.3%	36.0%
Total assets to total accruals (TATA)	42.1%	38.9%	31.4%	33.2%	38.4%
Debt/capital	50.4%	49.1%	50.7%	53.3%	53.4%
Asset turnover	42.3%	42.1%	41.7%	40.3%	42.1%

THE DOWNSIDE

EV-to-sales, ROA, cash flow to debt, total assets to total accruals, and buying stocks with the best percentage change in earnings per share all failed to beat the overall telecom sector's return. Yet it is when we look at buying stocks in the worst quintile of the composited value factors, price-to-cash flow and PE that the true horror story emerges.

First, none of these strategies beats an investment in 30-day U.S. T-bills—and *all* had maximum declines exceeding 97 percent. No doubt many of those companies that filed for bankruptcy found themselves in these very quintiles. Yet the base rates featured in Table 24.27 show how tricky this sector can be—usually, once you get out to the longer holding periods of seven and ten years, the base rates for success from the worst quintile fall close to zero. Yet here we see the worst quintile by Value Factor One actually beating the sector in 14 percent of all rolling ten-year periods, and the worst quintile by price-to-cash flow beating the sector in 30 percent of all rolling ten-year periods. No doubt this occurred at the tail end of the stock market bubble, but you can certainly see how it might be difficult for someone looking for telecom stocks to short to get a reliable measure by just looking at the base rates.

T A B L E 24.27

Worst Quintile: Summary Base Rate Information for All Rolling One-, Three-, Five-, Seven-, and Ten-Year Periods for the Telecommunication Services Sector's Worst Quintile (Strategies Benchmarked against the Returns of All Stocks in the Sector) December 31, 1967–December 31, 2009 (Strategies Sorted by Compound Return of the Best Quintile)

	Percent of time				
Strategy	1 year	3 years	5 years	7 years	10 years
Value Composite 1	41.7%	33.0%	22.0%	16.4%	14.0%
Price/cash flow	35.2%	31.9%	29.4%	29.9%	29.8%
Value Composite 3	37.9%	25.1%	15.0%	10.2%	6.9%
Value Composite 2	42.9%	30.9%	22.2%	16.6%	14.0%
Price/earnings	42.7%	33.6%	28.5%	17.1%	15.0%
EV/EBITDA	42.5%	36.6%	26.7%	15.6%	10.6%
Price/cash flow (free)	38.5%	32.3%	27.8%	18.0%	18.0%
Price/book	36.6%	32.1%	24.9%	19.2%	18.5%
Shareholder yield	33.4%	27.2%	25.3%	26.5%	31.5%
Dividend yield	46.2%	42.1%	33.4%	33.9%	38.9%
Price/sales	38.1%	31.3%	26.9%	25.6%	24.9%
EV/free cash flow	36.4%	32.1%	28.3%	20.1%	14.5%
3-mo. momentum	38.7%	30.4%	22.6%	14.9%	8.9%
6-mo. momentum	41.7%	35.1%	27.4%	21.8%	17.5%
9-mo. momentum	39.9%	31.5%	23.5%	16.8%	10.3%
NOA change	28.9%	13.8%	10.1%	6.6%	3.7%
Price/accruals	35.6%	33.6%	35.9%	30.8%	33.5%
12-mo. momentum	41.3%	33.0%	17.0%	11.4%	6.2%
Buyback yield	34.8%	25.1%	28.7%	30.1%	33.5%
ROE	37.0%	31.9%	20.4%	21.3%	17.5%
Debt change	31.8%	18.5%	11.9%	4.0%	0.7%
1-mo. momentum	44.7%	41.1%	29.8%	25.6%	22.7%
Sector benchmark	0.0%	0.0%	0.0%	0.0%	0.0%
Market cap	43.5%	39.8%	36.3%	30.3%	26.6%
EV/sales	44.3%	35.5%	28.7%	26.8%	23.9%
ROA	47.6%	54.9%	47.8%	44.5%	47.0%
Cash flow/debt	47.2%	40.6%	41.0%	38.4%	41.6%
EPS change	41.9%	42.1%	37.9%	31.5%	35.0%
Total assets to total accruals (TATA)	34.8%	24.9%	19.1%	15.6%	10.3%
Debt/capital	40.7%	29.4%	20.2%	10.7%	8.9%
Asset turnover	43.7%	37.0%	30.9%	20.4%	14.8%

IMPLICATIONS

The telecom sector offers disciplined investors an excellent return if they are willing to stick with those stocks with the best overall scores on the various composited value factors. Yet the sector has suffered extreme levels of volatility and some of the largest bankruptcies of any sector. Investors need to exercise extreme caution and *never* let their telecom portfolio drift into stocks that fall into the worst quintiles.

Telecom stocks that are the priciest ranked by any of the composited value factors, price-to-cash flow, or PE ratios should be avoided like the plague.

THE UTILITIES SECTOR

We wind up by moving from one of the most volatile sectors to the least—utilities. Many conservative investors are most comfortable in the placid waters of the utility sector. Historically, utilities have offered investors reasonable returns with much lower volatility and downside risk than any of the other nine sectors. Our analysis, featured in Table 24.28, shows that is absolutely true. While the sector itself returned a respectable average annual compound return of 11.25 percent over the 42 years of our study, investors could have done better by simply focusing on those utility stocks with the highest scores on any of the three composited value factors. An investor who diligently invested in the utility stocks that were in the best quintile of Value Factor Two or Three would have earned an average annual compound return of 16.01 percent. The standard deviation of return for Value Factor Two was slightly lower than that of Three, coming in at 14.51 and 14.60 percent, respectively. The high returns married to lower volatility gave each a Sharpe ratio of .75 or higher. Table 24.28 shows the returns for all the strategies tested. We see that buying those utility stocks in the best quintile of EV/EBITDA and price-to-cash flow round out the top five best-performing strategies. Table 24.29 shows the base rates for all strategies. The top three performing strategies also have excellent base rates, with all three beating the sector average in over 80 percent of all rolling one-year periods and in 100 percent of all rolling ten-year periods.

TABLE 24.28

Summary Results for Various Strategies Applied to the Utilities Sector (Strategies Benchmarked against the Returns of All Stocks in the Sector) December 31, 1967–December 31, 2009 (Strategies Sorted by Compound Return of the Best Quintile)

| | Geometric mean | | Best quintile | | | | | |
Strategy	Best quintile	Worst quintile	Standard deviation (%)	Sharpe ratio	Spread (best-worst)	Spread (best-benchmark)	Worst drawdown	Beta
Value Composite 2	16.01%	6.52%	14.51%	0.76	9.49%	4.77%	−32.96%	1.01
Value Composite 3	16.01%	7.00%	14.60%	0.75	9.01%	4.76%	−36.82%	1.02
Value Composite 1	15.63%	7.14%	14.90%	0.71	8.50%	4.39%	−36.92%	1.04
EV/EBITDA	15.55%	7.05%	16.91%	0.62	8.50%	4.31%	−55.79%	1.04

(continued on next page)

TABLE 24.28

Summary Results for Various Strategies Applied to the Utilities Sector (Strategies Benchmarked against the Returns of All Stocks in the Sector) December 31, 1967–December 31, 2009 (Strategies Sorted by Compound Return of the Best Quintile) *(Continued)*

	Geometric mean		Best quintile					
Strategy	Best quintile	Worst quintile	Standard deviation (%)	Sharpe ratio	Spread (best-worst)	Spread (best-benchmark)	Worst drawdown	Beta
Price/cash flow	14.91%	7.59%	15.20%	0.65	7.32%	3.67%	−39.99%	1.06
EV/free cash flow	14.74%	10.95%	16.01%	0.61	3.79%	3.50%	−45.03%	0.99
Shareholder yield	14.69%	7.95%	13.80%	0.70	6.75%	3.45%	−38.12%	0.96
Price/earnings	14.57%	8.15%	15.09%	0.63	6.42%	3.32%	−39.54%	1.05
Price/cash flow (free)	14.41%	10.30%	14.68%	0.64	4.11%	3.17%	−45.54%	1.02
Price/sales	14.35%	7.73%	16.21%	0.58	6.61%	3.10%	−50.16%	1.07
Price/accruals	13.92%	8.30%	15.08%	0.59	5.62%	2.67%	−43.00%	1.05
Price/book	13.38%	7.51%	16.43%	0.51	5.88%	2.14%	−47.80%	1.11
Debt/capital	13.24%	8.76%	16.43%	0.50	4.49%	2.00%	−47.80%	0.97
Buyback yield	13.03%	8.34%	14.11%	0.57	4.69%	1.78%	−44.22%	0.96
NOA change	12.85%	9.10%	14.02%	0.56	3.75%	1.61%	−47.06%	0.98
Market cap	12.76%	8.55%	13.46%	0.58	4.21%	1.51%	−39.39%	0.89
EV/sales	12.18%	9.25%	19.94%	0.36	2.93%	0.94%	−68.02%	1.09
Dividend yield	12.16%	8.09%	14.57%	0.49	4.07%	0.91%	−38.48%	0.99
Cash flow/debt	12.00%	10.48%	14.43%	0.49	1.52%	0.75%	−46.12%	0.95
Debt change	11.98%	10.06%	13.84%	0.50	1.91%	0.73%	−47.56%	0.97
3-mo. momentum	11.70%	10.06%	13.80%	0.49	1.64%	0.45%	−42.24%	0.94
6-mo. momentum	11.57%	10.43%	13.92%	0.47	1.14%	0.33%	−44.74%	0.92
Asset turnover	11.50%	9.98%	14.88%	0.44	1.52%	0.25%	−40.07%	0.94
ROE	11.42%	11.43%	15.20%	0.42	−0.01%	0.17%	−47.07%	1.00
Sector benchmark	11.25%	N/A	13.69%	0.46	N/A	N/A	−38.78%	N/A
Total assets to total accruals (TATA)	11.11%	8.38%	16.92%	0.36	2.74%	−0.13%	−47.42%	0.96
1-mo. momentum	10.94%	10.95%	13.86%	0.43	0.00%	−0.30%	−44.20%	0.97
9-mo. momentum	10.94%	10.96%	14.10%	0.42	−0.02%	−0.31%	−46.23%	0.91
EPS change	10.80%	11.96%	14.80%	0.39	−1.16%	−0.45%	−51.10%	1.03
ROA	10.65%	11.59%	14.24%	0.40	−0.93%	−0.59%	−44.45%	0.95
12-mo. momentum	10.32%	11.31%	14.27%	0.37	−0.99%	−0.93%	−49.92%	0.91

TABLE 24.29

Best Quintile: Summary Base Rate Information for All Rolling One-, Three-, Five-, Seven-, and Ten-Year Periods for the Utilities Sector's Best Quintile (Strategies Benchmarked against the Returns of All Stocks in the Sector) December 31, 1967–December 31, 2009 (Strategies Sorted by Compound Return of the Best Quintile)

	Percent of time				
Strategy	1 year	3 years	5 years	7 years	10 years
Value Composite 2	83.6%	94.0%	95.1%	98.6%	100.0%
Value Composite 3	81.4%	95.7%	97.3%	100.0%	100.0%
Value Composite 1	80.6%	96.0%	97.1%	100.0%	100.0%

(continued on next page)

T A B L E   24.29

Best Quintile: Summary Base Rate Information for All Rolling One-, Three-, Five-, Seven-, and Ten-Year Periods for the Utilities Sector's Best Quintile (Strategies Benchmarked against the Returns of All Stocks in the Sector) December 31, 1967–December 31, 2009 (Strategies Sorted by Compound Return of the Best Quintile) *(Continued)*

Strategy	Percent of time				
	1 year	3 years	5 years	7 years	10 years
EV/EBITDA	74.7%	88.1%	96.4%	100.0%	100.0%
Price/cash flow	76.5%	92.3%	100.0%	100.0%	100.0%
EV/free cash flow	68.0%	84.9%	90.6%	95.5%	98.3%
Shareholder yield	73.7%	91.9%	96.0%	100.0%	100.0%
Price/earnings	75.9%	91.5%	94.4%	98.1%	99.3%
Price/cash flow (free)	76.3%	92.3%	97.3%	98.3%	100.0%
Price/sales	71.3%	80.4%	90.1%	94.3%	96.8%
Price/accruals	70.4%	83.2%	96.2%	98.8%	100.0%
Price/book	66.6%	80.6%	91.7%	93.6%	97.3%
Debt/capital	55.9%	62.6%	73.1%	72.5%	75.6%
Buyback yield	60.1%	81.3%	85.2%	91.2%	94.6%
NOA change	71.1%	88.9%	93.5%	99.3%	100.0%
Market cap	64.8%	75.7%	83.6%	87.0%	89.9%
EV/sales	59.9%	68.9%	74.2%	78.2%	80.5%
Dividend yield	55.1%	63.2%	62.3%	57.1%	53.7%
Cash flow/debt	54.7%	62.6%	63.2%	60.0%	60.1%
Debt change	58.7%	67.9%	73.1%	73.5%	77.6%
3-mo. momentum	43.9%	47.0%	51.1%	54.5%	56.9%
6-mo. momentum	45.7%	50.4%	53.4%	55.5%	61.1%
Asset turnover	50.4%	56.0%	49.8%	56.4%	52.7%
ROE	52.4%	51.3%	54.7%	57.1%	59.9%
Sector benchmark	0.0%	0.0%	0.0%	0.0%	0.0%
Total assets to total accruals (TATA)	55.3%	62.1%	70.6%	75.8%	76.6%
1-mo. momentum	37.2%	40.2%	42.8%	50.0%	53.7%
9-mo. momentum	43.1%	45.1%	50.7%	56.4%	59.1%
EPS change	43.7%	47.0%	41.7%	39.3%	39.7%
ROA	47.6%	43.8%	40.4%	30.1%	22.2%
12-mo. momentum	43.7%	42.3%	48.7%	53.8%	53.0%

THE DOWNSIDE

Price momentum doesn't work very well in the utility sector, nor does buying those utility stocks with the best percentage increase in earnings per share. Total assets to total accruals and ROA also fail to beat the overall sector returns. Turning to the worst quintiles of the various composited value factors, we see that those stocks from the utility sector with the worst scores on any of the three composited value factors rarely beat the overall sector. All base rates are negative, and for those rolling periods of over three years, only in the single digits. Indeed, while relatively tamer than the worst value factor quintiles in the other sectors, we still see maximum declines of the utility stocks increase to more than 45 percent. Table 24.30 shows the base rates for the worst quintile.

T A B L E 24.30

Worst Quintile: Summary Base Rate Information for All Rolling One-, Three-, Five-, Seven-, and Ten-Year Periods for the Utilities Sector's Worst Quintile (Strategies Benchmarked against the Returns of All Stocks in the Sector) December 31, 1967–December 31, 2009 (Strategies Sorted by Compound Return of the Best Quintile)

Strategy	Percent of time				
	1 year	3 years	5 years	7 years	10 years
Value Composite 2	17.0%	5.1%	3.4%	1.7%	0.0%
Value Composite 3	14.2%	6.2%	3.8%	2.6%	0.5%
Value Composite 1	19.4%	6.4%	2.9%	1.9%	0.0%
EV/EBITDA	23.7%	16.4%	10.5%	8.1%	5.4%
Price/cash flow	28.1%	11.7%	7.2%	3.6%	1.0%
EV/free cash flow	36.8%	32.8%	28.3%	30.3%	30.0%
Shareholder yield	28.7%	15.1%	11.0%	3.6%	3.7%
Price/earnings	35.8%	24.7%	17.0%	9.7%	8.1%
Price/cash flow (free)	34.4%	33.4%	34.1%	29.9%	27.3%
Price/sales	23.5%	11.7%	6.1%	4.3%	0.0%
Price/accruals	28.9%	13.0%	5.8%	3.8%	2.5%
Price/book	34.8%	14.0%	11.7%	5.5%	4.9%
Debt/capital	36.2%	27.4%	20.2%	17.1%	12.6%
Buyback yield	34.6%	13.6%	11.9%	10.4%	6.2%
NOA change	34.4%	25.3%	20.0%	10.2%	8.9%
Market cap	30.6%	16.8%	19.1%	9.5%	3.7%
EV/sales	34.8%	35.3%	26.0%	25.1%	21.4%
Dividend yield	41.9%	34.9%	27.4%	22.3%	17.2%
Cash flow/debt	42.9%	47.7%	38.1%	28.2%	33.7%
Debt change	36.2%	27.2%	28.0%	28.4%	28.3%
3-mo. momentum	48.6%	50.6%	39.7%	24.4%	18.2%
6-mo. momentum	50.6%	54.0%	47.3%	32.9%	24.1%
Asset turnover	36.0%	28.7%	29.1%	30.1%	30.0%
ROE	53.8%	60.9%	56.7%	51.4%	50.2%
Sector benchmark	0.0%	0.0%	0.0%	0.0%	0.0%
Total assets to total accruals (TATA)	43.5%	42.1%	38.6%	32.7%	28.3%
1-mo. momentum	59.3%	63.2%	50.9%	33.6%	25.4%
9-mo. momentum	54.0%	58.1%	51.1%	35.8%	29.1%
EPS change	58.5%	64.9%	72.2%	74.2%	79.8%
ROA	57.1%	62.6%	59.2%	64.5%	62.6%
12-mo. momentum	53.8%	57.2%	51.3%	38.6%	34.5%

IMPLICATIONS

The utility sector is the most conservative of the 10 economic sectors. It has the lowest standard deviations of return and the smallest maximum declines. Yet investors can boost their returns from the sector by focusing on the composited value factors. Buying the quintile of stocks with the highest scores on composited Value Factor Two generated average annual compound returns of 16.01 percent and with a maximum decline of 33 percent. That's a very favorable risk and return profile when compared with an investment in the All Stocks universe, which, over the same period, earned an average annual compound return of 10.56 percent and had a maximum decline of 55 percent. It proves that utilities can offer excellent returns at much lower risk than an investment in the All Stocks universe.

Investors should also avoid utility stocks with factors in the worst quintile. As Table 24.30 shows, they all have very poor base rates and rarely beat the overall sector returns. Yet utility stocks in the worst quintiles aren't the catastrophic investments that bottom quintile stocks from the other sectors prove to be. Here, even bad investing is not punished as severely as in the other sectors. Even the *worst* quintiles in the utility sector outperform T-bills, something that the other sectors cannot claim.

SUMMARY AND IMPLICATIONS FOR ALL 10 ECONOMIC SECTORS

Now that we have looked at all 10 economic sectors, a very compelling narrative has emerged. One of the composited value factors, either one, two, or three, has been the best single strategy in six of the ten economic sectors and among the top five in every sector. Enterprise value when compared with free cash flow and sales is also at or near the top, as is buying those stocks with the highest shareholder yield. Across all 10 sectors, buying the stocks with these factors in the top quintile has outperformed the sector itself—and vastly outperformed the worst quintile, which normally underperforms an investment in the sector by a wide margin.

The three composited value factors add value, regardless of the volatility of the sector itself. Table 24.31 shows the 10 economic sectors ranked by their standard deviation of return over the entire period between December 31, 1967, and December 31, 2009. Note that higher risk is not always rewarded. The second-safest sector—consumer staples— offered the highest average annual compound return. And the third-safest sector—financials—offered the second-highest average annual compound return. Conversely, the *riskiest* sector—information technologies—had the *lowest* average annual compound return. These results are hardly consistent with the Capital Asset Pricing Model, which posits that higher risk leads to higher returns. Indeed, the best-performing sector level strategy—buying the quintile of energy stocks with the highest scores on composited Value Factor Three—was actually *less risky* than buying the overall energy sector. Buying utility stocks with the highest scores on composited Value Factor Two actually beat the best-performing strategy for the information technologies sector by 3 percent per year, with a nearly half as severe maximum decline.

Thus, appearances can be deceiving. If you asked the average investor what the best-performing sector was over the last 42 years, my guess is that the majority would say technology or telecom. I would seriously doubt many would guess consumer staples, but when you think about it, it does make sense. Industries that make goods and services that people *have* to buy, regardless of economic circumstances, are bound to do well whatever the economic conditions. The consumer staples sector is also filled with companies that have wide moats and world-recognized brands. Two of the biggest business advantages that company's can have are monopoly power or brand power with wide moats. While I am

T A B L E   24.31

Sectors Ranked by Standard Deviation of Return, Least to Most Risky, December 31, 1967, to December 31, 2009

Sector	Standard deviation	Return
Utilities	13.69%	11.25%
Consumer staples	15.76%	13.57%
Financials	17.74%	12.37%
Industrials	20.55%	9.82%
Materials	20.83%	11.59%
Telecom	21.44%	11.86%
Consumer discretionary	21.97%	9.60%
Health care	23.16%	10.55%
Energy	25.48%	11.57%
Information technologies	31.14%	7.29%

fairly certain that there are more than a few MIT students who are also working on schemes to disintermediate the tech powers-that-be, I doubt that there is a group of friends in a garage cooking up the next soft drink to knock Coke off its pedestal.

At the very least, we have seen that what works in the All Stocks universe also works quite well at the sector level. We have seen that what we should avoid investing in at the All Stocks universe level should also be avoided at the sector level. There are obviously a few caveats. For example, I have found that you can get much better returns from technology stocks if you let them find their way into a portfolio through the application of multifactor models applied to the All Stocks universe, rather than limiting yourself specifically to the tech sector. Tech stocks generally make it through on our growth screens, but as we have seen, the long-term data suggests that growth works best when tempered by a value governor to make sure we are not paying too much for growth. Thus, when we are buying tech stocks, they tend to also have reasonable value characteristics. This sector analysis has shown, perhaps above all, that you can generate excellent returns without taking on undue risk.

C H A P T E R

SEARCHING FOR THE IDEAL GROWTH STRATEGY

Facts do not cease to exist because they are ignored.

—Aldous Huxley

We've seen in earlier chapters that marrying good value characteristics with price momentum is an excellent way to find "cheap stocks on the mend." In this chapter we look at similar growth strategies from the All Stocks universe and then review how those growth strategies perform when selected from the Large Stocks, Small Stocks, and Market Leaders universes.

ORIGINAL STRATEGY USED PRICE-TO-SALES AS THE FINAL VALUE CONSTRAINT

Readers of earlier editions of this book might recall that the best growth strategy from the All Stocks universe consisted of stocks that met the following criteria:

- Be selected from the All Stocks universe.
- Price-to-sales must be below 1.5 at time of purchase.
- Earnings must be higher than those in the previous year.
- Three-month price appreciation must exceed the database average.
- Six-month price appreciation must exceed the database average.
- Buy the 25 or 50 stocks with the highest one-year price appreciation.

This strategy has continued to work well since the last edition of this book. An investment of $10,000 on December 31, 1963, in the 50 stocks that met the above criteria would have grown to $13,689,553 by the end of 2009, an average annual compound return of 17 percent. The 25-stock version of this strategy actually underperformed the 50-stock version over the same time period, turning $10,000 into $9,922,274, an average annual compound return of 16.18 percent. Nevertheless, both compare quite favorably with a similar investment in the All Stocks universe, where $10,000 invested over the same period grew to $1,329,513, an average annual compound return of 11.22 percent. Table 25.1 shows the summary data for each version of the strategy. Tables 25.2 and 25.3 show the base rates for each, and Tables 25.4 and 25.5 show the worst-case scenarios. In the tables and graphs, we will refer to this strategy by its abbreviation MF CSG Improved, which stands for Multifactor, Cornerstone Growth Strategy Improved.

T A B L E   25.1

Summary Annual Return and Risk Results Data: MF CSG Improved 25 Stocks, MF CSG Improved 50 Stocks, and All Stocks, January 1, 1964, to December 31, 2009

	MF CSG improved 25 stocks	MF CSG improved 50 stocks	All Stocks
Arithmetic average	19.61%	19.88%	13.26%
Geometric average	16.18%	17.00%	11.22%
Median return	23.74%	23.22%	17.16%
Standard deviation	23.99%	21.96%	18.99%
Upside deviation	13.82%	12.51%	10.98%
Downside deviation	17.31%	16.25%	13.90%
Tracking error	11.13	9.17	0.00
Number of positive periods	334	342	329
Number of negative periods	218	210	223
Maximum peak-to-trough decline	−62.95%	−59.20%	−55.54%
Beta	1.13	1.05	1.00
T-statistic (m = 0)	5.10	5.64	4.47
Sharpe ratio (Rf = 5%)	0.47	0.55	0.33
Sortino ratio (MAR = 10%)	0.36	0.43	0.09
$10,000 becomes	$9,922,274	$13,689,553	$1,329,513
Minimum 1-year return	−53.37%	−50.98%	−46.49%
Maximum 1-year return	120.32%	106.89%	84.19%
Minimum 3-year return	−23.48%	−19.53%	−18.68%
Maximum 3-year return	53.27%	50.86%	31.49%
Minimum 5-year return	−7.65%	−6.29%	−9.91%
Maximum 5-year return	40.72%	37.42%	27.66%
Minimum 7-year return	−1.76%	−0.92%	−6.32%
Maximum 7-year return	31.22%	31.51%	23.77%
Minimum 10-year return	5.05%	6.39%	1.01%
Maximum 10 year return	27.14%	27.64%	22.05%
Minimum expected return*	−28.38%	−24.04%	−24.73%
Maximum expected return†	67.60%	63.80%	51.24%

* Minimum expected return is arithmetic return minus 2 times the standard deviation.

† Maximum expected return is arithmetic return plus 2 times the standard deviation.

T A B L E 25.2

Base Rates for MF CSG Improved 25 Stocks and All Stocks, January 1, 1964, to December 31, 2009

Item	MF CSG improved 25 stocks beat All Stocks	Percent	Average annual excess return
Single-year return	375 out of 541	69%	6.73%
Rolling 3-year compound return	452 out of 517	87%	6.01%
Rolling 5-year compound return	462 out of 493	94%	5.67%
Rolling 7-year compound return	457 out of 469	97%	5.34%
Rolling 10-year compound return	433 out of 433	100%	5.12%

T A B L E 25.3

Base Rates for MF CSG Improved 50 Stocks and All Stocks, January 1, 1964, to December 31, 2009

Item	MF CSG improved 50 stocks beat All Stocks	Percent	Average annual excess return
Single-year return	421 out of 541	78%	6.90%
Rolling 3-year compound return	483 out of 517	93%	6.64%
Rolling 5-year compound return	485 out of 493	98%	6.45%
Rolling 7-year compound return	467 out of 469	100%	6.22%
Rolling 10-year compound return	433 out of 433	100%	6.05%

T A B L E 25.4

Worst-Case Scenarios: All 20 Percent or Greater Declines for MF CSG Improved 25 Stocks, January 1, 1964, to December 31, 2009

Peak date	Peak index value	Trough date	Trough index value	Recovery date	Decline (%)	Decline duration	Recovery duration
Apr–66	2.30	Oct–66	1.69	Jan–67	−26.50%	6	3
May–69	5.60	Jun–70	3.19	Jan–72	−43.14%	13	19
May–72	6.95	Sep–74	3.23	Jun–77	−53.54%	28	33
Aug–78	12.14	Oct–78	8.76	Mar–79	−27.83%	2	5
Feb–80	16.81	Mar–80	12.77	Jul–80	−23.99%	1	4
Nov–80	25.72	Feb–82	19.10	Nov–82	−25.75%	15	9
Jun–83	43.73	May–84	29.73	Dec–85	−32.01%	11	19
Aug–87	76.64	Nov–87	48.45	Mar–89	−36.78%	3	16
May–90	107.73	Oct–90	77.44	Feb–91	−28.12%	5	4
Jun–98	508.94	Aug–98	341.66	Jun–99	−32.87%	2	10
Aug–00	690.39	Sep–01	503.14	Apr–02	−27.12%	13	7
Apr–02	704.72	Feb–03	471.96	Aug–03	−33.03%	10	6
May–07	1,962.90	Feb–09	727.17	N/A	−62.95%	21	N/A
Average					−34.90%	10	11.25

T A B L E   25.5

Worst-Case Scenarios: All 20 Percent or Greater Declines for MF CSG Improved 50 Stocks, January 1, 1964, to December 31, 2009

Peak date	Peak index value	Trough date	Trough index value	Recovery date	Decline (%)	Decline duration	Recovery duration
Apr–66	2.15	Oct–66	1.64	Jan–67	−23.83%	6	3
Nov–68	4.70	Jun–70	2.85	Dec–71	−39.32%	19	18
May–72	5.87	Sep–74	2.89	Jun–76	−50.77%	28	21
Aug–78	10.97	Oct–78	7.96	Apr–79	−27.45%	2	6
Feb–80	15.33	Mar–80	11.93	Jul–80	−22.19%	1	4
Nov–80	23.13	Sep–81	18.12	Oct–82	−21.66%	10	13
Jun–83	39.41	May–84	28.32	Nov–85	−28.15%	11	18
Aug–87	72.80	Nov–87	47.82	Feb–89	−34.32%	3	15
May–90	100.04	Oct–90	73.22	Mar–91	−26.81%	5	5
Jun–98	539.62	Aug–98	379.44	Jun–99	−29.68%	2	10
Aug–00	715.72	Sep–01	571.07	Mar–02	−20.21%	13	6
Apr–02	810.38	Feb–03	571.95	Aug–03	−29.42%	10	6
May–07	2,396.76	Feb–09	978.00	N/A	−59.20%	21	N/A
Average					−31.77%	10	10.42

Since our research into the efficacy of composited factors—like the various value factor composites—we now have additional factors that might dramatically improve this model. For example, Value Composite One *beats* this strategy all on its own, with the top decile from All Stocks earning 17.18 percent per year over the same period. Let's see if we can improve the results to this growth strategy, first by simply substituting a value composite constraint in place of the price-to-sales ratio.

CHEAP STOCKS ON THE MEND WITH A NEW DEFINITION OF CHEAP

You will recall from Chapter Fifteen that the composited value factors combine several individual factors, which are assigned ranks. For this first look at our All Stocks growth strategy, we now include the composited Value Factor Two, which includes the following:

1. Price-to-book
2. Price-to-earnings
3. Price-to-sales
4. EBITDA/EV
5. Price-to-cash flow
6. Shareholder yield

For each combined group of factors, we assign a percentile ranking for each stock in the All Stocks universe on a scale of 1 to 100. If a stock has a PE ratio that is in the lowest 1 percent of the universe, it will receive a rank of 100; if a stock has a PE ratio in the highest 1 percent for the universe, it will receive a rank of one. We follow a similar convention for each of the factors—thus, if a stock is in the lowest 1 percent of the universe based on its price-to-sales ratio, it gets 100, if in the highest 1 percent, it gets a one. If a value is missing for a factor, we assign a neutral rank of 50. For shareholder yield, those stocks in the 1 percent of the universe with the *highest* yields will be ranked 100, whereas those within the lowest 1 percent will be ranked one. Once everything is ranked, we average across all factors and assign the stocks to deciles based upon their overall cumulative ranking on all factors. Those with the highest scores are assigned to decile 1, while those with the lowest scores are assigned to decile 10. This lets us get a much better picture of how the stock is scoring across all the value criteria, and, as we learned in Chapter Fifteen, leads to much better—and more consistent—returns than those generated by using any individual factor alone.

For our first test, we simply require the following:

- Be selected from the All Stocks universe.
- Fall in the top three deciles (top 30 percent) for composited Value Factor Two.
- Three-month price momentum must be greater than the database median.
- Six-month price momentum must be greater than the database median.
- Buy the 25 or 50 stocks with the best six-month price momentum.

Notice several additional changes from our first iteration of this cheap growth stocks on the mend strategy—in addition to using the more comprehensive value factor composite, we now require that three- and six-month momentum be greater than the database median as opposed to the database average. Using the more extensive CRSP database, we have found that using median price momentum generates more consistent results, as it has you fishing from the upper 50 percent of the universe. Conversely, the average can become quite skewed if a handful of stocks perform extraordinarily well or extremely poorly. Also note that the final factor is now six-month price appreciation rather than 12-month price appreciation. This is also the result of the additional data we were able to study from CRSP dataset. Over the 84 years of data available in CRSP, we saw that six-month price appreciation actually performs better than twelve-month price appreciation. Lets take a look at how these changes affect performance.

Table 25.6 shows the summary results for the 25- and 50-stock versions of the new Cheap Stocks on the Mend strategy. Quite an improvement! The $10,000 invested in the 50-stock and 25-stock versions of the strategy grows to $37,770,861 and $41,068,482, respectively, or an average annual compound return of 19.61 percent for the 50-stock version and 19.83 percent for the 25-stock version. Note that the standard deviation for both the 25- and 50-stock versions of the strategy are well below the original growth strategy, and that the 50-stock version's standard deviation of return of 18.06 percent is actually lower than that of the All Stocks universe's 18.99 percent. The lower risk married to the higher returns brings the Sharpe ratios for the 25- and 50-stock versions of the strategy in at very high readings of .76 and .81, respectively. Finally, note the minimum returns for the new version versus the original strategy: The minimum five-year return for the original version was a loss of 6.29 percent per year, whereas for the new 50-stock version it is a much lower loss of only 1.81 percent per year. Also noteworthy is that there are no negative returns over all rolling seven- and ten-year periods for either the 25- or 50-stock versions of the new strategy.

T A B L E   25.6

Summary Annual Return and Risk Results Data: Comp Value 2 in Top 3 Deciles, 3 and 6 Mo. Mom>Median, Top 25 by 6 Mo. Mom, Comp Value 2 in Top 3 Deciles, 3 and 6 Mo. Mom>Median, Top 50 by 6 Mo. Mom, and All Stocks, January 1, 1964, to December 31, 2009

	Comp value 2 in top 3 deciles, 3 and 6 mo. mom>median, top 25 by 6 mo. mom	Comp value 2 in top 3 deciles, 3 and 6 mo. mom>median, top 50 by 6 mo. mom	All Stocks
Arithmetic average	22.13%	21.58%	13.26%
Geometric average	19.83%	19.61%	11.22%
Median return	30.43%	29.61%	17.16%
Standard deviation	19.48%	18.06%	18.99%
Upside deviation	11.22%	10.51%	10.98%
Downside deviation	14.91%	13.94%	13.90%
Tracking error	8.51	7.84	0.00
Number of positive periods	356	362	329
Number of negative periods	196	190	223
Maximum peak-to-trough decline	−56.56%	−53.49%	−55.54%
Beta	0.93	0.87	1.00
T-statistic (m = 0)	7.02	7.40	4.47
Sharpe ratio (Rf = 5%)	0.76	0.81	0.33
Sortino ratio (MAR = 10%)	0.66	0.69	0.09
$10,000 becomes	$41,068,482	$37,770,861	$1,329,513
Minimum 1-year return	−50.01%	−46.27%	−46.49%
Maximum 1-year return	104.89%	92.53%	84.19%
Minimum 3-year return	−11.41%	−8.90%	−18.68%
Maximum 3-year return	57.22%	52.99%	31.49%
Minimum 5-year return	−2.75%	−1.81%	−9.91%
Maximum 5-year return	41.89%	40.24%	27.66%
Minimum 7-year return	0.23%	1.08%	−6.32%
Maximum 7-year return	32.94%	32.12%	23.77%
Minimum 10-year return	7.82%	7.70%	1.01%
Maximum 10 year return	30.06%	29.93%	22.05%
Minimum expected return*	−16.83%	−14.54%	−24.73%
Maximum expected return†	61.09%	57.70%	51.24%

* Minimum expected return is arithmetic return minus 2 times the standard deviation.

† Maximum expected return is arithmetic return plus 2 times the standard deviation.

BASE RATES, WORST-CASE SCENARIOS, AND BEST AND WORST RETURNS

Better yet, the base rates of the new 25- and 50-stock portfolios improve over the original strategy. As Table 25.7 shows, the 25-stock Cheap Stocks on the Mend strategy beats the All Stocks universe in 100 percent of all rolling three-, five-, seven-, and ten-year periods. The 50-stock version is nearly as good, beating the All Stocks universe in 99 percent of all rolling three-year periods, and in 100 percent of all rolling five- and ten-year periods. The new strategy also provides much better downside protection. The original version of the strategy had 13 separate declines of 20 percent or more between 1963 and 2009, whereas the new version has only 9. Tables 25.9 and 25.10 show the worst-case scenarios for the 25- and 50-stock versions of the strategy. In both instances, the worst drop occurred between October 2007 and February 2009. Review the tables for details on each strategy. Figure 25.1 shows the rolling excess return (alpha) of the strategy on a compound average annual return basis minus the return for the All Stocks universe for the 25-stock version of the strategy, and Figure 25.2 shows it for the 50-stock version.

T A B L E 25.7

Base Rates for Comp Value 2 in Top 3 Deciles, 3 and 6 Mo. Mom>Median, Top 25 by 6 Mo. Mom and All Stocks, January 1, 1964, to December 31, 2009

Item	Comp value 2 in top 3 deciles, 3 and 6 mo. mom>median, top 25 by 6 mo. mom beat All Stocks	Percent	Average annual excess return
Single-year return	465 out of 541	86%	9.03%
Rolling 3-year compound return	516 out of 517	100%	9.21%
Rolling 5-year compound return	493 out of 493	100%	9.22%
Rolling 7-year compound return	469 out of 469	100%	9.11%
Rolling 10-year compound return	433 out of 433	100%	9.04%

T A B L E 25.8

Base Rates for Comp Value 2 in Top 3 Deciles, 3 and 6 Mo. Mom>Median, Top 50 by 6 Mo. Mom and All Stocks, January 1, 1964, to December 31, 2009

Item	Comp value 2 in top 3 deciles, 3 and 6 mo. mom>median, top 50 by 6 mo. mom beat All Stocks	Percent	Average annual excess return
Single-year return	469 out of 541	87%	8.46%
Rolling 3-year compound return	512 out of 517	99%	8.82%
Rolling 5-year compound return	493 out of 493	100%	8.86%
Rolling 7-year compound return	469 out of 469	100%	8.77%
Rolling 10-year compound return	433 out of 433	100%	8.69%

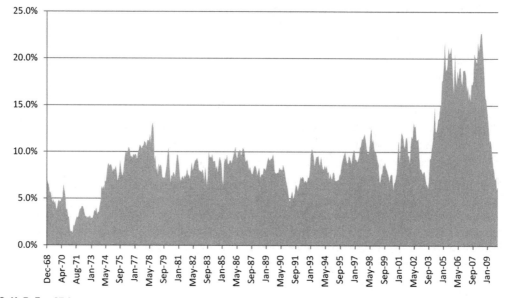

Five-year average annual compound excess (deficient) return comp value 2 in top 3 deciles, 3 and 6 mo. mom>median, top 25 by 6 mo. mom minus All Stocks, January 1, 1964, to December 31, 2009

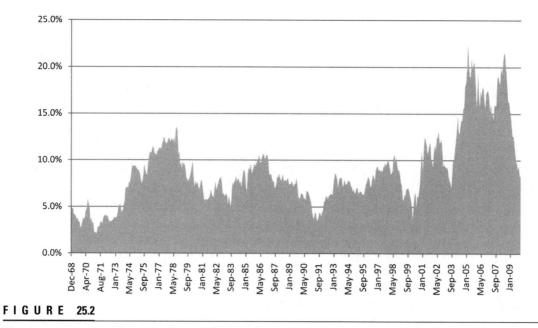

Five-year average annual compound excess (deficient) return comp value 2 in top 3 deciles, 3 and 6 mo. mom>median, top 50 by 6 mo. mom minus All Stocks, January 1, 1964, to December 31, 2009

TABLE 25.9

Worst-Case Scenarios: All 20 Percent or Greater Declines for Comp Value 2 in Top 3 Deciles, 3 and 6 Mo. Mom>Median, Top 25 by 6 mo. mom, January 1, 1964, to December 31, 2009

Peak date	Peak index value	Trough date	Trough index value	Recovery date	Decline (%)	Decline duration	Recovery duration
Apr–66	2.13	Sep–66	1.64	Apr–67	–23.05%	5	7
Nov–68	3.63	Jun–70	2.26	Jan–72	–37.57%	19	19
Apr–72	3.90	Sep–74	2.68	Apr–75	–31.26%	29	7
Aug–78	10.34	Oct–78	7.78	Jun–79	–24.80%	2	8
Aug–87	89.66	Nov–87	62.59	Jan–89	–30.19%	3	14
Sep–89	123.37	Oct–90	93.63	Mar–91	–24.10%	13	5
Jun–98	856.02	Aug–98	648.79	Dec–99	–24.21%	2	16
Apr–02	1,432.90	Feb–03	1,033.72	Sep–03	–27.86%	10	7
Oct–07	6,164.75	Feb–09	2,677.71	N/A	–56.56%	16	N/A
Average					–31.07%	11	10.38

TABLE 25.10

Worst-Case Scenarios: All 20 Percent or Greater Declines for Comp Value 2 in Top 3 Deciles, 3 and 6 Mo. Mom>Median, Top 50 by 6 Mo. Mom, January 1, 1964, to December 31, 2009

Peak date	Peak index value	Trough date	Trough index value	Recovery date	Decline (%)	Decline duration	Recovery duration
Apr–66	1.98	Sep–66	1.56	Mar–67	–21.14%	5	6
Nov–68	3.36	Jun–70	2.18	Jan–72	–35.02%	19	19
Nov–72	3.70	Sep–74	2.64	Apr–75	–28.67%	22	7
Aug–78	10.26	Oct–78	8.02	Jun–79	–21.76%	2	8
Aug–87	84.75	Nov–87	59.57	Jan–89	–29.72%	3	14
Sep–89	111.66	Oct–90	88.33	Mar–91	–20.89%	13	5
Jun–98	714.54	Aug–98	559.32	Dec–99	–21.72%	2	16
Apr–02	1,247.57	Feb–03	936.27	Aug–03	–24.95%	10	6
Oct–07	5,247.28	Feb–09	2,440.50	N/A	–53.49%	16	N/A
Average					–28.60%	10.22	10.13

Tables 25.11 and 25.12 show the best- and worst-case returns for a variety of holding periods. The best five-year return for both the 25- and 50-stock version of the strategy occurred in the period ending October 2007, when the 50-stock version of the strategy earned an average annual compound return of 40.25 percent, and the 25-stock version earned 41.89 percent. The worst five years for each occurred in the period ending November 1973, when the 50-stock version lost an average annual 1.81 percent, and the 25-stock version lost 2.75 percent. Table 25.13 shows the results for the each strategy by decade.

T A B L E   25.11

Best and Worst Average Annual Compound Returns for Monthly Data, January 1, 1964, to December 31, 2009

For any	1-year period	3-year period	5-year period	7-year period	10-year period
Comp value 2 in top 3 deciles, 3 and 6 mo. mom>median, top 25 by 6 mo. mom minimum compound return	−50.01%	−11.41%	−2.75%	0.23%	7.82%
Comp value 2 in top 3 deciles, 3 and 6 mo. mom>median, top 25 by 6 mo. mom maximum compound return	104.89%	57.22%	41.89%	32.94%	30.06%
Comp value 2 in top 3 deciles, 3 and 6 mo. mom>median, top 50 by 6 mo. mom minimum compound return	−46.27%	−8.90%	−1.81%	1.08%	7.70%
Comp value 2 in top 3 deciles, 3 and 6 mo. mom>median, top 50 by 6 mo. mom maximum compound return	92.53%	52.99%	40.24%	32.12%	29.93%
All Stocks minimum compound return	−46.49%	−18.68%	−9.91%	−6.32%	1.01%
All Stocks maximum compound return	84.19%	31.49%	27.66%	23.77%	22.05%

T A B L E   25.12

Terminal Value of $10,000 Invested for Best and Worst Average Annual Compound Returns for Monthly Data, January 1, 1964, to December 31, 2009

For any	1-year period	3-year period	5-year period	7-year period	10-year period
Comp value 2 in top 3 deciles, 3 and 6 mo. mom>median, top 25 by 6 mo. mom minimum $10,000 value	$4,999	$6,953	$8,700	$10,161	$21,223
Comp value 2 in top 3 deciles, 3 and 6 mo. mom>median, top 25 by 6 mo. mom maximum $10,000 value	$20,489	$38,864	$57,515	$73,392	$138,533
Comp value 2 in top 3 deciles, 3 and 6 mo. mom>median, top 50 by 6 mo. mom minimum $10,000 value	$5,373	$7,561	$9,129	$10,780	$21,002
Comp value 2 in top 3 deciles, 3 and 6 mo. mom>median, top 50 by 6 mo. mom maximum $10,000 value	$19,253	$35,809	$54,252	$70,270	$137,080
All Stocks minimum $10,000 value	$5,351	$5,379	$5,936	$6,330	$11,054
All Stocks maximum $10,000 value	$18,419	$22,734	$33,903	$44,504	$73,345

T A B L E 25.13

Average Annual Compound Rates of Return by Decade

	1960s*	1970s	1980s	1990s	2000s†
Comp value 2 in top 3 deciles, 3 and 6 mo. mom>median, top 25 by 6 mo. mom	18.97%	16.10%	25.01%	22.81%	16.17%
Comp value 2 in top 3 deciles, 3 and 6 mo. mom>median, top 50 by 6 mo. mom	17.85%	16.64%	24.01%	21.50%	17.50%
All Stocks	13.36%	7.56%	16.78%	15.35%	4.39%

* Returns for January 1, 1964, to December 31, 1969.
† Returns for January 1, 2000, to December 31, 2009.

Clearly, you can substantially improve your returns and lower your risk by using the new value factor composite along with six-month price momentum as the final sorting factor. Do note that if you are looking for a "pure play" growth strategy with a high correlation to the Russell growth indexes, this strategy is not for you. I have always looked at any strategy that uses price momentum as a final sorting factor as a "growth" strategy, since price momentum is one of the few growth factors that works with any consistency. However this new "growth" strategy correlates most highly with the Russell 2000 Value Index—at .9033. The next highest correlation is with the Russell 2000 at .891, making this much more of a core/value strategy, despite having price momentum as its final factor.

So now let's look at another strategy more highly correlated to the Russell growth indexes.

AN ALL STOCKS STRATEGY WITH A HIGHER CORRELATION TO GROWTH INDEXES

Our next strategy will make even greater use of the composite factors we have developed. To be included in the portfolio, a stock must:

- Be selected from the All Stocks universe.
- Annual percentage change in earnings per share must be greater than zero.
- Three-month price appreciation must be greater than the median for the universe.
- Six-month price appreciation must be greater than the median for the universe.
- The stock must be in the upper 50 percent of the Financial Strength, Earnings Quality and Value Composites (Value Composite Two for this test).
- Buy the 25 stocks with the best six-month price appreciation.

Let's call this strategy All Stocks Growth and review the results. A $10,000 investment on December 31, 1963, grows to $53,653,443 by the end of 2009, an average annual compound return of 20.53 percent. Risk is higher than with the Cheap Stocks on the Mend strategy, with a standard deviation of return of 24.83 percent and a maximum decline of

59.68 percent. The higher risk brings the strategy's Sharpe ratio to .63, behind the 25-stock Cheap Stocks on the Mend strategy's .76. This strategy also had a higher five-year maximum decline of –6.32 percent per year, which would have turned $10,000 invested five-years earlier into $7,217. That maximum five-year loss occurred in the period ending February 2009, at the bottom of the bear market—the Cheap Stocks on the Mend strategy actually earned money over the same period. Even so, when you look at Table 25.14, you'll see that –6.32 percent annual decline is still considerably better than the worst five-year period for the All Stocks universe, which lost an annual 9.91 percent. All the base rates for the All Stocks Growth strategy, featured in Table 25.15, were positive, with the strategy beating the All Stocks universe in 97 percent of all rolling five-year periods and in 99 percent of all rolling ten-year periods.

T A B L E 25.14

Summary Annual Return and Risk Results Data: All Stocks Growth and All Stocks, January 1, 1964, to December 31, 2009

	All Stocks Growth	All Stocks
Arithmetic average	24.28%	13.26%
Geometric average	20.53%	11.22%
Median return	28.07%	17.16%
Standard deviation	24.83%	18.99%
Upside deviation	15.30%	10.98%
Downside deviation	18.04%	13.90%
Tracking error	11.82	0.00
Number of positive periods	351	329
Number of negative periods	201	223
Maximum peak-to-trough decline	–59.68%	–55.54%
Beta	1.16	1.00
T-statistic (m = 0)	5.99	4.47
Sharpe ratio (Rf = 5%)	0.63	0.33
Sortino ratio (MAR = 10%)	0.58	0.09
$10,000 becomes	$53,653,443	$1,329,513
Minimum 1-year return	–53.65%	–46.49%
Maximum 1-year return	155.01%	84.19%
Minimum 3-year return	–21.04%	–18.68%
Maximum 3-year return	71.28%	31.49%
Minimum 5-year return	–6.32%	–9.91%
Maximum 5-year return	53.32%	27.66%
Minimum 7-year return	0.92%	–6.32%
Maximum 7-year return	42.16%	23.77%
Minimum 10-year return	2.48%	1.01%
Maximum 10 year return	39.85%	22.05%
Minimum expected return*	–25.38%	–24.73%
Maximum expected return†	73.94%	51.24%

* Minimum expected return is arithmetic return minus 2 times the standard deviation.
† Maximum expected return is arithmetic return plus 2 times the standard deviation.

T A B L E   25.15

Base Rates for All Stocks Growth and All Stocks, January 1, 1964, to December 31, 2009

Item	All Stocks Growth beat All Stocks	Percent	Average annual excess return
Single-year return	445 out of 541	82%	11.09%
Rolling 3-year compound return	496 out of 517	96%	10.39%
Rolling 5-year compound return	478 out of 493	97%	10.33%
Rolling 7-year compound return	458 out of 469	98%	10.32%
Rolling 10-year compound return	430 out of 433	99%	10.53%

WORST-CASE SCENARIOS AND BEST AND WORST RETURNS

Table 25.16 lists all declines greater than 20 percent for the All Stocks Growth strategy over the last 46 years. The strategy had 12 separate declines of 20 percent or more, with the last 2 exceeding 50 percent. Yes, this is a pure play growth strategy, with a correlation to the Russell 2000 Growth index of .924, but that's a pretty wild ride.

T A B L E   25.16

Worst-Case Scenarios: All 20 Percent or Greater Declines for All Stocks Growth, January 1, 1964, to December 31, 2009

Peak date	Peak index value	Trough date	Trough index value	Recovery date	Decline (%)	Decline duration	Recovery duration
Apr–66	2.35	Oct–66	1.76	Mar–67	−25.29%	6	5
May–69	5.52	Jun–70	3.52	Apr–71	−36.15%	13	10
May–72	7.68	Sep–74	4.73	May–75	−38.37%	28	8
Aug–78	18.01	Oct–78	12.82	Jun–79	−28.80%	2	8
Feb–80	25.61	Mar–80	19.61	Jul–80	−23.42%	1	4
May–81	37.84	Sep–81	30.13	Sep–82	−20.38%	4	12
Jun–83	73.57	May–84	55.08	May–85	−25.14%	11	12
Aug–87	161.59	Nov–87	109.48	Jan–89	−32.25%	3	14
Jun–90	230.48	Oct–90	177.66	Feb–91	−22.91%	4	4
Jun–98	2,026.40	Aug–98	1,444.99	Dec–98	−28.69%	2	4
Feb–00	5,594.93	Sep–01	2,711.72	Feb–05	−51.53%	19	41
Oct–07	9,016.71	Feb–09	3,635.30	N/A	−59.68%	16	N/A
Average					−32.72%	9.08	11.09

The best five-year return for this strategy occurred in the period ending February 2000, when the strategy earned an average annual compound return of 53.32 percent. The worst five-year return for the strategy occurred in the period ending February 2009, when the strategy lost an average annual 6.32 percent return. Tables 25.17 and 25.18 shows the best- and worst-case returns for other holding periods, and Figure 25.3 shows the rolling five-year excess return (alpha) of the strategy over the All Stocks universe. Table 25.19 shows the results by decade.

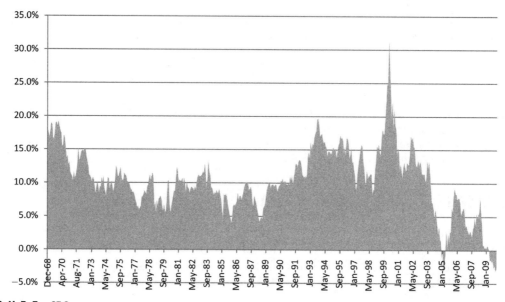

FIGURE 25.3

Five-year average annual compound excess (deficient) return All Stocks Growth minus All Stocks, January 1, 1964, to December 31, 2009

TABLE 25.17

Best and Worst Average Annual Compound Returns for Monthly Data, January 1, 1964, to December 31, 2009

For any	1-year period	3-year period	5-year period	7-year period	10-year period
All Stocks Growth minimum compound return	−53.65%	−21.04%	−6.32%	0.92%	2.48%
All Stocks Growth maximum compound return	155.01%	71.28%	53.32%	42.16%	39.85%
All Stocks minimum compound return	−46.49%	−18.68%	−9.91%	−6.32%	1.01%
All Stocks maximum compound return	84.19%	31.49%	27.66%	23.77%	22.05%

TABLE 25.18

Terminal Value of $10,000 Invested for Best and Worst Average Annual Compound Returns for Monthly Data, January 1, 1964, to December 31, 2009

For any	1-year period	3-year period	5-year period	7-year period	10-year period
All Stocks Growth minimum $10,000 value	$4,635	$4,922	$7,217	$10,660	$12,775
All Stocks Growth maximum $10,000 value	$25,501	$50,247	$84,732	$117,346	$286,133
All Stocks minimum $10,000 value	$5,351	$5,379	$5,936	$6,330	$11,054
All Stocks maximum $10,000 value	$18,419	$22,734	$33,903	$44,504	$73,345

T A B L E   25.19

Average Annual Compound Rates of Return by Decade

	1960s*	1970s	1980s	1990s	2000s†
All Stocks Growth	30.84%	16.02%	25.33%	34.81%	2.48%
All Stocks	13.36%	7.56%	16.78%	15.35%	4.39%

* Returns for January 1, 1964, to December 31, 1969.
† Returns for January 1, 2000, to December 31, 2009.

SMALL STOCKS DO SLIGHTLY BETTER

If we apply the Cheap Stocks on the Mend to the Small Stocks universe, returns improve slightly. Thus, the Small Stocks universe model is:

- Be selected from the Small Stocks universe (SS universe).
- Be in the top three deciles (top 30 percent) for the Value Factor Two composite.
- Three-month price momentum must be greater than the Small Stocks median.
- Six-month price momentum must be greater than the Small Stocks median.
- Buy the top 25 or 50 stocks with the best six-month price momentum.

Table 25.20 shows the summary results for the Small Stocks Growth strategy. Here you actually get a much better risk-adjusted return using the 50-stock version of the strategy. The $10,000 invested on December 31, 1963, grows to $44,705,480 by the end of 2009, an average annual compound return of 20.05 percent. All base rates for the 50-stock version of the strategy, featured in Table 25.21, are positive, with the strategy beating the Small Stocks universe in 100 percent of all rolling five- and ten-year periods. The base rates for the 25-stock version, featured in Table 25.22, are equally compelling.

T A B L E   25.20

Summary Annual Return and Risk Results Data: SS, Comp Value 2 in Top 3 Deciles, 3 and 6 mo. Mom>Median, Top 50 by 6 Mo. Mom, SS, Comp Value 2 in Top 3 Deciles, 3 and 6 mo. Mom>Median, Top 25 by 6 Mo. Mom, and Small Stocks, January 1, 1964, to December 31, 2009

	SS, comp value 2 in top 3 deciles, 3 and 6 mo. mom>median, top 50 by 6 mo. mom	SS, comp value 2 in top 3 deciles, 3 and 6 mo. mom>median, top 25 by 6 mo. mom	Small Stocks
Arithmetic average	22.06%	22.53%	13.94%
Geometric average	20.05%	20.18%	11.60%
Median return	30.81%	29.78%	19.28%
Standard deviation	18.21%	19.63%	20.31%
Upside deviation	10.62%	11.38%	11.87%
Downside deviation	14.20%	15.21%	14.83%
Tracking error	8.25	8.88	0.00
Number of positive periods	360	358	329

(continued on next page)

T A B L E   25.20

Summary Annual Return and Risk Results Data: SS, Comp Value 2 in Top 3 Deciles, 3 and 6 mo. Mom>Median, Top 50 by 6 Mo. Mom, SS, Comp Value 2 in Top 3 Deciles, 3 and 6 Mo. Mom>Median, Top 25 by 6 Mo. Mom, and Small Stocks, January 1, 1964, to December 31, 2009 *(Continued)*

	SS, comp value 2 in top 3 deciles, 3 and 6 mo. mom>median, top 50 by 6 mo. mom	SS, comp value 2 in top 3 deciles, 3 and 6 mo. mom>median, top 25 by 6 mo. mom	Small Stocks
Number of negative periods	192	194	223
Maximum peak-to-trough decline	−53.05%	−57.64%	−58.48%
Beta	0.82	0.87	1.00
T-statistic (m = 0)	7.48	7.08	4.38
Sharpe ratio (Rf = 5%)	0.83	0.77	0.32
Sortino ratio (MAR = 10%)	0.71	0.67	0.11
$10,000 becomes	$44,705,480	$47,002,323	$1,555,109
Minimum 1-year return	−46.23%	−51.47%	−46.38%
Maximum 1-year return	93.32%	102.46%	93.08%
Minimum 3-year return	−10.54%	−13.61%	−19.53%
Maximum 3-year return	52.56%	55.72%	34.00%
Minimum 5-year return	−1.98%	−2.27%	−11.75%
Maximum 5-year return	38.11%	39.44%	31.37%
Minimum 7-year return	1.96%	1.28%	−7.64%
Maximum 7-year return	33.31%	34.24%	27.35%
Minimum 10-year return	8.52%	8.57%	1.08%
Maximum 10 year return	31.15%	31.53%	24.47%
Minimum expected return*	−14.37%	−16.74%	−26.69%
Maximum expected return†	58.49%	61.79%	54.57%

* Minimum expected return is arithmetic return minus 2 times the standard deviation.

† Maximum expected return is arithmetic return plus 2 times the standard deviation.

T A B L E   25.21

Base Rates for SS, Comp Value 2 in Top 3 Deciles, 3 and 6 Mo. Mom>Median, Top 50 by 6 Mo. Mom and Small Stocks, January 1, 1964, to December 31, 2009

Item	SS, comp value 2 in top 3 deciles, 3 and 6 mo. mom>median, top 50 by 6 mo. mom Beat Small Stocks	Percent	Average annual excess return
Single-year return	456 out of 541	84%	8.20%
Rolling 3-year compound return	504 out of 517	97%	8.80%
Rolling 5-year compound return	493 out of 493	100%	8.98%
Rolling 7-year compound return	469 out of 469	100%	8.96%
Rolling 10-year compound return	433 out of 433	100%	8.91%

T A B L E 25.22

Base Rates for SS, Comp Value 2 in Top 3 deciles, 3 and 6 Mo. Mom>Median, Top 25 by 6 Mo. Mom and Small Stocks, January 1, 1964, to December 31, 2009

Item	SS, Comp Value 2 in Top 3 deciles, 3 and 6 mo. mom>median, top 25 by 12 mo. mom beat Small Stocks	Percent	Average annual excess return
Single-year return	460 out of 541	85%	8.17%
Rolling 3-year compound return	506 out of 517	98%	8.59%
Rolling 5-year compound return	493 out of 493	100%	8.77%
Rolling 7-year compound return	469 out of 469	100%	8.80%
Rolling 10-year compound return	433 out of 433	100%	8.80%

WORST-CASE SCENARIOS AND BEST AND WORST RETURNS

The 25-stock version of the strategy had 10 declines greater than 20 percent, with the worst being the 58 percent decline suffered between October 2007 and February 2009. Table 25.23 shows all other declines greater than 20 percent. Table 25.24 shows the worst-case scenarios for the 50-stock version of the strategy, and Tables 25.25 and 25.26 show the best and worst returns for both strategies over a variety of holding periods. Figures 25.4 and 25.5 show the rolling five-year average annual compound excess return (alpha) over the Small Stocks universe. Table 25.27 shows returns for both the 25- and 50-stock versions of the strategy by decade.

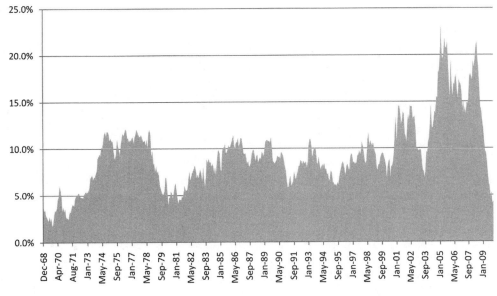

F I G U R E 25.4

Five-year average annual compound excess (deficient) return USA SS, comp value 2 in top 3 deciles, 3 and 6 mo. mom>median, top 25 by 6 mo mom minus Small Stocks, January 1, 1964, to December 31, 2009

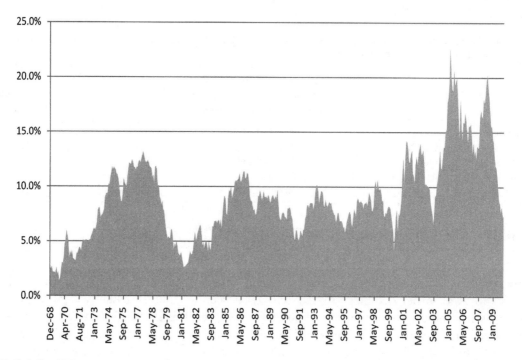

Five-year average annual compound excess (deficient) return USA SS, comp value 2 in top 3 deciles, 3 and 6 mo. mom>median, top 50 by 6 mo. mom minus Small Stocks, January 1, 1964, to December 31, 2009

T A B L E   25.23

Worst-Case Scenarios: All 20 Percent or Greater Declines for SS, Comp Value 2 in Top 3 Deciles, 3 and 6 Mo. Mom>Median, Top 25 by 6 Mo. Mom, January 1, 1964, to December 31, 2009

Peak date	Peak index value	Trough date	Trough index value	Recovery date	Decline (%)	Decline duration	Recovery duration
Apr–66	2.14	Sep–66	1.65	Apr–67	−22.74%	5	7
Nov–68	3.68	Jun–70	2.38	Apr–71	−35.27%	19	10
Apr–72	4.28	Sep–74	2.93	Apr–75	−31.56%	29	7
Aug–78	12.09	Oct–78	9.10	Jun–79	−24.68%	2	8
Jan–80	16.08	Mar–80	12.64	Jul–80	−21.39%	2	4
Aug–87	106.83	Nov–87	75.20	Oct–88	−29.61%	3	11
Jun–90	148.21	Oct–90	113.62	Mar–91	−23.34%	4	5
Jun–98	1,004.48	Aug–98	758.53	Dec–99	−24.48%	2	16
Apr–02	1,822.16	Feb–03	1,327.99	Sep–03	−27.12%	10	7
Oct–07	7,238.04	Feb–09	3,066.05	N/A	−57.64%	16	N/A
Average					−29.78%	9.2	8.33

TABLE 25.24

Worst-Case Scenarios: All 20 Percent or Greater Declines for SS, Comp Value 2 in Top 3 Deciles, 3 and 6 Mo. Mom>Median, Top 50 by 6 Mo. Mom, January 1, 1964, to December 31, 2009

Peak date	Peak index value	Trough date	Trough index value	Recovery date	Decline (%)	Decline duration	Recovery duration
Apr–66	1.99	Sep–66	1.58	Mar–67	−20.74%	5	6
Nov–68	3.53	Jun–70	2.35	Apr–71	−33.48%	19	10
Apr–72	4.04	Sep–74	2.86	Apr–75	−29.13%	29	7
Aug–78	11.64	Oct–78	9.08	Apr–79	−21.95%	2	6
Jan–80	15.30	Mar–80	12.24	Jul–80	−20.01%	2	4
Aug–87	97.23	Nov–87	68.39	Dec–88	−29.66%	3	13
Aug–89	129.29	Oct–90	102.60	Mar–91	−20.64%	14	5
Jun–98	854.85	Aug–98	669.87	Dec–99	−21.64%	2	16
Apr–02	1,552.01	Feb–03	1,157.58	Aug–03	−25.41%	10	6
Oct–07	6,010.50	Feb–09	2,821.79	N/A	−53.05%	16	N/A
Average					−27.57%	10.2	8.11

TABLE 25.25

Best and Worst Average Annual Compound Returns for Monthly Data, January 1, 1964, to December 31, 2009

For any	1-year period	3-year period	5-year period	7-year period	10-year period
SS, comp value 2 in top 3 deciles, 3 and 6 mo. mom>median, top 50 by 6 mo. mom minimum compound return	−46.23%	−10.54%	−1.98%	1.96%	8.52%
SS, comp value 2 in top 3 deciles, 3 and 6 mo. mom>median, top 50 by 6 mo. mom maximum compound return	93.32%	52.56%	38.11%	33.31%	31.15%
SS, comp value 2 in top 3 deciles, 3 and 6 mo. mom>median, top 25 by 6 mo. mom minimum compound return	−51.47%	−13.61%	−2.27%	1.28%	8.57%
SS, comp value 2 in top 3 deciles, 3 and 6 mo. mom>median, top 25 by 6 mo. mom maximum compound return	102.46%	55.72%	39.44%	34.24%	31.53%
Small Stocks minimum compound return	−46.38%	−19.53%	−11.75%	−7.64%	1.08%
Small Stocks maximum compound return	93.08%	34.00%	31.37%	27.35%	24.47%

T A B L E   25.26

Terminal Value of $10,000 Invested for Best and Worst Average Annual Compound Returns for Monthly Data, January 1, 1964, to December 31, 2009

For any	1-year period	3-year period	5-year period	7-year period	10-year period
SS, comp value 2 in top 3 deciles, 3 and 6 mo. mom>median, top 50 by 6 mo. mom minimum $10,000 value	$5,377	$7,160	$9,047	$11,459	$22,652
SS, comp value 2 in top 3 deciles, 3 and 6 mo. mom>median, top 50 by 6 mo. mom maximum $10,000 value	$19,332	$35,504	$50,257	$74,810	$150,597
SS, comp value 2 in top 3 deciles, 3 and 6 mo. mom>median, top 25 by 6 mo. mom minimum $10,000 value	$4,853	$6,447	$8,913	$10,935	$22,749
SS, comp value 2 in top 3 deciles, 3 and 6 mo. mom>median, top 25 by 6 mo. mom maximum $10,000 value	$20,246	$37,759	$52,716	$78,568	$154,973
Small Stocks minimum $10,000 value	$5,362	$5,210	$5,351	$5,733	$11,131
Small Stocks maximum $10,000 value	$19,308	$24,059	$39,129	$54,327	$89,249

T A B L E   25.27

Average Annual Compound Rates of Return by Decade

	1960s*	1970s	1980s	1990s	2000st
SS, comp value 2 in top 3 deciles, 3 and 6 mo. mom>median, top 50 by 6 mo. mom	19.15%	17.26%	24.41%	21.77%	17.44%
SS, comp value 2 in top 3 deciles, 3 and 6 mo. mom>median, top 25 by 6 mo. mom	19.86%	17.32%	25.40%	22.61%	15.83%
Small Stocks	15.39%	8.19%	16.46%	14.96%	4.95%

* Returns for January 1, 1964, to December 31, 1969.
† Returns for January 1, 2000, to December 31, 2009.

OTHER UNIVERSES AND WHICH MOMENTUM STRATEGY WILL BE RIGHT FOR YOU

Strategies similar to the ones we tested on the All Stocks universe work for the Large Stocks and Market Leaders universes as well, but they don't generate returns that are as high as those from All Stocks and Small Stocks. For example, the All Stocks Growth strategy does work when applied to the Large Stocks and Market Leaders universes, generating an average annual compound return of 13.93 percent and 14.37 percent, respectively. Both returns were well ahead of the returns for either universe alone, with the Large Stocks universe earning 10.20 percent and the Market Leaders universe earning 11.36 percent. You can improve performance for both the Market Leaders and Large Stocks universes by focusing on just the top two deciles of the Value Factor Two composite and then buying the 25 stocks with the best six-month price appreciation. There, Market Leaders' returns go up to 15.29 percent and Large Stocks to 14.81 percent. Keep in mind that this simple strategy is not highly correlated to the Russell Growth Indexes. Yet, at least for the Market Leaders group, requiring that the stocks from Market Leaders are in the top two deciles of Value Composite Two and then buying the 25 stocks with the best six-month price appreciation is among the best-performing strategies we've seen for Market Leaders, and the base rates are quite high, with the group beating the Market Leaders universe in 92 percent of all rolling five-year periods and in 100 percent of all rolling ten-year periods. They have the additional benefit of never having a rolling five-year return that was negative, and thus might be the right approach for more conservative growth investors yearning for downside protection with a portfolio of names with which they are familiar.

IMPLICATIONS

One of the very best ways to use price momentum is to marry it to a value constraint. In earlier editions of this book the price-to-sales ratio was the value filter, but since our research revealed the significant improvements that the composited value factors offer to both overall returns and volatility, we now use these composites in place of the price-to-sales ratio. And because we now have access to the CRSP dataset, we've also discovered that six-month price appreciation is a more effective final momentum filter than 12-month price appreciation. These two changes have significantly improved our returns for the Cheap Stocks on the Mend growth strategy. The portfolio does correlate more closely with core/value than it does with growth, so if you want to align your portfolios with the "style box" of pure growth, you are better off using the All Stocks Growth strategy.

C H A P T E R

SEARCHING FOR THE IDEAL VALUE STOCK INVESTMENT STRATEGY

The best way to manage anything is by making use of its own nature.

—Lao Tzu

In searching for the best value investment strategy, we follow the same methodology that we did with growth strategies in the last chapter, and make use of composited value factors. Here, we look at the All Stocks and Market Leaders universes. For these value strategies, our goal is to provide excellent returns at reasonable levels of risk. Therefore, we focus on strategies with better total returns than the universe from which they are derived, but that also have lower maximum declines, standard deviations of return, and downside risk. Let's start with a strategy that fishes from the All Stocks universe.

USING THE COMPOSITED FACTORS TO FIND A GREAT VALUE PORTFOLIO

Our first strategy requires that stocks meet the following criteria to be included in the portfolio:

- Be a member of the All Stocks universe
- Have annual earnings per share percentage change greater than zero
- Three- and six-month price appreciation must exceed the universe median
- Must be in the upper 50 percent of the combined composites of financial strength, earnings quality, and Value Composite Two
- Buy the 25 stocks with the best Value Composite Two scores

THE RESULTS

We start, as usual, on December 31, 1963, with a $10,000 investment. As Table 26.1 shows, this is an excellent All Stocks value strategy. Note that as we did when we went looking for the best growth strategies by including value factors, here we are also including some growth factors to enhance value, specifically by requiring positive earnings growth and three- and six-month momentum to be greater than the universe's median. This helps us avoid "value traps," or stocks that continue to decline in price. The $10,000 invested in this strategy grows to $43,868,549 by the end of 2009, an average annual compound return of 20 percent. The strategy also achieves our goal of having a lower maximum decline, standard deviation of return, and downside risk than the All Stocks universe itself. The excellent returns married to the lower standard deviation of return bring the strategy's Sharpe ratio to a very high .92, compared to .33 for the All Stocks universe. See Table 26.1 for all other relevant summary statistics. All base rates, featured in Table 26.2, are positive, with the strategy beating the All Stocks universe in 97 percent of all rolling three-year periods and in 100 percent of all rolling five- and ten-year periods.

T A B L E   26.1

Summary Annual Return and Risk Results Data: All Stocks Value and All Stocks, January 1, 1964, to December 31, 2009

	All Stocks Value	All Stocks
Arithmetic average	21.60%	13.26%
Geometric average	20.00%	11.22%
Median return	26.16%	17.16%
Standard deviation	16.34%	18.99%
Upside deviation	10.04%	10.98%
Downside deviation	12.99%	13.90%
Tracking error	8.70	0.00
Number of positive periods	376	329
Number of negative periods	176	223
Maximum peak-to-trough decline	−46.36%	−55.54%
Beta	0.77	1.00
T-statistic (m = 0)	8.18	4.47
Sharpe ratio (Rf = 5%)	0.92	0.33
Sortino ratio (MAR = 10%)	0.77	0.09
$10,000 becomes	$43,868,549	$1,329,513
Minimum 1-year return	−40.74%	−46.49%
Maximum 1-year return	80.82%	84.19%
Minimum 3-year return	−6.37%	−18.68%
Maximum 3-year return	46.99%	31.49%
Minimum 5-year return	−1.59%	−9.91%
Maximum 5-year return	37.30%	27.66%
Minimum 7-year return	2.97%	−6.32%
Maximum 7-year return	33.15%	23.77%

(continued on next page)

T A B L E 26.1

Summary Annual Return and Risk Results Data: All Stocks Value and All Stocks, January 1, 1964, to December 31, 2009 *(Continued)*

	All Stocks Value	All Stocks
Minimum 10-year return	9.24%	1.01%
Maximum 10-year return	30.52%	22.05%
Minimum expected return*	−11.08%	−24.73%
Maximum expected return†	54.29%	51.24%

* Minimum expected return is arithmetic return minus 2 times the standard deviation.
† Maximum expected return is arithmetic return plus 2 times the standard deviation.

T A B L E 26.2

Base Rates for All Stocks Value and All Stocks, January 1, 1964, to December 31, 2009

Item	All Stocks Value beat All Stocks	Percent	Average annual excess return
Single-year return	462 out of 541	85%	8.43%
Rolling 3-year compound return	501 out of 517	97%	8.95%
Rolling 5-year compound return	491 out of 493	100%	9.00%
Rolling 7-year compound return	467 out of 469	100%	8.96%
Rolling 10-year compound return	433 out of 433	100%	8.82%

WORST-CASE SCENARIOS AND BEST AND WORST RETURNS

This strategy suffered losses of more than 20 percent only four times since 1963. As Table 26.3 shows, the worst occurred during the most recent bear market when it lost 46.36 percent between October 2007 and February 2009. The four declines' average loss was 32.65 percent, and the average duration of the decline was 15 months. This compares quite favorably with the All Stocks universe, which suffered six declines greater than 20 percent over the same period, two of which were greater than 50 percent. Thus, this value strategy experiences significantly more reduced declines than an investment in the All Stocks universe itself.

T A B L E 26.3

Worst-Case Scenarios: All 20 Percent or Greater Declines for All Stocks Value, January 1, 1964, to December 31, 2009

Peak date	Peak index value	Trough date	Trough index value	Recovery date	Decline (%)	Decline duration	Recovery duration
Nov–68	3.45	Jun–70	2.32	Apr–71	−32.76%	19	10
Nov–72	3.95	Sep–74	3.08	Feb–75	−22.02%	22	5
Aug–87	102.79	Nov–87	72.50	Jan–89	−29.47%	3	14
Oct–07	5,155.70	Feb–09	2,765.28	N/A	−46.36%	16	N/A
Average					−32.65%	15	9.67

The strategy's best five-year return occurred in the period ending July 1987, when it earned an average annual return of 37.30 percent. (The *second*-best five years occurred in the period ending October 2007, when it earned 35.72 percent annually in the previous five years). The worst five years for the strategy occurred in the period ending November 1973, when it lost 1.59 percent a year. Tables 26.4 and 26.5 show the best and worst returns for other holding periods. Figure 26.1 shows the rolling excess (deficient) return (alpha) on an average annual compound basis for this All Stocks Value strategy, minus the return of the All Stocks universe. Table 26.6 shows the returns for the All Stocks Value strategy and All Stocks universe by decade.

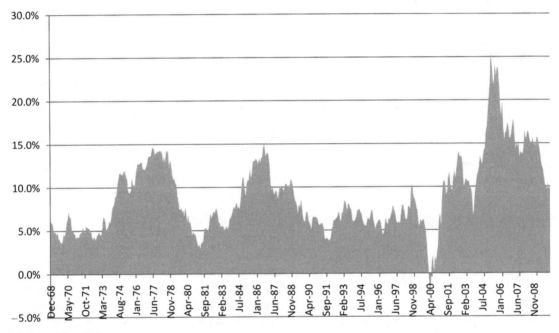

F I G U R E 26.1

Five-year average annual compound excess (deficient) return All Stocks Value minus All Stocks, January 1,1964, to December 31, 2009

T A B L E 26.4

Best and Worst Average Annual Compound Returns for Monthly Data, January 1, 1964, to December 31, 2009

For any	1-year period	3-year period	5-year period	7-year period	10-year period
All Stocks Value minimum compound return	−40.74%	−6.37%	−1.59%	2.97%	9.24%
All Stocks Value maximum compound return	80.82%	46.99%	37.30%	33.15%	30.52%
All Stocks minimum compound return	−46.49%	−18.68%	−9.91%	−6.32%	1.01%
All Stocks maximum compound return	84.19%	31.49%	27.66%	23.77%	22.05%

TABLE 26.5

Terminal Value of $10,000 Invested for Best and Worst Average Annual Compound Returns for Monthly Data, January 1, 1964, to December 31, 2009

For any	1-year period	3-year period	5-year period	7-year period	10-year period
All Stocks Value minimum $10,000 value	$5,926	$8,209	$9,228	$12,272	$24,201
All Stocks Value maximum $10,000 value	$18,082	$31,762	$48,791	$74,183	$143,495
All Stocks minimum $10,000 value	$5,351	$5,379	$5,936	$6,330	$11,054
All Stocks maximum $10,000 value	$18,419	$22,734	$33,903	$44,504	$73,345

TABLE 26.6

Average Annual Compound Rates of Return by Decade

	1960s*	1970s	1980s	1990s	2000s†
All Stocks Value	18.35%	17.47%	25.26%	19.05%	19.37%
All Stocks	13.36%	7.56%	16.78%	15.35%	4.39%

* Returns for January 1, 1964, to December 31, 1969.
† Returns for January 1, 2000, to December 31, 2009.

MARKET LEADERS VALUE STRATEGY

Many investors are uncomfortable with any strategy that buys stocks that are not well known or familiar to them. For example, the above All Stocks Value strategy is a fantastic performer, has excellent risk characteristics, and had only four declines of 20 percent or more in 46 years. Yet the portfolio is made up of a host of stocks that the average investor has probably never heard of, among them companies like Industrias Bachoco S.A.B., Endurance Specialty Holdings Ltd., China Yuchai International, and Domtar Corp. Hardly household names! The portfolio contains only a handful of stocks investors might be familiar with, such as paper and container maker Boise and health care provider Humana. That can be a real problem for investors, particularly when the portfolio is not performing well. Many investors prefer to own more well-known companies, and for those investors we offer a value strategy from the Market Leaders universe. You will recall that for a stock to be included in the Market Leaders universe, it must be a nonutility company that has a market capitalization greater than the average of the Compustat dataset; cash flow greater than the average; shares outstanding greater than average; and annual sales 50 percent greater than the average for the dataset. These requirements generate a universe of approximately 350 to 400 large, well-known companies from all over the world, as we allow the inclusion of American

Depository Receipts (ADRs) of foreign companies whose shares also trade in the United States.

For our first go around, we take a look at an improved version of a popular strategy from earlier editions of this book that buys market-leading companies with high shareholder yield. For this new version of the strategy, we continue the practice of adding a growth characteristic to a value portfolio to avoid any serious "value traps."

To be included in the strategy portfolio, a stock must meet the following characteristics:

- Be selected from the Market Leaders universe
- Three- and six-month price appreciation must be greater than the Market Leaders' median
- Buy the 25 stocks with the highest shareholder yield

THE RESULTS

The $10,000 invested on December 31, 1963, in this strategy grows to $6,168,039 by the end of 2009, an average annual compound return of 14.99 percent. That's considerably better than the $1,411,897 you'd have earned investing in the Market Leaders universe itself, which compounded at 11.36 percent per year. However, risk, as measured by the standard deviation of return as well as downside risk, was higher for this strategy—its standard deviation of return was 16.87 percent, and its downside risk was 12.62 percent. Nevertheless, its higher return brought the Sharpe ratio to .59, compared to .39 for the Market Leaders universe. As you can see from Table 26.7, the strategy's maximum decline was −57.92 percent compared with Market Leaders' −54.03 percent. This is a shift from our findings in earlier editions of this book, which found that the maximum decline of the strategy was lower than the Market Leaders universe. We also noted in earlier editions that this strategy never lost money in any five-year period, but now we have a five-year period with an average annual loss of −4.72 percent. There are two primary reasons for this. First is that the bear market of 2007−2009 was the worst since the Great Depression, and it was particularly hard on large-cap value stocks. The Russell 1000 Value index, for example, declined by 55.56 percent during the most recent bear market. The second reason is the result of our new approach to composited portfolio returns. By including the returns for portfolios starting in each month, we found some pockets of underperformance that the annual data missed. The number of rolling five-year periods with negative performance is actually quite small, however, with the strategy suffering negative five-year returns for the periods ending January, February, and March 2009 (near the bottom of the bear market), November 1973, and September and October 1974. Thus, out of 493 rolling five-year periods, six—just 1 percent—resulted in negative returns. The base rates for the strategy, featured in Table 26.8, are all positive with the strategy beating the Market Leaders universe in 90 percent of all rolling five-year periods and in 100 percent of all rolling ten-year periods.

T A B L E   26.7

Summary Annual Return and Risk Results Data: Market Leaders, 3 and 6 Mo. Mom>Median, Top 25 by Shareholder Yield and Market Leaders; January 1, 1964, to December 31, 2009

	Mareket Leaders, 3 and 6 mo. mom>median, top 25 by shareholder yield	Market Leaders
Arithmetic average	16.63%	12.82%
Geometric average	14.99%	11.36%
Median return	19.28%	14.62%
Standard deviation	16.87%	16.13%
Upside deviation	11.01%	10.00%
Downside deviation	12.62%	11.66%
Tracking error	6.36	0.00
Number of positive periods	352	335
Number of negative periods	200	217
Maximum peak-to-trough decline	−57.92%	−54.03%
Beta	0.97	1.00
T-statistic (m = 0)	6.22	5.10
Sharpe ratio (Rf = 5%)	0.59	0.39
Sortino ratio (MAR = 10%)	0.40	0.12
$10,000 becomes	$6,168,039	$1,411,897
Minimum 1-year return	−52.37%	−48.15%
Maximum 1-year return	63.15%	66.79%
Minimum 3-year return	−16.39%	−13.61%
Maximum 3-year return	42.36%	34.82%
Minimum 5-year return	−4.72%	−4.36%
Maximum 5-year return	38.58%	31.52%
Minimum 7-year return	0.36%	−2.93%
Maximum 7-year return	30.39%	24.56%
Minimum 10-year return	2.52%	1.01%
Maximum 10-year return	25.14%	19.69%
Minimum expected return*	−17.11%	−19.44%
Maximum expected return†	50.36%	45.07%

* Minimum expected return is arithmetic return minus 2 times the standard deviation.
† Maximum expected return is arithmetic return plus 2 times the standard deviation.

T A B L E   26.8

Base Rates for Market Leaders, 3 and 6 Mo. Mom>Median, Top 25 by Shareholder Yield and Market Leaders; January 1, 1964, to December 31, 2009

Item	Market Leaders, 3 and 6 mo. mom>median, top 25 by shareholder yield beat Market Leaders	Percent	Average annual excess return
Single-year return	346 out of 541	64%	3.60%
Rolling 3-year compound return	401 out of 517	78%	3.81%
Rolling 5-year compound return	443 out of 493	90%	4.07%
Rolling 7-year compound return	444 out of 469	95%	4.24%
Rolling 10-year compound return	433 out of 433	100%	4.36%

WORST-CASE SCENARIOS AND BEST AND WORST RETURNS

The strategy suffered six separate declines exceeding 20 percent. As you can see from Table 26.9, the largest decline of 57.92 percent was also the third longest, occurring during the 16 months between October 2007 and February 2009.

The best five-year period for the strategy occurred in the period ending July 1987, when it earned an average annual compound return of 38.58 percent over the previous five years. The worst five-year period for the strategy occurred in the period ending February 2009, when it lost 4.72 percent per year. Tables 26.10 and 26.11 show the best and worst returns for various other holding periods. Figure 26.2 shows the rolling five-year excess return (alpha) for the strategy minus the Market Leaders universes' returns. Table 26.12 shows the returns for the strategy and for the Market Leaders universe by decade.

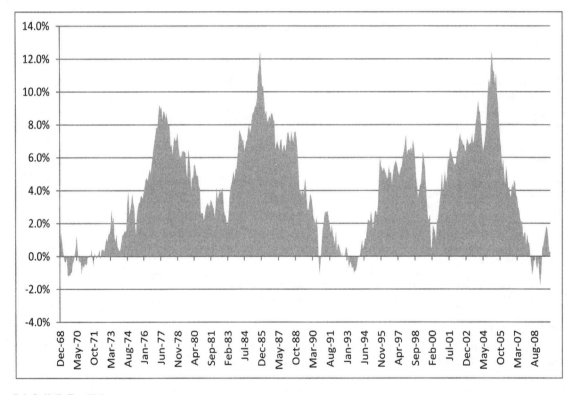

F I G U R E   26.2

Five-year average annual compound excess (deficient) return Market Leaders, 3 and 6 mo. momentum>median, top 25 by shareholder yield minus Market Leaders, January 1, 1964, to December 31, 2009

TABLE 26.9

Worst-Case Scenarios: All 20 Percent or Greater Declines for Market Leaders, 3 and 6 Mo. Mom>Median, Top 25 by Shareholder Yield, January 1, 1964, to December 31, 2009

Peak date	Peak index value	Trough date	Trough index value	Recovery date	Decline (%)	Decline duration	Recovery duration
Jan–69	1.97	Jun–70	1.29	Apr–72	−34.79%	17	22
Nov–72	2.18	Sep–74	1.56	May–75	−28.47%	22	8
Aug–87	33.04	Nov–87	22.73	Jan–89	−31.21%	3	14
Aug–89	40.10	Oct–90	29.88	Mar–91	−25.48%	14	5
May–02	302.21	Sep–02	236.73	Jun–03	−21.67%	4	9
Oct–07	728.90	Feb–09	306.71	N/A	−57.92%	16	N/A
Average					−33.25%	12.67	11.6

TABLE 26.10

Best and Worst Average Annual Compound Returns for Monthly Data, January 1, 1964, to December 31, 2009

For any	1-year period	3-year period	5-year period	7-year period	10-year period
Market Leaders, 3 and 6 mo. mom>median, top 25 by shareholder yield minimum compound return	−52.37%	−16.39%	−4.72%	0.36%	2.52%
Market Leaders, 3 and 6 mo. mom>median, top 25 by shareholder yield maximum compound return	63.15%	42.36%	38.58%	30.39%	25.14%
Market Leaders minimum compound return	−48.15%	−13.61%	−4.36%	−2.93%	1.01%
Market Leaders maximum compound return	66.79%	34.82%	31.52%	24.56%	19.69%

TABLE 26.11

Terminal Value of $10,000 Invested for Best and Worst Average Annual Compound Returns for Monthly Data, January 1, 1964, to December 31, 2009

For any	1-year period	3-year period	5-year period	7-year period	10-year period
Market Leaders, 3 and 6 mo. mom>median, top 25 by shareholder yield minimum $10,000 value	$4,763	$5,845	$7,851	$10,252	$12,824
Market Leaders, 3 and 6 mo. mom>median, top 25 by shareholder yield maximum $10,000 value	$16,315	$28,850	$51,117	$64,090	$94,166
Market Leaders minimum $10,000 value	$5,185	$6,448	$8,001	$8,122	$11,061
Market Leaders maximum $10,000 value	$16,679	$24,506	$39,355	$46,514	$60,354

TABLE 26.12

Average Annual Compound Rates of Return by Decade

	1960s*	1970s	1980s	1990s	2000s†
Market Leaders, 3 and 6 mo. mom>median, top 25 by shareholder yield	7.43%	11.53%	23.72%	18.86%	11.04%
Market Leaders	8.23%	7.32%	18.10%	16.54%	5.92%

* Returns for January 1, 1964, to December 31, 1969.
† Returns for January 1, 2000, to December 31, 2009.

SIMILAR TO RESULTS FOR MARKET LEADERS PURE SHAREHOLDER YIELD

While I have added the growth requirement that three- and six-month price appreciation must be greater than average, I should note that the return differences are very small between the strategy with that price momentum requirement and without it. Just buying the 25 stocks from the Market Leaders universe with the highest shareholder yield returns 14.87 percent over the same time period with similar levels of risk, and shareholder yield can be used on its own should you want to simplify the process. I like the idea of including at least one growth characteristic in what would otherwise be a pure value portfolio—just as I like including at least one value characteristic in what would otherwise be a pure growth portfolio—because I think they lead to better and more consistent overall returns. Yet, in this case the improvement to returns is a very small 12 basis points. I nevertheless think that if you are inclined to test your own investment strategies, you can improve your results by adding value components to growth strategies and growth components to value strategies.

IMPLICATIONS

Depending on your goals for the value portion of your portfolio, these two strategies are both attractive, solid performers. If you are willing to follow an all-cap strategy that might invest in unfamiliar companies, the All Stocks Value portfolio will be right for you. With only four drawdowns, none exceeding 50 percent, the strategy still managed to do vastly better than the All Stocks universe itself. It offers excellent risk-adjusted returns and very strong base rates. Of course, as noted, it does so buying names that are unfamiliar to the majority of investors. For investors who want to focus on bigger, better known stocks, the Market Leaders Value strategy might be best. It has excellent base rates and adds significant performance over the Market Leaders universe itself. While the strategy took a drubbing in the bear market of 2007–2009—with a drawdown of nearly 58 percent—prior to that it had never suffered a peak-to-trough decline exceeding 35 percent.

27 CHAPTER

UNITING THE BEST FROM GROWTH AND VALUE

What we learn from history is that we do not learn from history.
—Benjamin Disraeli

In this chapter we will look at uniting the best growth and value factors to produce a portfolio that we will call Trending Value. As you will recall from Chapter Twenty, price momentum proved to be an especially good way to identify both those stocks which go on to perform well and which go on to perform poorly, so we use six-month price appreciation as our growth factor. Let Table 27.1 serve as a reminder of the power of six-month price appreciation. (I've used the 1964–2009 period here so that we can have an apples-to-apples comparison with the value factor we use.) As you can see from the table, buying the stocks with the best six-month price appreciation from the All Stocks universe returned 14.52 percent a year, turning $10,000 invested on December 31, 1963, into $5,116,741 at the close of 2009, vastly better than the $1,329,513 you'd have earned from an investment in the All Stocks universe alone, which returned 11.22 percent a year over the same period. What's even more striking is the comparison to the performance of the 10 percent of stocks from All Stocks with the *worst* six-month price appreciation. Investing in the biggest six-month losers from All Stocks generated a paltry 3.67 percent a year over the same time period, turning $10,000 into a mere $52,419, considerably less than you would have earned from U.S. T-bills, where your $10,000 would have grown to $120,778, an average annual compound return of 5.57 percent.

T A B L E   27.1

Summary Annual Return and Risk Results Data: All Stocks 6-Mo. Momentum Decile 1, All Stocks 6-Mo. Momentum, Decile 10, and All Stocks, January 1, 1964, to December 31, 2009

	All Stocks 6-mo. momentum, decile 1	All Stocks 6-mo. momentum, decile 10	All Stocks
Arithmetic average	18.12%	7.06%	13.26%
Geometric average	14.52%	3.67%	11.22%
Median return	22.79%	7.09%	17.16%
Standard deviation	24.88%	25.37%	18.99%
Upside deviation	15.40%	17.25%	10.98%
Downside deviation	17.64%	17.53%	13.90%
Tracking error	10.79	9.88	0.00
Number of positive periods	337	305	329
Number of negative periods	215	247	223
Maximum peak-to-trough decline	−62.44%	−77.42%	−55.54%
Beta	1.20	1.26	1.00
T-statistic (m = 0)	4.57	1.83	4.47
Sharpe ratio (Rf = 5%)	0.38	−0.05	0.33
Sortino ratio (MAR = 10%)	0.26	−0.36	0.09
$10,000 becomes	$5,116,741	$52,419	$1,329,513
Minimum 1-year return	−54.29%	−56.18%	−46.49%
Maximum 1-year return	175.23%	107.23%	84.19%
Minimum 3-year return	−25.24%	−31.23%	−18.68%
Maximum 3-year return	59.15%	38.29%	31.49%
Minimum 5-year return	−9.05%	−21.12%	−9.91%
Maximum 5-year return	43.45%	26.10%	27.66%
Minimum 7-year return	−3.32%	−16.53%	−6.32%
Maximum 7-year return	33.36%	20.07%	23.77%
Minimum 10-year return	−0.29%	−7.42%	1.01%
Maximum 10-year return	29.64%	16.20%	22.05%
Minimum expected return*	−31.65%	−43.67%	−24.73%
Maximum expected return†	67.89%	57.79%	51.24%

* Minimum expected return is arithmetic return minus 2 times the standard deviation.
† Maximum expected return is arithmetic return plus 2 times the standard deviation.

THE PROBLEMS WITH PURE PRICE MOMENTUM

When I originally discussed the power of price momentum for selecting stocks which might go on to perform well and which might crash and burn, I also cautioned that it is a highly volatile strategy for the type of investor who could fall asleep on a rollercoaster. Tolerating upside volatility is one thing, but when a strategy moves against us it can be nearly impossible to stay the course. For example, many investors were drawn to momentum investing in the late 1990s, when the internet and tech bubble were in full swing: in 1999—the last and most explosive year of the bubble—buying the decile of stocks from All Stocks with the best six-month price appreciation soared by more than 100 percent! Those eye-popping returns led many investors to pile into pure momentum strategies and funds. The problem was that after the bubble burst in March 2000, the strategy proceeded to provide back-to-back losing years in 2000, 2001, and 2002, losing 17.72, 4.76, and 21.11 percent respectively. Other stocks did even worse, but even the most dedicated investor would have found it nearly impossible to stick with the strategy after three years of back-to-back disappointment. Thus, volatility is a real problem for what is an otherwise excellent long-term strategy.

UNITING VALUE AND MOMENTUM

One of the consistent themes of my research is the efficacy of uniting value and growth factors. Doing so allows you to smooth out the jags of a pure momentum strategy by tempering it with the best of value. Over long periods of time, the data proves conclusively that value trumps growth. Yet, there is also evidence that value strategies can get seriously out of sync during runaway bull markets. By definition, stocks that are very cheap in terms of PE, PSR, price to cash flow, EBITDA/EV, etc. are not going to be strong performers in markets that are defined by wild speculation in untested companies. In other words, when the market is in love with the *concept* of a company, as it was in the late 1990s with dot.com stocks, companies that have excellent financials and are modestly priced tend to be ignored. For example, the decile of stocks from All Stocks in Value Composite Two (those with the best valuations) went up a mere 4.12 percent in 1999, a year that saw the best decile from All Stocks by six-month price appreciation soar by more than 100 percent. Thus, what we will attempt with our next strategy is to find the best value stocks that are also trending up sharply in price, what we call Trending Value.

THE TRENDING VALUE PORTFOLIO

You will recall from Chapter Fifteen that combining several value ratios into a value composite leads to more consistent, higher returns than using any single value ratio alone. Table 27.2 compares the results for Value Composite Two buying those stocks with best six-month price momentum and to the All Stocks universe. On its own, buying the decile of stocks from All Stocks with the best Value Factor Two scores does significantly better than buying stocks with the best six-month price momentum. The stocks in decile one of Value Composite Two earned 17.30 percent a year, turning $10,000 invested on December 31, 1963 into $15,416,651. They also did so with less risk than the All Stocks universe, generating a very high Sharpe ratio of .72, and much better than buying the six-month price appreciators, whose higher risk generated a more disappointing Sharpe ratio of .38. Before we look at what happens when you *combine* these two factors, let's review how we create the value composites.

T A B L E   27.2

Summary Annual Return and Risk Results Data: All Stocks 6-Month Momentum, Decile 1, All Stocks VC 2 Decile 1, and All Stocks, January 1, 1964 to December 31, 2009

	All Stocks 6-Month Momentum, Decile 1	All Stocks VC2 Decile1	All Stocks
Arithmetic average	18.12%	19.00%	13.26%
Geometric average	14.52%	17.30%	11.22%
Median return	22.79%	22.74%	17.16%
Standard deviation	24.88%	17.10%	18.99%
Upside deviation	15.40%	11.32%	10.98%
Downside deviation	17.64%	12.81%	13.90%
Tracking error	10.79	8.10	0.00
Number of positive periods	337	368	329
Number of negative periods	215	184	223
Maximum peak-to-trough decline	−62.44%	−58.07%	−55.54%
Beta	1.20	0.81	1.00
T-statistic (m = 0)	4.57	6.95	4.47
Sharpe ratio (Rf = 5%)	0.38	0.72	0.33
Sortino ratio (MAR = 10%)	0.26	0.57	0.09
$10,000 becomes	$5,116,741	$15,416,651	$1,329,513
Minimum 1-year return	−54.29%	−48.60%	−46.49%
Maximum 1-year return	175.23%	77.27%	84.19%
Minimum 3-year return	−25.24%	−17.13%	−18.68%
Maximum 3-year return	59.15%	41.33%	31.49%
Minimum 5-year return	−9.05%	−3.65%	−9.91%
Maximum 5-year return	43.45%	35.99%	27.66%
Minimum 7-year return	−3.32%	−0.10%	−6.32%
Maximum 7-year return	33.36%	31.35%	23.77%
Minimum 10-year return	−0.29%	6.17%	1.01%
Maximum 10-year return	29.64%	29.77%	22.05%
Minimum expected return*	−31.65%	−15.20%	−24.73%
Maximum expected return†	67.89%	53.20%	51.24%

* Minimum expected return is arithmetic return minus 2 times the standard deviation.
† Maximum expected return is arithmetic return plus 2 times the standard deviation.

A REVIEW OF VALUE COMPOSITES

In this chapter, we use Value Composite Two, since it had the highest Sharpe ratio of the three value factor composites that we tested. We create the Value Factor Two composite by ranking the following factors:

1. Price-to-book
2. Price-to-earnings

3. Price-to-sales
4. EBITDA/EV
5. Price-to-cash flow
6. Shareholder yield

For the combined group of factors, we assign a percentile ranking (from 1 to 100) for each stock in the All Stocks universe. If a stock has a PE ratio that is in the lowest 1 percent of the universe, it receives a rank of 100; if a stock has a PE ratio in the highest 1 percent for the universe, it receives a rank of one. We follow a similar convention for each of the factors. Thus, if a stock is in the lowest 1 percent of the universe based on its price-to-sales ratio, it gets 100; if in the highest 1 percent, it gets a one. If a value is missing for a factor, we assign it a neutral rank of 50. For shareholder yield, those stocks in the 1 percent of the universe with the *highest* yields are ranked 100, whereas those within the lowest 1 percent are ranked one. Once all the factors are ranked, we add up all their rankings and assign the stocks to deciles. Those with the highest scores are assigned to decile 1, while those with the lowest scores are assigned to decile 10.

Thus the stocks in decile 1 would feature the best combined score and would have the lowest PEs, PSRs, and so on, while the stocks in decile 10 would have the *highest* PEs, PSRs, and so on. For this test, we concentrate on decile 1 of Value Composite Two.

THE TRENDING VALUE PORTFOLIO

This strategy hunts in the broadest of our universes, the All Stocks universe, which includes every stock with a market capitalization exceeding an inflation-adjusted $200 million. Thus, this will be an all-cap portfolio that can include any stock with a market capitalization above $200 million. To be included in this strategy, stocks must:

1. Be a member of the All Stocks universe
2. Be in decile 1 of the composited Value Factor Two (i.e., the 10 percent of stocks with the best valuation scores across the six value factors cited above)
3. Buy the 25 and 50 stocks with the best six-month price appreciation

Table 27.3 shows the power of combining Value Factor Two and six-month price appreciation. You'll recall that buying the 10 percent of stocks from All Stocks with the best six-month price appreciation earned 14.52 percent over the 46 years of the test, and buying stocks in decile 1 of Value Factor Two earned 17.30 percent. By marrying the two and buying the 25 stocks from decile 1 of Value Factor Two with the best six-month price appreciation, average annual returns jump to an eye-popping 21.19 percent, turning $10,000 into $69,098,587 between 1964 and 2009. What's more, risk and maximum declines drop as well. The 25-stock Trending Value portfolio had a standard deviation of return of 17.44 percent, some 1.55 percent below All Stocks' 18.99 percent. It also has a lower downside risk of 13.71 percent, compared with All Stocks' 13.90 percent. Those lower risk numbers push the Trending Value strategy's Sharpe ratio to .93, vastly better than the All Stocks' .33 and significantly ahead of decile 1 of Value Factor Two's Sharpe ratio of .72. On top of that, Trending Value's maximum decline of 50.55 percent is lower than All Stocks 55.54 percent.

T A B L E   27.3

Summary Annual Return and Risk Results Data: Comp Value 2 in Top Decile, Top 25 by 6 Mo. Mom, Comp Value 2 in Top Decile, Top 50 by 6 Mo. Mom, and All Stocks, January 1, 1964, to December 31, 2009

	Comp Value 2 in top decile, top 25 by 6 mo, mom	Comp Value 2 in top decile, top 50 by 6 mo, mom	All Stocks
Arithmetic average	23.04%	21.48%	13.26%
Geometric average	21.19%	19.85%	11.22%
Median return	29.20%	26.63%	17.16%
Standard deviation	17.44%	16.51%	18.99%
Upside deviation	10.60%	10.16%	10.98%
Downside deviation	13.71%	12.87%	13.90%
Tracking error	8.90	8.55	0.00
Number of positive periods	373	369	329
Number of negative periods	179	183	223
Maximum peak-to-trough decline	−50.55%	−49.64%	−55.54%
Beta	0.81	0.78	1.00
T-statistic (m = 0)	8.13	8.06	4.47
Sharpe ratio (Rf = 5%)	0.93	0.90	0.33
Sortino ratio (MAR = 10%)	0.82	0.77	0.09
$10,000 becomes	$69,098,587	$41,411,163	$1,329,513
Minimum 1-year return	−44.60%	−43.28%	−46.49%
Maximum 1-year return	93.05%	83.14%	84.19%
Minimum 3-year return	−4.50%	−8.13%	−18.68%
Maximum 3-year return	58.58%	52.03%	31.49%
Minimum 5-year return	0.15%	−0.64%	−9.91%
Maximum 5-year return	46.05%	38.85%	27.66%
Minimum 7-year return	3.97%	3.31%	−6.32%
Maximum 7-year return	35.88%	32.83%	23.77%
Minimum 10-year return	10.16%	9.04%	1.01%
Maximum 10-year return	30.04%	30.56%	22.05%
Minimum expected return*	−11.85%	−11.53%	−24.73%
Maximum expected return†	57.92%	54.49%	51.24%

* Minimum expected return is arithmetic return minus 2 times the standard deviation.

† Maximum expected return is arithmetic return plus 2 times the standard deviation.

For an investor who can commit to a five-year holding period, what's even more remarkable is that the Trending Value portfolio never had a five-year period in which it lost money, and it also had a significantly lower downside during all other holding periods. As you can see from Table 27.3, the 50-stock portfolio also performed very well, turning $10,000 into $41,411,163, an average annual compound return of 19.85 percent. As Tables 27.4 and 27.5 demonstrate, the base rates for both portfolios are overwhelmingly positive. The 25-stock version of Trending Value beat the All Stocks universe in 100 percent of all rolling five- and ten-year periods and in 99 percent of all rolling three-year periods. The base rates for the 50-stock version were nearly as good.

T A B L E   27.4

Base Rates for Comp Value 2 in Top Decile, Top 25 by 6 Mo. Mom and All Stocks, January 1, 1964, to December 31, 2009

Item	Comp Value 2 in top decile, top 25 by 6 mo. mom beat All Stocks	Percent	Average annual excess return
Single-year return	461 out of 541	85%	9.91%
Rolling 3-year compound return	513 out of 517	99%	10.38%
Rolling 5-year compound return	493 out of 493	100%	10.30%
Rolling 7-year compound return	469 out of 469	100%	10.11%
Rolling 10-year compound return	433 out of 433	100%	9.86%

T A B L E   27.5

Base Rates for Comp Value 2 in Top Decile, Top 50 by 6 Mo. mom, and All Stocks, January 1, 1964, to December 31, 2009

Item	Comp Value 2 in top decile, top 50 by 6 mo. mom beat All Stocks	Percent	Average annual excess return
Single-year return	447 out of 541	83%	8.33%
Rolling 3-year compound return	503 out of 517	97%	8.85%
Rolling 5-year compound return	492 out of 493	100%	8.88%
Rolling 7-year compound return	467 out of 469	100%	8.76%
Rolling 10-year compound return	433 out of 433	100%	8.56%

WORST-CASE SCENARIOS AND BEST AND WORST RETURNS

Table 27.6 shows all declines exceeding 20 percent for the 25-stock version of the portfolio, and Table 27.7 details them for the 50-stock version. The 25-stock portfolio lost 20 percent or more only four times in the last 46 years, with the worst being a loss of 50.55 percent between October 2007 and February 2009. The 50-stock version of the portfolio had five declines exceeding 20 percent, with the worst being a loss of 49.64 percent also occurring between October 2007 and February 2009.

T A B L E   27.6

Worst-Case Scenarios: All 20 Percent or Greater Declines for Comp Value 2 in Top Decile, Top 25 by 6 Mo. Mom, January 1, 1964, to December 31, 2009

Peak date	Peak Index value	Trough date	Trough Index value	Recovery date	Decline (%)	Decline duration	Recovery duration
Nov–68	3.38	Jun–70	2.31	Mar–71	−31.72%	19	9
Aug–87	106.17	Nov–87	74.65	Jan–89	−29.69%	3	14
Apr–02	1,679.68	Feb–03	1,273.11	Aug–03	−24.21%	10	6
Oct–07	8,688.72	Feb–09	4,296.64	N/A	−50.55%	16	N/A
Average					−34.04%	12	9.67

T A B L E   27.7

Worst-Case Scenarios: All 20 Percent or Greater Declines for Comp Value 2 in Top Decile, Top 50 by 6 Mo. Mom, January 1, 1964, to December 31, 2009

Peak date	Peak Index value	Trough date	Trough Index value	Recovery date	Decline (%)	Decline duration	Recovery duration
Nov–68	3.22	Jun–70	2.19	Mar–71	−31.91%	19	9
Nov–72	3.78	Sep–74	2.94	Feb–75	−22.22%	22	5
Aug–87	94.34	Nov–87	68.51	Jan–89	−27.38%	3	14
Apr–02	1,158.06	Feb–03	914.39	Jul–03	−21.04%	10	5
Oct–07	4,833.44	Feb–09	2,434.36	N/A	−49.64%	16	N/A
Average					−30.43%	14	8.25

As Tables 27.8 and 27.9 show, the worst five years for the 25-stock version of the strategy turned $10,000 into $10,074, a *gain* of 0.15 percent. The best five years for the 25-stock version turned $10,000 into $66,444, an average annual compound return of 46.05 percent. For the 50-stock version, the worst five years turned $10,000 into $9,686, an average annual loss of 0.64 percent, and the best five years turned $10,000 into $51,603, an average annual compound gain of 38.85 percent. Figure 27.1 shows the five-year average annual excess (deficient) return for the 25-stock version of Trending Value, and Figure 27.2 shows it for the 50-stock version. Table 27.10 shows the returns for each version of the strategy by decade along with the returns for the All Stocks universe.

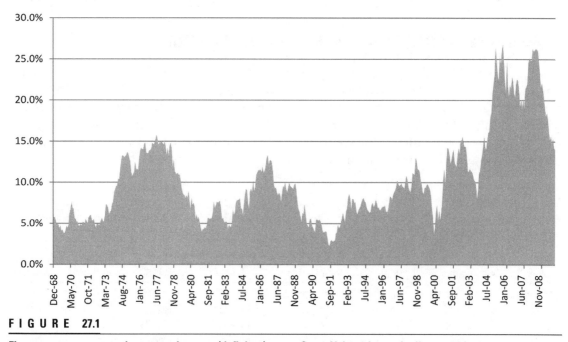

F I G U R E   27.1

Five-year average annual compound excess (deficient) return Comp Value 2 in top decile, top 25 by 6 mo. momentum minus All Stocks, January 1, 1964, to December 31, 2009

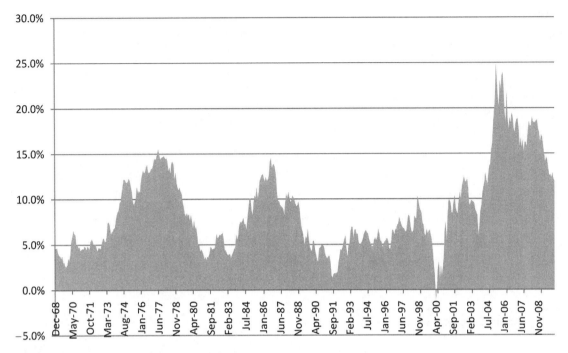

FIGURE 27.2

Five-year average annual compound excess (deficient) return Comp Value 2 in top decile, top 50 by 6 mo. momentum minus All Stocks, January 1, 1964, to December 31, 2009

TABLE 27.8

Best and Worst Average Annual Compound Returns for Monthly Data, January 1, 1964, to December 31, 2009

For any	1-year period	3-year period	5-year period	7-year period	10-year period
Comp Value 2 in top decile, top 25 by 6 mo. mom minimum compound return	−44.60%	−4.50%	0.15%	3.97%	10.16%
Comp Value 2 in top decile, top 25 by 6 mo. mom maximum compound return	93.05%	58.58%	46.05%	35.88%	30.04%
Comp Value 2 in top decile, top 50 by 6 mo. mom minimum compound return	−43.28%	−8.13%	−0.64%	3.31%	9.04%
Comp Value 2 in top decile, top 50 by 6 mo. mom maximum compound return	83.14%	52.03%	38.85%	32.83%	30.56%
All Stocks minimum compound return	−46.49%	−18.68%	−9.91%	−6.32%	1.01%
All Stocks maximum compound return	84.19%	31.49%	27.66%	23.77%	22.05%

T A B L E   27.9

Terminal Value of $10,000 Invested for Best and Worst Average Annual Compound Returns for Monthly Data, January 1, 1964, to December 31, 2009

For any	1-year period	3-year period	5-year period	7-year period	10-year period
Comp Value 2 in top decile, top 25 by 6 mo. mom minimum $10,000 value	$5,540	$8,709	$10,074	$13,132	$26,310
Comp Value 2 in top decile, top 25 by 6 mo. mom maximum $10,000 value	$19,305	$39,878	$66,444	$85,530	$138,284
Comp Value 2 in top decile, top 50 by 6 mo. mom minimum $10,000 value	$5,672	$7,755	$9,686	$12,562	$23,755
Comp Value 2 in top decile, top 50 by 6 mo. mom maximum $10,000 value	$18,314	$35,137	$51,603	$72,965	$143,947
All Stocks minimum $10,000 value	$5,351	$5,379	$5,936	$6,330	$11,054
All Stocks maximum $10,000 value	$18,419	$22,734	$33,903	$44,504	$73,345

T A B L E   27.10

Average Annual Compound Rates of Return by Decade

	1960s*	1970s	1980s	1990s	2000s†
Comp Value 2 in top decile, top 25 by 6 mo. mom	18.08%	18.85%	23.53%	22.05%	22.27%
Comp Value 2 in top decile, top 50 by 6 mo. mom	16.89%	18.09%	23.92%	19.20%	20.06%
All Stocks	13.36%	7.56%	16.78%	15.35%	4.39%

* Returns for January 1, 1964, to December 31, 1969.
† Returns for January 1, 2000, to December 31, 2009.

STYLE BOX INVESTING AND SOME OBSERVATIONS ON ANNUAL RETURNS

Morningstar Inc. has been extremely successful in promoting the idea of investing style boxes. It does excellent research and offers a fantastic amount of statistical information on a variety of stocks and mutual funds, and I highly recommend its services to do-it-yourself investors. Yet it has been *so* successful that many investors have been led to not think outside the proverbial box. I think that the Trending Value portfolio is a strong attempt to do just that. Normally, a portfolio in which the final criterion is price momentum is considered a growth-oriented investment. Yet because we limit ourselves to the top decile of All Stocks by Value Factor Two, the pool of stocks we select from are pure value stocks. Indeed, when you run a correlation of the portfolio against the various Russell indexes, its highest correlation is with the Russell 2500 Value index. Yet, a recent run of the strategy reveals four stocks out of the top 50 with market-caps exceeding $10 billion, traditionally considered to be large-cap stocks. While the overall average market-cap of this recently run portfolio is $3.2 billion—squarely in mid-cap territory—you should think of this as a portfolio that can fish anywhere in the market capitalization range. Historically, it has always led to the mid-cap value category, but that doesn't preclude it from being dominated by larger stocks sometime in the future. Here I offer the same caution for the Trending Value portfolio that I gave for the All Stocks Value portfolio in Chapter Twenty-Six—the portfolio is dominated by unfamiliar names. The handful of stocks that investors might know— Dillards, Federal-Mogul, Air-France, and Hitachi—are vastly overshadowed by virtual unknowns like IDT Corp, Uralsvyazinform JSC, Scailex Corp, and Scor S.E. ADS. Perhaps this is why the portfolio does as well as it does—for the most part, huge, well-known companies are not the engines of phenomenal year-in and year-out growth

Finally, let me offer a word about sticking to the strategy. Year-by-year results show how Trending Value is often out of sync with the overall market, something that is frequently difficult for investors to stomach. By examining Table 27.11, you can see that while there are years like 1972 and 1973 where Trending Value's performance would delight you, losing just 8.39 percent and 6.59 percent, respectively, compared to All Stocks stomach churning 27.46 and 26.33 percent losses, there are other times that might try your patience. Most notably that would have been in 1998 and 1999, the two biggest speculative years since 1967. During these two sizzling years, speculative stocks soared—the biggest six-month price appreciation gainers from All Stocks soared more than 100 percent, whereas the 25-stock version of Trending Value earned just 14.12 and 7.41 percent, respectively, in 1998 and 1999. Thus, while Trending Value is a great long-term strategy, my point is that by the end of 1999 you likely would have been deeply frustrated with its modest returns, especially as you watched other growth and momentum stocks soar.

T A B L E 27.11

Performance by Calendar Year

	Trending Value 25-stock Portfolio	Decile 1 Value Comp Two	Decile 1 All Stocks 6-mo. momentum	All Stocks
1964	24.61	23.75	16.16	16.47
1965	40.19	35.18	55.87	27.14
1966	−8.25	−11.03	1.22	−5.97
1967	56.90	51.23	76.01	49.80
1968	33.89	38.37	31.71	27.90
1969	−19.49	−23.82	−17.91	−20.45
1970	9.76	8.00	−17.38	−6.53
1971	17.65	16.33	26.28	18.14
1972	14.02	10.82	13.14	8.48
1973	−8.39	−21.68	−15.91	−27.46
1974	−6.59	−12.97	−26.46	−26.33
1975	49.70	64.06	36.23	45.86
1976	48.07	54.00	35.53	35.50
1977	16.84	11.72	14.36	6.99
1978	18.14	14.53	20.45	13.05
1979	45.89	35.89	63.27	35.40
1980	25.07	21.97	69.18	33.88

(continued on next page)

T A B L E   27.11

Performance by Calendar Year *(Continued)*

	Trending Value 25-stock Portfolio	Decile 1 Value Comp Two	Decile 1 All Stocks 6-mo. momentum	All Stocks
1981	12.88	16.31	−11.69	2.70
1982	35.66	29.86	33.10	24.73
1983	34.52	39.54	18.50	25.94
1984	20.24	19.93	−5.76	−1.34
1985	36.44	35.75	39.67	32.73
1986	27.33	24.09	19.11	12.70
1987	−3.87	0.20	0.94	−2.53
1988	29.45	26.23	17.32	22.49
1989	23.57	22.76	29.53	23.97
1990	−7.71	−14.02	−11.06	−13.53
1991	45.93	42.93	65.71	42.56
1992	30.65	24.07	11.02	14.64
1993	25.58	21.71	29.17	17.95
1994	−1.92	−0.18	−5.31	−2.41
1995	40.31	32.69	42.27	31.53
1996	32.06	23.52	14.21	17.94
1997	48.98	38.27	15.44	24.97
1998	14.12	1.79	16.73	1.63
1999	7.41	4.12	100.64	30.16
2000	20.56	21.86	−17.72	−8.80
2001	19.51	21.50	−4.76	4.25
2002	−2.08	−3.33	−21.11	−19.54
2003	74.37	58.22	59.72	52.99
2004	43.48	28.61	12.15	18.06
2005	32.47	15.65	13.91	7.67
2006	41.07	27.12	14.44	18.78
2007	29.02	−0.57	12.25	0.63
2008	−29.74	−35.47	−48.21	−40.38
2009	24.88	58.11	15.73	44.92
Minimum	−29.74	−35.47	−48.21	−40.38
Maximum	74.37	64.06	100.64	52.99
Average	23.11	19.51	18.21	13.42
Median	24.97	21.92	15.59	17.20
Standard deviation	21.22	22.34	29.72	21.59

As we saw in Chapters Two and Three, the single greatest threat to our success as investors is our own human nature. In hindsight, it may be easy to convince yourself that you would have stuck with this strategy and remained a systematic, dispassionate investor, but having lived through the period and working with many clients, I can tell you that the odds of this happening are small indeed. We are unfortunately our own worst enemies when it comes to letting a strategy work over the entire market cycle, and I urge every reader to contemplate this when the next "new, new" thing gets investors' imaginations ignited. It is at just those times that it can be the most difficult to stick with even the best of strategies.

IMPLICATIONS

Uniting the best of value and growth is a powerful way to get the best returns from the stock market. The ability to think outside the box and use strategies that have historically demonstrated consistently superior results is the key to long-term success, and the Trending Value strategy is an excellent approach when you're looking for strongly performing value stocks. You will likely recognize only a handful of stocks in the portfolio, but the strategy's underlying characteristics, strongly positive base rates, and downside advantages, are the keys to its success. If possible, with this and all the strategies featured in this book, try to review your results on a rolling basis and avoid making rash judgments in years like 1999—bubble markets rarely offer good direction for where the market will head over the next three or five years.

28 CHAPTER

RANKING THE STRATEGIES

I know of no way of judging of the future but by the past.
—Patrick Henry

It's time to rank all the strategies' returns on both an absolute and a risk-adjusted basis. As I note in the Introduction, I also present the returns for a variety of indexes and strategies on an inflation-adjusted basis to give you a sense of the real returns that they offer over longer periods of time. In order to compare apples to apples, I rank the strategies using the monthly return data between August 31, 1965, and December 31, 2009. This allows me to include all the strategies featured in various sections of the book. While it does not include the Great Depression, this 44-year period covers every other type of market environment. Booms, busts, manias, speculative fervor, a market crash, the biggest bull market in 70 years, the biggest bear market since the crash and Great Depression, and two other wicked bear markets are all woven into this 44-year market tapestry.

We begin this overview near the end of 1965. According to John Dennis Brown's *101 Years on Wall Street,* "In the record book, 1965 was another great year. The Dow ended up nearly 11 percent, closing on its very high, December 31. . . . Defense and space demands kept the aircraft and electronics soaring. Fairchild Camera was sensational, 27 to 165. Motorola added 109 points from 63. United Aircraft, 25 in 1964 and 50 in early 1965, reached 90 . . . [yet] the Consumer Price Index was rolling higher and the dollar was increasingly suspect. Military personnel in Vietnam totaled nearly 190,000, up tenfold during the year." Many of the huge gainers from the 1950s were still dominating trading, with Xerox, Polaroid, IBM, and Control Data still years away from the speculative highs they would achieve on their way to becoming members of the "nifty-fifty." The Nasdaq did not exist. Total volume had finally surpassed that of 1929. Computers still used punch cards, and even the most advanced lacked a fraction of the power we take for granted today. A tiny percentage of U.S. households owned stocks or mutual funds, and there was many a market participant who vividly and personally recalled the crash of 1929 and the ensuing depression of the 1930s.

We conclude this overview in 2009, the end of the first decade of the new millennium. While the decade served up the worst bear market since the Great Depression, the behavior of the market remains the same. Our world today looks little like the one in 1965, yet human beings—the agents of change in the marketplace—behave the same as well. For while the previous decades brought great change to the ways the markets operated, the one thing that did not change was human nature. We learned that firsthand with the speculative blow-off of the late 1990s and the resulting bear market of 2000–2002, where the reality of the marketplace ferociously reasserted itself. What's more, that first bear market of the new century proved a simple prelude to 2007–2009, the worst bear market since the 1930s, devastating investor's confidence in the equity markets and ushering in a whole new crop of fears that investors had not faced since the 1930s.

In the end, it is our consistent refusal to learn from history that condemns us to repeat it. While our situation and circumstances might change dramatically, *we* do not. It's that very fact that makes long-term data especially useful. By examining how investment strategies perform in many different market environments, we prepare ourselves for what might occur in the future. Undoubtedly, the top-performing companies and industries will change in years to come, but the underlying persistence of what works and what doesn't will continue. Thus, while I have no idea what the names of the winning and losing stocks of the future will be, I have a very good idea of what factors will define them. No doubt we will see new fads that will push individual stocks and industries to unsustainable highs, and commentators and investors will invent very exciting and seemingly plausible stories for why it is different "this time" for these new stocks and industries. Yet I believe—like *every time in the past*— that these story-stocks will go on to devastate investors as they crash back to earth. While I am not certain that we will again face a bear market of the ferocity of 2007–2009, we will inevitably experience regular bear markets that will try investors' patience and lead them to emotionally react to short-term conditions that, in the end, will cost them dearly in the long term. Our point is to review how all the strategies tested in this book have done over long periods of time and then use that information to guide us in the future. Let's look at the results.

THE RESULTS

This study of 44 years of monthly data proves that the market follows a purposeful stride, not a random walk. The stock market consistently rewards some strategies and consistently punishes others. The strategies found near the top or the bottom of our list all possess similar attributes that are easily identified. Each of the ten best-performing strategies, for example, includes relative strength criteria. Yet they are *always* tied to another factor, usually one requiring the stocks to be modestly priced in terms of how much you are paying for every dollar of sales, earnings, book value, or a combination of value factors. Most of the 10 worst-performing strategies buy stocks that investors have bid to unsustainable prices, giving them astronomical price-to-earnings, price-to-book, price-to-sales, or price-to-cash flow ratios, or are last year's biggest losers. With the exception of the disastrous performance of last year's biggest losers, all these factors usually reflect high hopes on the part of investors. History shows that high hopes are usually dashed and that investors are better off buying reasonably priced stocks with good relative strength.

Most of the best-performing strategies are riskier than the market as a whole, but a handful do *much better* than the market while taking only slightly more risk, or, in several cases, *less risk*. Most of the *worst*-performing strategies are actually considerably riskier than the best performing strategies. The results indicate that the market doesn't always award high returns to portfolios with higher risk. Indeed, you see when we sort the strategies by either downside risk or maximum decline that the *riskiest* strategies also have the highest downside risk and maximum declines, whereas many of the *lowest* downside risks belong to strategies that have historically done very well. The best-performing strategy from All Stocks is a good example—as you can see in Table 28.1, focusing on stocks from All Stocks that are in the first decile of Value Composite Two and then buying the top 25 stocks by six-month price appreciation compounded at 21.08 percent a year from August 31, 1965, through December 31, 2009, turning $10,000 into $48.2 million. Yet the standard deviation of return, downside risk, and maximum decline were all *less* than the All Stocks universe. Conversely, the *worst-performing* strategies from the All Stocks universe all had much *higher* standard deviations of return, downside risk, and maximum declines. Thus the empirical evidence does not support the idea central to the Capital Asset Pricing Model that posits that higher risk is rewarded with higher returns.

ABSOLUTE RETURNS

Table 28.1 ranks all the strategies by absolute return, and Figures 28.1 and 28.2 show the five best and five worst performers. The top eleven strategies by absolute return all come from the investable microcap universe and the Small and All Stocks universes—and all eleven use price momentum as the final factor. "Note: several of the strategies featured in the following tables are described in the additional material found at www.whatworkson-wallstreet.com." The top four strategies actually use the investable microcap universe (those stocks with inflation-adjusted market capitalizations between $50 million and $250 million) six of the remaining seven strategies come from the Small Stocks and All Stocks universes. One of the strategies, buying the stocks from All Stocks in decile 1 of Value Composite Two that have the best six-month price appreciation (the strategy we dubbed Trending Value in Chapter 27) has the highest correlation with the Russell 2500 Value index, making it a fairly pure play value strategy. Indeed, with the exception of All Stocks Growth, *all* eleven of the top-performing strategies have fairly restrictive value parameters built in, such as requiring the price-to-book ratio to be in the lowest 30 percent of the universe, the price-to-sales ratios to be lower than one, or a composite value score in the best 30 percent of the universe.

What's more, when we adjust for risk—as we will see in Table 28.3—the highest Sharpe ratios are all awarded to strategies with very strong value parameters. Thus, as we have found in every edition of this book, marrying value and growth factors offers the highest absolute returns—and often the highest risk adjusted returns as well—and is superior to pure growth strategies. The best-performing of the larger stock strategies is focusing on the Market Leaders in the top two deciles of Value Composite Two and then buying the 25 stocks with the highest six-month price appreciation. That strategy compounded at 15.34 percent and turned $10,000 into $5,585,470. As you can see from Table 28.1, All Stocks and Small Stocks dominate the returns ranked by absolute return. That makes a great deal of sense. Traditionally, smaller stocks have done significantly better than larger stocks, and that is proven out in the results featured here. As we see later in this chapter, what we want to look for are strategies that perform well when ranked on all of our criteria, and we want to focus on those that not only provide excellent absolute returns, but also offer great risk-adjusted returns, very high base rates, and the lowest maximum declines.

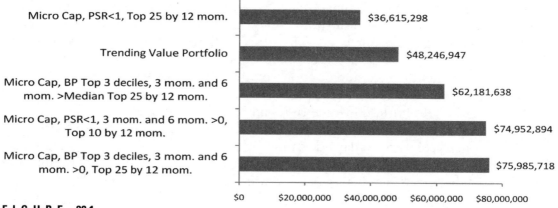

FIGURE 28.1

The five strategies with the highest absolute returns (duplicate strategies eliminated), August 31, 1965 to December 31, 2009

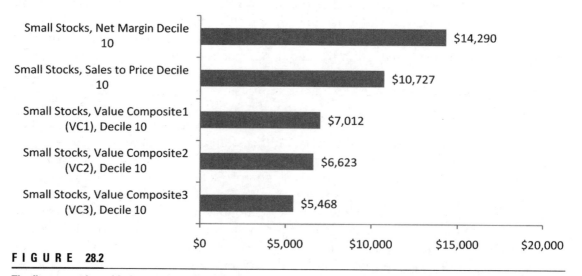

FIGURE 28.2

The five strategies with the worst absolute returns, August 31, 1965 to December 31, 2009

All Strategies for Monthly Data Series, August 31, 1965, to December 31, 2009. Strategies Sorted by Compound Average Annual Return

Strategy	Geometric mean	Standard deviation (%)	T-Statistic	$10,000 becomes	Sharpe ratio	Tracking error	Downside risk	Largest drawdown	Beta
Microcap, BP Top 3 deciles, 3 mom. and 6 mom. >0, Top 25 by 12 mom.	22.33%	20.38%	7.33	$75,985,718	0.85	9.73	14.88%	−53.89%	0.88
Microcap, PSR<1, 3 mom. and 6 mom. >0, Top 10 by 12 mom.	22.29%	27.57%	5.82	$74,952,894	0.63	15.14	18.65%	−57.64%	1.13
Microcap, BP Top 3 deciles, 3 mom. and 6 mom. >Median Top 25 by 12 mom.	21.78%	20.01%	7.29	$62,181,638	0.84	10.05	14.68%	−55.64%	0.85
Microcap, BP Top 3 deciles, 3 mom. and 6 mom. >0, Top 50 by 12 mom.	21.43%	19.17%	7.44	$54,772,842	0.86	8.86	14.46%	−55.26%	0.84
Trending Value Portfolio	21.08%	17.66%	7.87	$48,246,947	0.91	9.04	13.74%	−50.55%	0.81
Microcap, PSR<1, Top 25 by 12 mom.	20.33%	27.14%	5.47	$36,615,298	0.56	15.45	17.87%	−59.22%	1.09
All Stocks Growth	20.23%	25.16%	5.76	$35,282,794	0.61	12.00	18.09%	−59.68%	1.16
Small Stocks, VC2 in Top 3 Deciles, 3 and 6 mom.>Median, Top 25 by 6 mom.	19.85%	19.85%	6.79	$30,609,593	0.75	9.00	15.26%	−57.64%	0.87
Small Stocks, VC2 in Top 3 Deciles, 3 and 6 mom.>Median, Top 50 by 6 mom.	19.78%	18.42%	7.20	$29,832,100	0.80	8.38	14.24%	−53.05%	0.82
All Stocks, VC2 in Top Decile, Top 50 by 6 mom.	19.74%	16.70%	7.79	$29,366,965	0.88	8.69	12.89%	−49.64%	0.77
All Stocks, VC2 in Top 3 Deciles, 3 mom. and 6 mom. >Median, Top 25 by 6 mom.	19.54%	19.70%	6.75	$27,324,492	0.74	8.62	14.96%	−56.56%	0.92
Small Stocks, Value Composite3 (VC3), Decile 1	19.37%	18.92%	6.91	$25,670,891	0.76	7.95	14.21%	−59.68%	0.85
All Stocks, VC2 in Top 3 Deciles, 3 mom. and 6 mom. >Median, Top 50 by 6 mom.	19.36%	18.26%	7.12	$25,562,163	0.79	7.96	13.98%	−53.49%	0.86
Small Stocks, Value Composite2 (VC2), Decile 1	19.03%	18.14%	7.04	$22,566,623	0.77	8.29	13.73%	−60.05%	0.81
Small Stocks, EBITDA/ Enterprise Value Decile 1	18.96%	18.70%	6.85	$22,038,871	0.75	6.67	13.88%	−55.94%	0.86
Small Stocks, Value Composite1 (VC1), Decile 1	18.85%	19.37%	6.62	$21,149,675	0.72	7.86	14.51%	−60.23%	0.87
Small Stocks, PB in Top 3 Deciles, 3 mom. and 6 mom. >Median, Top 25 by SY	18.84%	16.35%	7.63	$21,049,215	0.85	9.66	13.37%	−49.20%	0.70
Small Stocks, PSR<1, 3 mom. and 6 mom. >0, Top 50 12 mom.	18.80%	23.29%	5.75	$20,778,182	0.59	9.96	17.00%	−56.62%	1.02
All Stocks, 3 mom. and 6 mom. >Median, Top 25 by SY	18.73%	17.05%	7.33	$20,230,058	0.81	8.40	13.50%	−52.27%	0.80
All Stocks, BP and 6 mom. >Median, Top 25 by BBY	18.59%	17.53%	7.11	$19,209,981	0.78	7.90	13.47%	−53.11%	0.83

(continued on next page)

T A B L E 28.1

All Strategies for Monthly Data Series, August 31, 1965, to December 31, 2009. Strategies Sorted by Compound Average Annual Return *(Continued)*

Strategy	Geometric mean	Standard deviation (%)	T-Statistic	$10,000 becomes	Sharpe ratio	Tracking error	Downside risk	Largest drawdown	Beta
Small Stocks, SY and 6 mom. >Median, Top 25 BP	18.49%	18.70%	6.72	$18,470,590	0.72	9.29	14.76%	−59.17%	0.81
All Stocks, PB in Top 3 Deciles, 3 mom. and 6 mom. >Median, Top 25 by SY	18.45%	15.48%	7.86	$18,224,488	0.87	9.24	12.11%	−47.66%	0.71
Small Stocks, BP and 6 mom. >Median, Top 25 BBY	18.44%	17.92%	6.94	$18,102,174	0.75	8.66	13.99%	−50.98%	0.79
Small Stocks, 3 mom. and 6 mom. >Median, Top 25 SY	18.37%	16.72%	7.33	$17,638,388	0.80	8.39	13.30%	−52.57%	0.75
Small Stocks, PB in Top 3 Deciles, 3 mom. and 6 mom. >Median, Top 25 by 12 mom.	18.34%	19.87%	6.36	$17,440,767	0.67	8.86	15.79%	−59.85%	0.87
Small Stocks, PB in Top 3 Deciles, 3 mom. and 6 mom. >0, Top 25 by 12 mom.	18.33%	19.79%	6.38	$17,383,935	0.67	8.84	15.48%	−59.65%	0.87
Small Stocks, PB in Top 3 Deciles, 3 mom. and 6 mom. >0, Top 25 by SY	18.28%	16.09%	7.54	$17,082,685	0.83	9.82	13.06%	−52.42%	0.69
Small Stocks, PB in Top 3 Deciles, 3 mom. and 6 mom. >0, Top 50 by 12 mom.	18.16%	18.42%	6.70	$16,333,580	0.71	8.31	14.70%	−56.04%	0.82
Small Stocks, PB in Top 3 Deciles, 3 mom. and 6 mom. >Median, Top 50 by SY	18.15%	17.08%	7.13	$16,290,759	0.77	9.00	13.91%	−49.60%	0.75
All Stocks, SY and 6 mom. >Median, Top 25 by BP	18.13%	18.42%	6.69	$16,166,786	0.71	9.02	14.13%	−58.68%	0.85
All Stocks, PB in Top 3 Deciles, 3 mom. and 6 mom. >Median, Top 25 by SY	18.02%	15.63%	7.63	$15,493,763	0.83	9.18	12.40%	−53.00%	0.72
Small Stocks, 3 mom. and 6 mom. >Median, Top 25 BP	18.00%	19.84%	6.27	$15,378,402	0.66	8.48	15.58%	−59.60%	0.88
Small Stocks, PB in Top 3 Deciles, 3 mom. and 6 mom. >Median, Top 50 by 12 mom.	17.97%	18.48%	6.62	$15,185,920	0.70	8.16	14.68%	−54.41%	0.82
All Stocks, PB in Top 3 Deciles, 3 mom. and 6 mom. >Median, Top 25 by 12 mom.	17.93%	19.93%	6.23	$14,973,336	0.65	8.57	15.68%	−60.95%	0.94
Small Stocks, 3 mom. and 6 mom. >Median, Top 50 BP	17.92%	18.75%	6.53	$14,890,544	0.69	7.63	15.01%	−56.80%	0.85
Small Stocks, PB in Top 3 Deciles, 3 mom. and 6 mom. >0, Top 50 by SY	17.85%	16.36%	7.28	$14,539,804	0.79	9.20	13.18%	−55.34%	0.72
Small Stocks, SY and 6 mom. >Median, Top 50 BP	17.84%	17.59%	6.85	$14,481,971	0.73	8.89	14.20%	−56.52%	0.77

(continued on next page)

All Strategies for Monthly Data Series, August 31, 1965, to December 31, 2009. Strategies Sorted by Compound Average Annual Return *(Continued)*

Strategy	Geometric mean	Standard deviation (%)	T-Statistic	$10,000 becomes	Sharpe ratio	Tracking error	Downside risk	Largest drawdown	Beta
All Stocks, SY and 6 mom. >Median, Top 50 by BP	17.82%	17.30%	6.94	$14,390,482	0.74	8.40	13.49%	−55.44%	0.81
All Stocks, BP and 6 mom. >Median, Top 25 by SY	17.77%	15.77%	7.48	$14,120,418	0.81	8.55	12.47%	−53.61%	0.74
All Stocks, PB in Top 3 Deciles, 3 mom. and 6 mom. >0, Top 25 by 12 mom.	17.74%	19.54%	6.27	$13,953,383	0.65	8.52	15.33%	−59.20%	0.92
All Stocks, PB in Top 3 Deciles, 3 mom. and 6 mom. >0, Top 50 by 12 mom.	17.71%	18.16%	6.64	$13,766,110	0.70	7.82	14.38%	−55.40%	0.86
Small Stocks, BP and 6 mom. >Median, Top 25 SY	17.64%	15.77%	7.44	$13,434,848	0.80	9.69	12.30%	−50.87%	0.68
All Stocks, 3 mom. and 6 mom. >Median, Top 50 by SY	17.54%	15.97%	7.33	$12,947,507	0.79	7.43	12.87%	−50.57%	0.77
All Stocks, PB in Top 3 Deciles, 3 mom. and 6 mom. >Median, Top 50 by SY	17.54%	15.84%	7.37	$12,923,562	0.79	8.80	12.68%	−49.30%	0.73
Small Stocks, Free CF to Enterprise Value Decile 1	17.54%	20.60%	5.95	$12,912,118	0.61	6.67	14.82%	−59.25%	0.95
Small Stocks, Earnings/ Price Decile 1	17.53%	19.58%	6.18	$12,875,519	0.64	7.56	14.34%	−56.31%	0.88
All Stocks, 3 mom. and 6 mom. >Median, Top 50 by BP	17.52%	18.53%	6.47	$12,808,436	0.68	7.29	14.79%	−57.03%	0.89
All Stocks, BP and 6 mom. >Median, Top 50 by BBY	17.51%	17.17%	6.88	$12,801,191	0.73	7.47	13.32%	−50.66%	0.82
All Stocks, PB in Top 3 Deciles, 3 mom. and 6 mom. >0, Top 50 by SY	17.51%	15.66%	7.43	$12,774,895	0.80	8.85	12.40%	−55.07%	0.72
Small Stocks, BP and BBY and 3 mom. >Median, Top 25 by 6 mom.	17.47%	20.09%	6.06	$12,575,407	0.62	7.75	15.78%	−59.70%	0.91
Small Stocks, BP and BBY >Median, Top 25 by 6 mom.	17.42%	20.49%	5.95	$12,337,258	0.61	7.83	15.96%	−61.12%	0.92
Small Stocks, Net Operating Cash Flow to Price Decile 1	17.39%	20.53%	5.92	$12,234,992	0.60	7.99	15.51%	−65.23%	0.92
All Stocks, PB in Top 3 Deciles, 3 mom. and 6 mom. >Median, Top 50 by 12 mom.	17.38%	18.29%	6.50	$12,174,722	0.68	7.84	14.52%	−55.95%	0.87
All Stocks, 3 mom. and 6 mom. >Median, Top 25 by BP	17.31%	19.66%	6.11	$11,864,813	0.63	8.34	15.30%	−60.50%	0.93
Small Stocks, BP and 6 mom. >Median, Top 50 BBY	17.30%	17.24%	6.79	$11,818,630	0.71	8.24	13.68%	−49.81%	0.77

(continued on next page)

T A B L E 28.1

All Strategies for Monthly Data Series, August 31, 1965, to December 31, 2009. Strategies Sorted by Compound Average Annual Return *(Continued)*

Strategy	Geometric mean	Standard deviation (%)	T-Statistic	$10,000 becomes	Sharpe ratio	Tracking error	Downside risk	Largest drawdown	Beta
Small Stocks, BP and SY >Median, Top 25 by 6 mom.	17.26%	19.40%	6.16	$11,646,050	0.63	7.72	14.98%	−59.63%	0.87
Small Stocks, 3 mom. and 6 mom. >Median, Top 50 SY	17.26%	15.94%	7.23	$11,629,675	0.77	7.97	12.74%	−50.21%	0.72
Small Stocks, BP and BBY and 3 mom. >Median, Top 50 by 6 mom.	17.24%	18.54%	6.38	$11,531,126	0.66	7.19	14.72%	−56.03%	0.84
All Stocks, Value Composite3 (VC3) Decile 1	17.20%	17.89%	6.54	$11,390,104	0.68	7.64	13.35%	−58.04%	0.85
Small Stocks, Sales to Enterprise Value Decile 1	17.13%	20.02%	5.97	$11,091,047	0.61	7.00	14.65%	−64.82%	0.91
All Stocks, Value Composite2 (VC2) Decile 1	17.12%	17.32%	6.69	$11,050,085	0.70	8.24	12.85%	−58.07%	0.81
All Stocks, BP and BBY >Median, Top 25 by 6 mom.	17.08%	20.38%	5.88	$10,877,510	0.59	7.81	15.49%	−61.21%	0.98
All Stocks, BP and BBY and 3 mom. >Median, Top 25 by 6 mom.	17.06%	20.05%	5.95	$10,767,673	0.60	7.67	15.37%	−61.21%	0.96
Small Stocks, BP and BBY >Median, Top 50 by 6 mom.	17.05%	18.91%	6.22	$10,728,796	0.64	7.19	14.91%	−56.68%	0.86
All Stocks, Value Composite1 (VC1) Decile 1	16.98%	18.32%	6.35	$10,468,074	0.65	7.62	13.56%	−57.78%	0.87
Small Stocks, BP and 6 mom. >Median, Top 50 SY	16.85%	15.48%	7.26	$9,965,964	0.77	9.51	12.06%	−48.74%	0.68
All Stocks, BP and SY >Median, Top 25 by 6 mom.	16.80%	19.04%	6.11	$9,754,288	0.62	7.31	14.56%	−59.75%	0.92
Small Stocks, Free Cash Flow to Price Decile 1	16.77%	20.92%	5.67	$9,674,166	0.56	7.61	15.32%	−63.76%	0.95
All Stocks, BP and BBY and 3 mom. >Median, Top 50 by 6 mom.	16.76%	18.58%	6.22	$9,622,609	0.63	6.62	14.32%	−56.58%	0.91
Small Stocks, BP and SY >Median, Top 50 by 6 mom.	16.68%	17.96%	6.36	$9,325,854	0.65	7.49	13.97%	−55.06%	0.81
All Stocks, BP and BBY >Median, Top 50 by 6 mom.	16.66%	18.91%	6.10	$9,264,340	0.62	6.66	14.46%	−57.24%	0.92
All Stocks, BP and 6 mom. >Median, Top 50 by SY	16.66%	15.13%	7.33	$9,260,473	0.77	8.74	11.78%	−51.23%	0.71
Combined Consumer Staples/Utilities Portfolio	16.56%	13.42%	8.10	$8,933,565	0.86	12.75	9.18%	−34.39%	0.52
All Stocks, EBITDA/ Enterprise Value Decile 1	16.46%	17.95%	6.29	$8,570,603	0.64	6.33	13.17%	−54.29%	0.88
All Stocks, BP and SY >Median, Top 50 by 6 mom.	16.35%	17.69%	6.33	$8,235,994	0.64	6.74	13.62%	−55.92%	0.86
All Stocks, Earnings/ Price Decile 1	16.11%	18.70%	5.98	$7,500,626	0.59	7.53	13.69%	−59.13%	0.89
All Stocks, Net Operating Cash Flow to Price Decile 1	16.00%	18.70%	5.94	$7,206,112	0.59	7.75	14.13%	−60.87%	0.89

(continued on next page)

All Strategies for Monthly Data Series, August 31, 1965, to December 31, 2009. Strategies Sorted by Compound Average Annual Return *(Continued)*

Strategy	Geometric mean	Standard deviation (%)	T-Statistic	$10,000 becomes	Sharpe ratio	Tracking error	Downside risk	Largest drawdown	Beta
All Stocks, Free CF to Enterprise Value Decile 1	15.90%	19.29%	5.78	$6,927,643	0.57	6.00	14.27%	−56.81%	0.95
All Stocks, Earnings Quality Composite Decile 1	15.79%	19.36%	5.72	$6,642,587	0.56	4.18	14.09%	−54.83%	0.98
Small Stocks, BP and 3 mom. and 6 mom. >Median, Top 25 12 mom.	15.76%	21.47%	5.30	$6,562,828	0.50	8.68	16.41%	−65.51%	0.95
All Stocks, Buyback Yield, Decile 1	15.74%	17.39%	6.22	$6,521,542	0.62	5.82	13.17%	−53.28%	0.86
Small Stocks, BP and 3 mom. and 6 mom. >Median, Top 50 12 mom.	15.62%	19.60%	5.63	$6,226,529	0.54	7.70	15.16%	−61.91%	0.88
Small Stocks, Buyback Yield, Decile 1	15.55%	18.17%	5.94	$6,074,251	0.58	6.33	13.90%	−54.20%	0.84
Small Stocks, Shareholder Yield, Decile 1	15.45%	15.96%	6.57	$5,834,309	0.65	8.20	12.42%	−55.73%	0.72
All Stocks, Sales to Enterprise Value Decile 1	15.44%	18.96%	5.71	$5,805,576	0.55	6.58	14.04%	−62.29%	0.93
All Stocks, Shareholder Yield, Decile 1	15.43%	15.43%	6.75	$5,792,778	0.68	7.67	11.90%	−54.70%	0.74
Market Leaders, Top 2 Deciles VC2, Top 25 by 6 mom.	15.34%	17.17%	6.14	$5,585,470	0.60	6.03	11.92%	−52.74%	0.98
All Stocks, Free Cash Flow to Price Decile 1	15.31%	18.99%	5.66	$5,539,519	0.54	7.32	14.20%	−61.66%	0.91
All Stocks, SY and 3 mom. and 6 mom. >Median, Top 50 12 mom.	15.08%	20.97%	5.20	$5,057,750	0.48	8.28	15.99%	−61.15%	1.00
All Stocks, BP and 3 mom. and 6 mom. >Median, Top 25 by 12 mom.	15.05%	22.01%	5.02	$5,010,429	0.46	9.15	16.69%	−68.16%	1.04
Market Leaders, 3 mom. and 6 mom. >Median, Top 25 by SY	15.02%	17.11%	6.05	$4,954,349	0.59	6.45	12.74%	−57.92%	0.97
All Stocks, Fin Strength Composite Decile 10	15.01%	17.05%	6.07	$4,923,801	0.59	4.25	12.74%	−50.82%	0.87
Market Leaders, Top 2 Deciles VC2, Top 50 by 6 mom.	15.00%	17.16%	6.03	$4,912,365	0.58	5.27	11.92%	−53.43%	1.00
Market Leaders, VC2>Median, Top 25 by SY	14.97%	17.25%	5.99	$4,847,391	0.58	6.60	12.80%	−58.21%	0.97
Small Stocks, SY and 3 mom. and 6 mom. >Median, Top 50 12 mom.	14.95%	21.24%	5.11	$4,809,289	0.47	7.83	16.12%	−58.10%	0.96
Cornerstone Value, Improved 25	14.94%	17.00%	6.05	$4,789,019	0.58	6.52	12.58%	−57.57%	0.96
Large Stocks, Buyback Yield, Decile 1	14.91%	16.40%	6.23	$4,738,299	0.60	5.68	12.03%	−51.56%	0.92
Large Stocks, 3 mom. and 6 mom. >Median, Top 25 by SY	14.85%	15.40%	6.54	$4,632,919	0.64	6.79	11.84%	−49.12%	0.84
Small Stocks, Sales to Price Decile 1	14.84%	22.46%	4.88	$4,618,693	0.44	8.79	16.13%	−70.68%	1.00
Market Leaders, Value Composite 2 Decile 1 (High)	14.84%	18.52%	5.62	$4,616,793	0.53	7.10	13.29%	−62.16%	1.05

(continued on next page)

T A B L E 28.1

All Strategies for Monthly Data Series, August 31, 1965, to December 31, 2009. Strategies Sorted by Compound Average Annual Return *(Continued)*

Strategy	Geometric mean	Standard deviation (%)	T-Statistic	$10,000 becomes	Sharpe ratio	Tracking error	Downside risk	Largest drawdown	Beta
Market Leaders, Shareholder Yield (%) Decile 1	14.72%	16.77%	6.04	$4,403,707	0.58	6.38	12.43%	−56.44%	0.95
All Stocks, BP and 3 mom. and 6 mom. >Median, Top 50 by 12 mom.	14.69%	19.99%	5.27	$4,359,495	0.48	7.64	15.33%	−64.48%	0.96
Small Stocks, 3 mom. and 6 mom. >0, ROE>avg, 50 best 12 mom.	14.66%	29.34%	4.11	$4,306,193	0.33	15.31	20.99%	−74.82%	1.24
Market Leaders, 3 mom. and 6 mom. >Median, Top 50 by SY	14.65%	16.32%	6.16	$4,289,473	0.59	5.09	11.94%	−56.33%	0.95
Large Stocks, BP and 6 mom. >Median, Top 25 by BBY	14.56%	16.52%	6.06	$4,140,567	0.58	6.42	12.45%	−53.90%	0.91
Cornerstone Value, Improved 50	14.55%	16.19%	6.16	$4,133,217	0.59	5.11	11.78%	−56.01%	0.94
Market Leaders, VC2>Median, Top 50 by SY	14.54%	16.51%	6.06	$4,101,645	0.58	5.23	12.12%	−57.42%	0.96
All Stocks, SY and 3 mom. and 6 mom. >Median, Top 25 by 12 mom.	14.50%	23.28%	4.68	$4,045,574	0.41	10.48	17.37%	−64.56%	1.08
Market Leaders, Value Composite 3 Decile 1 (High)	14.49%	18.29%	5.57	$4,028,546	0.52	6.90	13.18%	−60.13%	1.03
Large Stocks, Shareholder Yield, Decile 1	14.48%	15.08%	6.51	$4,021,172	0.63	7.17	11.08%	−52.66%	0.81
Small Stocks, Accruals to Price Decile 10	14.47%	22.86%	4.72	$3,992,730	0.41	7.93	16.12%	−66.72%	1.04
Market Leaders, EBITDA/ Enterprise Value Decile 1	14.39%	18.15%	5.56	$3,884,224	0.52	7.53	11.91%	−52.21%	1.01
Small Stocks, 6-Month Momentum, Decile 1	14.38%	26.32%	4.30	$3,857,815	0.36	11.03	18.35%	−63.10%	1.17
Small Stocks, SY and 3 mom. and 6 mom. >Median, Top 25 12 mom.	14.30%	23.54%	4.60	$3,745,468	0.40	9.92	17.71%	−63.04%	1.04
Small Stocks, BBY and 3 mom. >Median, Top 50 12 mom.	14.28%	24.14%	4.52	$3,722,115	0.38	9.42	17.71%	−58.74%	1.08
Market Leaders, Buyback Yield (%) Decile 1	14.28%	16.52%	5.97	$3,721,523	0.56	5.24	11.92%	−53.60%	0.96
Market Leaders, Value Composite 1 Decile 1 (High)	14.27%	18.69%	5.41	$3,705,032	0.50	6.75	13.35%	−60.56%	1.07
Small Stocks, Book to Price, Decile 1	14.26%	22.11%	4.77	$3,686,837	0.42	8.49	16.13%	−69.88%	0.99
All Stocks, 6-Month Momentum, Decile 1	14.24%	25.21%	4.38	$3,657,041	0.37	10.94	17.70%	−62.44%	1.20
Market Leaders, 3 mom. and 6 mom. >Median, Top 25 by VC2	14.23%	16.52%	5.95	$3,639,417	0.56	5.22	12.04%	−51.56%	0.96
Large Stocks, BP and BBY >Median, Top 25 by 6 mom.	14.21%	16.73%	5.88	$3,613,341	0.55	6.14	12.43%	−55.14%	0.93
Large Stocks, Value Composite2 Decile 1	14.20%	16.47%	5.95	$3,607,389	0.56	8.69	11.66%	−62.69%	0.85

(continued on next page)

All Strategies for Monthly Data Series, August 31, 1965, to December 31, 2009. Strategies Sorted by Compound Average Annual Return *(Continued)*

Strategy	Geometric mean	Standard deviation (%)	T-Statistic	$10,000 becomes	Sharpe ratio	Tracking error	Downside risk	Largest drawdown	Beta
Large Stocks, Value Composite3 Decile 1	14.17%	16.57%	5.91	$3,555,826	0.55	8.16	11.87%	−60.55%	0.87
All Stocks, Book to Price, Decile 1	14.13%	21.04%	4.91	$3,499,602	0.43	8.08	15.35%	−69.20%	1.01
Small Stocks, 60-Month Momentum, Decile 10	14.12%	24.83%	4.39	$3,496,345	0.37	9.51	16.70%	−69.84%	1.12
All Stocks, Accruals to Price Decile 10	14.10%	20.40%	5.01	$3,464,914	0.45	6.84	15.03%	−63.33%	1.00
All Stocks, Sales to Price Decile 1	14.06%	20.94%	4.91	$3,405,339	0.43	7.78	15.40%	−65.98%	1.01
Large Stocks, EBITDA/ Enterprise Value Decile 1	14.05%	17.01%	5.74	$3,397,255	0.53	8.34	11.45%	−52.85%	0.89
Large Stocks, 3 mom. and 6 mom. >Median, Top 25 by BP	13.97%	16.11%	5.98	$3,291,236	0.56	6.72	12.02%	−51.72%	0.88
All Stocks, 60-Month Momentum, Decile 10	13.88%	23.28%	4.51	$3,184,331	0.38	8.91	15.95%	−68.91%	1.12
Large Stocks, SY and 3 mom. and 6 mom. >Median, Top 25 by 12 mom.	13.86%	17.74%	5.50	$3,159,235	0.50	6.93	13.20%	−57.49%	0.98
Large Stocks, BP and BBY and 3 mom. >Median, Top 25 by 6 mom.	13.85%	16.62%	5.78	$3,143,237	0.53	6.19	12.45%	−53.96%	0.92
All Stocks, BBY and 3 mom. >Median, Top 50 by 12 mom.	13.83%	24.15%	4.41	$3,123,598	0.37	10.44	17.60%	−63.62%	1.14
Small Stocks, Dividend Yield, Decile 1	13.83%	14.83%	6.34	$3,118,403	0.60	11.50	11.66%	−62.48%	0.60
Market Leaders, Free CF to Enterprise Value Decile 1	13.75%	18.60%	5.26	$3,026,571	0.47	7.15	13.09%	−62.79%	1.05
Large Stocks, BP and 6 mom. >Median, Top 25 by SY	13.72%	14.84%	6.30	$2,990,404	0.59	7.53	11.21%	−52.63%	0.79
Market Leaders, Net Operating Cash Flow to Price Decile 1	13.72%	18.76%	5.21	$2,983,711	0.46	7.09	12.99%	−64.38%	1.06
Large Stocks, SY and 6 mom. >Median, Top 25 by BP	13.70%	15.69%	6.00	$2,962,965	0.55	7.77	11.11%	−53.62%	0.83
Small Stocks, Asset Turnover Decile 1	13.70%	21.31%	4.75	$2,962,382	0.41	5.93	14.98%	−64.74%	0.99
Small Stocks, BBY and 3 mom. >Median, Top 25 12 mom.	13.67%	26.48%	4.14	$2,935,937	0.33	12.09	19.40%	−63.25%	1.15
Market Leaders, Earnings/ Price Decile 1	13.67%	19.07%	5.13	$2,925,600	0.45	7.25	13.12%	−62.69%	1.08
Large Stocks, 3 mom. and 6 mom. >Median, Top 50 by SY	13.56%	14.90%	6.21	$2,804,780	0.57	5.91	11.29%	−48.95%	0.83
Large Stocks, BP and BBY and 3 mom. >Median, Top 50 by 6 mom.	13.54%	16.05%	5.83	$2,786,966	0.53	6.04	11.85%	−52.16%	0.89
Market Leaders, TATA Decile 10	13.54%	17.66%	5.40	$2,783,394	0.48	6.89	12.46%	−56.44%	0.99

(continued on next page)

TABLE 28.1

All Strategies for Monthly Data Series, August 31, 1965, to December 31, 2009. Strategies Sorted by Compound Average Annual Return (Continued)

Strategy	Geometric mean	Standard deviation (%)	T-Statistic	$10,000 becomes	Sharpe ratio	Tracking error	Downside risk	Largest drawdown	Beta
Large Stocks, BP and SY >Median, Top 25 by 6 mom.	13.53%	16.03%	5.84	$2,777,684	0.53	6.51	11.91%	−53.48%	0.88
Large Stocks, 6-Month Momentum, Decile 1	13.53%	22.36%	4.55	$2,777,019	0.38	10.95	16.05%	−59.80%	1.18
Large Stocks, Earnings/ Price Decile 1	13.52%	17.37%	5.47	$2,762,152	0.49	8.35	12.15%	−65.62%	0.91
Large Stocks, Net Operating Cash Flow to Price Decile 1	13.51%	16.45%	5.71	$2,758,118	0.52	8.12	11.75%	−62.15%	0.87
Large Stocks, BP and BBY >Median, Top 50 by 6 mom.	13.50%	15.99%	5.84	$2,747,543	0.53	5.91	11.73%	−52.86%	0.89
Cornerstone Value, 25 Div Yld	13.49%	17.22%	5.49	$2,731,351	0.49	7.91	12.25%	−65.01%	0.94
Large Stocks, BBY and 3 mom. >Median, Top 25 by 12 mom.	13.45%	19.45%	5.00	$2,691,570	0.43	8.42	14.25%	−59.35%	1.05
Large Stocks, Value Composite1 Decile 1	13.43%	16.90%	5.56	$2,673,161	0.50	8.28	11.99%	−61.86%	0.89
Market Leaders, Return 6 Month Decile 1	13.41%	18.27%	5.23	$2,652,260	0.46	8.67	12.99%	−58.00%	0.98
Large Stocks, BP and 6 mom. >Median, Top 50 by BBY	13.41%	15.86%	5.84	$2,643,957	0.53	5.79	11.87%	−51.52%	0.89
Small Stocks, Cash Flow to Debt (%) Decile 1	13.36%	20.72%	4.74	$2,595,632	0.40	5.50	14.25%	−54.47%	0.97
Market Leaders, PSR<avg, Top 25 by 12 mom.	13.35%	17.01%	5.50	$2,586,657	0.49	6.12	11.58%	−48.31%	0.97
Large Stocks, BP and 6 mom. >Median, Top 50 by SY	13.24%	14.94%	6.07	$2,474,341	0.55	6.73	11.03%	−51.38%	0.82
Market Leaders, 3 mom. and 6 mom. >Median, Top 50 by VC2	13.23%	16.11%	5.70	$2,469,214	0.51	4.25	11.75%	−51.88%	0.95
Large Stocks, Free CF to Enterprise Value Decile 1	13.20%	17.23%	5.39	$2,436,321	0.48	6.94	12.36%	−59.42%	0.94
Market Leaders, Accruals to Price Decile 10	13.17%	18.38%	5.12	$2,412,200	0.44	7.28	12.73%	−54.81%	1.03
Market Leaders, NOA Change (%) Decile 10	13.17%	16.62%	5.54	$2,411,698	0.49	5.24	12.18%	−52.95%	0.96
Market Leaders, Dividend Yield (%) Decile 1	13.13%	16.96%	5.43	$2,371,523	0.48	7.59	12.07%	−64.59%	0.93
All Stocks, Dividend Yield, Decile 1	13.12%	14.44%	6.19	$2,360,400	0.56	11.38	10.78%	−61.17%	0.61
Small Stocks, ROA Decile 1	13.10%	22.08%	4.48	$2,342,965	0.37	5.79	15.17%	−61.96%	1.03
Small Stocks, ROE Decile 1	13.08%	22.87%	4.37	$2,326,883	0.35	6.51	16.30%	−65.72%	1.07
All Stocks, BBY and 3 mom. >Median, Top 25 by 12 mom.	13.05%	26.62%	3.99	$2,299,944	0.30	13.18	19.36%	−66.50%	1.22
Market Leaders, Sales to Enterprise Value Decile 1	13.04%	17.27%	5.33	$2,288,339	0.47	6.08	12.05%	−51.07%	0.99
Large Stocks, BP and SY >Median, Top 50 by 6 mom.	12.99%	15.32%	5.85	$2,241,830	0.52	6.48	11.12%	−51.37%	0.84

(continued on next page)

All Strategies for Monthly Data Series, August 31, 1965, to December 31, 2009. Strategies Sorted by Compound Average Annual Return (Continued)

Strategy	Geometric mean	Standard deviation (%)	T-Statistic	$10,000 becomes	Sharpe ratio	Tracking error	Downside risk	Largest drawdown	Beta
Large Stocks, SY and 3 mom. and 6 mom. >Median, Top 50 by 12 mom.	12.95%	16.09%	5.61	$2,208,672	0.49	5.57	11.69%	−52.55%	0.91
Large Stocks, Book to Price, Decile 1	12.93%	18.43%	5.03	$2,190,230	0.43	8.42	13.15%	−67.47%	0.98
Market Leaders, Top 10 by PCF	12.89%	21.74%	4.46	$2,161,684	0.36	11.17	15.05%	−75.55%	1.15
Large Stocks, BBY and 3 mom. >Median, Top 50 by 12 mom.	12.87%	17.61%	5.20	$2,145,512	0.45	6.29	12.75%	−54.15%	0.98
Small Stocks, EPS Change (%) Decile 1	12.86%	23.35%	4.26	$2,132,696	0.34	6.88	16.63%	−64.25%	1.09
Large Stocks, SY and 6 mom. >Median, Top 50 by BP	12.85%	15.20%	5.84	$2,130,142	0.52	6.80	11.05%	−51.78%	0.83
All Stocks, TATA Decile 10	12.81%	22.21%	4.39	$2,093,156	0.35	6.24	16.30%	−69.09%	1.11
Market Leaders, PSR<avg, Top 50 by 12 mom.	12.79%	16.68%	5.39	$2,078,710	0.47	4.27	11.86%	−52.04%	0.99
All Stocks, Asset Turnover Decile 1	12.78%	20.14%	4.68	$2,071,598	0.39	6.01	14.37%	−62.08%	1.00
Large Stocks, Earnings Quality Composite Decile 10	12.76%	16.14%	5.52	$2,054,668	0.48	6.43	10.98%	−49.00%	0.89
Market Leaders, Return 12 Month Decile 1	12.71%	19.38%	4.78	$2,015,059	0.40	10.42	13.86%	−60.88%	1.00
Large Stocks, BBY >Median, Top 50 by DIVY	12.68%	14.43%	6.02	$1,990,472	0.53	9.40	9.88%	−55.30%	0.71
Market Leaders, Free Cash Flow to Price Decile 1	12.68%	19.44%	4.76	$1,990,354	0.40	7.79	13.81%	−65.82%	1.09
Large Stocks, 3 mom. and 6 mom. >Median, Top 50 by BP	12.67%	15.78%	5.59	$1,980,131	0.49	5.89	11.95%	−53.26%	0.88
Large Stocks, 60-Month Momentum, Decile 10	12.66%	19.36%	4.77	$1,972,949	0.40	8.55	13.16%	−65.10%	1.04
Small Stocks, TATA Decile 10	12.65%	24.78%	4.05	$1,968,047	0.31	8.55	17.54%	−70.06%	1.14
Large Stocks, Accruals to Price Decile 10	12.61%	16.08%	5.48	$1,935,038	0.47	7.47	11.20%	−53.48%	0.86
Large Stocks, BBY >Median, Top 25 by DIVY	12.60%	14.83%	5.85	$1,929,366	0.51	10.99	10.23%	−57.02%	0.68
Large Stocks, Sales to Enterprise Value Decile 1	12.49%	16.68%	5.28	$1,847,483	0.45	6.98	11.98%	−52.75%	0.91
Market Leaders, Sales to Price Decile 1	12.28%	18.76%	4.76	$1,696,417	0.39	6.96	13.60%	−58.12%	1.07
Market Leaders, Book/ Price Decile 1	12.21%	19.95%	4.53	$1,651,897	0.36	8.20	13.74%	−67.38%	1.12
Market Leaders, Debt Change (%) Decile 10	12.17%	17.29%	5.02	$1,628,137	0.41	4.69	11.68%	−48.85%	1.02
Small Stocks, 12-Month Momentum, Decile 1	12.14%	26.95%	3.76	$1,608,082	0.27	11.67	19.16%	−67.06%	1.20
All Stocks, 12-Month Momentum, Decile 1	12.14%	25.86%	3.84	$1,604,407	0.28	11.65	18.53%	−66.29%	1.22
Large Stocks, Free Cash Flow to Price Decile 1	12.11%	17.00%	5.07	$1,589,264	0.42	8.00	12.15%	−63.99%	0.90
Large Stocks, BP and 3 mom. and 6 mom. >Median, Top 50 by 12 mom.	12.10%	16.50%	5.19	$1,584,677	0.43	5.93	12.67%	−55.90%	0.92
All Stocks, ROE Decile 1	12.02%	21.00%	4.33	$1,534,842	0.33	6.32	15.04%	−63.88%	1.04

(continued on next page)

T A B L E 28.1

All Strategies for Monthly Data Series, August 31, 1965, to December 31, 2009. Strategies Sorted by Compound Average Annual Return *(Continued)*

Strategy	Geometric mean	Standard deviation (%)	T-Statistic	$10,000 becomes	Sharpe ratio	Tracking error	Downside risk	Largest drawdown	Beta
Large Stocks, BP and 3 mom. and 6 mom. >Median, Top 25 by 12 mom.	12.02%	17.80%	4.87	$1,534,382	0.39	6.98	13.72%	−59.99%	0.98
Large Stocks, 12-Month Momentum, Decile 1	11.93%	23.52%	4.00	$1,478,974	0.29	12.38	17.38%	−64.85%	1.21
All Stocks, NOA Change (%) Decile 10	11.83%	22.26%	4.11	$1,420,568	0.31	6.60	15.96%	−68.42%	1.11
Small Stocks, Operating Margin Decile 1	11.81%	16.07%	5.19	$1,409,381	0.42	8.78	12.59%	−53.55%	0.71
All Stocks, Depr Exp to Cap Exp Decile 1	11.81%	22.18%	4.12	$1,408,775	0.31	6.10	15.80%	−65.18%	1.11
Market Leaders, ROA Decile 1	11.77%	16.81%	4.99	$1,388,512	0.40	7.83	11.07%	−48.00%	0.91
All Stocks, ROA Decile 1	11.70%	20.84%	4.26	$1,368,925	0.32	6.09	14.34%	−58.45%	1.04
Small Stocks, Net Margin Decile 1	11.70%	17.63%	4.79	$1,349,305	0.38	7.06	13.28%	−52.87%	0.81
Small Stocks, Depr Exp to Cap Exp Decile 1	11.69%	24.23%	3.87	$1,346,569	0.28	8.72	16.91%	−69.57%	1.10
Large Stocks, TATA Decile 10	11.69%	18.44%	4.63	$1,343,540	0.36	7.11	13.59%	−69.58%	1.02
All Stocks, Cash Flow to Debt (%) Decile 1	11.65%	20.97%	4.22	$1,321,767	0.32	6.36	14.32%	−54.66%	1.04
Market Leaders, Net Margin Decile 1	11.63%	15.77%	5.19	$1,310,481	0.42	6.33	10.23%	−46.73%	0.89
Market Leaders, Asset Turnover Decile 1	11.60%	16.84%	4.92	$1,297,271	0.39	7.00	11.35%	−49.88%	0.94
Market Leaders, Operating Margin Decile 1	11.52%	16.92%	4.87	$1,256,293	0.39	6.91	11.37%	−57.34%	0.95
Large Stocks, Dividend Yield, Decile 1	11.42%	14.33%	5.52	$1,209,519	0.45	11.38	9.78%	−58.55%	0.64
Large Stocks, Fin Strength Composite Decile 10	11.37%	15.96%	5.05	$1,184,863	0.40	5.41	11.84%	−50.03%	0.90
SMALL STOCKS	**11.36%**	**20.60%**	**4.19**	**$1,180,447**	**0.31**	**N/A**	**14.87%**	**−58.48%**	**N/A**
All Stocks, Growth Composite Decile 1	11.34%	23.41%	3.86	$1,170,338	0.27	7.30	16.14%	−60.70%	1.17
Large Stocks, NOA Change (%) Decile 10	11.30%	17.23%	4.74	$1,150,579	0.37	5.62	12.79%	−58.76%	0.97
Market Leaders Universe	**11.27%**	**16.37%**	**4.91**	**$1,139,999**	**0.38**	**N/A**	**11.72%**	**−54.03%**	**N/A**
Large Stocks, Sales to Price Decile 1	11.25%	17.64%	4.63	$1,128,228	0.35	8.12	12.95%	−59.89%	0.94
Market Leaders, Depr Exp to Cap Exp Decile 1	11.21%	17.99%	4.55	$1,112,344	0.35	6.07	12.16%	−57.97%	1.03
Market Leaders, Cash Flow to Debt (%) Decile 1	11.04%	17.20%	4.64	$1,037,698	0.35	7.95	11.31%	−50.49%	0.93
Small Stocks, Debt Change (%) Decile 10	11.03%	23.89%	3.73	$1,034,729	0.25	7.52	16.54%	−67.10%	1.11
ALL STOCKS	**11.01%**	**19.26%**	**4.28**	**$1,025,389**	**0.31**	**N/A**	**13.94%**	**−55.54%**	**N/A**
Market Leaders, ROE Decile 1	10.95%	16.86%	4.68	$1,000,818	0.35	6.79	11.32%	−51.13%	0.94
Large Stocks, BP >Median, Top 25 by DIVY	10.87%	15.95%	4.85	$968,948	0.37	13.02	10.95%	−67.55%	0.65
Small Stocks, NOA Change (%) Decile 10	10.83%	25.57%	3.54	$953,378	0.23	10.03	17.67%	−75.46%	1.15
Large Stocks, Asset Turnover Decile 1	10.80%	16.79%	4.65	$943,969	0.35	6.91	11.53%	−54.64%	0.92
All Stocks, Operating Margin Decile 1	10.79%	16.23%	4.77	$939,035	0.36	8.00	12.27%	−55.56%	0.77
Large Stocks, BP >Median, Top 50 by DIVY	10.78%	14.73%	5.13	$935,732	0.39	12.26	9.93%	−62.19%	0.62
Market Leaders, Depr Exp to Cap Exp Decile 10	10.68%	18.29%	4.32	$897,158	0.31	6.43	12.73%	−55.30%	1.05
All Stocks, Debt Change (%) Decile 10	10.56%	22.46%	3.75	$856,482	0.25	6.45	15.85%	−66.25%	1.12
Large Stocks, Debt Change (%) Decile 10	10.35%	17.94%	4.27	$787,144	0.30	4.94	13.03%	−55.95%	1.03

(continued on next page)

T A B L E 28.1

All Strategies for Monthly Data Series, August 31, 1965, to December 31, 2009. Strategies Sorted by Compound Average Annual Return *(Continued)*

Strategy	Geometric mean	Standard deviation (%)	T-Statistic	$10,000 becomes	Sharpe ratio	Tracking error	Downside risk	Largest drawdown	Beta
Market Leaders, Asset Turnover Decile 10	10.35%	20.82%	3.86	$787,022	0.26	10.60	14.90%	−78.30%	1.10
Market Leaders, ROE Decile 10	10.34%	18.95%	4.11	$785,448	0.28	7.48	13.15%	−61.32%	1.07
All Stocks, Net Margin Decile 1	10.26%	17.31%	4.36	$758,759	0.30	6.52	12.92%	−53.32%	0.85
Market Leaders, Accruals to Price Decile 1	10.09%	16.55%	4.45	$710,389	0.31	5.80	12.40%	−51.92%	0.95
Market Leaders, Free CF to Enterprise Value Decile 10	10.07%	18.10%	4.15	$703,094	0.28	6.41	13.05%	−60.38%	1.03
Market Leaders, ROA Decile 10	10.06%	21.02%	3.76	$701,293	0.24	8.75	15.12%	−73.38%	1.18
LARGE STOCKS	10.06%	16.75%	4.39	$701,190	0.30	N/A	11.90%	−53.77%	N/A
Market Leaders, Cash Flow to Debt (%) Decile 10	9.98%	20.29%	3.82	$679,046	0.25	7.52	14.37%	−74.30%	1.16
Market Leaders, Net Margin Decile 10	9.79%	18.53%	3.99	$629,687	0.26	6.57	13.39%	−59.32%	1.06
Market Leaders, Free Cash Flow to Price Decile 10	9.75%	17.90%	4.08	$618,816	0.27	6.31	12.61%	−59.72%	1.02
Market Leaders, EPS Change (%) Decile 1	9.74%	18.26%	4.02	$616,058	0.26	6.36	12.65%	−53.81%	1.05
Market Leaders, Book/ Price Decile 10	9.66%	17.15%	4.17	$595,992	0.27	8.78	11.67%	−51.30%	0.90
Large Stocks, Depr Exp to Cap Exp Decile 1	9.61%	18.28%	3.97	$584,481	0.25	5.83	13.06%	−57.70%	1.03
Large Stocks, ROA Decile 1	9.55%	18.65%	3.89	$569,255	0.24	7.62	12.83%	−55.83%	1.02
Large Stocks, ROE Decile 1	9.44%	17.73%	3.99	$545,642	0.25	6.88	12.03%	−58.46%	0.98
Large Stocks, Growth Composite Decile 1	9.41%	19.70%	3.72	$538,900	0.22	7.25	13.65%	−57.48%	1.10
Market Leaders, Debt Change (%) Decile 1	9.40%	17.27%	4.06	$536,458	0.25	4.17	12.20%	−54.87%	1.02
S&P 500	9.33%	15.31%	4.41	$522,661	0.28	4.69	10.81%	−50.95%	0.88
Market Leaders, Operating Margin Decile 10	9.31%	18.06%	3.90	$518,265	0.24	6.81	12.25%	−54.95%	1.02
All Stocks, Asset Turnover Decile 10	9.07%	17.44%	3.92	$469,694	0.23	8.89	13.24%	−63.29%	0.80
Large Stocks, Operating Margin Decile 1	9.04%	16.97%	3.98	$463,704	0.24	8.24	11.87%	−59.83%	0.89
Large Stocks, EPS Change (%) Decile 1	8.96%	19.08%	3.65	$449,587	0.21	6.82	13.08%	−53.41%	1.07
Market Leaders, EBITDA/ Enterprise Value Decile 10	8.90%	19.44%	3.58	$438,867	0.20	8.62	13.33%	−65.29%	1.07
Market Leaders, EPS Change (%) Decile 10	8.83%	19.25%	3.58	$426,637	0.20	6.78	13.42%	−64.96%	1.11
Small Stocks, 60-Month Momentum, Decile 1	8.78%	24.09%	3.15	$416,618	0.16	8.19	16.97%	−68.08%	1.11
Large Stocks, Cash Flow to Debt (%) Decile 1	8.74%	20.00%	3.47	$410,961	0.19	8.78	14.33%	−71.34%	1.08
Market Leaders, Earnings/ Price Decile 10	8.74%	19.18%	3.56	$410,691	0.20	8.21	13.80%	−58.63%	1.06
Large Stocks, Book to Price, Decile 10	8.64%	22.02%	3.26	$394,329	0.17	10.68	15.65%	−70.70%	1.16
Market Leaders, Value Composite 1 Decile 10 (Low)	8.64%	17.55%	3.74	$394,035	0.21	9.28	12.06%	−57.66%	0.91
Small Stocks, Accruals to Price Decile 1	8.64%	23.17%	3.17	$393,912	0.16	6.08	16.04%	−64.22%	1.09
All Stocks, Accruals to Price Decile 1	8.60%	21.76%	3.27	$387,604	0.17	4.96	15.55%	−60.25%	1.11
Market Leaders, NOA Change (%) Decile 1	8.58%	17.67%	3.71	$384,987	0.20	5.85	12.51%	−53.01%	1.02

(continued on next page)

T A B L E 28.1

All Strategies for Monthly Data Series, August 31, 1965, to December 31, 2009. Strategies Sorted by Compound Average Annual Return *(Continued)*

Strategy	Geometric mean	Standard deviation (%)	T-Statistic	$10,000 becomes	Sharpe ratio	Tracking error	Downside risk	Largest drawdown	Beta
Market Leaders, Sales to Price Decile 10	8.57%	17.39%	3.74	$382,709	0.21	9.02	12.04%	-58.92%	0.91
Market Leaders, Sales to Enterprise Value Decile 10	8.53%	17.97%	3.65	$376,257	0.20	7.84	12.53%	-64.70%	0.99
Market Leaders, Return 12 Month Decile 10	8.52%	21.39%	3.26	$375,727	0.16	9.05	14.16%	-65.66%	1.20
Large Stocks, Net Margin Decile 1	8.48%	16.86%	3.79	$369,526	0.21	7.35	11.93%	-52.15%	0.91
Large Stocks, Accruals to Price Decile 1	8.41%	17.75%	3.64	$358,169	0.19	5.91	13.11%	-54.83%	1.00
Large Stocks, Asset Turnover Decile 10	8.34%	19.71%	3.38	$348,952	0.17	10.61	14.00%	-75.82%	0.99
All Stocks, 60-Month Momentum, Decile 1	8.31%	23.46%	3.07	$344,813	0.14	8.34	16.52%	-64.52%	1.15
Market Leaders, Return 6 Month Decile 10	8.30%	20.52%	3.28	$342,672	0.16	7.54	13.90%	-65.20%	1.18
All Stocks, Book to Price, Decile 10	8.13%	24.73%	2.95	$319,249	0.13	10.14	17.37%	-73.67%	1.19
Small Stocks, Book to Price, Decile 10	8.12%	26.81%	2.86	$318,580	0.12	10.66	18.70%	-74.79%	1.21
Large Stocks, Net Margin Decile 10	8.12%	20.22%	3.27	$318,114	0.15	8.72	15.64%	-82.79%	1.09
Large Stocks, Free CF to Enterprise Value Decile 10	8.09%	18.19%	3.48	$315,221	0.17	6.20	13.34%	-63.96%	1.02
Large Stocks, Growth Composite Decile 10	7.96%	17.87%	3.47	$298,449	0.17	6.10	12.65%	-63.64%	1.00
Large Stocks, ROE Decile 10	7.94%	19.80%	3.25	$296,059	0.15	8.83	14.89%	-79.66%	1.06
Market Leaders, Value Composite 2 Decile 10 (Low)	7.85%	18.03%	3.40	$284,927	0.16	9.13	12.77%	-60.68%	0.95
Small Stocks, Asset Turnover Decile 10	7.83%	17.68%	3.44	$282,317	0.16	8.57	13.11%	-62.16%	0.78
Market Leaders, TATA Decile 1	7.82%	18.06%	3.39	$281,123	0.16	5.78	12.75%	-56.09%	1.05
Market Leaders, Net Operating Cash Flow to Price Decile 10	7.80%	17.54%	3.45	$279,628	0.16	8.41	12.89%	-59.89%	0.94
Market Leaders, Value Composite 3 Decile 10 (Low)	7.71%	17.86%	3.38	$269,394	0.15	8.87	12.56%	-59.42%	0.95
Large Stocks, Free Cash Flow to Price Decile 10	7.57%	18.05%	3.31	$253,902	0.14	5.84	13.24%	-63.76%	1.02
Large Stocks, ROA Decile 10	7.53%	21.52%	2.99	$250,199	0.12	9.48	15.98%	-80.45%	1.17
Large Stocks, 60-Month Momentum, Decile 1	7.45%	24.18%	2.81	$242,263	0.10	11.56	17.28%	-76.08%	1.30
Large Stocks, EPS Change (%) Decile 10	7.44%	18.83%	3.18	$240,673	0.13	6.87	13.39%	-67.30%	1.05
Large Stocks, Depr Exp to Cap Exp Decile 10	7.41%	18.93%	3.16	$237,466	0.13	8.28	13.70%	-66.24%	1.02
Market Leaders, Shareholder Yield (%) Decile 10	7.25%	19.26%	3.07	$223,014	0.12	6.48	12.93%	-61.88%	1.11
Small Stocks, EPS Change (%) Decile 10	6.93%	26.17%	2.59	$194,631	0.07	9.57	17.98%	-72.16%	1.20
All Stocks, Free CF to Enterprise Value Decile 10	6.84%	23.07%	2.70	$187,800	0.08	6.88	16.53%	-66.73%	1.15
Large Stocks, Debt Change (%) Decile 1	6.83%	18.61%	3.00	$187,287	0.10	5.60	13.29%	-63.62%	1.06
All Stocks, Growth Composite Decile 10	6.80%	22.33%	2.72	$184,471	0.08	6.21	16.21%	-71.86%	1.12
Large Stocks, Operating Margin Decile 10	6.78%	20.52%	2.84	$183,358	0.09	8.98	15.79%	-85.76%	1.11

(continued on next page)

All Strategies for Monthly Data Series, August 31, 1965, to December 31, 2009. Strategies Sorted by Compound Average Annual Return *(Continued)*

Strategy	Geometric mean	Standard deviation (%)	T-Statistic	$10,000 becomes	Sharpe ratio	Tracking error	Downside risk	Largest drawdown	Beta
Market Leaders, Buyback Yield (%) Decile 10	6.76%	18.93%	2.94	$181,638	0.09	5.49	12.98%	−63.96%	1.11
Large Stocks, Fin Strength Composite Decile 1	6.53%	17.19%	3.03	$164,902	0.09	4.98	12.21%	−59.81%	0.98
Large Stocks, 12-Month Momentum, Decile 10	6.51%	22.24%	2.64	$163,990	0.07	10.54	15.59%	−69.38%	1.18
Large Stocks, Cash Flow to Debt (%) Decile 10	6.41%	20.05%	2.75	$156,826	0.07	9.13	15.32%	−77.96%	1.07
Small Stocks, Free CF to Enterprise Value Decile 10	6.39%	26.05%	2.46	$155,550	0.05	10.27	17.80%	−73.23%	1.18
All Stocks, Debt Change (%) Decile 1	6.24%	22.40%	2.57	$146,231	0.06	5.10	16.20%	−69.24%	1.14
Large Stocks, Earnings/ Price Decile 10	6.21%	21.66%	2.59	$144,339	0.06	9.86	16.15%	−79.88%	1.16
All Stocks, Free Cash Flow to Price Decile 10	6.09%	22.71%	2.51	$137,430	0.05	6.36	16.57%	−68.80%	1.14
Large Stocks, Net Operating Cash Flow to Price Decile 10	5.92%	21.36%	2.52	$127,975	0.04	9.69	15.95%	−77.33%	1.15
Large Stocks, TATA Decile 1	5.91%	19.50%	2.62	$127,540	0.05	6.92	13.88%	−58.61%	1.09
All Stocks, ROE Decile 10	5.83%	26.77%	2.32	$123,132	0.03	11.63	19.64%	−89.50%	1.28
All Stocks, EPS Change ($) Decile 1	5.70%	20.35%	2.51	$116,798	0.03	4.49	14.71%	−66.06%	1.03
Large Stocks, Earnings Quality Composite Decile 1	5.68%	19.03%	2.58	$115,851	0.04	6.29	13.88%	−61.33%	1.07
US 30 Day TBill USD	5.64%	0.82%	44.88	$113,721	0.78	16.78	0.00%	0.00%	NA
Large Stocks, Buyback Yield, Decile 10	5.61%	19.02%	2.56	$112,578	0.03	5.17	13.72%	−65.37%	1.10
All Stocks, 12-Month Momentum, Decile 10	5.60%	26.03%	2.27	$112,186	0.02	11.08	17.95%	−75.22%	1.25
Large Stocks, NOA Change (%) Decile 1	5.56%	19.86%	2.50	$110,113	0.03	7.68	15.13%	−78.05%	1.10
Small Stocks, Free Cash Flow to Price Decile 10	5.36%	25.22%	2.24	$101,397	0.01	9.24	17.66%	−72.60%	1.15
All Stocks, Earnings/ Price Decile 10	5.31%	26.92%	2.20	$99,120	0.01	10.86	19.18%	−82.14%	1.32
All Stocks, EPS Change ($) Decile 10	5.27%	21.52%	2.32	$97,542	0.01	5.97	15.56%	−67.86%	1.08
Small Stocks, Debt Change (%) Decile 1	5.25%	23.86%	2.24	$96,671	0.01	6.38	16.85%	−75.29%	1.12
Small Stocks, 12-Month Momentum, Decile 10	5.20%	27.41%	2.15	$94,641	0.01	11.34	18.74%	−79.12%	1.23
Large Stocks, Shareholder Yield, Decile 10	5.19%	19.86%	2.37	$94,131	0.01	5.56	14.16%	−68.49%	1.15
Large Stocks, EBITDA/ Enterprise Value Decile 10	5.15%	27.09%	2.16	$92,607	0.01	12.64	19.86%	−89.54%	1.27
Large Stocks, 6-Month Momentum, Decile 10	5.13%	21.92%	2.26	$92,064	0.01	9.50	15.36%	−68.85%	1.20
Small Stocks, Buyback Yield, Decile 10	5.10%	23.37%	2.22	$90,572	0.00	4.97	16.97%	−71.57%	1.11
All Stocks, Net Margin Decile 10	5.02%	27.68%	2.12	$87,544	0.00	12.89	20.52%	−93.05%	1.31
All Stocks, Buyback Yield, Decile 10	4.90%	21.95%	2.21	$83,448	0.00	4.55	16.05%	−70.91%	1.12
Small Stocks, Shareholder Yield, Decile 10	4.85%	24.17%	2.14	$82,837	0.00	5.60	17.29%	−74.59%	1.15
All Stocks, Depr Exp to Cap Exp Decile 10	4.78%	23.18%	2.15	$81,598	−0.01	7.33	16.83%	−71.68%	1.15
Small Stocks, Earnings/ Price Decile 10	4.74%	29.59%	2.05	$79,326	−0.01	13.76	19.79%	−82.67%	1.31
All Stocks, Sales to Enterprise Value Decile 10	4.73%	25.41%	2.09	$78,028	−0.01	12.11	19.83%	−92.02%	1.17
All Stocks, Shareholder Yield, Decile 10	4.71%	22.86%	2.13	$77,572	−0.01	5.24	16.41%	−72.38%	1.17
Large Stocks, EBITDA/ Enterprise Value Decile 10		23.89%	2.11	$76,893	−0.01	12.29	18.64%	−89.48%	1.25

(continued on next page)

T A B L E 28.1

All Strategies for Monthly Data Series, August 31, 1965, to December 31, 2009. Strategies Sorted by Compound Average Annual Return *(Continued)*

Strategy	Geometric mean	Standard deviation (%)	T-Statistic	$10,000 becomes	Sharpe ratio	Tracking error	Downside risk	Largest drawdown	Beta
All Stocks, Operating Margin Decile 10	4.58%	27.66%	2.02	$72,755	−0.02	13.01	20.58%	−93.34%	1.30
All Stocks, ROA Decile 10	4.57%	26.50%	2.03	$72,529	−0.02	12.64	20.00%	−91.36%	1.23
Large Stocks, Value Composite1 Decile 10	4.51%	22.73%	2.08	$70,595	−0.02	12.16	17.62%	−85.28%	1.16
All Stocks, Fin Strength Composite Decile 1	4.34%	22.71%	2.03	$65,775	−0.03	6.43	16.89%	−80.39%	1.14
Large Stocks, Sales to Price Decile 10	4.31%	22.46%	2.03	$64,848	−0.03	12.01	17.93%	−86.24%	1.14
Large Stocks, Value Composite3 Decile 10	4.30%	23.09%	2.01	$64,519	−0.03	12.20	17.76%	−85.90%	1.18
Large Stocks, Value Composite2 Decile 10	4.20%	23.29%	1.98	$61,850	−0.03	12.42	17.91%	−86.01%	1.19
Large Stocks, Sales to Enterprise Value Decile 10	4.07%	22.41%	1.97	$58,697	−0.04	11.73	17.95%	−87.97%	1.15
All Stocks, TATA Decile 1	4.05%	25.11%	1.91	$58,251	−0.04	8.27	17.43%	−77.80%	1.26
All Stocks, Earnings Quality Composite Decile 10	3.50%	25.15%	1.77	$46,045	−0.06	8.27	17.77%	−73.54%	1.26
Small Stocks, TATA Decile 1	3.47%	26.62%	1.76	$45,467	−0.06	9.13	17.98%	−81.88%	1.24
All Stocks, 6-Month Momentum, Decile 10	3.36%	25.74%	1.72	$43,236	−0.06	10.04	17.59%	−77.42%	1.26
Small Stocks, EBITDA/ Enterprise Value Decile 10	3.28%	28.75%	1.71	$41,748	−0.06	14.21	19.71%	−87.57%	1.24
Small Stocks, Depr Exp to Cap Exp Decile 10	3.27%	24.38%	1.71	$41,564	−0.07	7.93	17.26%	−72.64%	1.13
All Stocks, Net Operating Cash Flow to Price Decile 10	3.13%	26.48%	1.68	$39,130	−0.07	10.83	18.81%	−86.49%	1.29
All Stocks, Sales to Price Decile 10	3.11%	26.68%	1.67	$38,918	−0.07	13.37	19.84%	−91.41%	1.22
All Stocks, NOA Change (%) Decile 1	3.03%	25.34%	1.66	$37,546	−0.08	9.04	18.68%	−83.42%	1.26
Small Stocks, ROE Decile 10	2.66%	30.11%	1.59	$32,028	−0.08	14.66	20.33%	−91.45%	1.32
All Stocks, Value Composite1 (VC1) Decile 10	2.64%	28.25%	1.58	$31,727	−0.08	14.26	20.42%	−92.81%	1.30
Small Stocks, 6-Month Momentum, Decile 10	2.60%	27.07%	1.54	$31,163	−0.09	10.20	18.35%	−80.22%	1.24
Small Stocks, Sales to Enterprise Value Decile 10	2.52%	25.98%	1.52	$30,166	−0.10	12.13	19.40%	−91.71%	1.12
All Stocks, Net Operating Cash Flow to Price Decile 10	2.39%	28.72%	1.52	$28,474	−0.09	13.22	19.50%	−85.02%	1.27
All Stocks, Value Composite2 (VC2) Decile 10	2.29%	28.71%	1.50	$27,251	−0.09	14.39	20.45%	−92.67%	1.33
Small Stocks, Cash Flow to Debt (%) Decile 10	2.16%	29.59%	1.47	$25,817	−0.10	14.44	20.01%	−87.81%	1.29
All Stocks, Value Composite3 (VC3) Decile 10	2.13%	28.59%	1.46	$25,510	−0.10	14.26	20.42%	−92.77%	1.33
All Stocks, Cash Flow to Debt (%) Decile 10	2.08%	27.30%	1.43	$24,944	−0.11	12.49	20.25%	−92.73%	1.29
Small Stocks, NOA Change (%) Decile 1	1.84%	26.83%	1.37	$22,452	−0.12	9.65	19.34%	−85.63%	1.24
Small Stocks, ROA Decile 10	1.11%	29.56%	1.24	$16,282	−0.13	15.07	20.29%	−93.32%	1.26
Small Stocks, Operating Margin Decile 10	0.90%	29.92%	1.20	$14,869	−0.14	15.36	20.41%	−93.74%	1.28
Small Stocks, Net Margin Decile 10	0.81%	30.39%	1.19	$14,290	−0.14	15.58	20.58%	−94.14%	1.30
Small Stocks, Sales to Price Decile 10	0.16%	27.71%	0.98	$10,727	−0.17	13.99	20.00%	−93.67%	1.17
Small Stocks, Value Composite1 (VC1), Decile 10	−0.80%	29.92%	0.84	$7,012	−0.19	15.39	20.75%	−94.37%	1.28
Small Stocks, Value Composite2 (VC2), Decile 10	−0.92%	30.35%	0.82	$6,623	−0.20	15.42	20.90%	−94.46%	1.31
Small Stocks, Value Composite3 (VC3), Decile 10	−1.35%	30.18%	0.72	$5,468	−0.21	15.25	20.89%	−94.72%	1.30

THE DOWNSIDE

Three of the strategies we've outlined actually turned in negative results over the last 44 years. The booby prize goes to a Small Stocks strategy. Had you consistently invested in the stocks from the Small Stocks universe that fell into decile 10 of Value Composite Three—the 10 percent of Small Stocks with the *highest* PEs, price-to-book, and so on—you would have turned a $10,000 investment in 1965 into $5,468 by the end of 2009, a loss of 1.35 percent per year. You would have also had to face the ignominy of a maximum decline of 95 percent. Indeed, 54 of the strategies we tested had returns lower than an investment in U.S. T-bills. This means that you would have been better off making no investment at all rather than putting money into these losing stock strategies. It's a rogue's gallery of all the usual suspects—stocks that are the most expensive on all three of our value composites; those with the worst profit margins, the worst ROA and NOA; those with the highest sales-to-enterprise value and worst price-to-sales; and those that fall into the worst decile for price momentum. In every capitalization category, these stocks consistently end up near the bottom of the absolute return list and at the top of the risk and maximum decline lists. In virtually every market environment—save the most speculative—these are the toxic strategies you *must* avoid.

Also at the bottom of the lists are stocks with the *worst* scores on several of the accounting variables covered in Chapter Fourteen, such as TATA (total assets to total accruals), the Earnings Quality Composite, and the Financial Strength Composite. All these should raise red flags, helping you weed out stocks you own or are considering investing in. Now that we have 13 years of real-time returns that bear out the findings of our original backtests, there's still not a single compelling reason to be tempted to buy the most richly priced stocks, those with poor price momentum or those with balance sheet irregularities. All the strategies at the bottom of Table 28.1 have horrible long-term returns, high standard deviations of return, and huge maximum declines. Their stories may sound good, but the prospects for these stocks are always bad. The evidence is painfully clear—if you habitually buy stocks with good stories but the highest multiples, you'll do much worse than the market. And unless you are buying them at the end of a severe bear market, trying to bottom-fish stocks from the worst decile of six- or twelve-month price appreciation is also a loser's game, as is putting up with stocks that score poorly on our Financial Strength and Earnings Quality Composites.

In the absence of stories, investors look at the base rates. Table 28.2 shows the base rates for all of the strategies featured in Table 28.1. But let one dot-com stock in the door at the end of the 1990s, and many investors will jettison common sense and sound research, believing it's different this time. It isn't. I said this in the 1997 edition of this book, and I'll say it again today—tomorrow's hot "story" stocks may not be Internet darlings or large-cap tech stocks, but they have one thing in common—they *will* crash and burn. On the heels of the 2007–2009 bear market, we've also now learned what might be described as the opposite lesson—horrible bear markets lead many investors to shun the equity markets entirely, and history suggests that they too will go on to see disappointing returns. The lesson of the long-term data is unambiguous—find strategies that have great long-term returns, and *stick with them*.

T A B L E 28.2

Summary Base Rate Information for all Rolling One-, Three-, Five-, Seven-, and Ten-Year Periods, August 31, 1965, to December 31, 2009. Strategies Sorted by Compound Average Annual Return

Strategy	Percent of time				
	1 year	3 years	5 years	7 years	10 years
Microcap, BP Top 3 deciles, 3 mom. and 6 mom. >0, Top 25 by 12 mom.	78.89%	90.34%	98.94%	100.00%	100.00%
Microcap, PSR<1, 3 mom. and 6 mom. >0, Top 10 by 12 mom.	69.29%	88.93%	98.10%	99.11%	100.00%
Microcap, BP Top 3 deciles, 3 mom. and 6 mom. >Median Top 25 by 12 mom.	77.16%	90.14%	99.15%	100.00%	100.00%
Microcap, BP Top 3 deciles, 3 mom. and 6 mom. >0, Top 50 by 12 mom.	82.34%	93.36%	100.00%	100.00%	100.00%
Trending Value Portfolio	84.64%	99.20%	100.00%	100.00%	100.00%
Microcap, PSR<1, Top 25 by 12 mom.	72.55%	85.11%	95.77%	99.55%	99.76%
All Stocks Growth	81.57%	95.77%	96.83%	97.55%	99.27%
Small Stocks, VC2 in Top 3 Deciles, 3 and 6 mom.>Median, Top 25 by 6 mom.	83.30%	96.38%	100.00%	100.00%	100.00%
Small Stocks, VC2 in Top 3 Deciles, 3 and 6 mom.>Median, Top 50 by 6 mom.	83.69%	97.59%	100.00%	100.00%	100.00%
All Stocks, VC2 in Top Decile, Top 50 by 6 mom.	81.96%	97.18%	99.79%	99.55%	100.00%
All Stocks, VC2 in Top 3 Deciles, 3 mom. and 6 mom. >Median, Top 25 by 6 mom.	85.41%	99.80%	100.00%	100.00%	100.00%
Small Stocks, Value Composite3 (VC3), Decile 1	83.30%	94.16%	99.37%	100.00%	100.00%
All Stocks, VC2 in Top 3 Deciles, 3 mom. and 6 mom. >Median, Top 50 by 6 mom.	86.18%	98.99%	100.00%	100.00%	100.00%
Small Stocks, Value Composite2 (VC2), Decile 1	80.61%	93.36%	99.37%	99.78%	100.00%
Small Stocks, EBITDA/ Enterprise Value Decile 1	81.96%	95.17%	100.00%	100.00%	100.00%
Small Stocks, Value Composite1 (VC1), Decile 1	80.81%	92.56%	99.37%	100.00%	100.00%
Small Stocks, PB in Top 3 Deciles, 3 mom. and 6 mom. >Median, Top 25 by SY	75.05%	91.35%	97.46%	98.66%	100.00%
Small Stocks, PSR<1, 3 mom. and 6 mom. >0, Top 50 12 mom.	74.09%	89.13%	97.46%	98.89%	100.00%
All Stocks, 3 mom. and 6 mom. >Median, Top 25 by SY	77.35%	98.79%	100.00%	100.00%	100.00%
All Stocks, BP and 6 mom. >Median, Top 25 by BBY	79.46%	95.17%	99.79%	100.00%	100.00%
Small Stocks, SY and 6 mom. >Median, Top 25 BP	74.47%	89.94%	98.94%	98.44%	100.00%
All Stocks, PB in Top 3 Deciles, 3 mom. and 6 mom. >Median, Top 25 by SY	74.28%	93.16%	98.94%	98.66%	100.00%
Small Stocks, BP and 6 mom. >Median, Top 25 BBY	77.93%	95.17%	99.58%	100.00%	100.00%
Small Stocks, 3 mom. and 6 mom. >Median, Top 25 SY	74.86%	98.39%	100.00%	100.00%	100.00%

(continued on next page)

Summary Base Rate Information for all Rolling One-, Three-, Five-, Seven-, and Ten-Year Periods, August 31, 1965, to December 31, 2009. Strategies Sorted by Compound Average Annual Return *(Continued)*

Strategy	Percent of time				
	1 year	3 years	5 years	7 years	10 years
Small Stocks, PB in Top 3 Deciles, 3 mom. and 6 mom. >Median, Top 25 by 12 mom.	76.97%	93.76%	100.00%	99.55%	100.00%
Small Stocks, PB in Top 3 Deciles, 3 mom. and 6 mom. >0, Top 25 by 12 mom.	77.16%	91.55%	99.58%	99.55%	100.00%
Small Stocks, PB in Top 3 Deciles, 3 mom. and 6 mom. >0, Top 25 by SY	73.70%	91.35%	95.98%	98.44%	100.00%
Small Stocks, PB in Top 3 Deciles, 3 mom. and 6 mom. >0, Top 50 by 12 mom.	78.50%	94.37%	99.58%	99.55%	100.00%
Small Stocks, PB in Top 3 Deciles, 3 mom. and 6 mom. >Median, Top 50 by SY	75.05%	93.76%	98.73%	98.44%	100.00%
All Stocks, SY and 6 mom. >Median, Top 25 by BP	73.51%	90.34%	98.10%	98.44%	100.00%
All Stocks, PB in Top 3 Deciles, 3 mom. and 6 mom. >0, Top 25 by SY	74.09%	90.74%	97.25%	98.44%	100.00%
Small Stocks, 3 mom. and 6 mom. >Median, Top 25 BP	75.82%	88.33%	99.58%	99.55%	100.00%
Small Stocks, PB in Top 3 Deciles, 3 mom. and 6 mom. >Median, Top 50 by 12 mom.	77.35%	93.76%	99.79%	99.55%	100.00%
All Stocks, PB in Top 3 Deciles, 3 mom. and 6 mom. >Median, Top 25 by 12 mom.	80.61%	92.96%	99.58%	100.00%	100.00%
Small Stocks, 3 mom. and 6 mom. >Median, Top 50 BP	75.05%	92.96%	99.37%	99.33%	100.00%
Small Stocks, PB in Top 3 Deciles, 3 mom. and 6 mom. >0, Top 50 by SY	74.09%	89.54%	95.77%	99.33%	100.00%
Small Stocks, SY and 6 mom. >Median, Top 50 BP	72.36%	90.74%	97.25%	97.77%	100.00%
All Stocks, SY and 6 mom. >Median, Top 50 by BP	76.58%	92.76%	97.67%	98.22%	100.00%
All Stocks, BP and 6 mom. >Median, Top 25 by SY	71.40%	94.77%	99.37%	100.00%	100.00%
All Stocks, PB in Top 3 Deciles, 3 mom. and 6 mom. >0, Top 25 by 12 mom.	78.89%	90.34%	99.58%	99.55%	100.00%
All Stocks, PB in Top 3 Deciles, 3 mom. and 6 mom. >0, Top 50 by 12 mom.	79.46%	93.56%	99.58%	99.55%	100.00%
Small Stocks, BP and 6 mom. >Median, Top 25 SY	70.25%	89.34%	95.56%	99.11%	100.00%
All Stocks, 3 mom. and 6 mom. >Median, Top 50 by SY	78.12%	99.80%	100.00%	100.00%	100.00%
All Stocks, PB in Top 3 Deciles, 3 mom. and 6 mom. >Median, Top 50 by SY	75.62%	92.56%	98.52%	98.44%	100.00%
Small Stocks, Free CF to Enterprise Value Decile 1	73.51%	81.89%	83.93%	87.08%	92.01%

(continued on next page)

T A B L E 28.2

Summary Base Rate Information for all Rolling One-, Three-, Five-, Seven-, and Ten-Year Periods, August 31, 1965, to December 31, 2009. Strategies Sorted by Compound Average Annual Return *(Continued)*

Strategy			Percent of time		
	1 year	3 years	5 years	7 years	10 years
Small Stocks, Earnings/ Price Decile 1	76.01%	86.72%	91.12%	95.32%	99.52%
All Stocks, 3 mom. and 6 mom. >Median, Top 50 by BP	76.39%	90.95%	99.58%	99.55%	100.00%
All Stocks, BP and 6 mom. >Median, Top 50 by BBY	78.69%	95.98%	99.79%	100.00%	100.00%
All Stocks, PB in Top 3 Deciles, 3 mom. and 6 mom. >0, Top 50 by SY	73.32%	89.13%	97.04%	98.22%	100.00%
Small Stocks, BP and BBY and 3 mom. >Median, Top 25 by 6 mom.	74.86%	93.76%	99.15%	99.78%	100.00%
Small Stocks, BP and BBY >Median, Top 25 by 6 mom.	75.24%	93.36%	98.73%	99.33%	100.00%
Small Stocks, Net Operating Cash Flow to Price Decile 1	72.36%	82.29%	90.27%	93.99%	100.00%
All Stocks, PB in Top 3 Deciles, 3 mom. and 6 mom. >Median, Top 50 by 12 mom.	78.89%	93.56%	100.00%	100.00%	100.00%
All Stocks, 3 mom. and 6 mom. >Median, Top 25 by BP	73.70%	88.33%	96.19%	98.44%	100.00%
Small Stocks, BP and 6 mom. >Median, Top 50 BBY	74.09%	91.95%	99.37%	99.55%	100.00%
Small Stocks, BP and SY >Median, Top 25 by 6 mom.	76.78%	95.37%	98.73%	99.55%	100.00%
Small Stocks, 3 mom. and 6 mom. >Median, Top 50 SY	74.09%	97.18%	99.37%	100.00%	100.00%
Small Stocks, BP and BBY and 3 mom. >Median, Top 50 by 6 mom.	74.66%	93.96%	100.00%	100.00%	100.00%
All Stocks, Value Composite3 (VC3) Decile 1	79.27%	93.16%	97.89%	98.44%	99.52%
Small Stocks, Sales to Enterprise Value Decile 1	73.13%	86.92%	97.04%	99.78%	100.00%
All Stocks, Value Composite2 (VC2) Decile 1	75.43%	92.35%	97.89%	98.22%	99.52%
All Stocks, BP and BBY >Median, Top 25 by 6 mom.	78.89%	91.35%	96.19%	99.55%	100.00%
All Stocks, BP and BBY and 3 mom. >Median, Top 25 by 6 mom.	79.08%	92.15%	96.83%	98.89%	100.00%
Small Stocks, BP and BBY >Median, Top 50 by 6 mom.	74.66%	95.17%	99.58%	100.00%	100.00%
All Stocks, Value Composite1 (VC1) Decile 1	76.78%	92.76%	98.10%	98.44%	99.52%
Small Stocks, BP and 6 mom. >Median, Top 50 SY	67.95%	86.92%	94.08%	98.66%	100.00%
All Stocks, BP and SY >Median, Top 25 by 6 mom.	80.61%	93.16%	98.52%	100.00%	100.00%
Small Stocks, Free Cash Flow to Price Decile 1	68.33%	77.67%	86.05%	87.75%	90.56%
All Stocks, BP and BBY and 3 mom. >Median, Top 50 by 6 mom.	79.27%	96.58%	100.00%	100.00%	100.00%
Small Stocks, BP and SY >Median, Top 50 by 6 mom.	71.21%	94.16%	100.00%	100.00%	100.00%
All Stocks, BP and BBY >Median, Top 50 by 6 mom.	78.89%	94.37%	99.37%	100.00%	100.00%
All Stocks, BP and 6 mom. >Median, Top 50 by SY	68.52%	90.34%	97.67%	99.11%	100.00%
Combined Consumer Staples/Utilities Portfolio	65.07%	79.07%	84.99%	89.09%	97.09%
All Stocks, EBITDA/ Enterprise Value Decile 1	76.01%	87.32%	97.04%	99.78%	100.00%
All Stocks, BP and SY >Median, Top 50 by 6 mom.	77.54%	96.38%	100.00%	100.00%	100.00%
All Stocks, Earnings/ Price Decile 1	75.62%	85.11%	91.97%	95.77%	99.27%

(continued on next page)

Summary Base Rate Information for all Rolling One-, Three-, Five-, Seven-, and Ten-Year Periods, August 31, 1965, to December 31, 2009. Strategies Sorted by Compound Average Annual Return *(Continued)*

Strategy			Percent of time			
	1 year	3 years	5 years	7 years	10 years
All Stocks, Net Operating Cash Flow to Price Decile 1	72.17%	86.32%	90.70%	98.22%	99.76%
All Stocks, Free CF to Enterprise Value Decile 1	74.09%	81.29%	87.95%	87.75%	91.53%
All Stocks, Earnings Quality Composite Decile 1	83.69%	88.53%	94.29%	97.77%	100.00%
Small Stocks, BP and 3 mom. and 6 mom. >Median, Top 25 12 mom.	75.82%	87.12%	96.62%	98.00%	98.79%
All Stocks, Buyback Yield, Decile 1	83.11%	96.18%	99.15%	100.00%	100.00%
Small Stocks, BP and 3 mom. and 6 mom. >Median, Top 50 12 mom.	73.90%	93.56%	98.31%	98.00%	100.00%
Small Stocks, Buyback Yield, Decile 1	77.74%	95.98%	98.94%	99.78%	100.00%
Small Stocks, Shareholder Yield, Decile 1	70.25%	88.13%	94.93%	98.44%	99.27%
All Stocks, Sales to Enterprise Value Decile 1	73.51%	88.53%	97.25%	97.55%	98.79%
All Stocks, Shareholder Yield, Decile 1	74.47%	92.76%	98.10%	98.66%	99.52%
Market Leaders, Top 2 Deciles VC2, Top 25 by 6 mom.	72.94%	84.91%	91.97%	98.00%	100.00%
All Stocks, Free Cash Flow to Price Decile 1	71.40%	79.88%	91.97%	98.44%	100.00%
All Stocks, SY and 3 mom. and 6 mom. >Median, Top 50 by 12 mom.	76.58%	92.76%	95.98%	97.10%	98.31%
All Stocks, BP and 3 mom. and 6 mom. >Median, Top 25 by 12 mom.	74.86%	89.13%	93.23%	97.55%	98.55%
Market Leaders, 3 mom. and 6 mom. >Median, Top 25 by SY	65.64%	80.68%	91.75%	98.89%	100.00%
All Stocks, Fin Strength Composite Decile 10	83.11%	95.37%	97.04%	100.00%	100.00%
Market Leaders, Top 2 Deciles VC2, Top 50 by 6 mom.	75.24%	85.71%	92.60%	96.88%	99.76%
Market Leaders, VC2>Median, Top 25 by SY	66.03%	78.47%	88.37%	98.22%	100.00%
Small Stocks, SY and 3 mom. and 6 mom. >Median, Top 50 12 mom.	77.93%	94.16%	95.98%	96.88%	97.82%
Cornerstone Value, Improved 25	65.26%	82.09%	90.27%	98.44%	100.00%
Large Stocks, Buyback Yield, Decile 1	82.53%	92.96%	96.83%	99.55%	100.00%
Large Stocks, 3 mom. and 6 mom. >Median, Top 25 by SY	71.02%	91.35%	95.98%	97.77%	100.00%
Small Stocks, Sales to Price Decile 1	68.14%	68.41%	75.90%	75.50%	79.42%
Market Leaders, Value Composite 2 Decile 1 (High)	64.11%	71.23%	79.70%	92.87%	98.79%
Market Leaders, Shareholder Yield (%) Decile 1	64.88%	80.28%	91.33%	97.33%	100.00%
All Stocks, BP and 3 mom. and 6 mom. >Median, Top 50 by 12 mom.	75.82%	89.74%	97.04%	98.00%	100.00%
Small Stocks, 3 mom. and 6 mom. >0, ROE>avg, 50 best 12 mom.	64.49%	74.45%	82.88%	87.97%	94.19%
Market Leaders, 3 mom. and 6 mom. >Median, Top 50 by SY	67.31%	86.12%	98.10%	99.78%	100.00%
Large Stocks, BP and 6 mom. >Median, Top 25 by BBY	72.36%	90.14%	99.79%	99.55%	100.00%
Cornerstone Value, Improved 50	69.10%	84.91%	96.62%	99.11%	100.00%
Market Leaders, VC2>Median, Top 50 by SY	67.18%	80.08%	93.45%	100.00%	100.00%
All Stocks, SY and 3 mom. and 6 mom. >Median, Top 25 by 12 mom.	67.56%	83.90%	91.54%	95.99%	97.58%

(continued on next page)

T A B L E 28.2

Summary Base Rate Information for all Rolling One-, Three-, Five-, Seven-, and Ten-Year Periods, August 31, 1965, to December 31, 2009. Strategies Sorted by Compound Average Annual Return *(Continued)*

Strategy	Percent of time				
	1 year	3 years	5 years	7 years	10 years
Market Leaders, Value Composite 3 Decile 1 (High)	63.34%	67.81%	78.86%	91.31%	96.85%
Large Stocks, Shareholder Yield, Decile 1	74.47%	89.74%	96.83%	99.11%	99.76%
Small Stocks, Accruals to Price Decile 10	61.23%	69.01%	67.65%	70.16%	68.04%
Market Leaders, EBITDA/ Enterprise Value Decile 1	68.14%	77.67%	83.51%	93.54%	99.52%
Small Stocks, 6-Month Momentum, Decile 1	61.42%	72.64%	85.62%	91.09%	97.58%
Small Stocks, SY and 3 mom. and 6 mom. >Median, Top 25 12 mom.	72.17%	84.91%	91.75%	92.43%	97.09%
Small Stocks, BBY and 3 mom. >Median, Top 50 12 mom.	69.10%	81.69%	87.32%	93.54%	98.31%
Market Leaders, Buyback Yield (%) Decile 1	71.79%	86.92%	91.54%	95.10%	100.00%
Market Leaders, Value Composite 1 Decile 1 (High)	62.00%	70.62%	70.82%	87.97%	96.37%
Small Stocks, Book to Price, Decile 1	61.04%	68.61%	75.90%	89.98%	97.58%
All Stocks, 6-Month Momentum, Decile 1	62.38%	71.43%	85.41%	91.76%	97.09%
Market Leaders, 3 mom. and 6 mom. >Median, Top 25 by VC2	68.91%	78.87%	83.30%	93.10%	100.00%
Large Stocks, BP and BBY >Median, Top 25 by 6 mom.	77.35%	92.15%	100.00%	100.00%	100.00%
Large Stocks, Value Composite2 Decile 1	68.33%	82.70%	91.33%	95.99%	97.82%
Large Stocks, Value Composite3 Decile 1	69.10%	80.89%	93.02%	97.33%	97.82%
All Stocks, Book to Price, Decile 1	64.30%	73.64%	81.18%	92.43%	98.31%
Small Stocks, 60-Month Momentum, Decile 10	61.61%	71.63%	75.69%	78.17%	72.88%
All Stocks, Accruals to Price Decile 10	62.76%	76.46%	84.99%	85.52%	91.04%
All Stocks, Sales to Price Decile 1	66.79%	70.62%	74.42%	78.84%	88.62%
Large Stocks, EBITDA/ Enterprise Value Decile 1	72.36%	82.90%	90.27%	96.44%	99.52%
Large Stocks, 3 mom. and 6 mom. >Median, Top 25 by BP	68.14%	80.28%	96.41%	99.55%	100.00%
All Stocks, 60-Month Momentum, Decile 10	62.76%	69.42%	76.11%	77.73%	73.37%
Large Stocks, SY and 3 mom. and 6 mom. >Median, Top 25 by 12 mom.	71.21%	87.93%	95.98%	98.44%	100.00%
Large Stocks, BP and BBY and 3 mom. >Median, Top 25 by 6 mom.	75.43%	90.34%	100.00%	100.00%	100.00%
All Stocks, BBY and 3 mom. >Median, Top 50 by 12 mom.	66.41%	76.26%	82.88%	86.41%	95.40%
Small Stocks, Dividend Yield, Decile 1	55.28%	69.22%	71.88%	73.05%	87.17%
Market Leaders, Free CF to Enterprise Value Decile 1	62.96%	73.64%	87.53%	87.08%	90.56%
Large Stocks, BP and 6 mom. >Median, Top 25 by SY	63.72%	81.09%	95.98%	97.55%	98.31%
Market Leaders, Net Operating Cash Flow to Price Decile 1	60.65%	66.00%	73.78%	87.75%	97.09%
Large Stocks, SY and 6 mom. >Median, Top 25 by BP	68.91%	83.90%	92.81%	95.55%	99.03%
Small Stocks, Asset Turnover Decile 1	60.08%	62.98%	68.71%	71.71%	77.72%
Small Stocks, BBY and 3 mom. >Median, Top 25 12 mom.	63.34%	71.63%	77.59%	87.53%	95.64%

(continued on next page)

Summary Base Rate Information for all Rolling One-, Three-, Five-, Seven-, and Ten-Year Periods, August 31, 1965, to December 31, 2009. Strategies Sorted by Compound Average Annual Return *(Continued)*

Strategy	Percent of time					
	1 year	3 years	5 years	7 years	10 years
Market Leaders, Earnings/ Price Decile 1	61.42%	67.61%	65.12%	71.49%	64.65%
Large Stocks, 3 mom. and 6 mom. >Median, Top 50 by SY	65.45%	87.73%	93.02%	97.10%	100.00%
Large Stocks, BP and BBY and 3 mom. >Median, Top 50 by 6 mom.	72.55%	88.73%	98.94%	98.44%	99.03%
Market Leaders, TATA Decile 10	66.22%	74.85%	81.18%	83.07%	92.49%
Large Stocks, BP and SY >Median, Top 25 by 6 mom.	72.55%	88.73%	99.37%	98.66%	100.00%
Large Stocks, 6-Month Momentum, Decile 1	64.88%	74.04%	82.45%	86.41%	95.40%
Large Stocks, Earnings/ Price Decile 1	69.10%	73.84%	83.30%	89.09%	94.92%
Large Stocks, Net Operating Cash Flow to Price Decile 1	67.37%	73.84%	76.32%	87.53%	95.64%
Large Stocks, BP and BBY >Median, Top 50 by 6 mom.	72.36%	89.74%	98.10%	98.22%	98.79%
Cornerstone Value, 25 Div Yld	57.39%	65.19%	67.44%	72.38%	84.26%
Large Stocks, BBY and 3 mom. >Median, Top 25 by 12 mom.	64.49%	76.86%	86.47%	94.43%	96.37%
Large Stocks, Value Composite1 Decile 1	63.92%	75.65%	80.55%	89.98%	96.85%
Market Leaders, Return 6 Month Decile 1	62.57%	71.03%	83.72%	93.76%	96.85%
Large Stocks, BP and 6 mom. >Median, Top 50 by BBY	72.17%	88.33%	98.94%	98.89%	99.76%
Small Stocks, Cash Flow to Debt (%) Decile 1	53.74%	61.97%	69.98%	68.15%	62.71%
Market Leaders, PSR<avg, Top 25 by 12 mom.	67.18%	77.87%	84.78%	88.20%	98.31%
Large Stocks, BP and 6 mom. >Median, Top 50 by SY	63.92%	77.87%	93.87%	96.66%	96.85%
Market Leaders, 3 mom. and 6 mom. >Median, Top 50 by VC2	67.18%	75.45%	82.88%	91.54%	99.03%
Large Stocks, Free CF to Enterprise Value Decile 1	63.92%	78.47%	88.16%	92.65%	96.85%
Market Leaders, Accruals to Price Decile 10	59.69%	65.19%	72.94%	80.85%	91.53%
Market Leaders, NOA Change (%) Decile 10	61.80%	73.84%	79.07%	84.63%	85.47%
Market Leaders, Dividend Yield (%) Decile 1	55.66%	61.17%	67.23%	74.16%	85.96%
All Stocks, Dividend Yield, Decile 1	53.17%	69.42%	70.82%	72.38%	83.05%
Small Stocks, ROA Decile 1	57.01%	64.79%	69.13%	65.48%	60.05%
Small Stocks, ROE Decile 1	58.16%	62.17%	64.06%	59.69%	58.35%
All Stocks, BBY and 3 mom. >Median, Top 25 by 12 mom.	60.27%	64.79%	73.15%	81.51%	83.54%
Market Leaders, Sales to Enterprise Value Decile 1	63.53%	68.61%	75.05%	74.16%	81.36%
Large Stocks, BP and SY >Median, Top 50 by 6 mom.	67.18%	82.29%	95.56%	96.88%	98.55%
Large Stocks, SY and 3 mom. and 6 mom. >Median, Top 50 by 12 mom.	68.71%	87.32%	93.45%	97.33%	100.00%
Large Stocks, Book to Price, Decile 1	63.72%	72.23%	83.72%	89.31%	95.64%
Market Leaders, Top 10 by PCF	57.20%	62.78%	68.50%	81.51%	91.04%
Large Stocks, BBY and 3 mom. >Median, Top 50 by 12 mom.	69.67%	82.49%	92.18%	96.88%	99.76%

(continued on next page)

617

T A B L E 28.2

Summary Base Rate Information for all Rolling One-, Three-, Five-, Seven-, and Ten-Year Periods, August 31, 1965, to December 31, 2009. Strategies Sorted by Compound Average Annual Return *(Continued)*

Strategy	Percent of time				
	1 year	3 years	5 years	7 years	10 years
Small Stocks, EPS Change (%) Decile 1	58.54%	56.74%	63.00%	65.92%	66.59%
Large Stocks, SY and 6 mom. >Median, Top 50 by BP	65.26%	78.27%	91.97%	95.55%	97.82%
All Stocks, TATA Decile 10	68.91%	70.82%	69.13%	67.04%	77.00%
Market Leaders, PSR<avg, Top 50 by 12 mom.	64.11%	70.22%	73.15%	75.06%	80.15%
All Stocks, Asset Turnover Decile 1	59.50%	66.00%	74.63%	81.07%	86.20%
Large Stocks, Earnings Quality Composite Decile 10	71.79%	85.51%	88.79%	92.20%	99.76%
Market Leaders, Return 12 Month Decile 1	60.08%	66.00%	78.65%	83.07%	86.20%
Large Stocks, BBY >Median, Top 50 by DIVY	57.97%	69.62%	75.90%	84.19%	90.56%
Market Leaders, Free Cash Flow to Price Decile 1	58.35%	61.77%	69.13%	71.27%	72.88%
Large Stocks, 3 mom. and 6 mom. >Median, Top 50 by BP	62.38%	78.47%	87.95%	95.99%	99.76%
Large Stocks, 60-Month Momentum, Decile 10	60.84%	66.00%	75.26%	81.07%	92.01%
Small Stocks, TATA Decile 10	49.90%	56.14%	52.22%	53.90%	47.22%
Large Stocks, Accruals to Price Decile 10	62.57%	73.44%	74.84%	76.84%	88.14%
Large Stocks, BBY >Median, Top 25 by DIVY	55.66%	67.20%	72.73%	82.18%	87.17%
Large Stocks, Sales to Enterprise Value Decile 1	67.18%	72.84%	78.22%	81.96%	97.58%
Market Leaders, Sales to Price Decile 1	57.58%	53.32%	60.04%	57.02%	64.41%
Market Leaders, Book/ Price Decile 1	56.24%	55.53%	57.29%	64.14%	66.83%
Market Leaders, Debt Change (%) Decile 10	60.27%	64.59%	73.57%	79.73%	86.92%
Small Stocks, 12-Month Momentum, Decile 1	57.97%	57.14%	66.60%	69.27%	74.09%
All Stocks, 12-Month Momentum, Decile 1	59.50%	56.94%	69.98%	70.16%	78.21%
Large Stocks, Free Cash Flow to Price Decile 1	59.31%	64.39%	73.78%	83.52%	82.81%
Large Stocks, BP and 3 mom. and 6 mom. >Median, Top 50 by 12 mom.	61.61%	75.86%	85.62%	94.65%	100.00%
All Stocks, ROE Decile 1	58.54%	61.17%	64.90%	55.01%	48.43%
Large Stocks, BP and 3 mom. and 6 mom. >Median, Top 25 by 12 mom.	65.64%	77.46%	82.66%	93.32%	98.06%
Large Stocks, 12-Month Momentum, Decile 1	59.12%	69.22%	76.11%	78.40%	87.89%
All Stocks, NOA Change (%) Decile 10	58.16%	63.58%	67.65%	69.27%	75.30%
Small Stocks, Operating Margin Decile 1	46.64%	51.71%	58.14%	58.13%	58.11%
All Stocks, Depr Exp to Cap Exp Decile 1	57.39%	61.57%	60.89%	61.25%	71.19%
Market Leaders, ROA Decile 1	51.25%	45.67%	47.78%	52.78%	52.78%
All Stocks, ROA Decile 1	50.86%	50.91%	54.12%	52.34%	53.75%
Small Stocks, Net Margin Decile 1	49.52%	59.56%	61.10%	58.80%	57.38%
Small Stocks, Depr Exp to Cap Exp Decile 1	49.14%	50.10%	45.88%	39.64%	37.29%

(continued on next page)

Summary Base Rate Information for all Rolling One-, Three-, Five-, Seven-, and Ten-Year Periods, August 31, 1965, to December 31, 2009. Strategies Sorted by Compound Average Annual Return *(Continued)*

	Percent of time				
Strategy	**1 year**	**3 years**	**5 years**	**7 years**	**10 years**
Large Stocks, TATA Decile 10	62.38%	72.43%	76.96%	76.39%	80.63%
All Stocks, Cash Flow to Debt (%) Decile 1	47.22%	44.06%	52.22%	53.67%	56.42%
Market Leaders, Net Margin Decile 1	48.56%	52.11%	48.63%	54.79%	55.45%
Market Leaders, Asset Turnover Decile 1	49.33%	52.92%	54.76%	56.12%	67.07%
Market Leaders, Operating Margin Decile 1	45.68%	46.48%	45.03%	50.78%	53.27%
Large Stocks, Dividend Yield, Decile 1	48.37%	60.56%	61.95%	69.49%	78.69%
Large Stocks, Fin Strength Composite Decile 10	64.49%	74.04%	79.07%	79.96%	80.87%
SMALL STOCKS	0.00%	0.00%	0.00%	0.00%	0.00%
All Stocks, Growth Composite Decile 1	52.40%	53.92%	60.47%	61.92%	57.14%
Large Stocks, NOA Change (%) Decile 10	62.00%	66.40%	66.60%	65.92%	74.58%
Market Leaders Universe	0.00%	0.00%	0.00%	0.00%	0.00%
Large Stocks, Sales to Price Decile 1	58.16%	61.17%	65.12%	72.61%	77.48%
Market Leaders, Depr Exp to Cap Exp Decile 1	54.32%	61.37%	65.12%	70.16%	76.76%
Market Leaders, Cash Flow to Debt (%) Decile 1	46.45%	44.87%	36.36%	34.08%	33.90%
Small Stocks, Debt Change (%) Decile 10	47.60%	43.06%	37.42%	37.42%	38.26%
ALL STOCKS	0.00%	0.00%	0.00%	0.00%	0.00%
Market Leaders, ROE Decile 1	50.86%	43.86%	46.30%	44.32%	50.61%
Large Stocks, BP >Median, Top 25 by DIVY	48.56%	61.57%	57.29%	57.24%	69.01%
Small Stocks, NOA Change (%) Decile 10	49.33%	50.10%	46.09%	44.10%	39.71%
Large Stocks, Asset Turnover Decile 1	55.28%	60.97%	60.47%	62.36%	62.71%
All Stocks, Operating Margin Decile 1	49.14%	49.70%	55.39%	59.47%	55.69%
Large Stocks, BP >Median, Top 50 by DIVY	49.71%	56.34%	54.55%	60.58%	69.25%
Market Leaders, Depr Exp to Cap Exp Decile 10	45.30%	40.24%	38.27%	39.64%	39.47%
All Stocks, Debt Change (%) Decile 10	49.90%	50.30%	45.67%	41.43%	42.13%
Large Stocks, Debt Change (%) Decile 10	61.23%	59.36%	55.18%	46.33%	35.35%
Market Leaders, Asset Turnover Decile 10	51.25%	50.91%	56.45%	53.23%	49.15%
Market Leaders, ROE Decile 10	50.10%	45.67%	38.69%	36.08%	38.74%
All Stocks, Net Margin Decile 1	44.53%	54.33%	49.05%	50.11%	50.61%
Market Leaders, Accruals to Price Decile 1	42.61%	37.42%	39.96%	37.64%	25.42%
Market Leaders, Free CF to Enterprise Value Decile 10	44.91%	40.04%	39.75%	38.31%	33.41%
Market Leaders, ROA Decile 10	48.94%	34.00%	36.36%	37.42%	31.23%
LARGE STOCKS	0.00%	0.00%	0.00%	0.00%	0.00%

(continued on next page)

T A B L E 28.2

Summary Base Rate Information for all Rolling One-, Three-, Five-, Seven-, and Ten-Year Periods, August 31, 1965, to December 31, 2009. Strategies Sorted by Compound Average Annual Return *(Continued)*

Strategy	Percent of time				
	1 year	3 years	5 years	7 years	10 years
Market Leaders, Cash Flow to Debt (%) Decile 10	48.94%	52.11%	50.11%	47.88%	38.74%
Market Leaders, Net Margin Decile 10	47.41%	42.45%	40.38%	37.42%	44.07%
Market Leaders, Free Cash Flow to Price Decile 10	42.61%	34.00%	32.98%	27.17%	28.33%
Market Leaders, EPS Change (%) Decile 1	40.31%	32.39%	27.91%	22.49%	21.07%
Market Leaders, Book/ Price Decile 10	43.38%	38.43%	34.88%	35.19%	20.82%
Large Stocks, Depr Exp to Cap Exp Decile 1	51.25%	56.94%	51.16%	59.02%	62.95%
Large Stocks, ROA Decile 1	47.41%	43.26%	47.78%	46.10%	48.43%
Large Stocks, ROE Decile 1	53.93%	46.68%	46.93%	48.78%	52.06%
Large Stocks, Growth Composite Decile 1	46.26%	37.63%	36.79%	33.18%	30.51%
Market Leaders, Debt Change (%) Decile 1	38.39%	29.98%	22.20%	11.80%	1.69%
S&P 500	**41.65%**	**48.09%**	**45.67%**	**50.56%**	**48.18%**
Market Leaders, Operating Margin Decile 10	42.23%	37.63%	25.16%	26.50%	15.25%
All Stocks, Asset Turnover Decile 10	42.99%	43.06%	43.55%	43.65%	42.86%
Large Stocks, Operating Margin Decile 1	47.22%	44.47%	43.34%	42.98%	43.10%
Large Stocks, EPS Change (%) Decile 1	43.95%	33.40%	28.33%	25.84%	15.01%
Market Leaders, EBITDA/ Enterprise Value Decile 10	41.84%	31.99%	27.70%	26.95%	20.34%
Market Leaders, EPS Change (%) Decile 10	33.97%	24.75%	16.49%	10.24%	3.39%
Small Stocks, 60-Month Momentum, Decile 1	36.08%	32.80%	30.02%	24.28%	27.12%
Large Stocks, Cash Flow to Debt (%) Decile 1	45.68%	35.61%	34.04%	29.62%	15.98%
Market Leaders, Earnings/ Price Decile 10	40.69%	31.79%	28.12%	14.70%	8.72%
Large Stocks, Book to Price, Decile 10	47.41%	43.86%	39.11%	30.29%	20.82%
Market Leaders, Value Composite 1 Decile 10 (Low)	38.96%	33.40%	32.14%	25.17%	9.69%
Small Stocks, Accruals to Price Decile 1	39.54%	35.81%	33.40%	34.52%	23.00%
All Stocks, Accruals to Price Decile 1	38.58%	29.78%	21.78%	15.59%	7.51%
Market Leaders, NOA Change (%) Decile 1	35.51%	25.55%	16.07%	8.24%	1.69%
Market Leaders, Sales to Price Decile 10	40.88%	37.83%	30.87%	28.29%	9.93%
Market Leaders, Sales to Enterprise Value Decile 10	36.47%	33.80%	34.67%	33.63%	23.97%
Market Leaders, Return 12 Month Decile 10	33.21%	20.93%	13.11%	5.35%	1.45%
Large Stocks, Net Margin Decile 1	47.79%	34.00%	32.35%	32.07%	31.96%
Large Stocks, Accruals to Price Decile 1	36.85%	37.22%	34.88%	24.94%	15.25%
Large Stocks, Asset Turnover Decile 10	48.94%	44.27%	43.34%	38.31%	35.84%
All Stocks, 60-Month Momentum, Decile 1	37.43%	30.18%	26.85%	17.15%	15.50%

(continued on next page)

Summary Base Rate Information for all Rolling One-, Three-, Five-, Seven-, and Ten-Year Periods, August 31, 1965, to December 31, 2009. Strategies Sorted by Compound Average Annual Return *(Continued)*

Strategy		Percent of time				
	1 year	3 years	5 years	7 years	10 years
Market Leaders, Return 6 Month Decile 10	33.59%	13.28%	6.77%	1.34%	0.00%
All Stocks, Book to Price, Decile 10	42.61%	31.39%	26.00%	17.82%	9.69%
Small Stocks, Book to Price, Decile 10	41.65%	27.36%	21.35%	12.03%	5.57%
Large Stocks, Net Margin Decile 10	46.64%	45.27%	45.03%	36.30%	36.08%
Large Stocks, Free CF to Enterprise Value Decile 10	42.61%	34.00%	29.60%	26.95%	28.33%
Large Stocks, Growth Composite Decile 10	38.00%	34.00%	26.85%	22.49%	22.03%
Large Stocks, ROE Decile 10	45.49%	46.08%	35.94%	40.76%	42.86%
Market Leaders, Value Composite 2 Decile 10 (Low)	34.93%	32.19%	20.30%	11.58%	5.81%
Small Stocks, Asset Turnover Decile 10	35.12%	33.00%	19.66%	17.82%	9.44%
Market Leaders, TATA Decile 1	26.49%	8.85%	1.06%	0.00%	0.00%
Market Leaders, Net Operating Cash Flow to Price Decile 10	34.93%	28.17%	17.76%	14.25%	1.94%
Market Leaders, Value Composite 3 Decile 10 (Low)	34.36%	28.97%	20.30%	10.02%	4.84%
Large Stocks, Free Cash Flow to Price Decile 10	42.03%	29.58%	25.16%	16.70%	16.46%
Large Stocks, ROA Decile 10	46.26%	40.04%	28.33%	21.38%	20.34%
Large Stocks, 60-Month Momentum, Decile 1	43.38%	35.61%	29.60%	23.83%	20.82%
Large Stocks, EPS Change (%) Decile 10	38.39%	32.19%	25.79%	12.69%	8.96%
Large Stocks, Depr Exp to Cap Exp Decile 10	38.20%	30.58%	17.12%	7.13%	0.48%
Market Leaders, Shareholder Yield (%) Decile 10	21.88%	13.08%	3.17%	0.22%	0.00%
Small Stocks, EPS Change (%) Decile 10	32.05%	24.14%	17.76%	8.91%	4.84%
All Stocks, Free CF to Enterprise Value Decile 10	30.13%	16.10%	12.26%	5.57%	3.87%
Large Stocks, Debt Change (%) Decile 1	34.36%	22.74%	16.49%	9.58%	0.00%
All Stocks, Growth Composite Decile 10	28.60%	11.07%	5.92%	2.00%	0.00%
Large Stocks, Operating Margin Decile 10	43.95%	39.24%	22.41%	20.71%	12.83%
Market Leaders, Buyback Yield (%) Decile 10	23.22%	14.49%	4.44%	0.89%	0.00%
Large Stocks, Fin Strength Composite Decile 1	26.10%	12.27%	8.67%	3.79%	0.00%
Large Stocks, 12-Month Momentum, Decile 10	33.21%	14.29%	7.19%	4.01%	3.63%
Large Stocks, Cash Flow to Debt (%) Decile 10	38.96%	36.22%	29.18%	23.39%	16.95%
Small Stocks, Free CF to Enterprise Value Decile 10	29.37%	23.34%	18.18%	12.47%	8.96%
All Stocks, Debt Change (%) Decile 1	22.26%	8.05%	1.48%	0.00%	0.00%
Large Stocks, Earnings/ Price Decile 10	41.65%	30.18%	21.14%	15.81%	7.75%
All Stocks, Free Cash Flow to Price Decile 10	25.53%	10.87%	9.73%	6.01%	0.97%
Large Stocks, Net Operating Cash Flow to Price Decile 10	40.69%	22.94%	14.80%	7.35%	2.66%

(continued on next page)

T A B L E 28.2

Summary Base Rate Information for all Rolling One-, Three-, Five-, Seven-, and Ten-Year Periods, August 31, 1965, to December 31, 2009. Strategies Sorted by Compound Average Annual Return *(Continued)*

Strategy	Percent of time				
	1 year	3 years	5 years	7 years	10 years
Large Stocks, TATA Decile 1	27.06%	11.07%	5.71%	4.01%	0.00%
All Stocks, ROE Decile 10	36.28%	22.74%	18.60%	22.27%	25.67%
All Stocks, EPS Change ($) Decile 1	20.73%	11.27%	6.13%	2.90%	0.00%
Large Stocks, Earnings Quality Composite Decile 1	26.49%	14.69%	6.34%	0.89%	0.00%
US 30 Day TBill USD	33.21%	25.15%	23.89%	17.59%	17.68%
Large Stocks, Buyback Yield, Decile 10	27.26%	15.49%	4.23%	1.34%	0.00%
All Stocks, 12-Month Momentum, Decile 10	24.38%	7.65%	2.33%	1.56%	0.00%
Large Stocks, NOA Change (%) Decile 1	36.08%	23.34%	9.94%	6.46%	0.00%
Small Stocks, Free Cash Flow to Price Decile 10	27.26%	22.13%	16.07%	6.01%	1.69%
All Stocks, Earnings/ Price Decile 10	31.29%	16.30%	6.98%	0.89%	0.24%
All Stocks, EPS Change ($) Decile 10	21.31%	7.44%	6.55%	0.00%	0.00%
Small Stocks, Debt Change (%) Decile 1	22.46%	9.66%	2.11%	0.89%	0.00%
Small Stocks, 12-Month Momentum, Decile 10	20.92%	7.04%	3.38%	1.78%	0.00%
Large Stocks, Shareholder Yield, Decile 10	23.42%	13.08%	3.81%	1.56%	0.00%
All Stocks, EBITDA/ Enterprise Value Decile 10	30.13%	11.87%	6.98%	5.57%	1.94%
Large Stocks, 6-Month Momentum, Decile 10	28.98%	4.83%	1.27%	0.22%	0.00%
Small Stocks, Buyback Yield, Decile 10	16.51%	3.42%	0.85%	0.00%	0.00%
All Stocks, Net Margin Decile 10	37.04%	23.14%	20.30%	19.15%	20.82%
All Stocks, Buyback Yield, Decile 10	16.51%	2.41%	0.00%	0.00%	0.00%
Small Stocks, Shareholder Yield, Decile 10	18.43%	7.04%	2.54%	0.00%	0.00%
All Stocks, Depr Exp to Cap Exp Decile 10	26.30%	14.89%	8.03%	1.34%	0.00%
Small Stocks, Earnings/ Price Decile 10	29.37%	18.71%	10.15%	1.56%	0.24%
All Stocks, Sales to Enterprise Value Decile 10	32.44%	16.90%	16.07%	9.80%	7.02%
All Stocks, Shareholder Yield, Decile 10	19.58%	6.04%	1.06%	0.00%	0.00%
Large Stocks, EBITDA/ Enterprise Value Decile 10	34.36%	20.12%	15.86%	12.92%	6.30%
All Stocks, Operating Margin Decile 10	33.97%	19.32%	19.24%	18.71%	19.85%
All Stocks, ROA Decile 10	30.71%	18.51%	12.26%	9.58%	0.97%
Large Stocks, Value Composite1 Decile 10	37.24%	22.54%	14.80%	7.80%	2.18%
All Stocks, Fin Strength Composite Decile 1	16.89%	3.82%	0.00%	0.00%	0.00%
Large Stocks, Sales to Price Decile 10	38.00%	24.35%	12.05%	6.68%	2.18%
Large Stocks, Value Composite3 Decile 10	36.28%	23.14%	12.68%	7.57%	1.94%
Large Stocks, Value Composite2 Decile 10	36.28%	21.73%	12.90%	6.90%	2.18%

(continued on next page)

Summary Base Rate Information for all Rolling One-, Three-, Five-, Seven-, and Ten-Year Periods, August 31, 1965, to December 31, 2009. Strategies Sorted by Compound Average Annual Return *(Continued)*

Strategy	Percent of time				
	1 year	3 years	5 years	7 years	10 years
Large Stocks, Sales to Enterprise Value Decile 10	32.25%	20.32%	14.59%	8.69%	4.36%
All Stocks, TATA Decile 1	25.14%	7.24%	0.63%	0.00%	0.00%
All Stocks, Earnings Quality Composite Decile 10	26.10%	12.88%	2.54%	0.00%	0.00%
Small Stocks, TATA Decile 1	23.03%	8.45%	3.17%	1.34%	0.00%
All Stocks, 6-Month Momentum, Decile 10	14.78%	2.62%	1.06%	1.34%	0.00%
Small Stocks, EBITDA/ Enterprise Value Decile 10	23.61%	12.27%	4.86%	4.90%	1.21%
Small Stocks, Depr Exp to Cap Exp Decile 10	29.56%	19.92%	13.11%	4.45%	0.00%
All Stocks, Net Operating Cash Flow to Price Decile 10	28.02%	11.47%	1.90%	2.90%	0.00%
All Stocks, Sales to Price Decile 10	32.63%	22.13%	14.80%	7.80%	2.18%
All Stocks, NOA Change (%) Decile 1	24.38%	8.85%	1.69%	0.00%	0.00%
Small Stocks, ROE Decile 10	29.94%	25.96%	20.30%	17.59%	13.80%
All Stocks, Value Composite1 (VC1) Decile 10	33.59%	20.52%	12.05%	6.68%	0.24%
Small Stocks, 6-Month Momentum, Decile 10	11.32%	3.02%	1.06%	1.34%	0.00%
Small Stocks, Sales to Enterprise Value Decile 10	31.09%	18.31%	16.49%	10.69%	10.90%
Small Stocks, Net Operating Cash Flow to Price Decile 10	23.80%	10.26%	2.11%	0.67%	0.00%
All Stocks, Value Composite2 (VC2) Decile 10	32.44%	19.52%	10.57%	5.12%	0.24%
Small Stocks, Cash Flow to Debt (%) Decile 10	26.68%	17.10%	10.36%	2.45%	0.00%
All Stocks, Value Composite3 (VC3) Decile 10	31.67%	19.32%	7.40%	4.68%	0.24%
All Stocks, Cash Flow to Debt (%) Decile 10	25.34%	10.66%	5.71%	2.00%	0.00%
Small Stocks, NOA Change (%) Decile 1	25.53%	12.68%	6.13%	2.67%	0.00%
Small Stocks, ROA Decile 10	23.80%	11.07%	6.34%	6.24%	3.63%
Small Stocks, Operating Margin Decile 10	26.30%	17.91%	17.12%	11.80%	7.26%
Small Stocks, Net Margin Decile 10	28.60%	20.32%	18.60%	12.03%	7.99%
Small Stocks, Sales to Price Decile 10	30.71%	20.93%	16.70%	11.80%	8.47%
Small Stocks, Value Composite1 (VC1), Decile 10	28.21%	14.89%	9.73%	4.90%	0.97%
Small Stocks, Value Composite2 (VC2), Decile 10	28.79%	13.48%	8.88%	4.23%	0.48%
Small Stocks, Value Composite3 (VC3), Decile 10	27.64%	13.48%	7.40%	3.79%	0.48%

RISK-ADJUSTED RETURNS

Table 28.3 ranks the strategies by risk-adjusted return (Sharpe ratio), and Figures 28.3 and 28.4 show the five strategies with the highest and lowest risk-adjusted returns. Table 28.3 is a much more appropriate table for most investors to study when they're trying to decide which strategy is right for them. When you look only at absolute return, you're blind to how rocky the road ahead might be. In a perfect world, investors would simply stick with long-term strategies that had the best returns with the highest base rates, but we all know that we don't live in that world. Risk matters.

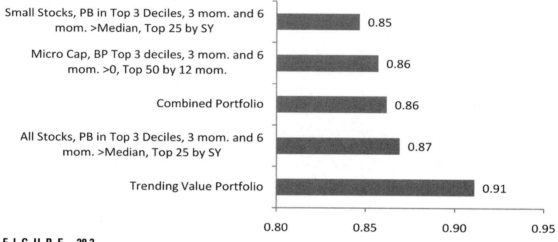

FIGURE 28.3

The five strategies with the highest risk-adjusted return (Sharpe Ratio), August 31, 1965 to December 31, 2009

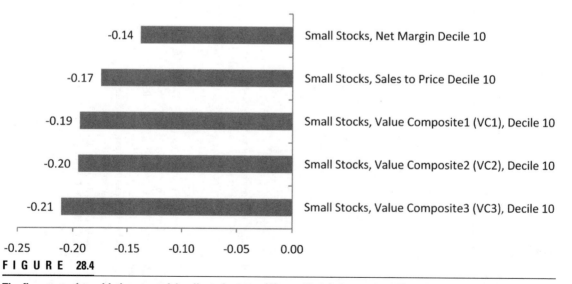

FIGURE 28.4

The five strategies with the worst risk-adjusted returns (Sharpe Ratio), August 31, 1965 to December 31, 2009

All Strategies for Monthly Data Series, August 31, 1965, to December 31, 2009. Strategies Sorted by Risk-Adjusted Return (Sharpe Ratio)

Strategy	Geometric mean	Standard deviation (%)	T-Statistics	$10,000 becomes	Sharpe ratio	Tracking error	Downside risk	Largest drawdown	Beta
Trending Value Portfolio	21.08%	17.66%	7.87	$48,246,947	0.91	9.04	13.74%	-50.55%	0.81
All Stocks, VC2 in Top Decile, Top 50 by 6 mom.	19.74%	16.70%	7.79	$29,366,965	0.88	8.69	12.89%	-49.64%	0.77
All Stocks, PB in Top 3 Deciles, 3 mom. and 6 mom. >Median, Top 25 by SY	18.45%	15.48%	7.86	$18,224,488	0.87	9.24	12.11%	-47.66%	0.71
Combined Consumer Staples/Utilities Portfolio	16.56%	13.42%	8.10	$8,933,565	0.86	12.75	9.18%	-34.39%	0.52
Microcap, BP Top 3 deciles, 3 mom. and 6 mom. >0, Top 50 by 12 mom.	21.43%	19.17%	7.44	$54,772,842	0.86	8.86	14.46%	-55.26%	0.84
Microcap, BP Top 3 deciles, 3 mom. and 6 mom. >0, Top 25 by 12 mom.	22.33%	20.38%	7.33	$75,985,718	0.85	9.73	14.88%	-53.89%	0.88
Small Stocks, PB in Top 3 Deciles, 3 mom. and 6 mom. >Median, Top 25 by SY	18.84%	16.35%	7.63	$21,049,215	0.85	9.66	13.37%	-49.20%	0.70
Microcap, BP Top 3 deciles, 3 mom. and 6 mom. >Median Top 25 by 12 mom.	21.78%	20.01%	7.29	$62,181,638	0.84	10.05	14.68%	-55.64%	0.85
All Stocks, PB in Top 3 Deciles, 3 mom. and 6 mom. >0, Top 25 by SY	18.02%	15.63%	7.63	$15,493,763	0.83	9.18	12.40%	-53.00%	0.72
Small Stocks, PB in Top 3 Deciles, 3 mom. and 6 mom. >0, Top 25 by SY	18.28%	16.09%	7.54	$17,082,685	0.83	9.82	13.06%	-52.42%	0.69
All Stocks, BP and 6 mom. >Median, Top 25 by SY	17.77%	15.77%	7.48	$14,120,418	0.81	8.55	12.47%	-53.61%	0.74
All Stocks, 3 mom. and 6 mom. >Median, Top 25 by SY	18.73%	17.05%	7.33	$20,230,058	0.81	8.40	13.50%	-52.27%	0.80
Small Stocks, VC2 in Top 3 Deciles, 3 and 6 mom.>Median, Top 50 by 6 mom.	19.78%	18.42%	7.20	$29,832,100	0.80	8.38	14.24%	-53.05%	0.82
Small Stocks, BP and 6 mom. >Median, Top 25 SY	17.64%	15.77%	7.44	$13,434,848	0.80	9.69	12.30%	-50.87%	0.68
Small Stocks, 3 mom. and 6 mom. >Median, Top 25 SY	18.37%	16.72%	7.33	$17,638,388	0.80	8.39	13.30%	-52.57%	0.75
All Stocks, PB in Top 3 Deciles, 3 mom. and 6 mom. >0, Top 50 by SY	17.51%	15.66%	7.43	$12,774,895	0.80	8.85	12.40%	-55.07%	0.72
All Stocks, PB in Top 3 Deciles, 3 mom. and 6 mom. >Median, Top 50 by SY	17.54%	15.84%	7.37	$12,923,562	0.79	8.80	12.68%	-49.30%	0.73
All Stocks, VC2 in Top 3 Deciles, 3 mom. and 6 mom. >Median, Top 50 by 6 mom.	19.36%	18.26%	7.12	$25,562,163	0.79	7.96	13.98%	-53.49%	0.86

(continued on next page)

T A B L E 28.3

All Strategies for Monthly Data Series, August 31, 1965, to December 31, 2009. Strategies Sorted by Risk-Adjusted Return (Sharpe Ratio) *(Continued)*

Strategy	Geometric mean	Standard deviation (%)	T-Statistics	$10,000 becomes	Sharpe ratio	Tracking error	Downside risk	Largest drawdown	Beta
Small Stocks, PB in Top 3 Deciles, 3 mom. and 6 mom. >0, Top 50 by SY	17.85%	16.36%	7.28	$14,539,804	0.79	9.20	13.18%	-55.34%	0.72
All Stocks, 3 mom. and 6 mom. >Median, Top 50 by SY	17.54%	15.97%	7.33	$12,947,507	0.79	7.43	12.87%	-50.57%	0.77
US 30 Day TBill USD	5.64%	0.82%	44.88	$113,721	0.78	16.78	0.00%	0.00%	NA
All Stocks, BP and 6 mom. >Median, Top 25 by BBY	18.59%	17.53%	7.11	$19,209,981	0.78	7.90	13.47%	-53.11%	0.83
Small Stocks, Value Composite2 (VC2), Decile 1	19.03%	18.14%	7.04	$22,566,623	0.77	8.29	13.73%	-60.05%	0.81
All Stocks, BP and 6 mom. >Median, Top 50 by SY	16.66%	15.13%	7.33	$9,260,473	0.77	8.74	11.78%	-51.23%	0.71
Small Stocks, PB in Top 3 Deciles, 3 mom. and 6 mom. >Median, Top 50 by SY	18.15%	17.08%	7.13	$16,290,759	0.77	9.00	13.91%	-49.60%	0.75
Small Stocks, 3 mom. and 6 mom. >Median, Top 50 SY	17.26%	15.94%	7.23	$11,629,675	0.77	7.97	12.74%	-50.21%	0.72
Small Stocks, BP and 6 mom. >Median, Top 50 SY	16.85%	15.48%	7.26	$9,965,964	0.77	9.51	12.06%	-48.74%	0.68
Small Stocks, Value Composite3 (VC3), Decile 1	19.37%	18.92%	6.91	$25,670,891	0.76	7.95	14.21%	-59.68%	0.85
Small Stocks, BP and 6 mom. >Median, Top 25 BBY	18.44%	17.92%	6.94	$18,102,174	0.75	8.66	13.99%	-50.98%	0.79
Small Stocks, VC2 in Top 3 Deciles, 3 and 6 mom.>Median, Top 25 by 6 mom.	19.85%	19.85%	6.79	$30,609,593	0.75	9.00	15.26%	-57.64%	0.87
Small Stocks, EBITDA/Enterprise Value Decile 1	18.96%	18.70%	6.85	$22,038,871	0.75	6.67	13.88%	-55.94%	0.86
All Stocks, SY and 6 mom. >Median, Top 50 by BP	17.82%	17.30%	6.94	$14,390,482	0.74	8.40	13.49%	-55.44%	0.81
All Stocks, VC2 in Top 3 Deciles, 3 mom. and 6 mom. >Median, Top 25 by 6 mom.	19.54%	19.70%	6.75	$27,324,492	0.74	8.62	14.96%	-56.56%	0.92
Small Stocks, SY and 6 mom. >Median, Top 50 BP	17.84%	17.59%	6.85	$14,481,971	0.73	8.89	14.20%	-56.52%	0.77
All Stocks, BP and 6 mom. >Median, Top 50 by BBY	17.51%	17.17%	6.88	$12,801,191	0.73	7.47	13.32%	-50.66%	0.82
Small Stocks, SY and 6 mom. >Median, Top 25 BP	18.49%	18.70%	6.72	$18,470,590	0.72	9.29	14.76%	-59.17%	0.81
Small Stocks, Value Composite1 (VC1), Decile 1	18.85%	19.37%	6.62	$21,149,675	0.72	7.86	14.51%	-60.23%	0.87

(continued on next page)

T A B L E 28.3

All Strategies for Monthly Data Series, August 31, 1965, to December 31, 2009. Strategies Sorted by Risk-Adjusted Return (Sharpe Ratio) *(Continued)*

Strategy	Geometric mean	Standard deviation (%)	T-Statistics	$10,000 becomes	Sharpe ratio	Tracking error	Downside risk	Largest drawdown	Beta
Small Stocks, PB in Top 3 Deciles, 3 mom. and 6 mom. >0, Top 50 by 12 mom.	18.16%	18.42%	6.70	$16,333,580	0.71	8.31	14.70%	-56.04%	0.82
Small Stocks, BP and 6 mom. >Median, Top 50 BBY	17.30%	17.24%	6.79	$11,818,630	0.71	8.24	13.68%	-49.81%	0.77
All Stocks, SY and 6 mom. >Median, Top 25 by BP	18.13%	18.42%	6.69	$16,166,786	0.71	9.02	14.13%	-58.68%	0.85
Small Stocks, PB in Top 3 Deciles, 3 mom. and 6 mom. >Median, Top 50 by 12 mom.	17.97%	18.48%	6.62	$15,185,920	0.70	8.16	14.68%	-54.41%	0.82
All Stocks, Value Composite2 (VC2) Decile 1	17.12%	17.32%	6.69	$11,050,085	0.70	8.24	12.85%	-58.07%	0.81
All Stocks, PB in Top 3 Deciles, 3 mom. and 6 mom. >0, Top 50 by 12 mom.	17.71%	18.16%	6.64	$13,766,110	0.70	7.82	14.38%	-55.40%	0.86
Small Stocks, 3 mom. and 6 mom. >Median, Top 50 BP	17.92%	18.75%	6.53	$14,890,544	0.69	7.63	15.01%	-56.80%	0.85
All Stocks, Value Composite3 (VC3) Decile 1	17.20%	17.89%	6.54	$11,390,104	0.68	7.64	13.35%	-58.04%	0.85
All Stocks, PB in Top 3 Deciles, 3 mom. and 6 mom. >Median, Top 50 by 12 mom.	17.38%	18.29%	6.50	$12,174,722	0.68	7.84	14.52%	-55.95%	0.87
All Stocks, Shareholder Yield, Decile 1	15.43%	15.43%	6.75	$5,792,778	0.68	7.67	11.90%	-54.70%	0.74
All Stocks, 3 mom. and 6 mom. >Median, Top 50 by BP	17.52%	18.53%	6.47	$12,808,436	0.68	7.29	14.79%	-57.03%	0.89
Small Stocks, PB in Top 3 Deciles, 3 mom. and 6 mom. >0, Top 25 by 12 mom.	18.33%	19.79%	6.38	$17,383,935	0.67	8.84	15.48%	-59.65%	0.87
Small Stocks, PB in Top 3 Deciles, 3 mom. and 6 mom. >Median, Top 25 by 12 mom.	18.34%	19.87%	6.36	$17,440,767	0.67	8.86	15.79%	-59.85%	0.87
Small Stocks, BP and BBY and 3 mom. >Median, Top 50 by 6 mom.	17.24%	18.54%	6.38	$11,531,126	0.66	7.19	14.72%	-56.03%	0.84
Small Stocks, 3 mom. and 6 mom. >Median, Top 25 BP	18.00%	19.84%	6.27	$15,378,402	0.66	8.48	15.58%	-59.60%	0.88
Small Stocks, Shareholder Yield, Decile 1	15.45%	15.96%	6.57	$5,834,309	0.65	8.20	12.42%	-55.73%	0.72
All Stocks, Value Composite1 (VC1) Decile 1	16.98%	18.32%	6.35	$10,468,074	0.65	7.62	13.56%	-57.78%	0.87
All Stocks, PB in Top 3 Deciles, 3 mom. and 6 mom. >0, Top 25 by 12 mom.	17.74%	19.54%	6.27	$13,953,383	0.65	8.52	15.33%	-59.20%	0.92
Small Stocks, BP and SY >Median, Top 50 by 6 mom.	16.68%	17.96%	6.36	$9,325,854	0.65	7.49	13.97%	-55.06%	0.81

(continued on next page)

T A B L E 28.3

All Strategies for Monthly Data Series, August 31, 1965, to December 31, 2009. Strategies Sorted by Risk-Adjusted Return (Sharpe Ratio) (Continued)

Strategy	Geometric mean	Standard deviation (%)	T-Statistics	$10,000 becomes	Sharpe ratio	Tracking error	Downside risk	Largest drawdown	Beta
All Stocks, PB in Top 3 Deciles, 3 mom. and 6 mom. >Median, Top 25 by 12 mom.	17.93%	19.93%	6.23	$14,973,336	0.65	8.57	15.68%	-60.95%	0.94
All Stocks, BP and SY >Median, Top 50 by 6 mom.	16.35%	17.69%	6.33	$8,235,994	0.64	6.74	13.62%	-55.92%	0.86
Small Stocks, Earnings/ Price Decile 1	17.53%	19.58%	6.18	$12,875,519	0.64	7.56	14.34%	-56.31%	0.88
Large Stocks, 3 mom. and 6 mom. >Median, Top 25 by SY	14.85%	15.40%	6.54	$4,632,919	0.64	6.79	11.84%	-49.12%	0.84
All Stocks, EBITDA/ Enterprise Value Decile 1	16.46%	17.95%	6.29	$8,570,603	0.64	6.33	13.17%	-54.29%	0.88
Small Stocks, BP and BBY >Median, Top 50 by 6 mom.	17.05%	18.91%	6.22	$10,728,796	0.64	7.19	14.91%	-56.68%	0.86
All Stocks, BP and BBY and 3 mom. >Median, Top 50 by 6 mom.	16.76%	18.58%	6.22	$9,622,609	0.63	6.62	14.32%	-56.58%	0.91
Small Stocks, BP and SY >Median, Top 25 by 6 mom.	17.26%	19.40%	6.16	$11,646,050	0.63	7.72	14.98%	-59.63%	0.87
Large Stocks, Shareholder Yield, Decile 1	14.48%	15.08%	6.51	$4,021,172	0.63	7.17	11.08%	-52.66%	0.81
Microcap, PSR#gt1, 3 mom. and 6 mom. >0, Top 10 by 12 mom.	22.29%	27.57%	5.82	$74,952,894	0.63	15.14	18.65%	-57.64%	1.13
All Stocks, 3 mom. and 6 mom. >Median, Top 25 by BP	17.31%	19.66%	6.11	$11,864,813	0.63	8.34	15.30%	-60.50%	0.93
Small Stocks, BP and BBY and 3 mom. >Median, Top 25 by 6 mom.	17.47%	20.09%	6.06	$12,575,407	0.62	7.75	15.78%	-59.70%	0.91
All Stocks, BP and SY >Median, Top 25 by 6 mom.	16.80%	19.04%	6.11	$9,754,288	0.62	7.31	14.56%	-59.75%	0.92
All Stocks, Buyback Yield, Decile 1	15.74%	17.39%	6.22	$6,521,542	0.62	5.82	13.17%	-53.28%	0.86
All Stocks, BP and BBY >Median, Top 50 by 6 mom.	16.66%	18.91%	6.10	$9,264,340	0.62	6.66	14.46%	-57.24%	0.92
Small Stocks, Free CF to Enterprise Value Decile 1	17.54%	20.60%	5.95	$12,912,118	0.61	6.67	14.82%	-59.25%	0.95
Small Stocks, BP and BBY >Median, Top 25 by 6 mom.	17.42%	20.49%	5.95	$12,337,258	0.61	7.83	15.96%	-61.12%	0.92
Small Stocks, Sales to Enterprise Value Decile 1	17.13%	20.02%	5.97	$11,091,047	0.61	7.00	14.65%	-64.82%	0.91
All Stocks Growth	20.23%	25.16%	5.76	$35,282,794	0.61	12.00	18.09%	-59.68%	1.16
Large Stocks, Buyback Yield, Decile 1	14.91%	16.40%	6.23	$4,738,299	0.60	5.68	12.03%	-51.56%	0.92
Small Stocks, Net Operating Cash Flow to Price Decile 1	17.39%	20.53%	5.92	$12,234,992	0.60	7.99	15.51%	-65.23%	0.92

(continued on next page)

All Strategies for Monthly Data Series, August 31, 1965, to December 31, 2009. Strategies Sorted by Risk-Adjusted Return (Sharpe Ratio) *(Continued)*

Strategy	Geometric mean	Standard deviation (%)	T-Statistics	$10,000 becomes	Sharpe ratio	Tracking error	Downside risk	Largest drawdown	Beta
Market Leaders, Top 2 Deciles VC2, Top 25 by 6 mom.	15.34%	17.17%	6.14	$5,585,470	0.60	6.03	11.92%	-52.74%	0.98
All Stocks, BP and BBY and 3 mom. >Median, Top 25 by 6 mom.	17.06%	20.05%	5.95	$10,767,673	0.60	7.67	15.37%	-61.21%	0.96
Small Stocks, Dividend Yield, Decile 1	13.83%	14.83%	6.34	$3,118,403	0.60	11.50	11.66%	-62.48%	0.60
All Stocks, Earnings/ Price Decile 1	16.11%	18.70%	5.98	$7,500,626	0.59	7.53	13.69%	-59.13%	0.89
All Stocks, BP and BBY >Median, Top 25 by 6 mom.	17.08%	20.38%	5.88	$10,877,510	0.59	7.81	15.49%	-61.21%	0.98
Small Stocks, PSR#gt1, 3 mom. and 6 mom. >0, Top 50 12 mom.	18.80%	23.29%	5.75	$20,778,182	0.59	9.96	17.00%	-56.62%	1.02
Market Leaders, 3 mom. and 6 mom. >Median, Top 50 by SY	14.65%	16.32%	6.16	$4,289,473	0.59	5.09	11.94%	-56.33%	0.95
Cornerstone Value, Improved 50	14.55%	16.19%	6.16	$4,133,217	0.59	5.11	11.78%	-56.01%	0.94
All Stocks, Net Operating Cash Flow to Price Decile 1	16.00%	18.70%	5.94	$7,206,112	0.59	7.75	14.13%	-60.87%	0.89
Large Stocks, BP and 6 mom. >Median, Top 25 by SY	13.72%	14.84%	6.30	$2,990,404	0.59	7.53	11.21%	-52.63%	0.79
All Stocks, Fin Strength Composite Decile 10	15.01%	17.05%	6.07	$4,923,801	0.59	4.25	12.74%	-50.82%	0.87
Market Leaders, 3 mom. and 6 mom. >Median, Top 25 by SY	15.02%	17.11%	6.05	$4,954,349	0.59	6.45	12.74%	-57.92%	0.97
Cornerstone Value, Improved 25	14.94%	17.00%	6.05	$4,789,019	0.58	6.52	12.58%	-57.57%	0.96
Market Leaders, Top 2 Deciles VC2, Top 50 by 6 mom.	15.00%	17.16%	6.03	$4,912,365	0.58	5.27	11.92%	-53.43%	1.00
Small Stocks, Buyback Yield, Decile 1	15.55%	18.17%	5.94	$6,074,251	0.58	6.33	13.90%	-54.20%	0.84
Market Leaders, Shareholder Yield (%) Decile 1	14.72%	16.77%	6.04	$4,403,707	0.58	6.38	12.43%	-56.44%	0.95
Large Stocks, BP and 6 mom. >Median, Top 25 by BBY	14.56%	16.52%	6.06	$4,140,567	0.58	6.42	12.45%	-53.90%	0.91
Market Leaders, VC2>Median, Top 25 by SY	14.97%	17.25%	5.99	$4,847,391	0.58	6.60	12.80%	-58.21%	0.97
Market Leaders, VC2>Median, Top 50 by SY	14.54%	16.51%	6.06	$4,101,645	0.58	5.23	12.12%	-57.42%	0.96
Large Stocks, 3 mom. and 6 mom. >Median, Top 50 by SY	13.56%	14.90%	6.21	$2,804,780	0.57	5.91	11.29%	-48.95%	0.83
All Stocks, Free CF to Enterprise Value Decile 1	15.90%	19.29%	5.78	$6,927,643	0.57	6.00	14.27%	-56.81%	0.95
Microcap, PSR#gt1, Top 25 by 12 mom.	20.33%	27.14%	5.47	$36,615,298	0.56	15.45	17.87%	-59.22%	1.09
Small Stocks, Free Cash Flow to Price Decile 1	16.77%	20.92%	5.67	$9,674,166	0.56	7.61	15.32%	-63.76%	0.95

(continued on next page)

T A B L E 28.3

All Strategies for Monthly Data Series, August 31, 1965, to December 31. 2009. Strategies Sorted by Risk-Adjusted Return (Sharpe Ratio) *(Continued)*

Strategy	Geometric mean	Standard deviation (%)	T-Statistics	$10,000 becomes	Sharpe ratio	Tracking error	Downside risk	Largest drawdown	Beta
All Stocks, Dividend Yield, Decile 1	13.12%	14.44%	6.19	$2,360,400	0.56	11.38	10.78%	-61.17%	0.61
Market Leaders, Buyback Yield (%) Decile 1	14.28%	16.52%	5.97	$3,721,523	0.56	5.24	11.92%	-53.60%	0.96
Large Stocks, Value Composite2 Decile 1	14.20%	16.47%	5.95	$3,607,389	0.56	8.69	11.66%	-62.69%	0.85
Market Leaders, 3 mom. and 6 mom. >Median, Top 25 by VC2	14.23%	16.52%	5.95	$3,639,417	0.56	5.22	12.04%	-51.56%	0.96
All Stocks, Earnings Quality Composite Decile 1	15.79%	19.36%	5.72	$6,642,587	0.56	4.18	14.09%	-54.83%	0.98
Large Stocks, 3 mom. and 6 mom. >Median, Top 25 by BP	13.97%	16.11%	5.98	$3,291,236	0.56	6.72	12.02%	-51.72%	0.88
Large Stocks, SY and 6 mom. >Median, Top 25 by BP	13.70%	15.69%	6.00	$2,962,965	0.55	7.77	11.11%	-53.62%	0.83
Large Stocks, Value Composite3 Decile 1	14.17%	16.57%	5.91	$3,555,826	0.55	8.16	11.87%	-60.55%	0.87
Large Stocks, BP and 6 mom. >Median, Top 50 by SY	13.24%	14.94%	6.07	$2,474,341	0.55	6.73	11.03%	-51.38%	0.82
All Stocks, Sales to Enterprise Value Decile 1	15.44%	18.96%	5.71	$5,805,576	0.55	6.58	14.04%	-62.29%	0.93
Large Stocks, BP and BBY >Median, Top 25 by 6 mom.	14.21%	16.73%	5.88	$3,613,341	0.55	6.14	12.43%	-55.14%	0.93
All Stocks, Free Cash Flow to Price Decile 1	15.31%	18.99%	5.66	$5,539,519	0.54	7.32	14.20%	-61.66%	0.91
Small Stocks, BP and 3 mom. and 6 mom. >Median, Top 50 12 mom.	15.62%	19.60%	5.63	$6,226,529	0.54	7.70	15.16%	-61.91%	0.88
Large Stocks, BBY >Median, Top 50 by DIVY	12.68%	14.43%	6.02	$1,990,472	0.53	9.40	9.88%	-55.30%	0.71
Large Stocks, BP and BBY and 3 mom. >Median, Top 25 by 6 mom.	13.85%	16.62%	5.78	$3,143,237	0.53	6.19	12.45%	-53.96%	0.92
Large Stocks, BP and SY >Median, Top 25 by 6 mom.	13.53%	16.03%	5.84	$2,777,684	0.53	6.51	11.91%	-53.48%	0.88
Large Stocks, BP and BBY and 3 mom. >Median, Top 50 by 6 mom.	13.54%	16.05%	5.83	$2,786,966	0.53	6.04	11.85%	-52.16%	0.89
Large Stocks, EBITDA/ Enterprise Value Decile 1	14.05%	17.01%	5.74	$3,397,255	0.53	8.34	11.45%	-52.85%	0.89
Large Stocks, BP and BBY >Median, Top 50 by 6 mom.	13.50%	15.99%	5.84	$2,747,543	0.53	5.91	11.73%	-52.86%	0.89
Market Leaders, Value Composite 2 Decile 1 (High)	14.84%	18.52%	5.62	$4,616,793	0.53	7.10	13.29%	-62.16%	1.05
Large Stocks, BP and 6 mom. >Median, Top 50 by BBY	13.41%	15.86%	5.84	$2,643,957	0.53	5.79	11.87%	-51.52%	0.89
Large Stocks, BP and SY >Median, Top 50 by 6 mom.	12.99%	15.32%	5.85	$2,241,830	0.52	6.48	11.12%	-51.37%	0.84

(continued on next page)

All Strategies for Monthly Data Series, August 31, 1965, to December 31, 2009. Strategies Sorted by Risk-Adjusted Return (Sharpe Ratio) *(Continued)*

Strategy	Geometric mean	Standard deviation (%)	T-Statistics	$10,000 becomes	Sharpe ratio	Tracking error	Downside risk	Largest drawdown	Beta
Market Leaders, Value Composite 3 Decile 1 (High)	14.49%	18.29%	5.57	$4,028,546	0.52	6.90	13.18%	-60.13%	1.03
Large Stocks, Net Operating Cash Flow to Price Decile 1	13.51%	16.45%	5.71	$2,758,118	0.52	8.12	11.75%	-62.15%	0.87
Market Leaders, EBITDA/ Enterprise Value Decile 1	14.39%	18.15%	5.56	$3,884,224	0.52	7.53	11.91%	-52.21%	1.01
Large Stocks, SY and 6 mom. >Median, Top 50 by BP	12.85%	15.20%	5.84	$2,130,142	0.52	6.80	11.05%	-51.78%	0.83
Large Stocks, BBY >Median, Top 25 by DIVY	12.60%	14.83%	5.85	$1,929,366	0.51	10.99	10.23%	-57.02%	0.68
Market Leaders, 3 mom. and 6 mom. >Median, Top 50 by VC2	13.23%	16.11%	5.70	$2,469,214	0.51	4.25	11.75%	-51.88%	0.95
Small Stocks, BP and 3 mom. and 6 mom. >Median, Top 25 12 mom.	15.76%	21.47%	5.30	$6,562,828	0.50	8.68	16.41%	-65.51%	0.95
Large Stocks, SY and 3 mom. and 6 mom. >Median, Top 25 by 12 mom.	13.86%	17.74%	5.50	$3,159,235	0.50	6.93	13.20%	-57.49%	0.98
Large Stocks, Value Composite1 Decile 1	13.43%	16.90%	5.56	$2,673,161	0.50	8.28	11.99%	-61.86%	0.89
Market Leaders, Value Composite 1 Decile 1 (High)	14.27%	18.69%	5.41	$3,705,032	0.50	6.75	13.35%	-60.56%	1.07
Large Stocks, SY and 3 mom. and 6 mom. >Median, Top 50 by 12 mom.	12.95%	16.09%	5.61	$2,208,672	0.49	5.57	11.69%	-52.55%	0.91
Cornerstone Value, 25 Div Yld	13.49%	17.22%	5.49	$2,731,351	0.49	7.91	12.25%	-65.01%	0.94
Market Leaders, NOA Change (%) Decile 10	13.17%	16.62%	5.54	$2,411,698	0.49	5.24	12.18%	-52.95%	0.96
Market Leaders, PSR#gtavg, Top 25 by 12 mom.	13.35%	17.01%	5.50	$2,586,657	0.49	6.12	11.58%	-48.31%	0.97
Large Stocks, Earnings/ Price Decile 1	13.52%	17.37%	5.47	$2,762,152	0.49	8.35	12.15%	-65.62%	0.91
Large Stocks, 3 mom. and 6 mom. >Median, Top 50 by BP	12.67%	15.78%	5.59	$1,980,131	0.49	5.89	11.95%	-53.26%	0.88
All Stocks, BP and 3 mom. and 6 mom. >Median, Top 50 by 12 mom.	14.69%	19.99%	5.27	$4,359,495	0.48	7.64	15.33%	-64.48%	0.96
Market Leaders, TATA Decile 10	13.54%	17.66%	5.40	$2,783,394	0.48	6.89	12.46%	-56.44%	0.99
Large Stocks, Earnings Quality Composite Decile 10	12.76%	16.14%	5.52	$2,054,668	0.48	6.43	10.98%	-49.00%	0.89
All Stocks, SY and 3 mom. and 6 mom. >Median, Top 50 by 12 mom.	15.08%	20.97%	5.20	$5,057,750	0.48	8.28	15.99%	-61.15%	1.00
Market Leaders, Dividend Yield (%) Decile 1	13.13%	16.96%	5.43	$2,371,523	0.48	7.59	12.07%	-64.59%	0.93

(continued on next page)

T A B L E   28.3

All Strategies for Monthly Data Series, August 31, 1965, to December 31, 2009. Strategies Sorted by Risk-Adjusted Return (Sharpe Ratio) *(Continued)*

Strategy	Geometric mean	Standard deviation (%)	T-Statistics	$10,000 becomes	Sharpe ratio	Tracking error	Downside risk	Largest drawdown	Beta
Large Stocks, Free CF to Enterprise Value Decile 1	13.20%	17.23%	5.39	$2,436,321	0.48	6.94	12.36%	-59.42%	0.94
Large Stocks, Accruals to Price Decile 10	12.61%	16.08%	5.48	$1,935,038	0.47	7.47	11.20%	-53.48%	0.86
Market Leaders, Free CF to Enterprise Value Decile 1	13.75%	18.60%	5.26	$3,026,571	0.47	7.15	13.09%	-62.79%	1.05
Small Stocks, SY and 3 mom. and 6 mom. >Median, Top 50 12 mom.	14.95%	21.24%	5.11	$4,809,289	0.47	7.83	16.12%	-58.10%	0.96
Market Leaders, PSR#gravg, Top 50 by 12 mom.	12.79%	16.68%	5.39	$2,078,710	0.47	4.27	11.86%	-52.04%	0.99
Market Leaders, Sales to Enterprise Value Decile 1	13.04%	17.27%	5.33	$2,288,339	0.47	6.08	12.05%	-51.07%	0.99
Market Leaders, Net Operating Cash Flow to Price Decile 1	13.72%	18.76%	5.21	$2,983,711	0.46	7.09	12.99%	-64.38%	1.06
Market Leaders, Return 6 Month Decile 1	13.41%	18.27%	5.23	$2,652,260	0.46	8.67	12.99%	-58.00%	0.98
All Stocks, BP and 3 mom. and 6 mom. >Median, Top 25 by 12 mom.	15.05%	22.01%	5.02	$5,010,429	0.46	9.15	16.69%	-68.16%	1.04
Market Leaders, Earnings/ Price Decile 1	13.67%	19.07%	5.13	$2,925,600	0.45	7.25	13.12%	-62.69%	1.08
Large Stocks, Sales to Enterprise Value Decile 1	12.49%	16.68%	5.28	$1,847,483	0.45	6.98	11.98%	-52.75%	0.91
Large Stocks, Dividend Yield, Decile 1	11.42%	14.33%	5.52	$1,209,519	0.45	11.38	9.78%	-58.55%	0.64
Large Stocks, BBY and 3 mom. >Median, Top 50 by 12 mom.	12.87%	17.61%	5.20	$2,145,512	0.45	6.29	12.75%	-54.15%	0.98
All Stocks, Accruals to Price Decile 10	14.10%	20.40%	5.01	$3,464,914	0.45	6.84	15.03%	-63.33%	1.00
Market Leaders, Accruals to Price Decile 10	13.17%	18.38%	5.12	$2,412,200	0.44	7.28	12.73%	-54.81%	1.03
Small Stocks, Sales to Price Decile 1	14.84%	22.46%	4.88	$4,618,693	0.44	8.79	16.13%	-70.68%	1.00
Large Stocks, BBY and 3 mom. >Median, Top 25 by 12 mom.	13.45%	19.45%	5.00	$2,691,570	0.43	8.42	14.25%	-59.35%	1.05
All Stocks, Book to Price, Decile 1	14.13%	21.04%	4.91	$3,499,602	0.43	8.08	15.35%	-69.20%	1.01
All Stocks, Sales to Price Decile 1	14.06%	20.94%	4.91	$3,405,339	0.43	7.78	15.40%	-65.98%	1.01
Large Stocks, BP and 3 mom. and 6 mom. >Median, Top 50 by 12 mom.	12.10%	16.50%	5.19	$1,584,677	0.43	5.93	12.67%	-55.90%	0.92
Large Stocks, Book to Price, Decile 1	12.93%	18.43%	5.03	$2,190,230	0.43	8.42	13.15%	-67.47%	0.98
Small Stocks, Operating Margin Decile 1	11.81%	16.07%	5.19	$1,409,381	0.42	8.78	12.59%	-53.55%	0.71
Market Leaders, Net Margin Decile 1	11.63%	15.77%	5.19	$1,310,481	0.42	6.33	10.23%	-46.73%	0.89
Small Stocks, Book to Price, Decile 1	14.26%	22.11%	4.77	$3,686,837	0.42	8.49	16.13%	-69.88%	0.99
Large Stocks, Free Cash Flow to Price Decile 1	12.11%	17.00%	5.07	$1,589,264	0.42	8.00	12.15%	-63.99%	0.90

(continued on next page)

All Strategies for Monthly Data Series, August 31, 1965, to December 31, 2009. Strategies Sorted by Risk-Adjusted Return (Sharpe Ratio) *(Continued)*

Strategy	Geometric mean	Standard deviation (%)	T-Statistics	$10,000 becomes	Sharpe ratio	Tracking error	Downside risk	Largest drawdown	Beta
Market Leaders, Debt Change (%) Decile 10	12.17%	17.29%	5.02	$1,628,137	0.41	4.69	11.68%	-48.85%	1.02
Small Stocks, Accruals to Price Decile 10	14.47%	22.86%	4.72	$3,992,730	0.41	7.93	16.12%	-66.72%	1.04
Small Stocks, Asset Turnover Decile 1	13.70%	21.31%	4.75	$2,962,382	0.41	5.93	14.98%	-64.74%	0.99
All Stocks, SY and 3 mom. and 6 mom. >Median, Top 25 by 12 mom.	14.50%	23.28%	4.68	$4,045,574	0.41	10.48	17.37%	-64.56%	1.08
Small Stocks, Cash Flow to Debt (%) Decile 1	13.36%	20.72%	4.74	$2,595,632	0.40	5.50	14.25%	-54.47%	0.97
Market Leaders, ROA Decile 1	11.77%	16.81%	4.99	$1,388,512	0.40	7.83	11.07%	-48.00%	0.91
Large Stocks, Fin Strength Composite Decile 10	11.37%	15.96%	5.05	$1,184,863	0.40	5.41	11.84%	-50.03%	0.90
Market Leaders, Return 12 Month Decile 1	12.71%	19.38%	4.78	$2,015,059	0.40	10.42	13.86%	-60.88%	1.00
Large Stocks, 60-Month Momentum, Decile 10	12.66%	19.36%	4.77	$1,972,949	0.40	8.55	13.16%	-65.10%	1.04
Market Leaders, Free Cash Flow to Price Decile 1	12.68%	19.44%	4.76	$1,990,354	0.40	7.79	13.81%	-65.82%	1.09
Small Stocks, SY and 3 mom. and 6 mom. >Median, Top 25 12 mom.	14.30%	23.54%	4.60	$3,745,468	0.40	9.92	17.71%	-63.04%	1.04
Large Stocks, BP and 3 mom. and 6 mom. >Median, Top 25 by 12 mom.	12.02%	17.80%	4.87	$1,534,382	0.39	6.98	13.72%	-59.99%	0.98
Large Stocks, BP >Median, Top 50 by DIVY	10.78%	14.73%	5.13	$935,732	0.39	12.26	9.93%	-62.19%	0.62
Market Leaders, Asset Turnover Decile 1	11.60%	16.84%	4.92	$1,297,271	0.39	7.00	11.35%	-49.88%	0.94
Market Leaders, Sales to Price Decile 1	12.28%	18.76%	4.76	$1,696,417	0.39	6.96	13.60%	-58.12%	1.07
All Stocks, Asset Turnover Decile 1	12.78%	20.14%	4.68	$2,071,598	0.39	6.01	14.37%	-62.08%	1.00
Market Leaders, Operating Margin Decile 1	11.52%	16.92%	4.87	$1,256,293	0.39	6.91	11.37%	-57.34%	0.95
Small Stocks, BBY and 3 mom. >Median, Top 50 12 mom.	14.28%	24.14%	4.52	$3,722,115	0.38	9.42	17.71%	-58.74%	1.08
Market Leaders Universe	**11.27%**	**16.37%**	**4.91**	**$1,139,999**	**0.38**	**N/A**	**11.72%**	**-54.03%**	**N/A**
All Stocks, 60-Month Momentum, Decile 10	13.88%	23.28%	4.51	$3,184,331	0.38	8.91	15.95%	-68.91%	1.12
Large Stocks, 6-Month Momentum, Decile 1	13.53%	22.36%	4.55	$2,777,019	0.38	10.95	16.05%	-59.80%	1.18
Small Stocks, Net Margin Decile 1	11.70%	17.63%	4.79	$1,349,305	0.38	7.06	13.28%	-52.87%	0.81
Large Stocks, BP >Median, Top 25 by DIVY	10.87%	15.95%	4.85	$968,948	0.37	13.02	10.95%	-67.55%	0.65
Small Stocks, 60-Month Momentum, Decile 10	14.12%	24.83%	4.39	$3,496,345	0.37	9.51	16.70%	-69.84%	1.12
Small Stocks, ROA Decile 1	13.10%	22.08%	4.48	$2,342,965	0.37	5.79	15.17%	-61.96%	1.03
All Stocks, 6-Month Momentum, Decile 1	14.24%	25.21%	4.38	$3,657,041	0.37	10.94	17.70%	-62.44%	1.20
All Stocks, BBY and 3 mom. >Median, Top 50 by 12 mom.	13.83%	24.15%	4.41	$3,123,598	0.37	10.44	17.60%	-63.62%	1.14
Large Stocks, NOA Change (%) Decile 10	11.30%	17.23%	4.74	$1,150,579	0.37	5.62	12.79%	-58.76%	0.97
Market Leaders, Top 10 by PCF	12.89%	21.74%	4.46	$2,161,684	0.36	11.17	15.05%	-75.55%	1.15

(continued on next page)

T A B L E 28.3

All Strategies for Monthly Data Series, August 31, 1965, to December 31, 2009. Strategies Sorted by Risk-Adjusted Return (Sharpe Ratio) *(Continued)*

Strategy	Geometric mean	Standard deviation (%)	T-Statistics	$10,000 becomes	Sharpe ratio	Tracking error	Downside risk	Largest drawdown	Beta
Large Stocks, TATA Decile 10	11.69%	18.44%	4.63	$1,343,540	0.36	7.11	13.59%	-69.58%	1.02
Market Leaders, Book/ Price Decile 1	12.21%	19.95%	4.53	$1,651,897	0.36	8.20	13.74%	-67.38%	1.12
All Stocks, Operating Margin Decile 1	10.79%	16.23%	4.77	$939,035	0.36	8.00	12.27%	-55.56%	0.77
Small Stocks, 6-Month Momentum, Decile 1	14.38%	26.32%	4.30	$3,857,815	0.36	11.03	18.35%	-63.10%	1.17
Large Stocks, Sales to Price Decile 1	11.25%	17.64%	4.63	$1,128,228	0.35	8.12	12.95%	-59.89%	0.94
Small Stocks, ROE Decile 1	13.08%	22.87%	4.37	$2,326,883	0.35	6.51	16.30%	-65.72%	1.07
Market Leaders, ROE Decile 1	10.95%	16.86%	4.68	$1,000,818	0.35	6.79	11.32%	-51.13%	0.94
All Stocks, TATA Decile 10	12.81%	22.21%	4.39	$2,093,156	0.35	6.24	16.30%	-69.09%	1.11
Market Leaders, Cash Flow to Debt (%) Decile 1	11.04%	17.20%	4.64	$1,037,698	0.35	7.95	11.31%	-50.49%	0.93
Large Stocks, Asset Turnover Decile 1	10.80%	16.79%	4.65	$943,969	0.35	6.91	11.53%	-54.64%	0.92
Market Leaders, Depr Exp to Cap Exp Decile 1	11.21%	17.99%	4.55	$1,112,344	0.35	6.07	12.16%	-57.97%	1.03
Small Stocks, EPS Change (%) Decile 1	12.86%	23.35%	4.26	$2,132,696	0.34	6.88	16.63%	-64.25%	1.09
All Stocks, ROE Decile 1	12.02%	21.00%	4.33	$1,534,842	0.33	6.32	15.04%	-63.88%	1.04
Small Stocks, 3 mom. and 6 mom. >0, ROE>avg, 50 best 12 mom.	14.66%	29.34%	4.11	$4,306,193	0.33	15.31	20.99%	-74.82%	1.24
Small Stocks, BBY and 3 mom. >Median, Top 25 12 mom.	13.67%	26.48%	4.14	$2,935,937	0.33	12.09	19.40%	-63.25%	1.15
All Stocks, ROA Decile 1	11.73%	20.84%	4.26	$1,368,925	0.32	6.09	14.34%	-58.45%	1.04
All Stocks, Cash Flow to Debt (%) Decile 1	11.65%	20.97%	4.22	$1,321,767	0.32	6.36	14.32%	-54.66%	1.04
ALL STOCKS	**11.01%**	**19.26%**	**4.28**	**$1,025,389**	**0.31**	**N/A**	**13.94%**	**-55.54%**	**N/A**
Market Leaders, Depr Exp to Cap Exp Decile 10	10.68%	18.29%	4.32	$897,158	0.31	6.43	12.73%	-55.30%	1.05
SMALL STOCKS	**11.36%**	**20.60%**	**4.19**	**$1,180,447**	**0.31**	**N/A**	**14.87%**	**-58.48%**	**N/A**
Small Stocks, TATA Decile 10	12.65%	24.78%	4.05	$1,968,047	0.31	8.55	17.54%	-70.06%	1.14
Market Leaders, Accruals to Price Decile 1	10.09%	16.55%	4.45	$710,389	0.31	5.80	12.40%	-51.92%	0.95
All Stocks, Depr Exp to Cap Exp Decile 1	11.81%	22.18%	4.12	$1,408,775	0.31	6.10	15.80%	-65.18%	1.11
All Stocks, NOA Change (%) Decile 10	11.83%	22.26%	4.11	$1,420,568	0.31	6.60	15.96%	-68.42%	1.11
All Stocks, Net Margin Decile 1	10.26%	17.31%	4.36	$758,759	0.30	6.52	12.92%	-53.32%	0.85
All Stocks, BBY and 3 mom. >Median, Top 25 by 12 mom.	13.05%	26.62%	3.99	$2,299,944	0.30	13.18	19.36%	-66.50%	1.22
LARGE STOCKS	**10.06%**	**16.75%**	**4.39**	**$701,190**	**0.30**	**N/A**	**11.90%**	**-53.77%**	**N/A**
Large Stocks, Debt Change (%) Decile 10	10.35%	17.94%	4.27	$787,144	0.30	4.94	13.03%	-55.95%	1.03
Large Stocks, 12-Month Momentum, Decile 1	11.93%	23.52%	4.00	$1,478,974	0.29	12.38	17.38%	-64.85%	1.21
S&P 500	9.33%	15.31%	4.41	$522,661	0.28	4.69	10.81%	-50.95%	0.88
Market Leaders, ROE Decile 10	10.34%	18.95%	4.11	$785,448	0.28	7.48	13.15%	-61.32%	1.07

(continued on next page)

All Strategies for Monthly Data Series, August 31, 1965, to December 31, 2009. Strategies Sorted by Risk-Adjusted Return (Sharpe Ratio) *(Continued)*

Strategy	Geometric mean	Standard deviation (%)	T-Statistics	$10,000 becomes	Sharpe ratio	Tracking error	Downside risk	Largest drawdown	Beta
Market Leaders, Free CF to Enterprise Value Decile 10	10.07%	18.10%	4.15	$703,094	0.28	6.41	13.05%	-60.38%	1.03
Small Stocks, Depr Exp to Cap Exp Decile 1	11.69%	24.23%	3.87	$1,346,569	0.28	8.72	16.91%	-69.57%	1.10
All Stocks, 12-Month Momentum, Decile 1	12.14%	25.86%	3.84	$1,604,407	0.28	11.65	18.53%	-66.29%	1.22
Market Leaders, Book/ Price Decile 10	9.66%	17.15%	4.17	$595,992	0.27	8.78	11.67%	-51.30%	0.90
All Stocks, Growth Composite Decile 1	11.34%	23.41%	3.86	$1,170,338	0.27	7.30	16.14%	-60.70%	1.17
Market Leaders, Free Cash Flow to Price Decile 10	9.75%	17.90%	4.08	$618,816	0.27	6.31	12.61%	-59.72%	1.02
Small Stocks, 12-Month Momentum, Decile 1	12.14%	26.95%	3.76	$1,608,082	0.27	11.67	19.16%	-67.06%	1.20
Market Leaders, EPS Change (%) Decile 1	9.74%	18.26%	4.02	$616,058	0.26	6.36	12.65%	-53.81%	1.05
Market Leaders, Net Margin Decile 10	9.79%	18.53%	3.99	$629,687	0.26	6.57	13.39%	-59.32%	1.06
Market Leaders, Asset Turnover Decile 10	10.35%	20.82%	3.86	$787,022	0.26	10.60	14.90%	-78.30%	1.10
Market Leaders, Debt Change (%) Decile 1	9.40%	17.27%	4.06	$536,458	0.25	4.17	12.20%	-54.87%	1.02
Small Stocks, Debt Change (%) Decile 10	11.03%	23.89%	3.73	$1,034,729	0.25	7.52	16.54%	-67.10%	1.11
Large Stocks, Depr Exp to Cap Exp Decile 1	9.61%	18.28%	3.97	$584,481	0.25	5.83	13.06%	-57.70%	1.03
Large Stocks, ROE Decile 1	9.44%	17.73%	3.99	$545,642	0.25	6.88	12.03%	-58.46%	0.98
All Stocks, Debt Change (%) Decile 10	10.56%	22.46%	3.75	$856,482	0.25	6.45	15.85%	-66.25%	1.12
Market Leaders, Cash Flow to Debt (%) Decile 10	9.98%	20.29%	3.82	$679,046	0.25	7.52	14.37%	-74.30%	1.16
Large Stocks, ROA Decile 1	9.55%	18.65%	3.89	$569,255	0.24	7.62	12.83%	-55.83%	1.02
Market Leaders, ROA Decile 10	10.06%	21.02%	3.76	$701,293	0.24	8.75	15.12%	-73.38%	1.18
Market Leaders, Operating Margin Decile 10	9.31%	18.06%	3.90	$518,265	0.24	6.81	12.25%	-54.95%	1.02
Large Stocks, Operating Margin Decile 1	9.04%	16.97%	3.98	$463,704	0.24	8.24	11.87%	-59.83%	0.89
All Stocks, Asset Turnover Decile 10	9.07%	17.44%	3.92	$469,694	0.23	8.89	13.24%	-63.29%	0.80
Small Stocks, NOA Change (%) Decile 10	10.83%	25.57%	3.54	$953,378	0.23	10.03	17.67%	-75.46%	1.15
Large Stocks, Growth Composite Decile 1	9.41%	19.70%	3.72	$538,900	0.22	7.25	13.65%	-57.48%	1.10
Large Stocks, EPS Change (%) Decile 1	8.96%	19.08%	3.65	$449,587	0.21	6.82	13.08%	-53.41%	1.07
Market Leaders, Value Composite 1 Decile 10 (Low)	8.64%	17.55%	3.74	$394,035	0.21	9.28	12.06%	-57.66%	0.91
Large Stocks, Net Margin Decile 1	8.48%	16.86%	3.79	$369,526	0.21	7.35	11.93%	-52.15%	0.91
Market Leaders, Sales to Price Decile 10	8.57%	17.39%	3.74	$382,709	0.21	9.02	12.04%	-58.92%	0.91
Market Leaders, NOA Change (%) Decile 1	8.58%	17.67%	3.71	$384,987	0.20	5.85	12.51%	-53.01%	1.02
Market Leaders, EBITDA/ Enterprise Value Decile 10	8.90%	19.44%	3.58	$438,867	0.20	8.62	13.33%	-65.29%	1.07
Market Leaders, EPS Change (%) Decile 10	8.83%	19.25%	3.58	$426,637	0.20	6.78	13.42%	-64.96%	1.11
Market Leaders, Sales to Enterprise Value Decile 10	8.53%	17.97%	3.65	$376,257	0.20	7.84	12.53%	-64.70%	0.99
Market Leaders, Earnings/ Price Decile 10	8.74%	19.18%	3.56	$410,691	0.20	8.21	13.80%	-58.63%	1.06

(continued on next page)

T A B L E 28.3

All Strategies for Monthly Data Series, August 31, 1965, to December 31, 2009. Strategies Sorted by Risk-Adjusted Return (Sharpe Ratio) *(Continued)*

Strategy	Geometric mean	Standard deviation (%)	T-Statistics	$10,000 becomes	Sharpe ratio	Tracking error	Downside risk	Largest drawdown	Beta
Large Stocks, Accruals to Price Decile 1	8.41%	17.75%	3.64	$358,169	0.19	5.91	13.11%	-54.83%	1.00
Large Stocks, Cash Flow to Debt (%) Decile 1	8.74%	20.00%	3.47	$410,961	0.19	8.78	14.33%	-71.34%	1.08
Large Stocks, Free CF to Enterprise Value Decile 10	8.09%	18.19%	3.48	$345,221	0.17	6.20	13.34%	-63.96%	1.02
Large Stocks, Asset Turnover Decile 10	8.34%	19.71%	3.38	$348,952	0.17	10.61	14.00%	-75.82%	0.99
Large Stocks, Growth Composite Decile 10	7.96%	17.87%	3.47	$298,449	0.17	6.10	12.65%	-63.64%	1.00
All Stocks, Accruals to Price Decile 1	8.60%	21.76%	3.27	$387,604	0.17	4.96	15.55%	-60.25%	1.11
Large Stocks, Book to Price, Decile 10	8.64%	22.02%	3.26	$394,329	0.17	10.68	15.65%	-70.70%	1.16
Market Leaders, Return 12 Month Decile 10	8.52%	21.39%	3.26	$375,727	0.16	9.05	14.16%	-65.66%	1.20
Market Leaders, Return 6 Month Decile 10	8.30%	20.52%	3.28	$342,672	0.16	7.54	13.90%	-65.20%	1.18
Small Stocks, Asset Turnover Decile 10	7.83%	17.68%	3.44	$282,317	0.16	8.57	13.11%	-62.16%	0.78
Market Leaders, Net Operating Cash Flow to Price Decile 10	7.80%	17.54%	3.45	$279,628	0.16	8.41	12.89%	-59.89%	0.94
Market Leaders, Value Composite 2 Decile 10 (Low)	7.85%	18.03%	3.40	$284,927	0.16	9.13	12.77%	-60.68%	0.95
Small Stocks, Accruals to Price Decile 1	8.64%	23.17%	3.17	$393,912	0.16	6.08	16.04%	-64.22%	1.09
Small Stocks, 60-Month Momentum, Decile 1	8.78%	24.09%	3.15	$416,618	0.16	8.19	16.97%	-68.08%	1.11
Market Leaders, TATA Decile 1	7.82%	18.06%	3.39	$281,123	0.16	5.78	12.75%	-56.09%	1.05
Large Stocks, Net Margin Decile 10	8.12%	20.22%	3.27	$318,114	0.15	8.72	15.64%	-82.79%	1.09
Market Leaders, Value Composite 3 Decile 10 (Low)	7.71%	17.86%	3.38	$269,394	0.15	8.87	12.56%	-59.42%	0.95
Large Stocks, ROE Decile 10	7.94%	19.80%	3.25	$296,059	0.15	8.83	14.89%	-79.66%	1.06
Large Stocks, Free Cash Flow to Price Decile 10	7.57%	18.05%	3.31	$253,902	0.14	5.84	13.24%	-63.76%	1.02
All Stocks, 60-Month Momentum, Decile 1	8.31%	23.46%	3.07	$344,813	0.14	8.34	16.52%	-64.52%	1.15
Large Stocks, EPS Change (%) Decile 10	7.44%	18.83%	3.18	$240,673	0.13	6.87	13.39%	-67.30%	1.05
Large Stocks, Depr Exp to Cap Exp Decile 10	7.41%	18.93%	3.16	$237,466	0.13	8.28	13.70%	-66.24%	1.02
All Stocks, Book to Price, Decile 10	8.13%	24.73%	2.95	$319,249	0.13	10.14	17.37%	-73.67%	1.19
Large Stocks, ROA Decile 10	7.53%	21.52%	2.99	$250,199	0.12	9.48	15.98%	-80.45%	1.17
Market Leaders, Shareholder Yield (%) Decile 10	7.25%	19.26%	3.07	$223,014	0.12	6.48	12.93%	-61.88%	1.11
Small Stocks, Book to Price, Decile 10	8.12%	26.81%	2.86	$318,580	0.12	10.66	18.70%	-74.79%	1.21
Large Stocks, 60-Month Momentum, Decile 1	7.45%	24.18%	2.81	$242,263	0.10	11.56	17.28%	-76.08%	1.30
Large Stocks, Debt Change (%) Decile 1	6.83%	18.61%	3.00	$187,287	0.10	5.60	13.29%	-63.62%	1.06
Market Leaders, Buyback Yield (%) Decile 10	6.76%	18.93%	2.94	$181,638	0.09	5.49	12.98%	-63.96%	1.11
Large Stocks, Fin Strength Composite Decile 1	6.53%	17.19%	3.03	$164,902	0.09	4.98	12.21%	-59.81%	0.98
Large Stocks, Operating Margin Decile 10	6.78%	20.52%	2.84	$183,358	0.09	8.98	15.79%	-85.76%	1.11
All Stocks, Growth Composite Decile 10	6.80%	22.33%	2.72	$184,471	0.08	6.21	16.21%	-71.86%	1.12

(continued on next page)

All Strategies for Monthly Data Series, August 31, 1965, to December 31, 2009. Strategies Sorted by Risk-Adjusted Return (Sharpe Ratio) *(Continued)*

Strategy	Geometric mean	Standard deviation (%)	T-Statistics	$10,000 becomes	Sharpe ratio	Tracking error	Downside risk	Largest drawdown	Beta
All Stocks, Free CF to Enterprise Value Decile 10	6.84%	23.07%	2.70	$187,800	0.08	6.88	16.53%	-66.73%	1.15
Small Stocks, EPS Change (%) Decile 10	6.93%	26.17%	2.59	$194,631	0.07	9.57	17.98%	-72.16%	1.20
Large Stocks, Cash Flow to Debt (%) Decile 10	6.41%	20.05%	2.75	$156,826	0.07	9.13	15.32%	-77.96%	1.07
Large Stocks, 12-Month Momentum, Decile 10	6.51%	22.24%	2.64	$163,990	0.07	10.54	15.59%	-69.38%	1.18
Large Stocks, Earnings/ Price Decile 10	6.21%	21.66%	2.59	$144,339	0.06	9.86	16.15%	-79.88%	1.16
All Stocks, Debt Change (%) Decile 1	6.24%	22.40%	2.57	$146,231	0.06	5.10	16.20%	-69.24%	1.14
Small Stocks, Free CF to Enterprise Value Decile 10	6.39%	26.05%	2.46	$155,550	0.05	10.27	17.80%	-73.23%	1.18
All Stocks, Free Cash Flow to Price Decile 10	6.09%	22.71%	2.51	$137,430	0.05	6.36	16.57%	-68.80%	1.14
Large Stocks, TATA Decile 1	5.91%	19.50%	2.62	$127,540	0.05	6.92	13.88%	-58.61%	1.09
Large Stocks, Net Operating Cash Flow to Price Decile 10	5.92%	21.36%	2.52	$127,975	0.04	9.69	15.95%	-77.33%	1.15
Large Stocks, Earnings Quality Composite Decile 1	5.68%	19.03%	2.58	$115,851	0.04	6.29	13.88%	-61.33%	1.07
All Stocks, EPS Change ($) Decile 1	5.70%	20.35%	2.51	$116,798	0.03	4.49	14.71%	-66.06%	1.03
Large Stocks, Buyback Yield, Decile 10	5.61%	19.02%	2.56	$112,578	0.03	5.17	13.72%	-65.37%	1.10
All Stocks, ROE Decile 10	5.83%	26.77%	2.32	$123,132	0.03	11.63	19.64%	-89.50%	1.28
Large Stocks, NOA Change (%) Decile 1	5.56%	19.86%	2.50	$110,113	0.03	7.68	15.13%	-78.05%	1.10
All Stocks, 12-Month Momentum, Decile 10	5.60%	26.03%	2.27	$112,186	0.02	11.08	17.95%	-75.22%	1.25
Small Stocks, Free Cash Flow to Price Decile 10	5.36%	25.22%	2.24	$101,397	0.01	9.24	17.66%	-72.60%	1.15
All Stocks, EPS Change ($) Decile 10	5.27%	21.52%	2.32	$97,542	0.01	5.97	15.56%	-67.86%	1.08
All Stocks, Earnings/ Price Decile 10	5.31%	26.92%	2.20	$99,120	0.01	10.86	19.18%	-82.14%	1.32
Small Stocks, Debt Change (%) Decile 1	5.25%	23.86%	2.24	$96,671	0.01	6.38	16.85%	-75.29%	1.12
Large Stocks, Shareholder Yield, Decile 10	5.19%	19.86%	2.37	$94,131	0.01	5.56	14.16%	-68.49%	1.15
Small Stocks, 12-Month Momentum, Decile 10	5.20%	27.41%	2.15	$94,641	0.01	11.34	18.74%	-79.12%	1.23
All Stocks, 6-Month Momentum, Decile 10	5.13%	21.92%	2.26	$92,064	0.01	9.50	15.36%	-68.85%	1.20
All Stocks, EBITDA/ Enterprise Value Decile 10	5.15%	27.09%	2.16	$92,607	0.01	12.64	19.86%	-89.54%	1.27
Small Stocks, Buyback Yield, Decile 10	5.10%	23.37%	2.22	$90,572	0.00	4.97	16.97%	-71.57%	1.11
All Stocks, Net Margin Decile 10	5.02%	27.68%	2.12	$87,544	0.00	12.89	20.52%	-93.05%	1.31
All Stocks, Buyback Yield, Decile 10	4.90%	21.95%	2.21	$83,448	0.00	4.55	16.05%	-70.91%	1.12
Small Stocks, Shareholder Yield, Decile 10	4.88%	24.17%	2.14	$82,837	0.00	5.60	17.29%	-74.59%	1.15
All Stocks, Depr Exp to Cap Exp Decile 10	4.85%	23.18%	2.15	$81,598	-0.01	7.33	16.83%	-71.68%	1.15
Small Stocks, Earnings/ Price Decile 10	4.78%	29.59%	2.05	$79,326	-0.01	13.76	19.79%	-82.67%	1.31
All Stocks, Sales to Enterprise Value Decile 10	4.74%	25.41%	2.09	$78,028	-0.01	12.11	19.83%	-92.02%	1.17
All Stocks, Shareholder Yield, Decile 10	4.73%	22.86%	2.13	$77,572	-0.01	5.24	16.41%	-72.38%	1.17
Large Stocks, EBITDA/ Enterprise Value Decile 10	4.71%	23.89%	2.11	$76,893	-0.01	12.29	18.64%	-89.48%	1.25

(continued on next page)

T A B L E 28.3

All Strategies for Monthly Data Series, August 31, 1965, to December 31, 2009. Strategies Sorted by Risk-Adjusted Return (Sharpe Ratio) *(Continued)*

Strategy	Geometric mean	Standard deviation (%)	T-Statistics	$10,000 becomes	Sharpe ratio	Tracking error	Downside risk	Largest drawdown	Beta
All Stocks, Operating Margin Decile 10	4.58%	27.66%	2.02	$72,755	-0.02	13.01	20.58%	-93.34%	1.30
All Stocks, ROA Decile 10	4.57%	26.50%	2.03	$72,529	-0.02	12.64	20.00%	-91.36%	1.23
Large Stocks, Value Composite1 Decile 10	4.51%	22.73%	2.08	$70,595	-0.02	12.16	17.62%	-85.28%	1.16
All Stocks, Fin Strength Composite Decile 1	4.34%	22.71%	2.03	$65,775	-0.03	6.43	16.89%	-80.39%	1.14
Large Stocks, Value Composite3 Decile 10	4.30%	23.09%	2.01	$64,519	-0.03	12.20	17.76%	-85.90%	1.18
Large Stocks, Sales to Price Decile 10	4.31%	22.46%	2.03	$64,848	-0.03	12.01	17.93%	-86.24%	1.14
Large Stocks, Value Composite2 Decile 10	4.20%	23.29%	1.98	$61,850	-0.03	12.42	17.93%	-86.01%	1.19
All Stocks, TATA Decile 1	4.05%	25.11%	1.91	$58,251	-0.04	8.27	17.43%	-77.80%	1.26
Large Stocks, Sales to Enterprise Value Decile 10	4.07%	22.41%	1.97	$58,697	-0.04	11.73	17.95%	-87.97%	1.15
Small Stocks, TATA Decile 1	3.47%	26.62%	1.76	$45,467	-0.06	9.13	17.98%	-81.88%	1.24
All Stocks, Earnings Quality Composite Decile 10	3.50%	25.15%	1.77	$46,045	-0.06	8.27	17.77%	-73.54%	1.26
Small Stocks, EBITDA/ Enterprise Value Decile 10	3.28%	28.75%	1.71	$41,748	-0.06	14.21	19.71%	-87.57%	1.24
All Stocks, 6-Month Momentum, Decile 10	3.36%	25.74%	1.72	$43,236	-0.06	10.04	17.59%	-77.42%	1.26
All Stocks, Sales to Price Decile 10	3.11%	26.68%	1.67	$38,918	-0.07	13.37	19.84%	-91.41%	1.22
All Stocks, Net Operating Cash Flow to Price Decile 10	3.13%	26.48%	1.68	$39,130	-0.07	10.83	18.81%	-86.49%	1.29
Small Stocks, Depr Exp to Cap Exp Decile 10	3.27%	24.38%	1.71	$41,564	-0.07	7.93	17.26%	-72.64%	1.13
Small Stocks, ROE Decile 10	2.66%	30.11%	1.59	$32,028	-0.08	14.66	20.33%	-91.45%	1.32
All Stocks, NOA Change (%) Decile 1	3.03%	25.34%	1.66	$37,546	-0.08	9.04	18.68%	-83.42%	1.26
All Stocks, Value Composite1 (VC1) Decile 10	2.64%	28.25%	1.58	$31,727	-0.08	14.26	20.42%	-92.81%	1.30
Small Stocks, 6-Month Momentum, Decile 10	2.60%	27.07%	1.54	$31,163	-0.09	10.20	18.35%	-80.22%	1.24
Small Stocks, Net Operating Cash Flow to Price Decile 10	2.39%	28.72%	1.52	$28,474	-0.09	13.22	19.50%	-85.02%	1.27
All Stocks, Value Composite2 (VC2) Decile 10	2.29%	28.71%	1.50	$27,251	-0.09	14.39	20.45%	-92.67%	1.33
Small Stocks, Sales to Enterprise Value Decile 10	2.52%	25.98%	1.52	$30,166	-0.10	12.13	19.40%	-91.71%	1.12
Small Stocks, Cash Flow to Debt (%) Decile 10	2.16%	29.59%	1.47	$25,817	-0.10	14.44	20.01%	-87.81%	1.29
All Stocks, Value Composite3 (VC3) Decile 10	2.13%	28.59%	1.46	$25,510	-0.10	14.26	20.42%	-92.77%	1.33
All Stocks, Cash Flow to Debt (%) Decile 10	2.08%	27.30%	1.43	$24,944	-0.11	12.49	20.25%	-92.73%	1.29
Small Stocks, NOA Change (%) Decile 1	1.84%	26.83%	1.37	$22,452	-0.12	9.65	19.34%	-85.63%	1.24
Small Stocks, ROA Decile 10	1.11%	29.56%	1.24	$16,282	-0.13	15.07	20.29%	-93.32%	1.26
Small Stocks, Operating Margin Decile 10	0.90%	29.92%	1.20	$14,869	-0.14	15.36	20.41%	-93.74%	1.28
Small Stocks, Net Margin Decile 10	0.81%	30.39%	1.19	$14,290	-0.14	15.58	20.58%	-94.14%	1.30
Small Stocks, Sales to Price Decile 10	0.16%	27.71%	0.98	$10,727	-0.17	13.99	20.00%	-93.67%	1.17
Small Stocks, Value Composite1 (VC1), Decile 10	-0.80%	29.92%	0.84	$7,012	-0.19	15.39	20.75%	-94.37%	1.28
Small Stocks, Value Composite2 (VC2), Decile 10	-0.92%	30.35%	0.82	$6,623	-0.20	15.42	20.90%	-94.46%	1.31
Small Stocks, Value Composite3 (VC3), Decile 10	-1.35%	30.18%	0.72	$5,468	-0.21	15.25	20.89%	-94.72%	1.30

In the real world, many investors check their portfolio's value *daily* and let the daily ups and downs inform their decisions, usually for the worse. In the real world, investors are far more frightened of short-term volatility then any rational economic model would suggest, but that very real fear must be accounted for in determining which strategy will be right for you. I have watched investors' reactions to short-term volatility over the last 14 years, and I can tell you that it is far more predictable than the markets' performance.

RANKING BY SHARPE RATIO

As you can see from Table 28.3, *all* the strategies with the best risk-adjusted returns include one or more value criteria. Value criteria act like a chaperone at a party, making sure that you don't fall for some sexy stock with a great story. They may keep you from having some short-term fun, but over time they keep you out of trouble by never letting you overpay for stocks. Except for the stocks selected from the Market Leaders universe, most of the stocks picked by these top-performing strategies aren't household names. They choose work-horses, not show horses. There are plenty of buyers for stocks with a hot story. That's exactly what pushes their prices to unsustainable levels. The workhorse stocks selected by most of the strategies with the highest risk-adjusted returns are companies like Great Lakes Dredge & Dock Corp. and HealthSpring Inc. Don't look for the chairmen of these companies on the cover of *Fortune* anytime soon.

The best-performing strategy on a risk-adjusted basis is also one of the best performers on an absolute basis—the Trending Value strategy. This strategy focuses on stocks from the All Stocks universe in the first decile of Value Composite Two—that 10 percent of stocks with the best scores on a variety of value and shareholder factors—and then buys the 25 with the best six-month price appreciation. The strategy earned an average annual compound return of 21.08 percent, turning $10,000 into $48.2 million dollars over 44 years, yet it had a standard deviation of return of just 17.66 percent. The high return married to the low standard deviation earned it a Sharpe ratio of .91, vastly higher than the All Stocks' Sharpe ratio of .31. The third best strategy by risk-adjusted return was one we were able to test back to 1927—focusing on the stocks from All Stocks that rank in the bottom 30 percent of the universe by price-to-book ratio, with three- and six-month price appreciation greater than the median and then buying the 25 stocks with the highest shareholder yield. Over the 1965–2009 period, this strategy earned an average annual compound return of 18.45 percent with a standard deviation of just 15.48 percent. That brought its Sharpe ratio in at .87—again, much higher than the All Stocks universe.

We also have data for this strategy from 1927 through 2009 and here we see that the longer-term data confirm the 44 years covered. Between December 31, 1927, and December 31, 2009, this strategy earned an average annual compound return of 15.43 percent, turning $10,000 into $1.3 billion. Over the longer term, it also had a lower standard deviation of return than All Stocks, 21.28 percent versus 23.25 percent for All Stocks.

Finally, the only strategy in the top 10 by risk-adjusted return that also had a maximum decline significantly better than the other strategies was the combined consumer staples and utility portfolio we reviewed in the additional material available online. This strategy is made up of the 25 stocks from the consumer staples sector with the highest shareholder yield and the 25 stocks from the utility sector with the highest scores on Value Composite 2. Over the 1965–2009 period, this 50-stock portfolio earned an average annual compound return of 16.56 percent, yet had a standard deviation of return of just 13.42 percent. That combination gave it a Sharpe ratio of .86, one of the highest of all of the strategies we tested. But the real appeal here is that the maximum decline for the strategy was just 34.39 percent, much lower than that for the other strategies as well as the All Stocks universe itself. Thus, this is a great choice for very conservative investors who nevertheless want to grow their portfolios with an investment in stocks. Yet, as Table 28.3 illustrates, there were 20 strategies that had higher risk-adjusted rates of return than U.S. T-bills. Conservative investors should focus on these strategies since they offer both excellent returns over the long-term and higher returns per unit of risk than even "riskless" U.S. T-bills.

THE DOWNSIDE

The five worst-performing strategies, as ranked by their Sharpe ratios, all come from the Small Stocks universe and have the *worst* scores on price-to-sales, profit margins, and our three value composites. The bottom 39 strategies all had *negative* Sharpe ratios, and the list is populated with the usual suspects—those with the worst scores on our value composites; the worst profit margins; the worst price appreciation; and the worst scores on our Earnings Quality and Financial Strength Composites. All the low Sharpe ratio strategies were outperformed by an investment in U.S. T-bills. With the exception of the poor price appreciation group, these stocks command unreasonably high prices for their underlying businesses, and their investors believe that trees really *do* grow to the sky. These companies' prices are based on hope, greed, or fantasies about a future that rarely comes to pass. VirnetX Holding Corp. might be a great software company, but is it really worth 8,231 times revenues? I think not. *It* may go on to meet these huge expectations, but the class of stocks with these characteristics will *not*, and investors should avoid them.

RANKING BY DOWNSIDE RISK

In the interest of space, we have featured additional tables for Chapter 28 in the supplemental material featured at www.whatworksonwallstreet.com. As Table 28.4 shows, when reviewing all the strategies by downside risk, it is interesting to note how well the broader indexes score. Nevertheless, there are 30 strategies with lower downside risk than the Market Leaders universe, the least risky of all of our universes. Once again, the consumer staples/utility strategy mentioned above ranked highest by downside risk as well as by absolute and risk-adjusted returns. It also had a low maximum decline of 34.39 percent. Investors who are concerned about a portfolio's downside should study this list very carefully, while keeping in mind that portfolios with low downside risk often have more limited upside potential. Studying the list will allow risk-adverse investors to focus on strategies with low downside risk that nevertheless have good average annual returns.

Another sensible thing for risk-averse investors to consider is where the strategy ranks compared to the All Stocks universe, as this is the broadest of all of the large universes I investigated. This gives you a greater number of strategies to choose from, while still investing in a portfolio with lower downside risk than the average stock.

STRATEGIES WITH THE HIGHEST DOWNSIDE RISK

It should come as no surprise that, much like the naughty child frequently found waiting outside the principal's office, strategies with the highest downside risk also have the worst real and risk-adjusted returns. At least they are *consistently* bad. All these strategies should be avoided, because the risk is just too high. You should never use a strategy with a downside risk much higher than the overall market's downside risk, except on those very rare occasions when their performance is so fantastic that it pushes the Sharpe ratio into the stratosphere. Unless the potential rewards of a strategy are vastly higher than the market, the emotional toll of high-risk strategies always outweighs their benefits. The best use of high-risk strategies is to blend them with lower-risk strategies, bringing overall risk to acceptable levels. See Figures 28.5 and 28.6 at www.whatworksonwallstreet.com.

RANKING BY MAXIMUM DECLINE

Finally, Table 28.5, featured in the supplemental material at www.whatworksonwall street.com, looks at how all the strategies rank by maximum decline over the last 44 years. With the exception of a long depression, every type of market is covered during this period, giving us a good sense for how bad things might get. Sixteen strategies had maximum declines of less than 50 percent, no small feat given that we are looking at a period that included the biggest market decline since the Great Depression. As already noted, the combined consumer staples and utility sector portfolio had the lowest maximum decline of 34.39 percent. What's interesting is that there are also several high-performing strategies near the top of the list—the All Stocks strategy that buys stocks with price-to-book ratios in the lowest 30 percent, good three- and six-month price appreciation, and the highest shareholder yields had a maximum decline of 47.66 percent, and the 50-stock version of Trending Value had a maximum decline of 49.64 percent. This indicates that you do not have to sacrifice high returns by focusing on strategies with low maximum declines.

STRATEGIES WITH THE HIGHEST MAXIMUM DECLINES

Surprise! All of the worst-performing strategies by maximum decline also wind up at the bottom of the barrel here: 18 strategies had maximum declines exceeding 90 percent! They are, yet again, the usual suspects—stocks with the worst scores on the value composites, the worst EBITDA-to-enterprise value, the worst price-to-sales ratios, and the worst margins. Of the broad universes, Small Stocks suffered the worst decline of 58.48 percent. I would recommend that as a proxy for a drop dead point. Only consider strategies with maximum declines less than that experienced by this most volatile of broad universes. Even when you eliminate strategies with maximum declines of over 59 percent, you still have many strategies to choose from, but you are avoiding those that are too volatile to stick with, as their volatility is simply too great. You can see that Figures 28.7 and 28.8 show the best and worst strategies by maximum decline at www.whatworksonwallstreet.com.

INFLATION-ADJUSTED RETURNS

I promised in the Introduction to include several examples of the real, or inflation-adjusted, returns for a variety of indexes and strategies. While the nominal returns featured here give you a good sense of the comparative advantage or disadvantage of the strategies tested, they ignore the often pernicious and eroding effects of inflation. Most investors have a very difficult time trying to weigh the effects of inflation, and we rarely pay as much attention to it as we should. You simply don't know how your investments have performed until you take inflation into account. For example, when reviewing nominal returns, you might look at a portfolio that doubled from $10,000 to $20,000 over 10 years. On the face of it, you'd be tempted to congratulate yourself on that 100 percent gain. Yet you have no way of knowing whether you have doubled your *purchasing power* unless you look at inflation. Thus, if $10,000 bought you 100 units of your favorite goods and services 10 years ago but now those same 100 units cost you $20,000, your net increase in purchasing power over the 10 years is zero. That means the real increase in your portfolio's value over the 10 years was zero, even though your nominal return was 100 percent. This seemingly simple concept is often difficult for investors to grasp. For example, our earliest tests in the book start in 1927 with $10,000. If we were to take the effects of inflation into account, you would have to adjust that figure to $122,299, since that is what you would have to have in the bank at the end of 2009 to equal the purchasing power of $10,000 in 1927! Something that cost $10,000 in 1927 now runs you more than $122,000. To put this in terms of return on investment, had you invested $10,000 in 1927 and it was now worth $122,000, your nominal return is a gain of 1,120 percent but your *actual gain* is zero, because you have gained nothing in purchasing power.

With this in mind, let's look at some inflation-adjusted returns. Table 28.6 shows the real returns for an investment in a variety of instruments between 1927 and 2009. Had you been an extremely conservative investor and kept your portfolio in U.S. T-bills, your 1927 $10,000 would have grown to only $16,256 by the end of 2009, a real average annual compound return of just 0.59 percent. In essence, you would not be much better off than you were in 1927, since your portfolio earned virtually nothing in 82 years. T-bills appeal to conservative investors over the short-term because there is no possibility of short-term loss. Yet look at what inflation did to the hapless T-bill investor—the maximum decline of the inflation-adjusted T-bill portfolio was 49 percent, the result of holding cash in an inflationary environment. That's hardly the risk-free investment it appears to be at first blush. James Grant, the editor of *Grant's Interest Rate Observer*, wryly noted that bonds often offer only "return free risks," and that is true for any of the fixed income alternatives featured here. After inflation is taken into account, intermediate and long-term U.S. government bonds earned only modest returns over the past 82 years, turning $10,000 into $60,942 and $64,028, respectively

T A B L E   28.6

Inflation-Adjusted Returns for Various Indexes and U.S. Bonds and T-Bills, December 31st, 1926, through December 31st, 2009

	Geometric mean (%)	Arithmetic mean (%)	Standard deviation (%)	Ending index value	Maximum decline (%)
Small Stocks REAL	7.53	9.95	23.16	$4,140,343.87	−82.36
All Stocks REAL	7.18	9.31	21.74	$3,151,789.66	−81.61
S&P 500 REAL	6.52	8.19	19.36	$1,894,850.36	−79.00
Large Stocks REAL	6.43	8.14	19.44	$1,767,734.68	−80.21
US LT Govt REAL	2.26	2.61	8.63	$64,028.45	−67.24
US IT Govt REAL	2.20	2.30	4.89	$60,941.70	−43.60
IA SBBI US 30 Day T-Bill REAL	0.59	0.60	1.82	$16,256.00	−48.76

As Table 28.6 illustrates, the inflation-adjusted returns for stocks are much better, with a $10,000 investment in the All Stocks universe growing to $3,151,790, a real average annual return of 7.18 percent. The same $10,000 invested in the Small Stocks universe grew to $4,140,344 over the same period, a real average annual compound return of 7.53 percent. Therefore, if you are interested in any meaningful long-term growth in your portfolio, you really have to consider stocks rather than fixed income alternatives. Table 28.7 shows the inflation-adjusted returns for a variety of the strategies we tested back to 1927. Yet again, as with the nominal returns, we see that the types of stocks you buy are vitally important to how you do over the long term. Look at the spread between buying the best 10 percent of stocks by six-month price appreciation versus the worst 10 percent—for the Small Stocks universe, the best six-month price performers turn $10,000 into $59.3 million, while the worst turn it into only $18,654. The same is true, to a lesser extent, for stocks with the best and worst shareholder and buyback yield—focusing on the best of them yields true wealth, whereas focusing on the worst leads to very modest returns.

Lest you think that inflation affects only very long-term results, lets take a look at a variety of our strategies from the shorter 44-year 1965–2009 time period. Here we see the same effects of inflation on returns. Table 28.8 shows the results. The best-performing strategies continue to do well, but note that real returns are considerably lower than nominal returns. Also note that maximum declines increase, since the period was marked by a fairly high inflation rate of 4.43 percent a year. Thus $10,000 in 1965 is equivalent to $68,000 at the end of 2009. Clearly, this matters in the real world—the house your parents might have bought in 1965 for $20,000 would now cost $139,000 if there were no real increase in value. That's why it is vital to keep inflation in mind when looking at your portfolio's returns.

T A B L E   28.7

Inflation-Adjusted Returns for Various Indexes and Various Deciles, December 31, 1926, through December 31st, 2009

	Geometric mean (%)	Arithmetic mean (%)	Standard deviation (%)	Ending index value	Maximum decline (%)
Small Stocks 6-mo. mom decile 1 REAL	11.03	13.80	25.42	$59,298,231.40	−71.68
All Stocks 6-mo. mom decile 1 REAL	10.72	13.28	24.54	$46,842,615.30	−72.55
All Stocks BBY decile 1 REAL	10.31	12.64	24.40	$34,443,445.11	−81.63
Small Stocks BBY decile 1 REAL	10.27	13.03	26.42	$33,294,740.23	−82.32
All Stocks SY decile 1 REAL	9.85	11.46	20.28	$24,398,288.41	−86.19
Small Stocks SY decile 1 REAL	9.79	11.56	21.03	$23,257,204.92	−88.71
Small Stocks REAL	7.53	9.95	23.16	$4,140,343.87	−82.36
All Stocks REAL	7.18	9.31	21.74	$3,151,789.66	−81.61
Small Stocks BBY decile 10 REAL	3.08	6.38	25.92	$124,156.51	−85.59
All Stocks SY decile 10 REAL	2.92	6.17	25.86	$109,148.55	−85.55
Small Stocks SY decile 10 REAL	2.82	6.52	27.54	$100,424.17	−86.60
All Stocks BBY decile 10 REAL	2.79	5.66	24.14	$98,497.92	−85.21
All Stocks 6-mo. mom decile 10 REAL	1.06	5.18	29.37	$23,922.66	−89.67
Small Stocks 6-mo. mom decile 10 REAL	0.75	5.27	30.77	$18,653.86	−90.13

T A B L E   28.8

Inflation-Adjusted Returns for Various Indexes and Strategies, December 31, 1965, through December 31, 2009

	Geometric mean (%)	Arithmetic mean (%)	Standard deviation (%)	Ending index value	Maximum decline (%)
Trending Value portfolio REAL	15.95	16.49	17.76	$7,055,392.80	−51.31
Value Comp 2 in top 3 deciles, 3 and 6 mo. mom>median, top 25 by 6 mo. mom REAL	14.47	15.59	19.77	$3,995,797.36	−57.23
Combined consumer staples/utility portfolio REAL	11.65	11.97	13.50	$1,322,013.86	−42.47
Market Leaders universe, Value Comp 2 in top 2 Deciles, top 25 by 6 mo. mom REAL	10.44	11.47	17.26	$816,791.30	−53.47
Market Leaders, Value Comp 2> median, top 25 by SY REAL	10.09	11.17	17.37	$708,858.25	−58.85
Market Leaders, 3 and 6 mo. mom>median, top 25 by Value Comp 2 REAL	9.38	10.40	16.62	$532,210.17	−52.31
Small Stocks REAL	6.64	8.63	20.68	$172,622.65	−70.96
Market Leaders universe USA REAL	6.55	7.74	16.48	$166,707.77	−54.73
All Stocks REAL	6.30	8.03	19.35	$149,947.82	−66.99
Large Stocks REAL	5.39	6.70	16.84	$102,538.53	−56.05

IMPLICATIONS

After weighing risks, rewards, and long-term base rates, two strategies emerge as the best overall—one for investors willing to take market risk and one for very conservative investors. The first is the Trending Value strategy that combines the best of value and the best of growth. It selects stocks from the All Stocks universe in decile 1 of Value Composite 2, and then buys the stocks with the best six-month price appreciation.

The second is the combined portfolio that draws from the consumer staples and utilities sectors and then buys the 25 stocks from consumer staples with the highest shareholder yield and the 25 stocks from the utilities sector with the best scores on Value Composite 2.

These two strategies consistently ranked at or near the top when ranked by absolute return, risk-adjusted return, downside risk, and maximum decline. Of course, there are many other excellent strategies that focus on different parts of the market, notably the Market Leaders strategies that focus on strong three- and six-month price appreciation and then buy the top stocks by either Value Composite 2 or by shareholder yield. The key is to use different strategies to cover various portions of the market. For example, if you built a portfolio that invested 25 percent in the Trending Value portfolio, 25 percent in the consumer staples/utilities portfolio, 25 percent in Market Leaders with good price appreciation and the highest scores on the Value Composite 2 and 25 percent in the Market Leaders with good price appreciation and the highest shareholder yield, you would end up with a portfolio that was roughly 55 percent larger-cap stocks and 45 percent small- and midcap stocks. Between 1965 and 2009, the blended portfolio's return was 16.56 percent, turning $10,000 into $8.9 million. This is roughly 9 times the return of an investment in the All Stocks universe, where $10,000 grew to $1 million. Yet the standard deviation of this combined portfolio was just 13.42 percent, considerably lower than All Stocks' 19.26 percent. What's more, the portfolio's 34 percent maximum decline was lower than all of our major universes. Its maximum decline over all rolling five-year periods was close to zero, compared with losses of between 4.36 percent per year and 9.91 percent for our major universes. Thus, by utilizing a variety of strategies with strong historical performance, you can build any number of portfolios that broaden your exposure to market capitalization classes, growth or value styles, or risk characteristics. You really no longer need to settle for portfolios that score poorly on any of the criteria we've reviewed in this chapter.

Finally, at the very least you can now see which types of stocks to avoid, You should *always* look at the historical record if you're tempted to take a chance on a glamour stock trading at high multiples. I remind you again: most of these stocks crash and burn. The data are unequivocal—if the only thing this book teaches you is to avoid these stocks, it will have served a useful purpose.

29
CHAPTER

GETTING THE MOST OUT OF YOUR EQUITY INVESTMENTS

To think is easy. To act is difficult. To act as one thinks is the most difficult of all.

—Johann Wolfgang von Goethe

Investors can learn much from the Taoist concept of Wu Wei. Taoism is one of the three schools of Chinese philosophy that has guided thinkers for thousands of years. Literally, Wu Wei means "to act without action," but in spirit it means to let things occur as they are meant to occur. Don't try to put square pegs into round holes. Understand the essence of a circle and use it as nature intended. The closest western equivalent is Wittgenstein's maxim: "Don't look for the meaning: Look for the use!"

For investors, this means letting good strategies work. Don't second guess them. Don't try to outsmart them. Don't abandon them because they're experiencing a rough patch. Understand the nature of what you're using and let it work. This is the hardest assignment of all. It's virtually impossible not to insert our ego or emotions into decisions, yet it is only by being dispassionate that you can beat the market over time.

Since I originally published this book in 1996, we've experienced the most tumultuous markets since the 1920s and 1930s. Stocks soared between 1996 and March 2000, creating a market bubble the likes of which we had not seen since the late 1960s and the roaring 1920s. This bubble led many investors to throw out the investing rule book. The more ridiculously overvalued a company was, the more it soared. Everyone talked of "the new economy" and how it *really* was different this time. Sticking with time-tested investment strategies during the stock market orgy was close to impossible. Month in, month out you had to stand on the sidelines, watching your reasonably priced stocks do nothing while the overpriced "story" stocks soared. And, as so often happens with stock market bubbles, just as the last sane investors capitulated and learned to love the stocks with the craziest valuations, along came the reckoning—all the previously gravity-defying stocks came crashing back to earth. Fortunes were lost and millions of investors lost their faith in the long-term potential of stocks. What's worse is that after recovering from the bear market of 2000–2003, a new bubble appeared in real estate markets and the debt used to finance them. This new bubble popped in an even more destructive fashion than that of the dot-com stocks earlier in the decade and brought worldwide markets close to the brink of collapse, ushering in the worst bear market for stocks since the Great Depression. Investors' faith in equity markets was almost completely destroyed by the great market crash of 2007–2009. The S&P 500's loss of 37 percent in 2008 was second only to its loss in 1931, when it plunged 43 percent. People were literally hoarding cash, terrified to make *any* investment in the stock market. And much as the bubble years gave birth to the idea that things really were different from the way they were in the past and we had emerged with a "new economy," the bust years also gave birth to the concept of "the new normal." To its advocates, the new normal meant that future returns would be permanently lower than they had in the past and that there was nothing we could do about it. Investors were desperate to avoid risk of any kind, and money poured out of equities and into bonds. The cover story in the September 2010 issue of *Institutional Investor* was titled "Paradise Lost: Why Fallen Markets Will Never Be the Same." The article's authors argued that, "The financial crisis has discredited free-market capitalism and given its state-driven counterpart a boost." Yet we are forever fighting yesterday's battle without paying attention to what we can *learn* from historical events.

In markets moving from extreme speculation to extreme despair, believing in Ockham's razor—that the simplest theory is usually the best—is almost impossible. We love to make the simple complex, follow the crowd, get seduced by some hot "story" stock, let our emotions dictate decisions, buy and sell on tips and hunches, and approach each investment decision on a case-by-case basis with no underlying consistency or strategy. On the flip side, when equity returns are horrible over a long period of time, we are far too willing to assume that stocks will never generate returns comparable to those of the past, abandoning them for less risky assets like bonds and money market funds. Even 14 years after the first edition of this book was published—showing decade upon decade of returns to a wide variety of strategies—people were still willing to throw the baby out with the bathwater and ignore the historical data because of short-term events, be they good or bad. No wonder the S&P 500 beats 70 percent of traditionally managed mutual funds over the long term.

A Taoist story is illuminating: One day a man was standing at the edge of a pool at the bottom of a huge waterfall when he saw an old man being tossed about in the turbulent water. He ran to rescue him, but before he got there, the old man had climbed out onto the bank and was walking alone, singing to himself. The man was astonished and rushed up to the old man, questioning him about the secret of his survival. The old man said that it was nothing special. "I began to learn while very young, and grew up practicing it.

Now, I'm certain of success. I go down with the water and come up with the water. I follow it and forget myself. The only reason I survive is because I don't struggle against the water's superior power."

The market is like the water, overpowering all who struggle against it and giving those who work with it a wonderful ride. But swimming lessons are in order. You can't just jump in; you need guidelines. Our study of the last 84 years with the CRSP dataset and the last 46 years with the Compustat suggests that to do well in the market, you must do what follows.

ALWAYS USE STRATEGIES

You'll get nowhere buying stocks just because they have a great story. Usually, these are the very companies that have been the *worst* performers over time. They're the stocks everyone talks about and wants to own. They often have sky-high price-to-earnings, price-to-book, and price-to-sales ratios. They're very appealing in the short term, but they're deadly over the long haul. You *must* avoid them. Always think in terms of overall strategies and not individual stocks. One company's data are *meaningless*, yet can be very convincing. Conversely, don't avoid the market or a stock simply because things have been bad over the short term. Few investors could see the compelling valuation of the overall stock market in March 2009, yet it was at this time that stocks were screaming buy and about to embark on a huge rally. At that time, if you had a simple rebalance strategy in place which allocated between stocks and other investments, the strategy would have *forced* you to buy more stocks.

But as Goethe's quote at the beginning of this chapter makes plain, acting is hard, and acting in line with what you think is almost impossible. If you can't use strategies and are inexorably drawn to the stock of the day, your returns suffer horribly in the long run. Remind yourself of what happens to these stocks by looking at charts of all the dot-com high flyers between 1998 and 2002 and the tables and charts for how value stocks came soaring back after the stock market bubble burst in 2000. If, try as you might, you can't stick to a strategy, put the majority of your money in an index fund and treat the small amount you invest in story stocks as an entertainment expense.

IGNORE THE SHORT TERM

Investors who look only at how a strategy or the overall market has performed recently are often seriously misguided by their focus on the short term. They wind up either ignoring a great long-term strategy that has recently underperformed or piling into a mediocre strategy that has recently been on fire. Over the last 15 years, I cannot count the number of times investors have gotten extremely excited about our strategies as they were doing well relative to their benchmark, nor can I count the number of times they have been despondent about short-term underperformance. Tragically, investors seem hardwired to inordinately focus on very short periods of time, often completely ignoring how the strategy has done over long periods of time. As investors, all of our information about returns is focused on *extremely* short periods of time. Just look at how much air time and column inches can be expended on why the stock market has gone up or down in a single day! However, over very short periods of time, the stock market is relatively impossible to forecast, yet when you extend your horizon, the market becomes far more understandable. As I mention in the introduction, if you look at the 50 worst rolling 10-year periods for the stock market, there is not a single instance when over the *next* 10 years the stock market failed to go up.

The point is that at some time in the future any of the strategies in this book will underperform the market, and it is only those investors who can keep their focus on the very long term who will be able to stick with them and reap the rewards of a long-term commitment. You should always guard against allowing what the market is doing today to influence the investments decisions you make. One way to do this is to focus on the *rolling batting average* of how your portfolio is performing versus its benchmark. Much as we focus on the rolling base rates for all the stock selection strategies we have tested in this book, you can do the same for your portfolio's performance versus its benchmark. When you look only at how your investment portfolio has performed for the last quarter, year, and three- and five-year period, you are looking at a tiny snapshot of time. Of course, this snapshot might delight you if you've done particularly well for that particular period, but it also might make you want to abandon your strategy if you've done poorly relative to other strategies. In both cases, I would argue that these snapshots are misleading. Let's look at a snapshot taken on December 31, 1999. An investor who had loaded up on pricey dot-com and tech stocks over the previous five years looks like a genius, and was no doubt planning for an early retirement. Conversely, an investor who had played it safe during those same five years and stuck to small-cap stocks and large-cap value fare would have been wincing with disappointment about his portfolio's prospects. Yet both snapshots were misleading. In a few short months, the tech-heavy portfolio went on to crash and burn, and the small-cap and large-cap value portfolio began to soar.

By focusing on how your portfolio is performing against a benchmark over *rolling* periods, you will get a much better sense of how you are actually doing. You will be much more likely to stick with a strategy that may be underperforming recently but has an outstanding win rate versus the market over all rolling periods. It gives you continuous feedback that allows you to take the hills and valleys with greater restraint than if you simply looked at a snapshot of time. It also gives you perspective by letting you put a strategy's recent performance into a historical context. With this information, you are much more likely to be able to stay the course.

Finally, this advice is equally useful after sharp drawdowns for stocks. In March 2009, I wrote a commentary for *Yahoo Finance* titled "A Generational Opportunity." In it, I argued that many investors were facing a once in a lifetime opportunity to purchase equities at valuations that we hadn't seen since the early 1980s. I urged middle-aged investors to increase the equity allocation of their portfolio to 70 percent to take advantage of the fear that permeated the markets. For the most part, the response I got was silence. People were so shell-shocked by the market declines over the previous 15 months that no amount of data would move them to take advantage of the situation. That's why ignoring the short term may be both the hardest—and best—thing you can do for the overall health of your portfolio.

USE ONLY STRATEGIES PROVEN OVER THE LONG TERM

Always focus on strategies whose effectiveness has been proven over a variety of market environments. The more time periods you can analyze, the better your odds of finding a strategy that has withstood a variety of stock market gyrations. Buying stocks with high price-to-book ratios appeared to work for as long as 15 years, but the fullness of time proves that it is not an effective strategy. Many years of data help you to understand the peaks and valleys of a strategy. What's more, sometimes a strategy might make intuitive sense, like buying stocks that have the greatest annual gain in sales, yet a review of the long-term data tells us that this is a losing strategy, probably because investors get so excited by those huge annual sales increases that they overprice the stocks accordingly. Using strategies that have not withstood the test of time will lead to great disappointment. Stocks change. Industries change. But the underlying reasons certain stocks are good investments remain the same. Only the fullness of time reveals which are the most sound. Remember how alluring all the dot-com stocks were in the late 1990s? Don't let the investment mania *de jour* suck you in—insist on long-term data that support your investment philosophy. Remember that there will *always* be current market fads. In the 1990s it was Internet and technology stocks; tomorrow it might be nanotechnology or emerging markets; but *all* bubbles get popped.

DIG DEEP

If you're a professional investor, make certain to test any strategy over as much time and as many seasons as possible. Look for the worst-case scenario, the time it took to recover from that loss, and how consistent it was against its relevant benchmark. Note the largest downside deviation it had against its benchmark, and be very wary of any strategy that wildly deviates from it. Most investors can't stomach being far behind a benchmark for long.

If you're an individual investor, insist that your advisor conduct such a study on your behalf, or do it yourself. There are now many Web sites where you can do this research. With all the tools now available to individual investors, there is simply no excuse for not doing your homework. A wonderful resource for individual investors is the American Association of Individual Investors. Its Web site (www.aaii.com) is chock full of helpful ideas as well as an entire section devoted to stock screening. Check the links at www.whatworksonwallstreet.com for any new sites that might turn up to aid you in your research.

INVEST CONSISTENTLY

Consistency is the hallmark of great investors and is what separates them from everyone else. If you use even a mediocre strategy *consistently*, you'll beat almost all investors who jump in and out of the market, change tactics in midstream, and forever second-guess their decisions. Look at the S&P 500. We've shown that it is a simple strategy that buys large capitalization stocks. Yet this one-factor, rather mediocre strategy still manages to beat 70 percent of all actively managed funds because *it never leaves its strategy*. Realistically consider your risk tolerance, plan your path, and then stick to it. You may have fewer stories to tell at parties, but you'll be among the most successful long-term investors. Successful investing isn't alchemy; it's a simple matter of consistently using time-tested strategies and letting compounding work its magic.

ALWAYS BET WITH THE BASE RATE

Base rates are boring, dull, and *very worthwhile*. Knowing how often and by how much a strategy beats the market is among the most useful information available to investors, yet few take advantage of it. Base rates are essentially the odds of beating the market over the time period you plan to invest. If you have a 10-year time horizon and understand base rates, you'll see that picking stocks with the highest multiples of earnings, cash flow, sales, or the lowest value composite scores has *very bad odds*. If you pay attention to the odds, *you can put them on your side*. You now have the numbers. Use them. Don't settle for strategies that may have done very well recently but that have poor overall batting averages. Chances are you'll be getting in just as those long-term base rates are getting ready to reassert themselves.

NEVER USE THE RISKIEST STRATEGIES

There is no point in using the riskiest strategies. They will sap your will, and you will undoubtedly abandon them, usually at their low. Given the number of highly effective strategies, always concentrate on those with the highest risk-adjusted returns.

ALWAYS USE MORE THAN ONE STRATEGY

Unless you're near retirement and investing only in low-risk strategies, always diversify your portfolio by investing in several strategies. How much you allocate depends on your risk tolerance, but you should always have some growth and some value guarding you from the inevitable swings of fashion on Wall Street. Once you have exposure to both styles of investing, make sure you have exposure to the various market capitalizations as well. A simple rule of thumb for investors with a time horizon of 10 years or more is to use the market's capitalization weights as guidelines. Currently, 75 percent of the market is large-cap and 25 percent is small- and mid-cap. That's a good starting point for the average investor. Unite strategies so that your portfolio can do much better than the overall market without taking more risk. Indeed, while this book covers only stocks that trade in the United States (with a reasonable number of them being American depository receipts of foreign-domiciled companies that offer shares to U.S. investors), you might think about having your portfolio aligned in a similar fashion to the MSCI All World Index. Currently, the United States makes up 35 percent of that index, with Japan, the United Kingdom, France, and Canada rounding out the top five. If you include the next five countries by market capitalization, Hong Kong,

Germany, Australia, Switzerland, and Brazil, you would cover 74 percent of the total market capitalization in the world. The point is, these strategies work *outside* the United States as well, and a well-diversified portfolio should reflect this. We have run tests similar to those in this book on the MSCI dataset that begins in 1970 and found that, for the most part, these strategies work equally well in foreign markets.

Additionally, you should have a plan for your *entire* portfolio, not just the equity portion. One of the simplest and most effective strategies for your entire portfolio is to rebalance your allocations to various styles and asset classes back to your target allocation at least once a year. If you are working with a financial advisor, he or she is probably already doing this for you, but if not, figure out what makes the most sense for you and then make sure that you *follow your allocation*. This effectively forces you to buy more of an investment style or an asset class when it has done poorly, and take money away from styles and asset classes that have performed well. It would have served you extraordinarily well near the bear market bottoms of the last decade because it would have forced you to move money from fixed income into equities at a time when most investors were fleeing the equity market. This would have allowed you to take advantage of the big move up from the market bottom. But it also would have served you well during the last market boom because it would have had you trim equity allocations and put additional money in fixed income and other assets. It's important to have a strategy for your entire portfolio.

USE MULTIFACTOR MODELS

The single factor models show that the market rewards certain characteristics while punishing others. Yet you're much better off using several factors to build your portfolios. Returns are higher, and risk is lower. You should always make a stock pass several hurdles before investing in it. The only exceptions to this rule are our composited factors like the Value Composite factors One and Two, the Composited Earnings Quality factor, and so forth. These are essentially multifactor models, requiring each stock to earn top scores in a wide variety of characteristics.

INSIST ON CONSISTENCY

If you don't have the time to build your own portfolios and prefer investing in mutual funds or separately managed accounts, buy only those that stress consistency of style. Many managers follow a hit-or-miss, intuitive method of stock selection. They have no mechanism to rein in their emotions or ensure that their good ideas work. All too often their picks are based on hope rather than experience. You have no way to *really* know exactly how they are managing your money, or if their past performance is due to the result of a hot hand unguided by a coherent underlying strategy.

Don't bet with them. Buy one of the many funds based on solid, rigorous strategies. If your fund doesn't clearly define its investment style, insist that it do so. You should expect nothing less.

THE STOCK MARKET IS NOT RANDOM

Finally, the data prove that the stock market takes purposeful strides. Far from chaotic, random movement, the market consistently rewards specific strategies while punishing others. And these purposeful strides have continued to persist well after they were first identified. We now have not only what Ben Graham requested—the historical behavior of securities with defined characteristics—but we also have a 14-year period since the first edition of this book in which we witnessed, in real time, the continued out performance of the top strategies and factors tested in 1996. We must let history be our guide, using only those time-tested methods that have proven successful. We know what is valuable, and we know what works on Wall Street. All that remains is to act upon this knowledge.

BIBLIOGRAPHY

Ambachtsheer, Keith P., "The Persistence of Investment Risk," *The Journal of Portfolio Management,* Fall 1989, pp. 69–72.

Arnott, Robert D., Kelso, Charles M., Jr., Kiscadden, Stephan, and Macedo, Rosemary, "Forecasting Factor Returns: An Intriguing Possibility," *The Journal of Portfolio Management,* Fall 1990, pp. 28–35.

Asness, Clifford S., "The Interaction of Value and Momentum Strategies," *Financial Analysts Journal,* April 1998.

Banz, R., and Breen, W., "Sample-Dependent Results Using Accounting and Market Data: Some Evidence," *Journal of Finance,* September 1986, pp. 779–793.

Barach, Roland, *Mind Traps: Mastering the Inner World of Investing,* Dow Jones-Irwin, Homewood, IL, 1988.

Basu, S., "The Relationship Between Earnings Yield, Market Value and Return for NYSE Common Stocks: Further Evidence," *Journal of Financial Economics,* June 1983, pp. 129–156.

Bell, David E., Raiffa, Howard, and Tversky, Amos, *Decision Making: Descriptive, Normative, and Prescriptive Interactions,* Cambridge University Press, Cambridge, U.K., 1988.

Bernstein, Peter L., *Capital Ideas: The Improbable Origins of Modern Wall Street,* The Free Press, New York, 1992.

Biggs, Barton, *Wealth, War and Wisdom,* John Wiley & Sons, New York, 2009.

Billett, Matthew T., Flannery, Mark J., and Garfinkel, Jon A., "Are Bank Loans Special? Evidence on the Post-Announcement Performance of Bank Borrowers" (November 26, 2001). *AFA 2002 Atlanta Meetings.*

Bjerring, James H., Lakonishok, Josef, and Vermaelen, Theo, "Stock Prices and Financial Analysts' Recommendations," *The Journal of Finance,* March 1983, pp. 187–204.

Blakney, R. B., *The Way of Life: A New Translation of Tao Te Ching,* New American Library Publishing, New York, 1983.

Bogle, John C., *Bogle on Mutual Funds: New Perspectives for the Intelligent Investor,* Irwin Professional Publishing, New York, 1994.

Bostrom, N., "Existential Risks: Analyzing Human Extinction Scenarios and Related Hazards," *Journal of Evolution and Technology*, Volume 9, Number 1, 2001.

Bradshaw, Mark T., Richardson, Scott A., Sloan, Richard G. "The relation between corporate financing activities, analysts' forecasts and stock returns," *Journal of Accounting and Economics,* 2006, pp. 53–85.

Brandes, Charles H., *Value Investing Today,* Dow Jones-Irwin, Homewood, IL, 1989.

Brealey, Richard A., *An Introduction to Risk and Return From Common Stocks,* Second Edition, MIT Press, Cambridge, MA, 1993.

Brealey, Richard A., "Portfolio Theory versus Portfolio Practice," *The Journal of Portfolio Management,* Summer 1990, pp. 6–10.

Brock, William, Lakonishok, Josef, and LeBaron, Blake, "Simple Technical Trading Rules and the Stochastic Properties of Stock Returns," *The Journal of Finance,* December 1992, pp. 1,731–1,764.

Bromberg-Martin, E., Hikosaka O., "Midbrain Dopamine Neurons Signal Preference for Advance Information about Upcoming Rewards," *Neuron,* Volume 63, Issue 1, July 2009, pp. 119–126.

Brown, John Dennis, *101 Years on Wall Street: An Investor's Almanac,* Prentice Hall, Englewood Cliffs, NJ, 1991.

Brown, Stephen J., and Kritzman, Mark P., CFA, *Quantitative Methods for Financial Analysis,* Dow-Jones-Irwin, Homewood, IL, 1987.

Brown, Stephen J., Leonard Stern School of Business, NYU and Goetzmann, William N., Yale School of Management, "Performance Persistence," Forthcoming, *Journal of Finance,* Vol 30 No 2, June 1995.

Browne, Christopher H., "Value Investing and Behavioral Finance," Columbia Business School Graham and Dodd Value Investing 2000, November 15, 2000.

Brush, John S., and Boles, Keith E., "The Predictive Power in Relative Strength & CAPM," *The Journal of Portfolio Management,* Summer 1983, pp. 20–23.

Brush, John S., "Eight Relative Strength Models Compared," *The Journal of Portfolio Management,* Fall 1986, pp. 21–28.

Casti, John L., *COMPLEX-ification, Explaining a Paradoxical World Through the Science of Surprise,* HarperCollins Publishers, New York, 1994.

Chan, Louis K., Hamao, Yasushi, and Lakonishok, Josef, "Fundamentals and Stock Returns in Japan," *The Journal of Finance,* December 1991, pp. 1,739–1,764.

Chan, Louis, K.C., and Lakonishok, Josef, "Are the Reports of Beta's Death Premature?" *The Journal of Portfolio Management,* Summer 1993, pp. 51–62.

Chancellor, Edward, *Devil Take the Hindmost: A History of Financial Speculation*, Plume Publishing, New York, 2000.

Chopra, Navin, Lakonishok, Josef, and Ritter, Jay R., "Measuring Abnormal Performance: Do Stocks Overreact?" *Journal of Financial Economics,* November 1992, pp. 235–268.

Cottle, Sidney, Murray, Roger F., and Block, Frank E., *Graham and Dodd's Security Analysis,* 5th ed. McGraw-Hill, New York, 1988.

Coulson, Robert D., *The Intelligent Investor's Guide to Profiting from Stock Market Inefficiencies,* Probus Publishing Company, Chicago, IL, 1987.

Dale, Richard, *The First Crash: Lessons from the South Sea Bubble,* Princeton University Press, New Jersey, 2004.

Damodaran, Aswath, *Investment Philosophies: Successful Strategies and the Investors Who Made Them Work,* John Wiley & Sons, Hoboken, NJ, 2003.

Dawes, Robyn M., *House of Cards: Psychology and Psychotherapy Built on Myth,* The Free Press, New York, 1994.

"Death of Equities," *Business Week,* August, 1979.

De Martino, B., D. Kumaran, B. Seymour, and R.J. Dolan, "Biases and Rational Decision-Making in the Human Brain," *Science* 313(5787) August 4th, 2006.

Dewdney, A.K., *200% of Nothing: An Eye-Opening Tour Through the Twists and Turns of Math Abuse and Innumeracy,* John Wiley & Sons, Inc., New York, NY, 1993.

Dimson, Elroy, Marsh, Paul, and Staunton, Mike, *Triumph of the Optimists: 101 Years of Global Investment Returns,* Princeton University Press, Princeton, NJ, 2002.

Douglas, A., "Last Chance to See," Ballantine Books, New York, 1990.

Dreman, David N., *Psychology and the Stock Market,* Warner Books, New York, 1977.

Dreman, David N., *The New Contrarian Investment Strategy,* Random House, New York, 1980.

Dreman, David N., "Good-bye EMH," *Forbes Magazine,* June 20, 1994, p. 261.

Dreman, David N., "Nasty Surprises," *Forbes Magazine,* July 19, 1993, p. 246.

Dreman, David N., "Choronically Clouded Crystal Balls," *Forbes Magazine,* October 11, 1993, p. 178.

Dunn, Patricia C., and Theisen, Rolf D., "How Consistently do Active Managers Win?" *The Journal of Portfolio Management,* Summer 1983, pp. 47–50.

Ellis, Charles D., "Ben Graham: Ideas as Mementos," *Financial Analysts Journal,* Volume 38, Number 4, July-August 1982.

Ellis, Charles D., and Vertin, James R., *Classics: An Investor's Anthology,* Dow Jones-Irwin, Homewood, IL, 1989.

Ellis, Charles D., and Vertin, James R., *Classics II: Another Investor's Anthology,* Dow Jones-Irwin, Homewood, IL, 1991.

Fabozzi, Frank J., Fogler, H. Russell, Harrington, Diana R., *The New Stock Market, A Complete Guide to the Latest Research, Analysis and Performance,* Probus Publishing Company, Chicago, IL, 1990.

Fabozzi, Frank J., *Pension Fund Investment Management,* Probus Publishing Company, Chicago, IL, 1990.

Fabozzi, Frank J., and Zarb, Frank G., *Handbook of Financial Markets: Securities, Options and Futures,* Dow Jones-Irwin, Homewood, IL, 1986.

Eugene, F., French, K., "The Cross-Section of Expected Stock Returns," *Journal of Finance,* Volume XLVII, Number 2, pp. 427–465, June 1992.

Faust, David, *The Limits of Scientific Reasoning,* University of Minnesota Press, Minneapolis, MN, 1984.

Ferguson, Robert, "The Trouble with Performance Measurement," *The Journal of Portfolio Management,* Spring 1986, pp. 4–9.

Ferguson, Robert, "The Plight of the Pension Fund Officer," *Financial Analysts Journal,* May/June, 1989, pp. 8–9.

Fisher, Kenneth L., *Super Stocks,* Dow Jones-Irwin, Homewood, IL, 1984.

Fogler, H. Russell, "Common Stock Management in the 1990s," *The Journal of Portfolio Management,* Winter 1990, pp. 26–34.

Freeman, John D., "Behind the Smoke and Mirrors: Gauging the Integrity of Investment Simulations," *Financial Analysts Journal,* November/December 1992, pp. 26–31.

Fridson, Martin S., *Investment Illusions,* John Wiley & Sons, Inc., New York, 1993.

Givoly, Dan, and Lakonishok, Josef, "Financial Analysts' Forecasts of Earnings: Their Value to Investors," *Journal of Banking and Finance,* December 1979, pp. 221–233.

Gleick, James, *Chaos: Making A New Science,* Viking Penguin, New York, 1987.

Graham, B., *The Intelligent Investor: A Book of Practial Counsel,* Harper & Row Publishers, 4th Edition, 1986.

Graham, B., Dodd, D., *Security Analysis: Principles and Techniques,* McGraw-Hill, New York and London, 1940.

Guerard, John, and Vaught, H.T., *The Handbook of Financial Modeling,* Probus Publishing Co., Chicago, IL, 1989.

Hackel, Kenneth S., and Livnat, Joshua, *Cash Flow and Security Analysis,* Business-One Irwin, Homewood, IL, 1992.

Hagin, Bob, "What Practitioners Need to Know About T-Tests," *Financial Analysts Journal,* May/June 1990, pp. 17–20.

Hanson, Dirk, *The Chemical Carousel: What Science Tells Us About Beating Addiction,* BookSurge Publishing, South Carolina, 2009.

Harrington, Diana R., Fabozzi, Frank J., and Fogler, H. Russell, *The New Stock Market,* Probus Publishing Company, Chicago, IL, 1990.

Haugen, Robert A., and Baker, Nardin L., "Dedicated Stock Portfolios," *The Journal of Portfolio Management,* Summer 1990, pp. 17–22.

Haugen, Robert A., "The Effects of Intrigue, Liquidity, Imprecision, and Bias on the Cross-Section of Expected Stock Returns," *Journal of Portfolio Management,* Summer 1996, pp. 8–17.

Hirshleifer, David, Hou, Kewei, Teoh, Siew Hong, and Zhang, Yinglei, "Do Investors Overvalue Firms With Bloated Balance Sheets?" *Journal of Accounting and Economics,* December 2004, pp. 297–331.

Hoff, Benjamin, *The Tao of Pooh,* Penguin Books, New York, 1982.

Hogan M., "*Modern Portfolio Theory Ages Badly—The Death of Buy and Hold,*" Barron's Electronic Investor, February 2009.

Ibbotson Associates, *Stocks, Bonds, Bills, and Inflation 1995 Yearbook,* Ibbotson Associates, Chicago, IL, 1995.

Ibbotson, Roger G., and Brinson, Gary P., *Gaining the Performance Advantage: Investment Markets,* McGraw-Hill, New York, 1987.

Ibbotson, Roger G., "Decile Portfolios of the New York Stock Exchange, 1967–1984," working paper, Yale School of Management, 1986.

Ikenberry, David, Lakonishok, Josef, and Vermaelen, Theo, "Market Under Reaction to Open Market Share Repurchases," July 1994, unpublished.

Jacobs, Bruce J., and Levy, Kenneth N., "Disentangling Equity Return Regularities: New Insights and Investment Opportunities," *Financial Analysts Journal*, May/June 1988, pp. 18–38.

Jeffrey, Robert H., "Do Clients Need So Many Portfolio Managers?" *The Journal of Portfolio Management*, Fall 1991, pp. 13–19.

Jones, Charles M. "A Century of Stock Market Liquidity and Trading Costs," Columbia University, May 22, 2002 version.

Kahn, Ronald N., "What Practitioners Need to Know About Back Testing," *Financial Analysts Journal*, July/August 1990, pp. 17–20.

Kahneman, D., "The Psychology of the Nonprofessional Investor," *Journal of Portfolio Management*, 1998.

Kahneman, D., Tversky A., "*Prospect Theory: An Analysis of Decision under Risk*," *Econometrica*, Vol. 47, No. 2. (Mar., 1979), pp. 263–292.

Keane, Simon M., "Paradox in the Current Crisis in Efficient Market Theory," *The Journal of Portfolio Management*, Winter 1991, pp. 30–34.

Keppler, A. Michael, "Further Evidence on the Predictability of International Equity Returns," *The Journal of Portfolio Management*, Fall 1991, pp. 48–53.

Keppler, A. Michael, "The Importance of Dividend Yields in Country Selection," *The Journal of Portfolio Management*, Winter 1991, pp. 24–29.

Klein, Robert A., Lederman, Jess, *Small Cap Stocks, Investment and Portfolio Strategies for the Institutional Investor*, Probus Publishing Company, Chicago, IL, 1993.

Knowles, Harvey C. III, and Petty, Damon H., *The Dividend Investor*, Probus Publishing Company, Chicago, IL, 1992.

Kritzman, Mark, "How To Detect Skill in Management Performance," *The Journal of Portfolio Management*, Winter 1986, pp. 16–20.

Kuhn, Thomas, S., *The Copernican Revolution: Planetary Astronomy in the Development of Western Thought*, Harvard University Press, Cambridge, MA, 1957.

Kuhn, Thomas S., *The Structure of Scientific Revolutions*, University of Chicago Press, Chicago, IL, 1970.

Kuhnen, Camelia M., Knutson, Brian, "The Neural Basis of Financial Risk Taking," *Neuron*, Vol. 47, 763–770, September 2005.

Lakonishok, Josef, Shleifer, Andrei, and Vishny, Robert W., "Contrarian Investment, Extrapolation, and Risk," working paper, June 1994.

Lawson, Richard "Measuring Company Quality," *The Journal of Investing*, Winter 2008, pp. 38–55.

Lee, Charles M.C., and Swaminathan, Bhaskaran "Price Momentum and Trading Volume," June 1998.

Lee, Wayne Y., "Diversification and Time: Do Investment Horizons Matter?" *The Journal of Portfolio Management*, Spring 1990, pp. 21–26.

Lefevre, Edwin, *Reminiscences of a Stock Operator*, George H. Doran Company, New York, 1923.

Lehrer, J., "Microscopic Microeconomics," *New York Times*, October 2010.

Lerner, Eugene M., and Theerathorn Pochara, "The Returns of Different Investment Strategies," *The Journal of Portfolio Management*, Summer 1983, pp. 26–28.

Lewis, Michael, *Moneyball: The Art of Winning an Unfair Game*, W.W. Norton & Company, New York, 2003.

Lo, Andrew W., and Mackinlay, A. Craig, *A Non-Random Walk Down Wall Street*, Princeton University Press, Princeton, NJ, 1999.

Lofthouse, Stephen, *Equity Investment Mangement, How to Select Stocks and Markets*, John Wiley & Sons, Chichester, England, 1994.

Lorie, James H., Dodd, Peter, and Kimpton, Mary Hamilton, *The Stock Market: Theories and Evidence*, Dow Jones-Irwin, Homewood, IL, 1985.

Loughran, Tim, and Ritter, Jay R., "The Operating Performance of Firms Conducting Seasoned Equity Offerings." *Journal of Finance*, Vol. 52 No. 4, December 1997.

Lowe, Janet, *Benjamin Graham on Value Investing, Lessons from the Dean of Wall Street*, Dearborn Financial Publishing Inc., Chicago, IL, 1994.

Lowenstein, Louis, *What's Wrong with Wall Street*, Addison-Wesley, New York, 1988.

MacLean, P.D., *The Triune Brain in Evolution: Role in Paleocerebral Functions*, Plenum Press, New York, 1990.

Maital, Shloml, *Minds Markets & Money: Psychological Foundation of Economic Behavior*, Basic Books, New York, 1982.

Malkiel, Burton G., *Returns from Investing in Equity Mutual Funds 1971–1991*, Princeton University, 1994.

Mandelbrot, Benoit, *The (mis)Behavior of Markets: A Fractal View of Risk, Ruin and Reward*, Basic Books, New York, 2004.

Martin, Linda J., "Uncertain? How Do You Spell Relief?" *The Journal of Portfolio Management,* Spring 1985, pp. 5–8.

Marcus, Alan J., "The Magellan Fund and Market Efficiency," *The Journal of Portfolio Management,* Fall 1990, pp. 85–88.

Mattlin, Everett, "Reliability Math: Manager Selection by the Numbers," *Institutional Investor,* January 1993, pp. 141–142.

Maturi, Richard J., *Stock Picking: The 11 Best Tactics for Beating the Market,* McGraw-Hill, New York, 1993.

McElreath, Robert B., Jr., and Wiggins C. Donald, "Using the COMPUSTAT Tapes in Financial Research: Problems and Solutions," *Financial Analysts Journal,* January/February 1984, pp. 71–76.

McQuarrie, Edward F. "The Myth of 1926: How Much Do We Know About Long-Term Returns on U.S. Stocks?" *The Journal of Investing,* Winter 2009, pp. 96–106.

Meehl, P., *Clinical versus Statistical Prediction: A Theoretical Analysis and Review of the Literature,* University of Minnesota Press, 1954.

Melnikoff, Meyer, *"Anomaly Investing," The Financial Analyst's Handbook,* edited by Sumner N. Levine, Dow Jones-Irwin, Homewood, IL, 1988, pp. 699–721.

Montier, James, *Behavioral Finance: Insights into Irrational Minds and Markets,* John Wiley & Sons, Ltd., West Sussex, England, 2002.

Montier, James, *Value Investing: Tools and Techniques for Intelligent Investment,* John Wiley & Sons, New York, 2009.

Murphy, Joseph E., Jr., *Stock Market Probability,* Revised Edition, Probus Publishing Company, Chicago, IL, 1994.

Nathan, Siva, Sivakumar, Kumar, and Vijayakumar, Jayaraman, "Returns to Trading Strategies Based on Price-to-Earnings and Price-to-Sales Ratios," *The Journal of Investing,* Summer 2001, pp. 17–28.

Neustadt, Richard E., *Thinking in Time: The Uses of History for Decision-Makers,* Free Press, NY, 1988.

Newbold, Gerald D., and Poon, Percy S., "Portfolio Risk, Portfolio Performance, and The Individual Investor," *Journal of Finance,* Summer 1996.

Nisbett, Richard, and Ross, Lee, *Human Inference: Strategies and Shortcomings of Social Judgement,* Prentice-Hall, Englewood Cliffs, NJ, 1980.

Nocera, J., "Poking Holes in a Theory on Markets," *New York Times,* June, 2005.

O'Barr, William M., and Conley, John M., *Fortune & Folly: The Wealth & Power of Institutional Investing,* Business-One Irwin, Homewood, IL, 1992.

O'Hanlon, John, and Ward, Charles W.R., "How to Lose at Winning Strategies," *The Journal of Portfolio Management*, Spring 1986.

Opdyke, Jeff D., and Kim Jane J., "A Winning Stock Pickers Losing Fund," *Wall Street Journal*, September 16, 2004.

Oppenheimer, Henry R., "A Test of Ben Graham's Stock Selection Criteria," *Financial Analysts Journal*, September/October 1984, pp. 68–74.

O'Shaughnessy, James P., "Quantitative Models as an Aid in Offsetting Systematic Errors in Decision Making," St. Paul, MN, 1988, unpublished.

O'Shaughnessy, James P., *Invest Like the Best: Using Your Computer to Unlock the Secrets of the Top Money Managers*, McGraw-Hill, New York, 1994.

O'Shaughnessy, James P., *Predicting the Markets of Tomorrow: A Contrarian Investment Strategy for the Next Twenty Years*, Portfolio Books, NY, 2006.

O'Shaughnessy, James P., *The Internet Contrarian*, April 1999.

Paulos, John Allen, *Innumeracy: Mathematical Illiteracy and Its Consequences*, Hill and Wang, New York, 1989.

Paulos, John Allen, *A Mathematician Plays the Stock Market*, Basic Books, New York, 2003.

Perritt, Gerald, W., *Small Stocks, Big Profit*, Dearborn Financial Publishing, Inc., Chicago, IL, 1993.

Perritt, Gerald W., and Lavine, Alan, *Diversify Your Way To Wealth: How to Customize Your Investment Portfolio to Protect and Build Your Net Worth*, Probus Publishing Company, Chicago, IL, 1994.

Peter, Edgar E., *Chaos and Order in the Capital Markets: A New View of Cycles, Prices, and Market Volatility*, John Wiley & Sons, New York, 1991.

Peters, Donald J., *A Contrarian Strategy for Growth Stock Investing: Theoretical Foundations & Empirical Evidence*, Quorum Books, Westport, CT, 1993.

Peterson, Richard, *Inside the Investor's Brain: The Power of Mind Over Money*, Wiley Trading, New York, 2007.

Pettengill, Glenn N., and Jordan, Bradford D., "The Overreaction Hypothesis, Firm Size, and Stock Market Seasonality," *The Journal of Portfolio Management*, Spring 1990, pp. 60–64.

Piotroski, Joseph D., "Value Investing: The Use of Historical Financial Statement Information to Separate Winners from Losers," *Journal of Accounting Research*, Vol 38, Supplement, 2000.

Reinganum, M., "Misspecificaiton of Capital Asset Pricing: Empirical Anomalies Based on Earnings' Yields and Market Values," *Journal of Financial Economics*, March 1981, pp. 19–46.

Reinganum, M., "Investment Characteristics of Stock Market Winners," *AAII Journal*, September, 1989.

"R.I.P. Equities 1982–2008: The Equity Culture Loses Its Bloom," *Institutional Investor's*, January 2010.

Ritter, Jay R., 1991, "The long run performance of initial public offerings," *Journal of Finance*, 46, pp. 3–27.

Santayana, G., "The Life of Reason: Phases of Human Progress," University of Toronto Libraries reprint, 2011. Originally published 1905.

Schwager, Jack D., *Market Wizards: Interviews with Top Traders,* Simon & Schuster, New York, 1992.

Schwager, Jack D., *The New Market Wizards,* Harper-Collins Publishers, New York, 1992.

Schleifer, Andrei, *Inefficient Markets: An Introduction to Behavioral Finance,* Oxford University Press, Oxford, England, 2000.

Spencer, J., Lessons from the Brain-Damaged Investor, *Wall Street Journal*, July 2005.

Sharpe, Robert M., *The Lore and Legends of Wall Street,* Dow Jones-Irwin, Homewood, IL, 1989.

Shiller, Robert J., *Market Volatility,* The MIT Press, Cambridge, MA, 1989.

Shiller, Robert J., *Irrational Exuberance,* Broadway Books, New York, 2001.

Siegel, Jeremy J., *Stocks for the Long Run: Second Edition, Revised and Expanded,* McGraw-Hill, New York, 1998.

Siegel, Laurence B., *Stocks, Bonds, Bills, and Inflation, 1994 Yearbook,* Ibbotson Associates, Chicago, IL, 1994.

Singal, Vijay, *Beyond the Random Walk: A Guide to Stock Market Anomalies and Low Risk Investing,* Oxford University Press, New York, 2004.

Smullyan, Raymond M., *The Tao is Silent,* Harper & Row, New York, 1977.

Speidell, Lawrence S., "The New Wave Theory," *Financial Analysts Journal*, July/August 1988, pp. 9–12.

Speidell, Lawrence S., "Embarrassment and Riches: The Discomfort of Alternative Investment Strategies," *The Journal of Portfolio Management*, Fall 1990, pp. 6–11.

Spiess, D. Katherine, Affleck-Graves, John, "The Long-Run Performance of Common Stock Following Debt Offerings," *Journal of Financial Economics*, 54 (1999), pp. 45–73.

Stowe, John D., McLeavey, Dennis W., and Pinto, Jerald E., "Share Repurchases and Stock Valuation Models," *The Journal of Portfolio Management*, Summer 2009, pp. 170–179.

Stumpp, Mark, and Scott, James, "Does Liquidity Predict Stock Returns?" *The Journal of Portfolio Management*, Winter 1991, pp. 35–40.

Taleb, Nassim Nicholas, *Fooled by Randomness: The Hidden Role of Chance in the Markets and in Life,* Random House, New York, 2001.

Tetlock, Philip, *Expert Political Judgment: How Good is It? How Can We Know?,* Princeton University Press, Princeton, NJ, 2006.

Thomas, Dana L., *The Plungers and the Peacocks: An Update of the Classic History of the Stock Market,* William Morrow, New York, 1989.

Tierney, David E., and Winston, Kenneth, "Using Generic Benchmarks to Present Manager Styles," *The Journal of Portfolio Management*, Summer 1991, pp. 33–36.

Train, John, *The Money Masters,* Harper & Row Publishers, New York, 1985.

Train, John, *Famous Financial Fiascos,* Clarkson N. Potter, New York, 1985.

Train, John, *The New Money Masters: Winning Investment Strategies of: Soros, Lynch, Steinhardt, Rogers, Neff, Wanger, Michaelis, Carret,* Harper & Row Publishers, New York, 1989.

Treynor, Jack L., "Information-Based Investing," *Financial Analysts Journal,* May/June 1989, pp. 6–7.

Treynor, Jack L., "The 10 Most Important Questions to Ask in Selecting a Money Manager," *Financial Analysts Journal,* May/June 1990, pp. 4–5.

"Trillion-dollar babies," *The Economist,* January 2010.

Trippe, Robert R., and Lee, Jae K., *State-of-the-Art Portfolio Selection: Using Knowledge-Based Systems to Enhance Investment Performance,* Probus Publishing Company, Chicago, IL, 1992.

Tsetsekos, George P., and DeFusco, Richard, "Portfolio Performance, Managerial Ownership, and the Size Effect," *The Journal of Portfolio Management*, Spring 1990, pp. 33–39.

Twark, Allan, and D'Mello, James P., "Model Indexation: A Portfolio Management Tool," *The Journal of Portfolio Management*, Summer 1991, pp. 37–40.

Tweedy, Browne Company LLC, *What Has Worked in Investing: Studies of Investment Approaches and Characteristics Associated with Exceptional Returns*, 1992.

Valentine, Jerome, L., CFA, "Investment Analysis and Capital Market Theory," *The Financial Analysts,* Occasional Paper Number 1, 1975.

Valentine, Jerome L., CFA, and Mennis, Edmund A., CFA, *Quantitative Techniques for Financial Analysis,* Richard D. Irwin, Inc., Homewood, IL, 1980.

Vandell, Robert F., and Parrino, Robert, "A Purposeful Stride Down Wall Street," *The Journal of Portfolio Management,* Winter 1986, pp. 31–39.

Vince, Ralph, *The Mathematics of Money Management,* John Wiley & Sons, New York, 1992.

Vishny, Robert W., Shleifer, Andrei, and Lakonishok, Josef, "The Structure and Performance of the Money Management Industry," in the *Brookings Papers on Economic Activity, Microeconomics,* 1992.

Watzlawick, Paul, *How Real Is Real? Confusion, Disinformation, Communication,* Vintage Books, New York, 1977.

Wilcox, Jarrod W., *Investing By the Numbers,* Frank J. Fabozzi Associates, New Hope, PA, 1999.

Williams, John Burr, Ph.D., "Fifty Years of Investment Analysis," *The Financial Analysts Research Foundation,* 1979.

Wood, Arnold S., "Fatal Attractions for Money Managers," *Financial Analysts Journal,* May/June 1989, pp. 3–5.

Zeikel, Arthur, "Investment Management in the 1990s," *Financial Analysts Journal,* September/October 1990, pp. 6–9.

Zweig, J., *Your Money and Your Brain,* Simon & Schuster, Reprint edition, September 2008.

INDEX